QUEBEC QUESTIONS

Second Edition

QUEBEC QUESTIONS

Quebec Studies for the Twenty-First Century

Edited by **Stéphan Gervais, Christopher Kirkey, and Jarrett Rudy**

Oxford University Press is a department of the University of Oxford.
It furthers the University's objective of excellence in research, scholarship,
and education by publishing worldwide. Oxford is a registered trade mark of
Oxford University Press in the UK and in certain other countries.

Published in Canada by
Oxford University Press
8 Sampson Mews, Suite 204,
Don Mills, Ontario M3C 0H5 Canada

www.oupcanada.com

First Edition published in 2011

Library and Archives Canada Cataloguing in Publication
Quebec questions : Quebec studies for the twenty-first century / edited by Stéphan Gervais, Christopher Kirkey, Jarrett Rudy. — Second edition.

Includes bibliographical references and index.
ISBN 978-0-19-901462-0 (paperback)

1. Québec (Province)—History. I. Gervais, Stéphan, 1968–, editor II. Kirkey, Christopher John, 1962-, editor III. Rudy, Robert Jarrett, 1970-, editor

FC2911.Q85 2016 971.4 C2015-907315-4

Cover image: Chris Forsyth, "The Montreal Metro Project – Jarry", 2014. chrismforsyth.com

Oxford University Press is committed to our environment. Wherever possible, our books are printed on paper which comes from responsible sources.

Printed and bound in Canada

1 2 3 4 — 19 18 17 16

Contents

Part C • Language

Part D • Citizenship

Part E • Quebec Models

Acknowledgements

Collectively, we would like to express our appreciation to many who share our enthusiasm for Quebec, its history, and its people. First off, editing a book that gathers such a great list of scholars is a unique privilege. We would like to thank them for sharing their expertise, giving us their confidence, and for responding quickly to our seemingly endless demands. We would also like to thank Oxford University Press (Canada) for continuing to recognize the tremendous value a multidisciplinary book focused on Quebec has. Most especially, we are grateful for all the efforts of the editorial team at Oxford, including Tamara Capar, Darcey Pepper, Ian Gibson, Katherine Skene, Leanne Rancourt, and Phyllis Wilson. It has been and remains a distinct privilege for the three of us to work on this project together, exchanging and assessing fresh ideas and perspectives. These countless *interchanges* have led to a close personal and professional friendship.

This book would never have been realized without the generous support, financial and otherwise, of several key offices. Above all else, significant support for the first edition was provided by the Ministère des Relations internationales du Québec. Specific funding was made available to the Institute on Québec Studies at SUNY Plattsburgh through a Québec Research Initiative grant.

The Government of Canada also provided important funding in the form of a conference grant to support an authors' colloquium in Montreal at McGill University. Further support for *Quebec Questions* was kindly provided by the Secrétariat aux Affaires intergouvernementales canadiennes (Programme de soutien à la recherche en matière d'affaires intergouvernementales et d'identité québécoise), the Association internationales des études québécoises (AIEQ), the Ministère des Ressources naturelles et de la Faune, the Ministère de la Justice, the Dean of Arts Development Fund at McGill University, the United States Department of Education, and the Centre de recherche interuniversitaire sur la littérature et la culture québécoises (CRILCQ).

We would like to acknowledge the extraordinary work of our translator, Cynthia Kelly, on 10 of the chapters in this volume. Her conscientious collaboration with the authors and editors brought great clarity to these texts. Ms. Kelly was backed by the invaluable talents of her colleagues Glenn Clavier, Maxine Cutler, and Donald McGrath, and by the sage linguistic advice of Brigitte Côté, Lisa Dillon, Cécile Latizeau, and Valerie Vanstone.

Many individuals have contributed over the years to giving us the personal and intellectual strength to cultivate our passion for Quebec. Of course, we will not be able to thank them all.

Stéphan would like to thank his parents, Louis Gervais and Lise Lafleur Gervais, for being such great role models, and especially his mother for valuing the power of education and teaching him to have, to rephrase a Quebec expression, a "quiet confidence" in himself. He also thanks his wife, Julie, for her love, passion, and inspiration. For this second edition, Stéphan would like to salute the unique intellectual inspiration that the late professor Roderick A. Macdonald has had on the study of Quebec, and also to salute the work and dedication of Robert Laliberté as a passionate ambassador of Quebec studies.

Chris remains deeply appreciative of the support provided to SUNY Plattsburgh's Institute on Québec Studies: Maria Beauséjour, Jean-Stéphane Bernard, Michel Constantin, Yanick Godbout, Michael Hawes, Patrick Hyndman, Robert Keating, Robert Laliberté, Jean-Claude Lauzon, Patrick Muzzi, John Parisella, Frédéric Tremblay, and Marc-André Thivierge have all proven over the years be to committed advocates for our program. An enormous debt of professional gratitude must be extended to John Ettling, president of SUNY Plattsburgh—from the moment he stepped onto the Plattsburgh campus back in 2004 he has consistently understood and championed the mission of the Institute on Québec Studies. Thank you, John! For initially instilling in him a sharp desire and appreciation for the study of Quebec, he would like to express gratitude to two special colleagues, Louis Balthazar and Alain-G. Gagnon. The friendship and professional collegiality extended by Stéphane Paquin,

Stéphane Roussel, Cheryl Gosselin, and Frédérick Gagnon have been nothing short of outstanding. Support, encouragement, and good humour from the Institute staff and faculty—most especially Amy Sotherden, Cherice Granger, Prem Gandhi, Matthew Smith, and Linda Bouvier—have been invaluable. Finally, Donna, Mackenzie, Cameron, Caroline, and Buddy have provided more time and patience in the pursuit of all things Quebec than one should rightly ask for let alone deserve.

Jarrett would like to thank his parents, Bob and Joan Rudy, for starting his interest in Quebec. He would also like to thank a number of other families who took him into their Quebec homes and taught him more about Quebec than any boy from Ontario could have hoped to learn. Important here are the Guindons of Saint-André-Avellin, the Nadeaus of Rivière-du-Loup, and the Groleaus of Sainte-Thècle. In the academic world, he would like to thank the members of the Montreal History Group for their intellectual support and their commitment to research that has gone a long way to making Quebec history a world-class field. Finally, he thanks his wife, Cynthia, for her love and patience.

This second edition of *Quebec Questions*, we believe, embodies the passion, commitment, and wide range of meaningful, interdisciplinary scholarship on Quebec that our late colleague Martin Lubin so thoroughly embodied. During a prolific career that spanned more than 40 years, Marty was a singular voice in the North American academic community, constantly encouraging instruction, research, and professional development by students and colleagues alike on questions that always informed our understanding and deepened our knowledge about Quebec. As co-editors of this volume, we remain guided by and grateful for his insights and deep personal affection for Quebec.

Contributors

Stéphan Gervais is the scientific coordinator at Quebec Studies and at the Centre for Interdisciplinary Research on Montreal (CIRM) at McGill University. His research interests include ethnocultural diversity, citizenship, and language issues in Canada. He is a founding member of *Globe : Revue internationale d'études québécoises*, and with Alain Beaulieu and Martin Papillon he recently edited the book *Les Autochtones et le Québec* (Presses de l'Université de Montréal, 2013). He is currently working on a book project on interdisciplinary perspectives on belonging and diversity in Quebec.

Christopher Kirkey is Director of the Center for the Study of Canada and Institute on Québec Studies at the State University of New York College at Plattsburgh, where he holds a concurrent position as full professor of political science. Previous academic and professional appointments include Adjunct Associate Professor at the School of International and Public Affairs at Columbia University (2001–3), Associate Professor of Political Science/Canadian Studies at Bridgewater State University (1993–2002), and Mine Action Scholar-in-Residence at the Canadian Department of Foreign Affairs and International Trade (1999–2002). A scholar of comparative foreign policy and international relations theory, his recent works include the co-edited Winter 2015 special issue on Quebec (with Cheryl Gosselin) of the *Journal of Eastern Townships Studies* (vol. 43); the co-edited special issue (with Michael Hawes) "CONNECT/Fulbright Canada—New Scholars Issue," of the *American Review of Canadian Studies* (vol. 44, no. 3, September 2014), the co-edited John W. Holmes issue (with Kenneth Holland), "Canada in Afghanistan," of *International Journal*; the co-edited Winter 2013 special issue (with Stéphan Gervais and Jarrett Rudy) of *Québec Studies*; the co-edited special issue (with Michael Hawes), "Canada in a Unipolar World? New Directions in Canadian Foreign Policy," of *Canadian Foreign Policy Journal* (vol. 18, no. 1, 2012), and the co-edited special issue (with André Senecal), "CONNECT—New Voices on Canada," of the *American Review of Canadian Studies* (vol. 42, no. 2, June 2012). He is currently working on several projects, including a book volume (co-edited with Michael Hawes) on *Canadian Foreign Policy in a Unipolar World* (Oxford University Press); co-editor (with Michael Hawes and Kenneth Holland) of upcoming special issues of *Canadian Foreign Policy Journal* and the *American Review of Canadian Studies*; and a co-edited special issue (with Tony McCulloch) of the *British Journal of Canadian Studies*. Dr. Kirkey serves on the editorial board of the *American Review of Canadian Studies, Québec Studies*, the *International Journal of Canadian Studies*, and is a member of the Fulbright National Student Screening Committee and the Fulbright Scholar Program on Canada for Research Chairs.

Jarrett Rudy is an associate professor in the Department of History and Classical Studies at McGill University. He teaches and researches nineteenth- and twentieth-century Quebec and Canadian social and cultural history. He is the author of *The Freedom to Smoke: Tobacco Consumption and Identity* (McGill-Queen's University Press, 2005) as well as articles in the *Journal of the Canadian Historical Association, Histoire sociale/Social History, Revue d'histoire de l'Amérique française, Globe : Revue internationale d'études québécoise,* and the *Canadian Historical Review*. He co-edits, with Magda Fahrni, the McGill-Queen's University Press series *Studies in the History of Quebec*, and is a member of the Montreal History Group. Currently he is writing a history of time telling in nineteenth- and twentieth-century Quebec.

Brett Rushforth is Kohlhagen Distinguished Associate Professor of history at the College of William and Mary. He is the author of *Bonds of Alliance: Indigenous and Atlantic Slaveries in New France* (University of North Carolina Press, 2012), and he is co-author, with Christopher Hodson, of *Discovering Empire: France and the Atlantic World* *from the Crusades to the Age of Revolution* (forthcoming from Oxford University Press).

Donald Fyson is a professor in the Département des sciences historiques at Université Laval and a specialist in eighteenth-, nineteenth-, and twentieth-century Quebec history. His current research projects include families and the law in Quebec, 1840–1920; penal justice in Quebec City, 1760–1965; capital punishment and imprisonment in Quebec, 1760–1960; and the legal and social effects of the British Conquest on Quebec.

Brian Young is an Emeritus Professor of History at McGill University. He is the author of many works on Quebec history, including *A Short History of Quebec* with John Dickinson. His most recent book is *Patrician Families and the Making of Quebec: The Taschereaus and the McCords* (McGill-Queen's University Press, 2014).

Micheline Milot is a professor in the Department of Sociology at the Université du Québec à Montréal (UQAM). She is the author of several works on religious pluralism and secularism.

Jocelyn Maclure is a professor in the Faculty of Philosophy at Université Laval, where he teaches ethics and political philosophy. His current work focuses on secularism and multiculturalism. He published, with Charles Taylor, *Laïcité et liberté de conscience* (Boréal, 2010) and *Quebec Identity: The Challenge of Pluralism* (McGill-Queen's University Press, 2003). He worked as an analyst and expert writer for the Bouchard–Taylor Commission on Accommodation Practices Related to Cultural Differences in 2007–8.

François Boucher is a postdoctoral research fellow at the Université de Montréal's Centre de recherche en éthique, where he also teaches legal and political philosophy. His current research focuses on multiculturalism and especially on religious diversity and political secularism. He completed his Ph.D. at Queen's University. His Ph.D. dissertation, "Open Secularism and the New Religious Pluralism," develops a liberal conception of secularism, drawing on Quebec's experience. He has recently published articles in *Criminal Law and Philosophy, Philosophy and Public Issues*, and *Revue Philosophique de Louvain.*

Yvan Lamonde is an Emeritus Professor of Literature and History at McGill University. Author of many works on Quebec intellectual history, including two volumes entitled *Histoire sociale des idées au Québec (1760–1919)* and two volumes entitled *La modernité au Québec (1919–1965)*, he was also the co-editor of *History of the Book in Canada.*

Germain Lacasse is an associate professor in the Department of Art History and Film Studies at the Université de Montréal. Specialist in the early years of cinema and on cinema production in Quebec, he has also been exploring the links between film and orality (he is part of a research team on the same topic). He has published extensively on these topics. Among his most recent publications are *Le bonimenteur de vues animées : Le cinéma muet entre tradition et nouveauté* (Nota bene, 2000) and *Le diable en ville : Alexandre Silvio et l'émergence de la modernité populaire à Montréal* (Presses de l'Université Montréal, 2012).

Andrew C. Holman is professor of History and Director of the Canadian Studies Program at Bridgewater State University in Massachusetts. He researches and writes on a variety of topics on the history of Canada, Quebec, and the United States, including the history of sport. He is author of several scholarly articles on the history of hockey and is editor of *Canada's Game: Hockey and Identity* (McGill-Queen's University Press, 2009).

Dominic Hardy is professor of the history and historiography of Quebec and Canadian art before 1900 at the Université du Québec à Montréal (UQAM). A specialist in Quebec and international caricature and graphic satire, he is the director of the Équipe de recherche en histoire de l'art and the Laboratoire numérique d'études sur l'histoire de l'art du Québec, both based at UQAM.

Chantal Bouchard is a linguist who teaches out of the French Language and Literature Department at

McGill University. She is the author of a book on the sociolinguistic history of Quebec (*Obsessed with Language*, Guernica, 2008) and she has also published a book on the linguistic changes of French during the revolutionary period and their consequences on the status of Quebec French: *Méchante langue : la légitimité linguistique du français parlé au Québec* (Presses de l'Université de Montréal, 2011).

Linda Cardinal is a professor in the School of Political Studies at the University of Ottawa and holder of the Research Chair on la Francophonie and Public Policy. Author of many publications on language, politics, linguistic minorities, and citizenship debates, she has recently co-edited two books: *State Traditions and Language Regimes* (McGill-Queen's University Press, 2015) and *Gouvernance communautaire et innovation au sein de la francophonie néobrunswickoise et ontarienne* (PUL, 2015).

Daniel Weinstock is the James McGill Professor in the Faculty of Law at McGill University where he is also the director of the Institute for Health and Social Policy. He has published many articles on a range of issues surrounding the normative foundations of public policy in a variety of domains, including language, education and childhood, and health.

Christopher M. Jones is a professor of French and Francophone Studies at Carnegie Mellon University. He has published regularly on Quebec popular music since 2000.

Denyse Baillargeon is a full professor of History at the Université de Montréal. Author of *Babies for the Nations: The Medicalization of Motherhood in Québec, 1910–1970* (Wilfrid Laurier University Press, 2009) and *A Brief History of Women in Quebec* (Wilfrid Laurier University Press, 2014), she is currently working on a study of the fundraising drives of the Hôpital Sainte-Justine, a pediatrics hospital in Montreal, between 1929 and 1970.

Raffaele Iacovino is an associate professor in the Department of Political Science at Carleton University. His research interests include Canadian and Quebec politics, federalism, citizenship and immigration, and citizenship education. He has co-authored, with Alain-G. Gagnon, *Federalism, Citizenship and Quebec: Debating Multinationalism* (University of Toronto Press, 2007).

Maryse Potvin is a political scientist, sociologist, and full professor of Education at the Université du Québec à Montréal. She is the head of the Observatoire sur la formation à la diversité et l'équité at UQAM and is in charge of the research axis on education and ethnic relations at the Centre d'études ethniques des universités montréalaises (CEETUM). She has published a number of books, including (with M. McAndrew and C. Borri-Anadon) *Le développement d'institutions inclusives en contexte de diversité : recherche, formation, partenariat* (Presses de l'Université du Québec, 2013) and *Crise des accommodements raisonnables : une fiction médiatique?* (Athéna, 2008). She has also published many book chapters, articles in scientific journals, and expert reports for, among others, the European Commission, the Bouchard–Taylor Commission, and various government departments.

Marie McAndrew is a full professor in the Department of Educational Administration and Foundations and is the chairperson of the Groupe de recherche immigration, équité, et scolarisation (GRIES) at the Université de Montréal. Her research interests include minority education, intercultural education, ethnic relations, and comparative educational policies.

Geneviève Audet is an associate professor in the Department of Administration and Foundations of Education at the University of Montreal. She holds a Ph.D. in psychopedagogy from the Université Laval and Université Paris VIII. She is also the coordinator of the Centre d'intervention pédagogique en contexte de diversité of the Commission scolaire Marguerite-Bourgeoys.

Mahsa Bakhshaei is a postdoctoral fellow with joint affiliation between McGill University (Department of Integrated Studies in Education) and University of California, Los Angeles (Graduate School of Education and Information Studies). She studies how immigrants and their children incorporate into social and educational bodies and the factors and dynamics influencing their achievement. Her research stands at the intersection of immigration studies and educational sociology, with a strong interdisciplinary scope. In her postdoctoral project, she is examining the educational achievement of South Asian-origin adolescents in Quebec and California.

Jean-François Gaudreault-DesBiens is Dean of Law and Canada Research Chair in North American and Comparative Juridical and Cultural Identities at the Université de Montréal. His scholarship focuses on federalism, fundamental freedoms, and the relations between legal traditions.

Éric Bélanger is professor in the Department of Political Science at McGill University and is a member of the Centre for the Study of Democratic Citizenship. His research interests include political parties, public opinion, voting behaviour, as well as Quebec and Canadian politics. He is the co-author, among other works, of a book on Quebec politics, *Le comportement électoral des Québécois* (Winner of the 2010 Donald Smiley Prize).

Chris Chhim is a Ph.D. candidate in the Department of Political Science at McGill University and is a member of the Centre for the Study of Democratic Citizenship. His research interests include regionalism, political parties, federalism, and Quebec politics.

Diane Lamoureux is a full professor in the Department of Political Science at Université Laval, where she teaches political philosophy. She is the author of many books and articles on the feminist movement in Quebec. Her research interests include citizenship and democracy issues in contemporary Western societies.

Peter Graefe is an associate professor in the Department of Political Science at McMaster University. His research on political economy and public policy has included work on Quebec's economic and social development policies, including policies to develop the social economy.

David Massell is a professor of History at the University of Vermont, where he teaches courses on the history of Canada, the United States, the North American environment, and North American Native peoples. He is the author of *Amassing Power: J.B. Duke and the Saguenay River, 1897–1927* (McGill-Queen's University Press, 2000). His second book, *Quebec Hydropolitics: The Peribonka Concessions of World War Two* (McGill-Queen's University Press, 2011), was shortlisted for both the Albert B. Corey Prize and the Canadian Political History Book Prize.

Antonia Maioni is professor of Political Science at McGill University and is also part of the Institute for Health and Social Policy. She has published widely in the fields of Canadian and comparative politics, with a particular focus on health and social policy.

Daniel Jutras is Dean of Law and holder of the Arnold Wainwright Chair in Civil Law at McGill University. His scholarship focuses on the distinctive aspects of Quebec's mixed legal culture, particularly in the law of contracts, civil liability, and procedure. He is currently working on a new edition of the seminal monograph on *Quebec Civil Law* originally published under the editorship of J. E. C. Brierley and R. A. Macdonald.

Martin Papillon is an associate professor in the Department of Political Science at the Université de Montréal. His work focuses on the governance of citizenship in pluralist societies. He has published analyses on modern treaties with Aboriginal peoples, the politics of Aboriginal participation in natural resources development, and on the intersection of Aboriginal and Quebec politics. He is the co-editor of *Federalism and Aboriginal Governance* (Presses de l'Université Laval) and *Les Autochtones et le Québec* (Presses de l'Université de Montréal).

Jody Neathery-Castro is an associate professor of Political Science, International Studies, and Women's and Gender Studies at the University of Nebraska-Omaha, where she teaches courses on comparative politics and gender issues. Her research interests include Quebec, French, and francophone politics and culture, with current work examining the role of culture in global trade.

Mark O. Rousseau is a professor emeritus of Sociology at the University of Nebraska-Omaha. He is the co-author of *Regionalism and Regional Devolution in Comparative Perspective* (Praeger, 1987). He has authored and co-authored numerous articles on French and Quebec political economy with recent work focused on Francophonie.

Louis Balthazar is Professor Emeritus at Laval University. He was, until 2013, co-president of the Center for US Studies, Raoul-Dandurand Chair, at the Université du Québec à Montréal. He has published extensively on US foreign policy, Canadian–American relations, Quebec nationalism, and other topics. Among his recent books are *Nouveau bilan du nationalisme au Québec* (VLB éditeur, 2013), *La politique étrangère des États-Unis : fondements, acteurs, formulations* with Charles-Philippe David and Justin Vaïsse (Presses de Sciences Po, 2008) and *Le Québec dans l'espace americain* with Alfred O. Hero, Jr. (Québec Amérique, 1999).

Michel Biron is a full professor of French and Quebec Literature at McGill University. Author of many works on Quebec literature, including *Histoire de la littérature québécoise* with François Dumont and Élisabeth Nardout-Lafarge (Boréal, 2007), he is currently working on a biography of the poet Saint-Denys Garneau (*De Saint-Denys Garneau ou le commencement perpétuel*, Boréal).

Sylvain Schryburt is an associate professor of Theatre at the University of Ottawa. Over the years he has been a member of the editorial board of *Revue Jeu* (2004–7) and editor in chief of *L'Annuaire théâtral* (2007–10). His contributions in the field of Quebec theatre history include a book (*De l'acteur vedette au théâtre de festival : Histoire des pratiques scéniques montréalaises*, Presses de l'Université de Montréal, collection "Socius") that was nominated for the Canada Prize in the Humanities (2013) and won the 2011–13 best book award from the *Société québécoise d'études théâtrales*. He is presently active in an interuniversity research group with a project called *Régimes socio-esthétiques du théâtre au Québec (1945–2015) : synthèse historique*. He is currently preparing a book that will conclude his research on the topic, entitled *Structure and Dynamics of the International Theatre Field (2000–2015)*.

General Introduction

Stéphan Gervais, Christopher Kirkey, and Jarrett Rudy

Since the 1960s the most basic question asked by Quebecers and other Canadians alike is "What does Quebec want?" This question has been central to any number of discussions about life in Quebec and in Canada. Over time and through numerous political crises, this question has transformed and many others have been added. Is Quebec distinct? What makes it distinct? Are its gender and class relations distinct? What of its political economy? What is Quebec culture, and how can this culture be protected? Is Quebec a nation? Who is included in this nation? Who supports Quebec sovereignty? What is its relationship with Canada? With the United States? What is Quebec's place on the international stage? In this era of globalization, it turns out that the issues raised by these questions have great currency elsewhere. What is the relationship between states and nations? How do we address national and cultural pluralism? What has been the impact of colonialism? In the end, it is no hyperbole to say that "Quebec questions" share much ground with debates taking place around the world.

This book brings together leading scholars from Quebec, the rest of Canada, and the United States to shed light on these and other "Quebec questions." Students should find these essays valuable for several reasons. First, the essays go beyond case studies to provide a broad overview of key issues, individuals, and events in understanding Quebec. Each contribution provides tools that allow students to expand their research on and interest in Quebec through further readings and bolded key terms. Second, as a multidisciplinary collection that spotlights research in history, sociology, literature, political science, the performing and visual arts, the law, film, and philosophy, this collection gives readers an entry into these disciplines and a sense of how different disciplines ask different questions about similar issues. With a sense of these various perspectives, students can develop a dynamic interdisciplinary approach to thinking about Quebec. And third, these chapters can provide a lens for comparative analysis as readers may see links between themes presented here and their readings and research on other places.

It is well known in the social sciences and humanities that questions are framed by the time and place of those who pose them, and there is no way we would want to hide this. Context is important. For example, two works published in 1969 by authors of different political interests both sought to explain the rising malaise in Quebec. In his classic *Quebec in Question*, Marcel Rioux argued that French Quebecers were becoming conscious of the fact that through a process of economic, political, and cultural colonization they had become a dominated ethno-class. By the late 1960s they were taking action to liberate themselves. In his anthology *French-Canadian Nationalism*, Ramsay Cook's goal was "to understand the complex minds and emotions of French Canadians as they debate the question that has been central to their entire history—*la survivance*." By explaining the central beliefs of French-Canadian nationalism, Cook also sought to provide a context for what was happening in the 1960s.[1]

Our own context in the early twenty-first century is decidedly different from that of 1969. In the aftermath of 11 September 2001, some have embraced an "us and them" world view, resulting in military engagements in Afghanistan and Iraq and questions as to whether people of Muslim and non-Judeo-Christian faiths should be able to immigrate to Western countries. Similarly, Quebecers have debated whether certain expressions of religious faith, such as wearing a hijab or kirpan, are compatible with "Quebec values." To some extent these debates have fuelled the fascination with cultural contact presented in this collection. They push us to think about the many ways in which different cultures make contact and about the resulting conflict, accommodation, assimilation, or hybridity. Questions of cultural contact highlight the dynamic nature of culture itself, casting doubt on the validity of an "us and them" perspective. They also sharpen our analysis of the power relations that have been so important to the study of Quebec since the late 1960s, as class and gender analysis came to the fore.[2] It is not surprising, then, that most of the articles here focus to some extent on contact among the diverse groups of people who have lived in Quebec.

The questions we ask here are also influenced by when we were born. As academics born in the 1960s and 1970s, we were not actors in the Quiet Revolution that culturally, economically, and politically transformed Quebec and which is discussed in many of the articles in this collection. We came of age following the Charter of the French Language (1977). For both the anglophone and francophone editors of this volume (the anglophones born in Ontario), the common public language in Quebec is French—indeed, it is the language of the majority. At the same time, Quebec is also home to people of diverse ethnic backgrounds and identities. For most of our adult lives there has been something close to peace between Quebec's linguistic communities. This does not mean there have been no conflicts. Nor does it mean that French will remain a vibrant language without a certain amount of vigilance. What it does mean is that concerns about the future of the French language are somewhat different than in 1969, when Rioux and Cook were writing.

Belonging to a post–Bill 101 generation has also affected how we answer the question "Who is a Quebecer?" For much of our adult lives, a significant part of the Quebec population has viewed the term *Quebecer* as referring to all people living in Quebec who choose to identify themselves as such. We share this view of an inclusive and civic national identity, although we are not seeking to imperialistically declare that everyone who has ever lived in what is Quebec today is a Quebecer.

Most of this volume focuses on the period following the creation of the Province of Quebec by British Royal Proclamation in 1763. There are several excellent surveys of Quebec history from pre-contact Indigenous peoples until today that should be read alongside this collection.[3] In terms of geography, *Quebec Questions: Quebec Studies in the Twenty-first Century* centres on the territory of the modern province of Quebec, though some articles explore Quebec's cultural, political, and economic relations with the broader international community.

We believe that *Quebec Questions* will prove useful to many around the world who look to study, teach, and conduct research on Quebec. Since at least the late 1970s, Quebec has increasingly become an object of study and a dedicated part of curricula in educational institutions far from its borders.[4] Interest was first fed through Canadian studies centres and especially French language and literature departments. It was further promoted though the establishment of the American Council for Québec Studies, the institutional and financial support of the Ministère des Relations internationales et de la Francophonie (Quebec Ministry of International Relations and La Francophonie), the foundation of the Association internationale des études québécoises (International Association for Quebec Studies),[5] and the increased emphasis recently given to Quebec by the Association for Canadian Studies in the United States.[6]

With established and growing interest in Quebec as a field of multidisciplinary (and increasingly interdisciplinary) study, we realized that an appropriate English-language text for students, teachers, and researchers featuring a comprehensive overview of Quebec simply did not exist.[7] Current English-language introductions to Quebec are grounded in distinct political science or historical perspectives; the most important include *Québec State and Society* by Alain-G. Gagnon; *The Québec Democracy* by Guy Lachapelle, Gérald Bernier, Daniel Salée, and Luc Bernier; *A Short History of Quebec* by John Dickinson and Brian Young; and *An Illustrated History of*

Quebec: Tradition and Modernity by Peter Gossage and J. I. Little.[8] While there is no question that these works serve as essential course materials for professors teaching Quebec politics and history, it is clear that present-day research and teaching on Quebec studies can also be served by a multidisciplinary volume. In addition, existing multidisciplinary texts dedicated to the study of Canada or Canada–US relations do not provide a substantive review of Quebec issues.[9]

This book is the direct result of a long conversation between the Quebec Studies Program at McGill University and the Institute on Québec Studies at SUNY Plattsburgh about how to address this specific need—a conversation that concluded with a joint commitment to craft a timely and comprehensive volume that, above all else, would teach Quebec studies to international, Canadian, and Quebec students. Specific discussions about this collection began when the Institute on Québec Studies convened a colloquium on 11 October 2006 called "The Future of Quebec Studies in the United States: Enriching a Vibrant Community" at the Weatherhead Center for International Affairs at Harvard University.[10] With the support of the Ministère des Relations internationales du Québec, the Government of Canada, the Association internationale des études québécoises, the Dean of Arts Development Fund at McGill University, and the Programme de soutien à la recherche en matière d'affaires intergouvernementales et d'identité québécoise, a contributors' conference was organized in Montreal in October 2008. For the conference we challenged authors to write "spirited surveys" of current research in their fields. Papers were discussed across disciplines—for example, a historian of New France was asked to comment on a paper on Quebec–US economic relations, and an art historian commented on the work of a specialist in Quebec diplomacy. In many ways, this mirrored our vision of interdisciplinary studies, where practitioners of different disciplines exchange insights on a common subject.

We have continued this interdisciplinary discussion in this second edition of *Quebec Questions*. Like the conference and the first edition, the second edition of *Quebec Questions* is organized to promote discussion across disciplines and to see readings in innovative ways. In the making of the first and second editions of *Quebec Questions*, we have been inspired by the concept of interdisciplinarity, as described by Julie Thomson Klein: "a means of solving problems and answering questions that cannot be satisfactorily addressed using single methods or approaches. Whether the context is a short-range instrumentality or a long-range reconceptualization of epistemology, the concept represents an important attempt to define and establish common ground."[11] Though somewhat reorganized, contributions are still divided into six interconnected thematic sections: memories, identities, language, citizenship, Quebec models, and Quebec international relations. These themes not only represent important current paths of research in Quebec, they also seek to provide scholars studying in other parts of the world with easy access for useful comparisons with Quebec. Each section begins with a brief introduction followed by essays. Accompanying most essays is a chronological timetable, a "Biography" of a notable person mentioned in the chapter, and a "Case Study"—an in-depth examination of a key event, all of which complement the narrative. In this second edition, readers will also discover Primary Source boxes. These primary sources provide a different perspective to the chapter. They allow readers to begin an active learning process and develop his or her own critical interpretations and deductions of issues introduced in the chapter. Each essay ends with study questions designed to promote classroom discussion, and a brief bibliography.

As a result of discussions with readers about the first edition and our own evolving interests, the second edition of *Quebec Questions* has changed in a number of ways. First, each chapter has been updated to take into consideration current events and recent scholarship. We have also added exciting chapters that deal explicitly with federalism and sovereignty. Questions around federalism and sovereignty were present in all the sections of the first edition (as in much of daily life in Quebec), but we felt they deserved their own entries. Finally, to expand the scope of this edition, we have added new contributions on sports, visual culture, and film. There are, of course, subjects that do not appear here: television and radio, new

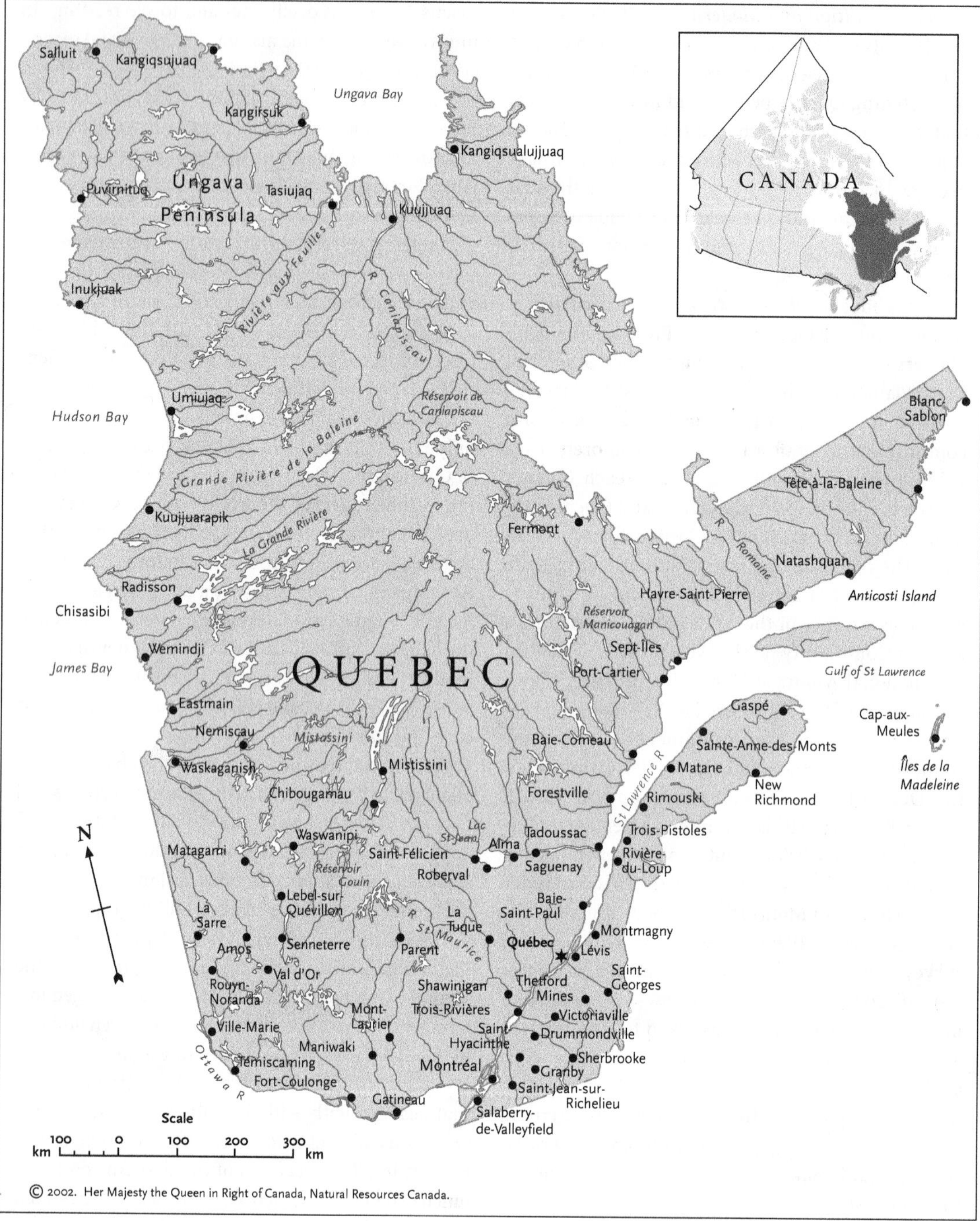
CANADA
QUEBEC
Ungava Bay
Hudson Bay
James Bay
Gulf of St Lawrence
Ungava Peninsula
Salluit
Kangiqsujuaq
Kangirsuk
Kangiqsualujjuaq
Puvirnituq
Tasiujaq
Kuujjuaq
Inukjuak
Rivière aux Feuilles
R. Caniapiscau
Umiujaq
Réservoir de Caniapiscau
Grande Rivière de la Baleine
Kuujjuarapik
La Grande Rivière
Radisson
Chisasibi
Wemindji
Eastmain
Nemiscau
Mistassini
Waskaganish
Mistissini
Chibougamau
Waswanipi
Matagami
Réservoir Gouin
Lebel-sur-Quévillon
La Sarre
Amos
Senneterre
Val d'Or
Rouyn-Noranda
Ville-Marie
Témiscaming
Fort-Coulonge
Ottawa R
Maniwaki
Mont-Laurier
Gatineau
Parent
La Tuque
St Maurice
Saint-Félicien
Lac St-Jean
Alma
Roberval
Saguenay
Tadoussac
Baie-Saint-Paul
Québec
Lévis
Montmagny
Shawinigan
Trois-Rivières
Thetford Mines
Saint-Georges
Victoriaville
Drummondville
Saint-Hyacinthe
Sherbrooke
Granby
Montréal
Saint-Jean-sur-Richelieu
Salaberry-de-Valleyfield
Fermont
Réservoir Manicouagan
Sept-Îles
Port-Cartier
Baie-Comeau
Forestville
St Lawrence R
Rivière-du-Loup
Trois-Pistoles
Rimouski
Matane
Sainte-Anne-des-Monts
Gaspé
New Richmond
Havre-Saint-Pierre
Natashquan
R. Romaine
Tête-à-la-Baleine
Blanc-Sablon
Anticosti Island
Cap-aux-Meules
Îles de la Madeleine
N
Scale
km 100 0 100 200 300 km

media, food culture, dance performance, journalism, minority cultures, and the cultural geography and historical demography of Quebec, to give but a few examples. Readers also might find that the book principally focuses on political, cultural, economic, and social elites and not enough on everyday people and how they contribute to Quebec society. As a one-volume project committed to providing contributing authors sufficient space to make substantial contributions, difficult decisions had to be made; we hope that this book can lead to further projects that bridge different parts of society.[12]

To conclude, the goal of this collection is not to launch a grand theory of Quebec society or to say "how it should be." As with the first edition, we remain committed to looking at the territory of Quebec and the population that lives there, asking a series of questions across disciplines to explore a set of themes we find useful. We trust that readers will be able to conceptually connect a variety of significant ideas and themes across disciplines. As co-editors of this project, we believe that available scholarly materials for students, professors, and researchers are key to promoting sustained curricular and research efforts in Quebec studies and thus expanding interest in Quebec. *Quebec Questions: Quebec Studies for the Twenty-first Century* is designed to serve this purpose.

Notes

1. First published in French as *La question du Quebec* (Paris: Seghers, 1969) and translated into English by James Boake (Toronto: James Lorimer, 1971); Ramsay Cook, ed., *French-Canadian Nationalism: An Anthology* (Toronto: Macmillan of Canada, 1969), 14.
2. For an impressive bibliography of this research, see John Dickinson and Brian Young, *A Short History of Quebec*, 4th ed. (Montreal and Kingston: McGill-Queen's University Press, 2008).
3. See Dickinson and Young, *A Short History of Quebec*, or Peter Gossage and J. I. Little, *An Illustrated History of Quebec: Tradition and Modernity* (Don Mills, ON: Oxford University Press, 2012).
4. See Fernand Harvey, "Le développement des études québécoises dans le monde," *Globe : Revue international d'études québécoises* 4, no. 2 (2001): 59–81.
5. The international network of academics formed by the Association internationale des études québécoises numbers close to 3,000 researchers.
6. See David Cameron, *Taking Stock: Canadian Studies in the Nineties* (Montreal: Association for Canadian Studies, 1996), and Patrick James and Mark Kasoff, eds., *Canadian Studies in the New Millennium* (Toronto: University of Toronto Press, 2008).
7. In French a number of works, published with an international audience in mind, have been published that offer a multidisciplinary introduction to Quebec civilization. See François Tétu de Labsade, *Le Québec : un pays, une culture*, 2nd ed. (Montreal: Boréal, 2000); Marcel Rioux, *Les Québécois*, 2nd ed. (Paris: Seuil, 1980); Jacques Bouchard, *Les 36 cordes sensibles des Québécois* (Montreal: Éditions Héritage, 1978); Marie-Christine Weidmann Koop, ed., *Le Québec aujourd'hui : identité, culture et société* (Sainte-Foy: Presses de l'Université Laval, 2003); and Robert Laliberté, ed., *À la rencontre d'un Québec qui bouge : introduction générale au Québec* (Paris: Comité des travaux historiques et scientifiques, 2009).
8. Alain-G. Gagnon, ed., *Québec State and Society*, 3rd ed. (Peterborough: Broadview Press, 2004); and Guy Lachapelle, Gérald Bernier, Daniel Salée, and Luc Bernier, *The Quebec Democracy: Structures, Processes & Policies* (Toronto: McGraw-Hill Ryerson, 1993). See footnote 2 for Dickinson and Young and Gossage and Little.
9. Patrick James and Mark Kasoff, eds., *Canadian Studies in the New Millennium*, 2nd ed. (Toronto: University of Toronto Press, 2013); David Taras and Beverly Rasporich, eds., *A Passion for Identity: Canadian Studies in the 21st Century*, 4th ed. (Toronto: Nelson Thomson Learning, 2001); Kenneth Pryke and Walter Soderlund, eds., *Profiles of Canada* (Toronto: Canadian Scholars' Press, 2003); and David Thomas and David N. Biette, eds., *Canada and the United States: Differences that Count*, 4th ed. (Toronto: University of Toronto Press, 2014).
10. The colloquium expressly focused on the identification and evaluation of the current state of teaching, research, publishing, and program activities on Quebec Studies in the United States.
11. Julie Klein, *Interdisciplinarity: History, Theory and Practice* (Detroit: Wayne State University Press, 1990), 196.
12. See Denise Lemieux, ed., *Traité de la culture* (Sainte-Foy: Presses de l'Université Laval, 2002), and the Quebec Government, "Observatoire de la culture et des communications," www.stat.gouv.qc.ca/observatoire/default_an.htm, to find research on these issues.

Part A
Memories

Introduction

A national past is alive in Quebec.[1] We see flashes of it in newspaper editorials, political speeches, debates about history curricula in schools, and even on Quebec licence plates, which announce *Je me souviens*—"I remember." But what is remembered? There is enormous debate about the past and "collective memory." How collective is memory? How can anyone really have a memory of events that occurred hundreds of years ago? How is collective memory produced? And what is the relationship between the production of historians and collective memory? Articles in this section implicitly and explicitly come up against these issues as they tell stories about Quebec's past.

Some authors present new interpretations based on a shift in perspectives—in a sense challenging collective memory. This is what Brett Rushforth does in his chapter on New France. While technically this chapter goes beyond the temporal boundaries of this volume, today the memory of New France profoundly shapes many Quebecers' sense of themselves, making questions about New France particularly important "Quebec questions." Rushforth presents a version of the history of New France that is innovative on at least two counts. First, he places European discovery of New France within a dynamic multinational Atlantic world where ships crossed the ocean far more frequently than previously thought and France's colonial eye went far beyond the St Lawrence Valley. Second, he evokes the work of a growing number of historians who have shown that Native peoples, for their own reasons, played a decisive role in France's imperial venture in North America. When the fate of the colony rides on the military force of Native allies—to the point that French laws did not apply to Natives and the Crown underwrote losses of French merchants to maintain positive economic relations with their Native allies—one has to think about the character of empire and how it was affected by local contexts. And, one might ask, how does seeing the Native and Atlantic contexts of New France relate to today's "collective memory"?

The second article in this section is more explicit about the impact of public memory on social and political relations today. Donald Fyson shows that numerous views about the impact of British Conquest on *les Canadiens* are front and centre in political debates today. Yet he also shows that in this case the relationship between the past (as historians understand it) and collective memory is tenuous at best. For example, professional historians no longer see the Conquest as a decapitation of the social structure of New France or as an event that brought enlightenment through the benevolence of the British Crown. Instead, their assessments are far more ambivalent and nuanced, as Fyson's article shows by looking at key areas of Canadiens' activity in the economy and their interaction with the new colonial state. Few historians, however, have given renewed attention to the immediate post-Conquest period, and the decapitation thesis dominates popular understandings of the Conquest in Quebec despite the findings of important published studies, including Fyson's own.[2]

There was no golden age when the past was not used to take political positions. In Brian Young's article on power relations in the period between the Lower Canadian Rebellions (1837–8) and Canadian Confederation (1867), Young finds uses of the past in numerous areas of power relations—from francophone–anglophone relations to the social relations of religion to gender relations. In the realm of politics, the claim of Lord Durham (whose report to the British Crown was supposed to explain and provide solutions to the problems that brought about the Rebellions) that French Canadians were a people without history still infuriates Quebecers today. In religion, it is hard to think of a more striking way of calling on the population to maintain Catholic tradition than through using the "old bones" of Bishop Laval, as Archbishop Elzéar-Alexandre Taschereau did in 1878. And patriarchy can be reinforced by calling on women to live up to the example set by the Virgin Mary. Yet Young's article demonstrates that memory is not the only way in which the past is active in today's political world. The past is part of our present through political structures, systems of land tenure, and the law. And ultimately power in Quebec, Young argues, has always been about more than the cultural clash of the national question—it is also about transforming class and ethnic relations and gender inequalities.

In recent years, few contemporary political debates have taken place so deeply in the shadow of the past as debates over the relationship between religion and the Canadian and Quebec states. Indeed, during the debates over reasonable accommodation and the Charter of Quebec Values, a Quebec past where the Roman Catholic hierarchy dominated the French-Canadian population was frequently evoked. Sociologist Micheline Milot's article looks at the long process by which Quebec and Canada stopped giving special rights to members of particular religious groups, a process she defines as "laicization." She argues that Quebec followed a timeline very similar (except in education) to that of other Canadian and American jurisdictions. Arriving earlier than elsewhere in the British Empire, the model of laicization in Quebec is rooted in the British domination of French Canada and colonial efforts to co-opt French-Canadian loyalty. Implicit and explicit freedom of religion and equality of worship rights were keystones that necessitated a neutral state, but not secular inhabitants.

In the last 30 years, this model of freedom and equality has been enshrined in human rights legislation, though during debates over reasonable accommodation and the Charter of Quebec Values some have attempted to push Quebec away from this long tradition. For these critics, the past is particularly important. Political philosophers Jocelyn Maclure and François Boucher call these critics "romantic conservatives" in their chapter on Quebec's "culture wars," and when Romantic Conservatives analyze the transition evoked by the Quiet Revolution from French-Canadian identity to Québécois identity, they see it as a story of loss. According to romantic conservatives, opposition to so-called reasonable accommodation and support for the Charter of Quebec Values were evidence of a "silent majority" taking a stand against enduring attacks on French-Canadian identity. Maclure and Boucher, however, see Quebec's current culture wars differently and take romantic conservatives to task for their belief in a silent majority. Rather than focusing on the return of the silent majority or a debate between ethnic and civic nationalism, they situate Quebec's culture wars as part of a discussion about pluralism and the place of religion within society. Maclure and Boucher show that groups who opposed reasonable accommodation and supported the Charter of Quebec Values were "strange bedfellows" that were not united by a homogeneous political philosophy. They also take romantic conservatives to task for their normative use of the past, a practice that, as we see in this section, has a long history in Quebec.

Notes

1. Recently, much fascinating research has pushed the study of memory in Quebec beyond "national" questions. See Steven High, Edward Little, and Thi Ry Duong, eds., *Remembering Mass Violence: Oral History, New Media and Performance* (Toronto: University of Toronto Press, 2014), and Steven High, *Oral History at the Crossroads: Sharing Life Stories of Survival and Displacement* (Vancouver: UBC Press, 2014). Notable "national" studies on memory in Quebec include Jacques Mathieu, ed., *La mémoire dans la culture* (Sainte-Foy: Presses de l'Université Laval, 1995); Patrice Groulx, *Pièges de la mémoire : Dollard des Ormeaux, les Amérindiens et nous* (Hull: Vents d'Ouest, 1998); and Colin Coates and Cecelia Morgan, *Heroines and History: Representations of Madeleine de Verchères and Laura Secord* (Toronto: University of Toronto Press, 2002). For a sociologist who asserts the importance of memory to the national project, see Jacques Beauchemin, *L'Histoire en trop : la mauvaise conscience des souverainistes québécois* (Montreal: VLB éditeur, 2002), and for an opposing view see Jocelyn Létourneau, *A History for the Future: Rewriting Memory and Identity in Quebec*, trans. Phyllis Aronoff and Howard Scott (Montreal and Kingston: McGill-Queen's University Press, 2004).
2. For a recent book on how young Quebecers understand Quebec's past, see Jocelyn Létourneau, *Je me souviens? Le passé du Québec dans la conscience de sa jeunesse* (Anjou, QC: Fides, 2014).

1 The Establishment of a French Empire in North America

Brett Rushforth, College of William & Mary

Timeline

1440s–80s Portuguese, French, and Italian explorations of eastern Atlantic.

1490s Columbus "discovers" Americas; cod fishing begins near Newfoundland.

1504 French reach Brazil and begin dyewood trade.

1524 Giovanni da Verrazzano explores the North American coast for François I.

1534–42 Jacques Cartier explores the St Lawrence Valley.

1555–65 Abortive French attempts to settle in Brazil and Florida.

1604 France establishes its first North American settlement at Port Royal.

1608 Champlain establishes Quebec.

1609–15 Champlain leads French-Native assaults against Iroquois.

1626–35 First French-Caribbean colonies settled at St Christophe, Martinique, and Guadeloupe.

1629–32 Quebec is taken over by British privateers and recovered by France.

1642 Jeanne Mance and Paul de Chomedey de Maisonneuve establish Montreal.

1649–66 Iroquois Wars—most Hurons are killed, captured, or scattered.

1663 Royal takeover of New France and Caribbean colonies.

1670s–80s French establish trade and mission posts in the Great Lakes region and the Mississippi Valley.

1689–1713 Imperial wars fought in North America; ending with Treaty of Utrecht.

1701 Great Peace of Montreal—treaty council confirming Iroquois neutrality.

1710s–40s Mesquakie (Fox) and Chickasaw Wars; Native slave trade expands.

1751 The Marquis de la Galissonière argues for Canada's continued importance to France.

1752 French-Odawa raid on Pickawillany begins an armed struggle for the Ohio Valley.

1754–63 France, Britain, and Spain battle around the globe in the Seven Years' War.

1755 France's native allies defeat General Braddock in the Battle of the Monongahela.

1759 Battle of the Plains of Abraham results in the surrender of Quebec.

1760 Montreal surrenders, completing the British victory in North America.

1763 Treaty of Paris confirms British control of Canada; French reclaim key Caribbean holdings.

Introduction

As part of a complex and competitive North American continent, Quebec is connected to Europe, Africa, the Caribbean, and Latin America by commerce, migration, cultural exchange, and shared environmental challenges. Far from new, these connections date to the first decades of exploration and settlement that initiated a French presence in North America. French settlers came to Quebec not to create an independent French outpost, but to establish one of many links in a trans-Atlantic network of settlements tied to an expanding global economy. Tracing these complex and cosmopolitan beginnings will help us understand Quebec's place in the global twenty-first century. But we must also remember the importance of Quebec's Native peoples to its history. Native peoples were both the lifeblood of New France's economy and the heart of its military defence, giving essential protection that allowed the colony to survive a century of colonial wars. Without their willing trade and military alliance there could have been no French presence in North America, and there would be no Quebec today. The households of Montreal and Quebec were also served by thousands of Native slaves, whose domestic and commercial labour subsidized the merchant community and propped up the status of town elites. Whether through labour, trade, diplomacy, or warfare, then, Native peoples helped lay the foundations of Quebec society. From the first voyages of exploration in the 1530s to the imperial warfare that gave Britain control of the region in 1763, Quebec was intimately tied to developments throughout Native North America and the Atlantic world.

Encounters and Discoveries

The earliest French activities in the Atlantic, like the colonialism that would follow, were part of a wider pattern of European expansion involving collaboration among investors, mariners, cartographers, and monarchs in most of Western Europe. French efforts to profit from New World discoveries, motivated by international competition, paradoxically relied on international connections for their success. In the fifteenth and sixteenth centuries it was difficult to disentangle the activities of one kingdom from those of another, not least because most Atlantic activity was private rather than state sponsored. Nearly a century before Columbus crossed the Atlantic, French mariners worked with Iberian partners to explore the eastern Atlantic, the first step in an incremental expansion that resulted in American discovery. In 1402, for example, a Norman captain, Jean de Béthencourt, worked alongside Portuguese mariners to map and conquer the Canary Islands, which were rich in dyes, fish, and enslavable labour. Rather than claiming the islands for the king of France, Béthencourt established his own fiefdom there, drawing heavy taxes from European settlers and merchants who profited from his conquest. Successes such as this inspired investors to take incremental risks, little by little venturing further into the Atlantic in search of new places and peoples. From the 1430s through the 1480s, Portuguese investors—famously including Prince Henry, "the Navigator"—sponsored the lion's share of these voyages, but French sailors and ships continued to play an important role even in ventures thought to be Portuguese or Spanish. Trading gold, bullock hides, ivory, and slaves between northwestern Africa and Europe, these voyages brought handsome returns to investors seeking Atlantic fortunes. Only by building on these more proximate successes could Christopher Columbus set a bolder course across the Atlantic. Columbus's accidental "discovery" of the Americas in 1492, followed by the more northerly explorations of John Cabot in 1497, set off a flurry of activity that shifted many French ships from African to trans-Atlantic trade.

News of Columbus's discovery spread rapidly in France, especially in port cities already linked to Iberian maritime activities. These connections immediately and extensively involved the French in New World commerce. Within a decade of Columbus's return to Europe, dozens of French ships—often with multinational crews—had sailed for the Americas. Extracting rich dyewoods from Brazilian forests, mostly with indigenous labour, French investors established a foothold in South America no later than 1504, alternately co-operating and competing with the Portuguese, who claimed Brazil as their exclusive territory. Norman craftsmen—such as the famous cloth makers of Rouen—used these new dyes to create highly desirable fabrics that were in demand by mid-century throughout Europe, Africa, and the Americas.

Although far less glamorous than Spanish gold or silver, the most profitable New World commodity in the first half of the sixteenth century was cod, which teemed in vast quantities off the coasts of Newfoundland. Often imagined as an English enterprise controlled by Bristol merchants, French ships actually dominated the industry in the sixteenth century, outnumbering English vessels at least three to one. After mid-century as many as 500 French ships sailed annually for the fisheries, returning with millions of pounds of dried fish that stocked French larders and stimulated the production of French merchandise. As in Brazil, Newfoundland fishing crews rarely had a single national identity: Basques, Italians, Portuguese, Azoreans, Normans, and Englishmen sailed, worked, lived, and died together.

The Spanish discovery of gold on the island of Hispaniola and their subsequent conquest of the Aztec and Incan empires brought fame and wealth to conquistador and crown alike, overshadowing earlier French activities and inspiring new ones. Envious of Spain's success—and fearful of the power a rival kingdom could derive from American wealth—the French Crown began to take an interest in the Americas, which had until the 1520s been largely left to private initiative. Only two years after learning of Spain's 1521 conquest of the gold-rich Aztec capital of Tenochtitlan, King François I commissioned an Italian mariner, Giovanni da Verrazzano, to explore the coast of North America. Hoping to find either a **Northwest Passage** through the Americas to Asia or another wealthy Native empire, Verrazzano found neither. Returning with a fairly detailed map of the North American coast and a description of coastal Native peoples, Verrazzano's voyage was only a limited success. A decade later, in 1534, Jacques Cartier obtained a similar commission, charged first with finding a passage to Asia and second with finding sources of wealth along the way. Cartier had much experience in American navigation. He had personally shipped fish from Newfoundland and dyewoods from Brazil, and he had good relationships with Basque, Spanish, Portuguese, and English sailors who had frequented the mouth of the Bay of St Lawrence since the 1490s. Cartier even kept a Brazilian Native girl, whom he had bought or kidnapped on an earlier dyewood expedition, at his home in St Malo.

Cartier's international experience qualified him to sail Atlantic waters and explore the lands west of Newfoundland, but he was ill-prepared for the complex cultural currents he would navigate through the indigenous world he encountered in North America. Like Europeans, Natives had their own political, military, and cultural structures that would shape French colonialism as much as those of the Old World. Cartier established a pattern of French–Native relations that would characterize the history of New France for more than two centuries. He first ignored Native peoples, then attempted to dominate them by force. Realizing that neither of these approaches could yield the results he needed, he settled on a policy of grudging co-operation that allowed Natives as much as the French to dictate the terms of their relationship.

Cartier and his contemporaries were initially quite dismissive of Native culture and accomplishments, calling Labrador "the land God gave to Cain" and its indigenous inhabitants "the sorriest folk . . . in the world."[1] Seeking passage through—rather than to—America, Cartier pried for geographical information about the hoped-for water route across the continent to the Pacific. When such information failed to materialize, he moved on. Frustrated by his inability to find a passage to Asia, Cartier turned to violence. Stopping to glean information from the people of Stadacona, near modern-day Quebec City, Cartier found them eager to trade. He was not interested. After a brief, tense exchange with their chief, Donnacona, Cartier seized the chief and his sons, threatening to kill anyone who tried to free them. Releasing the father, Cartier returned to France with the sons as proof of his explorations and as possible sources of information and leverage. But Cartier's original commission could not be achieved by random acts of violence, so he returned with his captives to the St Lawrence a year later, hoping that he could persuade their father to help him in exchange for their release. Naturally wary of the treacherous foreigners, Donnacona nevertheless accepted his sons' return and provided more information to Cartier. Heading farther up the St Lawrence, Cartier encountered the village of Hochelaga, on the island of modern Montreal, where he found a thriving village surrounded by vast corn fields. At Hochelaga, Cartier portrayed himself as the Natives' saviour ("one would have thought Christ had come down to earth to heal them"),[2] but in reality Natives often saved him and his crew from disaster, providing them with food, essential geographical information, and especially a life-saving herbal remedy for a scurvy outbreak that nearly killed all of Cartier's men.

French reaction to Cartier's discoveries was mixed, but by 1541 the French Crown sponsored a scheme to settle the St Lawrence Valley. Led by Cartier and his newly appointed superior, Jean-François de la Rocque de Roberval, the first French settlement in the St Lawrence was a short-lived failure. As they entered the Bay of St Lawrence they passed 13 ships: five Spanish, seven Portuguese, and one English. Cartier may have asserted exclusive right to the bay and the lands along the river that flowed into it, but his crew and the others he encountered there reflected the multinational nature of early Quebec exploration. Finding no diamonds, gold, or spices, the colony had to rely on trade with their Native neighbours, who were reluctant to welcome this settlement by people who had bullied and enslaved their kin. Within two years the enterprise folded and its few survivors returned to France. In the absence of precious minerals or easy routes to Asia, Cartier's successors instead tapped into the indigenous world of trade, providing France with valuable furs and skins that were in high demand in over-hunted Europe. Rather than dismissing or dominating Native peoples, the French could succeed only if they adapted to indigenous demands. Algonquians and Iroquoians would therefore play a prominent role in establishing permanent French settlement. Although it ended in short-term failure, what began as a mission to bypass North America sowed the seeds of French colonization that would grow in the seventeenth century.

In the second half of the sixteenth century French attention returned to the Newfoundland fisheries and Brazilian forests. In 1555, a French settlement near Rio de Janeiro on Brazil's Atlantic coast lasted only a few years before Portuguese competitors overcame a colony internally divided by religious conflict. Refugees from the Brazil experiment tried again in Florida, establishing two settlements to challenge the Spanish claim to North America's eastern seaboard. In 1565 the Spanish brutally crushed their French rivals in a one-sided campaign that left France with no permanent settlements in the Americas at the very time that Iberian New World expansion was reaching full stride. Spain found vast wealth in gold and especially silver, while Portugal's Brazilian settlers expanded the dyewood trade and built massive sugar plantations worked by both Native and African slaves. French involvement in the Americas continued for the final third of the sixteenth century in many uncoordinated but significant private ventures intent on extracting American resources. French port cities developed thriving industries associated with the New World, despite the absence of official or permanent French settlements there. These commercial connections, together with the geographical and nautical knowledge that made overseas commerce possible, created networks that would prove essential to

France's seventeenth-century expansion throughout the Atlantic world.

Creating New Societies

At the beginning of the seventeenth century, France—like England—took renewed interest in North America as a land of vast resources and a strategic site to harass their Spanish rivals. Unable to gain a foothold in Florida or other southern locations, France built on its long-standing presence in the St Lawrence Valley, exploring and eventually settling there at the same time the English were establishing their first permanent North American colony at Jamestown in Virginia. Both projects drew inspiration from the work of Richard Hakluyt, an English promoter of American colonization who spent significant time in France. American settlements, he wrote in the late sixteenth century, "will yelde unto us all the commodities of Europe, Affrica, and Asia, as farr as wee were wonte to travel, and supply the wants of all our decayed trades." Significantly, it would also "be a great bridle to the Indies of the Kinge of Spaine."[3] Hakluyt's time in France had convinced many that for all their differences, the two kingdoms shared these goals: grasping overseas riches and reining in their Spanish competitor.

The most important architect of France's seventeenth-century colonization in North America was Samuel de Champlain, a skilled cartographer whose account of a 1603 visit to Canada sparked a passion for exploring and settling the region. Characteristic of France's New World projects, Champlain's first interest in the Americas centred on the tropics, and his first voyage to the New World took him to the Caribbean and Mexico rather than to Canada. Acting in part the curious scholar and in part an unofficial spy against Spain, Champlain gleaned both experience and knowledge that laid the groundwork for his Canadian endeavours. Many other Frenchmen trolled Caribbean waters at the beginning of the seventeenth century, most of whom were pirates harassing Spanish ships sailing from Mexico and Panama. The island of Hispaniola (later to become Haiti and the Dominican Republic) was home to perhaps hundreds of French, English, and Dutch pirates, a population that would grow into a powerful force by the later seventeenth century.

Champlain's Caribbean voyage signalled the centrality of Spanish competition in French colonial beginnings, and his vision for Canada retained much of that character. Between 1603 and 1607 Champlain travelled three times to the St Lawrence Valley, gathering important information about the lands and peoples of the region and circulating his findings in accounts and maps, both published and unpublished. Champlain improved upon the sixteenth-century charts from Cartier's time, and he mapped islands and coastlines in modern Quebec and New England. But perhaps his most startling reports detailed a remarkable demographic shift over the past half century. Although the French presence in the St Lawrence Valley during the 1500s was limited and generally seasonal, it had profoundly affected the region's Native peoples. Between Cartier's departure in the 1540s and Champlain's arrival in the early 1600s, the Iroquoian people of Stadacona, Hochelaga, and other riverside villages had all but disappeared. Although little evidence survives to tell us why, the most likely explanation is a combination of disease brought by the Europeans and warfare sparked by competition for lucrative trade downriver. Whatever the cause, this depopulation opened opportunities for other Native peoples—the Montagnais, Algonquin, and Huron—to engage in French trade and to seek French alliances. During the 1580s and 1590s, as these groups solidified their trade relationship with the French, they also formed military partnerships. In the indigenous cultures of the northeastern woodlands, trade and alliance were inseparable. The friendship and trust that facilitated the exchange of goods also obliged mutual military protection in the face of common enemies. By 1600, French traders had established agreements with Montagnais, Algonquin, and Huron traders that, in exchange for furs, the French would give not only trade goods but also military assistance against their most feared enemies: the **Iroquois nations** south of the St Lawrence in modern New York. Attracted by trade, French adventurers were thus drawn into Native geopolitics. Indigenous commerce and alliance would dominate the colonial world of the seventeenth century.

In 1608, Champlain established a permanent settlement at Quebec from which he could trade with Native peoples and search for a passage to Asia. His original plans were fantastic, promising the French king massive revenue from a wide range of sources. In addition to millions of livres from eels, sturgeon, salmon, cow hides, and timber, the most dramatic revenue would come from levying customs duties on ships that sailed the St Lawrence to and from China, "which would surpass in value at least ten times all those levied in France, inasmuch as all the merchants of Christendom would pass through the passage."[4] The colony would also serve as an outpost in a great commercial war being waged by English and Flemish merchants, whose North American presence threatened to shut down France's very real profits from the cod and whale industries.

As for the country's Native peoples, Champlain's proposals ranged from paternalistic toleration of his Algonquian and Huron allies to unrestrained violence against his Iroquois enemies—a strategic rather than a moral distinction, as he believed that they all lived "like brute beasts" more than men, and that they were "given to revenge, and are great liars."[5] Attacking the Iroquois in 1609, 1610, and 1615, Champlain introduced a newly destructive form of warfare to a conflict that had remained in relative equilibrium throughout the known past: French, and then Dutch, guns and metal weapons rendered warfare more deadly and started the first American arms race.

As the decades wore on, Champlain found neither a passage to China nor vast wealth in eels, leaving him by the late 1620s in charge of a faltering settlement inhabited by fewer than 80 French colonists. Recognizing the settlement's weakness, and asserting older English claims to the St Lawrence based on their presence at the fisheries, a group of privateers took over Quebec in 1629 when Champlain surrendered without a fight. After three years of negotiations, France regained control of the settlement in 1632 with a mere 43 inhabitants. Bolstered by Champlain's arrival with supplies and settlers the following year, Quebec was still only a small collection of scattered buildings and just over a hundred French settlers when Champlain died there in 1635.

The fur trade provided an economic base for French expansion, growing steadily over the next generation. At the heart of the fur trade, of course, were the Huron, Montagnais, Algonquin, and other Native peoples who supplied the furs in exchange for European manufactured goods. Building on patterns of trade established in the 1500s, these peoples brought thousands of beaver pelts and many other animal skins to Quebec every year. The European goods they desired fit well within their own value systems, with the highest demand for practical items like wool cloth, metal cutting edges, and metal tips for arrows used for hunting as much as for war. But there was no denying the wartime advantage of iron weapons and guns, both of which remained in high demand in the face of Iroquois aggression.

Although undertaken for commercial profit, the colony at Quebec also had a religious purpose, supporters of which helped to fund the colony when commerce fell short. Although the **Jesuits** receive the most attention, many of the most influential religious figures in early New France were women. Two influential women arrived shortly after Champlain's death. The first, Marie Guyart (better known as Marie de l'Incarnation), arrived in 1639 following mystical visions of bringing Native children to Christ. She established a boarding school for French and Native girls, organized public relief efforts, and interacted intensively with her Native students' families. She learned to speak Algonquian and Iroquoian dialects and anticipated later Jesuit efforts by translating religious materials into both languages. Jeanne Mance, also moved by dreams of heavenly glory, arrived in New France in 1641 and helped to found Montreal (then called Ville-Marie) in 1642. Quebec's community of women, though small, stood at the heart of the colony's social and political world and left some of the best surviving descriptions of this period. Until the late 1600s French men would far outnumber French women in Canada, but this small and powerful cadre of women leaders were among the colony's most important founders. Between Marie de l'Incarnation's arrival and her death more than 30 years later, she and her Ursuline colleagues contributed to the colony's development at least as much as Champlain.

These women considered converting the Natives a genuinely sacred mission; others took a more secular approach, using Christianization as a means to a commercial end. For both reasons Quebec's administrators required Native people involved in French trade to host missionaries in their villages, and by the mid-1630s Jesuit priests were preaching Christianity to Algonquian and Huron villages some distance from Quebec. Living in a land controlled in every way by their Native hosts, Jesuits had no choice but to adapt. As one Jesuit wrote, "a missionary does not fear to make himself a savage, so to speak, with them, in order to make them Christians."[6] Living in Native villages, Jesuits witnessed firsthand the destruction wrought by European diseases like smallpox and influenza, which claimed thousands of lives across the St Lawrence and Great Lakes regions. Weakened by disease, the Hurons were ill-prepared to face an Iroquois threat that had been fuelled by French violence and rendered more deadly by Dutch weaponry. In the late 1640s, Iroquois warriors spread out across the Great Lakes region to attack their enemies, striking with special force against their Huron antagonists. Village after village fell under the onslaught, scattering survivors in all directions. They then turned to the Hurons' French allies, nearly destroying the tiny village of Trois-Rivières and threatening the survival of the whole colony. Although under threat themselves, Algonquins, Montagnais, and surviving Hurons fought alongside French militia to protect their fledgling settlements. But for their support, the French would most likely have been destroyed or forced to leave. As they had many times in the past, Native peoples proved essential to the colony's survival.

Yet within the larger world of French overseas expansion, the St Lawrence colony remained marginal at best. As Jesuits and a handful of fur traders struggled to survive in North America, costing most investors more than they earned, French investments in the Caribbean began to pay stunning dividends. With permanent settlements founded on St Christophe in 1626 and Martinique and Guadeloupe in 1635, French settlement in the Caribbean quickly outpaced and overshadowed activities in Canada. French settlement on these tiny islands more than doubled that of New France, and when slaves are included the ratio rises to four to one. But it was economic output that gave the Caribbean such an edge, with tobacco profits supplemented after the 1650s with rapidly growing revenues from sugar. Importing Native slaves from South America and African slaves through Dutch merchants, France's Caribbean colonies became intimately linked to Africa, which had its first French settlement in 1638 at the mouth of the Senegal River. This would grow into France's most important African colony, supplying slaves, animal hides, guns, ivory, and a little gold throughout the eighteenth century. By 1660, France had growing colonies in Senegal, Martinique, Guadeloupe, St Christopher, Guiana, St Domingue, and Canada.

Facing East, Facing West

Between 1660 and 1740, Canada grew more important to France and its expanding imperial ambitions. Despite a low population and an unstable economy, New France controlled access to the most strategic waterways in North America—the St Lawrence and Mississippi rivers and the Great Lakes—meaning that the colony could play a significant role in the **geopolitics** of empire. This role required the colony to develop along two different but complementary paths. Facing east toward the Atlantic, the colonial capital at Quebec became the key centre for French administration and the point of exchange for most French merchant ships coming from Europe or the Caribbean. Facing west toward the vast North American continent, Montreal became the primary site of trade and diplomacy with Native peoples. Exclusive suppliers of the colony's only profitable export—beaver pelts—Native nations also served as the colony's most important military defence against European rivals. The Atlantic and indigenous orientations of Quebec and Montreal worked in tandem to provide profits to France and allies to a strategic but always vulnerable colony.

In 1660 Canada's French population had not yet reached 3,000, dwarfed by the nearly 70,000 settlers in the English colonies just to the south. The colony's fur trade brought a few individuals great wealth but failed to provide significant returns to either the investment companies that controlled the colony or the French kingdom itself. A nearly constant state of war with the Iroquois threatened the colony's total ruin. Success elsewhere in the Atlantic world—in the French Caribbean as well as in Spanish, English, and Portuguese colonies—caught the attention of Louis XIV and his finance minister, Jean-Baptiste Colbert, prompting a plan to reinvigorate the French colonies and to channel their profits away from private individuals and toward the state. After assuming personal rule of France in 1661, as part of a larger restructuring of France itself, the king and his minister took direct control of France's overseas colonies from the private companies that had governed them since their inception. They appointed royal governors and *intendants* (civilian governors responsible for law and finance) to represent the king in the colonies, and a "sovereign" or "superior" council of local elites that answered to the *intendant*. Overturning an already successful Caribbean model, the Crown met great resistance to its intrusion there, but faltering Canada largely welcomed the move, receiving its first royal governor and seating its first superior council in 1663.

Colonists hoped that royal support could finally secure them from the Iroquois threat. As Canadian Pierre Boucher told Louis XIV during a 1662 visit to Paris, "we have an enemy who keeps us pent up in a little corner and prevents us from going about and making discoveries; and so he will have to be destroyed."[7] Over the next five years, Iroquois raids hit the French and their Native trading partners dozens of times, striking fear into colonists and interrupting the fur trade. Royal control of the colony brought with it the promise of French military support, which came slowly but surely. By 1666, two massive parties of French soldiers overwhelmed the easternmost Iroquois villages, destroying several Mohawk towns and impressing on the others the colony's increased power. Facing raids from French allies to the west and New England Natives to the east, the Iroquois agreed to a peace that lasted nearly 20 years.

Having provided a measure of security, the French Crown also began subsidizing migration to Canada by paying for the trans-Atlantic passage of workers, a few families, and a large group of single women. Within three years New France's population doubled, but in the long term as many as two-thirds of new migrants to Canada returned to France or headed for the warmer and more prosperous Caribbean. In France itself, potential migrants had many other options than North America: They could join the king's ballooning army or simply head south to Spain, paths taken by about half a million people in the seventeenth and eighteenth centuries. In contrast, a mere 10,000 colonists stayed permanently in Canada during the same two centuries. The colony's population reached 15,000 in 1700, but even with very high natural growth there was no chance of catching the English colonies, which the same year boasted more than 235,000 settlers and 30,000 slaves.

Nearly all French colonists lived in a narrow band of settlement described by an eighteenth-century visitor as "one continued village" stretching along the St Lawrence from Montreal to the settlement of Quebec (and a little beyond). At its east end, about 280 kilometres from Montreal, Quebec was the colonial capital and the centre of trans-Atlantic commercial and political activity. Home to about 2,000 people in 1700, Quebec grew to about 5,000 by the 1740s. With the highest proportion of French-born residents anywhere in the colony, and with a powerful merchant class tied to French port cities, Quebec was a thoroughly Atlantic town, oriented eastward toward France and the wider Atlantic world. Headquarters of the governor, *intendant*, and a superior council that served as both legislative body and appeals court, Quebec housed the colony's most influential families. Quebec's governors, *intendants*, bishops, and Atlantic merchants all moved readily between what were often temporary posts in Canada and those in the Caribbean or France. Situated where the St Lawrence narrows from a wide bay to a river, Quebec became the logical point to exchange French goods arriving on ocean-going vessels for North American commodities brought from Montreal and the West. To attract European goods and to find buyers for American furs and skins, the town's major merchants drew on trans-Atlantic family networks that linked ports in northern and western France with those in Canada, West Africa, and the Caribbean. Although France's

Atlantic colonies developed along distinct economic and social lines, familial and commercial ties wove a complex web of connection among them.

At the west end of the "continuous village" sat Montreal, the name of both a compact colonial town and the much larger island on which it was built. By the 1660s the town became the centre of the colony's fur trade. Initially this meant that Native traders brought their skins and furs to Montreal, but after the Iroquois scattered France's nearest allies, French traders ventured westward to meet the Natives in their own villages. From the 1660s to 1680s, French traders and missionaries established trading posts and missions near Native settlements throughout the western Great Lakes and upper Mississippi Valley. The Natives' culture of linking trade and diplomacy, which had drawn the French into war with the Iroquois, worked in France's favour in this case, making military allies of indigenous trading partners eager for European goods. By 1680 a powerful network of alliances had developed with key nodes of trade in modern Ontario, Michigan, Wisconsin, Illinois, and Indiana. These alliances demanded mutual cultural accommodation and innovation by both Natives and French. Native women married French men, creating exclusive, kin-based claims to French trade, a practice that helped the French gain support for their diplomatic agendas as well. Western posts were linked to the colony through Montreal, which remained the nerve centre of Native trade and diplomacy, if not always its geographic centre. Most fur-trade voyages were outfitted on the island with trade goods from the town's warehouses, which swelled with furs and the goods used to procure them. Most traders and contracted servants came from the parishes on and around the island; thus, over time, a significant proportion of the area's men had personal experience with Native trade, diplomacy, and sometimes warfare. Rather than a simple exchange of guns and alcohol for beaver pelts, by the early 1700s Native trade had matured and diversified. The most common exchange by far was of European cloth for the hides and furs of moose, deer, and other animals rather than beaver pelts.

Although colonial officials were pressured by their superiors to draw back from the West to the more defensible St Lawrence, Native allies made it clear that they would no longer travel all the way to Montreal for trade. They expected the French to come to them. To meet this request, and to prevent the English from taking their place in western trade, French officials established Detroit in 1701. Southern complements were founded along the Gulf of Mexico at Biloxi in 1699 and Mobile in 1702, from which the French built a southern alliance along much the same lines as in the Great Lakes. New Orleans would follow in 1718, and together they formed the separate but theoretically subordinate colony of Louisiana. With a longer growing season and excellent Mississippi delta soils, the site promised agricultural products as well as Native trade.

Despite the growth of trade, Canada still cost the French Crown more than it earned from taxes, rents, and other revenues. Wanting to avoid the expense of a large standing army, French officials began to subsidize the fur trade so the colony could benefit from the alliances that came with it. The strategy paid off during two successive imperial wars between France and England from 1689 to 1713. Vastly outnumbered by their English enemies, the French survived the wars only because allies came to their assistance in large numbers. Seeing the war as an opportunity to weaken their own enemies, especially the Iroquois, Natives joined the French in campaigns that struck English colonial towns and Iroquois villages along the New York and Maine frontiers. By 1696 the Iroquois agreed to make peace with New France and its Native allies and to remain neutral in future wars between France and England. The agreement was formalized at a massive conference that convened at Montreal in 1701. With over a thousand representatives from 38 Native nations, the negotiations enacted on a grand scale what had been occurring in Native villages all around the Great Lakes. French and Native customs merged, and innovative hybrids arose to bridge the divides among the many cultures present. Iroquois neutrality was neither complete nor perfect, but it proved important to New France's ability to battle the English to an inconclusive draw in 1713.

The following period of relative calm witnessed the colony's most sustained growth and stability, lasting through the mid-1750s. During these years

BIOGRAPHY

Philippe de Rigaud de Vaudreuil[8]

Philippe de Rigaud de Vaudreuil (ca. 1643–1725) was governor of New France from 1704 until his death in 1725. He was, according to his biographer, an "unspectacular" administrator with very limited education: He could not spell, his grammar was atrocious, and he owned only five books. But by mastering the indigenous and international worlds of New France he became a remarkably effective leader, successfully guiding the colony through a major war while expanding a Native alliance that would secure Canada for decades to come.

Louis-Philippe, eldest son of Philippe de Rigaud de Vaudreuil, governor general of New France. Louis-Philippe distinguished himself commanding warships in the *Marine royale française*. The portrait does not show the subject wearing the characteristic white cross of the Order of Saint-Louis, which means it probably predates 1721 when he was given that honour.

Library and Archives Canada, accession no. 1989-518-15; copyright expired

Born into a noble family from southern France, Vaudreuil gained distinction in European warfare as a member of Louis XIV's musketeers. In 1687, Vaudreuil translated his European experience into a post as commander of France's Canadian troops, a position that offered more upward mobility than he could hope for in Europe. When war with the Iroquois merged with the Nine Years' War in 1689, Vaudreuil's eventual success against a long-standing Iroquois enemy brought him prestige and earned him an appointment as governor of Montreal. In 1701, when western Native allies and the Iroquois met in Montreal to negotiate a truce and to guarantee Iroquois neutrality in imperial wars, Vaudreuil participated and as governor facilitated many of the local arrangements that made the conference a success. Because of his extensive military experience and his knowledge of Native diplomacy he was appointed governor of New France in 1704.

Vaudreuil's political enemies accused him of operating an illegal fur and alcohol trading business and of allowing widespread smuggling between Montreal and the English colony at Albany. The charges were likely true, but they illustrate the degree to which France's international objectives in Canada depended on maintaining good relations with Native peoples. French demand for furs was at an all-time low when Vaudreuil took office, threatening to undermine the diplomatic alliances that were linked to the fur trade. By bypassing normal channels, Vaudreuil was able to give Natives both a better price for their furs and alcohol, which was legally forbidden to them. By allowing French merchants to sell their furs to the English, Vaudreuil kept Natives coming to Montreal instead of Albany, securing for New France the alliances that allowed it to survive the War of the Spanish Succession intact.

Although he was frequently criticized, his strategy of working outside the law to facilitate Native alliances proved successful. During his governorship the French population of the colony almost doubled, from 16,000 to 30,000, and the colony entered its most sustained period of growth and stability. Vaudreuil's success brought prestige and opportunity to his family as they spanned the Atlantic in the French army and navy, and in the colonial administration of Louisiana, St Domingue, and New France. His son, Pierre, governed Louisiana in the 1740s and then became governor of New France in 1755 at the outbreak of the Seven Years' War (see Case Study box).

the colony grew to about 70,000 inhabitants (but fell much farther behind the British, who by mid-century had nearly 1.5 million colonists in North America). Sometimes called **the long peace** because of the absence of European wars, this was still a time of almost constant violence on New France's western frontier. A series of wars with the Mesquakie (or Fox) and Chickasaw nations kept French soldiers and Native allies engaged in war for most of these years. French households also began buying Native slaves, who performed domestic and other menial tasks. French demand for slaves complicated and often undermined the colony's diplomatic agenda in the West, even as it gave Native allies an opportunity to weaken their own indigenous enemies by selling them to the French. The slave population in Montreal and Quebec never approached the numbers found in the Caribbean, but several thousand slaves lived in the colony in the eighteenth century.

Despite the westward drift of trade and diplomacy, visitors to Montreal would have encountered hundreds, and at certain times of the year thousands, of Natives. Several Native villages, often called "missions" because they had a priest and a small chapel, dotted the island and the shores on either side of the St Lawrence. More than 2,000—and at times as many as 3,000—Natives lived in permanent settlements on and around Montreal, a number that in some years approached one-third of the island's French population. Natives from elsewhere in the St Lawrence and many from northern and western regions came annually to the town to meet with traders and conduct business. The governor and *intendant* would spend several weeks each summer in Montreal meeting with visiting Native delegations. The combined effect of these three types of Native presence—slaves, local residents, and periodic visitors—profoundly influenced Montreal. Someone passing through the merchant district in the 1740s would have found a Native slave in nearly half the households, Native boarders in several others, Native day labourers loading and unloading goods in merchants' warehouses, and Native hawkers selling meat and produce at the market square. Among them would have been a few dozen English captives, seized in raids on New England and New York, many of whom had adopted Catholicism and married into French families, and even a handful of enslaved Africans. It is impossible to gauge the numbers of these people, who were not counted in French censuses, but it is reasonable to estimate a summer non-French presence about equal to the French who permanently lived in the town.

Quebec and Montreal might have been the most important nodes of economic and political life in New France, but most French Canadians lived in rural villages along the St Lawrence. From a relatively small foundation this rural population grew quickly through large families with survival and life expectancy rates as high as any preindustrial society could

CASE STUDY

The Seven Years' War

Between 1689 and 1763, New France fought four major imperial wars that began in Europe but drew in competing colonies in the Americas. In the Nine Years' War (1688–97), a coalition of European nations joined to resist the expanding power of the French Louis XIV. In the War of the Spanish Succession (1701–14) the same coalition—minus Spain—fought to keep Louis XIV from making his grandson the king of Spain and thereby threatening all of Europe with the combined forces of France and Spain. In the War of the Austrian Succession (1740–48), France and Prussia fought England and the Netherlands over who would become the monarch of Austria. In the misnamed Seven Years' War (1754–63), France, England, and Spain squared off in a global contest that merged European territorial battles with a fight for overseas power in North and South America, India, and the Pacific Rim. The end of this war brought the end of French colonial rule in New France, as the colony was ceded to Britain in the 1763 Treaty of Paris.

In all of these wars, New France was called upon to attack England's interests in North America, raiding English settlements with Native allies and defending their own frontiers with local militia supplemented by a small number of French troops. In every case, the European treaties concluding these wars exchanged some colonial territories among European kingdoms but left others untouched. At the end of the War of the Spanish Succession, for example, Louis XIV yielded Acadia to Britain but made his grandson king of Spain. After the War of the Austrian Succession, Britain returned the captured fortress of Louisbourg to France in exchange for a French-controlled settlement in India. At the end of the Seven Years' War, France yielded Canada to Britain so it could recover the Caribbean islands of Guadeloupe and Martinique. In this respect, the end of French control in Canada was similar to many earlier bargains struck by European kingdoms. New France had finally lost the imperial game that had sustained its place in the French kingdom despite its drain on French finances. But in another respect the Seven Years' War was different. Although it became a global war—with fighting in the Americas, Europe, India, and the Philippines—it began in North America.

Even after New France's impressive performance during the first half of the eighteenth century, many compared the colony to France's Caribbean and African interests and found it wanting. In 1751 Canada's governor, the Marquis de La Galissonière, acknowledged the central imperial concern: "it cannot be denied that this colony has always been an expense to France, and that there is every appearance that it will long remain on the same footing." Colonies were supposed to make money for the mother country, but from the beginning the French Crown had lost more than it invested. Yet the governor reminded his superiors in France that preserving Canada was worth the cost, urging the king "to omit no means, and to spare no expense, to assure the preservation of Canada, since only through it can America be enslaved to English ambition; and the progress of their empire in that part of the world is what is most likely to give them the upper hand in Europe." By restricting the British colonies to the Atlantic seaboard, New France could keep them from the continent's vast resources and prevent their eventual expansion into Mexico, both essential to check British wealth and power.

According to the governor, the key to containing England's control of North America was the Ohio River Valley, which linked France's colonies in Canada and Louisiana and provided a barrier to English expansion. France and England both claimed the territory and had conducted trade there throughout the eighteenth century, but it remained under the control of independent Native "republics," as the French derisively called them. Native villages along the Ohio River, strategically placed to allow trade with both English and French colonies, drew suspicion as well as goods. One village in particular, called Pickawillany, began as a Miami settlement but quickly drew in a wide range of Natives with uncertain British and French allegiances. Growing in only one year from a small homogenous village into a large town with over 400 families, Pickawillany struck fear into the French for its potential to draw English influence into the Ohio Valley. Because trade and military alliance were so closely tied, France feared losing not only profits from the trade but their entire means of colonial defence. They responded with decisive force. Leading a group of Odawa, Métis, and French warriors, the Métis military commander Charles-Michel Mouet de Langlade crushed the town when many of its men were away hunting.

If Native trade in the Ohio Valley frightened the French, an armed attack there sounded alarm bells in the English colonies and put them on the

continued

defensive. When rumours spread about a French fort being built at the Forks of the Ohio (modern Pittsburgh, Pennsylvania), England responded with a reconnaissance mission. In 1754, an inexperienced George Washington marched to the Forks to monitor French activity. Before he could grasp the situation, Washington and his men fired on a French envoy and wounded him and several other men. One of Washington's allies, Tanaghrisson, killed a wounded French officer who had asked for quarter, hoping to spark a conflict that had already begun to smoulder. Tanaghrisson was successful. The French quickly retaliated, leading the governor of Virginia to warn of the total loss of North America and all its potential wealth unless the French could be chastened. Full-scale war broke out over control of the Ohio Valley, so central to the expansion and defence of both empires' North American holdings.

In North America, France won nearly all of the early campaigns, relying on Native warriors who killed or captured hundreds of British colonists in small but demoralizing raids all along the frontier. In a major victory for France, a force of western Natives and French soldiers routed General Edward Braddock and his army at Monongahela in 1755, eye-opening proof that indigenous ways of war could be highly effective against even a professionally led British army.

Through 1757 the war went well for France, which seemed in little danger of losing Canada during the conflict. Two things turned the tide: shifting British strategy and the loss of France's Native allies. First, in England, William Pitt began to devote remarkable sums of money to fight the war in North America, wielding the power of Britain's mighty navy and more than 40,000 ground troops to secure British colonies against New France's deadly attacks. Second, Louis-Joseph de Montcalm and other French military leaders alienated Native allies by treating them like subordinates and overturning previous promises of captives and looting—western Natives' primary reward for risking their lives to defend New France. Angry and insulted, the Odawas, Ojibwas, and other allies returned to their villages in the Great Lakes region, unwittingly taking the smallpox virus back to their villages. During the fall of 1757 hundreds died. Unwilling to take such risks again for so little reward, the colony's Native allies stayed home. The tide of the war turned permanently in 1758 when huge infusions of British troops met French soldiers minus their key allies. Forts fell quickly in a series of demoralizing British victories that culminated in the 1759 surrender of Quebec after the Battle of the Plains of Abraham, and the 1760 surrender of Montreal. The war ground on for three more years in Europe and Asia until, in 1763, France's crushing losses brought the parties to the negotiating table.

The British were unsure whether Canada was the best reward for defeating France, and they seriously considered returning the colony to French control. Like France, they recognized the superior position and profitability of the Caribbean, where they had taken several French and Spanish islands, and they worried about taking on a colony that was losing money. After long deliberation, Britain opted to retain control of Canada and return the sugar islands of Martinique and Guadeloupe to France (and Cuba to Spain). Britain's decision was based on the same strategic reasoning that had prompted France to invest in New France over the previous century. Both France and Britain viewed Canada as a strategic pawn in a global chess game where the reward was European, not colonial, power. Located to ensure access to the continental interior, the St Lawrence colony ensured Britain's control of the Great Lakes and Ohio River Valley, both of which were crucial to the security of Britain's North American colonies and to their future hopes of colonial expansion. The 1763 Treaty of Paris therefore ended French control of its former colony along the St Lawrence River. But no treaty could end the French presence there. Nearly all of the 70,000 French colonists remained, adapting to a new colonial regime but retaining many of their daily patterns of life.

hope for. With abundant land available even to relatively poor inhabitants, most families farmed their own land and lived free of the harsher demands of seigneurial life in rural France. Most of these people experienced the international aspects of New France only indirectly, when they bought French soap or drank brandy or rum. They would have seen Native people more often than French merchant ships or Caribbean plantations, but they likely did not understand how intricately their lives were bound to people they called *les sauvages*.

Thus for 150 years New France prospered by embracing its international and indigenous contexts, becoming a strategic node in a transnational web of empire that linked Europe, Africa, and the Americas long before anyone had coined the term *globalization*.

Questions for Critical Thinking

1. What role did New France play in the trans-Atlantic empire established by France from the sixteenth through the eighteenth centuries?
2. Discuss the importance of Native peoples in the history of New France. How did they shape the colony? How did the process of colonization affect them?
3. Should the Seven Years' War be considered a war of conquest in Canada? Who would favour and who would oppose this description and why? What historical evidence could help us answer this question?

Notes

1. Ramsay Cook, ed. and trans., *The Voyages of Jacques Cartier* (Toronto: University of Toronto Press, 1993), 10, 24.
2. Cook, *Voyages of Jacques Cartier*, 64.
3. Richard Hakluyt, "Discourse on Western Planting, Written in the Year 1584," in *Documentary History of the State of Maine*, ed. Charles Deane, vol. 2 (Cambridge: John Wilson and Son, 1877), 3.
4. Henry Percival Biggar, ed. and trans., *The Works of Samuel de Champlain*, 6 vols. (Toronto: The Champlain Society, 1971), vol. 2, 331.
5. Biggar, *Works of Samuel de Champlain*, vol. 1, 110–11.
6. Reuben Gold Thwaites, ed., *The Jesuit Relations and Allied Documents*, vol. 51 (Cleveland: Burrows Brothers, 1899), 265.
7. Pierre Boucher, *Histoire veritable et naturelle des moeurs & productions du pays de la Nouvelle France, vulgairement dite le Canada* (Paris, 1664).
8. Drawn from Yves Zoltvany, "Rigaud de Vaudreuil, Philippe de, Marquis de Vaudreuil," *Dictionary of Canadian Biography*, vol. 2 (Toronto: University of Toronto Press, 1969).

Select Bibliography

Anderson, Fred. *Crucible of War: The Seven Years' War and the Fate of Empire in British North America, 1754–1766*. New York: Vintage, 2001.

Boucher, Philip. *France and the American Tropics to 1700: Tropics of Discontent?* Baltimore: Johns Hopkins University Press, 2008.

Brandão, José António. *Your Fyre Shall Burn No More: Iroquois Policy toward New France and Its Native Allies to 1701*. Lincoln: University of Nebraska Press, 1997.

Cook, Ramsay, ed. *The Voyages of Jacques Cartier*. Toronto: University of Toronto Press, 1993.

Dechêne, Louise. *Habitants and Merchants in Seventeenth-Century Montreal*. Translated by Liana Vardi. Montreal: McGill-Queen's University Press, 1992.

Dickason, Olive P. *The Myth of the Savage and the Beginnings of French Colonialism in the Americas*. Edmonton: University of Alberta Press, 1997.

Eccles, W. J. *The French in North America, 1500–1783*. East Lansing: Michigan State University Press, 1998.

Fischer, David Hackett. *Champlain's Dream: The European Founding of North America*. New York: Simon & Schuster, 2008.

Gauvreau, Danielle. *Québec : une ville et sa population au temps de la Nouvelle France*. Québec: Presses de l'Université du Québec, 1991.

Grabowski, Jan. "The Common Ground: Settled Natives and French in Montreal." Ph.D. diss., Université de Montréal, 1993.

Greer, Allan. *The People of New France*. Toronto: University of Toronto Press, 1997.

Havard, Gilles. *Émpire et métissages : Indiens et Français dans le Pays d'en Haut, 1660–1715*. Paris: Presses de l'Université Paris-Sorbonne, 2003.

Lavallée, Louis. *La Prairie en Nouvelle-France, 1647–1760 : étude d'histoire sociale*. Montreal: McGill-Queen's University Press, 1992.

Mapp, Paul W. *The Elusive West and the Contest for Empire, 1713–1763*. Chapel Hill: University of North Carolina Press for the Omohundro Institute of Early American History and Culture, 2011.

Pope, Peter. *Fish into Wine: The Newfoundland Plantation in the Seventeenth Century*. Chapel Hill: University of North Carolina Press for the Omohundro Institute of Early American History and Culture, 2004.

Pritchard, James. *In Search of Empire: The French in the Americas, 1670–1730*. Cambridge: Cambridge University Press, 2004.

Richter, Daniel K. *Facing East from Indian Country: A Native History of Early America*. Cambridge, MA: Harvard University Press, 2001.

Rushforth, Brett. *Bonds of Alliance: Indigenous and Atlantic Slaveries in New France*. Chapel Hill: University of North Carolina Press for the Omohundro Institute of Early American History and Culture, 2012.

Taylor, Alan. *American Colonies*. New York: Viking, 2001.

Thornton, John. *Africa and Africans in the Making of the Atlantic World, 1400–1800*. Cambridge: Cambridge University Press, 1998.

Trigger, Bruce. *Natives and Newcomers: Canada's "Heroic Age" Reconsidered*. Montreal: McGill-Queen's University Press, 1985.

White, Richard. *The Middle Ground: Indians, Empires, and Republics in the Great Lakes Region, 1650–1815*. Cambridge: Cambridge University Press, 1991.

2 The Canadiens and the Conquest of Quebec: Interpretations, Realities, Ambiguities[1]

Donald Fyson, Université Laval/Centre interuniversitaire d'études québécoises

Timeline

1759 Defeat of French forces at the Battle of the Plains of Abraham and British occupation of Quebec City.

1760 Final surrender of French forces at Montreal; the fall of Canada.

1763 Treaty of Paris: Canada formally ceded by the French to the British. Royal Proclamation: creation of the Province of Quebec.

1764 Beginning of British civil administration of the new Province of Quebec.

1774 Quebec Act (fully in force from 1775).

1775 Beginning of the American War of Independence and invasion of Quebec.

1783 Treaty of Paris: end of American War of Independence; portion of Quebec south of the Great Lakes ceded to the new United States; arrival in Quebec of Loyalists (American colonists who remained loyal to the British Crown, known in the United States as Tories).

1791 Constitutional Act: Province of Quebec divided into two separate colonies (Lower Canada and Upper Canada, essentially the southern portions of modern-day Quebec and Ontario, respectively), each with an elected assembly.

The singular goodness and kindness with which we have been governed by His Most Gracious Majesty King George III since, by force of arms, we became subject to his dominion . . . will no doubt be sufficient to arouse your thanks and your zeal in support of the interests of the British Crown.

—Jean-Olivier Briand, bishop of Quebec, enjoining the Canadiens to resist the American invasion of 1775[2]

. . . the province . . . subjected to British empire, has been, since the period of subjugation, nothing other than a province of misfortunates and slaves . . . the conquering nation, by the hands of its national individuals, immediately invaded almost all of the positions in the conquered country; in other words, by this usurpation, the Canadiens were declared strangers, intruders, civil slaves, in their own country . . .

—Pierre Du Calvet, former magistrate imprisoned by Governor Haldimand, in *Appel à la justice de l'État*, 1784[3]

The Conquest took place a quarter millennium ago. For how many centuries will we still resent the British? . . . if there was the Conquest, there was also the 1774 Quebec Act, that guaranteed the Canadiens the maintenance of the Catholic religion and of the civil law . . . Quebec today is impregnated with English values, institutions, architecture . . . the heritage of that period is far from being exclusively negative . . .

—André Pratte, editor of *La Presse*, denouncing critics of Paul McCartney's show on the Plains of Abraham in 2008[4]

. . . whatever the revisionists say, the military conquest of New France by England and the avowed intent of the colonial power to assimilate the francophones can never be considered pleasant memories by the Québécois people. In our collective unconscious, the Conquest has the same meaning as a rape. Some act as if nothing happened and try to minimize the event, but others will never forget.

—Biz, member of the sovereignist rap group Loco Locass, *Le Devoir*, 2007[5]

Introduction

Despite the rhetorical certainty of those quoted at the beginning of this chapter, who span more than two centuries, the British Conquest of Quebec is a profoundly ambiguous event. Were the new British masters guided by kindness and gentleness toward their new subjects, as Briand suggests, or did the conquered **Canadiens** become slaves in their own land, as Du Calvet charged? Should today's francophone Quebecers stop making such a big deal out of the Conquest, as Pratte would like, or should they follow Biz in treating it as rape?

At its most basic, "the Conquest" (almost always capitalized) refers to the military defeat of the French and their Native allies by the British, first at the Battle of the Plains of Abraham in 1759, which led to the fall of Quebec City, and then at the final rendition of French forces at Montreal in 1760. This military victory gave Britain formal control over the former French colonial possessions in northeastern and central North America, part of what was known as New France (although in reality much of the "conquered" territory remained under Native control). In what is now Quebec (known then to the French as Canada), this was the end of what Europeans call the Seven Years' War, what Americans call the French and Indian War, and what is often called in Quebec *la guerre de la Conquête*, the War of the Conquest. The Conquest can also refer more generally to the transition of the colony and its Canadien population from one empire to another, including the military actions of 1759–60, the 1763 Treaty of Paris by which the French Crown formally ceded most of New France to the British, and the 1763 British Royal Proclamation that created the Province of Quebec. By extension, the decades following this event are often discussed in terms of "the effects of the Conquest," it being seen as the major traumatic event that shaped the colony's subsequent history. Indeed, according to a commonly held view, the Conquest founded modern Quebec: It was the point of departure of Quebec's contemporary history and the source of both Quebec's current unequal status within Canada and francophones' continuing status as a colonized people. One might almost talk of a continuous Conquest, right up to today. The Conquest, in short, is a very elastic concept.

The nature of the conquered entity is also open to interpretation. What exactly was conquered? New France? Canada? Quebec? The French? The Canadiens? None of these is particularly satisfying.

"New France" is too broad and "Canada" (as used by the French at that time) is too narrow. New France properly referred to the entirety of French possessions in North America at that time, including not only what is now central and maritime Canada but also what is now the Midwestern and (in part) Southern United States. Not all of this territory was conquered by the British. "Canada" referred primarily to the main French settlements in the St Lawrence

Valley, essentially the south of modern-day Quebec, along with their western hinterland, which was only part of what the British "conquered." Neither Canada (in its modern sense) nor Quebec existed at the time. The French officers and soldiers who defended the colony lost the battles, but they were not themselves conquered since most returned to France. Contrarily, some have long contended that it was not the Canadiens who were conquered, who lost the colony, but rather those same French. Finally, what of New France's Native populations, who were allied to the French but did not consider themselves to have been conquered by the British and remained largely independent nations for another half century?

As this chapter focuses on the effects of the Conquest on the francophone population of what is now Quebec, it adopts the shorthand "Conquest of Quebec." Although it is an anachronism, this term nevertheless has the satisfying effect of making clear that this series of events was not only the conquest of a historical political entity, but is also a locus of historical memory that belongs to a particular society.

The Conquest remains a significant subject of public interest and discourse in Quebec even today. For example, several years ago it appeared that the Conquest and other potentially conflictual events might be downplayed in a new high school history curriculum proposed by the Quebec government, with the Conquest integrated into a section entitled "The Accession to Democracy in the British Colony." A general public outcry and much-heated public debate ensued, leading to a partial government retreat on the matter. In 2008, the participation of the governor general, the Queen's representative in Canada, in the 400th anniversary celebrations of Quebec City was denounced by many Quebec nationalists as the very incarnation of the British Conquest. Even a concert by Paul McCartney on the Plains of Abraham was viewed by some as a "new conquest." In early 2009, plans to commemorate the 250th anniversary of the Battle of the Plains of Abraham with, among other things, a re-enactment and a masked ball, raised such a storm of protest that the re-enactment was cancelled and other events were substantially reshaped to avoid accusations of "celebrating" the French defeat. More generally, a keyword search in the electronic archives of major francophone Quebec newspapers for names, events, and dates related to the Conquest brings up hundreds of articles, editorials, and letters just over the last few years.[6] Many contain only passing references, but a substantial number take the Conquest as the central subject, as seen in the citations from Pratte and Biz above. It is a theme that regularly leads to flights of rhetorical excess, with hard language, such as "the holocaust of 1760," not uncommon. Most of the controversy stems from the widely divergent interpretations of the Conquest and their current political usage.

Interpretations of the Conquest

Most of the basic facts about the former French colony in the decades following the Conquest have been largely accepted, at least by professional historians, for quite some time (see the Case Study box). However, in interpreting the Conquest and its effects, there is and always has been far less agreement. Debates around Canadien adaptation to the new realities in the decades following the Conquest have long been a constant in Quebec and, indeed, Canadian history. Even the use of the term itself is contested. In French, at least, there are alternatives. *La Conquête* (or "the Conquest") is the standard historiographical term, used by almost all anglophone historians and in much of the French-language literature as well. But many writers, especially more nationalist ones, see the term as inherently adopting the perspective of the Conqueror—the British. As an editorialist for *Le Soleil* put it, it is a "contemptuous way of evoking the taking of possession of the soul and the body of an entire people."[7] For the French, after all, it was not a conquest. Since the nineteenth century, some francophone writers have instead used the term *la Cession*. For some, this was an attempt to soft-pedal the notion of conquest in the spirit of national reconciliation between French and English Canadians. For others, however, the term underscored the fact that it was not the Canadiens who lost the colony, but rather France, which ceded it to Great Britain. This drew on deep resentment in Quebec toward France for abandoning Quebec: first, by not sending

CASE STUDY

The Aftermath of the Conquest in Quebec

In the short term, the Conquest led to a series of dramatic and seemingly perilous changes for the European colony and its French inhabitants. The colony's name changed from Nouvelle-France (or Canada) to the Province of Quebec, and it became a royal colony under the direct control of the British Crown. New France had theoretically covered most of the interior of North America, down to Louisiana (though most of its territory was in practice largely controlled by France's Native allies), with its capital at Quebec City. As of 1763, the new Province of Quebec was limited to a small rectangle along the shores of the St Lawrence River. The colony's 65,000 or so francophone, Catholic inhabitants, or Canadiens, became subjects of the British Crown and were compelled to take an oath of allegiance. They had reason to be nervous about this transition. The British state was officially Protestant, anti-Catholic, and very publicly anti-French. The Catholic Church, which had dominated religion in New France, was thus in a precarious position. So too were elites such as seigneurs (major landowners) and nobles, who had depended on government patronage and support before the Conquest and were faced with a new colonial regime where traditional avenues of advancement, such as the army, were essentially closed to them. Canadien merchants were also concerned, especially those engaged in the import–export trade, mostly exporting furs and importing manufactured products and consumption goods. British imperial policies meant they could no longer trade directly with France. Even ordinary Canadiens had reason to fear. During the siege of Quebec, British forces had burned hundreds of farms in a deliberate policy of terror. In England and most of her American colonies, Catholics were excluded from most positions of public trust and subjected to many restrictions on their civil rights. Further, just a few years earlier in Nova Scotia, the British army of occupation had deported the entire Acadian (French-Catholic) population. Even private property was under threat. Though most was guaranteed under the terms of the 1760 articles of surrender, it appeared that the laws regulating property would be British. This, it was feared, would lead to the disappearance of the colony's landholding system, the seigneurial system, whereby the territory was divided into large landed estates owned by seigneurs and held by habitants, semi-independent farmers who worked for themselves but paid dues to the seigneurs. In short, the Conquest was a pivotal event in Quebec's history, rife with potential negative effects on the Canadien population.

The actual effects were more complicated. Overall, between 1759 and 1791, we can distinguish three major periods, each representing a major shift in British imperial policy toward the colony (see the timeline at the beginning of the chapter). First, the military regime, 1759–64: the period when the conquered colony was under military rule by the army of occupation, awaiting the outcome of the war elsewhere in the world and of the subsequent peace negotiations. This was a crucial period, since it established mutual expectations between the Canadiens and their new colonial masters. Overall, these expectations were positive. While the period was highly disruptive to the colony's former elites, who lost their positions of power, its broader effects on the Canadien population as a whole were perhaps less dramatic than what one might expect from the words *military regime*. Thus, much of the Canadiens' habitual referents were preserved: the Catholic religion, including the right of the Church hierarchy to exercise its functions; property rights, including the seigneurial system, the property of religious orders, and private property, including slaves; the right of Canadien merchants to continue operating; French civil law; even certain pre-Conquest structures of authority, such as the Canadien militia officers who ran the lower courts, Canadien bailiffs who essentially continued to act as the strong arm of the law, and Canadien notaries who continued to practise, though now with commissions granted by British military governors. There were of course some important changes, such as the dismantling of the French administrative system, which was replaced by military councils and tribunals, and the de facto abolition of the military functions of the militia and the disarmament of the population. But in their dealings with the Canadien population, the new British administrators most often communicated in French (the international language of the elite at the time). The Canadiens thus seemed to have had little fear of forced assimilation or (their other great fear) deportation.

Under the Royal Proclamation of 1763, however, largely implemented between 1764 and 1775, the official British policy was assimilation, with apparently significant restrictions on the religious and political rights of Canadiens (see the Primary Source box at the end of this chapter). The objective was to replace the French, Catholic colony with a British, Protestant one. To this end, British authorities envisaged a twofold approach: encourage British immigration, especially from the American colonies to the south, and assimilate the Canadiens. From this flowed measures such as the exclusion of Catholics from most high government offices; the wholesale replacement (in theory) of French civil and criminal law by English common and statute law; the intent to grant further land not in seigneuries but according to free and common socage (where farmers essentially owned their lands outright); the nomination of French-speaking Anglican curates with the express purpose of converting the Canadiens; the weakening of the Catholic Church by controlling its priests, no longer supporting its collection of revenues such as tithes, and abolishing the powerful male religious orders (the Jesuits and the Recollets); and even the amputation of the interior territory, which sought among other goals to sunder links between the Canadiens and their former Native allies in the interior.

Here was ample fodder to feed the fears of the Canadien population. However, put simply, this policy, designed in London, did not work. Few British colonists came to the colony, with semi-permanent immigration largely limited to colonial officials, American and British merchants eager to profit from the new opportunities of a colony suddenly open for trade, and a few artisans and labourers. The drying up of direct French immigration thus had little effect on the ethnoreligious composition of the colony's population. Further, almost all of the British settled in the three main towns—Quebec City (still the capital), Montreal, and Trois-Rivières—rather than in the rural areas of the colony, where 85 per cent or so of the population lived and which remained almost exclusively Canadien, at least until the mid-1780s. British imperial administrators on the spot found it more practical to attempt to solidify the loyalty of the Canadiens, notably their elites, by essentially putting aside the policies of assimilation and replacing them with a policy of appeasement, introducing flexibility as much as possible into their dealings with Canadiens and especially Canadien elites. For example, French civil law continued to hold sway de facto, with the tacit approval of the colonial administration, and early governors such as James Murray and Guy Carleton gave more support to the Catholic Church than to the fledgling Anglican establishment, as when they allowed the consecration of a new Catholic bishop in 1766. As well, from a purely practical point of view, administrators continued the practices of official bilingualism that were already initiated under the military regime, for example publishing all their official notices in both English and French and replying in French to correspondents who addressed them in that language.

continued

Finally, under the Quebec Act of 1774, appeasement became official imperial policy, despite secret instructions that appear to have preserved the idea of assimilation. Thus, from 1775 on, French civil law was definitively restored, though with some modifications; most of the religious and political restrictions on Catholics were lifted; Catholics were allowed to occupy almost any government position, with a number of Canadiens from the seigneurial class named to the colony's appointed legislature; the right of the Catholic Church to collect tithes was reaffirmed; and a significant part of the interior of the continent was reattached (formally, at least) to the colony (essentially, most of present-day southern Quebec and Ontario and the Great Lakes Basin). This was in part due to the troubles in the American colonies, which had been building toward revolution since the early 1770s. Britain thus found itself in the ironic position of having to count on the loyalty of its newly conquered Canadien subjects to counter the American subjects, largely on whose behalf the Conquest of Quebec had been undertaken 15 years before. This proved a very weak reed. When the American colonies launched their revolutionary war in 1775, one of their first military actions was to invade Quebec. Despite the efforts of Canadien religious leaders and most of the seigneurs, who were favoured by the Quebec Act, the Americans met little resistance from the Canadien population, although the Canadiens gave little active support either. The British defeat of the invasion was largely due to a combination of luck, American strategic problems, and the arrival of British reinforcements. Still, the spirit of the Quebec Act remained official policy through to 1791.

enough troops to defend New France during the war; then by not attempting to retake Canada once it had fallen to the British; and finally, at the 1763 peace talks, by giving up Canada in exchange for Guadeloupe, Martinique, and other considerations. Though not in common use today, *la Cession* is still used by some pre-eminent historians. Finally, since about the 1960s, some nationalist writers have used the term *la Défaite*, thus adopting the perspective not of the victors but rather of the vanquished and seeking to keep fresh the memory of an event that has become a cornerstone of the sovereignist trends in current Quebec nationalism. For example, it was used (though not capitalized) in the 1994 program of the Parti Québécois, the main Quebec sovereignist party, just before the 1995 referendum on Quebec independence. Scholarly use of this term is less frequent, however, and even in popular writing *la Conquête* remains by far the most usual term.

Whether called Conquest, Cession, or Defeat, the meaning of the event to the Canadien population is open to interpretation. Take, for example, the question of how ordinary Canadiens reacted to the change in allegiance. According to an older, nostalgic Tory school, epitomized by such historians as A. L. Burt or Donald Creighton, ordinary Canadiens were either indifferent to the change (since they were ignorant peasants) or, at best, passively contented to see French autocracy disappear and British liberties arrive. In contrast, according to neo-nationalist historians associated with the University of Montreal in the 1950s and 1960s, such as Michel Brunet and Maurice Séguin, ordinary Canadiens reacted by retreating into largely passive and defensive resistance to the hated Conqueror. The two views are of course incompatible. In them we see summed up the two basic competing interpretations: the beneficial Conquest and the disastrous Conquest—what one might call the "jovialist" and the "miserabilist" views. These two opposing views were present almost right from the start, as we can see in the quotations from Briand and Du Calvet, and continue to this day, as expressed by Pratte and Biz.

The "jovialist" notion that the Conquest was beneficial for the Canadien population has a long history, stretching back to the initial declarations of the first British administrators, such as James Murray. At first, Canadiens like Briand expressed it in vague terms as a way of coping with the fact of defeat and coming to terms with the new colonial masters. But the revolutions in Europe at the end of the eighteenth century provided a more potent argument with the development of the notion of the providential Conquest. The idea was simple: As revolution swept through France, conservative public figures in Quebec, such as Chief Justice William Smith or future Bishop Joseph-Octave Plessis, argued that by allowing the Conquest, God had miraculously preserved Quebec from the revolutionary and democratic horrors of its former motherland. This interpretation was taken up by the conservative, clerical historians of the nineteenth and early twentieth centuries, such as the abbé Henri-Raymond Casgrain. He wrote in 1891 that had New France remained French, it would have been subject to the abuses that destroyed France "until it had fallen, with this last, into the abyss of Revolution,"[8] and added, in a nod to social Darwinism, that the Conquest had weeded out the weaker elements of Quebec society.

By the second half of the twentieth century, this interpretation had largely declined, but another long-present variant continued. This interpretation had its roots in the British belief in the absolute superiority of their civilization: The Conquest had brought significant benefits to Quebec, such as parliamentary democracy, the printing press, a British-inspired entrepreneurial spirit, and so on. Often present in the writings of earlier generations of English-Canadian historians, in recent years this interpretation has largely disappeared from the historiographical landscape, at least in French, but is kept alive in the writings of historians like Marcel Trudel, who has written pieces with titles such as "The Conquest of 1760 also Had Its Advantages," as well as by anti-sovereignist editorialists such as Pratte.

In contrast, there is the "miserabilist" idea that the Conquest was a disaster for the Canadiens and subsequently the Quebec people. This too has long roots, associated with a nationalist interpretation of Quebec history that stretches back to writers such as Du Calvet and beyond. Its first real expression by a historian came from François-Xavier Garneau, often seen as the first influential francophone historian of Quebec, in the middle of the nineteenth century. Following the same line of argument as Du Calvet, Garneau declared that under the new British regime, "every day the Canadiens felt more and more the scope of the misfortune of foreign subjugation, and that the sacrifices they had made were nothing in comparison with the suffering and moral humiliation that was being prepared for them and for their posterity."[9] This notion of national disaster continued in the writings of the founder of scientific history in Quebec, the influential Lionel Groulx, in the first half of the twentieth century, to whom the Conquest was the "supreme catastrophe." It persisted in the writings of the historians of the neo-nationalist Montreal school in the 1950s and 1960s such as Brunet and Séguin, students of Groulx, and those of nationalist Marxists in the 1960s and 1970s such as Stanley Ryerson and Gilles Bourque. Ryerson and Bourque associated the colonialism inherent in the Conquest with the colonialism at that time being strongly contested elsewhere in the world, such as in Africa. Although now far less explicitly in academic circles, the "Conquest as disaster" idea still informs much of the discussion of Quebec history.

One aspect of the miserabilist view that deserves particular attention is the so-called **decapitation thesis**. In this view, dating back to Garneau and beyond, the Conquest led to the disappearance of the colony's francophone elites, most of whom left the colony after the Conquest. As sociologist Marcel Rioux wrote in 1969, "the habitants [farmers] and the curés [priests] remained alone (or almost alone) in Voltaire's acres of snow, coming to grips with the English, the long winters, poverty and survival. This was the beginning of Quebec's long hibernation . . ."[10]

Very much the minority opinion in Garneau's time and up to the early twentieth century (Groulx, for example, did not embrace the decapitation thesis), this view was revived in a more sophisticated form in the mid-twentieth century by Brunet, Séguin, and other neo-nationalist historians of the Montreal school. To explain why francophone Quebecers in the 1950s were economically dominated by their anglophone counterparts, they sought to portray pre-Conquest Canada as a normal society that had developed its own entrepreneurial class. But this class was suddenly cut off by the disaster of the Conquest. The entrepreneurs left, went bankrupt, or were simply shifted aside by the anglophone merchants (largely American and Anglo-Scottish) who were favoured under the new system. The Canadiens retreated into agriculture, leaving the economic field to the British. Thus the Conquest of 1759–60 led to the economic inferiority of francophone Quebecers two centuries later.

To this neo-nationalist version of the decapitation thesis, the Marxist historians of the 1960s and 1970s added the notion of class: The Canadiens, shorn of their bourgeoisie (the entrepreneurial class), became the working class, while the English merchants and administrators who came into the colony (these writers generally used English and British interchangeably) became the ruling class, a structure that has persisted in Quebec ever since. Class and ethnicity became one; to quote Rioux again, "all Quebec became a dominated ethnic class."[11]

The decapitation thesis did not go uncontested. Historians such as Fernand Ouellet and Jean Hamelin of Laval University argued instead that, first, there was no real entrepreneurial class in Canada before the Conquest, and second, the Canadiens could not adapt to the changes wrought by the Conquest largely because of cultural inadequacies inherited from the French regime, such as little entrepreneurial spirit. This view gained very few adherents in Quebec because it called into question the nature of current Quebec francophone society.

In current popular discourse on the effects of the Conquest, the disaster/decapitation thesis dominates. In major francophone newspapers over the last few years, perceptions of the Conquest, if not neutral, are almost always negative with few positive discussions. These negative portrayals of the Conquest range from general statements about its bad effects to hard-hitting attacks on the conquerors, such as this reference to "Dorchester and other 'conquerors' whose design [was] to annihilate the French-Canadian people, beginning with their language and their identity."[12] (Dorchester was one of the early governors of Quebec and an architect of the **Quebec Act**, which many historians consider one of the factors that allowed for Canadien cultural and linguistic survival.) The notion of a continuous Conquest, still resonating today, is a strong theme; as the leaders of a radical wing of the sovereignist Parti Québécois declared, "More than 250 years of domination have convinced us of the relentless desire of the governments that have dominated us and that still dominate us to update for their own period the fundamental aspects of the British conquest."[13] Or even more clearly, as one more radical sovereignist writer, René Boulanger, put it, "the Us of 1759 and that of 2006, is the same."[14] There are few who, like Pratte, venture to say that the Conquest was a good thing or tell francophone Quebecers to just "get over it."

Among professional historians, what largely gained sway in the last two or three decades was the notion that the Conquest led to rather less substantial change than was previously postulated. The notion of continuity was already present in the work of historians writing in the late nineteenth and early twentieth centuries, such as Thomas Chapais, but came into its own with the rise of historical study, beginning in the 1970s, that is less interested in politics than in broader social and economic conditions. For example, studies of Quebec agriculture or the **seigneurial system** in the eighteenth century rarely give 1759–60 as a pivotal date; instead, they tend to treat the entire century as a fairly unified period. A clear example is John Dickinson and Brian Young's *Short History of Quebec* (fourth edition, 2008), which, in striking contrast to previous works, includes both New France and immediate post-Conquest Quebec in a single period stretching from the 1650s to the 1810s. The Conquest, in effect, is eliminated as a major structural event.

Partly due to this perspective, until quite recently relatively few professional historians, whether francophone or anglophone, studied the effects of the Conquest as such, leaving thinking and writing about it to scholars in other fields or to the broader public. However, this began to change dramatically in the last few years, due in part to the public commemorations surrounding the 400th anniversary of the French founding of Quebec City (2008) and the 250th anniversaries of the Battle of the Plains of Abraham (2009) and of the Treaty of Paris (2013). This has spawned a raft of new publications, mainly in French although with some in English.[15] In these recent studies as well, one can still see the traces of the classic jovialist and miserabilist perspectives, although many historians have become more sophisticated and more aware of the complexities inherent to this period. The strong resonance of the Conquest with Quebec's current political status has also led some of this recent work to remain heavily shaped by contemporary political concerns, just like popular interpretations of the event. This new body of work does, however, include some exciting new developments, including a much better insertion of the Conquest and its after-effects into the broader histories of both the French and British empires, and a much greater interest in the effects of the Conquest on Aboriginal peoples.

Realities and Ambiguities

To put it mildly, opinions on the effects of the Conquest on the Canadien population vary. What then is the truth behind these different assertions? How can we reconcile them with reality as we know it, based on empirical historical research? There is as yet no definitive recent synthesis discussing the subject in depth; nor is there space in this chapter to examine all of the ramifications of the Conquest for the Canadien population. The main conclusion to emerge from recent empirical studies is that the effects of the Conquest were ambiguous and that neither the miserabilist nor the jovialist interpretation is persuasive. This can be illustrated by looking at two key themes: the economic effects of the Conquest on the Canadiens and the relationship of the Canadiens to political and state power in the post-Conquest period.

Economic Effects

As we have seen, the most fundamental debate on the economic effects of the Conquest on the Canadiens is that between continuity and change. The notion of a radical change long dominating and pushing the Canadiens back into agriculture was replaced more recently by the notion of continuity. This is largely a question of perspective. Clearly, there was little structural change in the colony's fundamental economic structures after the Conquest. The same products dominated (furs for the commercial economy, agricultural products such as wheat and livestock for the subsistence economy), and the relationship between the colony and its European metropolis remained one of subordination; the mercantilist principles favoured by both France and England allowed trade only within each empire, and each empire used colonies essentially as sources of raw materials. But detailed study reveals that the situation was much more complex.

For the economic elites of the French regime, it is clear that the Conquest was a short-term disaster. Many merchants had invested heavily in French paper money, which the French government largely refused to reimburse after the Conquest, leading to heavy losses. Canadien fur traders and import–export merchants, previously linked to French markets and credit networks that they knew well, suddenly found their French business links broken, since all transactions had to go through England or its possessions. They also had to compete with newly arrived British merchants (both from the American colonies and from Britain itself) with well-established credit and business relationships within the British Empire. As a result, over the decades following the Conquest, British merchants replaced Canadiens in the colony's international trade. Canadien seigneurs and nobles also feared for their prosperity and social status, since they were largely excluded from government and military positions. Even the Roman Catholic Church felt menaced, fearing the seizure of its properties by the Protestant English Crown. As a result, many French economic elites did indeed leave the colony and return to France soon after the Conquest.

As we saw, this return to France, evident in the contemporary records, led some historians to postulate the decapitation of Canadien society. However, the empirical data do not support this thesis, at least not in its more extreme form. Studies clearly show that most of the pre-Conquest elites, such as seigneurs and merchants, remained in the colony, especially those born there. They found it more profitable to deal with the new regime rather than leave for an uncertain future in France (see the Biography box on Luc de La Corne). The decapitation was thus at most a partial one, although a very real loss nevertheless. Those who remained had to work hard at adapting to their new situation. For example, Canadien fur merchants faced difficult times immediately after the Conquest, with many retiring from the trade and most no longer involved in international exchanges. However, by reorienting themselves to controlling the trade toward the interior of the continent, and especially through their relationships with the Native peoples who supplied the furs, Canadien merchants

BIOGRAPHY

Luc de La Corne

Luc de La Corne (1711–1784), generally known as La Corne Saint-Luc, is a good example of the adaptation of Canadien elites to British rule after the Conquest. Born in New France into a noble family, La Corne Saint-Luc had a profitable career as a colonial military officer and fur-trade merchant under the French regime. During the War of the Conquest, he used his extensive ties to Native groups, including his mastery of several Native languages, to lead Native allies into battle against the British, winning several notable successes. For these exploits, he was awarded the Croix de Saint-Louis (Cross of Saint-Louis), one of the highest honours available to nobles under the French. He fought in the final major battle between the British and the French in Quebec, the 1760 Battle of Sainte-Foy (near Quebec City), a French victory rendered irrelevant by the French government's failure to send enough reinforcements to follow up.[16]

Saint-Luc de La Corne—Anonymous, 1750–1761, 18th century. 4.5 x 3.4 cm

Source: © McCord Museum

One might expect that the Conquest represented disaster for La Corne Saint-Luc and that the British would have little desire to see him stay. His first inclination was indeed to return to France, as did a significant part of the French colonial nobility and officer class. He left Quebec in 1761, but the ship on which he was travelling, the *Auguste*, was wrecked off the northern tip of Nova Scotia, killing many Canadien nobles and officers and their families. La Corne Saint-Luc was one of the few survivors (he lost two children in the wreck, along with his eldest brother) and made his way back to Quebec. He later wrote a rousing and somewhat self-aggrandizing account of the wreck and his trip back, which was published in Montreal in 1778.

La Corne Saint-Luc stayed in Quebec and accommodated himself very well to the new regime. Although as a Catholic he could no longer hold a military or other official position, he remained one of the wealthiest Canadiens in the colony, with a fine house in Montreal, a retinue of slaves, and an expensive lifestyle. His main income still derived from trade, and despite not being a seigneur he was considered part of the seigneurial class, a group whom the British colonial administrators saw as natural allies. Two of La Corne Saint-Luc's daughters married British officers, and Governor Carleton (later Lord Dorchester) thought well enough of him to name him to the Legislative Council of Quebec in 1775. On 17 August 1775, with six fellow Canadien councillors, La Corne Saint-Luc took the oath specially designed for Catholics in the Quebec Act adjusted to the new regime. At the end of the 1760s, a decade after the Conquest, most canoes engaged in the fur trade leaving Montreal for the Western interior were still financed by Canadien merchants. It was not until the late 1770s, after the outbreak of the American War of Independence, that the arrival of a new set of British fur-trading merchants and changes in the organization of the fur trade itself led to British merchants almost completely replacing Canadien merchants, even in the interior trade. The change was thus gradual, giving Canadiens time to adapt.

that replaced the anti-Catholic measures in the Test Acts. In council he was an active member from the beginning, faithfully present at almost every session. He was also a staunch supporter of the French Party, which generally tended to support autocratic and conservative measures. La Corne Saint-Luc, for example, along with the other members of the French Party, voted in 1782 to refuse a law that would have introduced habeas corpus (the right to contest unwarranted imprisonment) into the colony. Further, when a habeas corpus law passed in 1784, he showed his religious conservatism by proposing a measure that would disallow the right to habeas corpus for members of religious orders who had taken vows—a measure that even the Catholic bishop of Quebec opposed.

La Corne Saint-Luc was not simply a British toady, and he acted against the interests of his former foes when it served his purposes. In the early 1760s he was accused of fomenting discord among France's former Native allies, who in 1763 rose against the British in Pontiac's Rebellion. Later in the fall of 1775, at the beginning of the American War of Independence when American troops invaded Quebec and Montreal was about to fall, La Corne Saint-Luc indirectly contacted the rebel general, Richard Montgomery, to offer secret terms of surrender—only a few weeks after he had been sworn in as a legislative councillor and taken an oath of loyalty to the king! Montgomery did not trust him, describing him as "a great villain and as cunning as the devil," and the Americans eventually imprisoned La Corne Saint-Luc for a short time in New York. After his release he again became a loyal British subject and participated with his Native allies in General John Burgoyne's ill-fated 1777 campaign against the rebels, which ended in disaster at Saratoga. Burgoyne in part blamed La Corne Saint-Luc for his defeat, describing him as "by nature, education, and practice, artful, ambitious, and a courtier." Burgoyne was not the only British official suspicious of La Corne Saint-Luc. Carleton's successor, Governor Haldimand, named him his aide-de-camp but was too suspicious of his changeable loyalties to promote him in the militia as he had requested. Indeed, La Corne Saint-Luc maintained commercial and personal links with France.

But this did not prevent La Corne Saint-Luc from benefiting from the British presence. All in all, for him the Conquest was no disaster, although it did significantly upend his life. Like many of his fellows, he became a staunch defender of the Quebec Act. In one of his last actions in the Legislative Council, he proposed a motion to the king for the preservation of the Quebec Act, which was then under fire from reformers, including some members of council. The motion in its original form stated that the council "wished nothing more strongly than to be able to transmit [the act] to posterity as a precious charter that will ensure the enjoyment of the privileges and the religion of the peoples of this province. [We are] convinced by the experience and the changes that have occurred since the Conquest that the Canadiens will live happily under this Act, and will be in short order indissolubly incorporated into the British nation."[17] On this, at least, he and Bishop Briand were in perfect harmony.

Canadien merchants also invested in seigneuries, which remained mostly in Canadien hands; even in 1791 less than a third of the colony's seigneuries had passed entirely or partially into British control, including that of the British Crown. As a result, two-thirds of the Canadien population had as their only seigneurs either Canadien elites or Catholic religious institutions (which owned a number of important seigneuries), and only about a sixth of Canadiens had as their only seigneur a member of the new British elite. Even in the cities, where the British population was concentrated, Canadiens dominated landholding. Since property was to become an increasingly lucrative source of income in the nineteenth century, Canadien property holders had good long-term prospects. Largely forced out of international trade by the competition of the new British merchants (although there did remain a few important Canadien import–export merchants), Canadien merchants also reoriented themselves toward internal trade: Even in the 1790s, half of those in the colony identifying themselves as merchants were Canadien.

The Canadiens thus adapted to the new economic order rather than withdrawing into agriculture, as was once thought. At the same time, the impact of the Conquest and the arrival of British merchants is undeniable and cannot be minimized. The situation was, in short, complex.

Political and State Power

When we look at Canadiens and the imperial transition from the perspective of political and state power, we again find ambiguity. From either a pro- or an anti-nationalist stance, the Conquest was a fundamental turning point in the relationship between Canadiens and the state, in the British colonial administration. Here again different historiographical visions clash. Notions of a reign of terror, of the crushing of Canadien rights, of their exclusion from power by an anti-papist government are expressed by historians such as Garneau, Groulx, Brunet, and those of the Marxist school. In contrast, notions of a benevolent dictatorship designed for an unenlightened people are found in Creighton, Burt, and others. But almost always, the post-Conquest Canadiens are presented as a people excluded from power, attached to their traditional institutions such as civil law and the French language, and hence firm in their rejection of British institutions. This characterization, whatever the underlying ideology, presents a fundamentally conservative view of Canadiens.

Indeed, the most persistent image is one of radical political change effected by the transfer of power from one crown to another, such as the abolition of French civil law under the 1763 Royal Proclamation (which led to very strong complaints) and the imposition of a British-dominated administration on the francophone population. Certainly, at a constitutional level, the change was clear: Through the Conquest and the change of allegiance, English public law (regulating the relationship between the Crown and its subjects, and including criminal law) replaced French. But more fundamentally, France and England, despite some apparent differences, were quite similar in political organization and operation, both being *ancien régime* states with an emphasis on elite rule, little popular participation in the structures of power, and strong co-operation between church and state. For the first 30 years of British rule, the political structures in Quebec were largely the same as under the French, with the colony ruled directly by a governor (under the French, a tandem of governor and *intendant*) aided by a council appointed from the colony's elites.

There was indeed significant continuity in how the colonial state dealt with the Canadien population. Take, for example, the administration of law. Even though French civil law was formally replaced by English common law in the 1763 Royal Proclamation, courts and notaries continued to follow French practices. The use of French civil law was acknowledged by British officials such as Lord Hillsborough, one of the principal architects of the Royal Proclamation, who wrote in 1768 that "it never entered Our Idea to overturn the Laws and Customs of Canada, with regard to Property."[18] Further, despite assertions by some historians, there is no evidence that the Canadien population boycotted the new courts of the British colonial administration or that they used the courts any less frequently than under the French regime. Many of the court officials were Canadien, although none of the judges were Catholics, and the courts operated in both languages. Even in the criminal courts, where English criminal law definitively replaced its French predecessor, the proceedings in most cases were similar to those under the French regime. Many court proceedings and documents were in French and jurors were drawn from both linguistic communities. Thus the Quebec Act of 1774 formalized a de facto situation when it restored French civil law (while maintaining English law for criminal cases). In the end, the British population of Quebec probably had to adapt to the legal traditions of the Canadiens as much as vice versa.

The same complexity is seen in the everyday administration of the colony. Despite early attempts to emulate British institutions, a significant part of local administration returned to French practices soon after the Conquest. For example, under the French regime the militia had been the principal means of organizing the population to do the bidding of the state, with every male of fighting age being enrolled. The residents of each parish were organized into one or more companies under the direction of a captain, who was also one of the principal agents of the colonial state for nonmilitary matters. The militia was abolished at the beginning of British civil administration in 1764 and replaced by a system of locally elected bailiffs. However, this system lasted only a decade, and the militia was restored in 1775 under the threat of American invasion. Once again, the militia captains served as government representatives in the rural parishes. Roads continued to be built and repaired under the existing French system of co-opting the labour of those who lived along them, under the supervision of an officer called the grand voyer, or chief roads inspector, a position retained from the French regime. Policing functions such as arrests were carried out by professional bailiffs who occupied essentially the same positions, and were often the very same men, as during the French regime. Even the Catholic parish was adopted as the basic administrative unit, an incongruous choice for a supposedly anti-Catholic empire where the Anglican Church was the official church.

If the nature of the colonial state did not change much, what of the persistent notion of the exclusion of Canadiens from power? The classic example, brought up again and again, is the 1763 Royal Proclamation. The proclamation, according to some interpretations, introduced anti-Catholic measures such as **Test Acts**, applied in England and in most of the American colonies, which required Catholics to renounce their faith if they wanted to participate in public administration.

It is undeniable that anti-Catholic measures were indeed enforced in the colony, but much qualification is needed. First, these measures did not specifically target the Canadiens as a conquered people with the object of crushing and assimilating them. They were rather an extension of the domestic and colonial policy of English anti-Catholicism, which was closely paralleled by anti-Protestant measures in France and in pre-Conquest New France. As well, the British colonial administrators quickly realized that in a colony that was over 95 per cent Catholic, excluding Catholics from all public functions was impossible. They thus found the means to circumvent the anti-Catholic measures. For example, Catholics were accepted on juries as early as 1764, while they were still excluded at least in part in England; Catholics were also permitted to serve in subordinate public positions, such as court personnel, notaries, and lawyers, and even in some important positions such as grand voyer. Further, a few francophones in the colony were Protestants, mostly Huguenots, officially banned but unofficially tolerated in New France; the British administrators placed several of them in high public office, notably as judges and magistrates. Finally, the whole policy of formal exclusion of Catholics from public life was abandoned from 1775 under the Quebec Act, which contributed to the American colonies' resentment of Britain and helped lead to the American War of Independence.

It is not enough, however, to say that the Canadiens could have access to all government positions from 1775; the important question is, did they?

Here again we find complexity. It is clear that the British significantly predominated the higher positions in the colonial administration: most often, two-thirds or more British to one-third or less Canadiens. However, two points are important to note. First, the British domination could be seen instead as the usual domination of metropolitans over colonials in both the French and British empires, including the American colonies. Public offices were often lucrative positions doled out as patronage to those who were well connected in the metropolis. Indeed, when the bureaucracies of Canada before the Conquest and Quebec after 1775 are compared, the proportion of high positions such as judgeships, seats on council, and the like that were held by people born in the colony (both British and French) is similar, about a third. Second, and more importantly, the further down one looks into the government bureaucracy, the more Canadiens one finds. Take for example the justices of the peace, the judges who dealt with most criminal cases and handled most local administration in the cities. As soon as the restrictions on Catholics were lifted, Canadiens were quickly in the majority in this important office. This meant that the public face of criminal justice and local administration in Quebec was at least as French as English; again, a most ambiguous situation for a conquered colony.

It must not be thought, however, that the French participation in administration was due to benevolence on the part of British administrators. It partly stemmed from conflicts within the British elite itself, divided between the governors, colonial administrators, and army on the one hand and the British merchants (who before 1775 included many Americans) on the other hand. Neither group appreciated the other: The governors, all former military officers with aristocratic views, disdained the merchants' commercial pursuits and sought to maintain autocratic control, while the merchants urged a more democratic form of government with the formation of a house of assembly (although to be reserved for Protestants only). In this context, Canadien elites, notably the seigneurs and nobles, became important allies of the governors. After all, they shared the same aristocratic and autocratic ideals. British governors kept French aristocratic traditions alive in the colony, living in the same residence as their French predecessors, the Château Saint-Louis in Quebec City; they were fond of French fashions and cooking, to the extent of importing French chefs; all spoke fluent French; and most attempted to reproduce some aspects of courtly life in the small elite society of Quebec City, with balls, banquets, and the like to which the seigneurs and nobles were invited. The wife of Guy Carleton, Lord Dorchester, the longest-reigning governor, had been educated in part in the court of Marie-Antoinette at Versailles. This partnership of British and French elites led to the British governors and their entourage becoming the firmest supporters of the rights of the Catholic Canadiens around what was known as the "French Party" (mostly composed of British administrators), which dominated the appointed colonial legislature through to the end of the 1780s.

But more importantly, the British had early learned that the best way to maintain effective control over a colony was to co-opt local elites and even popular classes into local government, while ensuring that ultimate power rested with British colonial administrators; this is the fundamental principle of "indirect rule." The English state used this model in England itself to administer local populations as well as in many of its other colonies. In Quebec, then, it was natural that colonial administrators would put local administration in the hands of the local population, including Canadiens. The importance here is that this principle created a political space that Canadiens, largely marginalized at the upper levels of political power, were able to occupy. For example, as noted above, in the first decade of British civil rule the colonial administration established a system of local officials in rural areas, the bailiffs. These were derived from the English system of parish constables, where every year heads of households elected one of their own to serve as constable (who was responsible for far more than just policing). The annual bailiff election records show that almost all the bailiffs were Canadien, and that Canadiens participated quite willingly in elections—in theory a new practice for them, though it also had roots in pre-existing forms of local governance such as parish assemblies. Thus, even ordinary Canadiens adapted rapidly to the new system.

Conclusion

Overall, the Conquest was and still is profoundly ambiguous. The effects of the Conquest and the regime change on the Canadien population varied considerably according to social group. Without doubt, the elites were far more affected than ordinary Canadiens, the farmers and other members of the popular classes. For the latter, life did not change dramatically; they were excluded from economic and political power before the Conquest and largely remained so after it. The new British masters preserved the same autocratic structures and, after a few years of uncertainty, confirmed the seigneurial system—some themselves became seigneurs. Socially and economically, the colony remained primarily agricultural. On the other hand, a new group of British, largely Anglo-Scottish elites arrogated to themselves a significant portion of the political and economic power previously held exclusively by the Canadien elites. It is nevertheless difficult to talk of any "decapitation" of Canadien society through the departure or decline of its elites; the great majority of them remained in the colony, and even in the immediate post-Conquest years retained considerable social and economic power, to which they added political power at both the colonial and the local level after 1775. What changed for them was their relative power; from essentially dominating under the French regime, these men had to cede much of their place to the new British elites. Further, by the end of the 1780s the Canadien population, both elite and popular class, once again faced challenges similar to those that had appeared so daunting in the 1760s. These challenges were a rapid influx of British Loyalist settlers from the former American colonies, a decline in the relative economic position of Canadien merchants, and a partial return in the 1790s and early 1800s to an official policy of cultural assimilation. But the more complicated, ambiguous legacy of the period of imperial transition up to the mid-1780s allowed them to adapt to the new regime and to survive the harsh impositions of colonialism that were to come in the nineteenth century, such as the military repression of the Rebellions of 1837–8 and the forced union with Upper Canada in 1841, with the express goals of submerging, assimilating, and anglifying the Canadien population. Still, both popular-class and elite Canadiens were not simply passive spectators of British domination: Both adapted themselves, pragmatically, to the new situation.

Nevertheless, the prime importance of the Conquest rests not only in its immediate effects but also in its long-term consequences. First, the Conquest evidently led to the integration of this francophone society into a larger anglophone milieu, first into the British Empire and then, progressively from 1841 onwards, Canada. This led to considerable and persistent interethnic tensions, expressed in dramatic events such as the Rebellions of 1837–8, the anti-conscription crises in Quebec during both World Wars, or the violent activities of the Front de libération du Québec in the 1960s and the subsequent October Crisis in 1970. Most significant is the key place that the Conquest holds in the collective memory and constructed identity of francophone Quebecers today: the sense of abandonment by France, still seen in the (now diminishing) popular phrase *maudit Français* ("damn Frenchman"); the continuing association of anglophones with the Conqueror; and finally, the profound sense of collective injustice that still pervades parts of Quebec society. Biz, quoted at the beginning of this chapter, was not wrong: The Conquest is indeed one of the founding moments in the collective memory of francophone Quebecers, one of the historic events that comes up again and again in public discourse (though whether it can be called "rape" is less clear). It is in this sense that the empirically verifiable effects of the Conquest on the Canadien population explored in this chapter are perhaps less important today than how the Conquest is perceived in contemporary Quebec's collective memory.

Primary Source

An Extract from the Royal Instructions to James Murray, the First Civil Governor of the British Colony of Quebec, 7 December 1763

The following extracts illustrate the lack of clarity in religious matters. Catholic worship was to be allowed, but only insofar as the laws of England permitted; those laws (notably the Penal Laws) placed severe restrictions on Catholicism and the conversion of the Canadiens to Protestantism was to be vigorously encouraged. In the end, governors such as Murray and his successor, Guy Carleton, largely ignored the religious provisions in their instructions, while the Quebec Act removed the limits placed on Catholic participation in institutions such as the governing council.

> 3. . . . You are forthwith to call Our said Council together, or such of them as can be conveniently assembled, and to cause Our said Commission to You to be read at such Meeting; which being done, You shall then take yourself, and also administer to Our Lieutenant Governors respectively, and to the Members of Our said Council, the Oaths . . . as also to make and subscribe, and cause them to make and subscribe the Declaration mentioned in an Act of Parliament made in the Twenty fifth Year of the Reign of King Charles the Second, intituled, "An Act for preventing Dangers which may happen from Popish Recusants."
>
> . . .
>
> 28. And whereas We have stipulated, by the late Definitive Treaty of Peace concluded at Paris the 10th Day of February 1763, to grant the Liberty of the Catholick Religion to the Inhabitants of Canada, and that We will consequently give the most precise and most effectual Orders, that Our new Roman Catholick Subjects in that Province may profess the Worship of their Religion, according to the Rites of the Romish Church, as far as the Laws of Great Britain permit; It is therefore Our Will and Pleasure, that you do, in all things regarding the said Inhabitants, conform with great Exactness to the Stipulations of the said Treaty in this respect.
>
> . . .
>
> 32. You are not to admit of any Ecclesiastical Jurisdiction of the See of Rome, or any other foreign Ecclesiastical Jurisdiction whatsoever in the Province under your Government.
>
> 33. And to the End that the Church of England may be established both in Principles and Practice, and that the said Inhabitants may by Degrees be induced to embrace the Protestant Religion, and their Children be brought up in the Principles of it; We do hereby declare it to be Our Intention . . . [that] all possible Encouragement shall be given to the erecting Protestant Schools in the said Districts . . . and also for a Glebe and Maintenance for a Protestant Minister and Protestant School-Masters; and you are to consider and report to Us, by Our Commissioners for Trade and Plantations, by what other Means the Protestant Religion may be promoted, established and encouraged in Our Province under your Government.[19]

Questions for Critical Thinking

1. Was the Conquest a disaster for the Canadien population of Quebec? Why or why not?
2. Why did the British treat the conquered Canadiens less harshly then had been feared?
3. What do Quebecers think of the Conquest today?

Notes

1. My thanks to Robert K. Whelan, Brian Young, and Thomas Wien for their comments. All translations in the text are my own. This is essentially the same text as was published in 2010, with only minor revisions and additions to take into account the recent historiography of the Conquest.
2. H. Tétu and C.-O. Gagnon, eds., *Mandements, lettres pastorales et circulaires des évêques de Québec*, vol. 2 (Quebec: A. Coté, 1888), 264–5.
3. Pierre Du Calvet, *Appel à la justice de l'État* (London, 1784), 135.
4. André Pratte, "Le calumet de paix," *La Presse*, 19 July 2008, A29.
5. Biz, "La célébration de l'aliénation Québécoise," *Le Devoir*, 22 December 2007, B5.
6. This is based on searches in the Eureka.cc database for articles from *Le Devoir*, *La Presse*, *Le Soleil* and *Le Droit*, and in canoe.ca for articles from the *Journal de Montréal* and the *Journal de Québec*, from the beginning of 2005 to mid-2009. Similar searches for more recent years show no tendency for this phenomenon to diminish.
7. Didier Fessou, "La Conquête, prise 2," *Le Soleil*, 18 December 2005, C1.
8. H.-R. Casgrain, *Guerre du Canada, 1756–1760 : Montcalm et Levis*, vol. 2 (Quebec: L.-J. Demers, 1891), 235.
9. François-Xavier Garneau, *Histoire du Canada depuis sa découverte jusqu'à nos jours*, vol. 2, 2nd ed. (Quebec: John Lovell, 1852), 378.
10. Marcel Rioux, *La Question du Québec* (Paris: Seghers, 1969), 41.
11. Ibid.
12. Francine Lavoie, "Un symbole de notre statut minoritaire," *Le Devoir*, 25 September 2007, A6.
13. Pierre Dubuc and Marc Laviolette, "Pour la relance du Parti québécois," *Le Devoir*, 19 May 2007, B5.
14. René Boulanger, *La bataille de la mémoire : essai sur l'invasion de la Nouvelle-France en 1759* (Quebec: Éditions du Québécois, 2007), 23.
15. In English, the two collections edited by Phillip Buckner and John Reid, given in the bibliography at the end of this chapter, provide the best overview of new work. There is a great deal of new work in French; see notably Laurent Veyssière and Bertrand Fonck, eds., *La guerre de Sept Ans en Nouvelle-France* (Québec: Septentrion/Paris: Presses de l'Université Paris-Sorbonne, 2011); Laurent Veyssière, ed., *La Nouvelle-France en héritage* (Paris: Armand Colin/Ministère de la Défense, 2013); Laurent Veyssière, Sophie Imbeault and Denis Vaugeois, eds., *1763 : Le traité de Paris bouleverse l'Amérique* (Québec: Septentrion, 2013); and Bertrand Fonck and Laurent Veyssière, eds., *La fin de la Nouvelle-France* (Paris: Armand Colin/Ministère de la Défense, 2013).
16. This biography of La Corne Saint-Luc is mainly based on the biography by Pierre Tousignant and Madeleine Dionne-Tousignant in the *Dictionary of Canadian Biography*, http://www.biographi.ca/en/bio/la_corne_luc_de_4E.html. For a more detailed treatment, see Marjolaine Saint-Pierre, *Lacorne Saint-Luc : l'odyssée d'un noble, 1711–1784* (Québec: Septentrion, 2013).
17. *Journals of the Legislative Council of Quebec*, 21 April 1784, Library and Archives Canada, R10808-4-X.
18. Adam Shortt and Arthur G. Doughty, *Documents Relating to the Constitutional History of Canada, 1759–1791*, 2nd ed. (Ottawa: J. de L. Taché, 1918), 297.
19. Ibid., 182–3, 191–2.

Select Bibliography

A significant part of the relevant historiography of the Conquest is in French and is not presented here. The older French-language historiography is partially summarized in English in Miquelon, Neatby, and Nish; for a French anthology, see Charles-Philippe Courtois, ed., *La Conquête : une anthologie* (Montreal: Typo, 2009). For recent French-language publications, see above, note 15.

Brunet, Michel. *French Canada and the Early Decades of British Rule, 1760–1791*. Ottawa: Canadian Historical Association, 1968. Available at www.collectionscanada.gc.ca/cha-shc/008004-111.01-e.php?q1=H&interval=100.

Buckner, Phillip, and John G. Reid, eds. *Remembering 1759: The Conquest of Canada in Historical Memory*. Toronto: University of Toronto Press, 2012.

———. *Revisiting 1759: The Conquest of Canada in Historical Perspective*. Toronto: University of Toronto Press, 2012.

Fyson, Donald. *Magistrates, Police, and People: Everyday Criminal Justice in Quebec and Lower Canada, 1764–1837*. Toronto: Osgoode Society/University of Toronto Press, 2006.

Igartua, José. "A Change in Climate: The Conquest and the Marchands of Montreal." *Historical Papers* (1974): 115–34.

Lawson, Philip. *The Imperial Challenge: Quebec and Britain in the Age of the American Revolution*. Montreal and Kingston: McGill-Queen's University Press, 1989.

Marshall, Peter. "British North America, 1760–1815." In *The Oxford History of the British Empire*, vol. 2, *The Eighteenth Century*, edited by P. J. Marshall, 372–93. Oxford: Oxford University Press, 2001.

Miquelon, Dale, ed. *Society and Conquest: The Debate on the Bourgeoisie and Social Change in French Canada, 1700–1850*. Toronto: Copp Clark, 1977.

Neatby, Hilda. *Quebec: The Revolutionary Age, 1760–1791*. Toronto: McClelland & Stewart, 1966.

———. *The Quebec Act: Protest and Policy*. Scarborough, ON: Prentice-Hall, 1972.

Nish, Cameron, ed. *The French Canadians, 1759–1766: Conquered? Half-Conquered? Liberated?* Toronto: Copp Clark, 1966.

Tousignant, Pierre. "The Integration of the Province of Quebec into the British Empire, 1763–91. Part I: From the Royal Proclamation to the Quebec Act." *Dictionary of Canadian Biography* IV (1979): xxii–xlix.

3 Thinking about Power in Post-Rebellion Quebec, 1837–1867

Brian Young, McGill University

Timeline

1774 Quebec Act is passed.

1791 Constitutional Act is passed.

1837–8 Rebellions in Lower and Upper Canada.

1839 Report of Lord Durham is released.

1840 Act of Union (Upper and Lower Canada) is passed.

1841 Registry Act (Lower Canada) is passed.

1838–41 Special Council (Lower Canada) is established.

1847 Responsible government is granted in Lower Canada.

1853–4 Establishment of faculties of law at McGill University and Université Laval.

1854 Seigneurial Act begins the process of dismantling seigneurialism in Lower Canada.

1854 Rome's Doctrine of Immaculate Conception is released.

1864 Charlottetown and Quebec Conferences on federation.

1866 Civil Code of Lower Canada takes effect.

1867 Canadian Confederation.

1975 Quebec Charter of Human Rights and Freedoms is adopted.

1982 Canadian Charter of Rights and Freedoms is adopted.

2000 Clarity Act is passed.

2001 Conrad Black renounces Canadian citizenship to sit in the British House of Lords.

2008 Cardinal Jean-Claude Turcotte renounces membership in the Order of Canada.

2013 2013 Parti Québécois government proposes to amend Quebec's 1975 Charter of Human Rights and Freedoms by adding a Charter of Values to limit the wearing of "conspicuous" religious symbols by state personnel; proposal dropped after defeat of government in the 2014 election.

Why, in 1878, would the most important religious leader in Canada, Elzéar-Alexandre Taschereau, organize an elaborate procession through the Quebec capital to rebury the bones of his predecessor Bishop François de Laval, who had been dead some 170 years? And, in a Victorian age that featured change, the photograph, the telegraph, and the Darwinian theory of evolution, what might explain his determination to impose the doctrine of Immaculate Conception (1854) across Catholic Quebec? From our standpoint in the twenty-first century, his concerns might seem like necrophilia, narcissism, or an anachronism from a more devout time. Or these actions might alert us to the fact that the cardinal, far from being pretentious, was living up to his reputation as a very practical "Prince" with Machiavellian goals, focused on wielding power and authority in Quebec society. Indeed, his connecting of the dots of memory around old bones of religious heroes and his aggressive campaign to control women, their sexuality, and their visions of conception illustrate the complexity of power in mid-nineteenth-century French Canada. Marx and Engels, now out of favour but seasoned observers nonetheless of matters of power, may not have had it entirely right, at least for the Quebec example, in arguing that by creating modern industry and world markets, the bourgeoisie had "conquered . . . exclusive political sway."[1] In this brief discussion we want to broaden our view of power to include priests, fathers, and yes, professors, journalists, and other purveyors of information.

Political interpretations of the mid-nineteenth century are readily available. Those that discuss Quebec—or Lower Canada, as it was known before Confederation in 1867—often use a neo-Marxist analysis to show the power of a developing professional and industrial bourgeoisie and its frequent use of police or the military to carry out state violence.[2] Politics in the sense of constitutions and parliaments will have an important place on the pages that follow, but if we look below the surface and think about the significance of old bones, Virgin Birth, or in our times power over the life of the unborn, we see that power in society is also hugely influenced by the Church, by law, and by gender and culture.

Eruption, Repression, and Reconciliation

Given the breadth of these power relations, historians try to organize their explanations by situating power into defined periods of time and space. Among the schemas used to define periods in Quebec's history are the following:

- constitutional landmarks in Canada's progress from colony to nation-state;
- the transition to modernity;
- the evolution of Lower Canada/Quebec from a feudal to an industrial economy; and
- the stages in the evolution of women's rights.

In all of these schemas, the Rebellions of 1837–8 in Lower Canada and the Canadian Confederation in 1867 are central events, making them useful bookends for examining how political, state, institutional, and family powers were transformed. The first decade, 1837–49, was characterized by eruption and repression. For eruption we have the Rebellions, the suspension of the Legislature and imposition of a Special Council, and later in the decade, the burning of the Parliament building in Montreal and publication of a manifesto of annexation to the United States. Repressive measures in the late 1830s and 1840s included imprisonment, exile, and execution of rebels or Patriotes, as they were called by the French Canadians. Also repressive, although Lord Durham would undoubtedly have denied it, was his report in 1839. Appointed governor to inquire into the Rebellions, he reduced French-Canadian nationality to the state of being "destitute" and its people as having "no history and no literature." By suspending the Patriote-dominated assembly following the Rebellions, the governor and his Special Council held direct power. Finally, the union of Lower Canada with Upper Canada in 1840 suggested the subordination and even assimilation of francophones into a larger English Canada.

As early as the mid-1840s, however, measures of reconciliation counterbalanced these tendencies. The state, whatever its historical suspicions of ecclesiastical power, enabled the Roman Catholic Church to increase its power in French Canada. Bicultural political alliances were also established. Francophone leaders such as Louis-Hippolyte LaFontaine and George-Étienne Cartier sought alliance with Upper Canadian, English-speaking Protestant counterparts like Robert Baldwin and Canada's first prime minister, John A. Macdonald. This coalition would play a central role in achieving **responsible government**, building a federal state, deconstructing **seigneurialism**, and fundamentally revising customary, mortgage, and contract law. At the same time, this group successfully marginalized liberals, Tories, nationalists, and religious zealots, both Protestant and Catholic.

It may also be useful to think of this pattern of eruption, repression, and reconciliation as recurring. Can it be compared, for example, to the period after the Conquest of 1759–60 or to the period marked by the independence movement and referendums in the last quarter of the twentieth century?

After the Conquest, repressive measures to deport French Catholics (as had been done with the Acadians in the Maritimes), to assimilate them, or to impose British law, institutions, and a Church of England Protestantism were quickly abandoned as impractical both for demographic reasons and out of respect for British liberties. Instead, the Quebec Act (1774) and Constitutional Act (1791) represented imperial recognition of French institutions and of a certain legal geography for French Canada, albeit always assuming that French Canadians would ultimately be a minority in the envisioned larger English-speaking Canadian state.

Can a similar pattern be seen in the aftermath of the narrowly failed 1995 referendum on Quebec sovereignty? Initial reactions of the Canadian federalist majority included the Clarity Act (2000), which gives Ottawa scrutiny over questions posed in future sovereignty referendums and over the validity of referendum results. More recently Ottawa has made gestures of reconciliation, including financial measures to give Quebec more autonomy in social programs, immigration, and health. In ways not always appreciated in Quebec, the federal government has recognized Quebec as a "nation," albeit a minority nation within a larger English-speaking Canada that defines itself as multicultural.

There is a final caveat to understanding power relations in both mid-nineteenth-century Canada and across the entire span of Canadian history from 1760 to the present. We must understand the centrality of the institutions of *ancien régime* France and, more important, the priority of the British constitutional and cultural systems over republican models erected in France and the United States. Any tendency to republican governance was purged by the abortive Rebellions of 1837–8 and by the failure of the short-lived American annexation movement. The parliamentary, party, and cabinet system; the established (state-supported) Roman Catholic and Anglican churches; and Quebec's judicial and administrative structures took their inspiration from Britain. British constitutional practice and its Canadian imitations were resolutely pragmatic, compromising, and much less theoretical than the models of intellectuals like Charles Louis de Montesquieu or Thomas Jefferson.

The dominance of British culture had strong implications for communication in Quebec. From our own school and tourist experiences with other languages, we know that mastery of language tilts power, be it that of a waiter or a judge! Checkmating of the nationalist movement, the subsequent reinforcement of British tradition, and the ongoing economic integration of Quebec with the dominant cultures in North America all meant increasing power for English as both a language and a way of thinking, even though the vast majority of Quebecers, then and now, were French-speaking.

Changing Forms of Political Power

Before the 1840s, Lower Canada was overwhelmingly rural, and imposing authority on its frequently unruly peasantry was a primary concern. Rural power in both New France and in Lower Canada had been concentrated in the hands of Crown officials and an aristocracy that exerted seigneurial control along the St Lawrence River and its tributaries. Other groups exercising significant power included the parish clergy and, in Montreal and Quebec City, the great merchants, whose wealth was derived from

BIOGRAPHY

George-Étienne Cartier

I first took up study of Cartier, a leading Montreal politician and a Father of Canadian Confederation, as a graduate student who was interested in industrialization and railways in Quebec. When I published what I thought was an innocuous study of his political defeat in the federal elections of 1872, I was shocked to receive a sharp rebuttal from Michel Brunet, nationalist historian at the Université de Montréal.[3] That episode brought home to me the complexity of issues around identity in Quebec and the sensitive relationship between history and the "National Question." My interest piqued, I set out to write a full biography of Cartier, poking at the vicissitudes of his career, his place among the Patriotes of 1837, and his role in founding what would become the Conservative Party. I was impressed by the complexity of his political milieu, his combination of being a francophone Montrealer and a pan-Canadian federalist, and his defence of the Catholic Church despite being a strong free thinker.

Portrait of George-Étienne Cartier, image 142 x 97 mm: on mount 181 x 130 mm Positive Paper Silver–albumen.

Notman & Son/Library and Archives Canada/C-06166

I was writing in the heyday of Pierre Elliott Trudeau, and I was struck by how these two Montreal politicians, albeit separated by a century, faced similar issues around individual mores, nationality, identity, and biculturalism. Cartier's own papers were largely destroyed following his death in 1873, but a few letters in archives in Montreal and Ottawa, the diaries of relatives, collections of his speeches, and the records of public debates in Ottawa and Quebec gave me adequate primary sources to construct a biography, *George-Étienne Cartier: Montreal Bourgeois*, published in 1981.

Cartier was born in Saint-Antoine sur Richelieu in 1814. His parents' decision to baptize him "George" in honour of King George III, rather than the French "Georges," was symptomatic of the politicization that would dog him throughout his life. At age 10 he was sent to the Collège de Montréal, a classical college run by the Sulpician priests. Trained in the law, in the 1830s Cartier was attracted to the Patriote cause of Louis-Joseph Papineau. He joined the Sons of Liberty and fought at the battle of Saint-Denis in October 1837; charged with treason, he fled to the United States.

With the annulment of the charges against him, Cartier was soon back in Montreal practising as a well-connected lawyer. He was an early supporter of Louis-Hippolyte LaFontaine and his alliance with anglophone reformers in Upper Canada. In 1848 he was elected to the Legislative Assembly, by 1854 he was in the cabinet, and two years later he was Canada's second-ranking politician as John A. Macdonald's French-Canadian lieutenant. In the administrative structuring of Canada in this period, Cartier played a major role in drafting legislation affecting education, municipalities, seigneurialism, and particularly the codification of Quebec civil law. Affable, capable in ethnic politics, and able to bridge the gap between religious minorities—Protestants in Lower Canada and Roman Catholics in the rest of Canada—he used his political connections well in acting for both the land interests of the Sulpicians and the industrial projects of the Grand Trunk Railway.

It was as a Father of Confederation that he takes his place in Canadian history. A conservative and a strong believer in the British balanced constitution, particularly its emphasis on an appointed upper house, he feared republicanism and American models that emphasized democracy or the "melting pot." As early as 1858 he adopted **federalism** as the best constitutional solution to Canada's political impasse, and his discourse bears comparison with that of Trudeau:

> . . . historical facts teach us that French-Canadians and English-speaking Canadians should have for each other a mutual sympathy, having both reason to congratulate themselves that Canada is still a British colony. . . . If we unite, we will form a political nationality independent of the national origin and religion of individuals.[4]

He agreed to sit in a coalition government in 1864 and represented Lower Canada at conferences in Charlottetown and Quebec City where the Quebec Resolutions were hammered out into what would become the British North America Act. After the Confederation of Canada in 1867, Cartier served in the first Macdonald government as Minister of Militia and Defence. By now, far from his Patriote sympathies in the Rebellions of 1837–8, Cartier insisted on a British aristocratic rank and in 1867 he was made a baronet. In the same year and, benefiting from the double mandate (the right to stand for office at two levels of government), "Sir" George-Étienne Cartier was elected to both the Canadian Parliament and the Quebec Legislative Assembly. His career, however, was winding down. As Quebec's most prominent federalist, he was unable to effectively defend a French-Canadian, Catholic identity in divisive issues like Catholic schools in New Brunswick and Riel's first rebellion in Manitoba (1869–70). Tension from **industrialization**, ethnic intolerance, and increasing British immigration weakened his projects for ethnic equality and for a federation in which French Canadians might jump at his cry of "All Aboard for the West." The rigidity of ultramontanist Catholic leaders like Bishop Ignace Bourget of Montreal and the rise of a liberal movement weakened his Montreal base of support. In the 1872 election, his enemies brought him down over his involvement in the Canadian Pacific slush fund.

These were the political ups and downs associated with hard-rock politics in Montreal. But his life had many other elements to interest the historian. A quintessential French Montrealer and political leader of Canada's most important and most bicultural city, he was on the cusp of French–English relations. To the chagrin of nationalists, Cartier was a committed anglophile, shopping for clothes and titles in London. A Gallican in his Catholicism, he was comfortable with the growth of the secular state. He had a positivist vision of a pan-Canadian society that, through a federal balance of powers and construction of a new "political nationality," might protect its political minorities. But competing visions were evident in his own home. His wife, Hortense Fabre, 14 years his junior, was connected to ultramontane clerics who were hostile to his religious tolerance and liberal social mores.

It is perhaps fitting that the anglophile Cartier died in May 1873 in London, seeking remedies for his kidney disease. His body was returned to Canada for a triumphant funeral in Notre Dame Basilica and burial in the parish cemetery Notre Dame des Neiges. He is memorialized in Montreal with a huge winged statue on Mount Royal (the base of the statue is now the site for intercultural smoking and drumming in Sunday afternoon "tam tam jams"). Hortense Fabre retired to France following Cartier's death and died in Cannes in 1898.

staple trades like furs, from importing goods from Britain and the Caribbean, or from trading locally in food, alcohol, or firewood. To give a face to these groups, we can think of Sir John Colborne, governor of British North America and representative of Queen Victoria during the Rebellions; Louis-Joseph Papineau, seigneur and leader of the Patriote movement; and Peter McGill, importer, banker, and land developer. (These men can be easily researched online through the website of the *Dictionary of Canadian Biography.*)

These groups—Crown officials, seigneurs, and merchants—lost power in the decades following 1837. The dismantling of the British mercantile system in favour of free trade encouraged Britain to step back from direct political control of the colony; Britain transferred power and the expenses of the colony from the governor and Colonial Office into the hands of Canadian authorities. The power exercised by governors like Colborne and his successors Lord Durham and Lord Elgin diminished after the 1850s. In the late 1840s, a half-century struggle between the legislature and executive for control over the taxation purse came to an end. The granting of responsible government, the development of party and cabinet systems, and the alliance of centrists in Upper and Lower Canada brought about the dependence of the executive branch on a binational majority in the legislative assembly. Papineau, leader of the movement for national liberation, anti-English, and elitist, could never aspire to majority status in this structure. Nor would Peter McGill and his generation of Tory and anti-French merchants remain important players in centrist politics and in establishing state structures to promote the railways and factories that would industrialize the St Lawrence Valley.

Let us briefly examine how political power evolved over the 1840s and 1850s. Martial law was proclaimed after the first Rebellion in 1837 and the assembly was suspended. After the second wave of Rebellions in 1838, harsher punishments were imposed. Some 850 Patriotes were arrested and 108 were court martialled, 99 of whom were condemned to death. Of these, 12 were actually hanged and 58 were deported to remote British penal colonies like Australia and Bermuda. The pain of this failure and punishment, and its heightening in Lord Durham's Report, has marked Quebec history ever since. Nationalist historian Maurice Séguin, for example, has not been alone in interpreting the period as "serfdom" under "British occupation."[5] Without doubt, the Rebellions facilitated a purging of nationalists, an accession to power by a new and biethnic group of moderates, and the expansion of conservative controls imposed by the Catholic Church. The Special Council, dominated by members of the anglophone elite, legislated for the colony between 1838 and 1841 and set in place a new institutional framework that included asylums, Catholic classical colleges, rural police, circuit courts, and literary societies. It began the breakdown of old seigneurial controls and the stranglehold of a religious order on land in Montreal, offering the city's landowners the right to commute their lands into freehold tenure. It further reassured capitalists through a Registry Act (1841), which forced the public registration of contracts such as land sales and mortgages. Finally, it accorded social and corporate powers to the Catholic Church, allowing existing religious communities to admit new members, permitting entry into Lower Canada of orders from France and Ireland, and exempting the property of religious institutions from taxes.

The Act of Union of 1840, one of Lord Durham's proposals, did permit a legislative assembly that would replace the Special Council. The assembly had 42 seats each for the newly named Canada East and Canada West (formerly Lower and Upper Canada), an apparent measure of equality that masked the fact that Canada East had a population of 650,000 compared to Canada West's 450,000. Power in this political structure inevitably shifted away from regional or nationalist parties to pragmatic, bicultural political alliances. Leaders like LaFontaine and Cartier found common ground with their Ontario counterparts around a program of canals, railways, and economic development. They agreed to leave provocative national issues such as schools and social institutions to separate, autonomous treatment in both Canada East and Canada West. This separation into provincial jurisdiction of controversial religious and social issues would be echoed later in Confederation. The formation of this centrist party, known first as the Reform Party and ultimately as the Conservative Party, coincided with the repeal of the British Corn Laws and Navigation Acts after 1846, as Britain embraced free trade and re-evaluated the worth of settler colonies like Canada. In 1847, Governor General Lord Elgin accepted the principle of responsible government, calling on LaFontaine and Robert Baldwin to form a government after they won an election majority. Passage of the Rebellion Losses Bill, which compensated Patriotes for their losses in the Rebellions, enraged the anglophone elite. In April 1849 they were at the core of an angry mob that torched the Parliament building in Montreal while other commercial leaders called for annexation to the United States.

Although politics in Lower Canada, or Quebec as it was known after Confederation in 1867, would remain deeply fractured, with strong liberal and nationalist tendencies, the LaFontaine–Cartier reformers kept themselves at centre stage. In the larger politics of Canada, they espoused liberal capitalism, free trade, and immigrant labour while at home they shored up their base by encouraging an expanding institutional and ideological place for the Catholic Church. They paid careful attention to regional concerns, subsidized local colonization and roads and railways into frontier zones, and used government patronage to good effect. Conscious of Lower Canada's sensitivities and power structures, they responded slowly to capitalist demands to dismantle seigneurialism, seeking support in particular from the Catholic clergy, proprietors of some of the largest seigneuries. They also understood the economic and regional importance in Montreal and the Eastern Townships of Quebec's English-speaking community, its conservatism, and its fears as an essentially Protestant minority. Reform leaders made important concessions; Quebec would be officially bilingual with English increasingly dominant in business and equal as a language in government and in the law. Speaking in English, moderates like Cartier emphasized their British loyalty, love of things British, and trust in the building of a bicultural, pan-Canadian state. They were also attentive to the future of English Montreal's McGill University and to English schools and benevolent and social institutions; and in the federation negotiations after the mid-1850s the Protestant minority was given assurances concerning its schools and rights to a fixed number of seats from the Eastern Townships.

Whatever its attraction to capitalists and central Canadian moderates, Confederation was never an easy sell in French Quebec or, for that matter, in parts of the Maritimes. Regionalism, increasing ethnic tensions, the concentration of power in Ottawa, and fears of being swamped by a Protestant and potentially racist English Canada tested federalist leaders like Cartier. While his opponents accused him of putting in place a legislative union rather than a federation and of leaving the French-Canadian population "fast asleep," Cartier, whatever his private cynicism, spoke of a political dream. In the old order, one's place depended on position in a hierarchy that was rooted in feudalism, while in the republican model, citizenship and constitutional rights guaranteed liberty and equality. Cartier suggested a third possibility, promoting a vision of identity and ultimately of sovereignty that was more layered, more intricate, and perhaps unattainable! He pointed to the model of existing autonomous jurisdictions in religious and ethnic matters such as education. He described the federation as potentially a new "political nationality" and, standing Durham on his head, described a society in which both French and English would remain intact and in which the common good would result from competition and imitation among races, nations, and religions:

> We would form a political nationality with which neither the national origin, nor the religion of any individual would interfere . . . We were of different races, not for the purpose of warring against each other, but in order to compete and emulate for the general welfare.[6]

At Confederation negotiations in Charlottetown and Quebec City in 1864, Lower Canadian delegates accepted a highly centralized state with protection of French-Canadian interests in Ottawa largely delegated to an upper house or senate that had no financial control and whose members were appointed for life. The financial terms of the British North America Act, which enacted Confederation, reinforced Quebec's subservience to Ottawa, since more than half of the province's income was a federal subsidy. Centralization was, however, entirely within the logic of Canadian capitalism, and the province's bankers, shippers, and industrial producers had access to strengthened, integrated markets. Quebec did retain much autonomy in powers that included education, social services, and natural resources. This would be important for the Church and for a local professional elite.

Power and the Church

Legislative politics and constructing the Canadian federation, as we have suggested by our reference to "old bones," were only pieces in Quebec's larger power puzzle. While the French and American republics and, to a lesser extent, English Canada emphasized the secular in modernizing and industrializing societies, Quebec took a distinct route. You may have noticed that the Roman Catholic Church, except for its parish role, was not particularly emphasized in our description of the dominant forces in Lower Canada before the Rebellions. True, the Church had been a loyal supporter of the Crown stretching back through the War of 1812 with the United States, through the horror for Catholics of the French Revolution, and through its comfortable connivance with both British and French officials across the eighteenth century. But the Church had had difficulty recruiting and training priests, and the peasantry had remained wary of the clergy's ambitions and controls. The Church's influence, however, had been particularly critical in the Rebellions of 1837–8, with bishops describing the insurrections as "criminal in the eyes of God." In rural parishes, the Church used its muscle to defuse unrest among the peasantry while priests from the Seminary of Montreal discouraged Montreal's growing Irish-Catholic working-class population from assimilating the Rebellions into their historical struggle against British exploitation. A grateful elite returned the favour in the 1840s, granting the Church power to develop schools, hospitals, and other social institutions for the Catholic population.

Membership of female religious communities, which had remained steady before 1840, doubled in the 1840s. Twelve male orders (most imported from Europe) were established in Quebec in the second half of the nineteenth century. The Church was given virtual autonomy in teaching Catholic children, training teachers, curricula, and textbooks, and powerful authority over the flow of information through books, clubs, and newspapers. Whereas only 36 per cent of the parishioners at Montreal's Notre Dame Basilica took Easter communion in 1839, virtually all of the Catholic population of the diocese of Montreal did so in the 1860s. With this expanded role, the Church used its power to push strongly in conservative directions, becoming more moralistic, more disciplinary of women, and emphasizing French Canada's separateness from the secular and materialistic culture of English-speaking North America. Adding to this growing moral and social authority, the Church, in the void left by the collapse of Papineau's Patriote movement, successfully portrayed itself as the primary defender of a French-Canadian nation. This orientation and insularity from North American society had effects stretching perhaps to the present in issues like immigration and integration. Catholic Quebec, with the singular exception of Irish Catholics, did not encourage a pluralist vision, tending instead to a defensive and exclusive corral protecting faith and nation. Intermarriage, American or English-Canadian trade unions, and Protestant university teachers posed difficulties, as we see below in the story of Elzéar-Alexandre Taschereau. Later in the century, newcomers such as Jews and other non-Catholic immigrants would gravitate to Protestant, English-speaking institutions. Nor was the Catholic Church immune from internal division between ultramontanists who believed in the superiority of the pope and those, led by the archbishop of Quebec, who gave predominance to the Church as a national institution.

CASE STUDY

The Consecration of Archbishop Taschereau, Quebec City, 20 March 1871

When I think of major ceremonial events that marked the immediate past, an Olympic opening, a Super Bowl game, or a royal marriage come to mind. Each had its pageantry, banners, fly-pasts, and rituals; its speeches, royal boxes, and "big shots"; its rock-star music and its rush of journalists and photographers. In their wake and in our cities and cupboards are stadiums, mementoes, and "royal" coffee cups. Similar public events were staged in nineteenth-century Quebec around events like the British victory at Waterloo, the opening of Montreal's Victoria Bridge, or the funeral of Albert, Prince Consort to Queen Victoria. Elzéar-Alexandre Taschereau was consecrated as archbishop in the Basilica of Quebec City on 20 March 1871. The extravagant ceremony included a papal bull; the display of coats of arms, uniforms, ecclesiastical robes, and flags; and the presence of bishops, justices, senators, and other notables from around the Atlantic world. Banquets, concerts, and symbolic processions through city streets and specially constructed triumphal arches culminated in a mass, communion, and bestowal of the ring and mitre on the new archbishop. The event was commemorated in paintings, special tokens, photos (thanks to new daguerreotype technology), and later, in front of the Basilica, a memorial statue of the archbishop.

Taschereau was a media star of his day, distinguished, cultured, and available for interviews and photos. The fourth generation in an aristocratic family, his father was both a judge and seigneur. While his brother chose law, rising to sit on the Supreme Court of Canada, Elzéar-Alexandre was drawn to the priesthood, the career of three of his uncles, including the bishop of Quebec. Trained in the classical-college tradition with an excellent education in the sciences, literature, and philosophy, he took a Grand Tour of Europe before being ordained a priest in 1842. Instead of serving as a parish priest, he spent his career as an intellectual and administrator; he taught at the Seminary of Quebec, took a doctorate in theology in Rome, and served as superior of the seminary and rector of Laval University.[7]

Occurring at the time of the new Quebec Civil Code, the Confederation of Canada, and the turbulence surrounding Louis Riel and the future of French Canadians in the West, his nomination as archbishop was part of the affirmation of a Quebec national identity rooted in the Roman Catholic Church, elite families, and historical legal, seminary, and convent institutions. His four-hour consecration was a major celebration. The Basilica was lavishly decorated for the occasion, with an artist from the *Illustrated News* capturing the scene for an audience throughout the British world. Journalists drew particular attention to the chandeliers above the altar from which hung the archbishop's coat of arms. The ceremony began with a triumphant procession that began next door to the Basilica at the Archbishop's Palace, but wound by a circuitous route past the city's most important institutions. It was officiated by the archbishop of Toronto who was seconded by eight bishops. Witnessing in front pews were 150 priests, the professoriate from Laval University, and political, diplomatic, and judicial notables. Among Taschereau notables present were his brother, Judge Jean-Thomas Taschereau, and Major Eugène-Arthur Taschereau, aide-de-camp to the lieutenant governor. After he was granted the ring, mitre, gloves, and pastoral baton of an archbishop, the bestowal of the kiss of peace from each of his episcopal colleagues, and the singing of a Te Deum, "His Grandeur" blessed the congregation:

continued

> A sentiment of profound respect marked each bowed head and a shiver of joy and of religious enthusiasm could be felt through the immense crowd. There was something infinitely solemn in this majestic benediction even if it had the familiarity of the blessing a father might give his children. It was in fact a moment of profound veneration and of the most respectful love typical of the great moments of affection stamped with the seal of religion.[8]

Taschereau used his office as archbishop and then as Canada's first cardinal (1886) to consolidate Roman Catholic institutions and to position the Church at the core of a French-Canadian national identity. He oversaw the establishment of some 40 new parishes, 30 missions, and regional classical colleges. He worked to strengthen Laval University as a Catholic university and introduced several teaching orders into Canada, including the Marist Brothers and the Clerics of Saint-Viateur. His funeral was held in the Basilica in April 1898, the same space where he had been consecrated archbishop and cardinal. The family biographer described the funeral ceremony as "the most impressive ever held in our country."[9] In 1923, with his nephew Premier Louis-Alexandre Taschereau looking on, a grateful province dedicated a statue in the archbishop's honour in the square in front of the Basilica. Designed and cast in bronze in Paris, the statue gave physical permanence to the ceremony and to his career in Church, seminary, and university. While the religiosity, emphasis on death, and masculine dominance in the Taschereau consecration perhaps differentiate it from Olympic opening ceremonies and Super Bowl victory celebrations, they are all examples of "theatre," as the wise Edward P. Thompson pointed out—spectacles that use public space to reinforce values and hierarchies.[10]

Power, Law, and Seigneurialism

Our discussion of power in mid-nineteenth-century Quebec must next consider the fundamental changes that occurred around historical systems of law and landholding. As a result of the Quebec Act (1774), the British had permitted jurisdiction of the family, social relations, and seigneurial lands to continue under French customary law, a system summed up in the sixteenth-century **Custom of Paris**. Our contemporary period can be described as "a charter age." Besides the expression of legal rights through the Canadian and Quebec Charters of Rights, there was heated debate in Quebec in 2014 over a proposed Charter of Values that would have seen the government imposing restrictions on religious symbols worn by public employees. The customary law of mid-nineteenth-century Quebec was different—it was less specific, less tightly written, and had more of a sense of historical maxims, what a sage called "the spirit of the centuries." Montesquieu used that same phrase in his *Spirit of the Laws* (1748), and other French legal thinkers related law to "natural order"; historian Bettina Bradbury alludes to the medieval hierarchies of that law, referring to the "superior chivalry of French law." At the time of the Rebellions, there was no official Lower Canadian version of the Custom.

Customary law in outlining seigneurialism did not give absolute rights in property, insisting instead on the priority of the family and of vulnerable widows or children. This clashed with the principles of a modern, capitalist state in which the individual can contract his labour or property apart from family needs and in which registered creditors have priority. A final frustration for those who favoured a rational, scientific, and uniform system was the fact that English (and sometimes American) common law applied in English-speaking regions. Wills, for example, could be prepared under the English system, while in the Eastern Townships a Vermont-style contract for the sale of a horse sealed by a handshake rather than a written agreement might be valid. Power and right in these polyjural situations was difficult to determine and remote from modern concepts of the law as an ordered and predictable science and discipline.

Since at least the beginning of the nineteenth century, feudal (and that is the correct term) institutions like customary law and seigneurialism in Lower Canada faced various attacks. These accelerated with capital accumulation in projects like railways or industries and with the prospect of geographical expansion into a broader Canadian state. Although wealthy English Quebecers had been major purchasers of seigneuries, their community regularly attacked it as obstructive to capitalist development. Seigneurialism applied to urban centres as well as the rural parishes, and the big industrial millers and land developers in Montreal chafed at its milling monopoly and its *lods et ventes* (sales taxes) on improvements. Capitalists and industrial producers demanded an end to seigneurial and customary rights in favour of a "free" market in land and labour. In the new legal and property regimes resulting from codifying the civil law and dismantling seigneurialism, individual rights, freedom of contract, and freehold property took precedence over family and community priorities that reached back to early Christian and medieval concepts of family and social relations. A universal education system; a province-wide judicial infrastructure of courthouses, jails, and police; new municipalities; and new forms of taxation were other pieces in this puzzle of changing relations of power.

The 1850s were a critical period in establishing what would become Quebec's legal foundations. Faculties of law, schools in which law would be treated as a scientific discipline, were established at McGill and Laval Universities in 1853–4. In 1854, the Seigneurial Act dismantled seigneurialism, taking land from its entwined and feudal context and making it a specific and distinct commodity that an individual could freely buy and sell. The most critical year was probably 1857, with Attorney General Cartier establishing a Codification Commission of three senior judges. Cartier pointed out that "the code will be written in both languages." The commission had power to determine which French laws were still in effect and how they had been affected by legislation since the Conquest. They would have huge influence in establishing new definitions of contract, of settling issues like divorce in Catholic society, and of reshaping the place of women. In 1866, one year before Confederation, the transformation of the Custom of Paris into the Civil Code was complete, and the Civil Code took effect in Quebec.

Power over Women

Gender is a fundamental locus of power relations, and the feminist movement has struggled to place this reality as central in the history of Quebec. Authors like Bettina Bradbury and Cecilia Morgan give particular importance to the mid-nineteenth century, emphasizing a slippage in the place of women—what Morgan and others call the "masculinization" of Canadian society after the Rebellions.[11] This could be seen in the factories, where women usually represented a reserve army of labour. Women who owned property could theoretically vote until 1849, when a law was rewritten to exclude them; women did not regain that right in Quebec provincial elections until 1940. Although few women had the right to vote, those who could played a decisive role in some urban ridings:

> . . . it is odious [Papineau argued for example] to see women dragged up to the hustings by their husbands, girls by their fathers, often against their will. The public interest, decency, and the modesty of the fair sex require that these scandals cease.[12]

In the same critical period in the mid-nineteenth century, administrative laws concerning registry, mortgages, and contracts were systematically adjusted to subordinate the rights of the wife to capitalist relations. Just as important as these changes in state regulation were private relations and legal and social customs that were deeply rooted in both Protestant and Catholic society in Quebec. To describe this power, we cannot do better than quote historian Bettina Bradbury:

> Power and rights were not evenly distributed at this time. In working-class families wage dependency locked wives and children to husbands and fathers in a relationship that

> was at once mutual and complementary, yet hierarchical and dependent. Women were legally incapacitated upon marriage. This meant that most had no rights to administer property or even their own wages.[13]

Law in Western society, whether English common law or the Custom of Paris, subjugated the wife to her husband. In Lower Canada and then Quebec, he had entire financial authority, he established the family home, he had rights to discipline his wife, and he had rights to infidelity as long as he did not bring a lover into the family home. Wives had always assisted their husbands in the boutiques, market stalls, and artisanal shops, and many operated businesses of their own such as grocery stores, taverns, and dressmaking shops. But a married woman who wanted to operate independently in trade and enter into contracts or hire employees could do so under article 179 of the Civil Code only with the formal authorization of her husband.

Historian Marta Danylewycz has pointed out that, as they were excluded from the professions, middle-class women had few work options outside marriage.[14] French-Canadian women increasingly turned to the convent for careers of authority and relative autonomy from male control; 25 female religious communities were established in Quebec in the second half of the nineteenth century. Women also faced strong moral and behavioural censure. While the world of law and university was increasingly influenced by rationalism and science, there

Primary Source

The Right of Widows to Vote by Petitioners to the House of Assembly, Lower Canada, 1828

That Mrs. widow Laperrière did tender to Mr. Scott, Returning Officer, her vote, under oath, which Mr. Scott did refuse to take and enregister . . . That the Petitioners saw with extreme concern and alarm this refusal to take a vote tendered under oath . . . That the Petitioners represent . . . that as the votes of the Widows were not taken, the return of Mr. Stuart is void, inasmuch as the free choice of all the electors was not made known.

That the Petitioners may presume to trouble the House with the reasons which they deem conclusive as to the right of Widows to vote; neither in men nor women can the right to vote be a natural right; it is given by enactment. The only questions are whether women could exercise that right well and advantageously for the State, and whether they are entitled to it. That the Petitioners have not learned that there exist any imperfections in the minds of women which place them lower than men in intellectual power, or which would make it more dangerous to entrust them with the exercise of the elective franchise than with the exercise of the numerous other rights which the law has already given them. That in point of fact women duly qualified have hitherto been allowed to exercise the right in question. That the Petitioners conceive that women are fairly entitled to the right if they can exercise it well. That property and not persons is the basis of representation . . . That the paying certain taxes to the State is also a basis of representation; for it is a principle contended for by the best Statesmen of England that there can be "no taxation without representation" . . . That it would be impolitic and tyrannical to circumscribe her efforts in society—to say that she shall not have the strongest interest in the fate of her country, and the security of her common rights.

Source: Petitioners to the House of Assembly, Lower Canada, 1828. From Margaret Fairley, *Spirit of Canadian Democracy* (Toronto: Progress Books, 1944), 62–3.

was growing cultural pressure on Catholic women to assume the mysticism, suffering, and obedience of models like Mary:

> Mothers, why not imitate the Blessed Virgin? a Montreal priest wrote in an 1871 sermon. . . . You sweep the floor, you cook the dinner, you mend your children's clothes, you keep things in good order in the house. Why not do all this in a spirit of love of God. All those actions the Blessed Virgin performed. There [*sic*] were very ordinary actions but they were sanctified by the spirit of love and charity which animated the Blessed Virgin.[15]

Conclusion

How can we relate these issues of power and authority to our own times and to other periods of Quebec history? Can we join the dots between the doctrine of Immaculate Conception as an example of nineteenth-century clerical power and Cardinal Jean-Claude Turcotte's decision in September 2008 to renounce his membership in the Order of Canada in protest against the naming to the Order of Henry Morgentaler? Morgentaler, who died in 2013, was a major force behind the liberalization of Canadian abortion laws and in giving women the power to determine the fate of a fetus they carry. As with the doctrines of the Virgin Birth and the Immaculate Conception, and the issues of secularism we saw in the 1850s, Cardinal Turcotte insists that power does not rest in the hands of individual mothers-to-be: "we are not masters of human life, it rests in the hands of God."

We also suggested that power in the mid-nineteenth century shifted from aristocrats and seigneurs to a new bourgeoisie that held power in government and business. Women and workers made little headway in the mid-nineteenth century, and most of their gains toward equality occurred in the twentieth century. But traditional hierarchies and forms of power are tenacious. In 2001, for example, Conrad Black, English-Quebec's most powerful capitalist native son (and well before he was convicted of fraud and sentenced to a term in an American jail), chose to renounce his Canadian citizenship so that he could sit in the British House of Lords as Lord Black of Crossharbour. And in 2014, Michaëlle Jean, Haitian-born and Canada's third female governor general, was awarded the Grand Cross, the highest distinction granted by France's Legion of Honor. For its part, Quebec remains uneasy in Confederation, regularly returning Parti Québécois governments to power that run on platforms of independence. We can conclude, then, that the nineteenth-century ideologies and forms of power we have examined here are not just nostalgic but real and ongoing.

Questions for Critical Thinking

1. What comparisons can be made between the themes developed here and other experiences across Canada in the same period?
2. Can you compare the role of the Catholic Church in Quebec to its place in France in the same period, in the United States, or in another country with which you are familiar?
3. Using the Notman Photographic Archive at the McCord Museum website, can you develop a portfolio of images that support or contradict the main arguments of this chapter?

Notes

1. See, for example Marx's *Communist Manifesto*, describing conditions in the very period we are examining!
2. Examples include Peter Gossage and J. I. Little, *An Illustrated History of Quebec: Tradition and Modernity* (Don Mills, ON: Oxford University Press, 2012); John Dickinson and Brian Young, *A Short History of Quebec* (Montreal and Kingston: McGill-Queen's University Press, 2008), 154–97; or Paul-André Linteau, Jean-Claude Robert, and René Durocher, *Quebec: A History, 1867–1929* (Toronto: Lorimer, 1983).

3. Brian Young, "The Defeat of George-Étienne Cartier in Montreal-East in 1872," *Canadian Historical Review* 51(4) (December 1970): 386–406. Excerpted in Marlene Shore, ed., *Reading Canada's History: The Contested Past* (Toronto: University of Toronto Press, 2002), 224–32.
4. Cited in J.- C. Bonenfant, "George-Étienne Cartier," *Dictionary of Canadian Biography*, http://www.biographi.ca/en/bio/cartier_george_etienne_10E.html. Cartier's ideology is most accessible in Joseph Tassé, ed., *Discours de Sir Georges [sic] Cartier* (Montreal, 1893).
5. Maurice Séguin, *L'idée d'indépendance au Québec : genèse historique*, (Trois-Rivières: Boréal, 1970), 250.
6. Cited in Brian Young, *George-Étienne Cartier: Montreal Bourgeois* (Montreal and Kingston: McGill-Queen's University Press, 1981), 81.
7. For his career, see the biography by Nive Voisine in the *Dictionary of Canadian Biography*, http://www.biographi.ca/en/bio/taschereau_elzear_alexandre_12E.html.
8. "Un sentiment de respect le plus marqué inclina toutes les têtes et l'on sentit comme un frémissement de joie et d'enthousiasme religieux agir sur l'immense assemblée. Il y avait là quelque chose d'infiniment plus solennel encore que cette bénédiction, pourtant si auguste du père de famille bénissant ses enfants. C'était une vénération plus profonde, un amour plus respectueux, comme toutes les grandes affections empreintes du sceau de la religion." *Le Nouveau Monde*, 21 March 1871.
9. Pierre-Georges Roy, *La famille Taschereau* (Lévis: Mercantile, 1901), "les plus imposantes qui aient jamais été faites dans notre pays," 137.
10. Edward Thompson, *Making History: Writings on History and Culture* (New York: New Press, 1994), 208.
11. Lykke de la Cour, Cecilia Morgan, and Mariana Valverde, "Gender Regulation and State Formation in Nineteenth-Century Canada," in *Colonial Leviathan: State Formation in Mid-Nineteenth-Century Canada*, ed. Allan Greer and Ian Radforth (Toronto: University of Toronto Press, 1992), 163.
12. Allan Greer, *The Patriots and the People: The Rebellion of 1837 in Rural Lower Canada* (Toronto: University of Toronto Press, 1993), 206.
13. Bettina Bradbury, *Working Families: Age, Gender, and Daily Survival in Industrializing Montreal* (Toronto: McClelland & Stewart, 1993), 220.
14. Marta Danylewycz, *Taking the Veil: An Alternative to Marriage, Motherhood, and Spinsterhood in Quebec, 1840–1920* (Toronto: McClelland & Stewart, 1987).
15. Cited in Brian Young, *In its Corporate Capacity: The Seminary of Montreal as a Business Institution, 1816–1876* (Montreal and Kingston: McGill-Queen's University Press, 1986), 155.

Select Bibliography

Bradbury, Bettina. *Wife to Widow: Lives, Laws, and Politics in Nineteenth-Century Montreal*. Vancouver: UBC Press, 2011.

Christie, Nancy, ed. *Transatlantic Subjects: Ideas, Institutions, and Social Experience in Post-Revolutionary British North America*. Montreal and Kingston: McGill-Queen's University Press, 2008.

Curtis, Bruce. *Ruling by Schooling Quebec: Conquest to Liberal Governmentality—a Historical Sociology*. Toronto: University of Toronto Press, 2012.

Danylewycz, Marta. *Taking the Veil: An Alternative to Marriage, Motherhood, and Spinsterhood in Quebec, 1840–1920*. Toronto: McClelland & Stewart, 1987.

Fecteau, Jean-Marie. *La liberté du pauvre : sur la regulation du crime et de la pauvreté au XIXe siècle québécois*. Montreal: VLB éditeur, 2004.

Greer, Allan, and Ian Radforth, eds. *Colonial Leviathan: State Formation in Mid-Nineteenth-Century Canada*. Toronto: University of Toronto Press, 1992.

4 That Priest-Ridden Province? Politics and Religion in Quebec

Micheline Milot, Université du Québec à Montréal

Timeline

1608 Foundation of Quebec City by Samuel de Champlain. French *ancien régime* alliance between the Catholic Church and the French state takes root in Quebec City.

1763 Treaty of Paris. After the British Conquest of 1759, France cedes New France to England. Catholic Church loses its status as the established Church.

1774 First constitution, the Quebec Act, grants Catholics freedom of worship and abolishes the requirement that Catholics take the Test Oath to hold public office.

1791 Constitutional Act marks the beginning of parliamentarianism and the division of Canada into two provinces. Section 21 stipulates that ministers of religions, be they Catholic or Anglican, cannot be elected as members of Houses of Assembly in either Upper or Lower Canada.

1832 House of Assembly of Lower Canada adopts legislation to guarantee persons professing the Jewish religion equal rights.

1854 Legislation to abolish financial privileges of Anglican Church is passed.

1866 Legislation on divorce is passed, despite the Catholic Church's resistance.

1867 Canada's Confederation. The Constitution Act (also called the British North America Act) is adopted; no privileges granted to churches, except for protection of school administration for minority populations of Protestants and Catholics in Quebec and Ontario.

1869 Catholic Church refuses to bury Joseph Guibord in a Catholic cemetery because he refused to renounce his membership in Institut canadien, which promoted liberal ideas.

1875 Judicial Committee of the Privy Council in London dismisses the Church's appeal in the Guibord case and orders that his remains be interred in a Catholic cemetery.

1901 Superior Court of Quebec rules in the *Delpit-Côté* case that the civil bond of marriage takes precedence over the religious bond.

1964 Ministère de l'Éducation du Québec is created. The state takes charge of education, but Catholic and Protestant churches still have a major role to play within government structures.

1968 A federal omnibus bill decriminalizes homosexuality and authorizes civil marriage.

1975 Quebec Charter of Human Rights and Freedoms is adopted by the National Assembly.

continued

As a supra-legislative instrument, this charter affords broad protection for equality and freedom of conscience and of religion.

1997 Quebec National Assembly obtains a constitutional amendment to repeal special protection for religious school administrations.

1999 A task force is created on religion in schools and recommends complete laicization of the school system.

2000 Law abolishes religious status of all public schools. Rights of churches within state structures are also abolished.

2005 Federal Civil Marriage Act recognizes civil marriages between same-sex spouses. There is strong opposition from some Catholic and Protestant groups.

2007 Consultation Commission on Accommodation Practices Related to Cultural Differences is established to shed light on the debate around accommodations granted on religious grounds in the public sphere.

2008 Religious courses in public schools are abolished in Quebec. A nonreligious course on ethics and religious culture becomes mandatory for all students.

2013 Debates around the Charter of Quebec Values, which affirmed the values of state secularism and religious neutrality and of equality between women and men, and provided a framework for accommodation requests (Bill 60).

For a long time, Quebec was perceived as "that priest-ridden province" in Canada, caught in the powerful grip of the Catholic clergy, which exerted its influence in all spheres of society and especially in political life. Was Quebec's situation exceptional compared with the United States or with Canada's anglophone provinces, which were predominantly Protestant? Was the Catholic Church more inclined than Protestant churches to impose religious norms on political power?

While the propensity of the Catholic Church to control politics in Quebec was undeniably strong, I submit that the situation was far more complex and nuanced. To this end, we will examine relations between Quebec's political, juridical, and religious institutions since the eighteenth century. At that time Quebec had to find ways of adapting to religious (albeit mainly Christian) diversity to facilitate political governance, as did the United States and Canada's anglophone provinces. All three of these societies went through a similar process; while they progressively recognized religious freedom and equality of worship (for all denominations), the state acted independently in relation to all churches. But Quebec is exceptional in North America for its unusually early adoption of explicit measures to safeguard tolerance.

The term *laicization* describes the process by which the Quebec state asserted itself and recognized religious freedoms, a process that differs from *secularization*. Here we are specifically addressing the process of laicization that has taken place since the British Conquest of New France in 1759. This date is important for our topic because it marks the end of the *ancien régime* in New France, under which a strict Catholic Church–French state alliance prevailed. What the Conquest itself meant to the French-Canadian population is a different topic and is dealt with extensively in Donald Fyson's article in this volume.

Secularization and Laicization

The place ascribed to religion in various societies has undergone major transformations over the past two centuries. On one level, everyday social and cultural norms around religion have changed, while on another level, public institutions and the state have made rules and protocols to both effect and prevent change. The term secularization has often been used in English to describe both levels of change. But in 1957, American sociologist Talcott Parsons proposed that in the United States the secularization of *values* or types of social behaviour be distinguished from the secularization of *institutional structures*. The notion of laicization allows us to define this second institutional level of change so that it is not confused with the first. Since this chapter specifically focuses on structures and institutional decisions, the term *laicization* will be used to more accurately identify the process being examined.

Secularization occurs when religion progressively loses its relevance as a social and cultural framework for defining moral values and social conduct. In a largely secular society, religion may still hold relevance for individuals and command social legitimacy, but it can no longer impose a single moral code prescribing norms for all members of that society. By contrast, laicization is a process by which the state deliberately distances itself from religion on an institutional level. Indeed, for the state to ensure that individuals and different religious convictions are treated equally (within prescribed legal limits), it must be free to formulate collective norms, and therefore no religion or set of convictions can be allowed to control the political order. Implicit in state independence is the dissociation of civil legislation from religious edicts. This dissociation demands that the state abstain from favouring or disfavouring one or several religions. In sum, I define **laicization** as in state-driven political and juridical adjustment process which, by virtue of guaranteeing equal justice for all, seeks to ensure freedom of conscience and religion under a state that is neutral with regard to different coexisting individual moral codes and beliefs about how to live a "good life"[1] in society.[2]

In this chapter, we will examine several political and juridical decisions that illustrate how equality of worship and freedom of conscience and religion were established, both through a framework of political neutrality and through a de facto (never constitutionally explicit) separation of Church and state in Quebec. With this historical background in mind, we will examine how these principles were developed up to the beginning of the twenty-first century.

From Tolerance to Law: 1759–1867

The colony of New France, as noted earlier, was an extension of the *ancien régime* in France in which the Catholic Church and the French state had forged a firm alliance. This model could not survive the British Conquest in 1759 and the new sociopolitical situation generated by a henceforth linguistically, religiously, ethnically, and culturally mixed society. On a political level, post-Conquest French Canada was subject to British governance, which maintained close ties with the Church of England (Anglicanism). But the newly conquered territory was exceptional for its time in that its political conflicts did not lead to entrenched religious conflicts or to the specific repression of any religion. In this sense, the new Province of Quebec was an extraordinary society in an era when religions in colonized territories were being politically repressed. Its departure from contemporaneous European models of relations between Church and state ushered in a novel approach to political regulation. These parameters for laicization were sketched out gradually in Quebec through a process that, in many ways, was unfolding ahead of its time.

Freedom of Worship

With the Royal Proclamation of 1763 (establishing a basis of government in the territories formally ceded by France to Britain in the Treaty of Paris), Catholic French Canadians became British subjects and as such their religious freedom was eventually protected under British law. This fundamental freedom, which some in Europe, torn apart by hundreds of years of religious wars, had long sought to establish, was entrenched in two constitutional acts adopted in the eighteenth century: the Quebec Act of 1774 and the Constitutional Act of 1791. The Catholic Church, which had been highly intolerant of Huguenots[3] and Jews under the French regime, was protected by the rights enshrined in these constitutional documents. The British government even granted the Catholic Church the right to collect its traditional tithes, thereby ensuring the clergy's subsistence and facilitating freedom of worship. Thus, the first cornerstones of laicization were set in

Primary Source

The Quebec Act, 1774
14 George III, c. 83 (U.K.)

V. And, for the more perfect Security and Ease of the Minds of the Inhabitants of the said Province, it is hereby declared, that his Majesty's Subjects, professing the Religion of the Church of Rome of and in the said Province of Quebec, may have, hold, and enjoy, the free Exercise of the Religion of the Church of Rome, subject to the King's Supremacy, declared and established by an Act, made in the first Year of the Reign of Queen Elizabeth, over all the Dominions and Countries which then did, or thereafter should belong, to the Imperial Crown of this Realm; and that the Clergy of the said Church may hold, receive, and enjoy, their accustomed Dues and Rights, with respect to such Persons only as shall profess the said Religion.

VI. Provided nevertheless, That it shall be lawful for his Majesty, his Heirs or Successors, to make such Provision out of the rest of the said accustomed Dues and Rights, for the Encouragement of the Protestant Religion, and for the Maintenance and Support of a Protestant Clergy within the said Province, as he or they shall from Time to Time think necessary and expedient.

VII. Provided always, and be it enacted, that no Person professing the Religion of the Church of Rome, and residing in the said Province, shall be obliged to take the Oath required by the said Statute passed in the first Year of the Reign of Queen Elizabeth, or any other Oaths substituted by any other Act in the Place thereof; but that every such Person who, by the said Statute, is required to take the Oath therein mentioned, shall be obliged, and is hereby required, to take and subscribe the following Oath before the Governor, or such other Person in such Court of Record as his Majesty shall appoint, who are hereby authorized to administer the same; *videlicet*,

"I A.B. do sincerely promise and swear, That I will be faithful, and bear true Allegiance to his Majesty King George, and him will defend to the utmost of my Power, against all traitorous Conspiracies, and Attempts whatsoever, which shall be made against his Person, Crown, and Dignity; and I will do my utmost Endeavor to disclose and make known to his Majesty, his Heirs and Successors, all Treasons, and traitorous Conspiracies, and Attempts, which I shall know to be against him, or any of them; and all this I do swear without any Equivocation, mental Evasion, or secret Reservation, and renouncing all Pardons and Dispensations from any Power or Person whomsoever to the contrary. So help me GOD."

place in the New World. Freedom of worship would no longer depend on the arbitrary benevolence of those controlling political governance. In other British territories and even in the United States, Catholics would not enjoy similar freedom for several decades.

This occurred within a context of political domination after a military conquest and at a time when religious pluralism was not yet widely tolerated. In the years following the Conquest, as a prerequisite to holding public office, the new British regime required Canadian Catholics to swear the Test Oath in which they renounced allegiance to the pope (along with the doctrine of transubstantiation and the cult of the Virgin). Over a decade after the **Test Oath** was proclaimed, the Quebec Act expressly abolished this practice. Under the act, only a simple oath of allegiance to the king was required for any British subject in Quebec to hold public office.

In the United States, the Religious Test was abolished when the First Amendment of the American

Constitution was introduced, but only within the federation, which meant that the Test continued to be mandatory in some states, such as Massachusetts, until 1821. The American approach to this tended to be steeped in ethical or philosophical justifications, like those of Thomas Jefferson, who held up tolerance as a virtuous and positive value that strengthened the social cement of the nation.[4] By contrast, in Quebec the British Crown's pragmatic political and economic concerns far outweighed its need for philosophical debate. Given that the former French colony occupied a strategic territorial position in North America and that maintaining the loyalty of its Catholic majority was crucial to ensuring the conquered territory's stability, British governors proceeded with care in matters of religion. Recognizing religious freedom as a right had the immediate advantage of currying favour with the population, but it also established an important benchmark and structured Quebec's development for years to come.

Equality of Worship

Abolishing the Test Oath was not just a religious matter, but also a question of juridical equality for the Crown's subjects. It marked a breakthrough in the progress of tolerance and began the process of ending deeply ingrained practices of discrimination. So while it was true that in practice British colonists could more easily attain high-ranking positions in the years that followed the Test Oath's abolition, this inequality was not so much a consequence of religious affiliation as it was the product of political domination.

At this point, equality of worship was still incomplete, since the state had reserved the right to support and maintain the Protestant clergy under section 36 of the Constitutional Act of 1791, an economic advantage that the Catholic Church did not enjoy. The Catholic Church had lost its civil recognition (London had prohibited any papal jurisdiction in the territories of the British Empire), but still had clear autonomy in internal ecclesial management and the right to collect its "accustomed Dues and Rights" (section 35) from its parishioners.

Gradually, equality of worship was written into nineteenth-century law. In 1832, the House of Assembly of Lower Canada passed An Act to Declare Persons Professing the Jewish Religion Entitled to All the Rights and Privileges of the Other Subjects of His Majesty in This Province. The Act of Union of 1840, joining Upper and Lower Canada, reiterated colonial state protections for freedom of worship. Under the Act of Union religions were to be treated without discrimination, and Lower Canada's Legislative Council and the House of Assembly were mandated accordingly:

> [No] Bill or Bills shall be passed containing any Provisions which shall in any Manner relate to or affect the Enjoyment or Exercise of any Form or Mode of Religious Worship, or shall impose or create any Penalties, Burdens, Disabilities, or Disqualifications in respect of the same... (Art. 42)

In 1851, the legislature of the United Province of Canada passed the Freedom of Worship Act, which more explicitly recognized equality of worship. Thus, despite the influence of Catholicism and the Church of England (the two majority faiths in Lower and Upper Canada, respectively), no political rights or official status was afforded to either as a state religion.

Separating Powers

In Quebec, as in the rest of Canada, no constitutional law proclaimed the separation of Church and state. However, the separation of powers was distinctly implied as a concept in Quebec's constitutions and legislation. In the Quebec Act of 1774, there was no mention of any established Church. Nonetheless, section 6 provided for the "accustomed Dues and Rights, for the Encouragement of the Protestant Religion, and for the Maintenance and Support of a Protestant Clergy." In reality, it was the Anglican Church (the Church of England) that benefited from this constitutional privilege. As a province of England (whose official church was ruled by the king), Quebec was being governed with an apparent bias. Without a clear separation between Church and state, the government lost credibility as an impartial entity capable of providing equal protection to persons of all faiths. For this reason, other Protestant denominations rallied to demand the abolition of Anglican economic privilege, which was supported by the Anglican Church itself. Consequently, the government adopted legislation in 1854 to eliminate the Anglican Church's economic privileges, a move that more clearly defined Church–state power relations.

The Constitutional Act of 1791 marked the beginning of a vital political phase because it introduced a parliamentary political system, based on the British model, in a colony still in the embryonic stages of becoming a democratic regime (which would take several decades to grow to maturity). Section 21 of the act, regarding representation by religious leaders in Canada's Houses of Assembly, stipulated

> That no Person shall be capable of being elected a Member to serve in either of the said Assemblies, or of sitting or voting therein, who shall be a Member of either of the said Legislative Councils to be established as aforesaid in the said two Provinces . . . who shall be a Minister of the Church of England, or a Minister, Priest, Ecclesiastic, or Teacher, either according to the Rites of the Church of Rome, or under any other Form or Profession of religious Faith or Worship.

Two provisions in this section of the Constitutional Act significantly influenced the development of relations between the churches and the state. First, the fact that no privileges were conceded to ministers of the Anglican Church in elective politics effectively separated the institutional role of politics from that of religion—a major break with the British model. Second, the disqualification from holding public office affected Anglican clergy as much as it did Roman Catholic clergy, thereby instituting equality between the churches in politics. It is also worth noting that none of the constitutions adopted in the eighteenth century made any specific explicit reference to God or contained any express provisions regarding the establishment or disestablishment of religion. Here we could say that there was a tacit or a de facto separation of powers.

Political Neutrality in Religious Matters

All of the New World societies were faced with the daunting challenge of ensuring that the sparks of dogmatic rivalries from Europe did not reignite in North America. There was a clear impetus to start fresh in the New World and construct politics on new foundations. But the scope of choices available for this construction was limited:

> Either the State would be constructed by borrowing its legitimacy from a source other than the insurmountable multiplicity of interpretations of the Sacred Text, or from one of these [interpretations]—a particular denomination, an interpretation that is controversial but provisionally dominant in terms of power relations—would seize control of [the state].[5]

Indeed, the state did not arbitrate in disputes between the existing dogmas and clearly did not rely on any of them to legitimize its authority. Instead, state legitimacy was largely determined by its willingness to act as a neutral authority in Quebec.

The first Neutrality Act was passed in the United States in 1794. This legislation clearly distinguished between the neutrality of the state and the freedom of its citizens, who were not required to observe moral neutrality. It also provided an innovative perspective in the Western world, although it did not prevent religion from holding considerable sway in American society. In Canada, this neutrality was established as much by what was contained in constitutions as by what was not, for it was through the state's constitutional recognition of religious freedom and equality of worship that various political bodies established a degree of neutrality. But it was also because the successive constitutions made no explicit reference to an official state religion that the government of Quebec was able to build credibility as a neutral entity. The abolition of the Anglican Church's financial privileges that began in 1854 was also a step toward political neutrality in state relations with different churches.

For years, of course, government neutrality was tested by French Canada's Catholic clergy, a formidable pressure group in its drive to influence politicians.

Through their near-monopoly over essential local services—notably schools, hospitals, and charities—Catholic religious communities played a central role in shaping the moral and cultural consciousness of Quebec's demographic majority. But government policy and juridical rulings clearly diverged from the Catholic Church's agenda, despite its best efforts to influence political decisions and preach moral prescriptions.

From the Canadian Federation to Quebec's Quiet Revolution

The Constitution adopted at the time of Confederation, on 1 July 1867, more clearly articulated the emerging tradition of religious tolerance and political neutrality and marked the birth of modern Canada. Four provinces were created by Confederation: Quebec, Ontario (these two having been the former Province of Canada), New Brunswick, and Nova Scotia. The British North America Act of 1867 (BNA Act) distributed powers in two tiers: a central federal authority and provincial authorities. The provinces acquired jurisdiction over social affairs, including education, civil law, and public health. The BNA Act, much like the constitutions that preceded it, did not provide a complete framework for relations between churches and the state. It did not mention the separation of Church and state, or laicism (or secularism), much less a union of Church and state, and made no reference to God. The 1867 Constitution Act relied *implicitly* on the principles of neutrality and the separation of the churches and the state. Nonetheless, it made provision for special protections that applied exclusively to the administration of Catholic and Protestant schools in minority contexts, both in Quebec and Ontario (this protection has not applied in Quebec since 1997). No financial support was guaranteed to Quebec's churches, the state did not promise to collect any taxes for redistribution to the religious communities, and there was no express provision regarding freedom of religion. However, prior legislation on freedom of worship was recognized under section 129 of the BNA Act. Measures prescribed by the Act of Union of 1840 regarding worship and religious groups therefore remained in effect for each province.

Blurred Boundaries between Politics and Religion

During the second half of the nineteenth century, French Canadians in Quebec expressed a particularly strong desire to ensure their survival as a cultural minority or "nation" in the Americas. French-Canadian national and clerical interests converged at a common crossroads:

> *Political* conservatism would strive to "conserve" [French-Canadian] nationality, language, laws, social mores and religion. *Religious* conservatism would strive to "conserve" an almost identical nationality and, most importantly, it would defend, in keeping with its spiritual and temporal interests, first religion, then language, laws and social mores.[6]

The Catholic Church's social "works" (like those of several other faiths in Quebec) were widespread, often highly efficient and a source of development, establishing its own schools, hospitals, farming co-operatives, journalism, and farmers' unions, effectively relegating the state to an auxiliary role in the areas of education, health, and social welfare. Things might have been different had the Quebec government taken charge of education and health institutions when the BNA Act gave it those powers. Later attempts at state intervention were rebuffed by the Church, which had invested extensively in these areas. Such was not the case in the English-speaking Protestant and Jewish communities of the same era in Quebec, where the institutional network for anglophones had been laicized for years. To create viable institutions within the province's faith-based social framework, anglophones had to maintain a peaceable coexistence with other faiths. Moreover, the (Protestant) anglophone bourgeoisie had established its power in business by keeping business matters clearly separate from religion, a materialism that the Catholic Church discouraged.

CASE STUDY

The Guibord Affair (1869–1875)

The Guibord Affair was a landmark event in Quebec's religious history. Joseph Guibord was a printer and a member of the Institut canadien in Montreal. Upon his death, the ultramontane Catholic bishop of Montreal, Msgr Bourget, refused to bury him in a Catholic cemetery, sparking a protracted series of sensational court battles. Repeated appeals by his widow culminated in a trial before the highest court in the land, the Judicial Committee of the Privy Council in London (there was no Supreme Court of Canada at that time).

Guibord's legal case held special significance because it took place at a time when the conservative forces of the Catholic clergy were virulently opposing liberal thinking. Thus, a simple dispute over refusing to bury a man created widespread controversy over both the dissemination of modern, liberal ideas in a very conservative society and the separation of Church and state. But to fully grasp what motivated the bishop's decision and the significance of the legal confrontation it provoked, some background is required on the Institut canadien and ultramontanism.

Institut canadien

The Institut canadien opened its doors on 17 December 1844 in Montreal. It was devoted to the free flow of ideas and was a gathering place for intellectuals, artisans, business employees, lawyers, and doctors who subscribed to the ever-expanding realm of liberal thinking in Quebec. Public lectures and intellectual debates were held there, it had a well-stocked library, and foreign newspapers were available to members and subscribers. Thanks to these resources, the men of the Institut canadien could follow events of the European revolutions, including the notable social unrest fomenting in France, or learn about the advent of democracy in several countries. Some of the more radical members rejected the Church's interference with freedom of thought and were even in favour of Quebec's annexation to the United States. It was not long before their overt liberal and annexationist ponderings caused the Conservative Party and the Catholic clergy to unite against them.

Ultramontanism

Ultramontanism was a Catholic doctrine that made its first appearance during the French Revolution and took root in Quebec between 1820 and 1830. Its followers categorically rejected any compromise between Catholicism and the modern thinking of liberalism. They even contended that religious society should entirely dominate civil society and that the state should submit to the Church. Of course, the ultramontanes firmly believed that the pope's authority was unassailable and his judgment infallible. Many of the initiatives launched by radical ultramontanes failed, but the ultramontane school of thought would continue to influence Quebec in various ways until the mid-twentieth century.

Msgr Ignace Bourget, the bishop of the diocese of Montreal from 1840 to 1876, was the most emblematic figure of Quebec ultramontanism. He believed that the existence of the Institut canadien and the new ideas that it promoted challenged the "absolute" authority of the Church and represented a threat to the faith of French Canadians. In fact, the Institut and the Church competed for public sympathy. Many Institut canadien members belonged to the Parti rouge, a political party that was promoting democracy and aiming to secure a dominant political influence over French-Canadian society. Meanwhile, under Msgr Bourget's leadership, the clergy's moral control over French Canadians was increasing substantially. It seemed that a confrontation was inevitable.

The Conflict

Msgr Bourget fought the Institut with threats in his sermons at various churches and even through edicts obtained from the Vatican. In 1858 the bishop succeeded in convincing 138 members to leave the Institut canadien. Rome condemned the Institut in 1868, placing its yearbook, printed by Joseph Guibord, on the Vatican's Index of Forbidden Books for its faithful. Msgr Bourget delivered the following edict:

> He who persists in the desire to remain in the said Institut or to read or merely possess the above-mentioned yearbook without being so authorized by the Church deprives himself of the sacraments at the hour of his death.[7]

Bourget was referring to the Catholic rite of "extreme unction," in which sacraments are administered to the gravely ill before death to absolve the faithful of all their sins. Prohibiting this essential sacrament to Catholics and thereby jeopardizing the peace of their immortal souls was a serious measure for the bishop to take, especially at this time in history.

In July 1869, with the support of Rome, the bishop proclaimed an ordinance against the Institut canadien, effectively discrediting it in the eyes of all Catholics. Four months later, on 18 November 1869, Joseph Guibord had a stroke and later died. But while Guibord was a member of the Institut, he was also a devout Catholic and not anti-clerical. Abbé André-Marie Garin, a missionary in northwestern Canada, had even entrusted Guibord with printing the catechism in an Aboriginal language in 1854. But Guibord refused to renounce his membership in the Institut. For this reason, the Church denied him its extreme unction, which meant that his body could not receive Catholic religious rites, including burial in a Catholic cemetery. This would be the last time Msgr Bourget would assail the Institut canadien.

The Legal Saga around the Refusal of Burial

Joseph Guibord's widow, Henriette Brown, and some of his friends subsequently launched legal proceedings against the bishop and the Fabrique de la Paroisse de Notre-Dame de Montreal (the organization that should have been responsible for Guibord's funeral) to appeal the refusal to bury Guibord. The case was heard before the courts of Quebec and was appealed as far as the Judicial Committee of the Privy Council in London. Years passed as the case went through the rigours of the legal system while Guibord's remains lay in a Protestant cemetery.

On 21 November 1874, five years after Joseph Guibord had died, the Judicial Committee ruled that the Catholic Church should not only bury Guibord in consecrated ground at a proper and convenient time,[8] but that it also defray all legal costs. When the belated burial was first attempted on 2 September 1875 at Côte-des-Neiges Catholic cemetery in Montreal, a crowd of Catholics prevented Guibord's remains from being interred. The undertakers involved in the second attempt came prepared with reinforcements, and on 16 November 1875, with the protection of 1,255 soldiers, a full six years after he had passed away, Joseph Guibord's remains were laid to rest. His grave was said to be covered with a protective layer of cement to prevent any desecration. Still determined to register the Church's disapproval, Msgr Bourget made use of the very last power at his disposal, deconsecrating the site of interment as prohibited to Catholics and separate from the rest of the cemetery.

Although the Church held that Catholic burials fell entirely under its jurisdiction, this event established the precedence of civil law over the laws of the Church—a major setback for a religious institution accustomed to controlling every aspect of its parishioners' lives, from cradle to grave.

Civil Law Puts a Damper on the Catholic Church's Social Control

Not surprisingly, the Catholic Church's attempts to orient social and political norms often ran afoul of the juridical interpretation of civil law. Among the many events illustrating a distancing of powers between Church and state was the famous Guibord Affair, described in detail in the Case Study box. In 1869, the bishop of Montreal, Msgr Bourget, refused to grant a Catholic cemetery burial to Joseph Guibord, who had worked for a group of liberal thinkers. The bishop was dealt a resounding blow when the Privy Council in London ruled against him on the matter. In its precedent-setting 1875 judgment, it deemed that cemeteries fell under civil jurisdiction even though churches held the right to keep civil status registries on behalf of the state. Other incidents clearly marked the divide between the aspirations of ecclesial powers and their denial by the civil state. In 1871 the Church tried influencing conservative members of the legislature directly, lobbying them to promote the "Catholic program" and commit to defending Catholic morals. The Church canvassed candidates in anticipation of the 1871 provincial election, and of the very few who signed on to the Catholic program only one managed to get elected.

In 1875, the government of Quebec took action to disentangle the Church from state affairs. In an amendment to the Quebec Election Act it prohibited "undue influence" (section 258) to eradicate intimidation, threats, or any other means of coercion being used by priests (the main targets of the legislation) to influence how their congregations would vote. In 1900 the moral ground held by Quebec's bishops shifted yet again when two Catholics were married by a Protestant pastor in the Delpit-Côté affair. The Catholic Church legally invalidated the marriage, but some months later the case was heard before the Superior Court of Quebec, where Justice J. S. Archibald stunned and overruled the bishopric. His ruling determined that marriage was governed primarily by *civil law* in Quebec. A hierarchy of jurisdiction over the religious aspect of marriage was thereby established by the court: The *form* of a ceremony would no longer determine the validity of a marriage contract. Notably, the government of Quebec did not invalidate the civil status of religious unions or introduce mandatory civil marriage, as was the case in France. Indeed, in Quebec, civil marriage was not instituted as such until 1969, meaning that until that time a religious ceremony was the only legal means of getting married.

From the Quiet Revolution to the Beginning of the Twenty-First Century

The *Quiet Revolution* is an expression that may require some clarification outside of Quebec. In fact, the "revolution" that began in 1960 did not involve the violent overthrow of a political regime, but a modernization of Quebec's institutions and the role of the state. After 15 years of an unusually authoritarian administration under Premier Maurice Duplessis, whose close connections with the Catholic Church greatly emboldened his style of governance, the province was breaking free of its political and religious constraints. Economic prosperity and ideas of social reform had already been remodelling institutional structures for some time in most Western societies. But in Quebec, reform happened so quickly that it seemed the province had made a radical, revolutionary break with past social and political patterns.

Following World War II, the modernization, industrialization, and urbanization of Quebec proceeded at a pace so accelerated that traditional frameworks founded on family and parish could not keep up with the new demands of modern living. Churches and congregations found it increasingly difficult to secure enough personnel and materials for the schools, hospitals, and charities they ran. The institutions they had been managing for over a century were quickly laicizing, a trend that soon came to be perceived as an unavoidable social necessity. But the laicization of institutions did not pit believers against nonbelievers, or liberal thinkers against Catholics. In fact, most of the writing and discussions about and initiatives in favour of laicization came from Catholic groups and even from within religious ranks, and it was these activities that led them to play an important role in Church renewal. In 1958, the Ministry of

Youth and Social Welfare was created, in 1961 the Hospital Insurance Act entered into force, and in 1964 the Ministry of Education was founded. From 1964 forward, a new middle class began to administer large institutions, taking over from clerics and members of religious orders, who were seeing their recruitment numbers plummet.

Schools: The Church's Bastion of Resistance

In Quebec the first real public debate on the roles of Church and state in education dates back to 1963, when the Royal Commission of Inquiry on Education in the Province of Quebec (called the Parent Commission) took place. Following the commission's recommendations, Bill 60, or An Act to Establish the Ministry of Education and the Superior Council of Education, was passed in 1964, bringing education under the provincial government's jurisdiction. Successive Catholic bishops had staunchly opposed the creation of this ministry since the end of the nineteenth century, fearing that if the state took control of education then "majority rule" would lead to a rapid laicization of the school system. The Assembly of Quebec Catholic Bishops lobbied the government to change Bill 60 so that the Church would be ensured of its right to continue administering its own schools. The resulting legislation, adopted six months later, was a compromise between state prerogatives and the interests of the Catholic Church: The Ministry of Education would oversee the administration of the school system, but the system would remain bi-denominational—Catholic and Protestant. The Catholic and Protestant churches were thereby seated in the upper echelons of the Ministry of Education and the Superior Council of Education, where they both served.

The discriminatory aspects of this faith-based arrangement soon came to light: Only two faiths had been given the right to a school system, and that system was out of step with the degree of secularization in Quebec society. Meanwhile, the groundwork that had been laid for policy orientations during the Quiet Revolution was already shaping areas such as cultural diversity, social integration, and equality among citizens. In 1999 widespread public debate over the place of religion in public schools was triggered by a report from the Task Force on the Place of Religion in Schools entitled *Religion in Secular Schools: A New Perspective for Quebec.* In its report, the task force recommended that the government laicize the entire public school system based on two considerations: the importance of recognizing fundamental human rights, and the need to adapt to the cultural and religious secularism and pluralism of Quebec's evolving social landscape. On 1 July 2000, all public schools in Quebec were laicized, and by 2008 religious instruction in Catholic and Protestant doctrine was abolished. The government introduced a mandatory new course on ethics and religious culture for all students to promote their understanding of various religious and secular world views while encouraging dialogue.

The Importance of Fundamental Human Rights

In the last quarter of the twentieth century, recognition for fundamental rights and freedoms progressed significantly, owing to the adoption of the Quebec Charter of Human Rights and Freedoms in 1975 (and the Canadian Charter of Rights and Freedoms in 1982). To a large extent, the moral foundations of a society shaped by long-standing Christian values were being rebuilt. Indeed, the value system expressed in the Charter became the touchstone of good citizenship. With the adoption of the Charter, equality and freedom of conscience and religion acquired supra-legislative status: No laws or public regulations could violate these principles.

Today, Quebec's justice system, like that of all contemporary democratic societies, is theoretically free of any expressly discriminatory provisions and does not favour any religious group. But in practice, religions and beliefs are treated differently and unequally because laws are uniformly enforced and designed for all citizens, regardless of the specific needs of particular groups. A rule or a universal law that applies uniformly to all members of society can have unintended discriminatory effects when, for example, restrictions affect the practice of one faith but not that of another. These are cases of "indirect discrimination." In Canada and in Quebec, a legal obligation exists to correct indirect discrimination:

> In certain cases, the obligation of accommodation forces the state, persons or private businesses to change norms, practices or legitimate and justified practices or policies, which apply to all without distinction, to take into account the particular needs of some (especially ethnic or religious) minorities.[9]

Reasonable accommodation is an instrument that promotes peaceable social negotiation and assists institutions and employers, encouraging them to adapt to social diversity.

This type of accommodation is not new and has established itself as a tradition in North America. However, in Canada and Quebec accommodation is a *legal obligation*—the equivalent of a conferred right to equality. Its underlying principle is that freedom of religion presupposes the right to freely practise a religion. But this practice may be infringed upon or restricted by general norms set in place for the majority. (A clear example of this is the general restriction on carrying weapons infringing on the Sikh practice of wearing a kirpan, a small knife.[10]) According to this juridical perspective, it is not enough to create theoretical rights; the state and its public institutions must ensure that reasonable accommodation is expressed in concrete policies and practices so that rights may be respected.

Debates on the Expression of Religious Affiliation in the Public Sphere

Quebec has therefore not experienced political debates on the separation of state and religion. However, a lively debate on secularism took place in Quebec between 2006 and 2014. It focused on the wearing of religious symbols in public institutions and their association with reasonable accommodations. The number of citizens displaying religious symbols is very low, and no real problems have been identified regarding the professionalism of the people wearing religious symbols. Yet some Quebecers would prefer to prohibit any display of religious affiliation in public institutions to assert the secular nature of state institutions. There are also those who object to the notion of overaccommodation with regard to the wearing of religious symbols (such as the Muslim hijab or the Sikh kirpan), adapting work schedules to religious practices, or providing spaces at work or school for prayer. The real fear was that the expression of identities and values that differ from those of the Christian and French-Canadian majority will harm Quebec's heritage of identity. National identity and accommodation have established themselves as a highly charged political issue.

Two government initiatives offered very different solutions to this debate. The first one took place in 2007, when the Quebec Liberal Party struck a Consultation Commission on Accommodation Practices Related to Cultural Differences.[11] The final report of the commission recognized the importance of the neutrality of the state and its institutions along with the equally important right to freedom of conscience and religion, which allows citizens to express their religious convictions provided that this expression does not infringe upon the freedoms of others. According to this secular state model—a model that historically prevails in Quebec—it is institutions and not individuals who are laicized.

The second government initiative took place in November 2013. The Parti Québécois government proposed a bill entitled "Charter Affirming the Values of State Secularism and Religious Neutrality and of Equality between Women and Men, and Providing a Framework for Accommodation Requests" (Bill 60).[12] Secularism, neutrality, and equality between women and men were associated with the need to preserve national identity against the values of minority religions. Bill 60 sought to make wearing religious symbols in all public institutions or institutions that receive funds from the state illegal.

This Parti Québécois bill gave rise to a strong polarization of opinions and a massive mobilization of very different social groups. In this clash, two models for accommodating religious diversity were opposed. The first is the model of laicism adopted in France, which prohibits wearing any religious symbol in public institutions and makes no religious accommodations in the workplace. From this point of view, the ban on religious symbols of minority religions, secularism, and national identity are closely linked. The second

BIOGRAPHY

Louis-Antoine Dessaulles (1818–1895)

Louis-Antoine Dessaulles was one of the many citizens of Lower Canada who significantly contributed to advancing modern ideas during the nineteenth century. Born in Saint-Hyacinthe on 31 January 1818, this intellectual was interested in politics but never held a prominent political position. It was as an activist that he distinguished himself and epitomized the political vibrancy of the era in which he lived. Indeed, tensions ran high during the second half of the nineteenth century as the free flow of liberal ideas made the conservative Catholic Church fear the worst for the future of the Roman Catholic religion and the French-Canadian nation.

Louis-Antoine Dessaulles, reproduction of an 1861 original print.

Studio Notman & Son, Montreal/Bibliotheques et Archives nationales du Quebec.

Inspired by the later work of the French writer Lamennais, Dessaulles was a polemicist renowned for his liberal spirit and anti-clericalism. A member of the Institut canadien, he served as its president three times between 1862 and 1867, delivering a number of lectures under its roof. At its inception, the Institut accepted only Catholics into its membership, but under Dessaulles's presidency men of other religious affiliations and atheists were also accepted. The ultramontane bishop of Montreal, Msgr Ignace Bourget, vehemently opposed the "religious mixing" within the Institut, which he perceived as a threat to the faith and the Catholic national identity of French Canadians.

Throughout his life Dessaulles stressed the importance of clearly separating Church and state and called for nonclerical, republican schools. In Quebec, as in Europe and the Americas, modern ideas were circulating as never before. The Vatican reacted by publishing Pope Pius IX's *Quanta cura*, an encyclical letter, and the Syllabus in 1864 denouncing the key "errors" of modernity, including a notable condemnation of the separation of Church and state.

Dessaulles's life story had its contradictions. For instance, although he was a staunch defender of "modern" freedoms, he owned a seigneury and thereby perpetuated the old seigneurial regime. He also extolled the virtues of universalism, human solidarity, and freedom of expression in his famous speech on tolerance in 1868. In fact, Dessaulles, who never denied that he was Catholic, deliberately included references to the Bible in this speech. Like a preacher, his discourse was based on the principles of Christian tolerance and charity. He hoped to teach religious authorities a lesson by using scripture to prove that religion and religious freedom were not incompatible. While he fought ultramontanism and was openly anti-clerical, he was not anti-religious. After Dessaulles's speech on tolerance was published in the yearbook of the Institut canadien in 1868, Msgr Bourget demanded that Rome place the publication in the Index of Forbidden Books and condemn the Institut. The next year, when Msgr Bourget refused to give Joseph Guibord a Catholic burial, Dessaulles ardently defended the civil burial rights and was a witness in the legal proceedings brought by Guibord's widow.

Dessaulles also belonged to the Parti rouge, a radical liberal party, and favoured annexing Quebec to the United States. To him, the American republic represented freedom from British royalty and was a truly democratic society in which Church and state were separated and the

continued

yoke of the Catholic Church carried no weight. Dessaulles published *Six lectures sur l'annexion du Canada aux États-Unis* in 1851. In his discussion of democracy, freedom, and religion he asserted that

> It was from the evangelical principle that all men are born equal that civilization drew a [fundamental] conclusion (a conclusion rejected by Ultramontanism in its stubborn interest and hunger for power), namely: that each individual possesses moral independence which results in his individual sovereignty as a member of society . . . . But man's individual and native sovereignty, inherent to his nature as a thinking being, *necessarily* flow from the sacred dogma of the *sovereignty of the people*, a dogma uncontested on the free soil of the American continent, even by the Catholic Hierarchy.

There is no doubt that Louis-Antoine Dessaulles contributed to the laicization that was already underway in Lower Canada. His battles, seen in the context of his era, presaged the current battles we see between people of faith and atheists, and battles for "laic democracy" (although this term was not used in Dessaulles's time). At the end of his 1868 speech on tolerance, Dessaulles categorically condemned intolerance and the submission of the mind as the "enemies" of democracy.

After some time spent in exile in Belgium and France, Louis-Antoine Dessaulles died in Paris in 1895.

follows the Quebec tradition of religious plurality and is supported by the Quebec Liberal Party. This model follows the recommendation of the Commission on Accommodation Practices discussed above. According to this model, the ban on wearing religious symbols is considered direct discrimination. The spring 2014 electoral campaign focused in large part on Bill 60, with the Parti Québécois government losing the election.

Conclusion

In Quebec, relations between religious tradition and the state have been defined more by praxis than by constitution. Indeed, most modern democracies today are founded on principles that dissociate the state from any specific religion or religious norms. From their inception, New World societies have grappled with issues around religious plurality, but mainly with regard to Christian plurality. These societies have become increasingly diversified as their citizens' ever-expanding world views have shaped institutions, laws, and public policies. Nonetheless, they still bear the imprint of their Christian heritage, and in Quebec some citizens would like these values to take precedence in areas such as societal development and the determination of individual rights. This view has fuelled a plethora of "rights" debates concerning abortion, gay and lesbian couples, and the wearing of religious symbols in public. Clearly, authorities in Quebec and North America are better equipped than they ever have been to tackle these controversies head on. Backed by the considerable gains of laicization, they should be implementing an ethic of recognition for the diversity of moral codes and religious beliefs that exist in our society.

Questions for Critical Thinking

1. What were the defining characteristics of the process of laicization undertaken by the state in Quebec?
2. Has the Catholic Church really been an influential power in all social and political aspects of life in Quebec?
3. How can we differentiate between processes of secularization and processes of laicization in democratic societies?

Notes

1. John Rawls, *A Theory of Justice* (Cambridge, MA: Harvard University Press, 1971).
2. Micheline Milot, *Laïcité dans le Nouveau Monde : le cas du Québec* (Turnhout, Belgium: Brepols, 2002), 34.
3. French Protestants who were members of the Reformed or Calvinistic communion of France in the sixteenth and seventeenth centuries. J.-L. Lalonde, *Des loups dans la bergerie : les protestants de langue française au Québec, 1534–2000* (Montreal: Fides, 2002).
4. D. Lacorne, "Tolérance, républicanisme et laïcité : l'exemple américain," in *Actualité de l'école républicaine?*, ed. P. Statius and P. Bachelard (Caen: Centre régional de documentation pédagogique, 1998), 85–93.
5. Guy Haarscher, *La laïcité* (Paris: Presses universitaires de France, 1996), 94.
6. Yvan Lamonde, *Histoire sociale des idées au Québec (1760–1896)* (Montreal: Fides, 2000), 319.
7. Jean-Roch Rioux, "Guibord, Joseph," *Dictionary of Canadian Biography*, originally accessed 10 April 2009, http://www.biographi.ca/en/bio.php?id_nbr=4470.
8. Lord Selborne, *Affaire Guibord : jugement des Lords du Comité Judiciaire du Conseil Privé sur l'Appel de Dame Henriette Brown vx. Les Curé et Marguillers de l'œuvre et de la Fabrique de Notre-Dame, au Canada*, 21 November 1874, 10.
9. José Woehrling, "L'obligation d'accommodement raisonnable et l'adaptation de la société à la diversité religieuse," *Revue de droit de McGill/McGill Law Journal* 43 (1998): 328, author's translation.
10. The case of Gurbaj Singh Multani is a classic illustration of general restrictions infringing on religious practice. This case began in Montreal in 2001 and wound up before the Supreme Court of Canada in 2006. See Chapter 17 for a discussion of this case.
11. The commission was co-chaired by Gérard Bouchard and Charles Taylor. Their final report is entitled *Building for the Future: A Time for Reconciliation* (2008). See the Case Study Box in Chapter 5.
12. See www.assnat.qc.ca/en/travaux-parlementaires/projets-loi/projet-loi-60-40-1.html.

Select Bibliography

Bramadat, Paul, and David Seljak, eds. *Christianity and Ethnicity in Canada*. Toronto: University of Toronto Press, 2008.

Carignan, P. *De la Charte québécoise des droits et libertés : origine, nature et défis*. Montreal: Thémis, 1989.

Hamelin, Jean, and Nicole Gagnon. *Histoire du catholicisme québécois. Le XXe siècle, t. I : 1898–1940*. Montreal: Boréal Express, 1984.

Lamonde, Yvan. *Histoire sociale des idées au Québec (1760–1896)*. Montreal: Fides, 2000.

Lemieux, L. *Histoire du catholicisme québécois. Les XVIIIe et XIXe siècles, t. I : Les années difficiles (1760–1839)*. Montreal: Boréal, 1989.

Lyon, David, and Marguerite Van Die, eds. *Rethinking Church, State and Modernity: Canada between Europe and America*. Toronto: University of Toronto Press, 2000.

Maille, Chantal, G. M. Nielsen, and D. Salée, eds. *Revealing Democracy: Secularism and Religion in Liberal Democratic States*. Brussels: P.I.E.-Peter Lang S.a, 2014.

Milot, Micheline. *Laïcité dans le Nouveau Monde : le cas du Québec*. Bibliothèque de l'École des Hautes Études, Section des sciences religieuses 115. Turnhout, Belgium: Brepols, 2002.

Rocher, Marie-Claude, and Catherine Drouin. *Un autre son de cloche : les protestants francophones au Québec*. Quebec: CEFAN, 1993.

Trudel, Marcel. *Mythes et réalités dans l'histoire du Québec*. Montreal: Hurtubise HMH, 2001.

Voisine, Nive. *Histoire de l'Église catholique au Québec (1608–1970)*. Commission d'étude sur les laïcs et l'Église. Première annexe au rapport. Montreal: Fides, 1971.

5 Quebec's Culture War: Two Conceptions of Quebec Identity

Jocelyn Maclure, Université Laval; and François Boucher, Centre de recherche en éthique, Université de Montréal

Introduction

Quebec society is not torn by public morality issues such as abortion, birth control, same-sex marriage, crime and punishment, and gun control. The pro-choice position on abortion is widely accepted, birth control is promoted and available, same-sex couples can marry, tough talk on "law and order" does not fly, and virtually no one thinks that most civilians should be allowed to carry guns in the street. While some Quebecers hold different views, few are ready to defend the conservative side on these issues. In light of the "culture wars" fought in the United States between progressivism and orthodoxy (following James Davison Hunter's terminology), it appears that the progressive agenda has carried the day in Quebec.[1] It would, however, be hasty to conclude that Quebec does not have its own "culture war." We want to suggest in this article that the debate over the meaning, contours, and fate of Quebec's collective identity is in some ways similar to the American culture wars, in its disagreements over world views, values, and political agenda.

We attempt to reconstruct the debate between two dominant current conceptions of Quebec identity, those with a significant number of adherents among intellectuals and opinion makers. (There are many conceptions of Quebec identity, some more widespread than others. We do not attempt to thoroughly map out all these conceptions here, and neither do we try to update the conceptual framework proposed in a previous book.[2]) The two dominant conceptions tend to give rise to conflicting political visions and programs and consequently to ethical and political disagreements, and therefore merit discussion.[3] We call these two conceptions the *romantic–conservative* and the *civic–pluralist* conceptions of Quebec identity.

Both conceptions originated in intellectuals' discussions about the meaning of Quebec identity in the aftermath of the 1995 referendum. They provided the basic framework within which questions of accommodation of religious minorities have been addressed since the mid-2000s. The term **religious accommodation** can be used in a narrow way to refer to the legal obligation of reasonable accommodation that "requires, in some cases, governments, persons and private corporations to modify legitimate norms, practices or policy, which are meant to apply to all individuals with no distinction, in order to take into account the particular needs of certain minorities, especially ethnic and religious ones."[4] Religious accommodation may also be defined more broadly as encompassing not only religious exemptions to general laws but also the whole range of measures adopted to enable individuals to freely practise their religion in various social contexts (the workplace, public institutions, and so on).

The two rival conceptions of Quebec identity played a significant role during the 2006–8 "reasonable accommodation crisis," which motivated the creation of the Bouchard–Taylor Commission (see the Case Study box), and in the debates on the terms of secularism that stormed Quebec's public sphere in the following years. The tension between those two conceptions reached a peak in 2013 during the controversy surrounding the

Parti Québécois's failed attempt to prohibit public sector employees (nurses in public hospitals, school teachers, clerks in the public administration, and so on) from wearing ostensible religious signs.[5]

We will first present the civic–pluralist conception, as the romantic–conservative is largely a reaction to it. Although this distinction somewhat resembles one more commonly made, between "ethnic" and "civic" nationalism, we argue that this more common distinction fails to grasp the substance of what is probably the most salient identity-related disagreement in Quebec today.

CASE STUDY

The 2007–8 Bouchard–Taylor Commission[6]

Summary of the Events

Following months of public discontent over the accommodation of religious minorities, on 8 February 2007 Quebec Premier Jean Charest announced the establishment of the Consultation Commission on Accommodation Practices Related to Cultural Differences. Since the recognition of an obligation to accommodate by Canadian and American courts, debates on the legitimacy of religious accommodations have continued both in political philosophy and in the public sphere, and the discontent had seized the general public through overwhelming media coverage. Cases such as the Supreme Court of Canada's decision to allow a young Sikh to wear his religious dagger (a kirpan) at school (the Multani affair—see Chapter 17) fuelled the controversy.

The Consultation Commission mandate included the following:

- taking stock of accommodation practices in Quebec
- analyzing the attendant issues, bearing in mind the experience of other societies
- conducting extensive consultation on this topic
- formulating recommendations to the government to ensure that accommodation practices conform to Quebec's values as a pluralistic, democratic, egalitarian society.

While it could have interpreted this mandate in the narrower sense of a strictly legal inquiry, the commission chose to address the broader issue of Quebec's sociocultural integration model. This audacious choice was consistent with the appointment of the commission's co-chairs, philosopher Charles Taylor and historian Gérard Bouchard, two leading intellectuals renowned for their work on identity and cultural diversity, among other things.

The investigation was based on different sources, including projects conducted by academic researchers, meetings with experts, and representatives of sociocultural organizations, but also—what came to be the most visible part of the commission—public consultations held all across Quebec. For weeks, Quebec's attention—through the press as well as live TV coverage—turned to the odyssey of these "two modern wise men" crossing the land in pursuit of the perceptions and opinions of the average citizen.

The subsequent work of the commission led to the publication of a thorough report named *Building the Future: A Time for Reconciliation*. While anchored in Quebec's situation, the report develops numerous concepts and tools that transcend the context in which they were formulated and are likely to enrich the debates on the challenges of cultural and religious diversity taking place all

continued

across the Western world. Therefore, one possible reason for the popular attention given to the commission is probably the notion that other societies facing similar fears and uncertainty could learn from a small, peripheral nation like Quebec.

The Two Sources of the Crisis

The commission's first conclusion was to confirm the asymmetry between the real scope and impact of cultural accommodations and the widespread popular perception of their effects. In addition to showing that the reasonable accommodation of minorities poses no threat to the foundation of collective life, the commission was able to prove that the degree of media coverage on reasonable accommodation did not correlate with a sudden increase in its practice. Perhaps the most shocking element discovered was that in 15 of the 21 cases at the core of the controversy, there were striking discrepancies between public perception and the facts. With these findings, it was then possible to characterize the crisis as a "crisis of perception."[7]

The second conclusion, however, tempers the idea of a political or media-led plot to foment public discontent, as the crisis of perception could not have caused such discontent without some sort of pre-existing widespread anxiety over the fate of Quebecers' shared identity. Many citizens, for instance, expressed anxiety over the possible loss of core values established during the Quiet Revolution, such as secularism and gender equality. The commission clearly pointed out the strangeness of a situation in which "the members of the ethnocultural majority are afraid of being swamped by fragile minorities that are worried about their future."[8] Although these concerns are rooted to some extent in the minority status of French-Canadian Quebecers in North America as a whole, it is nonetheless observable all across the Western world.[9]

The Three Social Norms of Quebec's Common Public Culture

One of the goals of the commission was to provide guidelines for reasonable accommodation, a task that involved for the most part a reconstruction of the values, norms, and institutions already present in Quebec's common public culture:

- The first element is the integration model: *interculturalism*. Often seen as distinct from Canadian multiculturalism, interculturalism aims to preserve Quebec's national character—for example, based on French as the common public language—while allowing and protecting cultural and ethnic diversity in conformity with liberal values. The focus is on integration, interaction, and sharing, whereas multiculturalism, as it is commonly interpreted, could be satisfied with a peaceful coexistence between hermetic communities.
- The second element relates to what the report calls "harmonization practices" and the need to negotiate when cultural customs or values conflict, rather than to launch a legal battle. The report characterizes the legal route as "codified" and "rigid" and as creating winners and losers. It recommends that a dispute be negotiated through the "citizen route" instead, which uses less formal procedures to reach a compromise that both sides are happy with. It thus offers an effective way to solve problems in accordance with the values of dialogue, negotiation, and reciprocity that we find at the centre of Quebec's integration model.
- The third element deals with deep-seated convictions, whether religious or secular. Behind any secular system there is a deliberate balance between four principles: the moral equality of persons, freedom of conscience, the separation of Church and state, and state neutrality with respect to

convictions of conscience. The commission argued in favour of a conception of the secular state that they call "open secularism." This system's primary virtue is to depart from a rigid model of secularism as seen in France, where the respect of the first two principles leads to actions directed against religion and its manifestations—as exemplified by the legislation that banned wearing visible religious symbols at school—a path that was deemed by the commission as incompatible with a true neutrality of the state, as well as with attaining integration through diversity.

Recommendations

While we have looked mainly at the conceptual content of the commission's report, it also includes the following practical recommendations:

- In response to possible clashes between accommodation and gender equality, the commission insisted in its first recommendation that, while general norms would exclude most instances of such conflict, all requests in the public service sector that would bestow upon women an inferior status to that of men were to be disqualified.
- Consistent with the guidelines for accommodation practices and in a spirit of reciprocity, it also stated that the practice of saying a prayer in some municipal council meetings should be abandoned and the crucifix, an explicit symbol of Christianity, should be removed from the wall of the Quebec National Assembly. It is to be noted that this recommendation was voted down unanimously by the members of the National Assembly a few minutes after they received the report, in an act that seems explicable only as a message to voters that accommodation issues are exclusively the concern of cultural minorities and will not require any change for the majority.
- In contrast, according to the commission's open interpretation of secularism and to be fair and inclusive, it recommended that society should respect dietary prohibitions of different cultures or faiths, and also allow the wearing of Islamic headscarves, Sikh turbans, or Jewish kippahs in class, in athletic events, and at work for most civil servants since the principles in these situations do not concern the separation of Church and state.
- Finally, it was reaffirmed that requests for legitimate accommodation must seek to protect or restore a right, such as time off for a non-Christian religious holiday, and that accommodation cannot be used to suppress someone else's rights. For example, a child cannot be denied the right to study science or to receive a life-saving blood transfusion in order to accommodate a parent's religious beliefs.
- In order to give more precise guidelines to legislators, civil servants, and concerned citizens, the report suggested that the Quebec government produce "a white paper on secularism" to review the tradition of open secularism in Quebec and ensure its clear articulation in debates to come. Fulfilling this recommendation does not yet appear to be on the government's agenda. Without agreed-upon, well-publicized guidelines to secularism, matters such as the wearing of the Islamic headscarf in the public sphere are still likely to launch heated debates.

Despite the work that is yet to be done to fulfill its recommendations, the commission was successful in ending the popular crisis surrounding the practice of accommodation.

The Debate between Civic Pluralists and Romantic Conservatives

The Civic–Pluralist View

The **civic-pluralist** conception of identity holds that all inhabitants of Quebec who recognize themselves as Quebecers *are* Quebecers.[10] Being a Quebecer is predicated upon neither French-Canadian origin nor assimilation to the majority. Identity choices are left to the individual—it is up to the newcomer to decide whether to keep aspects of his or her cultural origins alive or not. The emphasis is on the civic framework or "common public culture" that sets the terms of social co-operation. The civic-pluralist vision is at its core a *liberal* one: Individuals have basic human rights that limit what the state can do in the name of the common good (liberalism in this sense relates to the rights and freedoms of individuals, not necessarily leaning toward the left or right side of the political spectrum).[11]

There are debates and disagreements among civic pluralists. Some of these are **liberal neutralists** (or "difference-blind" liberals), believing that the state should guarantee the same basic individual rights to every citizen and adopt a "hands-off" approach to culture and identity. The state ought to fight against ethnic and religious discrimination and promote tolerance, but it should not put forward what has been called a "politics of recognition" or a policy of multiculturalism that confers special recognition and specific rights to cultural minorities.[12] As civic pluralists, they don't see cultural diversity as a threat that needs to be contained—quite the opposite, they most likely rejoice in the diverse lifestyles that immigration has brought to Quebec.[13] But they do not think that group-specific rights or policies should be designed for cultural minorities. They are not likely to support, for instance, religion-based accommodations in the workplace or in the delivery of public services. They see fairness as the identical treatment of all citizens by the state.[14] Citizens are free to engage in the cultural and religious activities of their choice in their private lives and in civil society, but the state should not implement policies and programs designed to support minority cultures.

On the other hand, some civic pluralists are **liberal multiculturalists.**[15] They think that fairness toward cultural and religious minorities sometimes necessitates differential treatment. Liberal multiculturalists favour, for instance, the reasonable accommodation of minority religious beliefs and practices and the recognition of the collective rights of Aboriginal peoples. The debate between liberal neutralists and liberal multiculturalists is a political philosophy debate; they differ on the meaning and conditions of social justice or fairness under conditions of cultural diversity.

For both liberal neutralists and liberal multiculturalists, Quebec identity is open to all Quebec citizens. Civic pluralists conceive cultural diversity as an asset for Quebec society. They see a multicultural Quebec society as good for the economy, the arts, and social interactions, insofar as new Quebecers are willing to lead their lives within the parameters of the common civic framework.

Civic pluralists (both liberal neutralists and liberal multiculturalists) are less likely to feel that Quebec identity is weak, fragile, threatened, and perhaps slowly disappearing. From their perspective, the Quiet Revolution succeeded in turning Quebec society into a strong, civic, outward-looking nation. They see Quebec society as strong enough to integrate and value cultural diversity. They see national identities as internally diverse and under continuous transformation. This vision is widespread among younger generations.

The Romantic–Conservative View

The **romantic-conservative** conception holds that the shift from French-Canadian identity to Quebec identity was not completely positive—something important was lost along the way. They believe that the "historical majority" (Quebecers of French-Canadian origins) somehow lost its political empowerment and assertiveness as it opened up to plurality. This, they argue, was caused not by conscious and voluntary decisions, but by a combination of the unhappy consciousness of a self-effacing majority that zealously wants to avoid xenophobia and ethnic nationalism and of the successful imposition of a pluralist ideology by the intellectual and political elites. Conservative nationalists therefore generally think that Quebecers of French-Canadian origin ought to start reasserting themselves and invite newcomers to rally behind them.[16] Romantic conservatives tend to worry about the fate of the older French-Canadian identity within the new civic Quebec identity.[17] In this regard, they are carrying out the legacy of the late sociologist Fernand Dumont.

The main contention of the romantic conservative seems to be that French Canadians (and those who assimilated to them) fought for their survival throughout history. They were the driving force behind the Quiet Revolution, but their affirmation and empowerment has somehow waned. They see political correctness and the prevailing pluralist ideology as preventing the "silent majority" from asserting itself and pursuing its legitimate goals and interests. The 2006–8 reasonable accommodation crisis as well as the Parti Québécois's Charter of Quebec Values are seen as romantic–conservative reactions against pluralism[18]—the majority allegedly has reasserted itself, shaken off political correctness, and loosened the grip of the pluralist ideology.

Why the majority is faced with this predicament is not clear. It is hard to pin down the argument made by romantic nationalists without reverting to philosophical concepts drawn from Hegel, Marx, and the Frankfurt School. They appear to argue that the self-consciousness of Quebecers seems to have been altered by a mix of superstructure and alienation/false consciousness. In this view, Quebecers' self-consciousness was influenced by the pluralization, fragmentation, and individualization of the superstructure, the general framework of society; this process is seen in many liberal, late-modern democracies. These forces make it difficult to maintain the republican idea of a people united by a shared vision of the common good.[19] The romantic conservative further argues that alienation and false consciousness have come into play; under the influence of a "cosmopolitan elite" promoting a pluralist ideology, Quebecers have been led to believe that they were xenophobic and not open enough to cultural diversity. Thus they would have internalized a distorted image of themselves and, in doing so, lost sight of their best self-interest.[20] In keeping with the "critique of ideology" program of the early Frankfurt School, romantic nationalists set themselves up to criticize the prevailing pluralist or cosmopolitan ideology and help the "silent majority" rediscover its voice.[21]

As we suggested in the introduction, the "civic–ethnic" nationalism distinction fails to capture the nature of the debate over Quebec identity. Conservative nationalists are not ethnic nationalists in the strictest sense. Ethnic nationalism is defined by the belief that ethnicity ought to be the sole criterion of citizenship. But romantic conservatives allow the possibility that newcomers can gradually come to identify with the experience and aspirations of the majority, that is, French Canadians. As Jacques Beauchemin writes:

> How should the idea of the Franco-Quebec majority be understood? Does it only include Quebecers of French-Canadian ancestry? They, as we know, have integrated [into their society] a great many individuals from other cultures who, for a very long time, have been part of the historical journey of French Canadians. It would not occur to us to consider the Ryans, Johnsons, Kellys and countless others in any other way. But we must also consider as an integral part of this majority those who, for one reason or another—such as language, cultural affinities or their belief in Quebec's common values—have boarded the train of Quebec history as it rolls along.[22]

The meaning of "boarding the train of Quebec's history" is, of course, very nebulous. One of the fault lines between romantic nationalists and civic pluralists most probably lies in what is expected from new Quebecers. Whereas conservative nationalists tend to favour a "cultural convergence" model of integration—which most probably involves substantial cultural assimilation on the part of the immigrant—pluralists or interculturalists will generally value and recognize cultural differences and leave identity choices to the immigrant.

Engaging Romantic–Conservative Nationalism

As readers may have guessed, we are engaged participants in this debate rather than neutral observers. We have tried to defend liberal pluralism both as a political philosophy and as an integration model for societies like Quebec. We now want to sketch out what we see as some of the most important problems in the romantic–conservative conception of Quebec identity.

First, we do not agree that the political affirmation process launched in the late 1950s has come to a halt. Conservative nationalists lose sight of one crucial sociological fact, one that is probably obvious to external observers of Quebec society: Nationalism is the dominant political paradigm in contemporary Quebec. To use a Wittgensteinian formulation, Quebec nationalism is a "background agreement" against which political disagreements are played out.

It is safe to say that an important majority of Quebecers and virtually all political leaders endorse the following two propositions: (1) Quebec is a nation and, as such, (2) it has a right to self-determination (which can take a variety of forms).[23] Accordingly, all significant political parties, including federalist ones, seek to consolidate or expand Quebec's political powers and claim to be the best defenders of Quebec's national interests. Take as a case in point the newspaper *La Presse*. The opinion section of *La Presse* is driven by a group of assertive and energetic federalist political writers who nonetheless all claim to be Quebec nationalists. And they are! One need not be a sovereignist to be a nationalist. These federalist–nationalists disagree with sovereignists on what political form best serves Quebec national interests, but they don't deny that Quebec is a nation that should enjoy much political autonomy. Anti-nationalist thought in Quebec is marginal. Who are its spokespersons? It dawned on us recently that the chapter on anti-nationalist thought among Quebec intellectuals in my 2000 book[24] was in fact an obituary!

It would perhaps help to distinguish here between an inflationist and a deflationist notion of nationalism. Here it is sufficient to note that the inflationist view holds, à la Ernest Gellner, that nationalism means that all nations should have their own state.[25] The deflationist view holds that nationalism lies in the identification with a distinct and bounded national identity and in the belief that nations have a right to some political autonomy.

We fail to see what facts derived empirically from the social sciences support the claim that Quebec nationalism, and in particular the political affirmation of francophone Quebecers, has stalled. One would want to ask romantic–conservative nationalists: Does the fact that Quebec sovereignty was not achieved prove that Quebec nationalism is on the back burner?[26] If so, this would mean that Quebec, Catalonia, and Scotland could effectively promote their own national identities and expand or consolidate their self-governing powers only if they secede and become fully sovereign countries—a statement that is empirically false.[27]

Second, the implicit philosophy of history that the romantic–conservative position seems to presuppose is suspect. It appears to be a teleological conception of Quebec history—a belief that we can discern in the past and the present the stages of a purposeful development process leading up to a final destination. Take, for instance, another quotation from Jacques Beauchemin:

> While subscribing to this conception of democracy, built on openness to minorities and the recognition of multiple identities, the first thing that the Franco-Quebec majority must do is to assert itself as a majority. A society, any society, cannot be constructed and advanced if it is not driven by the will of the majority, constituted as a political subject.
>
> The Quiet Revolution would not have been possible without the momentum garnered from the national awakening that occurred among Quebecers. In the same way, the future of Quebec, within the context of globalization and interdependence in which the fate of nations is playing out today, depends on its capacity to rally as a political subject, capable of speaking on [its own] behalf. . . .
>
> Quebecers must give themselves permission to do so. They must go back to their history,

> acknowledging the road [they have travelled] and, without any pangs of conscience, embrace their desire to extend it further. Essentially, this road remains that of the Franco-Quebec majority. [This majority] can legitimately wish to pave the way to Quebec's future constitution.[28]

What does it mean for Quebecers to "give themselves permission"? Should we not assume that they have already done so? If they have not, is it because they are blinded by false consciousness? And how are we to interpret the idea that Quebecers "must go back to their history, acknowledging the road [they have travelled] and, without any pangs of conscience, embrace their desire to extend it further" if not in terms of a philosophy of history predicated on the belief that Quebecers can extract from the past what they need to build their future?

What we ought to do here and now cannot really be directly inferred from the past. On the one hand, the past is rife with tensions and is interpreted in various, contested ways. Which events tell us what we must do now? Which interpretations of the past must we favour? On the other hand, and more importantly, just because *X* happened in the past does not imply that we need to pursue *X* or its correlates in the present or future. The fact that a nation was xenophobic at a given moment of its history obviously does not mean it ought to be the same in the present. The past simply does not generate that type of moral obligation.

Leaving aside the "was/ought" distinction that still keeps philosophers busy today, we can first note that the past cannot by itself provide us with the answers to our current challenges and predicaments. Moreover, it is hard to see the principle by which current generations would be morally obligated to simply reproduce the identity they inherited from their predecessors. It is precisely because we have to create a future for ourselves out of what we have inherited that we can enjoy a degree of freedom, that we can be the co-authors of our collective life. As the communitarian critics of liberalism have pointed out, it is true that identities do not emerge in a vacuum and are not strictly the result of autonomous will. We are "embedded" selves.[29] But the proposition that we are not free-floating agents is ontological; it describes a basic aspect of human nature. It is not a normative or a moral proposition—it does not prescribe how we ought to act. That identities are built with material inherited from the past does not generate a duty to be faithful to a given interpretation of our history. What we ought to do here and now does not mechanically unfold from what happened in the past. Invoking history can never replace reasoning together about what we want to become. Since normative judgments (what we should become) cannot be directly inferred from descriptive judgments (what happened in the past), conservative nationalists will have to provide their fellow citizens with reasons and arguments for their vision of the future.

The Debate over Religious Accommodations: The Strange Bedfellows Thesis

Earlier in this chapter we contested the idea that the francophone majority's political resolve faded as Quebec society opened itself to the world and became internally diverse. But conservative nationalists maintain that the recent commotion over the accommodation of religious minorities confirmed the identity-affirmation deficit of the majority and coincided with the beginning of its political reassertion.

The problem with this interpretation is that it greatly homogenizes the opposition to accommodating religious diversity. As we alluded to above, some liberal neutralists and civic nationalists are also opposed to the legal accommodation of minority religious beliefs and practices. However, their reasons are very different from those of the conservative nationalists. Their claim is that religious accommodations are incompatible with civic values such as gender equality, the separation of Church and state, fairness among co-workers, interculturalism, and so on. Such public values can be endorsed by all Quebecers *regardless of their cultural origins*. Many people who are generally well disposed toward cultural diversity and who favour interculturalism as an integration model nonetheless hold that the proper place of religion is in the private sphere and that no accommodations should be granted to the members of religious minorities.

Conservative nationalists see the reaction against religious accommodations as a reassertion of the historical majority's "identity," "culture," or "customs and ways." According to this view, Quebecers of French-Canadian origin would have seized the occasion of the reasonable accommodation debate to reassert themselves and stop bending too much in trying to accommodate immigrants. We would not want to deny that some Quebecers rebelled against religious accommodation because they saw it as a threat to the traditions and customs of the majority, but we think that a fair analysis of the debate leads us to conclude that the conservative reaction was considerably less prevalent than the civic or liberal critique of reasonable accommodation.[30]

These two often-stated but mutually incompatible positions show the heterogeneity of the opposition to religious accommodation:

1. It is only recently and as a result of painful struggles that Quebecers were able to achieve a true separation between the Church and the state. *Laïcité* (secularism) is one of the Quiet Revolution's greatest achievements. It is now threatened by the religious practice of minorities. They need to accept that religion, in Quebec, belongs to the private sphere. We should not let religion sneak back into the public sphere through accommodation measures.
2. Quebec is a Catholic (or, more inclusively, Christian) society. Catholicism is an integral part of Quebec history and identity. The Quiet Revolution threw the baby out with the bathwater. Catholicism ought to have a special status within our collective life. It cannot be put on a par with the other religions brought to Quebec through immigration.

These two positions are mutually incompatible. Normally at war with one another, liberal neutralists and conservative nationalists both found reasons to oppose religious accommodation, leaving civic pluralists caught in the middle. We call this the "strange bedfellows thesis" of the religious accommodation debate.[31]

This unlikely coalition of progressives and conservatives played an especially important role during the debates on secularism in Quebec that followed the Bouchard–Taylor commission. Quebec came to be divided between two sharply contrasted camps. On the one hand, proponents of a republican conception of secularism embraced the view that religion should in some contexts be privatized and that public institutions should not accommodate religious practices. They maintained that a strict separation of state and religion is necessary to protect individual freedom, equality, and social cohesion. On the other hand, proponents of an open or liberal–pluralist conception of secularism maintained that freedom and equality sometimes require special measures of accommodation for marginalized religious minorities facing various forms of discrimination and obstacles to full participation to society.

Several liberal–pluralist secularists expressed their views by publishing a manifesto in 2010 (*Manifeste pour un Québec pluraliste*), and proponents of a strict or republican conception of secularism replied a few weeks later with their own manisfesto (*Manifeste pour un Québec laïque et pluraliste*) (excerpts from both manifestos can be found in the Primary Source box). Interestingly, signatories of the second manifesto include important members of the Mouvement laïque Québécois (MLQ) who oppose the presence of religion in public life out of a commitment to difference-blind liberalism and an (arguably) anti-clerical view of the ills of religion, but it also includes prominent romantic–conservative figures, like Jacques Beauchemin, who seem to be saying that the authentic French and Catholic core of Quebec identity is threatened by openness to diversity. In 2013, those opponents to religious accommodation all supported Bill 60's proposed ban on wearing ostensibly religious signs by state employees.

Primary Source

Manifesto for a Pluralist Quebec *(Manifeste pour un Québec pluraliste)*

[The Quebec State] exercises its neutrality by abstaining from favouring or interfering with, directly or indirectly, a religion or a secular conception of existence, within the limits of the common good. This political orientation responds to the requirement of protecting freedom of conscience and its free expression as well as equality between citizens. This means that political and civic rights are not conditional upon the abdication of beliefs and of the practices of those who express them.

We can, however, witness the emergence, in Quebec, of the idea that publicly expressed religious belonging is, allegedly, detrimental to national identity, hence the necessity to adopt a charter of secularism. However, in practice, such a charter would primarily be a legal instrument forbidding the manifestation of adhesion to a religion in the public sphere and rejecting all demands of accommodation for a religious motive.

It is essential to agree on the meaning and scope of secularism; however, the blanket interdiction of any manifestation of religious belonging does not meet any social necessity. Such an interdiction would have a discriminatory effect since it would only target the believers of those religions that comprise clothing or alimentary prescriptions. But above all, it would be disproportionate compared to its objectives, especially that of ensuring the neutrality of public services.

Source: This manifesto was published in *Le Devoir* on 3 February 2010 and was written by Pierre Bosset, Dominique Leydet, Jocelyn Maclure, Micheline Milot, and Daniel Weinstock.

Manifesto for a Secular and Pluralist Quebec *(Manifeste pour un Québec laïque et pluraliste)*

For a society to be genuinely pluralist, that is, to respect all convictions in the domain of religion, it is necessary that the State and its institutions be committed to total neutrality with regard to these convictions. This neutrality means that the State recognizes and respects the freedom of all citizens to adopt and transmit their convictions to the extent that this freedom is exercised within the limits of the law.

Secularism enables us to manage social pluralism without requiring that the majority, which also partakes in pluralism, renounce its legitimate choices and without infringing upon anyone's freedom. Far from being a rejection of pluralism, secularism is its essential condition. It is the only path leading to a fair and equal treatment of all convictions because it neither favours nor accommodates any, whether atheist or religious. Pluralism, thus understood, belongs neither to minorities nor to the majority. Secularism is also an essential condition of equality between men and women.

The so-called "open" secularism, however, proves to be, in practice, a rejection of State secularism since it allows all forms of accommodation of public institutions with a religion or another [*sic*]. It therefore fails to respect the structuring principles of secularism, which are neutrality and separation between the State and the religious. The adjustments of "open" secularism converge with the objectives of conservative religious groups who want their principles

continued

to prevail over existing laws. At best, it is a case by case mode of management of freedom of religion within the public sphere, one that favours arbitrariness, but it certainly is not a theory of State secularism.[32]

Source: This manifesto was published in *Le Devoir* on 16 March 2010 and was signed by Daniel Baril, Marie-France Bazzo, Jacques Beauchemin, Paul Bégin, Henri Brun, Christian Dufour, Jacques Godbout, Jean-Claude Hébert, Yvan Lamonde, Bernard Landry, Julie Latour, Christiane Pelchat, and Guy Rocher.

Bill 60: Charter Affirming the Value of State Secularism and Religious Neutrality and of Equality between Women and Men, and Providing a Framework for Accommodation Requests

The purpose of this bill is to establish a Charter affirming the values of State secularism and religious neutrality and of equality between women and men, and providing a framework for accommodation requests.

. . .

Public bodies must, in the pursuit of their mission, remain neutral in religious matters and reflect the secular nature of the State. Accordingly, obligations are set out for personnel members of public bodies in the exercise of their functions, including a duty to remain neutral and exercise reserve in religious matters by, among other things, complying with the restriction on wearing religious objects that overtly indicate a religious affiliation. As well, personnel members of a public body must exercise their functions with their face uncovered, and persons to whom they provide services must also have their face uncovered when receiving such services.

Source: National Assembly of Quebec, www.assnat.qc.ca/en/travaux-parlementaires/projets-loi/projet-loi-60-40-1.html.

This coalition grew as liberal feminists joined it, fiercely opposing religious accommodation on the basis that several religious practices (but especially the practice of wearing the Islamic headscarf) reinforced patriarchal domination.[33] In other words, opposition to religious accommodation was constituted by romantic nationalists eager to protect the special and privileged place of Catholicism in Quebec's identity and public life, by liberal neutralists insisting that the state should not support or recognize *any* religion, and by liberal feminists who view all religions as historic tools of the subjection of women.

This unlikely alliance between liberal neutralists and conservative nationalists created the illusion of a self-conscious and united majority reasserting itself. This belief, however, is an illusion. The background political philosophies of the two camps are irreconcilable, as are the political prescriptions stemming from them. While they both provide reasons to oppose the accommodation of religious minorities' practices (such as wearing a hijab, kippah, or kirpan), they lead to contradictory positions with regard to public displays of Quebec's allegedly Catholic identity (such as the display of a crucifix at the National Assembly, just above the Throne of the Assembly's president). Thus, liberal neutralists and conservative nationalists were only able to make a common front in support of the Charter of Quebec Values because the Charter, despite being thought of as a charter of secularism, focused on banning minority practices and avoided taking a stance on questions that had an incidence on the treatment of Catholicism by the government. Indeed, it would not have made sense for liberal neutralists to accept the funding of religious schools or the legitimacy of a crucifix displayed as a state symbol in the legislative chamber, just as it would have put conservative nationalists at odds with their nostalgic commitments to oppose those elements.

Only the future will tell if the strategic alliance between liberal neutralists and romantic–conservative nationalists can survive its inherent tensions or if further social debates on secularism will bring their antagonistic foundations and political implications to the fore, rendering the coalition unmanageable. Refusing both difference blindness and romantic communitarianism, the civic–pluralist position seems to be more stable and it presents itself as the mean between neutral liberalism and romantic–conservative nationalism.

BIOGRAPHY

Charles Taylor[34]

Charles Taylor was born in 1931 in Montreal. Although he held the Chichele Chair in Social and Political Theory at All Souls College, Oxford, from 1976 to 1981, he taught for most of his career at McGill University. One of the few modern philosophers who dared to enter Quebec's political debate, he invested himself deeply in shaping Quebec's future. He ran for the (progressive, social democrat) New Democratic Party in four federal elections in the 1960s, participated in government consultations after the failure of the Meech Lake Accord for constitutional reform, and recently co-chaired the Consultation Commission on Accommodation Practices Related to Cultural Differences.

Charles Taylor in his office at McGill University. Taylor was awarded the Templeton Prize on 14 March 2007 as well as the Kyoto Prize in 2008.

Courtesy of Charles Taylor.

He holds a Ph.D. in philosophy from Oxford University. His thesis was published under the title *The Explanation of Behaviour* (1964). While more epistemological than his other writing, this book already presents a criticism of simplistic approaches to the human subject based only on brute facts and causal arguments and puts forth an explanation involving the deeper roots and motives for human actions. His work reached its peak with the publication of *Source of the Self* (1989), in which he examines the modern conception of "the subject," which he describes as the combination of the "value of ordinary life," centred on family, work, love, and so on, and of an "ethic of authenticity," an urge felt by each person to realize his or her own potential in a unique and authentic way.

Born from the union of an English-speaking Protestant and a French-speaking Catholic, and living in Quebec, Taylor's philosophy is sensitive to difference and to the importance of culture and language and their appropriate recognition—matters that post-World War II American liberal thinking tends to obscure. In his view, identity is a complex construction forged in dialogue and social interactions, involving "strong evaluations" that are not on par with more superficial and instrumental reasons for action. Thus, the "disengaged self"—the notion that one can fully define oneself through the exercise of one's rational faculties—is, according to him, a misconception.

Against this philosophical background, Taylor turned his focus to political philosophy and articulated a response to the framework set out by John Rawls in his famous book *A Theory of Justice*.

continued

Taylor's critique included an argument suggesting that the simplistic conception of the self found in liberal thinking is a consequence of the atomistic view borrowed from modern science. Yet, despite his appeal for a more holistic approach, Taylor (and most other so-called "communitarian" thinkers) does not repudiate liberalism as a whole and is in no way suggesting that the interests of the community have more weight than individual rights and freedoms. In fact, most of them even reject the "communitarian" denomination.

Taylor's contribution to the liberal-communitarian debate also includes a rejection of the dominant procedural theories of justice. These theories are based on the honourable idea that if a community proclaims *X* as good, all its members who do not accept *X* would be second-class citizens. Therefore, the state should limit itself in defining justice and make sure that everyone has the opportunity to pursue his or her goals, whatever they may be. This position is often presented as "the priority of the just over the good." While having some merits, these theories would abandon too much to achieve formal equality and individual freedom. Taylor points out that such a position presupposes a conception of "the good" and wants to reintegrate discussion of collective identity and common goals within debates on justice. Another of Taylor's concerns is that procedural liberalism ends up reducing politics to the judiciary process.

With that in mind, Taylor argues that the culture and language of some communities can be legitimately viewed as equally important to justice, Quebec being the prime example of a society that cannot bring itself to function under a purely procedural paradigm. As he observes, the political debate resulting from the emergence of "the good" alongside "the just" inevitably means that complex political disagreements cannot be solved by the simple application of a theory of justice such as Rawls's, and that difficult choices and sacrifices will have to be made.

While drawing heavily from continental European thinkers—including Rousseau, Herder, Hegel, Heidegger, and Merleau-Ponty—Taylor writes in the clear manner of Anglo-American philosophers and primarily for that audience, making him the ideal bridge-builder between these two great traditions of contemporary Western philosophy and, indeed, a central figure for any accurate understanding of a society such as Quebec that defines itself by referring to both traditions.

Conclusion

It is important to get a clearer view of the contrast between the civic-pluralist and the romantic-conservative conceptions of Quebec identity chiefly because this contrast generates substantial political disagreement about the nature of citizenship and integration. Those who adhere to the romantic-conservative view tend to favour a more conformist conception of the common public culture and a more assimilative integration model: Immigrants ought to endorse a particular interpretation of the past as well as a particular vision of the common good.

Those who hold the liberal and civic view defend a pluralist model of integration that seeks to strike an appropriate balance between respect for cultural diversity and the demands of social co-operation. Integration, seen from that standpoint, does not require assimilation. Liberals continue to debate among themselves about what form and degree of recognition and accommodation ought to be granted to cultural minorities. As it is solidly anchored in deep philosophical and political disagreements, Quebec's homebrewed "culture war" will most likely give intellectuals, elected officials, and citizens plenty of debate material in the years to come.

Questions for Critical Thinking

1. What are the positions in your own society about what should be expected or required from immigrants?
2. Where do the views of difference-blind liberalism and multicultural liberalism diverge? Which one is, in your opinion, the most congruent with the spirit of liberalism?
3. What is the role of political philosophy? Why, do you think, is Quebec society a fertile ground for political philosophy?

Notes

1. It will be interesting to see whether President Obama's more dialogue-based, less Machiavellian approach to politics will soften the edges of the culture wars in the United States. See William Saletan, "This Is the Way the Culture Wars End," *New York Times*, 21 February 2009, www.nytimes.com/2009/02/22/opinion/22saletan.html.
2. Jocelyn Maclure, *Quebec Identity: The Challenge of Pluralism* (Montreal and Kingston: McGill-Queen's University Press, 2003).
3. As John Rawls put it, "we turn to political philosophy when our shared political understandings, as [Michael] Walzer might say, break down, and equally when we are torn within ourselves." John Rawls, *Political Liberalism* (New York: Columbia University Press, 1993), 44.
4. José Woehrling, "L'obligation d'accommodement raisonnable et l'adaptation de la société à la diversité religieuse," *Revue de droit de McGill/McGill Law Journal* 43 (1998): 328, authors' translation.
5. In the fall of 2013, the Parti Québécois presented Bill 60 to the National Assembly. Named the *Charter Affirming the Values of State Secularism and Religious Neutrality and of Equality between Women and Men, and Providing a Framework for Accommodation Requests* and labelled as the Charter of Secularism or the Charter of Quebec Values, the bill contained several clauses seeking to assert the secular character of Quebec's government, the most controversial of which was the suggestion to forbid all public institution employees from wearing "ostensible" religious signs. The bill was not passed as the Parti Québécois lost the April 2014 provincial election to the Liberal Party, which was strongly opposed to Bill 60.
6. Prepared by François Côté-Vaillancourt, MA Candidate, Faculty of Philosophy, Université Laval.
7. Gérard Bouchard and Charles Taylor, *Building the Future: A Time for Reconciliation* (Québec: Gouvernement du Québec), 18.
8. Ibid.
9. Ibid., Chapter 9, Section C.
10. Since identities are in part matters of self-recognition and self-description, we must allow for the possibility that a Quebec *citizen* does not recognize him- or herself as a Quebecer. For example, think of someone who would describe him- or herself exclusively as a Cree, a Canadian, or a citizen of the world.
11. As Yael Tamir and David Miller have argued, liberalism and nationalism are not incompatible since the political community within which liberal institutions are set out is most commonly a *national* political community. We will not address here the liberal nationalists' additional argument that liberal institutions *necessitate* or *presuppose* the nation-state. It suffices for our purposes to point out that liberalism and nationalism are not logically incompatible. See Yael Tamir, *Liberal Nationalism* (Princeton, NJ: Princeton University Press, 1995); and David Miller, *On Nationality* (Oxford: Clarendon Press, 1995). For a critique of liberal nationalism, see Geneviève Nootens, *Désenclaver la démocratie : des huguenots à la paix des Braves* (Montreal: Québec Amérique, 2004).
12. Charles Taylor, *Multiculturalism and the Politics of Recognition* (Princeton, NJ: Princeton University Press, 1992); James Tully, *Strange Multiplicity: Constitutionalism in an Age of Diversity* (Cambridge: Cambridge University Press, 1995); and Will Kymlicka, *Multicultural Citizenship* (Oxford: Clarendon Press, 1995).
13. Jeremy Waldron, "Minority Cultures and the Cosmopolitan Alternative," *University of Michigan Journal of Law Reform* 25 (1991): 751.
14. Brian Barry, *Culture and Equality: An Egalitarian Critique of Multiculturalism* (Cambridge, MA: Harvard University Press, 2001).
15. We will not address here the debate over the similarities and differences between "multiculturalism" and "interculturalism." See Chapter 15 in this volume for Raffaele Iacovino's excellent presentation of the Quebec intercultural model of integration.
16. As we will see, this most probably means that immigrants should assimilate, but the formulations are usually very vague.
17. According to historian Éric Bédard, conservative nationalists are "as preoccupied with the defensive survival of Quebec as they are with the political status of Quebec." Their nationalism is driven by the "haunting anxiety of

seeing their culture disappear." Éric Bédard, "La colère 'bleue' des nationalistes," *Le Devoir*, 26 April 2007.

18. See the Case Study box on the Bouchard–Taylor Commission in this chapter.
19. For a clear and accessible analysis of these societal transformations, see Charles Taylor, *The Ethics of Authenticity* (Cambridge, MA: Harvard University Press, 1992).
20. The idea that Quebecers of French-Canadian origin are somehow alienated is a common theme among conservative nationalists in Quebec. See Maclure, *Quebec Identity*, Chapter 1.
21. The striking similarities between conservative nationalism and the Freudian-Marxism of some members (Marcuse, Fromm) of the early Frankfurt School never fail to surprise us.
22. Jacques Beauchemin, "La mauvaise conscience de la majorité franco-québécoise," *Institut du Nouveau-Monde*, accessed 13 September 2007, www.vigile.net/article4044.html; authors' translation. For Beauchemin, "alluding to Quebec's French-speaking majority is tantamount to designating the gathering of all those, old-stock French Canadians as well as travel companions, who feel they belong to Quebec not only from the point of view of the rights granted by citizenship but from the standpoint of the collective feeling which fuels solidarity and nurtures participation in a common adventure" (authors' translation). This is, again, very vague. We would need to know more about the meaning of "collective sentiment" and "common adventure" to tease out the real implications of Beauchemin's position.
23. Robert Bourassa's reaction after the failure of the Meech Lake Accord, as well as the conclusions of the Bélanger–Campeau Commission, were probably instrumental in the crystallization of that background consensus.
24. Jocelyn Maclure, *Récits identitaires : le Québec à l'épreuve du pluralisme* (Montreal: Québec Amérique, 2000). The English translation is cited in note 2.
25. Ernest Gellner, *Nation and Nationalism* (Ithaca, NY: Cornell University Press, 1983).
26. See Jacques Beauchemin, "La souveraineté au nom de la mémoire," in *Redonner sens à l'indépendance : Les intellectuels pour la souveraineté*, ed. Jocelyne Couture (Montreal: VLB éditeur, 2005).
27. Michael Keating, *Nation against the State: The New Politics of Nationalism in Quebec, Catalonia and Scotland*, 2nd ed. (New York: Palgrave Macmillan, 2001).
28. Beauchemin, "La souveraineté au nom de la mémoire," authors' translation.
29. Michael Sandel, *Liberalism and the Limits of Justice*, 2nd ed. (Cambridge: Cambridge University Press, 1998).
30. Maclure developed that position in "Le malaise relatif aux pratiques d'accommodement de la diversité religieuse : une thèse interpretative," in *L'accommodement raisonnable et la diversité religieuse à l'école publique : normes et pratiques*, ed., Paul Eid, Jean-Sébastien Imbeault, Marie McAndrew, and Micheline Milot (Montreal: Fides, 2008).
31. Maclure, *Quebec Identity.*
32. The excerpts from both manifestos were translated by the authors.
33. This position was best represented by the movement of the *Janettes*. For a summary of the Janettes' views, see their *Mémoire présenté par le mouvement des Janettes dans le cadre de la consultation générale et des audiences publiques tenues par la Commission des institutions de l'Assemblée nationale du Québec*, 18 December 2013, www.michelleblanc.com/wp-content/uploads/M%C3%A9moire-Mouvement-des-Janette-.pdf.
34. Prepared by François Côté-Vaillancourt, MA Candidate, Faculty of Philosophy, Université Laval.

Select Bibliography

Barry, Brian. *Culture and Equality: An Egalitarian Critique of Multiculturalism*. Cambridge: Polity Press, 2001.

Beauchemin, Jacques. *L'histoire en trop : la mauvaise conscience des souverainistes québécois*. Montreal: VLB éditeur, 2002.

Dumont, Fernand. *Raisons communes*. Montreal: Boréal, 1995.

Hunter, James Davison. *Culture Wars: The Struggle to Control the Family, Art, Education, Law, and Politics in America*. New York: Basic Books, 1992.

Kymlicka, Will. *Multicultural Citizenship*. Oxford: Clarendon Press, 1995.

Maclure, Jocelyn. *Quebec Identity: The Challenge of Pluralism*. Montreal and Kingston: McGill-Queen's University Press, 2003.

Taylor, Charles. *Multiculturalism and the Politics of Recognition*. Princeton, NJ: Princeton University Press, 1992.

Thériault, Joseph Ivon. *Critique de l'américanité : mémoire et démocratie au Québec*. Montreal: Québec Amérique, 2002.

Venne, Michel, ed. *Vive Quebec! New Thinking and New Approaches to the Quebec Nation*. Toronto: Lorimer & Company, 2001.

Part B
Identities

Introduction

This is the first of several sections in this collection that deals explicitly with questions of identity. Put most simply, identity can be defined as how we answer the question, "Who am I?" Until relatively recently the answer to this question was obvious. Yet increasingly, academics and others have conclusively demonstrated that our individual notions of identity derive from culturally specific social processes and practices.[1] Though we are not always completely conscious of it, our diverse relations with others, both within and outside our own culture, shape the way we understand who we are and who we aren't.

One's individual identity is multilayered: one has gender and sexual identities; class identity; racial, ethnic, and cultural identities (to name but a few!), all helping to shape one's personal identity. The elements that one shares with others create a collective identity. In creating personal identities we emphasize some parts of our personal stories and downplay others. Our identities are also subject to external pressures; other people have ideas about who we should be, and there may be a social price to pay if we don't live up to its changing norms of, for example, what a woman or a man should be or what beliefs a Quebecer should hold. Our identities frequently shape the way people treat us, and they influence the way we treat others.[2]

In recent years, one of the most important ways scholars have sought to understand Quebec identity is to think about what it has meant for a small francophone settlement to exist in the Americas. Historian Yvan Lamonde has been at the forefront of thinkers on this question. As we see in his chapter here, Lamonde argues that dominant francophone Quebec identities have been and still are deeply influenced by their "Americanicity." He thinks through the numerous ways in which Quebec identities have been influenced by belonging to the Americas, from the earliest French colonial settlement, to the US invasion during the War of Independence, to the ideological influence on the Patriote movement, to American controlling interests in Quebec industry, to US influence over Quebec fashion and style. Over time, certain aspects of American influence have been rejected while others have been accepted wholeheartedly. The result, Lamonde submits, is that Quebec identity is pluralistic and profoundly postmodern—a hopeful sign for the future of the increasingly pluralistic Quebec society. Lamonde also asks whether the majority of

Quebecers will take up the American passion for independence, in which case American influence on Quebec identity becomes even more fascinating.

In Germain Lacasse's chapter on the history of Quebec cinema, American influence on Quebec identity is also a central theme. The question of how Quebec can avoid domination by the American film industry is a constant preoccupation, from the earliest silent films arriving in Quebec with English subtitles to the recent trend of Quebec filmmakers leaving Quebec to make Hollywood films. Quebecers have adapted American films by having French commentaries done for silent films and later through dubbing Hollywood films into French. Others have used film to go beyond linguistically adapting American films. During the 1930s priests made documentaries to present and promote a rural, Catholic, French-Canadian nation, and during the 1960s experimental documentary and fictional filmmakers were important voices of Québécois nationalism. Though nationalism has been less of a force in Quebec films since the 1980 referendum on Quebec sovereignty, and the popularity of Quebec *auteur* films has varied over time during these years, readers from English-speaking Canada will be impressed by the continued vibrancy of Quebec films.

Lacasse notes that even though Quebec cinema has occasionally produced films stylistically for a French or European market, its critical success has come through creating a distinct Quebec style and tradition. According to the schema developed by Yvan Lamonde, this is another way in which Quebec identity and culture is fundamentally "of the Americas." And it has not only been artists and filmmakers that have exhibited a kind of *américanicité*. Some would use this term to explain the rise in popularity of hockey from its late nineteenth-century Montreal origins. Historian Andrew Holman tells us in the third chapter in this section that by the time of the Richard Riot in 1955, hockey was on the leading edge of the transformation in francophone Quebec identity. Indeed, the riot is seen by some as a harbinger of the Quiet Revolution. During the Quiet Revolution, the state became more active in the promotion of sport, sports associations became increasingly French-speaking and, since the 1970s, some sovereignists have called for the formation of a Quebec hockey team to participate in international matches. The proposal resurfaces from time to time, always creating controversy. Holman rightly notes that more than most cultural activities, sport has the ability "to express identity with . . . strength and raw emotion."

Of course, francophones were not the only people in Quebec who have used organized sports as performances of their identities. Indeed, lacrosse has long played an important role for Indigenous peoples in Quebec, and from the early nineteenth century men from the United Kingdom used organized sport in Quebec to perform middle-class masculine values.[3] Dominic Hardy's chapter on visual culture goes the furthest in conceptualizing how to think about the diversity of identities forming in what is now Quebec. He sets an agenda of exploring how art history has "configured the settler–colonial and Aboriginal traditions of visual culture" across this territory. Religious art, the politics of rural painting, the arrival of modernist art practices in Quebec, the satirical tradition of visual arts in the province, and the rise of abstraction and interdisciplinary visual arts all get their due consideration here. Broadly, Hardy unravels the ways in which artists gave their art meaning, exploring the training of artists and artistic conventions. He also highlights the importance of artistic intentions and reasons for production in understanding meanings of particular works: Was it created to help proselytize Indigenous peoples? Reassure English imperialists that French and English coexisted harmoniously in Quebec? Assert French-Canadian identity in the face of British assimilation efforts?

For Hardy, little Quebec culture production takes place in hermetically sealed ethnic silos. Indeed, artists project "identity markers" onto "people and places," giving them meaning. Indigenous peoples have been painted using European conventions, and recently Québécois artists have used Indigenous conventions in their art. Rather than creating some kind of postmodern pastiche, much artistic production in Quebec has been done as part of the settler–colonial occupation of the land. Hardy concludes that a better understanding of the role of Indigenous peoples in creating this art, how Indigenous artists have practised their craft, and how Indigenous art historians will conceptualize the field of Quebec art history will be some of the crucial issues undertaken by those studying Quebec visual art in the future.

Questions of identity are important because they have ethical, moral, and political implications. Indeed, in Quebec much rides on the question "Who am I?" This section largely focuses on how being part of the Americas has played a complicated role in constructing Quebec identities. Later sections will continue to investigate identity in Quebec through citizenship, language, and international relations.

Notes

1. On the rise of identity in the humanities and a useful critique, see Rogers Brubaker and Frederick Cooper, "Beyond Identity," *Theory and Society* 29 (2000): 1–47.
2. For those who would like to further explore issues of identity in Quebec, useful places to start are Mikhaël Elbaz, Andrée Fortin, and Guy Laforest, eds., *Les frontières de l'identité : modernité et postmodernisme au Québec* (Sainte-Foy: Presses de l'Université Laval and L'Harmattan, 1996); Jocelyn Létourneau, ed., *La question identitaire au Canada francophone : récits, parcours, enjeux, hors-lieux* (Sainte-Foy: Presses de l'Université Laval, 1994); and Bettina Bradbury and Tamara Myers, eds., *Negotiating Identities in 19th- and 20th-Century Montreal* (Vancouver: UBC Press, 2005). This introduction is indebted to Karine Hébert's contribution to Bradbury and Myers as well as Létourneau's introduction to his volume.
3. On "performance" of identity in Quebec, see Erin Hurley, *National Performance: Representing Quebec from Expo 67 to Céline Dion* (Toronto: University of Toronto Press, 2011); and Jarrett Rudy, *The Freedom to Smoke: Tobacco Consumption and Identity* (Montreal and Kingston: McGill-Queen's University Press, 2005).

6 Quebec's Americanicity

Yvan Lamonde, McGill University

Timeline

1774–5 American revolutionary propaganda distributed in Quebec and province invaded by American Revolutionary Army.

1791 England grants Lower Canada its House of Assembly.

1812 United States invades Canada for second time.

1830 Patriotes make increasing reference to US republican independence.

1837 US support for Patriote cause comes from inhabitants on Canada–US border, but not from American states or US federal government.

1838 Unsuccessful rebellion of some hundred exiled Patriotes originates in the United States.

1849 After resistance of 1837, Rebellion of 1838, and initiatives to repeal the Union of Upper and Lower Canada are all defeated, minority of francophone and anglophone Lower Canadians (British Tories and French-Canadian Democrats) draft plan for annexation to United States.

1859 Edmé Rameau de Saint-Père introduces notion that French Canada has spiritual or providential vocation in Americas.

1866 Abbé Henri-Raymond Casgrain grafts idea of moral vocation in Americas onto notion of providential vocation of French Canada.

1872 Trade Union Act recognizes the right of workers to associate in Canada, and US unions begin to organize in Canada and Quebec.

1896 In his book *L'avenir du peuple canadien-français*, Edmond de Nevers foresees "[North] American continental union" that would include "small nations."

1902 Msgr Adolphe Pâquet delivers his famous speech on the future of the French race in North America, breathing new life into Rameau de Saint-Père's vision, just as the Vatican begins to consider repudiating Catholic vocation of French Canadians in North America.

1928 Based on his observations of increased US investment and penetration of US business and media culture into Quebec, businessman Beaudry Leman says of American civilization, "We can't live with it and we can't live without it."

1945 Increasingly, French Canadians adopt materialist "American way of life," abandoning their ascetic spiritual self-image.

1961 Quebec's General Agency in New York (which hired its first Agent General in 1943) becomes General Delegation of Quebec in New York (now the Quebec Government Office in New York).

1970 More and more US counterculture is embraced in Quebec, and the place of Quebec in the Americas and Quebec's Americanicity are examined more intensively.

Quebec's **Americanicity** may seem obvious to a student from Boston or a professor from Seattle. Quebec is in North America; therefore, in the geographical sense of the word, it is **American.** It is "Americanized," hence it is "American." In contemplating the Declaration of Independence or the famous speech by Ralph Waldo Emerson, "The American Scholar,"[1] our student or professor might even conflate Canada's and Quebec's experiences with a wider emancipation process involving other societies in the Americas. They might consider for a moment, in the spirit of the Monroe Doctrine (1823) or of their compatriot John Louis O'Sullivan (1845), that the United States has a **Manifest Destiny**[2] in the Americas. But by the same token, our American scholars might well wonder what "destiny" the other societies of this hemisphere have followed. What destiny, what concept of their place, and what perception of their role might these societies, who share the continent of South and North America, have had in the past or have today?

Understanding the Americanicity of a society outside the United States but "inside" the Americas (a continent with a history that has not always been associated with or reduced to the US nation-state) requires us to embrace revelations and reorient our preconceptions about identity. With this in mind, let us start by trying to understand what is meant by *Americanization.*

Two Meanings of *Americanization*

The first meaning of *Americanization* dates back to America's earlier origins. In fact, all the societies that make up "the Americas" are new societies[3] in that they were shaped by the contact between European immigrants and the Aboriginal peoples of the continent.[4] All the colonial settlers had to adapt to the New World, its inhabitants, its climate, and its constraints. By taking up residence in the Americas, they became Americans. Most significantly, these newcomers (profoundly influenced by the Aboriginal peoples they met) underwent an Americanization that lasted fully two centuries before the United States was born.

The second meaning of Americanization lies in the United States' rise to power and its international expansionism at the end of the nineteenth century. The domination of Canada and other countries in the Americas by foreign US capital investment beginning around 1920; the spread of US culture throughout the Americas through technology and media such as the popular press; the near-monopoly of the US film industry after World War I; and the emergence after 1945 of the notion of an "American" way of life—these are all milestones in the process of Americanization. Indeed, the commanding power of the economy, military, technology, and media culture that flowed out of the United States has profoundly affected culture and behaviour in countries around the world.

Societies in the Americas have therefore undergone two forms of Americanization; but the second form cannot erase the historical and enduring first form. Indeed, US press, cinema, radio, architecture, television, diet, and attire—the second form—greatly contributed to the Americanicity of French Canada and Quebec. But Americanicity cannot be reduced to Americanization. In Quebec, as in Mexico (and here we have the full definition of Americanicity), there is a consciousness of belonging to the New World that precedes and transcends the relationship with the United

States, there is an attendant propensity to observe the political and cultural consequences of belonging to the American hemisphere, and all societies of the New World have the history of their relationships with the Old World, the memory of their "Europeanicity."[5] This said, the United States was the main catalyst in Quebec's historical relationships within the Americas for two reasons: its immediate geographic proximity as Quebec's neighbour and its very early and successful colonial emancipation, which later became a model for Europe and the Americas alike.[6]

Quebec's Americanicity and the War of Independence

The words *Quebec's Americanicity* convey an unfashionably historical phenomenon. French Quebec's long history of continental Americanicity began with the struggles of colonial settlers from France, who had to adapt to life in the New World. By the end of the eighteenth century, the telltale (political) signs of Americanicity were increasingly numerous. In 1774, 11 years after France ceded its American territory to England in the Treaty of Paris, the First Continental Congress (of what would become the United States) mandated Fleury Mesplet, a francophone printer in Philadelphia, to print pamphlets for distribution in the Province of Quebec. The pamphlets invited the inhabitants of Quebec to join the 13 American rebel colonies in their very just cause, urging, "your Province is the only missing link that remains to complete the strong and shining chain of their Union."[7] For six months, troops from the rebel colonies occupied Quebec before being pushed back from the shores of the St Lawrence River at Quebec City by the British regiments that arrived in the spring of 1776.[8] But by that time, there had been ample opportunity for the notion of American republicanism to be disseminated. In 1777, the governor of Britain's new colony recognized that "for years, the manner in which this people has been governed has not been sufficiently firm, whence the penetration of American ideas of emancipation and independence."[9] In the same vein, the bishop of Quebec City lamented the increased flouting of authority along with the subversive forces at work in 1790:

> have we not the right to blame the advancement of this spirit of liberty and independence among our [French] Canadians, [a spirit] initially brought to us through the distribution of Anglo-American manifestos at the beginning of the last war, and propagated through the multiplication and the licence of our newspapers and by the liberties taken in conversations about political affairs?[10]

The groundwork for US anti-colonial republican ideas was clearly being laid and would continue to influence political life in Lower Canada. This was particularly true after 1823, when Louis-Joseph Papineau came back disappointed from London, where he and John Neilson had gone on behalf of Lower Canada (now part of Quebec) to register their opposition to a prospective union with Upper Canada (now part of Ontario). By 1830, the Parti patriote, founded in 1826 (or the "Patriot Party" to its anglophone members, inspired by the US patriots of 1776), was making increasing reference to the success of American independence and the US model of republican government. The party was especially interested in applying the electoral model of the US state senates to the Legislative Council of Lower Canada. This was then the exclusive preserve of the British colonial authorities, who typically appointed anglophones who supported their policies, thereby giving the British the means to oppose legislation passed in Lower Canada's elected House of Assembly.

The Claws of the British Lion or the Talons of the American Eagle?

Louis-Joseph Papineau (see the Biography box) was not the only thinker to develop an "American" vision for the future of Lower Canada. Étienne Parent, editor of the Quebec City newspaper *Le Canadien*, was of the same mind in an editorial of 21 May 1831:

> There is not, to our knowledge, a French people in this Province, but rather a Canadian people, a religious and moral people, a people both loyal and liberty-loving, capable of enjoying these things; this people is not French, nor English, nor

> Scottish, nor Irish, nor Yankee, but Canadian. It can and must take pride in its origins and congratulate itself on its current union, which, we hope, will n'er be torn asunder by violence; yet the situation of this land, its statistics, its resources and a thousand other circumstances, must needs convince any attentive observer that (barring measures of violence and extermination) the people of Canada, embracing a vast share of the American hemisphere, has quite another destiny before it.

Nonetheless, Parent was not in favour of Lower Canada joining the American Union and compared Quebec's situation with that of Louisiana when it entered the Union in 1812. With this precedent in mind, Parent feared for the French language (doubting it would be used in Congress), for the legal system, and for some French colonial institutions like the seigneurial regime. Moreover, he predicted that if Lower Canada joined the Union, the ensuing flood of Americans pouring into Quebec would be so great that French Canadians would run the risk of losing "their political preponderance as a distinct people."

Parent, who would break ranks with Papineau and the Parti patriote in 1836, advised party members to spend more time studying the situation of Louisiana than that of Poland. On 22 February 1832, he wrote in *Le Canadien* that he did not believe

> a people of six thousand and some souls capable of maintaining its independence and its nationality. Assuredly not at the very doorstep of a powerful and enterprising nation. . . . It is for this reason that we have always maintained that the clear interest of England and of Lower Canada was that the nationality of the Canadian people be preserved and nurtured until it was in a state to defend itself from the encroachments of its neighbours.

The "Vocation" of French Canada in the Americas

The failure of the Patriote resistance in 1837, the Rebellion in 1838, the campaign to repeal the Union of Upper and Lower Canada proposed by Lord Durham, and the initiative to annex Lower and Upper Canada to the United States in 1849–50[18] elicited new questions: What would the destiny of French Canada be in the Americas? How would it deal with the presence and influence of the United States? Étienne Parent provided the first insight into both of these questions in his writings, and French author Edmé Rameau de Saint-Père examined them more thoroughly in a chapter about the moral and intellectual future of Canadians in the Americas in his book *La France aux colonies* (1859).

The notion of a collective **vocation** was embraced by French Canadians with relative ease, owing in part to the familiar foil of "American immorality." In *Le Canadien* of 28 November 1807, anticipating a change of allegiance, an anonymous author named "Canadiensis" wrote:

> If unfortunately, with the passing of time, Canada should fall under American domination, it would not be long before we felt the Americans' greed and monopolizing spirit, born in the bosom of commerce, and avaricious for all forms of power.

Thus, while the discourse around the new ruralist and agriculturalist vision for French Canadians was tinted with a degree of rosy Jeffersonianism, the Americans' spirit of debauchery, the poison of their "equality," and their mercantilism were typically condemned in the same breath. On 17 July 1837 in *Le Canadien*, Parent wrote that he expected no more from the Americans than "the sentiment that can result from a rule of arithmetic." By contrast, French Canadians had become a "providential people" (yet another familiar representation) uninfected by crass mercantilism and spared the horrors of the French Revolution, thanks to the prophylactic Conquest of the British.

In his book *La France aux colonies,* Rameau de Saint-Père proposed that

> national repulsion, better than a customs barrier, place an embargo on anything that remotely resembles Americanism at the border of Canada's land, that each person take heed and

BIOGRAPHY

Louis-Joseph Papineau (1786–1871)

Louis-Joseph Papineau, ca. 1852.

Photograph attributed to T.C. Doane/Library and Archives Canada/C-066899

Papineau would have been a George Washington or a Simón Bolivar if Lower Canada had succeeded in achieving independence in 1837 or 1838. But this was not to be and, for much of his political life, he in fact became the scapegoat for political failures, the frustrations of some, and the resentments of others. Today, Papineau is remembered as the greatest politician Lower Canada would see in the first half of the nineteenth century.[11] Indeed, his vision of Lower Canada's destiny in the Americas would be the most sustained and consistent of any politician, both before and after the resistance of 1837 and the Rebellion of 1838.

The son of Joseph Papineau (one of the members of the first House of Assembly of Lower Canada in 1792), Louis-Joseph Papineau was called to the bar in 1810, two years after he was first elected to the assembly. An articulate, self-assured orator, he was soon elected Speaker of the Assembly (1815) and took over as the clear leader of the Parti canadien (later the Parti patriote) in 1817. It was Papineau who, from 1815 to 1837, championed controversial parliamentary and constitutional struggles on behalf of the citizens of Lower Canada. His chief struggle was the demand that residents of Lower Canada enjoy the full range of freedoms that the British constitutional monarchy was required to afford its subjects. But Papineau's visit to London in 1823 opened his eyes to a number of discouraging circumstances: the British government's lack of interest in its colony, the social misery caused by industrialization, and the strategic waffling in the politics of the metropole. To his dismay, he found that the House of Commons Select Committee on the Civil Government of Canada conducted its affairs in much the same way in 1828. By 1831, Papineau was looking elsewhere for inspiration:

> it is therefore not to the mother country [England] any more than to the rest of Europe (where the social orientation is completely different and where the distribution of wealth is very unequal), that one must look for examples; it is instead to America, where one sees neither colossal fortunes nor degrading poverty, where men of genius move through the different ranks of society, unobstructed.[12]

Refusing to see the imperial, class-bound House of Lords reproduced in the colony, Papineau vigorously denounced Lower Canada's appointed (predominantly anglophone, British loyalist) Legislative Council and demanded that its members be elected. He was developing a vision for Lower Canadian society in the context of the Americas:

> There must needs be a king in Europe, where he is ensconced by monarchies. . . . The same does not apply here, for we do not have and cannot have an aristocracy; we have no need of these magnificent attributes. We do need a simple [form of] government, like that of the United States.[13]

In 1833, his criticism of the monarchy and the aristocracy led him to praise the American republic:

> Of all these governments, those whose regime is unrivalled in producing the most delightful fruits, have been [part of] the pure or slightly modified republicanism of the confederated states of New England. . . . [Republicanism] has produced, in its inhabitants' way of life, an improvement that is palpable and visible to this day.[14]

Papineau was certain that "before long, all of the Americas must be republican," later asserting confidently, "We need only be mindful of the fact that we are living in the Americas and mindful of how we have been living here." In 1834 he and other members of the Parti patriote drafted the famous Ninety-Two Resolutions, a political inventory of Lower Canada's grievances, demands, and aspirations, which were passed in the House of Assembly and submitted to the imperial government. Some of the Ninety-Two Resolutions (numbers 31, 41, 43, 45, 46, 48, 50, and 56) had obvious revolutionary overtones, presenting the United States as a democratic model for preventing abuses of power, underscoring social differences between England and the Americas, recalling the importance of representation by population, and evoking the imminent threat of annexation to the United States. The Russell Resolutions, London's response to these demands, categorically refused all of Lower Canada's resolutions.

Public outrage over the rejection of the Ninety-Two Resolutions and the popularity of Papineau's leadership during this period would be the most crucial factors in the months that followed. By May 1837 Papineau was keenly aware of both. Careful not to make any overt threats, he declared that if no significant changes were made, "the history of the former [American] plantations will once again [take its course], with the same inevitable result."[15] It was not long before these weighty words came to fruition.

The repression that followed the armed Patriote resistance of November 1837 forced Papineau and a number of Patriotes into exile in the United States. Papineau wrote to his friend, American historian George Bancroft, upon his arrival in the United States:

> [Our] society in the Americas is constituted differently from that of Europe. By all the laws of Nature, we are detached from Europe and attached to the United States, and our unanimous wishes call for this Union [with the United States].[16]

Papineau and his right-hand man, Edmund Bailey O'Callaghan, did not raise enough money to purchase arms and munitions for the Patriote cause, nor were they able to persuade the US authorities, including President Van Buren, to lend any form of support. The 1837 Patriote resistance and the Rebellion of 1838, from which Papineau publicly dissociated himself, subsequently met with defeat.

Worse yet, Papineau would see his attempts to oppose the union between Lower Canada and Upper Canada definitively quashed by a decree from London (following Lord Durham's 1839 *Report on the Affairs of British North America*). A proposal supporting Lower Canada's annexation to the United States, which he helped draft, also failed, since political backing from the colony's British Tories (disappointed by the repeal of the Corn Laws in 1846) and radical Whigs proved too limited and contradictory to move the initiative forward.

In February 1839, Papineau went to France under exile for his role in the Patriote cause. In 1845 he was pardoned and, upon his return to Lower Canada, re-entered political life, only to be marginalized by Louis-Hippolyte LaFontaine's "reformers." In 1854, Papineau left public life to develop his large estate, La Petite-Nation, a

continued

former seigneury that had just been abolished and re-established (with payment of compensation) as a freehold property.

The recent publication of Papineau's correspondence gives us a privileged glimpse into the intellectual and political development of a man who would remain a fierce proponent of the annexation of Lower Canada to the United States for the rest of his life. As of 1854, we see that Papineau did not embrace the emergent "mixed, neo-Canadian" national identity, preferring instead a mixed nationality of the Americas, which he called "Columbian" or "pan-American." He envisioned "a State of Quebec" within the Union; the annexed territory of Lower Canada would be twice the size of New York state and would constitute three states. Papineau supported annexation because he was convinced that the US style of federalism would be more open than that of Canada. Both before and after Canadian Confederation in 1867, annexationists in Lower Canada and (later) Quebec continued to be fascinated by the prospect of creating a flourishing state that would enjoy greater freedom from central authority. Shortly before his death, Papineau would speak of the same annexationist vision, in a "global confederation of the northern continent."[17]

> ward off the baneful contagion of this unwholesome civilization . . .

According to Rameau de Saint-Père, US civilization was based on "a lowly shopkeeper's calculations," the "worship of money," material well-being, and creature comforts. As to the moral future of French-Catholic Canada, he believed it would lie elsewhere:

> while in the United States, minds are being absorbed by the exhausting enterprises of business, industry and the worship of the golden calf, it is Canada's enterprise to build for herself, unselfishly and with a noble pride, the intellectual, scientific and artistic side of the American movement, preferably devoting herself to the worship of sentiment, thought and refined aesthetics.[19]

Conservative Catholic circles, eager to halt any annexation initiatives, wasted no time in transposing Parent's and Rameau de Saint-Père's spiritualist future into a Catholic future. Indeed, it was the Church's anti-annexationist discourse on the providential vocation of French Canadians in the Americas, used to spread the Catholic faith across the continent (reprised by Abbé Henri-Raymond Casgrain and in part by Edmond de Nevers, Msgr Louis-Adolphe Pâquet, Olivar Asselin, Victor Barbeau, and the Tory discourse calling for the promotion of traditional values), that would define French Canadians for an entire century.[20] This discourse continued in flagrant disregard of direct edicts handed down from the Vatican during the early 1920s (downplayed by the Catholic authority in Quebec at the time), which clearly stated that in Canada and the United States proselytizing was to be led by Irish anglophone Catholics. But these edicts went unheeded and the ideology of the "vocation of the French race in America" prevailed until the end of World War II.[21]

While Quebec's anti-American religious discourse was being undermined from within the Vatican hierarchy, it was also being challenged by the circumstances of the times. From 1830 to 1930, both in spite of and because of the "golden calf" ideology in the United States, hundreds of thousands of French Canadians emigrated to the land of factories and materialism in search of work; from 1872 onward, US labour unions would dominate Canadian and French-Canadian syndicalism; and the US culture of circuses, amusement parks (for example, Montreal's Sohmer Park 1889–1909), burlesque shows, silent motion pictures (1895), and the talkies (1929) reigned supreme. Commenting on the impact of American civilization in 1928, businessman Beaudry Leman declared, "We can't live with it and we can't live without it."[22]

Primary Source

After referring to a Hindu myth in which the creator Twashtri gives a woman to man who is unable to see her full potential, the author writes:

> Man could well state that he could not live without her, Twashtri informed him that he could neither be better off without her. As of which, man returned to the toils of life while murmuring:
>
> "May the Heavens help me, for I cannot live with her, nor without her!"
>
> Is this the state of our current standing with American civilization and should we conclude that we cannot live with or without it? It seems plausible in our prevailing circumstances, as we are driven towards progress, that we should preserve certain characteristics of our race within this predicament.

Source: Beaudry Leman, "Les Canadiens français et le milieu américain," *Revue trimestrielle canadienne*, 13, no. 55 (September 1928): 263–75.

Over the years, depictions of this evolving American civilization became increasingly prominent in the works of Quebec writers such as poet Alfred Desrochers and novelists Jean-Charles Harvey and Philippe Panneton (who went by the pen name "Ringuet"). Following World War II, the predominant American consumer society effectively supplanted the ideology of a French-Canadian, Catholic spiritual vocation in the Americas (see the Case Study box).

Writers and the Development of Americanicity

As World War II drew to a close, it was Quebec essayists and novelists who would detect contradictions and formulate entirely new representations of their cultural identities. It was during a polemical discussion with writers from France that Quebec novelist and publisher Robert Charbonneau first became conscious of belonging to the American continent: "We are not Frenchmen; our life in America, our cordial relations with our English-speaking compatriots and Americans, our political independence, have made us different." Charbonneau proposed that his fellow writers discover what it meant to be American by exploring "the American side as much as at the French side" and by sampling the vintages of both "the Californian vineyard of Mr. Steinbeck" and "the vineyard of Racine" in France.[23]

But it was French-Canadian essayist Jean Le Moyne who truly established Quebec's relationships with the Americas and with Europe as undisputed subjects of study. An avid reader of Henry James and F. Scott Fitzgerald, Le Moyne recognized that the Americas were invented by Europe and that, in his view, his people were very much connected with their "first-degree European relatives":

> . . . the Americas are an invention, the posterity of Europe, and in relation to Europe, American societies are without exception marsupial foetuses, unequally developed, but all attached to the teat. As Americans, nothing really distinguishes us but geography. Notwithstanding our European heredity, an irresistible differentiation has begun, occurring on all levels at the same time. We are slowly working on [developing] our difference, we are gradually crafting ourselves a new identity.[24]

Henry James showed Le Moyne that Americans had a "double identity," while F. Scott Fitzgerald taught him that "France is absent and the United

CASE STUDY

Americanicity and Postwar Consumption in Quebec

After the deprivation of the Depression and the rationing, scrimping, and saving that took place throughout World War II, consumer spending skyrocketed in North America in the postwar era. The United States, Canada's wartime ally, pumped an average of 74 per cent of foreign investment into the Quebec economy from 1945 to 1960. Simultaneously, US goods were consumed en masse, and with them came American influences and standards of living rose. For instance, during the same period, 64 per cent of feature films shown in Quebec theatres were made in the United States. In 1953, 34 per cent of Quebec households owned an automobile, and by 1960 49 per cent did. The car-to-person ratio was one car for every 15.2 people in 1939, which rose to one per 10.1 people in 1949, one per 9.1 people in 1954, and reached one per 6.3 people by 1959.

In 1953, 37.4 per cent of Quebec households owned an electric vacuum cleaner, compared with 57.8 per cent in 1960. These households, 82 per cent of which were already equipped with an electric washing machine in 1953, were even more likely to have one in 1960 (89 per cent). While most dwellings in Quebec contained an electric refrigerator in 1953 (68.4 per cent), this appliance had become the norm by 1960 (94 per cent). But for many households, the electric stove was the most striking new addition: Found in only 22.7 per cent of kitchens in 1953, it was in 50.2 per cent of them by 1960.

The boom in the ownership of communications and entertainment equipment generally progressed in keeping with the age of the medium. Telephone ownership grew from 52.5 per cent in 1941 to 77.2 per cent in 1951, and then to 84.3 per cent in 1960. Radios, found in 92.6 per cent of households in 1941, had a 97.3 per cent penetration rate by 1960. From a marketing perspective, television was a relatively fast-track technology.

Whereas radio took 15 years (1922–37) to reach most homes, television caught on in just four years: 9.7 per cent of households had a TV set in 1953, 27.8 per cent in 1954, 48.5 per cent in 1955, and 64.2 per cent in 1956.[25] With so many major everyday, domestic lifestyle changes in Quebec resembling those taking place in the United States, the question soon became, Is modernization synonymous with Americanization?

All told, retail sales leapt from $245.71 per person in 1941 to $600.86 in 1951 and had reached $781.19 by 1960. Another indicator of new levels of consumption was the rising number of advertising agencies, which grew from 22 Canada-wide in 1941 to 61 in 1961. Meanwhile, periodicals sold $100 million worth of advertising in 1948, compared with $300 million in 1960.[26] As these trends continued, the growing need to measure the Americanization of Canadian culture culminated in the Royal Commission on National Development in the Arts, Letters, and Sciences (also known as the Massey Commission), held from 1949 to 1951.[27]

The clear acceptance of consumerism and an "American" way of life was significant on two levels in Quebec. First, it tended to narrow the gap between middle-class and working-class perceptions of the United States and Americanization.[28] Second, the self-representation of French Canadians as the standard-bearers of spiritualism and Catholic asceticism became both anachronistic and contradictory after the cumulative effects of the Depression and World War II turned them into "materialists." Once again, French Canada would embark on a quest for its destiny in the Americas.

States is far away" from Quebec. Above all, Le Moyne admitted that he no longer believed that French Canadians could ever entirely define themselves in French

> because of one overriding fact: the invention and the form of the Americas are not French. As a result, we are subjected to an osmotic pressure that no fortifications could contain. The only obstacle [to this pressure], given [Quebec's] geographic location and indistinct borders, would be the one thing that we will never have: large numbers.[29]

The writers and critics who followed Le Moyne on his imaginary "Oregon trail" (to the "great American promised land") would recast this ambiguity and contribute to naming the variable that is Quebec identity. This literary journey was unfolding around 1970, at a time when the US counterculture had reached Quebec and the beat generation was being expressed by poets and writers.[30] This was also the era of bohemian "Californian dreaming" in the Quebec novel.[31]

Playwright Jacques Languirand explored the symbolic and political relationship of Quebecers of French-Canadian ancestry with the Americas, and how the repressed aspects of their Americanicity manifested themselves:

> To be frank, I had the impression that the more French Canada defined itself as being independentist-separatist at a conscious level, the more it became annexionist at a subconscious level.[32]

Jacques Godbout investigated the cultural aspects of this double identity, relating it (like Le Moyne) to Quebec's relationships with France and with America. His 1965 novel *Le couteau sur la table* (*Knife on the Table*) begins by taking a stand: "rather than being *French*, in a very personal way, we now prefer to be *ourselves*, in French." Godbout's abiding fascination for this American vein of identity and Quebec's collective imaginings come to life in his novels, essays, and in his film *Will James*.

Essayist Jean Larose, who has looked closely at the challenge of being French or francophone in the Americas, has commented, "it is easy, crossing Washington Square [in New York City] or Place du Panthéon [in Paris], to imagine that we have found peace in our mixed identity." Larose regards Quebecers' indecision about their identity as rich in potential and holds that Quebecers of French-Canadian origin must move away from their double negation (being neither French nor American) and toward a double assertion of self.[33]

In 1995 the study of Americanicity in Quebec literature was authoritatively established with the publication of Jean Morency's brilliant work *Le mythe américain dans les fictions d'Amérique : de Washington Irving à Jacques Poulin*, in which Morency evokes the imaginary realm common to culturally dualistic American societies that belong to both "the European sphere and that of the New World [which is] in the process of inventing itself." To Morency "the splendid autonomy of the continental imagination" was revealed in the grand narrative of "an intellectual history [involving] the metamorphosis of humankind upon contact with the American continent." On her part, Louise Vigneault has made an American reading of the art of the two painters.[34]

A current perspective on Quebec's Americanicity is found in the surveys and reflections of Guy Lachapelle and Gilbert Gagné. Guy Lachapelle surveyed Quebecers' feelings about belonging to Canada and the Americas and their perceptions of the United States. Overall, he found that Quebecers jealously guard their language and universal health care system; favour continental economic relations; and have joined the US media and business culture, adopting and often adapting US content, formulas, and formats. Gilbert Gagné has examined the effects of globalization on Quebecers' perceptions of the United States and, in particular, on strategies to promote and defend cultural difference and diversity.[35]

Obstacles to Engaging with the Concept of Americanicity in Quebec

Perceptions of Quebec's relationship to the Americas, and especially Quebec's relationship with the United

States, are not unanimous. For instance, anti-capitalist and socialist Quebecers may identify with Latin American experiences, but these may not be the sole or the most vital way for them to remember that they belong to the *entire* American continent and to embrace their Americanicity.[36] On the other side of the same fence, José Marti in Cuba (*Nuestra America*, 1891), José Vasconcelos (*La Raza Cósmica*, 1925) and Leopoldo Zea in Mexico, and Domingo Faustino Sarmiento in Argentina are Latino thinkers and writers of the Americas who have sought to further articulate this multilayered relationship.

Historically, there are five main reasons why Quebecers of French-Canadian ancestry have not been able to fully accept or engage with the concept of Americanicity. First, it is not easy to grasp that Americanicity flows from everyday lived experiences rather than being consciously or intelligibly pondered. For Quebecers to accept their Americanicity they would have to acknowledge Quebec's similarities and differences vis-à-vis an entire continent. It would mean confronting the fact that, like the societies that surround it, Quebec is also a "new society," shaped by various waves of immigration (1815, 1900, 1945, and 1970 until today), that did not opt for the US melting pot or for Canadian multiculturalism, but for a policy of integrative interculturalism that is still in its ill-defined infancy.[37]

Second, since the 1930s, francophilia (exaggerated veneration for France and all things French) has overshadowed Quebec's American origins. For Quebecers of French-Canadian ancestry to engage with the concept of their Americanicity, they would have to accept their Europeanicity, and particularly the traditional relationships that Quebec has been maintaining with France, Britain, and Rome and the Vatican. My mnemonic formula for this *external* heritage is $Q = -F + GB + US^2 - R$, as explained in my book *Allégeances et dépendances*.

Third, even after 1945, embracing Quebec's Americanicity would have undermined the notion of "French America," whereby the French race had an exclusive, providential vocation in the Americas. Being a francophone meant being a good French-Canadian Catholic. Significantly, this "American" Francophonie was often ignored in academe, except in discussions of French-Canadian emigration to the United States since 1830. But resistance to embracing Americanicity abated in Quebec after the Estates General of French Canada (1967). At these meetings it became clear that francophone Quebecers and French Canadians outside of Quebec had different interests and, for the most part, these groups would no longer be represented by the same organizations. The notion of "French Canada" subsequently began its decline[38] and took on another meaning for those who began to call themselves "Québécois"—no longer Frenchmen and Frenchwomen living in the Americas, but the francophones of the Americas.[39] From this point on in Quebec's development, the notion of French America could no longer be contemplated as anything but a curious cultural artifact.

Fourth, although for years openly accepting Quebec's Americanicity was perceived as a tacit endorsement of annexationism, this perception has also clearly fallen by the wayside. After over a quarter-century of promoting free trade in the Americas as an economic imperative, both the Parti Québécois and the Liberal Party of Quebec have established the conviction among Quebecers that it is possible to be continentalist without being annexationist.

Fifth, recognizing that Quebec belongs to the American continent does not mean that Quebecers unconditionally accept all of the ideological positions, economics, technology, and military stances that define the United States, nor does it mean that they reject their ties with Europe. In fact, on both counts, some measured resistance to embracing Americanicity remains.

Understanding Quebec's Americanicity requires us to break free of our preconceptions, a notion that is itself characteristic of the American experience. But the notion of breaking free is complicated by Quebec's status within Canada. It would seem that placing any conceptual distance between Quebec and France or England requires a reconceptualization of Quebec's relationship with Canada. It is not my contention that sovereignty is a prerequisite for recognizing Quebec's Americanicity. I would simply suggest that for Quebecers to recognize themselves as full-fledged denizens of the Americas, cultural and political choices will have to be made.

One thing is certain: The heritage of Americanicity is worth knowing, recognizing, and metabolizing properly if Quebec's self-image is to be commensurate with reality. Understanding Quebec's Americanicity means situating our identity within postmodernism, in the plural, without giving up anything of ourselves, and embracing the broad diversity of heritages that enrich a new, intercultural generation of Québécois citizens.

Questions for Critical Thinking

1. What is the difference between "Americanization" and "Americanicity"?
2. What kept the notion of the "vocation of the French race in the Americas" alive, and why did this notion lose its relevancy?
3. What were the components of Quebec's new "destiny" in the Americas?
4. Why has it been so difficult for some Quebecers to accept or engage with the concept of their Americanicity?

Notes

1. This speech was translated in Quebec by Sylvie Chaput (Quebec: Éditions du Loup de gouttière, 1992).
2. An expression coined by O'Sullivan in the *Washington Democratic Review* (Summer 1845), which he founded in 1837; Y. Lamonde and Louis-Georges Harvey, "Origines et formes diverses du 'destin manifeste' dans les Amériques : les Papineau et la *United States Democratic Review* de Washington et New York," *Les Cahiers des Dix* 67 (2013) : 25–73.
3. Gérard Bouchard, *Genèse des nations et cultures du nouveau monde : essai d'histoire comparée* (Montreal: Boréal, 2001).
4. The first studies on Quebec's Americanicity predate 1992, the 500th anniversary of Columbus's discovery of the Americas. For the moment, these studies borrow little from New American Studies, a field that provides greater perspective on the Eurocentric narrative of the Americas and is mindful of the place of the Aboriginal peoples of the Americas' pre- and post-Columbian history. For a pioneering study, see Denys Delâge, "L'influence des Amérindiens sur les Canadiens et les Français au temps de la Nouvelle-France," in *L'acculturation, Lekton* 2, no. 2 (automne 1992): 103–91. His article was translated into English and published as "Aboriginal Influence on the Canadians and French at the Time of New France," in *Aboriginality and Governance: A Multidisciplinary Perspective*, ed. Gordon Christie (Penticton, BC: Theytus Books, 2006), 79–139. The original French version of this article is available online on the website Les Classiques des sciences sociales: http://classiques.uqac.ca/contemporains/delage_denys/delage_denys.html.
5. In the United States, the work of Henry James provides an apt illustration of this last point. For a breakthrough on Quebec relations with South America, see Maurice Demers, *Connected Struggles: How Cultural and Religious Diplomacy Influenced Canada–Mexico Relations* (Montreal and Kingston: McGill-Queen's University Press, 2014); also Marie Couillard and Patrick Imbert, eds., *Les discours du Nouveau Monde au XIXe siècle au Canada français et en Amérique latine* (New York and Ottawa: Legas, 1995).
6. This concept is developed in Yvan Lamonde, *Allégeances et dépendances : histoire d'une ambivalence identitaire* (Quebec: Nota bene, 2001), chapitre II. For a bibliographical update on studies in Quebec's Americanicity, see Yvan Lamonde, "Les appropriations culturelles du nouveau continent au Québec (1800–1960)," in *Québécois et Américains : la culture Québécoise aux XIXe et XXe siècles*, ed. Gérard Bouchard and Yvan Lamonde (Montreal: Fides, 1995), 395–418.
7. "Aux habitants de la province de Québec," 26 October 1774, in Gustave Lanctôt, *Le Canada et la révolution américaine (1774–1783)* (Montreal: Beauchemin, 1965), 281–91, author's translation.
8. For an examination of writing on the American presence in the eighteenth century, see Pierre Monette et al., *Rendez-vous manqué avec la révolution américaine : les adresses aux habitants de la province de Québec* (Montreal: Québec Amérique, 2007).
9. Governor Carleton to Lord Germain, 9 May 1777, in *Documents Relating to the Constitutional History of Canada, 1759–1791*, Part II, ed. Adam Shortt and Arthur G. Doughty (Ottawa: Printed by J. de L. Taché, 1918), 676.
10. Yvan Lamonde, *Histoire sociale des idées au Québec, I : 1760–1896* (Montreal: Fides, 2000), 31–3, author's translation.
11. The Quebec expression "avoir la tête à Papineau" evokes the reverence many Quebecers had for Papineau's intelligence. The English equivalent of this expression would be "a true Einstein."

12. "Correspondance de *La Minerve*." L.-J. Papineau, *La Minerve*, 17 February 1831.
13. Ibid.
14. "Correspondance de *La Minerve*." L'hon. Orateur L.-J. Papineau, *La Minerve*, 21 January 1833, author's translation.
15. Louis-Joseph Papineau, *Procédés de l'assemblée des électeurs du comté de Montréal*, Montreal, May 1837, 11, author's translation.
16. The references to the documents of this period may be found in Lamonde, *Allégeances et dépendances*, 38–40, 44–6.
17. Yvan Lamonde, "Introduction," in Louis-Joseph Papineau, *Lettres à ses enfants*, vol. I: 1825–1854, ed. Georges Aubin and Renée Blanchet (Montreal: Les Éditions Varia, 2004), 22–4; Yvan Lamonde and Jonathan Livernois, *Papineau : erreur sur la personne* (Montreal: Boréal, 2012).
18. Henry David Thoreau would tour through Lower Canada six years thereafter. See the most recent version of *A Yankee in Canada* (1856), and *Excursions*, ed. Joseph J. Moldenhauer (Princeton, NJ: Princeton University Press, 2007).
19. Edmé Rameau de Saint-Père, *La France aux colonies* (Paris: Jouby, 1859), 269.
20. For information on their writing and positions, see Lamonde, *Allégeances et dépendances*, 59–82.
21. On this question, see chapter V, "Rome et le Vatican : la vocation catholique de l'Amérique française ou de l'Amérique anglaise?" in *Allégeances et dépendances*, ed. Lamonde.
22. Beaudry Leman, "Les Canadiens français et le milieu américain," *Revue trimestrielle canadienne* 14, no. 5 (September 1928): 263–75.
23. Robert Charbonneau, *La France et nous : journal d'une querelle* (Montreal: L'arbre, 1947), 23, 32, 34, 40, 49, 53.
24. Jean Le Moyne, "Ringuet et le contexte canadien-français," *Revue dominicaine* (février 1950): 83.
25. Jean-Pierre Charland, *Système technique et bonheur domestique : rémunération, consommation et pauvreté au Québec (1920–1960)* (Quebec: Institut québécois de recherche sur la culture, 1992), 147, 148, 150, 152, 156; Yvan Lamonde and Pierre-François Hébert, *Le cinéma au Québec : essai de statistique historique (1896 à nos jours)* (Quebec: Institut québécois de recherche sur la culture, 1981), 165.
26. Jean-Guy Daigle and Luc Côté, "La sollicitation marchande dans la vie privée : les annonces du jeudi dans les quotidiens québécois (1929–1957)," *Recherches sociographiques* 33, no. 3 (1992): 369–406; from the same authors, see "Publicité de masse et masse publicitaire dans la presse quotidienne au Québec (1929–1957)," in *La culture inventée : les stratégies culturelles aux XIXe et XXe siècles*, ed. Pierre Lanthier and Guildo Rousseau (Quebec: Institut québécois de recherche sur la culture, 1992), 247–66.
27. Paul Litt, *The Muses, the Masses, and the Massey Commission* (Toronto: University of Toronto Press, 1992).
28. Yvan Lamonde, "Le regard sur les Etats-Unis : le révélateur d'un clivage social dans la culture nationale Québécoise," *Journal of Canadian Studies/Revue d'études canadiennes* 30, no. 1 (printemps 1995): 69–74.
29. Jean Le Moyne, "Lectures anglaises," in *Convergences* (Montreal: Hurtubise HMH, 1977), 27.
30. For two different readings of the beat generation, see Pierre Nepveu, *Intérieurs du nouveau monde : essai sur les littératures du Québec et des Amériques* (Montreal: Boréal, 1998), and Jean-Sébastien Ménard, *Une certaine Amérique à lire : la beat generation et la littérature québécoise* (Montreal: Nota bene, 2014).
31. René Labonté, "Québec-Californie : la Californie à travers la fiction Québécoise," *French Review* 62, no. 5 (April 1989): 803–14.
32. Jacques Languirand, "Le Québec et l'américanité," in *Klondyke* (Montreal: Cercle du livre de France, 1971), 219–37; repris dans *Études littéraires* 8, no. 1 (April 1975): 143–57.
33. Jean Larose, *La petite noirceur* (Montreal: Boréal, 1987), 70–1, 192, 175–6; *L'amour du pauvre* (Montreal: Boréal, 1989), 94.
34. Jean Morency, *Le mythe américain dans les fictions d'Amérique : de Washington Irving à Jacques Poulin* (Québec: Nuit blanche éditeur, 1995), 11–12, 17, 225–6; see also Yvan Lamonde, "Pour une étude comparée de la littérature québécoise et des littératures coloniales américaines," *Journal of Canadian Studies/Revue d'études canadiennes* 32, no. 2 (été 1997): 72–8; Jean-François Chassay, *L'ambiguïté américaine : le roman québécois face aux Etats-Unis* (Montreal: XYZ, 1995); and Louise Vigneault, *Espace artistique et modèle pionnier: Tom Thomson et Jean-Paul Riopelle* (Montreal: Hurtubise, 2011).
35. For Guy Lachapelle's recent research on Quebec's contemporary Americanicity and Gilbert Gagné on cultural aspects of free trade exchanges, see Guy Lachapelle, ed., *Le destin américain du Québec : américanité, américanisation et anti-américanisme* (Québec: Presses de l'Université Laval, 2010).
36. On the subject of the anti-Americanism of *Parti pris* and *Socialisme* in postwar Cuba and during the war in Vietnam, see Lamonde, *Allégeances et dépendances*, 97. For information on the anti-Americanism of prominent essayist and union activist Pierre Vadeboncoeur, and on the resistance of sociologist Fernand Dumont, see ibid., 104–7.
37. François Rocher, Micheline Labelle, Ann-Marie Feld, and Jean-Claude Icart, *Le concept d'interculturalisme en contexte québécois : généalogie d'une néologisme* (Montreal-Ottawa: UQÀM-Université d'Ottawa, Centre

de recherche sur l'immigration, l'ethnicité et la citoyenneté, 21 December 2007), report submitted to the Bouchard-Taylor Commission.

38. The decline of French Canada is brilliantly analyzed by Marcel Martel. His work, *Le deuil d'un pays imaginé : rêves, luttes et déroute du Canada français. Les rapports entre le Québec et la francophonie canadienne (1867–1975)* (1997) is summarized in a brochure: *French Canada: An Account of its Creation and Break-up, 1850–1967* (Ottawa: Canadian Historical Association, 1998).

39. Guy Rocher, "Les conditions d'une francophonie nord-américaine originale," in his, *Le Québec en mutation* (Montreal: Hurtubise, 1973), 89–107.

Select Bibliography

Bouchard, Gérard. *Genèse des nations et cultures du nouveau monde : essai d'histoire comparée.* Montreal: Boréal, 2000.

Chassay, Jean-François. *L'ambiguïté américaine : le roman québécois face aux Etats-Unis.* Montreal: XYZ, 1995.

Demers, Maurice. *Connected Struggles: How Cultural and Religious Diplomacy Influenced Canada-Mexico Relations.* Montreal-Kingston: McGill-Queen's University Press, 2014.

Lachapelle, Guy, ed. *Le destin américain du Québec : américanité, américanisation et anti-américanisme.* Québec: Presses de l'Université Laval, 2010.

Lamonde, Yvan. *Allégeances et dépendances : histoire d'une ambivalence identitaire.* Quebec: Nota bene, 2001.

———. "Les appropriations culturelles du nouveau continent (1800–1960)." In *Québécois et américains : la culture québécoise aux XIXe et XXe siècles*, edited by Gérard Bouchard and Yvan Lamonde, 395–418. Montreal: Fides, 1995.

Morency, Jean. *Le mythe américain dans les fictions d'Amérique : de Washington Irving à Jacques Poulin.* Quebec: Nuit blanche éditeur, 1995.

Nepveu, Pierre. *Intérieurs du Nouveau Monde : essai sur les littératures du Québec et des Amériques.* Montreal: Boréal, 1998.

Rocher, Guy. "Les conditions d'une francophonie nord-américaine originale." In *Le Québec en mutation,* 89–107. Montreal: Hurtubise, 1973.

7

Quebec Cinema: Telling Pictures

Germain Lacasse, Université de Montréal

Timeline

1896 First Cinématographe Lumière screening at the Palace Concert Hall on St Lawrence Street in Montreal, June 27.

1897 Viscount d'Hauterives makes his debut as Quebec's first French film lecturer (travelling showman/projectionist) and continues his work until 1906.

1906 Opening of the Ouimetoscope, the first permanent moving picture theatre in Montreal. Léo-Ernest Ouimet begins to produce silent film newsreels. Film venues spread quickly across Quebec and a number of them employ French-language film lecturers, including Alex Silvio, who continues his work until 1930.

1913 Creation of the Board of Censors of Moving Pictures of the Province of Quebec. Legendary for its strict standards, the board is replaced by the far less strict Cinema Supervisory Board in 1967.

1920 Establishment of Associated Screen News, a prolific studio that produces documentary films until 1972, including the famous documentary *Canadian Cameos.*

1922 Release of *Madeleine de Verchères* by Joseph-Arthur Homier and Emma Gendron, Quebec's first feature-length fictional film (regrettably lost to history).

1925 Catholic priest Albert Tessier shoots his first documentary films, providing his own live commentary during screenings across the province.

1930 Montreal cinemas begin to screen French-language talking motion pictures (talkies), which would claim a large share of box-office sales in the decades to come.

1932 Gordon Sparling makes *Rhapsody in Two Languages,* an avant-garde documentary about Montreal produced by Associated Screen News.

1937 Catholic abbot Maurice Proulx finishes *En pays neufs,* the first feature-length documentary film with sound to be made in Canada.

1939 Foundation of the National Film Board (NFB), then based in Ottawa.

1941 Vincent Paquette, the NFB's first francophone filmmaker, is hired.

Creation of the Service de ciné-photographie (SCP) by the government of Quebec. The SCP distributes government documentary films and those acquired from priest filmmakers.

1944 Establishment of Renaissance Films by Joseph Alexandre DeSève, who immediately produces *Le Père Chopin* by Fédor Ozep, a drama that is performed in formal, academic French.

1945 American producers bring dubbed French-language offerings to the movie market.

1946 Québec Productions Corporation is founded by Paul L'Anglais.

1949 Paul L'Anglais produces *Un homme et son péché* (*A Man and His Sin*), a film performed in vernacular Québécois French and directed by Paul Gury.

1952 Release of *Tit-Coq*, by playwright Gratien Gélinas, about which René Lévesque writes, "Canadian cinema is coming out of the caves."

1956 The NFB establishes its offices in Montreal, where master animator Norman McLaren goes to work. The board also hires a number of young francophones.

1957 The newspaper *Le Devoir* publishes articles denouncing discrimination against francophones at the NFB, setting off a larger campaign in the French-language press referred to as "the NFB affair."

1958 Release of *Les raquetteurs* by Michel Brault and Gilles Groulx, a short film that marks the advent of direct cinema.

1959 Death of Quebec Premier Maurice Duplessis, whose long tenure in office is dubbed "la Grande Noirceur" or "the Great Darkness."

1963 Release of *Pour la suite du monde* (*For Those Who Will Follow*) by Pierre Perrault and Michel Brault, the first direct cinema feature film and the first Quebec film in competition at the Cannes Film Festival.

Release of *À tout prendre* (*Take It All*) by Claude Jutra, an avant-garde autobiographical feature film that marks the birth of modern fictional cinema in Quebec.

1964 The French section of the NFB is officially established.

Release of *Le chat dans le sac* (*Cat in the Sack*), an identity-based fictional film that Gilles Groulx makes by hijacking a documentary project at the NFB.

Release of *Trouble-fête* by Pierre Patry, produced by Coopératio, an independent film co-operative.

1967 Creation of the Canadian Film Development Corporation (CFDC), a federal organization dedicated to funding Canadian film production.

Release of *De mère en fille (From Mother to Daughter)* by Anne Claire Poirier, the first Quebec feature film to be made by a woman at the NFB.

1968 Release of *Valérie* by Denis Héroux, the first of a long series of lucrative erotic films.

1970 Release of *Les Mâles (The Males)* by Gilles Carle, which becomes an international success.

1971 Release of *Mon oncle Antoine (My Uncle Antoine)* by Claude Jutra, now renowned as one of the greatest films ever made in Quebec or in Canada.

1972 Release of *La vie rêvée (Dream Life)* by Mireille Dansereau, the first feature fictional film to be made in Quebec's private film industry by a woman.

1974 *Les Ordres (Orderers)* by Michel Brault, a dramatization of the events of the 1970 Quebec October Crisis, wins Best Director Award at the Cannes Film Festival.

continued

The Apprenticeship of Duddy Kravitz by Ted Kotcheff wins a Golden Bear Award at the Berlin International Film Festival.

1976 The Parti Québécois, founded in 1968 by René Lévesque, triumphs in Quebec's provincial election.

Release of *L'eau chaude, l'eau frette* (*Hot Water, Cold Water*) by André Forcier, marking the beginning of the filmmaker's singular, prolific, and poetic body of cinematic work.

1977 Creation of the Institut québécois du cinéma (IQC) by the provincial government to provide financial support to Quebec cinema.

1980 The first referendum on Quebec sovereignty is held and the sovereignty option is rejected.

Release of *Les bons débarras* (*Good Riddance*) by Francis Mankiewicz, written by Réjean Ducharme, which goes on to win eight Genie Awards.

1981 Release of *Les Plouffe* (*The Plouffe Family*) by Gilles Carle, the first of many productions that turned television series into feature-length films.

1983 CFDC becomes Telefilm Canada; IQC becomes Société générale du cinéma du Québec (SGCQ), thereby consolidating support for the film industry from both the federal and provincial governments.

Sonatine by Micheline Lanctôt wins the Silver Lion at the Venice Film Festival.

1984 Release of *La femme de l'hôtel* (*A Woman in Waiting*) by Léa Pool, marking the beginning of the woman filmmaker's personal and impressive body of work.

1986 Release of *Le déclin de l'empire américain* (*The Decline of the American Empire*) by Denys Arcand. It is a huge success in Quebec and wins the International Critic's Prize at the Cannes Film Festival.

1987 *Un zoo la nuit* (*Night Zoo*) by Jean-Claude Lauzon is released as the opening film at the Cannes Film Festival's Directors' Fortnight.

Release of *Train of Dreams* by John N. Smith, the first film made by an anglophone Quebecer to receive the Prix Léo-Ernest Ouimet-Molson for best feature film.

1990 Release of *Une histoire inventée* (*An Imaginary Tale*) by André Forcier, the filmmaker's first commercial success.

1992 Release of *Manufacturing Consent: Noam Chomsky and the Media*, a documentary by Peter Wintonick that is translated into 12 languages and wins 20 international prizes.

1995 The second referendum on Quebec sovereignty is held, and the sovereignty movement registers another defeat.

Release of *Yes Sir! Madame* by Robert Morin and *Le confessional* (*The Confessional*) by Robert Lepage, two major works on identity in Quebec.

1997 Release of *Les Boys* (*The Boys*) by Louis Saïa, a sports comedy that establishes a "franchise."

2003 A banner year for Quebec film audiences, who are treated to *La grande séduction* (*Seducing Doctor Lewis*) (Jean-François Pouliot), *Gaz bar blues* (Louis Bélanger), *Mambo Italiano* (Émile Gaudreault), *Les Invasions barbares* (*The Barbarian Invasions*) (Denys Arcand) and many others.

2005 Release of *Les états Nordiques* (*Drifting States*) by Denis Côté, a singular, experimental, and eclectic film.

2006 Release of *Rechercher Victor Pellerin* (*Missing Victor Pellerin*) by Sophie Deraspe, an unsettling, skilfully crafted quasi-mockumentary.

Release of *Bon cop, Bad cop*, by Éric Canuel, a bilingual police comedy that soon becomes the top-grossing movie in the history of Canadian cinema.

2007 Release of *Continental, un film sans fusil (Continental, a Film without Guns)* by Stéphane Lafleur, who revives poetic realism.

In May, the Action democratique du Québec party introduces draft legislation to promote the dubbing industry in Quebec and restrict the distribution of films not made in French and not subtitled or dubbed in French. The bill is not adopted.

2009 Release of *J'ai tué ma mère (I Killed My Mother)* by Xavier Dolan, who wins three prizes at the Cannes Film Festival at just 20 years of age.

2010 *Les Cahiers du cinéma* publishes a feature piece on a "Renewal" of Quebec cinema.

Release of *The Trotsky* by Jacob Tierney, which is a huge success and stirs up controversy about the place of anglophone and first-generation/immigrant filmmakers in Quebec cinema.

2012 Release of *La mise à l'aveugle (Small Blind)* by Simon Galiero, who also publishes an acerbic critique of the "Renewal" filmmakers mentioned in *Cahiers du cinéma.*

Release of *Monsieur Lazhar* by Philippe Falardeau, which earns an Oscar nomination.

Release of *Rebelle* (*War Witch*) by Kim Nguyen, an international success that receives a tepid reception in Quebec.

2013 Quebec filmmakers Philippe Falardeau, Denis Villeneuve, Jean-Marc Vallée, and others are making movies in the United States.

2014 Xavier Dolan wins the Jury Prize at the Cannes Film Festival for his film *Mommy,* whose characters distinguish themselves by speaking working-class Québécois French.

Introduction

From its inception, Quebec cinema has been defined by five adjectives that have laid the groundwork for its history and identity: minor, oral, documentary, direct, and national. In retrospect, it is stunning to recall that filmmaking was sidelined as a *minor* media art for over half a century in Quebec for reasons largely beyond the control of its makers. The first films were made on shoestring budgets by marginalized communities in a regional vernacular with no connection to the international market. Constantly struggling for recognition[1] under the mammoth dominance of foreign films and some weighty authorities, Quebec filmmakers had to devise efficient ways to interpret, assert, and distinguish themselves in their work. So it was that language, speech, songs, and other forms of *oral* expression became and remained vital tools in their craft.[2] The unfavourable market conditions they faced also meant that fictional film production was low and came late. By contrast, but for the same reasons, a tradition of unscripted content drawn from everyday life in **documentary cinema** began. It was only during the Quiet Revolution that Quebec cinema finally got its footing: fictional film could at last be made freely, and documentary films grew from strength to strength with the advent of **direct cinema.**[3] This distinctive attribute of filmmaking in Quebec (*direct* cinema), along with the groundwork of its (minor, oral, documentary, and direct) attributes that were established by previous generations, built up what many have called a *national* cinema.[4]

There is some debate as to whether the word *national* applies to the films that filmmakers from anglophone, Indigenous, first-generation/immigrant[5] and other communities have been making in Quebec for decades now. In answer to such debates, Michel Biron has observed that "national consciousness coexists with a multicultural experience that forces it to redefine itself" in Quebec.[6] Indeed, the relevance of each attribute of Quebec cinema to the abundant assortment of fictional films we have seen in recent years is necessarily relative. However, the success of Quebec cinema, both at home and abroad, has been predicated on how these distinguishing attributes have come together and evolved over time.

This chapter will discuss the historical thread informed by these attributes and take a careful look at a few elements that historians tend to neglect, such as the periods of cinematic development that preceded the Quiet Revolution, the "national" films made by priest filmmakers in Quebec from 1930 to 1960, and popular cinema as a telling part of the overall corpus of Quebec film.

American Silent Films with French Commentary

Language issues came to light from the time the very first unilingual English-language films were screened before enthusiastic francophone audiences in Quebec in the summer of 1896. Silent films were brought in by small show-business entrepreneurs from the United States, England, and France, many of whom spoke little or no French. Those who could speak French were quick to achieve great success, as evidenced by the Viscount d'Hauterives, who wowed crowd after crowd with his oratory talent for "film lecturing."[7] During the 10 years he toured Quebec with a film projector that he called the "Historiographe," his public grew accustomed to watching film screenings with French commentary—entertainment deemed far superior to the rival unilingual British and American silent moving picture show experiences. Once cinema had grown popular enough for exclusive movie theatres to stay afloat, dozens of "scopes" (or "moving picture halls") opened within a few years in Montreal and elsewhere in Quebec. Commentators, known as film lecturers, stood and spoke to audiences at the front of theatres near the screens—a trend that continued until the advent of the "talkies" around 1930. Alex Silvio was the most popular film lecturer in the history of Quebec, enjoying a prosperous career from 1908 to 1932. So widely was he esteemed that, by the mid-1920s, he was managing five movie theatres, and the films he lectured about became major attractions. Although cinema had become extremely popular, most films still came from outside of Quebec and were made in English. Therefore, oral commentary provided audiences with a much-needed translation (into French) of the intertitle cards in silent films while adding a little local colour to the viewing experience.

It was also at this time that the documentary tradition in Quebec was born. Léo-Ernest Ouimet, the first owner of a moving picture theatre in Quebec, decided he wanted to show his growing audiences films that were different than the ones he had shipped in from abroad. So in 1906 he began producing some short documentaries. At first Ouimet himself, then his employees, went out to film events that were important or popular at the time, such as *L'incendie de Trois-Rivières* (a fire in Trois-Rivières, 1908), *Les fêtes du Tricentenaire de Québec* (tercentenary celebrations in Quebec City, 1908), *Le congrès eucharistique de Montréal* (a Eucharistic conference in Montreal, 1910), and many others. Through his association with the French film firm Pathé he became the chief Canadian distributor of newsreels, for which he opened theatres in several major cities across Canada.

Encouraged by Ouimet's success, other aspiring filmmakers enthusiastically embarked on some attempts at producing fictional films, the most significant among them being the collaboration between photographer and playwright Joseph-Arthur Homier and Emma Gendron. Between 1922 and 1925, their films *Oh! Oh! Jean, Madeleine de Verchères,* and *La drogue fatale* all did well in Montreal and across the province, but they were no match for the near-monopoly that Hollywood had held over the Canadian market since 1908.

Local entrepreneurs were also confronted with another daunting adversary: the francophone Catholic clergy. The Church had been demonizing cinema from the time the first moving picture theatre opened in 1906, observing that not only were American films unquestionably racy at the time, but people were flocking to see them on Sunday—"the Lord's Day." Indeed, going to the pictures had become an essential part of a growing popular culture that embraced modernity, refusing and rejecting the clerical–nationalist elite. In the end, the Catholic Church did not succeed in having moving picture venues shut down on Sundays, but it did contribute to the creation of a provincial censorship board in 1913 (the Board of Censors of Moving Pictures of the Province of Quebec), which it controlled until the 1960s and which was proud to be recognized as one of the strictest censorship bodies in the world.[8] Caught between Hollywood's market domination and the Catholic Church's moral scrutiny, Quebec cinema remained a minor player in the film industry at this time. Still in its infancy, local filmmaking struggled to find its voice in Quebec, but at least it was struggling in French.

Conservative Catholic Cinema

Léo-Ernest Ouimet launched the first cinematic period in Quebec with his silent newsreel documentaries, but the next historical period of cinema clearly belonged to the Catholic Church. After the arrival of sound film (the "talkies"), the Church's control over both film distribution and production remained almost absolute for about three decades throughout Quebec. **Catholic cinema** was largely produced and directed by priest filmmakers who were motivated by Pope Pius XI's new cinema policy, which encouraged Catholic clergy and Church activists to develop Christian propaganda.[9] Albert Tessier, a priest and history teacher in Trois-Rivières, and Maurice Proulx, an abbot and agronomy professor in Quebec City, had already made some amateur films by the time the papal encyclical *Vigilanti Cura* was issued in 1936. The Vatican's new position encouraged them to develop their filmmaking activities. Their brethren, including Louis-Roger Lafleur, Jean-Philippe Cyr, Thomas-Louis Imbeault, Léonidas Larouche, and many others also became filmmakers in their own right. These efforts expanded thanks to the wholehearted support of the Quebec government and the ultraconservative Union Nationale party, both headed by Quebec Premier Maurice Duplessis. The notoriously authoritarian Duplessis served two terms in office, from 1936 to 1939 and from 1944 until his death in 1959. During his extraordinarily long tenure as provincial premier, Church and state enjoyed an unusually close relationship. The Duplessis government forged a steadfast alliance with the Catholic Church as both sought to safeguard a traditionalist ideology of family-farm economics and rigorous Catholicism. Duplessis therefore provided government funding for the production and distribution of films that promoted the ideas and projects related to this shared ideology.

Albert Tessier (1895–1976) was the leading light and propagandist in this conservative Catholic school of cinematic thought. In 1937 Tessier became an itinerant province-wide supervisor for domestic science schools (for young single ladies, Écoles d'enseignement ménager), and his travels throughout Quebec allowed him to film farm life, peasant traditions, and religious and historical celebrations, as we see in films such as *Cantique du soleil* (hymn of the sun, 1935), *Hommage à notre paysannerie* (an homage to our peasantry, 1938), and *Credo du paysan* (the peasant's credo, 1942).[10] He edited and screened his own films, providing live commentary much like the more colourful film lecturers of the first days of Quebec cinema would do. In his filmmaking Tessier was especially attentive to the framing and quality of his shots. Editing and action were secondary considerations that simply served to illustrate his oral commentary. Later, soundtracks were added to some of his films so they could be disseminated by the Service de ciné-photographie that the provincial government had established in 1941. Tessier shot over 70 films and lectured at over 5,000 film screenings in the course of his career. The generation that followed him would marginalize his accomplishments, eager to escape any reminder of traditionalist conservatism. But Tessier's pioneering role in Quebec cinema has since been acknowledged with the creation of the Prix Albert-Tessier (a Government of Quebec film award).

The other leading figure in the conservative Catholic cinematic school of thought was Maurice Proulx, an abbot and professor who learned about filmmaking so that he could produce teaching materials for his agronomy classes. Between 1933 and 1937 he followed and filmed a group of French-Canadian settlers who were out clearing land to make way for new farming villages in Abitibi West. From the resulting footage, he made the first feature-length documentary film in Quebec, *En pays neufs* (1937), a truly epic tale of provincial twentieth-century rural development. By today's standards the film seems inordinately long, but its images are of high quality and were, after all, designed to serve as illustrations to accompany propagandist commentary for the promotion of rural settlement. Later Proulx devoted his filmmaking career to didactic works in praise of farm life that also provided descriptions of modern agricultural techniques, such as *Défrichement motorisé* (about motorized land clearing, 1946), *La culture de la betterave à sucre* (about beet crops, 1949) and *Le tabac jaune du Québec* (about yellow tobacco, 1951).[11]

Like other filmmakers, a substantial number of Proulx's films dealt with religious subjects. Quebec cinema from this era resembled a Vatican filmography, with works like Thomas-Louis Imbeault and Léonidas Larouche's *Noces sacerdotales de Mgr Eugène Lapointe* (depicting Monsignor Eugène Lapointe's ordination, 1936), Tessier's *Le Miracle du curé Chamberland* (on Father Chamberland's miracle, 1938) and Proulx's *La béatification de Mère d'Youville* (recording the beatification of Mother d'Youville, 1960). Though it is true that concepts of sovereign nationhood were not yet widespread during this era, it would not be an exaggeration to say that the Duplessis government's vision of provincial nationalism was consecrated through the school of conservative Catholic cinematic thought.

Around the same time there were some documentary filmmakers working with institutions outside of the Catholic Church in Quebec. Associated Screen News, a major documentary and promotional film company, began operations in 1922. Its *Canadian Cameos* series, produced mainly by Gordon Sparling, was known and well received in a number of countries. Filmmakers like Jean Palardy and Vincent Paquette also worked for the National Film Board (NFB) in Ottawa, which was founded in 1939. However, the Duplessis government limited the distribution of films from the NFB, an organization it purported was a hotbed for communists.

This cinematic period also saw the genesis of a commercial Catholic–secular fictional film corpus. Production of these works was prolific, their distribution superior, and their conservation a success, especially as compared to the silent era. In large part, Catholic–secular fictional films owed their existence to the new boom in French-language films that came about with the arrival of French-language talkies (talking motion pictures). In fact, it was the distribution of French-language talkies in Quebec that helped establish the France-Film company in 1932 and later the far-reaching influence of its second director, Joseph Alexandre DeSève.[12] Closely affiliated with Quebec's Catholic clergy, DeSève had ambitious fictional Catholic film projects in mind for his company. World War II temporarily derailed his projects, but at the end of the hostilities DeSève got his entreprise back on track, financing several films including *Le gros Bill* (by René Delacroix, 1949), *Le petite Aurore l'enfant martyre* (*Little Aurore's Tragedy*, by Jean-Yves Bigras, 1952), and *Tit-Coq* (by René Delacroix and Gratien Gélinas, 1953). With the possible exception of *Tit-Coq* (a film primarily focused on psychology), DeSève opportunistically capitalized on the values promoted by the Quebec Catholic clergy: faith, submission, and resignation.

Paul L'Anglais was another prominent backer of national Catholic fictional film projects. L'Anglais began his career in radio, where he launched many highly successful radio dramas. Based on these radio dramas he created a series of films, which he shot around 1950, including *Un homme et son péché* (*A Man and His Sin*, by Paul Gury, 1949) and *Le curé de village* (also by Paul Gury, 1949). As was the case with DeSève (with whom L'Anglais often collaborated), the aesthetics of L'Anglais's films were rudimentary but adroitly captured the small-town spirit and family values prevalent in a Quebec that was changing but still compliant with traditional Catholic morals. L'Anglais and DeSève produced the first major body of fictional films in Quebec—a significant achievement outside of Hollywood movie circuits. Both focused on making films about national subjects with many featuring a popular vernacular, and in both cases their aesthetic contributions to Quebec cinema might best be described as minor or negligible. This shortcoming was duly noted by the next generation, who took some radical measures to correct it.

The Quiet Revolution and Direct Cinema

During the 1950s, while these filmmakers and directors were trying their hand at cinematic fiction, young people in universities and colleges were being exposed to their films through the Catholic film clubs established on campuses. The Duplessis regime monitored the circulation of ideas closely but was unable to stem the popularity of modernity, which it held suspect. Frustrated by their anti-intellectual, authoritarian society, the students of the next generation came to admire foreign films, even though they often only saw their censored versions.

In 1956, when the NFB was established in Montreal, many of these students applied for jobs there. From the moment they were hired it forever changed their lives and the face of filmmaking in Quebec. As part of a new francophone group of NFB employees, Michel Brault, Marcel Carrière, Gilles Groulx, Claude Jutra, Pierre Perrault, and Arthur Lamothe (among others) were fascinated by the documentaries of anglophone filmmakers at the NFB, who were experimenting with the latest "candid eye" trend. The idea was to try to capture everyday scenes by shooting in a quasi-improvised fashion, then edit the resulting footage to express the essence of the subject as much as that of the shoot itself. In 1958 the new francophone group went out to film a snowshoeing tournament in Sherbrooke, surreptitiously slipping into the crowd for some closer shots, but rather than focus on the athletic feats of the participants they filmed the gestures that expressed the redundant aspects of the event. The resulting film was a scathing critique of a Quebec hopelessly trapped in its traditions. But above all it also represented an aesthetic innovation that marked the history of film: direct cinema.[13]

These filmmakers built up their analysis and techniques by using and refining lightweight, mobile equipment to shoot diverse facets of life in Quebec, from the solemn to the trivial, which became the subject of film classics such as *La lutte* (*Wrestling*, by Michel Brault, Claude Jutra, and Marcel Carrière, 1961), *Golden Gloves* (by Michel Brault and Gilles Groulx, 1961), *Pour la suite du monde* (*For Those Who Will Follow*, by Michel Brault and Pierre Perrault, 1963), and *Bucherons de la Manouane* (*Manouane River Lumberjacks*, by Arthur Lamothe, 1962). The works made by the filmmakers who followed in their footsteps offered more social commentary, as was the case in *On est au coton* (*Cotton Mill*, by Denys Arcand, 1970), *Un pays sans bon sens!* (by Pierre Perrault, 1970), and *24 heures ou plus . . .* (by Gilles Groulx, 1972).

But this radical innovation was not achieved without a fight. The young francophone filmmakers working with the NFB, who wanted creative licence over what and how they filmed, were stopped short by their anglo-Canadian bosses. Enthusiastic and keenly aware that they were participants in a sweeping social transformation in Quebec, these filmmakers refused to have their work scrutinized and be condemned to a minority status by what they viewed to be foreign and colonial authorities. Following some very public outcry in the French-language press about their internal struggles against NFB management (see the 1957 entry on the timeline at the beginning of this article), a new studio was consequently founded and became known as the "French team" at the NFB. In the same spirit, the NFB put together a bold program of social activist cinema:

> *Challenge for Change/Société nouvelle* had the primary goal of having the working classes film, view, and re-edit the images shot of themselves, by themselves, in order to build a community-based activism. This was accomplished by screening the finished films and videos in union halls and community centres.[14]

Anglophone and francophone filmmakers alike continued to use the new lightweight video technology in many of their film shoots to produce salient works that highlighted major social issues. For example, Fernand Dansereau exposed the human side of

Primary Source

The Poetic Documentary

Pierre Perrault writes about *Pour la suite du monde* (For Those Who Will Follow):

> I [wanted to] spell it out [for the community I was writing in, Île-aux-Coudres]: *This film will not be a documentary.* Out of caution. Or out of ignorance. Because how can we know in advance what reality has in store for us? What the film has in store for reality?
>
> I write that we are going to *fictitiously provoke a return of [the beluga] fishing [or whaling industry].* Not to be outdone.
>
> I add, very candidly, that *each episode will be invented, imagined and performed by the people of the island [Île-aux-Coudres] themselves.*
>
> I figured I might as well admit right away that I did not know what I was doing. At least [I did] not [know] yet. I reread these lines and cannot help but smile at my own naiveté. My intuition was trying to get a handle [on the situation]. Clumsily! How could I have known what this film would become before I did it? One thing is certain, I put my trust in [people's] voices. I had put their incomparably thick skin to the test. I offered them a theatre stage because they knew how to stage their storytelling voices. And is eloquence not the very substance of theatricality? I therefore proposed that some activity accompany their storytelling, a feat for their thick skin, a great opportunity to lyricize, verbalize, and brag.
>
> Of course my entire project relied on the two men who served as the pillars of the film: Alexi and Grand-Louis. Especially regarding one activity: beluga fishing. But how to define or predict what was going to happen? Would we succeed in making more than one documentary about fishing? And this kind of fishing, what was it going to precipitate between the fishermen? And, especially, what kind of adventure was it going to be? I did not dare, I did not know how, to predict it. And timidly, I was proposing to myself . . . that I would *fictitiously provoke the return of beluga fishing.* Not admitting the fanciful [nature of the] plan:

severe unemployment, low wages, and poverty in his film *Saint-Jérôme* (1970), and Kathleen Shannon documented the daily struggles of a Jamaican single mother and her need for daycare in *Mothers Are People* (1974).

The Quiet Revolution and direct cinema defined a historic cinematic period that saw the most remarkable production and corpus of documentary films in the history of Quebec cinema. Although comparatively fewer fictional works were produced during this period, slowly but surely fictional production consolidated its status. There is not much doubt that it sprang from the same soil as documentary film and its experiments. Some theoreticians called it "direct fiction" film, since its scenarios were rudimentary, improvisation was encouraged and detectable, shoots were often done outdoors with small crews, traces of the editing process were frequently visible, and colloquial language was prominently featured, all in a clear effort to accentuate a resolutely modern aesthetic. The subjects of these fictional films were as innovative and experimental as their techniques and aesthetic sensibility. They featured quests for personal and social identity (*Le chat dans le sac/Cat in the Sack*, Gilles Groulx, 1964), the sexual revolution (*À tout prendre/Take It All*, Claude Jutra, 1963), political change (*Le révolutionnaire/The* that of filming reality, in person. And still, to this day, thirty years later, I do not undertake a new film without misgivings. What if reality refused to cooperate? So I was taking my own self for a work of fiction, for a director. The river, the shoals, the *drives* of iceflows in the March currents—can we not say that it was all a stage? The decor was therefore not fictitious. We did know something about it: The water was glacial, the wind strong, the clay slippery and the boat nooses heavy as we reached out with them at tide's end. So what would we accomplish there? I felt a little guilty to be a filmmaker. It was as though I could not really admit what my intentions were. Yet, I did not have the least urge to manipulate reality. To tell a story. To write a romance. Already, I am asserting my wish to let reality choose for me. It is their fishing that interests me. Their beluga, in the flesh, and the blood and the snow. Might as well add this: *each anecdote* (the word is inaccurate, I admit, I should have said "episode," "event" . . .) *will be invented, imagined and performed by people from the island.*

Here I am stepping away from the role of director. Transferring these machinations off of my shoulders, onto theirs. They will be in charge of the film. They will invent it, imagine it, perform it. I admitted part of it was performance. Without daring to assert that that [particular] part is part of life. I did not dare to say so. Perhaps I did not know. But in reality, they did not so much perform and invent a film as they did live a fishing expedition. Or perhaps they lived their lives. And in a low-key way, as though to minimize the staging [factor] that threatens the film, I add a few more words into the sentence: *performed by people from the island who will, in a way, be called upon to live their own legend.*

Live or relive? But I wrote *live.* And that is the real gist [of the matter]. If I had chosen to engage them in some activity that was not in their nature, in an activity that they would have had to imagine, invent, [or] perform, I now know that I would have been courting catastrophe. If the film [seemed] authentic, [and] credible, it was because they lived fishing instead of performing it. That, in my view, is the amazing result of this beautiful adventure. The unhoped-for miracle! Unexpected! The result that surpasses expectations.

Revolutionary, Jean-Pierre Lefebvre, 1965), social strife transfigured (*L'eau chaude l'eau frette/Hot Water, Cold Water,* André Forcier, 1976), historical criticism (*Mon oncle Antoine/My Uncle Antoine,* Claude Jutra, 1970); *La mort d'un bûcheron/The Death of a Lumberjack,* Gilles Carle, 1974), and political criticism (*Les orders/Orderers,* Michel Brault, 1974). Anglophone filmmakers in Quebec produced work that was less politically charged but nonetheless innovative in its style and discourse, as seen in Paul Almond's sensitive study of a woman's changing psyche in *Isabel* (1968) and Ted Kotcheff's captivating depiction of Montreal's Jewish community in *The Apprenticeship of Duddy Kravitz* (1974).

Quebec's decidedly stylized and innovative fictional cinema was not left alone to fend for itself commercially during the Quiet Revolution. Quebec businesses began to see it as a potentially good investment, their interest bourgeoning as the momentum of sovreignist nationalist sentiment grew. The federal and provincial governments also provided increased financial support to Quebec cinema, going on to respectively found the Canadian Film Development Corporation (CFDC) in 1967 and the Institut québécois du cinéma (IQC) in 1977. Steeped in an era of sexual liberation, these elements also led to the development of a considerable corpus of erotic film that followed international trends. Filmmaker

CASE STUDY

The NFB Affair: A Press Campaign for the NFB French Team

In 1957 a very public debate took place in Montreal about what came to be known as "the NFB affair," a series of events that had a major effect on cinema in Quebec and Canada and whose repercussions would be felt for years to come. On 26 February 1957, journalist Pierre Vigeant of *Le Devoir* wrote a short article on the injustices that French Canadians had to endure at the National Film Board of Canada (NFB). These injustices had already been the subject of two editorials by André Laurendeau but only got worse when the NFB relocated to Montreal the previous year.[15] Vigeant's article set off an intense two-month press campaign that would involve several other newspapers. In the hailstorm of articles that followed, it was revealed that francophones at the NFB, even those who were bilingual (a job requirement), were systematically being paid less than their unilingual anglophone colleagues who occupied equivalent job positions. Therefore, the chances for job advancement were almost nil for francophones, whose films made up just 7 per cent of all NFB output. Moreover, all film scripts had to be written in English so that management could understand them, and many francophones were limited to the positions of assistants or translators. Francophones experienced daily slights that were simply inadmissible and whispered about how the British sense of "fair play" was being used between employees as a cover for the constant shoddy treatment they received. Between 1952 and 1956 total production at the NFB (over four years) was 1,109 films; only 69 of them were made in French. There was no recognition whatsoever at the NFB that French-Canadian culture was part of a multifaceted Canadian culture: Management and anglophone producers claimed the right to define what culture was, be it in Quebec or in Acadia (the other major francophone region of Canada).

To the young francophone intellectuals who had just been hired at the NFB, their situation seemed symptomatic of a larger Canadian reality. Francophones were being told that they should not fool themselves: They were not going to be allowed to excel in their field or advance in their profession; the status of the francophone community would not change in relation to the anglophone majority. Francophone employees were experiencing the same tensions and forms of oppression that were playing out on the political stage, but NFB management had exacerbated the situation by creating a rivalry between filmmakers from the two groups.

Although the NFB's mandate was to promote Canadian unity, behind closed doors domineering colonialist, racist, and linguistic discrimination toward francophone employees clearly indicated that management was intolerant of the presence of a minority culture. As one of the filmmakers flatly stated:

> The truth, what no one has ever in fact admitted at the NFB, and no one has ever actively recognized, is that two cultures exist, each with different approaches to self-expression. . . . We are like Lazarus, picking crumbs off the floor, under some rich man's table. . . . In fact, a very colourful expression was found to describe the "maladjusted" French Canadians: they were *dead wood* or *not well integrated* into the NFB. A French Canadian intellectual was for them a kind of strange beast, from another planet.[16]

The other French-language newspapers soon expressed their support for the *Le Devoir* article.

La Presse, the biggest newspaper at the time, assigned journalist Roger Champoux to write a series of "objective" articles on the situation at the NFB. In one of Champoux's articles there was even an interview with film producer and distributor Joseph-Arthur DeSève, who lent the francophones at the NFB some firm support:

> Asking that we be allowed to work—within the necessary administrative framework, that goes without saying—but in accordance with our mindset and our culture is not, as far as I know, a demand for some [sort of] privilege but rather an elementary recognition of each person's right to self-expression.[17]

In the end, the journalistic pieces that appeared in *La Presse* regarding this issue were attempts to defuse the ever-growing sentiment of public dissatisfaction, but fell far short. The goal was also perhaps to show that the NFB should not be allowed to fire Roger Blais, who was its most outspoken and outstanding francophone film director.[18] Of course, the NFB's final decision to fire Blais amounted to throwing more fuel on the fire. French-language newspapers intensified their demands and received a flood of supportive comments. Consequently, the NFB was forced to take immediate action.

On 23 April 1957, Guy Roberge became the first French Canadian to be appointed as Canada's government film commissioner, in which capacity he ran the National Film Board. Pierre Vigeant commented on the situation: "The first reform that we expect the new Commissioner to make is to found a French section. That would be the natural course of action in a bicultural organization."[19] This statement marked the end of the press campaign, but it still took years before the independence of francophones at the NFB was officially recognized. In 1959, Fernand Dansereau, Bernard Devlin, Léonard Forest, and Louis Portugais became the executive producers of the French team with limited but real decision-making authority. In 1962, the independence of the team was further consolidated with the nomination of Pierre Juneau as the francophone section director. From this moment forward, there were two distinct entities at the NFB, each with their own administration, somewhat analogous to the division of authority at Radio-Canada/CBC, which had (and still has) both an English and a French network. The French section of the NFB led to the founding of a "French team"—two words that would have special resonance for the group that went on to develop direct cinema, which relied on the ability of a film crew ("équipe" or "team" in French) to blend into a community and reflect its reality in its own language.

Today, the NFB is a very different organization than what it used to be, but the small group of French-Canadian employees exposed the oppression that they had suffered and was a crucial element in the wider struggle to have Québécois culture recognized—a culture that has continued to evolve since that time, within Canada, or despite it. Today the enemy is elsewhere, in the "globish" culture, as the business community says, where cinema from Quebec or from Canada does not count for much. Pierre Véronneau, a Quebec cinema historian who was director of research at the Cinémathèque québécoise for almost half a century, provides another perspective on the NFB affair in his writing. In fact, the title of his book could be used as a guide for fights to come: *Résistance et affirmation*.[20]

Denis Héroux made a name for himself with *Valérie* (1968), *L'initiation* (1969), and many other films that rode the same Romanesque-erotic wave. But Claude Fournier's *Deux femmes en or* (*Two Women in Gold*, 1970) was the runaway success of this era—a blockbuster that turned the audience's desires into gold for the filmmaker.

At the same time that women were the subjects and objects of commercial film projects, they were making their own films and constructing a school of feminist thought that was immersed in the effervescence of an emerging feminist movement. Their outstanding works included radical documentaries like *Les filles du Roy* (*They called us "Les filles du Roy,"* 1979) and *Mourir à tue-tête* (*A Scream from Silence*, 1974) by Anne Claire Poirier, as well as innovative fictional films like *La vie rêvée* (*The Dreamed Life*, 1972) by Mireille Dansereau and *La cuisine rouge* (1979) by Paule Baillargeon and Frédérique Collin, which demanded women's liberation rather than Quebec's liberation as a nation at the time. The concept of "nation" nonetheless pervaded Quebec films of the 1960s, whose male and female creators would subsequently be among the most outspoken disseminators of the campaign for Quebec sovereignty and later among the critics of its defeat. Quebec cinema had become a modern national cinema for many. But the movement that inspired it lost steam after the first referendum defeat in 1980, and the government that had first stepped forward to support it financially and legally remained a government still within a province that was governed by Canada.

Post-Referendum and Postmodern Cinema

On one hand, the referendum defeat in 1980 left organizers of the sovereignty movement confounded and many filmmakers disillusioned and cynical. On the other hand, business was booming for Quebec cinema. By the 1980s filmmaking in the province had become institutionalized and had strong legal and financial government support. Filmmaking had grown from scattered artisanal projects into a full-fledged industry (as Gilles Marsolais writes), and filmmakers adapted their inspiration to the prevailing conditions.[21] A gradual parting of ways between the nationalist sovereignty movement and Quebec's cinematic industry thereby ensued as fate had dealt each entity two very different hands. Quebec cinema's subsequent **postmodern** turn redefined its relationship with the past, making it more intertextual and intermedial. Bill Marshall has summed up the new political and social climate of this period as follows:

> Denys Arcand's *Le déclin de l'empire américain [The Decline of the American Empire]* (1986) and *Jésus de Montréal [Jesus of Montreal]* (1989) inaugurated, at the end of the 1980s, a cinema preoccupied less by national self-definition, assertion, and creation than by the awareness of a Quebec inserted in global flows of culture and communication.... These "world" developments and their accompanying cultural shifts would remain on the agenda despite the resurgence of Quebec nationalism after the collapse of the Meech Lake Accord in 1990.[22]

As part of these "global flows," ambitious feature film/television mini-series were coproduced between France and Quebec, dramatizing literary classics like *Maria Chapdelaine* (Gilles Carle, 1983), *Bonheur d'occasion* (*The Tin Flute*, Claude Fournier, 1983) and *Le matou* (*The Alley Cat*, Jean Beaudin, 1985). All of these works acknowledged Quebec's national oppression, but they nonetheless requested that actors express themselves in "international French" (thus expunging Quebec's regional/national vernaculars) for the market in France—right décor, wrong language. Made-for-television productions that targeted Quebec's domestic market, while less ambitious, were generally more relevant to Quebecers. For instance, Robert Ménard's *T'es belle Jeanne* (*You're Beautiful, Jeanne*, 1988) was a compassionate tale of disability and rehabilitation, while Paule Baillargeon's *Sonia* (1986) was a journey into the life of an artist who is losing her memory.

Quebec's anglophone fiction filmmakers, who were less concerned than their francophone counterparts with national sovereignty issues during this period, studied Quebec's growing cultural diversity with great acuity of vision. John N. Smith's *Sitting in Limbo* (1986) and *Train of Dreams* (1987) are two cases in point, with the latter film winning the Prix Léo-Ernest Ouimet-Molson. Conversely, the zeitgeist films made by Quebec francophones at this time had a cynical edge about nationalism. It was this cynicism that made them hugely successful both at home and abroad, as evidenced by Denys Arcand's *Le déclin de l'empire américain* (*The Decline of the American Empire,* 1984). Arcand's bitter portrayal of the retreat of self-absorbed intellectuals after the 1980 referendum defeat in Quebec struck a powerful chord with audiences.

Like Arcand, other filmmakers from the Quiet Revolution were focusing on issues that were more personal than they were political: Jacques Leduc's *Trois pommes à côté du sommeil* (*Three Apples,* 1989) alternated between fictional and documentary film in a retrospective featuring the women he loved; Jean-Pierre Lefebvre ambitiously attempted to blur the boundaries between real and imagined worlds in *Le fabuleux voyage de l'ange* (*The Fabulous Voyage of the Angel,* 1991); Marc-André Forcier continued producing magic realist films with *Au clair de la lune* (1984) and *Kalamazoo* (1988), in which his bemused poetry often veered into Chaplinesque sadness; and Gilles Carle put his critical sense of irony aside to produce his thriller *La guêpe* (*The Wasp,* 1986) and his facile comedy *La postière* (*The Postmistress,* 1992).

A gust of fresh inspiration came from some new sources, like the theatre and artisanal cinema in the early 1990s, when playwright Robert Lepage made the move to film. Catalyzing his considerable talents, he told his postmodern philosophical and political stories with superior technical and pictorial inventiveness. His movie *Le Confessionnal* (*The Confessional,* 1995) recounted a Quebec family's speedy transition from conservative 1950s Quebec to the secular, permissive society it became in the 1990s; while *La face cachée de la lune* (2003) focused on the particularly contemporary story of a man pondering the relativity of knowledge and the fragility of human existence.

Impressive young francophone directors also made their mark with their sure-footed talent. Miles away from past issues of Quebec identity, Denis Villeneuve travelled to Jamaica for his psychodrama *REW FFWD* (1994), Manon Briand's bicycle courier raced against mid-life in *2 secondes* (*2 Seconds,* 1998), and François Girard introduced audiences to an eccentric anglophone Canadian icon in his unconventional biopic *Trente deux films brefs sur Glenn Gould* (*Thirty-Two Short Films about Glenn Gould,* 1993). Around the same time the exceptionally talented Léa Pool was taking a vibrantly personal approach in her films, in contrast to the social justice films made by women in the 1960s. Pool, who began her career in the 1980s, soon established herself as one of Quebec's foremost filmmakers with moving works like *La femme de l'Hôtel* (*A Woman in Waiting,* 1984), *Anne Trister* (1986), and *Emporte-moi* (*Set Me Free,* 1998). Also making his mark was the young and exceptionally gifted Jean-Claude Lauzon. Tragically, Lauzon was killed in a plane crash in northern Quebec, leaving only a few films to posterity. Of all the films he produced, *Léolo* (1992) towers above the rest in its truculent poetics, revealing the inner musings of a child who escapes into a fantasy world to avoid his morbid reality.[23]

As Quebec cinema became more industrial in its approach, artisanal production was marginalized but still generated some surprising works that reached audiences. The most interesting among them were thought provoking and asked highly relevant questions about the existence of film as an entity, as was the case in Jean Beaudry and François Bouvier's *Jacques et novembre* (*Jacques and November,* 1984), Pierre Goupil's *Celui qui voit les heures* (1985), and Olivier Asselin's *La liberté d'une statue* (*A Statue's Liberty,* 1990). These artisanal movies addressed the narrow detours of both human existence and the film industry on which their fragile creativity depended.

In the category of artisanal activist filmmaking, the next generation came from the world of video devices, which offered less expensive and restrictive technology. Robert Morin emerged as the most singular and disturbing artisanal activist filmmaker, inspired by live methods to create works like *Le voleur vit en enfer* (*The Thief Lives in Hell,* 1984) that were as political as they were intensely self-referential. In a similar vein, Morin himself played a bilingual "split subject" character in his off-the-wall, ferocious satire *Yes Sir! Madame* (1995).

Quebec's commercial cinema quickly dropped its nationalist discourse and moved on to comedy, which had become the preferred genre in box-office sales among the general public. The hapless heroes in these top-selling comedies spoke vernacular Québécois French and were caught up in screwball intrigues that often turned burlesque, as in *Les Boys* (Louis Saïa, 1998), or grotesque, as in *Angelo, Fredo et Roméo* (Pierre Plante, 1995). The demands of audiences and the commercial market were not only reshaping the content of productions, but also changing the relative status of genres. Although the undeniable legacy of documentary cinema was intact, it lost the preponderant position it had occupied since the beginning of Quebec cinema. In what historian Marcel Jean calls the "documentary film crisis" of the 1980s, activist cinema was overrun by made-for-television hybrid productions in which documentary blurred into fictional film, as was the case in *Le million tout puissant* (*Almighty Million*, Michel Moreau, 1985) and *La guerre oubliée* (*The Forgotten War*, Richard Boutet, 1988). The historian remarked that a number of first-person film essays were being produced around the same time, including *Journal inachevé* (*Unfinished Diary*, Marilú Mallet, 1982), *Voyage en Amérique avec un cheval emprunté* (*Travels in America with a Borrowed Horse*, Jean Chabot, 1987), and *Alias Will James* (Jacques Godbout, 1988). Jean also underscored the links these films had with past documentary film techniques:

> When they put their own gaze front and centre, when they place themselves between the camera and the subject they are addressing and when they integrate fictional sequences, the documentary filmmakers of the 1980s gave characters the chance to talk... and categorically refused to claim objectivity, the myth that was completely destroyed with the appearance of direct cinema.[24]

Postnational Cinema in an Era of Globalization

By the year 2000 it seemed as though Quebec was entering its golden age of cinema: The quantity of films had increased and stabilized, audience attendance had reached new heights, and a number of films were receiving prestigious nominations and awards. In 2003, *La grande seduction* (*Seducing Doctor Lewis*, Ken Scott), *Mambo Italiano* (Émile Gaudreault), *Les invasions barbares* (*The Barbarian Invasions*, Denys Arcand), and *Gaz Bar Blues* (Louis Bélanger) were all commercial triumphs and attracted considerable audiences in a variety of film genres. Owing to its limited scope of influence, Quebec cinema was still a minor player in international cinema, but the quality of the work being produced was unquestionable. The years ahead would see the growth of a widening gap between the quality of top films and their degree of commercial success. Many new filmmakers became known for their original works (*La moitié gauche du frigo*/*The Left-Hand Side of the Fridge*, Philippe Falardeau, 2000; and *Rebelle*/*War Witch*, Kim Nguyen, 2012), but even when they won numerous awards at film festivals in Quebec and abroad their local success remained modest. This gap between the quality of the film and its commercial success has only widened over time and constitutes one of the abiding preoccupations of the current cinematic period. Those in the film industry continue to wonder whether Quebec can keep its francophone filmmakers and whether they will continue making world-class films in French.

Denis Villeneuve (*Maelström*, 2001) and Jean-Marc Vallée (*C.R.A.Z.Y*, 2005), who were very busy and successful in Quebec around the beginning of the millennium, are now making American films in Hollywood (*Prisoners*, 2013; *Dallas Buyers Club*, 2013). Is working in the United States the ultimate goal of Quebec filmmakers, or is it simply part of a normal career path for a profession in which Hollywood has been the gravitational centre for well over a century? Quebec audiences certainly never lost their voracious appetite for Hollywood films, and demand for dubbed French versions (oral translation) of these films has consequently remained high. One provincial political party in Quebec even tried to protect the francization of the film market and the dubbing industry for Hollywood films in Quebec in June 2007 (but to no avail).[25] Some Quiet

Revolution filmmakers known for championing the French language and Quebec culture are still active, but their inspiration seems blunted, diluted, and contrived. For instance, Denys Arcand's films have placed among the top selections at major film festivals (*Les invasions barbares/The Barbarian Invasions,* 2003), but Arcand seems to have fallen into a repetitive rut of pretentious cynicism (as in *Le règne de la beauté/The Reign of Beauty,* 2014). Marc-André Forcier is still producing magic realist films, but he too seems to be repeating himself (*Je me souviens,* 2009; *Côteau rouge,* 2011).

Quebec's newest edition of films, which reflect the director's creative vision to the point that they are seen as the film's creative origins, or *auteur* fiction filmmaking, was announced in 2010 as the "Renewal" ("new wave," or "mouvée").[26] As these Renewal filmmakers embarked (and continue to embark) on their hopeful careers, the financial exposure taken on for their films was (and remains) perilously high given the marked decline in box-office sales in Quebec and the industry's ongoing minor-league position within a globalized distribution system. Within Quebec, this situation has meant that "Renewal" films have had little presence. New names in the spotlight include Denis Côté, Sophie Deraspe, Rafaël Ouellet, Stéphane Lafleur, and more recently the young prodigy Xavier Dolan. Educated in film programs that are now well established (in colleges, universities, and institutes), these filmmakers are masterful with their tools, their aesthetic erudition, and personal creativity, and they know how to work within modest budgets. Being relatively recent newcomers to the industry also means that they may attach less importance to outdated obsessions or to issues like Quebec's national identity than their elders do.

These days activist filmmakers who are part of the Renewal view the issue of Quebec's national identity as secondary, being far more interested in other social issues. More aesthetically oriented Renewal filmmakers are far more interested in experimentation and ignore the issue of identity entirely. Denis Côté, the latest standout aesthetics-oriented filmmaker from the Renewal, is a case in point, as his camera's gaze literally keeps the audience at a distance from his marginalized characters (*Curling,* 2010; *Vic et Flo ont vu un ours/Vic and Flo Saw a Bear,* 2013). In 2006, Sophie Deraspe threw audiences a curve ball with her quasi-mockumentary about a wily painter, *Recherche Victor Pellerin* (*Missing Victor Pellerin,* 2006), then came back with another twist in *Les signes vitaux* (*Vital Signs,* 2009), in which a disabled woman volunteer tells lies to bring relief to ailing people. These two filmmakers shared an ethos of ambiguity with Rafaël Ouellet, who reserved all moral judgment in showing us the sacrifice made by a young girl who has been betrayed by an older adult woman in *Derrière moi* (*Behind Me,* 2008) and the quest of a teenage girl who felt smothered in her small town in *New Denmark* (2009). Musician and filmmaker Stéphane Lafleur took a similar approach, reviving poetic realism in *Continental, un film sans fusil* (*Continental, a Film without Guns,* 2007) and *En terrains connus* (*Familiar Grounds,* 2011), circling banal facts and gestures slowly to reveal buried tenderness. And last but certainly not least in the Renewal movement of aesthetic filmmaking there is Xavier Dolan. At 25 years of age, he received the 2014 Cannes Film Festival Jury Award for his film *Mommy,* in which he revitalized the Quebec tradition of bringing together visually mesmerizing innovation and vernacular orality.

Robert Morin is part of the more socially conscious side of Quebec's Renewal. Morin kept his activist focus after moving to film from an early career as a videographer in the 1980s. In his drama *Le Nèg* (*The Negro,* 2002) he exposed the disquieting dynamics of small-town racism, and in *Papa à la chasse aux lagopèdes* (*Papa Goes Ptarmigan Hunting,* 2008) he revealed the treachery of financial speculation. Like Denis Côté, Morin has often preferred to create his movies outside of institutional funding sources rather than make any compromises in his film projects (which he has always managed to disseminate through various channels). Morin's work inspired the work of younger filmmakers interested in Quebec's social issues, such as Simon Lavoie and Mathieu Denis, who expressed their concern for the survival of francophone culture in Quebec in *Laurentie* (2011); Sébastien Pilote, who explored the ups and downs of consumerism in *Le vendeur*

(*The Salesman,* 2011); and Simon Galiero, who took a sardonic look at class struggle in *La mise à l'aveugle* (*Small Blind,* 2012).

The enormous expansion of fictional film production during this **postnational cinematic** period relegated documentaries to a less visible role. But many documentarians pursued their analytical work often in a much freer and more critical way than they could have done in fiction. For example, André-Line Beauparlant reported on patriarchal violence in *Trois princesses pour Roland* (*Three Princesses for Roland*) in 2001, Ève Lamont denounced industrial agriculture in *Pas de pays sans paysans* (*Fight for True Farming*) in 2005, Richard Brouillette presented his depiction of new globalized capitalism in *L'encerclement* (*Encirclement*) in 2008, and Hugo Latulippe investigated the future of the Quebec Francophonie in *République : Un abécédaire populaire* (*Republic: A Popular ABC*) in 2011.

Some mainstream movie theatre owners have been very vocal in their claims that *auteur* filmmaking was ruining Quebec's film industry because they felt that its unusual, complicated, and sometimes depressing storylines were scaring away audiences. This view of Quebec *auteur* film meant that its distribution was limited in comparison to homegrown popular comedies. Indeed, the sequels to a number of famous popular comedies that poked fun at serious subjects were released during this period of postnational cinema. Émile Gaudreault was the champion of this genre with *Mambo Italiano* (2003) and *De père en flic* (*Father and Guns,* 2009). As ever, the *Les Boys* (*The Boys*) sequels were both guaranteed financial successes and guaranteed creative washouts, relying far too heavily on a facile, ongoing obsession with our national sport. Louis Saïa's mainstream comedy *Les dangereux* (2002), while at least as shoddy, had the merit of proving that even in this (often) lucrative market niche a big-budget fiasco could lose a whopping $7 million. So it may be that putting all of Quebec's eggs into the mainstream comedy basket could be ill advised.

Is it the content of films that causes box-office sales to drop, and should Quebec filmmakers be re-examining the content of the films they are making? Are filmmakers out of step with the times in a globalized, culturally diversifying Quebec? In 2010 Jacob Tierney, the anglophone filmmaker who wrote and directed the hit feature comedy *The Trotsky,* gave his opinion on this subject and stirred up some controversy in the process:

> Quebec cinema is white, white, white. It's homogeneous! It's embarrassing. Look at the films that are being made in Quebec: 1981, *C.R.A.Z.Y.*, Polytechnique . . . These are good films, but they are all focused on the past. It's a glorification of nostalgia. As though everything was more interesting before. There is something unhealthy about that.[27]

Tierney's concern was that the cultural diversity of Quebec is not accurately reflected in the content of Quebec cinema. (Tierney himself makes a conscious effort to include characters from different communities in his filmmaking.) The concern he raises gives all Quebec filmmakers something to think about in the future. What will the most interesting films look like in the years ahead?

Tierney also claimed that "Anglos and immigrants are ignored in Quebec's film reality." As far as anglophones not being part of the province's film reality, the filmmaker was perhaps forgetting that Quebec can boast an incredibly impressive list of world-renowned, award-winning anglophone filmmakers, including Norman McLaren, Gordon Sparling, and Bonnie Sherr Klein. It is also worth noting that the number of notable "immigrant" filmmakers is growing in Quebec, including names like celebrated Egyptian-born activist documentarian Tahani Rached (*Haïti-Québec/Haiti-Quebec,* 1985), Chilean-born Patricio Henríquez (*Le dernier combat de Salvador Allende/The Last Stand of Salvador Allende,* 1998), and Chinese-born Zhimin Hu (*A Cold Summer Night,* 2015), not to mention organizations like Les Films de l'Autre, which bring together filmmakers of all origins.[28]

Over the past decade, Quebec has also seen Indigenous filmmakers make their mark in documentary filmmaking. Wapikoni Mobile is a mobile studio that has been showcasing poignant, healing, and haunting works, like those of Kevin Papatie (*L'amendement/The Amendment*, 2007) and Réal Junior Leblanc (*L'enfance déracinée/Uprooted Generation*, 2013). In 2011, Yves Sioui-Durand of the Huron-Wendat Nation released *Mesnak*, the first-ever feature film to be made by an Indigenous person in Quebec (2011).[29]

Of course, the question remains: Is anybody watching the films being made in Quebec? Much has been made of the notorious gap that exists between the growing number of movies being produced and plummeting audience attendance. But it seems that this gap may not be attributable to the films themselves, as some would have us believe. The fragmentation of film distribution is far more likely the determining factor. Today, films are available through a variety of mobile devices, which means they can be watched anytime, anywhere. Some filmmakers are even integrating other people's recorded phone footage into their own films, which they then disseminate widely across a number of new media platforms. Dominic Gagnon did this with his films *RIP in Pieces America* (2010) and *Pieces and Love All to Hell* (2011). So, despite frequent reports of its imminent demise, film in Quebec, as elsewhere, is being watched and is continuing.

Conclusion

In 2013, 27 feature-length fictional films were made in Quebec. This number is impressive, but distribution has now fallen off to the point that, in many cases, the biggest viewership for Quebec's homegrown films is located outside of Quebec. This apparent incongruity between supply and demand has led to two main types of debates that are as revealing as they are worrisome. As mentioned earlier, there are commercial film promoters who criticize *auteur* cinema, claiming that it scares away audiences with its deeply personal or pessimistic storylines. But there are also filmmakers and critics who say that *auteur* films are what makes Quebec cinema vibrant and original—a legacy we should be promoting and a standard we should uphold.

Beyond the debate about the viability of *auteur* films, there are complaints about the *auteurs* themselves. Some critics in the industry believe that there is a sphere of *auteurs* that tends to seek validation by fixating on incongruous passing trends in aesthetics rather than considering the possibility of making movies that reflect the realities of their own communities. Simon Galiero is the most outspoken critic in this area:

> How is it, then, that the same type of [aesthetic] representation can be so widespread under the aegis of what has been called "auteur cinéma"[30] . . . It is therefore no surprise to find, among the filiation of this cinema, faces that have also become banal and even annoyingly predictable. . . . And it is even less of a surprise to observe that some of the most glorified headlines of the "mouvée du renouveau"[31] are also among the most active on Facebook and Twitter, where they spend their time on self-promotion, relaying all the most fashionable jack-asseries like parakeets, displaying their simulated marginality. Magnificent specimens whose conversations are peppered with the preoccupations of daytraders.[32]

When Galiero's film *La mise à l'aveugle* (*Small Blind*, 2012) came out shortly after he wrote these lines, it was based on the popular social cinema of the 1970s, which he associated especially with Gilles Carle and André Forcier.

Clearly, there are two overarching approaches to cinema in Quebec: One is rooted in addressing social issues and the other is more focused on asking artistic/technical questions (and sometimes doing formal research). During the Quiet Revolution, young filmmakers found ways of using technology (rather than inventing it) to talk about their community, give that community a voice, and disseminate that voice to the world, showing how Quebecers honestly saw themselves. Of course no generation is quite like the last, and the intrinsic importance of the international film industry is unprecedented for this generation and may be for those that follow. But in the new debates about approaches to Quebec cinema, it would be worthwhile to consider what was learned during the Quiet Revolution so that the essence of cinema can be passed on to future generations of Quebec, shaping the cinema of tomorrow. Regardless of what future Quebecers choose to call themselves (or Quebec for that matter), making films right here and staying attuned to who we are becoming will extend the art beyond our times. Time and resources permitting.

BIOGRAPHY

Pierre Perrault: Filmmaker and Writer (1927–1999)

Pierre Perreault's work spans over a half-century of history. From literature, film, and theatre to poetry and radio, his multiple forms of expression remain unparalleled in any artistic or cultural landscape the world over. At a time when Quebec was still heavily influenced by foreign cultural references, Perrault inspired an authentic sense of Québécois self-awareness and self-assertion. True to the spirit of famous explorers like Jacques Cartier, who inspired him deeply, he travelled the length and breadth of the land to describe it with words from the people of Quebec. His work was beyond monumental and remains deeply relevant, not only because it lends itself generously to a viewing and listening audience, but chiefly because it invites us to reflect on what place we occupy in this world.

A lawyer by trade, Perreault made his debut on the airwaves of Radio-Canada in the 1950s, writing and recording no less than 800 radio shows. Fascinated by the potential that lay in recording devices and inspired by the conversations of the sailors, fishers, and hunters who were living on the shores of Quebec's St Lawrence River, he succeeded in introducing himself into the everyday lives of these people to record them. For the first time in Quebec history their voices were being documented, along with his own poetic commentary. This discovery of voice was a turning point. It revealed the exceptional qualities of a literature based on a sense of orality still imbued with the know-how of local inhabitants who found their own words to talk about the place they called home.

From radio Perrault moved to film, where his radiophonic and poetic approach lay the groundwork for a voice-oriented kind of cinema. He dove in, swept up in the direct cinema adventure of the 1960s. Transported by his thirst to discover Quebec, Perrault remained faithful to the colourful characters he had encountered during his career in radio, including Alexis Tremblay and Grand-Louis Harvey of Île-aux-Coudres, two absolutely inexhaustible storytellers whose fabulous yarns verged on the epic. In his filmmaking, he invited them to participate in an activity, a quest, a trip or to go hunting and succeeded in getting them to forget his camera was present. Perrault would draw them out with scenarios that he skilfully developed, film after film. This was how, with the co-operation of the other inhabitants of Île-aux-Coudres, he made his film trilogy *Pour la suite du monde* (*For Those Who Will Follow,* 1963), *Le règne du jour* (*The Times That Are,* 1967), and *Les voitures d'eau* (*The River Schooners*, 1969). He thus made a name for himself both in Quebec and in France as the representative of a new style of filmmaking in which characters had a voice and directed themselves. By presenting Île-aux-Coudres as the microcosm of a nation undergoing deep changes, Perrault opened the door for Quebec cinema to join a style of young national cinematography that was emerging throughout the globe.

At a time when Quebec was struggling to define itself and make its voice heard, Perrault expanded his horizons to explore the question of national identity in Quebec, in the belief that it was important to encourage awareness and express his passion for his country. To make his symphonic film/poem *Un pays sans bon sens!* (1970), he added a whole host of voices—people from every social, cultural, and linguistic background he could find—to the fabulous yarns that he gleaned from the Île-aux-Coudres storytellers. This resolutely modern, poetic, and political film was a groundbreaking piece of work, not only in Perrault's own filmography but also in the entire filmography of Quebec and Canada. The film led him to continue in the same vein and give other communities a voice. His quest for identity was experienced in different ways, according to whether subjects were Acadian (*L'Acadie, l'Acadie?!?/Acadia, Acadia?!?* 1971), Abitibian (*Un royaume vous attend/A Kingdom Awaits You,* 1976), or Indigenous (*Le goût de la farine/The Taste of Flour,* 1977).

Like his human characters, animals were also omnipresent in Perrault's movies. From belugas to muskox, mice to caribou, and pigs to moose, animals were all incarnations of nature in Quebec and of its inhabitants. By observing behaviour in the animal kingdom, Perrault attempted to draw insightful conclusions, as evidenced by the devastating film in which a hunted moose became the hunter (*La bête lumineuse/Shimmering Beast,* 1982). With this film, Perrault's work laid bare a stark human truth, showing the extent to which the cruelty of the animal world applied to our own. Perreault knew that, sooner or later, his rank among the hierarchy of the other occupants of the land would become clear. After all, that was how the survival of the species worked. That was the conclusion he arrived at in his very last film (*Cornouailles,* 1994) where, seeking to define the relationships that humans have with the land, he was confronted with the millenarian presence of the muskox in northern Quebec—yet another metaphor for the country and the survival of the human race. In this episode, the eternal silence of the onlooking muskoxen forced Perrault to fall back on his own voice and the poetic commentary that defined his first cinematic works.

Perrault's long, poetic, radiophonic, cinematic, and literary expedition led him from Île-aux-Coudres to Bretagne, from Acadia to Abitibi, and from the North Shore to northern Quebec. His journeys left to Quebec one of the most groundbreaking, contemporary, and compelling works of its time.

Questions for Critical Thinking

1. How has orality been a defining feature of Quebec cinema?
2. What has been the foremost aesthetic film style in Quebec cinema? Describe its characteristics.
3. Do you think that innovative aesthetics-based filmmaking has brought more to Quebec cinema than activist filmmaking?

Notes

1. Michèle Garneau studied this aspect of Quebec cinema in great depth in her doctoral dissertation: "Pour une esthétique du cinéma québécois" (Ph.D. diss., Université de Montréal, 1997).
2. I have studied this distinguishing feature of Quebec cinema in various publications, which have been summed up in the article "L'accent aigu du cinéma oral," in *Le cinéma au Québec : tradition et modernité,* ed. S.-A. Boulais (Montreal: Fides, 2006).
3. Quebec directors described direct cinema as a filmmaking technique that attempts to eliminate the distance between protagonists and spectators. Gilles Marsolais published the most authoritative study on direct cinema: *L'Aventure du cinéma direct revisitée* (Laval: Les 400 coups, 1974 and 1997).
4. Historian Yves Lever's book, *Histoire générale du cinéma au Québec,* first released in 1988 and re-edited in 1995, is an exhaustive reference. An excellent, more current, work has been produced by Bill Marshall, *Quebec National Cinema* (Montreal and Kingston: McGill-Queen's University Press, 2001).

5. The term *immigrant* is used here to describe Quebec filmmakers who were born in a foreign country and whose work is often reflective of their life experiences.
6. Although Biron's remarks pertain to Quebec literature, they ring just as true in the field of film. Germain Lacasse, *L'Historiographe : les débuts du cinématographe au Québec* (Montreal: Cinémathèque québécoise, 1984).
7. Journalists called the small film projection houses "scopes," taking their inspiration from the suffix of Léo-Ernest Ouimet's Ouimetoscope cinema.
8. Yves Lever, *Anastasie ou la censure du cinéma au Québec* (Montreal: Septentrion, 2008).
9. The papal encyclical *Vigilanti Cura* was published in June 1936 by Pope Pius XI.
10. René Bouchard, *Filmographie d'Albert Tessier* (Montreal: Boréal, 1973).
11. Marc-André Robert, *Dans la caméra de l'abbé Proulx* (Montreal: Septentrion, 2013).
12. Yves Lever, *J.A. De Sève : diffuseur d'images* (Montreal: Les éditions Michel Brûlé, 2008).
13. Gilles Marsolais describes the technique and spirit of direct cinema as follows: "As its name indicates, this kind of cinema captures live footage ('on the ground'—outside the studio), conversation, and gestures, using equipment (a camera and tape recorder) [that is] synchronous, light, and easy to handle, it is a cinema that establishes 'direct' contact with man, that tries to 'stick to what is real' as best it can (given that this entire enterprise requires mediation)." Gilles Marsolais, *L'aventure du cinéma direct* (Paris: Seghers, 1974), 22 (author's translation).
14. Scott Mackenzie, *Screening Québec: Québécois Moving Images, National Identity, and the Public Sphere* (Manchester: Manchester University Press, 2004), 149.
15. André Laurendeau, "L'Office national du film et les Canadiens français," *Le Devoir*, 24 February 1954, 4; "Les Canadiens français et l'Office national du film," *Le Devoir*, 17 February 1956, 4.
16. Anonymous (one of the "not well integrated" francophone employees), "La déclaration Lortie : un aveu I," *Le Devoir*, 6 March 1957; "La déclaration Lortie : un aveu II," *Le Devoir*, 7 March 1957.
17. Roger Champoux, "Notre équipe est excellente : donnons-lui totale liberté d'agir," *La Presse*, 4 April 1957 (author's translation).
18. Pierre Vigeant, "Blocs-notes : le limogeage de M. Roger Biais à l'ONF," *Le Devoir*, 4 April 1957.
19. Pierre Vigeant, *Le Devoir*, 23 April 1957.
20. Author's translation of the book title *Resistance and Self-Assertion*. Véronneau's book is available in French only on the Cinémathèque québécois website: http://collections.cinematheque.qc.ca/publications/les-dossiers-de-la-cinematheque/no17-resistance-et-affirmation-la-production-francophone-a-l-onf-1939-1964-histoire-du-cinema-du-quebec.
21. Gilles Marsolais, *Cinéma Québécois : de l'artisanat à l'industrie* (Montreal: Tryptique, 2011).
22. Bill Marshall, *Quebec National Cinema* (Montreal and Kingston: McGill-Queen's University Press, 2001), 283.
23. *Léolo* was screened at Cannes Classics in 2014 in a retrospective that highlighted Lauzon's originality and his place in history.
24. Marcel Jean, *Le cinéma québécois* (Montreal: Boréal, 1991), 104.
25. Malorie Beauchemin and Nathaëlle Morissette, "Doublage made in Québec : la riposte d'Hollywood redoutée," *La Presse*, 7 June 2007.
26. Jean-Pierre Sirois-Trahan, "Le mouvée et son dehors : renouveau du cinéma québécois," *Les Cahiers du cinema*, October 2010, 76–78.
27. Nicolas Bérubé, "Jacob Tierney : 'Les anglos et les immigrants sont ignorés,'" *La Presse*, 6 July 2010, accessed 9 February 2015, www.lapresse.ca/cinema/nouvelles/201207/17/01-4548729-jacob-tierney-les-anglos-et-les-immigrants-sont-ignores.php.
28. Les Films de l'Autre, "À propos," accessed 9 February 2015, http://lesfilmsdelautre.com/?page_id=5#.
29. Wapikoni Mobile films may be viewed at www.wapikoni.ca.
30. Our quotes and punctuation.
31. A reference to Renewal or "new-wave" filmmakers.
32. Simon Galiero, "Du cinéma d'auteur et du 'renouveau' dans le cinéma québécois," *Liberté* 299 (2013): 27–9. The title alludes to the Sirois-Trahan article quoted above; Galiero did the same in an interview published in *24 Images* 161 (2013), author's translation.

Select Bibliography

Alemany-Galway, Mary. "The New Québécois Cinema: Postmodernism and Globalization." *Nouvelles vues sur le cinéma québécois* 2 (2004). www.cinema-quebecois.net/edition2/hors_dossier_alemany_galway_b.htm.

Baby, François. "Pierre Perrault et la civilisation orale traditionnelle." In *Dialogue Cinéma canadien et Québécois*, edited by Michael Dorland et al. Montreal: Médiatexte Publications et Cinémathèque québécoise, 1993.

Bouchard, René. *Filmographie d'Albert Tessier*. Montreal: Boréal, 1978.

Bouchard, Vincent. *Pour un cinéma léger et synchrone! : invention d'un dispositif à l'Office national du film, à Montréal*. Villeneuve-d'Ascq (Nord): Presses universitaires du Septentrion, 2012.

Boulais, Stéphane-Albert, ed. *Le cinéma au Québec : tradition et modernité*. Montreal: Fides, 2006.

Carrière, Louise. *Femmes et cinéma québécois.* Montreal: Boréal, 1983.

Chabot, Claude, et al. *Le cinéma québécois des années 1980.* Montréal: Cinémathèque québécoise, 1989.

CinémAction, No. 40. *"Aujourd'hui le cinéma Québécois."* Paris and Montreal: Cerf/OFQ, 1986.

Collectif. "Imaginaires du cinéma Québécois." *Revue belge du cinéma* 27, Bruxelles, 1989.

Cornellier, Bruno, ed. "Parole, culture orale et cinéma Québécois." *Nouvelles vues* 1 (Winter 2004). http://cinema-quebecois.net/01_hiver_2004/accueil.html.

Coulombe, Michel, and Marcel Jean. *Dictionnaire du cinéma Québécois.* Montreal: Boréal, 2006.

Denault, Jocelyne. *Dans l'ombre des projecteurs : les québécoises et le cinema.* Sainte-Foy: Presses de l'Université du Québec, 1996.

Dérives, No. 52. *"Cinéma québécois, nouveaux courants, nouvelles critiques."* Montreal: 1986.

Fournier-Renaud, Madeleine, and Pierre Véronneau. *Écrits sur le cinéma : bibliographie québécoise 1911–1981.* Montreal: Cinémathèque québécoise, 1982.

Froger, Marion. *Le cinema à l'épreuve de la communauté : le cinéma francophone de l'Office national du film 1960–1985.* Montreal: Presses de l'Université de Montréal, 2010.

Garel, Sylvain, and André Paquet, eds. *Les cinémas du Canada.* Paris: Centre Georges Pompidou, 1992.

Garneau, Michèle. "Pour une esthétique du cinéma Québécois." Ph.D. diss., Université de Montréal, 1997. wwwlib.umi.com/cr/umontreal/fullcit?pNQ35591.

Green, Mary Jean. "Towards Defining a Postcolonial Quebec Cinema: The Films of Claude Jutra." *Québec Studies* (Spring 2003): 1–13.

Helfield, Gillian. "I'y ava't un' fois (Once Upon a Time): Films as Folktales in Québécois Cinéma Direct," In *Folklore/Cinema: Popular Film as Vernacular Culture,* edited by Sharon Sherman and Mikel Koven. Logan: Utah State University Press, 2007.

Jean, Marcel. *Le cinéma québécois.* Montreal: Boréal, 1991.

Lacasse, Germain. *Le bonimenteur de vues animées : le cinéma "muet" entre tradition et modernité.* Québec and Paris: Nota bene et Méridiens Klincksieck, 2000.

———. "Le cinéma oral au Québec." In *Le cinéma au Québec : tradition et modernité,* edited by S.-A Boulais. Montreal: Fides, 2006.

———. *Histoires de scopes : le cinéma muet au Québec.* Montreal: Cinémathèque québécoise, 1988.

———, J. Massé, and B. Poirier. *Le diable en ville : Alexandre Silvio et l'émergence de la modernité populaire au Québec.* Montreal: Presses de l'Université de Montréal, 2012.

Lever, Yves. *Histoire générale du cinéma au Québec.* Montreal: Boréal, 1988.

Mackenzie, Scott. *Screening Québec: Québécois Moving Images, National Identity, and the Public Sphere.* Manchester: Manchester University Press, 2004.

Marshall, Bill. *Quebec National Cinema.* Montreal and Kingston: McGill-Queen's University Press, 2001.

Marsolais, Gilles. *L'aventure du cinéma direct.* Paris: Seghers, 1974; new edition, 2002.

Noguez, Dominique. *Essais sur le cinéma québécois.* Montreal: Éditions du jour, 1971.

Poirier, Christian. *Le cinéma Québécois : à la recherche d'une identité?* Sainte-Foy: Presses de l'Université du Québec, 2004.

Scheppler, Gwenn. "Je suis le premier spectateur : l'œuvre de Pierre Perrault ou le cinéma comme processus." Ph.D. diss., Université de Montréal, 2009.

Tremblay-Daviault, Christiane. *Un cinéma orphelin : structures mentales et sociales du cinéma québécois 1942–1953.* Montreal: Québec Amérique, 1981.

Véronneau, Pierre. *Histoire du cinéma au Québec II : cinéma de l'époque duplessiste.* Montreal: Cinémathèque québécoise, 1979.

Warren, Paul. *Pierre Perrault, cinéaste-poète.* Montreal: L'Hexagone, 1999.

Weinmann, Heinz. *Cinéma de l'imaginaire québécois, de la petite Aurore à Jésus de Montréal.* Montreal: L'Hexagone, 1990.

8

Sport and Identities in Quebec

Andrew C. Holman, Bridgewater State University

Timeline

1807 The Montreal Curling Club is founded by Scottish merchants and soldiers. The Quebec Curling Club is founded in 1821.

1856 Formation of the Montreal Lacrosse Club by English-speaking bourgeois, including Dr. George Beers, a founder of the National Lacrosse Association of Canada (1867) and the author of *Lacrosse: The National Game of Canada* (1869). The first francophone lacrosse club was le Champlain de Québec, founded in 1868.

1875 First recorded indoor hockey match is played at the Victoria Skating Rink in Montreal. Two years later the rules of the game are codified when they are published in the *Montreal Gazette*.

1881 The Montreal Amateur Athletic Association is founded and is the first multi-sport organization in the country. Until World War I, it is the most important institution of its sort in Canada.

1894 Foundation of l'Association athlétique d'amateurs nationale to promote sports for French-Canadian youth. The group constructs a sports centre that opens its doors on 12 December 1918 under the name Palestre Nationale.

1909 Founding of the Canadiens Hockey Club representing francophone Montreal. The only original member of the National Hockey League (1917) still in existence, it holds a record of 24 Stanley Cup championships.

1944 Suzanne Thouin is the first French Canadian to win the Canadian Junior Ladies' Figure Skating Championship.

1955 On March 17, the crowd at the Montreal Forum riots to protest NHL President Clarence Campbell's banning of Maurice Richard for punching a referee in a mélee in an earlier game against Boston. The event ends when Richard, in a statement made by radio, calls for calm. Richard scored 544 goals in 978 NHL games and led the league in scoring in five seasons over an 18-year career.

1968 Montreal obtains a Major League Baseball franchise, the Expos, named in honour of the World Exposition that the city hosted in 1967. The team plays its first game in Jarry Park against the St. Louis Cardinals on 14 April 1969 and moves to the Olympic Stadium in 1977. The franchise moved to Washington, DC, in 2005.

1976 Montreal hosts the XXI Summer Olympic Games, which includes 92 nations and 6,084 athletes competing in 21 sports. The event prompted Montreal to construct several world-class sporting venues, including the Olympic Stadium, the Velodrome (now repurposed as the Biodome), and the Claude Robillard Centre.

1992 Sylvie Fréchette wins the first of her two Olympic medals in synchronized swimming, a gold in Barcelona and a silver in Atlanta in 1996.

1999 After only four seasons of competition, the Rouge et Or from l'Université Laval is the first francophone university football team to win the Vanier Cup, the Canadian intercollegiate championship.

Introduction

Few cultural activities in the modern Western world have the ability to express identity with the strength and raw emotion of organized sports. For both athletes and followers, sports invite (and sometimes insist upon) allegiance, the taking of sides. Who are we for? Who are we against? And by extension, who are we? For many, sports have been a means of creating a sense of self since they were children; over time, simple play became infused with the messages and the meanings of modern civic life. Sport is more than child's play, a pastime, or empty games. Sport matters. As a generation of social scientists have argued, sport reflects modern society's triumphs and ills and reveals the often divisive relationships between its constituent parts. Sport can be a vehicle for community and consensus, but just as often it creates and broadens the social fissures—race, social class, gender, nation, and others—that keep us apart.

It is more than a little surprising, then, that scholars of Quebec—a society preoccupied with questions about selfhood—had for so long given so little attention to the role that sport has played in articulating identities there. "Québécois historians, and especially university professors," Université du Québec à Montréal scholar Gilles Janson wrote in 2003, "consider the subject trivial and unworthy of interest."[1] Janson could not make that claim so strongly today; in the past 10 years scholars have begun to look upon sport more seriously as a meaningful window on Quebec questions. Sport is now visible in growing numbers of scholarly books and journal articles on university library shelves and on the syllabuses of university and college courses.

This chapter examines aspects of the history of sport in Quebec, from its origins as a series of anglo-elite gentlemanly pastimes to its place as a vector for national affirmation among francophones and others in the province. The chapter shows that sport has been implicated in the turbulent political culture of Quebec since the mid-nineteenth century. Sport has been a site where the interests of Quebec's First Nations, anglophone, francophone, and immigrant communities have been articulated—sometimes in consensus, sometimes in conflict. Sport reflects the complex ethnic history and cultural present of the province. In Quebec, sport is at once a catalyst, a proxy, and a mirror for the national question.

Sport in Quebec Today

First, some definition is in order. When we refer to modern sport, we are talking about those activities that, as American sport historian Steven Riess has it, are "competitive contests governed by customs or rules that require physical activity and skills."[2] Though the ancestors of Quebecers have for centuries engaged in physical activities that derived from life in a rough, rural, settler society—hunting, fishing, equestrian events, and blood sports[3]—what concerns us in this chapter are organized sporting events that accompanied the rise of urban, industrial society. In these modern sports, athletes compete against themselves, other individuals, a standing record, or as members of teams. Included are those who compete as amateurs for their own pleasure and professionals who perform sport for compensation and the advancement of a business.

Like their neighbours across North America, Quebecers compete in a wide variety of sports at all levels—from youth house leagues to elite, high-performance competitions to adult recreation "ligues de has-beens." Today, the province is home to three big-league professional franchises (Major League Soccer's Montreal Impact, the National Hockey League's Montreal Canadiens, and the Canadian Football League's Montreal Alouettes) and one minor-professional baseball team (Quebec City's Capitales).[4] Quebec is home to a universe of amateur competitors, organized and governed by Sports-Québec, a private nonprofit federation of 62 provincial sport organizations (PSOs) that range from badminton to water polo. The federation runs the annual Quebec Games, a 40-year-old multisport festival that gathers the province's budding sportsmen and women. It provides athletic scholarships and promotes elite athletes in their competitions in the rest of Canada and abroad. The bulk of Sports-Québec's generous funding comes from the state: In 2011–12 the government of Quebec spent more than $65 million to develop "sports excellence."[5] Here, competitive sport is supported at an impressively high level—higher, athletic officials and politicians in the province are fond of acknowledging, than in any other Canadian province. Success has been the result. In Canada's entry to the 2012 Summer Olympic Games in London, for example, Quebec athletes composed 24 per cent of the country's delegation and were among the nation's highest achievers.[6] And in collegiate sport, Quebec universities and CEGEPs rank among the best nationally in a wide variety of men's and women's activities. Sport is a vibrant part of Quebec's cultural fabric, a means of collective expression and a symbol of a modernizing nation.

CASE STUDY

Francophone Football's Not-so-Quiet Revolution

Following a decisive 33–7 playoff loss to Université Laval in early November 2011, Gerry McGrath, the football coach at Montreal's anglophone Concordia University, strayed uncharacteristically from the sort of benign postgame responses that sportsmen normally give to media questions. For McGrath, his team's defeat (its seventh straight loss to the Rouge et Or) was predictable—the field was deplorably tilted against his Stingers. "Everywhere you turn (Laval, Montréal, and Sherbrooke) have a huge advantage in resources, facilities, financially, and geographically (for recruiting purposes)," McGrath told the *Montreal Gazette*. "And I don't know if we share the same values."[7]

McGrath's concern referred not just to the mercurial rise of competitive football teams among francophone universities in Quebec, but to the *way* they rose to success. From the birth of Canadian "rugby football" at McGill University in 1874 until 1996, Quebec university football had been strictly an affair among anglophone students and the smattering of francophones who gravitated to McGill, Concordia, and Bishop's to play the game. But in 1996 Laval took up football with purpose and a unique funding structure: a $2 million budget administered by a private-sector corporate body that functions at arm's length from the school and dwarfs its competitors in its ability to raise money, recruit players, and distribute scholarships. Similar structures were established at both Montréal and Sherbrooke, which now provide francophone athletes with robust programs in their own language.

continued

The results have been stunningly impressive—between 1996 and 2013, Laval has won its conference 12 times (nine straight since 2005) and the national championship Vanier Cup eight times. For their part, the Carabins of Université de Montréal were not far behind, posting winning records in 10 of the 12 seasons since their inauguration in 2002, one conference title, and in 2014 a Vanier Cup national championship.[8] "The average football program in Canada has two or three coaches and a budget of about $400,000," former University of Western Ontario football coach and athletic director Darwin Semotiuk complained about Laval in 2009. "How do you expect people to compete with a team that is spending four or five times that amount?"[9]

Even in the world of sports, talk about "values" and fairness in twenty-first-century Quebec touches sensitive nerves and stirs up centuries-old antagonisms. It did not take long for francophone critics to respond to McGrath's lament. It rang hollow to some that anglophones might complain about the situation given the monopoly they held on university football for so long. In a province that is 85 per cent French-speaking, the emergence of francophone football should be celebrated, not denigrated, according to one long letter that two Quebec football fans wrote to Quebec City's *Le Soleil:* "As Maurice Richard made professional hockey change in his day, football has required a figure of French prowess to end the English stranglehold on Québec university football. Rouge et Or football has become that guide." Now, they continued, "young French-speaking university students from places such as St-Michel-de-Bellechasse, Québec, La Tuque, Saint-Flavie, Lévis, L'Islet [and] Brossard" play the game. To lament that development is at best bad faith and at worst "*presque raciste*." Perhaps, these fans argued, the anglophone schools should consider cutting one of their programs to better fit the demographic reality and a new era of Quebec football that is here to stay.[10]

Victorian Origins: Gentlemanly Sport

Quebec sport is marked today by francophone direction and state support, but its origins were considerably different. Organized sport got its start in the mid-nineteenth-century private clubs of elite anglophone Montreal. Victorian Montreal was host to Canada's first industrial revolution, a process that expanded the city's working class impressively and created a new white-collar stratum of managers, bankers, professionals, and others who had enough expendable income, leisure time, and the need for "rational recreation": spirited competitive sports that could test their mettle and teach the allegedly Protestant moral values of self-control and fair play. Here the first sports that drew popular support were themselves British imports—curling, cricket, soccer, rugby, and golf—the "garrison games," whose origins carried with them the political stamp of empire. In 1807, anglophone merchants established the Montreal Curling Club, a cricket club in 1829, and the Royal Montreal Golf Club in 1873.

But by the 1860s anglophone sportsmen in Montreal had begun to move away from that inheritance. Whether sportsmen of the era recognized it or not, their move constituted a sort of "sporting declaration of independence"—a sign that (on the playing fields anyway) these Canadians wished to keep British influence at arm's length and establish new, *continental* identities. For some, doing so meant embracing the game that had become an American obsession—baseball; in Montreal, a total of 21 different teams swung the bat as early as 1887.[11] But for many others, that meant appropriating First Nations activities and remaking them as proper, orderly, gentlemanly (and white) pursuits: snowshoeing, lacrosse, and hockey—sports that became quintessential *Canadian* sports. Members of the Montreal Snow Shoe Club formally coalesced in 1843, identifiable by the blue woolen toques they chose to adorn their heads. Organized hockey, heir to a variety of ball and stick games including those played by Aboriginals in Canada, was first played in 1870 at McGill University, but most conspicuously in 1875 when a *Montreal Gazette* reporter recorded the game organized by James Creighton and a cohort of young anglophone professionals and McGill students on the Victoria Skating Rink. Two years later the same newspaper made Creighton's game *the* game of hockey by publishing his version of its rules.[12] By the mid-1880s the Montreal game gave rise to the Amateur Hockey Association of Canada (1886), whose players after 1893 competed for the Dominion Championship: the Stanley Cup.[13] But it was lacrosse that captured this appropriation most vividly. Bourgeois Montrealers formed a Montreal Lacrosse Club (MLC) in 1856, and the sport quickly caught fire. When the National Lacrosse Association was formed in that city in 1867, there were 15 playing clubs; that number turned into 56 by 1893. In 1869, Montreal dentist George Beers, a goaltender for the MLC, published a thick manual on the sport that declared it "Canada's National Game"—and the label stuck. In all of this, as historian Gillian Poulter notes, anglophone white lacrosse players imposed order and gentlemanly virtue on the First Nations game, "appropriating and secularizing what had been a significant aboriginal ritual" and making it (and themselves) "Canadian."[14] While Aboriginal players continued to practise the rituals of and play the "indigenous game" in Haudenosaunee communities south and west of Montreal, by the 1880s the white version of the game had almost fully eclipsed its Aboriginal forebear in the popular press.[15]

Lacrosse team, Montreal, QC, 1878 (Notman & Sandham). © McCord Museum

By the 1880s anglophone sports clubs in Montreal were thick on the ground. In 1871, 42 sports clubs played 10 different sports. But by 1887, 142 clubs were playing 17 different sports, and by 1894, 294 were playing 23 sports.[16] The highlight of the winter sporting season was the Montreal Winter Carnival, 1883–9, an annual week-long celebration of Quebec's nordicity that presented fancy skating, tobogganing, snowshoe "tramps," and a hockey tournament to thousands of spectators, many of them from Europe and the United States.[17] Organizationally, ground zero within the city was the Montreal Amateur Athletic Association (MAAA), a multisport governing body whose members paid annual fees and bound themselves together with a formal constitution and a code of ethics that required all its athletes to remain amateur always and in every sport and to never compete against professionals. The MAAA was the most powerful sporting organization in all of Canada until the Athletic War of 1906–9 augured the demise of amateur ideal in sports and undermined the MAAA's mission. For more than half a century, the **amateur ideal** reigned in Montreal. Only the Shamrocks, lacrosse and hockey teams composed of Irish-origin working-class Montrealers, whose aggressiveness on the field and rink, willingness to play for pay, and remarkable success on the field and ice challenged the bourgeois code of sport for sport's sake.[18]

"Emparons-Nous du Sport": French-Canadian Clubs Take Hold

If the impetus for organized sport in Quebec had its genesis in the anglophone circles of friends and associates in Montreal business offices and clubs and among students at McGill, it did not remain there exclusively for very long. French-Canadian sporting clubs first appeared in dribs and drabs in the middle decades of the nineteenth century: Montreal showshoeing clubs Le Trappeur and Le Canadien, for example, and the Champlain Lacrosse Club of Quebec, founded in 1868 to compete against anglophone and First Nations teams. Still, before 1890 French-Canadian sport was, as Janson writes, "un phénomène marginale,"[19] conditioned by the inaccessible nature of anglophone clubs, the expense of sporting equipment, and the fear circulated by some francophone Roman Catholic clergy that sport might lead to assimilation or cultural contamination and thus risk Catholic morality and modesty.[20]

In the following decade, sport began to shed its bourgeois character in cities across Canada and become a mass phenomenon and sank its roots more deeply in francophone Quebec. Now, after some trial and error, petit bourgeois Montrealers established a lasting federation of francophone sport clubs, placing organized sport on a permanent footing in French-Canadian culture. The first attempts to establish francophone sport federations were modelled on the athletic unions in France. In Montreal, the Association nationale de gymnastique du Canada took form in 1892, seeking to unite French-Canadian lacrosse, showshoeing, target shooting, gymnastics, fencing, and other clubs numbering between 400–500 members. But it soon failed for want of funding and insufficient patronage, and because of the tendency for its members to trickle away to anglophone clubs. Similar fates met the École nationale de gymnastique et d'art militaire and the Association athlètique d'amateurs Canadiens-Français (AAAC-F), both of which were organized in Montreal in the early 1890s, the latter done so avowedly to rival the MAAA along ethnic lines. If nothing else, these false starts succeeded in cultivating interest and laying the seed. In 1894 that spirit took root in the Association athlètique d'amateurs Le National (AAAN), the first permanent multisport francophone governing body in the province that gathered together a variety of clubs (cycling, gymnastics, baseball, croquet, lacrosse, handball, hockey, and others) and even opened its door to women. "The first goal of the National was patriotic," writes Janson. Though initially it struggled financially, by 1918 its members had succeeded in building a handsome clubhouse, which took on the name Palestre Nationale, a label that stuck to it until the club ceased all of its activities in 1978.

In the same decade that gave rise to multisport francophone organizations such as the AAAC-F and the AAAN, French-language sport journalism emerged as well, both the inspiration and the product of a new sporting enthusiasm among French Canadians. The first of the these publications, the *Courrier Athlètique*, appeared in August 1892, and shortly thereafter sports columns appeared in the French-language newspapers *La Presse* and *La Patrie*. "**Emparons-nous du sport**" became the *cri de coeur* among sports journals and organizers.[21] Perhaps the most vibrant (if short lived) of these periodicals was *Le Sport Illustré*, which lasted only six issues in 1899 but loudly contradicted the prevailing impression that athletics was the dominion of anglophone sportsmen. French Canadians, editor A. Marion declared, were Canada's first athletes. "As if *la raquette*, before becoming the snowshoe that today the English clubs put on to do the sporty tour of the Mountain here, this winter, had not carried our fathers ten times to the conquest of Hudson Bay!"[22] (see the Primary Source box). The successes of the AAAN's senior lacrosse and hockey teams emboldened AAAN President François-Xavier Dupuis to claim at the club's annual banquet in 1895: "Everything indicates that French Canadians are in matters of sport, as in all other spheres of human activity, not inferior to other races."[23] In their bombast, francophone editors and club organizers wished to develop French-Canadian patriotism, and they saw rivalry with anglophone sportsmen as a means to an end. In reality, co-operation among English- and

Primary Source

The Prospectus of *Le Sport Illustré*

Le Sport Illustré is more than sport reported; it is sport in action, it is sport by example, it is almost sport triumphant.

What obstacles, what prejudices it had to overcome in Canada . . . It hasn't been our position to say that sport was an English institution; that those among our compatriots whom it has been able to support blushed at their French ancestry.

As if the French regime in Canada had not itself been a sporting epic registered in the records at Boston, at Detroit and throughout the entire course of the Mississippi to New Orleans!

As if there had never been in Manitoba and throughout the Northwest a race of Métis, claiming by its very existence, and especially by its language, that it was born of a race of *coureurs de plaines*, as French as they were sportsmen.

As if *la raquette*, before becoming the snowshoe that today the English clubs put on to do the sporty tour of the Mountain . . . had not carried our fathers ten times to the conquest of Hudson Bay!

As if the industrial sport of timber rafting on the tributaries of the Ottawa and onto the rivers of Michigan were not done almost exclusively by people who speak French! . . .

As if the 65th, in its long marches to the Northwest, had to borrow an idiom other than their own to sing the sporting songs that led them to victory at Frenchman's Butte.

As if lacrosse, so long the sceptre of the English sports royalty in our country, was not a French game brought here by Champlain!

As if the National had to renounce some article of its religious or patriotic faith in order to snatch from the English clubs this past year the champion's title they held for many years.

As if the Montferrands, Duchênes, Merciers, Laberges, Vincents, Beaudrys, Pichés, Cyrs, Barrés, had not on any occasion, in their respective sports, paid homage to their national family through the successes they achieved, either in Montreal, on the Ottawa, on the Yukon!

It is finished . . . finished forever, this tradition . . . we allowed to grow around the French name . . . while we, sons of the discoverers, conquerors and colonizers of this country, were reduced to watching the sports frolicking among the other races over the fences of their exercise fields.

It is finished, thanks to these snowshoeing, fencing, tobogganing, rowing, swimming, lacrosse, shooting, baseball, fishing and hunting clubs, which have given rise in our province, in recent years, a patriotic initiative to many a fellow.

. . . It is finished, thanks above all to the wide publicity that our daily newspapers have given to sport in general and most particularly to the athletic games that, renewed from ancient Greece, modified with Christian mores, are still the most powerful factor of national vigour.

. . . [O]ur journal . . . will be [the movement's] indefatigable propagator. In this role . . . the "Sport Illustré" will . . . reclaim [for French Canadians] the honour of the right to march at the head of the troops of the first line, sound the charge, bugle in one hand and sword in the other.

The Editor

Source: A. Marion, "Prospectus," *Le Sport Illustré* 1, no. 1 (10 June 1899): 2

French-speaking sportsmen in these years was more characteristic. In hockey, historian Michel Vigneault argues that French Canadians first entered the game in the 1890s in Montreal with the support of Irish-Catholic students who studied and played together at the same classical colleges.[24]

By the start of the twentieth century, the closed, robust world of Montreal sport had started to open and expand. First, sport spread beyond its urban, Anglo confines to all parts of the province, where it animated and enthralled the masses. Though, as sports journalists loudly proclaimed, sport had long existed in nascent form across the province, it pervaded Quebec society by the 1940s and 1950s, spread through municipalities and local businesses that sponsored teams and clinics, and especially after 1930 through the Church-run *Oeuvres des patronages* (or *patros*, youth clubs) and *Oeuvres des terrains de jeux*, (OTJs, playground organizations) that dotted the province. "OTJs were the agencies that had the greatest influence on organized sport in Quebec," Jean Harvey writes. They were the places where generations of francophone children first learned sports such as hockey, baseball, and swimming.[25]

Sport crossed gender lines, too. Born as an expression of manly virtue, sport in Quebec, as elsewhere, gradually became embraced by women (to the objection of clergymen and lay moralists everywhere, and in the face of what contemporaries felt was a special bias against women's athletics in Quebec). Though ladies' golf clubs had been established at Quebec and Montreal as early as 1892, and women's hockey clubs in Trois-Rivières, Montreal, Lachute, and Quebec City in the 1900s, it took until the 1930s and 1940s for Quebec women to make their mark outside the province. And they did, for example, in the feats of St Lawrence River distance swimmer Daisy King Shaw (1928); pedestrian Mlle L. Gallipeau (10-mile race, 1929), sprinter Hilda Strike (1932 Olympic relay silver medallist), and figure skater Suzanne Thouin (National Junior Champion, 1944).[26] Still, before the 1970s women athletes received little systemic support and even less coverage in the Quebec newspapers.

Hockey: *Pas Comme Les Autres*

One mark of the early history of sport in Quebec was its ubiquity: Quebecers organized, played, watched, and reported on a wide variety of athletic events. By the 1890s, however, one sport eclipsed all others (and continues to do so today). Birthed and raised in Montreal, hockey has been invested with special meaning for Quebecers, and the locus of this obsession is the Montreal Canadiens. From the club's creation in 1909 until at least the 1980s, the Montreal Canadiens professional hockey club was a metonym for Quebec and an emblem for French-Canadian culture within Canada. "Qu'est que c'est le Canadien de Montreal?" sport sociologist Fannie Valois-Nadeau asks in a recent essay: "A team, a business, a cult object, a collective memory and an inheritance. Perhaps a bit of all of these."[27] To these, theologian Olivier Bauer adds: "a religion."[28] Generations of scholars and journalists have written a great deal about the sociopolitical basis for the Canadiens' historical popularity within Quebec. Not only were the Canadiens perennially competitive during the 1920s to the 1970s, but they featured French-Canadian stars in whom ordinary spectators could see themselves: Georges Vézina in the 1920s, Aurèle Joliat in the 1930s, Émile Bouchard, Bernard Geoffrion, Jean Béliveau, Henri Richard, Guy Lafleur, and others in the 1940s, 1950s, 1960s, and 1970s. By the 1920s, the exploits of the Canadiens were delivered to households across Quebec via radio and, after 1952, through the miracle of television, where the dulcet tones of announcer René Lecavalier described the team's every play on the popular show *Soirée du Hockey*, broadcast on Saturday nights. The appeal of the Canadiens and their French-Canadian players rested also in the economic context of the times. In the years before the Quiet Revolution, when Quebec's economy was dominated by Anglo-Canadian and American capitalists, French Quebecers saw themselves as an economic underclass, "hewers of wood and drawers of water" for the strangers whose English-speaking businesses ran the province. French Canadians found it difficult to advance in this economy, to win—but on the ice, at least symbolically, their fortunes fared better. The Canadiens carried the hopes of the Québecois nation, and when they were victorious so too were all Quebecers.

The star that shone brightest was Maurice "Rocket" Richard, a feisty and determined skater who played 18 seasons in the NHL, leading it in goal scoring for five of them. His play was so central to the Canadiens' success that he was routinely targeted by other teams, taunted verbally with racist slurs, and physically fouled. A spirited player, he often responded to these trespasses with anger and on-ice violence, a trait that landed him in hot water with the NHL league office and its president, Clarence Campbell. But it also deepened the sense of persecution that French Canadians felt for and through him. A national hero in Quebec, he is celebrated in statuary and popular literature, not least in the universally known children's story *Le Chandail* (*The Hockey Sweater*) by Roch Carrier, in which all the hockey-playing children in his town wore Canadiens uniforms emblazoned with the famous number 9: "we were five Maurice Richards taking [the puck] away from five other Maurice Richards."[29] In 1996, when the Canadiens held an elaborate ceremony to close down their home rink, the 70-year-old Montreal Forum, Richard was the last among a parade of players to be announced to the home crowd, who greeted him with a 15-minute standing ovation that ended only when the Rocket, embarrassed at his fame, repeatedly asked them to stop. When he died in 2000, the province staged a state funeral for him, and 115,000 mourners filed past his coffin on display in the Bell Centre, the successor of the Forum.[30]

Richard generated many vivid memories for the Canadiens' faithful at the Forum, but one of the most recounted involved a game in which he didn't play at all. It has become known as the **Richard Riot**. On 13 March 1955, the Rocket was cut on the head by a high stick from a Bruins player in a game at the Boston Garden. In the heat of the moment (and in the wake of verbal and physical abuse), Richard snapped. When a linesman attempted to restrain him, Richard punched the official, committing one of hockey's few cardinal offences. Richard was ejected from the game, but the real contention came days later. After interviewing the principals involved in the altercation, Campbell banned Richard for the remainder of the 1954–5 NHL season as well as the playoffs. The decision set off a welter of protest, particularly among French-speaking Montrealers, who interpreted the decision as yet another racist insult to the French-Canadian people and their hero. Two days later, on 17 March, the intrepid Campbell proceeded to his regular seat in the Forum midway through the first period of the Canadiens game against the Red Wings. It did not take long for events to erupt. Once identified by the partisan crowd, Campbell was first booed, then pelted with eggs and tomatoes and shoved. Shortly thereafter an irate fan set off a tear-gas bomb, causing the Montreal fire chief to evacuate the building and end the game. But the mob was not finished. Demonstrators took to the streets for hours outside the Forum, smashing store windows, looting, overturning cars, and chanting "*À bas Campbell.*" The Richard Riot resulted in $100,000 in damages and the arrest of dozens of the Rocket's supporters.[31] The dust settled only when Richard took to the airwaves to make a public plea for a return to order. But the anger—with Campbell, with the NHL, and more generally with the Anglocentric economic system (and its political allies in the government and the Church in Maurice Duplessis's Quebec) that conspired to keep ordinary Quebecers "down on the farm" remained and festered. Historians see *l'Affaire Richard*, like the Asbestos Strike of 1949, as a harbinger of the end of an era called the Great Darkness and the coming of a Quiet Revolution that, after 1960, ushered in a new, more urgent self-awareness and confidence among Quebecers determined to become "*maîtres chez nous.*"[32]

The Quiet Revolution and the New Politics of Sport

It is no coincidence, perhaps, that Quebec sport's own great awakening happened even as the whole province underwent the considerable economic, political, ideological, and social changes that historians call the Quiet Revolution, a sweeping transformation defined by a new territorial nationalism, a desire to secularize

Montreal Canadiens Maurice Rocket Richard (9) victorious with teammate Bernie "Boom Boom" Geoffrion (5) after scoring a goal against the Toronto Maple Leafs, 17 November 1954. Getty/Hy Peskin

the public sphere, the elevation of the French language, and the use of the provincial state to support francophone enterprise and social mobility. Sport reflected this grand change and was one of its many cultural beneficiaries. In sports the change was visible in two dramatic ways.

First, in the 1970s and 1980s the levers of control over sports organizations (many of them creations of Anglo-Montrealers) increasingly fell into the hands of francophone Quebecers. **Francization** took hold of organized sport as it did other realms of Quebec public life. In 1963, 52 per cent of Quebec sports clubs were francophone affairs, but by 1973 that number had risen to 80 per cent, four years before Bill 101 redrew linguistic power relations in the province. Moreover, francophone athletes stepped out of the shadows and into the foreground in the 1960s, 1970s, and 1980s. At the 1928 Olympic Games in Amsterdam (summer) and St Moritz (winter), the names of Quebec medallists were distinctly Anglo sounding: Philip Aaron Edwards, Alexander S. Wilson, Walter Spence, Maurice E. Letchford, and Donald Stockton. Sixty-four years later, the names of Quebec medallists at Barcelona and Albertville had a more Gallic ring: Guillaume Leblanc, Sylvie Fréchette, Isabelle Brasseur, Frédérick Blackburn, Sylvie Daigle, Laurent Daignault, Sylvain Gagnon, Nathalie Lambert, and Annie Perreault, among others.[33] As in so many other realms, French became the *lingua franca* of the sports field, rink, and court.

Second, the provincial state gradually came to see sport as worthy of support and cultivation. Before 1950, historian Jocelyn East tells us, government interventions into sport were virtually non-existent, save for the ephemeral Provincial Sports Council, created in 1939. But by the 1960s and 1970s, the massive expansion of the state (in health, education, and welfare) spurred the co-option of organized sport. Quebec governments began to look upon physical education, fitness, and sport as important civic virtues and avenues toward modernization. Sport became secularized and a recognized part of the services that should be provided by a modern welfare state. On the local level, recreation programs run by municipal governments and professionally trained physical educators gradually elbowed out Church-run sports programs. Provincially, the government created the Office of Leisure and Sport in 1964 (a portfolio raised in 1980 to the level of a ministry), and in 1968 a Commission on Youth, Leisure, and Sport was enacted, whose report resulted in the creation of the Confédération des sports du Québec (later renamed Sports-Québec), with a budget that by 1975 had grown to $1.9 million.[34] The era of the Quiet Revolution, Jean Harvey and Lucie Thibault write, was the "apogee" of provincial sponsorship, the outcome of a transition in sport from private- and church-based organization before the 1960s to state-based locus that has been in place ever since.[35]

Une Équipe Nationale?

"Like participation in world's fairs, the possession of a flag and anthem, and the sending of diplomatic representatives abroad," historian Barbara Fields tells us, "sport . . . shape[s] the form and images of nations as they enter the international order."[36] In Quebec, the Quiet Revolution's impetus to project Quebec into the world had an unmistakable effect on sport. Quebec's awakening involved a push by the government to promote and expand an international personality of its own, one distinct from Canada. Acting upon a doctrine first asserted in 1965 by Education Minister Paul Gérin-Lajoie, Quebec began to sign international education and cultural agreements (within the province's constitutionally assigned jurisdiction) with foreign nations and established its own delegations in several foreign capitals and commercially important cities.[37] Sport was implicated in this agenda.

In a way, sport has already for some time been an unofficial means of projecting Quebec internationally, and athletes its de facto diplomats: When Quebecers compete abroad (and especially when they succeed), "Quebec" is projected, even when the team uniform says something else. This sort of representation was true for four-time Olympic speed skating medallist Gaétan Boucher; world champion and two-time Olympic gold medallist in biathlon Myriam Bédard; figure skaters Joannie Rochette, Isabelle Brasseur, David Pelletier, and Josée Chouinard; cyclist and cross-country skier Pierre Harvey; Major League Baseball pitcher and Cy Young Award winner Eric Gagné; motorcar racers Gilles Villeneuve (1950–1982) and Jacques Villeneuve; and divers Sylvie Bernier and Alexandre Despatie, among others.

But alongside this sort of representation there has emerged since the 1970s a repeated call for a formal

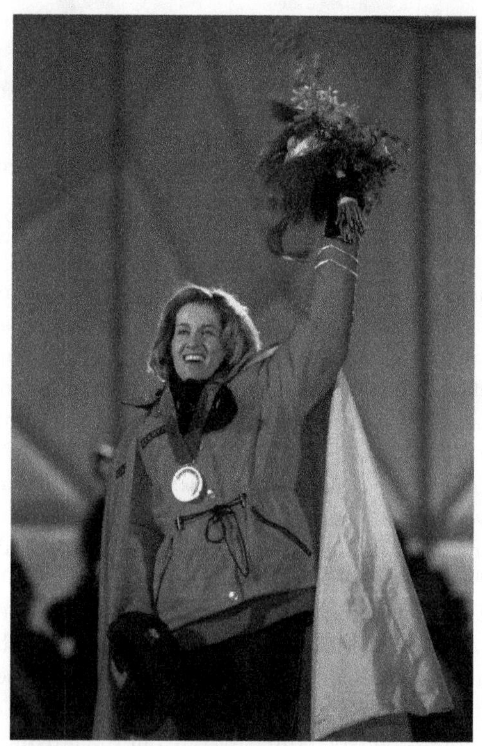

Myriam Bédard receives the gold medal for the women's 7.5-kilometre biathlon at the 1994 Lillehammer Winter Olympics. Getty/Clive Brunskill

BIOGRAPHY

Myriam Bédard and the Politics of International Sport

International athletes never ask to become cultural diplomats; they are assigned that role, whether they like it or not. Fans and journalists stamp their heroes with the maple leaf and the fleur-de-lis. For Quebec's international athletes, this creates an uncomfortable duality. Perhaps the most telling example of this involves Olympic hero Myriam Bédard, whose unexpected success in the early 1990s in a nontraditional Canadian sport, biathlon, brought her into public prominence.

Born near Quebec City in 1969, Bédard was a gifted athlete from an early age. She was naturally adept on skis and, at age 15, became a cadet with the Canadian Armed Forces and learned the skills of a sharpshooter. She quickly achieved success, winning a junior national title in biathlon in 1987. That same year she joined Canada's national biathlon team, on which she remained until 1998. Bédard's star shone brightest in the early 1990s, when she won medals in the Biathlon World Cup events in 1991 and 1993, but especially for her bronze medal in the 15-kilometre biathlon at the Winter Olympics in Albertville, France, and her two gold medals (in 7.5-kilometre and 15-kilometre events) two years later at the Lillehammer Games. In 1994 she was awarded the Lou Marsh Trophy as Canada's Sportsperson of the Year. She was inducted into Canada's Sports Hall of Fame in 1998, the first biathlete to achieve that honour.[38] "In Quebec," the *Montreal Gazette* noted in 2007, "Bédard was for more than a decade viewed as a female Maurice Richard . . . carrying the hopes of a people on her back."[39]

Bédard was hardly prepared for the spotlight. After her victory in Albertville the English-Canadian media initially saw in her the perfect, innocent sports hero for Canada. "Her blue eyes sparkled, she giggled," the *Winnipeg Free Press* reported on Bédard's appearance at the medal ceremony. Then the trouble started. Bédard stepped off the podium and into the arms of her excited family, including "her father, Pierre . . . clutching a miniature fleur-de-lis flag." Rumours of her support for Quebec separatism prompted one reporter to ask her if her feat was a victory for Canada or for Quebec. Bédard's answer was honest if impolitic: "I don't want to pronounce myself on that. I don't want to say that I'm more Quebecer than Canadian. It's a medal for both of them."[40] Reporters pushed further, asking if she would compete for Quebec at future Olympics, given the chance. Her response was telling: "I don't have that feeling of Canada and the flag, and all of those things."[41] By 1994, Bédard seemed much better prepared for the postcompetition media rush. Perhaps two years' time had given her enough pause to consider what audiences expected to hear from a Canadian Olympic champion. On the medal podium in Lillehammer, she wept openly as she sang along to the playing of "O Canada." By 1998, when she made a public appearance on Parliament Hill in Ottawa as host of that year's Canada Day ceremony, her public transformation was complete.

Still, the episode underlines the conundrum that is foisted upon these athletes. It is not fair. As *Toronto Sun* columnist Steve Buffery noted, "Anyone in Bédard's shoes pretty well has to keep mum on the issue. If she 'pronounces' herself as a proud Canadian, she'll get crucified by a large segment of the Quebec media."[42] And vice versa. Quebec's sports diplomats carry an uncommon burden.

Quebec national team made up of elite Quebec athletes in a variety of international competitions. The aim here is a formal representation of the Quebec nation. The practice is not entirely new. Team Quebec has for some time competed against teams from other Canadian provinces in the Canada Summer Games, and in myriad youth sport tournaments that pit Canadian and American regions against one another. Quebec has also, since 1987, entered a sport delegation in the quadrennial Jeux de la Francophonie, a goodwill sports-and-culture gathering among the world's French-speaking nations.

What Quebecers have not yet done is establish a Quebec national team at the highest levels of sport and, specifically, in the one sport that matters most: hockey. An **Équipe-Québec** has been loosely pinned to the politics of the sovereignist movement since the early 1970s and, ironically, sprang from the epic eight-game Canada–Russia Summit Series of 1972. "At that time," separatist Quebec City lawyer Guy Bertrand remembered, "we . . . were impressed by the Series's strength to unite a people. In the same way, a Quebec hockey team could give us a *rejouissance nationale*."[43] In 1976 Bertrand made a formal plan, creating the Comité Équipe-Québec, for which he was spokesperson. But the initial idea foundered when Hockey Canada resisted and the Lévesque government's referendum on political sovereignty in 1980 failed.

Still, it didn't die. In 2006, prompted by Canadian Prime Minister Stephen Harper's statement in Parliament that Quebecers form "a nation within a united Canada," Bertrand revived the campaign. With the 2008 IIHF World Tournament in Quebec City approaching, he beseeched the prime minister to convince Hockey Canada and the IIHF to allow it, citing a fall 2006 Léger Marketing poll in which 72 per cent of Quebecers supported the idea of a Team Quebec for the 2008 World Championship. As with earlier attempts, the notion of a Team Quebec separate from (and potentially competing against) Team Canada in IIHF competitions raised uncomfortable questions. Would Quebec automatically be given a spot in the elite division? Would it need the consent of Hockey Canada? Would Québécois players choose to play for Quebec and not for Canada? In the end, no Team Quebec was entered into the 2008 World Championship, an outcome that did not sit well with hockey-mad Quebecers.

Today, the issue remains alive and unresolved. In the summer of 2013, Parti Québecois Premier Pauline Marois declared her interest in seeing the Équipe-Québec project come to fruition and appointed a commission to prepare a feasibility study for the establishment of national teams in both soccer and hockey. And in June 2013 a Quebec national soccer team played in the International Peoples, Cultures and Tribes Tournament in Marseille, France.[44] Whatever its outcome and whatever its merits, the quest for an Équipe-Québec is not a capricious endeavour and shows no signs of fading away.

Questions for Critical Thinking

1. What does the following claim mean? "In Quebec, sport is at once a catalyst, a proxy, and a mirror for the national question."
2. "A team, a business, a cult object, a collective memory . . . an inheritance" and "a religion." Explain why the Montreal Canadiens have become such an important source of national feeling in Quebec. Is this a unique phenomenon?
3. For or against? Which argument would you make regarding a Quebec national team that could compete in international competitions, such as the World Cup of soccer or the Olympics?

Notes

1. Gilles Janson, "Le sport au Québec, un champ de recherche méprise," *Bulletin d'histoire politique* 11, no. 2 (Winter 2003): 9.
2. Steven A. Riess, "Preface," *Major Problems in American Sport History*, 2nd ed. (Stamford, CT: Cengage Learning, 2015), xvii.
3. The first horse racing courses were built by British soldiers on the Plains of Abraham garrisoned at Quebec City in 1764, and a Quebec Turf Club was founded in 1789. See Donald Guay and Jocelyn East, eds., *Chronologie des sports* (Quebec: Secretariat au loisir et au sport, July 2003). On blood sports in Canada more generally, see

Colin D. Howell, *Blood, Sweat and Cheers* (Toronto: University of Toronto Press, 2001), ch. 1; on blood sport in working-class Montreal, see Peter DeLottinville, "Joe Beef of Montreal: Working-Class Culture and the Tavern, 1869–1889," *Labour/Le Travail* 8/9 (1981/82): 9–40.

4. Visit the team websites at www.impactmontreal.com/en, http://canadiens.nhl.com, http://en.montrealalouettes.com, and www.capitalesdequebec.com. Accessed 30 November 2014.
5. "Quebec Government Wishes Home-Grown Athletes the Greatest Success," Relations internationales et Francophonie Québec, accessed 9 August 2012, www.mri.gouv.qc.ca/en/salle-de-presse/actualites/11016; S. Robertson, "Government Commitment: Developing an Integrated Sport System in Quebec," *Coaches Report* 10, no. 2 (Fall 2003): 8–14. Sports-Québec makes a special claim to "promote the interests of francophones to the Canadian sport community." See Sports-Québec, accessed 20 October 2012, www.sportsquebec.com.
6. They could claim all or part of 5 of Canada's 18 medals. The 281-member Canadian Olympic delegation included 41 women and 26 men from Quebec.
7. Randy Phillips, "Something Must Change, Stingers Coach Says," *Montreal Gazette*, 7 November 2011.
8. Herb Zurkowsky, "Carabins Take Vanier Cup," *Montreal Gazette*, 30 November 2014.
9. Mark Cardwell, "Laval's Field of Dreams," *University Affairs*, 9 November 2009.
10. Daniel Proulx and Jean Poiré, "Football universitaire québécois : les universités francophones sont-elles avantagées?" *Le Soleil*, 28 November 2011.
11. Alan Metcalfe, "The Evolution of Organized Physical Recreation in Montreal, 1840–1895," *Histoire sociale/Social History* 11, no. 21 (1978): 149. Baseball thrived in the Eastern Townships in the 1880s and 1890s. See D. Morrow and K. Wamsley, eds., *Sport in Canada: A History*, 2nd ed. (Don Mills, ON: Oxford University Press, 2010), 102.
12. "Hockey," *Montreal Gazette*, 4 March 1875; "Hockey on Ice," *Montreal Gazette*, 1 February 1877.
13. See John Chi-kit Wong, *Lords of the Rinks: The Emergence of the National Hockey League, 1875–1936* (Toronto: University of Toronto Press), chs. 1 and 2.
14. Gillian Poulter, "Snowshoeing and Lacrosse: Canada's Nineteenth-Century 'National Games,'" *Culture, Sport, Society* 6, no. 2/3 (Summer/Autumn 2003): 304.
15. On Indigenous lacrosse, see Allan Downey, "Engendering Nationality: Haudenosaunee Tradition, Sport, and the Lines of Gender," *Journal of the Canadian Historical Association* 23, no. 1 (2012): 319–54.
16. Metcalfe, "The Evolution of Organized Physical Recreation in Montreal," 149.
17. Sylvie Dufresne, "Le Carnaval d'Hiver de Montréal, 1883–1889," *Urban History Review* 27 (1996): 173–90.
18. See John Matthew Barlow, "'Scientific Aggression': Irishness, Manliness, Class, and Commercialization in the Shamrock Hockey Club of Montreal, 1894–1901," in *Coast to Coast: Hockey in Canada to the Second World War*, ed. John Chi-kit Wong (Toronto: University of Toronto Press, 2009), 35–85.
19. A big exception to this generalization was Louis Cyr (1863–1912), a native of Saint-Cyprien-de-Napierville who, from 1885 to 1906, performed astounding feats of strength for audiences in Canada, Europe, and the United States. Cyr's athletic events were more theatre than sport, since weightlifting had not yet been standardized as a competition. See Morrow and Wamsley, *Sport in Canada*, 127–30.
20. See Jean Harvey, "Sport and the Quebec Clergy, 1930–1960," in *Not Just a Game*, ed. Jean Harvey and Hart Cantelon (Ottawa: University of Ottawa Press, 1988), 81. For a revision of Harvey's argument about clerical influence, see Jocelyn East, "L'institutionalisation du sport au Québec de 1900 a 1967," *Stadion* 31, no. 2 (2005): 273–92.
21. Gilles Janson, *Emparons-nous du sport : les Canadiens français et le sport au XIXe siècle* (Montreal: Guérin, 1995).
22. A. Marion, "Prospectus," *Le Sport Illustré* 1, no. 1 (10 June 1899): 2.
23. Author's translation. "Le club national," *La Presse*, 3 April 1895.
24. See Michel Vigneault, "La Naissance d'un sport organisé au Canada : le hockey à Montreal, 1875–1917" (Ph.D. diss., Université Laval, 2001).
25. Harvey, "Sport and the Quebec Clergy," 81.
26. See M. Ann Hall, *The Girl and the Game: A History of Women's Sport in Canada* (Peterborough: Broadview Press, 2002), 37, 66, 82, 105.
27. Fannie Valois-Nadeau, "Le Canadien de Montreal comme objet populaire : représentations de la tradition," in *Le Canadien de Montréal : Une légende repensée*, ed. A. Laurin-Lamothe and N. Moreau (Montreal: Presses de l'Université de Montréal, 2011), 75.
28. Olivier Bauer, *Hockey as a Religion: The Montreal Canadiens* (Champaign, IL: Common Ground Publishing, 2011).
29. Roch Carrier, *The Hockey Sweater and Other Stories* (Toronto: House of Anansi, 1979), 78.
30. See Benoît Melançon, *The Rocket: A Cultural History of Maurice Richard* (Vancouver: Greystone Books, 2009).
31. Melançon, *The Rocket*, 123–9; and Sidney Katz, "The Strange Forces behind the Richard Hockey Riot," *Maclean's*, 17 September 1955.
32. See Peter Gossage and J. I. Little, *An Illustrated History of Quebec: Tradition and Modernity* (Don Mills, ON: Oxford University Press, 2013), 230–1.
33. Guay and East, *Chronologie des sports.*

34. Roger Boileau and Donald Guay, "Pratiques corporelles, reflet de mutations sociales : le cas de Québec," in *La Culture du Sport au Québec*, ed. Jean-Pierre Augustin and Claude Sorbets (Talence: Maison des Sciences de l'Homme d'Aquitaine, 1996), 127.
35. Jean Harvey and Lucie Thibault, "Politique du sport et restructuration de l'Etat-providence au Canada," in *La Culture du Sport au Québec*, ed. Jean-Pierre Augustin and Claude Sorbets (Talence: Maison des Sciences de l'Homme d'Aquitaine, 1996), 94.
36. Barbara Keys, *Globalizing Sport: National Rivalry and International Community in the 1930s* (Cambridge, MA: Harvard University Press, 2006), 17.
37. David Meren, *With Friends like These: Entangled Nationalisms and the Canada-Quebec-France Triangle, 1944–1970* (Vancouver: UBC Press, 2012).
38. "Myriam Bedard," Canada's Sports Hall of Fame/Pantheon des sports canadiens, accessed 21 October 2012, www.sportshall.ca/honoured-members/27548/myriam-bedard.
39. "Quebec Heroine Transcended Her Sport," *Montreal Gazette*, 3 January 2007.
40. "Bedard Claims Biathlon Bronze," *Winnipeg Free Press*, 20 February 1992.
41. Steve Buffery, "Biathlon Blues," *Toronto Sun*, 3 July 1998.
42. Ibid.
43. Telephone interview, Guy Bertrand, Quebec City, 4 September 2013.
44. Ronald King, "Équipe Québec : l'idée fait son chemin," *La Presse*, 20 June 2013. The tournament was not recognized by FIFA, nor is Équipe-Québec formally affiliated with that governing body.

Select Bibliography

Augustin, Jean-Pierre, and Claude Sorbets, eds. *La Culture du Sport au Québec*. Talence: Maison des Sciences de l'Homme d'Aquitaine, 1996.

Bélanger, Anouk. "The Last Game? Hockey and the Experience of Masculinity in Quebec." In *Sport and Gender in Canada*, edited by P. White and K. Young, 292–309. Don Mills, ON: Oxford University Press, 1999.

East, Jocelyn, "L'Institutionalisation du Sport au Québec de 1900 a 1967." *Stadion* 31, no. 2 (2005): 273–92.

Melançon, Benoît. *The Rocket: A Cultural History of Maurice Richard*. Vancouver: Greystone Books, 2009.

Poulter, Gillian. *Becoming Native in a Foreign Land: Sport, Visual Culture and National Identity, Montreal 1840–1885*. Vancouver: UBC Press, 2009.

Guay, Donald. *La Conquête du Sport : le sport et la société québecoise au XIXe siècle*. Montréal: Lanctôt éditeur, 1997.

Harvey, Jean. "Whose Sweater Is This? The Changing Meanings of Hockey in Quebec." In *Artificial Ice: Hockey, Culture, and Commerce*, edited by D. Whitson and R. Gruneau, 29–52. Toronto: Broadview/Garamond, 2006.

Janson, Gilles. *Emparons-nous du sport : les Canadiens français et le sport au XIXe siècle*. Montreal: Guérin, 1995.

Laberge, Suzanne. "Sociology of Sport in Quebec: A Field Deeply Rooted in Its Society." *Sociology of Sport Journal* 12, no. 2 (June 1995): 213–23.

Wolofsky, Sandy. "Is It the Poutine? How Quebec Is Producing a Powerhouse of Freestyle Skiers." *Ski Racing*, 30 January 2012, 42–44.

9 Shared Territories: Key Issues in the History of Visual Arts in Quebec, 1600–1960

Dominic Hardy, Université de Québec à Montréal

Timeline

1615–70s French Recollet, Jesuit, and Sulpician missionaries work with images in the St Lawrence Valley and Great Lakes First Nations territories.

1639 Arrival of the Ursuline order of nuns at Quebec; encounters between European and Aboriginal women and weaving practices.

1670–1 Sojourn of Recollet painter Claude François (Frère Luc) at Quebec.

1700–30 Planning and construction of Ursuline Convent at Quebec; decorative sculptures (retable, tabernacle, sculpted furnishings) by Pierre-Noël Levasseur.

1776–80 François Baillargé is the first Quebec-born artist to be sent to Paris for academic training in architecture, sculpture, and painting.

1790s Montreal emerges as an important centre of artistic production and as a key destination for immigrant artists.

1817–20 Shipment to Quebec City of the religious paintings gathered in post-revolutionary France by Pierre Desjardins, destined for the churches of Lower Canada.

1820–60 Continued immigration to Quebec of European artists (France, Great Britain, and Central Europe).

1860 Foundation of Art Association of Montreal.

1883 Opening of the school of the Art Association of Montreal.

1918 Avant-garde journal *Le Nigog* establishes beachhead for modernist practices in Quebec.

1923–4 Founding of the École des beaux-arts de Québec and the École des beaux-arts de Montréal.

1935 Foundation of the École du meuble de Montréal.

1939 Foundation of the Contemporary Arts Society in Montreal.

1948 *Refus Global* and *Prisme d'Yeux* manifestos are released.

Introduction: Visual Arts in the Middle Ground

European **visual culture** was established on the territories that eventually became "Quebec" with the definitive arrival of a sustained French program of colonization at the beginning of the seventeenth century. In the visual arts, as in the rest of Quebec and Canadian history, the travels of Samuel de Champlain to Quebec's Atlantic and river shores starting in 1603 form a useful point of departure for any narrative of what will become Quebec's art history.

It is at first a story of the way a represented place and its people became part of the European imaginary. Early representations of land formations, flora, fauna, and inhabitants were chiefly deployed, from Champlain's time and throughout the French regime, via the conventions of cartography and illustrated materials (books and prints) published in Europe, or via the largely symbolic and schematic treatments of place that we find in the religious paintings that were eventually destined for Quebec churches and altars.

In his *Voyages*, published from 1604 onward, Samuel de Champlain's keen textual observations and

Primary Source

The Encounter between Visual Cultures

Letter from Charles Garnier to his brother, Father Henri de Saint-Joseph, from Teanaustayae, ca. 1645

In this letter to his brother, sent from the Jesuit mission at Teanaustayae (near present-day Hillsdale between Barrie and Penetanguishene, Ontario), Garnier explains the type of religious images (typically small paintings showing scenes of the life of Jesus, members of the Holy family, or figurative representations of the soul) that he would like sent to him to support his proselytizing work among the Hurons. In reading the letter, we come to understand that Garnier sees certain accommodations as being necessary to the figurative conventions of Catholic religious iconography if he is to take full advantage, in an Aboriginal cultural context, of the images' powers of persuasion. Along with other writings of the period (for example, by Recollet Father Gabriel Sagard (ca. 1590–1640) and the Jesuit Relations), this source gives us some understanding of what was at stake in the encounter between Aboriginal and European visual cultures in the seventeenth century.[2] Toward the end of his letter, Father Garnier establishes a list of the desired characteristics of the images he would like to have shipped to him:

> 1st that The Figures appear very much as they appear in the Images of Polsnam and even of Huré[3]
>
> 2nd that they should not be of profile but that we see the whole Face and having open eyes; these Images please those who look at them and that there not be too much shadow on the body
>
> 3rd that there not be too great a confusion of Figures and that they not be too covered with clothing but that a part of the body appear unveiled.
>
> 4th Well brushed and straight hair pleases them far more than curly hair, and it is best that they not be bald, and that they have no beard.
>
> 5th The best would be that there be little or no trees flowers and animals to distract.
>
> 6th that Our Saviour Our Lady and the blessed be quite white.

interpretations of his encounters with the continent, its places, and people, coupled with his cartographic expertise, allow us to understand how this European imaginary both encoded and decoded its "New World." The conventions of travel narrative and graphic representations of the spaces of commercial exploration were combined in a strategic address to a multilayered home readership comprising both Champlain's state patrons and an ever-burgeoning reading class.[1]

Although the seventeenth century was witness to a rise in painted landscape representations, especially in Northern Europe, the vagaries of *enracinement* and the stealthy growth of the colony throughout the century did not provide the necessary conditions for the emergence of a landscape practice in Quebec. But the colonial structure established here by France was nonetheless centred on a strong visual culture attached to religious life. The materiality of this visual culture is exemplified by colonial architecture, by the sculpted and painted decorations imported or made in the colony for its churches, and by the imported printed religious imagery destined for private and public worship and for the conversion of the Aboriginal populations.

Today, Quebec art history is in the early stages of investigating its historiographical structures to understand how it has configured the settler–colonial

7th that the drapery be of a vivid colour such as of a fine red or a fine blue, of a fine Scarlet, or even of cloth with figures and blended with the brightest colours. Yellow and green please them not at all on clothes.

8th It would be best that they have the head uncovered, rather than covered with clothes as Our Lady often has, and these circles of Light or glory that are put around the head of Our Saviour and Our Lady seem to them as hats, but these lights made as rays do yet please them. I would like to have a blessed Soul coming down from the Sky white as snow and that there come out of its body a Light, and that it be covered with a nice clothing of a vivid colour that would leave a part of its body honestly uncovered, that it would have a serene and laughing face and that it would gaze amiably on those that look at it, as in inviting them to the Sky that it would show with one hand with this written beneath the Image *nec oculos vidit &c.* but excuse me my desires are ever growing if it must still be that I explain to you how I would wish that the Damned Soul that I spoke of earlier could be made if it depended on me I would desire that it appeared grilled and blackened by flames that would rise above the head from behind, and that the whole of the void in the Image be filled with flames, and even some flames in the front here and there that would not cover it too much, eyes Sparkling and that the mouth should be open as a person who screams out aloud, that at the back of the mouth appear a few flames, ditto that they come out of the nose and the ears, and the eyes, all the face scrunched up, the hair on end, the two hands tied with burning iron, and the feet too, and another iron chain burning at the middle of the body: a frightful Dragon coiled around the body that would bite at the ear, but that this Dragon have horrible scales, and not a pretty blue as I have seen, two mighty and fearful demons at its two sides that tear at the Body with two harpoons of iron, and another above that wants to take him by the hair. My very dear brother forgive me for asking so much of you, but Our Saviour will be your reward . . .

Source: This excerpt is a free translation based on the text "Lettre de saint Charles Garnier à son frère, le père Henri de Saint-Joseph, carme, de Teanaustayae, sans date (1645?)." Charles Garnier, *Lettres de saint Charles Garnier à son frère le père Henri de Saint-Joseph*, Québec, s.n., 1931, 30–2. I have tried to preserve the rhetorical flavour of the original. The full text of the original letter is reproduced in François-Marc Gagnon's *La conversion par l'image* (Montreal: Bellarmin, 1975).

and Aboriginal contributions to traditions of visual culture across its territories. Ultimately, this configuration attends to questions of identity and the identity markers projected onto the people and places represented by the visual. The aim of this chapter, which will concentrate on painting, textile arts, sculpture, and graphic arts (leaving architecture aside), is to provide an overview of select historical contexts through which these questions can be imagined for studies that will have to be carried out in the coming years.

Religious Art in New France

It is worth remembering that the members of the Recollet and Jesuit orders who accompanied Champlain on his first missions were themselves part of recently formed organizations, working during the early stages of the Counter-Reformation. In reaction to the often iconoclastic reforms of the emergent Protestant churches in sixteenth-century Europe, the Catholic Church convened the Council of Trent (1545–63), through which it affirmed and defined both pedagogical and liturgical uses for images, notably in the campaigns of proselytization undertaken on the European mainland.

The work that could be accomplished with images was, in this respect, tributary of the same forces that had done so much to propel the ideas of the Reformation across Europe in the first place. In the century following the development of the printing press, printed graphic arts (woodcuts, metal engraving, and etching) emerged with their own rich repertoires of visual codes that could organize and present the complex narrative iconographies of the Old and New Testaments, the stories of Jesus's life and death, and the lives of saints and figures of salvation and damnation. These visual vocabularies of proselytization and worship that were developed in Church painting, sculpture, architecture, and decorative arts were disseminated through the production of autonomous, collectible prints or in illustrated books. The mobility of the printed image would prove to be paradigmatic for the exporting of visual culture into Europe's "New World."

Fanning out across their European homelands and across the globe in the wake of European military and commercial exploration, both the Recollets (founded in 1583 as a new branch of the twelfth-century Dominicans) and Jesuits (founded in 1540) were among the most militant proponents of efforts undertaken to bring wayward populations to the Catholic Church's vision of Christendom. As France undertook to establish settlements along the northeast Atlantic coast and the shores of the St Lawrence River after 1600, both Recollets and Jesuits accompanied the voyages of Pierre Du Gua de Monts and Champlain with the aim of converting the Aboriginal Nations with which they set up trading and cultural relationships. Both orders would use small mobile imagery—engravings and small paintings on copper constituting especially portable and therefore useful artistic forms for this purpose—to position a Christian world view of Catholic **iconography** against Aboriginal cosmology and spiritual practices. The imagery would also serve in the pastoral care of the French settlers and their families and for the eventual Aboriginal converts, whose nomadic life would ultimately be transformed in the communal settlements established by the missionaries after 1650.

At the same time, the Recollets and Jesuits seem to have entertained differing conceptions of the Aboriginal visual cultures they encountered. Recounting his 1623–4 sojourn among the people whom the French called the Huron, then established in the region around present-day Midland, Ontario, the Recollet Father Gabriel Sagard wrote, "They like painting, and succeed at it fairly industriously, for people who have no art nor proper instruments, and nevertheless make representations of men, of animals, of birds and other grotesques; as much in carving in stone, wood and other similar materials, as in flat painting upon their bodies, that they do, not in order to be idolatrous; but to please the eye, embellish their peace pipes and tobacco-bowls, and to decorate the entrance to their huts."[4]

The impression given by the Jesuit Father Paul Le Jeune in the late 1630s is quite different. In being attentive to Algonquin use of imagery in healing practices, for example, Le Jeune appears to discount any sense of the aesthetic pleasure noted by Sagard:

> His brother-in-law came to tell him that he'd thought that his niece would heal if she was made to lie on a sheep-skin, decorated with various

figures . . . so a thousand grotesques are painted, canoes, oars, animals and suchlike, the Fathers who had not yet given instruction to this girl, mentioning that this remedy is useless but that it must be tried. The sick girl lies down on these paintings, and receives no real healing. Another charlatan gave his opinion that if the sick one was given a white sheet at bedside, on which men dancing and singing would be painted, then the sickness would go. They fall over themselves in painting men on a sheet; but they can only make scribbles, such good painters as they are; and this remedy succeeds no better than the first.[5]

If these observations are important to us as eyewitness reports, the story of the alternating reception and resistance to Aboriginal visual culture that they tell is of course partial—focusing on the Europeans' response to what they see as unusual ways of making images. Yet within Sagard's account of his journey and, later, throughout the annual Jesuit *Relations*, the vision we have of *Aboriginal* responses to *European* visual culture—much of which operated on transformations that depended on the depth of the Aboriginal cosmological structures already in place—allows us to recognize the agency at work in Aboriginal appropriations of European spiritual and visual practices. At the same time, these practices undergo modifications as they are adapted to be used in these territories that constitute, from the time of contact onward, what Richard White has called the "Middle Ground," a large geopolitical region that is also the site of far-reaching social and cultural transactions throughout the seventeenth and eighteenth centuries.[6] Art historians Janet Berlo and Ruth Phillips have drawn on this concept in their discussion of Eastern Woodlands Aboriginal artistic practices, and Ruth Phillips has examined in detail the interactions between Aboriginal artists and the nuns at the Ursuline Convents at Trois-Rivières and Quebec City in the early eighteenth century.[7]

The arrival of the nuns of the Ursulines and the Augustine orders in 1639 signalled a significant transfer of artistic expertise into the colony at a time when most artistic productions needed for religious or domestic use had to be imported.[8] The Ursulines effectively established what could be considered the first teaching workshop for the visual arts in New France. The order's co-founder, Marie Guyart (1599–1672), came from a family of textile designers and producers long active in Tours, a site of royal tapestry patronage. Before taking her vows and becoming Marie de l'Incarnation in 1633, Guyart had managed the family textile firm.[9] At the fledgling convent in Quebec City—a building that would twice be entirely destroyed by fire, in 1650 and 1686, before being definitively established at its present site from 1687 onward—Marie de l'Incarnation would supervise the nuns' twin mandate: to educate the young women of French and Aboriginal families and, as Ruth Phillips notes, to ensure "the production of magnificent altar cloths and vestments, heavily embroidered in glass beads, silk, and gilt thread with pictorial scenes and

Figure 9.1 Workshop of the Ursulines of Quebec. Nativity Altar Cloth. Musée des Ursulines de Québec. Collection du Monastère des Ursulines de Québec.

CASE STUDY

Rereading the Records in Quebec Visual Arts

How can Quebec art history be reconfigured to appropriately reflect Aboriginal contributions? This case study suggests that a consideration of recent art-historical texts, artworks, and museum installation practices may provide a starting point. To show how this might be possible, let's consider two examples of historical *discontinuity* side by side. Problems that challenge the historian's search for explanations sometimes prove to be the most productive.

In the private chapel of the Ursulines in Quebec City, visitors can see a painting that has become foundational for studies in Quebec art history. Known today as *La France apportant la foi aux Hurons de la Nouvelle-France*, the painting shows a royal female figure presenting a painting of the Holy Family (Christ and his parents with Saint Anne and the Holy Spirit) to a kneeling Aboriginal person, held to be of the "Huron" Nation (today Huron-Wendat) in the foreground (Figure 9.2).[15] To the sides, the receding hilly landscape frames a body of water that extends to the horizon and through which French sailing ships are seen to be travelling. Their exact affiliation (whether to the Crown or a noble house) is unknown. Above is another holy family group, this time including a representation of God the Father, which looks down on the scene below—and is pointed to by the royal female figure, generally agreed to be Anne of Austria, who did a great deal to support the establishment of Quebec through the sponsorship offered by Louis XIII and herself in the 1630s. At left, small wooden houses adorned with crosses suggest the dwellings built by Jesuit missionaries on their travels through the *pays d'en haut* to Sainte-Marie among the Hurons, which is in present-day Midland, Ontario. The buildings are familiar from an engraving by Grégoire Huret commemorating the martyrdom of the Jesuit fathers Gabriel Lalemant and Jean de Brébeuf, events that preceded the massacre of the Hurons by the Iroquois and the Jesuit repatriation of Huron survivors to the Quebec area in 1650.

A reading of the Jesuits' journal for 1666 indicates that a painting was commissioned at the request of the Huron-Wendat, who gave presents for a work that would show "how they embraced the faith." Beyond these few indices, we have no idea who painted this work or when. Indeed, there is no trace of its presence in Quebec before an inventory of the Ursuline possessions made in the early 1800s. It is supposed that the painting had been held by the Jesuits until their expulsion from Canada following the Conquest (the order was entirely suppressed by the Church from 1773 to 1814, and the "last Jesuit in Canada," caretaker of the order's legacy, died in 1802). But nothing was certain about the work's history before it entered the historiography of parish

Figure 9.2 Unidentified French artist, *La France apportant la foi aux Hurons de Nouvelle-France*. Musée des Ursulines de Québec. Collection du Monastère des Ursulines de Québec.

histories and the art history developed by pioneer Gérard Morisset from the 1930s onward. Long attributed to Claude François (1610–1685), the Recollet father known as Frère Luc, who sojourned in Canada in 1670–1, its attribution became definitively uncertain with the painstaking research and rereading of sources carried out by François-Marc Gagnon into the missionary uses of images. The attribution to an "unknown French artist" has now stood unchallenged since 1983, despite several re-examinations of the file. Like the paintings of the *Fonds Desjardins*, it occupies an unstable, unfixable place in history, but a dense and constantly revisited place in historiography.

Such rereadings are at the heart of the enterprise of Quebec art history, and here too artists and institutions play a role. In 2006, the Montreal Museum of Fine Arts (MMFA) acquired *Trappers of Men*, a vast painting by contemporary Cree artist Kent Monkman.[16] This painting appropriates and modifies an emblematic nineteenth-century landscape of American art by Albert Bierstadt, peopling the foreground with an array of Western artists, from Piet Mondrian to Edward Curtis to Jackson Pollock, whose modes of representation are challenged by the Aboriginal figures who are actively setting out visual and spatial information through their own modes of representation, and by the Venus-like Miss Chief Eagle Testickle, who rises from the lake framed by the foreground shore and the distant majestic Rockies.

As the first work by a contemporary Aboriginal artist to be acquired by this institution for many years—despite the emergence of a thriving network of contemporary Aboriginal art practice across Canada since the 1970s—*Trappers of Men* ushered in the institution's rereading and performance of itself as a place open to critical, postmodern, settler-colonial critique. In the planning of the new Québec and Canadian Art Pavilion, the MMFA turned to Monkman once again, commissioning a work (*The King's Beavers*, 2011)[17] that would comment on and fill the gaps in its own collection in order to address the visual culture of the moment of colonial encounter in the seventeenth century (Figure 9.3). Installing the work at the entrance to a gallery christened Founding Identities, the MMFA also placed the video work *Portrait in Motion* (2002) by Nadia Myre[18] in proximity to two works by Joseph Légaré: *Martyre de Françoise Brunon-Gonannhatenha* of 1828 and *View of Québec City from Pointe de Lévy* of 1840. The conjoined temporalities conjured up by such placements are as good a place as any for the difficult yet rewarding work of making sense of—and for making meaning out of—the visual arts that have been made on and for the territories and people gathered today under the name of Quebec.

Figure 9.3 Kent Monkman, *The King's Beavers*. Montreal Museum of Fine Arts, Purchase, 1980.3

flowers, which they supplied to churches in Québec and elsewhere"[10] (Figure 9.1). The visual splendour of the surviving textile pieces gives us a sense of the spectacular nature of colonial visual culture in Quebec, not only for liturgical services but also on ceremonial and processional occasions at which the French and Aboriginal elites were present in the colony's public sphere.[11]

By the early eighteenth century, Aboriginal and Ursuline women artists engaged in exchanges of motifs and artistic expertise. The Ursuline nuns began producing **souvenir arts** employing bark, moose hair, and porcupine quill techniques and distinctive floral motifs that, as Phillips has shown, became key commodities both in the organization of the economic welfare of monastic and Aboriginal communities and in the circulation of signs of "Indianness" for settler-colonial and European consumption.[12]

In contrast to the public uses of visual culture were other more private and devotional uses. Ariane Généreux has shown how New France became a market for small religious works painted on copper, a type of production that by the mid-seventeenth century was widely consumed in Northern Europe, particularly in Flanders and France.[13] The intimate scale of these paintings made them apt, as we've already seen, for missionary work. But they were also well adapted to private religious life and for the moments of deep spiritual engagement characteristic of the religious fervour and mysticism prevalent in France in the first half of the seventeenth century. In this respect, the material life of certain religious artworks of the European cultural community can be understood as a gateway to a realm of mystical experiences. In this realm, an equally important order of nonmaterial visual imagery is produced. In turn, such visionary experiences find their way into the diaries and letters of figures such as Marie de l'Incarnation.[14] They also find their echo in Aboriginal spiritual practices.

Landscapes and Identities, 1759–1867

A century and a half after Champlain, British military artists who served with the invading forces of 1759–63, or in the subsequent colonial administrations, developed an extensive topographical watercolour iconography that has become a significant documentary and aesthetic record of early Quebec and Canadian history. Many of these artists were trained at the Royal Military Academy at Woolwich by British landscape artist Paul Sandby (1730–1809). Their images of the St Lawrence Valley's landmarks (Montmorency Falls and the Citadel at Quebec, Montreal from St Helen's Island, the shores of the Great Lakes, and Niagara Falls) helped to develop an international visual identity for Quebec. Watercolours, paintings, and prints of these landmarks fed a growing and vibrant middle-class audience, women and men who positioned themselves as both producers and consumers of **landscape** representations that articulated ideological, subjective, and economic relationships to place and places in Britain and throughout its growing empire.

These representations also carried strong aesthetic codes for their audiences, being designed in accordance with contemporary ideas of the picturesque or the sublime. The series of engravings by Richard Short (active 1754–60) published in London in 1760, among the very earliest of these images, shows strategic sites of the French civil and religious administration after the British bombardments of the 1759 campaign, echoing the growing taste for representations of ruins, both real and imaginary, in a society driven by a passion for archaeological discoveries and historicist fantasies of the antique and medieval worlds.[19] At the same time, the topographer watercolourists such as Thomas Davies (ca. 1737–1812), James Peachey (d. 1797), and George Heriot (1759–1839, also deputy postmaster general of British North America from 1799–1816) fed a public appetite for images of the newest territorial acquisition in Britain's overseas empire.[20]

These images were destined to augment the picturesque repertoire available to the British spectator/reader, and also to confirm the orderliness of British imperial reconstruction following the Conquest, seen throughout this iconography as resulting in a harmonious balance of pastoral settings and commercial and administrative urban centres. In this balance, a cast of British expatriate ladies and gentlemen, imperial officers, merchants, and their families were positioned in harmonious coexistence with Canadian (that is, French-speaking) and Aboriginal subjects.

Thomas Davies's work is emblematic of this approach to landscape. Whether in the wake of conquest or on the eve of the political reorganization of the colony as it acquired directly elected legislative assemblies, Davies harnessed his capacity for topographical accuracy. His work was designed to faithfully portray Quebec's landscape icons to a firm demonstrative visual structure in which the choice of point of view and the shaping of landforms conveyed strong decorative accents to the overall compositions.

These structures reinforced the dynamics of British, Canadian, and Aboriginal spectatorship. Davies shows his figures in contrasting modes of engagement with the land, either active or passive as the situation demands. The somewhat forlorn Aboriginal onlooker in Davies's 1790 view of Montmorency appears to have drifted across time from the couple who witnessed history rather as a pair of disporting Renaissance figures in his 1760 *A View of Fort La Galette*.[21] The emblematic uses of such figures made by Champlain at the outset of the colonial experience have not diminished; the figures have simply migrated into the fictions organized by the artist for the viewer in his pictures' respect for the conventions used to create a credible suggestion of perspectival space.

The fact that the application of these conventions to representations of Quebec's iconic spaces takes place under British domination creates a key historiographical issue, for the introduction of this visual behaviour appears to conform to the paradigm of rupture that is attached to the Conquest and the cession of the colony to the British. This rupture introduces other political motifs that Canadien artists and writers would eventually address through reference to land and figural identities. While this became especially clear for Canadien artists in the wake of the failed 1837–8 Rebellions, other ruptures had an impact on the political organization of cultural life and artistic training.

The reorganization of the colony's administrative and legal structures in the early 1790s took place in the context of the French Revolution. For the Canadien clergy, the execution of King Louis XVI and the destruction of Church privilege, property—and life—along with the introduction of a form of democratic representation for Quebec, led to a reassessment of the clergy's leadership role even as it continued to co-operate with the governing British administrators. Throughout this period the Church expanded as the francophone, Catholic Canadien population increased and new parishes were established. Expatriate European painters such as Louis Dulongpré (1759–1843) and William Berczy (1744–1813) were highly active, while the sculpture workshops led by François Baillargé (1759–1830) at Quebec and Louis Quévillon (1749–1823) around Montreal established near monopolies on their respective regions, even as post-revolutionary loyalist settlement in Quebec and Lower Canada brought a wave of immigration that was not only British and American but also European in origin. Artist–artisans such as Georg and Daniel Finsterer, active in the parishes of the Richelieu valley, emerged from the ranks of German soldiers loyal to Britain and demobilized after the Revolutionary War to become important church decorators in the Richelieu valley region.[22]

The Lower Canada artistic market chiefly paid tribute to the activities of the governor general, the political administration, and the Church. It had yet to develop the density required to establish and sustain centres for the training of artists and the collecting of their works, the kinds of institutions that had already been set up in the United States following European models in the wake of that country's independence. Nonetheless, the need to offer training to artists, and particularly painters, outside of the workshop system was more and more acutely felt. The career of self-taught artist Joseph Légaré (1795–1855) points both to this need and to what could be done in colonial circumstances to mitigate the absence of artistic institutions.

Légaré, who had briefly attended the Petit séminaire de Québec as a teenager, was trained as a housepainter and glazier. In 1817 he came into contact with the 180 works of what Laurier Lacroix has called the *Fonds de tableaux Desjardins*. This was a group of mostly seventeenth- and eighteenth-century French paintings or copies after Italian originals that were "rescued" from the iconoclasm of the French

Revolution. Their rescue was the initiative of the priest Philippe-Jean-Louis Desjardins (1753–1833) who, working with his brother Louis-Joseph Desjardins (1766–1848), destined these works for export to Quebec at the close of hostilities between Britain and France, a development that would await the end of the Napoleonic era.[23] Paintings that had been removed wholesale from French churches during the revolution, hidden away and discounted as copies or as second-rate works in the early nineteenth-century art system, acquired a new status when they were sold in Quebec for dispersal among the growing number of churches in Lower Canada, where supply could not keep pace with demand. The Desjardins paintings, most of them long kept in deleterious conditions, were soon being restored and copied by painters such as Joseph Légaré and Yves Tessier. Légaré developed his entire career in the "visual laboratory" of this kind of work: With no teaching institutions available anywhere in Canada during his time, he learned through practices of retouching, repairing, copying, and adapting to local conditions and needs.[24] Légaré also had access to the extensive collection of European prints available at the Séminaire de Québec.

Légaré enjoyed rapid success as a supplier of religious paintings. By 1819 he was obliged to take on an apprentice, Antoine Plamondon (1804–1895), who went to France from 1826 to 1830 in search of academic training. Once he was established at Quebec, Plamondon hired Théophile Hamel (1817–1870) in 1834. Hamel in turn travelled to France, Italy, and Belgium for his own training (1843–6). The pattern of early skill development in the workshop of an established artist followed by further study abroad became the standard form of professional art education in nineteenth-century Quebec.

Légaré also initiated an individual form of politically engaged, landscape-based history painting that contributed to the nationalist discourses circulating in Lower Canada before and after the 1837–8 Rebellions. In 1840, when Lord Durham published his report advocating a fusion of the two Canadas to ensure the minority status and the eventual full linguistic and cultural assimilation of the French Canadians—a people whom Lord Durham claimed had no culture and no history—Légaré provided a response in his *View of Quebec City from Pointe de Lévy* (Figure 9.4).[25] The painting exemplified Légaré's thoughtful articulation of a wide range of sources and styles and showed how he could set up different cultural codes to play off of one another. In the lush, highly contrasted foreground the setting is a clearing atop a hill in Lévis looking across the St Lawrence toward l'Anse-au-Foulon, the British-built citadel and the French-Catholic spires of the colonial capital (adapted from an early nineteenth-century engraved view of Quebec). In the distance are the hills of Montmorency. In the foreground a habitant couple are gazing, on our behalf, toward the city: We know that they are habitants by their identity markers, their clothes—he with red toque and *ceinture fléchée*, she demure in a gathered shawl. Their Lévis is a lush forested and agricultural world inspired by any number of seventeenth-century pastoral scenes. Quebec is as distant to them as the furthest Montmorency hills that lie beyond, and both are rendered with the same topographical precision and in the same cool palette, with its overtones of watercolour application. It is as though the visual traditions of the Baroque landscape associated with mainland Europe are established as the historical order that is appropriate to the habitant, while the hybrid colonial urban–territorial reality is rendered according to the visual codes of topography and watercolour that are so closely associated with the British presence.

Légaré explored this articulation of identities further in his enigmatic work *Landscape with Monument to Wolfe*, likely to have been made around 1845.[26] Once again a lush setting, in this case a riverside clearing, in which a languid yet vigorous-looking Aboriginal man reclines against a thick forest backdrop, is placed in contrast with a cool visual symbol of British presence: an unlikely stone monument to James Wolfe, the victorious general killed in the Battle of Quebec. Légaré again combined sources, this time in specific seventeenth-century Italian representations of ancient Roman mythology, in order to set up the allegorical structure of his work. Through cultural productions such as this painting, the polemical journalism of the late 1830s and 1840s, and the publication of François-Xavier Garneau's *Histoire du Canada*, the period of the Rebellions and the union

Figure 9.4 Joseph Légaré, *View of Quebec City from Pointe de Lévy.* Montreal Museum of Fine Arts, Purchase, 1980.3

of the Canadas has often been seen as ushering in a somewhat tragic awareness and resolve. It is also the period in which graphic satire definitively arrives in Quebec, with the first satiric journals published at Quebec (*Le Fantasque*, 1837) and Montreal (*Le Diable Bleu*, 1843; *Le Charivari canadien*, 1844). Légaré was a friend of Napoléon Aubin (1812–1890), publisher of *Le Fantasque*, and would respectively be the butt and the initiator of visual satires printed and painted in 1849–50. *Landscape with Monument to Wolfe* may well be one of Quebec society's rare satiric history paintings.[27]

A more overtly tragic and indeed Romantic conception of history is given by Antoine Plamondon's 1838 portrait of Zacharie Vincent (1815–1886), a young man from the Huron-Wendat Nation established at Lorette, today Wendake, north of Quebec City.[28] Plamondon gave the work the title of *Le dernier des Hurons*, in echo of James Fenimore Cooper's *Last of the Mohicans* (1826, published in a French edition that same year). Displayed at Quebec in 1838, the work caused a small sensation, serving as inspiration for one of Garneau's most celebrated poems. The portrayals in paint and verse confirmed a strong association through projection of the Canadiens onto Aboriginal identity and nationhood, all within the parameters of an English-speaking empire. Ironically, the painting was purchased by Lord Durham, who by taking it with him on his return to Britain also removed any possibility of inserting the painting into ensuing discourse—except through the echo of Garneau's words. The painting came back to Canada when a Toronto family purchased it at auction in the 1980s.

Plamondon's portrayal of Zacharie Vincent set up a double bind in its fiction of a man who was "the last of his kind," a personifying trope that is all too familiar in European conceptions of the historical outcomes of Aboriginal civilization. But Vincent had children and was part of a community that thrives today. He became a painter in his own right. As

Louise Vigneault has shown, he can be understood today through his career-long production of a range of remarkable self-representations that articulated the identities of the hybrid Huron-Wendat/British subject to that of an artist who painted himself and who, toward the end of his life, commissioned photography of himself in this role.[29] The performance of identity in nineteenth-century art is today a growing area of research because it provides ways of assigning artistic agency to endeavours that have until recently been overlooked in the construction of "national" narratives for Quebec art history, and because it provides paths of continuity to concerns that are present in contemporary Aboriginal visual arts in which performance is both an artistic strategy and one of the key topics of representation.

Similar patterns of engagement can be followed through visual culture from the work of Légaré. His young habitant couple belong to a family of vigorous types; the young Aboriginal man reclining in contemplation of the distinctly reedy James Wolfe has his counterpart in the attractive young farmer who reclines in a field in Légaré's 1834 *Le Canadien*, a painting whose design was transposed into the masthead of the nationalist newspaper of the same name. From the 1840s through the 1860s, Dutch immigrant artist Cornelius Krieghoff (1815–1872), working first at Montreal and then at Quebec, became a one-man industry producing snowy genre landscapes inhabited by bucolic Canadien and stoic Aboriginal men, women, and children. By century's end, at the hands of Henri Julien (1852–1908) and Frederick Simpson Coburn (1871–1960), the young nationalist had turned into the aged habitant figure, a solid and sensible elderly man who ranged through the forest carrying water or re-enacting the glory days of the Rebellions. He sometimes sat in the corner of parlours as young people danced at *réveillon* festivities under the watchful eyes of parents and parish priests.

Artists known especially for their contributions to Canadian Impressionism, like Marc-Aurèle de Foy Suzor-Côté (1869–1937), or who were working in monumental or Symbolist "Rodinesque" public sculpture such as Louis-Philippe Hébert (1850–1917) and Alfred Laliberté (1878–1953), also devoted much of their work to creating collectible bronze representations of this habitant figure, emblematic of the *bon vieux temps* and suitable for display in the bourgeois home. Each of these artists also worked at furthering an iconography of "Indians in the forest," which was in keeping with European and North American conceptions of Aboriginal identity as associated with nature, violence, adventure, and a forlorn physical nobility. One of Julien's habitant designs, the *Vieux de '37*, was similarly evocative of forest and violence, for it showed an elderly man with pipe, toque, *ceinture fléchée*, rifle, and gunpowder pouch tramping on an imagined invisible path through woods of some sacred battle memory from the Rebellions. Created in 1904 for a private collector, this image became emblematic of the entire genre following the publication of the posthumous retrospective *Album Julien* in 1917 and through the ensuing efforts of anthropologist and ethnologist Marius Barbeau to make Julien's work better known in the 1930s and 1940s. The image was recuperated by the Front de Libération du Québec during the October Crisis of 1970 and can today be found on countless apparel items and Internet websites celebrating Patriote ideology.

Quebec Visual Arts in an International Framework, 1860 to Today

The visual arts in colonial Quebec saw a form of progress in which expertise was developed locally as far as possible given the circumstances. Artists were coming from elsewhere to provide the necessary resources for visual arts production in Quebec: the British topographic painters, Dulongpré and Berczy, and later a series of German-born academic artists. Cornelius Krieghoff sold his genre paintings of Canadiens and Aboriginal men and women to an eager legion of British officers stationed in colonial Quebec. William Raphael (1833–1914) and Otto Jacobi (1812–1901) came to a Montreal that was, in the early 1860s, in the grips of its rapid transformation into the business (if not the political) capital of Canada on the eve of Confederation.

Innovations in artistic training and practices also emerged in Quebec in the context of new visual technologies. The Scottish-born entrepreneur William Notman (1826–1891) played a key role in this transformation by gathering painters and photographers together in the production of portrait and landscape visual imagery at the photographic studio that he opened in Montreal in 1856. In 1860 Notman hosted the founding meeting of the Art Association of Montreal (AAM), today's Montreal Museum of Fine Arts. Notman's firm rapidly opened branches across Canada and the United States and was pivotal in establishing a new realm of landscape imagery for Canada from the 1870s onward through its work with (and on) the Canadian Pacific Railway. The affiliation of Notman's artists to Canada's Rockies proved to be meaningful as part of the English-Canadian search for a "national" landscape imagery. In one respect, while this quest eventually led subsequent artists to the woodlands of the Precambrian Shield, the near North, and the Arctic, it also set up a site of distinction from French-Canadian artistic interpretations of and interactions with landscape that were largely focused on the pastoral *arrière-pays* of Quebec or on the transformations of Quebec's rural and urban spaces. The art world of Montreal was perhaps already too complex by 1900 to be reduced to this sort of distinction.

At the Art Association's school, William Brymner (1855–1925) was busy training generations of artists in both academic foundations and in the necessity to confront contemporary art ideas and forms. He encouraged his students to make the trek to Europe—and as the early twentieth century found more and more Montreal women enrolled in the AAM school, they too would follow Brymner's advice. Art history has conferred on them a role in the emergence of **modernist** practices in Quebec visual arts, from Helen McNicoll (1879–1915), who like James Wilson Morrice (1865–1925) came from a well-to-do family and settled overseas before World War I, to the generation of Prudence Heward (1896–1947), Lilias Torrance Newton (1896–1980), and the other members of what has become a quasi-mythical entity in Quebec and Canadian art history, the "Beaver Hall Group."

Among the francophone artists, brothers Adrien Hébert (1890–1967) and Henri Hébert (1884–1950; both were sons of Louis-Philippe Hébert, sculptor of the national figures that adorn the façade of the National Assembly in Quebec) were also part of the efforts to translate modernist practices into Quebec artistic circles in the early twentieth century. As Esther Trépanier has shown, all of the artists working in Quebec in the interwar years were at work in an environment that was more and more influenced by the growth of professional art criticism.[30] While Quebec artists were aware of the developments in European modern art that have since become signposts in art-historical conceptions of the avant-garde—Fauvism, Cubism, Futurism, Dada, and Surrealism—they were on the whole more interested, as were many other artists in Europe and the Americas in this period, in preserving an engagement with conventional forms and topics as a way of participating in the wider discussions about national and international visual culture.

Quebec continued to enjoy strong immigration throughout the early twentieth century, not only from Britain and France but also increasingly from Central and Eastern Europe and Italy. Artists who were active in the multilayered émigré Jewish community of Montreal, notably in the 1930s, also made important contributions to Quebec modernist practices. Regina Seiden (1897–1991), Louis Mulhstock (1904–2001), Jack Beder (1910–1987), Alexander Bercovitch (1891–1951), Sam Borenstein (1908–1969), Harry Mayerovitch (1910–2004), and, in the 1940s, Ghitta Caiserman (1923–2005) and Alfred Pinsky (1921–1999) were all active in fashioning representations of urban life, first of all in Depression-era Montreal (from the speakeasies and jazz clubs to the alleys around the Main and the paths on Mount Royal).

Muhlstock, Mayerovitch, and Caiserman made and published drawings and prints in keeping with the socialist engagement of much illustration and caricature circulating in the North American political press after 1900. In this they joined the satiric tradition established by Napoleon Aubin in the 1830s. In later nineteenth-century Montreal, Henri Julien drew illustrations and caricatures for the *Canadian Illustrated News* (1873 to 1883) and in the satirical journals of Hector Berthelot (1843–1895) before joining the *Montreal Daily Star* in 1888. Julien remained with the *Star* until his death in 1908, contributing reportage illustrations to the paper throughout these years but drawing cartoons only in 1899. In taking over from Julien in the satirist's chair at the *Star* in late 1899, Arthur George Racey (1870–1941) was Montreal's first daily caricaturist. Like Julien (and later Muhlstock, Mayerovitch, and Caiserman), newspaper caricaturists such as Albéric Bourgeois (1876–1962, at *La Presse* from 1905 to 1957) and Robert LaPalme (1908–1997) also sustained other artistic practices, Bourgeois as a landscape watercolourist and LaPalme as a muralist and designer of book covers and theatre posters.

Throughout World War II a group of artists was moving toward an attempt at and an unrestrained embrace of forms of abstraction—choosing to adapt to their local conditions an exploration that was taking place elsewhere in Western art at a time of new (and catastrophic) ruptures in Western politics and culture. Founded in 1939 by John Lyman, already a veteran of modernism in Montreal, this group would come to include Paul-Émile Borduas, Fritz Brandtner, Louis Muhlstock, Jori Smith, Goodridge Roberts, and Alfred Pellan. In 1948, Borduas and a group of seven women and seven men, artists and writers to whom Borduas acted as mentor, joined in publishing the manifesto *Refus Global.* The group included Françoise Sullivan, who contributed an essay, "La Danse et l'espoir," to the main text. Marcelle Ferron, Madeleine Arbour, Jean-Paul Riopelle, Jean-Paul Mousseau, and Claude Gauvreau were also among the members. With its specific condemnation of the influence of the Catholic Church in its co-operation with the reactionary government of Maurice Duplessis (premier from 1936–9 and 1944–59), and of the persistence of a ruralist, habitant mentality, *Refus Global* called for personal and social liberation—"*place à la magie.*"

As a result of the manifesto, Borduas lost his teaching position at the École du meuble and embarked on an artistic journey, first to New York and then to Paris where he died in 1960, only five years after his teacher and mentor Ozias Leduc (see the Biography box). Borduas left a body of work in abstraction that can be understood as exploration and research that was at once intellectual and painterly. He moved from an early *automatiste,* surrealist exploration of subconscious workings, through graphic and painted marks, to a problematic founded in figural struggles between heavily impastoed, architectonic dark and light surfaces. His painting *L'étoile noire* (1957) has become emblematic of the work carried out by Borduas during his final years.[31]

Many of the *Refus Global* group enjoyed rich and varied careers and went on to earn the highest honours bestowed by the Quebec government, as the era of the Quiet Revolution and its aftermath came retrospectively to see *Refus Global* as the first trumpet blast in Quebec's cultural coming of age. Public artworks by Marcelle Ferron, Madeleine Arbour, and Jean-Paul Mousseau have become part and parcel of the Montreal urban experience in the early twenty-first century.

In 2015, Françoise Sullivan is still painting, 67 years after photographer and fellow signatory Maurice Perron captured her choreography *Danse dans la neige* (1948, based on improvisations developed during 1947–8) as a single, interdisciplinary moment of artistic liberation.[32] This interdisciplinarity has become a hallmark of Quebec visual arts ever since. Crucially, *Danse dans la neige* (Figure 9.5) is also still fundamentally engaged with identity

Figure 9.5 Françoise Sullivan, *Danse dans la neige*, #1-17, 1948. Collection of Vivian and David Campbell, Promised Gift to The Art Gallery of Ontario, Toronto.

BIOGRAPHY

*Ozias Leduc**

Ozias Leduc (1864–1955) has a special place in the coming of age of Quebec culture in the post-Confederation era. As art historian Laurier Lacroix reminds us in *Ozias Leduc: An Art of Love and Reverie*, "his work is the link between two centuries of artistic production in Quebec."[33] This artist from Mont Saint-Hilaire, whose practice was as coherent as it was diverse, was both the inheritor of a long tradition of religious painting and the precursor of painterly modernism in Quebec. Leduc was a painter of important church decors, works in still life and landscape, and allegories and portraits, all of which allow us today to identify him as an important proponent of a Symbolist approach in the history of Quebec art. He was also the mentor of painters such as Jean-Paul Riopelle (1923–2002) and Paul-Émile Borduas (1905–1960), artists who spearheaded the veritable paradigm shift toward lyrical abstraction that Quebec art underwent starting in the 1940s. In all his artistic projects, Leduc strove for an ideal in which the stirrings of the soul and the beauty of matter would come together in the act of painting.

At the Normal School in his home town, the young Leduc's talent was noticed early on by a teacher who encouraged him to develop his skills by giving him images to copy. He established his studio, Correlieu, in 1880. In 1886 he became the apprentice of one of the period's most important church decorators, Luigi Capello (1843–1902). Throughout his lifetime, Leduc worked in a Quebec cultural sphere that was marked by the considerable influence of the Catholic Church. Church commissions were still a significant source of income for talented painters. Yet, even as Leduc perfected his skills with the first of these commissions, he was also beginning to transpose Capello's teaching to the more intimate scale of the easel. Slowly but surely, Leduc explored and affirmed his artistic and spiritual identity through the attention he paid to the technical aspects of painting. For Leduc, the mastery of paint was an essential part of the power of any painting, the material itself part of the very meaning of a work of art. This emphasis speaks to a key tenet of artistic modernity—the autonomy of artistic practice.

In 1897, thanks to the sponsorship of his parish priest, Leduc was able to travel to Europe to perfect his training—a rite of passage for almost all Quebec artists of this period. Studying in Paris for a year, Leduc discovered painters working in a wide range of styles and subject matter. He bought books and visited museums. The trip was a turning point: The debates of the artistic avant-gardes nourished his ideas, allowing him to reflect on his own artistic practice and to shape his identity as a painter.

Returning to Saint-Hilaire, Leduc proposed an original iconographic program for his parish church, complementing the traditional imagery of the life of Christ with representations of the seven sacraments (Baptism, Eucharist, Reconciliation, Confirmation, Marriage, Holy Orders, Anointing of the Sick).[34] In planning these large panels, Leduc's emphasis on drawing and design was reinforced by his use of colour as the organizing principle of light. His iconographic imagination showed both extensive learning and simplicity of purpose, each element taking its place in an idealized setting in what Lacroix has called a "spiritual poetry."[35]

This thoughtful planning was also evident in his secular work, always marked by his quest to understand the fundamentals of things and of beings. His portraits, especially those of people he admired, translated the humanity of his sitters. Having committed himself to an ideal of communication, Leduc tried to show in his paintings the benefits of knowledge. This is particularly evident in his studies of adolescents engaged in the act

continued

of reading, such as the National Gallery of Canada's *The Young Student*.[36] The surface textures, the subtle intensities of Leduc's lighting, the poses of the readers all accentuate the effect of absorption that transcends the world depicted in the painting to capture the attention of the viewer. The same is true with Leduc's still-life works, of which several are veritable enigmas in which the painter invites us to reflect with him on the very nature of painting, on the act of creation, and on the role of the artist. Many of Leduc's landscapes, such as *L'heure mauve* (Figure 9.6) and *Gilded Snow*,[37] are meditations on the mysteries and creative power of the timeless Monteregian mountain that gives its name to his village, Mont Saint-Hilaire.

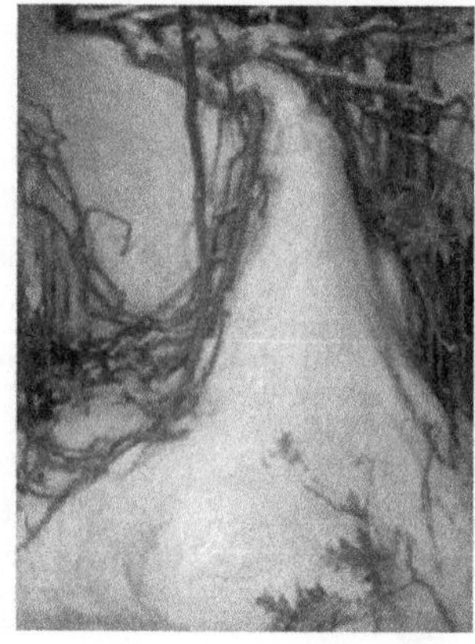

Figure 9.6 Ozias Leduc, *L'heure mauve (Mauve Twilight)*, 1921.

Throughout his career, Leduc constantly sought to achieve this ideal of an equilibrium between ethics and aesthetics. His philosophical engagement was largely founded in the principles of Thomas of Aquinas, very much in vogue among both Church and secular intellectuals throughout this period; it was nurtured by his own intellectual curiosity and by an allegiance to the three transcendentals (the good, the true, the beautiful). This quest for deeper knowledge was to be achieved through art itself and also through an engagement with an artistic community—friends, writers, architects, musicians, and other artists who shared this ideal. In 1918, Leduc was a founder of and contributor to the art journal *Le Nigog*, which opposed regionalist tendencies and sought to open Quebec art to ideas of the avant-garde. Leduc was also committed to the life of his village (he was elected alderman in 1924). He earned the status of a respected elder to whom both the clerical elite and the young avant-garde artists could turn for guidance.

If Leduc's fusion of spiritual and formal concerns links him to the international Symbolist movement, their most articulated statement came in his religious work. Lacroix sees the decor of the church of Notre-Dame-de-la-Présentation in Shawinigan-Sud as the artist's testament: "his ideas on the nature of religious decoration became more rigorous. He established iconographic programmes that enabled him to adapt the most abstract theological message to the particular conditions of the faithful."[38] The mandate to communicate knowledge that Leduc had adopted early in his career found its apotheosis in these narrative frescoes, for the parishioners themselves became integrated within the artist's iconographic program.

All his life, Leduc sought to transmit his vision of the world and to share his knowledge and his love of learning. For almost a century, coinciding with the era of Quebec's most profound social transformations, Ozias Leduc sought to communicate what it is that art has to tell us about the soul:

> Art, what is it? Art is the sound of all that vibrates. It's the sound of a bell, of a cymbal, of a harp, of a violin.
>
> A sound expressive of emotion, a sound that is deep, rhythmic, punctuated, thread; a sound that engages our whole being, our whole self.
>
> A sound that comes from the sensibility of he who sets it in motion, that comes also from metal and its alloy. Gold and silver, elements of the living instrument.
>
> An individual sound, one that comes from the personality of the artist.
>
> A sound, effect of a tool as well.
>
> Art is the sound of a soul.[39]

* Written in collaboration with Nathalie Miglioli.

(artistic, personal, community) and place (snowy hillsides of Otterburn Park in the suburban pastoral belt east of Montreal in the St Lawrence Valley). These might be snowy hillsides depicted by Suzor-Côté, or indeed by Krieghoff before him. The habitants have all disappeared, and as for Aboriginal presence, Louise Vigneault has shown how, in the context of the *automatiste* movement, Borduas's and Riopelle's identity projections adopted and adapted Aboriginal referents. This still leaves open the questions of Aboriginal agency, participation, and contribution to Quebec visual arts and of the role that will be played in the future by Quebec Aboriginal scholars in renewing accounts of artistic practices in the history of Quebec society.

Questions for Critical Thinking

1. This chapter presents introductory statements about Aboriginal visual culture in Quebec for two main periods: (1) the era that begins just after contact with Europeans and closes with Confederation, and (2) the period of contemporary art (which could be said to begin after about 1960). What do you think accounts for the gaps in the record between these two periods?
2. Three documentary sources from French missionaries are cited in this chapter. Given what they tell us about different attitudes toward certain kinds of representation, how can we fit the missionaries' statements into an overall set of ideas about what art is supposed to do in our society? How do their statements measure up to what we know about the different artistic choices made by artists working in Quebec in the twentieth and twenty-first centuries? What is the role of identity in these choices, and what forms of identity are at stake?
3. This chapter has also presented information about the participation of women in the formation of Quebec visual culture from the time of the Ursuline nuns right up to today. What does each of the accounts of women's involvement in the arts tell us about access to training? What kinds of infrastructure seem to be necessary to sustain visual arts practice?

Notes

1. François-Marc Gagnon, *Hommes effarables et bestes sauvaiges : images du Nouveau Monde d'après les voyages de Jacques Cartier* (Montréal: Boréal Express, 1986); Gagnon, *La conversion par l'image : un aspect de la mission des jésuites auprès des indiens du Canada au XVIIe siècle* (Montréal: Bellarmin, 1975).
2. See Gabriel Sagard, *Le grand voyage du pays des Hurons : suivi du Dictionnaire de la langue huronne*, ed. Jack Warwick (Montréal: Presses de l'Université de Montréal [Bibliothèque du Nouveau Monde], 1998 [1632]). An electronic version of this edition is widely available. An examination of Sagard's text for its reading of Aboriginal women's visual culture can be found in Laurier Lacroix, "L'art des Huronnes vu par le frère récollet Gabriel Sagard en 1623–1624," *Cahiers des Dix* 66 (2012): 323–38.
3. "Polsnam" may be the Italian painter Scipione Pulzone (active from 1569–98), who was closely linked to the Jesuits in the sixteenth century. See Jean-François Palomino, "Cartographier la terre des païens : la géographie des missionnaires jésuites en Nouvelle-France au XVIIe siècle," *Revue de Bibliothèque et Archives nationales du Québec* 4 (2012): 12, n 9. A *Lamentation on the Body of Christ* (1593) is in the collection of the Metropolitan Museum of Art in New York (www.metmuseum.org/collection/the-collection-online/search/437342). "Huré" is the French engraver Grégoire Huret (1606–1670). His celebrated imagery of the martyrdom of the Jesuit fathers Brébeuf and Lalement is discussed at length by François-Marc Gagnon in *La conversion par l'image*. See also Emmanuelle Brugerolles and Guillet David, "Grégoire Huret, dessinateur et graveur," *Revue de l'Art* 1 (1997): 9–35, www.persee.fr/web/revues/home/prescript/article/rvart_0035-1326_1997_num_117_1_348339.
4. Gabriel Sagard, *Le grand voyage du pays des Hurons*, ed. Réal Ouellet, with introduction and notes by Réal Ouellet and Jack Warwick (Montreal: Bibliothèque québécoise, 2007 [1632]), 173; author's translation.
5. *Relation de ce qui s'est passé en la Nouvelle-France en l'an 1636* (Paris, 1637), *Early Canadiana Online*, http://eco.canadiana.ca/view/oocihm.94031/3?r=0&s=1, cited in Gagnon, *La conversion par l'image*, 24, n 37; author's translation.
6. Richard White, *The Middle Ground: Indians, Empires and Republics in the Great Lakes Region, 1650–1815* (Cambridge: Cambridge University Press, 1991).

7. Janet C. Berlo and Ruth Phillips, *Native North American Art* (Oxford: Oxford University Press, 1998); Ruth Phillips, *Trading Identities: The Souvenir in Native North American Art from the Northeast, 1700–1900* (Montreal and Kingston/Seattle: McGill-Queen's University Press/ University of Washinton Press, 1998).
8. Christine Turgeon, *Le fil de l'art : les broderies des Ursulines de Québec* (Quebec: Musée du Québec/Musée des Ursulines de Québec, 2002).
9. Marie-Emmanuel Chabot, "Guyart, Marie, called Marie de l'Incarnation," in *Dictionary of Canadian Biography*, vol. 1 (Toronto/Sainte-Foy: University of Toronto Press/ Presses de l'Université Laval, 2003), accessed 14 December 2014, www.biographi.ca/en/bio/guyart_marie_1E.html.
10. Phillips, *Trading Identities*, 106.
11. Laurier Lacroix, *Les arts de la Nouvelle France* (Quebec: Musée national des beaux-arts du Québec/Les publications du Québec, 2012), 57–9.
12. Phillips, *Trading Identities*.
13. Ariane Généreux, "Les huiles sur cuivre en Nouvelle-France au XVIIe siècle : circulation et usages," (master's thesis, Université du Québec à Montréal, 2010), www.archipel.uqam.ca/id/eprint/2843.
14. In the twenty-first century, American scholars have claimed for early American cultural history Ursuline visual and textual practices that were bound up with francophone territorial settlement in early colonial North America. See Frances Pohl, *Framing America* (New York: Thames and Hudson, 2012 [2002]).
15. The definitive historiographical account of this painting remains Gagnon and Lacroix's 1983 article "*La France apportant la foi aux Hurons de Nouvelle-France* : un tableau conservé chez les Ursulines de Québec," *Journal of Canadian Studies* 18, no 3 (Fall 1983): 5–20. For a representation of this work and the restoration process it has undergone at the Centre de conservation du Québec, see the CCQ website: www.ccq.gouv.qc.ca/index.php?id=100&no_cache=1&tx_mcccfrechercheavancee_pi1%5Bress_uid%5D=271.
16. Kent Monkman (Cree/Métis), *Trappers of Men*, 2006, acrylic on canvas, wood frame, 262 x 415 x 9 cm, Montreal Museum of Fine Arts, purchase, Horsley and Annie Townsend Bequest, anonymous gift and gift of Dr. Ian Hutchison, 2006.87, http://educart.ca/oeuvre-artwork/2006_87-eng.
17. Kent Monkman (Cree/Métis), *The King's Beavers*, 2011. Acrylic on canvas, 243.8 x 213.4 cm, Montreal Museum of Fine Arts, gift of the artist and W. Bruce C. Bailey in honour of Nathalie Bondil to mark the 150th anniversary of the Montreal Museum of Fine Arts, 2011.401, http://educart.ca/oeuvre-artwork/2011_401-eng.
18. Nadia Myre (Algonquin Nation Kitigan Zibi Anishinabeg), *Portrait in Motion*, 2002. Mini DV transferred to DVD, framed glass plate (screen), 1/5 Screen: 64.5 x 31.4 x 3.8 cm; time: 2 min, 21 s (nonstop). Montreal Museum of Fine Arts, purchase, the Museum Campaign 1998–2002 Fund, 2009.59.1, http://educart.ca/oeuvre-artwork/2009_59_1-eng.
19. A full set of the Short engravings is held at Montreal's McCord Museum, www.mccord-museum.qc.ca/scripts/search_results.php?Lang=1&artist=00675.
20. Gerald E. Finley, *George Heriot, Postmaster Painter of the Canadas* (Toronto: University of Toronto Press, 1983).
21. *A View of Fort La Galette, Indian Castle, and Taking a French Ship of War on the River St. Lawrence, by Four Boats of One Gun Each of the Royal Artillery Commanded by Captain Streachy*, 1760. Watercolour over graphite on laid paper, 38.3 x 58.9 cm, National Gallery of Canada (no. 6271), purchased 1954, www.gallery.ca/en/see/collections/artwork.php?mkey=3756.
22. Marilou Desnoyers, "Le décor sculpté de l'église Sainte-Marguerite de Blairfindie : une œuvre palimpseste et pluridiscursive," (master's thesis, Montréal, Université du Québec à Montréal, 2013).
23. Laurier Lacroix, "La révolution française et le renouveau de la peinture d'histoire au Bas-Canada," in *La circulation des œuvres d'art/The Circulation of Works of Art in the Revolutionary Era 1789–1848*, ed. Roberta Panzanelli and Monica Preti-Hamard (Presses universitaires de Rennes/Institut national d'histoire de l'art/ Getty Research Institute, 2007), 249–66.
24. John R. Porter, *Joseph Légaré 1795–1855 l'oeuvre : Catalogue raisonné* (Ottawa: National Gallery of Canada, 1977); Mario Béland, ed., *Peinture au Québec 1820–1850 : Nouveaux regard, nouvelles perspectives* (Québec: Musée du Québec, 1991); Lacroix, "La révolution française."
25. Joseph Légaré, *View of Quebec City from Pointe de Lévy*, ca. 1840–2. Oil on canvas, 90 x 120 cm, Montreal Museum of Fine Arts, purchase, gift of the Succession J. A. DeSève and Horsley and Annie Townsend bequest, 1980.3, http://educart.ca/oeuvre-artwork/1980_3-eng.
26. Joseph Légaré, *Landscape with Monument to Wolfe*, ca. 1845. Oil on canvas, 131.3 x 174.6 cm, Musée national des beaux-arts du Québec, 1955.109, www.mnbaq.org/collections/oeuvre/paysage-au-monument-a-wolfe-2522. Didier Prioul, "Joseph Légaré, Paysagiste" (Ph.D. diss., Université Laval, 1991).
27. The satiric thesis is argued by Suzanne Simoneau, "Joseph Légaré, un ironiste militant : contexte et portée satirique du *Paysage au monument à Wolfe*," (master's thesis, Université du Québec à Montréal, 2014).
28. David Karel, Marie-Dominic Labelle, and Sylvie Thivierge, "Vincent, Zacharie," in *Dictionary of Canadian Biography*, vol. 11 (Toronto/Sainte-Foy: University of Toronto Press/Presses de l'Université Laval, 2003), accessed 20 December 2014, www.biographi.ca/en/bio/vincent_zacharie_11E.html.
29. Louise Vigneault and Isabelle Masse, "Les autoreprésentations de l'artiste Huron-Wendat Zacharie Vincent (1815–1886) : icônes d'une gloire politique et spirituelle," *Journal of Canadian Art History/Annales d'histoire de l'art canadien* 33, no. 2 (2011): 41–70.

30. Esther Trépanier, *Peinture et modernité au Québec 1919–1939* (Montréal: Nota bene, 1998).
31. Paul-Émile Borduas, *L'étoile noire/The Black Star,* 1957. Oil on canvas, 162.5 x 129.5 cm, Montreal Museum of Fine Arts, gift of Mr. and Mrs. Gérard Lortie, 1960.1238. The MMFA provides a presentation of the work on its Virtual Museum website at https://educart.ca/oeuvre-artwork/1960_1238-eng.
32. The work was the subject of a retrospective entitled *Saisons Sullivan* and presented by Louise Déry at the Galerie de L'UQAM in 2007. For images of the choreography and a discussion of the exhibition, see Gilles Lapointe, "Françoise Sullivan et Marion Landry," *Spirale* [online edition], www.spiralemagazine.com/parutions/217/portfolio/pfolio_01.html.
33. Laurier Lacroix, "Introduction," in *Ozias Leduc: A Work of Love and Reverie,* ed. Laurier Lacroix (Montreal Museum of Fine Arts/Musée du Québec, 1996), 22. This text, prepared in collaboration with Nathalie Miglioli, is greatly indebted to Lacroix's definitive study.
34. Lacroix, *Ozias Leduc,* 105.
35. Ibid., 108.
36. Ozias Leduc, *The Young Student,* 1894. Oil on canvas, 36.7 x 46.7 cm, National Gallery of Canada, www.gallery.ca/en/see/collections/artwork.php?mkey=1361.
37. Ozias Leduc, *Mauve Twilight,* 1921. Oil on paper, mounted on canvas, 92.4 x 76.8 cm, Montreal Museum of Fine Arts, www.virtualmuseum.ca/edu/ViewLoitLo.do%3Bjsessionid=C981A1807143A96EAAE16F-321C9003AF?method=preview&lang=EN&id=5537; Ozias Leduc, *Gilded Snow,* 1916. Oil on canvas, 137.8 x 77.2 cm, National Gallery of Canada, www.gallery.ca/en/see/collections/artwork.php?mkey=13507.
38. Lacroix, *Ozias Leduc,* 226.
39. Ozias Leduc, "L'art, qu'est-ce?" (Bibliothèque et Archives nationales du Québec MSS 327). Cited in Lacroix, *Ozias Leduc,* 227.

Select Bibliography

Béland, Mario, ed. *Painting in Quebec, 1820–1850: New Views, New Perspectives.* Quebec: Musée du Québec, 1991.

Des Rochers, Jacques, ed. *Quebec and Canadian Art: The Montreal Museum of Fine Arts' Collection.* Vol. 1. Montreal: Montreal Museum of Fine Arts, 2011.

Gagnon, François-Marc. *La conversion par l'image : un aspect de la mission des jésuites auprès des indiens du Canada au XVIIe siècle.* Montreal: Bellarmin, 1975.

———. *Hommes effarables et bestes sauvaiges : images du Nouveau Monde d'après les voyages de Jacques Cartier.* Montreal: Boréal Express, 1986.

Karel, David, ed. *Dictionnaire des artistes de langue francaise en Amérique du Nord : peintres, sculpteurs, dessinateurs, graveurs, photographes, et orfèvres.* Québec/Sainte-Foy: Musée du Québec/Presses de l'Université Laval, 1992.

Lacroix, Laurier. *Les arts de la Nouvelle France.* Quebec: Musée national des beaux-arts du Québec/Les publications du Québec, 2012.

Mirzoeff, Nicholas. *An Introduction to Visual Culture.* London: Routledge, 1999.

Mitchell, W. J. T. *Picture Theory: Essays on Verbal and Visual Representation.* Chicago: University of Chicago Press, 1995.

Phillips, Ruth. *Trading Identities: The Souvenir in Native North American Art from the Northeast, 1700–1900.* Montreal/Seattle: McGill-Queen's University Press/University of Washington Press, 1998.

Reid, Dennis. *"Our Own Country Canada": Being an Account of the National Aspirations of the Principal Landscape Artists in Montreal and Toronto, 1860–1890.* Ottawa: National Gallery of Canada, 1979.

Trépanier, Esther. *Femmes artistes du XXe siècle au Québec : œuvres du MNBAQ.* Quebec: Musée national des beaux-arts du Québec, 2010.

———. *Jewish Painters of Montreal: Witnesses of Their Time, 1930–1948.* Montreal: Éditions de l'Homme, 2008.

———. *Peinture et modernité au Québec, 1919–1939.* Montreal: Nota bene, 1998.

Turgeon, Christine. *Le fil de l'art : les broderies des Ursulines de Québec.* Quebec: Musée du Québec/Musée des Ursulines de Québec, 2002.

Vigneault, Louise, and Isabelle Masse. "Les autoreprésentations de l'artiste Huron-Wendat Zacharie Vincent (1815–1886) : icônes d'une gloire politique et spirituelle." *Journal of Canadian Art History/Annales d'histoire de l'art canadien* 33, no. 2 (2011): 41–70.

Villeneuve, René. *Baroque to Neo-Classical: Sculpture in Quebec.* Ottawa: National Gallery of Canada, 1997.

Part C
Language

Introduction

In a book that identifies key "questions" to better understand Quebec, it seems quite obvious that a few of these questions should be related to language. In fact, one could ask if a book about Quebec's history and society could *not* have a section dedicated to the question of language. Quebecers are admittedly obsessed with language.[1] The situation in the early twenty-first century, characterized by linguistic peace, contrasts sharply to that of only a few decades ago. The presence of the French language in North America has always been an object of curiosity and fascination.

In his 1831–2 tour of America that led to the publication of the book *Democracy in America*, French thinker Alexis de Tocqueville wrote:

> Canada piques our curiosity keenly, [as] the French nation has kept itself intact there. They have the customs and language of the century of Louis XIV.[2]

Language has always been a central theme of debate and discussion within the different political and social circumstances of New France, the Province of Quebec, Lower Canada, United Canada, Quebec, and Canada. For example, language was one of the first matters raised by the newly elected members in both the Lower Canada Parliament (1792–3) and the 1867 Dominion of Canada House of Commons. Parliamentarians pondered what the language of debates and laws within parliamentary and political institutions should be. Although the questions have differed from one century to the next, the importance of language in both Quebec and Canadian history has been constant. Examining the language theme in the context of Quebec raises questions that relate to all of the themes in this book: memory, identity, citizenship, Quebec models, and Quebec in the international sphere.

Much of the international interest in Quebec focuses on language. It is striking to see, for example, in academic writings on language and society, how often Quebec is used as a case study for language policy and planning, language conflict, language and identity, bilingualism and bilingual education, language and ethnicity, language rights, linguistic minorities, language and nationalism, and second language acquisition.[3]

Following a multidisciplinary approach, this section examines the topic of language through the lens of a sociolinguist, a political scientist, a philosopher, and a specialist in popular music. These different approaches provide us with insightful perspectives on the situation of the French language and language dynamics in Quebec and in Canada. They also raise important questions about identity and culture, and individual, collective, and minority rights.

The section begins with Chantal Bouchard's sociolinguistic examination of French in Quebec. To paraphrase sociolinguist J. A. Fishman, it seeks to answer the question, Who speaks (or writes) what language (or what language variety) to whom, when, and to what end?[4] Bouchard asks: Is Quebec French considered the equivalent of Parisian French? And how has the perception of French changed over time? The reader gains a historical overview of the perceived quality of French in Quebec. Starting with the French regime, Bouchard shows that various European observers perceived French in New France to be very similar to metropolitan French, differing only in vocabulary. This perception would, however, change. In the nineteenth century, Europeans and Canadians (descendants of French settlers in New France) called New World French "gobbledygook." What explains this change from "pure" language to "corrupt" language usage? Why did this devaluation occur? Bouchard shows how key political and historical moments influenced this perceptual transformation. For example, how did the Conquest and the British regime affect language? Ties with France gradually waned, and French in Quebec was isolated and threatened. Bouchard asserts, for example, that the linguistic insecurity of francophone Quebecers began in 1841, with the Union of Upper and Lower Canada. She evaluates the extent to which periods of anglicization in the sociolinguistic history contributed to self-depreciation.

Linda Cardinal's chapter looks at language policy choices made over the years in Quebec and Canada. While discovering the importance of the French and English languages, readers discover how the choices and decisions made over language were influenced by political events, culture, history, and power relations. The author demonstrates how language policy brings to the forefront the importance and the role of a key actor: the state. In the adoption of language legislation, Cardinal argues, solutions have been crafted over the years (in the context of Quebec and more broadly Canada) to solve language conflicts and inequalities, and to determine the use and status of both French and English. We discover how, within the Canadian federation, Canada and Quebec have resorted either to territoriality or to personality principles in their crafting and implementation of successive language legislative initiatives. Cardinal's article provides a nuanced approach toward understanding the fundamental milestones of both Canadian and Quebec language regimes. Stressing the forces of competition and collaboration, Cardinal's contribution offers a complex portrait of the evolution of language issues while simultaneously providing a detailed analysis of the most salient current and prospective language planning and policy matters in Quebec.

Daniel Weinstock focuses on Quebec language policy issues from a political philosophy perspective. This contribution is part of a rich body of scholarly literature on language and diversity that has been advanced by Canadian political philosophers such as Charles Taylor, Will Kymlicka, and James Tully. To contextualize the Quebec situation, Weinstock examines a variety of language-related challenges for Quebecers and Catalans. Weinstock's main question is, How can language policies favour a popular convergence around a regional majority language, which is itself a minority language in the larger regional context? Francophone Quebecers faced the dilemma of opting either for a laissez-faire approach that might jeopardize the vitality of their language, or for a legislative approach that aims to protect the language but risks infringing on individual rights. This building tension between collective and individual rights raises the question: Can a society with strong collective goals be liberal?

French in Quebec has always been much more than a medium of communication. It was a central part of Canadian and French-Canadian identity and culture. With the Quiet Revolution and the decline of Catholicism, French became even more important to the new Quebec identity, becoming the focus of political life in the 1960s as campaigns for new language laws began what Weinstock calls the "politics of language." Weinstock points out that interpretations of the language debate in Quebec vary greatly. Indeed, how do the perspectives of Canadian francophones, anglophones, and allophones inside Quebec vary and compare to each other and to those of Canadians outside Quebec? Weinstock suggests two important concepts for understanding this situation from the perspective of political philosophy: identity and liberal justice. French as the official and common public language helps to establish French as a new pillar of territorially based Quebec identity; but to non-francophone Quebecers, the mandatory use of French might seem exclusionary. Weinstock reflects on how language policies can achieve balance and justice. Finally, he considers how perceptions of language policies in Quebec have changed. What could explain the linguistic peace in Quebec for the last 20 years? Why are anglophones and allophones not contesting Bill 101, as they did when the law was adopted in 1977? Weinstock suggests that the key lies in identity issues around questions such as who is a Quebecer, and who is a francophone?

We then shift focus to language and identity issues as expressed in Quebec music and song lyrics. What is the importance of language in defining a Quebec song? Christopher Jones asks, What is unique about popular music in Quebec in the North American context, and how does popular music shape the way Quebecers think about themselves? Jones starts his musical journey of periods, genres, and celebrities in 1945 when Félix Leclerc and Raymond Lévesque, the first icons of Quebec *chansons* (French songs whose lyrics are most important) made their mark on the public sphere. He notes several factors in the emergence of these unique Quebec voices in *chansons*: radio and television programs devoted to *chansons*, popular venues, contests, and the influence of key individuals. We discover that the road to the recognition of Quebec's voice in *chansons* first passed through Paris.

Jones then takes us to the 1960s and the Quiet Revolution, examining the role of songwriters in this time of intense social change. In a period that poet Roland Giguère calls "*l'âge de la parole,*" we find, not surprisingly, a boom in Quebec *chansonniers* (songwriters) and a proliferation of popular music houses called *boîtes à chansons*. Songwriters lent their voices to the evolving discourse on nationalism, identity, and language. We also find an American influence in the 1950s and 1960s, and the *chansons* of this era shared the popular success and spirit of the *yé-yé* movement. Like Quebec literary writers, by the end of the 1960s Quebec songwriters had to choose between standardized French or the colloquial Québécois *joual*. Songwriters in the 1960s and 1970s felt the pulse of Quebec society and contributed to its nationalism, and a new generation of bands took over from the *chanson* pioneers. These artists benefited from government policy in the 1970s that mandated a high level of French-language content on the radio.

The 1980s brought tough economic times and a post-referendum effect, which caused national identity and language concerns to play a smaller role in Quebec popular culture. English lyrics with little Quebec specificity became common. In the 1990s, the Quebec music scene expanded into hip-hop, country, and Anglo rock. The *chanson* tradition was revived with the work of bands like Les Colocs, who integrated various musical genres with playful French lyrics containing popular Québécois colloquialisms. Jones's chapter shows how a Quebec-based musician belongs to a diverse, multilingual community of musical genres where French is key.

The music scene faces many of the same French-language questions that Quebec society does: Is French, as the common public language of Quebec, encompassing Quebecers of all origins? Will French be the medium that can promote interactions among all Quebecers for the development of Quebec society? Who can be identified as a francophone artist?

The chapters in this section on language illustrate for readers a range of important historical and contemporary episodes focusing on Quebec's "language journey." We clearly discover, following the claim of sociolinguist Florian Coulmas, that "every language is a social product, and every society constitutes itself through language."[5] Tensions, conflicts, and polarized identities are a part of the Quebec language narrative. As Quebec author Sherry Simon has observed in her work on Montreal, public language "has always been more than information: it has been a battleground."[6]

Notes

1. Taken from Chantal Bouchard's book title: *Obsessed with Language: A Sociolinguistic History of Quebec* (Toronto: Guernica, 2008).
2. Alexis de Tocqueville, to his mother, 19 June 1831, Yale Tocqueville collection.
3. See, for example, Chrstina Brett Paulston and G. Richard Tucker, *Sociolinguistics: The Essential Readings* (Toronto: Wiley-Blackwell, 2003), and Florian Coulmas, ed., *The Handbook of Sociolinguistics* (Toronto: Wiley-Blackwell, 1998).
4. J. A. Fishman, "The Sociology of Language," in Pier Paolo Giglioli, ed., *Language and Social Context* (Harmondsworth, England: Penguin, 1972), 46.
5. Florian Coulmas, "Sociolinguistics," in Mark Aronoff and Janie Rees-Miller, ed., *The Handbook of Linguistics* (Oxford: Blackwell, 2003), 563.
6. Sherry Simon, *Translating Montreal: Episodes in the Life of a Divided City* (Montreal and Kingston: McGill-Queen's University Press, 2006), 215.

10 The Sociolinguistic History of French in Quebec

Chantal Bouchard, McGill University

Timeline

1763 Treaty of Paris: France cedes Canada to England. After surrender of New France three years earlier, most schools close their doors.

1791 Constitutional Act: Canada is divided into two provinces: Lower Canada, which is mainly French, and Upper Canada, which is mainly English.

1831 Étienne Parent relaunches newspaper *Le Canadien* under the motto "Our Institutions, Our Language and Our Laws!" Alexis de Tocqueville comments on language of French Canadians.

1837 Patriote rebellion violently repressed by the British army.

1840 Union Act unites Upper and Lower Canada, further to the recommendation of Lord Durham, who also advised the linguistic assimilation of French Canadians. Section 41 (repealed only eight years later) makes English the only official language of the United Province of Canada.

1867 British North America Act: Section 133 institutes bilingualism in Canada's federal Parliament, Quebec's legislature, and in courts of every province.

1902 Société du parler français au Canada is founded and begins to publish *Bulletin du parler français au Canada* as well as organize large-scale "congresses" on the French language. (The first takes place in 1912; the fourth, and last, in 1956.)

1937 Second Congress on the French Language: Participants call for creation of Office de la langue française and the Comité permanent de la survivance française is established.

1961 One year after Liberal Party of Jean Lesage is elected and the Quiet Revolution begins, Office de la langue française is created.

1968 Gendron Commission of Inquiry on the Position of the French Language is struck. St Leonard school crisis begins.

1974 Bill 22 adopted by the Liberal government of Robert Bourassa, proclaiming French as the official language of Quebec.

1977 René Lévesque's Parti Québécois government adopts Bill 101, Charter of the French Language, and founds Conseil de la langue française, the Commission de toponymie, and Commission de protection de la langue française.

2001 Commission of the Estates General on the Situation and Future of the French Language in Quebec, chaired by Gérald Larose, tables its report.

If ever there was one central issue, one nerve centre, in Quebec history, it would be language. The French language that was transplanted to the banks of the St Lawrence River in the early seventeenth century thrived there unhindered until the middle of the eighteenth century. At that time, it was the language of the Canadiens, the name given to the French colonists who were born in New France. It was also the same prestigious parlance spoken not only in Paris and in all of France's major cities, but also in cultivated circles throughout Europe. It was after 1763, when the colony was ceded to Britain in the Treaty of Paris, that the trouble with language began.

The Paradox of *Bon Usage* and Devaluation

After the British takeover, with each passing era, perceptions of the French language changed remarkably among Quebecers of French-Canadian (Canadien) origin. For years now I have studied their political, economic, and social history, asking questions about how this history has shaped linguistic identity. One question I have asked is why francophone Quebecers in the 1950s and 1960s were so negative in their opinions about the French they spoke. Through my research, I was able to convincingly demonstrate that their opinions were directly linked to the development of a negative self-image, which began to emerge toward the end of the nineteenth century.[1] My political, economic, and social analyses proved this point.

Politically, I found that French Canadians saw themselves as a dominated, poor, and ignorant people, condemned to a mediocre destiny. This collective identity had been forged over time by a sequence of weighty events (the British Conquest, the Rebellions of 1837–8 and the ensuing repression, the Durham Report, the Union Act, and Canadian Confederation). Each of these events disempowered French Canadians and underscored their political status as a minority people.

Economically, I found that their most striking change in self-image came with a massive change of vocations and context. As the population grew and arable farm land became correspondingly scarce, the province's peasant farming class, the **habitants**, flocked to the city to take on jobs and underwent a large-scale proletarization. These erstwhile farmer–landowners, who had not been rich but had enjoyed relative independence up to that point, thereby became dependent, waged urban labourers and employees at the service of their English bosses. The undereducation of the peasant and working classes was clearly not conducive to their social mobility. Neither was the fact that anglophones controlled the industrial and business sectors. These factors only exacerbated the feeling among French Canadians that they were being blocked at every turn, caught in an inferior social position from which they were ill equipped to break free.

Socially, this decline in class status followed the same downward curve as opinions on language, with both reaching their lowest point around 1950–60. Newspapers, books, and public presentations about language fed much of my post-Conquest analysis. But I was not able to examine opinions on language prior to 1840 since the first documentation of this kind appeared around that time. Therefore, it is impossible to know first-hand what the Canadiens of 1800 might have thought about their language and whether they deemed it legitimate or not. This said, there are many documents dating from the time of New France and the first decades of the British regime, written by foreigners who were merely passing through. By all of these visitors' accounts, the French spoken in New France was faithful to the ***bon usage*** (correct use of language) for that era and judged in a very positive light. Differences were remarked upon in some cases, but mostly pertaining to vocabulary. Neither pronunciation nor syntax seemed to diverge from the **norm**. A few concurrent usages were noted, but these simply reflected language variations that also existed in France. It was toward the mid-nineteenth century that a negative discourse about the language of the Canadiens began to surface and would virtually establish itself as the rule. Erudite French-Canadian "men of letters" began to disparage the language of their compatriots in their writings on the subject—and they were not alone in their opinions. The British, the Americans, and Anglo-Canadians also heaped derogatory criticisms on the language spoken by French Canadians, often claiming it was nothing but a French *patois* (dialect). As comment upon comment accumulated, the French spoken in Quebec was devalued. Within little more than half a century, how could such a remarkable reversal of opinion have occurred?

Certainly, after the Conquest, the British presence in Quebec had been making its mark on the language of the Canadiens. But how could a few dozen borrowed English words lead to such a dramatic loss of status, especially at a time when borrowings from English were common enough in France? To answer this question it is important to understand the importance of contact with France. When contact was broken, the linguistic changes taking place in France no longer had any direct bearing on the inhabitants of its former colony. Consequently, it took less than two generations for Canadien French to lose its legitimacy—an abrupt, if not brutal, turn of events. Certainly, no other rational explanation for this reversal of opinion may be found by examining the internal development of French in Quebec. There is, in fact, every reason to believe that the early Canadiens were very conservative in their language use. We may surmise that between 1793 and 1830 a trickle of anglicisms likely found their way into common parlance, but such utterances were still relatively limited. It also appears that the departure of a large segment of the upper class during the 1763 regime change in Quebec fostered the dissemination of some popular or provincial vocabulary, to the detriment of normative or *bon usage* French words.[2] However, on the whole these changes were too modest to account for the loss of legitimacy suffered by French in Quebec, as manifested in the criticisms of the French-Canadian, British, and American intelligentsia.

In any event, these exceptional anglicisms and incorrect locutions should not have sufficed to discredit the language of French Canadians such that it could be justifiably labelled a "French-Canadian *patois*," as the British and Americans would unrelentingly claim. As for the unfavourable opinion of French-Canadian men of letters, my research has shown that two main factors came into play. First, they feared that anglicization, which was spreading throughout the nineteenth century, would bastardize French (and they soon launched an ambitious newspaper campaign against it). Second, their perception of deviations from the *bon usage* was predicated on the normative standard of contemporaneous Parisian French. Since, as I have previously pointed out, Canadian French had evolved very little since 1763, it had to be the changes in Parisian usage that ultimately produced these perceived deviations. It was this historical progression that the intellectual elite of 1840 failed to acknowledge and elucidate to others.

What, in fact, have intellectuals said about the "deviations" that occurred from 1763 to 1840? Through its research (in the early twentieth century), the Société du parler français au Canada (SPFC) established that many of the Canadianisms in Quebec pronunciation and vocabulary were in fact archaisms with respect to normative French. In other words, as abundantly illustrated by Jules-Paul Tardivel, they were very much in keeping with the *bon usage* of their time.[3] SPFC researchers Adjutor Rivard and Louis-Philippe Geoffrion also highlighted the etymological similarities between France's regional vernaculars and the Quebec lexicon. In fact, claims that French has remained in a very pure state in Quebec, and that Canadien French is the language of the *Grand Siècle* of Bossuet and Racine, are not hard to find. Defenders of Canadien French would say that it remained "legitimate" because it complied with the *bon usage* of the eighteenth century and that of the *ancien régime*. Viewed in this way, the linguistic conservatism of French Canadians was eminently praiseworthy, buttressed by the indisputable prestige of French literature and culture during this period and by a widespread distrust of the innovations of the Republic, the Empire, and (in literary matters) Romanticism.

But it is here that we encounter the thorny notion of "legitimacy." Louis Fréchette, Arthur Buies, and many other writers and intellectuals ridiculed such claims, saying their proponents were "puffed up with crass ignorance."[4] These detractors (and like-minded critics in the nineteenth century) argued that conformity to contemporary standards was the sole measure of **linguistic legitimacy**; hence any of the archaisms, anglicisms, or other uses of their compatriots' language that these men perceived as being inaccurate were judged illegitimate.

As for vocabulary, over the years the question of legitimacy has focused minds, intellectual or not, on various categories of Canadianisms and has been addressed somewhat differently. While everyone agrees that anglicisms should be rejected in French, positions on other categories have varied considerably. Because the first systematic research into the origins of Canadianisms began only in the twentieth century, distinctions remain unclear between archaisms that were part of the norm in the seventeenth

Primary Source

Arthur Buies, "Chronique"

There is one thing that is perpetually hurting us, and it is not necessarily limited to the correct use of the French language, nor the intimacy we share with it, but that we live in an English country, an English environment, and are surrounded by English speakers. What is absolutely French in the province of Quebec are the traditions, the character, the type, the uniqueness, the way of thinking, acting and feeling in the manner of the old Gauls. What is least French is the language. The majority of public figures, of professional men, and of all those who partake in any type of active career, know less French than English, using the latter regularly while remaining oblivious to their abundant use of English words, expressions, and sentences. I would even state, and may the entire law society descend upon me in a disparaging manner or burn me at the stake for it, that generally speaking, our lawyers (who are the traitors—the scoundrels—regardless of party membership) speak neither English, nor French, preferring an unyielding jargon that we only understand because we have grown accustomed to it, and now have a better understanding of what they mean than what they say. Keep in mind that I speak of virtuous men, men of value (if we turn a blind eye to the schemes of the profession). I speak of intelligent, cultured, educated, knowledgeable men, who will leave their mark in any country, or in any advanced society throughout civilization. But what can I say? It is not their fault; we must blame the world we live in. The constant use of French and English perverts both languages; and of course, the one that suffers the most from this bastardization is the one that is afforded less value in everyday settings. Here, commerce, industry, finance, arts, trades, as well as our education system, our habits, even the way we greet one another or how we blow our noses, is in English. How will our language survive all of these external influences continually berating, enveloping, and suffocating it? How can these men allow thousands of everyday occurrences [to] slowly chip away at it? It would be a miracle if it was otherwise, but to then conclude that we must irrationally allow things to continue in this manner, *sinere res radere ut cadunt,*[5] would be misleading. There is an abyss which I am personally determined to cross, and I want to convince my compatriots to join me in this endeavour. If we succumb, oh well, we'll succumb, but it will not be without the utmost effort, and if we must hear "*fines Canadie*"[6] in French, may it be, like Kosciuszko, with our weapons in hand. Alas! We have lost the spirit of the French language, but should we not attempt to find it again, as we still have the time, the ability, and most of all, the willingness to take up the task?

Source: Arthur Buies, "Chronique," *L'Électeur,* 21 January 1888, 1, 4.

and eighteenth centuries, provincialisms brought over from Poitou or Normandy, and neologisms of form or meaning created to name the discoveries of the New World. What we do know, as evidenced by the Quebec newspaper columns on the French language at the end of the nineteenth century, is that people tended to reject a word or expression when they discovered its "Canadian" origins and realized that it competed with or deviated from standard language use. Similarly, language columnists typically accepted only Canadianisms that expressed concepts exclusive to North America. In short, the scope for lexical creativity remained exceedingly narrow in Quebec until 1900.

The paradox before us is astonishing. After just two generations a language variety that had changed very little was almost entirely devalued. The political and economic circumstances of French Canadians weighed significantly in the balance, since the prestige of a language variety is inextricably linked to the social position of its speakers, or, as Pierre Bourdieu would say, "a language is worth what those who speak it are worth."

The Impact of the Conquest

In 1763 New France was ceded to England in the Treaty of Paris. The population of the colony, some 65,000 souls of French origin, was entirely French-speaking since emigration conditions and the situation in the colony did not allow for the transmission of any other European languages at the time. Linguistic unity was achieved quickly and without the need for any intervention, since *patois d'oïl* and the other languages spoken in eighteenth-century France died out with the first generation of Canadiens.

What sort of French did Quebecers speak as new British subjects? Various sources provide valuable insight into this question. By way of comparison, we may look at the comments made by foreign visitors to New France and (later) to the Province of Quebec under the British regime. About a dozen descriptions of New France are left to us by these foreigners, providing telling observations about the language spoken by French Canadians.[7] The concordance between their comments is remarkable, as all agreed that the Canadiens spoke a very pure French with no accent and that there were no *patois* in Canada. Even the Marquis de Montcalm remarked that "the peasants speak French very well."[8] Another dozen or so accounts from foreign visitors[9] were written about the province under British rule from 1763 to 1853, essentially confirming observations from the previous period but including a few remarks on the influence of English. With the passage of time, this influence would become more pronounced.

Toward the beginning of the nineteenth century, the archaizing (increasingly outdated) characteristics in Canadian French are first mentioned, and they too became increasingly pronounced over time. By 1833, Isidore Lebrun spoke of the "strong imprint of the refugee style"[10] in Quebec. He was referring to the style of exiled Protestant writers who, cut off from the evolution of the language in France, used turns of phrase and expressions that seemed outmoded in the mother country. In an article that appeared in an 1850 edition of the *Revue des Deux Mondes*, writer Théodore Pavie undoubtedly best articulated the feeling that must have overtaken most cultivated Frenchmen when they recognized jargon among Canadiens that had not been used for a generation or two in France:

> They speak an old and relatively inelegant French; their thick pronunciation, devoid of accentuations, is not so far removed from that of the Lower Normans. Talking with them, one soon realizes that they were separated from us before the period in which everyone in France began to write and engage in discussion.[11]

The historic period alluded to here was, of course, that of the French Revolution. Jean-Jacques Ampère, who was also a writer, struck another note entirely in his comments, expressing his pleasant surprise at overhearing local lingo in Montreal that appeared to come straight out of Molière's time.

Observations about pronunciation and accents followed a similar path. Many of the pronunciations generally used in Quebec had come to be associated with popular or regional uses in France, and owing to their exclusion from the "sophisticated" register of France, they came to be regarded as archaisms of pronunciation. But no major differences in pronunciation between the social strata were apparent within Quebec, where society was not highly stratified at that time. During the first half-century of the English regime, after the departure of the French elites, this relative similarity in pronunciation was even more apparent. By the first half of the nineteenth century, comparisons with the accent from Normandy had become increasingly frequent. In her detailed and comprehensive study of observations written by foreigners in the seventeenth, eighteenth, and nineteenth centuries, Marie-France Caron-Leclerc found that few concrete examples of pronunciation were given to substantiate these comparisons. Moreover, Caron-Leclerc has rightly underscored the fact that, in the eighteenth and nineteenth centuries, the slightest departure from the reference accent was considered to be either Norman or Gascon. The so-called "Gascon" accent was undoubtedly a catch-all category for the full range of accents in the Midi region (in the south of France). The "Norman" accent was used in reference to all of the supposed provincial accents in northern France. These somewhat impressionistic accounts from the first half of the nineteenth century show that foreigners perceived a difference in Canadian pronunciation that was usually somewhat analogous to that found in the cities of northwestern France. "[They] speak French with the Norman accent of the middle classes,"[12] said Tocqueville of Quebec lawyers, aptly capturing the essence of an accent not of the Norman peasants but of the inhabitants of Norman towns and villages. It should be pointed out that accents in Quebec at that time had likely not reached present-day levels of homogeneity, whereby only a few characteristics now enable us to distinguish between regional varieties. In short, some accents most likely incorporated traits of pronunciation that had become archaisms in the reference French of the times (but had survived in Quebec and the provinces of France), which led foreigners to conflate Canadian and Norman accents.

Ideally, to complete this sociolinguistic overview and gain some insight into French at the beginning of the nineteenth century, we would listen to what the Canadiens themselves had to say about the language they were speaking. But since few metalinguistic documents predate 1840, Jacques Viger (1787–1858) (the first mayor of Montreal and a learned scholar), provides us with one very instructive and exceptionally nonjudgmental resource. In 1810, Viger set about compiling a collection of French-Canadian neologisms, including variants in pronunciation, new accepted meanings for existing French words, and borrowings from English and Amerindian languages.[13] Since this collection was only published a century later, it could not have influenced the perception that Viger's contemporaries had of their language. Nonetheless, it does show that, in certain circles, Canadians were aware of the original nature of their French.

Scholars studying sociolinguistics can now describe with some accuracy the language spoken by French Canadians in the early nineteenth century. As to their vocabulary, it seems that the consequences of the Conquest, notably the departure of the French elite and the collapse of the education system (which caused a dramatic drop in literacy rates), led to a reduction in lexical variation. Claude Poirier has pointed out that popular language clearly gained ground as many words found in the writings of New France disappeared and were replaced by competing regional or popular expressions.[14] Also, from 1763 onward, as British and French-Canadian populations mingled, an increasing number of English borrowings were added to the original lexical base. The vocabularies of politics and the law were the first to be affected, since French Canadians had to adapt to these new institutions, but some observations show English words from other language categories were also being borrowed with increasing frequency in everyday language.

The Peculiarities of Canadien French

The vocabulary of Canadianisms used by the Canadiens may be classified into a number of subsets, depending on their origins. In the original lexical base of French origin, there are *archaisms*, words from standard seventeenth- and eighteenth-century French that fell out of use in France but remained current in Quebec. There are *provincialisms*, words or expressions brought over by the colonists from their various provinces of origin. Also worth noting, within the vocabulary of French origin are scores of existing words that took on one or more new meanings. In many cases, these were the *semantic neologisms,* which assigned new meanings to flora and fauna whose names, in France, designated other, often similar, species.

Certainly it was natural that a population transplanted to a new continent and living in circumstances very different from those of their ancestors would feel the need to coin words to designate new things and concepts with *morphological neologisms.* A wide variety of geographic, climatic, and cultural phenomena would be named in this way. The Canadianisms of the New World also included a major class of words, called *borrowed neologisms.* These were words borrowed from foreign tongues, the oldest of which came from Amerindian languages. While *Amerindianisms* were not numerous, they established themselves in the language very quickly. Most provided names for plants and animals, although some pertained to elements of material culture.

Of course the largest class of *borrowed neologisms* was English borrowings. Within this class, it is important to distinguish between words or expressions that constitute *formal borrowings,* whose form is English but meaning is not, and those that are *semantic borrowings,* whose form is French but whose meaning is English. Also included in this category are *calques,* which result from the translation of the elements of a compound word or expression.

English borrowings only gradually made their way into Canadien French and, apart from neologisms, have been the only class of words to undergo constant development since 1763. By contrast, a number of archaisms, provincialisms, and Amerindianisms progressively faded out of use. Before the nineteenth century drew to a close, a whole host of Amerindianisms had been dropped from Canadien French. As for archaisms and provincialisms, harsh condemnations from language columnists likely contributed to their gradual demise and to the pursuant adoption of words from standard French. However, with the founding of the Société du parler français au Canada in 1902, a movement was launched to rehabilitate archaisms and provincialisms, which were declared legitimate because they were French in origin. English borrowings, for their part, would remain subject to general reprobation, and they continue to be perceived today as the chief threat to the quality of French in Quebec.

The Self-Consciousness of Language (1841–1842)

For some 80 years after France broke contact with its former colony, French in Quebec evolved in a vacuum. In reality, apart from the growing influence of English, little had changed, although pronunciation undoubtedly became more uniform. For most French Canadians, whose literacy rate remained markedly low, language transmission had been oral. Under the French regime, overall literacy was 23 per cent and as high as 45 per cent in Quebec City, but by 1779 it had fallen to 13 per cent and had inched up to 27 per cent by 1849.[15] Only a few men of letters, such as Michel Bibaud and Jacques Viger, seem to have been aware of specific and manifest divergences between the French spoken in Quebec and that spoken among the educated classes in France. It was therefore in a context of sheltered ignorance that a small textbook for college students suddenly questioned the legitimacy of Canadian usage of French and gave rise to a controversy that would have enduring repercussions. Published by Abbé Thomas Maguire in 1841, the *Manuel des difficultés les plus communes de la langue française, adapté au jeune âge, suivi d'un recueil de locutions vicieuses*, was a sort of dictionary of language problems. From this time forward, Quebec's own francophone elite, Anglo-Canadians, the British, and the Americans would question the legitimacy of Canadian French with growing stridency and regularity. In fact, this very public rejection of the language spoken by Quebecers would mark a point of origin for the insecurity about language that would follow in Quebec.

BIOGRAPHY

Abbé Thomas Maguire

Abbé Thomas Maguire, the author of the *Manuel* that sparked the language debate, was born in Philadelphia in 1774 to parents of Irish and British origin. His family settled in Halifax in 1776 (at the time of the American War of Independence) since his parents were United Empire Loyalists. At the age of 13, Maguire was sent to Quebec City to study under the Jesuits, with whom he completed his education. Ordained into the priesthood, he was appointed curate of the parish of Notre-Dame de Québec and then served various other parishes. In 1828, he was appointed principal of Collège de Saint-Hyacinthe, and was later sent on a mission to France to resolve a problem regarding funds that belonged to several religious communities that were confiscated during the French Revolution. He stayed in France for six months. A year after returning to Quebec, Abbé Maguire left his position at Collège de Saint-Hyacinthe and settled in Quebec City, where he taught philosophy at the seminary. He was subsequently named chaplain to the city's Ursuline Order of nuns, a position he would hold until his death in 1854. In 1829 he went on another European assignment, this time in Rome. Abbé Thomas Maguire published several works on Catholicism. The *Manuel des difficultés*, which appeared in 1841, was his last publication.

Abbé Jérôme Demers

The Abbé Jérôme Demers was the author of "Remarques sur le 'Manuel des difficultés les plus communes de la langue française,'" which appeared in the *Gazette de Québec* in April and May of 1842. Born in Saint-Nicolas, Quebec, to a farming family in 1774, he studied first at the Petit Séminaire de Québec and then in Montreal before returning to Quebec City and the Grand Séminaire. Demers began teaching before completing his studies and became director of the Petit Séminaire in 1802. There, until 1849, Demers was by turns director, superior, and procurator, while continuing to teach and produce student textbooks, of which there was great need at the time. For 50 years he devoted himself almost exclusively to the education of young people and thereby helped train a large segment of the French-Canadian elite during the first half of the nineteenth century. Narcisse-Eutrope Dionne, who devoted a monograph to the controversy surrounding Maguire's *Manuel*, wrote that the reach of Demers's authority was considerable, well beyond the Petit Séminaire:

> How could things have been otherwise when he was known to have trained 10 bishops, 200 priests, 60 lawyers, 40 doctors, 30 notaries, and when the list of his former pupils included Quebec notables like Louis-Joseph Papineau, Jacques Labrie, Louis Moquin, Joseph Parent, René-Édouard Caron, Joseph Lagueux, Augustin-Norbert Morin, Zéphyrin Nault, Pierre Chauveau, Jean-Thomas Taschereau, Joseph Cauchon and Octave Crémazie? So you see, it is hardly surprising that the advice of the Abbé Demers was considered equivalent to that of an oracle—his word was law.[16]

Jérôme Demers died in 1853.

Comparing the Protagonists

It is striking to note that the two main protagonists in this debate were born in the same year, received very similar educations in most of the same institutions (the Petit Séminaire and the

Grand Séminaire in Quebec City), and must have known one another. The tone of their attacks and retorts even suggests a possible mutual dislike. As to their perceptions of language, two biographical details may have played a role in their respective positions. First, Maguire's mother tongue was English, and he had spent a significant amount of time in Paris. These factors probably enabled him to be more detached in his appraisal of the language spoken by French Canadians. Second, Demers came from a modest background but was renowned for his vast erudition. Having never left the province, he had to rely on books published in France for his authoritative knowledge of standard French. Indeed, he made abundant use of such sources in his *Gazette* articles.

Inside the Debate

Now for a closer look at some of the other authors who commented on the debate that pitted Maguire against Demers. The editor of the *Gazette de Québec* penned several lines at the end of Demers's last letter as an introduction to the article that appeared in *Le Canadien.* He also wrote an editorial note in support of Demers's position on the use of the Amerindianism *atoca* (cranberry), citing an excerpt from a dictionary. The author of these editorial remarks was most likely Ronald Macdonald. Born in Prince Edward Island in 1797, Macdonald began his studies in a Quebec City seminary at the age of 15 and must have studied under none other than Jérôme Demers.

Étienne Parent, editor of *Le Canadien*, contributed much more substantially to the debate. He wrote an article directly critiquing Maguire's *Manuel,* making no allusions to Demers's letters. The article argued in favour of many of the Canadianisms condemned by Maguire. Born to a farming family in 1802, Parent studied at the Collège de Nicolet and then at the Grand Séminaire in Quebec City. He soon became a journalist and spearheaded many debates, all of which focused on the defence of the French-Canadian nation. Although an ally of Papineau and the Parti patriote, he rejected calls for rebellion. In 1831 he relaunched the newspaper *Le Canadien* and gave it its celebrated motto: "Our Institutions, Our Language and Our Laws!"[17]

Michel Bibaud was the last, but not the least ardent debater, to pronounce on Maguire's *Manuel* and the polemics surrounding it. Born in 1782 to a Côte-des-Neiges farming family, he studied at Montreal's Collège Saint-Raphaël, initially devoting himself to teaching. He launched his career in journalism at *Le Spectateur canadien* and helped to found *L'Aurore* in 1817. *L'Aurore* was the first paper to publish a column discussing the French language, written by a French Canadian. In it, Bibaud denounced borrowings from English. He then wrote for *Le Spectateur canadien* (which merged with *L'Aurore*) until 1822 and also published numerous school textbooks and authored the first book of poetry in Quebec's literary history, *Épîtres, satires, chansons, épigrammes, et autres pièces de vers*, released in 1830. Bibaud founded several monthly papers, notably *La Bibliothèque canadienne* in 1825 and *Le Magasin du Bas-Canada* in 1832. In 1842 he established *L'Encyclopédie canadienne, journal littéraire et scientifique,* which featured his critique of Maguire's *Manuel* and of the polemics that pitted Maguire against Demers. Throughout his long career, Bibaud strove to enhance the cultural enlightenment of French Canadians. His background differed from those of the other protagonists in the language debate. He was the only Montrealer among them and the only one with no connection to a seminary in Quebec City. By the time Maguire's *Manuel* appeared, Bibaud had been writing articles on Canadian French for 20 years, persistently criticizing the anglicization of the language, especially in the field of law.

Case Study

The Origin of Doubt about French in Quebec: Maguire versus Demers

Some 80 years after relations with France were broken off, only a few French-Canadian men of letters seem to have been aware of the discrepancies that were beginning to appear between the French spoken in Canada and that spoken by the educated class in France. Oblivious to this ever-widening divide, Abbé Thomas Maguire published a small textbook for college students that questioned the legitimacy of some Canadian French and thus unwittingly unleashed a storm of polemics whose repercussions would shape a generation of thought. Published in 1841, the *Manuel des difficultés les plus communes de la langue française, adapté au jeune âge, suivi d'un recueil de locutions vicieuses* was a sort of dictionary of language problems. In it, Maguire addressed a variety of linguistic issues, from idioms and difficult conjugations to shades of meaning between words. Most of the entries were merely explanations based on similar textbooks, dictionaries, and grammar books from France. But Maguire's *Manuel* differed from these publications in that it often adopted a peremptory tone and denounced language usage that could be collectively described as "Canadianisms." This term encompassed a multitude of linguistic sins, including variant pronunciations, morphosyntactic variations, French-Canadian neologisms, formal and semantic borrowings from English, archaisms, provincialisms, nautical terms whose meanings had been stretched, and words or expressions from popular vernacular.

A few weeks after Maguire's *Manuel* was released, an anonymous author published a long article in the pages of the *Gazette de Québec* criticizing it. Maguire wrote a reply and the anonymous author, who would soon be revealed as the Abbé Jérôme Demers, responded in kind. The editor of the *Gazette de Québec* appended to the end of Demers's response a commentary by Étienne Parent, the editor of another newspaper, *Le Canadien*. It was at that point that Michel Bibaud commented on the debate and on the *Manuel* in several issues of his new monthly newspaper entitled *L'Encyclopédie canadienne*.[18]

Historical context also played an important role in this language debate. For French Canadians demanding truly representative democracy, 1837–8 was a pivotal time in their political agitating. Louis-Joseph Papineau's Parti patriote led the people into a rebellion that was violently repressed by the British army. In the wake of this devastating civil unrest, the British government sent Lord Durham to conduct an inquiry. In an infamous report, Durham recommended that the two colonies of Upper and Lower Canada be united for the avowed purpose of making the French Canadians a minority, the better to shepherd their linguistic assimilation toward English. His description of French Canadians as "a people with no history, and no literature" shocked and offended the province's educated elite, particularly Étienne Parent, who published his translation of Durham's report in the pages of *Le Canadien* newspaper. Despite the opposition of most members of the French-Canadian educated class—including journalists, politicians, and legal experts—the Act of Union of Upper and Lower Canada was adopted in 1840 by the British Parliament. Section 41 of the enabling legislation made English the only official language of the United Province of Canada, a provision that would not be repealed until 1848. The dramatic failure of the 1837–8 rebellion had so weakened the position of French Canadians that they were unable to muster any effective opposition to the new political structure that had made them a minority. A morose atmosphere of collective defeat and bleak prospects for the nation weighed heavily in the years that followed.

continued

In these disheartening circumstances, the publication of a work that denounced—often in highly condescending terms—many of the most current linguistic habits of French Canadians (thereby attacking one of the building blocks of their identity) was perceived as a slap in the face. Maguire's *Manuel* effectively confirmed Lord Durham's views by characterizing French Canadians as ignoramuses who could not even master their mother tongue. Worse, by denying legitimacy to most Canadianisms, this publication essentially stripped French Canadians of their right to linguistic creativity. At a time when French Canadians, sorely tried by political events, were struggling to define themselves within a state structure not of their choosing and were feeling threatened by the minority status it had imposed upon them, this sudden attack on *their* French hit a raw nerve.

Language Laws and Language Battles

The creation of the Office de la langue française in 1961 was the Quebec government's response to an increasingly urgent popular demand. The idea behind this demand was first articulated at the second Congress on the French Language in 1937, when the Société du parler français au Canada recommended that a government body be created to address the deterioration it had observed in the quality of French in Quebec. But it was only after World War II that Quebec francophones seriously considered using their government as an instrument in the service of their language. It was then that a new kind of consciousness grew among French Canadians regarding their cultural dispossession and linguistic alienation. This consciousness reached unprecedented levels in 1960, culminating in a state of crisis and the public debates that raged over ***joual***.[19]

Despite the efforts that were made to promote French in Quebec, the language seemed to be steadily deteriorating. French-Canadian society had undergone profound changes since the latter part of the nineteenth century. The anglicization of culture and language in Quebec started with the transition from a rural/agricultural to an urban/industrial society, and continued to manifest itself increasingly in a pervasively English environment, among a population whose levels of education remained limited until the 1960s.

During the 1920s and 1930s, in an effort to legitimize Canadian French and to combat the myth of a French-Canadian *patois*, the members of the SPFC celebrated the virtues of the peasant language as an expression of the nation's values, emphasizing how unaffected it had been by the "sin" of anglicization in the "language of the cities." After World War II, as the exodus from the countryside to the city continued in Quebec, a potentially catastrophic situation had to be confronted once again, according to some authorities: In a nutshell, French was dying out in Canada.[20]

Newspaper columnists, educators, journalists, and writers all persistently sounded the alarm. In 1952, at the third Congress on the French Language, the seemingly unstoppable deterioration of the language was highlighted yet again, making past remedies (individual efforts and education) appear increasingly futile. The decisive year for changing the attitudes of opinion leaders appears to have been 1956. It was then that the fourth Congress called for the establishment of an Office du vocabulaire français in Quebec's Department of Public Instruction. From that time on, the discourse from all sides in colloquia, congresses, reports, conferences, and newspaper articles invariably called on the Quebec government to take decisive action to promote French. But these appeals were met with political inertia. The failure of Premier Maurice Duplessis's government to act exasperated a generation of young intellectuals who were growing increasingly impatient with the social obstacles imposed on francophones.

In October 1959, jouurnalist André Laurendeau sparked a virulent debate on the controversial subject of *joual*. In a letter to the newspaper *Le Devoir* regarding the quality of the French spoken by the teenagers he knew, he lamented that "almost all of them speak *joual*."[21]

A Catholic brother and teacher, operating under the pen name of Frère Untel (later translated as "Brother Anonymous" in English) concurred on this point in another letter to the editor: "Our pupils talk *joual*, they write *joual*. . . . *Joual* is their language." Brother Anonymous continued: "I hear talk of a Provincial Office of Linguistics. I am all for it. THE [FRENCH] LANGUAGE IS PUBLIC PROPERTY and the State should protect it as such."[22]

This exchange between Laurendeau and Brother Anonymous prompted an extraordinarily spirited reaction. A shock wave ran through the public, as though the very act of naming *joual*, the cultural outcome of generations of hard urban living, had crystallized the long-standing apprehensions of the francophone intellectual elite. It had also heightened a consuming collective consciousness regarding the gravity of the situation.

In the early 1960s, the Lesage government announced that it was creating a Ministry of Cultural Affairs. Journalist Gérard Fillion commented on this plan as follows:

> The government has just announced the creation of a Ministry of Cultural Affairs. This is all well and good. But by what concrete measures does the Quebec State intend to protect the French language—the same way it proposes to put an end to forest depletion and water pollution? . . . It should know in advance that [whatever] concrete measures it does adopt, however rigorous they may be, they will resonate deeply with both the people and the intellectual class.[23]

Faced with the fact that the many measures taken by civil society groups and movements to promote French in the early twentieth century had failed to slow its perceived degradation, on 24 March 1961 the Quebec government created the Ministry of Cultural Affairs and the Office de la langue française (OLF). In an era when some people even questioned whether "Quebec French" could be considered French at all, the Quebec government appeared to be the only body powerful enough to rectify this situation. The first step it took was having the OLF "define a linguistic model." Public pressure continued for the government to address the cause–effect relationship between the status of the language and the inferior economic and social position of French Canadians. However, at its inception the OLF had no means by which to address these causes of linguistic deterioration that were so integrally linked to the inferior status of French. Plainly, there was much work to be done before the government would be able to turn the tide in linguistic development.

The debate about *joual* served to expose the imbalance between the strength of English in relation to French, showing that despite Quebec's strong francophone majority, English was continuing to gain ground. In the late 1960s, the realization grew among Quebec francophones that the anglicization of immigrant children via the school system also seriously threatened their majority status. The Catholic–Protestant division imposed by the education system had long segregated students according to their religious backgrounds. Newcomers from southern Europe, being mostly Catholic, generally sent their children to French-language Catholic schools, whereas new Quebecers of most other religious affiliations attended English-language Protestant schools, which were more open to religious diversity. A Catholic English-language system also served many Quebecers of Irish origin. Until 1930, immigrant children were divided almost equally between English-language and French-language schools. But some 30 years later, in 1961, over 90 per cent of children of immigrant origin were being educated in English. Montreal had long been 65 per cent francophone, but English was disproportionately represented everywhere—in business, in public signage, and in the workplace. In many of Montreal's neighbourhoods it was difficult to find services in French. English was an essential qualification for employment, even for subordinate positions, and the average income of unilingual francophones was lower than that of all other social groups, including immigrants. The prospect of Quebec's metropolis being overrun by the English language was perceived as a real and present danger for the future of francophone society in Quebec and for the survival of its culture.

In 1968, against this volatile backdrop, a controversy broke out regarding the schools of St Leonard, Montreal. The local school board had decided to eliminate their bilingual curriculum and offer French-only courses. This move prompted anglophone Quebecers and immigrant associations to launch a broad-based protest movement, and the ensuing battle remained heated for months on end. Various francophone groups supported the school board's decision and broadened their lobby for new regulations to require that immigrants to Quebec attend French-language schools. Quebec's Union Nationale government reacted by adopting Bill 63, effectively making language of instruction a matter of free choice, but this law did not resolve the problem. It was not until Bill 22 was adopted in 1974 by Robert Bourassa's Liberal government that more effective measures were taken to integrate foreign-born students into francophone society. Bill 101, adopted in 1977 by the Parti Québécois government under the leadership of René Lévesque, would further strengthen these measures.

Bill 22, which became the Official Language Act, made French the official language of the Quebec government. Bill 101, which became the Charter of the French Language, was more ambitious and much wider in scope, seeking to make French the common public language of all Quebecers.

Quebec French Comes into its Own

For years, in other Canadian provinces, francophone Quebecers had witnessed the unremitting erosion of French-Canadian communities that had assimilated to English in droves. Even in their majority position in Quebec francophones recognized that their demographic predominance was seriously threatened and, overcome with an intense feeling of linguistic alienation, reacted by trying to take control of all the political ground at their disposal.

Still working through this difficult process, francophone Quebecers (and the rest of the Western world) experienced faster and more pervasive communications through modern technology. First radio, then (especially) television, brought the news of the day into homes in the most remote regions of the countryside, establishing widespread daily contact with standard French. Moreover, as trips and visits abroad increased and more francophone immigrants and travellers came to Quebec, Quebecers began to break out of the isolation they had experienced since the late eighteenth century. In Quebec as elsewhere, all of these phenomena led to a relative levelling of dialects. Many of the traits of pronunciation and some of the vocabulary, including borrowed English words or local, twentieth-century vocabulary, that had previously characterized Quebec French were gradually replaced by their standard French equivalents from one generation to the next. And as might be expected, broad swaths of vocabulary pertaining to traditional peasant life fell into disuse because of urbanization and the modernization of agricultural techniques.

These transformations had an even greater effect on the entire panoply of words influenced by English. Indeed, everyday Quebec French of the 1960s was teeming with these *formal borrowings* or *loan words* from English, which, being *doubly* stigmatized, were ripe for elimination. De-anglicizing Quebec French undoubtedly brought it more in line with standard French, even though standard French (in France) had paradoxically begun to borrow more and more from Anglo-American vocabulary. Semantic borrowings from English accounted for another source of divergence from standard French and were a growing trend among the increasingly bilingual francophone Quebecers. More recently, over the past two decades, I have observed a sharp rise in the use of *faux amis* ("false cognates") in France, particularly in the nation's newspapers and electronic media. A recent study conducted by Marie-Éva de Villers, who systematically compared the vocabulary used in the French newspaper *Le Monde* with that used in several Quebec dailies, indicated that over 80 per cent of their content shared the same lexical usages.

As for the Quebec print media, recently created neologisms formed the largest category of nonstandard usage. We may therefore infer that, when it comes to naming new objects and concepts, francophone Quebecers are now allowing themselves a greater margin of lexical innovation than they did in the past. Other indicators show that while the resemblance between spoken French in Quebec and Europe has increased, in recent decades certain facets of Québécois pronunciation and vocabulary have also acquired a legitimacy that they never enjoyed before. Far from being signs of linguistic regression, over time they have come to be valued as positive, identity-enriching social assets. In fact, observations of diction among Quebec radio and television anchors (the standard-bearers of oral French) reveal phonetic traits distinctive to Quebec, traits that used to be systematically eradicated in the media.

It seems that francophone Quebecers, heartened by 40 years of collective successes, now have a much higher opinion of their distinctive culture and language, a positive sense of their identity, and are therefore exercising some autonomy vis-à-vis the prevailing normative reference. This new linguistic norm has yet to be clearly defined, and its departures from the European standard are neither numerous nor very pronounced. But simply put, a distinctly Québécois variety of French now exists and its use is socially valued, a fact that will doubtless have a formative effect on the future development of the language.

Some might contend that current prevailing trends—the relative levelling of dialects and the emergence of a new linguistic norm for Quebec—are potentially contradictory. In fact, this is not so: The reason Quebecers can allow themselves to appreciate a distinctly Québécois variety of French today is that Quebec usage is now close enough to other varieties of French that it will not lead to misunderstandings and is not becoming a distinct language, contrary to the fears voiced half a century ago. Simply put, Quebec's language policy, combined with developments in communications technology, has actually succeeded in turning the tide in linguistic development.

French as a Common Public Language

Over 25 years after the adoption of the first measures to make French the official language of Quebec and to integrate immigrants into French-language schools, a 1997 report by the Conseil de la langue française, *Le français, langue d'usage public au Québec*, noted that while French had indeed become the language of public life in Quebec, it remained weak in some areas, including the workplace. Moreover, the report held that the level of francization among newcomers to the province was not yet satisfactory.

The findings in this report for Quebec as a whole may seem reassuring since they showed that 88 per cent of Quebecers were using French in their public activities. But predictably, a regional breakdown of statistics for respondents who used French almost exclusively or as the main language of their public life dropped to 78 per cent in the Greater Montreal area and to 71 per cent for the Island of Montreal. Clearly, Greater Montreal is the place where the stakes are highest, where the vast majority of anglophone Quebecers live, and where most immigrants have settled. The behaviour of these two groups will therefore determine whether French will progress, stagnate, or regress as the common language of Quebec in the future.[24]

If the current behaviour of younger generations of allophone and anglophone Quebecers is any indication, the public use of French has a good chance of gaining ground in Quebec's metropolitan area, since these young people now far outnumber their parents in their mastery of French. In fact, 80.8 per cent of young adult anglophones now have a fluent command of the language.[25] However, the new immigrants who settle in Montreal each year, many of whom do not speak French upon arrival, must also be factored into the linguistic equation. In most other regions of Quebec, where French predominates, these linguistic shortcomings may be addressed through varying degrees of institutional involvement, but half-measures will not suffice in the Greater Montreal area where newcomers are more likely to choose English over French for a multitude of reasons. Failure to integrate newly arrived Quebecers into the francophone community is likely to have lasting, long-term repercussions. Therefore, it is no longer enough to send foreign-born children to French-language schools. Quebec must also promote and protect classes for learning French as a second language for adult immigrants as an equally important part of consolidating the use of French as the language of public life.

Conclusion

From 1760 to 1960, the sociolinguistic history of Quebec followed a long downward spiral of degradation. With Quebec's loss of political status, insecurity about the French language grew increasingly strong. By contrast, since the 1970s French has seen a steady improvement in its status within Quebec society. Language legislation has successfully mitigated the sense of alienation it was designed to address. In 2010, francophone Quebecers have a much higher opinion of their language, which they now regard as being legitimate. The fact that newcomers now adopt French as the language of their public lives is accepted as a matter of course. But given that some stagnation in the everyday use of French has been observed in recent years (especially in Montreal), francophone Quebecers are still on their guard. Without fail, each new statistical report on language is immediately and meticulously analyzed. Each line is sure to be dissected, scrutinized, and commented on. Indeed, it may truly be said that very few societies in the world are as passionate about language issues as Quebec, because language indisputably remains one of Quebec's most distinguishing cultural characteristics.

Questions for Critical Thinking

1. How can we account for the differences between standard French and the French spoken in Quebec over the years?
2. Francophone Quebecers had a very negative opinion of their language from about 1850 to 1960. What social factors contributed to this opinion?
3. To what can we attribute the much more favourable opinion that francophone Quebecers now have of their language at the beginning of the twenty-first century?

Notes

1. See Chantal Bouchard, *Obsessed with Language: A Sociolinguistic History of Quebec* (Toronto: Guernica, 2008).
2. See Claude Poirier, "Une langue qui se définit dans l'adversité," in *Le français au Québec : 400 ans d'histoire et de vie*, ed. Michel Plourde (Montreal: Fides/Les publications du Québec, 2000), 111–22.
3. Tardivel delivered a lecture to this effect in 1901. Jules-Paul Tardivel, *La langue française au Canada* (Montreal: Cie de publication de la Revue canadienne, 1901), reproduced in *Le Devoir*, 22 June 1912.
4. Louis Fréchette, *La Patrie*, 4 August 1874.
5. Translation: "allowing things to be as they are."
6. Translation: "Make sure that the boundaries of (French) Canada are known"; that is to say, maintain a clear demarcation line on the linguistic front between English and French Canada.
7. All of these observations may be found in Marie-France Caron-Leclerc, "Les témoignages anciens sur le français du Canada (du XVIIe s. au XIXe s.) : édition critique et analyse" (Ph.D. diss., Université Laval, 1998).
8. Louis-Joseph de Montcalm, *Journal du marquis de Montcalm* [témoignage de 1756], in Caron-Leclerc, "Les témoignages anciens," 65.
9. John Lambert, *Travels through Canada* . . . [témoignage de 1807], in Caron-Leclerc, "Les témoignages anciens," 73–4.
10. Isidore Lebrun, *Tableau statistique et politique des deux Canadas* [témoignage de 1833], in Caron-Leclerc, "Les témoignages anciens," 101.
11. Théodore Pavie, "L'Amérique anglaise en 1850," *Revue des Deux Mondes* 8, 15 December 1850, 992, in Caron-Leclerc, "Les témoignages anciens," 116.
12. Alexis de Tocqueville, in Caron-Leclerc, "Les témoignages anciens," 90.
13. Jacques Viger, "Néologie canadienne ou dictionnaire des mot créés en Canada et maintenant en vogue;—des mots dont la prononciation et l'orthographe sont différentes de la prononciation et orthographe françaises, quoique

employés dans une acception semblable ou contraire, et des mots étrangers qui se sont glissés dans notre langue," in *Bulletin du parler français au Canada* VIII (1909–1910).

14. Claude Poirier, "Une langue qui se définit dans l'adversité," in *Les français au Québec*, ed. Plourde, 111–22.
15. Claude Galarneau, "Évolution de l'alphabétisation au Québec," in *Les français au Québec*, ed. Plourde, 103.
16. Author's translation. Narcisse-Eutrope Dionne, *Une dispute grammaticale en 1842* (Quebec: Typ. Laflamme & Proulx, 1912), 34.
17. "Nos institutions, notre langue et nos lois!"
18. Demers's first letter to the *Gazette de Québec* appeared on 23 April 1842. Maguire's reply was published on 28 April, and Demers's final text came out in early May. Michel Bibaud's commentaries in *L'Encyclopédie canadienne* appeared in Book 1, Volume 3 (May 1842), Volume 4 (June 1842), Volume 6 (August 1842), and Volume 7 (September 1842). Bibaud also reprinted the article from *Le Canadien* in Volume 9 (November 1842).
19. *Joual* is the name given to the type of working-class language developed in cities among former peasants who became urban labourers and worked under anglophone bosses around the end of the nineteenth century. The progressive anglicization that characterized *joual* reached its apex in the 1960s, when heated debates over its legitimacy led writers like Michel Tremblay to reclaim and celebrate this popular vernacular in their various works. With the language laws of the 1970s, the adoption of French as the common language of public life, and vastly improved levels of education overall, the anglicization of French has subsided significantly in Quebec.
20. Pierre Baillargeon, "Quelle langue parlons-nous?" *La Patrie*, 26 October 1947.
21. André Laurendeau, "La langue que nous parlons," *Le Devoir*, 21 October 1959.
22. Jean-Paul Desbiens (Frère Untel), "Je trouve désespérant d'enseigner le français," letter to the editor, *Le Devoir*, 3 November 1959. For English translation, see Frère Untel, *The Impertinences of Brother Anonymous*, trans. Miriam Chapin (Montreal: Harvest House, 1962). Upper case typography has been used as in the original French version.
23. Gérard Fillion, "Le règne du joual-vapeur," *Le Devoir*, 23 November 1960.
24. Paul Béland, *Le français, langue d'usage public au Québec en 1997*, rapport de recherche (Quebec: Conseil de la langue française, Gouvernement du Québec, 1999).
25. Madeline Gauthier and Mégane Girard, *Caractéristiques générales des jeunes adultes de 25–35 ans au Québec* (Quebec: Observatoire Jeunes et société, Institut national de la recherche scientifique, prepared for Conseil supérieur de la langue françaises, May 2008), 89.

Select Bibliography

Bouchard, Chantal. *Méchante langue : la légitimité linguistique du français parlé au Québec*. Montreal: Presses de l'Université de Montreal, 2011.

———. *Obsessed with Language: A Sociolinguistic History of Quebec*. Toronto: Guernica, 2008.

Corbeil, Jean-Claude. *L'embarras des langues*. Montreal: Québec Amérique, 2007.

Gendron, Jean-Denis. *D'où vient l'accent des Québécois? Et celui des Parisiens?* Sainte-Foy: Presses de l'Université Laval, 2008.

Georgeault, Pierre, and Michel Pagé, eds. *Le français, langue de la diversité québécoise*. Montreal: Québec Amérique, 2006.

Mougeon, Raymond, and Édouard Béniak, eds. *Les origines du français québécois*. Sainte-Foy: Presses de l'Université Laval, 1994.

Plourde, Michel, ed. *Le français au Québec : 400 ans d'histoire et de vie*. Montreal: Conseil supérieur de la langue française/Fides, 2008.

Stefanescu, Alexandre, ed. *Le français au Québec : les nouveaux défis*. Montreal: Fides, 2005.

Villers, Marie-Éva de. *Le vif désir de durer*. Montreal: Québec-Amérique, 2005.

11 Language Politics and Language Policies in Quebec and in Canada

Linda Cardinal,[1] University of Ottawa

Timeline

1774 Quebec Act guarantees freedom of religion in province of Quebec and restores French civil law while maintaining English criminal law.

1791 Constitutional Act divides Province of Quebec into Upper and Lower Canada. In Lower Canada, English and French are used in the Legislative Assembly and bills are prepared in both languages. In Upper Canada, French has no official status.

1839 Lord Durham presents his *Report on the Affairs of British North America*, which recommends uniting the two provinces in order to assimilate French Canadians into English culture.

1840 Section 41 of Act of Union provides that all records and proceedings of Parliament of the United Province of Canada be in English only.

1867 Section 133 of the British North America Act permits the use of French and English in parliamentary debates and in all federal courts, and for provincial statutes and in provincial courts in Quebec.

1870 Manitoba Act establishes dual system of Protestant and Roman Catholic schools. It also states that both English and French can be used in the Legislative Assembly as well as before the courts. Records and journals of the legislature must be prepared and all laws must be published in both languages.

1871 Common Schools Act provides for free education in New Brunswick but abolishes public support of denominational schools.

1877 Northwest Territories Act is amended to specify that both English and French may be used in the Legislature and before the courts.

Both languages shall be used in records, journals, and orders.

1890 Official Language Act in Manitoba provides that English be the only official language of that province. Public funding of Catholic schools is abolished.

1892 French is abolished de facto in Northwest Territories Legislative Assembly. In the following years, it is gradually abolished as the language of instruction in the region.

1910 In Quebec, the Lavergne Act is passed, the first act regulating the use of French. It requires that bus, train, and tram tickets be printed in both English and French.

1912 In Ontario, Regulation 17 limits the use of French as a language of instruction to first

continued

two years in elementary schools. It is amended one year later to permit French as a subject of study for one hour per day.

1916 English is made the only language of instruction in Manitoba.

1931 English is made the only language of instruction in Saskatchewan.

1936 Premier Duplessis, leader of the Union Nationale (UN), and his government adopt legislation stipulating that only the French text of Quebec legislation is authoritative.

1951 Debut in Montreal of Radio-Canada, the French-language television network of the Canadian Broadcasting Corporation.

1956 Premier Duplessis appoints the provincial Royal Commission of Inquiry on Constitutional Problems.

1960 Founding of Rassemblement pour l'indépendance nationale (RIN), which advocates for political independence for Quebec and French as the sole official language of Quebec.

Election of Premier Jean Lesage and a Quebec Liberal Party (QLP) majority government.

1961 Creation of the Office de la langue française. Lesage government establishes Quebec's first Department of Cultural Affairs within the new office.

1962 RIN's pamphlet, *Le bilinguisme qui nous tue*, argues that bilingualism in Montreal is inherently unequal, and the strength of English is a threat to French language and culture.

1966 QLP loses Quebec elections to UN government under the leadership of Daniel Johnson.

1968 Quebec establishes the Commission of Inquiry on the Position of the French Language and French Language Rights in Quebec (Gendron Commission).

Ontario amends its Education Act to recognize the existence of French-language elementary schools and to authorize the creation of French-language high schools.

Saskatchewan Education Act is modified to allow for the establishment of designated schools that can teach as much as 80 per cent in French.

1969 Official Languages Act declares that English and French enjoy equal status, rights, and privileges in Parliament and the Government of Canada.

Quebec adopts Bill 63, which makes English schools available to any child upon the parents' request. Curricula and examinations must ensure a working knowledge of French for all Quebec children attending English schools.

1970 QLP returns to power under the leadership of Robert Bourassa. FLQ October crisis.

Bill 113 restores the status of French as a language of instruction in Manitoba.

1974 National Assembly of Quebec adopts Bill 22. French is proclaimed the official language of the province.

1976 Parti Québécois (PQ) forms a majority government under the leadership of René Lévesque.

1977 Bill 101, also known as the Charter of the French Language, is adopted.

1981 An Act Recognizing the Equality of the Two Official Linguistic Communities in New Brunswick is adopted.

1982 Government of Canada and nine provinces agree on repatriating the Canadian Constitution. The Charter of Rights and Freedoms is enshrined in the new Constitution Act. The Charter incorporates language rights of the Official Languages Act and new rights related to official language minority education.

1983 Quebec adopts Bill 57, which recognizes bilingualism in English-language schools, hospitals, and social service agencies.

1986 Ontario adopts the French Language Services Act, ensuring that government services are offered in French in 25 designated areas.

1988 In Alberta, the Language Act reaffirms unilingual English nature of the province while recognizing the right to use French in the legislature and before certain courts.

Alberta School Act recognizes francophones' right to instruction in French.

1993 QLP majority government adopts Bill 86, stating that French must predominate on all public signs, posters, and commercial advertising.

1998 In *Reference re Secession of Quebec*, the Supreme Court of Canada rules on whether Quebec has the right to unilateral secession, identifying protection of minorities as the underlying constitutional principle.

2001 Publication of the report of the Commission of the Estates General on the Situation and Future of the French Language in Quebec.

2002 PQ majority government adopts Bill 104, modifying Bill 101, that stipulates that pupils attending private English-language schools can no longer enrol automatically in public English-language schools. Bill 104 also establishes that special permissions for attending public English-language schools no longer implies a right to attend an English-language school will be conferred on descendants.

2010 QLP majority government adopts Bill 115, which reinstitutes transfers from private English-language schools to public English-language schools.

Introduction

Language policy choices are far from neutral. Power relations between language groups influence those choices. Political and normative debates on language policies are linked to concrete political issues. States need to provide solutions to these political issues to bring about linguistic peace in one form or another. Language policy choices are made at critical junctures. For example, globalization represents a critical juncture that informs changes, but the shape they take is embedded in existing traditions, such as liberalism in the United States and federalism and political compromise in Canada.[2] In other words, state traditions inform policy pathways.

In discussing the crucial role that language, in particular English and French, has played and continues to play in both Canadian and Quebec politics, especially in Quebec, this chapter shows that much history, tradition, and politics lie behind language policy choices in both societies. Canadians like to think that they are a tolerant people and that they respect diversity—qualities they see as part of their political culture—yet language policy is also the result of power politics. There is nothing "natural" about the recognition of diversity or the promotion of languages. Language policy choices require formal state intervention and require adopting language legislation.[3] Language laws also interact with planning and policymaking in numerous spheres of government intervention, such as the economy, education, health, immigration, and justice. Those are strategic sectors for promoting language. Sociolinguists advocate an integral or holistic approach to language policy choices, including planning.[4] Those choices, as already mentioned, are informed by institutional traditions linking the **language regime** to the history of state intervention in any given polity. These choices also interact with two principles recognized internationally: personality and territoriality.[5] The **personality principle** is based on the idea that individuals have rights, including the right to speak the language of their choice, in particular when in contact with their government. In contrast, the **territoriality principle** is based on the idea that a language is a collective good that needs to be protected or reinforced on its own territory.

Students of nationalism agree that the territoriality principle is more effective for accommodating linguistic and national minorities.[6] However, language policies often borrow from both the territoriality and the personality principles. A language policy may be premised on the ideal of individual rights (the personality principle) but may only apply in certain areas where numbers warrant (the territoriality principle). This is a negative use of the territoriality principle; a more positive use would be to provide some form of territorial devolution or confer a special status on a particular group. Such a situation, however, may create minorities within the minority. In a liberal framework, language policies that reinforce the language of a majority on a given territory should at least recognize rights to services of its internal minorities.

While sociolinguists provide valuable information about the process of language planning and policymaking, scholars of nationalism and political theorists debate the best ways to recognize the demands of linguistic and national minorities.[7] Political economists argue that language policy choices are also informed by power relations.[8] Finally, historical institutionalists study the role of state traditions in determining language policy choices.[9] While attempting to bridge these differing analytical tools, this chapter argues that the recognition of both English and French as **official languages** in Canada, and that of French as the only official language in Quebec, are informed by political debates that go back, at the very least, to the eighteenth century, when Britain conquered New France. Debates on the future of French in both Canada and Quebec are particularly lively in Quebec, where the French-speaking population constitutes the largest French national group in North America but remains a minority on the continent. For any student interested in sociolinguistics, nationalism studies, policy studies, or political theory, the role of state traditions such as federalism or political compromise in Quebec and Canada also represent key elements for explaining language policy choices in both jurisdictions.

The chapter is divided into three sections. First, it briefly surveys the status of English and French in Canada and Quebec, looking at the most recent language data published by Statistics Canada. Second, it proposes some milestones for understanding language politics in Canada and its impact on Quebec's language policy choices. Third, it discusses language politics in Quebec and the role of state traditions in the development of its own language regime within the federation. In conclusion, the chapter identifies some of the most pressing language issues that could be addressed by both the Canadian and the Quebec states.

English and French in Canada and Quebec

As in the case of the United States and other parts of the world, a diversity of mother tongues form Canada and Quebec's linguistic landscape. According to Statistics Canada, of the 1.27 million immigrants who arrived in Canada from 2006 to 2011, 77 per cent had a mother tongue other than English or French—notably Chinese languages, Italian, German, Punjabi, Spanish, Arabic, Tagalog, and Urdu (see Table 11.1). This growing linguistic diversity is felt in metropolitan areas especially: In Montreal, 24 per cent of the population has a mother tongue other than French or English; in Toronto, the figure is 45 per cent; and in Vancouver, 43 per cent. Italian, Arabic, and Spanish are the leading languages among Montreal's allophones (those whose mother tongue is neither French nor English); Chinese languages, Italian, and Punjabi dominate allophones in Toronto; and Chinese languages, Punjabi, and Tagalog dominate in Vancouver.

Table 11.1 The Most Common Nonofficial Mother Tongues, 1971, 2001, 2006, and 2011

	1971			2001			2006			2011		
Mother Tongues	Number	Percentage of Nonofficial Mother Tongues	Percentage of All Mother Tongues	Number	Percentage of Nonofficial Mother Tongues	Percentage of All Mother Tongues	Number	Percentage of Nonofficial Mother Tongues	Percentage of All Mother Tongues	Number	Percentage of Nonofficial Mother Tongues	Percentage of All Mother Tongues
Chinese languages	95,915	3.4	0.4	872,400	16.4	2.9	1,034,090	16.4	3.3	1,072,555	16.3	3.2
Italian	538,765	19.2	2.5	493,985	9.3	1.7	476,905	7.6	1.5	407,490	6.2	1.2
German	558,965	19.9	2.6	455,540	8.5	1.5	466,650	7.4	1.5	409,200	6.2	1.2
Punjabi	..	..	..	284,750	5.3	1.0	382,585	6.1	1.2	430,705	6.5	1.3
Spanish	23,950	0.9	0.1	260,785	4.9	0.9	362,120	5.8	1.2	410,670	6.3	1.2
Arabic	28,520	1.0	0.1	220,535	4.1	0.7	286,785	4.6	0.9	327,870	5.0	1.0
Tagalog	..	..	..	199,770	3.7	0.7	266,440	4.2	0.9	327,450	5.0	1.0
Portuguese	85,845	3.1	0.4	222,855	4.2	0.8	229,280	3.6	0.7	211,335	3.2	0.6
Polish	136,540	4.9	0.6	215,010	4.0	0.7	217,605	3.5	0.7	191,650	3.0	0.6
Urdu	..	..	..	86,810	1.6	0.3	156,415	2.5	0.5	194,000	3.0	0.6
Ukrainian	309,890	11.0	1.4	157,385	3.0	0.5	141,805	2.3	0.5	111,450	1.7	0.3

Source: Statistics Canada, Censuses of Population, 1971, 2001, 2006, and 2011. Catalogue no.98-314-XBC, accessed 22 April 2014, www.statcan.gc.ca/tables-tableaux/sum-som/l01/cst01/demo11a-eng.htm.

Table 11.2 Population by Mother Tongue, Canada, Provinces and Territories, 2011

	Total	English	French	Nonofficial language	English and French	English and Nonofficial Language	French and Nonofficial Language	English, French, and Nonofficial Language
Canada	**33,121,175**	**18,858,980**	**7,054,975**	**6,567,685**	**144,685**	**396,330**	**74,430**	**24,095**
Newfoundland and Labrador	509,950	497,565	2,480	8,790	465	585	45	25
Prince Edward Island	138,435	127,635	5,195	4,860	445	260	35	10
Nova Scotia	910,615	836,090	31,110	37,090	3,030	2,855	315	130
New Brunswick	739,900	479,935	233,530	18,395	6,580	1,115	245	90
Quebec	7,815,955	599,230	6,102,210	961,700	64,800	23,435	51,640	12,950
Ontario	12,722,065	8,677,040	493,300	3,264,435	46,605	219,425	13,645	7,610
Manitoba	1,193,095	869,990	42,090	256,500	3,800	18,940	1,425	365
Saskatchewan	1,018,310	860,500	16,280	129,035	1,730	9,850	750	175
Alberta	3,610,180	2,780,200	68,545	698,930	8,410	49,970	2,945	1,185
British Columbia	4,356,210	3,062,430	57,280	1,154,220	8,600	68,800	3,345	1,530
Yukon	33,655	28,065	1,455	3,625	140	335	20	15
Northwest Territories	41,035	31,375	1,080	8,045	75	445	15	5
Nunavut	31,765	8,925	435	22,070	10	320	5	0

Source: Statistics Canada, "Population by Mother Tongue and Age Groups (Total), 2011 Counts, for Canada, Provinces and Territories," *Language Highlight Tables, 2011 Census*. Catalogue no. 98-314-XWE2011002, released 24 October 2012, accessed 23 April 2014, www12.statcan.gc.ca/census-recensement/2011/dp-pd/hlt-fst/lang/Pages/highlight.cfm?TabID=1&Lang=E&Asc=1&PRCode=01&OrderBy=999&View=1&tableID=401&queryID=1&Age=1.

Despite the demographic importance of these communities, not all languages have official status in Canada. For historical, social, and political reasons that we will explore later, English and French are Canada's two official languages—Aboriginal languages in the territories also have official status with English and French. Briefly, in Nunavut Inuktitut is an official language; in the Northwest Territories, official Aboriginal languages are Chipewyan, Cree, Gwich'in, Inuinnaqtun, Inuktitut, Inuvialuktun, North Slavey, South Slavey, and Tåîchô; in Yukon, the Official Languages Act recognizes the existence of numerous Aboriginal languages.

French is the mother tongue of 21.3 per cent of the Canadian population (7,054,975 people), compared with 56.9 per cent (18,858,980 people) for whom English is the mother tongue (see Table 11.2). Most people whose mother tongue is French live in Quebec, where they make up 86 per cent of the population (6,102,210 people). Approximately 1 million people whose mother tongue is French live outside Quebec.

French in Quebec is protected by the provincial government's Charter of the French Language, Bill 101.[10] Federal legislation on official languages protects French in the rest of Canada, and likewise promotes English in Quebec. Both French and English are official languages of New Brunswick, but elsewhere in Canada measures to promote French are limited. In 1986, Ontario adopted the French

Language Services Act, which provides French-language services in designated areas where French is the mother tongue of either 5,000 people or 10 per cent of the local population. But overall, there are many challenges to the promotion of French outside Quebec. Rates of assimilation in some parts of the country are as high as 70 per cent (the rate of assimilation is determined by subtracting the number of people who speak French at home from those who claim French as their mother tongue). In Ontario and New Brunswick, where there are significant concentrations of people whose mother tongue is French, 42.8 per cent and 11.6 per cent of French speakers, respectively, spoke English most often at home. In British Columbia the rate is 71.8 per cent, and in Alberta 65.1 per cent.

In Quebec, in 2011, data revealed that for the first time since 1931 the proportion of Quebecers with French as their mother tongue has dropped below 80 per cent. While figures such as this play on the linguistic insecurity of French Canadians, the data also show that 27.3 per cent of allophones in Quebec use French at home, which is encouraging. In contrast, the use of English is threatened neither in Quebec nor in Canada. Furthermore, in Quebec the language rights of individuals whose mother tongue is English are protected by both the Quebec and federal governments.

In Canada, speakers of nonofficial languages, or *allophones*, might receive some services in their mother tongues at the local level, but these languages are not promoted as intensely as English or French. This does not mean that nonofficial languages are not valued. However, especially outside of Quebec, most speakers of nonofficial languages eventually adopt English as their home language. Similarly, French is adopted as the language spoken at home by many allophones in Quebec. However, in 2011, while 19.8 per cent of Canadians declared a nonofficial language as their mother tongue, there is considerable movement toward English; 66.3 per cent of Canadians (21,975,690) use English at home (compared to the 56.9 per cent [18,858,980] whose mother tongue is English—see Table 11.3).

Since 1971, English has made net gains everywhere in Canada, and the situation is not about to change. Despite its multicultural and bilingual character, the country appears to be reaching a cap for bilingualism, except in Quebec, where English is more and more popular among the French-speaking population. When examining bilingualism in Canada, we find that 17 per cent of Canadians could conduct a conversation in both English and French in 1996—an increase from 12 per cent in 1951. But the data from the 2006 and 2011 censuses show that French–English bilingualism is stagnating, as Canadians fluent in both languages remains at 17.5 per cent (see Table 11.4). While a significant portion of the Canadian population declares itself favourable to official languages, only 8.9 per cent of English Canadians are able to conduct a conversation in both French and English. Outside of Quebec, 6 per cent of anglophones and 6 per cent of allophones consider themselves fluent in English and French.[11] There is a big gap between the number of francophones (87 per cent) and the number of anglophones (6 per cent) who can use both official languages. But the rate of bilingualism among anglophones in Quebec is quite high, at 67.8 per cent. However, does this mean that those same persons can sustain a conversation in French? It is difficult to evaluate adequately the proficiency level of French among English-speaking students in Quebec.[12]

Language Policy Choices in Canada: Some Milestones

After the Conquest of New France by Britain,[13] the Quebec Act of 1774 guaranteed French Canadians the right to maintain their own legal system, the Civil Code; to practise their religion, Catholicism; and to keep the seigneurial system of land ownership. The French language was not recognized in any formal way, but it was entwined with all these institutions. Almost 20 years after the adoption of the Quebec Act, the status of French was first tested in 1791 when Loyalists fleeing the American War of Independence pressured the British crown to partition the Province of Quebec into Lower Canada and Upper Canada. Loyalists were invited to immigrate to Upper Canada where land was more readily available

Table 11.3 Population by Language Spoken Most Often at Home, Canada, Provinces, and Territories, 2011

	Total	English	French	Nonofficial Language	English and French	English and Nonofficial Language	French and Nonofficial Language	English, French, and Nonofficial Language
Canada	**33,121,175**	**21,457,075**	**6,827,865**	**3,673,865**	**131,205**	**875,135**	**109,705**	**46,325**
Newfoundland and Labrador	509,950	502,475	1,145	5,005	245	1,035	15	35
Prince Edward Island	138,435	132,200	2,465	2,925	270	545	15	20
Nova Scotia	910,615	868,765	15,940	18,510	1,815	5,295	120	175
New Brunswick	739,900	512,115	209,885	9,310	6,235	2,020	175	155
Quebec	7,815,955	767,415	6,249,085	554,400	71,555	43,765	100,110	29,625
Ontario	12,722,065	10,044,805	284,115	1,827,870	37,955	509,100	6,375	11,845
Manitoba	1,193,095	1,007,330	17,950	125,285	2,485	38,935	635	490
Saskatchewan	1,018,315	938,170	4,295	59,240	855	15,360	205	190
Alberta	3,610,185	3,095,255	24,690	379,545	4,945	102,995	1,115	1,640
British Columbia	4,356,205	3,506,595	16,685	670,100	4,700	155,065	930	2,130
Yukon	33,655	31,025	815	1,240	110	445	5	10
Northwest Territories	41,040	36,485	550	3,615	45	335	0	15
Nunavut	31,765	14,440	250	16,820	5	250	5	0

Source: Statistics Canada, "Population by Language Spoken Most Often and Regularly at Home, Age Groups (Total), for Canada, Provinces and Territories," *Language Highlight Tables, 2011 Census*. Catalogue no. 98-314-XWF2011002, released 24 October 2012, accessed 23 April 2014, www12.statcan.gc.ca/census-recensement/2011/dp-pd/hlt-fst/lang/Pages/Highlight.cfm?TabID=1&Lang=E&PRCode=01&Age=1&tableID=403&queryID=1.

and the landowners among them could control a legislative assembly—which they believed to be their right—and form a political majority. In contrast, those who went to Lower Canada had to collaborate with French Canadians. French-Canadian landowners were not excluded from participating in politics and constituted the majority of elected officials in the Lower Canadian Assembly.[14]

Since the British ruled the Empire, which now included Lower Canada, it was their prerogative to impose its language, as in Ireland at the time. However, French speakers, who formed the majority, took for granted that their language should prevail in the new assembly.[15] After fierce debates, French was accepted as the language of the assembly and has remained so to this day, despite the continuing presence of representatives of the English-speaking communities.[16]

In 1840, following rebellions against corruption and lack of representative government in both Lower and Upper Canada, Britain suspended both assemblies, created the United Province of Canada, and prohibited the use of the French language in the new legislature. The episode marks Canada's first official language policy, though it was disregarded by French-Canadian representatives who continued to use their language to conduct affairs in the new legislature. In comparison with the Quebec Act, which can be interpreted as a form of accommodation, the aim of the new language policy of United Canada was the assimilation of French Canadians. Given tensions within the new legislature, both parties agreed that a new structure of government was required.

In 1867 Canada became a federation of four provinces: New Brunswick, Nova Scotia, Ontario,

Table 11.4 English-French Bilingualism among Anglophones and Allophones (Single Mother Tongue), Canada, Provinces, Territories, and Canada less Quebec, 1996 to 2011

	Anglophones				Allophones			
	1996	**2001**	**2006**	**2011**	**1996**	**2001**	**2006**	**2011**
Regions	Percentage							
Canada	**8.8**	**9.0**	**9.4**	**8.9**	**11.2**	**11.8**	**12.1**	**11.7**
Newfoundland and Labrador	3.5	3.7	4.3	4.2	6.7	6.5	6.8	5.9
Prince Edward Island	7.2	8.3	9.2	9.2	11.6	9.7	9.1	6.6
Nova Scotia	5.7	6.4	7.1	7.1	9.0	10.6	9.9	8.7
New Brunswick	14.0	15.0	16.0	14.9	15.7	17.5	16.9	14.4
Quebec	61.7	66.1	68.9	67.8	46.7	50.4	50.2	49.9
Ontario	8.1	8.2	8.4	8.0	6.3	6.8	6.6	6.0
Manitoba	6.3	6.5	6.5	6.3	2.5	2.9	2.8	2.5
Saskatchewan	3.7	3.6	3.7	3.4	1.9	2.0	2.1	2.1
Alberta	5.1	5.3	5.4	5.0	3.9	4.1	4.1	3.9
British Columbia	5.7	6.0	6.6	6.2	4.3	4.4	4.5	3.9
Yukon	7.3	7.3	8.0	9.6	6.2	8.0	9.7	7.6
Northwest Territories	6.2	7.0	7.7	7.7	2.5	3.1	3.7	7.6
Nunavut	8.5	7.2	7.9	7.2	0.6	0.7	0.9	0.7
Canada less Quebec	**6.9**	**7.1**	**7.4**	**7.4**	**5.3**	**5.7**	**5.6**	**5.5**

Source: Statistics Canada, Censuses of Population, 1996 to 2006, accessed 6 March 2009, www12.statcan.ca/english/census06/analysis/language/tables/table_17.htm, and Statistics Canada, Census of Population, 2011, *Focus on Geography Series*. Catalogue no.98-314-XWE2011004, released 2 February 2012, accessed 23 April 2014, www12.statcan.gc.ca/census-recensement/2011/as-sa/fogs-spg/select-Geo Choix.cfm?Lang=Eng&GK=PR.

and Quebec. Federalism is an important state tradition in Canada. According to most experts, it makes the Canadian political system distinct from Great Britain's despite Canada's adoption of the Westminster model.[17] In Canada, federalism is informed by political compromise. It represents a specific practice of brokerage politics between elites that enables the country to evolve or transform itself incrementally. In the area of language, political compromise and federalism involve the coexistence of more than one type of language policy in Canada.[18] For example, Article 133 of the British North America Act (the Canadian Constitution from 1867) recognized that French or English can be used in parliamentary debates in both the federal and Quebec legislatures, that laws will be published in both languages federally and in Quebec, and that French and English are the languages of both federal and Quebec courts. Article 133 also guaranteed English speakers the constitutional right to use English in the new Quebec Parliament. However, there was no equivalent protection for the French-speaking populations living in the other founding provinces—Nova Scotia, New Brunswick, and Ontario. A few years later, French was prohibited in the legislatures of most English-speaking provinces and in their education systems. In these provinces, the Orange Order and the Canada First movement advocated for one language and one culture and were among the most popular and successful groups to influence language policies.[19]

From 1840 to after World War II, language politics remained intense in Canada. In the 1960s, Quebec's political parties, media, and social movements demanded that the federation be redesigned on the basis of a new equal partnership between

English-speaking and French-speaking Canadians. Within this new context, the country witnessed its most important debates on the future of French since the prohibitive movements of the nineteenth century.

Thus, following much political debate and study, in 1963 the Canadian government created the Royal Commission on Bilingualism and Biculturalism (better known as the B&B Commission) to examine the situation between the two founding peoples and make recommendations to improve it. Liberal leader and Canadian Prime Minister Lester B. Pearson appointed two co-chairs, André Laurendeau from Quebec and Davidson Dunton from Ontario, and 10 commissioners.[20] The commission published its first report in 1965 but concluded its work in 1970. It revealed important discrepancies between French- and English-speaking communities, especially in education and the workplace, where past discrimination against French Canadians was documented and acknowledged. The commission made several important recommendations to redress the situation, some of which were accepted by the newly elected Liberal prime minister, Pierre Elliott Trudeau. It thus laid the foundation of Canada's contemporary linguistic regime.

CASE STUDY

The Royal Commission on Bilingualism and Biculturalism: A Meeting of the Two Solitudes[21]

In 1962, Social Credit Members of Parliament Réal Caouette and Gilles Grégoire, questioning the Diefenbaker government on bilingualism in Canada, underlined the fact that English and French didn't enjoy equal status. They demanded that a Royal Commission on bilingualism and on French-Canadian participation in the civil service be established.[22] The proposition was ignored until 1963 when the newly elected Liberal government of Lester B. Pearson appointed André Laurendeau, editor in chief of the newspaper *Le Devoir*, and Davidson Dunton, president of Carleton University, as co-chairs of the Royal Commission on Bilingualism and Biculturalism. Laurendeau was a committed French-Canadian nationalist. In 1942 his campaign against conscription led him to enter provincial politics under the Bloc populaire banner, but his career as a member of the Quebec legislature lasted only three years. He resigned his seat in 1947 to join *Le Devoir*, Quebec's nationalist newspaper. Dunton was an English Quebecer. After working for the *Montreal Star*, he became editor of the *Montreal Standard* in 1938. By the end of World War II he was appointed the first full-time chair of the Canadian Broadcasting Corporation (CBC).[23] He left the CBC after 13 years to become president of Carleton University. Ten other members were appointed to the commission, which held 23 regional public meetings across the country, attracting more than 10,000 people. The co-chairs also met with provincial premiers and received many written submissions.

The Royal Commission's mandate was an ambitious one:

> to inquire and report upon the existing state of bilingualism and biculturalism in Canada and to recommend steps to develop Canadian Confederation on the basis of an equal partnership between the two founding races, taking into account the contribution made by the other ethnic groups to the cultural enrichment of Canada.[24]

Three questions were raised at the beginning of each public meeting: "Can English-speaking and French-speaking Canadians live together, and do they want to? Under what new conditions? And are they prepared to accept those conditions?"[25]

More specifically, since the B&B Commission it can be said that Canada has witnessed three generations of more positive language policies derived from 1969, 1982, and 1988 initiatives. The 1969 Official Languages Act marked the first generation. It was the federal government's first major step toward **institutional bilingualism** in federal institutions. Informed by the personality principle described above, the aim of the new legislation was for all federal departments and agencies to become fully bilingual; government services across the country were to be offered in both official languages and a fair share of public service employment was to be accessible to francophones. The act also created the position of commissioner of official languages to watch over the application of the act and to investigate citizens' complaints of non-compliance with the act. The commissioner reports annually to Parliament.

A second generation of language planning and policymaking began in 1982, when Canada patriated its Constitution and adopted a Charter of Rights and Freedoms. The latter gave constitutional status to the French and English languages in bilingual institutions and education. Institutional bilingualism was

Released on 1 February 1965, the preliminary report described a country that was undergoing the worst crisis in its history. French Canadians "did not occupy in the economy, nor in the decision-making ranks of government, the place their numbers warranted."[26] English Canadians did not understand what was going on in Quebec and expressed satisfaction with the status quo. The commission published its findings in six volumes from 1967 to 1970. Book I, *The Official Languages*, introduces the concept of the bilingual district, where services would be provided in both languages where an English- or French-speaking minority formed at least 10 per cent of the local population. It also recommended that the Constitution be modified to recognize explicitly that English and French are Canada's two official languages.[27]

Book II, *Education*, recommended measures to give Canadians more opportunity to become bilingual. It suggests that the study of the second official language be mandatory for all students.[28] It also made recommendations for the extension of educational rights for official language minorities. Book III, *The Work World*, made suggestions aimed at putting an end to the domination of English in the federal administration and in the Canadian Forces. The last three volumes were *The Cultural Contribution of Other Ethnic Groups* (1969), *The Federal Capital* (1970), and *Voluntary Organizations* (1970).

Four decades later the commission's effects are still felt in today's society. Some recommendations never materialized. Bilingual districts were abandoned as soon as Book I was released. But it did achieve some substantial results. The Official Languages Act was adopted in 1969, giving equal status to English and French. The Official Languages in Education Program was established in 1970 to encourage provinces to offer courses in the other official language. These initiatives had important consequences, contributing to national unity. More specifically, the Official Languages in Education Program provided language training to successive generations of young Canadians who would become more aware and hopefully more supportive of their country's linguistic duality. It can be concluded that the Royal Commission on Bilingualism and Biculturalism made a significant contribution to the development of the contemporary Canadian language regime.

given a stronger status. Federal institutions would now provide services in both official languages, as indicated in articles 16 to 20 of the Charter. Article 23 states that "parents belonging to a linguistic minority have the right to have their children educated in the minority language, in homogeneous schools which they (official language communities) can manage, where numbers warrant." This article is particularly important for French-speaking minorities outside Quebec, because it repairs nineteenth- and early twentieth-century injustices wherein they lost their rights to education in their language. Likewise, English-speaking Quebecers benefit from article 23.

At the time, the government of Quebec did not find the adoption of the Official Languages Act to be sufficient for the protection of the French language in Quebec. However, it did not oppose its adoption. In 1982, the Quebec government refused to sign the Charter. The context was different than at the time of the B&B Commission when the province was governed by the Liberal Party; in 1982, the governing party was the Parti Québécois. In power since 1976, the Quebec government held a referendum in 1980 asking Quebecers to give its government a mandate to negotiate the province's political independence from, while maintaining an economic association with, the rest of Canada. The majority of the population voted "no" after Prime Minister Pierre Trudeau, speaking for the federal government, promised a new Constitution that included a charter to meet Quebec's needs within the federation. The Constitution was thus patriated from Westminster two years after the first sovereignty referendum in Quebec. The Charter was adopted, but at the time the Quebec government believed that it did not respond adequately to its demands. For example, it did not recognize Quebec's specific needs and demands for a special status within the federation. For the Quebec government, the Charter limited the legislative powers of Quebec's National Assembly, the province's legislature. For example, while article 23 of the Charter was welcomed by official language minorities, it was criticized severely by the Quebec government because it invalidated its own legislation toward English speakers.[29]

More than 30 years later successive Quebec governments of different parties have refused to sign the 1982 Constitution. At time of writing this chapter, the coming to power of a new Liberal government in Quebec has led to renewed discussions on whether it would sign the Constitution. In the rest of Canada, debates about whether Quebec was right in not signing the Constitution remain important and are often emotional.[30] The adoption of the Constitution by the Quebec government is still considered necessary for Canadian unity despite the fact that most Canadians have learned to live with the awkwardness of the situation.

A third generation of language policy began in 1988 with the adoption of a new Official Languages Act, in which the federal government added two new components to its approach. The act had to be redesigned in order to comply with the Charter. First, the act now recognizes the right of civil servants to work in the official language of their choice (part IV). Second, and more importantly for our argument, the new act states the following:

> The Government of Canada is committed to (a) enhancing the vitality of the English and French linguistic minority communities in Canada and supporting and assisting their development; and (b) fostering the full recognition and use of both English and French in Canadian society (section 41, part VII).

This section is another example of how legislation designed to benefit official language minorities can conflict with language policies adopted by the provinces. Section 41 allows the Canadian government to intervene in areas of provincial jurisdiction, which means that provinces lose some control over their policies. However, language rights in Canada are increasingly part of intergovernmental relations, where there is tentative recognition in each province of the need to respect official language minority communities in areas important for the sustainability of their communities, such as education, employment, health, immigration, and justice. Federalism allows the development of different language policies, but the case of section 41 invites more collaboration. In 2005, the 1988 Official Languages Act was amended to add to section 41 the requirement that the Canadian government take "positive measures" to promote the development of official languages communities. The Canadian government does not define what it means by "positive measures," but Canadians were given the right to take the government to court if they believe that the Canadian government did not do so. This means that the courts could eventually be asked to define the concept of positive measures.

Language Politics in Quebec: The Difficult Road to Linguistic Peace

In Quebec, more than anywhere else in Canada, language politics has been a key dimension of contemporary politics. Language policy choices in Quebec are a significant case study of how the personality principle (individual rights) interacts with the territoriality principle (collective rights) and federalism.

While the Canadian approach is informed by federalism, political compromise, and the personality principle, the Quebec government takes a different course. Since 1969, one of the effects of the Official Languages Act in Quebec has been to recognize that English is a minority language in Quebec while guaranteeing the presence of French speakers in the federal civil service. As already mentioned, the personality principle implies that all Canadians have linguistic rights as individuals. Since 1969 the development of bilingualism in the federal public service (that is, institutional bilingualism) has been based on the personality principle. This means that all Canadians, including Quebecers, can receive governmental services in the official language of their choice. However, in Quebec the personality principle is deemed insufficient to protect French and transform power relations between French and English speakers in the province. Furthermore, under section 41 the federal government has the obligation to enhance the development of English-speaking minority communities in Quebec, a section that was not well received in Quebec at the time of adoption.

In contrast, most Quebec governments operate under the assumption that Quebec represents a distinct nation within Canada.[31] This explains why collective rights or the territoriality principle is so important in Quebec, especially to protect the French language. However, before the 1960s, aside from the Lavergne Law, the Quebec government did little to promote French within the province.[32] The Canadian government provided some accommodating measures like bilingual postage stamps (1927), banknotes (1936), and bank cheques (1945),[33] but these measures served to promote bilingualism in federal institutions. It did not necessarily contribute to the enhancement of the French language in Quebec.

Starting in the 1960s the situation changed dramatically. The Quebec government became more and more concerned with the status of the French language within its own province. The context of the B&B Commission raised consciousness about the situation of the French language in Canada generally. National liberation and civil rights ideals were also popular at the time. Intellectual circles were inspired by several African nations' demands for the right to self-determination.[34] For example, the new political magazine *Parti pris*, an openly left-wing magazine, called for an independent and socialist Quebec. Most activists, including a new generation of politicians like René Lévesque, were also convinced that French was doomed outside of Quebec, especially in the context of the B&B Commission that had showed how French Canadians in Quebec were discriminated against within their own province. For them, it was time to adopt more radical measures to protect and promote the French language in Quebec. This new generation called on the Quebec government to intervene and adopt a new language regime that would provide the needed linguistic security to pursue its own development as a French-speaking nation, whether inside or outside the federation.

It is in this context, characterized by the need for radical change in many circles, that the government departed from its pre-1960s laissez-faire approach to language and embarked on a new kind of activism. However, the Quebec government did not embrace the territoriality principle from the start. For example, in 1961 the Quebec government adopted legislation that created both the Office de la langue française (Office for the French Language) and the Ministry of Cultural Affairs. The Office de la langue française was given the mandate to define a standard that would help promote the specificity of the French language in Quebec as well as internationally. The new institution would have an impact on the status of French within civil society even though it was not a tool for increasing the legal status of the language. At the time, French in Quebec was not seen as "proper" French in comparison with the French spoken in France. For others, this particular French, also called *joual* (a language spoken by the working class) was a source of pride (see Chapter 10 in this volume). The creation of the Office de la langue française did not resolve the debate on what constitutes a good French spoken in Quebec, but it did lead to the creation of important tools for monitoring the sociolinguistic situation of French in Quebec.

With the creation of the Office de la langue française, the Quebec government announced the formation of two commissions that would also have a decisive impact on the status of the French language. First, in 1963, the government created the Royal Commission of Inquiry on Education in the Province of Quebec, commonly known as the Parent Commission after its chairperson, Alphonse-Marie Parent, the rector of Laval University. The Parent Commission was not a commission on language per se, but commissioners called for measures to promote education among French Canadians. They also showed concern for the linguistic integration of immigrants in the French-speaking school system. These immigrants preferred bilingual schools where children could also be taught in English. In 1968, the Gendron Commission on the situation of the French language and on linguistic rights in Quebec called for the development of a language regime that would make French the common language for all Quebecers. The Gendron Commission led to the 1969 adoption of An Act to Promote the French Language in Quebec (Bill 63). The act promoted French by insisting that English schools provide French training to their pupils, especially immigrants. However, most actors considered Bill 63 too tame. It did not include measures to ensure the promotion of French. Following the 1974 recommendations of the Gendron Commission, the Quebec government took a bolder approach and adopted Bill 22, which made French the official language in Quebec. Finally, the 1977 adoption of Bill 101 confirmed that French was the language of the workplace and became the cornerstone of Quebec's approach to language policy.

Bill 101 is distinct from Canadian language laws because it provides a legislative basis for the collective dimension of language. Unlike the Canadian language regime, which grants linguistic rights to individuals, the Quebec approach links language to territory and grants the majority a collective right to use the language. Bill 101's collective dimension is visible in its preamble, which claims that the majority of the Quebec population speak French and that the language is an expression of its identity.

Bill 101 led to major debates on the legitimacy of a language law that conferred collective rights to its population.[35] It had an important effect on the anglophone community in Quebec.[36] Between 1971 and 1981, approximately 225,600 anglophones left the province for other parts of Canada or the United States, and a further 124,400 left between 1981 and 1991. The anglophone population appears to have stabilized since 2001.

Since the adoption of Bill 101, most English speakers who stayed in Quebec have learned to live with the legislation and have adapted to the new context.[37] With Bill 101, they also became Anglo-Quebecers, meaning that, as a group, they could no longer take the English language for granted as the norm in Quebec. The Quebec government guaranteed their rights to education as well as health and social services in English, but after years of domination over the French-speaking population they were to be recognized as a minority and began to organize on that basis. Following the 1982 re-election of the Parti Québécois government, a group of anglophones created Alliance Quebec with the goal of engaging in a constructive dialogue with the French-speaking majority. Soon it was fighting fierce legal battles against Bill 101. The anglophone-based Equality Party was formed in 1988 to run candidates in provincial elections. It radicalized some members of the English-speaking population against Quebec's language laws, though some dubbed it a party of "angryphones."[38] Furthermore, in the event of separation from Canada the Equality Party supported partitioning the province. Prominent activists such as former Liberal Cabinet Minister Reed Scowen were adamant in promoting English in Quebec despite the fact that English speakers widely used French in obtaining public services.[39] In the 1989 election, four Equality Party candidates were elected to the Quebec National Assembly. The party is no longer active, but some of its members are still involved in public debates or court cases against Bill 101. Most Anglo-Quebecers now support the Quebec Liberal Party.

Another effect of Bill 101 was felt at the Canadian level, especially at the level of the federal government. Following the adoption of Bill 101, Anglo-Quebecers (but also francophones outside of Quebec) were encouraged to use the courts to fight for their language rights. The federal government established and fully funded a Court Challenges Program in 1978; it is well known that, although this program addresses language and equality rights in general across Canada, it was established mainly to help the anglophone minority in Quebec fight Bill 101.[40] For some anglophone activists, the judicial process could lead to a reaffirmation of the individual rights of English speakers in Quebec.

Since the 1970s more than 40 court cases dealing with language issues have been fought in Canada, and the role of the Supreme Court of Canada has been a delicate one. Many battles were won in the name of anglophones in Quebec, but the Supreme Court has also played a key role in helping Quebecers and Canadians see the legitimacy of Bill 101 while addressing aspects that it deemed unconstitutional. For example, the law's section on using only French in legal texts conflicted with article 133 of the British North America Act and was quickly amended by the Quebec government.[41] The Supreme Court confirmed that article 133 could not be modified unilaterally by the Quebec government; all parties involved at the time of the adoption of the article had to agree to its modification.

Another example comes from the battle over article 23 of the 1982 Charter of Rights and Freedoms. Article 23 invalidated Bill 101's restrictive provisions for the education of English-speakers' children in public schools and extended to all Canadian anglophones the right to have their children educated in English.[42] In contrast, the Supreme Court confirmed the legitimacy of Bill 101's requirement that children of immigrants attend French public schools—there is no freedom of choice possible for immigrants in Quebec attending public schools. In a brief to the United Nations Educational, Scientific and Cultural Organization (UNESCO), the Canadian government also recognized that this was a necessary measure because of the unique situation of French in Canada and in North America.[43] There is, in fact, no freedom of choice in public schools for immigrants elsewhere in Canada. Outside of Quebec, immigrants have to attend English schools even if they want to send their children to French public schools.

Nevertheless, in the year 2000 political and economic pressures on immigrants and francophone Quebecers to learn English has led some immigrant and francophone parents to challenge Bill 101 in the courts to obtain the right to send their children to English public schools. Since 2005, the Supreme Court has addressed this issue in three cases: *Gosselin*, *Solski*, and *Nguyen*.[44] In *Gosselin*, it rejected the principle of freedom of choice in education for French speakers; Bill 101 legitimately restricts francophones to studying in the French public school system. However, in *Solski* the Supreme Court determined that a child whose mother tongue was not English who had previously received the major part of his or her education in English had the right to attend an English school. It also established that the "major part" of a child's previous education should be measured subjectively as well as quantitatively. Finally, in 2009 in *Nguyen*, the Supreme Court ruled unconstitutional a provision of Bill 101 (added in 2002) to further regulate access to English schools for non–English speakers. This new section did not recognize time spent in a non–state-funded private school in qualifying for an English school.[45] The Supreme Court gave Quebec one year to redraft this provision in keeping with its more subjective approach in assessing a child's previous education. Since then debate has continued. In 2010 the Quebec Liberal government adopted Bill 115, reinstating transfers from private English-language schools to public English-language schools, and in 2012 the minority PQ government proposed Bill 14

BIOGRAPHY

Camille Laurin[49]

The life and times of Camille Laurin (1922–1999), chief architect of the Quebec Charter of the French Language, provide a useful lens through which to view the complex process of modernization in Quebec during the latter half of the twentieth century. Catholicism, nationalism, and Freudian psychiatry constitute a triad of Laurin's salient formative influences, which at various stages had a profound impact on his core economic, social, and political beliefs. The theme of continuity and change is central to understanding the intellectual odyssey of Camille Laurin. Beginning as an insular, clerical, conservative French-Canadian nationalist, he became a secular, statist, Québécois neo-nationalist public intellectual and a Parti Québécois (PQ) government cabinet minister.

Camille Laurin entering the National Assembly in Quebec City on 27 April 1977 to introduce the government's French-language law.

The Canadian Press/Louise Bidault

Laurin was born in 1922 in Charlemagne, then a small French-Canadian village at the extreme east end of the Island of Montreal, coincidentally only a few months before René Lévesque, the father of the contemporary Quebec sovereignty movement. At that time the Roman Catholic Church and its health, educational, and social welfare institutions dominated French-Quebec society. Anglo-Canadian and US capital dominated the primary natural resources and the rapidly growing secondary manufacturing sectors of the Quebec economy. The Laurin family were devoutly Catholic in a community where social ties developed principally around the Church and numerous religious holidays. Laurin's father, Eloi, a director of the local branch of the Provincial Bank of Canada, was a *petit bourgeois* French-Canadian economic nationalist, a fervent supporter of *achat chez nous*—buy goods and services from *our own* French-Canadian merchants, not from *them*, the non-French Canadian non-Catholics—and an ardent defender of the French language. A long-time Quebec Liberal Party militant, in 1935 Eloi shifted his allegiance to Paul Gouin's l'Action libérale nationale, which advocated the nationalization of hydroelectricity; he detested Duplessis. It was Paul Gouin, son of former Quebec premier Lomer Gouin and grandson of Honoré Mercier, another former premier and a member of the French-Canadian "big bourgeoisie," who financially enabled Eloi's son Camille to continue his education from 1937 to 1941 at L'Assomption College. This school catered to children of less-well-off French-Canadian merchants, workers, and farmers.

In his fourth year of classical college, at the behest of Abbé Armand Trottier, Camille joined St Mary's English Academy, a literary and oratory student club. His speech topics—in English—included "School and Immorality," "Struggles for Our Language," and "Immigration Is Detrimental to Us." This was his introduction to the English language and civilization. In 1940, Camille composed a song that contained the lyrics, "My dear friends, hang on to our language, let us never obey our oppressors, from our ancestors it is saintly heritage, our young hearts must remain French." Meanwhile, in the classrooms and corridors of this classical college student Camille heard and did not disagree with lavish praise heaped upon both the Francisco Franco and Philippe Pétain fascist corporatist regimes in Spain and France.

His admission to the University of Montreal School of Medicine was delayed one year because he was not adequately prepared at L'Assomption College in the basic physical sciences. In 1947, Laurin became director of the university's student journal *Quartier Latin*. In these pages, perspectives of the emerging post–World War II French-Canadian intelligentsia on Catholic social action were presented. Laurin wrote that neither Marx, Dewey, nor Freud were enemies of French Catholics. Frequent themes that Laurin addressed included "The Role of the Church in Society," "Secularization of Education," "Workers' Conditions," "Social Policy," "Political Future of Quebec and Canada," and "International Issues." As director of the *Quartier Latin*, Laurin was also preoccupied with the journal's use of proper French—that worthy cause of the greatest French university in North America.

Although French-Canadian nationalists (including Laurin) generally conflated anti-communism, defence of Catholicism, anti-conscription, and anti-English Canada themes, Laurin at this time wrote that French-Canadian nationalism was too much grounded in the traditional values of language and religion. To be relevant in the future, French-Canadian nationalism would have to refocus on new social values and the economic development of society. French-Canadian nationalism would continue to believe in a collective cultural and Catholic mission, but Laurin thought it necessary to focus largely on issues such as workers' salaries, collective bargaining, housing, social insurance, taxes, popular education, and recreation.

In 1949, during his fifth and final year of general medicine at the University of Montreal, he decided to specialize in psychiatry rather than clinical medicine. In 1950 he did a 12-month residency in psychiatry at Queen Mary Veterans Hospital in Montreal. He chose Queen Mary because he judged that anglophone hospitals were more advanced than francophone institutions, with more emphasis on psychological causes than the physical and physiological roots of mental disorder stressed in French hospitals in Quebec. To realize his dream of becoming a fully accredited psychoanalytic psychiatrist he had to pursue further study in the United States or Europe, because in Montreal francophone psychiatrists were resistant to modern trends in the field. In French Quebec generally at this time, mental illness was widely stigmatized. Quebec was also far behind in teaching methods in psychiatry and in-patient care in psychiatric hospitals. Thus, Laurin began to see himself as a future psychiatrist, teacher, administrator, and reformer of Quebec psychiatry.

Despite decades of use in Europe and the United States, even the most advanced thinkers among French-Quebec psychiatrists feared Freud's theories. In Laurin's eyes, Freud was a genius; his discoveries were essential to understanding and treating the human mind. He went to Boston until 1952, when US conscription laws forced him to go to France to complete the arduous prerequisites to full certification as a psychotherapist. In 1957 he returned to Quebec to start a practice at the age of 35.

Catholic, nationalist, and Freudian psychoanalytic cross-currents intertwine in Laurin's analysis of what ailed the French-Quebec people and what could be done to cure this collective disorder. He believed that the French Québécois suffered a deep and collective sense of powerlessness that only the liberating gesture of political independence would be able to correct. He saw his own Québécois people as sad, passive, resigned to their fate, and discouraged. The healthy part of their personality was affected by a significant loss of self-confidence and the sense of always being a small cog in the grand scheme of things. The remedy could only be the establishment of a strong Quebec state to overcome the enduring effects of the British Conquest.

In a sense, the story of modern Quebec is the story of Camille Laurin writ large.

to reinforce Bill 101, though the bill died when the PQ were defeated in 2014.

Another example of a measure that led to fierce court battles is the section of Bill 101 that made French the exclusive language of public and commercial signs. The measure was meant to transform corporate names and commercial signage in Montreal, which was almost exclusively in English.[46] In 1988 the Quebec government was summoned by the Supreme Court to relax its restriction on other languages on signs because it was argued that it did not respect freedom of expression.[47] This judgment was not popular among the majority of Quebecers. Many mobilized and publicly protested, leading the government of Quebec to not comply with the Supreme Court judgment and to be denounced vigorously in English Canada while being applauded at home. In 1993, a Liberal government under Robert Bourassa adopted Bill 86, which allowed signage in other languages but required that French predominate.

The debate over language in Quebec is far from over. Informed by so much history and politics, Quebec's language regime is unique in Canada. Today, the tensions between the personality and the territoriality approaches to language policy remain important. The recognition of the French language as an important marker of identity and as the common language for all Quebecers is still a key dimension of the province's territorial approach. Language planning and policymaking in Quebec is about how to maintain the status of French as a majority language in its territory. Finally, in understanding language politics in Quebec, it is also important to acknowledge both the crucial role of the Quebec state and that of the Supreme Court of Canada in the development of the province's language regime. Important court cases led to changes to Bill 101, but it remains a fundamental law that aims to reassert French majority control over the province and to end discrimination against French speakers. It is still contested by some English-speaking activists who believe that it is illiberal legislation, especially in education. For them, freedom of choice should trump preservation of the French language. For others, living in Quebec as a linguistic minority involves important soul searching, but they recognize that English is not in the least threatened in the province.[48]

Conclusion: The Future of Language Politics in Quebec

This chapter has discussed briefly the politics of language and language policies in Quebec and in Canada. It first commented on the most recent data on language in Canada with a particular focus on Quebec. It also discussed the status of both English and French in the federation. It then presented the context in which language policy choices evolved in Canada. This was followed by a discussion of language politics in Quebec and its impact on the status of anglophones and francophones in the province.

Overall, this sociopolitical, institutional, and historical discussion of language politics in both Canada and Quebec shows how the principles of personality and territoriality can guide the language policy choices of governments. The Quebec government is influenced by the territoriality principle because of its concern for the status of French in its territory. As for the Canadian government, it has chosen the personality principle as a guide for the development of institutional bilingualism.

Our discussion also helps understand the impact of the state tradition of federalism on the development of distinctive language regimes. Federalism is conducive to the adoption of different language policies from one province to the other. However, we have seen that those distinct language regimes need to comply with the Constitution. The role of the courts in clarifying the legitimacy of language policy processes, especially on how governments should treat their minorities, is thus important.

Finally, one particularity of the language debate in Canada and in Quebec is that these tensions between Canada's and Quebec's language regimes have framed our normative understanding of how law should relate to issues of language and identity. Many internationally renowned authors such as Will Kymlicka and Charles Taylor are from Canada and Quebec (see the Biography box in Chapter 5). Their works on the politics of recognition inform the debate on the accommodation of linguistic and national minorities internationally. Building on the contrast between the personality and territoriality principles, they have further contrasted individual and collective rights, the just and the good, and liberalism and communitarian theories in order to address demands for minority recognition. While Kymlicka, for example, understands society as a context of choice in which individuals choose what they need to advance their conception of the good life,[50] Taylor argues that a conception of the good at the level of the state can also guide action.[51]

Applied to the Canadian and Quebec contexts, such debate leads to the question of whether it is just for the Quebec government to legislate in favour of French speakers.[52] While Taylor proposes a nonutilitarian approach to language and society, others have suggested that a state should legislate only to increase the salience of a language as a means of communication, not as a collective good. There is no ultimate resolution to such debate, except that any purely utilitarian attitude toward language seems to undermine its importance in one's identity, and that power relations will determine which principles might be the most appropriate for linguistic peace.[53]

One of the most pressing issues in Quebec today is to better understand how the equilibrium between francophone and anglophone Quebecers is affected by the growing use of English as an international lingua franca. Given its location on the North American continent, will Quebec remain a predominantly French-speaking province? While knowledge of French is increasingly important for the anglophone population, there is also pressure to use English in the workplace and in the public sphere. Furthermore, in 2006 it was shown that French-speaking immigrants might face language discrimination since they do not have access to jobs requiring bilingual skills.[54] In 2008 a study published by the Conseil supérieur de la langue française on the linguistic behaviour of young Quebecers revealed that many people whose first language is French did not feel the fight for French to be a priority.[55] This is a blow to older activists who remain convinced that the language is fragile and its protection needs constant vigilance.

We might also ask, how is the changing demography in Quebec affecting the vitality of the French language? How do immigrants negotiate their identity in the ongoing competition between French and English in the workplace, especially in Montreal? Given the growing immigrant population in Quebec, more research should be done to survey if or how they gradually come to define themselves as francophones or Quebecers.

Finally, there is still some debate in Canada on the need for federal language legislation to acknowledge the predominance of Bill 101 in its dealings with Quebec. Conflicts between federal and provincial legislation need to be resolved; some suggest that Bill 101 be given constitutional status to confirm its importance and affirm its role as a fundamental tool for linguistic peace in Canada and in Quebec.[56] Quebec remains convinced that its own language regime is necessary for the protection and the promotion of the French language in its territory.

Questions for Critical Thinking

1. What is the status of English and French in Canada and in Quebec? Explain why Canada has adopted both English and French as official languages.
2. What has been the impact of the Supreme Court of Canada on Bill 101?
3. Discuss possible impacts of globalization on the future of French in Canada and in Quebec.

Notes

1. I would like to thank the editors of the book for their suggestions and Simon Letendre and Marc Prévost from the School of Political Studies at the University of Ottawa for their assistance.
2. Linda Cardinal and Selma K. Sonntag, eds., *State Traditions and Language Regimes* (Montreal and Kingston: McGill-Queen's University Press, 2015).
3. Jean-Claude Corbeil, *L'embarras des langues : origine, conception et évolution de la politique linguistique québécoise* (Montreal: Québec Amérique 2007), 24, and Jean Laponce, *Loi de Babel et autres régularités des rapports entre langue et politique* (Quebec: Presses de l'Université Laval, 2007).

4. Colin H. Williams, "Language Policy and Planning Issues in Multicultural Societies," in *Linguistic Conflict and Language Laws: Understanding the Quebec Question*, ed. Pierre Larrivée (Basingstoke, England, and New York: Palgrave Macmillan, 2003), 1–56.
5. Kenneth McRae, "The Principle of Territoriality and the Principle of Personality in Multilingual States," *International Journal of the Sociology of Language* 4 (1975): 35–45.
6. Rainer Bauböck, "Autonomie territoriale ou culturelle pour les minorités nationales?" in *La constellation des appartenances : nationalisme, libéralisme et pluralisme*, ed. A. Dieckhoff (Paris: Presses de Sciences Po, 2004), 317–70.
7. For an overview of those debates, see Selma K. Sonntag and Linda Cardinal, "State Traditions and Language Regimes: Conceptualizing Language Policy Choices," in *State Traditions and Language Regimes*, ed. Linda Cardinal and Selma K. Sonntag, 3–28.
8. Abram de Swaan, *Words of the World: The Global Language System* (Cambridge: Polity Press, 2001).
9. See John Loughlin, "Les changements de paradigmes de l'État et les politiques publiques envers les minorités linguistiques et culturelles en Europe de l'Ouest," in *La gouvernance linguistique : le Canada en perspective*, ed. J.-P. Wallot (Ottawa: Presses de l'Université d'Ottawa, 2005), 19–38.
10. Gouvernement du Québec, Charter of the French Language, www2.publicationsduquebec.gouv.qc.ca/dynamicSearch/telecharge.php?type=2&file=/C_11/C11_A.html.
11. C. Michael MacMillan, "Resolving the Language Question: The Impact of the Bi & Bi Commission," *Canadian Issues/Thèmes canadiens* (Fall 2003): 39–43.
12. Patricia Lamarrre, "L'enseignement du français dans le réseau Anglophone," in *Le français au Québec : les nouveaux défis*, ed. A. Stefanescu and P. Georgeault (Montreal: Fides, 2005), 553–68.
13. See Chapter 2 for an analysis of the impact of the Conquest.
14. Pierre Tousignant, "Problématique pour une nouvelle approche de la constitution de 1791," *Revue d'histoire de l'Amérique française* 27 (1973): 181–234.
15. Ibid.
16. These debates are illustrated in the famous Charles Huot painting entitled *The Language Debate*, which is installed above the Throne of the President of Quebec's National Assembly; see www.assnat.qc.ca/en/abc-assemblee/organisation-travaux-assemblee/symboles.html#Debate.
17. David E. Smith, "The Westminster Model in Ottawa: A Study in the Absence of Influence," *British Journal of Canadian Studies* 15, no. 1–2 (2002): 54–64; and David E. Smith, *Federalism and the Constitution of Canada* (Toronto: University of Toronto Press, 2010).
18. Linda Cardinal, "Linguistic Peace: A Time to Take Stock," *Inroads* 23 (2008): 62–70; Linda Cardinal, "State Tradition and Language Regimes in Canada," in *State Traditions and Language Regimes*, ed. Linda Cardinal and Selma K. Sonntag (Montreal and Kingston: McGill-Queen's University Press, 2015), 29–44.
19. Carl Berger, *The Sense of Power: Studies in the Ideas of Canadian Imperialism, 1867–1914* (Toronto: University of Toronto Press, 1970).
20. Graham Fraser, *Sorry, I Don't Speak French: Confronting the Canadian Crisis that Won't Go Away* (Toronto: McClelland & Stewart, 2006).
21. Prepared by Simon Letendre, School of Political Studies, University of Ottawa.
22. Fraser, *Sorry, I Don't Speak French*, 31.
23. James H. Marsh, "Dunton, Arnold Davidson," *Canadian Encyclopedia*, www.thecanadian encyclopedia.ca/en/article/arnold-davidson-dunton/, accessed 7 March 2009.
24. Royal Commission on Bilingualism and Biculturalism, *Report of the Royal Commission on Bilingualism and Biculturalism. Book I: The Official Languages* (Ottawa: The Commission, 1967), xxi.
25. Fraser, *Sorry, I Don't Speak French*, 43.
26. Gertrude Laing, "Royal Commission on Bilingualism and Biculturalism," *Canadian Encyclopedia*, originally accessed 7 March 2009, http://www.thecanadianencyclopedia.ca/en/article/royal-commission-on-bilingualism-and-biculturalism/.
27. Royal Commission on Bilingualism and Biculturalism, *Report, Book I: The Official Languages*, 147.
28. Royal Commission on Bilingualism and Biculturalism, *Report, Book II: Education* (Ottawa: The Commission, 1968), 302.
29. Garth Stevenson, *Community Besieged: The Anglophone Minority and the Politics of Quebec* (Montreal and Kingston: McGill-Queen's University Press, 1999).
30. Ron Graham, *The Last Act: Pierre Trudeau, the Gang of Eight, and the Fight for Canada: The History of Canada* (Toronto: Allen Lane Canada, 2011).
31. The recognition or formalization of this assumption that Quebec is a nation has become a formal constitutional demand by the Quebec government, especially since the 1960s. Quebec wants its right to self-determination to be formally recognized in the Canadian Constitution. In 2006, the Canadian government confirmed that Quebecers form a distinct society within a united Canada in a declaration by the Canadian Parliament. The declaration is a symbolic form of recognition since it did not lead to its incorporation in the Constitution, nor did it involve any devolution of new powers to the Quebec government. The 2006 declaration might be viewed as a first gesture confirming the right to self-determination of Quebecers by the Canadian Parliament. However, it is still not sufficient as a measure for the Quebec government to sign the Constitution. Furthermore, Quebec remains convinced that its own language regime is necessary for the protection and the promotion of the French language in its territory.

32. The Lavergne Law, passed in 1910, was the first piece of legislation addressing language adopted by the Quebec government. It required public service organizations to provide services in French and English.
33. Linda Cardinal and Martin Normand, "Des accents distincts : les régimes linguistiques ontarien et québécois," in *Les relations Ontario-Québec : un destin partagé*, ed. J. F. Savard, A. Brassard, and L. Côté (Montreal : Presses de l'Université de Montréal, 2011), 135.
34. According to Corbeil (*L'embarras des langues*, 519), the publication in 1959 of Albert Memmi's *Portrait of the Colonized* had an important impact in Quebec.
35. Pierre Larrivée, "Anglophones and Allophones in Quebec," in *Linguistic Conflict and Language Laws: Understanding the Québec Question*, ed. Pierre Larrivée (Basingstoke, England, and New York: Palgrave Macmillan, 2003), 163–87; and Stevenson, *Community Besieged*.
36. Garth Stevenson, "English-Speaking Québec: A Political History," in *Québec: State and Society*, ed. A.-G. Gagnon (Peterborough: Broadview Press, 2004), 329–44. See also G. Chambers, "Les relations entre anglophones et francophones," in *Le Français au Québec : 400 ans d'histoire et de vie*, ed. M. Plourde (Quebec: Conseil supérieur de la langue française and Fides, 2000), 319–25.
37. Michael Stein, "Changement dans la perception de soi des Anglo-Québécois," in *Les anglophones du Québec de majoritaires à minoritaires*, ed. G. Caldwell and É. Waddell (Quebec: Institut québécois de recherche sur la culture, 1982), 125–6.
38. Larrivée, "Anglophones and Allophones in Quebec," 177–8.
39. Ironically, for someone who wanted the expansion of English in Quebec, Scowen now lives in Toronto and has a chronicle in French on the Ottawa French national radio once a month. See also Stevenson, *Community Besieged*, 206.
40. Linda Cardinal, "Le pouvoir exécutif et la judiciarisation de la politique au Canada : une étude du programme de contestation judiciaire," *Politique et Sociétés* 20, no. 2–3 (2000): 4–65.
41. See *Attorney General of Quebec v. Blaikie et al.*, [1979] 2 SCR 1016; completed in 1981: [1981] 1 SCR 312.
42. See *Attorney General of Quebec v. Quebec Protestant School Boards*, [1984] 2 SCR 66.
43. François Cardinal, "Ottawa défend la loi 101 devant l'UNESCO," *Le Devoir*, 1 July 2000.
44. *Gosselin (Tutor of) v. Quebec (Attorney General)*, [2005] 1 S.C.R. 238, 2005 SCC 15; *Solski (Tutor of) v. Quebec (Attorney General)*, [2005] 1 S.C.R. 201, 2005 SCC 14; *Nguyen v. Quebec (Education, Recreation and Sports)*, [2009] 3 S.C.R. 208, 2009 SCC 47.
45. The concept of non–state-funded private schools may read as a strange concept for non-Quebecers. One must understand that in Quebec private schools can either be partly state funded or non–state funded. When state funded, private schools make a commitment to teach state accredited programs and provide some teaching of French. Non–state-funded private schools do not have those requirements.
46. Marc V. Levine, *The Reconquest of Montreal: Language Policy and Social Change in a Bilingual City* (Philadelphia: Temple University Press, 1990).
47. *Ford v. Quebec (Attorney General)*, [1988] 2 S.C.R. 712.
48. Leigh Oakes and Jane Warren, *Language, Citizenship and Identity in Quebec* (Basingstoke, England: Palgrave Macmillan, 2007).
49. The following was originally written by the late Professor Martin Lubin and published in the first edition of *Quebec Questions*. Sources: J.-C. Picard, *Camille Laurin : l'homme debout* (Montreal: Boréal, 2003); R. Filion, *Une saison chez Camille Laurin: carnet d'un compagnon de route* (Montreal: Isabelle Quentin, 2005).
50. Will Kymlicka, *Finding Our Way* (Toronto: Oxford University Press, 1998).
51. Charles Taylor, *Reconciling the Solitudes: Essays on Canadian Federalism and Nationalism* (Montreal and Kingston: McGill-Queen's University Press, 1994).
52. On this question, see Daniel Weinstock's chapter in this book.
53. Astrid von Busekist, "Cannibales et gourmets : quelques recettes d'équilibre linguistiques," in *Politiques et usages de la langue en Europe*, ed. M. Werner (Paris: Éditions de la Maison des sciences de l'homme, 2007), 101–20; and Cardinal, "Linguistic Peace."
54. Paul Morissette, "Quand la politique officielle bute sur la réalité," *Le Devoir*, 24 August 2006.
55. Nathalie St-Laurent, *Le français et les jeunes* (Québec: Conseil supérieur de la langue française, 2008), 28.
56. John Richards, "Breaking the 'Vicious Cycle': A Retrospective and Prospective Examination of Quebec/Canada Relations," in *Quebec and Canada in the New Century: New Dynamics, New Opportunities*, ed. M. Murphy (Kingston: Institute of Intergovernmental Affairs, 2007), 233–56.

Select Bibliography

Bauböck, Rainer. "Autonomie territoriale ou culturelle pour les minorités nationales?" In *La constellation des appartenances : nationalisme, libéralisme et pluralisme*, edited by A. Dieckhoff, 317–70. Paris: Presses de Science Po, 2004.

Berger, Carl. *The Sense of Power: Studies in the Ideas of Canadian Imperialism, 1867–1914*. Toronto: University of Toronto Press, 1970.

Busekist, Astrid von. "Cannibales et gourmets : quelques recettes d'équilibre linguistiques." In *Politiques et usages de la langue en Europe*, edited by M. Werner, 101–20. Paris: Éditions de la Maison des sciences de l'homme, 2007.

Cardinal, Linda. "Linguistic peace: A time to take stock." *Inroads* 23 (2008): 62–70.

———. "Le pouvoir exécutif et la judiciarisation de la politique au Canada : une étude du programme de contestation judiciaire." *Politique et Sociétés* 20, no. 2–3 (2000): 4–65.

———. "State Tradition and Language Regime in Canada." In *State Traditions and Language Regimes*, edited by Linda Cardinal and Selma K. Sonntag, 29–44. Montreal and Kingston: McGill-Queen's University Press, 2015.

———, and Martin Normand. "Des accents distincts : les régimes linguistiques ontarien et québécois." In *Les relations Ontario-Québec : un destin partagé*, edited by J.-F. Savard, A. Brassard, and L. Côté, 131–58. Montreal: Presses de l'Université de Montréal, 2011.

Corbeil, Jean-Claude. *L'embarras des langues : origine, conception et évolution de la politique linguistique québécoise.* Montreal: Québec Amérique, 2007.

Fraser, Graham. *Sorry, I Don't Speak French: Confronting the Canadian Crisis that Won't Go Away.* Toronto: McClelland & Stewart, 2006.

Gouvernement du Québec. *La langue française au Québec : quelques repères.* 2008. www.spl.gouv.qc.ca/fileadmin/medias/pdf/400ans_quelquesreperes2.pdf.

Graham, Ron. *The Last Act: Pierre Trudeau, the Gang of Eight, and the Fight for Canada: The History of Canada.* Toronto: Allen Lane Canada, 2011.

Kymlicka, Will. *Finding Our Way.* Toronto: Oxford University Press, 1998.

Laponce, Jean. *Loi de Babel et autres régularités des rapports entre langue et politique.* Quebec: Presses de l'Université Laval, 2007.

Larrivée, Pierre. "Anglophones and Allophones in Quebec." In *Linguistic Conflict and Language Laws: Understanding the Quebec Question*, edited by Pierre Larrivée, 163–87. Basingstoke, England, and New York: Palgrave Macmillan, 2003.

Levine, Marc V. *The Reconquest of Montreal: Language Policy and Social Change in a Bilingual City.* Philadelphia: Temple University Press, 1990.

Loughlin, John. "Les changements de paradigmes de l'État et les politiques publiques envers les minorités linguistiques et culturelles en Europe de l'Ouest." In *La gouvernance linguistique : le Canada en perspective*, edited by J.-P. Wallot, 19–38. Ottawa: Presses de l'Université d'Ottawa, 2005.

MacMillan, C. Michael. "Federal Language Policy in Canada and the Quebec Challenge." In *Linguistic Conflict and Language Laws: Understanding the Quebec Question*, edited by Pierre Larrivée, 87–117. Basingstoke, England, and New York: Palgrave Macmillan, 2003.

———. "Resolving the Language Question: The Impact of the Bi & Bi Commission." *Canadian Issues/Thèmes canadiens* (2013): 39–43.

McRae, Kenneth. "The Principle of Territoriality and the Principle of Personality in Multilingual States." *International Journal of the Sociology of Language* 4 (1975): 35–45.

Oakes, Leigh, and Jane Warren. *Language, Citizenship and Identity in Quebec.* Basingstoke, England: Palgrave Macmillan, 2007.

Richards, John. "Breaking the 'Vicious Cycle': A Retrospective and Prospective Examination of Quebec/Canada Relations." In *Quebec and Canada in the New Century: New Dynamics, New Opportunities*, edited by M. Murphy, 233–56. Kingston: Institute of Intergovernmental Affairs, 2007.

Smith, David E. *Federalism and the Constitution of Canada.* Toronto: University of Toronto Press, 2010.

———. "The Westminster Model in Ottawa: A Study in the Absence of Influence." *British Journal of Canadian Studies* 15, no. 1–2 (2002): 54–64.

Sonntag, Selma K., and Linda Cardinal. "State Traditions and Language Regimes: Conceptualizing Language Policy Choices." In *State Traditions and Language Regimes*, edited by Linda Cardinal and Selma K. Sonntag, 3–28. Montreal and Kingston: McGill-Queen's University Press, 2015.

Stein, Michael. "Changement dans la perception de soi des Anglo-Québécois." In *Les anglophones du Québec de majoritaires à minoritaires*, edited by G. Caldwell and É. Waddell. Québec: Institut québécois de recherche sur la culture, 1982.

Stevenson, Garth. *Community Besieged: The Anglophone Minority and the Politics of Quebec.* Montreal and Kingston: McGill-Queen's University Press, 1999.

Swaan, Abram de. *Words of the World: The Global Language System.* Cambridge: Polity Press, 2001.

Taylor, Charles. *Reconciling the Solitudes: Essays on Canadian Federalism and Nationalism.* Montreal and Kingston: McGill-Queen's University Press, 1994.

Tousignant, Pierre. "Problématique pour une nouvelle approche de la constitution de 1791." *Revue d'histoire de l'Amérique française* 27 (1973): 181–234.

Williams, Colin H. "Language Policy and Planning Issues in Multicultural Societies." In *Linguistic Conflict and Language Laws: Understanding the Quebec Question*, edited by Pierre Larrivée, 1–56. Basingstoke, England, and New York: Palgrave Macmillan, 2003.

12 The Politics of Language: Philosophical Reflections on the Case of Quebec

Daniel Weinstock, McGill University

Introduction

Language politics has been at the centre of political debate in Quebec for the past 40 years. The centrality of language politics is easy to understand. Quebec is home to a majority of the French speakers residing in Canada and in North America. But francophones are a minority in the Canadian federation. Within North America and the Americas generally, they represent a very small fraction of the total population.[1] Furthermore, English within the Canadian federation is the language of the erstwhile conqueror, a fact that has been enshrined in many of the political institutions around which the Canadian federation was created.

Quebec's language debates have provided an interesting and fertile laboratory for political philosophers. Most societies do not need to engage in language politics at all. That is, in most countries a majority language achieves institutional dominance without the need for any special policies. It is understood by everyone that when one moves, say, to France, French will be the language of instruction used in schools, the language in which one will be addressed in courts, and so on.

Things are different for societies such as Quebec, Catalonia, and a number of others. Catalan speakers and French-speaking Quebecers constitute a majority within a territory, but each of these territories is embedded within a larger political entity (Spain, Canada) in which the majority speaks another language. They therefore cannot simply expect that, as a matter of course, all those who come to their society will converge on their language. In the absence of deliberate policy, such as an official language policy, it may seem just as natural for a new arrival to Quebec or to Catalonia to speak and transact business in English or in Spanish, since these are the majority languages of Canada and Spain.

Quebecers and Catalans are thus faced with a dilemma. They could allow all inhabitants of their territories to speak whatever language they want and risk seeing their own language eroded by the assimilative pressures of the broader society's language. Or they can enact mildly coercive legislation aimed at securing their language and run the risk of being viewed as illiberal.

This chapter looks at the language debate within Quebec as a political philosopher might. The aim is not to provide readers with historical insight into the evolution of language policy in Quebec,[2] but rather to see whether a convincing **liberal democratic** rationale can be provided for language policies such as Quebec's attempt to protect a vulnerable language without wholesale breaches of individual rights. The arguments canvassed and considered in what follows are therefore not necessarily the arguments that were actually presented at crucial junctures by the main protagonists on either side of Quebec's language saga. Rather, they are reconstructions aimed at couching those debates in the terms of the most prominent contemporary political philosophies.

Language and Identity

Debates about language policy crystallize a number of broader political and philosophical debates that have been at the heart of Quebec's political and intellectual evolution over the past 40 years or so.

For most French-speaking Quebecers, the survival of the French language is central to the survival of Quebec as a distinct community within Canada and North America. The centrality of language for survival is due to the fact that French has become central to the *identity* of Quebecers.

For much of its history French Canada was held together by the predominant place of the Catholic religion and its accompanying values and institutions within the lives of French Canadians both inside Quebec and in the rest of Canada. French-speaking Catholics were among the most devout people on the planet, a fact to which Quebec's architecture and place names still bear eloquent witness. Until the 1950s, the survival of French-Canadian identity was tied to the survival of a community bound together first and foremost by the values, symbols, and institutions of the Church. The refusal to allow non-Catholic immigrants into Catholic schools, which were most often de facto francophone, could be seen as part of this survival strategy. Though it might have meant that more children would have been integrated into the *French-speaking* community through the school system, it also would have carried the risk of watering down the *Catholic* identity.

Things changed dramatically with the Quiet Revolution. Voices urging for the liberalization and deconfessionalization of French-Canadian society had always been present in Quebec society, but in the course of one generation they became dominant. Catholicism receded from the forefront of the identity of Quebecers. The self-understanding of Quebecers became much more pluralistic. The identity of Quebecers would from then on have to encompass a great many values and ways of life, rather than being tightly defined around a single religion.

As well, a French-speaking economic and political class emerged, intent on using the levers of provincial power in Quebec to give institutional weight to the existence of a distinctive society within North America. A territorially concentrated identity was needed, one that might be shared by all people within Quebec, to replace the old, territorially dispersed French-Canadian identity that spanned almost the entire breadth of the country from the Atlantic provinces to Alberta. This identity would have to be one that all of Quebec inhabitants could adhere to, regardless of religion.

Language was well suited to replace Catholicism as a pillar of a new, territory-based Quebec identity. It unites a vast proportion of the society's inhabitants, regardless of religion or ethnic background. Further, it can more easily be used by the Quebec state as the focus for nation-building than religion ever could be. Indeed, a liberal democracy such as Quebec can insist on its citizens acquiring some competency in the French language without damaging its liberal–democratic status as a society that respects, protects, and promotes its citizens' individual civil and political rights. "Thicker" aspects of identity, such as religion, are in this regard far more problematic. Today, and indeed since the 1960s, the survival of Quebec increasingly hangs upon the ability of its society and institutions to integrate immigrants, and it is much easier to have them share a linguistic identity than a religious one.

The growing centrality of language to Quebec identity explains the intensity of feeling that has surrounded rights-based challenges to the language law. "*Ne touchez pas à la loi 101*" has become a potent political rallying cry in Quebec, pointing to the fact that the legal tools that have been enacted to protect the French language, in addition to the language itself, have themselves become central to the way in which Quebecers have come to identify themselves.

BIOGRAPHY

Children of Bill 101 (Les Enfants de la Loi 101)

Children of Bill 101 (*Les enfants de la loi 101*) refers to the children who began their education under the language regime instituted by the Parti Québécois government in 1977. Bill 101 required that all Quebecers, except those whose parents were educated in English in Quebec, be schooled in French. The first children who entered the Quebec school system under this law are in their late 30s today. They serve as an important barometer of the success of Quebec's language policies. Like many modern societies, Quebec depends significantly on immigration (Quebec takes in roughly 45,000 immigrants every year[3]). The degree to which the education provisions of Bill 101 succeed in protecting the existence of a French-speaking society in Quebec therefore depends in great measure on the Children of Bill 101.

It is therefore not surprising that they have been intensely studied by researchers attempting to chart the course of the future of Quebec society. The evidence so far provides cause both for optimism and for concern among those who seek to protect and promote French in Quebec.

On the one hand, it is quite clear that the vast majority of the Children of Bill 101 exit the Quebec school system fluent in French, and are thus capable of functioning with ease in a French-speaking public environment. The sights and sounds of young Quebecers of various ethnic backgrounds speaking in perfect French in school grounds and parks, comfortable with the idiomatic particularities of Quebec French, are everywhere in areas where many immigrants live, especially in the Greater Montreal area. There is thus reason for optimism that the language law is succeeding in creating French speakers out of children of very different linguistic backgrounds.

On the other hand, the attitude of new Quebecers schooled under Bill 101 is quite different from that of "old stock" French-speaking Quebecers. Studies show that while the latter identify with the French language, in the sense that they view it as a non-negotiable part of their identities, newer Quebecers have a more instrumental attitude not just toward French but toward language in general. They often speak three (or more) languages: their heritage language, that of their parents; French, which they acquire in school; and English, which they pick up from the pervasive North American culture (evidence shows they do this more readily than their francophone Quebecer counterparts). Given the range of languages in their repertoire, it is thus not surprising that they identify less with any one language. It is also not surprising that the linguistic choices that they make outside the public sphere vary. For example, they may choose to speak their mother tongues in private, domestic contexts but choose English when the time comes to select colleges and universities.

Thus, the Children of Bill 101 speak French fluently, but they have less of an identity stake in its survival than do the French speakers who trace their origins in Quebec back through the centuries.

For some, this is not a cause for concern. The goal of language policy is, in their view, to make French the language of the *public* sphere. And to the degree that the Children of Bill 101 can function comfortably in French in public and commercial contexts, they view this goal as being amply achieved by the language law.

Others are less sanguine. They point out that if the proportion of Quebecers who have a more instrumental attitude toward French increases, especially in and around Montreal, a tipping point may be reached where they will decide on instrumental grounds to use English more in

continued

public. They therefore find the present language laws insufficiently robust. Some believe that the education laws should apply not only to primary and secondary schools, but to Quebec's CEGEPs as well (CEGEPs are Quebec's equivalent of American junior colleges). Others think that preference should be given to immigrants to Quebec whose first language is French, or who speak a language that is sufficiently close to French to make it more likely that they will identify with the French language.

Does the linguistic and sociological study of the Children of Bill 101 foster optimism or pessimism about the success of Quebec's language laws? It all depends on what the ultimate goal of these laws is taken to be. There can be no doubt that the requirement that immigrants and francophones educate their children only in French within the public school system increases the likelihood that French will continue to thrive in the province. Some proponents of the language laws think that this is all that can reasonably be achieved. Others aspire to firmer guarantees and hope to strengthen the language laws to come as close as possible to securing the future of the French language against all possible cultural and linguistic threats.

Which of these two views will prevail among the intellectual and political elites of Quebec? It is impossible to answer this question with any degree of certainty. What is certain is that the emergence of the Children of Bill 101 will not mark the final episode in Quebec's ongoing language saga.

Language and Justice

Some evidence suggests that most French-speaking Quebecers think that language debates are an important stake in identity. English-speaking Quebecers and immigrants, as well as many outside observers, tend to view the language debates in Quebec from the point of view of *liberal justice*. They ask themselves how a liberal democracy committed to the protection of individual and minority rights should view the central issues in the formation of language policy. They have often been harsher in their judgment of Quebec's language laws than French-speaking Quebecers have been, because of the apparent conflict between measures intended to protect the French language and individual liberty.

The questions that the lens of liberal justice forces us to address concern the degree to which the state can use both incentives and coercion to alter the linguistic choices that citizens make for themselves and for their children. To what degree can a just society limit individual rights to achieve a collective end such as language protection? This question is at the heart of the debate about Quebec's language laws, which has been couched in terms of liberal justice.

Liberalism is perhaps above all else a theory of limited government. Liberals believe that the state should not interfere with the choices made by individuals unless there are weighty reasons to do so. There are debates among liberals about what those reasons might be. Some argue that the role of the state should be limited to securing physical safety and property rights. Others argue for a more expansive role for the state, because individuals interacting freely in their own self-interest cannot be relied upon to generate certain goods such as clean air and water, health-care institutions, and the like. These are known as **public goods**, that is, goods that everyone wants but that people tend not to be sufficiently motivated to create on their own.

The default liberal view would therefore be that language choice should be left to individuals. Parents should be able to school their children in the language of their choice, and all should be able to do business in whatever language they see fit. The very notion of a state having an "official language" seems suspect, on a par with its having an established religion. The only acceptable posture for the state to adopt with respect to language would be **benign neglect**.

Is anything wrong with this view? A complicating factor is that whereas the state does not have to privilege any one religion, it cannot avoid taking sides when it comes to language: It uses language to frame legislation, courts and public schools must operate in a common language, and so on. It cannot hope to treat all the languages spoken in its territory equally. It must pick some subset of the languages that are spoken and communicate with all its citizenry in those languages.

Many things follow from this. If the state chooses to communicate with its citizens in the language of the majority, fairness dictates that it provide members of linguistic minorities and immigrants with the means to achieve competency in that language; linguistic ghettos make it difficult to achieve a shared linguistic identity across the state's territory. But they are also bad for those stuck within them, who are prevented from achieving the political and economic opportunities that competency in the dominant language affords.

So the state must make language training in the dominant language available and accessible. But must it make it mandatory? After all, if minority-language speakers are provided with the opportunity to learn the dominant language, and are made aware of the disadvantages of not doing so, should they not be free to bear those disadvantages if they so choose?

Reflecting on the case of Quebec shows that we cannot answer this question in the abstract. As we have seen, Quebec is a province within Canada. Canada is a bilingual country within which French speakers are outnumbered in a ratio of approximately three to one. Quebec's French speakers represent a tiny fraction within largely English-speaking North America. What's more, though French is a "global" language, in the sense that it is spoken throughout the current and former colonies of France, it is not, as English is, a "language of **globalization**."

The speakers of a majority language in other parts of the world can make their language dominant without making it mandatory since they are confident that minority-language speakers and immigrants will see it as being in their interest to acquire proficiency in the dominant language. Their language does not have to compete with any other language for pre-eminent status within the same territory, nor does it have to withstand the pressure of a continent massively dominated by another language. True, no language in the world is completely immune from the prominence of English as the language of global commerce and science. But most often English becomes the *de rigueur* second language rather than replacing the other language.

French speakers in Quebec can have no such confidence. Choosing English rather than French, for example as the language of instruction for their children, does not consign immigrants or minority-language speakers to a linguistic ghetto from which it would be rational for them to want to escape. Rather, it locates them within the national and continental majority. Even if the Quebec state were to generously provide immigrants with the means to learn French, it might be more rational for them to integrate into the English-speaking community.

Given the context of French in Canada and North America, it is thus easy to see why French-speaking Quebecers intent upon making French a chief pillar of a shared post-religious, territory-based identity would *want* to make French mandatory by enshrining it in an official language law such as Bill 101. But is it *just* for them to do so? After all, the linguistic map of the world is changing all the time as people respond to different incentives. Though the disappearance of a language may cause regret, it does not always call for state action. The disappearance of a language does not always constitute an *injustice*.

According to the renowned Canadian philosopher Charles Taylor, the decision by the Quebec state to make French mandatory as the language of education, public communication, and business does not represent the kind of major departure from the standards of liberal democracy that would require special justification. As long as it protects its citizens' fundamental civil and political rights and freedoms—the right to bodily integrity, the freedoms of religion and of conscience, the right to equal participation in the institutions of democratic self-government—Quebec, in Taylor's view, acts within an appropriate discretionary range by limiting its citizens' language rights.[4]

According to Will Kymlicka, whose theories of minority rights have attained global prominence, the value that liberal justice ascribes to individual choice makes sense only if value is also ascribed to the "contexts of choice" that individuals require to exercise their capacity for choice. It is because they are members of "societal cultures," that is, of societies affording them a full range of choices across the full range of fields of human endeavour, that individuals are capable of choosing one thing over another. Members of minority societal cultures need to be able to protect themselves against external pressures that would push them toward assimilation. For Quebecers, this means protecting themselves against the assimilative pressure of English by enacting legislation that makes linguistic integration mandatory.[5]

A third approach would view language as a kind of public good. In this view, French-speaking Quebecers have a problem of collective action with respect to their language. Each francophone would rather have business transactions and official state communications conducted in French. But this preference is not unconditional. People will act on this preference on condition that enough of their fellow citizens do so as well. If this condition is not significantly fulfilled, too few speakers of the language will remain to keep it viable. In the absence of their fellow citizens' assurance that they too will choose French, it will be rational for each French speaker to "defect" to English, with all of the advantages of that choice in Canada and North America.

By backing the use of French with the force of law, the state in effect provides the required assurance. In so doing, it provides a public good that is structurally analogous to clean air. Someone who owns a factory that emits toxic gases might choose to pay the costs of limiting the emissions only if assured that other factory owners were doing the same; otherwise he or she would incur an economic disadvantage relative to them. Most people would say it is the state's responsibility to ensure collective action among factory owners to limit emissions. Similarly, the state can also be seen as responsible to ensure a public good such as language.

So far we have seen that the default presumption of a liberal theory of justice on language—benign neglect—is not so simple for a language that, like French in Quebec, is subject to assimilative pressures. First, the Quebec state can't simply assume that its minority-language population and immigrants will acquire French on their own; it must take steps to make language training available and accessible. Second, there are several arguments to the effect that justice permits making French mandatory.

But making French mandatory does not necessarily mean making it *exclusive*. The status of French as the official language in Quebec does, however, make it exclusive in several domains. For example, schooling is unilingual for French-speaking Quebecers and for immigrants, and many state institutions function in French only. But are there any reasons to prohibit institutional bilingualism? At first glance, the requirement that children receive their instruction in French and that French be used on all commercial signs and in all government communication is not incompatible with bilingualism. Children could, after all, be educated in bilingual schools, and signage and official communication could be in both English and French.

According to many sociologists, economists, and linguists, like Jean Laponce, the ensuing asymmetrical bilingualism would mean the disappearance of French over time. Bilingualism in Quebec would inevitably be asymmetrical by virtue of the dominance of English in Canada, and more largely in North America. Given this asymmetry, there would always be more reason for francophones to use English than for anglophones to use French. The natural tendency would therefore be for communication between anglophones and francophones to occur in English. Over time, this would lead to English dominance in all public interactions. French would become "folklorized," that is, relegated to the private and cultural spheres. The lowly status to which French has fallen in places like Louisiana and the struggle it faces merely to maintain viability in other parts of Canada suggest that this understanding of asymmetrical bilingualism might very well be borne out by the facts.

In general, then, many researchers in the area of language believe that it is difficult for languages to coexist peacefully in the same territory. In situations of asymmetrical bilingualism, the dominance of the "weaker" language can be assured only by being engineered through state action. In the absence of state action, the "stronger" language will naturally achieve the dominant position. The intermediate position—institutional bilingualism—is in their view inherently unstable and will in time enshrine the dominance of the stronger of the two languages.

All of the arguments that have been canvassed above have been subjected to vigorous scrutiny and debate. Clearly, however, their cumulative effect is to suggest that achieving justice in language policy is a more complicated matter than simply allowing people to make unconstrained linguistic choices for themselves and for their children.

Who Is a Quebecer?

In retrospect, many of the conflicts that arose in the years following the adoption of Bill 101 can be seen as pitting against each other the two perspectives developed above. French-speaking Quebecers tend to view the protection of the French language as a necessary condition for the survival of Quebec as a distinct society. Many anglophones and immigrants tend to view the laws enacted to achieve that protection as antithetical to liberal rights and freedoms.

Over time, the conflict has significantly abated. Successive legal challenges have somewhat softened the law. For example, whereas the law originally banished English entirely from commercial signs, in its present form it merely requires that French be clearly dominant.

But the "linguistic peace" that has characterized Quebec since about 1995 may also be due to the fact that the opponents of Bill 101 and its effects have come to realize that they actually stand to significantly benefit from them. Through being required to attend French schools, immigrant children emerge from school fluently bilingual, as do the children of anglophone Quebecers who, though they are entitled to attend English schools, are increasingly being sent to French schools by their parents.

Paradoxically, francophone children arguably do less well than their anglophone and immigrant counterparts. They are required to attend French schools exclusively. But whereas the other children attending French schools acquire proficiency in at least one other language at home, French-speaking children have little access to languages other than French. The cost of protecting the French language in North America may ultimately be the limitation of the linguistic horizons of francophone children.

Challenges to the language law in years to come are therefore likely to emanate from within the francophone community, torn between its desire to protect the French language and the inevitable desire to prevent their children from being at a competitive disadvantage in a globalized economy compared to their English and immigrant counterparts.

Some francophone commentators have sounded an alarm, claiming that the language law is not having its desired effect and that the dominance of French is still fragile, especially on the Island of Montreal. They have noted that though immigrants and anglophones acquire competency in French through the school system, this competency does not translate into a choice to use French outside of contexts in which it is required by law. Their fears echo the predictions of sociolinguists that have just been mentioned, according to which asymmetrical bilingualism may not be stable. Thus, in its short-lived stint in government from 2012 to 2014, some members of the Parti Québécois proposed that the ban on access to public anglophone educational institutions for francophones and immigrants be extended to **CEGEPs** (CEGEPs are Quebec's equivalent of American junior colleges). It is important to note that the purpose of the proposed extension of the language provisions of Quebec's language laws was not to increase linguistic competence, but to foster greater socialization on the part of immigrants into francophone society.

Primary Source

Mandatory Francophone CEGEPs: For an Enlightened Debate

Conrad Ouellon, president of the Conseil supérieur de la langue française:

> The question of whether the requirement to attend francophone educational institutions should be extended to CEGEPs has been at the heart of certain political debates. On this topic, a number of arguments concerning allophones that are put forward in media seem incorrect. The first holds that young immigrants who attend anglophone CEGEPs are more likely to undergo linguistic transfer toward English. That is, they are according to this argument more likely to adopt English as a new language in the home. The second argument claims that attendance in an anglophone CEGEP promotes the integration of immigrants into anglophone spheres of work and public life.
>
> Though they are based on data collected by Statistics Canada in recent censuses, these arguments do not paint an accurate picture of the situation. Certain variables ought to have been considered in the interpretation of these data. We could mention the origin of immigrants. If instead of comparing the linguistic transfers toward English of all students having attended CEGEP, with no distinctions between countries of origin, we group them according to different categories of such countries, for example anglotrope (allophones with a non-Latin mother tongue or who do not come from countries of the international *Francophonie*) and francotrope (allophones with a Latin mother tongue or arriving from countries of the international *Francophonie*), [then the] results are quite different. Indeed, we discover that CEGEP attendance has almost no effect on linguistic transfer. Even though the raw data from Statistics Canada show that allophones who have attended CEGEP are most likely to undergo linguistic transfer, this phenomenon is due not to attendance in an anglophone CEGEP, but to their country of origin. It is this factor that, from the outset, determines whether they will be more likely to attend an anglophone CEGEP. This same logic applies to the second argument, which has to do with workplace language. We note that CEGEP attendance has little effect on the use by immigrants of French or of English at work. In this case as well, it is country of origin that matters most.
>
> Now that we have evaluated both arguments, the question that we must ask ourselves is the following: how to convince these anglotrope immigrants, who have a tendency to integrate into anglophone educational and professional milieu, to learn and to use French in the common public life of Quebec? That is the real debate. But one thing is certain: it is imperative that immigrants integrate into life in French in order to ensure better social cohesion in Quebec.

Source: Conrad Ouellon, "L'obligation du cégep de langue française : pour une argumentation éclairée," www.cslf.gouv.qc.ca/publications/pubf305/f305.pdf.

These challenges raise important questions. What indicators should be used to determine whether the language law has been effective? Is acceptable linguistic integration marked by an individual being proficient enough in French to use it in public? Or does it also require that he or she use French in private life? Has integration failed if English (or some other language) is spoken at home? Does successful integration require that first-generation immigrants achieve fluency in French, or does it suffice that children of the second generation do so?

Different answers to these questions yield dramatically different pictures of the linguistic situation of the province. Focusing on the private linguistic choices of recent arrivals, for example, produces a picture quite different from that which emerges from looking at how well they can function in French in public settings such as workplaces, courts, legislatures, and schools. Choices of indicators are moreover likely to be highly ideologically motivated.

How will Quebec's language laws evolve over the years to come? The focus of legislation will undoubtedly vary, depending on which picture of the linguistic situation holds sway among decision makers. But as long as French remains as central a pillar of the Québécois identity as it presently is, there will always be policies designed to protect the language against the enormous pressures that it must withstand in North America and on the global stage.

CASE STUDY

Important Legal Challenges to the Charter of the French Language

The Charter of the French Language, Bill 101, was adopted by the National Assembly of Quebec in 1977. It very quickly became the object of legal challenges, and the Supreme Court of Canada had to render decisions on numerous occasions on the constitutionality of its various provisions. These legal challenges were and continue to be fraught with political tensions.

Before the adoption of the Charter of Rights and Freedoms in 1982, the British North America Act provided only a fairly narrow basis on which to challenge Bill 101. The BNA Act requires that all legislation enacted in Quebec be published in both English and French. Accordingly, the first legal challenge to Bill 101 produced the Supreme Court of Canada's decision that the provision that all Quebec legislation be published only in French was unconstitutional.

The 1982 Charter, and in particular section 23 of the Charter, provided opponents of the language law with a broader basis upon which to challenge Bill 101. Section 23 ensures the education rights of francophone minorities in English Canada and of anglophone minorities in Quebec. The educational provisions of Bill 101 restricted access to English schools to children of parents who had themselves been educated in English in Quebec. On the basis of section 23, the Supreme Court decision in the case of *Attorney General of Quebec v. Quebec Protestant School Boards* extended access to English schools to all children of parents educated in English anywhere in Canada.

In 1988, the Supreme Court issued a decision that Bill 101's requirement that outdoor commercial signs be exclusively in French was unconstitutional. It argued that a less stringent requirement, that French clearly predominate on commercial signs, would be acceptable. The Liberal provincial government of the time, headed by Robert Bourassa, invoked the "notwithstanding clause" of the Canadian Constitution in order to keep the law unchanged. The notwithstanding clause allows legislatures to override Charter provisions for five years. The use of this clause of the Constitution sent shockwaves through the rest of Canada. It is widely credited with having caused the failure of the Meech Lake Accord, a set of constitutional amendments designed to secure Quebec's acceptance of the 1982 Constitution. (The Constitution had been adopted in 1982 without Quebec's consent.) The use of the notwithstanding clause to uphold the linguistic privileges of the majority,

continued

contrary to Charter rights, was seen by many in the rest of Canada as unreasonable and dampened the enthusiasm for constitutional reconciliation with Quebec.

An era of relative linguistic peace in Quebec followed the rendering of these decisions on commercial signage and on the language of instruction. Many parents, both immigrant and anglophone, began to see the benefits of their children being educated in French.

A spate of recent cases, however, may reignite political unrest around the language law. In *Solski (Tutor of) v. Quebec (Attorney General)*, decided in 2005, the Supreme Court ruled that the provision of Quebec's language law that grants eligibility to attend English schools to children whose parents had received the "major part" of their education in English in Canada should not be read in a strict quantitative manner. According to the judgment, it might suffice to qualify a child for English instruction that a "significant" part of the parents' education had been in English. They would thus signal their commitment to minority-language instruction and be eligible for such instruction under section 23 of the Charter.

In 2002, Quebec introduced legislation designed to close loopholes in the language law on access to English schools. That loophole allowed children to become eligible for English education by spending at least a year in an unsubsidized (private) English school. (Schools receiving no subsidies are not subject to the language law.) Bill 104 sought to close that loophole. The Quebec Court of Appeal struck the bill down as unconstitutional, and the case of *Nguyen v. Quebec (Education, Recreation and Sports)* was heard by the Supreme Court in 2008. The decision in 2009 decreed that the time that a child spent in a private English school should be taken into account in assessing his or her eligibility for admittance into a public English school.

Taken together, these two decisions broaden the category of children admissible for English instruction. However, the Supreme Court has rejected other appeals aimed at loosening the strictures on the language of instruction. In *Gosselin (Tutor of) v. Quebec (Attorney General)*, the Supreme Court rejected the claim made by a group of francophone parents that under the Charter equality rights they should be able to choose to send their children to English schools. The Supreme Court's decision rested on interpreting the language law as not excluding categories of children from English instruction, but rather protecting the rights of the anglophone community.

Given the growing awareness among francophone parents of the competitive disadvantage that their children's education gives them in a globalized economy that functions largely in English, this challenge is unlikely to be the last one to come from the francophone community. It may be that the 20 years or so of linguistic peace in Quebec is more fragile than previously thought.

Questions for Critical Thinking

1. How much do you identify with your mother tongue? How much does it matter to you that your children and grandchildren speak it fluently?
2. Do you think it is fair for the government of Quebec to require its immigrants to send their children to French schools when English schools are available?
3. Do you think that the French language would survive in North America in the absence of legislation such as Bill 101?

Notes

1. Francophones represent around 2 per cent of the total population of the Americas. See C. Frechette, *Les enjeux et défis linguistiques de l'intégration des Amériques* (Québec: Conseil de la Langue française, 2001), 8.
2. See Chapters 10 and 11 for the history of the language debates.
3. See the Quebec government website for recent numbers: www.micc.gouv.qc.ca/fr/recherches-statistiques/stats-immigration-recente.html.
4. Charles Taylor, *Reconciling the Solitudes: Essays on Canadian Federalism and Nationalism* (Montreal and Kingston: McGill-Queen's University Press, 1993).
5. Will Kymlicka, *Finding Our Way: Rethinking Ethnocultural Relations in Canada* (Toronto: Oxford University Press, 1998).

Select Bibliography

Bouchard, Chantal. *Obsessed with Language: A Sociolinguistic History of Quebec*. Montreal: Guernica, 2008.

Carens, Joseph H. ed. *Is Quebec Nationalism Just? Perspectives from English Canada*. Montreal and Kingston: McGill-Queen's University Press, 1995.

Commission des États Généraux sur la situation et l'avenir de la langue française au Québec. *Le français, une langue pour tout le monde*. Quebec: Gouvernement du Québec, 2001.

Conseil supérieur de la langue française. *Le français et les jeunes*. Quebec: Gouvernement du Québec, 2008.

Fraser, Graham. *Sorry, I Don't Speak French: Confronting the Canadian Crisis that Won't Go Away*. Toronto: McClelland & Stewart, 2006.

Georgeault, Pierre, and Michel Pagé, eds. *Le français, langue de la diversité québécoise*. Montreal: Québec Amérique, 2006.

Handler, Richard. *Nationalism and the Politics of Culture in Quebec*. Madison: University of Wisconsin Press, 1988.

Kymlicka, Will. *Finding Our Way: Rethinking Ethnocultural Relations in Canada*. Oxford: Oxford University Press, 1998.

———, and Alan Patten, eds. *Language and Political Theory*. Oxford: Oxford University Press, 2003.

Laponce, Jean. *Loi de Babel et autres régularités des rapports entre langue et politique*. Sainte-Foy: Presses de l'Université Laval, 2006.

Levine, Marc V. *The Reconquest of Montreal: Language Policy and Social Change in a Bilingual City*. Philadelphia: Temple University Press, 1991.

Maclure, Jocelyn, and Alain G. Gagnon, eds. *Repères en mutation : identité et citoyenneté dans le Québec contemporain*. Montreal: Québec Amérique, 2001.

Taylor, Charles. *Reconciling the Solitudes: Essays on Canadian Federalism and Nationalism*. Montreal and Kingston: McGill-Queen's University Press, 1993.

13 Popular Music in Quebec

Christopher Jones, Carnegie Mellon University

Timeline

1920s–1930s Mary Travers ("La Bolduc") pens many songs, often topical, humorous, and using informal language.

1940 Roland "Soldat" Lebrun evokes sacrifices of war.

1945 Country stars Willie Lamothe, Paul Brunelle, and Marcel Martel begin their careers.

Late 1940s Opening of clubs Au Faisan Doré in Montreal and Chez Gérard in Quebec City, showcasing French *chansonniers.*

1950 Félix Leclerc invited to Paris by Jacques Canetti.

1956 Concours de la Chanson Canadienne ("Canadian Song Contest") showcases many new (French) Canadian songwriters.

1958 Cabaret Chez Bozo groups Jean-Pierre Ferland, Claude Léveillée, Clémence Desrocher, and Raymond Lévesque, all of whom would have sustained careers.

1962 *Yé-yé* magazine and *Jeunesse d'aujourd'hui* (*Youth Today*) TV show address new teen pop market.

1970s Folk movement strengthens; blues/rock of Offenbach and Michel Pagliaro.

1972 Beau Dommage, Les Séguin, Harmonium, and Octobre shift from folk and country to progressive rock.

1974 At Superfrancofête, 100,000 hear Félix Leclerc, Gilles Vigneault, and Robert Charlebois.

1976 At Saint-Jean-Baptiste concerts, 400,000 hear *chansonniers* and bands on Mont-Royal.

1978 Luc Plamondon's rock opera *Starmania is* a hit in France and Quebec.

1980s Punk, disco, and *retrenchement* during economic and spiritual crisis.

1988 First *FrancoFolies de Montréal,* a francophone song festival.

1993 Les Colocs' first album exemplifies a certain Montreal Plateau existence.

1999 The hip-hop of Dubmatique makes the radio (briefly).

1990s Western-themed festivals expand.

2001 *Spin* magazine tags Montreal as "the next big scene" for international anglophone rock.

2003 First *Star Académie* TV talent competition is held.

2002 Pierre Lapointe and Arianne Moffat are new genre-bending stars.

2004 Loco Locass *Amour oral* album is released, their second major rap success.

2007 Arcade Fire and Simple Plan bring international success for Anglo bands.

Introduction

The production and consumption of popular music in Quebec expanded enormously during the second half of the twentieth century. This echoed a trend found elsewhere in the Western world where—along with television—song came to prominence as a mass cultural phenomenon. Aspects of this development in Quebec were nevertheless unique, as the musical explosion paralleled closely the social, economic, and political transformations discussed elsewhere in this volume. In the process, the production of French-language popular music came increasingly under local control; also, many artists abandoned Parisian and American conventions in favour of language inflection and imagery of clearly local origin. A significant number of artists also identified closely with the movement through the Quiet Revolution toward sovereignty, up to the failed referendum of 1980.[1] The subsequent maturing of the Quebec music industry involved a conscious adoption of American production standards for mainstream pop, the refinement of pop and rock sensibilities and musical skills, and a diversification of marginal genres (punk, metal, hip-hop). Influences also expanded to include other francophone music and those emanating from immigrant communities in a burgeoning multicultural society and from world youth cultures increasingly available via electronic means.

This chapter is a brief history of the periods, genres, and major figures of popular music in Quebec since World War II, as well as of the development of the music industry and the organs, history, and importance of public policy. We address, among others, the following questions: What is unique about popular music in Quebec in the North American context? What are the major influences on the development of this music? What special challenges do musicians in Quebec face? How does popular music shape the way Quebecers think about themselves?

1945–1958: Quebec Song Emerging

Quebec in 1945, despite its growing industrialization and urbanization, remained under the moral authority of the Catholic Church and the economic control of a primarily English-speaking upper class, with a francophone political class unable or unwilling to effectively change the status quo. Culturally, the Catholic influence could be extremely constraining; Simone de Beauvoir's 1959 interview for Radio-Canada, for example, was pulled from the air under pressure from the archbishop of Montreal, no doubt for its frank discussion of atheism and feminism. Intellectuals in Quebec were well aware that they were at a disadvantage in the repressively conservative environment of the Duplessis years, known as *la grande noirceur* ("the Great Darkness") in history books, with Paul-Émile Borduas's *Refus global* (*Total Rejection*) manifesto of 1948 being a memorable indicator of the level of discontent with the status quo among artists and intellectuals.

The music industry had relatively little local autonomy. Local affiliates of large American companies commissioned and promoted French versions of American hits, often in mainstream crooner or country styles. The market for songs authored in French by Canadians was almost nonexistent, as the songwriter Fernand Robidoux emphasized: "R.C.A. Victor . . . obstinately refused the songs from Quebec that I suggested. Anything that came from us, by us, for us, had no importance whatsoever."[2] Change was on the way, however.

Country music was emerging as a viable genre with the original recordings of Willie Lamothe, Marcel Martel, and Paul Brunelle building on the popular though rather musically limited wartime recordings of Roland "Soldat" Lebrun, like "L'Adieu du soldat" ("The Soldier's Goodbye") or "Courageux canadiens" ("Courageous Canadians"): "Dear Canadians keep your courage / If one day you are called / Come combat those savages / To keep our liberty."[3] If Martel was a rather plain songwriter and singer, inspired more by the Appalachian tradition, he as well as Lamothe and Brunelle saw themselves as Western (country) entertainers and built careers based on quality recordings and live performances. Their writing had both humour and variety, and they made recordings using the latest techniques.[4] Lamothe's "Je chante à cheval" ("I Sing on Horseback") became the title of a documentary on his life and presaged the continuing fascination in Quebec with the myth of the West and its culture.

Folk music, descended from its Celtic origins in the west of France and from the British Isles, had many active practitioners, especially in the Gaspé and

BIOGRAPHY

Félix Leclerc

Félix Leclerc (1914–1988) was a poet, novelist, playwright, actor, and singer-songwriter. He began work in radio and theatre as early as 1934 and wrote his first song that year.[7] His fame as a songwriter, however, came first during his sojourn in Paris beginning in 1950, where he had been invited to record and perform by the French impresario Jacques Canetti based on a homemade demo of Leclerc's "Le train du nord" ("The Northern Train"), a song about a conductor bored with his existence: "On the train to Saint-Adèle / Was a man who wanted to get off / But try getting off / When the train's going fifty miles an hour / and what's more you're the conductor."[8]

Félix Leclerc.

National Film Board of Canada. Phototheque/ Library and Archives Canada/ PA-107872.

These narrative songs with rural settings found few fans among Quebec city-dwellers. In Paris, however, he was billed as "The Canadian," and his roughhewn persona and poetic songs were attractive both for their exoticism and their quality. That Canetti subsequently discovered Jacques Brel and nurtured Georges Brassens furnishes two points of comparison for the songs of Leclerc. In North America of 1950 the comparisons are fewer; some of Woody Guthrie's work is possibly relevant—or, a decade later, Bob Dylan, Phil Ochs, and other singer-songwriters of the 1960s folk revival.

The notion that life in Quebec could be the stuff of popular song was a key realization for Leclerc. He was not the only songwriter in Quebec creating in this way (Oscar Thiffault and Willie Lamothe, for example, were also fruitful in folk and country at this time), but Leclerc was the only one touring Europe and recording in France.

Acadian peninsulas to the east. Oscar Thiffault was a prolific writer in the folk tradition, primarily by writing new words for traditional melodies. Several of his songs entered into cultural history, like "Le rapide blanc" ("The White Express"), which tells an amusingly risqué story of a train-man's wife receiving a visitor while the train-man is at work. The *violoneux* ("fiddler") had long been a part of the folk tradition, and Jean Carignan's exceptional career was getting underway during this period.

Roger Chamberland dates the beginnings of Quebec *chanson*[5] to the extensive creations and popular success of Mary Travers, known as "La Bolduc," in the 1920s and 1930s.[6] It was in postwar Quebec that *chanson* saw its first full flowering, though two of its important practitioners took a detour through Paris. Both Félix Leclerc (see the Biography box) and Raymond Lévesque spent the early 1950s in France, returning to Quebec only after attaining success on the other side of the Atlantic. In Montreal, the cabarets Le Faisan doré and Le Saint-Germain-des-Prés, after having welcomed Parisian ***chansonniers*** (singer–songwriters) like Charles Aznavour and Marcel Mouloudji, began to feature homegrown talent. The appearance of television and radio shows dedicated to Quebec song showcased the variety of songwriting and performing talent and encouraged others to begin a musical career. Perhaps of most importance for the latter was the Concours de la chanson canadienne ("Canadian Song Contest") on Radio-Canada in 1956. The culmination of this period occurred (or the next one began) when Clémence Desrochers, Jean-Pierre Ferland, and Claude Léveillée, among others, gathered around the club Chez Bozo in central Montreal in 1959, performing songs that

By 1953 his success began to grow in Quebec and he began performing there regularly. He continued to write for the theatre and for television and turned down offers (like the *Ed Sullivan Show* and Las Vegas) that could have made him more money, but these styles of show business were at odds with his personality and values. He naturally gravitated toward the *chansonnier* ("songwriter") group beginning to emerge in the late 1950s and 1960s, having little in common with the American teen pop-inspired *yé-yé* groups of that period. The *chansonniers* saw him as the godfather of Quebec song, as he is still considered today.

In 1970, after a period in Switzerland, he installed himself in Quebec again, building a house with his own hands on Île d'Orléans along the St Lawrence River near Quebec City, and began to participate in the movement toward independence that was then gathering momentum. Songs like "L'alouette en colère" ("The Angry Lark") were poetic expressions that resonated with many Quebecers: "I have a son stripped of everything / Like his father before him / Watercarrier, wood-cutter / Renter and unemployed / In his own country / He has nothing left / but the pretty view of the river / and his native language / which is not recognized." In 1974 Leclerc appeared on stage with Gilles Vigneault and Robert Charlebois at the Superfrancofête before 100,000 people. This performance—and especially the rendering of Raymond Lévesque's "Quand les hommes vivront d'amour" ("When Mankind Will Live on Love")—represented a meeting of both minds and generations and a cathartic moment in the nationalist movement, a movement that appeared to be inexorable until its first defeat in the referendum of 1980. During the 1970s Leclerc found himself in an almost continuous round of creation, recording, touring, collaborations, and official honours. After 1980, he worked primarily on writing projects in his Île d'Orléans home until his death in 1988.

Leclerc is remembered in both France and Quebec in many ways, not least in the annual music awards given out at the ADISQ gala (the Quebec equivalent of the American Grammy Awards) named after him in 1979. There is no higher honour in Quebec popular music than receiving a "Félix".

combined a cabaret-derived French musical foundation with Quebec themes and images.

Richard Baillargeon sees the 1950s as the last period in which pop music (primarily crooners and early rock 'n' roll) was on an equal footing with folk, country, and the early cabaret-style *chanson*. In the 1960s, with its increasing openness to Anglo-Saxon–dominated pop and rock influences, folk and country—perceived as premodern in a rapidly modernizing Quebec—would be pushed to the margins.[9]

1959–1968: *Chanson* and *yé-yé*

Maurice Duplessis died in 1959. In the 1960s, Liberal Jean Lesage is credited with initiating many of the reforms that characterized the Quiet Revolution. Other chapters in this volume deal with aspects of this period in depth, but it is worth recalling the breadth and rapidity of the change. In 10 years, 49 new governmental institutions were created, nearly equalling the number in the previous century.[10] Virtually overnight the Catholic Church lost its hold on health, education, and local government. The drop in both the birth and marriage rates, and the rise in the divorce and abortion rates, foreshadowed profound demographic changes. The residents of Quebec ceased to consider themselves *Canadiens* ([French] Canadians) and adopted the term *Québécois* to name themselves and to describe everything emanating from their territory, including songs.[11]

It was the continuation of the *chanson* tradition that was most closely associated with the Quiet Revolution, by both explicit reference to it and by association through participation in mass gatherings with national implications. Its primary institution was the *boîte à chanson* (song club), the successor to the 1950s Montreal and Quebec City cabarets like Chez Bozo, where Jean-Pierre Ferland got his start. The *boîte à chanson* developed a countercultural mystique with improvised decors where song lyrics were sung over simple musical settings, usually on guitar or piano, for audiences of college students. The songs' imagery often drew on a real or imagined rusticity associated with *québécitude* ("Quebecness," the nature of being of Quebec). These associations carried within them the seeds of their own destruction, if we consider the modernizing drive of the Quiet Revolution, but had parallels elsewhere in North America, notably in the hippie and back-to-the-land movements in the American 1960s, which occurred simultaneously with the folk revival.

A generation of remarkable artists emerged during this period, notably Gilles Vigneault, Robert Charlebois, and Louise Forestier, while others, like Félix Leclerc and Jean-Pierre Ferland, continued to work and, especially in Ferland's case, evolve. Vigneault, close to the Jacques Brel–Léo Ferré model of creation and performance, nevertheless wrote a number of songs anchored in Quebec life that touched Quebecers deeply. The godfather of the winter leitmotif songs, his "Mon pays" ("My Country") poetically mixed the imagery of the white north (including the immortal line "My country isn't a country, it's winter") with a subtle evocation of the emerging solidarity and identity among the Quebecers involved in the nationalist thrust. For an in-depth analysis of the song's lyrics and its metaphoric character, visit the *Encyclopedia of Music in Canada*.[12]

The *chanson* evolution did not define popular music in Quebec during this period, however; simultaneously a pure pop movement known as *yé-yé* echoed the French equivalent and its imitations of the fluffier side of American and British hit parades. It was quite probably *yé-yé* that offered the richer training ground for all aspects of the music business, from promotion to electric guitar and drumming techniques.[13] In *yé-yé* many bands sang in English and covered American hits. In important cases—the band Les Gants Blancs becoming the blues/rock powerhouse Offenbach, for example—the *yé-yé* apprenticeship led to extended careers, with bilingual or exclusively French song creation and an attention to *québécitude* at the later stages. Although the nationalist movement was important to some, the children of the 1950s working class were not nostalgic about Quebec, which for them connoted hunger and misery in a not-so-distant past.[14] Their modernizing heroes were Elvis Presley, James Dean, and perhaps the French rocker Johnny Hallyday; such glamour and wealth seemed available only in English and American contexts.

Michel Louvain, beginning in 1958, bridged the gap between crooners and bands, basing his career on television exposure and attracting crowds of screaming teenagers (a phenomenon unknown in the *chanson* tradition); Michèle Richard was his female equivalent. It is *yé-yé* as well that initiates the televised presentation of artists via lip-synching to their recordings, a practice associated with Dick Clark's *American Bandstand* in the United States. From 1962 to 1974 *Jeunesse d'aujourd'hui* (*Youth Today*) ran a half-hour *yé-yé* showcase corresponding roughly to the Golden Age of *yé-yé*, though the latter portion of that period is most commonly described as the union of *chanson* and *yé-yé* into a Quebec rock movement where this division has lost most of its meaning.[15]

The bands had names like Les Classels, Les Sinners, César et les Romains, and Les Baronets and took their inspiration from the Beatles, the Mamas and Papas, the Shadows, and so on. Les Classels combined white suits with white wigs and songs like "Ton amour a changé ma vie" ("Your Love Changed My Life") rendered in a classic Philadelphia doo-wop style. Les Baronets' rendering of the Beatles's "Love Me Do" as "C'est fou mais c'est tout" ("It's Crazy But It's Everything") involved harmony singing while prancing through some basic choreography in rose-coloured suits of the British mod style.

There were those in the *yé-yé* movement who had their 15 minutes of fame and moved on quickly to another life. A few, like Renée Martel, returned to her father Marcel's roots and began a long and successful career in country music. The Mississippian Nanette Workman managed to follow her unlikely success in *yé-yé* with stints in France and the UK before returning to Quebec in the late 1970s to make several disco recordings, including the local version of the international hit "Lady Marmelade," remembered primarily for its line "Voulez-vous coucher avec moi ce soir?" Others graduated into the Quebec rock movement taking shape in the 1970s as band members, leaders, songwriters, and impresarios.

1968–1980: Rock and Nationalism

Many use "May 1968," the shorthand designation for the student revolt, as a historical breaking point in France. In Quebec it could have been October 1970, when the Front de Libération du Québec took the British diplomat James Cross and Labour Minister Pierre Laporte hostage, eventually killing Laporte. During the crisis the federal government imposed martial law and military occupation in Quebec. Historically there appeared to be a crescendo of nationalist fervour developing through the crisis that culminated in the electoral victory of René Lévesque and the Parti Québécois in 1976, followed by the defeat of the referendum on negotiating **sovereignty** for Quebec in 1980. This defeat stopped the music, in several senses of that expression.

What are collectively known as the "language laws" emerged during this period, culminating in the Charter of the French Language in 1977, which would radically change language use in Quebec. French became the official language of Quebec and the language of the workplace and school for most residents and virtually all immigrants.[16] This ended more than 200 years of English dominance among workplace elites and free choice of language of education. Of equal importance to musicians was the setting of radio quotas for francophone and Canadian content (65 per cent and 35 per cent, respectively) in Quebec, established at the federal level in 1973.

The musical equivalent of October 1970 (ignoring for the moment the progressive rock group Octobre, which took its name from the political events) was Robert Charlebois' series of *L'Osstidcho* revues beginning in the fall of 1968, which announced (some even say caused) the merging of the *chanson* and *yé-yé* genres into a North American blues and country–rock mainstream (see the Case Study box). As musical foundations moved further from cabaret tendencies toward blues, rock, and country mixtures, the language of Quebec as well as English mixtures began to appear in the lyrics. Québécois (the French spoken in Quebec) and the Montreal street variant *joual* seemed to adapt themselves more readily to the rhythms of rock than European French. As Luc Plamondon—who became famous as a lyricist for Diane Dufresne and for musicals—commented (without apparent regard for political correctness), "We're like ten years ahead of them [the French] when it comes to the Americanization of French."[17]

CASE STUDY

Osstidcho

If the logjam (to use a Quebec-appropriate metaphor) of 1960s popular music caused by the split between *yé-yé* and *chanson* was indeed as severe as Robert Giroux and others claim, Robert Charlebois acted as the stick of dynamite that opened the cultural flow again.[18] *Osstidcho*, his multiperformer, multimedia revue that was first presented in 1968, presented new possibilities in popular music in Quebec.

Charlebois had training as both an actor and a musician and combined appearances in film with album production during a mid-1960s *boîte à chanson* period. He also began collaborating on revues, including (somewhat ironically) *Yé-yés versus chansonniers* in 1965 and *Terre des bums* (*Land of the Bums*) in 1967.[19] Trips to the West Indies and especially to California (at the height of the "flower power" period) changed him both philosophically and musically: *Osstidcho* was conceived of as a "happening" in the Californian sense, with all that implies in terms of spontaneity and improvisation.[20] The revue had three separate runs beginning in May 1968, continuing with *Osstidcho King Size* in September (which toured outside of Montreal), and with *L'Osstidcho meurt* (*Osstidcho Dies*) in January 1969 being the necessary end before it ossified into something permanent and rehearsed.[21] *Osstidcho* is taken to be a short form of *hostie de show*. The name was full of significance in a Quebec that was in the process of losing its religion: *hostie* means "host," in the sense of the "body of Christ" used in communion, but is also a common blaspheme in Québécois (along with several other key words in Catholic ritual). Thus *hostie de show* would mean something like "showbiz communion," with its blasphemous usage muddying the waters even further or adding to its resonance, depending on your point of view.

The revue itself was a hybrid, but one Charlebois had been working up to by mixing songs sung with Louise Forestier and his companion Mouffe (Claudine Monfette), humorous monologues by Yvon Deschamps, and music by the group Free Jazz of Quebec. The participants made mistakes and joked about them on stage, and early on the shows were endearingly

If Charlebois opened the door for a more North Americanized popular music scene in Quebec, most artists did not follow his genre-bending *Osstidcho* example, but rather chose a primarily blues–rock or country–rock vein and stuck to it. Among the latter were Les Séguin and Beau Dommage, while Harmonium mixed *chanson* and progressive orchestral rock.

In the blues–rock vein, Michel Pagliaro and the bands Offenbach and Corbeau began productive careers during this period. Pagliaro, who is still active more than 40 years later, began his formal apprenticeship during the *yé-yé* period with Les Chanceliers. He turned toward American-style rock as he began his solo career in 1968 and managed to record successfully in both English and French, as well as working as a producer in Quebec and in France.

Offenbach, created in part from the *yé-yé* group Les Gants Blancs, had a long itinerary marked by failed efforts to reach an English market, some instability in band membership (though one of the faithful was Willie Lamothe's son Michel), and an early indifference to their blues orientation in Quebec, where folk and country–rock dominated the early part of this period. Once Pierre Harel joined the group and began to write French lyrics, they found an audience and defined a certain sort of approach with songs like "Calîne de Blues" ("Calling the Blues") and "Le blues me guette" ("The Blues Is After Me").

unpredictable. What made them electrifying were two things: the use of relaxed Québécois French, *joual*, and even English in the song lyrics, and the mixing of rock, psychedelia, jazz, and soul into a soup that defied the characterization of the previously segregated *chanson* and *yé-yé* production in the 1960s.

It is important to realize that Charlebois broke not only the stylistic music taboos separating *chanson* and *yé-yé* production, but also ridiculed the aura of near-holiness that surrounded some of the early *chansonnier* reverence for rural and traditional imagery. This reverence, while invigorating to some extent in its local orientation, unfortunately recalled the rural Catholic nationalism promoted by Maurice Duplessis at a time when the majority of Quebec workers had long since migrated to the cities into a working class beginning to organize to exercise its power.[22]

Thus, in "Demain l'hiver" ("Tomorrow It's Winter"), Charlebois takes neither himself nor Gilles Vigneault's "Mon pays" seriously (the latter certainly the more serious crime):

> Tomorrow it's winter, I could care less
> I'm heading south, to the sun
> To bathe in the sea
> I'll think of you
> While I'm planting my toes in the soft sand[23]

The songs "California" and "Lindberg" are more closely linked to the revue, however, with the latter becoming a somewhat unlikely hit, with its rather tenuous relationship to the famous pilot (note the different spelling of the name), an intro of free jazz and sound effects, trumpet and sax improvisations throughout, and lyrics by Claude Péloquin, including a chorus whose primary component is a list of airline companies.

As his career progressed, he came to lean increasingly on collaborations with lyricists, including Mouffe, Marcel Sabourin, and Réjean Ducharme, and even used poems by Gilles Vigneault and Arthur Rimbaud, but he has managed to maintain a freewheeling atmosphere that was still identifiably Charlebois—the Charlebois forever linked to *L'Osstidcho*.

This period is often called the Golden Age of Quebec song, and in terms of its mass appeal there is little question: Market share for Quebec song jumped from 10 per cent in 1970 to 25 per cent, then returned to 10 per cent by the end of the decade.[24] The expansion was helped by public policy decisions like the Canadian and French-language broadcast quotas instituted in 1973 and the general movement toward self-governance and self-awareness epitomized by the ascendance of the Parti Québécois.

Large outdoor events like the Superfrancofête in 1974 (featuring Charlebois, Leclerc, and Vigneault) were mass celebrations that consecrated *chanson* as the voice of the people and defined its newfound reach. During Saint-Jean-Baptiste celebrations in 1976, the year that the Parti Québécois would come to power bearing hopes for progress toward independence, two concerts on Mont-Royal in the centre of Montreal grouped Vigneault, Charlebois, Léveillée, Ferland, and Deschamps on the first day, and the new generation including Raoul Duguay, Beau Dommage, Octobre, and Harmonium on the second. Over the two days, 400,000 people attended. This event seemed to define for the foreseeable future that popular music was the primary expression of an emerging sovereign and francophone society.[25] The movement seemed unstoppable. It proved not to be, neither politically nor in the dominance of the *chanson* heritage within Quebec popular music.

1980–1999: Crisis and Recovery

If the Mont-Royal concerts of June 1976 represented an apotheosis, they were simultaneously a turning point. In November, when the Parti Québécois achieved electoral victory, the oppositional role played by the *chansonniers* and new rockers was no longer necessary—their party had won. It was less attractive for artists to be attached to the new establishment than to the rising opposition. The PQ in power necessarily began to make decisions that alienated some of its base, like freezing salaries in the public sector (in 1982) as the recession lingered from the late 1970s, and presenting a 1980 referendum question that seemed fairly toothless to many: A "Yes" victory would merely allow the government to begin negotiations toward a sovereignty whose character had yet to be defined. When even this mild initiative was voted down, the ideological link of Quebec *chanson* to the nationalistic project went on indefinite hiatus along with the project itself, which lost ground in the "me-first" 1980s when social goals were replaced by individual ones: "a 'loft' downtown, a BMW, and a vacation house in Magog."[26]

The primary reasons for the ensuing crisis in the music industry were not political, however, but economic. A worldwide energy crisis and ensuing recession, followed by a reorganization of the music industries with the advent of CDs and music videos, combined to cause a flight from regional markets by the major record labels. It is into this void that a combination of public subsidies and local initiatives gave rise to a local music industry that had not fully existed before, with Audiogram and its retail, distribution, and concert arms becoming the poster child for success.[27] Available funding was nevertheless limited, and the insularity of small markets meant that new artists had difficulty breaking in. A music-industry trade group—ADISQ—was founded in 1979 and increasingly made its influence felt on issues such as subsidies and regulation in the following decade, as well as organizing the Félix awards that filled a need for Quebec-specific recognition of musical accomplishment.[28]

Of the two genres that appeared during this decade—punk and disco—the latter proved to be ephemeral, while the punk anti-establishment ethos has not only endured but turned up as an influence among contemporary artists as diverse as Mara Tremblay and Les Cowboys Fringants. Neither genre (nor the various other "waves" of the period) offered much continuity to either *chanson* or the first wave of Quebec rock practitioners, who in some cases went away quietly while others (Michel Rivard, Pierre Flynn of Octobre, Diane Dufresne [doing Bowie-esque shows], and Claude Dubois) continued solo careers as established stars. Artists attaining new prominence in this period worked primarily in the rock vein; these included Paul Piché and Daniel Lavoie. The Manitoban Lavoie produced a remarkable album—*Tension, Attention*—in 1983, featuring one of the first successful integrations of synthesizers, electronica, and timely lyrics.

The 1980s also saw the consecration of Luc Plamondon as a creator of musicals in French with the huge success in Paris of *Starmania*, in collaboration with the composer Michel Berger. The show became a launching pad for new and existing Québécois artists (including Dufresne, Fabienne Thibeault, and Nanette Workman) and continues to be performed in French and English to this day.[29]

By the 1990s, a brief flirtation with synth-bands like Lili Fatale gave way to a host of fresh new voices in rock/*chanson* (Jean Leloup), mainstream rock (Éric Lapointe, France D'Amour, Les Respectables), new country (Bourbon Gautier, Gildor Roy, Steve Faulkner), folk (La Bottine Souriante), fledgling hip-hop recordings, and artists like the collective Les Colocs. Les Colocs represented a kind of urban vitality and stylistic eclecticism, including brass-driven swing and blues that set them apart from most everything that had come before but somehow evoked life in the vibrant Plateau Mont-Royal neighbourhood where founder André "Dédé" Fortin and several others lived.

Quebec popular song during the 1990s regained its pre-1980 vigour and managed to compete with imports in terms of quality while offering a diverse palette of genre and influence to local fans. Music grounded in folk origins found renewed life at the end of the decade. Following in the footsteps of the international success of La Bottine Souriante (The Smiling Boot), were groups like La Volée de Castors (The Flock of Beavers), the a cappella group Les Charbonniers de l'Enfer (The Coalmen of Hell), and especially Mes Aïeux (My Ancestors), whose song "Dégénérations" manages to chronicle five generations of change in land ownership, work, family, and music in eight short verses.[30]

1999 to Today: The Challenges of Pluralism

Pluralism is commonly applied to political discourse or to ethnic and cultural diversity. The latter sense certainly has relevance for the current discussion, but a diversity of genres and of distribution and support structures within the music industry also partly characterize the twenty-first century in popular music, with manifestations and consequences just beginning to be understood. This trend, of course, does not date from 1999 but traces its roots to the 1980s implosion and rebuilding of the Quebec music industry with diminished regard for the importance of *chanson* and increased insertion into a global pop mainstream. Certain characteristics of the twenty-first century evolution, however, are indicative of a true pluralism, one that includes strong genre/fan identification and scenes with their own internal logic and continuity and lines of influence that owe little to the history of Quebec song. This pluralism is tending to escape from the confines of the local music industry itself, including a diminishing role for the trade group ADISQ and the instruments and beneficiaries of public policy. Three examples of this are hip-hop, country, and Anglo rock from Montreal.

Hip-Hop

I chose 1999 as the jumping-off point for pluralism because it is the year of the first commercially successful hip-hop release in Quebec, Dubmatique's 1999 album *La Force de Comprendre* (*The Strength to Understand*). Dubmatique combined the strengths of its French influences (IAM and MC Solaar among them) with accessible refrains and French lyrics (written by members OT MC and Disoul) that are comprehensible from Senegal to Paris.

Hip-hop in Quebec was already 10 years old, but early practitioners of black Caribbean origin rapped primarily in English and recorded rarely in a Canadian context where black musicians were virtually invisible to the music industry.[31] The passage from imitation of African-American musicians in English to self-expression in French was cathartic. SP (Sans Pression) describes the defining nature of that moment:

> When I did shows [in French], it was fire, man. After that I could never go back to English.[32]

After Dubmatique's success, major recording labels signed several other acts, including Muzion and Sans Pression, who were much harder; mixed creole, the Montreal dialect *joual*, and French; and were commercially not what the major labels had hoped for. By 2004 major label interest had all but evaporated and acts were primarily self-promoting and recording, with the exception of Loco Locass, three white rappers from Quebec City who signed to Audiogram for their second album and managed significant sales. Though there has since been an uptick in hip-hop–related activity, the scene suffers from a lack of radio exposure and support of the industrial infrastructure. There is nevertheless enormous energy, though sometimes rather unfocused, in live events, the shows on community radio, the two active websites dedicated to Quebec hip-hop, and the strong cultural identification through dress and speech.

Country

Country, or Western, in Quebec has prospered almost entirely without critical and media support, in a system of Western and agricultural festivals where country artists appear and often hawk their wares from suitcases on the street. The festival at Saint-Tite is the largest of these, drawing more than

500,000 fans who mostly travel in RVs to a village of 4,000 inhabitants. There are Félix awards for country music, but the winners never appear on the televised part of the ceremony—a symbolic illustration of the tenuous relationship between country and the popular music industry. Country repertoires may include American songs in English, but excellent writers (such as Paul Daraîche, Gildor Roy, Bourbon Gautier, and Steve Faulkner) continue to work in French in the tradition of the early, very popular pioneers like Willie Lamothe. Critics, when they mention country at all, point to excessive sentiment, simplistic structures, and outlandish cult apparel (cowboy hats and boots and fringed clothing) as reasons to ignore the genre, though one or more of these characteristics could be applied to various other genres equally well. Although Quebec is an overwhelmingly urban and industrialized society, country music projects mythical, preindustrial, rural values that resonate with a mostly white working-middle-class audience for whom the benefits of a modern multicultural social environment are not clear. The Saint-Tite organizers know exactly what they're doing: "We are not simple organizers. Every autumn we become the creators of a fantasy world, the world of the Far West."[33]

Anglo Rock

In 2005 a *Spin* magazine article entitled "The Next Big Scene: Montreal" detailed the bands and clubs in a vibrant and mostly English-language rock scene.[34] Two years later I picked up a copy of the *Observer Music Monthly* in London to see one of these bands on the front cover with the headline "Could Arcade Fire Be the Best Band in the World?" In the related story, band leader Win Butler described how he came to Montreal (via Houston and Philips Exeter): "I felt like I discovered Montreal . . . I never even looked at this place on the f—map, there's this great weird city, and it's full of arts and culture, and I was so shocked."[35] But the Montreal Anglo bands do not all involve Americans: Simple Plan is a five-piece band of all native Quebecers, including three born in Montreal; Sam Roberts is a West Island (of Montreal) native; The Stills met at art school in Montreal; and The Dears are a changing cast around black Montrealer Murray Lightburn, who says: "We all have strong feelings for Montreal—I often feel I have to go back to my birthplace before I can give birth to new songs."[36]

How these comments and occurrences fit into the history and future of Quebec popular music requires some background about population and language trends. Quebec is commonly divided into three components: the capital (Quebec City), the metropolis (Montreal), and the regions (essentially all the rest). Of a total population of approximately 8 million, nearly half live in the Montreal area, the cultural and economic engine, with popular song being no exception. The Island of Montreal is also the only area where French is not the native language of the majority and where bilingualism or multilingualism is the norm.[37] The practical effect for musicians is that they can live in Montreal bilingually (or even without French altogether) and participate in a globalized pop environment with a local club base as an incubator, but otherwise almost entirely without local industrial support or subsidy. The reach of the most successful of these bands, who are signed to multinational labels (Arcade Fire, Simple Plan), reaches the entire anglophone market (i.e., the whole world). Montreal thus becomes just another of the magnet North American cities—Austin, San Francisco, Vancouver, Boston—which are not music-industry centres like New York, Los Angeles, and London, but which draw artists and musicians to their cultural diversity and thriving arts communities. Unfortunately, linking this status to the Quebec nationalistic project, which has always assumed the French language as a given, and to the increasingly monolingual ROQ (rest of Quebec) is uncomfortable, since it diminishes Montreal's role as the Québécois cultural capital. The most friction may come from a critical establishment, coupled with government and industry figures, that has invested heavily in a certain version of the history of Quebec popular song, a version defined a priori as francophone and in which the Montreal Anglos are difficult, if not impossible, to place.

Other Trends

An interesting sidelight is the rebirth of a pop–*chanson* split (recalling *yé-yé–chanson*) following the success of the *Star Académie* television talent shows (loosely based on the French *Star Academy* and *American Idol* shows), which have produced a series of young pop stars dependent on a market and an industry that struggles to find a second act for them. Among participants who have subsequently produced at least two albums (one is subsidized for winners) are Émily Bégin, Marie-Élaine Thibert, Marie-Mai Bouchard, Wilfred Le Bouthillier, Cornelieu Montano, Stéphanie Lapointe, Martin Giroux, Marc-André Fortin, and Maxime Landry,[38] while 2012 winner Jean-Marc Couture seems likely to join this group.

Its title notwithstanding, the FrancoFolies song festival in Montreal has long included a "multicultural" stage, where artists of ethnic origin but local residence, as well as artists from **la Francophonie** (the French-speaking world), have performed, singing often in languages other than French. The festival's only requirement is that performers speak French on stage, not that they sing in French.[39] This aspect of the festival is intended to reflect the multicultural nature of contemporary Quebec society and has included Montrealers Bïa, who is Brazilian and sings in five languages, singer Eméline Michel from Haiti, the accordion player and *merengue* artist Joachim Diaz from the Dominican Republic, and many others.

In spite of the impact of pluralism beginning to manifest itself, the *chanson* tradition is alive and well, with new artists integrating a wide spectrum of influence from country (Vincent Vallières), French cabaret (Pierre Lapointe), or rock/electronica/rap (Arianne Moffat). The language used varies from Lapointe's near-Parisian to Vallières's relaxed Québécois (recalling Charlebois or Lucien Françoeur).

Quebec Identity

Those of us listening to English-language popular music may find the national origins of artists a curiosity (Björk from Iceland, or the Sri Lankan/London background of M.I.A.), but we don't necessarily imagine that such artists are important for the national self-image of their countries of origin. They cross national borders in the process of the consumption of music in a globalized but primarily English-language popular music industry. Quebec popular music in French, however, is principally consumed in Quebec, with a small additional penetration of certain artists into other francophone countries such as France or Belgium. The net effect of local consumption is that there is a strong component of cultural identification between Quebec popular musicians and their fans, which has a nationalistic overtone that is quite independent of whether a given song has an overtly political message.

Gilles Vigneault's song "Mon pays c'est l'hiver" ("My Country Is Winter"), often considered to be Quebec's unofficial national anthem, is a good example of this. There is no specific mention of Quebec in the song, but some of the imagery is so strongly related to Quebec cultural (and climatic!) experience that the song had an immediate emotional impact on Quebecers of the Quiet Revolution period and became part of that social and political constellation.

There have always been, and continue to be, artists that both celebrate and critique Quebec explicitly, however. The rappers Loco Locass are the most vocal and visible defenders of the cause of sovereignty in Quebec today, while the alt-rock-folk-country Les Cowboys Fringants constantly turn a satirical if affectionate eye on things Québécois, in songs like "Québécois de souche," where they take on the contradiction between white Quebecers who clamour for ethnic purity while slaughtering the French language in daily life.

The use of French, in and of itself, is an affirmative act with political connotations in North America, and francophone Quebecers live this out every day. Songwriters are no exception; Michel Rivard's "Le Cœur de ma vie" ("The Heart of My Life") is perhaps the most eloquent musical statement of that reality, with the central metaphor establishing his French language as both love interest and foundation for his very existence.

Primary Source

There is nothing quite like listening to music in a club or concert setting, and for fans the best time for this in Quebec is during the festival season, when the FrancoFolies (in June) and many other festivals occur in Montreal, Quebec City, Granby, and Abitibi. For international (that is, mostly Anglo) indie rock, POP Montreal is now also a major destination in September, and Heavy Montréal keeps metal fans happy in August. But if you're unable to make the trip, browsing the listings and visiting artist websites and YouTube channels can point you in the direction of artists to support by purchasing their recording either in digital or CD formats. If you're ambitious enough to want to follow up on artists mentioned here, there are many general and genre-specific websites as well as selected recordings and bibliography:

Encyclopedia of Music in Canada:
www.thecanadianencyclopedia.ca/en/article/encyclopedia-of-music-in-canada
A website that includes historical and current aspects of popular, folk, religious, concert, and other forms of music in Canada.

Québec Info Musique:
www.qim.com
A useful website and database of articles about Quebec music and artists.

La Parolier – Section Québécoise:
www.leparolier.org/quebecois/quebecois2.htm
Information about Quebec artists can be found via alphabetical links that lead to lists of artists' names. Clicking on a name calls up biographical information, as well as a discography that can be browsed by scrolling down.

Hip-Hop Franco:
www.hiphopfranco.com
Find songs and information about hip-hop bands in Quebec.

Vibration Country:
www.vibrationcountry.com
Find out more about Quebec country music artists.

Conclusion

In 2014 the music industry worldwide is in crisis, with the only winners being the stockholders of the new streaming services that are now monopolizing all growth in music distribution (cannibalizing both physical and digital sales), with minimal return to creators or producers of music itself. If this is true in the United States, it is worse in Quebec in that none of the streaming services are based on Canadian soil or have any obligation to include Canadian or Quebec content. The net effect of this on the music industry could well be worse than the devastating effect of digital piracy. This is a cause for deep concern, and not just for Quebecers (or musicians, for that matter), but we can only hope that innovations allowing for the continuing production of popular music in French in North America will emerge.[40]

The sonic record of Quebec popular culture is vital and varied, a remarkable accomplishment when we consider that its total population in 1941 was 3.3 million, and even today is only 8.1 million, with approximately 80 per cent of those being first-language French speakers.[41] As reference points, the population of the state of Massachusetts is 6.5 million, and Pennsylvania 12.5 million.[42] This smallness, and the struggles to define and maintain a separate identity in a great North American sea of primarily Anglo-Saxon culture, have given Quebec popular music a dynamism that it might not otherwise have had. If cultural historians tend to overemphasize this separateness, however, the musicians themselves rarely do: Most recognize that along with their *québécitude* comes a healthy dose of *américanité*. Songwriters from Willie Lamothe to Charlebois to Atach Tatuq's Egypto have acknowledged, even embraced, the triumvirate of primary cultural sources for their music: North America, France, and Quebec itself.

The increasing fluidity of music distribution systems abetted by the Internet (while not without its downside, as noted above) has made even this expanded vision of influences seem quaint, however. Young musicians have easy access to **world music** *and* the music of the world, both live in concert and through sites like YouTube or sites dedicated to local genre audiences such as Hip-Hop Franco and Découvertes Country (Country Discoveries). It is unlikely that the music of Quebec will become *less* diverse any time soon: the genre mixing and expansion of influences reflects not only the increased modes of access but also the nature of Quebec society itself, especially in Montreal, where multilingualism and ethnic diversity is a fact of daily life. The culinary metaphor for Quebec music will never be a steak dinner, but rather a traditional dish like the *tourtière* (meat pie): You're never quite sure what went into it, but the combination tastes good, and you can't get it anywhere but Quebec.

Questions for Critical Thinking

1. What social and historical factors influenced the flowering of Quebec music in the 1950s and 1960s?
2. How is each of these languages important in the Quebec musical context: French, English, and Haitian creole? (Other languages can be added to this list, of course.)
3. What special challenges do musicians in Quebec face in developing careers within the music industry, especially in light of new streaming technologies?

Notes

1. Christopher Jones, "Song and Nationalism in Quebec," *Contemporary French Civilization* 24, no. 1 (2000): 21–36.
2. Bruno Roy, *Panorama de la chanson au Québec* (Montreal: Leméac, 1977), 40.
3. Roland S. Lebrun, *Héritage québécois*, MCA, 1991.
4. Catherine Lefrançois, "La chanson country-western au Québec : état de la question et pistes musicologiques," *Quebec Studies* 45 (2008): 29–42. Lefrançois does an interesting study of the use of reverb in several early country songs, as an illustration of the fact that country artists were not behind other popular artists of the day in adopting new technologies.
5. The word *chanson*, in French, is literally translated as *song* in English. The connotations in French, however, are different enough—a greater emphasis on lyrics, authorship, an anti-pop penchant—that *chanson* is not used in the generic sense but rather to describe a specific current within the larger history of popular song.
6. Roger Chamberland and André Gaulin, *La chanson québécoise : de La Bolduc à aujourd'hui* (Montreal: Nuit blanche éditeur, 1994), 21.
7. Robert Thérien and Isabelle D'Amours, *Dictionnaire de la musique populaire au Québec, 1955–1992* (Quebec: Institut québécois de recherche sur la culture, 1992), 64.
8. This lyric translation and all other translations in this chapter are the responsibility of the author. French lyric sources include album covers, Roger Chamberland and André Gaulin's anthology *La chanson québécoise : de La Bolduc à aujourd'hui*, and online sources verified against the original recordings where possible.
9. Richard Baillargeon and Christian Côté, *Destination Ragou : une histoire de la musique populaire au Québec* (Montreal: Éditions Triptyque, 1991), 48.
10. M. Durand, *Histoire du Québec* (Paris: Éditions Imago, 1999), 124.
11. Claude Gauthier's song about a lumberjack rebelling against his British boss, "Le grand six-pieds" ("The Big Six-Footer"), originally included the line "*Je suis de nationalité / Canadienne-française*" ("I'm of French-Canadian nationality"), which by 1965 he was singing as "*nationalité québécoise-française*" and by 1970 simply as "*nationalité québécoise*" (Chamberland and Gaulin, op. cit., 110).
12. Hélène Plouffe, Suazanne Thomas, Stephen Willis, "'Mon Pays,'" *Encyclopedia of Music in Canada*, www.thecanadianencyclopedia.com/index.cfm?PgNm=TCE&Params=U1ARTU0002417.
13. Robert Léger, *La chanson québécoise en question* (Montreal: Québec Amérique, 2003), 47.

14. Renée-Berthe Drapeau, "Le *yé-yé* dans la marge du nationalisme québécois (1960–1974)," in *La chanson prend ses airs*, ed. R. Giroux (Montreal: Éditions Triptyque, 1993), 135.
15. Ibid., 141.
16. For more details about the Charter of the French Language please see Chantal Bouchard's article in this section (Chapter 10).
17. *Pour une chanson* (television series), Productions SDA Ltée, 1985.
18. The subsection on page 58 of the following book begins with the title "*Chanson* polarized: *yé-yés* against *chansonniers*." Robert Giroux, Constance Havard, and Roch Lapalme, *Le guide de la chanson québécoise* (Montreal: Éditions Triptyque, 1996), 58.
19. *Terre des bums* is an ironic riff on *Terre des hommes* (*Land of Men/Man and His World*), the theme for Expo '67, the world's fair of that year in Montreal.
20. Sylvain Cormier, "Essai—Ce show que l'on qualifia d'ossti," *Le Devoir*, 7 June 2008.
21. Bruno Roy, *L'Osstidcho ou le désordre libérateur* (Montreal: XYZ éditeur, 2008), 88.
22. Durand, *Histoire du Québec*, 110.
23. Robert Charlebois, *Robert Charlebois (collection Québec Love)*, Gamma AGEK-2201, 1993.
24. Jacques Aubé, *Chanson et politique au Québec (1960–1980)* (Montreal: Éditions Triptyque, 1990), 58.
25. Robert Léger, *La chanson québécoise en question* (Montreal: Québec Amérique, 2003), 94.
26. Giroux, Havard, and Lapalme, *Le guide de la chanson québécoise*, 129.
27. Line Grenier, "Aftermath of a Crisis: Quebec Music Industries in the 1980s," *Popular Music* 12, no. 3 (1993): 211.
28. Ibid., 214.
29. Giroux, Havard, and Lapalme, *Le guide de la chanson québécoise*, 152.
30. In French this title represents the homonyms *dégénération* ("degeneration") and *des générations* ("[several] generations").
31. Roger Chamberland, "The Cultural Paradox of Rap Made in Quebec," in *Black, Blanc, Beur: Rap Music and Hip-Hop Culture in the Francophone World*, ed. A Durand (Lanham, MD: Scarecrow Press, 2002), 126.
32. SP, personal interview with author, 2007.
33. Saint-Tite, *Historique du Festival Western de Saint-Tite*, accessed 8 December 2008, www.festivalwestern.com/historique.
34. Rodrigo Perez, "The Next Big Scene: Montréal," *Spin* 21, no. 2 (2005): 61–5.
35. Paul Morley, "Could Arcade Fire Be the Best Band in the World?" *Observer Music Monthly* 43 (March 2007): 30.
36. Tim Jonze, *The Dears*, accessed 10 October 2008, http://timjonze.googlepages.com/dearsdazed.
37. The Hull/Gatineau area opposite Ottawa, as well as a few pockets in the Eastern Townships, are the only other areas where bilingualism effectively persists as a daily fact of life.
38. Information on the current competition can be accessed at www.staracademie.ca.
39. The exception to this rule is anglophone artists, who have been excluded since the beginning. French-speaking artists often perform songs in English. I saw the French artist Laurent Voulzy perform a medley of 1960s American pop songs to close his set in 2003.
40. The author (as a songwriter) receives daily mailings from ASCAP, one of the two major American performance rights societies, with links to articles of interest. Recently, the content of each mailing has been preceded by this text: "Tech companies and criminals have made billions supporting the illegal exploitation of our cultural past while ruthlessly pursuing the dismantling of incentives creators need to fashion our cultural future." ASCAP Daily Brief, retrieved 17 July 2014.
41. Quebec statistics taken from the Banque de données des statistiques officielles sur le Québec, accessed 16 July 2014, www.bdso.gouv.qc.ca/docs-ken/multimedia/PB01662FR_TSC2014M07F00.pdf.
42. State populations taken from US Census Bureau statistics, accessed 23 January 2009, www.census.gov/popest/states/NST-ann-est.html.

Select Bibliography

Alix, Yves. "Restructuration de l'industrie de la musique et transformation du produit musical." In *La Chanson en question(s)*, edited by R. Giroux, 55–65. Montreal: Éditions Triptyque, 1985.

Aubé, Jacques. *Chanson et politique au Québec (1960–1980)*. Montreal: Éditions Triptyque, 1990.

Baillargeon, Robert, and Christian Côté. *Destination Ragou : une histoire de la musique populaire au Québec*. Montreal: Éditions Triptyque, 1991.

Beauvoir, Simone de. "Simone de Beauvoir censurée." Radio-Canada, 1959. Accessed August 2008. http://archives.radio-canada.ca/arts_culture/litterature/clips/2015.

Chamberland, Roger. "The Cultural Paradox of Rap Made in Quebec." In *Black, Blanc, Beur: Rap Music and Hip-Hop Culture in the Francophone World*, edited by A. Durand, 124–37. Lanham, MD: Scarecrow Press, 2002.

———, and André Gaulin. *La chanson québécoise : de La Bolduc à aujourd'hui*. Montreal: Nuit blanche éditeur, 1994.

Cormier, Sylvain. "Essai—Ce show que l'on qualifia d'ossti." *Le Devoir*, 7 June 2008.

Drapeau, Renée-Berthe. "Le *yé-yé* dans la marge du nationalisme québécois (1960–1974)." In *La chanson prend ses airs*, edited by R. Giroux, 115–30. Montreal: Éditions Triptyque, 1993.

Durand, Marc. *Histoire du Québec*. Paris: Éditions Imago, 1999.

Giroux, Robert, Constance Havard, and Roch Lapalme. *Le guide de la chanson québécoise*. Montreal: Éditions Triptyque, 1996.

Grenier, Line. "Aftermath of a Crisis: Quebec Music Industries in the 1980s." *Popular Music* 12, no. 3 (1993): 209–27.

Jones, Christopher. "Song and Nationalism in Quebec." *Contemporary French Civilization* 24, no. 1 (2000): 21–36.

Jonze, Tim. *The Dears*. Accessed 10 October 2008. http://timjonze.googlepages.com/dearsdazed.

Lefrançois, Catherine. "La chanson country-western au Québec : état de la question et pistes musicologiques." *Quebec Studies* 45 (2008): 29–42.

Léger, Robert. *La chanson québécoise en question*. Montreal: Québec Amérique, 2003.

Morley, Paul. "Could Arcade Fire Be the Best Band in the World?" *Observer Music Monthly* 43 (March 2007): 30–9.

Perez, Rodrigo. "The Next Big Scene: Montréal." *Spin* 21, no. 2 (2005): 61–5.

Pour une chanson. Television series. Productions SDA, 1985.

Roy, Bruno. *L'Osstidcho ou le désordre libérateur*. Montreal: XYZ éditeur, 2008.

———. *Panorama de la chanson au Québec*. Montreal: Leméac, 1977.

Saint-Tite. *Historique du Festival Western de Saint-Tite*. Accessed 8 December 2008. www.festivalwestern.com/historique.

Straw, Will. *L'industrie du disque au Québec*. www.arts.mcgill.ca/programs/ahcs/html/Straw/Traite.pdf.

Thérien, Robert, and Isabelle D'Amours. *Dictionnaire de la musique populaire au Québec, 1955–1992*. Quebec: Institut québécois de recherche sur la culture, 1992.

Recordings

Atach Tatuq. *Deluxxx*. AT Music ANUCD001, 2005.

Beau Dommage. *Beau Dommage*. EMI 724387523425, 1974.

Bel-Air (Les). *Les grands succès country*. Disques mérite, 1970.

Charlebois, Robert. *Robert Charlebois (collection Québec Love)*. Gamma AGEK-2201, 1993.

Colocs (Les). *Les Années 1992–1995*. BMG, 2001.

Cowboys Fringants (Les). *La Grand-Messe*. Disques La Tribu, TRIICD-7233, 2004.

Déry, Marc. *Marc Déry*. Audiogram, ADCD-10121, 1999.

Harmonium. *Si on Avait Besoin D'une Cinquième Saison*. Polygram, 8339902, 1975.

Lamothe, Willie. *Les Grands du Country*. BMG Musique Québec, 1995.

Lapointe, Pierre. *Pierre Lapointe*. Disques Audiogramme, 2004.

Lavoie, Daniel. *Tension, attention*. Kébec-Disc KD-584, 1983.

Lebrun, Roland S. *Héritage québécois*. MCA, 1991.

Lelièvre, Sylvain. *Ses Plus Belles Chansons*. Kébec-Disques, KDC 672, 1991.

Loco Locass. *Amour oral*. Disques Audiogramme, 2004.

Mes Aïeux. *En Famille*. Disques Victoire VIC2-1871, 2004.

Moffat, Ariane. *Aquanaute*. Disques Audiogramme, 2002.

Muzion. *Mentalité Moune Morne*. BMG 74321-65673-2, 1999.

Offenbach. *L'Ultime Offenbach*. Disques Helena, 2007.

Parent, Kevin. *Pigeon D'argile*. Tacca, TACD 4507, 1995.

Rivard, Michel. "Le Cœur de ma vie." Released as a single in 1989; it appears on the album *Michel Rivard* (Audiogram, ADCD-10034, 1989).

Sans Pression. *514-50 Dans Mon Réseau*. Les Disques Mont Real, MRLCD-5069, 1999.

Séguin (Les). *Récolte de rêves*. Disques Musi-Art, 1995 (reissue).

Tremblay, Mara. *Le Chihuahua*. Audiogram ADCD 10120, 1999.

Vallières, Vincent. *Chacun dans son espace*. Productions BYC, BYCD 130, 2003.

Vigneault, Gilles. *Gilles Vigneault (Collection Émergence)*. Sony Musique C2K 91053, 1995.

Part D
Citizenship

Introduction

Since the conclusion of the late war, we have been happy in considering you as fellow-subjects; and from the commencement of the present plan for subjugating the Continent, we have viewed you as fellow-sufferers with us.

—Second Continental Congress,
"Letter to the Inhabitants of Canada," 29 May 1775[1]

First we must secure once and for all, in accordance with the complex and urgent necessities of our time, the safety of our collective "personality." This is the distinctive feature of the nation, of this majority that we constitute in Quebec—the only true fatherland left us by events, by our own possibilities, and by the incomprehension and frequent hostility of others.

—René Lévesque, *An Option for Quebec*[2]

I have always opposed the notions of special status and distinct society. With the Quiet Revolution, Quebec became an adult and its inhabitants have no need of favours or privileges to face life's challenges and to take their rightful place within Canada and the world at large.

—Pierre Elliott Trudeau, *The Essential Trudeau*[3]

Throughout their history, the people of Quebec have often questioned their allegiances. Political leaders and other elites have variously tried to convince Quebecers that they should express their nationality and citizenship within the United States of America, within Canada, or within an independent Quebec. So what have Quebecers decided? How have they expressed their desires for citizenship over the years? What does it mean to be a Quebec citizen? How does the French language relate to citizenship in Quebec? Are there distinct civil, political, and social rights for women, immigrants, and Aboriginal peoples? Does citizenship in Quebec accommodate differences?

The concept of citizenship is broad. Political scientist Jane Jenson writes, "the word does define societal boundaries, distinguishing insiders from outsiders, 'we' from 'they.'"[4] T. H. Marshall[5] provides a classic definition of citizenship, defined through its civil, political, and social aspects, while others reflect on different understandings, such as those highlighted by Daniel Weinstock: status, rights, democracy, practices, and identity.[6]

Historian Denyse Baillargeon begins our exploration of citizenship in this section of *Quebec Questions* by examining women's civil, political, and social journey in twentieth-century Quebec. Baillargeon explores how the road travelled by Quebec women, especially French-Canadian women, is measured. How did women in early twentieth-century Quebec live under the yoke of the Church and the state? For example, Baillargeon examines the arguments of political leaders and the Catholic Church over female waged labour. While many of these arguments in Quebec echoed those in other Western societies, Baillargeon argues that disputes took on a "distinct" and "patriotic" form in Quebec—one concerned with the survival of French Canadians as a people and the preservation of their "true" identity. Nationalist leaders and church representatives loudly and clearly proclaimed that women had a maternal vocation. As a minority within both Canada and North America, French Canadians attributed great importance to this vocation and the fertility rate. Many French-Canadian women chose not to work for wages, choosing instead a religious life. Why? What role did these women play in pre-Quiet Revolution Quebec? Consider that in Quebec there were 18 nuns for every 1,000 women in 1941.[7] What was their impact on laywomen and on the state? How can we evaluate their contribution from a feminist perspective?

Baillargeon then addresses the legal status of married women in Quebec, examining the individuals and organizations that fought for universal suffrage, a right that was obtained at the provincial level in 1940. The female presence in the labour market is another good indicator of the citizenship status of women. Baillargeon provides excellent documentation and analysis from the end of World War II to the current situation. We discover the issues and battles that feminists took to the public and private spheres to bring about legal, political, and social change. She ends by exploring the recent relations between Quebec nationalists and Quebec feminists. Do nationalists and feminists share views on how citizenship practices in Quebec can be inclusive for all citizens? How does the Quebec state respond to these issues?

This question leads us to the contribution of Raffaele Iacovino, who focuses his inquiry on Quebec policies on ethnocultural diversity. Since the 1960s, Quebec has established many regulations, policies, and laws framing citizenship practices. Iacovino examines the Quebec Ministry of Immigration, created in 1968, which sought to control the selection and integration of immigrants to Quebec. What pushed the Quebec state to fight for this power? Immigration is a shared jurisdiction under the BNA Act; how do Canada and Quebec share these powers? As this chapter shows us, Quebec challenged Canada on this issue. Some categorize this confrontation as minority versus majority nationalism. Quebec has struggled for the recognition of a "differentiated citizenship"[8] for itself within the Canadian framework. By examining the laws and policies adopted to manage diversity, Iacovino explores whether this Quebec model conflicts with the broader Canadian model. What are the principal values of the Quebec model, known as *interculturalism*? How has the model of interculturalism evolved? In addressing these questions, Iacovino reveals rich insights into how Quebec frames citizenship. What are the rights and responsibilities of individuals within Quebec? He describes the notion of a common public culture in Quebec. What are its principles? What could unite all Quebecers in the interests of social harmony and cultural preservation?

These questions bring us to Maryse Potvin's chapter on interethnic and race relations in Quebec. How do Quebecers of all origins live together? How can we characterize the state of interethnic relations in Quebec? From a sociological perspective, Potvin examines changes in intercultural and race relations in Quebec since the 1960s. How could we assess the Quebec state's performance in promoting equality for all Quebecers? Beyond the official Quebec state discourse, can we discern socioeconomic gaps between different minority and racialized groups and francophone Quebecers? Potvin appraises Quebec's public policies that attempt to end discrimination, racism, and ethnic inequalities. In Quebec, societal tensions have recently shifted from linguistic to religious ones, and religious diversity in public spaces has become a central issue. This current chapter helps the reader interpret some recent key political events that have had important impacts on interethnic and race relations in Quebec, including the Bouchard–Taylor Commission and the debate on "reasonable accommodation" (2006–8), as well as the Charter of Quebec Values (2013–14). In sum, Potvin's chapter forces us to contemplate some of the most important challenges ahead in Quebec in terms of interethnic and race relations, including the pivotal importance attached to the roles and responsibilities of Quebec in promoting and realizing the successful social and economic integration of immigrants and racialized minorities.[9]

Next is Marie McAndrew, Geneviève Audet, and Mahsa Bakhshaei's chapter on immigration and diversity in Quebec schools. Schools contribute greatly to the formation of citizenship. How does the school system participate in managing diversity in Quebec? Can Quebec find a balance between its collective goals, such as preserving French as a common public language, and its desire to promote immigration, respect for diversity, and individual rights? The authors look at the effect of immigration policies since the 1960s on French-language schools in Quebec. Through the analysis of policy statements, they explore how interculturalism is enacted within the education system.

The authors examine how the linguistic debate affects the integration of immigrants in the school system. How did the 1977 Charter of the French Language affect the numbers of allophone students in French-language schools? The authors illustrate how the debate over diversity in Quebec schools has recently polarized into two competing concepts: secularization and preserving a traditional identity. How can we assess linguistic integration in Quebec schools? What does recent data tell us about the equality of opportunity and the academic success of students from all ethnic backgrounds? How are intergroup inequities, such as the disparity in secondary school graduation rates, fought? The authors close by suggesting that full recognition of pluralism in Quebec's schools is a work in progress. Quebec teachers and school administrators have much in common with their Canadian colleagues in the challenges of successfully integrating intercultural perspectives into the curriculum. Nevertheless, the authors state that the identity issue of "majority fragility" is specific to Quebec society.[10]

The next article in this section, focusing on the topic of federalism, is offered by law professor Jean-François Gaudreault-DesBiens. Depending on the commentator, federalism in Canada—in particular the dynamics associated with and arising from intergovernmental relations—has been characterized according to a seemingly endless variety of conceptual labels, including asymmetrical, centralized, competitive, co-operative, collaborative, decentralized, open, renewed, and so on. Gauldreault-DesBiens invites the reader to consider how Quebec has and continues to evaluate the experience of Canadian federalism. When looking to define the term, one may easily agree that the concept of federalism is a legal term referring to an "organization of government in which the authority to govern is divided between a central (national) government on the one hand, and a number of constituent regions, provinces, states, or other territorially distinct political authorities on the other hand."[11] The legal and political cornerstone of federalism is generally recognized to be grounded in and based on a country's constitution. Former professor of Canadian constitutional law Gérald A. Beaudoin argues that federalism "is the most fundamental and most discussed aspect of the Canadian Constitution. In principle, no level of government in a federation is subordinate to any other: each is sovereign in its sphere, and their activities are coordinated.

The citizen is subject to two governments, two legislative authorities. Both governments act directly on the citizen."[12]

Canadian federalism, a key variable of the citizenship equation in Quebec and Canada, needs to be viewed and understood, according to Gaudreault-DesBiens, in a decidedly larger and more fulsome context. It is necessary to enlarge our scope of scholarly inquiry to extend beyond a strict legal or constitutional analysis of federalism. Gaudreault-DesBiens echoes political scientists Richard Simeon and Ian Robinson's affirmation that "federalism should be described not so much as a steady state but as a process."[13] The intellectual path of the article brings us beyond the power of the federal government to make laws for peace, order, and good government or the division of powers between federal and provincial governments (sections 91 and 92 of the British North America Act). Gaudreault-DesBiens embraces a broad analysis of the Canadian federal regime by including political and sociological approaches to his analysis of Quebec's views on federalism. He claims that in Quebec, a nationalist vision frames and dominates the evaluation of the Canadian federal experience. Additionally, beliefs, opinions, and conjectures are part of this nationalist discourse that is "constitutive of a pathological prism when it comes to evaluating how federalism fares in protecting or accommodating the province's interests." In a brilliant exercise that offers a complex and well-articulated analysis of Quebec's experience within the Canadian federation, Gauldreault-DesBiens further identifies some key issues that are likely to have a significant impact on the evolution of Canadian federalism—from a Quebec perspective—in the years to come.

Following pioneering works by Vincent Lemieux, Kenneth McRoberts, and Maurice Pinard on political attitudes and voting behaviour in Quebec, Éric Bélanger and Chris Chhim look at national identity issues in Quebec and popular support for sovereignty among Quebecers. Bélanger and Chhim, drawing on a range of public opinion polling data, specifically examine the political realities of the Canadian and Quebec context. Their chapter echoes the analysis of political scientists James Bickerton and Alain-Gagnon: "What most differentiates Canada from other modern federations such as the United States, Australia and Germany, is that this country continues to constitute an ongoing experiment in competing state and nation-building projects. This has been illustrated by the historical prominence of regional protest parties primarily in Western Canada, and a nationalist movement and parties in Quebec."[14] In using public opinion poll results, readers are offered fresh insight on Quebec identity and the way that "best describes how they think of themselves" (1996–2014) as well as their "feelings of attachment to Quebec and to Canada" (1980–2014). Bélanger and Chhim also look carefully at polling results for those expressing support for sovereignty (1988–2014) to compare and interpret these numbers alongside public opinion poll results supportive of the idea of Quebec as a "country." When looking at the realities of Quebec politics, many actors differ on the relative importance to ascribe to sovereignty—this reality, Bélanger and Chimm suggest, has been and continues to be reflected in political preferences and formal voting patterns. This contribution to the volume also raises key questions for Quebec's political future. Has a "post-sovereignty era" effectively started in Quebec, or as political scientist Alain Noël has recently suggested, does Quebec remain "a small nation with an uncertain political status. When all is said and done, this founding question remains, and it conditions much of the rest."[15]

The chapters in this section reveal how challenges surrounding citizenship in Quebec are important to all Quebecers. As in most Western societies, Quebec is a pluralistic society striving to find a balance between common collective characteristics and respect for the diversity of individuals and cultural groups. Tensions, conflicts, and disagreements are all part of the decision-making process in a community. The notion of citizenship has been, is being, and will be re-examined. One can only hope that the Quebec democracy will encourage this debate, allowing all Quebecers to collectively determine a uniquely Quebec way of life.

Notes

1. The full text of this letter can be found at http://lincoln.lib.niu.edu/cgi-bin/amarch/getdoc.pl?/var/lib/philologic/databases/amarch/.5722.
2. René Lévesque, *An Option for Quebec* (Toronto: McClelland & Stewart, 1968), 21.
3. Pierre Elliott Trudeau, letter to Lucien Bouchard, originally published in the *Montreal Gazette*, 17 February 1996; reprinted in *The Essential Trudeau*, ed. Ron Graham (Toronto: McClelland & Stewart, 1998), 161.
4. Jane Jenson, "Recognizing Difference: Distinct Societies, Citizenship Regimes and Partnership," in *Beyond the Impasse: Toward Reconciliation*, ed. Roger Gibbins and Guy Laforest (Montreal: IRPP, 1998), 215–39.
5. Thomas H. Marshall, *Class, Citizenship, and Social Development: Essays* (Garden City, NY: Doubleday, 1964).
6. Daniel Weinstock, "Citizenship and Pluralism," in *Blackwell Guide to Social and Political Philosophy*, ed. R. L. Simon (Malden, MA: Blackwell, 2002), 239–70.
7. Danielle Juteau and Nicole Laurin, *Un métier et une vocation : Le travail des religieuses au Québec de 1901 à 1971* (Montreal: Presses de l'Université de Montréal, 1997), 2.
8. This term is attributed to Iris Marion Young.
9. See the following publication of the Commission des droits de la personne et des droits de la jeunesse: www.cdpdj.qc.ca/Publications/memoire_politique-immigration_resume.pdf.
10. Between 2004 and 2008, Quebec admitted an average of approximately 45,000 immigrants per year, most of whom (86.9 per cent) chose to live in the metropolitan area of Montreal. For comparison, Toronto is the home of 68.3 per cent of foreign-born Ontarians.
11. Peter Cane and Joanne Conaghan, *The New Oxford Companion to Law* (Oxford: Oxford University Press, 2008).
12. Gerald Hallowell, *The Oxford Companion to Canadian History* (Toronto: Oxford University Press, 2004).
13. Richard Simeon and Ian Robinson, "The Dynamics of Canadian Federalism," in *Canadian Politics*, 5th ed., ed. James Bickerton and Alain-G. Gagnon (Toronto: University of Toronto Press, 2009), 155.
14. James Bickerton and Alain-G. Gagnon, "Federal Adaptation and the Limits of Hybridity," in *Routledge Handbook of Regionalism and Federalism*, ed. John Loughlin, John Kincaid, and Wilfried Swenden (Florence, KY: Routledge, 2013), 173.
15. Alain Noël, "Quebec," in *The Oxford Handbook of Canadian Politics*, ed. John C. Courtney and David E. Smith (New York: Oxford University Press, 2010), 106.

14 Quebec Women of the Twentieth Century: Milestones in an Unfinished Journey

Denyse Baillargeon, Université de Montréal

Timeline

1893 Montreal Council of Women founded, consisting mainly of English Montreal's charitable or educational women's organizations. It also had individual members, including some francophones.

1897 National Council of Jewish Women of Canada founded, consisting mainly of Quebec Jewish women's organizations, much like its largely anglophone counterpart (see above).

1902 Coloured Women's Club founded by Anne Greenup and six other black American women to aid the black population of Montreal.

1907 Fédération nationale Saint-Jean-Baptiste founded, an umbrella group for francophone women's associations.

1908 École d'enseignement supérieur pour jeunes filles, the first classical college for francophone women, opens its doors (later to become Collège Marguerite-Bourgeois in 1926).

1913 Montreal Suffrage Association founded by Carrie Derick, a professor of genetics at McGill University.

1915 Cercles de Fermières organization founded by Quebec's minister of agriculture to educate rural women about agricultural production methods.

1917 Mothers of soldiers and military nurses are granted the right to vote at the federal level.

1918 Federal Act to Confer the Electoral Franchise upon Women is passed.

1919 An Act to Provide for Fixing a Minimum Wage for Women is passed in Quebec.

1922 Provincial Franchise Committee founded by Marie Lacoste Gérin-Lajoie, Thérèse Casgrain, and Mrs. Walter Lyman.

1924 Matchwomen at E.B. Eddy Company in Hull walk out in wildcat strike.

1927 Fondation de l'Alliance canadienne pour le vote des femmes au Québec founded by Idola St-Jean.

1928 Supreme Court of Canada denies women the right to be senators, ruling that whereas the British North America Act states that Senate seats are open to all "persons," women are not "persons" in the eyes of the law.

1929 Privy Council in London overturns the Supreme Court's decision, recognizing that women are indeed "persons" and may therefore sit as senators.

Commission on the Civil Rights of Women (called the Dorion Commission after its president, Charles-Édouard Dorion) is struck. Provincial Franchise Committee becomes League for Women's Rights and is presided over by Thérèse Casgrain.

1930 Cairine Wilson of Montreal becomes the first woman appointed to the Senate in Ottawa.

1931 Further to the Dorion Commission's recommendations, married women receive the legal right to keep the wages they earn.

1934 Married women can open their own bank accounts in Quebec.

1937 Some 5,000 female French-Canadian, Jewish, and immigrant garment-industry workers unite to strike in Montreal.

Fédération catholique des institutrices rurales de la province de Québec, first rural schoolmistresses' organization, founded by Laure Gaudreault.

An Act Respecting Assistance to Needy Mothers is adopted in Quebec to assist single mothers, most of them widows.

1940 Quebec grants women the right to vote and run in provincial elections.

1941 Quebec women law graduates are admitted to the provincial Bar and are thus permitted to practise law in the province.

Quebec women are permitted to vote in municipal elections provided they meet voter eligibility criteria.

1942 Quebec women are granted the right to become school board commissioners.

1943 Federal government opens daycare centres in Montreal to encourage mothers to join the war effort.

1945 Federal Family Allowance program is introduced, leading to conflict with Quebec over cheques being issued to mothers instead of fathers.

1952 Men and many women employees go on strike at the French-Canadian department store Dupuis Frères.

1954 A double standard in the Civil Code of Quebec is abolished. Previously, a husband could obtain a legal separation if his wife committed adultery, but a wife could not separate from an adulterous husband unless he kept his mistress in the family dwelling.

1961 Bérengère Gaudet becomes the first woman notary in Quebec. Marie-Claire Kirkland-Casgrain becomes the first woman to sit in Quebec Legislative Assembly.

1962 Married women are granted the right to become teachers with the Montreal Catholic School Commission.

1964 Bill 16 abolishes married women's legal incapacity and mitigates the principles of paternal authority and of marital powers of husbands.

1965 Conference called "La femme du Québec: hier et aujourd'hui" held, concluding with a vote to found the Fédération des femmes du Québec.

1966 Fédération des femmes du Québec (FFQ) is founded.

Association féminine d'éducation et d'action sociale is founded, comprising Cercles d'économie domestique and L'union catholique des femmes rurales. Both organizations were created in 1945 following a rift within Cercles de Fermières.

1967 Royal Commission on the Status of Women in Canada is established, chaired by Florence Bird.

continued

Indian Rights for Indian Women founded by Mary Two-Axe Early, a Mohawk woman from Kahnawake.

1968 Act Respecting Divorce is adopted in Quebec, authorizing civil marriage and divorce in the province.

1969 Providing information on contraceptives is decriminalized in Canada. Hospitals are authorized to provide abortions sanctioned by a therapeutic abortion committee comprising at least three physicians.

Montreal Women's Liberation Movement is founded.

All Aboriginal citizens are granted the right to vote in Quebec.

"Partnership of acquests" replaces "community of property" as the legal matrimonial property regime.

Front de libération des femmes du Québec (FLF) is founded and its *Manifeste des femmes québécoises* is disseminated.

1970 Demonstration organized by the FLF on 10 May (Mother's Day) to demand free and accessible abortion.

1971 Federal legislation on unemployment insurance is amended to provide 17 weeks of maternity leave, granting new mothers 60 per cent of their salary for 15 weeks.

1972 Centre des femmes is founded in Montreal, offering abortion services and publishing its *Manifeste pour une politique de planification des naissances* to advocate for a family-planning policy in Quebec.

1973 Government of Quebec creates the Conseil du Statut de la femme. Claire L'Heureux-Dubé becomes the first woman to be appointed judge to the Superior Court of Quebec. She later becomes the first woman to sit on the Quebec Court of Appeal (1979) and then the first woman judge from Quebec appointed to the Supreme Court of Canada (1987).

Bertha Wilson was the first woman judge appointed to the Supreme Court (in 1982). L'Heureux-Dubé was the second woman appointee, but the first woman from Quebec.

1974 Lise Bacon, Quebec Liberal cabinet minister, tables plan to introduce government daycare, mainly for low-income families. Quebec Native Women's Association founded (later to become Quebec Native Women Inc.).

1975 Quebec Charter of Human Rights and Freedoms is adopted, prohibiting all forms of discrimination.

1977 Principle of "parental authority" replaces "paternal authority" in the Civil Code of Quebec.

1978 Conseil du statut de la femme publishes a comprehensive policy entitled "Pour les Québécoises; égalité et indépendance."

Quebec's Minimum Wage Act guarantees women the right to take 18 weeks of maternity leave and prohibits firing women who take it.

First family-planning clinics with abortion services, called "Lazure clinics," are founded.

Regroupement des femmes québécoises is founded.

Government of Quebec adopts maternity allowance program to cover the two-week waiting period not covered by the federal program.

The CALACS network (Centres d'aide et de lutte contre les agressions à caractère sexuel) is established to address issues around sexual assault.

Provincial Act Respecting Child Day Care is passed, and the Office des services de garde is created to implement and fund daycare services in homes, schools, and daycare centres.

1979 Regroupement provincial des maisons d'hébergement et de transition pour femmes victimes de violence conjugale is founded to help women victims of domestic violence.

1980 Quebec's Bill 89 establishes equality between spouses in administration of assets and in children's education.

1982 Quebec Charter of Human Rights and Freedoms is amended to accommodate affirmative action programs. Charter requires future legislation to comply with the principle of equality between the sexes, prohibiting discrimination against pregnant women and sexual harassment.

1988 Supreme Court decriminalizes voluntary interruption of pregnancy, declaring section 251 of the Criminal Code of Canada unconstitutional. Therapeutic abortion committees are no longer legal in Canada.

1989 Quebec's Act Respecting Economic Equality of the Spouses is proclaimed, providing for equal sharing of family patrimony between spouses after a marriage is dissolved, whatever matrimonial regime a couple chooses.

In *Daigle v. Tremblay*, the Supreme Court rules that a fetus is not a legal person and that third persons cannot prevent a woman from having an abortion.

On 6 December, 14 young women are gunned down at École Polytechnique de Montréal by a deranged man who accuses them of being feminists.

1990 A conference called "Femmes en tête" celebrates the fiftieth anniversary of Act Granting Women the Right to Vote in Quebec.

Unpaid parental leave of 34 weeks is introduced in Quebec for parents of newborns or adopted children.

1992 Conference called "Un Québec féminin pluriel" is organized by the FFQ to discuss and develop an inclusive feminist social project.

1995 FFQ organizes the Bread and Roses march in Quebec.

Government of Quebec authorizes automatic collection of alimony payments.

1996 Quebec's Pay Equity Act is adopted.

1997 New family policy measures include $5-a-day daycare program, network of early childhood centres, and a parental insurance program to replace income during parental leaves.

Parental leave increased from 34 to 52 weeks.

1998 Midwifery is legalized in Quebec.

1999 Juanita Westmoreland-Traoré becomes the first black woman judge appointed to the Court of Quebec.

2000 First World March of Women to protest poverty and violence against women is held.

2004 Quebec Court of Appeal rules that same-sex couples have the right to marry in Quebec.

Introduction

> *Like the children, women in Quebec seem never to have been just persons. They are pawns in the game, ornaments or slaves, means to pleasure, temptations to sin, instruments for the production of children, members of a labour force, but not quite people. Now that they are becoming recognized as people they are making a revolution in Quebec.*
>
> —Miriam Chapin[1]

This telling quote shows how for many years women in Quebec, particularly those of French-Canadian origin, were perceived as creatures entirely subjugated by the Church and confined to their families. According to Miriam Chapin, it was not until the mid-1950s that women were recognized as persons and began effecting radical social change that would herald the Quiet Revolution of the 1960s. Today, women in Quebec, and particularly francophone women, have something of a reputation for their self-assurance, their independence from men, and the breadth of their egalitarian aspirations. According to many observers, Quebec women are more militant than their counterparts in other parts of North America, Europe, and particularly France. Indeed, Quebec's "masculinist" movement, which agrees with this view, has virulently denounced the "excesses" of **feminism**.[2] It is true that Quebec feminism appears very dynamic, compared to that of other Western societies. Clearly, women in Quebec enjoy more advanced and generous social legislation and family policies (for example, daycare and parental leaves) than do other Canadian women, and that some rights (such as the right to abortion, for which feminists fought fiercely in the 1970s) are less violently challenged in Quebec than elsewhere in North America. So it is no wonder that the very women who used to be disparaged as the least emancipated of their kind in North America are now seen as the wave of the future.

But this straightforward black-and-white portrayal of Quebec women is ripe for a nuanced critique and, even more, for a re-examination in light of its historical complexities. How should we measure the road travelled by Quebec women, especially French-Canadian women, during the twentieth century? What meandering turns did it take? How did their journey relate to the changes taking place in Quebec society? This chapter attempts to address these and other questions. While focusing on the place and role of women in the private and public spheres before and after World War II, we also pay particular attention to the "national question" in Quebec, which strongly influenced gender relations and explains much about why the province's women came to win their freedom.

1900–1940: Women under the Yoke of Church and State?

Waged Labour

In the early twentieth century, Quebec was well on its way to becoming an industrialized society. In fact, from 1921 onward, most of the population would live in the cities, notably in Montreal, the province's cosmopolitan hub, industrial heartland, and largest urban centre. At the turn of the century, attracted by urban job opportunities (particularly in domestic and unskilled factory work), single female city dwellers between the ages of 15 and 30 outnumbered their male counterparts. Generally speaking, single, young female workers of that era would leave the workforce as soon as they married, as the notion of a married woman holding down a salaried job was heartily condemned in Quebec. Estimates indicate that before the 1940s less than 5 per cent of married women held down jobs outside of the home. However, many housewives did odd jobs at home, a strategy that reconciled their domestic responsibilities with the need to supplement the family purse. As the railway system expanded, the **sweating system** that flourished in the garment industry also recruited women in rural regions, where specialization and commercialization in agriculture had created more free time for farm women. As shown in Table 14.1, 1910 marked the beginning of an era in which a growing proportion of single, young women also found work in offices, businesses, and in the professions available to them at the time: teaching and nursing.

Light industries and offices in early twentieth-century Quebec were quick to take advantage of women's cheap labour, but the presence of single, young women in these contexts was perceived as a "social problem" or a threat to women's moral integrity until the 1920s. In fact, although women were working under truly deplorable conditions, reformers, intellectuals, clerics, and even male labour organizers were more inclined to question the legitimacy of the female workforce than to denounce its low wages and shameless exploitation. After World War I, waged labour for single, young women became more widely accepted, but that of married women (while a very marginal phenomenon) continued to be met with staunch opposition, with some workers' organizations going so far as demanding their dismissal. Tolerated rather than truly accepted, women's waged labour was the subject of renewed attacks during the Depression of the 1930s when thousands of men became unemployed. It was against this backdrop that Joseph-Napoléon Francoeur, a member of the provincial legislature, tabled a bill (which never became law) calling for "women and young girls asking for work to prove that they really needed to do so."[3]

Table 14.1 Distribution of the Female Workforce by Professional Sector and Proportion of Women in the Workforce in Quebec as a Whole, 1911–41 (%)

Sectors of activity	1911	1921	1931	1941
Professions and administration	11.1	19.3	14.7	13.9
Business	4.1	4.9	5.3	5.4
Employees	58.1	51.8	61.7	60.2
Offices	4.2	10.6	10.5	10.5
Services	53.0	39.3	49.7	48.7
Transportation and communications	0.9	1.9	1.5	1.0
Workers	24.5	21.3	16.5	19.1
Others	2.2	2.7	1.8	1.4
% of women in the workforce	16.9	18.4	21.0	24.4

Source: G. Bernier and R. Boily, eds., *Le Québec en chiffres de 1850 à nos jours* (Montreal: ACFAS, Collection by GRÉTSÉ, 1986), 204.

Opposition to waged labour for women, particularly married women, resonated powerfully throughout the Western world. Everywhere women's integration into the workforce was perceived as a threat both to men's privilege and to their patriarchal authority within the family. In Quebec, however, this opposition was magnified by fears about the survival of French Canadians as a people. At a time when thousands of francophone Quebecers had left for the United States and when the constitutional rights of francophones (especially those concerning education) were habitually violated in anglophone-majority provinces, traditional nationalists (including a large proportion of Catholic clergymen) believed that the continued existence of the French-Canadian nation was in jeopardy. As a minority in anglophone Canada's inhospitable political landscape, francophone Quebecers had great difficulty influencing any major decisions in Ottawa—decisions that would determine the future of the country. Even in Quebec, where francophones constituted the majority, they were economically dominated by the anglophone elite, which used its capital holdings to lord over the province's economic development. Traditional nationalists therefore held that industrialization was not only tangible proof of francophone subordination, but was also an Anglo-Saxon importation that was sapping the roots of French-Canadian society. They contended that industrial work and the urban way of life ran contrary to the fundamental values and the very identity of French Canadians, as represented in the triptych of Language, Faith, and Rural Vocation. So, as the countryside emptied to fill factories in the city, traditional nationalists looked on with great trepidation—especially when it came to women workers.

Motherhood First

Far from being a homogeneous or monolithic political block, Quebec nationalists of this era had various opinions about how French Canadians ought to assert their nationhood. Opinions sometimes differed over what measures might best safeguard the people's future, but they were unanimous on one point: French-Canadian mothers were the cornerstone of francophone survival in North America, and anything that might divert them from that mission had to be vigorously denounced. As the purveyors of language and tradition, it behooved women to ensure the reproduction of the "race" (the French-Canadian people), both biologically and culturally. Nationalists, and clerics in particular, were constantly reminding women of their overriding duty to be fruitful and multiply. Troubled equally by industrialization and the shrinking proportion of francophones in Canada, both the Catholic Church and the nationalists believed they could count on the proverbial high francophone fertility rate that had supposedly existed since the era of New France to maintain the proportion and standing of French Canadians within the Canadian political landscape and even gain back some ground—the better to propagate their high spiritual values.

Table 14.2 General and Total Fertility Rates* for Quebec and Ontario, 1901–41

Year	General Fertility Rate,† Quebec	General Fertility Rate,† Ontario	Total Fertility Rate,‡ Quebec	Total Fertility Rate,‡ Ontario
1901	160	108	N/A	N/A
1911	161	112	5.4	3.6
1921	155	98	5.3	3.2
1931	116	79	4.0	2.6
1941	102	73	3.4	2.4

* Fertility rates measure live births to women aged 15 to 49.
† Fertility rate per 1,000 women in a given year.
‡ Average number of children that may be born to a woman over her lifetime (based on the fertility rates from that year).
Source: J. Henripin, *Tendances et facteurs de la fécondité au Canada* (Quebec: IQRC, 1989), 21; J. Henripin, *Naître ou ne pas naître* (Quebec: IQRC, 1989), 35.

Studies have shown that the so-called "Revenge of the Cradle,"[4] to borrow the title of the famous natalist speech given by Father Louis Lalande in 1918, never actually took place. For while Father Lalande and other nationalists were extolling the virtues of large families, these were already a minority, as only 20 per cent of married women born in 1887 gave birth to more than 10 children. In reality, fertility rates for Quebec women had been constantly decreasing since the latter third of the nineteenth century, and dropped off even more sharply during the 1920s, as shown in Table 14.2.

But compared to the rest of Canada, to Ontario, or to anglophone Quebec, French-Canadian families in Quebec were in fact bigger. Quebec francophone women born in 1903 had an average of 5.1 children, versus 4.4 children for Quebec women as a whole and 3.4 for Canadian women. Despite the Catholic Church's firm condemnation of contraception, the data show that its use was nonetheless becoming more widespread, especially in the cities, where difficult economic conditions were leading more couples to restrict the size of their families. The same trend continued during the Depression, as revealed in numerous testimonies from women who tried (though not always successfully) to limit their number of pregnancies.

While the ideal of the large family was far from being realized, it nonetheless epitomized the traditional nationalist concept of the place and role of women in society: maternity—"holy and fruitful maternity,"[5] to quote Henri Bourassa (who founded the nationalist daily *Le Devoir*)—represented the primary if not the sole legitimate function women could perform. Wanting to escape procreation, or simply wanting to pursue other interests, defied the grand design of Providence, which had crafted "Woman's nature" for this purpose. This discourse on the maternal vocation of women was certainly not exclusive to Quebec nationalists—it was widespread in the Western world and was even endorsed by feminists to back their political demands. But in Quebec, where the national question had become an obsession, confining women to the domestic sphere where they would devote themselves exclusively to motherhood was undoubtedly expressed much more fervently; the repercussions were seen in the small proportion of married women in the workforce and a relatively slow decline in the fertility rate.

Nuns and Feminists

The predominance of the Catholic Church is often cited to explain Quebec's comparatively high fertility rate. But was the Church alone also responsible for Quebec women's remarkable number of religious vocations? The number of religious communities swelled from 15 in 1850 to 80 in 1941, and the exceptionally high proportion of nuns among single women over the age of 20, 9 per cent in 1921, set a record for its time in the Western world. Clearly, entering the cloister was a path that many young women in Quebec chose during this period. Often from large families, where Catholic precepts about reproduction were strictly obeyed and where religious practices were intense, these women (many of them very young) undoubtedly entered this life to answer God's calling. At the same time, for many the religious life was also likely a vehicle for upward social and intellectual mobility, or a way to escape poverty and the physical travails of maternity. Quebec nuns could work in a variety of administrative capacities within their communities and were among the first women to gain access to higher education (often studying at American Catholic universities) and to professions that were difficult for laywomen to practise.

The role played by nuns in Quebec was considerable. Under the cover of their habits they commanded a legitimacy that was denied to laywomen. Nuns founded and directed countless convent schools for girls, established and ran most of Quebec's major hospitals, and by the mid-nineteenth century were attempting to minister to the needs of poor urban populations by significantly multiplying their works of assistance. It may be said without exaggeration that women's religious communities established (sometimes with little or no government funding) the first health-care, social assistance, and education network for girls in Quebec,[6] a network that they ran until the mid-1960s.

The impressive magnitude of the nuns' activities was a direct consequence of the Quebec government's reluctance to intervene in education and social welfare, areas regarded by the Catholic Church as its exclusive preserve. In the Church's view, dispensing charity within a religious framework was the best way to help the destitute while preserving the Christian family and social order—the foundations of the French-Canadian nation. It was just as crucial to the Church to keep the upper hand in education, a highly sensitive social nerve centre in which young minds could be shaped according to Catholic ideals. Since any state incursion into these areas was deemed by the Church to be an attack on the Catholic character of francophones, it resolutely opposed mandatory school attendance until it was finally introduced in 1943. This said, Quebec state liberalism was very much at home with the Church's ambitions to expand the domain of its ministry and, although the government continued to increase funding to health and social assistance institutions run by the Church until the 1960s, the state took great care not to dispense any services directly to the public.

Nuns were both the spearhead and linchpin of the Church's front-line operations; the institutions founded by the nuns allowed the Church to reach Quebec's entire Catholic population and provide free health care, relief, succour, and education in environments that honoured its doctrine. The position of nuns in relation to the ecclesiastic authorities was therefore somewhat ambiguous. On one hand, these communities of women enjoyed considerable autonomy in directing their congregations and institutions, and many nuns occupied positions and assumed functions and responsibilities that would have been inaccessible to them as laywomen. On the other hand, their range of power was limited by that of the prevailing male clerical authorities, which they had to obey. Their social and educational activities were performed under the banner of "spiritual maternity" and at least partly served to strengthen the Church's control over souls. So donning the habit may have opened many doors to these women, but whether it paved the way to their emancipation is less certain, given that these opportunities were available to them only if they abided by the decrees of the bishopric and assumed an eminently feminine and maternal identity.

The vibrancy of religious communities also had negative repercussions on the lives of francophone laywomen. Nuns, owing to their quasi-monopoly over social and educational services for girls, reserved administrative positions for each other within their institutions, thereby blocking the way for their "worldly" lay sisters. For a time, nuns also represented a large proportion of nurses and teachers in Quebec, thereby further restricting laywomen's access to these female professions as well. Moreover, by working for free, in the name of their apostolic mission, nuns reinforced the idea that nursing and education were women's "vocations," for which wages could be justifiably very low. Consequently, francophone women in these professions earned comparably less than did anglophone women. By multiplying their charitable social work, women's religious communities similarly limited the spheres in which middle- and upper-class women could practise philanthropy, a form of social engagement which, among Quebec anglophones as elsewhere in the Western world, was a hotbed for feminism. The founding of Hôpital Sainte-Justine in 1907 by a group of upper-class French-Canadian women and of Assistance maternelle in 1912, a French-Canadian charity that provided succour to poor mothers in Montreal, were therefore exceptional feats.

Historian Micheline Dumont contends that, during the first decades of the twentieth century, entering a religious order was the only way in which French-Canadian women could challenge traditional roles without confronting Quebec's **patriarchal society**. But feminist historians have also recognized that the prevalence of the nuns probably delayed the formation of francophone feminist organizations. As early as 1893, anglophone women from Montreal had founded the Montreal Local Council of Women (MLCW), a local branch of the National Council of Women of Canada (NCWC), which was established the same year. The MLCW brought together anglophone women's organizations and individuals of all religious affiliations and attracted some francophone members, who were active for some time and even held administrative positions. But the ethnic tensions that were exacerbated around the beginning of the twentieth century and the hostility of the Catholic clergy (which disapproved of Catholic women's membership in groups dominated by Protestants) contributed in equal parts to the departure of francophone women from the MLCW. In 1907, these women went on to found their own organization, the Fédération nationale St-Jean-Baptiste (FNSJB).

The ethnic and religious schisms in Montreal's feminist forces did not prevent the two (francophone and anglophone) majority groups from working together on a number of social issues. In 1922, the Provincial Franchise Committee (directed by Marie Lacoste Gérin-Lajoie, president of the FNSJB) united francophone and anglophone women to campaign for the right to vote at the provincial level, a right that had been granted to women at the federal level in 1918. In this case, however, these feminists' requests were rejected by male politicians, secure in the conviction that they were acting with the Church's sanction. The Catholic clergy and the nationalists, who already regarded the FNSJB with great suspicion, opposed women's suffrage with all their might and even alleged that it violated Catholic doctrine. These men believed that giving women the vote would divert them from their primary mission in life—the reproduction of the "race"—and would give them a power that could undermine patriarchal relationships within the family. It was not until 1940 (despite vehement opposition from the clergy) that the newly elected Liberal Party of Quebec, prompted by lobbying from Thérèse Casgrain, made good on a campaign promise to grant women citizens the vote.[7]

Among its other initiatives, the FNSJB, allied with other francophone and anglophone organizations, succeeded in lobbying the government for a commission of inquiry, the Dorion Commission, to examine the legal status of married women at the beginning of the 1930s. The commissioners, a constellation of prominent legal experts and ardent nationalists, rejected most of their requests to change legislation, arguing that the Civil Code of Quebec, inherited from France, was one of the cornerstones on which the nation had been built and that most of its provisions (especially those entrenching the legal incapacity of married women and the marital powers of fathers) were emanations of Divine Law. Therefore, the provincial government only amended legislation to recognize married women's ownership of their wages, essentially preserving the spirit and the letter of the Civil Code, and with it, the nationalist notion of French-Canadian women's place and duties to nation and family.

BIOGRAPHY

Thérèse Forget Casgrain (1896–1981)

Thérèse Forget Casgrain was the daughter of Lady Blanche MacDonald and Sir Rodolphe Forget, a Montreal lawyer, wealthy financier, and a Conservative member of the House of Commons from 1904 to 1917. She was also the mother of four children and the wife of Pierre Casgrain, a Liberal member of Parliament in Ottawa (1917–1941) before he was appointed to the Superior Court of Quebec. But, more importantly, she was one of the most tireless activists of her day.

Mme Marie Thérèse (Forget) Casgrain
Library and Archives Canada/ PA-126768

As a member of Montreal's elite bourgeoisie who had been immersed in the world of politics since childhood, Casgrain undoubtedly possessed the credentials required for a lengthy career as an activist, a role she fulfilled in every sense of the word. In the early 1920s she took up the struggle for women's suffrage, working with the Provincial Franchise Committee. She was part of the first delegation of feminists to travel to Quebec City to attempt to convince Premier Alexandre Taschereau to grant women the right to vote. In 1929, following her presidency of the Provincial Franchise Committee, she founded the League for Women's Rights, which continued to lobby the provincial government, shoulder-to-shoulder with Alliance canadienne pour le vote des femmes (founded by Idola Saint-Jean) until 1940, when the franchise was won.

Representing another cause championed by the league, Casgrain appeared before the Dorion Commission in 1929, demanding that the Civil Code of Quebec be changed to remedy the unequal legal status of married women. In 1926, she founded the Young Women's League, a non-denominational organization that encouraged engagement in social causes among young women. Throughout the 1930s, while continuing to lobby for the vote, Casgrain hosted *Fémina*, a radio program for women. In 1937, she publicly sided with striking Montreal garment workers and later went on to publicize the plight of rural schoolmistresses, whose working conditions were particularly appalling.

Thérèse Casgrain played a pivotal role in the battle for women's suffrage. Through her position as vice-president of the National Federation of Liberal Women of Canada and supported by some 40 delegates, she succeeded in having women's suffrage incorporated into the Liberal Party's platform at its 1938 provincial convention. Once elected in 1939, the new provincial Liberal government, led by Adélard Godbout, made good on its platform promises, despite the Catholic Church's protestations.

Casgrain waged a war on two fronts when the lobby to have Family Allowance cheques issued to mothers was launched. She led a campaign on the issue in Quebec while bringing a rain of protest to bear in Ottawa on Canadian Liberal Prime Minister William Lyon Mackenzie King, who ultimately reversed his decision and issued the Family Allowance benefits to mothers instead of fathers in Quebec.

During World War II, Casgrain helped to launch the Wartime Prices and Trade Board, an organization that aimed to stem inflation through price and wage controls, and went on to establish the board's Consumer Branch, which organized rationing across Canada. Driven by the conviction that women should exercise not only their right to vote but also their eligibility to hold public office, she ran in a 1942 by-election as an

continued

independent Liberal candidate for Charlevoix-Saguenay, a riding which both her father and husband had represented. Although defeated, she remained undaunted; during the 1940s and 1950s Casgrain stood as a candidate in nine elections, both federal and provincial, without ever being elected. As of 1946, she ran as a candidate under the banner of the Co-operative Commonwealth Federation (CCF), a social democratic party founded in the 1930s, which she felt was more deeply committed to pursuing the common good than were the conventional parties. In 1948 she became a CCF vice-president and in 1951 she became the leader of the party's Quebec wing, making her the first Canadian woman to hold such a position.

In the early 1960s, Casgrain helped found the Civil Liberties Union, over which she presided for a number of years. As the founder of the Quebec chapter of the Voice of Women (1961), a women's organization that works for world peace, she took part in many international conferences. Her peace activism even led to her arrest and detention for several hours during a demonstration against nuclear arms held in front of the NATO offices in Paris in 1964. The following year, to celebrate the twenty-fifth anniversary of women's suffrage legislation in Quebec, she initiated the organization of a two-day conference entitled "La femme du Québec : hier et aujourd'hui." The conference was the catalyst for the foundation of the Fédération des femmes du Québec, an umbrella organization that comprised some 30 groups from the francophone and anglophone communities at its inception. In 1970, Casgrain was appointed to the Canadian Senate by the Liberal government of Pierre Elliott Trudeau, nine months before her seventy-fifth birthday—the mandatory age of retirement for a senator. To a journalist who questioned her ability to achieve very much in the Senate in the little time she would serve, she apparently replied, "Young man, you might be surprised to learn what a woman can do in nine months!"[8]

Casgrain's spirited candour was an integral part of her personality: "I was always picking fights with everyone. I suppose that's what kept me in form," she wrote in her autobiography. Indeed, even after retiring from the Senate she continued to advocate for the rights of consumers (a cause she had supported as president of the Quebec branch of the Consumers' Association of Canada in 1969) and she lobbied for the abolition of mandatory retirement. In 1970 she publicly endorsed the application of the War Measures Act during the October Crisis, and in 1980 she backed the "No" camp in the referendum on sovereignty, stances which some Quebecers had difficulty forgiving.

Throughout the twentieth century, Casgrain took on many a battle, not only for women but also for the underprivileged, for human rights, and for world peace. Defining herself as a humanist, she actively fought against all forms of injustice, receiving scores of honours for her work. The contribution she made to the advancement of women and social causes likely makes her one of the most famous and highly respected feminists of her time. "A woman in a man's world," she was committed and tenacious to the very end.

From 1940 to 2000: A "Quiet Revolution" for Quebec Women

Mothers and Workers

Although 1960–70 is the decade generally associated with deep structural transformations and the state takeover of strategic sectors (like education and health) in Quebec, many sociocultural changes occurred as early as World War II. The labour shortfall during the war ushered in an era that was radically different from the Depression, as married women were called upon to join the workforce to support the war effort. This federal appeal to women angered

Primary Source

"Idola Saint-Jean Argues for the Franchise in Quebec"

Extract of a 1931 Radio Address

Ladies, Gentlemen,

Tomorrow the Legislature will for the fifth time receive a bill demanding suffrage for the women of this province. A just and legitimate demand which, if it is finally realized, will put the women of Quebec on equal footing with their sisters in the other eight provinces of Canada.

The women of Quebec were the first on the scene and as one looks back to the early pages of our history, we find them working with ardour at the admirable work of colonization.

In all aspects of social life, they have been the valiant companions of men, always at work, giving the best of themselves to build a country destined to play a great role in the history of the world.

Let our legislators, when they are called tomorrow to vote yes or no on whether we will be admitted to full participation in our political life, remember that, in 1705, the first cloth manufactory in Canada was founded by a woman, Madam de Repentigny; let them recall the work of Marie Rollet, the great mistress of our Canadian farmers, who brought to our country the first plough. Then there was Jeanne Mance who set herself up as the municipal treasurer of Ville-Marie and found the necessary money to bring in a regiment charged with the defence of the colonists against the devastating attacks of the Iroquois. The founders of the first hospitals, the founders of the first schools, were they not, these women, whom we have the honour of calling our ancestors, the equivalent of Ministers of Commerce, Ministers of Education, and I dare say, Ministers of Finance, filling these offices, in such a way, thanks to their organizational and economizing skills, as to even give pointers to a large number of men?

. . .

We women have not lost our abilities, it seems to me, ladies and gentlemen, one finds us today in all the areas of charity and work. Economic conditions throw us into industry, into commerce, into education, in a word into all spheres of activity. As we have to work to live, then, why are we condemned to occupy only the subordinate positions? Why not allow us access to the professions and also the parliaments which make the laws that affect the woman as much as the man? Why, I ask you, Gentlemen, should we not bring to bear our qualities as teachers when a law concerning our schools is being discussed? Why should mothers not have the right to vote when the House studies a law concerning the welfare of the child, of the family, etc.? Are those not the problems that a woman will always understand better than a man?

Think about all these women, Gentlemen, and let your vote tomorrow be liberating. In the interests of all of us rather than of all men, generously open the door of the political and professional arena to women who will learn to stay in public life, as they are in private life, the descendants of the Jeanne Mances, the Marguerite Bourgeoises, the Madeleine des Verchères and all the others who contributed to the development of our country. Since all the professional women and the legion of women who work are unanimous in reclaiming their political rights and their right to unrestricted work, do not take responsibility any longer, Gentlemen, for keeping them on the sidelines of the political and professional life of their province that they love and the welfare of which they want to serve.

Source: Beth Light and Ruth Roach Pierson, eds., *No Easy Road: Women in Canada, 1920s to 1960s* (Toronto: Hogtown Press, 1990), 365–6.

traditional nationalists, who were convinced it would jeopardize the very existence of the family and believed society's morals were being eroded by married women who were deserting hearth and home. In truth, Quebec nationalists and the federal authorities were equally committed to the traditional provider–homemaker family model. The federal government saw the presence of married women in factories as a strictly temporary measure and expected that gender roles would return to "normal" once the war was over. Indeed, many women did lose their jobs when munitions factories closed after the war, but their return to the home front proved to be just as temporary. By the late 1940s, more and more mothers were returning to work after they had raised their families. As the trend continued in the following decades, the percentage of employed married women soared from 17 per cent in 1951, to nearly 49 per cent in 1971, and shot up again to 62 per cent in 1981.[9] By the 1970s, even mothers of young children were working outside of the home—as 80 per cent of them do in Quebec today.

Also during World War II, the federal Family Allowance program began. Introduced in 1945, the program was designed to boost postwar consumer spending and coax married women back to full-time homemaking. But when Family Allowance cheques were issued to mothers rather than to the male "head" of the household, Quebec nationalists protested; they viewed the program as a sacrilegious attack on the principle of paternal power, as established in the Civil Code of Quebec. Swayed by political pressure from the nationalists, the federal government agreed to make an exception for Quebec and pay the benefits to fathers. But this time, the nationalists would not carry the day. Thérèse Casgrain led a coalition of women's groups and unions that successfully argued that an article of the Civil Code gave married women a tacit mandate to manage the everyday affairs of the family, and that paying Family Allowance benefits to mothers was consistent with this mandate.

Fewer Children, Fewer Parishioners

As in the rest of North America, postwar Quebec experienced a **baby boom**, but it did not see higher fertility rates; more couples got married at this time, and thus more children were born during this period, with the average number of children per family remaining at approximately four between 1946 and 1960. From the beginning of the 1960s, fertility rates continued to drop sharply and, by 1966, Quebec women had the lowest fertility rates in Canada, a statistical distinction they have maintained ever since.[10] Until the contraceptive pill was introduced, most Catholic couples in Quebec relied on the Knaus-Ogino Rhythm Method, widely taught in marriage preparation courses organized by the Jeunesse ouvrière catholique féminine (JOCF), or on the Sympto-Thermal Method taught by the Service de régulation des naissances (Seréna), an organization founded in 1955 by a couple seeking to reconcile Church precepts with a humanist perspective on reproduction. Since these two groups were offshoots of the Catholic Church, the Church was indirectly contributing to lowering fertility rates, although it also expressed many reservations about the wide dissemination of these methods. The pill was strictly prohibited by the papal encyclical *Humanae vitae* in 1968, but this prohibition went unheeded and, by the end of the 1960s, the pill had become Quebec's most popular means of contraception.

Significantly destabilized by the shock of postwar sociocultural changes (and particularly by the rise of consumerism), the Church's authoritarianism met with more and more overt challenges. Its ascetic, moralistic position on reproduction accelerated the spiritual defections that had been taking place since the 1950s. The downturn in religious fervour was evident in waning attendance at Sunday mass and in women's declining interest in joining religious communities. In fact, although the absolute numbers of nuns continued to increase until the mid-1960s, from the 1940s onward their growth rate declined relative to that of laywomen. In the latter half of the 1960s, membership in women's religious communities dropped by 14 per cent, owing to numerous departures.

Workers and Feminists

While the decline in the numbers of nuns and parishioners was another manifestation of the

Church's unpopularity, it also reflected the new opportunities available to women in civil society at a time when big capital and the state were clamouring more loudly than ever for an abundant female workforce. After World War II, Quebec's economic development required more women to fill positions in the service sector and to do office work. The creation of a host of social programs caused both the provincial and especially the federal public service sectors to grow at an unprecedented rate, attracting an ever-increasing proportion of women workers. Moreover, during the 1960s the government of Quebec became much more interventionist, amplifying trends from previous decades and effectively eliminating some vocations. From state intervention in the economy and culture to state-run health care, social welfare, and education, the "social project" of the Quiet Revolution (fuelled by a new nationalism that had been gestating for a decade or more) took over several sectors that previously had been the purview of the Church. Under the welfare state, French Canadians began to redefine themselves as a secular Québécois nation. Looking back, Quebecers began to regard the charity-driven religious management of the Church's institutions as the amateur bunglings of a bygone era in which the state had recused itself of its putative social responsibilities. Government intervention, by contrast, seemed to bear the hallmark of competency and expanded social justice. The Quebec government changed the rules of the game accordingly, placing health care and schools under the authority of male administrators, while laywomen gradually replaced religious staff, whose numbers were dwindling dramatically.

The increased presence of laywomen in service-related jobs, facilitated by greater access to schools and universities for girls and single, young women, fostered a feminist consciousness that would come into its own in the latter half of the 1960s. During the 1960s, as the secular nationalism of the Quiet Revolution emerged, a new kind of women's movement also clearly entered the public arena. After they had won the vote in 1940, women's social and political activism certainly did not disappear, as evidenced by the dynamic family movements they led, the consumer advocacy and anti-nuclear groups they founded, and the unions that a few women labour organizers fought to establish. Nearing the end of the 1950s (as Miriam Chapin observed), Quebec women had set the scene for yet another radical departure. In the 1960s many new feminist organizations were created with the primary goal of denouncing sexist oppression and discrimination and promoting women's independence in all aspects of social, economic, and political life. As feminists struggled for greater sexual freedom during this period, the decriminalization of abortion became their predominant demand.

The fight for abortion rights figured prominently in Quebec throughout the 1970s, but was not championed by all feminists and their organizations because opinions were divided. Two organizations that represented the reformist fringe of the new feminist movement (both founded in 1966) did not take up the cause immediately: the Fédération des femmes du Québec (FFQ) and the Association féminine d'éducation et d'action sociale (AFÉAS). The FFQ was an umbrella organization that brought together anglophones and francophones, and its activities typically focused on lobbying for legislation to guarantee equality between men and women in all areas. The AFÉAS, whose membership mainly consisted of rural women, concentrated its efforts on social and political activism and training for women. Neither group questioned liberal capitalist society nor believed that patriarchy perpetuated sexist discrimination and subordination. At the opposite end of the political spectrum, the Montreal Women's Liberation Movement (1968), the Front de libération des femmes du Québec (FLF, 1969), Centre des femmes (1972), and a myriad of smaller feminist groups that emerged in the early 1970s believed that patriarchy was the root cause of women's oppression and that women's liberation hinged on the eradication of men's control over women's bodies—meaning their maternity and their sexuality.[11] These groups and their members would go on to lead the struggle for decriminalized, free, and accessible abortion in the years to come.

Feminists set their sights on a wide range of other major issues during the 1970s, including ending physical and sexual violence against women and systemic discrimination against women in the workplace, establishing daycare and parental leave, the recognition of women's work within the family, and the equality of spouses in marriage.[12] Some feminist analyses partly attributed the advances made in these areas to the institutionalization of feminism that occurred with the birth of the Conseil du statut de la femme du Québec (CSF), created by the government of Quebec in 1973 as an advisory body on the status of women. With this institutionalization came the fear that feminism would be politically co-opted. At the same time, as grassroots feminist organizers were obtaining government funding to establish a growing multitude of women's groups and shelters, a number of feminists said that these social responsibilities, which should have been shouldered by all of society, had been unloaded onto the backs of "feminist cheap labour."[13] This kind of statement clearly shows the complexity of the dialogue between feminists and the state. Later, feminists would see that more women delegates in political parties, women members of legislatures, or even women ministers did not always facilitate this dialogue, as those who declared themselves feminists were frequently torn between personal convictions and party allegiances.[14]

The relationships that have developed between feminism and nationalism over the past decades in Quebec have proved to be just as complex. Broadly speaking, many francophone feminist activists have been drawn to the promise of the nationalist movement, seeing in its promotion of a more assertive, modern Quebec a reflection of their own hoped-for emancipation. The new Quebec nationalist movement certainly had everything to gain by winning over feminists (a growing social force) and in fact showed a degree of openness toward them.[15] But at times, the notion of a woman's place and role espoused by the nationalist social project was at odds with the feminist vision and caused considerable tensions between the two groups. Frequently during the 1980s and 1990s, spokespeople for the Parti Québécois (the province's main sovereignist party) and nationalist conservatives alike voiced their concern that Quebec francophones were a shrinking minority within Canada and North America, denouncing the low fertility rates in Quebec, and proposing natalist policies, some of which even aimed to get women back into the home. During the 1995 referendum campaign, Quebec Premier Lucien Bouchard himself publicly expressed his dismay that "white women" in Quebec were not producing enough children.

While contemporary nationalists can no longer use the moral authority of the Catholic Church to force women to have larger families, they nonetheless continue to be deeply concerned about the issue of reproducing the "race." While nationalist feminists have railed against the nationalist–natalist discourse, some of their own nationalist positions have created new rifts within feminist ranks and been roundly condemned by minority women's organizations.[16] Since the 1980s, the ethnocultural reconfiguration of the population and the dismantling of the welfare state have presented major challenges for Quebec feminists. How can the movement sustain itself in the absence of an interventionist government? How will it bring all Quebec women together? Nationalists are asking themselves similar questions. Recently, spokespersons from both nationalist and feminist movements declared that equality between men and women was one of the most "fundamental values" in Quebec. Will this unifying idea bring the two movements closer together? The answer may lie in the context that elicited their declarations—a highly publicized provincial consultation commission, known as the Bouchard–Taylor Commission, that was followed by a hot debate about the adoption of a Charter of Quebec Values.

The hearings of the consultation commission (2007–8), created to clarify Quebecers' views on the government's cultural policies, showed that some nationalists and feminists harboured deep-seated apprehensions about the potential for religious fanaticism and sexist oppression among new Quebecers. Similar views were held in 2013–14 by representatives of both groups while the minority government of the Parti Québécois, led by Pauline Marois, the first female premier in Quebec history, proposed the adoption of a Charter of Quebec

Values to enforce equality between men and women and, to this effect, ban the wearing of any "ostentatious" religious clothing or symbols, like a hijab, by government employees. Because the Quebec Liberal Party won the election in April 2014 the charter was never adopted, but the controversy it provoked (the Fédération des femmes du Québec, it must be said, having strongly denounced the project) demonstrates that the whole matter remains a thorny issue. After years of struggle against Church and patriarchy, devout religion and gender-specific traditions are seen by many in Quebec as inherently oppressive anachronisms that continue to haunt their collective memory. Therefore, taken in context, when feminists and nationalists agree on Quebec's "fundamental values" it does not so much indicate a newfound unity but more likely a shared malaise about the new cultural and social landscape both must face in the future. Today, as before, feminists and nationalists will have to grapple with issues that are as likely to unite them as they are to tear them apart.

CASE STUDY

The Yvette Affair

The Yvette affair provoked a flood of commentary from the moment it began during the campaign for the 1980 Quebec referendum on sovereignty. Portrayed by the media either as a backlash against feminists or as a federalist strategy to secure the victory of the "No" camp, it was one of the most remarkable events of the campaign—a genuine turning point, according to many observers. The quantity of ink that flowed in the press over the Yvette affair at the time, and the number of occasions on which it has been revisited for some 30 years now, clearly show that issues about the status of women are eminently political. The Yvette affair also shows how women's issues can be exploited for a wide variety of partisan purposes.

On 6 March 1980, Lise Payette, then minister responsible for the status of women in the Parti Québécois government of René Lévesque, called a press conference to report on the progress of women's issues under her government. During the press conference, the minister read an excerpt from a story in an elementary schoolbook. The story depicted a sweet, docile, and dutiful little girl named Yvette, who was always keen to help her mother. Yvette's brother, Guy, on the other hand, was an ambitious, daring young boy who played a variety of sports. The minister concluded by announcing, "I am here to tell you that the days of Yvette are over!" By this, she meant that the days of being docile and submissive were over for Quebec women, who were on the road to equality. A few days later, at a rally for the "Yes" camp (in favour of Quebec sovereignty), she asserted that women and anglophones were the two groups most resistant to Quebec sovereignty. To drive home her point—that women's fears about Quebec's future were based in their conditioning as subordinates—she reread the passage about Yvette and her brother and then said, "Let us have the courage to leave our prisons of fear behind." For Payette, the feminist and nationalist causes had become one, and women had to emancipate themselves both as women and as Quebecers. Later, responding to a question from the audience, she quipped that Claude Ryan, the leader of the Liberal Party and head of the "No" camp, was very fond of "Yvettes," since they were opposed to sovereignty, adding that Ryan was married to an "Yvette."

continued

Payette had just committed a monumental political gaffe, particularly since Madeleine Ryan, who was indeed a housewife, was also deeply committed to a number of social causes. Naturally, the newspapers had a field day: In *Le Devoir*, editor Lise Bissonnette berated Payette, contending that the minister's words were an attack on all housewives.

But the Yvette affair did not end there. Toward the end of March, at a brunch in Quebec City for the female members of the Liberal Party, participants wore buttons marked "Yvette," clearly embracing the moniker that Lise Payette had considered to be an insult. Some journalists noted that Payette's blunder had revitalized the federalist "No" camp, which had been somewhat apathetic and lacklustre up until that point, and had given it ammunition that it very ably exploited.

Journalists continued to run stories about the federalists using the Yvette affair as a campaign strategy to win over a segment of voters (especially women). At the beginning of April the affair took another turn, as over 14,000 women attended a rally held at the Montreal Forum. In the media, particularly in *Le Devoir*, the rally was depicted not as a political event orchestrated by the "No" camp against sovereignty, but rather as an impromptu gathering of "everyday" women, housewives who felt targeted by Minister Payette's words and were showing how fed up they had become with feminists. Above all, contended Lise Bissonnette, the event's social significance lay in the fact that "thousands of women . . . did not identify with the discourse of 'liberation,' and even felt slighted and ridiculed by the [feminist] movement, which was telling them their everyday lives were a dreary monotony from which they had to either escape at all costs—or amount to nothing."[17] Bissonnette believed that these women had flocked to the Forum not to hear "No" camp speeches, but rather to express their discontent with feminists. She went on to rebuke the Liberal Party and the "No" camp for exploiting the anti-feminist backlash and manipulating women by inviting one and all to attend a mass event at the Forum that night.

The fact that, like Bissonnette, many journalists emphasized the anti-feminist angle of this story is most certainly symptomatic of the exasperation and anxiety that 10 years of feminist demands had elicited in some segments of Quebec—and among some members of the media. In the Yvette affair, the "national question" was once again inextricably linked to women's issues, creating activist amalgams—feminist sovereignists; anti-feminist federalists—which surely ran contrary to the convictions of some female Liberal leaders, who were every bit as feminist as Minister Lise Payette but served the "No" camp very well. Indeed, Payette's gaffe has often been cited as a major reason that the bid for Quebec sovereignty was lost in the 20 May 1980 referendum. With the help of massive media coverage, her few words put wind in the sails of the Liberal "No" camp and turned the tide against a very strong "Yes" camp that had seemed bound to sail on to victory.

Questions for Critical Thinking

1. Why were there many nuns in Quebec during the first half of the twentieth century, and what was their impact on laywomen's involvement in social causes and feminism?
2. How did the "national question" in Quebec influence the paths feminists took in the twentieth century?
3. How is the road travelled by French-Canadian women similar to and different from that travelled by other North American women?

Notes

1. Miriam Chapin, *Quebec Now* (Toronto: Ryerson Press, 1955), 96.
2. Mélissa Blais and Francis Dupuis-Déri, eds., *Le mouvement masculiniste au Québec* (Montreal: Les Éditions du remue-ménage, 2008).
3. Marie Lavigne and Jennifer Stoddart, "Ouvrières et travailleuses montréalaises,1900–1940," in *Les femmes dans la société québécoise*, ed. Marie Lavigne and Yolande Pinard (Montreal: Boréal Express, 1977), 111.
4. In Quebec, the expression "Revenge of the Cradle" conveyed the conviction that only a high fertility rate had allowed French Canadians to survive as a people, despite the British Conquest and the massive arrival of immigrants from England that began in the nineteenth century.
5. In Henri Bourassa's words, "la sainte et féconde maternité," in his editorial "Le suffrage féminin," *Le Devoir*, 30 March 1918, 1.
6. Boys were taken care of separately by male religious communities.
7. Given that at this point in history federal law did not extend Canadian citizenship to persons of Asian descent and that Aboriginal people were treated as perpetual minors under the Indian Act, women and men in these groups, as well as incarcerated individuals, had to wait longer to obtain this right.
8. Quoted in the "Biographie" page of the Fondation Thérèse F. Casgrain website, www.fondationtheresecasgrain.org/bio.html, author's translation.
9. Francine Barry, *Le travail de la femme au Québec : l'évolution de 1940 à 1970* (Montreal: PUQ, 1977), 20; The Clio Collective, *Quebec Women: A History* (Toronto: Canadian Scholars Press, 1990), 482.
10. Since the early 1980s, the synthetic fertility index has remained between 1.4 and 1.6. Michel Venne, ed., *L'annuaire du Québec 2004* (Montreal: Fides, 2003), 148.
11. Louise Toupin, "Les courants de pensée féministe," *Version revue du texte Qu'est-ce que le féminisme? Trousse d'information sur le féminisme québécois des 25 dernières années*, 1997, accessed 21 October 2008, http://netfemmes.cdeacf.ca/documents/courants0.html.
12. Bill 16, passed in 1964 on the initiative of Marie-Claire Kirkland-Casgrain (the first woman MLA), had already abolished the legal incapacity of married women but fell short of ensuring full equality between spouses within the family.
13. See Chapter 20 in this volume.
14. Marie-Claire Kirkland-Casgrain was elected in 1961 in a by-election, becoming the first female member of the provincial legislature. In the general election of 1976, five women were elected. By 1985 this figure had climbed to 15, and by 2003 it stood at 38—the highest number of women members of the legislature ever elected in Quebec. In the general election of December 2008, 37 women won seats, occupying 30 per cent of the legislature, while in 2012 and 2014, 36 and 34 women were elected, respectively. Marie-Claire Kirkland-Casgrain was also the first woman to head a provincial ministry. It was not until 1981 that two women occupied positions as ministers. Current figures are the highest ever, with 13 women occupying cabinet positions in a cabinet comprising 27 members (almost half of all members). See the National Assembly of Quebec's website, accessed 6 August 2014, www.assnat.qc.ca. It should also be noted that in June 2007, a woman, Pauline Marois, became the leader of the Parti Québécois who won the general election of September 2012. She thus became the first female premier in the history of Quebec, but her minority government did not last: The Quebec Liberal Party won the election in April 2014, while Marois lost her own riding.
15. In the 1960s, radical nationalists could be sexist and even misogynist. Women were perceived by many of the men in these movements as obstacles to the Quebec liberation movement. Moreover, their speeches and writing often referred to "conquering" and "taking" Quebec as a man would a woman—and this included raping her. S. Lanthier, "L'impossible réciprocité des rapports politiques et idéologiques entre le nationalisme radical et le féminisme radical au Québec : 1962–1972" (master's thesis, Université de Sherbrooke, 1998).
16. Women from a variety of minority communities have struggled for a voice in Quebec's mainstream feminist movements. Although it is beyond the scope of this article to retrace the history and name all of the groups that have made major contributions to the advancement of feminism in Quebec, we would like to mention the Quebec Native Women's Association (founded in 1974), the Montreal Regional Committee of the National Congress of Black Women of Canada (1974), the South Asian Women's Centre (1981), Collectif des femmes immigrantes du Québec (1983), Association de défense des droits du personnel domestique de Montréal (1976), and its daughter organization the Centre des femmes d'ici et d'ailleurs (1984).
17. Lise Bisonnette, "L'appel aux femmes," *Le Devoir*, 9 April 1980, 8; author's translation.

Select Bibliography

Auger, Geneviève, and Raymonde Lamothe. *De la poêle à frire à la ligne de feu : la vie quotidienne des québécoises pendant la guerre 39–45.* Montreal: Boréal Express, 1981.

Baillargeon, Denyse. *Babies for the Nation: The Medicalization of Maternity in Quebec, 1910–1970.* Waterloo, ON: Wilfrid Laurier University Press, 2009.

———. *A Brief History of Women in Quebec.* Waterloo, ON: Wilfrid Laurier University Press, 2014.

———. *Making Do: Women, Family and Home in Montreal during the Great Depression.* Waterloo, ON: Wilfrid Laurier University Press, 1999.

Barry, Francine. *Le travail de la femme au Québec : l'évolution de 1940 à 1970.* Montreal: PUQ, 1977.

Boyer, Kate. "Re-Working Respectability: The Feminization of Clerical Work and the Politics of Public Virtue in Early Twentieth-Century Montreal." In *Power, Place and Identity: Historical Studies of Social and Legal Regulation in Quebec,* edited by T. Myers et al., 151–68. Montreal: GHM/MHG, 1998.

Charles, Aline. *Travail d'ombre et de lumière : le bénévolat féminin à l'hôpital Sainte-Justine 1907–1960.* Edmond-de-Nevers Collection no 9. Quebec City: IQRC, 1990.

Clio Collective. *Quebec Women: A History.* Toronto: Canadian Scholars Press, 1990.

Dandurand, Renée. *Le mariage en question : essai socio-historique.* Quebec City: IQRC, 1988

Danylewycz, Marta. *Taking the Veil: An Alternative to Marriage, Motherhood, and Spinsterhood in Quebec, 1840–1920.* Toronto: McClelland & Stewart, 1987.

Dufour, Andrée, and Micheline Dumont. *Brève histoire des institutrices au Québec de la Nouvelle-France à nos jours.* Montreal: Boréal, 2004.

Dumont, Micheline. *Le féminisme québécois raconté à Camille.* Montreal: Les Éditions du remue-ménage, 2008.

———. "The Origins of the Women's Movement in Quebec." In *Challenging Times: The Women's Movement in Canada and the United States,* edited by *Constance* Backhouse and David H. Flaherty, 72–89. Montreal and Kingston: McGill-Queen's University Press, 1992.

———. *Les religieuses sont-elles féministes?* St-Laurent: Bellarmin, 1995.

———, and Nadia Fahmy-Eid. *Les couventines : l'éducation des filles au Québec dans les congrégations religieuses enseignantes, 1840–1960.* Montreal: Boréal, 1986.

———, and Louise Toupin. *La pensée féministe au Québec.* Montreal: Les Éditions du remue-ménage, 2003.

Fahmy-Eid, Nadia, and Micheline Dumont, eds. *Maîtresses de maison, maîtresses d'école : femmes, famille et éducation dans l'histoire du Québec.* Montreal: Boréal Express, 1983.

Fahrni, Magda. *Household Politics: Montreal Families and Postwar Reconstruction.* Toronto: University of Toronto Press, 2005.

Forget, Nicolle. *Thérèse Casgrain : la gauchiste en collier de perles.* Montréal: Fides, 2013.

Gauvreau, Danielle, Peter Gossage, and Diane Gervais. *La fécondité des Québécoises, 1870–1970 : d'une exception à l'autre.* Montreal: Boréal, 2007.

Gauvreau, Michael. "The Emergence of Personalist Feminism: Catholicism and the Marriage Preparation Movement in Quebec." In *Household of Faith: Family, Gender and Community in Canada, 1760–1969,* edited by Nancy Christie, 319–47. Montreal and Kingston: McGill-Queen's University Press, 2002.

Lacelle, Nicole. *Entretiens avec Madeleine Parent et Léa Roback.* Montreal: Les Éditions du remue-ménage, 1988.

Lamoureux, Diane. *Citoyennes? Femmes, droit de vote et démocratie.* Montreal: Les Éditions du remue-ménage, 1989.

———. *Fragments et collage : essai sur le féminisme québécois des années 1970.* Montreal: Les Éditions du remue-ménage, 1986.

———. *L'amère patrie : féminisme et nationalisme dans le Québec contemporain.* Montreal: Les Éditions du remue-ménage, 2001.

Lamoureux, Jocelyne, Michèle Gélinas, and Katy Tari. *Femmes en mouvement : trajectoires de l'Association féminine d'éducation et d'action sociale, AFÉAS, 1966–1991.* Montreal: Boréal, 1993.

Laurin, Nicole, Danielle Juteau, and Lorraine Duchêsne. *À la recherche d'un monde oublié : les communautés religieuses de femmes au Québec de 1900 à 1970.* Montreal: Le Jour éditeur, 1991.

Lavigne, Marie, and Yolande Pinard, eds. *Travailleuses et feminists : les femmes dans la société québécoise.* Montreal: Boréal, 1983.

Lévesque, Andrée. *Making and Breaking the Rules: Women in Quebec, 1919–1939.* Toronto: McClelland & Stewart, 1994.

———, ed. *Madeleine Parent, Activist.* Toronto: Sumach Press, 2005.

Malouin, Marie-Paule. *Le mouvement familial au Québec : les débuts : 1937–1965.* Montreal: Boréal, 1998.

Marshall, Dominique. *The Social Origins of the Welfare State: Quebec Families, Compulsory Education, and Family Allowances, 1940–1955.* Translated by Nicola Doone Danby. Waterloo, ON: Wilfrid Laurier University Press, 2006.

Myers, Tamara. *Caught: Montreal's Modern Girls and the Law, 1869–1945.* Toronto: University of Toronto Press, 2006.

Piché, Lucie. *Femmes et changement social au Québec : l'apport de la Jeunesse ouvrière catholique féminine 1931–1966.* Québec: Presses de l'Université Laval, 2003.

Sineau, Mariette, and Évelyne Tardy. *Droits des femmes en France et au Québec, 1940–1990.* Montreal: Les Éditions du remue-ménage, 1993.

Tardy, Évelyne, and André Bernard. *Militer au féminin dans la Fédération des femmes du Québec et dans ses groupes affiliés*. Montreal: Les Éditions du remue-ménage, 1995.

Tardy, Évelyne, Manon Tremblay, and Ginette Legault. *Maires et mairesses : les femmes et la politique municipale.* Montreal: Liber, 1997.

Tremblay, Manon. *Québécoises et représentation parlementaire.* Sainte-Foy: Presses de l'Université Laval, 2005.

———. "Quebec Women in Politics: A Reappraisal." In *Rethinking Canada: The Promise of Women's History*, edited by Veronica Strong-Boag, Mona Gleason, and Adele Perry, 377–93. Don Mills, ON: Oxford University Press, 2002.

15 Between Unity and Diversity: Examining the "Quebec Model" of Integration

Raffaele Iacovino, Carleton University

Timeline

1968 Quebec's Union Nationale government creates the Ministry of Immigration. A Quebec Immigration Service had been housed in the Ministry of Cultural Affairs since 1965.

1971 Lang-Cloutier Agreement, the first federal-provincial agreement on immigration, allows representatives of Quebec to work in Canadian embassies and to advise Canadian immigration officers stationed abroad about Quebec's unique social conditions.

1973 Andras-Bienvenue Agreement slightly expands the role of Quebec agents abroad, allowing them to direct interviews with immigration candidates. Agents would be more active in the selection process and in making recommendations to visa officers.

1975 Quebec enacts a statutory Bill of Rights entitled Charter of Human Rights and Freedoms, which takes precedence over all provincial legislation. While most bills of rights in North America cover civil and political rights, the Quebec Charter is unique in that it offers some important social and economic protections.

1977 Quebec enacts the Charter of the French Language, also known as Bill 101. In its preamble, it resolves "to make of French the language of Government and the Law, as well as the normal and everyday language of work, instruction, communication, commerce and business."

1978 The Cullen-Couture Agreement (the Quebec-Canada Accord in Matters of Immigration and Selection of Foreigners) grants Quebec a greater role in selecting immigrants. Quebec could select desirable candidates from its own network of offices abroad, and could control temporary worker and student immigration. Federal government retained control over borders and admitting and selecting refugee claimants. Quebec had to still abide by the categories of immigrants defined by federal legislation—independent immigrants, family-class immigrants, and individuals in distress.

1981 Parti Québécois government of René Lévesque releases first major policy statement on Quebec's approach to integration, entitled *Autant de façons d'être Québécois : Plan d'action à l'intention des communautés culturelles*, developing and building on the idea of "cultural convergence" as compromise between cultural pluralism and protection of the French language and culture in Quebec.

1990 Quebec Liberal Party of Robert Bourassa releases the most comprehensive policy guide on immigrant integration to date, entitled *Au Quebec pour bâtir ensemble : Énoncé de politique en matière d'immigration et d'intégration*. Most closely associated with the model of interculturalism, the policy statement introduced two key concepts—"moral contract" and "common public culture"—in shifting toward a more culturally pluralist approach.

1991 Gagnon-Tremblay–McDougall Accord (Canada-Quebec Accord Relating to Immigration and Temporary Admission of Aliens). This accord is the most recent and remains in force. Quebec received exclusive responsibility in three areas of permanent immigration: total volume for its territory; selection of candidates that seek settlement in Quebec (except for refugee and family reunification claimants); and management and follow-up of sponsorship arrangements and their duration, according to criteria established by federal legislation.

2000 Le forum national sur la citoyenneté et l'intégration, an attempt to explore questions around citizenship and diversity in Quebec, launched by Parti Québécois. It was heavily criticized for what was perceived to be foregone conclusions in the consultation document. It left very little trace of integration discourse in Quebec, other than the idea of internal citizenship for Quebec to facilitate its integration efforts.

2001 Estates General on the Situation and Future of the French Language in Quebec (Larose Commission) recommends the establishment of formal internal citizenship for Quebec to clearly indicate that it is a society with distinct social needs centred on the primacy of the French language.

2004 *Des valeurs partagées, des intérêts communs*, the latest policy blueprint, is released by Quebec Liberal Party government of Jean Charest. It returns to principles established in the 1990 document. It comments on the new importance of security interests and adds more specific anti-discrimination measures.

2008 Commission de Consultation sur les pratiques d'accommodement reliées aux différences culturelles (Bouchard–Taylor Commission) is established to study the legal practice of reasonable accommodation in Quebec. The commission widened its mandate to examine cultural diversity. Among its conclusions, the commission recommended more formal definition of interculturalism by the state, and generally advocated a return to synthesis and reciprocity to regulate cultural interactions.

Introduction: Diversity and Cultural Pluralism

Diversity

Like most contemporary societies, Quebec must reconcile its past with its future to form an identity that will define public life and anchor its integration policies. Francophone Quebecers have a minority collective identity in Canada as a whole, but a majority in Quebec, which includes a bounded territory, democratic institutions, its own internal diversity claims, and policy levers that qualify it as a host society. Quebec is at once responsible for the flourishing of its uniqueness, which draws upon its French-Canadian heritage, while debating the limits and possibilities of various other cultural influences and accepting cultural pluralism in defining the terms of belonging. Quebec is thus both an *object* of diversity management while making accommodation claims as a national minority, and also a site of diversity, a *host society* that is responsible for managing sociocultural difference. This is the sociopolitical context for managing diversity in Quebec.

Although immigration is a shared jurisdiction in Canada, Quebec has negotiated a comprehensive bilateral arrangement with the federal government that allows for much discretion in selecting and integrating immigrants. Quebec thus frames the norms of collective life through a set of policies meant to integrate newcomers and bolster democratic participation. However, in attempting to carve out a "citizenship space" in the larger Canadian context,

Quebec has not left to chance the protection and flourishing of its francophone collective identity; certain collective goals cannot coexist with an unqualified commitment to **cultural pluralism** on one end, and a neutral, civic, or universal conception of liberal citizenship on the other.[1] The limits and constraints of such an environment have led to a model called *interculturalism*, which is distinct from the Canadian policy of multiculturalism.

The concept of diversity requires further clarification. As Daniel Weinstock[2] has highlighted, contemporary liberal societies must first address *axiological pluralism,* which consists of the diversity inherent in a free and democratic society, the result of the multitude of differences produced by the freedoms of association, thought, and expression—essentially, identities that emerge out of life choices. Second, *cultural pluralism* refers to groups that seek recognition by the larger society on the basis of their cultural, linguistic, ethnic, religious, or national differences. While axiological pluralism explores the extent to which the state may justifiably intervene in shaping these life-affirming choices, a commitment to cultural pluralism involves finding a balance between the identity-based claims of groups, the terms of integration with the wider political community, and bases of social cohesion. The latter manifestation of diversity is explored here.

More specifically, the focus is on an even smaller slice of this complex tapestry in looking at Quebec's response to *ethnocultural diversity.* Indeed, cultural differences are not the only manifestation of politically salient diversity in Quebec. National minorities such as Aboriginal peoples or the anglophone minority in Quebec enjoy some recognition by the state as historical collectives rather than as the result of recent immigration.[3] Moreover, other forms of pluralism in which groups make accommodation demands on the larger society include identities of gender, sexual orientation, urban versus rural lifestyle, class, and so on.

Quebec is a particularly interesting case because it has charged itself with these questions as a substate national minority. It has devised its own model of interculturalism as an alternative approach to Canadian multiculturalism and the traditional American melting pot. As such, it is a case worthy of assessment on its own terms, particularly since it has acquired many of the powers for recruiting, selecting, and integrating immigrants; has committed significant resources to a wide network of immigration offices abroad; and has consistently shown a desire to craft its own boundaries of belonging to Quebec society.

Citizenship and Cultural Pluralism

Responses to diversity range from outright **cultural assimilation** to the complete exclusion of culture from the public sphere; most liberal democracies have attempted to strike a balance between unity and recognizing difference and have dismissed cultural assimilation as morally excessive, seeking to rethink the terms of integration for minority cultures with two broad objectives. First, they foster and promote cultural diversity as important in itself, drawing upon both the norms of tolerance and the benefits of intercultural exchange as the basis for social cohesion. Second, members of minority cultural groups are deemed more likely to integrate effectively if they can be recognized by the larger community without a wholesale shedding of their particular identities. A commitment to equal conditions of membership requires some acknowledgement that such groups need to maintain the integrity of their cultural attachments, since imposing a majority culture would require a much more difficult transition. The basic thrust here is to avoid the shock of cultural distance and the possibility of such groups closing themselves off to the wider society. As such, public institutions ought to recognize this fact and not be heavily slanted toward sustaining the collective integrity of the majority culture at the expense of minority contributions, as a matter of equality.[4]

A commitment to cultural pluralism implies that citizenship—the rights, responsibilities, terms of membership, and nature of entitlements, as well as expectations of democratic participation—should not simply recognize people as undifferentiated individuals, where culture is merely a private concern and not a matter for state intervention. As illustrated below, the spectrum of policy options for integration in Quebec have generally fallen within these parameters since the **Quiet Revolution**. A commitment to cultural pluralism has ranged from moderate to more robust versions, determined by the need to maintain the integrity of the minority nation in the face of evolving challenges. Prior to exploring these debates, the following section will provide a brief overview of immigration and integration in Quebec.

Ethnocultural Diversity and Quebec

Following World War II, an increase of immigrants from Southern and Eastern Europe prompted Quebec to think about how their francophone culture could survive and flourish in North America.[5] As the birth rate declined among francophones, most immigrants adopted English,[6] threatening the demographic weight of francophones in both Quebec and Canada. This renewed interest in the social and political consequences of immigration coincided with the onset of a more positive and open attitude toward the role and contributions of cultural minorities in Quebec.

Several events precipitated this shift in thinking. First, the horrors of World War II caused the Catholic hierarchy in Rome, and subsequently the clergy in Quebec, to re-evaluate its social doctrine on relations between ethnoreligious groups. Second, French-Canadian nationalists began to view new arrivals as potential allies in developing an identity that would willingly disengage from the British Empire. Third, more liberal thinkers associated with the Quebec Liberal Party began to explore and develop ideas about the economic benefits of immigration.[7] Moreover, new international human rights standards, coupled with Quebec's specific demographic, economic, and identity-related concerns, fostered growing interest in immigration policy.

Quebec gradually accepted that it required policy instruments appropriate to its status as a French-speaking host society, and it could no longer leave these matters to Ottawa. In 1968, a Ministry of Immigration was created,[8] and between the 1970s and the 1990s the Quebec state secured increasing powers of selection and integration in a series of bilateral agreements with the federal government.

In 1991, the two parties signed the Canada–Quebec Accord Relating to Immigration and Temporary Admission of Aliens (Gagnon-Tremblay–McDougall Accord), the most comprehensive agreement to date. The accord stipulates that the federal government is responsible for annual volume to Canada, criteria of residency, categories of immigrants, criteria for family sponsorship and assisted relative cases, and asylum claims. Quebec has exclusive responsibility in three domains relative to permanent immigration:

- Total volume for its territory
- The selection of candidates that seek settlement in Quebec (except refugee and family reunification claimants)
- The management and follow-up of sponsorship arrangements and their duration, according to the criteria established by federal legislation

In terms of temporary immigration, Canada must receive Quebec's consent in issuing work permits, issuing student permits and admitting international students (except those participating in a Canadian assistance program with developing states), and the authorization for a visitor to Quebec to receive medical treatment. In short, while Canada sets the broad guidelines, including selection criteria, Quebec enjoys much latitude in how it chooses to meet its own needs, including altering the relative weight of priorities.[9] Moreover, Quebec immigration officials review files of applicants, interview them, and ultimately grant approval for entrance, clearly demonstrating that it is the Government of Quebec that admits applicants, not the Government of Canada, to help alleviate potential confusion among immigrants about the society into which they are expected to integrate.

Immigration is intimately linked with controlling and developing the boundaries of identity in any democratic political community; thus the state expects to be able to develop and enact what Michael Sandel has termed "formative projects"[10] without the added burden of having to constantly justify them within a larger political association. Quebec has largely achieved this, although without formal constitutional recognition as a host society. The Canadian Constitution recognizes Quebec as a province equal in status to the others, and the Canadian Charter of Rights and Freedoms is meant to apply from coast to coast. Canada is officially a multicultural country within a framework of bilingualism. Belonging in Canada is thus formally defined through the choice of language (French or English) and the capacity to maintain one's particular cultural attachments. The idea of a different set of rights and responsibilities for citizens of Quebec, therefore, is developing outside of the formal structures of Canadian citizenship. There is no recognition of Quebec as a distinct host society, or a provision acknowledging its particular model of integration. The next section looks more closely at the extent to which Quebec, notwithstanding its greater institutional leverage, still faces distinct challenges in the Canadian context.

Immigration and Political Community in Quebec

Assessing the immigration and integration policies of particular societies serves somewhat as a lens into the priorities, principles, and norms in its framing of citizenship—the bases of belonging and the obligations expected of its members. In a minority nation such as Quebec, where immigration is a shared jurisdiction, control over these policies carries a dual purpose.

First, immigration addresses various social and economic needs; thus it is a function common to most advanced capitalist political economies. Second, control over selecting and integrating immigrants reflects a desire, unique to minority nations, for a measure of self-determination, or more minimally, autonomy, so that it may maintain and develop its society for future generations according to its collective needs. Joseph Carens states this feature of immigration succinctly:

> The degree of openness to immigrants, the criteria of selection and exclusion, the kinds of adaptation, and the degree of conformity to the dominant population expected of new arrivals and their descendants—all these factors indicate something about who belongs, what is valued, and what membership and citizenship mean.[11]

Indeed, Quebec has always seen itself as a constituted political community, a "societal culture"[12] within Canadian federalism—a vision often pitted against a pan-Canadian project based on provincial equality, bilingualism, and multiculturalism as the foundations for citizenship. Quebec must thus constantly justify its role as a primary host society, since this can never simply be assumed as long as the minority nation is within an alternative host society that simultaneously frames the boundaries of citizenship.

In the 1960s, a new era of rapid modernization through increased state intervention resulted in a profound transformation of politically salient identity in Quebec. Quebec moved to structure its national identity along civic and territorial lines. Previously, the nation of French Canadians had been defined along ethnic lines, based largely on Catholicism and the French language and culture.[13] Indeed, in what is characteristic of most ethnically based collective movements, immigrants were viewed as somewhat threatening to the integrity of the nation and a challenge to French-Canadian culture and institutions; thus foreign influences were shunned in a defensive posture of survival. With a more open, inclusive, and territorial conception of belonging, however, Quebec defined itself not only as a society open to immigration for instrumental reasons, but as one that began to embrace the contributions of immigrants. A policy document from 1990 nicely captures this point:

> The social and cultural impact of immigration is certainly more difficult to determine when demographic, economic and linguistic indicators, on their own more easily quantifiable, are called into question. Nevertheless, the number of examples of Quebecers that have come from abroad and have enriched Quebec's culture and institutions; have allowed this society to be appreciated abroad and, inversely, have sensitized this society to important if sometimes misunderstood realities, speaks largely to the significance that immigration can represent with regards to sociocultural dynamism and openness to the world.[14]

The next section traces the various attempts to address the terms of integration since the early 1980s.

The Evolution of the "Quebec Model" of Cultural Pluralism

The Canadian Context: Competing Projects and Ambiguous Citizenship

A persistent problem for Quebec is that despite its efforts to implement a coherent integration policy and to frame Canadian citizenship in differentiated terms, many newly arrived immigrants and even established ethnocultural groups continue to identify primarily with the markers of Canadian citizenship. Competing interpretations of political community create both a sense of ambiguity for new arrivals and a challenge for public policy that most nation-states do not face.[15]

Canada is responsible for granting formal citizenship status, which is broadly based on multiculturalism within a bilingual framework, a Charter of Rights and Freedoms, and provincial equality.[16] Aside from administrative agreements with Quebec, Canada does not formally endorse constitutional asymmetry.[17] Many initiatives of the Quebec government that bear upon citizenship continue to be viewed with suspicion by ethnocultural community leaders.[18] They see the initiatives either as hidden projects for assimilation contrary to Canadian pluralism or as nationalist ploys to further sever ties with Canada, rather than as genuine efforts to integrate immigrants into a distinct democratic space.[19] The Charter of the French Language, for example, seeks social cohesion and integration; but for a time it was rejected and viewed as the imposition of a majority language in what is formally a bilingual country, as an illegitimate instrument to establish linguistic peace, or as the means of doing away with the use of English altogether.[20]

Indeed, the basic idea behind Canadian multiculturalism is that all cultural identities could participate equally in social and political spheres. Culture is constitutionally recognized and protected, and no official culture forms the basis of citizenship. The key element in this discussion is multiculturalism's inherent centralizing effect. By not differentiating between various forms and manifestations of politically salient collective identities—historical national minorities, the majority nationalist identity, and ethnocultural groups—all "cultural claims" are treated equally and their primary reference is the bundle of rights granted by the central government.[21]

Multiculturalism as one of the pillars of Canadian citizenship is thus not merely a commitment to a model of cultural pluralism—it also represents the nonrecognition of majority culture as a structuring principle for political life in Canada. Indeed, successive Quebec governments have viewed the policy as a nation-building device meant to undermine the primacy of any particular collective grouping that claims the right to govern a separate democratic political community, or host society, as part of the federal framework.

With the larger context established, we now turn to the ways in which Quebec has grappled with these internal challenges over time. Indeed, the obstacles confronting Quebec have not prevented governments from engaging in much soul-searching about the terms of belonging to Quebec society, as illustrated in the series of policy statements and formal consultative commissions devoted to this issue. Rather than muddling through specific policy programs on ethnocultural diversity management, certain documents that provide a lens into the broad framework through which Quebec has addressed these questions and illustrate the evolution of a model that is specific to Quebec have been selected.

Managing Diversity in Quebec

While integration involves many policy areas, including education, training and employment, and poverty alleviation, this section looks at the broad orientations of the terms of integration developed in a series of policy statements and official commissions of inquiry. The aim here is to highlight the general contours of citizenship in official discourse as a window into the values, identities, and norms that guide integration policies.

Before examining the ideas that have shaped the Quebec model, however, the two foundations of the larger framework within which interculturalism has been developed must be highlighted. First, in 1975 Quebec enacted its own Charter of Human Rights and Freedoms, the guarantor of fundamental rights that has since been upheld as a foundational initiative by subsequent Quebec governments. A second structuring instrument is the Charter of the French Language (1977), which explicitly links integration with the public use of French. This Charter affirms that protecting the French language and allowing it to flourish are not merely the responsibility of the francophone majority, but are fundamental to the rights and responsibilities of belonging in Quebec.

In 1981 the Quebec government published *Autant de façons d'être Québécois*,[22] which is a founding document of Quebec interculturalism. Recall that an actual law outlining the model of interculturalism was never formulated. In 1990, the government produced a more comprehensive policy statement on immigration and cultural pluralism, *Au Québec pour bâtir ensemble*.[23] Subsequently, two other less successful attempts to structure Quebec citizenship are examined: *Le forum national sur la citoyenneté et l'intégration* (2000) and the final report of the Larose Commission (2001)[24] on the future of the French language in Quebec. A more recent policy statement, *Des valeurs partagées, des intérêts communs* (2004), the final report of the Consultation Commission on Accommodation Practices Related to Cultural Differences (the Bouchard–Taylor Commission, 2008), and the very recent attempt to introduce a more comprehensive and controversial Charter of Quebec Values round out the overview.

Primary Source

B. Integration and Interculturalism: A Model to Be Clarified

The 11 proposals below allow us to define Québec interculturalism even more precisely.

1. Québec as a nation, as recognized by all Québec political parties and the federal government, is the operational framework for interculturalism.
2. In a spirit of reciprocity, interculturalism strongly emphasizes interaction, in particular intercommunity action, with a view to overcoming stereotypes and defusing fear or rejection of the Other, taking advantage of the enrichment that stems from diversity, and benefiting from social cohesion.
3. Members of the majority ethnocultural group, i.e., Quebecers of French- Canadian origin, like the members of ethnocultural minorities, accept that their culture will be transformed sooner or later through interaction.
4. Cultural and, in particular, religious differences need not be confined to the private domain. The following logic underpins this choice: it is healthier to display our differences and get to know those of the Other than to deny or marginalize them.
5. The principle of multiple identities is recognized, as is the right to maintain an affiliation with one's ethnic group.
6. For those citizens who so wish, it is desirable for initial affiliations to survive, since ethnic groups of origin often act as mediators between their members and society as a whole. A general phenomenon arises in this regard: almost without exception, each citizen integrates into society through a milieu or an institution that serves as a link, e.g., the family, a profession, a community group, a church, an association, and so on.

7. Multilingualism is encouraged at the same time as French as the common public language. The debate that opposes the language of identity and the common language (as a simple communication tool) is hardly promising. What is important, first and foremost, is the broadest possible dissemination of French, in whatever form.
8. To facilitate the integration of immigrants and their children, it is useful to provide them with the means to preserve their mother tongue, at least at the outset. This helps them to mitigate the shock of immigration by affording them a cultural anchor. It is also a means of preserving the enrichment that stems from cultural diversity.
9. Constant interaction between citizens of different origins leads to the development of a new identity and a new culture. This is what has been happening in Québec in recent decades without altering the cultural position of the majority group or infringing on the culture of minority groups.
10. Under a recent, highly promising orientation from the standpoint of pluralism, the groups present in Québec define themselves with reference to common, often universal, values stemming from their history rather than their ethnic traits. Québec is thus part of an international trend whereby societies choose to integrate diversity in light of shared values.
11. The civic and legal dimensions (and everything that concerns, in particular, non-discrimination) must be regarded as fundamental in interculturalism.

Source: G. Bouchard and C. Taylor (Co-Commissioners), *Building the Future: A Time for Reconciliation* (Quebec: Commission de consultation sur les pratiques d'accommodement reliées aux différences culturelles (abridged version), 2008), 40–2.

Autant de façons d'être québécois : Énoncé de politique en matière d'immigration et d'intégration (1980)

In 1981, following a series of consultations with representatives of cultural communities that were recognized as interlocutors in defining the Quebec democratic space, the first policy blueprint emerged. Three objectives were outlined:

- Ensuring the preservation, specificity, and development of cultural communities
- Sensitizing francophone Quebecers to the place of cultural communities in developing a common heritage
- Promoting the integration of the cultural communities in Quebec society, especially in the sectors where they were underrepresented, particularly in the public service

The document acknowledges the salience of framing integration such that minority cultures are protected and refers to the various measures undertaken previously to ensure their integrity, including programs such as Centre d'orientation et de formation des immigrants (COFI) and Programme d'enseignement des langues d'origines.[25] Moreover, it encourages cultural exchanges with countries of origin and minority-language instruction, and even proposed subsidizing such programs.

As an overarching blueprint, the theme of the document is *convergence*, emphasizing the promotion of markers of belonging around the majority group. Integration is thus defined as a process where newcomers are expected to eventually converge toward Quebec's francophone culture, in effect acknowledging the existence of majority/minority dynamics in the process of integration. While it does not advocate outright cultural assimilation, since the contribution of minority cultures is explicitly valued, the overriding theme is that belonging in Quebec means proceeding toward the identity markers of the established majority culture. As such, it does not limit integration to language acquisition merely in an instrumental sense or in strictly public terms.

This approach rests on a hierarchy of cultures in Quebec, with an established majority culture as the basis for integration. It nevertheless represents a watershed in diversity management in Quebec, particularly in intercommunity relations. The document is replete with references to the past and expected future contributions of minority cultural groups to Quebec's development. Quebec identity is thus to become open to much more influence by minority cultural groups integrating into its society; the document includes concrete recommendations for increasing allophones' accessibility to public service jobs, for services better adapted to immigrants' specific needs, and for financial assistance to minority cultural community associations. The Ministry of Immigration was renamed the Ministry of Immigration and Cultural Communities, which signalled a greater awareness of the specific needs of newcomers.

While explicit references to meeting the particular needs of members of minority cultures represent a modest pluralist turn, the strong language of cultural convergence resulted in a model that placed most of the responsibility to integrate and adapt onto the minority groups themselves—to integrate into a Quebec identity still defined largely as an expression of francophone culture. The majority was thus limited to demonstrating a greater sensitivity to the difficulties encountered by newcomers, and that this would contribute to more effective efforts at integration. While the government demonstrated a firm intention of establishing a propitious environment for accommodating minority cultures, the expectation of unity around an established core dampened the pluralist intentions of the approach.

Finally, the policy statement clearly demarcates Quebec as a host society, embedded in but distinct from the Canadian policy of multiculturalism, and states its divergence from the American melting pot. In 1990, Quebec would once again tackle these questions in a more comprehensive model.

Au Quebec pour bâtir ensemble : Énoncé de politique en matière d'immigration et d'intégration (1990)

This document outlines three fundamental principles of Quebec's approach to integration. Quebec is to be

- a society in which French is the common language of public life;
- a democratic society where the participation and the contribution of everyone is expected and encouraged; and
- a pluralist society open to multiple contributions within the limits imposed by the respect for fundamental democratic values and the necessity of intercommunity exchange.

The policy statement remains to this day the one most closely associated with the Quebec model of interculturalism. The basic thrust is that the integration of immigrants or minority cultures into the larger society is to be a reciprocal endeavour—a *moral contract* between majority and minority groups, with the aim of establishing a *common public culture.* It emphasizes that the responsibility for integration belongs to all Quebecers, not merely immigrants.

The first principle reaffirms the primacy of French as the common public language in Quebec. Language is described not merely in terms of its instrumental function, but as a symbolic identity marker. New arrivals and minority cultures signal their willingness to belong to the Quebec political community by embracing French and engaging with its flourishing collective. However, the document insists that linguistic assimilation is not the aim, and individual choice of language in private life is encouraged. The mutual recognition inherent in the notion of a **moral contract** also requires that the host society provide the necessary resources for French-language instruction and adoption throughout Quebec.

Second, regarding democratic participation, the model invokes the importance of social justice and equality of opportunity laid out in the Quebec Charter of Human Rights and Freedoms. The host society is also called upon here to help alleviate socio-economic and cultural barriers to strengthen the avenues of participation for neo-Quebecers. Integration into democratic life is thus a two-way street and involves more than an expectation that immigrants make an effort to learn about the values and institutions of the larger society.

Third, the principle of intercultural dialogue indicates a willingness to move toward greater pluralism. An intercultural turn is evident here, since the model shifts toward cultural exchange that would transform both the minority and majority cultures in forging a common public culture. Without denying the importance of the francophone heritage in fostering this common identity space, the model nevertheless turns away from the language of convergence and stresses reciprocal exchange. Cultural contact becomes the basis for new common references and a new identity for the larger community—a "fusion of horizons" through open dialogue and participation. Thus, a main pillar of the model discourages cultural enclosure and isolation. There is no cultural recognition outside of a democratic imperative—it is an outcome of participation and deliberation, the result of contributing to a common public culture that is open to change.

Much like its predecessor, this approach explicitly maintains a strong distinction from Canadian multiculturalism. Despite its many similarities to multiculturalism, interculturalism differs in that it links cultural recognition to the act of participation and deliberation. It is this emphasis on a responsibility to participate in public life, contributing through the lens of one's particular culture in a reciprocal exchange with other minority groups as well as the majority which is overtly acknowledged, that most fully characterizes the model.

CASE STUDY

Au Quebec Pour Bâtir Ensemble : Énoncé de politique en matière d'immigration et d'intégration/Building Quebec Together: Policy Statement on Immigration and Integration (1990)

Until the 1960s, francophone Quebec society was not perceived as open to immigrant integration, and francophone Quebecers were considered either as a majority group within Quebec or as part of a larger ethnocultural group that spanned Canada. The larger Canadian community was responsible for citizenship, and immigrants to Quebec were for the most part integrated into the anglophone community, particularly in Montreal. Following the Quiet Revolution, the Quebec state assumed a more activist role in constructing the boundaries of belonging and membership in Quebec society and made it clear that immigration and integration were significant to the future of francophone Quebec.

In 1991 the Quebec government published an unprecedented and comprehensive policy statement of its fundamental motivations, justifications, and visions regarding immigration, including selection and integration. For the first time, the government clearly linked immigration to the challenges inherent in the development of Quebec. The importance of this document cannot be overstated—it was an exercise in systematic and coherent introspection that we rarely get from governments, and it lays bare all of the challenges confronting a minority nation that does not fully control the policy levers of citizenship. It is a statement about what a society stands for, where it came from, and where it wants to go. Essentially, the way a society frames immigrant integration is a lens into its fundamental notions of justice—the rights of and the responsibilities expected of all citizens. After having negotiated with the federal government extensive powers in selecting and integrating immigrants, Quebec suddenly began to act like, and become, a host society. This is still a work in progress and social debates still rage in Quebec, but this was the first formal attempt to outline the main orientations of the state in a policy area

continued

that is unlike most others, in that it explicitly and quite self-consciously seeks to answer questions about belonging.

For intercommunity relations specifically, the document spells out three broad objectives. First, it aims to develop the tools to ensure that newcomers and their cultural communities better know and understand Quebec society. Second, it promotes pluralism as an integral aspect of Quebec society. Third, it seeks to provide the foundations for a rapprochement between members of the cultural communities and the majority community. These rather ambitious issues would set the tone of the approach established by the policy statement, in the sense that integration was everybody's business, not an unwarranted burden placed exclusively in the hands of newcomers.

Quebec's position on immigration included a commitment to a flourishing francophone society, with an emphasis on economic prosperity accompanied by values such as family reunification and international solidarity. Quebec thus concerned itself with establishing the admission criteria for both independent and temporary immigration. Moreover, Quebec made a commitment to be more involved in political asylum claims, particularly in reception services. Quebec would also determine levels of immigration appropriate to its needs and capacities as a host society, an issue that has been firmly entrenched in political debates to this day.

For integration, Quebec's primary goal is to develop resources for newcomers and members of ethnocultural minorities to learn French and to promote its use. Moreover, the policy statement called for the host society to be more open to the full participation of such groups in the economic, cultural, political, and institutional life of Quebec. Finally, the state would intervene directly in ensuring harmonious relations among ethnocultural groups of all origins.

Perhaps more importantly, the statement explicitly links Quebec's particular development challenges as a "distinct society" (the common terminology at the time) with immigration, and links it with four major challenges in its future: demographic concerns, economic prosperity, the perpetuation of French as a majority language, and an opening to the world. The Quebec state for the first time laid out a framework for belonging that would form the backbone of debates about Quebec identity for years to come—even the recent Bouchard-Taylor Commission refers to this statement in outlining its model of Quebec interculturalism. The policy statement produced a new area of comparative inquiry as well, loosely labelled "integration within a minority nation," and examination of its similarities to and compatibilities and competition with Canadian multiculturalism has blossomed into a full-blown interdisciplinary field of research. Suddenly, questions about immigration and integration came to be centred on Quebec society as a point of reference.

It is in this document that Quebec introduces the notion of a "moral contract"—a reciprocal obligation between minority groups and the majority group. The moral contract comprises three main orientations for Quebec's model of integration:

- A society in which French is the common language of public life
- A democratic society where all members are expected and encouraged to participate and contribute
- A pluralist society that is open to multiple contributions within the limits of a respect for fundamental democratic values and the necessity of intercommunity exchange

The model goes on to stress that the three themes of this moral contract involve rights and responsibilities for both immigrants and the host society—again, successful integration involves society as a whole. The state is responsible for making available to all the tools needed for successful integration according to the moral contract. Immigrants would thus understand this distinct society into which they were integrating, and Quebecers would accommodate efforts at integration, including committing resources for them, and would be aware of the rights and responsibilities that they freely and proudly took upon themselves as fundamental values and principles. Through such a framework, the objective was to foster an evolving and plural "common public culture" distinct from past attempts to define a national culture as a site of integration and as a dominant pole of cultural convergence.

Source: Government of Quebec, *Au Quebec Pour Bâtir Ensemble : Énoncé de politique en matière d'immigration et d'intégration* (Quebec: Direction des communications du ministère des Communautés culturelles et de l'Immigration du Quebec, 1991).

Forum national sur la citoyenneté et l'intégration (2000)

While the 1990 policy statement attracted much attention, several events resulted in a shift in the government's discourse. The Parti Québécois took power in 1994 and launched a referendum on sovereignty that resulted in a very close loss, leaving ethnocultural groups with a sense of resentment. At the same time, integration and diversity under this government shifted toward a discourse centred on citizenship, universal markers of identity, and essentially a more civic conception of belonging. The immigration and integration portfolio dropped references to cultural communities and was renamed the Ministry of Immigration and Citizen Relations. The idea was to establish more inclusive criteria for membership, stressing formal equality rather than the recognition of cultural differences.[26] In short, this period was characterized by a retreat from interculturalism. One concrete measure in applying this approach was the cancellation of the COFI program, which was seen as promoting cultural enclaves rather than facilitating integration.

In this context the Quebec government launched the *Forum national sur la citoyenneté et l'intégration* in 2000. The forum's rationale is outlined in the first section, where the challenges, principles, and issues surrounding Quebec citizenship and integration are highlighted. Challenges included rapid technological change, population movements, intensification of negotiations with Aboriginal peoples, and increased urbanization and cosmopolitanism. Moreover, it examined the fundamental tension and resulting ambivalence in a situation where Canada and Quebec engage in overlapping efforts at integrating newcomers. Indeed, this is taken as a clear obstacle to the host society effectively integrating newly arrived citizens. Generally, the report makes little mention of a commitment to cultural pluralism, proposing a new civic contract in place of cultural reciprocity:

> Whether it involves the promotion and the protection of rights, establishing one's civil status, or even the framework for information exchanges that touch individuals and their private lives, the mission of the different branches of the Ministry of Immigration and Citizen Relations converge toward an appreciation of the value of Quebec's civic heritage.
>
> Moving away from an approach that categorizes citizens according to their ethnic origins or their migratory paths, the Government of Quebec chooses to adopt an inclusive approach that ties together the various ministries and public institutions. A person that has arrived as an immigrant is thus no longer considered through the status of his/her origin, but rather through his/her status as a citizen in relations with the state.[27]

The consultation document was heavily criticized for its slant toward a Quebec citizenship that would reinforce common identity references and cohesion. Citizenship is thus defined in its transcendental function, as an institution meant to overcome rather than accommodate particular identities. As it was conceived, citizenship was not open to diverse contributions in determining the orientations of Quebec society. Jocelyn Maclure, for example, criticized the exercise as a veiled promotion of sovereignty rather than a serious debate about integration and the markers of belonging in Quebec.[28] In other words, this was an exercise in large-scale consultation and deliberation about the boundaries of Quebec citizenship in which some of the conclusions were predetermined. In the end, the forum was generally viewed as a missed opportunity, and it never quite achieved guidepost status for meeting the challenges of managing diversity.

Report of the Larose Commission on the Future of the French Language in Quebec (2000)

The idea of a public consultation that would contribute to formalizing Quebec citizenship was not abandoned. Indeed, in the Estates General on the Situation and Future of the French Language in Quebec, language was explicitly linked with citizenship. The French language was seen as the bond that holds public life together—a condition of democratic participation and a necessary vehicle for attaining equality—and thus the primary marker of Quebec citizenship. In this light, the commission described the foundations of an active citizenship in Quebec, expressed through a common language and a set of democratic values and institutions, as well as a common heritage. Moreover, it identified the cultural contributions of all Quebec's constituent groups as integral to Quebec identity. It also suggested a move away from multiculturalism toward interculturalism, signalling somewhat of a return to the discourse of a distinct approach. This passage from the report nicely captures the concerns and conclusions of the commission:

> Bringing together the values, knowledge, and institutions of the Quebec people, channelling artistic, intellectual, material activities and production, as well as original symbols, Quebec culture lies naturally at the heart of its identity, and consequently, at the heart of Quebec citizenship. In effect, citizenship can be seen as the recognition of belonging to a nation, to a community of people that make the choice to live together within a common culture.
>
> The concept of citizenship is not well served by a demographic discourse that slices society into three ethnolinguistic categories: francophones, anglophones, and allophones, with the latter having become the group upon which the weight of safeguarding the French language has been placed. These categories, which give the image of a fragmented and polarized society, ought to be denounced when they move beyond the realm of statistical categories. Leaving behind the defensive attitude of minorities and rejecting the divisive and ethnic character of multiculturalism, the Quebec nation rests increasingly on the binding potential of a common culture, as the fruition of the creativity of all its members, to raise the level of consciousness with regard to sharing a single citizenship.[29]

All citizens of Quebec are expected to contribute to the flourishing of the French language, particularly in the face of constant pressures from expanding globalization. The commission recommended the formalization of an internal citizenship for Quebec as the most effective way to address growing concerns over language.

The commission's recommendations, however, said very little about relations with minority cultural communities and the role of minority languages in fostering Quebec identity. It continued along a civic path, where language was to trump all differences and serve as both a condition for participation and the basis for social cohesion. Most critics decried the overly stringent association of language and Quebec citizenship, as though Quebec did not contain historically protected minority languages on its territory. Also, the report failed to rally a consensus. Its recommendations, like the forum preceding it, never quite caught on, and most observers continued to point to the Quebec Charter of Human Rights and Freedoms, the Charter of the French Language, and the 1990 policy statement as the main structuring principles of Quebec's approach to diversity management.

Des valeurs partagées, des intérêts communs (2004)

The return to power of the Quebec Liberal Party in 2003 marked another shift in emphasis. Most notably, the government dropped references to citizenship and returned to "cultural communities" as its preferred designation. The name of the ministry was again changed to Immigration and Cultural Communities.

A return to the "moral contract" was one of many elements borrowed from the 1990 statement, and few innovations were included except for a note on the prominence of national security in a post–9/11 context. Moreover, the document rejected the Parti Québécois's use of the language of citizenship, strong insistence on unity, and the development of a primary allegiance and loyalty toward Quebec. Finally, the policy statement sought to more concretely raise awareness of the importance of intercultural communication, suggesting the targeting of specific areas in which such tensions might emerge, including schools, workplaces, civil society, government institutions, relations between landlords and tenants, and finally in situations particularly conducive to racial profiling. Overall, however, the policy statement is largely a return to the principles outlined in 1990 and represents a severing with suggestions for internal citizenship that arose in the intervening years.

Consultation Commission on Accommodation Practices Related to Cultural Differences (Bouchard–Taylor Commission, 2008)

While it does not enjoy the force of a governmental policy statement, the recommendations of the Bouchard–Taylor Commission constitute the most comprehensive account of Quebec interculturalism to date:

> Often mentioned in academic papers, interculturalism as an integration policy has never been fully, officially defined by the Quebec government, although its underlying principles were formulated long ago. This shortcoming should be overcome, all the more so as the Canadian multiculturalism model does not appear to be well adapted to conditions in Quebec. . . . According to the descriptions provided in scientific documentation, interculturalism seeks to reconcile ethnocultural diversity with the continuity of the French-speaking core and the preservation of the social link. It thus affords security to Québecers of French-Canadian origin and to ethnocultural minorities and protects the rights of all in keeping with the liberal tradition. By instituting French as the common public language, it establishes a framework in society for communication and exchanges. It has the virtue of being flexible and receptive to negotiation, adaptation and innovation.[30]

The report refines and provides coherence to many of the established principles around which the preceding debates had evolved. Several distinctive normative and descriptive features merit further discussion.

First, the commission clearly stipulates that the nation of Quebec constitutes the operational framework for interculturalism. This is an essential attribute of the model—it is meant for this political community in its particular set of circumstances. The framework is clearly distinct from Canadian multiculturalism, even though it acknowledges that the model of multiculturalism has itself changed in the direction of social cohesion and unity in the past 30 years.[31] The authors note four particularly salient conditions: a much stronger language-related anxiety in Quebec, existential anguish over its minority status, the fact that there is no longer a dominant majority ethnic group in Canada, and finally that there is much less concern in Canada for maintaining a founding culture and more for promoting national unity. The commissioners conclude, without delving deeply into the politics of multiculturalism as it relates to Quebec, that the models represent distinct attempts to apply a pluralist philosophy.

Second, the model is lauded for its ability to adapt to a variety of influences on Quebec identity, due to the principle of intercultural reciprocity. As such, a static conception of an existing culture as a centre of convergence, and of a civic space situated above the reach of cultural influence, is not in keeping with a model of interculturalism. A commitment to cultural pluralism does not confine cultural differences to the private sphere.

Finally, and most significantly, the commissioners proposed that to alleviate ambiguity the National Assembly of Quebec should adopt an official text on interculturalism, whether a statute, statement, or declaration. Following extensive public consultations, this would serve as a social blueprint to provide continuity and overarching identity to Quebec in its capacity as a host society—an effective reference point and coherent guide for public and community interveners. Moreover, it could promote awareness and teaching about the value of cultural pluralism, which might help reduce racism and other forms of ethnocultural discrimination. Like Canadian multiculturalism, interculturalism could eventually become a national symbol and a core value.

The recommendations of the commission, however, were largely ignored. By the time the Charter of Quebec Values[32] entered the scene, the dismissal of the commission's basic call for continuity was complete. Indeed, both the Liberal Party and the Parti Québécois (PQ) initially responded with a series of ad hoc and disjointed proposals that seemed to be motivated by short-term political considerations in place of a serious commitment to the commission's findings.

In March 2010, the Liberal government proposed Bill 94 in the National Assembly, titled An Act to Establish Guidelines Governing Accommodation Requests within the Administration and Certain Institutions, which prohibited the covering of one's face when communicating with a public agent for reasons of security, communication, or identity. This was soon followed by the introduction of a "Values Pledge" for newcomers, which compelled newcomers to sign a statement affirming their commitment to the "common values of Quebec society" to be eligible for settlement services—a clear rejection of the spirit of reciprocity inherent in the model of interculturalism.

The PQ, both in opposition and in government, sought to take this rupture much further. While in opposition, the PQ tabled Bill 195, the Quebec Identity Act, which sought to add a preamble to the Quebec Charter of Human Rights and Freedoms that would safeguard equality between the sexes, affirm the secular nature of public institutions, the predominance of the French language, and the protection of Quebec culture. It also called for proof of French proficiency and knowledge of Quebec culture to obtain a citizenship certificate required for the exercise of certain political rights, such as running for office in provincial, municipal, or school board elections. Again, this initiative catered to a view of integration that sought to more explicitly stem perceived cultural fragmentation and asserted a more hegemonic conception of majority–minority relations.

The initiatives described above, however, would pale in comparison to the magnitude of the PQ's attempt to inject some closure to the issue of cultural and religious pluralism with their proposal to enact a comprehensive Charter of Quebec Values during its short stint as a minority government. The Charter sought to instill a more restrictive brand of secularism and to provide a more predictable framework with which to interpret accommodation requests by proposing amendments to the Quebec Charter of Human Rights and Freedoms to include interpretive clauses affirming the "values of equality between women and men, the primacy of the French language as well as the separation of religions and State and the religious neutrality and secular nature of the State." However, the initiative also included language permitting exceptions for the "emblematic and toponymic elements of Québec's cultural heritage that testify to its history," in effect providing greater latitude to officials to recognize the collective cultural rights of the majority.

The Charter also sought to assert a restrictive form of secularism that would prohibit "personnel members of public bodies" from expressing religious beliefs as well as wearing conspicuous religious symbols such as clothing, headgear, and jewellery, replete with illustrated examples delineating what would be considered conspicuous and what would not. With regard to accommodation claims, the bill listed a series of normative guideposts meant to serve as an interpretive framework. While most are predictable—human rights, gender equality, prohibitive costs, performance, and health and safety considerations—the list nevertheless permitted authorities substantial discretion in denying accommodation requests:

> When an accommodation request on religious grounds is submitted to a public body, the public body must make sure that . . . the accommodation requested does not compromise the separation of religions and State or the religious neutrality and secular nature of the State.

Contrary to the moderation and continuity promoted by the Bouchard–Taylor Commission through interculturalism and **open secularism**, the Charter would have provided public officials with much leverage to disengage from Quebec's now long-standing commitment to pluralism. Absolutist secularism that restricts religious expression as well as an ambiguous allowance for contingencies deemed to pertain to Quebec's cultural heritage clearly establish the normative primacy of the dominant culture.

The orientations of Quebec society on this question are still very much in the air. Although the Charter of Quebec Values was killed with the majority Liberal Party victory in the April 2014 elections, with a promise to eventually revisit the question of cultural and religious accommodations, it is too early to interpret whether or not the sentiments that nourished it remain strong or whether new initiatives will reassert Quebec's commitment to interculturalism.

BIOGRAPHY

Gérald Godin: Father of Quebec Interculturalism

> I have learned to understand (immigrants) through my profession, to appreciate more profoundly who they were here in Quebec, thus to increasingly love them. In this sense, it's a new phase of Quebec nationalism, a much more open nationalism that is more conducive to respecting others that are here and to ensure that every one of them can contribute to the construction of the country. In the beginning, we believed that we would build the country practically alone; now, we believe we must do it with others.[33]

Gérald Godin.

Bibliotheque et Archives Nationales du Quebec/ Gabor Szilasi

While Gérald Godin's influence on the intellectual life of Quebec is difficult to capture in a brief synopsis—he was an accomplished politician, poet, essayist, novelist, songwriter, painter, and journalist—it is his enduring mark on Quebec's early debates on immigration and integration policy that would have a profound and lasting impact. Godin was a pioneer in Quebec's continuing social and political debates on cultural pluralism. For Godin the humanist, culture was paramount in building a forward-looking and confident Quebec society. Ever the artist, Godin infused political life with an open affirmation of difference, justice, and knowledge as universal and human values, injecting the strategic and rational world of politics with a gentle and serene sensibility. In his view, the affirmation of Quebec as a confident and strong nation went hand in hand with the promotion, recognition, and respect of the plurality of cultures on Quebec soil.

Godin's quest began with his elegant appeal for a Quebec literature to replace traditional French-Canadian literature, which he believed stifled creativity, belonged to the past, and failed to reflect the artistic expression inherent in a modern, flourishing, and new Quebec society open to the world. It was a call for liberation in Quebec—a sense of "artistic decolonization" away from the dogma of the past.

His entrance into politics was marked by a bold initiative. Against most strategic and calculated advice, he ran in the 1976 provincial election for the Parti Québécois in a multiethnic neighbourhood—against the leader of the opposition, Robert Bourassa—rather than in one of the "safe" ridings usually reserved for high-profile candidates such as himself. He diligently met the people of the riding, learned about their interests and identities, and extolled a vision of a new, exciting future for Quebec—and surprisingly defeated Robert Bourassa as part of the Parti Québécois victory. He would go on to win three more elections for the PQ.

continued

In 1980–1 he served as minister of immigration, and at his insistence as the newly named minister of immigration and cultural communities from 1981–5. Here his legacy is felt to this day. Godin viewed building a new Quebec as inextricably linked to welcoming and fully integrating the diverse contributions of newly arrived citizens. He became the strongest advocate of the value of difference in his government and party, often at odds with factions that promoted ethnic allegiance in pursuing independence, particularly his colleague Jacques Parizeau, who at times openly speculated that sovereignty might be legitimately determined by francophones alone. Godin thought Quebec culture and society would inevitably benefit from the contribution of a diversity of cultures, and that this should be embraced rather than rejected as a threat to the sovereignty movement. This was the birth of Quebec interculturalism. It is through Godin's vision for Quebec that the seeds of a "common public culture" approach to immigration were sown—the value of cultural exchange and the capacity to respect and recognize others. From literature characterized by an independence of spirit, to Quebec national affirmation, to the politics of embracing difference, Godin's vision for Quebec was nourished by a common element, a quiet collective confidence that signalled a coming of age for Quebec, a new beginning and a thorough and genuine curiosity about the needs and aspirations of people from all walks of life.

The questions of integration and ethnocultural relations lie deep in the heart of Quebec identity, as they ask citizens to understand their place in the political project that is under construction, constantly changing, challenged at many turns, and always the subject of passionate debates. Godin found it particularly difficult to make a case for cultural pluralism as a member of a political party that has traditionally elicited strong negative reactions from new Quebecers, the ethnocultural and linguistic minorities. Moreover, he took control of the dossier of immigration and integration soon after the referendum, which had caused many rifts and persisting tensions between the francophone majority and ethnocultural minorities. Godin's deft touch was all the more remarkable in those circumstances.

Indeed, until the Quiet Revolution Quebec was not always the most hospitable place for immigrants: Montreal was, for the most part, a divided city, linguistically and culturally; very few immigrants lived in Quebec's regions; and socio-economic and cultural forces fostered strong xenophobic tendencies. Moreover, federal policies were assimilationist and did not address Canadian dualism. By the end of the 1960s, francophone Quebec would reject its minority status and begin to affirm itself as a majority nation that could be a host society in its own right, with inclusive citizenship practices that would no longer threaten the existence of the nation. Integration became a key aspect of this project, encompassing concerns about Quebec's demographic weight in Canada, social and economic integration, and the place of religious and ethnic minorities in Quebec.

From 1968–81, much effort of the Quebec state was devoted to concluding bilateral agreements with the federal government to transfer some authority to Quebec. When Godin became minister of immigration and cultural communities in 1981, he made full use of Quebec's new powers and launched a series of programs aimed at fostering cultural convergence. The ministry's name change was accompanied by three fundamental objectives under Godin's leadership: maintaining and developing cultures of origin, promoting integration and the full participation of cultural communities in the wider society, and encouraging exchange between minorities and the larger francophone majority. The list of initiatives was long: financing cultural community organizations that provided services and activities for members, subsidizing the construction or renovation of cultural centres, funding the media development for cultural groups, providing heritage language retention programs, and so on.

In 1983 Godin was asked by Premier René Lévesque to review the Charter of the French Language, a difficult task that could alienate both nationalists, who saw it as an untouchable text, and the anglophone and allophone minorities, who were increasingly mobilizing against the perceived bureaucratic and unreasonable rigidities of the law. This was soon after Canada had patriated its Constitution without Quebec's consent, an act seen by many nationalists as a betrayal. Godin the nationalist and pluralist again struggled to reconcile seemingly clashing ideals. Throughout 1983 Godin held tension-filled public consultations on the future of the Charter.

The status of the anglophone minority was particularly challenging—a minority, yet historically dominant, which was linked to the wider Canadian political community. Godin's vision was to grant the anglophone minority a particular status as a cofounding people of Quebec—a historical national group and not an ethnocultural group among others. He made the case that the anglophone community in Quebec, unlike wider North American and global structural forces, should not in itself be considered threatening to a vibrant francophone Quebec. Its institutions should not be held responsible for the fears of linguistic assimilation that precipitated language legislation in the first place. This vision represented a new course that was never publicly stated in Quebec, much less by the PQ.

Godin once again laid the foundation for a new basis of rapprochement between the linguistic communities in Quebec. Some concrete results of his intervention include a measure of institutional bilingualism for anglophone schools, hospitals, and social service agencies, while ensuring the continuation and improvements of francization in the workplace. Godin also proposed reciprocal arrangements on minority-language education with other provinces that provided it for their French-speaking minorities, which ended the impasse between Quebec and other provinces on this matter.

In 1984 Godin co-organized the Breakthrough Conference with the Jewish community, which an unprecedented 20 PQ ministers attended. It addressed many issues that concerned the Jewish community, including health, education, senior citizens, employment, youth, and the like. One result was a generous program of subsidies for not only Jewish schools, but Greek, Armenian, and Chinese schools as well. In his five or so years at the helm of what can be called Quebec's "identity portfolio," his capacity to apply the deft touch of a humanist in addressing political challenges is evident in the myriad testimonials on his behalf from all parts of Quebec society—and most would agree that Gérald Godin can indeed be called a prominent founder of contemporary Quebec.

Source: Adapted from Lucille Beaudry, Robert Comeau, and Guy Lachapelle, *Gérald Godin : Un poète en politique* (Montréal: Éditions de L'Hexagone, 2000).

Conclusion

This chapter has outlined the main tenets of a "Quebec model" of diversity management and how it has evolved. On a unity-diversity continuum, Quebec has for the most part leaned toward unity. This is not surprising, since the goal has primarily been to carve out a citizenship space within the larger Canadian associative community. Over the years and due to the shifting priorities of successive governments, the model has been slightly altered in emphasis, vacillating between social cohesion and unified citizenship, and more pluralistic notions of belonging that allow for much more public recognition of the distinctiveness of ethnocultural groups. These shifts in emphasis, however, have been rather modest, and the model's main premises have stood the test of time as a uniquely Quebec approach to the question of cultural diversity.

Quebec governments have consistently rejected the Canadian policy of multiculturalism as inadequate for protecting the collective goals of Quebec and its ability to manage its unique sociocultural characteristics. Indeed, one of the forgotten yet salient points in the persistent debate about the differences between interculturalism and multiculturalism is the fact that Quebec has consistently and forcefully attempted to develop its own model to fit its particular sociological challenges. While the policies may overlap to some extent, particularly since they are both committed to cultural pluralism, interculturalism is a unique approach that is meant to serve as an alternative to multiculturalism—a reference of sorts that delineates Quebec citizenship.

At the very least, Quebec's activities in recruitment, selection, and integration reveal a distinct normative framework for diversity management, and perhaps it will be formally recognized as a constitutive aspect of Quebec society. For students interested in the management of ethnocultural diversity, the Quebec case offers a unique lens into an alternative approach, a genuine national model of diversity management emerging from a rich body of policy statements, commissions of inquiry, and public policies. The traditional American melting pot model, inspired by republican principles, and the Canadian policy of multiculturalism have been explicitly rejected in what can be considered Quebec's own interpretation of the rights and responsibilities that follow in the complex entanglement of culture and citizenship. This is an achievement that cannot be ignored.

Questions for Critical Thinking

1. Provide a brief overview of Quebec's approach to the management of cultural diversity. In what ways is it distinct from or similar to Canadian multiculturalism? What explains the fact that Quebec has adopted its own approach to cultural diversity?
2. Explain the difference between the concepts of cultural synthesis and cultural convergence in the elaboration of the Quebec model over the past 30 years.
3. Why is the idea of citizenship invoked in discussions about immigrant integration and ethnocultural diversity management? How would you justify or reject the case for internal Quebec citizenship?

Notes

1. A commitment to cultural pluralism implies that the state makes special provisions or allows certain legal accommodations for cultural groups as constitutive sociopolitical entities that are recognized as such in public institutions. Traditional liberal citizenship, on the other hand, recognizes individuals as the primary units of public recognition through a set of rights, entitlements, and responsibilities.
2. Daniel Weinstock, "La citoyenneté comme réponse aux problèmes du pluralisme des sociétés modernes," in *Les enjeux de la citoyenneté : Un bilan interdisciplinaire* (Laboratoire de recherche, Immigration et métropole, June 1998), 75.
3. See Leigh Oakes and Jane Warren, *Language, Citizenship and Identity in Quebec* (London: Palgrave Macmillan, 2007).
4. See Will Kymlicka for a groundbreaking theoretical contribution on the importance of recognizing culture(s) as integral to the liberal project, *Multicultural Citizenship* (Oxford: Oxford University Press, 1995).
5. See Chapter 16.
6. See Chapter 17.
7. Fernand Harvey, "L'Ouverture du Quebec au multiculturalisme (1900–1981)," *Études Canadiennes/Canadian Studies* 21, no. 2 (1986): 222.
8. See Martin Pâquet, *Toward a Quebec Ministry of Immigration, 1945 to 1968*, Canada's Ethnic Groups Series, Booklet 23 (Ottawa: Canadian Historical Association, 1997).
9. J. Carens, "Immigration, Political Community and the Transformation of Identity," in *Is Quebec Nationalism Just?*, ed. J. Carens (Montreal and Kingston: McGill-Queen's University Press, 1995), 26.
10. M. Sandel, *Democracy's Discontent* (Cambridge, MA: Harvard University Press, 1996), 6.
11. Carens, "Immigration, Political Community and the Transformation of Identity," 20.
12. Will Kymlicka defines "societal culture" as "a culture which provides its members with meaningful ways of life across the full range of human activities." Kymlicka, *Multicultural Citizenship*, 76.

13. See Fernand Harvey, "La question de l'immigration au Quebec : genèse historique," in Harvey et le Conseil de la langue française, *Le Quebec français et l'école à clientèle pluriethnique : Contributions à une réflexion*, Coll. Documentation du Conseil de la langue française (Quebec: Éditeur officiel du Quebec), 29.
14. Gouvernement du Quebec, *Au Quebec pour bâtir ensemble : Énoncé de politique en matière d'immigration et d'intégration* (Ministère des communautés culturelles et de l'immigration du Quebec, Direction des communications, 1990), 15; author's translation.
15. Jean-François Lisée, *Sortie de secours* (Montreal: Boréal, 2000). Lisée argues that among allophones (citizens whose mother tongue is neither French nor English), 51 per cent identified themselves as Canadian in 1979, while that number rose to 70 per cent in 1999. Lisée attributes this to an aggressive symbolic initiative by the federal government to tout the merits of Canadian citizenship in relation to the sovereignty movement in Quebec. See also Micheline Labelle and Daniel Salée, "Immigrant and Minority Representations of Citizenship in Quebec," in *Citizenship Today: Global Perspectives and Practices*, ed. T. A. Aleinikoff and D. Klusmeyer (Washington: Carnegie Endowment for International Peace, 2001).
16. See Alain-G. Gagnon and Raffaele Iacovino, *Federalism, Citizenship and Quebec: Debating Multinationalism* (Toronto: University of Toronto Press, 2007), for elaboration on these principles.
17. Constitutional asymmetry refers to a legal framework in which some member-states enjoy different sets of jurisdictions vis-à-vis the others in the federal division of powers between the central government and the provinces.
18. Micheline Labelle and Joseph J. Lévy, *Ethnicité et enjeux sociaux : Le Quebec vu par les leaders de groupes ethnoculturels* (Montréal: Liber, 1995).
19. For more on the phenomenon in which minority nations seek to create a separate democratic space vis-à-vis the majority nation, through concurrent and evolving nation-building processes, see G. Bourque, "Between Nations and Society," in *Vive Quebec: New Thinking and New Approaches to the Quebec Nation*, ed. M. Venne (Toronto: James Lorimer and Company, 2001).
20. Labelle and Salée, "Immigrant and Minority Representations of Citizenship in Quebec."
21. For an excellent overview of the Canadian policy of multiculturalism, see Citizenship and Immigration Canada's website devoted to the topic at www.cic.gc.ca/english/multiculturalism/citizenship.asp.
22. Marcel Gilbert, *Autant de façons d'être Québécois : Plan d'action à l'intention des communautés culturelles* (Quebec: Ministry of Communications, Direction générale des publications gouvernementales, 1981).
23. Gouvernement du Quebec, *Au Quebec pour bâtir ensemble.*
24. Gouvernement du Quebec, *Le français, une langue pour tout le monde : Rapport de la Commission des États généraux sur la situation et l'avenir de la langue française au Quebec* (Quebec: Gouvernement du Quebec, 2001).
25. Centre d'Orientation et de Formation des Immigrants was meant to provide French-language instruction as well as to provide basic transitional services for newcomers, while Programme d'enseignement des langues d'origine was a program devoted to the maintenance of languages of origin through educational programs specific to particular cultural groups and generally targeted to children.
26. Micheline Labelle, "La politique de la citoyenneté et de l'interculturalisme au Quebec," in *Les identités en débat : intégration ou multiculturalisme?*, ed. H. Greven-Borde and J. Tournon (Paris: L'Harmattan, 2000), 269–94.
27. *Forum national sur la citoyenneté et l'intégration : document de consultation* (Quebec: Ministère des Relations avec les citoyens et de l'immigration, September, 2000), 20; author's translation.
28. Jocelyn Maclure, "Commission nationale sur la citoyenneté : pour une politique des relations civiques," *Le Devoir*, 8 August 2001, A7.
29. *Le français, une langue pout tout le monde : une nouvelle approche stratégique et citoyenne* (Quebec: Commission des États généraux sur la situation et l'avenir de la langue française au Quebec, 2001), 14; author's translation.
30. Gerard Bouchard and Charles Taylor, *Building the Future: A Time for Reconciliation, Commission de Consultation sur les pratiques d'accommodement reliées aux différences culturelles* (Quebec: Gouvernement du Quebec, 2008), 21.
31. See Will Kymlicka, *Finding Our Way: Rethinking Ethnocultural Relations in Canada* (Toronto: Oxford University Press, 1998); and Y. Abu-Laban and Christina Gabriel, *Selling Diversity: Immigration, Multiculturalism, Employment Equity and Globalization* (Peterborough: Broadview Press, 2002).
32. Official title: Québec, projet de loi no. 60, *Charter Affirming the Values of State Secularism and Religious Neutrality and of Equality between Women and Men, and Providing a Framework for Accommodation Requests*, Première Session, Quarantième Législature, Éditeur officiel, 2013, www.assnat.qc.ca/en/travaux-parlementaires/projets-loi/projet-loi-60-40-1.html.
33. Lucille Beaudry, Robert Comeau, and Guy Lachapelle, *Gérald Godin : Un poète en politique* (Montreal: Éditions de L'Hexagone, 2000), 106.

Select Bibliography

Blad, Cory, and Phillipe Couton. "The Rise of an Intercultural Nation: Immigration, Diversity and Nationhood in Quebec." *Journal of Ethnic and Migration Studies* 35, no. 4 (2009): 645–77.

Carens, Joseph H. "Cultural Adaptation and the Integration of Immigrants: The Case of Quebec." Chapter 5 in *Culture, Citizenship and Community: A Contextual Exploration of Justice as Evenhandedness*. Oxford: Oxford University Press, 2000.

Dupré, Jean-François. "Intercultural Citizenship, Civic Nationalism and Nation-Building in Quebec: From Common Public Culture to Laïcité." *Studies in Ethnicity and Nationalism* 12, no. 2 (2012): 227–48.

Gagnon, Alain-G., and Raffaele Iacovino. *Federalism, Citizenship and Quebec: Debating Multinationalism*. Toronto: University of Toronto Press, 2007.

Gervais, S., D. Lamoureux, and D. Karmis. *Du tricoté serré au métissé serré? La culture publique commune au Québec en débats*. Québec: Presses de l'Université Laval, 2008.

Iacovino, Raffaele. "Canadian Federalism and the Governance of Immigration." In *The Politics of Immigration in Multi-level States: Governance and Political Parties*, edited by E. Hepburn and R. Zapata-Barrero. Basingstoke, England: Palgrave Macmillan, 2014.

Joppke, Christian, and Ewa Morawska. "Integrating Immigrants in Liberal Nation-States: Policies and Practices." In *Toward Assimilation and Citizenship*, edited by C. Joppke and E. Morawska. New York: Palgrave Macmillan, 2003.

Juteau, Danielle. "The Citizen Makes an Entrée: Redefining the National Community in Quebec." *Citizenship Studies* 6, no. 4 (2002): 377–94.

Karmis, Dimitrios. "Pluralism and National Identity(ies) in Contemporary Quebec: Conceptual Clarifications, Typology, and Discourse Analysis." In *Quebec: State and Society*, 3rd ed., edited by Alain-G. Gagnon, 69–96. Peterborough: Broadview, 2004.

Kymlicka, Will. "The Unhappy Marriage of Federalism and Nationalism." Part Two in *Finding Our Way: Rethinking Ethnocultural Relations in Canada*, 127–81. Toronto: Oxford University Press, 1998.

Labelle, Micheline, and François Rocher. "Debating Citizenship in Canada: The Collide of Two Nation-Building Projects." In *From Subjects to Citizens: A Hundred Years of Citizenship in Australia and Canada*, edited by P. Boyer, L. Cardinal, and D. Headon, 263–86. Ottawa: University of Ottawa Press, 2004.

McAndrew, Marie. "Quebec's Interculturalism Policy: An Alternative Vision." In *Belonging? Diversity, Recognition and Shared Citizenship in Canada*, edited by Keith Banting, Thomas J. Courchene, and F. Leslie Seidle, 143–54. Montreal: IRPP, 2007.

Oakes, Leigh. "French: A Language for Everyone in Quebec?" *Nations and Nationalism* 10, no. 4 (2004): 539–58.

16 Interethnic Relations and Racism in Quebec

Maryse Potvin, Université du Québec à Montréal

Timeline

1701 The Great Peace of Montréal is signed between France and 39 Aboriginal nations to end their conflicts.

1709 New France legalizes slavery through an ordinance from Intendant Raudot. Practised since the beginning of seventeenth century under Code Noir (adopted by France in 1685), slavery would continue under the British regime in Quebec until it was abolished in 1833.

1759 Conquest of Quebec results in British dominance over the French population, which is five times more numerous.

1816–51 Canada's first wave of massive immigration brings nearly 1 million British, Scottish, and Irish immigrants to Quebec City, Montreal, and other Atlantic ports.

1839 Lord Durham's *Report on the Affairs of British North America* recommends that British immigration be increased in Canada to speed cultural and linguistic assimilation of French Canadians.

1874–9 Deep recession causes massive exodus of French Canadians to the United States. Between 1880 and 1890, nearly 150,000 (or 11.3 per cent of Quebec's population) leave the country. Between 1840 and 1930, 1 million emigrate southward.

1879–1914 Dominion Lands Act (free land grants, 1872), John A. Macdonald's National Policy (1879), and the Sifton Plan (1896) are part of the largest push in Canada's history to increase immigration. Immigrants are sought to colonize the West, set up farms, provide cheap labour in industrial Ontario and Quebec, build Canada's national railway, and establish national infrastructure.

1880–5 Immigration policy restricts and excludes Asians (especially Chinese and Japanese) through quotas and taxation, and subsequently prohibits their entry into Canada outright (through legislation affecting Japanese immigration applicants in 1908 and the Chinese Immigration Act of 1923).

1923 After World War I, Canada's federal government passes the Empire Settlement Act to pursue its development of the West through immigration.

1939–45 During World War II thousands of Jewish refugees, seeking refuge from Nazism, are turned away from Canada. When Japan joins the war, Canadians of Japanese ancestry are interned in work camps or deported, and their property confiscated.

1946–61 Many Italian and British immigrants settle in Quebec, followed in numeric importance

continued

by Germans, Austrians, French, Greeks, and Jews from various countries (including numerous Holocaust survivors).

1947 First federal Citizenship Act creates the legal status of "Canadian Citizen," but it is still based on an ethnic conception of "nation" and the importance of preserving cultural homogeneity.

1952 Immigration Act establishes framework for managing immigration and grants major discretionary powers to immigration officers in selection of candidates. Eligibility and exclusion criteria remain unclear.

1956 Federal regulation clearly establishes hierarchy of ethnic preferences for Canadian immigration policy. Canada decides to prioritize immigrants from Commonwealth and northern European countries; then Eastern Europe; followed by southern Europe, Middle East, and Latin America; and finally Asia and Africa.

1962 New regulations abrogate preferential provisions for British, French, or American immigration candidates and replace them with "objective" selection criteria, based on applicants' education level, employability, and professional and technical qualifications.

1967 Abolition of all preferential (or discriminatory) immigration provisions.

1968 "St Leonard School Crisis" is triggered when a suburban Montreal school board decides to do away with bilingual classes and replace them with classes taught in French. Creation of Quebec's first Ministry of Immigration (MIQ).

1971 Multiculturalism Policy of Canada is passed.

1975 Quebec's Charter of Human Rights and Freedoms is adopted, establishing fundamental rights of citizens as inalienable principles that take legal precedence over all other legislation.

1977 Charter of the French Language (Bill 101) is passed, establishing links between integration of immigrants and the province's common public language.

1982 Canadian Charter of Rights and Freedoms is entrenched in the Canadian Constitution. Multiculturalism is integrated into the Charter.

1986 Federal Employment Equity Act is adopted, introducing the term *visible minority* and forcing companies under federal jurisdiction to adopt an equity plan for some target groups, including women, visible minorities, and Aboriginal peoples.

1988 Canadian Multiculturalism Act is passed.

1990 Gagnon-Tremblay–McDougall Accord gives Quebec exclusive jurisdiction over integration and selection of "independent immigrants."

Policy Statement on Immigration and Integration is adopted. It is subsequently updated in the government's 2004 Action Plan, which best describes the Quebec model of interculturalism.

Oka standoff becomes a political crisis over Aboriginal land claims that lasts three months, pitting the Mohawk Nation and its allies against governments of Quebec and Canada.

1995 Referendum on Quebec sovereignty: the "No" side wins by a narrow majority of 50.58 per cent. That very evening former Premier Jacques Parizeau blames some "ethnic votes" for the defeat of the "Yes" camp.

2005 Canadian government passes *Canada's Action Plan Against Racism*, presented as a pan-governmental effort to combat racism.

2006–8 Reasonable accommodation crisis. On 8 February 2007, Consultation Commission on Accommodation Practices Related to Cultural Differences (also known as the Bouchard-Taylor Commission) is struck. It files its final report on 19 May 2008.

2008 The Quebec government unveils *Diversity: An Added Value: Government Policy to Promote Participation of All in Québec's Development*, which focuses on fighting discrimination based on sex, age, disability, social condition, sexual orientation, colour, and ethnic or national origin.

2009 Bill 16, An Act to Promote Action by the Administration with Respect to Cultural Diversity, is tabled, immediately contested, and indefinitely shelved.

2013–14 The Parti Québécois minority government, elected in September 2012, proposes Bill 60, Charter Affirming the Values of State Secularism and Religious Neutrality and of Equality between Women and Men, and Providing a Framework for Accommodation Requests. This bill, more than the reasonable accommodation crisis, generates tensions and creates a deep division within society until the 7 April 2014 elections. Religious minorities are particularly targeted and subjected to racializing slips in some discourses as well as acts of intimidation (death threats, vandalism against places of worship, altercations, and so on).

2014 The Parti Québécois suffers a major defeat in the provincial election despite rather favourable polls for its "Secular Charter" (Bill 60).

Introduction

Contrary to some received wisdom, Quebec has never been a homogeneous society. It is true that Quebecers of French-Canadian origin currently account for 78 per cent of the population (out of more than 8 million inhabitants), that 80 per cent of Quebecers speak French at home, and 80 per cent claim to be Catholic.[1] But historically, Quebec (and Canadian) society has been shaped by successive waves of population settlement, beginning with the Aboriginal peoples, followed by French and then British colonizers, and sustained by an increasingly diversified combination of newcomers.

Although Quebec's population has grown increasingly diverse and recent governments have adopted an inclusive public discourse (backed by a substantial battery of measures to promote equality), there are still major gaps between this "official" normative discourse on the one hand and the reality of intergroup relations and their mutual representations on the other hand. Persistent instances of social malaise and **racializing discursive "slips"** have been observed vis-à-vis immigration and the integration of newcomers to Quebec. Our hypothesis is that these instances of malaise seem to be linked to the fragile status of francophone Quebecers as a majority group and their attachment to the gains of "modernity" in Quebec—the secularization of institutions, movements toward gender equality, and the entrenchment of French as the common public language.

This chapter sets forth some explanatory hypotheses about the gaps between official normative discourses and popular/media discourses in Quebec. It provides a snapshot of diversity and ethnic relations in the province, and more specifically examines racism in its shifts, empirical forms, and manifestations in social practices and discourses,[2] particularly in public debates that sometimes morphed into crises. As examples, we will explore debates over "reasonable accommodation" and the Charter of Quebec Values. The chapter also resituates the influence of Quebec–Canada relations within the problematics of racism in Quebec and the "fragile" dual majority/minority identity status of francophone Quebecers of French-Canadian origin that permeates the province's social discourse on ethnic relations. It concludes with an appeal to bring broad-based civic education to a variety of settings in Quebec.

Ethnic Diversity and Intergroup Relations

Ethnic pluralism, or *pluriethnicity*, is inherent to the history of Quebec and Canada. This land of Aboriginal peoples and French and British colonizers has also been a land of hope and sanctuary for many subsequent waves of immigrants since the eighteenth century: United Empire Loyalists, black Americans using the Underground Railroad to escape slavery, the Irish fleeing the Great Potato Famine of 1847, the Chinese seeking work, and the Jewish people escaping pogroms and political problems in Eastern Europe. Other more recent waves of immigration have followed.

However, many groups of immigrant origin were victims of classic racism, "nativism,"[3] and open, **systemic discrimination** until the 1960s. Black and Aboriginal peoples could be legally enslaved between 1709 and 1834, an episode of history that was long hidden by historians.[4] Canadian immigration policy was openly discriminatory until 1967, as its entry criteria effectively excluded or restricted the migration of many individuals of what we now call visible minority groups. The policy specified that British and American immigrants were to be sought first, followed by northern Europeans. Southern Europeans were only somewhat tolerated, and citizens from other continents were entirely undesirable. This institutionalized hierarchy of ethnic preferences led, over time, to the exclusion of non-whites, to selective recruitment measures, and to quotas on applicants from Asia and the Indian subcontinent.

In 1967, the federal government abrogated all preferential and discriminatory provisions based on race, religion, culture, language, and national origin and replaced them with "objective" selection criteria (for example, education, occupational qualifications, experience), which were to be applied to all prospective newcomers. Canada would be one of the first (and only) countries to have a selective immigration policy based on a periodic analysis of the economic and demographic needs of the provinces. The face of Quebec and the rest of Canada would quickly diversify as a result.[5] The number of immigrants of European origin decreased, whereas those from "developing countries" increased. At the time of the 2011 National Household Survey, 12.6 per cent of the population of Quebec was of immigrant origin (foreign born) and 9.8 per cent identified themselves as "visible minorities."[6] The Montreal region was the place of residence for 89.6 per cent of Quebecers of immigrant origin and 90.2 per cent of those from visible minority groups. In Montreal, immigrant denizens made up 23 per cent of the population and 20 per cent were visible minorities, a group that had grown by 30 per cent since 2001. Of all the visible minority groups, 60 per cent were immigrants. Black Quebecers represented the largest visible minority group in the province: Most lived in Montreal and 4 out of 10 were born in Canada. Most Quebec citizens of Arab and Latin American origins also lived in Montreal and registered the fastest growth of any community (an increase of over 50 per cent in both cases).

Normative Discourse and Social Realities

Following World War II, immigration and the development of human rights at an international level forced democratic countries to adopt legislation and other measures to combat discrimination and inequalities. In the same spirit, since the 1970s Quebec has clearly been developing an inclusive "official" normative discourse on diversity and implementing a series of measures to defend human rights and facilitate the integration of newcomers to the province.[7] Despite this systemic and inclusive adaptation to diversity, a significant gap remains between normative discourse and the reality of intergroup relations and mutual representations. Three factors partly explain this gap: the shifts that have taken place in contemporary racism, the paradoxical situation of racism in Quebec, and the dual majority/minority status of francophone Quebecers.

Racism: Shifts, Mechanisms, and Processes

Today, racism is a paradoxical reality. While "classic racism," based on biological materialism (peoples' physical attributes), has been discredited, there has been a resurgence in racism since the 1980s, notably in societies where anti-racist movements have progressively weakened[8] (as was the case with the labour movement in Europe). While these social and political struggles ran out of steam, a retreat into identity and the rise of populist figures took place. These elements came to typify a global shift in racism.[9]

But shifts in racism have also been attributable to its illegality and its illegitimacy in this era of human rights. Since World War II, systematized racism in the form of ideas, theories, and doctrines based on the presumption that "races" were unequal has been replaced by a more implicit neo-racism of human rights, recentred around the dual theme of identity and difference and founded on ostensibly more legitimate differentiation criteria.[10] Neo-racism's ideological terms changed (*culture* replaced *race*) along with its manifestations and discursive modes, which were implicit, indirect, and symbolic. The targets of neo-racism (those in the minority) were no longer constructed as biologically inferior, but as "unassimilable," irreducible, or natural carriers of pathological differences, much as the presumed "races" of yesteryear were.

Neo-racism continues to combine two processes: the differentiation and the "inferiorization" of the Other, with difference (for example, mores and beliefs) being constructed as a marker of social inferiority.[11] These indissociable processes, combined with sociohistorical realities, have allowed racism to adapt to modernity.[12] Today, the process of domination–differentiation–inferiorization is no longer used to justify colonization[13] or the economic exploitation of immigrant workers, but serves instead to establish the inferiority of certain cultural practices as "medieval" or "barbaric" in order to preserve "historically acquired rights," democratic values, or national unity. It is founded on the presumption that peoples or "nations" exist rather than on the presumption that "races" exist. Its manifestations in popular discourses clearly illustrate these shifts. The processes of neo-racism often appear to be natural reactions coming from citizens who are "legitimately" defending themselves against the "imposition," by minorities, of cultures perceived as "unassimilable" into the majority culture, which would erode historically acquired "rights," the order of things, a national identity, or the presumed unity of a people.

Contemporary neo-racism presents itself as being egalitarian, democratic, and respectable. It condemns flagrant forms of racism, deemed to be socially unacceptable from a human rights perspective, finding its justifications in irreproachable arguments drawn from universalist and liberal concepts.[14] Therefore, neo-racism is not simply a reaction to migrations and demographic changes, but much more a result of cultural shifts and of global issues. In an age of mass media and new communications technologies, neo-racism appears as a byproduct of the mediatization of power relations between groups in a context of globalization (neocolonialism), and therefore of North–South relations and the prejudices and inequalities that these relations generate. Neo-racism tends to spread in symbolic and imagination-based modes, divorced from any real contact with members of different groups. Thus, neo-racism cannot be eliminated using institutional correctives alone. The subjective elements of negatively constructing the Other will always escape state control, but they contribute just as much to making racism a "social fact" that acts upon intergroup relations in many forms (prejudices, discrimination) and draws upon many sources (for example, economic and historical differences).

While the manifestations and victims of racism have changed over the course of history, its structure, function, and *mechanisms* have stayed the same. Racism remains a process: the construction of irreducible differences prompted by power relations and serving to justify inferiorizing the Other to legitimate domination.[15] The underlying justifications are often emotional—based on feelings that privileges, prestige, property, security, or identity are being threatened. These feelings lead to the desire to destroy, inferiorize, or exclude the threat to defend a real or potential personal "entitlement." Differentiation and inferiorization operate based on sociocognitive mechanisms,[16] which we have identified inductively and defined and systematized in our numerous discourse analyses as follows:

- *Negative dichotomization* (Us–Them)
- *Inferiorization* of the Other
- *Generalizations* about an entire group
- *Self-victimization*
- *Catastrophism*
- *Demonization* of the Other
- The *desire to expel* the Other ("Go back to where you came from")
- *Political legitimation* (one of the upper echelons of neo-racism)[17]

These discursive mechanisms may be understood as echelons of racism, which are often linked to one another and which harden gradually within the same discourse.

The effects of discrimination on society and its manifestations in society are many and may be fraught with ambiguity. For example, spatial segregation, which may be a strategy of social mobility among some groups, may not always be attributed to discrimination but may result from it. Likewise, "ethnic businesses," school failure, or socioeconomic disparities may fuel racism or veer toward its production without being clearly attributable to it. Affirmative action programs or the obligation to make reasonable accommodations for various groups may correct the effects of discrimination or feed the ills that they are claiming to combat. Racism (or neo-racism) may be an instrumental cause or effect in many social phenomena. Its visibility and intensity fluctuate according to economic times, political events, everyday relationships, social sectors of life, and public debates.

A Paradoxical Situation in Quebec

The changes that have taken place make it difficult to paint a clear picture of the state of racism in the province.[18] Overall, the situation is paradoxical. Viewed from one perspective, there is no racist political party in Quebec and racist violence is relatively rare. The extremist or neo-Nazi groups who kept police busy between 1989 and 1996 have almost all disappeared, as have most of the anti-racist groups that fought against them. Racism and xenophobia are less present in Quebec's public debates than they are in Europe, where extreme right-wing parties are part of the political scene. Human rights jurisprudence has developed exponentially, but cases of violations cited by the Commission des droits de la personne et des droits de la jeunesse (CDPDJ) are relatively rare and few appear before the courts. Similarly, only rarely are major racist incidents the subject of public inquiries (as was the case in Montréal-Nord in 2008).[19] The number of Quebecers who openly call themselves racists has decreased and, in the aggregate, data on social mobility among some Quebecers of immigrant origin has been, in general, relatively positive, although it varies from one group to another.[20]

But viewed from another perspective, there has been a radicalization of alarmist discourse regarding religious symbols and demands for religious accommodation for some 10 years, even if public opinion polls or complaints filed with the CDPDJ do not paint an accurate picture of what racism and discrimination entail. Moreover, according to the Conseil de Presse du Québec, it received no complaints during the crisis of reasonable accommodation.[21] Mutual representations between groups and everyday relationships in different sectors of society are therefore difficult to measure. From the 1970s until the debate around "reasonable accommodation" (2006–8), polls indicated that the public's attitudes toward immigration and diversity were increasingly favourable, but public behaviour did not reflect this trend. Hate-mongering websites were proliferating on the Internet, cultural conflicts within institutions flared, racist conduct was taking place in the job and housing markets and in schools, and inequalities persisted for some minorities at the same time that these opinion polls were conducted. And no indicators seemed to allow us to predict the intergroup perceptions and racializing discursive "slips" in recent public debates about religion, which have morphed into "social crises."[22]

As in other egalitarian societies, the paradox in Quebec lies in the conflict between a system of democratic values and a system of complex, interrelating historical oppressions and expressions of racism (in forms that are analytically interrelated but empirically scattered). In this conflictual coexistence of systems, which affects some groups differently (Jewish, black, Muslim, youth, women), many forms of discrimination are often present at the same time: Their patterns intersect, and it is difficult for researchers or judges to pinpoint whether racism, sexism, or classic discrimination may be involved in some situations.

By and large, social practices in the media and in the housing and job markets have escaped state control. In the job market, for example, unequal (often systemic) gaps between groups have usually been measured in terms of differential market access and integration experienced by foreign-born Quebecers, but also in terms of the differential distribution of status and of unequal opportunities between "white" and "non-white" Canadians. A segmentation and a dual stratification (ethnic and social) of the job market have long been observed:[23] since 1971, census data have shown a persistent trend toward an overrepresentation of visible minorities in both reduced- and high-qualification level jobs. This polarized job market profile reflects the bimodal nature of immigration in Canada (the effect of selection policies) and the dual bilinguistic job market (posing problems for those who are not linguistically qualified) in Quebec, both of which are difficult to separate from the phenomenon of racial discrimination.

Statistical analyses show enduring disparities between groups, which have been apparent in income gaps between foreign-born and native-born Canadians for two decades, in the declining economic well-being of newcomers, and in increased inequalities for some visible minorities.[24] The *Ethnic Diversity Survey* (EDS) conducted in 2002 by Statistics Canada revealed that incomes of members of certain visible minorities (notably black Canadians) were substantially lower and their poverty levels higher than those among Canadians of "white" European ancestry. Employment rates and incomes among visible minorities have tended to increase with the duration of their residency in Canada, but gaps in relation to other Canadians have widened over time.[25] People from visible minorities groups were better educated on average than the population as a whole, but given the same level of education they had higher rates of unemployment and lower rates of representation in senior positions and in the public service. Quantitative studies in Quebec that adopted a so-called "residual" approach to discrimination observed "unexplained gaps" in income, unemployment, and employment among black Quebecers after controlling for a set of variables.[26]

Similarly, second-generation Quebec youth from visible minority groups have difficulties getting and keeping jobs—difficulties that are not attributable to insufficient academic qualifications or occupational skills. These youth were not foreign born, were fluent in French and familiar with job market practices, and their credentials were recognized.[27] Objectively speaking, their employment profiles were similar to or better than those of other young Quebecers: On average, their academic records, graduation rates, and levels of bilingualism or trilingualism were equal or superior to those of young Quebecers as a whole.[28] Nevertheless, their unemployment rates were markedly higher and they found they had to contend with prejudices from prospective employers.

Racism and Dual Majority/Minority Status among Francophones

Racism has also been the product of the historical Quebec–Canada relations surrounding the recent transition of francophones in Quebec from a minority status (French Canadians) to a majority status (Quebecers or Québécois). The age-old rivalry between francophones and anglophones in Canada has regulated relations between ethnic groups, still defined and stratified within a "vertical mosaic."[29] Power relations and competition between the two "founding peoples," tinged with neo-racism,[30] have had some notable repercussions on the way that both majorities have addressed immigration and Aboriginal issues.

We may recall that in 1960s Quebec, when ethnic and class boundaries separated francophones and anglophones, some French Canadians took a dim view of immigrants, who tended to integrate into the anglophone community in hopes of boosting their social mobility. At that time, anglophones "attracted" more immigrants because they controlled the economy and job market in Montreal, lived in the best neighbourhoods, and enjoyed a level of prestige unequalled in the rest of Canada. They also had well-developed and attractive institutions for integrating immigrants into their community.[31] French Canadians, who defined themselves as a dominated and exploited "minority," therefore perceived immigration as a threat that the government of Quebec was not controlling. For these reasons, with a view to planning its own development, Quebec decided to involve itself in the process of selecting and integrating immigrants *into the francophone majority.* Immigration thereby became a major political issue and was perceived as a means of countering the demographic and linguistic decline of francophones in North America.

From that point forward, the sociological transition of francophones to the status of a "majority people" oriented a civic, intercultural, and inclusive dominant normative discourse vis-à-vis the integration of immigrants *into the majority.*[32] With this change of status and with the Parti Québécois taking office in 1976, normative discourse progressively dissociated itself from its former militant, anti-colonial rhetoric. Critical perspectives on relations of oppression and power essentially disappeared from social discourse by the end of the 1980s, in the wake of rising neoliberalism. The focus shifted from denouncing the "oppressive relationships" suffered by minority groups (including even francophones of French-Canadian origin, who felt historically victimized) to integrating minorities into the new francophone-majority society. The discourse of "national liberation" as a minority people progressively made way for a discourse of national assertion as a majority.

From the 1980s until 2006, during public consultations on a political project intended to be "anti-racist," the subject of racism in Quebec faded from normative discourse, appearing as a marginal matter in official government policies, one that a more voluntarist integration policy would surely resolve. Successive governments would become increasingly reticent and guarded about taking action when accusations of racism were periodically directed at Quebec by the rest of Canada. In fact, for a long time, in the various halls of government, recognizing the existence of racism through public policy seemed tantamount to admitting that the Quebec model of integration had failed.

In a social and political context that had profoundly changed over the course of the 1990s, racism took on new forms in public debates. Owing to the successive failures that had marked the constitutional debate for 30 years, and to the many racializing discursive "slips" in Quebec–Canada relations since 1995,[33] Quebec nationalism was no longer driven by the same social aspirations or the project of modernization that began during the Quiet Revolution. The spectre of "referendum repeats" and the fear that integrating immigrants or meeting their demands for accommodation would cause francophone Quebecers to disappear as a people seemed to foster a return to conservative nationalism, "guarded" and victimizing.[34] At the same time, the referendums and constitutional failures that periodically exacerbated tensions between Canada's two majority groups had consequences for ethnic minorities in Quebec, who often found themselves stuck in the middle of debates and conflicts between the two "founding peoples," much as Canada's Aboriginal peoples had been. Gone unchecked, this "sandwiching" of Others sometimes made them easy targets for venting or scapegoating.[35] This tendency surfaced near the end of the 1980s in the xenophobic overtones of the documentary film *Disparaître* in 1989. Similarly, when the "No" side narrowly won the 1995 referendum, Quebec Premier Jacques Parizeau publicly blamed some "ethnic votes" for the defeat of the "Yes" side.

The "crisis of reasonable accommodations" from 2006 to 2008 would further illustrate how Quebec–Canada power relations negatively influenced the treatment of ethnic minorities, as we show in the following section. This crisis re-emerged in 2013–14 when the minority Parti Québécois government of Pauline Marois proposed, for clientelistic purposes, a Charter of Quebec Values (or the Secular Charter; Bill 60) with the intention, in the view of many observers, of reviving the sovereignist "flame" by feeding francophones' sense of threatened identity.[36]

BIOGRAPHY

Juanita Westmoreland-Traoré: Blazing a Trail for Human Rights

In Quebec, Juanita Westmoreland-Traoré is known mainly as the province's first judge of African-Canadian descent. In the rest of Canada, she is known for being the first—and to date the only—black dean of a Canadian law faculty. But these achievements are only a small part of her career path and social activism, which have been guided by a deep devotion to defending the rights and dignity of her fellow citizens.

Juanita Westmoreland-Traoré, Officer of the Ordre national du Québec.

The Canadian Press/Photo Windsor Star–Scott Webster

Quebec-based lawyer Juanita Westmoreland-Traoré was born in Verdun (on the Island of Montreal), a second-generation Quebecer whose English-speaking parents originated from Guyana, South America. As a teenager, young Juanita was steeped in the excitement of the anti-discrimination and civil rights movements of the 1950s, working as the secretary of her high school's Negro Citizenship Association. These were the awe-inspiring days of America's black civil rights movement. Hopeful black students were risking their lives to enrol in white schools and universities. Martin Luther King and his Southern Christian Leadership Conference were taking unprecedented stands to demand civil rights, like the year-long bus boycott in 1955 after Rosa Parks was arrested for refusing to give up her bus seat to a white person. These courageous movements made a lasting impression on the girl from Verdun. She was particularly influenced by Thurgood Marshall, lead counsel for the National Association for the Advancement of Colored People, who in 1967 became the first black person to be appointed as a US Supreme Court judge. Westmoreland-Traoré resolved to follow in Marshall's footsteps, aspiring to use the law as a tool for social action in the cause of underprivileged and defenceless people. After earning a law degree at Université de Montréal and a State Doctorate in Public Law at Université de Paris II, she was called to the Quebec Bar in 1969, specializing in immigration and citizenship, human rights, and family law.

Within the first few months of her career as a newly minted lawyer, Westmoreland-Traoré's skills were put to the test. It was 1969 and she was one of two black lawyers practising in Quebec (the other was her uncle). Some students at Sir George Williams (later Concordia) University had been charged with illegally occupying and ransacking the campus computer centre. They had occupied the premises in protest against the trivializing approach that the university administration had taken regarding some allegations of racism. As part of a team of defence attorneys, Westmoreland-Traoré helped have these students acquitted of 11 of the 12 charges filed against them in what would become a landmark case.

Not surprisingly, the determined lawyer's pursuits quickly diversified. In addition to her private practice she was an assistant professor at the Université de Montréal's Faculty of Law, and then a half-time professor in the Department of Legal Science at Université du Québec à Montréal. It was around this time that she became a member of the Office de la protection des consommateurs du Québec and served as a commissioner on the Canadian Human Rights Commission.

Westmoreland-Traoré also found time to write several significant articles in the *Revue du Barreau* and for the Presses de l'Université de

continued

Montréal. She collaborated on the *Rapport sur les attentes de la Communauté noire relatives au système d'éducation publique* for the Conseil supérieur de l'Éducation du Québec, and worked with the implementation committee for the *Plan d'action en faveur des communautés culturelles.* In 1985, Westmoreland-Traoré played a major role in establishing the Conseil des communautés culturelles et de l'immigration du Québec, which she chaired for five years. During her term of office at the Conseil, she was active in the development of the 1986 *Declaration by the Government of Quebec on Ethnic and Race Relations*, which committed the government of Quebec to recognize and promote the right to nondiscrimination for minorities in fulfillment of its responsibilities under international conventions.

In the 1990s, her career rose to new heights within Canada and abroad as she became the Ontario Employment Equity Commissioner for five years and subsequently worked in Haiti as an advisor to the United Nations' Truth and Justice Committee. Becoming dean of the University of Windsor's Faculty of Law and then a Quebec Court judge in the Criminal and Penal Division and the Youth Division, she also marked two more firsts for African-Canadians in Quebec.

As a judge, Westmoreland-Traoré has made noteworthy rulings setting pioneering precedents in the area of discrimination. For instance, in a 2005 ruling she acquitted a young black man charged with drug possession for the purposes of trafficking on the grounds that the city of Montreal's police department had used an illegal method of racial profiling. Before this case, no Quebec tribunal had ruled in this way on this kind of case.

The list of honours bestowed upon Westmoreland-Traoré is long and substantial. She has been appointed as an officer of the Ordre national du Québec and received honorary doctoral degrees from both the University of Ottawa and Université du Québec à Montréal. She holds a medal from Université de Montréal for her extraordinary contribution to human rights; the Canadian Jewish Congress's Alan Rose Award for human rights; the Jackie Robinson Achievement Award, conferred on black individuals who are models of success and contribute to their community; the Canadian Bar Association's Touchstone Award for her outstanding contribution to the promotion of equality in Canada's legal community; the Mérite Christine-Tourigny, awarded by the Quebec Bar for her social involvement and contributions to the advancement of women in the legal profession; and the Droits et Libertés award from Quebec's Commission des droits de la personne et des droits de la jeunesse for her unflagging commitment to the fight against discrimination, on the occasion of the sixtieth anniversary of the Universal Declaration of Human Rights.

Behind all of these honours lies the public's appreciation for Juanita Westmoreland-Traoré's resolute devotion to fighting discrimination on many fronts, from community to institutional settings. At the community level, she has served as legal counsel to the Congress of Black Women of Canada, the Black Community Centre, and the Association québécoise des organismes de Coopération internationale. She has travelled to observe trials and elections for the international missions organized by Ligue des droits et libertés, Centre d'information et de documentation sur l'Afrique australe, and the South Africa Education Fund. She has worked with Centraide of Greater Montreal, sat on the Canadian Civil Liberties Association board of directors, served on the Canadian Human Rights Foundation executive, acted as a panellist with the Canadian Council on Social Development Court Challenges Program, presided over the Montreal Regional Committee of the National Congress of Black Women, been a member of the Consultative Committee on Education of the National Judicial Institute, sat on the board of directors of the Canadian Institute for the Administration of Justice, and chaired the Canadian Association of Provincial Court Judges' Equality and Diversity Committee.

Throughout her long career, Westmoreland-Traoré was often struck by the dearth of resources for judges in cases that involved diversity and equality. With this in mind, during her tenure on the board of directors of the Canadian Chapter of the International Association of Women Judges, she co-coordinated the publication of a judicial guide to these issues that encourages judges to carefully consider social context as a matter of course when interpreting the law—a practice that Westmoreland-Traoré holds to be crucial to the balanced evolution of Canada's jurisprudence. The guide contains dozens of articles on doctrine and jurisprudence. It addresses grounds for discrimination, such as race, age, disability, and impoverishment (drawn from human rights legislation), as factors that intersect within a social context to produce social inequality between citizens of the same country.

Juanita Westmoreland-Traoré has used her renown and resources to raise awareness about the unstable living conditions faced by poor and vulnerable citizens (especially women and children) in Quebec, Canada, and abroad. Having seen the ravages of poverty, war, genocide, and crimes against humanity, she has worked ardently to make her voice heard in some of the world's most respected organizations.

The following analysis presents the broad outlines of our expert report on the media treatment and opinion discourses surrounding reasonable accommodations, which was drawn up at the request of the Bouchard–Taylor Commission.[37] We highlight first the key devices and practices used by the print media during "event-based coverage" at the time of the reasonable accommodations crisis in 2006 and 2007, and next the neo-racist rhetorical devices used in the opinion discourses of editorialists, columnists, intellectuals, or readers when analyzing their texts in the print media. More specifically, our study analyzed both event-based coverage by journalists (451 articles) and a corpus of opinion discourses (654 editorials, columns, letters by intellectuals and readers) in Quebec's five major newspapers: *Le Devoir, La Presse, Le Journal de Montréal, Montreal Gazette,* and *Le Soleil.* We then establish some links with the recent crisis surrounding the Charter of Quebec Values (or the Secular Charter) in 2013–14.

The "Reasonable Accommodation" Debate of 2006–8

Reasonable accommodation is a legal concept specific to Canada and is based on the jurisprudence of the Supreme Court in matters of indirect discrimination and human rights. The 1985 decisions of *O'Malley v. Simpsons-Sears* and *Bhinder v. Canadian National Railway* established the concept of reasonable accommodation and defined its scope. This obligation requires that norms, practices, or institutional or organizational policies be adapted in function to the needs of certain persons on the basis of their handicap, religion, or other motives to avoid or counter a discriminatory situation pertaining to them. However, this obligation no longer applies if it causes the employer an "excessive constraint," such as infringing on the rights of others, endangering personal safety, affecting the institution's basic missions, or involving excessive costs.

The reasonable accommodations debate, which lasted over two years in the Quebec media (2006–8), revealed a steep gap between, on the one hand, normative and legal discourse on pluralism and human rights, and on the other hand social and populist discourse on these issues in public opinion. This "crisis" highlighted the state of ethnic relations, mutual intergroup perceptions, and specific sensitivities related to the still-recent transition of francophones to a majority status in Quebec. It particularly demonstrated the perception gap between Quebecers in Montreal and Quebecers in other regions, as well as the dearth of knowledge among some of the public about the realities of immigration and the measures and infrastructure implemented in matters of integration and human rights. It also opened a forum for populist and racist discourses, which were often used unconsciously in public and journalistic opinion.

The debate began to crystallize in the media in March 2006[38] and morphed into a "crisis" by January 2007. In a context of media one-upmanship and proliferating racializing discourses, on 8 February 2007, as a matter of apparent urgency and at the beginning of his election campaign, Premier Jean Charest struck the Consultation Commission on Accommodation Practices Related to Cultural Differences (also known as the Bouchard–Taylor Commission). Many Quebecers said they had the impression that they had been transported back in time "to Quebec pre-1977, when the French-Canadian nation saw itself as being homogeneous and experienced its relationship to the Other in terms of an identity-based threat."[39]

In this debate, the juridical–political apparatus and normative discourse were called into question and virulently criticized by a host of citizens and journalists. Quebec's Charter of Human Rights and Freedoms, Canada's Charter of Rights and Freedoms, and the obligation of making reasonable accommodation were presented as unidirectional legal instruments in human rights jurisprudence that forced public institutions to always accept requests for accommodation from minority groups, and even to grant them privileges. Journalists set about scrutinizing public policies on immigration and integration and their application, looking for a fight. During the debate, media confusion over the concept of reasonable accommodation and its objectives, limitations, and application led some citizens and municipal politicians to request that governments change the Charters, or even abolish them, in response to this "state of emergency"[40] and to the "injustice" done to Quebec's majority group.

Media Strategies

The role of the media was central in turning this debate into a social crisis, through its strategies and selective coverage of social discourses.[41] Some of the media's processes, **framing**, and staging around "reasonable accommodations" allowed it to set the political agenda and generate a state of "moral panic."[42] Some journalists contributed to fuelling the pervasive confusion by conflating "reasonable accommodation" (which is an obligation and a remedial measure used to address a discriminatory situation) with voluntary adjustments or private agreements that did not result from the violation of a fundamental freedom. Indeed, over 75 per cent of the "incidents" reported by journalists regarding "reasonable accommodations" between March 2006 and April 2007 were private agreements or anecdotal current events that they blew out of proportion.

Some newspapers went out of their way to break one news story after another, thereby elevating a collection of anecdotal events to the rank of a "social crisis." Using a sweeping array of public opinion polls about "racism among Quebecers," daily spot polls, and "exclusive news investigations," these newspapers began constructing issues, "storytelling," and "**agenda setting**" for public debate, forcing politicians and citizens alike to take a stand on a number of questions. Their over-the-top magnification of events had a huge influence on the public and the political agenda during this period.

The way journalists framed their stories (their "angle") and the importance they attributed to some points of view allowed them to influence the public's understanding of the issues. Two ways of framing stories were unmistakably used by the media: a legal–juridical frame and a dramatic–conflictual frame. The legal–juridical frame, which was the starting point for most "breaking" news stories, misled the public or, at the very least, fed public confusion by erroneously associating private agreements with reasonable accommodations. Requests for accommodation were often presented from the angle of "privileges" or "abuses" rather than presenting a citizen's right to equality or to negotiated agreements.[43] In the race for fresh content, the dramatic–conflictual frame, be it real or imagined, was used in polarized interpretations of events. The angle of polarization between minority and majority groups intimated that some minorities enjoyed privileges and threatened common values, thereby engaging readers of the majority group in a victimizing reading of events.

Event-Based Coverage and Opinion Discourses in the Print Media

With respect to event-based coverage, the analysis reveals that the media contributed to exacerbating popular prejudices toward certain minorities by covering events in the following ways:

- Publishing images of the minority members of religious minority groups—Muslim women wearing niqabs or burkas; Ultra-Orthodox Jews (Hasidim)
- Running headlines and leads that featured populist quotes from the right-wing Action démocratique du Québec (ADQ) party, which later became the Coalition Avenir Québec (CAQ)
- Conducting daily spot polls, often from a victimizing point of view—"Are you fed up with . . . ?"
- Mainly quoting people who viewed themselves as victims
- Participating in herd behaviour (in print, television, radio, and on the Web), in which media responded to each other
- Producing copious amounts of "exclusives" and "breaking news" stories in competition with other newspapers, upping the ante in front-page headline news and media hype
- Passing off hypothetical, fictitious events[44] as examples of social deviancy, antisocial behaviour, or nonconformity to majority-group norms, thereby building momentum for what is called a "deviancy amplification spiral" in moral panic theory
- Providing disproportionately extensive coverage of a small-scale phenomenon (there were only a handful of bona fide cases of reasonable accommodations at the time)
- Staging the defining issue of the election campaign

Indeed, the debate was used as a "hot-button" issue and a decorative prop in staging the 2007 February–March provincial election campaign. Constantly solicited to comment on "breaking news," obliging politicians helped to artificially prolong the media-driven debate. Politicians hazarded opinions without investigating the veracity of the facts related by journalists or distinguishing anecdotal information from real cases of accommodation. "Breaking news" could therefore be used as a kind of litmus test to judge the competency of public figures.

At this time, numerous journalists attributed the rise in popularity of the ADQ to the populist positions taken in the debate by its leader, Mario Dumont. Claiming to speak on behalf of the majority, daring to "say out loud what everyone is thinking," Dumont politically legitimated populist discourse by constantly accusing his political adversaries of being "lax" on the issue of reasonable accommodation, by favouring a "hard-line" approach, and by making striking declarations such as "We cannot defend our identity with one knee [already] on the ground."[45] This type of legitimation became commonplace and even banal in the media, whereas one year earlier the issue would not have found a public tribune. Letters to the editor made ample use of Dumont's populist expressions—"wear the pants," "one knee [already] on the ground," and "bending to the demands of minorities"—which were reprised in scores of articles on current events.

Our analysis of opinion discourses—based on a corpus of 654 editorials, columns, and letters to the editor from intellectuals and readers published in Quebec's five major newspapers—revealed that populist and neo-racist discursive mechanisms were explicitly and implicitly present in half of the texts. Any of the eight discursive mechanisms specified in our analytical grid could be found in 14 per cent of the editorials/columns and 52 per cent of letters from readers.[46] Some opinion discourses combined a range of discursive mechanisms from our grid:

1. An Us–Them *negative dichotomization* ("They come to our country to impose their ways on us")
2. *Generalizations* about all immigrants or all members of a minority ("They're not integrating into society"; "They're all fundamentalists")
3. *Inferiorization* of the Other ("They're still living in the Middle Ages")
4. *Self-victimization* ("one knee [already] on the ground"; loss of power and identity; "They come along and impose their customs on us/get privileges")
5. *Catastrophism* (state of emergency; conspiracy theories; "Things will only get worse")
6. *Demonization* (invasion; the Other being "unassimilable" to democratic values; "They are strange, unpredictable, and worrisome")

7. Justification for the *desire to expel* the Other ("Go back to where you came from")
8. Appeals for *political legitimation* (through elected ADQ politicians or municipal representatives, like those in Hérouxville, who proposed that a "code of conduct" for immigrants be adopted)

The momentum of these discursive mechanisms drove the issue into an upward spiral, from one echelon to the next between March 2006 and April 2007, as though their almost banal presence in the media had legitimated taking a harder line.

Among the opinion discourses of newspaper editors, columnists, and intellectuals, these mechanisms were most often found in articles about Hasidic Jews. Negative dichotomization tended to be used to contrast majority values (defined as those of Quebec's "citizens" or "society") with those of the Hasidic Jewish community, notably in the area of gender equality (which was posited as irreducible and non-negotiable) to demonstrate that the community had not adapted to a "modern" way of life. Derision was frequently used by these journalists and intellectuals, along with absurd humour and extreme examples, to denounce the potential escalation of "hare-brained" requests and to weigh up the "limits" that had been breached. Many associated making "reasonable accommodations" with "fundamentalism," contrasting the progression of religious fundamentalisms in the public sphere with the "laxity" of Quebecers regarding requests made by minorities. For some, this contrast implicitly expressed victimhood or catastrophism. The following extract from a column by Michel Vastel illustrates some of these mechanisms:

> Months ago, our political leaders—the leader of the Parti Québécois in particular—should have put a stop to the unreasonable demands of a few very vocal minorities. They had a historic duty to defend Quebec, as it exists everywhere, not only in the City of Montreal or in Westmount. All we got was subservience. But beyond these political squabbles, we are nevertheless brave people! We are racist and we don't hide it when others crowd in and mess things up . . . the majority of new Quebecers (74%) and old-stock Quebecers (83%) are fed up with so-called "reasonable accommodations" . . . The message to the political elites and government leaders is now clear: the majority doesn't want any more reasonable accommodations (author's translation).[47]

More readers than columnists wrote about feeling their values and cultural points of reference were being threatened and that they, as members of the majority, had been wronged by minorities, who would "abuse" the "laxity" of "Quebecers," or by judges, politicians, or institutions that would "unduly" grant "privileges" to the minorities, whom these readers perceived to be "fundamentalist." We observed a sense of distance and powerlessness in relation to the political and juridical authorities that were purportedly making disembodied decisions contrary to "popular will." The federal and provincial Charters of human rights and the power of judges were sharply criticized in two contradictory tendencies of popular discourse: The Charters seemed to be allowing what they forbade by granting rights to people whose collective religious beliefs ran contrary to individual rights and the choices of the "majority." Many blamed judges, the Supreme Court, or the Charters for this situation and questioned their ability to serve the population. Whereas some argued in favour of amending the Charters, others questioned the soundness of their principles and their adequacy for dealing with present-day realities.

Dominant representations of the Other in this racializing discourse saw a major Us–Them dichotomization. Among readers, "Them" generally referred to recent immigrants and foreigners, often amalgamated as Sikh, Muslim, and even Islamic fundamentalists. A number of opinion discourses about religious minorities also depicted "Them" as "fundamentalists" and singled them out as causing various kinds of social unrest around identity in a context of destabilizing international events. The rigidity of the "precepts" in these communities was often contrasted with the hard-fought "rights and freedoms" historically acquired by native-born civil society and social movements. Some made the distinction between "good immigrants" who "wanted" to integrate into society (by becoming "just like Us") and "bad immigrants" (who demanded accommodation and were therefore seen to be refusing Quebec's "common values"). Those who wished to continue to live "as they did in their own country" were not part of "Us."

CASE STUDY

Adopting a Quebec Policy to Fight Racism in a Context of Crisis

Until recently, the issues of racism and discrimination were practically absent from "official" normative discourse in Quebec. The government's *Policy Statement on Immigration and Integration* in 1990 and its *Policy on Educational Integration and Intercultural Education* in 1998 devoted only a few lines to racism and framed the issue as a potential individual transgression rather than a systemic phenomenon. Portions of Quebec's anti-poverty legislation (Bill 112) and its National Strategy to Combat Poverty and Social Exclusion targeted "immigrants" and "visible minorities" as "vulnerable groups," but did not discuss the sociological mechanisms that interlink racism, discrimination, social inequalities, and exclusion. There has been a reticence or guarded attitude in Quebec toward dealing directly with racism, naming it, and introducing it into public policies as an issue to combat. There has also been a fragmentation of provincial initiatives, instead of a systemic, coherently applied approach, based on the effectiveness of human rights regarding equity, equality, diversity, and anti-poverty issues.[48]

Institutional responses regarding these issues have remained ambivalent and often circumstantial or sporadic. Generally speaking, racism elicits a reaction from Quebec's public authorities when it leads to excessive racializing discursive "slips" (as occurred in public debates around reasonable accommodation) or to violence, but it is often treated as a marginal, individual loss of control, as though it was not an issue that plays out every day as the cause or effect of social inequalities. Consequently, the struggle against racism and discrimination has been left to the field of law and to the legal apparatus, but has not become part of public discourse or of a coherent overall policy to more comprehensively address the mechanisms that perpetuate discriminations and unequal power relations.

During the summer of 2006, the Quebec government struck a parliamentary commission to address racism and discrimination. The commission launched public consultations based on a document entitled *Towards a Government Policy to Fight against Racism and Discrimination*, the provincial follow-up document to the federal government's 2005 *Canada's Action Plan Against Racism* (itself much awaited and called for by numerous groups and observers after the World Conference on Racism, Racial Discrimination, Xenophobia and Related Intolerance in Durban, South Africa, in 2001). Nevertheless, because of the media crisis and the populist political "slips" on "reasonable accommodation," which shook Quebec from 2006 until 2008, it was not until after the Consultation Commission on Accommodation Practices Related to Cultural Differences (the Bouchard–Taylor Commission) that a government policy was adopted in this area. Indeed, in November of 2008, a few days before a provincial election was called, the Liberal government of Quebec launched *Diversity: An Added Value: Government Policy to Promote Participation of All in Québec's Development*. This policy promoted equal opportunity and the fight against discrimination, a component that was neglected in the 1990 *Policy Statement* and in government actions during the intervening years but that was largely "euphemized" in this policy.[49] The new policy proposed a

continued

comprehensive approach built around three main orientations:

1. Recognizing and combating prejudices and discrimination by ensuring that all citizens are educated about their rights
2. Renewing practices through real equality and the full participation of all citizens in Quebec's economic, social, and cultural development by promoting access to and advancement in employment
3. Coordinating efforts to ensure coherence and complementarity in government programs

This policy provides an action plan, which includes 21 measures and associates all government bodies and ministries in this approach, covering education and awareness raising, prevention, redress of injury to rights, mobilization of institutions and diversity management, victim support, and the suppression of racist violence.

At the same time as this policy was released, the CDPDJ held extensive public consultations on "racial profiling" and systemic discrimination. The commission tackled this problem in the wake of the Montréal-Nord events in 2008, when an altercation with police led to the shooting death of a Latino youth followed by a spectacular riot in this underprivileged neighbourhood. Furthermore, the CDPDJ had received approximately 60 complaints regarding racial profiling in Quebec, conducted a number of surveys, and presented about a dozen profiling cases before the Tribunal des droits de la personne. The report from this consultation, published in 2011, contains close to a hundred recommendations, but almost none of them were followed up, even though some referred to measures set out in the 2009–14 action plan, *Diversity: An Added Value*.

In order to implement this action plan, notably to deal with certain religious issues (including the wearing of the niqab in communications between citizens and the state), the minister of immigration tabled Bill 16, An Act to Promote Action by the Administration with Respect to Cultural Diversity, on 22 September 2009, which quickly rekindled the controversy around "reasonable accommodation." The bill was meant to ensure that government bodies establish and follow accountability directives and rules on "diversity management" to set a good example by integrating Quebecers of all origins and providing high-quality services to an increasingly diversified clientele. Some accused the Charest government of placing religious freedom above gender equality. The Conseil du statut de la femme, for example, viewed this bill as an unlimited obligation imposed by the state to adapt to diversity. The Conseil pointedly remarked that the government had not placed any demands on new Quebecers and religious minorities to respond in kind by adapting to Quebec society. Others even saw the bill as a setback or a reversal of the "moral contract" between two parties (minorities and the majority), as described in the 1990 *Policy Statement*. The Conseil du statut de la femme proposed a number of amendments, asserting that the principles of secularism, gender equality, and the promotion of the French language must guide the interpretation of this bill. In the end, this initiative was shelved. Because the issue has not been settled, the recommendations of the Bouchard–Taylor Commission have also been shelved.

When the Parti Québécois came to power in 2012 it quickly proposed a project for a Secular Charter of Quebec Values, which exclusively targeted the wearing of religious symbols (and not racism within society) and which included certain articles that contradicted the Canadian and Quebec Charters of Rights and Freedoms. The two former co-chairs of the Bouchard–Taylor Commission, Gérard Bouchard and Charles Taylor, vehemently denounced this charter project. Taylor saw it as "an absolutely terrible act of exclusion . . . something we would expect to see in Putin's Russia."[50] Bouchard, for his part, argued that the Parti Québécois government was "stirring up primal and irrational fears among a segment of the population (about a grand Islamic plot secretly at work in Quebec, our society's takeover by Muslims: 'they refuse to assimilate,' 'they impose their values,' 'they don't respect our laws,' 'they're invading us.')"[51] Finally, the charter was abandoned when the Liberals won the election in April 2014.

Letters by readers often included many racializing mechanisms, such as negative dichotomization marked by inferiorization ("Do we have to go back to the Middle Ages because one particular group still wants to live this way?"[52]), the desire to expel ("Immigrants who want to stay in Quebec should adapt to our customs, not the opposite. If they can't accept this, they should go back where they came from"[53]) or inferiorization, demonization, and self-victimization:

> We have become racists because of a radical left-wing government wanting to impose changes based on the desires of some bottom rung immigrants. They come from the streets in their country, they are either thieves or sick, and they are imposed upon us. They receive social security cheques, but continue to steal. They have often been deported from other countries, but we welcome them here.[54]

There was also a perception that the Charters had violated the rights of some (the majority) to create privileges for others (the minority), rather than protecting rights (equality) as the central value of Quebec's collective identity. In some discourses, we observed an inversion of the Charters' values for the purposes of "delegitimating" and inferiorizing the "Other." The refusal to accept divergence and the demand for "loyalism" (or for a presumably consensual social conformity) therefore displaced respect for rights and freedoms. The equality of individuals was replaced by the conviction that favouritism was being shown to certain groups and an injustice perpetrated on other citizens; the "inclusive Us" became a drive for homogeneity. Racializing discursive mechanisms were based on the conviction that they represented the "universal" and on a stereotypical and even mythical representation of those who stood accused of opposing it.

The Crisis Triggered by the "Charter of Quebec Values" in 2013–14: Prolongation of the Reasonable Accommodation Crisis

In the years following the reasonable accommodation crisis, this issue resurfaced a number of times and there was little action on the recommendations in the Bouchard–Taylor report (see the Case Study box). Like the Action démocratique du Québec (now the CAQ), which had radicalized its discourse for clientelistic purposes during the 2007 electoral campaign (enabling it to acquire the status of Official Opposition in the National Assembly), the Parti Québécois attempted to recover the CAQ's right-wing votes by proposing a "Secular Charter" (Bill 60) aimed at banning the wearing of "conspicuous" religious symbols in the civil service. In 2013, Bill 60, entitled Charter Affirming the Values of State Secularism and Religious Neutrality and of Equality between Women and Men, and Providing a Framework for Accommodation Requests, targeted not only the president of the National Assembly, judges, prosecutors, police officers, and prison guards, as recommended in the Bouchard–Taylor report, but also extended the ban to educators and monitors in daycare centres, primary and secondary school teachers, and public sector employees in government organizations, hospitals, social service centres, and colleges and universities. The debate quickly focused on "gender equality" and particularly targeted Muslim women wearing hijabs.

With Bill 60, piloted by the minister responsible for democratic institutions, Bernard Drainville, the government brewed an extremely tense and divisive public debate that lasted several months, from summer 2013 until the elections on 7 April 2014. The debate led to the creation of two highly polarized camps as well as spontaneous citizen movements. There ensued a proliferation of racializing "slips" and insults, even death threats, among the population, which were expressed mainly through social media.[55] Several former sovereignist premiers, public figures (such as Gérard Bouchard and Charles Taylor), and organizations (such as the Commission des droits de la personne, the Barreau du Québec, the Association québécoise d'établissements de santé et de services sociaux, the Fédération des femmes du Québec, the Fédération des chambres de commerce du Québec, universities, and many others) opposed the charter because of its potentially discriminatory effects, and many campaigned against it in various forums. Most pronounced themselves in favour of the recommendations in the Bouchard–Taylor report, that is, a ban on the wearing of religious symbols only by those with the power to exercise restraint (police, judges,

Primary Source

Bill 60: Charter Affirming the Values of State Secularism and Religious Neutrality and of Equality between Women and Men, and Providing a Framework for Accommodation Requests

Explanatory Notes (pp. 2–3)

The purpose of this bill is to establish a Charter affirming the values of State secularism and religious neutrality and of equality between women and men, and providing a framework for accommodation requests.

A further purpose of the bill is to specify, in the Charter of Human Rights and Freedoms, that the fundamental rights and freedoms guaranteed by that Charter are to be exercised in a manner consistent with the values of equality between women and men and the primacy of the French language as well as the separation of religions and State and the religious neutrality and secular nature of the State, while making allowance for the emblematic and toponymic elements of Québec's cultural heritage that testify to its history.

Public bodies must, in the pursuit of their mission, remain neutral in religious matters and reflect the secular nature of the State. Accordingly, obligations are set out for personnel members of public bodies in the exercise of their functions, including a duty to remain neutral and exercise reserve in religious matters by, among other things, complying with the restriction on wearing religious objects that overtly indicate a religious affiliation. As well, personnel members of a public body must exercise their functions with their face uncovered, and persons to whom they provide services must also have their face uncovered when receiving such services.

The same rules apply to other persons, in particular to persons who exercise judicial functions, or adjudicative functions within the

prosecutors). Otherwise, the ban explicitly involved a suspension of the rights and liberties protected by the Quebec Charter of Human Rights and Freedoms for electoral purposes. As Jocelyn Maclure argues:

> The time is long over when the Parti Québécois was dominated by intellectuals and elected officials who tried to show that nationalism and independence were compatible with the recognition of cultural and religious diversity. Its supporters now favour a secularism that's more apt to curtail freedom of religion and equality regarding access to employment and services on behalf of the concept (mistaken, in my opinion) of the neutrality of the State. The party also includes nationalists who believe that the "historic majority," apathetic for too long, must now assert itself and impose its will on minorities.[56]

Other organizations and prominent public personalities, including the Syndicat de la Fonction publique du Québec; former Supreme Court justice Claire L'Heureux-Dubé; Janette Bertrand, a well-known Quebec TV personality who started the "Janette movement"; and others campaigned in favour of it. According to a CROP survey conducted on 17 and 21 October 2013, 50 per cent of respondents supported the charter project (more than 60 per cent in the francophone group), while only 41 per cent opposed it. This support would hold steady at around 50 per cent in the weeks ahead, based on various polls, thereby dividing the population in two.[57]

This crisis would again open the way for racializing discourses, more specifically within the camp of those "in favour" of the charter. During an electoral campaign brunch on 30 March 2014, Premier Pauline Marois and Janette Bertrand, president of administrative branch, and to personnel members of the National Assembly.

The bill defines, in the Charter of Human Rights and Freedoms, what constitutes an accommodation resulting from the application of the Charter, and sets out the conditions for granting such an accommodation. An analytical framework is also provided to facilitate the handling of accommodation requests submitted to public bodies on religious grounds.

Public bodies are required to adopt a policy to implement the prescriptions of the bill.

The Act respecting the National Assembly is amended to specifically grant the Assembly the power to regulate the wearing of religious symbols by Members, and grant the Office of the National Assembly the power to approve the presence of a religious symbol in the premises of the Assembly.

Chapter II (pp. 5–6)

Duties and Obligations of Personnel Members of Public Bodies

Division I

Duties of Neutrality and Reserve in Religious Matters

3. In the exercise of their functions, personnel members of public bodies must maintain religious neutrality.
4. In the exercise of their functions, personnel members of public bodies must exercise reserve with regard to expressing their religious beliefs.

Division II

Restriction on Wearing Religious Symbols

5. In the exercise of their functions, personnel members of public bodies must not wear objects such as headgear, clothing, jewellery or other adornments which, by their conspicuous nature, overtly indicate a religious affiliation.

Source: Text is available at www.assnat.qc.ca/en/travaux-parlementaires/projets-loi/projet-loi-60-40-1.html.

the "Janettes," maintained that "*fundamentalists*" were "*threatening*" Quebec society by "*chipping away at*" certain rights and therefore posing a risk to gender equality.[58] Their comments illustrate the presence of discursive dichotomization mechanisms (Us–Them), but especially of catastrophism, demonization of the Other, and self-victimization as member of the majority group. To explain her decision to found the "Janette movement" and her defence of the charter, Janette Bertrand had this to say: "When I saw women on television, young women wearing veils who called themselves feminists, I said to myself: I have to do something."[59] She went on to explain: "Medicine tells us that prevention is important. So we're taking preventive action. We think there's a danger here; we can name names, but we won't. It's dangerous, so let's prevent it by having a charter."[60]

Using personal experience to support her alarmist vision, she told the audience that a "very respectable" Algerian man had told her that Muslim fundamentalists, "the Muslim Brothers, . . . in all countries make small demands, small demands, small demands"[61] to obtain religious accommodations. She then gave a hypothetical example, based on catastrophism, to justify the charter's adoption:

> I live in a building with a swimming pool. I swim once a week for aquafit class. And then two men arrive, and they're upset at the sight of two women in the pool—me and my friend. They go away. Let us then imagine these men go to see the owner, who is very happy to have a lot of rich McGill students there. And then they ask, well we want to have a day (when women aren't allowed). And then, in a few months, they're the

> only ones who can use the pool. Well that's it, the chipping away of rights that we're scared of, and that's what will happen if there's no charter.[62]

Parti Québécois leader Pauline Marois supported and legitimated Bertrand's comments. Recalling the debate on the establishment of Islamic courts in Canada, Marois affirmed that, regarding the threat of fundamentalism,

> It's not a significant threat for us at the moment, but the fact it's not a significant threat doesn't mean there's no need for prevention. . . . There was the Bouchard–Taylor Commission, there were various different occurrences when they wanted to adopt reasonable accommodations in our institutions, in our schools, in our hospitals. I didn't dream that. We've been working on these issues for 5, 6, 7 years, so there must be a problem somewhere! So we, on our part, think we have to take the bull by the horns.[63]

On 5 April, the prime minister even maintained that those fired from the public service for refusing to remove their religious symbol would be "helped" by the government to find comparable jobs in the private sector—an uncompromising position that excluded all exceptions for workers hired before this charter's adoption. However, on 7 April 2014 the sovereignist Parti Québécois government lost the election to the Liberal Party far more decisively than the polls had predicted partly because of this crisis.

Conclusion

This chapter has shown that there is a major gap between the development of Quebec's inclusive and pluralistic official discourse on one hand, and the persistence of exclusion and discrimination (in addition to public debates tinged with fears over identity and racializing discourses) on the other hand. We have also seen that because racism is constantly shifting, it is difficult to measure progress in ethnic relations.

The debates around "reasonable accommodation" and the Secular Charter (Bill 60) revealed that the normative and juridical discourse meant to be inclusive and egalitarian does not seem to have entirely penetrated the fabric of Quebec society, as demonstrated by the persistence of a misunderstanding in public opinion of the concept of reasonable accommodation in the application and the respect of human rights. These two debates, which morphed into a crisis, testified to something of a backlash against this normative and legitimate discourse by leaving the floor wide open for racializing discourses whose mechanisms inverted the values entrenched in both the federal and provincial Charters of Human Rights and Freedoms. Major "Us–Them" boundaries and guarded conceptualizations about Quebec identity persist to this day in some sectors of Quebec public opinion. In the first accommodations crisis, the controversy was initially engaged through one-upmanship in the media, then in the political arena with racializing "slips" from some elected officials (such as Hérouxville's municipal code of conduct and the political legitimation of populist fears and discourses by the leader of the ADQ), which allowed racializing discourses to spiral within a few weeks beyond several echelons of racism and affected social cohesion in Quebec. In the second crisis, the political legitimation of the Secular Charter, clumsily proposed by the government and including discriminatory articles, attested to the government's entire responsibility for generating the crisis for electoral purposes.

These two crises were not merely sudden expressions of exasperation that involved the scapegoating of religious minorities. Beyond fears about the rise of religious fundamentalism leading to conflicts and terrorist acts in different countries, they were also a *symptom* of the fragility of Quebec's identity as a national entity (as a people). This fragility has been caused by social and economic upheaval in a context of globalization, which draws upon the historical malaise created by competitive relations between Quebec and the rest of Canada over the allegiance of immigrants, in matters both linguistic and symbolic. This malaise (related to the fragility of the majority status of francophones) was reflected in a series of insecurities in opinion discourses: fears of losing the recent gains of Quebec's modernity (for example, gender equality, francization); fears regarding the majority's ability to see themselves as an inclusive Us and to successfully integrate immigrants; fears of being called "racist" by the rest of Canada[64] and the world; and, in sum, fears about the success or failure of the Quebec model of integration. These fears were manifested in discourses that favoured "abolishing" the charter, and that strongly opposed Canadian multiculturalism and the "power of judges" who decide "against the majority" in democracy. These catastrophic discourses victimize the majority group, which is supposedly threatened by "religious fundamentalists" who wish to "impose their law," receive "privileges," and multiply their "excessive demands."

According to many front-line workers in education and social services, reasonable accommodations are generally well managed day to day in communities. The gap between reality and perception was striking in these debates, and education concerning not only respect for human rights and accommodations in various work settings, but also in relation to "diversity," conflict management, and citizenship demonstrates their particular importance in contexts of crisis and heightened tensions.

Whereas these debates have shown how tensions can rise very quickly during identity crisis situations, very few measures regarding prevention and the education and sensitization of people of all ages and in all sectors of social life have been implemented since the Bouchard–Taylor Commission. Accordingly, a coherent public policy on diversity, equity, and inclusion must articulate government and community actions from a very concrete perspective of social *co-responsibility* and legal obligations for citizens and for all social, economic, and political actors (including private businesses and labour organizations, municipalities, and regions). It must count on the support of sectors that influence "equal opportunities" for minorities (employment, education, media, housing), as well as on the changing attitude of the majority (through education and training) and on the development of a feeling of belonging to a common society, one beyond an inward-looking tribal consciousness. The increase in partnerships, sponsorships, and settings for *collective action* and amicable social gatherings, where citizens from all origins can develop relationships of mutual understanding and social solidarity around common causes, is also at the base of a participative public culture common to all, which must be based upon local dynamism so that the gap can decrease between the normative discourse and social practices.

Questions for Critical Thinking

1. What is contemporary neo-racism?
2. What kinds of neo-racist discursive mechanisms have we seen manifested in social discourses?
3. In what ways did the dual majority/minority status of Quebec francophones permeate the public debates on religious symbols and reasonable accommodations, which re-emerge periodically in Quebec?
4. Are these debates good indicators of the state of ethnic relations and reciprocal representations in Quebec?

Notes

1. *The Evolving Linguistic Portrait*, 2006 Census, Catalogue no. 97-555-XWE2006001; Ministère des Relations avec les citoyens et de l'Immigration, *Données sur la population recensée en 2001 portant sur la religion : analyse sommaire*. Direction de la population et de la recherche, 27 May 2003.
2. Marc Angenot defines *social discourse* as "the aggregate of all that is said and written in a state of society, to the extent that this aggregate does not appear to be composed of *random* statements, but of [statements] governed by conventions, held within ideological configurations" (author's translation). See M. Angenot, "Théorie du discours social," *Contextes*, no. 1, Discours en contexte (September 2006), accessed 15 August 2008, http://contextes.revues.org/51.
3. Nativism was an ideology that aimed to favour those born in Canada and exclude foreigners.
4. Marcel Trudel, *Deux siècles d'esclavage au Québec* (Montreal: Hurtubise HMH, 2004); Brett Rushforth,

"'A Little Flesh We Offer You': The Origins of Indian Slavery in New France," *William and Mary Quarterly* 60, no. 4 (October 2003): 777–808.

5. Ethnic diversity is measured in three (self-declared) categories in the Canadian Census: foreign-born (immigrant), visible minority, and ethnic origins (ancestry). Second-generation Canadians are counted through a question about their parents' country of origin.
6. *Visible minority* is an official term from the Employment Equity Act (1986). It refers to "persons, other than Aboriginal peoples, who are non-Caucasian in race or non-white in colour." In the 2006 census, this category included persons of Chinese, South Asian, Black, Filipino, Latin American, Southeast Asian, Arab, West Asian, Korean, and Japanese origin.
7. Here are some examples of this official discourse: Quebec's Charter of Human Rights and Freedoms (1975) and Charter of the French Language (1977), which established links between the integration of immigrants and the recognition of minorities and Quebec's common public language; the Commission des droits de la personne et des droits de la jeunesse and the Tribunal des droits de la personne; the Affirmative Action Program; major developments in legislation and jurisprudence in this area; and the adoption of official policies, including the recent policy to fight against racism and discrimination (2008) (see "Adopting a Quebec Policy to Fight Racism in a Context of Crisis" in this chapter).
8. Michel Wieviorka, *L'espace du racisme* (Paris: Le Seuil, 1991).
9. Pierre-A. Taguieff, *La force du préjugé* (Paris: La Découverte, 1987); Pierre-André Taguieff, ed., *Dictionnaire historique et critique du racisme* (Paris: Presses universitaires de France, 2013); Martin Barker, *The New Racism* (London: Junction Books, 1981); and many others.
10. Étienne Balibar, "Y-a-t-il un 'néo-racisme'?" in *Race, Nation, Classe : les identités ambiguës*, ed. E. Balibar and I. Wallerstein (Paris: La Découverte, 1988); Pierre-André Taguieff, *Face au racisme 2 : analyses, hypothèses, perspectives* (Paris: La Découverte, 1991); Taguieff, *La force du préjugé*.
11. Colette Guillaumin, *L'idéologie raciste : genèse et langage actuel* (Paris: Mouton, 1972).
12. Alain Touraine, "Le racisme aujourd'hui," in *Racisme et modernité*, ed. M. Wieviorka (Paris: La Découverte, 1993).
13. John Rex and David Mason, eds., *Theories of Race and Ethnic Relations* (Cambridge: Cambridge University Press, 1986); Balibar and Wallerstein, *Race, Nation, Classe*.
14. In fact, democratic and universalist values, as entrenched in the Charters of Canada and Quebec, were inverted for the purpose of inferiorizing the Other (perceived as being barbaric, particularistic, or communitaristic). Maryse Potvin, "Les dérapages racistes à l'égard du Québec au Canada-anglais depuis 1995," *Politique et Sociétés* 18, no. 2 (1999): 101–32; Maryse Potvin, "Some Racist 'Slips' about Quebec in English Canada between 1995 and 1998," *Canadian Ethnic Studies* 32, no. 2 (2000): 1–26.
15. Albert Memmi, *Le racisme* (Paris: Gallimard, 1982, 1994).
16. These are sociocognitive (social and cognitive) mechanisms because they appeal simultaneously to people's personal reasoning abilities and draw upon the political, ideological, historic, social, economic, or cultural determinants that are specific to a given context.
17. See Potvin, "Les dérapages racistes," and "Some Racist 'Slips' About Quebec"; Maryse Potvin, *Crise des accommodements raisonnables : une fiction médiatique?* (Montreal: Athéna, 2008); Maryse Potvin et al., *Les médias écrits et les accommodements raisonnables : l'invention d'un débat* (Montreal, January 2008), www.accommodements.qc.ca/documentation/rapports/rapport-8-potvin-maryse.pdf.
18. Maryse Potvin, "Racisme et discrimination au Québec : réflexion critique et prospective sur la recherche," in *Racisme et discrimination : permanence et résurgence d'un phénomène inavouable*, ed. Jean Renaud, Annick Germain, and Xavier Leloup (Québec: Presses de l'Université Laval, 2004), 172–96. See also the first mapping of racism in different sectors of social life in Quebec: Marie McAndrew and Maryse Potvin, *Le racisme au Québec : éléments d'un diagnostic*, Collection Études et Recherches no. 13, Ministère de l'Immigration et des Communautés Culturelles (Quebec: Éditeur officiel du Québec, 1996).
19. A number of investigations were conducted in 1980–90. Most notably, the Commission des droits de la personne et des droits de la jeunesse has investigated racial discrimination experienced by Haitian nurses (1992–3) and by black taxi drivers (1982–5), along with some blunders committed by police (*Bellemare* and *Yarovski Reports*, 1987 and 1992).
20. Jean Renaud et al., *Ils sont maintenant d'ici : les dix premières années au Québec des immigrants admis en 1989*. Études, Recherche et Statistiques no. 4 (Quebec: Ministère des Relations avec les citoyens et de l'Immigration, 2000).
21. Potvin, *Crise des accommodements raisonnables*.
22. Racializing "slips" occurred in dealings with Aboriginals during the Oka standoff of 1990, between Quebecers and citizens in the rest of Canada after Quebec's referendum in 1995 (Potvin, "Les dérapages racistes," and "Some Racist 'Slips' About Quebec"; Maryse Potvin et al. "Du racisme dans les rapports entre groupes nationaux au Canada et en Belgique?" *Revue canadienne des études ethniques* 36, no. 3 (2004): 25–60), and with religious minorities during the debate around "reasonable

accommodations" between 2006 and 2008 (Potvin, *Crise des accommodements raisonnables*).

23. John Porter, *The Vertical Mosaic* (Toronto: University of Toronto Press, 1965).
24. Statistics Canada, *The Deteriorating Economic Welfare of Immigrants and Possible Causes: Update 2005*, research document by G. Picot and A. Sweetman, Analytical Studies Branch Papers Series, Catalogue no. 11F0019MIE, issue no. 262. Business and Labour Market Analysis Division, Statistics Canada, and School of Policy Studies, Queen's University (Ottawa: Industry Canada, June 2005). Earnings are less in the second generation whose fathers come from the Caribbeans, Central America, South America, or Oceania; A. Aydemir, W. H. Chen, and M. Corak, *Intergenerational Earnings Mobility among the Children of Immigrants in Canada*. Analytical Studies Branch, Research Paper no. 267 (Ottawa: Statistics Canada, 2014).
25. Jeffrey G. Reitz and Rupa Banerjee, "Racial Inequality, Social Cohesion and Policy Issues in Canada," in *Belonging? Diversity, Recognition and Shared Citizenship in Canada* (Montreal: Institute for Research on Public Policy, 2007).
26. Renaud et al., *Racisme et discrimination*; Victor Piché and Jean Renaud, "Immigration et intégration économique : peut-on mesurer la discrimination?" in *Annuaire du Québec 2003*, eds. Roch Côté and Michel Venne (Montreal: Fidès, 2002), 146–51. In connection with the theory of human capital, investigations of this type provide clues about the existence of "probable" discriminations, observed when discrepancies between groups cannot be explained based on differences in controlled variables (for example, age, gender, education, professional credentials, language proficiency, qualifications). These studies take into account indicators such as income, unemployment, type of employment, and education to explain discrimination, which is presented as an "unexplained discrepancy" between groups.
27. Monica Boyd, "Variations in Socioeconomic Outcomes of Second Generation Young Adults," *Canadian Diversity*, Thematic issue: *The Experiences of Second Generation Canadians* 6, no. 2 (Spring 2008): 20–4; Maryse Potvin, Nancy Venel, and Paul Eid, eds., *La 2e génération issue de l'immigration : une comparaison France-Québec* (Montreal: Athéna, 2007); Marie McAndrew et al., *La réussite scolaire des jeunes des communautés noires au secondaire* (Montreal: Immigration et métropoles, 2005).
28. Marie McAndrew, Jacques Ledent, Jake Murdoch, and Rachid Ait-Said, *La réussite scolaire des jeunes Québécois issus de l'immigration* (Montréal: Centre Métropolis du Québec (CMQ-IM), 2012); Commission des droits de la personne et des droits de la jeunesse, *Profilage racial et discrimination systémique des jeunes racisés : rapport de la consultation sur le profilage racial et ses conséquences* (Montreal: CDPDJ, May 2011); James L. Torczyner et al., *L'évolution de la communauté noire montréalaise : mutations et défis* (Montreal: Consortium de McGill pour l'ethnicité et la planification sociale stratégique, 2010).
29. Porter, *The Vertical Mosaic*.
30. Potvin, "Les dérapages racistes...", and "Some Racist 'Slips' About Quebec"; Potvin et al., "Racisme et discrimination au Québec."
31. Marc V. Levine, ed., *The Reconquest of Montreal: Language Policy and Social Change in a Bilingual City* (Philadelphia: Temple University Press, 1990).
32. Maryse Potvin, "Discours publics et discriminations au Québec," *Les Cahiers du 27 juin* 2, no. 2 (Winter–Spring 2005): 47–52; Maryse Potvin, "Racisme et discours public commun au Québec," in *Du tricoté serré au métissé serré? La culture publique commune au Québec en débats*, ed. Stéphan Gervais, Dimitrios Karmis, and Diane Lamoureux (Québec: Presses de l'Université Laval, 2008), 227–48.
33. Potvin, "Les dérapages racistes...," "Some Racist 'Slips' About Quebec...," and "Racisme et discrimination au Québec...."
34. Notable articles include those by Mathieu Bock-Côté and by some young conservatives in the nationalist review *L'Action Nationale* since about 2005.
35. Some of the racist "slips" regarding the constitutional crisis are described in Potvin, "Les dérapages racistes...," "Some Racist 'Slips' About Quebec," and "Racisme et discrimination au Québec."
36. See the film *La charte des distractions* online at http://chartedesdistractions.com; see also Michel Seymour, *Le Projet de loi 60 et les signes ostentatoires*, brief submitted to the Commission parlementaire sur le projet de loi 60, December 2013; and Jocelyn Maclure, "Charte des valeurs québécoises—Le jeu dangereux du Parti québécois," *Le Devoir*, 23 August 2013.
37. Potvin, *Crise des accommodements*; Potvin et al., *Les médias écrits*.
38. The debate had reappeared every so often since 1985, but generally concerned bona fide cases of reasonable accommodation (in the legal sense of the term). From 2006 onward, following the Supreme Court judgment that allowed a baptized Sikh student to wear a kirpan to a Quebec public school, media headlines were flooded with "breaking news," incorrectly categorized as cases of "reasonable accommodation," thereby creating confusion and intolerance in public opinion (Potvin, *Crise des accommodements raisonnables*); Gérard Bouchard and Charles Taylor, *Building the Future: A Time for Reconciliation* (Quebec: Government of Quebec, 2008), 15–17.
39. The reference to 1977 pertains to the year that the Charter of the French Language (Bill 101) was implemented. Marie McAndrew, "Pour un débat inclusif sur l'accommodement raisonnable," *Revue Éthique publique* (2007).

40. In January 2007, the municipal council of Hérouxville (a small municipality, population 1,300) adopted a "code of conduct" that was designed for potential immigrants to the town. The code prohibited public stoning, female excision, and the wearing of burkas. Drafted by André Drouin (a municipal councillor who became a major media figure), the "code of conduct" drew comments from around the globe, and on 5 February 2007 Drouin asked the premier of Quebec to declare a state of emergency. Five neighbouring towns asked their municipal and provincial governments to review the Canadian and Quebec Charters.
41. Our study constructed two analytical grids to examine factual media coverage on one hand (451 articles) and opinion discourses on the other hand (654 editorials, columns, and letters from intellectuals and readers) in Quebec's five major newspapers (Potvin, *Crise des accommodements raisonnables*; Potvin et al., *Les médias écrits*).
42. Stanley Cohen, *Folk Devils and Moral Panics* (London: MacGibbon and Kee, 1972).
43. At least six times *Le Journal de Montréal* used the angle of "privileges" accorded to Jews in breaking news. For example, on 17 May 2006, its headline read: "Special Privilege for Jews—Charest Government Is Accommodating" (a news story about a Jewish daycare centre—a "CPE"). On 18 May 2006, it read: "Quebec City Ignores the Charter" (to open the Jewish daycare centre). On 25 May 2006, page 2 read "Quebec City Keeps Code of Silence about Two CPEs," with the subtitle "Jewish Community *Favoured* by Process." On 19 November 2006, page 9 read: "Laval CLSC. Preferential Treatment for a Jew." This article recounted an incident from the day before in which a Jewish man jumped a queue in a health-care centre so that he could keep Shabbat. On 15 December 2006, *Le Journal* set off the "CLSC de Ste-Thérèse de Blainville affair" (page 3) with the headline "Reasonable Accommodations—Special Privileges for Jews." The subtitle underscored the fact that "Nurses Must Bend to Their Demands to Provide Care to Patients from the Community." Here we see a mechanism of victimization among the majority group as well as a generalization of the so-called demands of "all Jews." In many instances, persons belonging to the minority groups being discussed have little or no voice. All headlines are the author's translations.
44. Some anecdotes were presented as "abusive" demands on institutions when no such demands had actually been made by the minorities concerned. Such was the case for the "directive" handed down by Montreal's police service and by Quebec's chief electoral officer on the issue of whether Muslim women wearing niqabs could vote with their faces covered.
45. As another example, on 17 November 2007 *Le Journal de Montréal* quoted Mario Dumont in a lead headline: "Reasonable Accommodations—'We are slipping into abuses of the Charter,'" with the subtitle "Leader of the ADQ judges some concessions to minorities to be worrisome." The lead caption in the article reinforced this generalizing and negative angle: "Accommodations made for ethnic and religious minorities defy common sense, according to Mario Dumont." The article began with a quote from Dumont, who played up the victimization of the majority group: "While a young Sikh is walking around with his dagger at school, the majority of Quebecers can no longer use the word 'Christmas.'" The linkage of these kinds of quotes clearly oriented public debate: "If a majority of citizens defends values that are its own, that does not constitute a racist attitude or a singular phenomenon in the modern world." Quebec society was defined as being "generous" in this article, reinforcing the notion that minorities were receiving "privileges" and that in exchange they had to respect "our values": "The police haven't gone and kidnapped anyone in the world to force them to come and live in Quebec," Dumont contended. All quotes are the author's translation.
46. Opponents of reasonable accommodation did not all use racializing discursive mechanisms. For example, 79 per cent of the 391 letters from readers we analyzed expressed opposition, but 202 letters (52 per cent of the corpus) contained racializing discursive mechanisms. For more detailed data and numerous excerpts illustrating these mechanisms, see Potvin, *Crise des accommodements raisonnables*.
47. Michel Vastel, "Mario Dumont avait raison," *Journal de Montréal*, 20 January 2007, 26.
48. Potvin, "Discours publics et discriminations au Québec," and "Racisme et discours public commun au Québec."
49. Potvin, "Racisme et discours public commun au Québec".
50. Jessica Nadeau, "Charte des valeurs québécoises—Une fuite mal reçue," *Le Devoir*, 21 August 2013.
51. "Charte des valeurs : Gérard Bouchard accuse le gouvernement de mentir aux Québécois," Radio-Canada, 10 January 2014, accessed July 16, 2015, http://ici.radio-canada.ca/nouvelles/politique/2014/01//10/004-charte-laicite-audiences-reactions-gerard-bouchard.shtml.
52. Pierre Murray, "Simple question de respect," *La Presse*, 28 September 2006, A19.
53. Ginette Fortin, "Le policier chanteur," *Le Journal de Montréal*, 29 January 2007, 26.
54. Sylvain Paquet, "Autres pays, autres mœurs," *Le Journal de Montréal*, 16 January 2007, 21.
55. Watch a documentary about the Charter and reactions to it: *La charte des distractions*, www.youtube.com/watch?v=uc0e-C9jFpk.
56. Maclure, "Charte des valeurs québécoises."
57. Louise Leduc, "L'appui à la charte est maintenant majoritaire," *La Presse*, 3 March 2014.
58. Tommy Chouinard, "Charte : 'Il y a un danger,' dit Janette Bertrand," *La Presse*, 30 March 2014.

59. Mélanie Paré, "Janette Bertrand vilipende les 'intégristes,'" *Le Devoir*, 30 March 2014.
60. Ibid.
61. Chouinard, "Charte : 'Il y a un danger,' dit Janette Bertrand."
62. Paré, "Janette Bertrand vilipende les 'intégristes.'"
63. Chouinard, "Charte : 'Il y a un danger,' dit Janette Bertrand."
64. The rest of Canada has a long history of accusing Quebec (and the sovereignty movement) of racism. These accusations are perceived by many Quebecers as a denigration of the national character of francophones in Quebec (initiated by the dominant anglophone group in Canada) and an attempt to reduce francophones to the status of "just another minority."

Select Bibliography

Abella, Irving, and Harold Troper. *None Is Too Many: Canada and the Jews of Europe, 1933–1948*. Toronto: Lester & Orpen Dennys, 1982.

Abu-Ladan, Yasmeen, and Daiva Stasiulis. "Ethnic Pluralism under Siege: Popular and Partisan Opposition to Multiculturalism." *Canadian Public Policy* 18, no. 4 (1992): 365–86.

Anctil, Pierre, Norma Ravvin, and Sherry Simon. *New Readings of Montreal Yiddish*. Toronto: University of Toronto Press, 2007.

Balthazar, Louis. *Bilan du nationalisme au Québec*. Montreal: Éditions l'Hexagone, 1986.

Berthelot, Jocelyn. *Apprendre à vivre ensemble : Immigration, société et éducation*, 2nd ed. Montreal: Éditions Saint-Martin, 1991.

Bissoondath, Neil. *Selling Illusions: The Cult of Multiculturalism*. Toronto: Penguin, 1994.

Bouchard, Gérard, and Charles Taylor (Commission de consultation sur les pratiques d'accommodement reliées aux différences culturelles). *Fonder L'avenir : Le temps de la réconciliation*. Abridged report. Quebec: Gouvernement du Québec, 2008.

Commission Gendron. *Rapport de la commission d'enquête sur la situation de la langue française et sur les droits linguistiques au Québec*, Vol III. Quebec: Éditeur officiel, 1972.

Coutu, Michel, and Pierre Bosset. "La Charte des droits et libertés de la personne et culture publique commune au Québec : une quasi absence?" In *De tissé serré à métissé serré? La culture publique commune en débats*, edited by Stéphan Gervais, Dimitrios Karmis, and Diane Lamoureux, 183–206. Quebec: Presses de l'Université Laval, 2008.

Drouilly, Pierre. "Le référendum du 30 octobre 1995 : une analyse des résultats." In *L'année politique au Québec, 1995–1996*, edited by Robert Boily. Montreal: Presses de l'Université de Montréal, 1996.

Juteau, Danielle. "L'État et les immigrés : de l'immigration aux communautés culturelles." In *Minorités et État*, edited by P. Guillaume, J. M. Lacroix, J. Zylberberg, and R. Pelletier, 35–50. Bordeaux, France and Quebec: Presses universitaires de Bordeaux and Presses de l'Université Laval, 1986.

———, and Marie McAndrew. "Le multiculturalisme canadien et l'intégration 'à la québécoise' : est-il possible de dépasser leurs limites?" Unpublished paper, 1998.

Labelle, Micheline. *Racisme et antiracisme : discours et déclinaisons*. Quebec: Presses de l'Université du Québec, 2011.

LaFerrière, Michel. "Les idéologies ethniques de la société canadienne : du conformisme au multiculturalisme." In *Le facteur ethnique aux États-Unis et au Canada*, edited by Monique Lecomte and Claudine Thomas, 203–12. Lille, France: Presses universitaires de Lille, 1983.

Levine, Marc V., ed. *The Reconquest of Montreal: Language Policy and Social Change in a Bilingual City*. Philadelphia: Temple University Press, 1990.

McRoberts, Kenneth. *Misconceiving Canada: The Struggle for National Unity*. Toronto: Oxford University Press, 1997.

Meisel, John, Guy Rocher, and Arthur Silver. *As I Recall—Je me souviens bien*. Montreal: Institut de recherche en Politiques publiques, 2000.

Ministère des communautés culturelles et de l'immigration. *La politique québécoise du développement culturel*. 2 vols. Quebec: Éditeur officiel, 1978.

———. *Au Québec pour bâtir ensemble : énoncé de politique en matière d'immigration et d'intégration*. Quebec: MCCI, 1990.

Palmer, Howard, ed. *Immigration and the Rise of Multiculturalism*. Toronto: Copp Clark, 1975.

Piché, Victor, and Danièle Laliberté. *Portrait statistique de la nouvelle immigration à Montréal*. Working document of the Société des transports de la Communauté urbaine de Montréal (STCUM). Montreal: STCUM, 1987.

Porter, John. *The Vertical Mosaic*. Toronto: University of Toronto Press, 1965.

Potvin, Maryse. "The Reasonable Accommodations Crisis in Quebec: Racializing Rhetorical Devices in Media and Social Discourse." *International Journal of Canadian Studies* 50 (2014).

———. *Crise des accommodements raisonnables : une fiction médiatique?* Montreal: Athéna, 2008.

———. *Les médias écrits et les accommodements raisonnables : l'invention d'un débat. Analyse du traitement médiatique et des discours d'opinion dans les grands médias québécois sur les situations reliées aux accommodements raisonnables, du 1er mars 2006 au 30 avril 2007.* Report to the Commission de consultation sur les pratiques d'accommodement reliées aux différences culturelles. Montreal, 7 January 2008, www.accommodements.qc.ca/documentation/rapports/rapport-8-potvin-maryse.pdf.

———. "Racisme et discours public commun au Québec." In *De tissé serré à métissé serré? La culture publique commune en débats,* edited by Stéphan Gervais, Dimitrios Karmis, and Diane Lamoureux, 227–48. Quebec: Presses de l'Université Laval, 2008.

———. "Discours publics et discriminations au Québec." *Les Cahiers du 27 juin* 2, no. 2 (Winter–Spring 2005): 47–52.

———. "Racisme et discrimination au Québec : réflexion critique et prospective sur la recherche." In *Racisme et discrimination : permanence et résurgence d'un phénomène inavouable,* edited by J. Renaud, A. Germain, and X. Leloup, 172–96. Quebec: Presses de l'Université Laval, 2004.

———. "Some Racist 'Slips' About Quebec in English Canada between 1995 and 1998." *Canadian Ethnic Studies/Revue canadienne des études ethniques* 32, no. 2 (2000): 1–26.

———. "Les dérapages racistes à l'égard du Québec au Canada-anglais depuis 1995." *Politique et Sociétés* 18, no. 2 (1999): 101–32.

———, Anne Morelli, and Laurence Mettewie. "Du racisme dans les rapports entre groupes nationaux au Canada et en Belgique?" *Revue canadienne des études ethniques/Canadian Ethnic Studies* 36, no. 3 (2004): 25–60.

Rioux, Marcel. *La Question du Québec.* Montreal: L'Hexagone, 1974, 1987.

Royal Commission on Bilingualism and Biculturalism (B&B Commission). *Preliminary Report* (1965); *The Official Languages* (1967); *Education* (1968); *The Work World* (1969); *The Cultural Contribution of the Other Ethnic Groups* (1969); *The Federal Capital* (1970); *Voluntary Associations* (1970). Ottawa: Queen's Printer.

Stein, Michael. "Changement dans la perception de soi des Anglo-Québécois." In *Les anglophones du Québec : de majoritaires à minoritaires,* edited by Gary Caldwell and Eric Waddell, 111–30. Quebec: Institut québécois de recherche sur la culture, 1982.

Taguieff, Pierre-André, ed. *Dictionnaire historique et critique du racism.* Paris: Presses universitaires de France, 2013.

Taylor, Charles. "The Politics of Recognition." In *Multiculturalism and the "Politics of Recognition,"* edited by A. Guttman, 25–73. Princeton, NJ: Princeton University Press, 1992.

Thériault, J. Yvon. "L'individualisme démocratique et le projet souverainiste." *Sociologie et sociétés* 26, no. 2 (Autumn 1994): 19–32.

Trudel, Marcel. *L'esclavage au Canada français : histoire et condition.* Quebec: Presses de l'Université Laval, 1960.

Waddell, Eric. "L'État, la langue et la société : les vicissitudes du français au Québec et au Canada." In *Les dimensions politiques du sexe, de l'ethnie et de la langue au Canada,* edited by Alan C. Cairns and Cynthia Williams. Ottawa: Commission royale sur l'avenir économique et les perspectives de développement du Canada, 1986.

Williams, Dorothy W. *The Road to Now: A History of Blacks in Montreal.* Montreal: Véhicule Press, 1997.

17 Immigration and Diversity in Quebec's Schools: An Assessment

Marie McAndrew, Université de Montréal; Geneviève Audet, Université de Montréal; and Mahsa Bakhshaei, McGill University–University of California, Los Angeles

Timeline

1969 First welcoming classes for students of immigrant origin are introduced in the Commission scolaire de Montréal.

1977 Bill 101 is adopted, requiring newcomers to attend French-language schools.

1978 Heritage language program (Programme d'enseignement des langues d'origine à l'école publique—PELO) is established.

1982 Grid is developed for the elimination of discriminatory stereotypes included in teaching materials across Quebec.

1985 Report by the Committee on Quebec Schools and Cultural Communities introduces the term *intercultural education*.

1990 *Let's Build Québec Together: Vision: A Policy Statement on Immigration and Integration* outlines the Quebec government's immigration policy orientation and Quebec model of integration and diversity relations.

Gagnon-Tremblay–McDougall Accord on immigration gives Quebec exclusive jurisdiction in selection of independent immigrants and in linguistic and economic integration of all newcomers to Quebec.

1994–5 Muslim girl wearing a hijab is expelled from public school in Montreal, generating wide public debate.

1995 Intercultural awareness enters into approval criteria for teacher education programs in universities.

1996 *Learning from the Past: Report of the Task Force on the Teaching of History* (the Lacoursière Report) recommends fostering openness to teaching international history and improving students' knowledge about the contribution of Aboriginal peoples and cultural communities to Quebec's history.

1998 Major educational reform takes place in Quebec's education system, introducing new programs more open to diversity.

Confessional school boards become linguistic school boards (although individual schools may remain confessional).

A School for the Future: Policy Statement on Educational Integration and Intercultural Education is adopted, introducing diversification in reception services, providing guidelines for reasonable accommodation, and bringing intercultural education to all regions of Quebec.

continued

1999 *Religion in Secular Schools: A New Perspective for Québec* (also known as the Proulx Report) on the place of religion in schools forms the basis of establishing nondenominational schools and implementing a new course in ethics and religious culture, but its recommendations are implemented only in 2005 and 2008, respectively.

2006 Supreme Court of Canada rules in *Multani* case, granting a Sikh student the right to wear his kirpan according to specific guidelines to ensure the safety of his fellow students.

2007 Advisory Committee on Integration and Reasonable Accommodation in the Schools tables its report, *Inclusive Québec Schools: Dialogue, Values and Common Reference Points* in November 2007, providing an overview of the situation, defining guidelines for action, and instituting conflict resolution processes.

2008 Bouchard–Taylor Commission presents its report on accommodation practices related to cultural differences. But due to a lack of consensus between proponents of pluralism, of strict secularism, or of a return to a traditional definition of Quebec identity, most recommendations are shelved.

2013 The Department of Education widens its funding formula, aiming at learning of French among newcomers, to include, among other things, longer-term support for immigrant-origin students experiencing difficulties and better recognition for their heritage languages.

2014 Evaluation Report of 15 years of implementation of the *Policy Statement on Educational Integration and Intercultural Education* is published, confirming that major frameworks and objectives are still relevant but that new challenges must be better addressed.

Quebec independentist government's short-lived project of a Charter of Quebec Values initiates heated debate, especially regarding the proposed ban on civil servants wearing religious gear and symbols.

Introduction

Regardless of the complexity of their ethnic relations, all immigrant-receiving societies share common challenges. Quebec is no exception. It must ensure the linguistic, social, and economic integration of newly arrived Quebecers while effecting major change in the host society itself. For the past 50 years in Canada (and in the United States), these two objectives have given rise to numerous recurring debates in education milieus. For students of immigrant origin and their families, school is often the primary vehicle of social mobility; recognizing ethnocultural diversity (in both schools and society) has become a crucial tool for ensuring equal opportunity. Modern public schools shape the culture of tomorrow as well as defining the identities and attitudes of our future citizens. They must therefore perform a delicate balancing act, determining the respective positions of various languages and cultural heritages while emphasizing the common values of citizenship.

The case of schools in Quebec is particularly revealing. For while Quebec society resolutely strives to be modern in its active commitment to immigration and in its search for a conciliatory middle path between assimilation and **multiculturalism**, it remains fragile. This fragility lends complexity to the challenges in the linguistic, academic, and social integration of newcomers. Indeed, exposure to diversity is a more recent phenomenon in Quebec (at least for much of the francophone community) than it is in other North American contexts. All these factors make for remarkably dynamic policy formulation, program design, and social action, but they have also generated numerous tensions.

English-language schools are also characterized by cultural diversity in Quebec; however, our focus here is on French-language schools, attended by 90 per cent of Quebec's students, including the vast majority of allophone students[1] and students of immigrant origin.[2]

Major Policy Frameworks

Immigration Policy and Its Impact on Schools

Since the late 1960s, Quebec, more than any other Canadian province, has sought to play a major role in immigration, a shared jurisdiction between the federal and provincial governments under the Canadian Constitution. In essence, Quebec's interest in this area was motivated by the same factors that guided the development of its language policy: the assimilation of most **immigrants** into the anglophone community and the impact of this assimilation on the demolinguistic equilibrium in Montreal.[3] Gradually, a series of agreements culminated in the Canada–Quebec Accord Relating to Immigration and Temporary Admission of Aliens (the Gagnon-Tremblay–McDougall Accord), which enshrined Quebec's exclusive jurisdiction in selecting "independent" immigrants (who account for 65 per cent of total movement) and over the linguistic and economic integration of all newcomers to Quebec.

Quebec's involvement in immigration follows principles fairly similar to those in Canadian immigration policy and is currently characterized by three goals.[4] First, given the feared economic consequences of a demographic deficit and an aging population, Quebec is targeting a gradual increase in intake so that it will ultimately receive 25 per cent of total immigration to Canada. Currently, Quebec falls well short of that mark; in 2011, it received only 19.2 per cent of Canada's immigrants. However, with an average intake of some 47,710 immigrants over five years, for its population of 8 million Quebec has a significant immigration rate compared with other jurisdictions (see Table 17.1).

Table 17.1 Gross Immigration Rates in Six Jurisdictions* (2011)

Jurisdiction	Immigration as a Percentage of the Total Population
Canada	0.72
Quebec	0.65
United States	0.34
California	0.56
New York	0.76
Australia	1.01

*Measured solely on the basis of permanent admissions as a percentage of the total population.

Second, Quebec's selection policy attempts to balance competing selection criteria: the recruitment of French-speaking immigrants, the contribution of immigration to economic development, the promotion of family reunification, and the commitment to international solidarity. The combined complexity of these criteria has led to a highly diversified immigrant population both in terms of language skills and national origin. Indeed, within the selection grid, prior knowledge of French is not an eliminatory criterion, although currently over 61.7 per cent of admitted immigrants already speak some French. In addition, 80 per cent of immigrants now come from regions other than North America or Europe. The five largest immigrant groups (from Algeria, Morocco, France, China, and Colombia) account for less than 36 per cent of all entrants, which explains the heterogeneity of most multiethnic classrooms.

Third, the primary goal of both the federal government's and Quebec's immigration policy is permanent settlement. Citizenship may be acquired very quickly (after three years), which contributes to the significant political influence of minorities in society generally and in the education system in particular.

Successive waves of immigration have shaped the school population,[5] which now comprises over 142,000 students (14.2 per cent of the total school population) whose first language is not English, French, or an Aboriginal language. Students of immigrant origin (those born abroad or with at least one parent born abroad) now number over 237,000 (23.7 per cent) of Quebec's total school population.

While most immigrants typically settle in Montreal, Montreal-born francophones tend to move to the suburbs and often enrol their children in private schools. Consequently, in Montreal's public French-language schools, 54.8 per cent of students do not speak French as their first language and 70.8 per cent

Table 17.2 Percentage of Students Whose First Language or Language Spoken at Home Is Neither French (Quebec) nor English (Rest of Canada and the United States) in Five Major North American Cities*

Montreal French-language schools (2013)	Toronto English-language schools (2011)	Vancouver English-language schools (2013)	New York English-language schools (2012)	Los Angeles English-language schools (2012)
54.8	53.0	60.0	49.0	65.0

*First language: Montreal; students who have a language other than English as their mother tongue or as the primary language spoken at home: Toronto; students who speak a language other than English at home: Vancouver, New York, and Los Angeles.

are of immigrant origin. In this respect, Montreal is on par with averages for large cities in Canada and the United States (see Table 17.2). In almost half of Montreal schools, students of immigrant origin account for the majority of the population, and one out of four schools have an immigrant population of over 75 per cent.

Interculturalism and Intercultural Education: A Long-Standing Normative Commitment

Quebec **interculturalism** may be described as the quest for a middle path between Canadian multiculturalism and French Jacobinism. Canadian

Primary Source

Extracts from *A School for the Future: Policy Statement on Educational Integration and Intercultural Education—A New Direction for Success*

The principles for action proposed here for Québec schools dealing with ethnocultural, linguistic and religious diversity are derived from the basic principles of education itself and from government policy statements concerning the integration of immigrants into Québec society. . . .

Equal Opportunity

The role that schools play, and must continue to play, in promoting equal opportunity for all is closely related to their vocation itself, which concerns instruction, socialization and certification. . . . The schools have an obligation to fulfill their mission with all students, whatever their characteristics (ethnic origin, mother tongue, social condition, sex, religion, etc.). This obligation follows from the principle of equal opportunity for all . . . Equal opportunity implies not only ensuring that all students have access to the basic educational services, but also providing special conditions or compensatory measures (for example, help learning French) if students require them. This is consistent with the principles of equity and non-discrimination and of accepting and respecting otherness and rejecting intolerance, ethnocentrism and all other expressions of discrimination. To apply this principle, schools have to recognize students for who they are, with their similarities and differences, their shared and particular characteristics. . . .

Proficiency in French, the Language of Public Life

The school is the main, although not the sole, institution responsible for ensuring that students learn and use French, the language of public life, with which Quebecers of all origins can communicate and participate in the development of Québec society. Educational institutions should be capable of turning out students who are proficient in the multiculturalism has been criticized for essentializing cultures and for isolating them from each other. Conversely, French Jacobinism, by relegating diversity to the private sphere, is not entirely compatible with the recognition of pluralism, an ideal widely embraced in Quebec.[6]

In the 1980s, following the publication of *A Cultural Development Policy for Quebec* and *Quebecers, Each and Every One*, the government adopted an approach of intercultural rapprochement between individuals whose membership in clearly distinguishable groups was taken for granted. The idea was to create a culture of convergence, centred on a traditional but modern francophone culture and enriched by the province's various minority **ethnic groups**, which are called "cultural communities" in Quebec.

With *Let's Build Québec Together: Vision: A Policy Statement on Immigration and Integration* (adopted in 1990 and still in effect), an expanded recognition of cultural hybridity began to emerge. This document acknowledged both plurality as a fundamental aspect of Quebec culture and the right of Quebecers of all origins to express their cultures "within the limitations imposed by the respect for fundamental democratic values and the need for intergroup exchanges." The policy statement expressly identified gender equality, respect for children's rights, nonviolence, and Quebec's societal choices (including language rights) among the democratic values to be promoted. It also called for the full participation and the equal contribution of all citizens, specifically those of immigrant origin.[7]

The *Policy Statement on Educational Integration and Intercultural Education*, published in 1998 by the Department of Education, followed a similar path.[8] Intercultural education was defined as learning how

use of this basic tool of communication, whether French is their mother tongue, as it is for the majority, their second language, as it is for Anglophones and some allophones, or their third language, as it is for certain children of immigrants, who generally do not speak it at all on their arrival. The education system should take the appropriate measures to fulfill this expectation by providing students in French-language institutions with a solid grounding in the language of instruction and giving students in English-language institutions quality instruction in the second language. Acquiring proficiency in French and using it can help students from other backgrounds surmount their marginalization and develop a sense of membership and participation in Québec society.

Education for Citizenship in a Democratic, Pluralistic Society

Seeking and promoting shared values contributes to the development and consolidation of a democratic society that accepts all its members as full participants. Citizenship education aims to make these values an integral part of a society characterized by democratic traditions and institutions, respect for individual rights and a commitment to live together in mutual respect for individual and group differences. Schools have a responsibility to promote citizenship education in order to prepare students, both young and adult, to play an active role in Québec democracy by adopting its values, codes and norms, knowing its key institutions, and exercising the rights and responsibilities of citizens in a democratic society. Citizenship education focuses on both knowledge and experience, and is grounded not only in the curriculum but also in democratic practices, in the schools and outside them. In this sense it extends into the life of the immediate community and more generally into social, economic and cultural life.

Source: Ministère de l'Éducation du Québec, *A School for the Future: Policy Statement on Educational Integration and Intercultural Education—A New Direction for Success* (Quebec: Government of Québec, 1998), 6–8.

to live together in a democratic, pluralist, French-speaking society. Ways to promote the normative recognition of diversity made up a significant part of the statement and were essentially governed by the same parameters set forth in 1990: protecting individual rights and Quebec's linguistic choices, and ensuring that institutions can operate smoothly. This document stands out for its complex treatment of the concept of culture. It urges that instead of essentializing differences, teachers should regard ethnic identity as only one among many factors influencing integration and academic success.

The 1998 policy statement specifically highlighted three key challenges in intercultural education: (1) integrating people of various ethnocultural origins at all levels of employment in the education system; (2) providing training and professional development of teaching staff; and (3) implementing a pluralist transformation of the formal and real curriculum. This last objective was at the crux of most debates regarding the policy statement. Indeed, the tension between common values and the recognition of diversity is evident throughout the document, which underwent a mostly cosmetic rewrite in French aimed at addressing the sensitivities of more nationalist segments of Quebec society.

Although the 1998 policy statement was adopted about 20 years ago, its principles still form the basis of the Department of Education initiatives and have significantly influenced statements formulated by school boards with the highest concentration of students of immigrant origin. However, while the policy statement was meant to extend the recognition of diversity to milieus that do not experience diversity daily, progress on that front has been limited. A recent evaluation of the implementation of the policy confirms that its major framework and objectives are still considered relevant by school principals, pedagogical advisors, and university and community stakeholders in a context where immigration has been significantly on the rise in the province. Overall, initiatives put in place by the ministry are appreciated, although some respondents complained that projects are often short-lived and not sufficiently funded. Others identified everlasting issues such as providing sufficient support for the learning of French in milieus where the presence of immigrant students is more limited, as well as supporting significant school–family–community relationships in multiethnic milieus. Some challenges are also more relevant today than they were 20 years ago, such as the professional integration of the growing number of immigrant-origin teachers, as well as intercultural rapprochement between students attending pluriethnic and homogeneous schools.[9]

Public Debate

Language and the Educational Integration of Immigrants

Before the enactment of Bill 101 in 1977, over 80 per cent of newly arrived immigrants chose English-language schooling, since English was the dominant language of business and French-language institutions were not especially open to cultural diversity. Thus, immigrant schooling profiles became the central focus of the language debate in the 1970s, which pitted proponents of mandatory French-language education for immigrants against supporters of free choice.

This round of Quebec's language debates was settled with the enactment of Bill 101, the Charter of the French Language. The bill's main purpose was to make French the common language of public life. It also made French-language schools mandatory for all francophone and allophone students while preserving the historical right of the anglophone community and anglicized immigrant communities to attend English-language institutions. As a result, over 85 per cent of allophone students and more than 90 per cent of students of immigrant origin now attend French-language schools. In fact, today the French school system in Montreal is more multiethnic than the English school system.[10]

In public debates over the integration of students of immigrant origin, the prominence of language issues, although still significant, has faded steadily since 1977.[11] From 1977 to the end of the 1980s, public concern focused more specifically on whether immigrant students were learning French and whether their families were actively or passively resisting attendance at French-language schools. Nonetheless, a growing consensus (corroborated by ministerial exam results) emerged during this period that young immigrant students were in fact becoming reasonably fluent in French. Moreover, changes in immigration, newly dominated by more francophile groups, such as Haitians, Vietnamese, and Latin Americans, helped reduce resistance to attending French-language schools.

In the early 1990s, the focus of public debate shifted to the use of French and attitudes toward the language. Three issues were central to this debate: (1) how concentrations of ethnic groups affected the linguistic environment in schools; (2) whether students of immigrant origin were choosing to attend English- or French-language CEGEPs[12] (not governed by Bill 101 and therefore subject to individual choice); and (3) the extent to which using French in schools would affect longer-term linguistic practices among allophones. Although numerous studies and reports yielded mainly positive findings regarding these issues, attendant controversies remained heated until the late 1990s. During this time, a relatively large wave of young anglophone or anglophile immigrants arrived from South Asia and Hong Kong (following political changes in that region).

Since the 2000s, under the combined effect of an unprecedented wave of francophone immigration from North Africa and an international malaise spawned by the events of 11 September 2001, the language debate has faded in prominence. Issues around the culture and, especially, the religion of newcomers have captured media attention and generated public concern. But public apprehensions about language have not yet entirely disappeared, particularly on the ground.

Cultural and Religious Diversity in Schools

For almost a decade, Quebec has indeed been involved in another heated controversy over "reasonable accommodation."[13] The debate has centred on the place of ethnocultural diversity within Quebec identity. The controversy was set in motion by a Supreme Court of Canada decision in April 2006 regarding a student who wore a Sikh kirpan to his public school (see the Case Study box). This incident spiralled into a crisis that encompassed a raft of other identity-related issues, many of which were expressed at the fall 2008 hearings of the Consultation Commission on Accommodation Practices Related to Cultural Differences (the Bouchard–Taylor Commission) set up by the Quebec government to manage the crisis. Although the controversy seemed to cool down after 2009, it was given a new impetus in 2014 when the Parti Québécois (PQ) minority government proposed to adopt a Charter of Quebec Values (also referred to as *Charte de la laïcité*/Secularism Charter). Two elements of this proposed charter enjoyed a wide consensus in Quebec society: proclaiming Quebec's secular nature and establishing further guidelines for reasonable accommodation in public institutions. But the last element, which would have banned the wearing of religious symbols and gear by civil servants, harshly divided the Quebec population. The proposal gave rise to many ethnocentric and racist slips but was short-lived because the Liberals defeated the PQ in the April 2014 election, thus killing the proposed bill.[14]

CASE STUDY

The Right to Wear the Kirpan

One of the events fuelling the debate around "reasonable accommodation" was the Supreme Court's decision of 2 March 2006 that authorized a Sikh student to wear his kirpan[15] to a Quebec public school. The *Multani* decision was widely misunderstood and in some cases condemned

continued

outright. The events that triggered this controversy, the court decisions it generated, and the subsequent place of religious diversity in schools that was envisioned had profound impacts on stakeholders in education and the public alike.

Gurbaj Singh Multani is a baptized orthodox Sikh (about 10 per cent of Sikhs in Canada are orthodox). As such, he strictly adheres to the tenets of the Sikh religion and wears a ritual dagger, the kirpan, which symbolizes the purity of the faith and his commitment to defend it. Multani, 12 years old at the time of the incident, belonged to a predominantly anglophone community, but under Bill 101 attended a French-language school. Ethnocultural diversity in this school, attended mostly by francophone students, was a relatively recent phenomenon. On 19 February 2001, the kirpan that Multani was wearing inside his clothes slipped out accidentally in the schoolyard. On 21 December 2001, as a reasonable accommodation of Multani's religious convictions, the Commission scolaire Marguerite-Bourgeoys (CSMB) sent a letter to his parents stating that he could wear the kirpan at school provided it was sealed inside his clothing. This solution, widely applied across Canada, had been previously adopted following an Ontario Superior Court decision in the early 1990s. Multani and his parents accepted these terms. However, on 12 February 2002, the governing board of the school (wielding considerable decision-making power in Quebec), comprising predominantly francophone school parents, refused to approve the accommodation. The board deemed that wearing a kirpan violated the school's code of conduct, which prohibited carrying weapons and dangerous objects. On 19 March 2002, after much equivocation and internal tension, the CSMB's elected Council of Commissioners concurred with the governing board and rejected the initial accommodation for the kirpan. The family was asked to have their son wear a symbolic pendant or a nonmetallic kirpan. On 25 March 2002, Multani's father filed a motion with the Superior Court of Quebec, requesting that this decision be declared void and of no effect. On 17 May 2002 the motion was granted, and Gurbaj Singh Multani was allowed to wear his kirpan. However, in a dramatic turn of events two years later (in 2004), the Quebec Court of Appeal overturned the Superior Court's judgment, citing security issues and the importance of following common rules, such as reasonable limits on the right to express religious beliefs. Some considered this ruling to be an indicator of an emerging culture in Quebec courts in which the values of good citizenship were taking precedence over the culture of personal rights that (it was claimed) epitomized Canadian jurisprudence. In 2006, the Supreme Court of Canada reversed the Court of Appeal decision, upholding the original 2001 proposal that the student be allowed to wear his kirpan securely fastened inside his clothes, provided that Multani not surrender it at any time, that its loss be immediately reported to school authorities, and that school staff be authorized to verify that all of these conditions were being followed.

The Supreme Court decision belongs to a vast body of jurisprudence on reasonable accommodation that has been building since 1985. It is now recognized that when an apparently neutral standard or practice is applied to all the people within an institution it may, in some instances, infringe on equality or fundamental rights or freedoms of some individuals, including religious freedoms. In such cases, the courts have consistently sought compromises negotiated in good faith between the parties, called "reasonable accommodations." While such compromises may exempt a person from certain standards or practices, they must still ensure the smooth operation of institutions.

It was not the concept of reasonable accommodation in itself that made the ruling in the *Multani* case significant, but rather that for the first time this concept was applied to a school as a service provider for students and their families. The judges of Canada's highest court were asked to reflect on this accommodation's compatibility with the school's complex mandate of preparing future citizens for life within society. The Supreme Court rejected the CSMB's argument that the kirpan was a symbol of violence, based both on a lack of proof and because it showed a lack of consideration for Canadian multicultural values and a disrespect for the Sikh faith. The court reminded Canadians that schools are a place for meeting and dialogue and must be founded on principles of tolerance and impartiality. Since leading by example is the best way to promote respect for constitutional rights within a democratic society, the court reiterated that institutions and teachers are therefore bound to respect students' rights and provide an education that is free of prejudice, bias, and intolerance.

While some politicians and editorial writers welcomed the nuanced reasoning of the Supreme Court ruling, it was nonetheless misunderstood and in some cases very poorly received by a vocal segment of the population in Quebec. Negative public opinion was divided into three camps. One camp recognized the legitimacy of reasonable accommodations in general, but disagreed with the court's opinion that kirpans pose little danger. A second camp attacked the ruling as a classic example of the impasse created by the federal multiculturalism policy and its negative impact on Quebec. They noted that while in principle the court recognized the importance of common civic values, in practice reasonable accommodations consistently favoured the rights of individuals or specific cultural communities, thereby factionalizing society, even within schools where, of all places, developing social cohesion should be paramount. A third camp took advantage of the decision to make overtly anti-immigration or discriminatory remarks, primarily in blogs and open online letters not published in newspapers, against some religious groups. The fact that the family of the Sikh student and the spokesperson of his community spoke only English also fuelled tensions by linking language issues to religious issues.

The shockwave created by the *Multani* decision led the Department of Education to relaunch a series of measures aimed at recognizing diversity. These measures had been most intensely implemented during the 1995 "hijab crisis" (in which a girl was expelled from a public school for wearing a hijab), but were less actively implemented by the end of the decade. Two measures were particularly noteworthy. First, a training unit for school principals that focused on consideration for cultural and religious diversity was updated and a training campaign, led by a team of educational instructors, has been implemented since 2008. Second, in the fall of 2006 the Department struck the Advisory Committee on Integration and Reasonable Accommodation in the Schools, comprising representatives from various areas of the education system, including school boards, parents' committees, professional associations, and unions. The advisory committee's report, submitted in November 2007, included an update that set the record straight on the frequency and nature of requests for accommodation. It also reiterated and strengthened existing guidelines for recognizing diversity, proposing some practical ways to foster harmonious negotiations between schools and parents.

As the process of adapting schools to diversity continues, three issues have been broadly debated in public by two distinct groups: one championing strict secularism (inspired by France) and the other a return to a "traditional" Quebec identity. The pro-secularist group strongly opposed students and teachers wearing the Muslim veil. After a major controversy in this issue emerged in 1994–5, the consensus seemed to be that the practice would be tolerated within the guidelines defined by the Commission des droits de la personne et des droits de la jeunesse that equal access to school activities would not be compromised and that freedom of choice for students and their parents would be preserved. Indeed, at the Bouchard–Taylor Commission hearings in 2008 these guidelines were reiterated by official educational bodies, but were still largely absent from the briefs of ordinary citizens, who often drew direct connections between wearing the Muslim veil and women's oppression. Moreover, given the relative success in recruiting teachers and student teachers of all origins and religious persuasions, the question of whether teaching staff should be allowed to wear religious symbols is now central to current public debate. The commission's report, which expressed some openness to this position, attracted many negative comments, while the Charter of Quebec Values reinforced the position of those who consider that school, as reflected by its main agents, should be a totally neutral space.

The chief focus for those championing a return to Quebec's "traditional" identity was the threat they perceived in the new Ethics and Religious Culture Program. This program was the culmination of a secularization process initiated in 1998 that transformed confessional school boards into English- and French-language school boards. In the fall of 2008 it replaced the Catholic, Protestant, and Moral Education Programs (the latter choice being the only alternative for non-Christian students up to that point). The new Ethics and Religious Culture Program was criticized for placing all religions on an equal footing and ignoring both the central role that the Catholic religion had played in the development of Quebec and its contemporary demographic weight. Traditionalists also argued that teaching religion from a cultural perspective could constitute an infringement on the religious freedom of young children, who would be unable to distinguish the facts presented on various religions from the beliefs that their parents wished to instill in them.

On the whole, the briefs submitted and the positions taken publicly at the Bouchard–Taylor Commission's hearings cast the role of the education system in transforming Quebec's identity in a positive light. Even the most apprehensive or negative participants at the commission's hearings often mentioned that the "children of Bill 101" bore little resemblance to them, since this new generation has lived and breathed diversity. Indeed, a number of young people spoke out at the hearings to remind their elders to practise more moderation in their assertions about other cultures. Opinion polls during the Charter of Quebec Values controversy also showed that there was a generation gap in the support for the project, which was not popular among young people, even when they were francophone or lived in a homogenously francophone region.

Programs and Measures

Reception Services for Newly Arrived Immigrants

In contrast to the model prevailing in the rest of Canada, which places students lacking host-language proficiency directly into regular classes but provides ESL (English as a second language) support, Quebec has opted for a closed "welcoming class" model. The first welcoming classes, introduced in 1969, reflected the view that the best way for allophone students to learn French was through a systematic and structured approach, not by merely exposing them to the language in regular classes (an approach that often suffices when the target language is clearly dominant in society). Welcoming classes enjoy a reduced student/teacher ratio. The language learning program is well developed and includes a component on the life and culture of the host society. In outlying regions, if there are too few allophone students to warrant a separate class, they attend regular classes but receive FSL (French as a second language) support. In 2011, some 20,000 students attended welcoming classes or were provided with linguistic support.[16]

Until very recently, heritage languages were not recognized as having any role in the various measures adopted for teaching French to newly arrived immigrants.[17] However, since 1977 Quebec has offered a heritage languages program, known by its French acronym PELO (Programme d'enseignement des langues d'origine), for allophone students who have mastered French. The program was originally designed to reassure Quebec's older, established cultural communities that multilingualism was a valued complement to efforts in promoting the French language. In 2012–3, 15 heritage languages were taught to some 7,250 students, but the program is less popular than might be expected owing to the resistance of public school teachers and to the schooling choices of highly committed allophone parents, who would rather enrol their children in private trilingual schools that are partially funded by the government of Quebec. The program also suffers from a lack of focus. While research indicates that this approach is most effective when the host language is learned simultaneously with the heritage language, the PELO program is not available to new arrivals still attending welcoming classes, and it targets elementary school students, whereas problems in mastering French arise mainly at the secondary school level.

After the publication of the Quebec government's *Policy Statement on Educational Integration and Intercultural Education* in 1998, welcoming programs and other measures evolved significantly. Observers had noted that the 10 months that students were to spend in a welcoming class tended to be extended, which caused some concern regarding the social integration of newcomers into schools. Therefore, various innovative models have been explored in recent years to help immigrant students make the transition from welcoming classes into regular classes. These models may involve partial immersion in regular classes tackling less linguistically demanding subjects, team teaching between teachers from welcoming classes and heritage language classes, or placing allophone students in regular classes with linguistic support.

Nevertheless, a recent evaluation of the various programs aiming at the mastery of French among allophone newcomers concluded that there was much resistance to the diversification of the formula, especially within boards where the presence of immigrant students was a large and a long-standing phenomenon, and tended to cling to the closed-class formula. Thus, in many settings, the integration of newcomers was found lacking and some degree of segregation of welcoming classes was deplored. In milieus that have fewer immigrants, innovative practices were more widespread but proper funding was often lacking. Following this report, the ministry of education significantly changed its funding formula for the teaching of French to newcomers, allowing for better support in homogeneous milieus, longer-term programs for immigrant-origin students still experiencing difficulties, and better recognition of heritage languages.

Adapting to Pluralism

In Quebec's elementary and secondary school programs, there are many points of entry for promoting intercultural, **anti-racist**, or citizenship education. These points may be found both in the general aims of the curriculum and in the detailed descriptions of targeted student competencies, in broad areas of learning, and in various academic subjects.[18] The learning area entitled Citizenship and Community Life, which comprises the teaching of geography, history, and citizenship education, has the greatest number of stated commitments to providing education on diversity. Moreover, all three of these subjects involve a common educational aim: "openness to the world and respect for diversity." Other broad areas of learning like media literacy, environmental awareness, and consumer rights and responsibilities include elements related to intercultural education, such as awareness of the interdependence of all peoples and the consequences of globalization on the distribution of wealth, as well as the ability to recognize stereotyped media messages. There are also three targeted student competencies that contribute to intercultural education that must be taught in all programs: "To exercise critical judgment," which teaches the recognition of prejudices and the importance of putting opinions in perspective; "To construct his or her identity," which requires students to recognize their cultural roots and acknowledge those of others; and "To cooperate with others," which encourages respect for difference, developing openness to others, and constructively embracing pluralism and nonviolence.

Through the Ethics and Religious Culture Program, students also learn about major world religions such as Islam, Buddhism, Hinduism, and Sikhism, although the primary emphasis is on Christian and Aboriginal traditions. The program targets two complementary aims: acknowledging each student's sense of belonging or not belonging to a religious tradition and promoting the sharing of values and involvement in co-operative projects in a pluralist society. Students learn to weigh ethical questions, demonstrate their understanding of religious phenomena, and discuss these topics with people who do not necessarily share their own beliefs.

For these ambitious programs to succeed, bias-free teaching material had to be produced to properly reflect diversity. Quebec's track record in this regard, though not without its flaws, has been improving.[19] Beginning in 1982, an approval process for teaching materials was implemented to ensure that designs and depictions of ethnocultural minorities were not discriminatory. By the late 1980s, minorities were included more in the materials' content and overt stereotypes had been eliminated. At that point, the qualitative treatment of diversity required that omissions and more subtle ethnocentric biases be addressed. Several studies conducted in the 1990s showed that although textbooks during this period generally promoted cultural diversity, they often folklorized various cultures and portrayed "them" as outsiders to the target readership. In addition to underplaying the contribution of minority groups to Quebec society, the presentation of non-Western civilizations (especially the Muslim world) was stereotypical. Further to the implementation of the educational reform in 1998, no studies on the evolution of the treatment of cultural, religious, and ethnic diversity in teaching materials have been conducted. However, an examination of some of the history books in current use indicates that there are increased international perspectives on non-Western societies and cultures, and Quebec-based perspectives on Aboriginal cultures and groups of immigrant origin. A recent study also noted significant progress in depictions of Islam and the Muslim world, although the contribution of the Muslim community in Canada and Quebec is still insufficiently recognized.

Teachers also need training to be able to adapt fully to the new diversity in schools. In this area, reviews are more mixed.[20] Since 1995, the Department of Education has made intercultural awareness activities an early requirement for teacher training programs, and its framework of competencies for educators contains at least three activities that incorporate an intercultural or anti-racist perspective. A recent portrait of intercultural training in Quebec has stressed that the faculties of education of the 12 Quebec universities have introduced mandatory courses on ethnic diversity, inequality, and discrimination, and developed adapted approaches to teaching. Many other courses, especially those preparing future teachers to teach history, religious culture, and ethics or French to allophone students also address these issues. But the report also concluded that current efforts are insufficient or, at least, that their impact on future teachers is not always conclusive. Different courses across Quebec developed without clear objectives or a common definition of knowledge, skills, and attitudes to develop among future schoolteachers. This was partially caused by the lack of commitment of the Department of Education. Intercultural teaching often lacks status, especially in universities situated in homogeneous regions where often only one isolated course is offered. Also, teaching competencies in intercultural matters are not always adequately reinforced during internships within regular schools.

The Department of Education, school boards, various government bodies like the Commission des droits de la personne et des droits de la jeunesse, and some community organizations also offer in-service training for teaching staff on topics such as intercultural communication, intervention in multiethnic schools, prevention of racism, relations with parents, and reasonable accommodation. However, none of this training is mandatory, and it has been criticized for preaching to the converted—that is, to teachers already making major efforts to adapt to cultural diversity.

Other initiatives, aimed at increasing the representation of minority students in teacher training through university education faculties and later among future school teaching staff, are beginning to bear fruit.[21] This positive development is partly because of the efforts of these bodies to update equal opportunity plans in recruitment and employment. It is also due to the growing presence of qualified francophones in recent waves of immigration, many of whom take up teaching when they encounter obstacles to practising the professions for which they were initially trained.

Outcomes

Linguistic Integration

Overall, three decades of concerted efforts in linguistic integration in Quebec schools have borne positive results.[22]

In terms of students' command of the French language, a cohort study of youths who started secondary school from 1998 to 2000 found that students of immigrant origin had an average success rate of 69.8 per cent in French compared to 72.0 per cent for Quebec students overall. But these findings should be considered with two caveats in mind. First, because this exam is administered at the end of secondary school, the participation rate for students of immigrant origin was 5 points lower than that of the student population as a whole. Second, success on the exam does not reliably indicate that students have mastered French at the level of complexity required for scholastic success, as indicated by other research on students' linguistic competencies and by the perceptions of teachers, who have identified many of these students' shortcomings.

As for language use in school, the impact of mandatory French-language schooling seems to be well established. A 1999 study conducted in 20 Montreal multiethnic elementary and secondary schools confirmed this fact, at a time when the sociolinguistic context was clearly less favourable than it is today. Languages of origin aside, in elementary schools the relative strength of French over English varied from 70 per cent to 100 per cent. For secondary schools, the respective rates were 59.9 per cent to 99.3 per cent. Overall, the level of French-language use observed among students was thus much higher than expected, that is, higher than their parents' recorded linguistic behaviour (as reported in the Canadian census). Interviews with students also revealed that the most successful approaches to promoting French were those that complemented (and did not oppose) the competencies that students already possessed in other languages.

The choice of language of instruction at the CEGEP level has also been closely studied over the years, since some view it as an important predictor of future behaviour among young people. The statistics indicate a stepwise progression. In the late 1980s, the first allophone student cohorts educated entirely in French chose French-language CEGEPs in over 70 per cent of cases. In the years that followed, that percentage decreased each year, reaching 53.6 per cent in 1999. Since then, the percentage of allophone students choosing French-language CEGEPs has steadily increased, and by 2010 this figure had reached over 68 per cent. Currently there is no consensus as to why students choose English-language CEGEPs. While some see cause for concern in this choice, viewing it as long-term predictor of language habits, others argue that it is chiefly strategic.

As for the longer-term impact of French-language schooling, a study conducted by the Conseil supérieur de la langue française among a large sampling of anglophones and allophones aged 20 to 35 showed that French was used by 65 per cent of those who had attended French-language schools as the predominant language of their public lives, but by only 36.5 per cent of those educated in English-language schools. Moreover, these positive results did not include young immigrants whose first language was French and whose numbers are increasing. Census data from 2011 on the language most frequently spoken in the home indicate that French is more popular among foreign-born allophone youth in the 15–24 age bracket than it is in older age brackets.

Still, for those who believe that multilingualism will eventually lead to the dominance of English,[23] statistics on the substantial maintenance of languages of origin and the significant ongoing use of English may be read more pessimistically.

Equal Opportunities and Academic Success

The issues of equality of opportunity and of academic success have long been the poor cousins of the debate on the educational integration of youth of immigrant origin in Quebec. But after 2000, these issues gained prominence in public debates.

A recent study indicates that, in relation to the school population as a whole, students born abroad or whose parents were born abroad entered secondary school with greater academic delay, which continued to accumulate even when they started at the usual age of entry.[24] They were less likely to obtain a secondary school diploma after five years (46.5 per cent versus 55.4 per cent) or even after seven years of schooling (61.1 per cent versus 68.2 per cent). Fewer of these students took ministerial exams and, as noted above, they had slightly lower mean results in French, but their marks in math and science were higher than those of longer established students. Moreover, immigrant-origin students show greater resilience since they pursued CEGEP-level studies in proportions slightly higher to that of their third-generation-plus peers (57.7 per cent versus 56.5 per cent).

Among the many factors influencing academic success, five were especially important: gender, whether a student was born in Canada or abroad, entry level in the school system, cumulative delay during schooling, and to a lesser extent socioeconomic status. As regards intergroup differences, an older study also documented an especially dramatic situation among students from black communities. After seven years of secondary school (which should last five years in Quebec), their graduation rate was 17 percentage points lower than that of the overall population and, among students of West Indian origin whose first language was English or Creole, only 4 out of 10 students graduated from secondary school. These data provide some insight into the prevalent feeling of alienation among this segment of the population.

After the publication of the aforementioned study and its wide dissemination within educational milieus and the communities concerned, a number of measures specifically targeting the black community were implemented under the aegis of a Department of Education follow-up committee. Moreover, the government bodies responsible for implementing intervention strategies in underprivileged milieus are now analyzing the specific needs of ethnic communities and developing interventions that are adapted to their situations.

Intercultural Relations at School: Teachers, Parents, and Students

Promoting the recognition of diversity in Quebec schools remains a work in progress.[25] But noteworthy progress has been made, including the many initiatives designed to better adapt schools to their communities. In a survey of all Quebec school principals carried out in 2007, over 25 per cent stated that they had implemented various measures on their own initiative and reported over 1,000 successful examples of "best practices." The survey also showed that requests for accommodations have remained stable for the previous three years and that schools were not as ill-equipped as previously reported, having acquired the necessary tools to cope with community and parental pressures. Thus, on average, 50 per cent of these requests were accepted, slightly less than 25 per cent refused, and alternative solutions were found in just over 25 per cent of cases. Significantly, despite widespread stereotypes, requests for accommodation do not come exclusively from newly arrived immigrants or Muslims.

Nevertheless, a number of stakeholders in education still harbour reservations about the impact of adapting to diversity. In the short term, they are worried about the potential conflicts between some of the accommodation measures taken and the requirements of the Education Act regarding school attendance, academic programs, or student safety. They also question whether providing "too much" accommodation could have longer-term consequences on sharing common values, creating social cohesion, or ensuring a broader inclusion of minority youth. In recent years, in Quebec as elsewhere, Muslims have become emblematic figures for many people's fears surrounding cultural and societal identity.

Meanwhile, although many teachers do address human rights and intercultural relations issues in their classrooms on an ad hoc basis, some research indicates that many others still resist introducing a full-scale intercultural perspective into the curriculum.[26] Many teachers look to integrate students into the host and school cultures and to ensure academic success. As a result, differences are often implicitly recognized by teachers who adapt teaching strategies to their students. But expressly acknowledging differences by making changes to programs and instructional content is a rarer occurrence. Anti-racist interventions mainly consist of crisis management and ad hoc conflict resolution. Course material on racism also tends to focus on events elsewhere in the world rather than the dynamics experienced within the province or within schools. It is true that many of these findings could be applied to any multiethnic society. But other research analyzing the discourse of Quebec teachers of French-Canadian origin shows varying degrees of defensiveness related to their minority status in Canada and within North America or their concerns as a fragile majority (one that has fought long, hard battles to achieve linguistic and economic recognition, even within Quebec). Thus, adapting to diversity is seen by some teachers as a threat to "traditional" Quebec identity. Their discourse also conveys civic concerns and stresses the need to defend values such as gender equality and democracy.

Research among youth generally confirms this glass half-empty/half-full assessment. High school students generally share the values of "liberal individualism" and "democratic egalitarianism." Primarily, these students identify as youth and maintain a critical distance from the values of their parents, notably in interethnic relations. The students of immigrant origin feel strongly about being part of Quebec society, albeit less so than third-generation students. Overall, both groups converge more than they diverge in their opinions on priority social problems and their definition of citizenship. Where differences exist, they are more likely linked to socioeconomic status than to ethnic identity.[27]

These positive trends do not mean that the blueprint (implicit among many proponents of Bill 101) to turn the children of immigrants into *Québécois d'abord et avant tout* (Quebecers first and foremost) has actually come to fruition. Actually, many studies show that identifying as a Quebecer still ranks lower than identifying as a Canadian for most of these allophone "children of Bill 101." Some nationalist public figures believe that this trend reflects Quebec's ambiguous political status within Canada and can only be rectified if Quebec achieves its independence. Others view this situation differently. They contend that Canadian identity is positively linked with cultural and linguistic diversity, whereas a Quebec identity continues to be associated more exclusively with a French-Canadian heritage. Thus, many youth of immigrant origin who conduct their public lives in French and enthusiastically embrace many aspects of Quebec culture and possess little knowledge of other Canadian provinces still tend to identify as Canadians first and foremost, an identity that they view as being more open and civic minded and hence more apt to include them.[28]

BIOGRAPHY

Lise Coupal: Just an Ordinary Teacher?

Born in 1953 to a middle-class family, Lise Coupal grew up in Villeray, a working-class francophone neighbourhood in Montreal. From as far back as she can remember, she dreamed of becoming a teacher. Following her studies at CEGEP Ahuntsic, she attended the Faculty of Education at Université du Québec à Montréal, where she earned her bachelor's degree in 1980. After working for a few years as a preschool teacher for four-year-olds in a community setting, she joined the Protestant School Board of Greater Montreal as a welcoming class teacher for immigrant children in 1988. When Quebec's confessional school boards became linguistic school boards, she began teaching regular classes with the Commission scolaire de Montréal.

Lise Coupal in her classroom.

Photographer: Michel La Veaux. Les Films du 3 Mars.

Since 2000, Coupal has taught Grade 1 at École Barthélemy-Vimont, one of Montreal's most multiethnic schools, where she plans to spend the remainder of her teaching career. Every year Coupal says she relives the special magic of Grade 1, the year when she believes the metamorphosis in students

continued

is most remarkable. She also feels that teaching in a multiethnic setting is easier than in a more homogeneous student population. Coupal particularly appreciates the respect that parents and children show the teachers and the importance they ascribe to education.

Transforming a public institution like a school into a welcoming, pluralistic learning environment does not just happen from the top down. It requires patience and persistence from a host of front-line participants. Lise Coupal, also known as "Madame Lise," is a teacher who possesses both of these qualities in abundance. In fact, when she and her 20 students starred in a film called *La classe de Madame Lise*, it won the 2006 award for best documentary at the Jutras (Quebec's modest equivalent of the Oscars). Here is our adaptation of what *La Presse* (North America's foremost French-language daily) had to say about Madame Lise's classroom.

The Incredible Madame Lise

In Lise Coupal's classroom, you won't find many Carolines or Jean-Mathieus. The desks in her class are occupied by students with names like Adnan, Noura, Furkans, Tajinder, Sumbbal, and Hatyum. Documentary filmmaker Sylvie Groulx followed this École Barthélemy-Vimont elementary school teacher and her class of about 20 first-grade students throughout the school year in Montreal's Parc-Extension neighbourhood. In her film, *La Classe de Madame Lise,* she showed that when you learn your ABCs with Madame Lise, you also learn a great deal about different cultures.

"I've never had a White Catholic class with names like Bouchard or Tremblay," says Lise Coupal. Seated in her classroom in front of some Lilliputian desks, this devoted teacher speaks with pride about her school, where cultures mix like the multicoloured lines on the students' little rulers.

"When Sylvie Groulx walked into the school yard she was impressed by the number of nationalities she found, all together in one place," says Lise Coupal. She reaches into the closet and takes out an imposing calendar of the cultural and religious holidays celebrated by her students. École Barthélemy-Vimont brings together students of almost 80 different ethnic origins, who speak in 30 different languages.

The small film crew came to visit Lise Coupal's class about 30 times between September and June. "After a while, the students and I forgot about the camera completely," says Coupal. A very discreet cameraperson succeeded in capturing some precious private moments between the teacher and her students who were experiencing difficulties.

"I knew when I came here that people would see my method and criticize it," she says. "But I decided to take the plunge just the same." Although, as she says, she plays the role of nurse, psychologist, and mother for her students, her real challenge remains teaching French and reading. "The biggest challenge comes when parents don't speak French," she explains. "In those kinds of cases, I ask their older brothers or sisters to be my interpreters." Some of Lise Coupal's students go to school on Saturdays to learn their parents' languages, like Chinese. Others study Arabic, Vietnamese, or Spanish at noon hour.

"What I like about first grade is discovering reading. I have the privilege of being part of this important moment in their lives," says Coupal.

It has been said that École Barthélemy-Vimont is one of the most underprivileged schools in one of Montreal's most violent neighbourhoods. "I don't believe that there is any more violence here than there is elsewhere," says Coupal. "That would be a distorted image of the neighbourhood."

Coupal once turned down an offer to go teach elsewhere. After 18 years of teaching, she has difficulty understanding why young people become violent. "When children come to my class they aren't violent. Why does it change when they turn 14 or 15? I often ask myself that question."

When you meet her, it is easy to guess why Lise Coupal was chosen for a documentary film. Madame Lise is the ideal school teacher. Smiling, affectionate, strict but not disagreeable. With her, anyone would want to get an "A" in every subject.

"Today," says Coupal, "I have a great deal of difficulty hearing close-minded ideas about immigrants."

Conclusion

Quebec's traditionally homogeneous French-language education system has undergone some radical changes over the past 30 years and continues to be shaped by public policies geared toward promoting French and openness to ethnocultural diversity. The province has come a long way and now compares favourably with other immigrant-receiving societies. Nevertheless, many challenges lie ahead. Among other things, the marginalization of some ethnic groups, and most especially that of the black community, must be better understood and actively prevented. Adapting to religious diversity, still a source of tension for some, will also have to be further addressed. Quebec's educational system is relatively well positioned to meet these challenges now that it can draw upon the major policy frameworks developed by the government and upon the expertise developed by many front-line participants. Still, given the current context, in which intercultural conflict is growing in many areas around the globe and in which globalization could jeopardize some gains (notably regarding language rights), only time will tell to what extent the theories of the optimists or of the pessimists will prevail.

Questions for Critical Thinking

1. To what extent should diversity be taken into consideration in schools?
2. What do you think are the main strengths and weaknesses of the measures taken in the integration of immigrant students and in intercultural education?
3. What results have been achieved in the integration of immigrant students and in intercultural education?
4. Do you think that Quebec's experience in adapting to ethnocultural diversity is specific to the context and challenges of its society? How are Quebec's experiences similar to or different from those in the United States or the rest of Canada?

Notes

1. Students whose first language is neither French nor English.
2. Under Bill 101, in addition to the traditional anglophone community, English-language schools are also attended by students from Quebec's established communities of immigrant origin, the majority of whom are at least third-generation denizens. However, the transformation of English-language institutions (through the introduction of French-immersion schools, among other things), which took place in the wake of the new linguistic dynamics in Quebec, would clearly warrant further attention as a case study unto itself.
3. See Chapters 11 and 12.
4. Ministère de l'Immigration et des Communautés culturelles, *Let's Build Québec Together: Vision: A Policy Statement on Immigration and Integration* (Montreal: Direction des communications, 1990); Statistics Canada, *Immigration and Ethnocultural Diversity in Canada: National Household Survey,* (Ottawa: Statistics Canada, 2011); Ministère de l'Immigration et des Communautés culturelles, *Caractéristiques de l'immigration au Québec : statistiques* (Quebec: Government of Quebec, 2011).
5. Ministère de l'Éducation, du Loisir et du Sport, *Portrait statistique 2011–2012 des élèves issus de l'immigration* (Quebec: Government of Quebec, 2014); Comité de la gestion de la taxe scolaire de l'Ile de Montréal, *Portrait socioculturel des élèves inscrits dans les écoles publiques de l'île de Montréal,* 2014.
6. Danielle Juteau, Marie McAndrew, and Linda Pietrantonio, "Multiculturalism à la Canadian and intégration à la Québécoise: Transcending their limits," in *Blurred Boundaries: Migration, Ethnicity and Citizenship,* ed. Rainer Bauböck and John Rundell (Aldershot, England: Ashgate, 1998), 95–110; Daniel Salée, "The Quebec State and the Management of Ethnocultural Diversity: Perspectives on an Ambiguous Record," in *Belonging? Diversity, Recognition and Shared Citizenship in Canada,* ed. Keith Banting, Thomas J. Courchene, and Leslie Seidle (Montreal: IRPP, 2007), 105–42.
7. For an overview of policy development and the surrounding debates, see Chapter 15.
8. Ministère de l'Éducation du Québec, *A School for the Future: Policy Statement on Educational Integration*

and Intercultural Education—A New Direction for Success (Quebec: Government of Quebec, 1998); Marie McAndrew, *Immigration et diversité à l'école : le débat québécois dans une perspective comparative* (Montreal: Presses de l'Université de Montréal, 2001); Ministère de l'Éducation, du Loisir et du Sport, *La politique d'intégration scolaire et d'éducation interculturelle (1998). Rapport d'évaluation* (Quebec: Government of Quebec, 2014).

9. John R. Mallea, *Quebec's Language Policy: Background and Responses* (Quebec: CIRB, 1977); Marc V. Levine, *The Reconquest of Montreal: Language Policy and Social Change in a Bilingual City* (Philadelphia: Temple University Press, 1990).
10. Ministère de l'Éducation, du Loisir et du Sport, *Portrait statistique 2011–2012 des élèves issus de l'immigration.*
11. Marie McAndrew, "La loi 101 en milieu scolaire : impacts et résultats," *Revue d'aménagement linguistique* (Autumn 2002): 69–82; Marie McAndrew, "Le remplacement du marqueur linguistique par le marqueur religieux en milieu scolaire," in *Ce qui a changé depuis le 11 septembre 2001 : les relations ethniques en question,* ed. Jean Renaud, Linda Pietrantonio, and Guy Bourgeault (Montreal: Presses de l'Université de Montréal, 2002), 131–48.
12. Between secondary school (which ends at about age 16) and university, Quebec's school system provides an intermediate academic institution commonly referred to as CEGEP (collège d'enseignement général et professionnel) where most students study between the ages of 16 to 18. CEGEPs are somewhat akin to US community colleges, although according to international standards they do not constitute a form of postsecondary education.
13. It is through this concept (now tainted by its overuse in the media) that Canadian jurisprudence has designated exceptions to be granted by public and private institutions to handicapped persons or members of minority groups for whom apparently neutral or universal standards and practices effectively constitute a form of indirect discrimination.
14. Gérard Bouchard and Charles Taylor, *Building the Future: A Time for Reconciliation* (Quebec: Consultation Commission on Accommodation Practices Related to Cultural Differences [CCAPRCD], 2008); Jocelyn Maclure, "Le malaise relatif aux pratiques d'accommodement de la diversité religieuse : une thèse interprétative," in *L'accommodement raisonnable et la diversité religieuse à l'école publique : normes et pratiques*, ed. Marie McAndrew et al. (Montreal: Fides, 2008), 215–42; Assemblée nationale, *Projet de loi no 60 : Charte affirmant les valeurs de laïcité et de neutralité religieuse de l'État ainsi que d'égalité entre les femmes et les hommes et encadrant les demandes d'accommodement* (Quebec: Government of Quebec, 2013).
15. A kirpan is a metal dagger with a curved blade. Kirpans vary in length, but may be several centimetres long and are carried in a scabbard attached to a belt worn over the shoulder.
16. McAndrew, *Immigration et diversité*; Ministère de l'Éducation, du Loisir et du Sport, *Portrait statistique 2011–2012 des élèves issus de l'immigration.*
17. McAndrew, "Ensuring Proper Competency in the Host Language: Contrasting Formula and the Place of Heritage Languages," *Teacher College Review* 111, no, 6 (2009): 1528–54; Françoise Armand and Zita DeKoninck, *Portrait des services d'accueil et d'intégration scolaire des élèves issus de l'immigration* (Quebec: Ministère de l'Éducation, du Loisir et du Sport, 2012).
18. Ministère de l'Éducation du Québec, *Quebec Schools on Course: Educational Policy Statement* (Quebec: Government of Quebec, 1997); Ministère de l'Éducation du Québec, *Quebec Education Program: Preschool Education—Elementary Education* (Quebec: Government of Quebec, 2001); Ministère de l'Éducation du Québec, *Quebec Education Program: Secondary School Education, Cycle One* (Quebec: Government of Quebec, 2004); Ministère de l'Éducation, du Loisir et du Sport, *Establishment of an Ethics and Religious Culture Program: Providing Future Direction for all Quebec Youth* (Quebec: Government of Quebec, 2005).
19. McAndrew, *Immigration et diversité*; Béchir Oueslati, "The Evolution of the Coverage of Islam and Muslim Cultures in Quebec French-Language Textbooks since the 1980s," in *Islam and Education in Pluralistic Societies: Integration and Transformations. Final Report on the Workshop Held at the University of Montreal,* ed. Marie McAndrew, Patrice Brodeur, and Amina Triki-Yamani (2008).
20. Maryse Potvin, Marie McAndrew, and Fasal Kanouté, *L'éducation antiraciste en milieu francophone montréalais : bilan critique*, Chair on ethnic relations: Université de Montréal (2006); Marie McAndrew, Julie Larochelle-Audet, Corina Borri-Anadon, and Maryse Potvin, "Pre-Service Teacher Training in Ethno-Cultural, Religious and Linguistic Diversity Offered by Québec Universities: A Quantitative and Qualitative Portrait," in *Education's Role in Preparing Globally Competent Citizens,* ed. Nikolay Popov, BCES Conference Books, 12 (Sofia: Bulgarian Comparative Education Society, 2014), 108–13.
21. Fasal Kanouté, Janine Hohl, and Nathalie Chamlian, "Les étudiants allophones dans les programmes de premier cycle de la Faculté des sciences de l'éducation de l'Université de Montréal," in *L'intégration des minorités visibles et ethnoculturelles dans la profession enseignante,* ed. Donatille Mujawamariya (Outremont: Les Éditions Logiques, 2002) 183–201.
22. Marie McAndrew, Jacques Ledent, Jake Murdoch, and Rachid Ait-Said, *La réussite scolaire des jeunes québécois issus de l'immigration au secondaire* (Quebec: MELS,

2011); McAndrew, "La loi 101 en milieu scolaire"; Marie McAndrew, Mathieu Jodoin, Michel Pagé, and Josefina Rossell, "L'aptitude au français des élèves montréalais d'origine immigrée : impact de la densité ethnique de l'école, du taux de francisation associé à la langue maternelle et de l'ancienneté d'implantation," *Cahiers québécois de démographie* 29, no. 1 (2000): 89–118; Gérard Pinsonneault, Marie McAndrew, and Jacques Ledent, *Le cheminement et le choix linguistique, au cégep et à l'université, des élèves du secondaire français issus de l'immigration, cohortes 1998–1999 et 1999–2000* (Quebec: MELS, 2012).

23. Catherine Girard-Lamoureux, *La langue d'usage public des allophones scolarisés au Québec* (Quebec: Conseil supérieur de la langue française, 2004); Statistics Canada, *Population selon la langue parlée le plus souvent et régulièrement à la maison, groupes d'âge (total), pour le Canada, les provinces et les territoires*, highlight tables (2011).

24. Marie McAndrew, Bruce Garnett, Jacques Ledent, Charles Ungerleider, Maria Adumati-Trache, and Rachid Ait-Said, "La réussite scolaire des élèves issus de l'immigration : une question de classe sociale, de langue ou de culture?" *Éducation et Francophonie* 36, no. 1 (2008): 177–96; McAndrew et al., *La réussite scolaire des jeunes québécois issus de l'immigration au secondaire.*

25. Advisory Committee on Integration and Reasonable Accommodation in the Schools, *Inclusive Québec Schools: Dialogue, Values and Common Reference Points* (Quebec: MELS, 2007); Marie McAndrew, "The Muslim Community and Education in Quebec: Controversies and Mutual Adaptation," in *Islam and Education in Pluralistic Societies*, ed. McAndrew et al.

26. Potvin, McAndrew, and Kanouté, *L'éducation antiraciste en milieu francophone montréalais*; Diane Gérin-Lajoie, *Le discours du personnel des écoles sur la diversité de la clientèle scolaire*, 60th ACELF Congress, 2007; Marie McAndrew, *Fragile Majorities and Education: Belgium, Catalonia, Northern-Ireland, and Quebec* (Montreal and Kingston: McGill-Queen's University Press, 2013).

27. Michel Pagé, Marie McAndrew, and Mathieu Jodoin, *Vécu scolaire et social des élèves scolarisés dans les écoles secondaires de langue française de l'île de Montréal* (Quebec: Ministère des Relations avec les citoyens et de l'Immigration du Quebec, 1997); Anne Laperrière and Patrick Dumont, *La citoyenneté chez de jeunes Montréalais : vécu scolaire et représentations de la société* (Montreal: GREAPE, Université de Montréal, 2000).

28. Marie-Hélène Chastenay and Michel Pagé, "Le rapport à la citoyenneté et à la diversité chez les jeunes collégiens québécois : comment se distinguent les deuxièmes générations d'origine immigrée?" in *Les deuxièmes générations en France et au Québec*, ed. Nancy Venel, Paul Eid, and Maryse Potvin (Montreal: Athéna, 2007); Maryse Potvin, "Second Generation Haitian Youth in Quebec: Between the 'Real' Community and the 'Represented' Community," *Canadian Ethnic Studies* 31, no. 1 (1999): 43–73.

Select Bibliography

Advisory Committee on Integration and Reasonable Accommodation in the Schools. *Inclusive Québec Schools: Dialogue, Values and Common Reference Points.* Report submitted to the Minister of Education, Recreation and Sports. Quebec: Government of Québec, 2007.

Bouchard, Gérard, and Charles Taylor. *Building the Future: A Time for Reconciliation.* Quebec: The Consultation Commission on Accommodation Practices Related to Cultural Differences, 2008.

McAndrew, Marie. "The Education of Immigrant Students in a Globalized World: Policy Debates in a Comparative Perspective." In *Global Understandings: Learning and Education in Troubled Times*, edited by M. Suarez-Orozco, 232–55. Berkeley/London/New York: University of California Press/Ross Institute, 2006.

———. *Fragile Majorities and Education: Belgium, Catalonia, Northern Ireland, Quebec.* Montreal and Kingston: McGill-Queen's University Press, 2013.

Ministère de l'Éducation du Québec. *A School for the Future: Policy Statement on Educational Integration and Intercultural Education—A New Direction for Success.* Quebec: Government of Québec, 1998.

Ministère de l'Immigration et des Communautés Culturelles. *Diversity: An Added Value: Government Policy to Promote Participation of All in Québec's Development.* Quebec: Direction des politiques et programmes d'intégration, de régionalisation et de relations interculturelles, 2008.

———. *Let's Build Québec Together: Vision: A Policy Statement on Immigration and Integration.* Montreal: Direction des communications, 1990.

18 Canadian Federalism and Quebec's Pathological Prism

Jean-François Gaudreault-DesBiens, Université de Montréal

Timeline

1867 British North America Act (now the Constitution Act, 1867) is signed, creating the Canadian federation with a division of powers that is still applicable today.

1883 *Hodge v. The Queen:* Judicial Committee of the Privy Council confirms that provinces do not act as delegates or agents of the federal government when legislating, and their legislative power is plenary in their areas of jurisdictions.

1976 Election of the Parti Québécois (PQ); for the first time, a secessionist party holds power in Quebec City.

1977 Charter of the French Language: French language's status is significantly reinforced, and the use of languages other than French in advertisements is submitted to new restrictions. French's position as the province's official language is reiterated; it had first been affirmed in the 1974 Official Language Act (Bill 22).

1980 First referendum on sovereignty-association in Quebec; Canadian Prime Minister Pierre Trudeau promises constitutional changes but remains ambiguous as to their exact nature; the "no" side wins.

1980–2 Frequent constitutional conferences are held around a project of patriating the Canadian Constitution and the inclusion in that Constitution of a charter of rights; provinces are divided.

1981 *Re: Resolution to Amend the Constitution:* Supreme Court of Canada confirms that, absent a constitutional amendment formula in the British North America Act, the federal government may legally take steps to unilaterally patriate the Canadian Constitution from the United Kingdom, but that since provincial powers are affected by the constitutional amendments envisaged, constitutional conventions require that a substantial degree of provincial consent be obtained prior to proceeding further; federal government returns to the negotiation table, where it and nine provinces agree on a final draft; Quebec refuses to sign the agreement.

1982 Constitution Act, 1982, enters into force against Quebec's objections, but Quebec is legally bound nonetheless; contains the Canadian Charter of Rights and Freedoms.

1982 *Reference re: Amendment to the Canadian Constitution:* Supreme Court of Canada confirms that Quebec does not have a veto over the constitutional amendments effected by the Constitution Act, 1982.

1984 Election of Brian Mulroney as prime minister of Canada; Mulroney wants Quebec to return to the constitutional fold with "honour and enthusiasm."

1985 Election of Liberal Premier Robert Bourassa after nine years of PQ government.

1987 Meech Lake Accord is signed, though it must be passed by the federal Parliament and provincial legislatures; Quebec is recognized as a "distinct society."

1990 Collapse of the Meech Lake Accord; creation of the Bloc Québécois.

1992 Charlottetown Accord: Quebec is recognized as a distinct society in a constitutional amendment proposal with a broader scope than simply meeting Quebec's demands; collapse of the Charlottetown Accord after referendums held in Quebec and in the rest of Canada.

1994 Election of PQ Premier Jacques Parizeau.

1995 Referendum on sovereignty-partnership; a thin margin of voters reject the proposal.

1998 *Reference re Secession of Quebec*: Supreme Court specifies the basic rules applicable in the case of a provincial unilateral declaration of independence.

1999 Adoption of An Act Respecting the Exercise of the Fundamental Rights and Prerogatives of the Québec People and the Québec State.

2000 Final adoption of the Clarity Act by both chambers of Parliament.

2006 Election of Stephen Harper as prime minister of Canada; motion to recognize Quebecers as a nation.

Introduction

On what basis is Canadian federalism evaluated in Quebec? This is the question that this chapter seeks to explore. It argues that while many variables come into play in such an evaluative process, some "reasoning templates" consistently bend this process in a way that tends to yield unfavourable results for Canadian federalism. The central thesis underlying this chapter is that the nationalist agenda that dominates and frames, for all practical purposes, provincial political discourse in Quebec is constitutive of a pathological prism when it comes to evaluating how federalism fares in protecting or accommodating the province's interests. It is intentional that I have used the word *pathological*, since the prism in question indeed induces many Quebecers to grasp some legitimate manifestations, expressions, or expectations related to federalism as dysfunctions, if not diseases.

This thesis should not be construed as an indictment of Quebec nationalism, but as a study of some epistemological obstacles upon which analyses of federalism elaborated through a nationalist prism may stumble; in this respect, Quebec nationalism arguably fares neither better nor worse than other democratic nationalisms. It is worth noting, moreover, that the representation of Quebec nationalism in certain expressions of majoritarian federalism in Canada could also be subjected to an analysis akin to that made in this chapter.[1]

Evaluating Federalism

Federal regimes purport to reconcile many different often conflicting values: unity and diversity, autonomy and solidarity, and so on. In so doing, they may fall prey to political agendas systematically seeking to privilege one particular value at the expense of all others. Although prioritizing a single value over competing ones tends to undermine, if not contradict outright, the logic of equilibrium arguably underlying federalism, it is nevertheless observable in various forms in many federations.

The values so frequently promoted become focal points from which to evaluate the evolution of a given federation. In the 1980s political scientist Richard Simeon published a seminal article in which he noticed that some recurring unbalances could arise in federal regimes that risked undermining support for them.[2] Examining which normative criteria were used in evaluating the successes or failures of federations, he argued that federal systems tended to be evaluated from three distinct standpoints.

The first is the political communities that citizens primarily identify with, which may be the broader federal polity or a particular federated unit.[3] From this standpoint, a federation will be evaluated in light of its ability to maintain a balance between the powers respectively held by the federal community and the federated communities. In such a case, a particular communitarian perspective becomes constitutive of an evaluative prism. This angle of approach thus looks at the success (or lack thereof) of federalism through the prism of a political identity deemed primordial. For example, in Belgium the Flemish tend to identify more with their institutional community than with the broader Belgian federation, while Walloons historically identify more with the central state, although their primary political identification may be changing in reaction to Flemish nationalism and the increasing decentralization process in Belgium.

A second common vantage point is democracy: A federation will be evaluated according to its ability to foster democracy. Again, views on this question may differ significantly. For some, federalism undermines democracy because it frustrates majority rule as a result of the institutionalized fragmentation of the global polity that it operates. For others it promotes democracy because it ensures the existence of constitutionally protected federated units that are arguably closer to citizens, thus enabling the latter to be more involved in the self-government of their community. As they relate to questions pertaining to the meaning of federal citizenship and the basic socio-economic rights that all citizens can expect to enjoy in a federation, debates in Canada regarding the potential involvement of the federal government in the elaboration of social policies, irrespective of the constitutional basis upon which such involvement may rely, reveal the influence of conflicting conceptions of the relation between federalism and democracy.

The third standpoint is functional effectiveness. In a nutshell, this perspective induces those who adopt it to evaluate federalism according to its ability to optimize the allocation of resources and the distribution of public goods. Does federalism enhance or reduce the ability of governments to enact responsive public policies? Which level of government is best able to deliver services in a particular area? The functionalist perspective, which is rational, systemic, and citizen centred, tends to emphasize a federal regime's toolbox role and evaluates its performance accordingly, but it often underestimates the significance of intangible variables like identity that the communitarian perspective tends, on the contrary, to overemphasize. This perspective has had a significant influence in the United States, particularly after World War II.

Relying on Simeon's analytical framework, dominant attitudes toward federalism in Quebec can be characterized as being anchored in a communitarian perspective; hence the methodological nationalism that frames political discourse, be it secessionist or federalist. However, this communitarian perspective may not enjoy the dominance it once exercised, primarily as a result of the rise of a more individualistic and universalistic culture that some attribute to the expanding influence of the rights culture and multiculturalist ideology that followed the adoption of the Charter of Rights and Freedoms in 1982. This hypothesis is perhaps counterintuitive given the official rejection of that Charter in most Quebec political circles, but a serious case can be made in its favour. Recent debates shed light on the existence of possible cracks in the dominant communitarian narrative and on the increasing influence of other perspectives, including functionalist ones.

The Centrality of Post–Quiet Revolution History

Attitudes toward federalism in Quebec cannot be understood without briefly looking back at the historical context in which they were formed. Leaving aside the regularly rehashed episodes of the British Conquest or the 1837–8 Rebellions, to name but a few, more recent events have shaped perceptions of Canadian federalism. When focusing on recent *formal* constitutional developments, the picture indeed appears bleak to many Quebecers.

Since the Quiet Revolution of the 1960s, all provincial political parties, whatever their persuasion, have embraced a nationalist agenda that posits Quebec as the one and only home of the French-speaking majority of the population (as opposed to the broader and relatively borderless French-Canadian identity that dominated before), and that the Quebec government bears a special responsibility to affirm the distinct identity of the "Quebec nation." This set the stage for what effectively led to a political, cultural, and spatial transformation of identity for a majority of Quebecers. Quebec's national affirmation has, to a great extent, been orchestrated through the creation of a centralized state endowed with the mission of ensuring the preservation and the flourishing of the only predominantly francophone society in North America.

In addition to preserving this unique identity, the state's actions had to mirror, even to increase, this prescribed and normative uniqueness. I use the words *prescribed* and *normative* on purpose to draw attention to some assumptions that inspired, and still inspire, the apprehension of "national identity" in Quebec's state-building project. Essentially, this national identity has been depicted as "a natural, organic and archaic entity, rooted in a past that inevitably calls for continuity in the future,"[4] a future for which the state bears the ultimate responsibility. In other words, this Quebec identity has been depicted as being forever fixed in its essential characteristics. As the Quebec state became its protector and promoter, the *interests of the government of Quebec* were soon equated with the *interests of Quebecers* themselves.

Nationalist discourses increasingly depicted the federal government as the government of the "rest of Canada," which, as such, rarely acts in the interests of Quebecers, or worse tends to wilfully act *against* their interests. To a large extent, the federal government has seen its legitimacy melting away like snow under the sun, even when it acted within the limits of its constitutional powers. Canadian federalism was in turn assigned the sole mission of being economically "profitable"; the federalist Bourassa government was a main proponent of this view.[5] This is further evidence of the strong influence of the communitarian perspective on the performance evaluation of Canadian federalism in Quebec.

While legitimate in some regards, this perspective nevertheless raises problems from the standpoint of federal theory, as it induces citizens to conceptualize the identities of the federation and of the federated political communities as hardly compatible, thereby inciting citizens to choose one over the other. The embrace of a strong nationalist agenda by all political parties thus launched a zero-sum game under which federal "gains" tended to be construed as Quebec "losses," thus fostering a discourse of victimization fuelled by constitutional developments since the early 1980s.

The first and most important of these developments was the adoption of the Constitution Act, 1982, which was the culmination of a process of patriation of the Canadian Constitution. The Constitution Act, 1982, includes the Canadian Charter of Rights and Freedoms, which sets human rights–based limits on governmental action and establishes a regime of constitutional supremacy.

Two main objections were raised in Quebec against the Constitution Act, 1982. The first concerned the very nature of the constitutional amendments brought about by this act. In a nutshell, Quebec argued that it unduly reduced its legislative powers, particularly in the field of language. Indeed, the minority-language rights applicable in the field of education that are contained in the Canadian Charter were a partial response to Quebec's Charter of the French Language, which was adopted a few years before and which imposed stricter conditions on access to English schools in the province. Other rights or freedoms contained in the Canadian Charter, such as freedom of expression, could also be used (and were actually used) to challenge provisions of the Charter of the French Language. Moreover, the Constitution Act, 1982 failed to grant Quebec a veto over future amendments affecting its jurisdictions.

Finally, emphasizing multiculturalism as a principle of interpretation of the Canadian Charter was perceived as a further rejection of Quebec's particular conception of federalism, which primarily envisages Canada as a compact of two nations: one French-speaking and the other English-speaking.

The second objection had to do with the process that led to the adoption of the Constitution Act, 1982, in the context of which Quebec ended up isolated in its rejection of this new constitutional instrument. It was indeed adopted against the will of René Lévesque's secessionist government after the collapse of an alliance of provinces opposed to the constitutional package then proposed by Pierre Trudeau's federal government. In the nationalist narrative, which has also been adopted by federalist parties in Quebec, the province's isolation resulted from a plot of the federal government and the other provinces that culminated in the "night of the long knives." In the weak version of this narrative, this outcome demonstrates that Quebec's unique concerns within the Canadian federation always tend to be taken lightly. In the strong version, this episode is seen as evidence that the province's status in Canada is trivialized and Quebec is not treated in the way it sees itself, as a nation. Instead, it is dealt with as a mere province among others.

Even though it remains unclear how, in 1982, the PQ's secessionist government could have agreed to a constitutional amendment package that, if accepted by Quebec, could have destroyed its dream of creating a new nation-state, the nationalist narrative has had, and continues to have, a tremendous impact on Quebec politics. As of today, no Quebec government, secessionist or federalist, ever formally endorsed the Constitution Act, 1982, and the lack of a formal constitutional recognition of Quebec's nationhood remains an open sore for many Quebecers.

It is this sore that later constitutional developments sought to cure. The first salve came in 1987 with the Meech Lake Accord, which sought to bring Quebec back into the constitutional fold. This accord essentially sought to ensure that interpretations of the Constitution, including the Charter, be consistent with the recognition of Quebec as a distinct society. Such a formal recognition was one of the essential conditions for Quebec to sign the Constitution Act, 1982. Other features of the accord were a provincial veto over certain types of constitutional amendments; a provincial right to opt out, with compensation, from any federal program in a field under exclusive provincial jurisdiction; the recognition of increased provincial powers in the field of immigration; and a guarantee that the three Supreme Court justices appointed from Quebec would be selected from a list submitted by the Quebec government.

In spite of having been approved by the federal government and all provincial governments in 1987, the Meech Lake Accord collapsed in 1990 after two of the constitutionally required legislative assemblies failed to ratify it. This failure provoked a seismic shift in Canadian politics. It triggered the creation of the separatist Bloc Québécois, paving the way for a second referendum on sovereignty in 1995. It was also perceived by a significant number of Quebecers as a rejection of their unique identity. Moreover, it led in 1992 to the tabling of a further constitutional amendment project, the Charlottetown Accord, which sought both to recognize Quebec as a distinct society and to address the underinclusiveness for which the Meech Lake Accord had been criticized, notably by integrating an interpretive clause designed to enhance the protection of Aboriginal rights.

The Charlottetown Accord was defeated in two simultaneous referendums held in the fall of 1992, one under federal law and the other under Quebec law. This outcome, which was construed by many as a reciprocal rejection of Quebec and the rest of Canada, was followed in 1994 by the election of a Parti Québécois government, which in 1995 held a referendum where Quebec voters narrowly rejected secession from Canada. Following this near-death experience, the federal government asked the Supreme Court for an advisory opinion on a potential unilateral declaration of independence by Quebec. In 1998, the court opined that even though a unilateral declaration of independence would be illegal both under Canadian and international law, a clear majority on a clear question in favour of independence would trigger a duty to negotiate on the part of other constitutional actors.[6] Absent a negotiated outcome, the court alluded to the possibility—not the legality—of effecting a unilateral declaration of independence with the international community as the ultimate arbiter. Both the federal government and the Quebec government claimed victory after the court's opinion, and both were eventually compelled to formally position themselves vis-à-vis the court's requirements: the federal government with the so-called Clarity Act, and the PQ-led Quebec government with An Act Respecting the Fundamental Rights and Prerogatives of the Québec People and the Québec State.

Since then, the only formal constitutional development, beyond numerous judicial decisions, that has taken place was the recognition of Quebecers as forming a nation in a motion adopted by the House of Commons in 2006 at the initiative of the Conservative government of Stephen Harper. This political recognition fell short of what many Quebecers were expecting—that is, a *formal* constitutional recognition of their national status within Canada.

Reasoning Templates and the Evaluation of Canadian Federalism

The discussion above draws attention to the influence, often implicit or subdued, of **reasoning templates**.[7] These templates consist of basic intellectual and cognitive preconceptions that inform how one understands and interprets reality. Arguably, at least three qualitatively different, although interrelated, types of templates play a role in influencing how Quebecers tend to perceive Canadian federalism: historical, ideological, and juridical.

BIOGRAPHY

The Unknown Constitutional Soldier, or the Decline of Heroic Political Figures

These days, we often hear politicians saying that they are uninterested in discussing, let alone actively pursuing, constitutional reforms, and that instead their preference is to concentrate on "real things," such as the economy. Even nationalist politicians from Quebec shy away from seriously entertaining the idea of proposing substantial constitutional reforms, knowing that it would not resonate well elsewhere in Canada. Only secessionists who generally get a good return on their investment in any constitutional crisis seem happy to talk about such reforms, provided that the ones contemplated are radical enough. In any event, they are not currently particularly prone to seriously promoting their option given the relatively weak support for it in the population, preferring instead to emphasize their ability to form a "good government."

That a country is no more able nor willing to hold a discussion about its foundational legal framework—the basic rules of the *vivre-ensemble*—is perhaps regrettable, but there is no indication that this situation will change in the near future. As a result, public debate in Quebec about constitutional issues remains polarized around the federalism/secession dichotomy, which now mainly serves a local electoral purpose—that is, dividing the vote between the federalist Liberals and the secessionist PQ. The Coalition Avenir Québec continues to attempt to sneak in between the two by appropriating the popular rhetoric of a-constitutionalism and declaring itself ready to address "important things." Ultimately, we might have to seriously consider the possibility that the population of Quebec indeed considers that a constitutional reform is not an "important thing," or, alternatively, that former politicians' obsession with formal constitutional law is not a passion shared by the population anymore.

In sum, we are light years away from the fierce debates that took place between 1960 and 1995 on the reform of Canadian federalism so as

continued

to better grasp Quebecers' sense of nationhood. Most importantly, since the 1995 referendum there has hardly been a personality important enough to warrant a full-fledged profile in this chapter. Lucien Bouchard and Jacques Parizeau are long gone, and so are the key players of the great constitutional reform attempts of the 1970s and 1980s, such as Pierre Trudeau, René Lévesque, Robert Bourassa, Jean Chrétien, or Brian Mulroney.

Perhaps political actors with a lower profile should then be considered? Think, for example, of Stephen Harper, who became prime minister in 2006. Although his election was supposed to herald a new era of "federalism of openness" and in spite of the fact that his government tabled a motion in the House of Commons recognizing Quebecers as forming a nation, his government's policies have hardly had any impact on the way Quebecers envisage federalism. Actually, even when they sharply fell under federal jurisdiction, many of these policies only increased the antagonism or indifference of the population of Quebec toward federalism, since the values that inspired them were often seen as antithetical to those shared by the majority of Quebecers.

The only serious contender remains, from my perspective, someone who has possibly been vilified like no other before in Quebec. Yet that person's political actions have arguably had a lasting impact on the shape of constitutional debates, for better or for worse depending on one's opinion. That person is Stéphane Dion. After the collapse of the Meech Lake Accord, and particularly after having been recruited by Prime Minister Jean Chrétien to become his minister of intergovernmental affairs, this former political science professor from the Université de Montréal became one of the leading proponents of federalism in Quebec, who was constantly on the front line to refute arguments diminishing the achievements of federalism, whether they emanated from mere nationalists or from outright secessionists. He notably had epic epistolary debates with Lucien Bouchard, then premier of Quebec, stressing that if Canadian federalism may sometimes be theoretically problematic, it works most of the time rather well in practice. Dion himself sought to demonstrate that when he struck an agreement with then-Quebec Minister of Education Pauline Marois on a bilateral constitutional amendment that effectively abolished public denominational schools in the province.

It is perhaps as the father of the Clarity Act that Dion will be most fully remembered, again for better or for worse. The Clarity Act, which sought to give meaning, from the standpoint of Parliament, to the requirements set forth by the Supreme Court in the *Secession Reference* of 1998, was arguably a game changer. First, the government of Quebec's call for popular mobilization against it failed, which prompted Premier Bouchard's resignation. Second, the act's emphasis on the need for clarity in referendums on secession has influenced to some extent similar processes elsewhere, such as the 2014 vote held in Scotland. Third, it has placed Quebec secessionists on the defensive in spite of their constant denunciation of the act as distorting the Supreme Court's opinion in the *Secession Reference* and as illegitimately restricting Quebec's alleged right to external self-determination.

Whatever one thinks of Dion's political views and actions, it is hard to deny the impact he had in shaping the contemporary debate on federalism and nationalism in Quebec. As constitutional debates were quieting down, Stéphane Dion eventually turned his political attention to environmental issues, and his brief and lacklustre tenure as leader of the Liberal Party of Canada, as well as that party's electoral difficulties, forced him to adopt a much lower political profile.

Thus, more than the presence of any "strong" constitutional actor deserving to be profiled in this section, it is rather the absence of any such actor that has been striking in the last decade or so. No politician with a clear will to launch and implement an arguably much-needed constitutional reform has emerged in federalist circles; nor has any politician with some stature emerged from within the ranks of the secessionist movement. We might surmise that this is due to the creation of a new taboo in Canadian and Quebec constitutional politics, that of constitutional reform. Some public intellectuals, like André Pratte on the federalist side and Mathieu Bock-Côté on the nationalist-secessionist perspective, have to a certain extent animated public debates in the province, but their influence is hardly comparable to that of their predecessors, such as Claude Ryan or Fernand Dumont. Clearly, heroic figures are a thing of the past in the field of constitutional politics. This is why the most appropriate person to profile in this section is perhaps "the unknown constitutional soldier," who can either represent the absent figure on which I just shed light or the relatively anonymous one who tirelessly works to make the federal regime work, but who does so in the shadows to which constitutional discussions are now relegated.

Historical Templates

Historical templates are distinct from mere historical events. Indeed, these templates serve as a backdrop against which particular historical events are themselves interpreted and assessed; as such they give meaning to these events, and in this way can be said to participate in what sociologist Fernand Dumont called a nation's "identity reference."[8] An important historical template as far as Quebecers' perceptions of Canadian federalism are concerned is the so-called **compact theory**,[9] whose resilience is hardly questionable. There are actually two main versions of this theory. The first depicts the Canadian federation as a compact of equal provinces; over the years it has regularly fuelled the "provincial rights" agenda of some provinces outside of Quebec. The second version, which remains salient in Quebec but which has practically disappeared elsewhere, holds that Canada is a compact of two founding nations, an English-speaking one and a French-speaking one, with the second concentrated in Quebec. With the constitutional enshrinement of Aboriginal rights, a modified version could hold that Canada incorporates three founding nations.

The "two nations compact" theory continues to significantly influence political discourse in Quebec. The province's unending quest for a formal recognition of its unique identity within Canada does not primarily stem from concerns relating to a more efficient allocation of powers or to a better redistribution of resources. It essentially emanates from a self-perception, shared by a huge number of Quebecers, that their province should be granted a distinct status both by virtue of its role as the main *foyer* of French-speaking Canadians and because it constitutes, as such, a political community presenting the archetypal characteristics of a nation.

Ideological Templates

The way in which many Quebecers evaluate Canadian federalism is deeply influenced by the ideological template of **methodological nationalism**. Discussing how methodological nationalism has informed the epistemology of social sciences in the modern era, sociologist Andreas Wimmer and anthropologist Nina Glick Schiller identify three distinct features of this ideological template: (1) ignorance of or wilful blindness about the influence of the nation-state model on the structure of political thought and discourse; (2) "naturalization" of this model and of national narratives, without problematizing them further; and (3) territorial limitation of the political identity, referring to analytical frameworks that are for all relevant purposes determined by the projected boundaries of the national community.[10]

These characteristics of methodological nationalism are observable in Quebec's dominant political discourse. They are predictably exacerbated in the secessionist narrative, which is permeated by a rhetoric that represents Quebec's accession to statehood as the natural or normal fate of the province as a political community and of the Quebec people as an organic entity. Although the assumption that each nation must possess its own state is highly questionable, as well as is the idea that there are "normal" (that is, independent) and "abnormal" (nonindependent) nations, it is another assumption about the "predetermined" fate of the Quebec people that sheds a better light on how secessionists use narratives of Manifest Destiny. More specifically, this assumption relates to the organic depiction that is given of the Quebec people as a kind of natural, almost prepolitical, entity and to the essentialist vision of identity upon which this depiction relies. Indeed, secessionist discourse often posits that by voting "yes" to Quebec independence, Quebecers would then "say 'yes' to themselves." In a way, this amounts to equating the accomplishment of each individual Quebecer's inner self to Quebec's accession to statehood. According to that view, a "yes" vote—and only a "yes" vote—in a referendum on independence could be construed as the expression of the community's soul, evincing some kind of historical meeting of minds between individual voters sharing a common essence, memory, and geographically bounded territory. The thinkers of Quebec's new conservative "identity nationalism" promote that view to various extents, which somehow assumes that there is an "authentic" way of being a Quebecer.[11] Methodological nationalism thus tends to view as expressions of false consciousness claims seeking to relativize the importance of nationhood in one's individual and political identity. Moreover, it dismisses the possibility of claiming multiple concurrent political allegiances. Monological nationalism thus supplements methodological nationalism. As such, methodological nationalism entails a strong adherence to homogenous representations of cultures, identities, and the political communities allegedly bearing such identities.[12] It is also often a fellow traveller to Jacobin republicanism, which under the guise of universalism seeks to erase or at least obscure any form of internal diversity. Recent debates about the Charter of Quebec Values tabled by the PQ government in 2013, which would have sought to ban ostentatious religious signs, have revealed the possible links between methodological nationalism and Jacobin ideologies: Under the guise of promoting a "one law for all" approach, the government's project was indirectly promoting a "one identity for all" approach.

In any event, such monism is hard to reconcile with federalism, which to a certain extent seeks to institutionalize pluralism, and constitutionally enshrines the existence of various levels of political communities whose objectives may sometimes converge and at other times diverge. That being said, even nonsecessionist Quebecers embrace methodological nationalism; to use a hockey metaphor, it has until recently set the rules of the rink on which provincial politicians must skate. We will see below that in the constitutional field this ideological template triggers what could be characterized as jurisdictional fetishism in addition to encouraging legal formalism and overestimating the law's ability to effectively translate political claims for recognition into normative terms. Legal formalism refers here to approaches solely focusing on formal expressions of the law—constitutions, statutes, or cases—as opposed to approaches also taking into consideration how the law is concretely received by its addressees and how it tangibly affects people's behaviour.

Juridical Templates

Although their impact is neglected in most political analyses, juridical preconceptions prevalent in Quebec also arguably contribute to skepticism toward Canadian federalism. It bears noting in this respect that not only lawyers but also nonlawyers may share such preconceptions, as both groups evolve in a particular legal culture that influences, to various degrees, their vision of the law and their expectations about it.[13]

One such preconception is tied to the province's connection to the **civil law** tradition. Contrary to the law of other provinces, which is entirely anchored in the common law tradition, Quebec law is said to be mixed in that its private law is linked to France's civil law tradition while its public law is associated with Britain's common law tradition. What is critically important for the sake of this discussion is that the primary source of law in the civil law tradition is legislation. There is thus a strong emphasis in that tradition on enacted law, which implies a formalization of legal norms through authoritative texts formally adopted by a particular legislature. As well, the civil law's emphasis on enacted law as representing the "will of the people" increases the importance of an explicit political assent to the rules that bind citizens together. This stands in contrast with the common law tradition, where the primary source of law can be found in judicial decisions.

Even though the modes of production of law in the two traditions have significantly converged, these archetypes remain relevant because they still shape visions of what the law is, what it does, and what it can do. As such, a jurisdiction's affiliation to a given legal tradition may partly explain the prevalence of particular regulatory strategies.[14]

My argument here is, first, that such expectations and strategies are more likely to be focused on and to mobilize formal law in jurisdictions that have an affiliation with the civil law tradition than in others without any such affiliation. Indeed, the civil law tradition, particularly in the French expression that Quebec has inherited, tends to privilege a more text-centred and top-down conception of the law over a more experiential one, as is often the case in common law jurisdictions, especially in the United States. For the purpose of the discussion, *formal law* is understood as referring to norms that are formalized through a text that is deemed to pre-exist the adjudication of cases, and which are expressed in constitutions, legislation, or delegated legislation.

Second, this emphasis on formal law in Quebec legal culture and constitutional thought encourages a disconnection between the political and legal reality of federalism, on the one hand, and the perception that Quebecers may have of that reality on the other. Indeed, the grip of legal formalism arguably influences the citizens' assumptions about what formal law can do while potentially blinding them to what less-formalized expressions of the law actually do. Recent debates over religious accommodation exemplify this attitude. Indeed, these debates revealed a belief in the power of general legislative interventions over judicial decisions made on a case-by-case basis to solve societal problems. Yet what many citizens saw as much-needed legislative clarifications were often mere codifications of regularly applied judicial doctrines. Finally, it may induce them to project unrealistic expectations onto the text of the law and to privilege symbols over tangible, if less spectacular, accomplishments.

Two main dynamics are at play. One lies in what could be called a *fetishism of the form*, which is closely tied to the symbolism often characterizing politics of recognition. This fetishism helps create illusions as to the formal law's ability to translate recognition claims and identities themselves, in all their complexities.[15] An interesting illustration of this can be found in the government of Quebec's recurring demand for a formal constitutional recognition of the province's distinct identity or nationhood. Such recognition would be a way to explicitly accommodate the province's "difference," although its tangible impact would, in all likelihood, be rather minimal. For instance, the Meech Lake Accord's "distinct society" clause, which would have taken the form of an interpretive clause of the Canadian Charter of Rights and Freedoms, would have created no new substantive rights for Quebec. Moreover, such recognition would have essentially codified a practice that the Supreme Court of Canada itself launched in the early days of its interpretation of the Charter—that is, taking into account, without always making it a determinant variable, Quebec's particular historical trajectory and cultural circumstances.[16]

My point is not to say that such demands of formal recognition on the part of a federated unit like Quebec are illegitimate or useless. On the contrary, they are easily understandable as a means to increase the level of cultural security of recognition seekers, even when the strategies chosen essentially revolve around symbolic solutions. Ignoring the relevance of symbolic solutions (or blindly refusing to consider them to be, to a significant extent, symbolic) risks exacerbating the alienation felt by those recognition seekers. I simply want to stress that the overarching importance given to the fulfillment of that need is to some extent troubling, especially in light of the actual condition of Quebec society today. Indeed, it seems hardly disputable that this society is already extremely dynamic *without* any formal recognition of its distinctiveness or nationhood. It is as if the fact of the actual blossoming of Quebec as a predominantly French society within the Canadian federation was deemed "unpleasant"[17] under the lens of methodological nationalism and, *a fortiori*, under a secessionist prism. In a way, it is as if Quebec's particular experience, including its achievements, could not be authentic or real without a constitutional form to contain it.

In the face of such circumstances, to what extent can we not explain, at least in part, Quebec's thirst for formal recognition by its affiliation to a formalist legal tradition—the civil law? As well, can we not attribute the difficulties that the rest of Canada experiences in trying to understand why such recognition is so important to Quebecers to its affiliation to a tradition that values experience over form? It is hard, in my view, not to concur with Rod Macdonald, who argued that "whatever the value of . . . explicit accommodation strategies, they rest on an outmoded conception of law and legal-constitutional process that presumes the state to be the centre of legal discourse, and to have a monopoly on the creation of legal and constitutive political norms."[18] Yet the demand for such formal strategies remains a central component of Quebec's political claims.

The second dynamic that I wish to highlight is that of "identitization" of formal law. It is closely related to the phenomenon of *jurisdictional fetishism* that pervades Quebec's legal culture and dominant constitutional thought, and which leads to the elevation of provincial areas of jurisdiction to the status of sacred cows that cannot be affected by any constitutional reform. Quebec's quest to have its distinct identity constitutionally recognized, combined with the already mentioned equation of *Quebecers'* interests to those of the *government of Quebec,* also contributes to amplify this phenomenon.[19] To the extent that all of the Quebec government's actions are deemed to promote the flourishing of the province's distinct identity, it is not surprising that, through a quasi-osmotic process, many Quebecers tend to defend provincial areas of jurisdiction which have no or very little identity-related content, exactly as if these areas of jurisdiction dealt with subjects considered essential for the preservation and the flourishing of Quebec's identity. This approach has induced the emergence of what can be characterized as a form of "narcissism of small differences"[20] in Quebec's legal culture and dominant constitutional thought. Through this narcissistic lens, Quebec's slightest difference, even if purely administrative, is vested with an identity dimension. Therefore, any federal intervention, as minimal as it may be, in a jurisdictional area where this small difference is deemed to be expressed risks being depicted as raising an existential question for the protection of Quebec's identity. From the perspective of federal theory, such an attitude obscures one of the central features of federalism—that is, that far from being solely a mechanism designed to accommodate diversity, federalism inherently implies a certain level of integration and unity. As much as it must respond to identity-related concerns, it cannot solely respond to such concerns.

In the end, while it is true that some federal assertions of power inspired by efficiency concerns may end up negating the dynamics inherent in federalism, the nationalist agenda in Quebec also ends up undermining the idea of a balanced conception of federalism. It does so by systematically overemphasizing diversity over all competing values and by breeding and feeding a pathological prism that induces Quebecers to envisage federalism as a zero-sum game. From that perspective, in a context like Quebec, where the performance evaluation of Canadian federalism is inextricably tainted by the successes or failures of the province's general politics of recognition, the possibility of tangible attitudinal changes seems remote.

CASE STUDY

Whither the Tower of Pisa? Federalism at the Supreme Court of Canada

Although the patriation of the Canadian Constitution against the objections of the Quebec government outraged a great number of Quebecers and triggered initiatives seeking to mitigate the damage that had been done, this event merely added fuel to a simmering fire originally ignited by the Supreme Court of Canada's interpretation of the division of powers between the federal government and the provinces.

A short glimpse into constitutional law is warranted here. The Constitution Act, 1867 (formerly known as the British North America Act of 1867), which laid the foundation of the Canadian federation, gave very broad powers to the federal government to such an extent that political theorist K. C. Wheare refused, on the basis of an analysis of these formal powers, to characterize Canada as having a federal constitution even though he recognized that, in practice, the country indeed possessed a federal form of government.[21] Wheare particularly had in mind the federal power to disallow provincial legislation, which is no longer used. Moreover, the variety of powers allocated to the federal Parliament were very broadly worded, such as the power to enact laws "for the peace, order, and good government of Canada," and this only increased fears that provinces would be treated as subordinate orders of government by the federal Parliament. In the *Hodge* case of 1883,[22] however, the Judicial Committee of the Privy Council, which was Canada's ultimate court of appeal until 1949, soon assuaged these fears by stating that provinces were sovereign in their areas of jurisdiction and not mere delegates of the federal government. In the decades that followed, the Privy Council, much to the dislike of foremost Canadian constitutional law scholars like Frank Scott or Bora Laskin (the latter would serve as the future chief justice of Canada, occupying this position when the patriation-related references were heard), gave a rather balanced interpretation to the division of powers by significantly narrowing the scope of some broad federal powers, such as the commerce clause, and by construing broadly competing provincial jurisdictions, such as that over property and civil rights.

When appeals to the Privy Council ceased, the Supreme Court of Canada became the last resort. It assumed this new role when Premier Maurice Duplessis was still leading the province of Quebec, and in a series of judgments the court often relied upon the division of powers to strike down Quebec laws targeting minorities or restricting fundamental freedoms, often under the guise of protecting the fabric of Quebec society. Reacting to such decisions, Duplessis coined the metaphor of the Tower of Pisa to describe the attitude of the Supreme Court of Canada toward Quebec, a metaphor that still has currency in nationalist circles. That being said, it is primarily from the late 1960s to the end of the 1980s that the Supreme Court's case law began to really bend in favour of the federal government, largely under Justice Laskin's intellectual influence; as a disciple of legal realism, he valued efficiency (and centralization) over other concerns like diversity.[23]

However, around the mid-1990s and thanks to a revival of the principle of federalism as a normative standard, the Supreme Court returned to a more balanced conception of federalism.[24] Some recent illustrations of this approach can be found in cases as diverse as *Pelland*[25] (dealing with a federal-provincial chicken marketing scheme), *Canadian Western Bank*[26] (addressing the interplay of federal and provincial rules in the banking sector), *NIL/TU,O*[27] (examining the regulation of labour relations in an agency delivering services to Aboriginal families), *Reference re: Assisted Human Reproduction*[28] (scrutinizing a federal statute regulating assisted reproduction), *PHS Community Services Society*[29] (dealing with the regulation of a safe injection facility), or *Reference re: Securities Act*[30] (assessing a federal attempt to regulate the securities market), to name but a few.

What looks like a judicial revival of federalism does not mean that the Supreme Court systematically adopts "decentralizing" solutions[31]—in any event, the intellectual value of abstract analyses about "centralization" or "decentralization" is dubious at best[32]—nor does it mean that its judges all share the same "balanced" conception of federalism. What it means is that possibly more than ever the court seems inclined to impose in its division of powers case law a requirement of proportionality upon all federal actors. While emphasizing the increasing complementarity of both

continued

regulatory levels under the guise of co-operative federalism, however vague this principle remains, and thus privileging the "double aspect" doctrine of interpretation of the division of powers over its "watertight compartments" rival, the court has kept affirming the importance of maintaining an equilibrium between the two levels of government, in addition to stressing the need to allow both of them a tangible regulatory space.[33]

Attention to the co-operative dimension of federalism is also paid in recent cases not directly dealing with the division of powers but with issues of significant constitutional importance for provinces, and particularly Quebec, such as the appointment of Supreme Court justices and Senate reform. In *Reference re: Supreme Court Act*, ss. 5 and 6,[34] the court practically constitutionalized the mode of appointment of its Quebec justices and emphasized the need to obtain the provinces' assent to change the mode of appointment of senators in *Reference re: Senate Reform*.[35] Interestingly, in these cases the court did not resort to the federal principle to justify its findings, since this principle applies symmetrically to all provinces. It looked instead for other justifications, such as the need for its Quebec justices to have an understanding of the civil law and of "Quebec values," and to the Senate's role as providing a "sober second look" at the issues considered in Parliament. This seemingly strategic avoidance of the federalism principle allows the Supreme Court the possibility of effectively carving out a special status for Quebec, not unlike that which was claimed by the province during the Meech Lake saga.

In spite of the resilience of the Tower of Pisa metaphor in nationalist discourse, it appears harder and harder to sustain. So, this begs the question: Whither the Tower of Pisa?

Conclusion

The picture that I have painted in this chapter was inspired by the overwhelming role that nationalist narratives have played, and still play, in framing the dominant discourse on federalism in Quebec. Granted, the real picture is more complex. There are some who amplify the pathological prism highlighted in this chapter to reject Canadian federalism outright. There are others, arguably a minority, who reject any expression of Quebec nationalism, be it as a result of an intrinsic distaste for all sorts of nationalisms or of an adhesion to a competing pan-Canadian nationalist narrative. There are still others, arguably the majority, who try to reconcile Quebec nationalism with Canadian federalism, in spite of the latter's rather loaded history and of its sometimes dysfunctional modes of operation. Many of these critics feel that they are in a situation of "internal exile" within Canada as a result of the events that took place since 1982.[36] However, nationalism informs in one way or another most of these positions. This begs the question as to how it will evolve, particularly in light of recent debates over identity, which have revealed deep fractures within the nationalist movement, particularly as to what being a Quebecer means. They have also shed light on the return of a more conservative and ethnocentric type of nationalism—"identity nationalism"—that competes with the more civic brand of nationalism that had dominated since the launching of the Quiet Revolution. The debate that was prompted by the former PQ government's Charter of Quebec Values provided a telling illustration of the divisions within nationalist ranks, but it remains to be seen if and how such divisions will also affect the nationalist framework through which Canadian federalism is evaluated.

A further trend to watch is the relative lack of interest of younger generations for identity politics. One might surmise that the growth of individualism and cosmopolitism, as well as an increasing skepticism toward nationalist metanarratives, could soften the grasp of the often monolithic representation of Quebec interests that stems from the "community perspective" historically adopted in the province. Mobilization of citizens around nationalist causes could also be made more complicated. This, however, could very well happen without a greater emotional or political investment in Canada on the part of Quebecers. Indeed, even if a large number of them have a positive opinion of Canada, their primary community of identification is Quebec, which explains why nationalist sentiments, even when they seem to be shifting, will always inform in one way or another their evaluation of the performance of the Canadian federation. In a way, many Quebecers envisage the Canadian federation as a contingent political community—that is, one that is neither impossible nor necessary as far as Quebec's fate is concerned. At the same time, federalism is seen as an existential precondition of Quebec's adhesion to Canada. Yet, given the intrinsic complexity of this political regime and the likely resilience of the pathological prism that accompanies Quebec nationalism, it will always remain a hard sell.

Questions for Critical Thinking

1. If you live in a federation (or a quasi-federation), what is your own perception of the relationship between federated entities and the central government representing the federal polity? From which standpoint do you tend to assess that relationship? Are there competing standpoints? If you don't live in a federation, try to imagine how one can negotiate between two distinct political identities, sometimes converging, sometimes diverging, within the same country.
2. Could Quebec's methodological nationalism be construed as a reaction to another expression of nationalism, that of the English-speaking majority outside Quebec, which tends to instrumentalize the federal government for its own purposes?
3. To what extent is a formal constitutional recognition of Quebec needed to protect the province's distinct identity within the Canadian federation?

Notes

1. On majoritarian federalism, see Alain-G. Gagnon, André Lecours, and Geneviève Nootens, eds., *Les nationalismes majoritaires contemporains : identité, mémoire, pouvoir* (Montreal: Québec Amérique, 2007).
2. Richard Simeon, "Criteria for Choice in Federal Systems," *Queen's Law Journal* 8 (1983): 131.
3. Ibid., 133.
4. Jocelyn Létourneau, "Le lieu (dit) de la nation : essai d'argumentation à partir d'exemples puisés au cas québécois," *Revue canadienne de science politique* 30 (1997): 55, 68; author's translation.
5. Since the Quiet Revolution, governments formed by the Quebec Liberal Party have played a significant role in "normalizing" that type of nationalist discourse. In this respect, it is interesting to compare the various reports submitted by the constitutional committees of the Quebec Liberal Party since the late 1970s and the political positioning of Liberal governments over the years, the latter generally being much more nationalist than the former.
6. *Reference re Secession of Quebec*, [1998] 2 S.C.R. 217.
7. On such templates, see Jean-François Gaudreault-DesBiens, "Underlying Principles and the Migration of Reasoning Templates: A Trans-Systemic Reading of the *Quebec Secession Reference*," in *The Migration of Constitutional Ideas*, ed. Sujit Choudhry (Cambridge: Cambridge University Press, 2006), 178.
8. Fernand Dumont, *Genèse de la société québécoise* (Montreal: Boréal, 1993), 237–8.
9. See A. Silver, *The French-Canadian Idea of Confederation, 1864–1900* (Toronto: University of Toronto Press, 1982).
10. Andreas Wimmer and Nina Glick Schiller, "Methodological Nationalism and Beyond: Nation-State Building, Migration and the Social Sciences," *Global Networks* 4, no. 2 (2002): 301, 303–8.
11. The most articulate of these conservative thinkers is arguably Mathieu Bock-Côté; see *Fin de cycle : aux origines du malaise politique québécois* (Montreal: Boréal, 2012).
12. On the tensions between monist ideologies and federalism, see Jean Leclair, "Le fédéralisme comme refus des monismes nationalistes," in *La dynamique confiance-méfiance dans les démocraties multinationales : le Canada sous l'angle comparatif*, ed. Dimitrios Karmis and François Rocher (Québec: Presses de l'Université Laval, 2012), 209.
13. Lawrence Friedman, *The Legal System: A Social Science Perspective* (New York: Russell Sage Foundation, 1975).
14. Jean-François Gaudreault-DesBiens and Noura Karazivan, "The 'Public' and the 'Private' in the Common

Law and Civil Law Traditions and the Regulation of Religion," in *Religion in Public Spaces: A European Perspective*, ed. Silvio Ferrari and Sabrina Pastorelli (Farnham, England: Ashgate, 2012), 93.

15. I elaborate on this in Jean-François Gaudreault-DesBiens, "The Fetishism of Formal Law and the Fate of Constitutional Patriotism in Communities of Comfort: A Canadian Perspective," in *Ties That Bind: Accommodating Diversity in Canada and the European Union*, ed. Jon Erik Fossum, Paul Magnette, and Johanne Poirier (Brussels, Bern, and Berlin: P.I.E. Peter Lang, 2009), 301.
16. This was done even in cases where provisions of the Charter of the French Language were struck down by the Supreme Court. Indeed, the court recognized that Quebec could legitimately restrict constitutionally entrenched fundamental freedoms in view of protecting its linguistic visage, provided it did so in a proportionate way.
17. Unpleasant facts are those that contradict one's ideological preconceptions: Max Weber, *Le savant et le politique : une nouvelle traduction*, trans. Catherine Colliot-Thélène (Paris: La Découverte, 2003), 96.
18. Roderick A. Macdonald, "The Design of Constitutions to Accommodate Linguistic, Cultural and Ethnic Diversity: The Canadian Experiment," in *Dual Images: Multiculturalism on the Two Sides of the Atlantic*, ed. Kalman Kulcsar and Denis Szabo (Budapest: Royal Society of Canada and Institute for Political Science of the Hungarian Academy of Sciences, 1996), 52, 53.
19. This dynamic was arguably amplified after the events that surrounded the enactment of the Constitution Act, 1982. It is eloquently captured in the declaration by Claude Ryan, then leader of the Official Opposition (the Quebec Liberal Party), before the National Assembly in 1981: "We must conclude with much firmness that each time the National Assembly is impacted in its essential prerogatives, it is the people of Quebec itself which is affected. Remaining indifferent to encroachments on the National Assembly's powers is being indifferent to, or taking lightly, the aspirations and the fundamental reality of the people of Quebec" (author's translation of "Nous devons conclure avec beaucoup de fermeté que chaque fois que l'Assemblée nationale est atteinte dans ses prérogatives essentielles, c'est le peuple du Québec lui-même qui est atteint. Être indifférent à une atteinte faite aux pouvoirs de l'Assemblée nationale, c'est être indifférent ou traiter à la légère les aspirations et la réalité fondamentale du peuple québécois lui-même"). See Assemblée nationale du Québec, *Journal des débats* XXV (1), 30 September 1981, 23. While the opposition of the National Assembly to a constitutional project is indeed a sign of the existence of a serious political problem that should not be taken lightly, the assumptions underlying Ryan's declaration, which very few political actors in Quebec would dare challenge, must be questioned to some extent. First, it relies on an idealized picture of representative democracy that equates the will of the people with the will of its elected representatives. While this image continues to inform political theory, the least that can be said is that it deserves to be nuanced in light of the actual practice of representative democracy. Second, it seems to assume that decisions of elected representatives are the only ones that may claim some form of political legitimacy. Again, this is going too fast: There are many alternative forums where democratic deliberation may be exercised by citizens, a phenomenon whose importance has grown since the early 1980s, notably as a result of the emergence of the type of constitutionalism that the Constitution Act, 1982 brought about. See Pierre Rosanvallon, *La contre-démocratie* (Paris: Éditions du Seuil, 2006). Finally, while Ryan may have been justified to say what he said in 1981, one who would be tempted to say the same thing today had better take into consideration, as far as the legitimacy of the Constitution Act, 1982 is concerned from Quebec's perspective, the phenomenon of the legitimization of constitutions through practice—that is, through the daily use of constitutional provisions by citizens. In this respect, there is no difference in the use of the Constitution Act, 1982 between Quebecers and other Canadians. See Joseph Raz, "On the Authority and Interpretation of Constitutions: Some Preliminaries," in *Constitutionalism: Philosophical Foundations*, ed. Larry Alexander (Cambridge: Cambridge University Press, 1998), 152, 173–4; in the Canadian context, see Jean-François Gaudreault-DesBiens, "Memories," *Supreme Court Law Review*, 2nd Series 19 (2003): 219.
20. Sigmund Freud, "Civilization and Its Discontents," in *Civilization, Society and Religion: Group Psychology, Civilization and its Discontents and Other Works* (London and New York: Penguin Books, 1985), 251.
21. Kenneth C. Wheare, *Federal Government*, 4th ed. (Oxford: Oxford University Press, 1963), 19–20.
22. *Hodge v. The Queen*, [1883] 9 A.C. 117 (J.C.P.C.).
23. See Jean Leclair, "The Supreme Court's Understanding of Federalism: Efficiency at the Expense of Diversity," *Queen's Law Journal* 28 (2003): 411.
24. See Jean-François Gaudreault-DesBiens, "The 'Federal Principle' and the Legacy of the *Patriation* and *Quebec Veto* References," *Supreme Court Law Review* 54 (2011): 78.
25. *Fédération des producteurs de volailles du Québec v. Pelland*, [2005] 1 S.C.R. 292, 2005 SCC 20.
26. *Canadian Western Bank v. Alberta*, [2007] 2 S.C.R. 3, 2007 SCC 22.
27. *NIL/TU,O Child and Family Services Society v. B.C. Government and Service Employees' Union*, [2010] 2 S.C.R. 696, 2010 SCC 45.
28. *Reference re Assisted Human Reproduction Act*, [2010] 3 S.C.R. 457, 2010 SCC 61.

29. *Canada (Attorney General) v. PHS Community Services Society*, [2011] 3 S.C.R. 134, 2011 SCC 44.
30. *Reference re Securities Act*, [2011] 3 S.C.R 837, 2011 SCC 66.
31. See, for example, *Quebec (Attorney General) v. Lacombe*, [2010] 2 S.C.R. 453, 2010 SCC 38.
32. See Robert Howse, "Federalism, Democracy, and Regulatory Reform: A Skeptical View of the Case for Decentralization," in *Rethinking Federalism: Citizens, Markets, and Governments in a Changing World*, ed. K. Knop et al. (Vancouver: UBC Press, 1995), 273. However, see also Gérard Bélanger, "The Theoretical Defence of Decentralization," in *The Case for Decentralized Federalism*, ed. R. Hubbard and G. Paquet (Ottawa: University of Ottawa Press, 2010), 68.
33. The recent case of *Quebec (Attorney General) v. Canada (Attorney General)*, 2015 SCC 14, in which the Supreme Court rejected the Quebec government's bid to prevent the destruction of the Quebec-related data contained in the dismantled long-gun registry, shows that the principle of co-operative federalism does not constrain the otherwise valid exercise of a particular legislative competence.
34. *Reference re Supreme Court Act, ss. 5 and 6*, [2014] 1 S.C.R. 433, 2014 SCC 21.
35. *Reference re Senate Reform*, [2014] 1 S.C.R. 704 , 2014 SCC 32.
36. The expression "internal exile" was coined by political scientist Guy Laforest, "L'exil intérieur des Québécois dans le Canada de la Charte," *Constitutional Forum* 16, no. 1–3 (2007): 63.

Select Bibliography

Gagnon, Alain-G. *La raison du plus fort : plaidoyer pour le fédéralisme multinational.* Montreal: Québec Amérique, 2008.

Gat, Azar (with Alexander Yakobson). *Nations: The Long History and Deep Roots of Political Ethnicity and Nationalism.* Cambridge: Cambridge University Press, 2013.

Handler, Richard. *Nationalism and the Politics of Culture in Quebec.* Madison: University of Wisconsin Press, 1988.

Karmis, Dimitrios, and Wayne Norman, eds. *Theories of Federalism: A Reader.* New York: Palgrave Macmillan, 2005.

Laforest, Guy. *Trudeau and the End of a Canadian Dream.* Montreal and Kingston: McGill-Queen's University Press, 1995.

Lajoie, Andrée. *Jugements de valeurs.* Paris: Presses universitaires de France, 1997.

Létourneau, Jocelyn. *Que veulent vraiment les Québécois?* Montreal: Boréal, 2006.

Morissette, Yves-Marie. *Le Renvoi sur la sécession du Québec : bilan provisoire et perspectives.* Montreal: Éditions Varia, 2001.

Reuchamps, Min. *L'avenir du fédéralisme en Belgique et au Canada : quand les citoyens en parlent.* Brussels: Peter Lang, 2011.

Saywell, John. *The Lawmakers: Judicial Power and the Shaping of Canadian Federalism.* Toronto: Osgoode Society for Canadian Legal History/University of Toronto Press, 2004.

Schapiro, Robert A. *Polyphonic Federalism: Toward the Protection of Fundamental Rights.* Chicago: University of Chicago Press, 2009.

Scott, Kyle. *Federalism: A Normative Theory and its Practical Relevance.* New York: Continuum, 2011.

Tushnet, Mark, Thomas Fleiner, and Cheryl Saunders, eds. *Routledge Handbook of Constitutional Law.* London: Routledge, 2013.

Yack, Bernard. *Nationalism and the Moral Psychology of Community.* Chicago: University of Chicago Press, 2012.

19 National Identity and Support for Sovereignty in Quebec

Éric Bélanger and Chris Chhim, McGill University

Timeline

1864 Quebec conference on proposal for federation of British North America adopts Quebec resolutions, outlining the main provisions of the federal constitution for Canada.

1867 British North America (BNA) Act comes into effect.

1948 Quebec adopts its own official flag; first province to do so.

1960 Jean Lesage becomes premier, beginning the "Quiet Revolution." Rassemblement pour l'indépendence nationale (RIN) is established.

1967 René Lévesque publishes *Option Québec*, leaves the Liberal Party, and forms Mouvement Souveraineté-Association (MSA), then the Parti Québécois (PQ) a year later.

1970 Robert Bourassa becomes premier. PQ wins second-largest share of popular vote.

October Crisis: Front de libération du Québec (FLQ) kidnaps and kills Pierre Laporte. War Measures Act is proclaimed.

1976 Lévesque becomes premier and forms the first PQ government.

1977 Charter of the French Language is adopted.

1980 Referendum on sovereignty-association is held; 40 per cent vote in favour.

1981 Federal government and all provinces except Quebec agree to a new constitutional amending formula and the Charter of Rights and Freedoms, which protects English-language education in Quebec.

1990 Meech Lake Accord, recognizing Quebec as "distinct society," unravels as Manitoba and Newfoundland refuse to ratify it. Lucien Bouchard resigns from the federal government and forms the Bloc Québécois.

1995 Referendum on sovereignty is held; 49.4 per cent vote in favour.

1998 Supreme Court rules that Quebec has no automatic right to secede, but that the federal government would have to negotiate if a "clear majority" of Quebec voters supported sovereignty.

2000 *Clarity Act* imposes rigid conditions on Quebec's ability to secede.

2006 Canada's Parliament recognizes that "the Québécois form a nation within a united Canada."

Introduction

For several decades, two sociopolitical realities have characterized and shaped Quebec's political life. The first is its status as a majority French-speaking region in a largely English-speaking North American continent. The second is its being part of the Canadian federation. In their own way, both realities have helped define contemporary Quebec and offer important insights to better understand the political dynamics of this province.

The consequences of Quebec's place within a federal framework, as well as its linguistic minority status, can be felt on various levels. For citizens of Quebec, these consequences can be reflected in their political attitudes. Are Quebecers' feelings of cultural identity and belonging just limited to the province's borders? Or are Quebec's citizens also attached to the Canadian federation? The same question could just as well be asked of Quebecers concerning what they think about the political status of the province. At what point do the inhabitants of this majority francophone society decide that they are better off governing themselves and becoming politically independent? And how do Quebec's relations with the rest of Canada affect Quebecers' opinions with regard to their province's political future?

Quebecers' political attitudes[1] have varied over time, seeming to principally hinge on relations between the francophone majority in Quebec and the anglophone majority in the rest of Canada. Looking back at history, we see that changes in this dynamic have contributed to the ebb and flow of not only Quebecers' feelings of identity, but also their attachment to Canada and even their support for independence. In short, political relations between these two communities have sometimes led to tensions that can have lasting effects on Quebecers' feelings of nationalism and identity.

These are the questions that will be explored in this chapter. To do this, we use public opinion data[2] that track the evolution in Quebecers' feelings of identity as well as their degree of attachment to both Quebec and Canada. Other polling data will be used to show Quebecers' opinions toward the national question, which has been at the heart of many political debates in the province for the past half-century. This portrait of Quebecers' political attitudes[3] will allow us to draw some conclusions about the current state of the political debate in Quebec regarding the independence movement, as well as recent political developments on the provincial level.

Identity and Attachment

It is important to note that identifying oneself as a Quebecer is a relatively recent development. The terms used to describe present-day Quebecers' feelings of identity have greatly changed over the past few decades and reflect changing sociopolitical conditions throughout the province's history. From the start of European settlement until the Quiet Revolution in the 1960s, a vast majority of those living in what we currently call Quebec were of French ancestry and first identified themselves as "Canadiens," then "French Canadians," to distinguish themselves from the other large cultural group of the time, the "English Canadians" (who were mostly of English descent). With the creation of the Canadian federation in 1867, some chose to identify simply as "Canadian" without any reference to their ethnic origin.

The public opinion data that exist on ethnic identity in Quebec only date back to the beginning of the 1970s. Nonetheless, the available data,[4] which cover a period of 30 years (1970 to 2001), illustrate a revealing trend. In 1970, 34 per cent of francophones stated that they identified as Canadian, whereas 44 per cent identified instead as French Canadian. In 2001, these proportions were no more than 13 per cent and 30 per cent, respectively. That being said, the dynamics behind these declining identities are not the same. In its own way, each trend reflects important political events that happened during the time as well as the rise of a "Quebec identity," properly speaking. Within the data, we also see that Canadian identity had fallen to 16 per cent by the middle of the 1970s, coinciding with the rise of the Parti Québécois to power and a large increase in the proportion of francophones who reported identifying as "Québécois" (from 21 per cent in 1970 to 36 per cent in 1977). The percentage of people who identify as French Canadian remained stable over the same period. Only starting at the end of the 1980s, during the linguistic and constitutional crises that gripped Quebec, does the number of francophones identifying as French Canadian decline to 28 per cent, while those identifying as Québécois jumps to 59 per cent. These proportions remain relatively stable into the early part of the twenty-first century.

How can we explain this gradual transition to an identity that is primarily Québécois? The rise of a distinct Quebec identity corresponds with the birth of the modern-day independence movement during the Quiet Revolution. The active state apparatus that guided the political and economic developments of the time also turned into a new locus for nationalist mobilization. The Quebec state became a *national* state that was an instrument of emancipation. As such, it was seen as necessary for the province to have as much control as possible over its affairs to best defend its inhabitants' interests.[5] This evolution in sociopolitical thought during the 1960s, which would come to claim the "freeing" of Quebec francophones from their dominance by English Canadians, was also fuelled by the nationalists' embrace of decolonization ideologies.[6] The ultimate goal of this nationalist movement was the accession of Quebec to the status of a sovereign nation, where a majority francophone collectivity is consolidated within a given territory. In addition, over time, belonging to this francophone collectivity would be more linked to using the French language in public life as opposed to being of French-Canadian heritage. This shift from narrow ethnicity-based membership partly reflects the influence of immigration on Quebec's sociodemographic dynamics. Thus, identifying more and more as Québécois can be seen as the expression of a political nationalism founded on the idea of present-day Quebec being the home of a French-speaking majority. This is not to say that the identity debate is now entirely devoid of any hint of ethnicity. But despite the recent controversies surrounding reasonable accommodations and secular values, it remains that much effort has been put into making language the main marker of Québécois identity over the last half-century.

Although francophones are a majority within Quebec, they nonetheless also live under a federal system where political powers are split between the provincial government and the central government in Ottawa. This multilevel governance can have the effect of creating two identities, one Québécois and the other Canadian, which may not necessarily be mutually exclusive and in fact simultaneously coexist within individuals. Some researchers have already observed this phenomenon of **nested identities** in nonsovereign nations, including Quebec.[7] Recent data shown in Figure 19.1 illustrate this trend for the period 1996–2014.

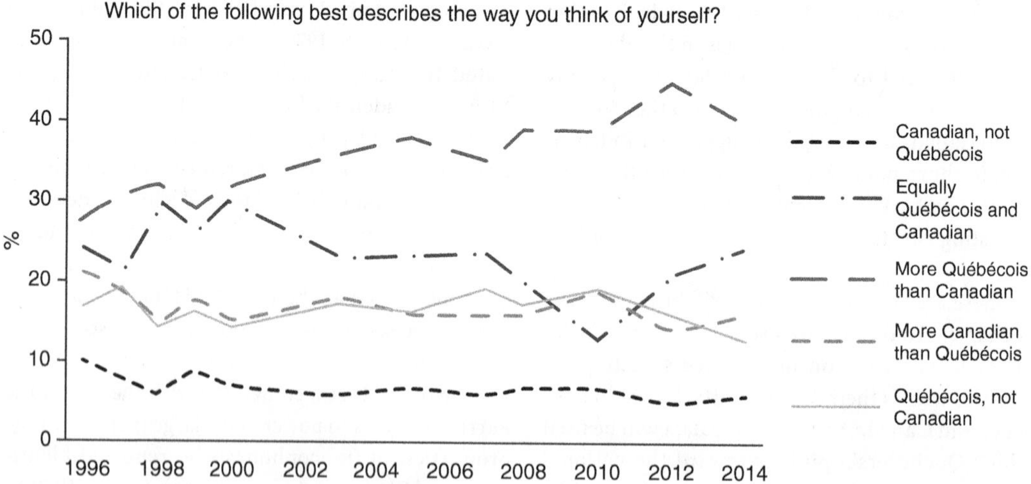

Figure 19.1 Quebecers' "Nested Identities," 1996–2014.

As these data demonstrate, the most often mentioned category is "Québécois first, but also Canadian," followed by "equally Québécois and Canadian." We also see that the least mentioned categories are the two most exclusive categories ("Québécois only" and "Canadian only"). Quebecers' multiple identities seem to be relatively stable across time. One exception is a rise in the proportion of individuals who consider themselves Québécois first but also Canadian, mostly at the expense of those who see themselves as equally Québécois and Canadian—although the gap between these two identities has started to narrow in the last couple of years. It seems, therefore, that the phenomenon of multiple identities continues in Quebec. Approximately three-quarters of the citizens polled chose one of the three categories where the two identities coexist to some degree.

Another noteworthy indicator of Quebecers' feelings of identity is their degree of attachment to both Quebec and Canada. Even if most Quebecers continue to identify at least partially as Canadian, their degree of attachment to Canada can be considered as a more emotional indicator of identity. Figure 19.2 presents public opinion data about this topic for the period 1980–2014. The same phenomenon of nested identities can be observed here. Attachment to Quebec is very high (on average, about 90 per cent of respondents report being attached to Quebec). With regard to Canada, there is clearly less attachment, but it remains relatively high (on average 70 per cent). Yet over the long term we notice some noteworthy fluctuations. While attachment to Quebec was stable during the 1980s, attachment to Canada declined because of the bitter constitutional debates that took place during this period (for example, patriation of the Constitution without Quebec's participation, along with the failure of the Meech Lake Accord being seen as a rejection of Quebec by the rest of the country). In the years following the 1995 referendum we see a narrowing of the gap between these two attachments, to the point where both curves almost touch in 2001. The gap then widens once again and returns to levels similar to the early 1990s. However, while moving in parallel, both attachment levels fell during the first decade of the twenty-first century, although attachment to Canada shows what may be the beginning of a new increase starting in 2014.

These findings about Quebecers' feelings of identity reveal that the last quarter of the twentieth century bore witness to some important changes. The province's inhabitants gradually abandoned

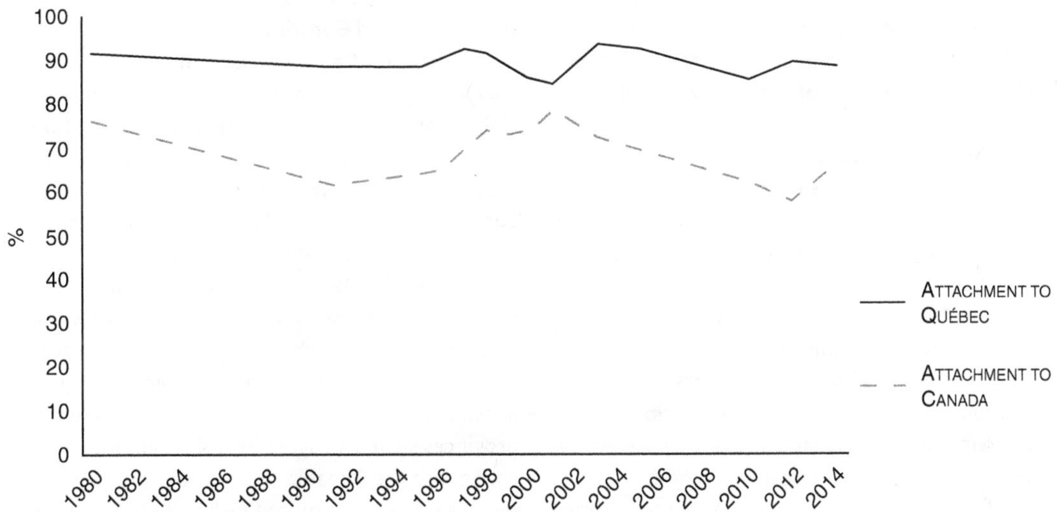

Figure 19.2 Quebecers' Feelings of Attachment, 1980–2014.

their French-Canadian identity for a Québécois one. Although largely dominant, this new label does not exclude a Canadian identity or being attached to Canada itself. Thus, Quebecers' feelings of identity express a strong Quebec nationalism, but one that is also attached to Canada. From an identity point of view, while the language and constitutional debates could have pushed Quebecers away, the fact of remaining within the Canadian federation helped Quebecers foster a degree of attachment to Canada, in spite of everything. As historian Jocelyn Létourneau argues, remaining in the federation has allowed Quebecers to advance as a collectivity and now (for the most part) participate in the Canadian federation; the resulting sense of identity appears as "ambivalent" in nature precisely because it aims at reconciling autonomy (its Québécois-ness) and integration (its Canadian-ness).[8] That being said, the data also suggest a certain decline in the relevance of the identity question over the last decade.

CASE STUDY

The 1995 Referendum on Quebec Sovereignty

Some might see the evening of 30 October 1995 as the end of a tumultuous chapter in Quebec–Canada relations. After an eventful referendum campaign, 50.6 per cent of Quebecers voted "No" to the accession of Quebec to the status of a sovereign country. The 1995 referendum was the second vote on sovereignty in the province's history and was the culmination of tensions that were building for years between the provincial and federal governments.

For those sympathetic to the sovereignist cause, repatriating the 1982 Constitution without Quebec's consent highlighted the province's vulnerability in the Canadian federation. Although the Supreme Court of Canada ruled that the Constitution Act, 1982 would apply to Quebec without the consent of the Quebec National Assembly, feelings of rejection and betrayal would continue to spoil Quebec–Canada relations. When Robert Bourassa became premier of Quebec in 1985, he made five demands to then–Prime Minister Brian Mulroney for Quebec to sign on to the Constitution: explicit recognition of Quebec's distinct society, increased powers over immigration, provincial input in nominations to the Supreme Court of Canada and the Senate, limitations on federal spending power, and a veto over any future constitutional changes. Eager to bring Quebec into the Constitution "with honour and enthusiasm," Mulroney convened a meeting of all provincial premiers in the spring of 1987 where all of Quebec's demands were accepted. The result of this meeting was the Meech Lake Accord. The 10 provincial governments had three years to ratify the accord in their respective legislatures, but the process failed on 22 June 1990 because of opposition in Newfoundland and Labrador and Manitoba.

Rejection of the Meech Lake Accord soured Quebec–Canada relations and drove the Quebec National Assembly to set up the Commission on the Political and Constitutional Future of Quebec (the Bélanger–Campeau Commission), which was charged with investigating the constitutional options available to Quebec. Released on 27 March 1991, the commission's report recommended that the Quebec and federal governments consider ways to renew the Canadian federation. Otherwise, a referendum would be held no later than 26 October 1992 on either a new arrangement with the federal government or the independence of Quebec. Mulroney's response to the Bélanger–Campeau report was to call another meeting of provincial premiers in Charlottetown. There the provinces signed an agreement that, among other changes to the Canadian federation, would notably give a special status to Quebec (but only in the fields of language, culture, and civil law). Unlike the Meech Lake Accord, this new constitutional reform project would be subject to a nationwide referendum. Ultimately, mostly because of factors unrelated to Quebec (such as Mulroney's low popularity as well as an economic recession), the Charlottetown Accord was defeated on 26 October 1992, with 54.3 per cent of Canadian voters refusing to accept the proposed reforms.

The failure of the Charlottetown Accord pushed Quebec further down the path toward a second referendum on sovereignty (the province had already voted in a first independence referendum on 15 November 1980). Two years after Charlottetown, the Parti Québécois came into power with a majority government, under the leadership of Jacques Parizeau, creating an opportune moment for the sovereignty project. Although support for sovereignty when the PQ came to power was around 40 per cent (and lower than it had been during the Meech Lake and Charlottetown periods), the PQ government introduced the *Loi sur l'avenir du Québec* (Bill 1) on 6 December 1994. The bill established the Quebec National Assembly's authority to officially declare Quebec's sovereignty following a popular vote.

The polls, however, continued to reveal Quebecers' hesitation toward independence. Even the head of the Bloc Québécois, Lucien Bouchard, said that he was not comfortable with the sovereignist project as proposed by the Parizeau government. Instead, he said that a "turn" was necessary if the referendum was to be a success for the sovereignists. For Bouchard, Quebec sovereignty should be accompanied by an offer for an economic and political partnership with the rest of Canada. This forced Parizeau to change his strategy via a tripartite agreement, signed on 12 June 1995 (see the Primary Source box). This agreement brought together Jacques Parizeau from the Parti Québécois, Lucien Bouchard from the Bloc Québécois, and Mario Dumont from Action démocratique du Québec to form a coalition around a common project that would "unite as many Quebecers as possible on a clear, modern and open proposal." Thus, Bouchard's "turn" slightly modified the referendum project by reframing it as one more focused on renewing Quebec's partnership with the rest of Canada rather than Quebec separation.

After the tripartite agreement was signed, some polls showed that support for the "Yes" camp started to rise. The unveiling of the referendum question and the decision to hold the referendum on 30 October 1995 only added to the commotion surrounding the campaign. The question that would be posed to the voters was the following: "Do you agree that Quebec should become sovereign after having made a formal offer to Canada for a new economic and political partnership within the scope of the bill respecting the future of Quebec and of the agreement signed on June 12, 1995?"

Jean Chrétien, prime minister of Canada at the time, immediately attacked the constitutionality of the sovereignty project. According to those in the federalist camp, there is no provision in the Canadian Constitution allowing for the unilateral secession of Quebec. Chrétien made it clear that a "Yes" victory would not be seen as a proclamation of independence, but rather as a consultative plebiscite. While the sovereignists were emphasizing Quebec independence as a way for the Quebec people to emancipate themselves, the federalists were bringing up more practical considerations, such as splitting up investments and the national debt. For federalists, it was not necessarily a given that an independent Quebec would automatically be part of existing international treaties such as NAFTA or that it could continue to use the Canadian dollar. In addition, businesspeople feared that a "Yes" victory would destabilize international financial markets.

These arguments appeared to slightly weaken the "Yes" side, which seemed to be plateauing out in the public opinion polls. However, in the middle of the campaign it was announced that Lucien Bouchard, and not Jacques Parizeau, would act as head negotiator of the partnership agreement with the rest of Canada mentioned in the referendum question. The immense popularity of Bouchard

continued

revitalized the "Yes" camp to the extent that three days before the referendum, the "No" forces decided to hold a rally at the Place du Canada in Montreal. Brian Tobin, Canadian minister of fisheries and oceans at the time, played a large role in the organization of the so-called "Unity Rally," at which notable politicians such as Prime Minister Jean Chrétien, leader of the Progressive Conservative Party of Canada Jean Charest, and leader of the Quebec Liberal Party Daniel Johnson, all made appearances. While the actual number of attendees is unknown, estimates vary between 30,000 and 150,000 people. The Unity Rally indeed influenced the referendum result by unexpectedly harming the "No" camp. While a majority of the rally participants were from Montreal and surrounding areas, many Quebecers instead perceived this gathering as a mass invasion of people from the rest of Canada suddenly descending upon and occupying downtown Montreal.

The results were tight right up until the final moments. With a participation rate of 93.5 per cent of the voting population, 50.6 per cent of Quebecers voted "No" to the possibility of a new economic and political partnership with the rest of Canada. The referendum evening was not only catastrophic for the sovereignist cause, but also for the political career of Jacques Parizeau. The day after his controversial speech, in which he attributed the sovereignist defeat to "money and some ethnic votes," Parizeau resigned from his positions as a member of the National Assembly (MNA) for l'Assomption, leader of the Parti Québécois, as well as premier of Quebec. Parizeau's departure paved the way for Lucien Bouchard to step in and take over the reins as leader of the PQ and provincial premier.

The negative yet close result of the 1995 referendum has had long-term consequences for Quebec–Canada relations. Notably, the federal government put together a political strategy to avoid a third referendum. The first part of this strategy (often called "Plan A") sought to raise the visibility of the federal government in the province, for example by sponsoring various sporting and cultural events. However, this sponsorship program led to abuses that were brought to light during the Gomery Commission hearings in 2004–5. The other part (often called "Plan B") aimed to impose judicial measures to diminish the Quebec government's capacity to declare its independence. The government asked the Supreme Court of Canada to give its opinion on whether a unilateral declaration of independence was legal on the basis of three questions that touched upon both Canadian and international law. On 20 August 1998, the Supreme Court of Canada made its decision in *Reference re Secession of Quebec*; regarding independence, it attributed legality to Ottawa and legitimacy to Quebec. The judgment served as the inspiration to establish the **Clarity Act**, which became law on 29 June 2000. The law states that any future question that deals with the secession of a province must be formulated in a "clear" manner and should also obtain the support of a "clear" majority of the electorate.

Primary Source

Excerpt from the Tripartite Agreement of 12 June 1995

The Referendum Mandate

Following a "Yes" victory in the referendum, the National Assembly, on the one hand, will be empowered to proclaim the sovereignty of Quebec, and the government, on the other hand, will be bound to propose to Canada a treaty on a new economic and political partnership, so as to, among other things, consolidate the existing economic space. The referendum question will contain these two elements.

Accession to Sovereignty

Insofar as the negotiations unfold in a positive fashion, the National Assembly will declare the sovereignty of Quebec after an agreement is reached on the partnership treaty. One of the first acts of a sovereign Quebec will be ratification of the partnership treaty.

The negotiations will not exceed one year, unless the National Assembly decides otherwise. If the negotiations prove to be fruitless, the National Assembly will be empowered to declare the sovereignty of Quebec without further delay.

The Treaty

The new rules and the reality of international trade will allow a sovereign Quebec, even without a formal partnership with Canada, continued access to external markets, including the Canadian economic space. Moreover, a sovereign Quebec could, on its own initiative, keep the Canadian dollar as its currency.

However, given the volume of trade between Quebec and Canada and the extent of their economic integration, it will be to the evident advantage of both states to sign a formal treaty of economic and political partnership.

The treaty will be binding on the parties and will specify appropriate measures for maintaining and improving the existing economic space. It will establish rules for the division of federal assets and management of the common debt. It will create the joint political institutions required to administer the new economic and political partnership, and lay down their governing rules. It will provide for the establishment of a Council, a Secretariat, an Assembly and a Tribunal for the resolution of disputes.

As a priority, the treaty will ensure that the partnership has the authority to act in the following areas:

- Customs union;
- Free movement of goods;
- Free movement of individuals;
- Free movement of services;
- Free movement of capital;
- Monetary policy;
- Labour mobility;
- Citizenship.

In accordance with the dynamics of the joint institutions and in step with their aspirations, the two member-states will be free to make agreements in any other area of common interest, such as:

- Trade within the partnership, so as to adapt and strengthen the provisions of the Agreement on Internal Trade;
- International trade (for example, to establish a common position on the exemption with respect to culture contained in the WTO Agreement and NAFTA);
- International representation (for example, the Council could decide, where useful or necessary, that the partnership will speak with one voice within international organizations);
- Transportation (to facilitate, for example, access to the airports of the two countries or to harmonize highway, rail or inland navigation policies);
- Defence policy (for example, joint participation in peacekeeping operations or a coordinated participation in NATO and NORAD);
- Financial institutions (for example, to define regulations for chartered banks, security rules and sound financial practices);
- Fiscal and budgetary policies (to maintain a dialogue to foster the compatibility of respective actions);
- Environmental protection (in order to set objectives in such areas as cross-border pollution and the transportation and storage of hazardous materials);
- The fight against arms and drug trafficking;
- Postal services;
- Any other matters considered of common interest to the parties.

Support for Sovereignty

Nationalist sentiment has clearly surfaced at specific points in Quebec's history. In the early nineteenth century, the nationalist movement drew strength from the events leading up to the Lower Canada Rebellions of 1837–8. These armed uprisings stemmed from the British refusal to give certain democratic rights demanded by the parliamentarians of the Parti patriote in Lower Canada (which roughly corresponds to the part of the St Lawrence Basin within Quebec's borders). These rights mostly concerned ensuring responsible government where executive power would truly rest in the hands of elected representatives. While democratic grievances were the main source of conflict, some members of the Parti patriote dreamed of making Lower Canada a true independent republic. This dream quickly disappeared following the failure of the rebellion, but returned during the Quiet Revolution and led to two referendums on Quebec sovereignty held toward the end of the twentieth century.

The re-emergence of the independence movement in the wake of large-scale political and administrative reforms in the 1960s had its roots in the socioeconomic inequalities of the time. French Canadians generally lived in worse economic conditions than those of the province's anglophone minority, earning lower salaries and not having access to managerial positions in large companies, which were mostly controlled by the English-Canadian economic elite. Partially because of these reasons, there was (at the very least on a symbolic level) an inferior status given to both French Canadians and their language. While the latter situation dated back to at least 1850,[9] the depreciation toward the French language in Quebec became politically salient during the nationalist revival that accompanied the 1960s. Indeed, these ethnic grievances fanned the flames of popular support for the idea of political independence and the creation of René Lévesque's Parti Québécois.

The other two historic moments for the Quebec independence movement were the 1980 and 1995 referendums on the accession of Quebec to the status of a sovereign state. While the independentists lost the first referendum with only 40.4 per cent support for their project, the second one had a significantly closer result, with 49.4 per cent of Quebecers supporting the idea of a **sovereignty-partnership** with the rest of Canada. According to political scientist Guy Laforest, these two referendums can be seen as modern-day "democratic rebellions" similar in spirit to the armed rebellions of the previous century.[10] This imagery highlights the fact that both referendums are still about the same struggle for greater political freedom for Quebec, but are fought in another time by different partisans and, of course, via very different means.

Yet we note that the Quebec population does not seem to be entirely convinced of the benefits of independence. There is still some hesitation, notably regarding the economic viability of independence in the medium to long term. In addition, the old ethnic grievances that fanned the flames of sovereignty support during the 1970s and 1980s have largely been assuaged by political and economic advances made since the Quiet Revolution. Even concerns over the future of the French language, although still very present, have for the most part been eased thanks to the effects over the past 50 years by the federal government to advance the role and place of French in Canadian society, and most especially the adoption of stringent provincial language laws.[11]

What is the current state of support for sovereignty in Quebec? While public opinion data are quite varied, we focus on the two questions that polling firms most often ask Quebecers to give a systematic portrait of how support has changed over time.[12] The first question we look at is one that makes a direct reference to Quebec sovereignty.[13] The exact wording of this question varies according to the survey firm, but typically is as follows: "If a referendum on the sovereignty of Quebec were held today, would you vote for or against Quebec sovereignty?" Figure 19.3 presents the annual averages from 1988–2014 for the answers given to this question.

Figure 19.3 demonstrates how support for sovereignty can be influenced by political developments. While support for sovereignty in 1988 averaged around 32 per cent, it doubled over the next two years, peaking at 66 per cent in 1990, the year when tensions surrounding the Meech Lake Accord were at their highest. In short, about two out of every three

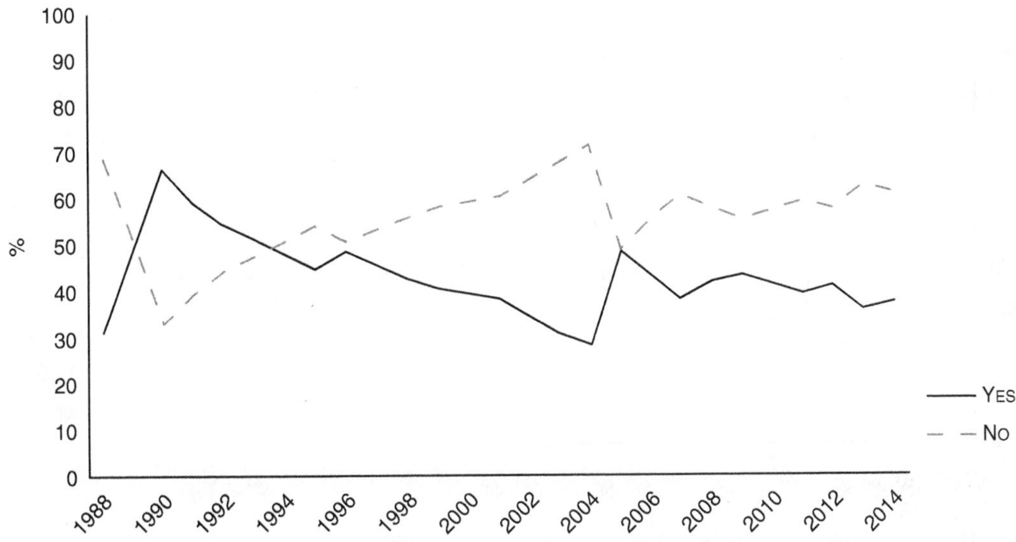

Figure 19.3 Support for the "Sovereignty" Project, 1988–2014.

Quebecers in 1990 were favourable to sovereignty. This support gradually diminished over the following five years, to 45 per cent on average in 1995. After a slight rebound following the second referendum (49 per cent support in 1996), the sovereignty option continued its slow decline until 2005, when the **sponsorship scandal** erupted (and returned to 49 per cent on average). The effect of the sponsorship scandal on support for Quebec sovereignty was, however, short-lived, as support thereafter fell to around 40 per cent. Thus, two external shocks can explain, at least in part, the surges in support: the failure of Meech Lake and the sponsorship scandal. Otherwise, one can observe a slow decline, with a little over one-third of Quebecers being favourable to the sovereignty project at the end of the period being covered.

The second question often asked of Quebecers references the idea of making Quebec into a "country." This is an important distinction, especially since the Parti Québécois officially abandoned the notion of "sovereignty-partnership" with the rest of Canada in 2005. The CROP survey firm has asked this question in a systematic manner since 2007, and the typical wording is as follows: "If a referendum were held today asking if you want Quebec to become a sovereign country, would you vote yes or no?" Very similar questions referencing the notion of a country have also been asked going as far back as 1970. As shown in Figure 19.4, support for Quebec being a country was only at 13 per cent at the beginning of this period. It reached 35 per cent in 1979, the eve of the first referendum, but fell to 17 per cent in 1985 during the post-referendum demobilization phase. Support for making Quebec into a country rose sharply to 61 per cent in 1990 before falling to the 40 per cent range. The data indicate that support for the project of making Quebec into a country has essentially remained stable during the 1990s and 2000s (note that the sponsorship scandal did not seem to have as big an effect on support for Quebec as a country as it did for that of "Quebec sovereignty") but has started to slightly dip in the early 2010s.

A comparison of the two figures shows that the two support curves change in relatively similar ways over time, but that support for the idea of Quebec as a "country" is slightly lower than that for "sovereignty." Even larger differences in support levels appear when more "hard" terms are used to describe the

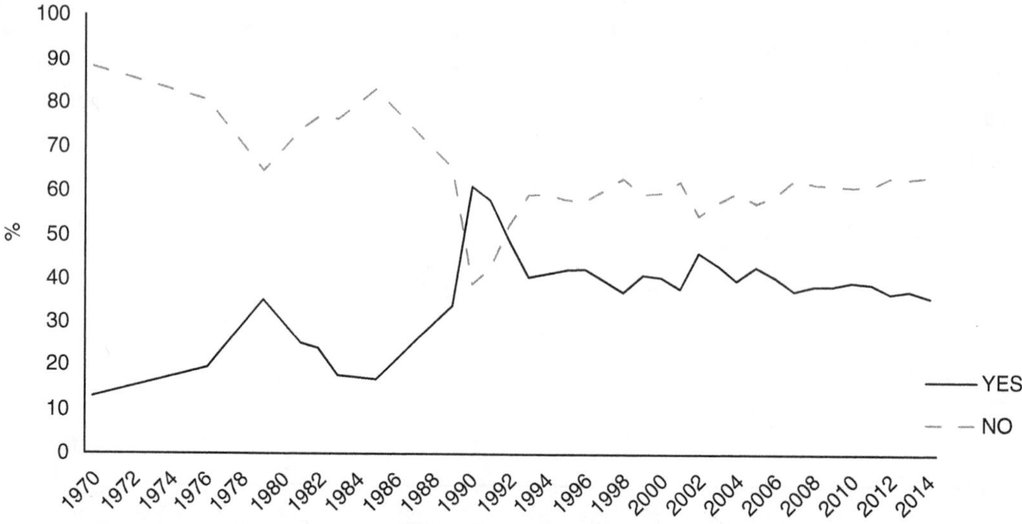

Figure 19.4 Support for Making Quebec a "Country," 1970–2014.

sovereignist project. Table 19.1 shows to what extent Quebecers can be sensitive to the wording of questions about the political future of their province. The possibility of some sort of association with the rest of Canada, or just the offer of a free trade agreement with the rest of Canada, generates the highest level of support within the population. Support strikingly diminishes, however, once the term "sovereignty" is replaced with "independence."[14] When the question refers to a "completely independent" country without any mention of maintaining any sort of link with the rest of Canada, support is at its lowest (there is a 15 percentage point difference between this question and the first question).[15]

Table 19.1 Opinions on Quebec's Political Future According to Question Wording

Question	% Who Would Vote "Yes"
If a referendum were held today on the same question that was asked in 1995, that is, **sovereignty with an offer of partnership** with the rest of Canada, would you vote "Yes" or would you vote "No"?	49
If a referendum were held today asking you if you wish Quebec to accede to the status of a **sovereign country, without the offer of a partnership**, but with a free trade agreement to be subsequently proposed to the rest of Canada, would you vote "Yes" or would you vote "No"?	47
If a referendum were held today asking you if you wish Quebec to accede to the status of an **independent country, without the offer of a partnership**, but with a free trade agreement to be subsequently proposed to the rest of Canada, would you vote "Yes" or would you vote "No"?	40
If a referendum were held on the following question, "Do you want Quebec to become a **completely independent country**," would you vote or be tempted to vote "Yes" or "No"?	34

Source: Portraits of Canada Survey, 2005.

These figures suggest that Quebecers have a clear preference for maintaining some kind of link with the rest of Canada and therefore are more resistant to the idea of complete political and economic separation for their province. These observations complement data presented earlier showing Quebecers' overall identification with and attachment to Canada. That being said, it is possible that a certain confusion within the sovereignist movement also explains such differing reactions to the wording of both survey and referendum questions. For example, according to data from Matthew Mendelsohn, 26 per cent of Quebecers believed that the "sovereignty-partnership" offered during the 1995 referendum meant that Quebec would remain a province of Canada, but with more powers.[16] These observations show how choices over rhetoric made by political actors on both sides of the sovereignty debate can influence public opinion in nontrivial ways.

BIOGRAPHY

Biography: Lucien Bouchard

Born on 22 December 1938 in Saint-Cœur-de-Marie in the Saguenay-Lac-Saint-Jean region, Lucien Bouchard was raised in a Catholic family of modest means. Considering that education was highly valued in his family, it is no surprise that his three brothers acquired their doctorate degrees in various academic specialties. From his beginnings as a lawyer to his final days as Quebec premier, Bouchard had a significant impact on the political development and constitutional future of Quebec.

After obtaining a law degree from Université Laval, Bouchard practised as a lawyer in Chicoutimi until 1985. During these years he was also charged with various responsibilities in the public service. He is notably known for his role as chief prosecutor for the Commission d'enquête sur l'exercice de la liberté syndicale dans l'industrie de la construction (Cliche Commission) from 1974–5. The commission investigated allegations of corruption in the construction industry in Quebec and uncovered criminal elements present in four unions of the Conseil provincial du Québec des métiers de la construction.

In addition, in 1975 Bouchard was a member of the Commission d'étude et de consultation sur la révision du régime des négociations collectives dans les secteurs public et parapublic (the Martin–Bouchard Commission), which sought to renew public sector employees' system of collective bargaining. During the first referendum on Quebec sovereignty in 1980, Bouchard supported the "Yes" camp. Two years later, he was a lawyer representing the government of Quebec in front of the Supreme Court of Canada arguing against the repatriation of the Canadian Constitution.

In 1984 Bouchard participated in the election campaign for a Progressive Conservative government. The new prime minister, Brian Mulroney, a former classmate from Université Laval, named him to various official positions, notably as Canadian ambassador to France (1985–8), Quebec lieutenant, and minister of the environment. He was elected as the member of Parliament (MP) for Lac-Saint-Jean for the first time in June 1988 during a by-election and re-elected during the 1988 general election.

Although a nationalist, he approved the Meech Lake Accord negotiated by Mulroney because he believed that its main clauses were enough to satisfy Quebec's grievances. However, on 22 May 1990 he resigned from his cabinet post for the Progressive Conservative Party and later became an independent MP in reaction to the refusal of Newfoundland and Labrador and Manitoba's provincial legislatures to ratify the Meech Lake Accord. In July 1990, Bouchard

continued

was named member of the Commission on the Political and Constitutional Future of Quebec (the Bélanger–Campeau Commission), established by the Quebec government and charged with the task of enumerating Quebec's available options following the failure of Meech Lake. Later that same month, Bouchard was part of eight independent MPs who regrouped themselves into the newly formed Bloc Québécois (BQ). In June 1991, he officially became leader of the new party.

During the federal election on 25 October 1993, Lucien Bouchard was re-elected, this time as a BQ MP for Lac-Saint-Jean. With 54 MPs, the BQ had become the Official Opposition in the House of Commons and Lucien Bouchard was named Leader of the Official Opposition. Approximately one year later tragedy struck when he had to be hospitalized for phlebitis. Doctors later discovered that Bouchard suffered from a flesh-eating bacteria, and his condition deteriorated to the point where his left leg had to be amputated. With the news of Bouchard's illness and amputation made public, Canadian politicians of all stripes offered their support to Bouchard in an exceptional moment of nonpartisan unity.

After returning to politics in the spring of 1995, Bouchard signed the tripartite agreement with Jacques Parizeau's PQ and Mario Dumont's ADQ before actively joining the referendum campaign for the coming fall. After the victory of the "No" vote and Parizeau's resignation, Bouchard was the only candidate to succeed him. He became leader of the PQ on 27 January 1996 and premier of Quebec two days later. He was formally elected as an MNA one month later during a by-election in the riding of Jonquière.

With his arrival as provincial premier, Bouchard put the sovereignty issue on the back burner. At the end of 1996 he declared that "winning conditions" would be necessary for holding a third referendum. Instead of actively fighting for Quebec sovereignty, he focused on cutting back public spending as a way to breathe new life into the province's economy. Most notably, Bouchard introduced a "zero deficit" plan for a balanced budget by the end of the century. The resulting cuts greatly affected public services, especially in the area of health care. Yet despite its objective of trimming down public spending, Bouchard's first mandate also saw the introduction of new social programs, the most notable including the creation of Emploi-Québec (1998), the Pay Equity Act (1997), the establishment of educational childcare facilities (1997), and the Public Prescription Drug Insurance Plan (1997). In November 1998, Bouchard's PQ government was re-elected for a second mandate. Although Bouchard had tried to avoid the national question, he nonetheless had to deal with certain constitutional problems. Following the signing of the Calgary Declaration (which made reference to Quebec's "unique character") without Quebec's consent and the adoption of the Clarity Act, the Bouchard government passed An Act Respecting the Exercise of the Fundamental Rights and Prerogatives of the Québec People and the Québec State (Bill 99) in December 2000, which reiterated Quebec's fundamental right to decide its own future.

On 11 January 2001 Lucien Bouchard announced that he was leaving politics, giving two official reasons: the fact that he was unable to bring about the winning conditions necessary for Quebec sovereignty and the fact that he wanted to spend more time with his family. Even after his resignation Bouchard continued to be influential in Quebec political life. Most notably, on 19 October 2005 he signed the *Pour un Québec lucide* manifesto with 11 other prominent Quebecers. The manifesto criticized the province's "refusal to change" and the fact that the social discourse in Quebec is dominated by various pressure groups, such as labour unions. Supporters of the manifesto (dubbed "lucides") were concerned with two large problems confronting Quebecers over the coming decades: the size of the public debt and demographic decline. As a solution, they advocated more openness toward the private sector and a major reform of the taxation system. Lucien Bouchard has been and remains a prominent public figure dedicated not only to the political future of Quebec but also the preservation of Quebec identity in Canada.

Conclusion: A "Post-Sovereignty" Era?

From this foray into Quebecers' attitudes toward their identity, attachment, and independence we can draw a number of conclusions. First, we see that since the beginning of the 1990s there is some stability with regard to how Quebecers identify themselves, their attachment to Quebec and Canada, and their support for sovereignty. Although the trends have been relatively stable over the past 25 years, leading those in the sovereignty movement to hope that it will be able to one day capitalize on these base levels of support, the fact remains that there has been little real change in public opinion. We even observe a slight decline in sovereignty support following the poor performance of the Bloc Québécois during the 2011 federal election and the Parti Québécois's short but controversial minority government from 2012–4. Therefore, we can say that public opinion on the national question shows more stagnation than anything else, particularly since the beginning of the 2000s (but with the brief exception of the sponsorship scandal in 2004–5).

Does this overall stagnation reveal something about the current political juncture, or is it the reflection of a trend? Although prudence is always advised when discussing these kinds of questions, it seems that we are witnessing a trend. As we have seen, many Quebecers still report being sovereignist when asked by various polling firms. But such an affirmation seems more and more to be attributable to a sort of automatism, or even worse, devoid of meaning. (Political scientist Jean-Herman Guay even goes so far as to argue that in Quebec sovereignists are now like Catholics: they still claim to be but many have stopped practising.[17]) It might also be the case that some citizens, while resolutely sovereignist, would rather invest their energy in other priorities, at least for the time being. Other voters seem to completely reject the old labels of "federalist" and "sovereignist." Voting behaviour patterns in the 2014 provincial election even suggest that the youngest generation may have abandoned both the PQ and the national question debate altogether, something which, if confirmed in the next few elections, would constitute a radical shift from the last half-century in Quebec's political history.[18]

Overall, it seems that Quebecers are currently demobilized over the national question, similar to how they were during the 1980s right before the linguistic and constitutional crises erupted. Today, it seems that many of the ethnic grievances that fed nationalist sentiment 50 years ago have gone away with the sociopolitical evolution of the province. What is more is that since the 2000s Quebec–Canada relations have been calm, absent of any serious political conflicts.

On the basis of similar observations, journalist Alain Dubuc calls the current period "post-sovereignist."[19] Former PQ minister François Legault, head of the Coalition Avenir Québec created in 2011, essentially makes the same observation as Dubuc by proposing a temporary moratorium on the national question. According to these observers of Quebec political life, the Quebec population is currently ready to move on to things other than attaining more political independence for the province (at least for now). While it may be too early to tell if they are correct in their appraisal of the political situation in Quebec and the opinion of Quebecers, it would be hazardous to conclude that the national question is no longer important.

Even if we can see the failure of the "No" side in the 1995 referendum as the end of a chapter in the Canadian constitutional odyssey, what still remains unresolved is the larger question of Quebec's place in the federation. While some federalists outside of Quebec may consider the case of the province's political future closed, other important grievances remain and stem from a collection of historical and political events, of which the repatriation of the Canadian Constitution in 1982 without Quebec's consent is just the most striking example. As shown through public opinion data, many Quebecers have a double identity that allows them to identify as both Canadian and Québécois. Yet it seems regrettable that instead of directly addressing the source of discontent for many of these Quebecers who still identify to a certain degree with Canada, measures such as the *Reference re Secession of Quebec* and the Clarity Act only further box in the province and exacerbate Quebec–Ottawa tensions. The fact that popular support for sovereignty has not been high over the past few years does not mean that there is no more potential for serious tensions between Quebec and Ottawa to re-emerge. In fact, this is not entirely out of the question, especially if the rest of Canada is perceived as moving away from Quebec. By disinteresting itself from the concerns of this province, the rest of the country could very well be seen as alienating Quebec. The debate over the national question in Quebec is also likely to be influenced by the efforts of other independence movements around the world in the first half of the 2010s, most notably those in Scotland and Catalonia. In the long run, these various factors could open the door once again to the return of the sovereignty movement and the rise of nationalist sentiment in Quebec.

Questions for Critical Thinking

1. In your opinion, is it legal and/or legitimate for Quebecers to unilaterally decide to separate from Canada?
2. Given the defeats of the 1980 and 1995 referendums, do you think that a third referendum could happen in Quebec?
3. What influence could the attitudes of young Quebecers toward the national question have on the future of the sovereignty movement?

Notes

1. Political attitudes are individuals' expression of favour or disfavour toward some political object. See Roger Tourangeau and Mirta Galesic, "Conceptions of Attitudes and Opinions," in *The SAGE Handbook of Public Opinion Research*, ed. Wolfgang Donsbach and Michael W. Traugott (Thousand Oaks, CA: SAGE Publications, 2008), 141–54.
2. Public opinion data refer to the measurement of attitudes via a survey from a sample of the population. See Murray Goot, "Mass-Observation and Modern Public Opinion Research," in *The SAGE Handbook of Public Opinion Research*, ed. Donsbach and Traugott, 93–103.
3. Note that all public opinion data presented in this chapter include responses from non-Francophone Quebecers.
4. Maurice Pinard, Robert Bernier, and Vincent Lemieux, *Un combat inachevé* (Sainte-Foy: Presses de l'Université du Québec, 1997), 90; Matthew Mendelsohn, "Measuring National Identity and Patterns of Attachment: Quebec and Nationalist Mobilization," *Nationalism and Ethnic Politics* 8, no. 3 (2002): 78.
5. Louis Balthazar, *Nouveau bilan du nationalisme au Québec* (Montreal: VLB éditeur, 2013).
6. Sean Mills, *The Empire Within: Postcolonial Thought and Political Activism in Sixties Montreal* (Montreal and Kingston: McGill-Queen's University Press, 2010).
7. Mendelsohn, "Measuring National Identity and Patterns of Attachment."
8. Jocelyn Létourneau, *A History for the Future: Rewriting Memory and Identity in Quebec* (Montreal and Kingston: McGill-Queen's University Press, 2004).
9. See Chapter 10 in this volume.
10. Guy Laforest, "One never knows . . . Sait-on jamais?" in *Quebec and Canada in the New Century: New Dynamics, New Opportunities*, ed. Michael Murphy (Montreal and Kingston: McGill-Queen's University Press, 2007), 53–81.
11. On these various conclusions, see Matthew Mendelsohn, "Rational Choice and Socio-Psychological Explanation for Opinion on Quebec Sovereignty," *Canadian Journal of Political Science* 36, no. 3 (2003): 511–37.
12. The selection of these questions and surveys was done through the website of Claire Durand, professor of sociology at the Université de Montréal, accessed 1 August 2014, www.mapageweb.umontreal.ca/durandc/souverainete/recherche_souverainete.html. We updated the data to 2014 ourselves.
13. From this compilation, we exclude surveys also making reference to "sovereignty-association," "sovereignty-partnership," "separation," "independence," or "country." This exclusion mostly explains why the data presented in Figure 19.3 only start at 1988.
14. Note that the only difference between the second and third question in Table 19.1 is the replacement of the term "sovereign" with "independent." For these two questions, the survey sample was randomly divided in two: one-half was asked the second question while the other half was asked the third question.
15. See also the longitudinal study by François Yale and Claire Durand, "What Did Quebeckers Want? Impact of Question Wording, Constitutional Proposal and Context on Support for Sovereignty, 1976–2008," *American Review of Canadian Studies* 41, no. 3 (2011): 242–58.

16. Mendelsohn, "Rational Choice and Socio-Psychological Explanation for Opinion on Quebec Sovereignty."
17. In Paul Journet, "La souveraineté, le projet d'une génération?" *La Presse*, 7 April 2012, 2.
18. Katia Gagnon, "Génération 'Non,'" *La Presse*, 2 June 2014, A2.
19. Alain Dubuc, *À mes amis souverainistes* (Montréal: Les Éditions Voix Parallèles, 2008).

Select Bibliography

Bouchard, Lucien. *On the Record.* Toronto: Stoddart, 1994. Published in French under the title *À visage découvert.*

Cardinal, Mario. *Breaking Point.* Montreal: CBC/Bayard Canada Books, 2005. Published in French under the title *Point de rupture.*

Dubuc, Alain. *À mes amis souverainistes.* Montréal: Les Éditions Voix Parallèles, 2008.

Gagné, Gilles, and Simon Langlois. *Les raisons fortes : nature et signification de l'appui à la souveraineté du Québec.* Montréal: Presses de l'Université de Montréal, 2002.

Gagnon, Alain-G., ed. *D'un référendum à l'autre : le Québec face à son destin.* Québec: Presses de l'Université Laval, 2008.

Hébert, Chantal, and Jean Lapierre. *The Morning After.* Toronto: Knopf, 2014. Published in French under the title *Confessions post-référendaires.*

Pinard, Maurice, Robert Bernier, and Vincent Lemieux. *Un combat inachevé.* Sainte-Foy: Presses de l'Université du Québec, 1997.

Part E
Quebec Models

Introduction

The fifth part of *Quebec Questions* speaks directly to Quebec's distinctive style and form. Titled "Quebec Models," this section presents contributions on how Quebec has developed unique approaches and policies to a variety of significant social and economic matters. The central analytical questions that permeate each of these essays are: Why has Quebec chosen to carefully craft a unique, context-specific approach? What factors and personalities have shaped the agenda? Has this pursuit of an identifiably Quebec-style model benefited Quebecers? What have been the most significant impacts, if any, of these Quebec models?

Diane Lamoureux's examination of feminism in Quebec makes it clear that the Quebec feminist movement is, from the outset and for a variety of reasons, "exceptional within North America." Most strikingly, this movement is still extremely active. It has not, unlike in the United States, been reconceptualized and institutionalized in the framework of higher education, nor has it undergone pervasive fragmentation. It has changed over time, Lamoureux writes, most notably in the expanding agenda of Quebec feminism, increased majority representation of francophone women, and the increasing success of feminist-sponsored legislation and corresponding policies. This contribution sketches "the robust constitution of feminism" *à la Québécoise*, underscoring the much needed and pivotal roles that women have played in advancing Quebec society.

Peter Graefe, in his examination of social and economic development in Quebec, provides compelling evidence that politics—as fashioned and championed by the push and pull of political parties and leaders, the business community, labour, and various interest groups—is pivotal to any understanding of Quebec's development model. The principal model of development for Quebec, we learn, emerged in the Quiet Revolution of the 1960s and to this day maintains significant resonance. Yet as Graefe importantly underscores, since the government of Robert Bourassa Quebec's model of social and economic development—in which the state's institutional machinery is purposely constructed, centrally positioned, and administratively geared first and foremost toward providing an expansive range of significant social and economic benefits that are anticipated/expected by individuals—has undergone a movement toward neoliberalism, and its social consensus is thereby challenged. The core issue in determining how Quebec today organizes economic and social policy, Graefe suggests, focuses on the relationship between "individuals and society," and more specifically "the role of the state." The Quebec model, "distinct in North America in its adoption of stakeholder partnerships and community development," is increasingly subject to neoliberal forces—forces that are set to continue in the absence of "well-organized and well-articulated counterpropositions."

Hydroelectricity—its development and use—is yet another seminal issue that further distinguishes Quebec. Author David Massell walks us through the history of hydroelectric power in Quebec throughout the twentieth century, stressing first the role of private enterprise, then examining the establishment of the colossus public corporation Hydro-Québec, and finally the eventual nationalization of the industry. Driven by "practical and ideological" considerations, Quebec's hydroelectric footprint has not, Massell informs us, been without controversy. As that footprint has sought to grow ever larger since the 1970s, with varying degrees of success, voices of concern—notably those of Quebec's First Nations communities—have repeatedly arisen. More often than naught, negotiated agreements have been and continue to be struck between Quebec and a variety of First Nations Cree and Innu groups, effectively facilitating the further economic development of hydro power in exchange for financial compensation, business partnerships, employment opportunities, creation or expansion of public services in the north, and enhancement of First Nations' "title and rights to their ancestral lands." The story of hydroelectricity in Quebec has been and will continue to be, this chapter tells us, one of fundamental "human struggle to contest and control the province's hydro sector."[1]

Health care has been driven and shaped, author Antonia Maioni reminds us, by political, social, economic, and medical factors that have combined to produce a distinctive Quebec approach to health-care policy and services. The historical development of health care in Quebec is positioned against a backdrop of federal and provincial personalities, policies, and institutions. This overview effectively demonstrates that the planning and delivery of health care in Quebec is decidedly different from that in the rest of Canada and in the United States. The negotiation of physicians' fees, the implementation of medical insurance, and the general relationship between the state and the medical community all illustrate this point. Maioni does point out, however, that private health care has recently made important, albeit selective and incomplete, inroads in Quebec—the lasting impact of which, given Quebec's particular approach to health care, largely remains to be determined. The necessary curative "prescription for the Quebec health-care system," Maioni observes, faces a formidable range of contemporary public health challenges.

The final contribution in this section, provided by Daniel Jutras, focuses on the foundations, evolution, and application of Quebec's legal tradition. This tradition, we learn, has been and remains decidedly different, effectively constituting a distinct model for Quebec's legal identity. Jutras underscores, in a rich analysis tracing the multicentury development of Quebec's legal system, two pivotal points: First, "Quebec's roots are found in the French civil law tradition," and second, Quebec's current legal order is of a clearly mixed character, having been informed and profoundly shaped by the English common law tradition. The interplay of civil and common law traditions in Quebec, Jutras writes, can be most closely explained by the historical, political, and social forces that shaped Quebec and Canada, most significantly during the seventeenth and eighteenth centuries. Quebec's attachment to the French legal tradition of civil law was not "displaced" or marginalized with the onset of English rule in 1760. Indeed, the Quebec Act of 1774—unquestionably one of the most significant political instruments in the history of the province—while introducing English common law simultaneously sought to explicitly recognize and restore the centrality of civil law in Quebec. This hybrid or mixed legal model in Quebec, in which civil law would be "reaffirmed at each stage of the construction of Canada in constitutional documents of 1791, 1840, and 1867," continues today to provide Quebec with a distinct legal order. The hybridity of Quebec's legal system, arguably the most visible element of which rests in the 1991 Civil Code of Quebec, will continue to guarantee that the province will follow a distinctive legal model in Canada, North America, and the broader international community.

Note

1. For the most comprehensive scholarly examination of the seminal 1975 James Bay Northern Quebec Agreement, please consult Hans M. Carlson, *Home is the Hunter: The James Bay Cree and Their Land* (Vancouver: UBC Press, 2008), 202–59.

20 The Paradoxes of Quebec Feminism

Diane Lamoureux, Université Laval

Timeline

1966 Fédération des femmes du Québec (FFQ) formed.

1969 Montreal Women's Liberation Movement is founded.

Front de libération des femmes is founded.

1970 First pro-choice demonstration in Quebec takes place on Mother's Day.

1972 Centre des femmes is established.

Teach-in on feminism held at Université du Québec à Montréal, bringing together academics and activists.

1974 *Nous aurons les enfants que nous voulons* manifesto is published.

1975 Centre de santé des femmes is established.

First battered women's shelter opens; managed by feminists.

1975 Bookstore Librairie des femmes d'ici opens.

1976 Publishing house Les Éditions du remue-ménage is created.

Play *La nef des sorcières* is performed at Théâtre du Nouveau Monde.

First issue of the radical feminist newsletter *Les Têtes de pioche* is released.

Debates are held and speakers featured at the first anniversary of Librairie des femmes d'ici.

1977 First issue of *Pluri-elles*, a liaison newsletter for women's groups, is released and later becomes *Des luttes et des rires de femmes* (also a feminist collective).

Play *Les fées ont soif* is performed, leading to general protest and mobilization of Catholic groups.

Coop-femmes, Quebec's first francophone lesbian group, is founded.

1978 Coordination nationale pour l'avortement libre et gratuit is founded and mobilizes a large pro-choice movement.

Conseil du statut de la femme releases its *Pour les Québécoises : Égalité et Indépendance* report on improving the status of women in Quebec.

1980 *La Vie en rose*, a high-circulation feminist magazine, launches its first issue (final issue released 1987).

1982 *Amazones d'hier, lesbiennes d'aujourd'hui*, a radical lesbian magazine, launches its first issue (final issue released 1992).

First annual Journées de visibilité lesbienne is held.

1984 Quebec feminist magazine *Marie-Géographie* publishes its first issue (final issue released 1987).

Projet Gilford, a multidisciplinary feminist and lesbian activity centre, is established.

1985 Network of women's centres L'R des centres de femmes du Québec is founded.

1988 Book fair La Foire internationale du livre féministe is held in Montreal.

1989 Record-breaking number of pro-choice demonstrations held in support of Chantal Daigle.

Fourteen women gunned down in anti-feminist Montreal Massacre at École Polytechnique.

Association canadienne-française pour l'avancement des sciences creates a Feminist Studies section.

1990 Conference Les 50 heures du féminisme is held to celebrate the fiftieth anniversary of women's suffrage legislation in Quebec.

1992 Pour un Québec féminin pluriel conference is held.

1995 Bread and Roses March takes place.

1998 Némésis, a feminist alter-globalization group, is formed.

2000 FFQ organizes the year 2000 World March of Women.

Radical feminist magazine *Les sorcières* launches its first issue.

2003 Penser enfin une démocratie avec les femmes conference is held, linking women's equal political representation with electoral reform.

FFQ's young feminists hold the Colloque des jeunes féministes.

2005 *La Vie en rose* publishes a special issue.

2008 Toujours RebELLES—Waves of Resistance Pan-Canadian Young Feminist Gathering is held.

2009 Conference to mark the twentieth anniversary of the Montreal Massacre.

2011–3 États généraux du féminisme.

2013 Divisions among feminists regarding the Charter proposed by the Parti Québécois that would have banned public servants from displaying religious symbols in the workplace.

Introduction

Feminism shows every sign of being alive and well to this day throughout Quebec. With its thousands of groups, a solid capacity to mobilize its forces and attract a new generation of feminists, and an impressive ability to influence public debate, the Quebec feminist movement is often the envy of women from other countries and sometimes the bane of masculinists in its own backyard[1] (who see in it a [post]modern resurgence of matriarchy). It has even succeeded in motivating Quebec's political elites to declare, in a rare show of unanimity, that equality between women and men is now an integral part of "Quebec's values."[2]

This notion that equality has already been achieved in Quebec has generated an anti-feminist sentiment and movement. It is also deployed in a racist manner by some politicians who take advantage of it to distinguish the Québécois (who have reached equality) from "others," mainly immigrants of Arabic or Muslim background, which thereby perpetuates the myth of white men saving brown women from brown men.

Quebec's situation is exceptional within North America in that elsewhere on the continent feminist ideas and practices had their heyday in the 1970s, only to see the resultant poles of reflection move into university subjects such as Women's Studies and Gender Studies thereafter. Today in much of North America there is little connection between the ideas expressed in academic discussions and the practices developed in women's groups. Perhaps in this respect the comparatively small-scale institutionalization of feminist studies in Quebec universities represents an advantage for the feminist cause, in that it remains well connected to movements on the ground. The other element that distinguishes the feminist movement in Quebec is its sustained ability to rally a united front, whereas in the rest of Canada and the United States feminist movements have been forced to contend with attacks from neoconservative and religious fundamentalist currents and consequently have suffered widespread fragmentation over the past 15 years or so.

The robust constitution of feminism in Quebec has been the fruit of long, hard work and dedication. For more than 40 years the demands made by women's groups for gender equality and women's liberation not only have changed the course of women's and men's lives in Quebec, but also have succeeded

Primary Source

Excerpt from États généraux du féminisme

The feminist idea of society is ambitious as it is not limited to equality, and hopes to eliminate all forms of domination, inequality, and privilege between men and women, as well as between women and between peoples.

To Build a Feminist Society

A significant shift has emerged through the *États généraux* as feminists embrace and are inspired by the guidelines and actions outlined by other social groups working toward community mobilization.

The proposals from this assembly are ambitious because they suggest a drastic break from current systems perpetuating inequalities. Feminists are calling all social groups to question their current understanding of democracy, gender relations, and capitalism's part in reinforcing major societal problems. The *États généraux* further encourages all social groups to review their strategies in order to focus their efforts more efficiently on tackling the systems in place upholding inequality. In doing so, they will be able to see the interactions between the different systems of oppression in a global perspective. In this context, the *États généraux* call upon all social movements to create and reinforce lasting alliances with the feminist movement.

. . .

We have established our vision for the future. We have reached the end of a long process. And yet, this is where the real work begins. We have weaved networks and webs of solidarity through meetings, speaking tours, and discussions. These deliberations give us the necessary strength to now take action.

Our movement's next chapter has begun. Our ideas can transform a world marked by divisions, injustices, and inequalities. We firmly believe that feminism offers a vision of hope for in legislating change to eradicate legal discrimination against women (by reforming family law, the legal status of women, and labour legislation) and in instituting new wide-ranging public policies (such as daycare, parental leaves, pay equity, family planning services, and battered women's shelters). It is because of feminism that some Quebec women have broken through glass ceilings to establish themselves in a variety of professional fields, dramatically transforming both public and private life in the process.

Regrettably, for years the movement has mainly involved women from Quebec's "majority group," often called "les Québécoises de souche."[3] But, little by little, Quebec's "minority" women have come to play a larger part in the mainstream movement. Feminist Aboriginal women, who have developed a movement unto themselves with their own distinct dynamics, have also carved out a place for themselves within the movement, signing a solidarity declaration with Quebec's largest feminist umbrella organization, the Fédération des femmes du Québec (FFQ) and co-organizing the États généraux du féminisme conference. Anglophone women have been active in promoting feminism since its inception in Quebec but, as a group, no longer play the predominant role they once did in the early twentieth century. Immigrants and women from ethnocultural communities have become more and more involved with the Bread and Roses March and the World March of Women since the struggle against violence and poverty allowed women of all ethnic backgrounds to fight together.

In the past years, we have seen successful Quebec-wide meetings, like that organized by the FFQ's young feminist committee in 2003, or the Quebec-initiated Toujours RebELLES—Waves of Resistance Pan-Canadian Young Feminist Gathering, held in 2008.

this world in search of liberty, equality, peace, justice, and solidarity.

Our feminist idea of society rests on the firm conviction that all women have their place in society. It is essential that we leave no one behind in this great march toward equality. Neither violence against women nor any patriarchal practices belong in this vision. The slogan for the World March of Women is "As long as all women are not free, we will march."

We call on this movement to denounce and further challenge the logic of capitalism and its incapacity to answer humanity's needs as it exploits our bodies and our lands. Our movement is an ecological one, as we belong to the earth and have an obligation to take care of it for the following generations. Our movement seeks to break free from ideas of exclusion and domination present at home as well as internationally. Our movement hopes to build an equal partnership with the Aboriginal peoples and nations in Quebec and around the world. As our destiny is intertwined with theirs, our actions should be as well. One individual did not shape the feminist movement; it has always been a plural struggle. It is one of our greatest strengths as we are called upon to learn from each other and to find a common ground while acknowledging our differences. It is now our turn to put this strength into action. Let us turn our hopes and ideas into new projects and strategies.

. . .

We are calling upon women, feminists, women's groups, collectives, status of women committees, as well as individuals and groups committed to bringing this feminist vision into action. Social transformation will be led by, with, and for women, and ultimately, for society overall. Today, we are thousands; tomorrow we will all be one. . . .

Sources: *Cahier du Forum* (États généraux du féminisme conference, Université du Québec à Montréal, 14–17 November 2013), 23, www.etatsgenerauxdufeminisme.ca/images/documents/Cahier%20du%20Forum%20-%20complet.pdf; "Une société féministe à construire," *Bilan de comité d'orientation : États généraux de l'action et l'analyse féministes, 2011–2013,* 8–10, www.etatsgenerauxdufeminisme.ca/images/documents/Bilanpol-FINALv4.pdf.

From 2011 to 2013, the discussions that led to the États généraux du féminisme conference, which took place in November 2013, strove to establish an agenda for the Quebec feminist movement over the next 20 years and mobilized women's groups of all stripes and all activist sectors throughout the province.

These kinds of events, along with steady enrolment in feminist studies programs, are clearly demonstrating that feminism was not just a cause taken up by one or two generations. Instead, it is quite naturally being championed by the next—if only because gender inequalities and patriarchy have continued to feed revolt and anger among younger and older women alike.[4]

In this look back at the recent history of Quebec feminism, I will highlight the fascinating paradoxes it presents: the importance of the reformist pole and the concurrent presence of a radical pole; the provision of services and the work to politicize and mobilize; the cultural homogeneity of the movement and its openness to pluralism; and the collective public movement and the individual lifestyle transformations it has introduced into women's private lives. Through each of these paradoxes, it will become apparent that Quebec feminism is not a uniform, monolithic movement but one that continues to be enriched by unsuspected resources and undercurrents.

The 1970s: Separate Paths

The 1970s have been lauded by some as the golden age of feminism in Quebec, as in many other parts of the Western world.[5] Three major elements set this decade apart: the drive of some governments to "modernize" by updating family law to suit new social realities; the new cohort of reformist feminists who were willing to work with their respective governments; and the emergence of a more radical feminist fringe that raised new issues and developed terms of engagement in the struggle.

This remarkable generalized trend in North America and Western Europe was accompanied in Quebec by the dynamics of the Quiet Revolution—a vast state-engineered modernization of Quebec society through a movement that had been building for two decades. The Quiet Revolution began with the election of the provincial Liberal Party under Jean Lesage in 1960 and continued until the Quebec referendum of 1980. Although women were not the first to be invited to the table during the Quiet Revolution, their influence was undeniable. Using the Quiet Revolution as a jumping off point, this chapter focuses on the reconfiguration of the reformist feminist current and the emergence of radical feminism in Quebec. But first, let us revisit one vital event in feminist history.

Quebec passed legislation granting eligible women citizens the right to vote in 1940 (the last province in Canada to do so). As in many other parts of the world, this landmark victory led to a relative post-suffrage lull among Quebec's feminist groups. But while activity waned in these groups, scores of women continued putting feminism into practice in labour organizations, pacifist movements, university communities, and professional groups. So in demonstrable ways the feminist movement did continue, building expertise in various areas, but was less visible for many years.

Fast-forward to the effervescent years of the Quiet Revolution. In 1965, women decided to rally together to celebrate the twenty-fifth anniversary of suffrage legislation. It was an occasion for feminists to stand together once again and boost the movement's visibility. It was also a chance to make the most out of having a newly elected female provincial cabinet minister and of the Quebec government's new openness to significantly change the legal status of married women[6] and guarantee equal scholastic opportunities for girls and boys.[7]

Former suffragettes like Thérèse Casgrain, labour organizers like Madeleine Parent, young academics like sociologist Monique Bégin, committed pacifists like Simone Monet-Chartrand and Laurette Sloane, and a host of other women (mostly from the Greater Montreal area) came together for the twenty-fifth anniversary celebrations. They would all take part in founding a new feminist lobby group, the Fédération des femmes du Québec (FFQ), that would take advantage of the winds of change at both the federal and provincial levels to promote women's rights.[8] The FFQ was similar to some of Quebec's past feminist organizations in that it set out to bring anglophones and francophones together and to provide a coordinating structure for the political representation of Quebec women to public authorities. For this reason, the FFQ was predominantly constituted by organizations, though individual women could also hold membership.

Being the last women in Canada to receive the vote in provincial elections, these women had learned valuable lessons from the suffrage movement. They had also seen how particularly reactionary the Quebec provincial government had been compared with the Canadian government, which had been engaged in the process of building the welfare state since the end of World War II. This process gained momentum and integrity at the end of the 1960s, when Prime Minister Trudeau's Liberal Party government presented its "just society" political platform. As the Liberal Party's progressive policies continued to win favour with feminists, it was not surprising, during the 1980 referendum campaign on sovereignty, to see the (officially nonpartisan) FFQ discreetly support the Liberal-backed "Yvettes" movement.[9] Moreover, the sitting FFQ president, Sheila Finestone, would later go on to become a Liberal member of Parliament.

The Quiet Revolution also brought major transformations to rural areas, leading women in these communities to feel that their organizations were due for some major change as well. In 1966, the same year that the FFQ was founded, the Association féminine d'éducation et d'action sociale (AFÉAS)[10] was established. AFÉAS was the product of a merger between the Union catholique des femmes rurales and the Cercles d'économie domestique. In the beginning, AFÉAS was more conservative than the FFQ and defended "feminine specificity," an approach predicated on the role of rural women within the family. However, AFÉAS quickly shifted its political orientation to suit the changing needs of its members. Many of the association's members were de facto partners or "co-operating spouses" in their husbands' family businesses (farms, professional occupations, or small businesses), often receiving no financial consideration. During the 1970s, after access to separation and divorce was expanded and the influence of the Catholic Church on social mores had broken down, some of these former "homemakers" were getting separated and divorced—and losing everything they had worked for in the process. AFÉAS vigorously lobbied to have the legal status of "co-operating spouses" recognized and fought for them to receive a more equitable share of the family patrimony.[11]

Soon enough, the separate political lobbying of the FFQ and AFÉAS became so similar that their efforts fell "into sync," and their combined impetus prompted the Quebec government to take a comprehensive look at the status of women, close on the heels of an identical initiative taken by the federal government. Consultation on Carrefour 75 process (the Quebec government's initiative to celebrate International Women's Year declared by the UN) was subsequently launched, along with the consultations that culminated in the *Pour les Québécoises : égalité et indépendance* report. It was these consultations that would later serve as the basis for substantive legislative reform to improve the status of women in Quebec.

As this reformist pole of feminism established itself, another more radical current was also developing, demanding women's "liberation."

> What was obvious for the women's liberation movement at the end of the 1960s was the radical will to break with everything it found in the present: there was no acknowledgement of the legitimacy of earlier feminist currents. On the contrary, feminists now considered it a priority to mark a break with earlier women's movements.[12]

This radical new kind of feminism included the belief that women-only organizations were needed if feminist struggles were to succeed. Furthermore, since there was a perception that women's legal equality had been achieved but that de facto equality had yet to be realized, "women's liberation" came to trump "equality" as the radical movement's chief imperative. "Liberation" was the only demand deemed to be truly radical, as it marked a dramatic departure from past feminist movements, like that of the suffragettes, which were indiscriminately labelled as "bourgeois" or "reformist"—supreme insults in the radical feminist political epithets of the times.[13]

Into this era of radicalism two major radical feminist organizations were born. The Montreal Women's

Liberation Movement (MWLM) was founded mainly by anglophone women students from McGill University, and the Front de libération des femmes (FLF) was founded mainly by francophone women, and most members of both groups subscribed to the tenets of radical Quebec nationalist currents.[14] Instead of addressing the issues of discrimination against women and equal opportunity as past groups did, these two groups drew their inspiration from radical American feminism, which held that women's exploitation and oppression were caused by a sexist, materialist, male-dominated social system—the patriarchy. Since these radical groups distrusted capitalist, patriarchal governments, they placed no faith in legislative change but introduced consciousness-raising activities for women and staged direct action events to unmask the various manifestations of women's oppression. Some of these actions included occupying taverns (to condemn their long-standing men-only rule), occupying the jury bench during the court case of Lise Balcer[15] (to protest the fact that women could not legally serve as jurors),[16] and disrupting proceedings at the Salon de la femme, a women's trade show (to denounce the diktats of the fashion and beauty industries).

It was not long before the MWLM and the FLF added their voices to those calling for the decriminalization of abortion, which was already included in the recommendations of the federal government's Royal Commission on the Status of Women (the Bird Commission).[17] But this was only the beginning of their involvement in the struggle for abortion rights. Both organizations operated referral and transportation services for women to get safe abortions in New York state, where legislation was more liberal at the time, and worked with qualified physicians in Montreal who were willing to provide clandestine abortions. These services became part of their shared tradition of direct action.

Quebec's radical feminist current was also committed to linking women's liberation with the drive for Quebec sovereignty. This commitment was clearly expressed in one slogan from that era:

> No women's liberation without the liberation of Quebec, no liberation of Quebec without women's liberation![18]

As with most social movements during the Quiet Revolution (including community, student, and union movements), the scope of this feminist current's actions was resolutely Québécois[19] and not Canadian. A particularly striking example of this tendency was the FLF's refusal to join a radical Canadian feminist initiative in its pan-Canadian feminist caravan to promote abortion rights in 1971.

When the FLF was dissolved in 1972, the Centre des femmes was quick to take up the mantle of its pro-choice activities, particularly through its abortion referral services. Some Centre activists began organizing homemakers in low-income neighbourhoods and set up daycare facilities so that mothers of young children could pursue their professional aspirations,[20] while others worked in solidarity with labour struggles or defended the rights of social assistance recipients—more often than not, women. One of the most important activities of the Centre des femmes was publishing its radical feminist newsletter, *Québécoises deboutte!*

The Centre des femmes ceased operations in 1975 and was replaced by more specialized organizations loosely connected by an intergroup structure.[21] Taking advantage of a window of opportunity afforded by Carrefour 75, women's groups established a wide array of organizations throughout Quebec, setting up bookstores, publishing houses, newspapers, battered women's shelters, women's health centres, community women's centres, nonunion women's labour groups, labour union status-of-women committees, and lesbian organizations. Most of these organizations identified with radical feminism, and their early combined physiognomy remains intact in Quebec to this day: Together, they form a highly decentralized movement stretched out in a capillary fashion across the province, often dispensing services to a population larger than the membership of its collectives, each of which use consensus decision making on an independent basis but still have a remarkable ability to rally their numbers to organize common-front initiatives.[22] It has been through this physiognomy that a wide spectrum of ideological currents have grown and blossomed in Quebec over the years.

Certainly, no survey of Quebec radical feminism would be complete without mentioning two influential newsletters that drew attention to the ideological currents of the late 1970s and early 1980s: *Les Têtes de pioche*,[23] which aimed to be the standard-bearer of radical feminist thinking, and *Amazones d'hier, lesbiennes d'aujourd'hui* (AHLA), which defended the ideas of radical lesbianism. *Les Têtes de pioche* was created as a reaction to a tendency it perceived in part of the Quebec feminist movement to dilute women's struggles among other social struggles. Its goal was to disseminate the ideas developed by radical American feminists and to promote the full independence of the women's movement from patriarchal institutions, be they left-wing political groups, governmental organizations, or unions. As for AHLA,[24] it defended lesbian autonomy from the feminist movement and the idea that the constructed social nomenclatures of "men" and "women" only hold meaning within a heterosexual political, economic, ideological, and social matrix.

Feminist Confluences: 1980–1995

By reconfiguring as a vast network of small collectives working on specialized issues (linked by issues and region), the Quebec women's movement not only laid solid foundations for feminist ideas but also effectively ensured the wide dissemination of these ideas throughout Quebec society. This reconfiguration transformed mindsets, but that was not all. It also meant that the "feminist" movement became the "women's" movement, it allowed for the development of service provision, and it ensured greater social visibility for feminist ideas. The ideological boundaries between the radical current and the reformist current, which had structured much of 1970s feminism, were significantly blurred in the process.

The transition from a "feminist" movement to a "women's" movement took place gradually and almost imperceptibly through the provision of services and the dissemination of the movement across Quebec.[25] In a way, women's groups had become women's "unions," representing the interests of women as a social category, but women's groups were also charged with the responsibility of "managing" women. These roles were constructed on two levels: At the first level, women's groups were essentially constituted to represent women's interests but within the government's established parameters of interest-group policy management; at a second level, the government would use the expertise of women's groups to translate feminist demands into public policies. These dynamics explain why some feminists ended up working in government offices or (through political parties) entered government itself.

The struggle for abortion rights was a case in point, as the Comité de lutte pour l'avortement libre et gratuit and some women's centres that provided abortion services agreed to work with civil servants from the Ministère de la Santé and the Ministère des Affaires sociales[26] to set up services in some CLSCs[27] and to partner with the Centre de santé des femmes de Montréal as an accredited abortion facility.[28] Groups for the prevention of violence against women also organized workshops designed for civil servants from the Ministère de la Justice and various police forces to formulate intervention protocols for partner violence. Yet other women's groups contributed to drafting the Quebec government's policy on pay equity.

The drive to provide services to women was congruent with a desire not to await the downfall of the patriarchal system to improve women's lives in the here-and-now. Still, ambivalence about choosing this path was evident and surfaced in three core points of tension: program funding and political activism, the transition from activism to employment, and the subordinate integration of women's groups within the state apparatus. Underlying all of these tensions was the fact that these services were often bogged down in their everyday concerns and had little capacity to innovate.

This brings us to the first point of tension: funding and political activism. Simply securing government funds (often piecemeal, short term, and in competition with other groups) for the survival of these services was an exhausting exercise in itself, leaving little time or energy for mobilization. So base groups attempted to remedy this situation by forming noncompetitive Quebec-wide coordinating structures (according to type of service) to establish leverage through collective bargaining with the government rather than undergo case-by-case evaluations.

The second point of tension—concerning the transition from activism to employment—was twofold. First, the relative distance between "permanent" employees and "clients" could undermine democracy within women's groups.[29] Second, their political logic was partially replaced by therapeutic logic. Instead of using a political analysis of the patriarchal social structures causing women's problems, groups began to focus on finding solutions for individual women within the framework of existing social systems, reducing their broader focus to a case-by-case therapeutic analysis (with all of its inherent political limitations).

The third point of tension was that these services, which were primarily state funded, served as smokescreens for public sector inaction, allowing the government to buy social services at a discount. This type of transaction was the epitome of neoliberal logic: The state had ensured that civil society would shoulder the burden of social solidarity. Thus feminist-initiated social service provision and its ambivalent position—between direct action activism and subordinate integration into public policy initiatives—effectively contributed to blurring the boundaries between the radical and reformist currents discussed earlier.

From 1980 to 1995, the visibility of feminism increased considerably in the public space. The many factors that contributed to this visibility included legal gains (which demonstrated feminists' ability to influence public policy) and a widespread media presence. This media presence was enhanced by the dissemination of "writing in the feminine"[30] as a new generation of female authors emerged, adopted feminism to varying degrees, and managed to have their work published. All of this was made possible because feminist publishers like Les Éditions du remue-ménage and La pleine lune led the way, but also because many publishers had decided to produce "women's collections" to keep up with the new competition(!). The same pattern was seen throughout the creative arts. Not only were more women gaining prominence in theatre, dance, and visual arts, but the venues dedicated to women's creation were also growing and developing (such as Powerhouse Gallery, now called La Centrale, and Théâtre Expérimental des Femmes, which later became L'Espace Go). In print, *La Vie en rose,* a high-circulation feminist magazine, not only influenced the mass media, which began covering feminist issues, but also influenced mainstream women's magazines, which began to venture beyond the subjects of fashion, beauty, and cooking to maintain their readerships. Landmarks that promoted and generated creation, such as Maisons de femmes, feminist bookstores, and women's cafés, dotted the urban landscape.

In 1989, the Quebec feminist movement was thrust more squarely into the media spotlight both at home and abroad by two incidents. The first occurred when the abortion rights[31] of a Quebec woman named Chantal Daigle were violated.[32] For weeks on end, the media focused on Daigle's harrowing (and highly saleable) personal narrative with rapt attention as pro-choice forces rallied feminist lawyers, health-care advocates, performers, artists, and activists, setting records for the number and breadth of demonstrations they held. The second incident occurred a few months later, when 14 women, most of them engineering students, were gunned down at École Polytechnique by a man who "accused" them of being feminists. Of course, the media provided extensive coverage of the incident and of the plethora of feminist events held in Quebec[33] and around the globe that denounced the anti-feminist, misogynist nature of the "Montreal Massacre."[34] But in an effort to "balance" coverage, feminist expertise on male violence was ignored.

Clearly, reporting on feminist issues did not make the Quebec media pro-feminist. In fact, the recurring message during this period was that feminism had lost its relevance. According to this distilled postfeminist reasoning, the feminist movement had been necessary in the 1960s and 1970s when discrimination against women was blatant and prevalent in almost all aspects of society; but since the proper laws had been put in place and society had changed for the better, feminism was no longer necessary; therefore, anyone who still believed feminism to be necessary was just going to drag society into a messy war of the sexes that would be a lose–lose proposition for men and women alike.[35]

Against this backdrop of neoliberal politics and "postfeminist" media messages, the 1990 Les

50 heures du féminisme conference (organized by Relais-femmes to celebrate the fiftieth anniversary of suffrage legislation), was planned as an opportunity for the feminist movement to take stock of past struggles and practices and look to the future. However, history would take an unexpected turn when relations between the "majority" "Québécoises de souche" feminist groups and those from "minority" cultures became a central concern. In this case, the object of concern was not past struggles between the two groups,[36] but the very controversial Lise Payette, who had been chosen as a figurehead for the event. Payette was a media celebrity who polarized opinion on several fronts. Certainly no one questioned her feminist convictions. She had denounced injustices against women and taken action to effect change both during her career as a radio and television host and as a provincial cabinet minister. Controversy had swirled around Payette over her role in the Quebec nationalist movement and the Yvette affair in 1980, but that was of relatively little concern in 1990. It was her prominent role as a writer and narrator of the documentary film *Disparaître* that exposed her to more damning criticism. The premise of the documentary was that the French-Canadian nation was losing ground in Canada (demographically, socially, and politically) to the anglophone majority because of Quebec's low birth rate and insufficient measures to ensure that immigrants to Quebec would learn French. A number of women's groups who regarded the film as being xenophobic vigorously protested Payette's presence at the conference and promised to boycott it if the organizing committee did not reverse its decision to reserve a place of honour for Payette. The decision was not reversed, Payette continued as a figurehead of the event, and the boycott was carried out.

The Payette controversy brought about a major paradigm shift in relations between majority-group and minority-group women in the Quebec feminist movement. Fortunately, the matter was not completely swept under the rug. In fact, it formed the basis of another meeting to adopt the Québec féminin pluriel[37] platform, an attempt (years after the *Manifeste des femmes québécoises*[38] was drafted to address the issue of the intersectionality of oppressions[39]) to pave the way for a new kind of feminism in Quebec, one that would actively welcome a diversity of women. These kinds of ideas opened a new chapter in the development of Quebec feminism, although they did not heal all wounds. Only a few months later, when the Meech Lake Accord was rejected by some Canadian provinces,[40] the wounds were reopened as discussions about the Accord between feminists in Quebec and feminists from "Canada-outside-of-Quebec,"[41] and also among feminists within Quebec, caused major rifts once again. During the 1995 sovereignty referendum campaign, relations fared no better when the FFQ decided to support the "Yes" camp (in favour of Quebec sovereignty) despite an embarrassing public declaration from Lucien Bouchard, leader of the federal Bloc Québécois, that Quebecers constituted "one of the White races [in the world] that [was] producing the fewest number of children." Even greater damage was done on the evening of the referendum when the results were known and Quebec nationalist Premier Jacques Parizeau made an infamous speech blaming the defeat of his sovereignist forces on "money and some ethnic votes."

Since 1995: Social Justice for All

The most recent period of Quebec feminism began with the Bread and Roses March in 1995. Organized on the initiative of the FFQ, this march allowed feminist forces to remobilize women at a crucial juncture in the history of Quebec and of Quebec feminism. Indeed, the repercussions of this march and especially the defeat of the sovereignty movement in the Quebec referendum a few months later marked important turning points in Quebec politics. Moreover, the Quebec government was progressively relinquishing its long-held vision of the welfare state (an ideal championed by the Quebec nationalist movement since the Quiet Revolution), and adopting the prevailing North American neoliberal approach. The repercussions of the government's actions were acutely felt in the women's movement as political opportunity structures were shutting down and the possibilities of influencing the political agenda were growing slim. Consequently, the terms of polemic engagement between the state and the women's movement changed, and unlike the preceding period, polemics started to overshadow co-operation.

Oddly enough, things seemed to have started well in 1995. The anti-poverty measures proposed by women at the Bread and Roses March were warmly received by the public and by some female cabinet ministers in the Quebec government. Not only were the women who participated in the march greeted at the Quebec National Assembly in 1995 by a number of members of the assembly, but their demands were partially met.[42] However, one year later, in 1996, the winds of politics had shifted. The government flatly refused to add the notion of "zero poverty"[43] to its "zero deficit" policy, and this refusal led to a major rift between the government and women's groups. With divisions in the air on a number of fronts, some Quebec feminists started to explore (and revisit) the rudiments of **intersectionality**.

The concept of the intersectionality (or the integrative nature) of issues of class, race, and gender implicitly informed the development of Quebec feminism's radical currents in the 1970s, as mentioned earlier, and was more explicitly present in the issues raised by the Québec féminin pluriel conference, which recognized the need to take the diversity of women's situations into account to develop a truly inclusive feminism.[45] But it was not until after 1995, through its growing involvement in the struggle against neoliberal policies, that the Quebec women's movement could take in the magnitude of what intersectionality would demand and see the limitations intrinsic to a brand of feminism that focused solely on gender issues.

In 2000, the World March of Women (WMW) was launched with the goal of uniting the women's movement around two issues: violence against women and poverty. Mobilizing the entire women's movement in Quebec over a period of almost three years, the WMW was an opportunity to create a new form of activism for the movement while extending the increasingly intersectional register of its concerns. The WMW not only provided an opportunity to develop internationalism within the Quebec feminist movement, but also raised awareness about the need to integrate issues of race, class, and gender into strategies of struggle against social inequalities. This lesson was valuable, since the WMW was immediately followed by the first World Social Forum, held in Porto Alegre, Brazil, to which the FFQ was invited, having established an international presence through its organization of the WMW and especially through its significant presence and mobilization activities for the massive demonstrations in Quebec City around the 2001 Summit of the Americas (convened by politicians for the purpose of making North and South America free trade areas).

CASE STUDY

The Bread and Roses March

We need roses
A breather, a break
We need bread
Take our hand
We now stand taller
Than we seem to you
We want peace
For the world that we have made.[44]

The Bread and Roses March played a major role in constructing the physiognomy of Quebec's present-day feminist movement. The organizers chose the name of the march very consciously. By borrowing the early twentieth-century American socialist feminist slogan, "Bread and Roses," they aimed to underscore a new orientation within the Quebec women's movement toward broader social issues. In fact, the march was a vehicle for linking issues beyond gender and class, including ethnocultural diversity. In this way, it was designed to mend some of the wounds left by the 1990 Les 50 heures du féminisme conference and was an extension of the remedial Pour un Québec féminin pluriel conference. This event subsequently empowered the vision behind the World March of Women and generally made it easier for broad sectors of the women's movement to join alter-globalization struggles and the fight against neoliberalism.

The beauty of this form of mobilization was that it not only allowed many people to participate, but also offered the possibility of getting involved in different ways at different levels. A substantial proportion of the marchers were employees from women's groups or belonged to labour union status-of-women committees, and some were retired. Grassroots women's groups were extensively mobilized to prepare the event and greet the marchers.

From 26 May to 4 June 1995, 850 women marched across Quebec and on to Quebec City to deliver nine main demands on various issues. Over those 10 days the marchers not only received support from women's groups but were resoundingly cheered on by the general public. The day they converged on Quebec City, over 20,000 people were waiting to join them in delivering their demands to the government. With a referendum on sovereignty just a few months away, the marchers reaped the benefits of a vibrant political atmosphere and made some positive gains. The demands they presented covered a variety of issues.

The first demand proposed the introduction of "a system for automatically collecting support payments through source deductions." Women's groups had been making this demand for over a decade because separation or divorce (situations affecting a good half of married women) often led to marked impoverishment for women, partly owing to the lax administration and application of court rulings on the collection of child support. On 11 May 1995, shortly before the march began, the Quebec government adopted a bill addressing this problem.

The second demand, "a tuition freeze and larger bursaries for students," had been a recurring issue in student struggles since 1968 in Quebec, as the government had never been willing to apply the Parent Commission's recommendations on educational reform, which called for a gradual phase-out of tuition fees. It took a wave of student strikes in 1996 for the government to commit to a tuition freeze, which was maintained until 2007. But the fact remained that since the 1970s the bursary portion of the loans-and-bursaries pie had been shrinking, creating correspondingly bigger student loans. This trend became the central issue in the 2005 general strike by students, who opposed even more restricted access to higher education for lower-middle-income and low-income Quebecers and burdensome debt for many students upon graduation.

The third demand called for "the creation of at least 1,500 units of social housing annually," a recurring appeal made by women's groups and the housing rights movement. During this period, the rental vacancy rate in cities was low, causing rents to increase. Indeed, one year before the march the government had promised to build 1,200 social housing units, then failed to fulfill its promises. The marchers wanted immediate action, but in the end reached an agreement that 60 of the planned units would be reserved, with community support, for women with specific challenges such as drug addiction or psychiatric disorders.

The fourth demand sought to establish "access for all women to general and vocational training programs and services, accompanied by adequate financial support, with a view to helping them join or return to the labour market." This demand was in keeping with the "workfare" philosophy promoted by the Quebec government, which aimed to reduce the number of people on social assistance. Here again, the gains were minimal: In every nontraditional vocational training

continued

program, the government simply reserved one-third of the positions to women.

The fifth demand, "a social infrastructure programme, with jobs open to women," was inspired by a federal government infrastructure program that had created employment by investing in built environments and roadways. The women's movement wanted a similar program to be set up, but in the social sector, so that women would be more likely to be hired for the jobs that were created. The government responded to this demand by effectively hijacking it. Although most of the members on the advisory committee it set up to study social infrastructures were representatives from women's groups, the committee's work was partially short-circuited when the 1996 Socio-Economic Summit established a social economy committee, into which the bulk of relevant budget allocations were subsequently channelled.

The sixth demand called for "a retroactive reduction of the length of sponsorship from 10 to 3 years for immigrants sponsored by their husbands, and access to social programmes for immigrant women subjected to spousal or family violence." This demand forced Quebec to use the full measure of its immigration powers. It also highlighted the fundamentally sexist nature of Canadian immigration legislation: There is a heavy bias in the criteria used to determine an immigrant's category ("independent" or "sponsored"), which results in men obtaining "independent immigrant" status over women. Many women therefore have no choice but to be sponsored by their husbands. During the sponsorship period, this means they have no access to social programs or French-language proficiency training. It follows that sponsored women become increasingly dependent on their husbands, which reinforces patriarchal structures and makes it practically impossible for them to escape from situations of partner and family violence. In this matter, the government met the marchers' demand and shortened the sponsorship period from 10 years to 3.

The seventh demand also involved a long-standing issue for the women's movement: "a proactive Pay Equity Act." The net impact of the march was to spur on the movement for pay equity itself, since the mechanisms for introducing such legislation and labour committees were already in place but had been stalled since 1992. In the fall of 1996, the Pay Equity Act was finally adopted, thanks to sustained activist pressure. It took the June 1996 vigil in Quebec City, in which women formed a human chain around the National Assembly, to finally force the government to pass its legislation.

The eighth demand for the "application of the Labour Standards Act for all participants in employability measures" was similar to the fourth demand in that the women's movement was not challenging the philosophy of workfare, but merely seeking to adjust it. At first the government committed in principle to meet the demand, but in practice, subsequent amendments to the act respecting income security made this commitment meaningless. The living conditions of people on social assistance deteriorated substantially as a result.

The ninth demand, a "raise in the minimum wage above the poverty line ($8.15 an hour)" met with partial success. Although the government did not accept the underlying principle of the demand (that full-time paid employment enabled people to overcome poverty), it did raise the minimum wage to $6.45 per hour—the largest increase that had been seen in many years.

The Bread and Roses March breathed new life into the struggle for women's rights and helped to establish the women's movement as a key proponent in the fight against poverty. The fight would continue in the years that followed, as neoliberalism made the rich richer and the poorest in society, among whom women were overrepresented, poorer still. Buoyed by the success of the march, the Quebec delegation at the NGO meeting of the UN World Conference on Women in Beijing launched the idea of a World March of Women, a dream that would become a reality in 2000.

In Quebec City, the women's movement held a full day of panels the day before the opening of the People's Summit (an alternative to the Summit of the Americas) organized by a coalition of unions, community and feminist groups, and international solidarity organizations. The anti-FTAA (Free Trade Area of the Americas) struggle was presented in information sessions in many local women's groups. New

BIOGRAPHY

Michèle Asselin

Michèle Asselin's activism exemplifies that of thousands of feminists like her working in women's groups throughout Quebec. You could say she has made Quebec women's groups her career, as they have formed the backdrop to her entire professional life. In contrast to the ideologically entrenched feminist approaches of the 1970s, Asselin built up her understanding of feminism through her own careful circumspection about the issues she tackled in her activism.

Michèle Asselin (left) receives the Prix québécois de la citoyenneté 2008 (Quebec's 2008 citizenship award) from the provincial minister of immigration and cultural communities, Yolande James. Asselin's award acknowledged her work as president of the Fédération des Femmes du Québec in the fight against racism.

After studying community organizing at Université du Québec à Montréal, Michèle Asselin worked as the coordinator of the Centre d'éducation et d'action des femmes de Montréal (CEAF). Founded in 1972, this centre in the Ste-Marie–St-Jacques riding of Montreal is a good example of how local roots and networking have served the Quebec women's movement. Although mainly concerned with popular education, CEAF also offers a range of services for women in this underprivileged neighbourhood (such as Internet access and a drop-in daycare service). It was instrumental in developing a local community health service centre, introducing social housing resources for single mothers, and setting up a popular local daycare centre, which was then integrated into the CPQ (Centres de la petite enfance, or early childhood agency) network. The centre has a reputation for promoting grassroots politicization as part of its mandate of popular education, organizing, for example, workshops on such topics as the impact of neoliberal globalization on women and the Déclaration citoyenne, in which women envisioned the kind of city they wished to live in. Moreover, it was CEAF that established a structure for coordinating women's centres across Quebec: L'R des centres de femmes du Québec (*R* stands for *regroupement* or *grouping*).

Not surprisingly, after working for several years as the coordinator at CEAF, Michèle Asselin went on to become the coordinator of L'R des centres de femmes du Québec, a position she held for some 15 years. It was during her tenure as CEAF coordinator that Asselin sat on the Coalition des femmes pour l'accès à l'égalité, on the advisory board for women's programs at the Commission de la formation professionnelle de Montréal, and on the board of directors at Relais-femmes (an organization that links feminist researchers and women's groups). Her work was a reflection of the areas in which women's groups played an

continued

active role in Quebec at the time: group-to-group networking, advocacy for equality rights policies (with government and paragovernmental organizations), and linkages between feminist researchers at universities and women's groups.

When Asselin was the coordinator of L'R des centres de femmes du Québec (1988–2003), the group was very active on several fronts: ensuring that women were participating in regional development structures; establishing the Equal Access to Decision-Making program to increase the number of women holding key positions in local and municipal governing bodies; and mobilizing to fight both neoliberal globalization and poverty. Again, Asselin's work embodied the ever-expanding gamut of the feminist movement's priorities of the times, including participating in government consultations on women's equality and rallying wider forces for new civil rights and public policies. While she was coordinating L'R des centres de femmes du Québec, she was also involved in organizing Les 50 heures du féminisme (a conference to celebrate the fiftieth anniversary of legislation on women's suffrage in Quebec).

This was a pivotal period in the relationship between women's groups and the Quebec government. From the outset, the women's movement had a polemical relationship with the state apparatus: While it was well aware of the government's shortcomings when it came to promoting gender equality, it intended to take full advantage of favourable "structures of political opportunity" to influence these policies in a positive manner. However, by 1996 the neoliberal watershed established by successive "cost-cutting" government administrations (irrespective of the party in power) progressively closed political opportunities for grassroots organizations and radicalized the women's movement.

An early example of this radicalization was the Bread and Roses March, which promoted the movement's anti-poverty agenda with a specific (but not exclusive) focus on poverty affecting women. The march inaugurated two crucial linkage initiatives within the women's movement. The first was the link women made between their struggles with the fight against neoliberal globalization. This led the movement to establish an enduring association with the Collective for a Law on the Elimination of Poverty (comprising community and union organizations), then with the Réseau de vigilance (an umbrella group of feminist, union, community, and environmental organizations that were taking a stand against neoliberal policies and against the Charest government itself), and to participate in the 2001 People's Summit and the 2007 Forum social québécois. The second linkage initiative made connections between local, national, and international feminist struggles during the NGO Forum at the UN World Conference on Women in Beijing; the organization of the year 2000 World March of Women; the various editions of the World Social Forum; and the adoption of the Women's Global Charter for Humanity in 2005.

Throughout Michèle Asselin's presidency at the FFQ from 2003 to 2009, she was confronted with a multitude of challenging issues: carving out a place in the movement for Aboriginal and minority-culture women; creating a cohesive local, national, and international approach to the movement's activities; repositioning the FFQ politically on local and global issues; and combating the united forces of neoliberalism and neoconservatism, along with the rise of masculinism.

Under her tenure, Asselin initiated a major reorganization of the FFQ. Among other achievements, a committee of immigrant and racialized women was struck, and a collaborative agreement was signed with Quebec Native Women. She took a proactive role in the FFQ political platform review at home, maintained a dynamic presence abroad, and ensured much greater autonomy for the World March of Women (as an independent but affiliated entity), both within francophone spaces and at the World Social Forum. Michèle Asselin also distinguished herself as a vocal defender of free access to abortion and an expert builder of coalitions to maintain and expand women's rights.

feminist collectives linked with the alter-globalization current, such as Némésis[46] or the group publishers of the magazine *Sorcières*, also participated, developing women-only activities and an explicitly feminist alter-globalization perspective.

At this juncture, many women saw a logical link between their own struggles and the struggle against neoliberalism and were inspired to participate in anti-poverty coalitions like the Réseau de vigilance or the Coalition pour un Québec sans pauvreté. Some even went on to found a new political movement called Option citoyenne, which would later become the provincial Québec solidaire party.[47] These feminists, who had worked to build a women's movement that would include all women, went on to constitute a "social justice project" that would include all members of society. This project would emphasize the integral links between the issues of gender, race, and class.

The struggle against neoliberalism also stimulated the emergence of new collectives of young women who identified as radical feminists and had various ties with anarchism.[48] In addition to these currents, more radical feminists joined the movement through meetings like Rencontres des féministes radicales (2003, 2008), the conference held for young feminists by the young women's committee of the FFQ (2003),[49] and the Canada-wide RebELLES conference (2008).

This intersectional focus has been significantly strengthened through the debates that led to the États généraux du féminisme conference in November 2013, a convention that brought more than 800 women together after months of intense debates within diverse women's groups throughout the province. In addition to aligning itself with the Forum pour un Québec féminin pluriel, the presentation text for this convention emphasizes the importance of situating women's struggles within the larger context of struggles against neoliberal capitalism that "threatens social benefits and public services, weakens democratic spaces, and renders women's living and working conditions precarious,"[50] and against conservative values that advocate for a return to the traditional heterosexual family unit.

Conclusion

Feminism in Quebec has developed in a protean fashion in environments and communities so diverse that it would be impossible to draw up an exhaustive list of them all. In studying Quebec feminism, we could single out specific ideological currents, detail issues, or conduct a survey of women's groups. In so doing, however, we would be overlooking one essential point: It was through feminism that women began to trust each other and initiate a mutually inclusive dialogue. Be they scholars or dropouts, rich or poor, city or country dwellers, "Québécoises de souche" or more recent citizens, through feminism women recognized in each other their positions as active participants in a shared "herstory." Women also attained the status of "speaking beings," a status previously denied them because so many people claimed not to understand what they were talking about. "What on earth could they still want?" had become the familiar dismissive refrain. Women began to speak out and speak to each other, even though this new speech act fell on the deaf ears of those who dominated them. "Feminism" is the name of this act and of the diverse movements that it empowered, movements to establish gender equality, to subvert the place that society had assigned to women, and to position the disputes between the sexes at the very heart of the body politic. Using the word in the plural, "feminisms," would more faithfully represent the diversity of the practices and reflections within these movements of resistance and of critical thought.

These feminist achievements have led to a backlash on two fronts. On the one hand is the idea that feminism has already been achieved in Quebec and that feminist struggles are therefore old fashioned, even conservative. On the other hand, an antifeminist backlash has been developed over the years. It first manifested itself publicly during the massacre at Montreal's École Polytechnique in 1989 along with the outpouring of support the murderer received; this has led to the development of a men's rights movement that argues that it is now men who are oppressed in Quebec. As a result, feminists must work for the improvement of all women's living conditions while defending themselves against the attacks and threats of men's rights activists.[51]

Epilogue: Quebec and the United States

The Quebec women's movement developed its own distinctive traits and, harking back to the 1960s, developed dynamics that were different from those that prevailed in the United States. Indeed, in the 1980s Quebec feminists were not forced to confront any major hostilities, in sharp contrast to the situation in the United States, where the defeat of the Equal Rights Amendment and the concurrent rise of the conservative and religious right (fighting abortion and gay rights) impeded feminist mobilization and meant that the women's movement was constantly on the defensive. The "sex wars" of the 1980s (debating issues around pornography) further split the US movement. The fact that in Quebec the feminist movement's confrontation with the combined forces of neoliberalism and neoconservatism occurred only after 1995 has afforded feminists the opportunity of becoming better equipped to resist and organize against these highly anti-feminist trends in contemporary politics. The election of Conservative governments in Ottawa since 2006 has considerably strengthened the groups that oppose abortion on demand ("pro-life" movements). While their hostility has not achieved the same force as that of their American counterparts, they are nevertheless increasingly engaging in forms of harassment in front of abortion clinics and now disseminate their propaganda in schools more widely.

Questions for Critical Thinking

1. What were the differences between reformist feminists and radical feminists in the 1970s?
2. To what can we attribute the ability of the Quebec women's movement to mobilize its forces?
3. What kinds of issues reshaped the Quebec women's movement in the 1990s?

Notes

1. Masculinist thought differs from other currents of thought regarding masculinity in that masculinists believe that men in Western societies are dominated by women. Consequently, they contend that they must organize, as women have, to struggle against the discrimination to which men are purportedly being subjected. This current is particularly active in Quebec, and its key points of contention are high rates of suicide among young men, dropout rates among male youth, violence against men, and the experiences of separated or divorced fathers who have lost custody of their children. Their lobby is particularly insistent on this last point and has had some success with public authorities. For more information, see the collective work edited by Mélissa Blais and Francis Dupuis-Déri, *Le masculinisme au Québec : l'antiféminisme démasqué* (Montreal: Les Éditions du remue-ménage, 2008; new edition, revised and expanded, 2015).
2. See my chapter "Comment l'égalité entre les femmes et les hommes est devenue une 'valeur fondamentale' de la société Québécoise," in *À la recherche d'un Québec qui bouge*, ed. Robert Laliberté (Paris: Centre des travaux historiques et scientifiques, 2009).
3. A colloquial name for women from Quebec's majority group of French-Canadian ancestry. This expression denotes the concepts of "founding people" or "old-stock Quebecers" and is not universally embraced.
4. Although Denyse Baillargeon, in Chapter 14, documents major gains in the women's movement, there is still significant social inequality between men and women in employment, wages, violence, reconciling work–family commitments, and domestic work, to name but a few examples.
5. I have discussed this question in a much more detailed fashion in *Fragments et collages* (Montreal: Les Éditions du remue-ménage, 1986).
6. The legal equality of married women, a demand that the Quebec feminist movement began making at the beginning of the twentieth century, was incorporated into the Fédération nationale Saint-Jean-Baptiste's platform by Marie Gérin-Lajoie. Although in 1964 Bill 16 was the first step to achieving equality of legal status between men and women in Quebec, it would not be until the Civil Code of Quebec was reformed in 1980 that gender equality came into effect.
7. Educational reform was one of the major initiatives of the Quiet Revolution. The Parent Commission, established to examine this issue, included a common school curriculum for female and male students among its recommendations.

8. Around the mid-1960s, when Pierre Elliott Trudeau, Jean Marchand, and Gérard Pelletier (who were associated with opposition to the Duplessis regime in Quebec) became part of the federal Lester B. Pearson government, far-reaching changes were effected in this area. Under pressure from many women's groups, the Pearson government established a Royal Commission on the Status of Women, chaired by journalist Florence Bird, with research services headed by the commission's executive secretary, Monique Bégin. Established in 1967, the commission submitted its report in 1970 and drafted a set of recommendations for the equal treatment of women in law, education, pay, and employment opportunities, calling for improved access to abortion and many other services and programs. The recommendations were much the same as the demands of the reformist feminist component of the movement, which was lobbying for equal opportunities between women and men within the existing social system.
9. During the 1980 referendum campaign on sovereignty in Quebec, the federalist "No" camp mobilized thousands of women under the moniker of "Yvettes" to oppose sovereignty in Quebec. (See "The Yvette Affair" in Chapter 14).
10. For a history of AFÉAS, see Jocelyne Lamoureux, Michèle Gélinas, and Katy Tari, *Femmes en mouvements : trajectoires de l'Association féminine d'éducation et d'action sociale* (Montreal: Boréal, 1993).
11. The legal term used in Quebec for the total family assets acquired or used during a marriage or civil union.
12. Dominique Fougeyrollas-Schwebel, "Feminism in the 1970s," in *Political and Historical Encyclopedia of Women*, ed. Christine Fauré (New York: Routledge, 2003), 426.
13. See, for example, Zillah Eisenstein, *The Radical Future of Liberal Feminism* (Boston: Northeastern University Press, 1981). Ironically, since large sections of radical feminism were heavily influenced by liberalism, it would be more appropriate to acknowledge the "Liberal Future of Radical Feminism."
14. The history of the FLF and that of the Centre des femmes, as well as the reproduction of the magazine *Québécoises deboutte!* are addressed in Véronique O'Leary and Louise Toupin, *Québécoises deboutte!* 2 vols. (Montreal: Les Éditions du remue-ménage, 1982–3).
15. Lise Balcer was infamous for her indictment as a member of the FLQ (Front de libération du Québec) in trials arising from the kidnapping and death of Pierre Laporte.
16. This direct action event is analyzed in detail in Marjolaine Péloquin, *En prison pour la cause des femmes* (Montreal: Les Éditions du remue-ménage, 2007).
17. A recommendation that was not adopted by the federal government, which opted to authorize abortion in hospitals (conditional on the sanction of a therapeutic abortion committee) if the life or health of a mother or fetus were in jeopardy.
18. Author's translation of the original French slogan: "Pas de liberation des femmes sans Québec libre, pas de Québec libre sans la liberation des femmes!"
19. During the Quiet Revolution, French Canadians in Quebec began to call themselves "Québécois," a name that referred to the territory of the province of Quebec, the only province in which francophones made up the majority of the population. Today this word has come to include any resident of Quebec, regardless of language group.
20. These popular community daycare centres, managed by staff and parents, were the precursors to Quebec's current Centres de la petite enfance (CPEs) (early childhood centres).
21. Member organizations of this "intergroupe" included Centre de santé des femmes du Plateau–Mont-Royal, Comité de lutte pour l'avortement libre et gratuit, Théâtre des cuisines, and Les Éditions du remue-ménage. The proliferation of women's groups during this period soon made the "intergroupe" obsolete as a coordinating structure, and its operations were therefore partly transferred to *Pluri-elles*, a liaison newsletter for independent women's groups that would in turn become an independent feminist newsletter and collective under the name of *Des luttes et des rires de femmes.*
22. This impressive capacity for mobilization has been demonstrated in the fight for abortion rights, feminist counteractions to the Montreal Massacre at École Polytechnique, the organization of the fiftieth anniversary of suffrage legislation (*Les 50 heures du féminisme)*, the *Pour un Québec féminin pluriel* conference, and the Bread and Roses March and the World March of Women in 2000.
23. The complete collection of this magazine may be found in *Les Têtes de Pioche* (Montreal: Les Éditions du remue-ménage, 1980).
24. An excellent analysis of this collective may be found in Louise Turcotte's article "Itinéraire d'un courant politique : le lesbianisme radical au Québec," in *Sortir de l'ombre : histoires des communautés lesbienne et gaie de Montreal*, eds. Irène Demczuk and Frank W. Remiggi (Montreal: VLB éditeur, 1998).
25. I discuss these issues in Chapter 7 of *L'Amère patrie* (Montreal: Les Éditions du remue-ménage, 2001).
26. This process began in 1977 and results were apparent during the 1980s and beyond.
27. Centres locaux de services communautaires (CLSCs) (Local Community Service Centres in English) were established in the 1970s within the framework of universal and public health-care insurance coverage. These individual clinics brought together medical, social, and community services and developed the preventive and curative concept of health care of the period.
28. See Louise Desmarais, *Mémoires d'une bataille inachevée* (Montreal: Trait-d'Union, 1994).

29. See Nancy Guberman et al., *Les défis des pratiques démocratiques dans les groupes de femmes* (Montreal: Saint-Martin, 2001).
30. *"L'écriture au féminin"* is based on the important locution *"au féminin,"* used to indicate a woman-centred cultural perspective that gained currency in Quebec's feminist discourse in the late 1970s and early 1980s. In 1980 it appeared in a text by lesbian feminist writer Nicole Brossard and was incorporated into the name of an important Montreal conference in 1982, "Emergence d'une culture au féminin."
31. In a landmark decision in January 1988, the Supreme Court of Canada permanently struck down criminal prohibitions on abortions on the basis that they were unconstitutional.
32. A pregnant Quebec woman whose violent ex-boyfriend temporarily prevented her from getting an abortion by serving her with a civil injunction, which was overturned by the Supreme Court of Canada, thereby setting a vital precedent in Canadian law. See Desmarais, *Mémoires d'une bataille inachevée.*
33. Most of the feminist reactions to this event in Quebec were compiled in a publication edited by Marie Chalouh and Louise Malette, *Polytechnique, 6 décembre* (Montreal: Les Éditions du remue-ménage, 1990).
34. December 6, the date of the Montreal Massacre, continues to be commemorated every year by feminists in Quebec.
35. This was the message conveyed by Roch Côté in *Manifeste d'un salaud* (Terrebonne: Le portique, 1990), and by Denise Bombardier in *La déroute des sexes* (Paris: Seuil, 1993).
36. This retrospective analysis was compiled in Femmes en tête, *De travail et d'espoir* (Montreal: Les Éditions du remue-ménage, 1990).
37. The minutes from this meeting are published in *Pour un Québec féminin pluriel* (Montreal: Les Éditions Écosociété, 1994).
38. The *Manifeste des femmes québécoises* was written by Quebec nationalist feminists.
39. This notion was developed in the United States to better problematize the overlapping or "integrative" oppressions that women experience. See Kimberlé Crenshaw, "Mapping the Margins: Intersectionality, Identity Politics and Violence against Women of Color," *Stanford Law Review* 43 (1991): 12–41.
40. According to the overriding formula stipulated in the Canadian Constitution Act of 1982, the Meech Lake Accord, which was drawn up in 1987, had to be ratified by all provinces and territories by 1990. Such was not the case, as Newfoundland retracted its ratification and Manitoba refused to ratify the Accord.
41. Although most authors take a Canada-centric view with expressions like "Quebec and the *rest* of Canada," in this case I am mirroring this expression to underscore an opposite perspective.
42. There was a marked contrast between the situation in 1995, when the march was positively received by the government, and that of 1996 (the referendum and the zero-deficit Socio-Economic Summit had been held in the interim). In 1995, the government established an advisory committee on social infrastructure whose members included some of the march's founding organizers, whereas in 1996 it raised minimum wage by a meagre $0.10 per hour.
43. This policy demand was originally championed by the Collective for a Law on the Elimination of Poverty and was delivered during the 1996 Socio-Economic Summit, where the notion "zero poverty" was adopted by the FFQ and Front d'action populaire en réaménagement urbain (FRAPRU).
44. Author's free translation of an excerpt from the chorus of the march's theme song, "Du pain et des roses," lyrics by Hélène Pedneault. The slogan "Bread and Roses" was originally part of an English-language poem (which also became a song), inspired by the 1912 Lawrence Textile strike in Lawrence, Massachusetts. Printed with permission from Fondation Léa-Roback.
45. To the notion of intersectionality we could add that of seriality, developed by Iris Marion Young; see "Gender as Seriality" in her *Intersecting Voices* (Princeton, NJ: Princeton University Press, 1997).
46. For a history of this group, see Anna Kruzynski, "De l'opération SalAMI à *Némésis*," *Recherches féministes* 17, no. 2 (2004): 227–62. For an overview of the ideas behind the magazine *Sorcières*, see Mélissa Blais, Laurence Fortin-Pellerin, Ève Marie Lampron, and Geneviève Pagé, "Pour éviter de se noyer dans la (troisième) vague : réflexion sur l'histoire et l'actualité du féminisme radical," *Recherches féministes* 20, no. 2 (2007): 141–62.
47. Françoise David, long-time president of the FFQ, helped found the Option citoyenne movement and would become the female spokesperson (there is also a male spokesperson) of the provincial party, Québec solidaire, in 2006. See Chapter 21 in this volume.
48. See Émilie Breton, Julie Grolleau, Anna Kruzynski, and Catherine Saint-Arnaud Babin, "Mon/notre/leur corps est toujours un champ de bataille," *Recherches féministes* 20, no. 2 (2007): 113–39.
49. See Elsa Beaulieu and Barbara Legault, "The Making of," in *Dialogues sur la troisième vague féministe,* ed. Maria Nengeh Mensah (Montreal: Les Éditions du remue-ménage, 2005).
50. États généraux du féminisme conference, Université du Québec à Montréal, 14–17 November 2013, 24, www.etatsgenerauxdufeminisme.ca/images/documents/Cahier%20du%20Forum%20-%20complet.pdf.
51. A man linked to men's rights movements has already been convicted for having iterated death threats to feminist activists. In addition, some men's rights activists attempt to disrupt some feminist activities.

Select Bibliography

Beauchamp, Colette, ed. *Pour un Québec féminin pluriel.* Montreal: Les Éditions Écosociété, 1994.

Dumont, Micheline. *Le féminisme raconté à Camille.* Montreal: Les Éditions du remue-ménage, 2008.

———, and Louise Toupin, eds. *La pensée féministe au Québec.* Montreal: Les Éditions du remue-ménage, 2003.

Dufour, Pascale, and Isabelle Giraud. *Dix ans de solidarité féministe.* Montreal: Les Éditions du remue-manage, 2010.

Femmes en tête. *De travail et d'espoir.* Montreal: Les Éditions du remue-ménage, 1990.

Lamoureux, Diane. *L'Amère patrie.* Montreal: Les Éditions du remue-ménage, 2001.

———. *Fragments et collages : essai sur le féminisme québécois des années 1970.* Montreal: Les Éditions du remue-ménage, 1986.

Mensah, Maria Nengeh, ed. *Dialogues sur la troisième vague féministe.* Montreal: Les Éditions du remue-ménage, 2005.

O'Leary, Véronique, and Louise Toupin. *Québécoises deboutte!* Vol. 1. Montreal: Les Éditions du remue-ménage, 1982.

21 The Politics of Social and Economic Development in Quebec

Peter Graefe, McMaster University

Timeline

1960 Quebec election on 22 June, which is believed to mark the launch of the Quiet Revolution.

1976 Parti Québécois wins election and forms government on 15 November.

1981–2 Major recession pushes PQ government to rein in public spending; sparks conflict with public sector unions.

1985 Quebec Liberal Party wins provincial election on 2 December based on promises of significant economic liberalization.

1995 Marche du Pain et des Roses (Bread and Roses March Against Poverty and Violence), 26 May–4 June.

1996 Conférence sur le devenir social et économique du Québec, 18–20 March.

1996 Sommet sur l'économie et l'emploi, 30 October–1 November.

2003 Election of Quebec Liberal Party on 14 April, which is believed to mark a shift to a more neoliberal style of governing.

2012 Mass student strike of university and college students—the "Maple Spring."

In the spring of 2012, students at many of Quebec's colleges and universities suspended their studies and went on strike against the government's plan to raise tuition rates toward the Canadian average. On 22 March, the Day of Action, 300,000 of the province's 400,000 full-time students participated in the strike. The strike began as a dispute about how the costs and benefits of education should be shared between individuals and society, but soon became a larger debate about public services and the role of the state.[1] The more radical student association CLASSE (Coalition large de l'Association pour une solidarité syndicale étudiante) put out a radical manifesto[2] (see the Primary Source box) and organized a series of massive street demonstrations, including four with over 200,000 marchers. Students who disagreed with the strike wore a green square (les carrés verts) and argued that since people enriched themselves through education, they should pay more of the cost up front and presumably lower taxes. This corresponded to the calls of business and corporate leaders for more user fees, fewer public services, and lower taxes.

All democratic societies debate how they will organize economic and social policy to secure growth and equity, although not always as openly as in this case. This particular debate was the latest in a long

Primary Source

Share Our Future: The CLASSE Manifesto

This is the meaning of our vision, and the essence of our strike: it is a shared, collective action whose scope lies well beyond student interests. We are daring to call for a different world, one far removed from the blind submission our present commodity-based system requires. Individuals, nature, our public services, these are being seen as commodities: the same tiny elite is busy selling everything that belongs to us. And yet we know that public services are not useless expenditures, nor are they consumer goods.

Together we have realized that our underground wealth cannot be measured in tons of metal, and that a woman's body is not a selling point. In the same way, education cannot be sold; it ought to be provided to each and every one of us, without regard to our immigration status or our condition. Our aim is for an educational system that is for us, that we will share together.

Because education is a training ground for humanity, and because humanity does not bow to economic competitiveness, we refuse to allow our schools to bend under the weight of well-stocked portfolios. Together, we call for an egalitarian school system that will break down hierarchies, one that will pose a threat to all those men and women who still think they can rule over us with a free hand.

In providing everyone with the resources they need to develop their full capacities, we will succeed in creating a society where decision-making and the ways in which we organize our lives with one another are shared. This is the heart of our vision. Education is not a branch of the economy, nor is it a short-term training service. Our educational system, which is at the root of all knowledge, can allow us to pave the way towards freeing society as a whole; it can provide a liberating education that will lay the foundation for self-determination.

We believe that if our educational system is to be seen as a space where universal knowledge is shared, it must banish all forms of gender-based discrimination and domination. And yet a woman in the current educational system walks a path just as difficult as the one she walks in today's society. It is futile to believe that unequal status is no longer reproduced in the halls of academe: we are disgusted to see that the professions traditionally associated with women are still undervalued, and that it is still mostly women who study for these professions. We women are numerous in Bachelor's-level classrooms, but how many of us climb to the highest rungs of the academic ladder?

We are against prolonging this discrimination against women as well as against people who are in any way shunted aside by society. Our aim is to make our educational system well and truly a space where equality reigns and differences are respected. Our fervent wish is for an educational system that allows each and every one of us to blossom.

In choosing to strike, we have chosen to fight for these ideas. We have chosen to create a power relationship, the only mechanism that will allow us to tip the scales. *Sharing* this responsibility together, we can accomplish a great deal: but in order to do this we have to speak up, and speak up forcefully. History has shown us eloquently that if we do choose hope, solidarity, and equality, we must not beg for them: we must take them. This is what we mean by *combative syndicalism*. Now, at a time when new democratic spaces are springing up all around us, we must make use of these to create a new world. Now is no time for mere declarations of intent: we must act. In calling for a social strike today, we will be marching alongside you, people of Quebec, in the street tomorrow. In calling for a social strike today, we hope that tomorrow, we will be marching, together, alongside the whole of Quebec society.

Together, we can rebuild
Share our future

Source: Coalition large de l'Association pour une solidarité syndicale étudiante, *Share Our Future: The CLASSE Manifesto*. Available at www.stopthehike.ca/2012/07/share-our-future-the-classe-manifesto.

series in Quebec about how to reform the institutions inherited from the Quiet Revolution of the 1960s, pitting supporters of **economic liberalism**[3] (the "carrés verts") against supporters of **social democracy** (the "carrés rouges"). Yet to look at this as simply a running debate is problematic on two fronts. First, the fact that the debate recurs, and is thus in a sense unresolved, does not mean that important changes in the **development model** have not occurred over the past quarter century. Second, while a debate nominally occurs between equals each trying to convince others that their position is strongest, the setting of a development model comes not only from rational argument, but also through social power and the contest of different social actors (business, unions, students, social movements, interest groups).

This chapter seeks to describe the major features of Quebec's development model since 1960, with particular emphasis on the competing programs to transform it over the last three decades. After a very brief background on Quebec's economy and a discussion of development models, it considers the development model that came out of the Quiet Revolution of the 1960s, the model that continues to serve as the backdrop for contemporary debates. Since the 1980s, the strongest challenge to the model has come from employers' associations, who have advanced a neoliberal model. While this latter model was in part resisted in the 1990s by counterproposals of "progressive competitiveness" and partnership, it gained traction with the election of a Liberal provincial government in 2003, and was not greatly dislodged by the post-2008 financial crisis or the Liberals' loss of power between 2012 and 2014. While the future remains open, it would appear that the actors who had successfully championed alternatives to neoliberalism have been weakened and are now less able to develop imaginative counterproposals for Quebec's development.

Background

There is not space here to give a comprehensive survey of economic and social indicators (although see Table 21.1), but suffice it to say that Quebec boasts a

Table 21.1 Quebec–United States Comparison of Selected Indicators (adjusted, after-tax 2007 figures)

Economic Indicators	Quebec	United States
Poverty rate	9.5% (MBM)*	15.9%
Labour force participation rate	65.2% (04/14)	62.8% (06/14)
Annual hours of work	1,789	1,790
Wages (weekly) average	CDN$843.46 (04/14)	US$843.53 (06/14)
Women's wages as a percentage of men's wages (full-time, full-year workers)	0.77	0.81
Union density		
Total	39.5%	11.3%
Public sector	82.0%	35.3%
Private sector	25.5%	6.7%
Distribution of disposable/aggregate income (by household)		
Lowest quintile	5.7%	3.2%
Second quintile	11.5%	8.5%
Third quintile	16.8%	14.5%
Fourth quintile	24.0%	23.0%
Highest quintile	42.1%	50.9%

* Quebec poverty number is for Market Basket Measure.

Sources: US Bureau of Labor Statistics; Institut de la Statistique Québec, 2011; Statistics Canada, 2008; Survey of Labour and Income Dynamics 2009.

modern and diversified economy. If Quebec were a country, its economy would rank roughly fortieth in size in the world, and its per capita GDP would rank it as the twenty-eighth richest country in the world.

Quebec's economy has traditionally relied on natural resource extraction and primary processing, particularly in forestry and mining. More recently, it has used its significant hydroelectric resources to promote energy-intensive primary metal manufacturing (aluminum and magnesium). These resource-based activities have been grafted onto the more diverse economy of Montreal, which was the major financial hub in British North America and Canada into the mid-twentieth century, as well as the cradle of Canada's industrial revolution in the nineteenth century. The reliance on primary exports has given a boom–bust character to Quebec's economy, while declining manufacturing has contributed to a pattern of lower wages and higher unemployment than the Canadian average. Successes in higher-end manufacturing and financial services have not had sufficient employment effects to erase this disadvantage, although unemployment and poverty have fallen in recent years toward the Canadian average after being structurally higher through most of the 1970s to 1990s.

How one characterizes Quebec's performance is heavily politicized. Some have pointed out that Quebec is falling behind, with its per capita GDP being lower than every state in the United States. Others point out that this reflects the presence of more wealthy individuals in the United States, but that the standard of living of the bottom 50 per cent of Quebec's population is in fact higher than the bottom 50 per cent in the United States, and that a good portion of the overall income gap reflects Quebecers choosing to work fewer hours. From this perspective, Quebecers have a high standard of living. For our purposes, it is enough to note that Quebec has developed an advanced capitalism that is slightly more redistributive and egalitarian than the American variant, and which has delivered relatively high standards of living despite levels of poverty and unemployment that reflect the difficulties of transforming a resource-based economy.[4]

What Are Development Models?

To speak of development models is to argue that capitalism has a geography and a history. While capitalism now spans the globe and disciplines economic activity with the rigours of competition and profit, the manner in which capitalist economies are organized differs across countries and over time. Many things vary, even among the advanced industrial countries, such as labour markets (degree of unionization, extent of regulation of working conditions), financial institutions (type of banking system, design of central bank), taxation (levels and structure), and social provision (size of the welfare state, design of programs). There are many ways to put together a capitalist economy, and this has led to attempts to differentiate national capitalisms and to periodize changes within capitalism (e.g., Keynesianism, neoliberalism).

The distinction between capitalist models is not an abstract academic exercise. Differences in the organization of capitalism have tangible impacts on how people live. They affect who gets what through such things as wage rates, degrees of job stability, ability to take time to care for young children or elderly relatives, access to income when injured or unemployed, and ability to have a voice in the workplace. The definition of development models is therefore bound up in power relations between political actors, each vying to advance forms of economic organization that advance their own interests. And the play of power is complex, as part of it involves convincing others that a given form in fact represents the common interest, or of making partial compromises to bring others to accept a particular form of development.

In a capitalist system, society relies heavily on the owners of large pools of capital (that is, capitalists) for major decisions about investment and production. Where firms invest and how they produce will affect things like the number and quality of jobs or the amount of pollution in a community. Capitalists therefore have great power in shaping development models, since they can invest elsewhere if wage levels or regulations are making them unprofitable. Nevertheless, there is room for negotiation, in part since different capitalists may have different interests,[5] and in part because other interests in society can organize to extract concessions over aspects of the development model or to propose positive-sum compromises.[6] Capitalist societies are not just about capitalism, however. A series of other cultural understandings, for instance about the appropriate roles of men and women, about what forms of sexuality are deemed acceptable, or about who is deemed to be a full citizen or a second-class citizen, are also the subject of ongoing negotiation and struggle and affect the economic and social policies that are adopted.

Development Models in Quebec

The Quiet Revolution[7]

Current debates about Quebec's development model invariably refer back to the economic nationalism and welfare-state building of the Quiet Revolution of the 1960s. In the 1940s and 1950s, a number of sectors of Quebec society, including francophone capitalists, the labour movement, intellectuals, and the middle classes, came to criticize the Quebec government's liberal economic policies on several grounds. First, while the economy grew strongly over the period, this growth was weaker than in neighbouring Ontario and was insufficient to prevent unemployment from increasing. The province's rapid urbanization and industrialization also created social problems because the provincial government hesitated in regulating the labour market or in developing a modern welfare state. Second, control of the economy rested largely in the hands of anglophones, leaving the francophone majority without much say over private investment decisions affecting their society's development. This lack of control was worsening as the concentration of economic activity into larger corporations made it difficult for francophone capitalists, who were most present in smaller-scale economic activities, to get into the game. Third, the pattern of ownership translated into a labour market where francophones were excluded from higher-order management jobs.

This coalition of business, labour, intellectuals, and the middle class managed to replace the Union Nationale government with a Liberal one in the 1960 election. The new administration embarked on an aggressive strategy of state-building to respond to the three concerns discussed above. To respond to the first challenge, the government adopted labour legislation and social policies to bring Quebec into line with those across the industrialized West in those years. It also invested heavily in public infrastructure to maintain high employment levels. To meet the challenge of economic control, it developed a series of investment vehicles and sector-specific state corporations (in forestry, petroleum, aluminum, and so on) to consolidate francophone holdings, upgrade the industrial structure, and create pools of capital to aid francophone capitalists to succeed in mergers and acquisitions. These tools helped to overturn some of the underrepresentation of francophones at the commanding heights of the economy, and the expansion of the state as a whole provided high-quality professional jobs for francophones. However, real incursions into the world of work to overcome the linguistic inequality in the labour market would have to wait until the 1970s with Bill 22 in 1974 and Bill 101 in 1977, and their measures to "francize" the workplace by making French the language of work, with exceptions for head offices, research centres, and small firms.

Already by the early 1970s, this development model was under criticism from various quarters. Quebec nationalists in the Parti Québécois (PQ) felt that the reforms had not gone far enough in transferring economic control to the francophones and in ensuring that foreign investment served national interests. They therefore looked to France's postwar planning institutions and called for greater control over investment and a larger state presence through public enterprises. The labour unions, influenced by the radicalism of the late 1960s, developed socialist critiques of the existing model. These emphasized how the state intervention of the 1960s served the interests of capitalists and strengthened American imperialism rather than leading to balanced economic development that reduced inequalities between the rich and poor and between anglophones and francophones. Meanwhile, community organizations and women's groups criticized the bureaucratic nature of the new welfare state, its failure to adequately address continued poverty and exclusion, as well as its silence on key questions such as violence against women.

Faced with these calls for greater state regulation, as well as an overall uneasiness with the growth of state intervention post-1960, the business community responded by creating its own peak association, the Conseil du patronat du Québec (CPQ). The CPQ proposed a counterstrategy of increased economic liberalism, extolling the contribution of capitalist competition to the spread of mass consumption (such as having a car in every driveway) and dismissing the idea that economic control was largely out of the hands of francophone Quebecers.

Faced with these divergent views, the Liberal government of 1970–6 and the PQ government elected in 1976 largely followed the course of the Quiet Revolution, with the Liberals giving more space to economic liberalism and the PQ implementing more moderate demands of the unions, community organizations, and women's groups in terms of greater union rights and labour market regulations, some recognition of the role of co-operatives and community organizations in regional development, and a modest extension of women's rights. By the time it took office, the PQ no longer wished to emulate France's economic planning, but it did believe that economic competitiveness required government policies to aid firms in acquiring new technologies, undertaking research and development, or developing export markets.

The decision of the US Federal Reserve in 1979 to break inflation by dramatically increasing interest rates, and its effect of creating a hard recession across the Western industrialized countries, was strongly felt in Quebec. Given that Quebec embarked on building its welfare state a decade later than elsewhere, it was left holding a significantly greater debt that would have to be financed at a significantly higher interest rate. This, coupled with significant job losses in the manufacturing sector, depressed state revenues, increased costs, and ultimately produced a budgetary crisis. This allowed the employers' associations to make a plausible case that the interventionist strategy of the Quiet Revolution had run its course. They felt that the public had unrealistic expectations about what sort of public services the state could afford and that an in-depth reworking of the state–economy relationship was required. The CPQ argued that taxes and spending needed to be cut, particularly through aggressive cuts in government programs and through imposing user fees for public services.

On the other hand, the union federations proposed **concertation** ("concerted action") as a way out of the impasse: having the state bring together economic stakeholders to find collective and positive-sum solutions to problems of industrial or regional decline. This was particularly the strategy of the largest union federation, the Fédération des travailleurs et travailleuses du Québec (FTQ). It had moved from its radical discourse of the early 1970s to embrace the Swedish idea of bargaining between employers, unions, and the state to set economic and social policy.

The PQ government wavered between these two options up to its defeat in the 1985 election. On the one hand, it unilaterally reopened public sector contracts to cut wages and strip out benefits and adopted punitive features targeted at young people on social assistance. On the other hand, it experimented with concertation, for instance by creating the Table national de l'emploi. But the overall impression was one of muddling through rather than of bold departures.

New Directions under the Bourassa Liberal Government, 1985–1994

The election of a Liberal government headed by Robert Bourassa in 1985 at first appeared to signal a clear choice. Upon taking office, Bourassa set up working groups, whose recommendations rehearsed the mantras of significantly reducing state expenditures, privatizing most state-owned corporations, and significantly reducing the regulatory burden. While these were perhaps close to his preferences, Bourassa was too cautious to adopt such radical proposals; program cuts would draw the opposition of those who relied on those programs, while early attempts at privatization ran into concerted union campaigns to ensure that unionized jobs were not replaced by nonunionized ones in the process.

Bourassa's government nevertheless set a course of restraining the growth of public expenditure and of reducing state ownership. Faced with a worsening balance sheet in the early 1990s as a result of a North American economic downturn and the Bank of Canada's high interest rate policy, restraint in public spending became more severe. At the same time, the social assistance (or welfare) program was restructured to reduce benefits but increase the number of subsidized work placements in the private and community sectors, a move that drew strong opposition from welfare rights organizations.

This overall shift, which could be described as "neoliberal," nevertheless developed some unusual trappings at the turn of the 1990s.[8] Across fields, the government experimented with new forms of partnership and concerted action. Recognizing that market mechanisms alone could not be counted on to ensure a smooth restructuring of the Quebec economy, the government launched a cluster strategy and a provincial training board (the Société québécoise de développement de la main d'oeuvre—SQDM). The cluster strategy adopted the premise that firms working in similar industries might increase their competitiveness from sharing information or developing partnerships to overcome common problems (training, research and development, relationships between firms and suppliers, and so on). Thus, the government created roundtables of key firms in various industrial sectors. The idea behind the training boards was that employers and employees shared an interest in creating a skilled labour force, and giving employers and unions responsibility for governing training initiatives would lead to better training and force these "social partners" to overcome their differences.

The impetus for supporting partnerships is difficult to pin down. Partly it reflected bureaucratic learning about industrial strategies being used elsewhere and their applicability to smooth economic adjustment in Quebec. They could also build on certain partnership initiatives outside of the state, such as union–business–community alliances in the Partenaires pour l'emploi (Partners for Jobs), an attempt to bring stakeholders together to fight unemployment. Finally, the failure of the Meech Lake constitutional amendment in 1990, and the resurgence of Quebec nationalism that followed from this, forced the Bourassa government to develop a broader national consensus to maintain legitimacy in its ongoing negotiations with the federal government. This too favoured initiatives that married a commitment to economic liberalism with the development of social partnerships.

These programs certainly reached out to the union federations, who were proposing stronger union–management partnerships as part of a program of "progressive competitiveness." In their view, Quebec could continue to be competitive in industries that paid high wages and offered good working conditions provided that employers were required to work in partnership with unions, both at the level of the plant and at the level of industry sectors. These partnerships would pay off, because they would allow firms and workers to identify positive-sum compromises to increase productivity while maintaining employment levels in well-paid jobs. Similar positive-sum compromises were envisioned in other areas, such as community development efforts in impoverished neighbourhoods.

The government's experiments with partnerships went beyond the economic realm to influence social policy. This reflected the strength of the women's movement and community organizations. These groups recognized that the Bourassa government wished to save money by cutting health and social services and by downloading responsibility for social programs onto community organizations. But rather than simply opposing this move, they applauded the idea of removing bureaucracy to empower service users and better respond to their needs. However, they argued that for community organizations to play an empowerment role, they needed stable, recurrent funding to enable service users and providers to identify priorities and innovative solutions. They also argued that the community sector and women's organizations needed formal representation in decision-making structures so that they would be true partners in the governance of health and social services, rather than simply subcontractors.

The Parti Québécois in Power 1994–2003: The Referendum and After[9]

The election of a PQ government in 1994 opened the possibility of a further shift from economic liberalism. Having promised a referendum on sovereignty within a year of taking office, the PQ had an interest in assembling as broad a coalition as possible to ensure the sovereignty option won. This meant presenting a vision of an independent Quebec that was highly inclusive. This was a tricky game for the PQ, since they also needed to reassure the business community that its position would be protected in an independent Quebec and that trade and investment liberalization agreements with the United States (such as the North American Free Trade Agreement) would continue to apply. It managed to square the circle, at least for the referendum campaign, by drawing on the unions' progressive competitiveness—making the case that national economic competitiveness under globalization required the nation to mobilize all of its resources, thereby necessitating both a labour-business partnership and compensatory measures to ensure no one was left behind.

Following the loss of the 1995 referendum, the PQ government was forced to regroup and develop solutions to the persistent double-digit unemployment rate and large budget deficits. The business community made it clear that it would not invest in Quebec, given the unresolved nature of Quebec's national status, unless the deficit was tamed through spending cuts. A straightforward strategy of making deep cuts to government programs was not open to the PQ as it would impose too many costs on its political base (unions, community organizations, women's groups). Instead, it convened a summit of economic stakeholders in an attempt to tackle the twin problems of unemployment and deficit spending (see the Case Study box).

CASE STUDY

The 1996 Social and Economic Summits

In calling major social actors together for an economic summit in March 1996, the Quebec government was hardly modest in its ambitions: "The pact at the base of our society is broken: we must reinvent it." Faced with recurrent budget deficits and high rates of unemployment and poverty, the government called on social partners to develop new solutions. These reached beyond the employers and unions to include representatives of student, women's, and community organizations. The summits were called in part in response to union demands for concerted action, but the participation of business came with a bottom line: namely, balancing the budget in two years without increasing taxes. The union federations were not particularly opposed to this approach, although they wanted meaningful job-creation commitments from the government and the private sector. Their modest bargaining position reflected the sense that many of their members favoured reducing the deficit. In addition, the summits represented an example of the social partnership that they wished to see repeated, so the very fact of holding one was a victory.

The process of balancing demands was nevertheless more tricky than simply bringing the employers and unions to agreement, as the women's and community groups had their own demands. The women's movement had held a widely covered Bread and Roses March against violence and poverty in 1995. The march built on several years of organizing and popular education around a different model of development. Rather than leaving development to the private decisions

continued

of capitalists, as in the business associations' view, or of emphasizing partnerships enabling Quebec firms to compete without downgrading wages and working conditions, as in the unions' plan, the march proposed development on the basis of meeting the basic needs of all Quebecers. The march's first demand was to create and solidify "social infrastructures" that created jobs and met needs. The idea was to take women's often precarious, unpaid, or underpaid work in community organizations and to properly recognize it by providing stable funding to the organizations. Since many community organizations relied on social assistance recipients and on subsidized work placements to keep their programs running, there was an existing funding stream that could be converted into support for permanent and sustainable work. Alongside the social infrastructures, the march also emphasized anti-poverty strategies, including higher minimum wages and the stronger enforcement of minimum labour standards.

The women's movement's call for social infrastructures is often confused with a parallel call for investment in the **social economy** (economic ventures that prioritize social goals over profit) that came from other parts of the community sector. Partisans of the social economy argued that both economic and social development could be advanced by experimenting with new forms of not-for-profit organization that mixed social goals with market activity. An example would be a community restaurant in a poor neighbourhood serving inexpensive meals. The restaurant could simultaneously provide people in poverty with access to food and sociability; provide food preparation and service training to the unemployed; and create a small number of jobs for the managers of the enterprise. In addition, such enterprises could democratize their activity by providing worker and user input through a community board of directors and participatory forms of management.

The summit in March 1996 gave rise to an agreement on deficit reduction, albeit on a four-year timeline rather than the proposed two years. It also set up working groups to explore avenues of job creation, which were to report back to the October summit. One of these groups was on the social economy and provided an opportunity for more entrepreneurial parts of the community sector to advance a series of community economic development projects, although in the process the program of social infrastructures proposed by the women's movement was marginalized.

The October summit was less harmonious. The unions and employers were again ready to pay tribute to joint action, and parts of the community sector were overjoyed with the prominence given to the social economy as an example of how to bring different social actors together around job creation. Women's and anti-poverty groups nevertheless felt that their concerns were ignored and made a show of leaving the table before the summit ended. This dissent was somewhat deflected by an agreement at the summit to set up a $250 million anti-poverty fund to support community initiatives to help the jobless find work. The veneer of consensus hid the fact that the plan for job creation was long on good intentions but short on firm commitments. This meant that eliminating the deficit would ultimately rely on program cuts rather than on increased tax revenue from the newly employed. Since that logic led to the downsizing of the public sector workforce, the union leadership came under strong criticism from their members.

The 1996 summits therefore can be seen in two different ways. In one reading, they confirm Quebec's exceptionalism (at least in North America) in that difficult economic decisions about public finances and employment were made by consensus between social actors. In the process, actors discovered new approaches to social and economic development, such as those represented by the social economy. As part of the behind-the-scenes negotiations, Quebec's family policy, including universal low-cost childcare, an enriched child tax credit, and improved parental leaves, was also given the green light. In another reading, however, the summits represent the conversion of the Parti Québécois to a neoliberal platform of cuts to state programs and regulations, and highlight its ability to co-opt the unions and other social democratic actors by appealing to their nationalism with the argument that getting state finances in order will ensure a winning referendum. In this second reading, the summits were a first step in breaking links between the PQ and social democratic actors, preparing the way for the former's loss in the 2003 elections and the schism in the nationalist movement between the PQ and Québec solidaire.

The 1996 summits set the tone for the remainder of the PQ's term in office. It was attentive to the business community, yet invested strategically in the social economy and progressive competitiveness. This mix of supporting business while experimenting with partnerships and social innovation was marketed by the PQ as "the Quebec model," but it remained a difficult political sell. While the PQ was attentive to business demands, the employers' federations preferred the Liberals. And while the PQ argued that Quebec had a more progressive model than the neoliberal one found elsewhere in Canada or the United States, an increasing number of activists in the unions and in women's and community movements found the government closed to their demands when they might offend the business community. For example, many feminists lost faith in the PQ when the latter responded to a demand for higher minimum wages with a paltry hike of 10 cents an hour.

In its later years in office, the PQ increasingly looked to European debates about the knowledge-based economy to navigate this tension. This involved pairing market liberalization through reduced regulation and rates of taxation with social policies favouring social cohesion. The latter included an anti-poverty law binding current and future governments to develop poverty-reduction plans, but also enriched child benefits, core funding for community-based advocacy organizations, and continued support for experiments with social entrepreneurship. In the process, there was less use of concertation, and indeed the PQ wound down the SQDM in favour of a less powerful roundtable of economic partners. The government also revamped the regional health boards, reducing the seats available to the community and women's movements. For the most part, the PQ did not roll back these bodies, but neither did it move them forward, causing the project of concertation to lose steam.

The Charest Liberals and the Attack on "Corporatism"[10]

Although the PQ government eliminated the deficit, cut taxes and regulation, and started to experiment with public–private partnerships in delivering state services, it was not embraced by business interests. The employers' federations were unhappy that the government did not use all of its fiscal room to cut taxes, but also spent on initiatives like a universal low-cost childcare program, and that it reformed the labour code to protect a larger number of workers. This impatience led them to undertake new initiatives, including creating a free market think tank, the Montreal Economic Institute, to foster public acceptance of market solutions to public problems, and flirting with the Action démocratique du Québec (ADQ) party, which was offering a far more neoliberal platform of policy reform than the usual party of business, the Quebec Liberal Party.

The Liberals nevertheless won a majority in the 2003 provincial election, positioning themselves as more moderate than the ADQ yet fresher than a tired PQ government worn down by a decade in power. Once elected, the Liberals introduced neoliberal reforms that challenged the ethos of social consensus that stretched back to the later Bourassa period, and in some ways back to the Quiet Revolution. These included diminishing stakeholder involvement in a series of institutions of concertation such as local and regional health boards and local development boards. This was premised on the idea that concertation did not promote positive-sum compromises, but instead created a "corporatism" that prevented necessary changes by allowing groups to protect their narrow self-interests. The government also changed a key section of labour legislation to make it easier for firms to get rid of existing unions in cases where work was subcontracted, and it unilaterally rearranged union representation in the health sector. The Liberals also tried to roll back the highly popular \$5 per day daycare program by proposing measures to significantly increase the daily rate for those with higher incomes. This was beaten back by a wave of protests (although the daily rate did increase to \$7), but the government allowed the private sector to increase its share of the daycare market relative to not-for-profit providers. Another controversial aspect of the government's agenda was to engage in public–private partnerships to deliver public services, despite concerns about their cost effectiveness.

These initiatives provoked large-scale mobilizations led by the labour movement, as well as a student strike (over cuts in student loans and bursaries) that shut down parts of several universities in February and March 2005. These mobilizations damaged the government's popularity and indicated that the appetite for a large-scale replacement of existing institutions with neoliberal ones was limited. The government thereafter decided to pursue a less radical course of reform, premised on incremental changes, such as increasing the role of the private sector in the management of public infrastructure via public–private partnerships, and slowly opening the door to for-profit providers of medical services. The language about uprooting the corporatist interests inhibiting change largely disappeared. Re-elected as a minority government in 2007 and as a majority in 2008, the Liberal government continued to slowly advance neoliberal reform. While the 2008 recession pushed the government to embrace deficit spending (albeit modestly, compared to neighbouring jurisdictions), the need to return to a balanced budget has provided the pretext for public sector austerity. This time around, the emphasis is on both limiting the growth of public spending and increasing user fees for public services.

Unions and other social movements organized in 2010 to oppose such fees (like higher electricity prices and a health tax), and this fed into the 2012 student strike in opposition to increased tuition fees. The student strike polarized Quebec society, and when the Liberal government was replaced by a PQ minority government in the fall of 2012, it was felt that there might be a change of course. The PQ had spoken in favour of a tuition freeze and had campaigned on environmental issues. While the PQ showed some social democratic signs in increasing the number of daycare spaces, raising the minimum wage, and reducing the health tax and electricity increases, it did backtrack on tuition (indexing fees to the cost of living in 2013) and stepped back from environmental commitments when they conflicted with natural resource development megaprojects. The general emphasis on budgetary austerity persisted and has been extended by the Liberal majority government elected in April 2014.

While the union federations and various social movements (women and students) were relatively successful in slowing the Liberal Party's reform agenda since 2003, they have proven relatively weak in either reversing it or proposing an alternative. Those on the political left who had been dissatisfied with the PQ government crystallized into a new political party, Québec solidaire (QS). While Québec solidaire has been the most successful left-wing alternative yet to the PQ, it drew fewer than 4 per cent of the votes in the 2007 and 2008 elections, electing its first member, Amir Khadir, in 2008. In 2012 it added a second member, and in the 2014 election, with 7.6 per cent of the votes, it elected a third. The originality and creativity that marked the alternative development strategies in the 1990s (progressive competitiveness, partnership, social infrastructures, and a social economy) were also largely absent from both the PQ and QS platforms. Neither party promised much to rebuild concertation, nor did they emphasize community action or the social economy.

This loss of creativity results from the demobilization of the labour and women's movements. Twenty years have passed since the crafting of progressive competitiveness strategies, but the union movement has not updated them or replaced them with a new approach. As a result, it remains on the defensive, trying to wring concessions from the government of the day or gains from concertation in the partnership forums in which it has a seat. In protecting past gains, the union movement comes to be seen, unfairly, as aiding "insiders" at the expense of helping "outsiders" who never benefited from the pay and protection of a unionized job. The unions' image problem has been compounded by corruption scandals in the construction industry, which included ties with high-ranking FTQ officials.

For the women's movement, which does not have a base of dues payers like the unions and which

BIOGRAPHY

Françoise David

Françoise David is a fascinating figure in a discussion of Quebec's development, as the public associates her with a feminist and social democratic vision of Quebec's future. Through her trajectory, we see both how the women's and community movements have shaped development, and how they are currently at a political impasse.[11]

Québec solidaire co-leader Françoise David takes part in an anti-poverty protest in front of the Congress Centre in Quebec City on 15 June 2009.

Francis Vachon/TCPI/The Canadian Press

David was born in 1948 into an upper-middle-class family. She enjoyed a privileged childhood, but grew up with a sense of responsibility for those less fortunate. This desire to help others led to the decision to study social work and community organizing at university during the late 1960s, a time when there was a radicalization of the community sector that was innovating in developing new services such as community health or childcare clinics that were not being offered by the public sector. As these services matured, the community sector and the state entered into tense negotiations over their funding and governance—the state wanting to bring them into the public sector and community organizations wishing to preserve their more responsive and democratic character while receiving state support.

David's experience of this period is somewhat singular, as she belonged to the Marxist-Leninist group En Lutte ("In Struggle") until its implosion in 1982. Like other Maoist parties of the time, it demanded intense loyalty to the organization and its line of analysis, as well as the dedication of several hours a day (above and beyond full-time work) to popular education, outreach, and recruitment. When the group imploded, many members disappeared for several years into wrenching self-questioning: How did their search for social justice lead to blind commitment to an anti-democratic and hierarchical organization? This was the case for David, who faced the additional challenges of a marital breakdown and caring for a young child.

She emerged from this period of introspection in 1987 to become coordinator of L'R des centres de femmes du Québec, the provincial network of women's centres. Women's centres vary from place to place depending on the priorities of local women, but offer a mix of support services, education, and collective action (demonstrating, lobbying, participating in governance structures, and so on). They tend to work with poor and isolated women and thus focus on poverty and violence. L'R brought together 53 of these centres at its founding in 1985 (its membership now surpasses 100) to strengthen the centres in negotiating with the state (by speaking with a common voice and sharing strategies between localities) and to allow them to pool resources by acting as a clearinghouse for expertise and education.

In the late 1980s and early 1990s, L'R broadened the Quebec women's movement's thinking, pushing the idea that women's centres were not just about meeting *social* needs but also about *economic* activity. The centres employed people, produced goods and services (such as meals in a collective kitchen or the repair of damaged clothes for resale), and provided support and training for those in crisis, enabling them to return to employment more quickly or with better skills.

continued

In 1992, David became a vice-president of the Fédération des femmes du Québec (FFQ), the umbrella organization of women's organizations, which was at a low point as many women's organizations felt it did little for them. The FFQ nevertheless renewed itself at its 1993 convention by positioning itself as the voice of women who were poor, excluded, or faced discrimination, and in 1994 the organization elected David as president. She oversaw the organization of the Bread and Roses March against violence and poverty in the summer of 1995, which imported much of L'R's thinking about the economic contributions of meeting social needs, particularly in its headline demand to invest in "social infrastructures" that aimed to meet the needs of people in poverty by addressing unpaid or underpaid work.

The march was a high point for the FFQ's program, but its voice became increasingly marginal given demands for cutting state spending and lowering taxes. David continued to lead the FFQ until 2001; under her leadership it organized the World March of Women in 2000. On the one hand, this march was a success, allowing the Quebec women's movement to work with women from around the world and to bring out over 40,000 people for its local march. On the other hand, the march demonstrated the near-complete closure of the PQ government to the FFQ's demands. Many feminist activists grew disillusioned with the PQ government to the point of looking for a political alternative, but there were also tensions within the FFQ: Women across the province had burned themselves out to organize the 2000 march, and for what?

Upon leaving the FFQ, David nevertheless continued to advocate for development to fight poverty and briefly headed the group Au bas de l'échelle, which was pressuring the state to protect vulnerable workers by improving labour standards. Here she had more success than with the World March, with the PQ government agreeing to extend the application of standards to more workers and to improve standards to remedy a number of abuses.

Nevertheless, her disappointment with the PQ led her to explore the creation of a left-wing alternative to it, starting with the publication of a personal manifesto,[12] followed by the creation of the Option Citoyenne (Citizen's Option) and its merger with another left-wing party to form Québec solidaire, of which she is co-spokesperson. In this role she participated in the televised leaders' debates during the 2012 and 2014 elections. This party has proven more responsive than the PQ to the demands of the women's and community movements, but has had limited electoral success, although David was elected in the riding of Gouin in 2012 and re-elected in 2014. It remains to be seen whether building an alternative to the PQ strengthens the place of feminist and social democratic ideas in Quebec, or whether it weakens the incentive of the PQ to respond to them.

has a harder time maintaining its autonomy from the state given its reliance on government money, the task of maintaining mobilization has been challenging. After the success of the 1995 march and the central role in organizing the inaugural World March of Women in 2000, there has been some burnout as well as internal disagreements over strategy (Was the 2000 march worth the effort expended?) and program (Does the focus on women's poverty address the needs of middle-class women? Does it disempower women in poverty by portraying them as victims?). The movement continues to place poverty and violence at the centre of their demands on the state and is particularly concerned with the uneven impact of austerity on women, both as users of public services and as public employees. As with the unions, this remains more reactive than proactive. In this context, the slow but steady progress of economic liberalism, started under Bourassa, has continued under subsequent PQ and Liberal governments. It faces constant opposition, but no well-organized and well-articulated counterpropositions.

Conclusion

As this chapter has demonstrated, however, the future remains open. Over time, social actors change their strategies about how to achieve development, and their relative influence waxes and wanes. Quebec adopted a particular set of institutions in the 1960s, and these have been reworked over time. Sometimes this reform has followed the liberal blueprint of reducing state social provision and strengthening state protection of private property rights. Other times this reform has had a more social democratic cast in fostering the participation of a wider set of interests through concertation or in supporting social provision via social infrastructures and the social economy. Organized interests have been crucial players in generating and publicizing ideas for reform, but elections have also been significant as switching points for choosing some ideas over others. The push and pull of conflict in setting the development model has created a Quebec model that is distinct in North America in its adoption of stakeholder partnerships and community development (although this distinction is eroding with time) as well as its lower rates of inequality, but that remains distinctively North American from a European perspective in its economic liberalism.

Quebecers have important choices to make in the coming years. It would be presumptuous and arrogant to claim that there is only one path to choose. Quebec could follow the North American path in adopting a market liberalism that allows the decisions of capitalists, responding to the whip of market competition, to set the course for competitiveness and relies on individuals to look after their own welfare. Or it could supplement private decision making with economic policies favouring a wider participation of stakeholders, empowering community-based development, and expanding public policies that enable people to adapt by protecting them against emerging social risks. Academics can certainly debate the trade-offs involved in any model, but ultimately it will be the Quebec people who will decide through the demands and negotiations of their collective actors (employers' associations, unions, community groups, social movements, and so on) and through the ballot box.

Questions for Critical Thinking

1. This chapter portrays social and economic development in Quebec as a debate between social democracy and liberalism, but claims that similar debates are common to most societies. How does the debate in Quebec, both in its evolution over time and in its current form, compare to the debate in your society?
2. The development plans of various social actors (women's movement, labour movement, employers' associations) were discussed in this chapter. How do these plans differ or overlap? What are their respective primary goals? Are there collective actors holding similar ideas in your society?
3. Looking across the half-century covered in this chapter, how important were elections and political parties in setting the Quebec development model, and how important was social pressure brought to bear by collective actors such as employers' associations, the women's movement, and unions?

Notes

1. Eric Pineault, "Quebec's Red Spring: An Essay on Ideology and Social Conflict at the End of Neoliberalism," *Studies in Political Economy* 90 (2012): 29–56.
2. Coalition large de l'Association pour une solidarité syndicale étudiante, *Share Our Future: The CLASSE Manifesto*. Available at www.stopthehike.ca/2012/07/share-our-future-the-classe-manifesto.
3. *Economic liberalism* refers here to a policy of leaving economic decision making to individual property owners and limiting state intervention to the protection of property rights and the enforcement of contracts. This can be confusing for American audiences, where the use of *liberalism* is often used in the opposite sense of state interventions to counter market inequality. Where economic liberalism is most concerned with the freedom of individuals to enjoy their property, social democrats are more concerned with creating a basis of equality so that all citizens can effectively enjoy their rights and fulfill

their duties, and in extending the realm of decisions over which citizens exercise democratic choice.

4. See Pierre Paquette, "Relever les vrais défis," in *Agir maintenant pour le Québec de demain,* ed. Luc Godbout (Lévis: Presses de l'Université Laval, 2006), 49–66; and Alain Noël, "Quebec's New Politics of Redistribution," in *Inequality and the Fading of Redistributive Politics,* ed. Keith Banting and John Myles (Vancouver: UBC Press, 2013), 256–82.
5. Low-wage employers are more concerned about the minimum wage than high-wage ones. Firms who rely solely on the domestic market will be less in favour of free trade than firms who are large exporters. The insurance industry will be less opposed to anti-pollution measures than the automotive and oil and gas industries.
6. For instance, workers may agree to actively help increase productivity on the assembly line in return for better wages.
7. This section draws on Kenneth McRoberts, *Quebec: Social Change and Political Crisis,* 3rd ed. (Toronto: McClelland & Stewart, 1988); William D. Coleman, *The Independence Movement in Quebec, 1945–1980* (Toronto: University of Toronto Press, 1984); and Alain-G. Gagnon and Mary Beth Montcalm, *Quebec: Beyond the Quiet Revolution* (Toronto: Nelson, 1990).
8. See Dorval Brunelle and Benoît Lévesque, "Free Trade and Quebec Models of Development," in *Whose Canada? Continental Integration, Fortress North America and the Corporate Agenda,* ed. Ricardo Grinspun and Yasmine Shamsie (Montreal and Kingston: McGill-Queen's University Press, 2007), 391–406.
9. For a fuller treatment, see Daniel Salée, "Transformative Politics, the State, and the Politics of Social Change in Quebec," in *Changing Canada: Political Economy as Transformation,* ed. Wallace Clement and Leah Vosko (Montreal and Kingston: McGill-Queen's University Press, 2003), 25–50; and Peter Graefe, "The Dynamics of the Parti Québécois in Power: Social Democracy and Competitive Nationalism," in *Challenges and Perils: Social Democracy in Neoliberal Times,* ed. William K. Carroll and R. S. Ratner (Halifax: Fernwood, 2005), 46–66.
10. For fuller treatments, see Jane Jenson, "Rolling Out or Back Tracking on Quebec's Child Care System? Ideology Matters," in *Public Policy for Women,* ed. Marjorie Griffin Cohen and Jane Pulkingham (Toronto: University of Toronto Press, 2009), 50–70; Rachel Laforest, "The Politics of State/Civil Society Relations in Quebec," in *Quebec and Canada in the New Century,* ed. Michael Murphy (Kingston: Institute of Intergovernmental Relations, 2005), 177–98; and Christian Rouillard, Éric Montpetit, Isabelle Fortier, and Alain-G. Gagnon, *Reengineering the State: Toward an Impoverishment of Quebec Governance* (Ottawa: University of Ottawa Press, 2006).
11. See also Françoise David, "Life of Solidarity: Reflections on a Life in Politics," *Canadian Dimension* 41, no. 2 (2007): 31–7.
12. See Françoise David, *Bien commun recherche : une option citoyenne* (Montreal: Écosociété, 2004).

Select Bibliography

Brunelle, Dorval, and Benoît Lévesque. "Free Trade and Quebec Models of Development." In *Whose Canada? Continental Integration, Fortress North America and the Corporate Agenda,* edited by Ricardo Grinspun and Yasmine Shamsie, 391–406. Montreal and Kingston: McGill-Queen's University Press, 2007.

Coleman, William D. *The Independence Movement in Quebec, 1945–1980.* Toronto: University of Toronto Press, 1984.

David, Françoise. *Bien commun recherché : une option citoyenne.* Montreal: Écosocieté, 2004.

———. "Life of Solidarity: Reflections on a Life in Politics." *Canadian Dimension* 41, no. 2 (2007): 31–7.

Gagnon, Alain-G., and Mary Beth Montcalm. *Quebec: Beyond the Quiet Revolution.* Toronto: Nelson, 1990.

Graefe, Peter. "Quebec Nationalism and Quebec Politics from Left to Right." In *Transforming Provincial Politics,* edited by Bryan Evans and Charles Smith. Toronto: University of Toronto Press, 2015.

———. "Whither the Quebec Model? Boom, Bust and Quebec Labour." In *Boom, Bust and Crisis,* edited by John Peters, 125–41. Halifax: Fernwood, 2012.

Jenson, Jane. "Rolling Out or Back Tracking on Quebec's Child Care System? Ideology Matters." In *Public Policy for Women,* edited by Marjorie Griffin Cohen and Jane Pulkingham, 50–70. Toronto: University of Toronto Press, 2009.

Laforest, Rachel. "The Politics of State/Civil Society Relations in Quebec." In *Quebec and Canada in the New Century,* edited by Michael Murphy, 177–98. Kingston: Institute of Intergovernmental Relations, 2005.

McRoberts, Kenneth. *Quebec: Social Change and Political Crisis,* 3rd ed. Toronto: McClelland & Stewart, 1988.

Noël, Alain. "Quebec's New Politics of Redistribution." In *Inequality and the Fading of Redistributive Politics,* edited by Keith Banting and John Myles, 256–82. Vancouver: UBC Press, 2013.

Rouillard, Christian, Éric Montpetit, Isabelle Fortier, and Alain-G. Gagnon. *Reengineering the State: Toward an Impoverishment of Quebec Governance.* Ottawa: University of Ottawa Press, 2006.

Salée, Daniel. "Transformative Politics, the State, and the Politics of Social Change in Quebec." In *Changing Canada: Political Economy as Transformation,* edited by Wallace Clement and Leah Vosko, 25–50. Montreal and Kingston: McGill-Queen's University Press, 2003.

22 A Question of Power: A Brief History of Hydroelectricity in Quebec

David Massell, University of Vermont

Timeline

1895 Entrepreneurs harness the waterpower of Niagara Falls, New York, inaugurating an era of large-scale hydroelectric energy development in North America.

1898 Quebec enters the age of hydroelectricity when Shawinigan Water and Power Corporation launches construction of a dam at Shawinigan Falls on Saint-Maurice River.

1910 With the organization of Hydraulic Service, the government of Quebec definitively abandons outright sales of waterpower in favour of leases and royalty taxes, and thus begins serious regulatory efforts in the hydro sector.

1934 Under intense political pressure to better regulate the "electrical trust," Liberal administration of Louis-Alexandre Taschereau agrees to the formation of an Electricity Commission to study province-wide nationalization.

1944 Government of Quebec under Liberal Adélard Godbout expropriates assets of Montreal Light, Heat and Power Consolidated, which become the property of the newly formed Quebec Hydro-Electric Commission, or "Hydro-Québec."

1960 Jean Lesage's Liberal Party defeats the Union Nationale and advances reforms of the Quiet Revolution.

1962 Just two years into his mandate, Lesage calls a snap election on full-scale nationalization of the remaining private electric utilities. Under the campaign slogan of "*Maîtres chez nous,*" the Liberals are victorious.

1963 On 1 May, Hydro-Québec takes possession of Quebec's remaining private electrical utilities at a cost of some $600 million.

1969 "Manic-5" is completed, a multiple-arched dam on Manicouagan River that stirs pride and joy in French Quebecers.

1971 Liberal Premier Robert Bourassa launches the "project of the century," the James Bay Hydroelectric Project.

1975 By the James Bay and Northern Quebec Agreement (JBNQA), Quebec's Cree and Inuit attempt to settle traditional land claims covering two-thirds of the province of Quebec while allowing construction of the James Bay Project to proceed.

2002 Cree Grand Chief Ted Moses and Parti Québécois Premier Bernard Landry sign La Paix des Braves, which resolves Cree court litigation over the JBNQA and permits the development of Rupert and Eastmain rivers, while assuring joint Cree–Quebec management and shared profits from mining, forestry, and hydroelectricity on traditional Cree territory.

Introduction

Turbines and transmission lines, volts and kilovolts, kilowatts and megawatts. These are but some of the technical terms used to describe and measure the production and flow of electrical energy—from distant waterfall to home refrigerator, air conditioner, or personal computer. And such technical terms speak correctly to the fact that the history of **hydroelectricity** is, to some extent, a story of science and technology applied to the natural world, ever since Thomas Edison patented a practical incandescent light bulb in 1880 and industrialists pioneered large-scale electrical generation at Niagara Falls in the following decade. Still, technophobes may relax and humanists rejoice. For the central term in our chronology is neither tailrace nor kilowatt-hour—it is simply *power.* One needn't master the difference between volts and watts to grasp the human history of electricity in Quebec. *Power* means more than energy; it denotes a source of authority and strength and the capacity to act. In French, the noun *pouvoir* doubles as the crucial verb "to be able." In English, similarly, the term connotes not only a means of supplying energy, but also, to quote *Webster's New Collegiate Dictionary,* "possession of control, authority, or influence over others . . . physical might . . . political control or influence."[1]

The story of power in Quebec is not merely one of technological achievement, but of a century's power struggle over the most crucial and contested of Quebec's natural resources. At the dawn of the hydro age, English speakers, especially Americans, dominated this industry in their scramble for hydro sites and corporate profits on the northern resource frontier. By the middle of the twentieth century, French Canadians contested Anglo control of hydroelectric energy production, both as a practical means of meeting rising consumer demand for electricity at reasonable rates and as a proud symbol of surging francophone influence, instrumental (as René Lévesque put it) in "the economic re-conquest of Quebec." As the century turned, Aboriginal people—Crees, Inuit, and Innu—had themselves challenged the status quo.

The Importance of Hydroelectricity to Quebec

That our focus should be *hydro*electricity (power generated by falling water, as opposed to oil-fired or coal-fired thermal energy or nuclear energy) is due to the geographic makeup of Quebec. Ninety percent of the province's territory is the rocky, granitic Canadian Shield. As historians Albert Faucher and Maurice Lamontagne point out, this terrain made Quebec a coal-starved province, whose late nineteenth-century industrial development was long hampered by (among other things) the lack of this essential fossil fuel of the Industrial Revolution.[2] Through the 1920s, industry lagged behind neighbouring Ontario, and Quebec's populace outside Montreal remained largely rural and poor, tempted to migrate southward to the burgeoning mill towns of New England.

Meanwhile, the province's abundant falling waters, or "white coal," made hydroelectricity Quebec's major energy substitute and industrial saving grace. Humans had long used waterpower to mill grain into flour or saw wood into boards with water wheels and pulleys. As hydro*electric* technology emerged in the 1890s—dams, powerhouses, transmission lines—and was demonstrated at Niagara Falls (deemed "the great modern experiment in hydroelectric engineering"),[3] it promised to correct this provincial imbalance, bolster urban industry, and slow the hemorrhage of French Canadians to the United States. A full 12 per cent of Quebec's surface area is water, and the province holds 3 per cent of the planet's fresh water reserves. Moreover, many of Quebec's best, high-volume waterpower sites are situated along the southern fall line of the Canadian Shield (along the Ottawa, Saint-Maurice, and Saguenay rivers, as well as the St Lawrence River itself) within transmission distance of the fertile and populous St Lawrence Valley as well as New England and Ontario markets. This lends a natural advantage to the development of this resource. The Canadian Shield also offers natural storage of water in its myriad lakes (which regulates

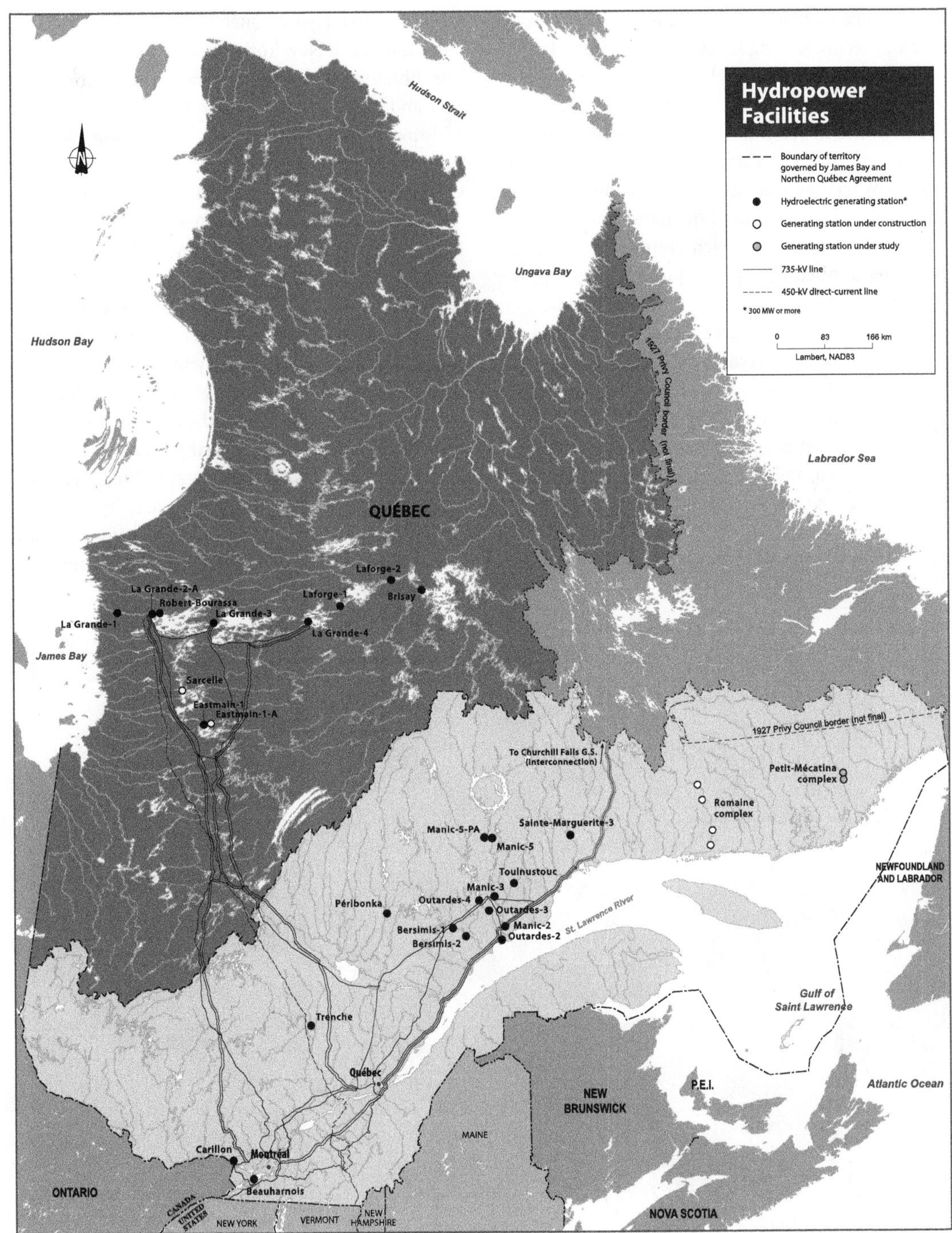

Figure 22.1 Map of Quebec and surrounding regions.

Source: Hydro-Québec

the flow of a river across the seasons) as well as excellent and secure footing for the construction of dams.

Quebec's hydro-rich landscape has proved an extraordinary gift to the province. By the end of the 1920s, Quebec was already the leading hydroelectric producer in Canada, ahead of Ontario; by mid-century, Quebec accounted for over one-half the hydroelectric output of the nation (itself among the world's most hydro-rich countries) and could be safely dubbed by Hydro-Québec as "the power province": "the world's most richly endowed region in hydro-electric resources."[4] By 2015, Quebec's Crown corporation Hydro-Québec, with assets of some $75 billion and 20,000 employees, can claim the honour of being Canada's largest electric utility, bearing the most extensive transmission network in North America, and being among the planet's largest producers of hydroelectric power. With the capacity to generate over 36,000 megawatts (a megawatt is one million watts; a light bulb burns in a range of 40–100 watts), Hydro-Québec can serve nearly four cities the size of New York, or six the size of Toronto. The Romaine River project, now under construction and slated for completion by 2020, will add an additional 1,500 megawatts of production capacity. Producing far more energy than its population can use, Quebec has been able to export power for significant profit since the 1970s to consumers in New York, New England, Ontario, and New Brunswick (some 20 per cent of Quebec's power is exported). Large quantities of inexpensive hydro power have also allowed Quebec to manufacture the power-intensive metals aluminum and magnesium for export. Hydroelectricity constitutes some 96 per cent of the electricity produced in Quebec (in the United States the figure is 7 per cent); 2 per cent is derived from nuclear power and 2 per cent from thermal plants and wind power (the latter likely to grow in importance in coming years). Thus electrical development and hydroelectric development are practically synonymous in the province. In sum, the

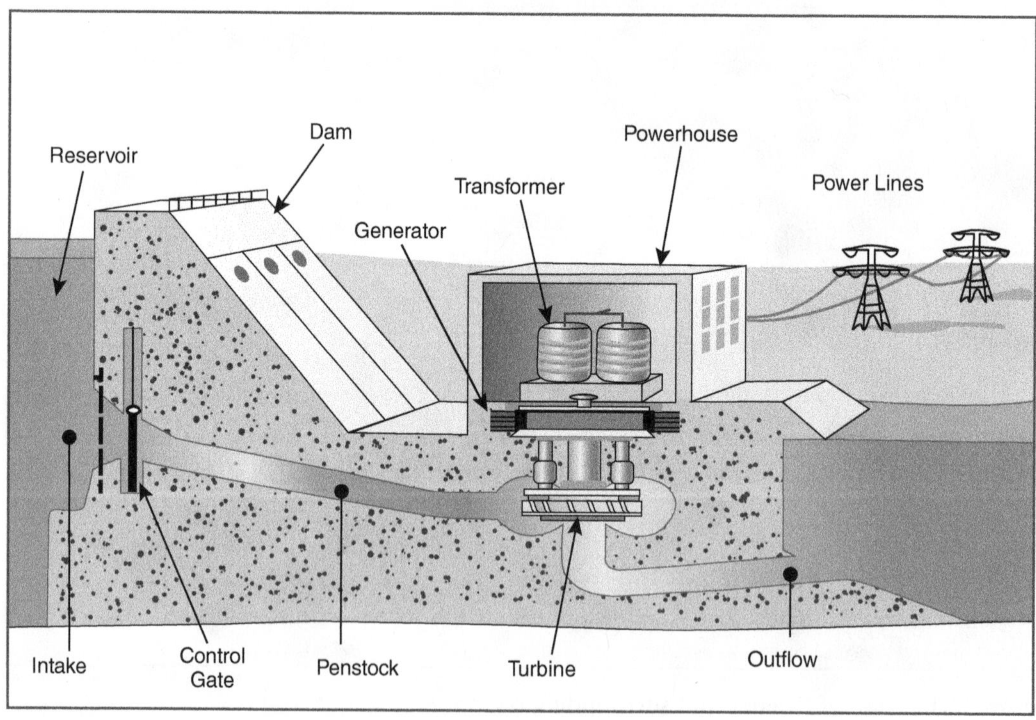

Figure 22.2 Inside a hydropower plant.

"generosity of Nature," according to Laval University economist Jean-Thomas Bernard, has produced in Quebec a set of circumstances "unique in the world." The result, as Hydro-Québec's former president and CEO Thierry Vandal has put it, is that Quebec is "the land of large dams."[5]

Anglo Dominance of the Hydro Sector

That hydroelectric production was dominated early on by an English-speaking elite should not surprise students of Quebec history. This was a province of Canada whose majority French-speaking populace owned and controlled but a small fraction of its factories, wealth, and resources well into the twentieth century. In the hydro sector, moreover, such were the fixed or overhead costs of dams, power stations, and transmission lines that Canada's anglophone bourgeoisie was itself largely displaced by wealthier American capitalists who were hustling to first acquire and develop, and then profit from, the continent's most promising hydro sites. Quebec's provincial government, meanwhile, dominated by French Canadians and certainly the constitutional owner of provincial lands, lacked the funds to engage in large-scale dam building and was content to leave the task to private enterprise. "I'd rather import American dollars," said Premier Louis-Alexandre Taschereau repeatedly in the 1920s, "than export Canadians to the United States."

A case in point is the Saguenay River, which was dominated by America's tobacco baron, James "Buck" Duke. Invited by Canadian entrepreneurs to take an interest in damming the massive Saguenay on the eve of World War I, Duke quickly seized control of the enterprise for himself, working through local agents to buy up waterpower sites and farm lands, and selecting a political ally in Quebec City–based paper producer William Price. Through Price, Duke secured generous concessions from the Quebec government of Taschereau to impound Lac Saint-Jean as a holding reservoir. Duke's chief engineer, William States Lee, hailed from the Carolinas, like Duke himself. The price tag of Duke and Price's Isle Maligne dam—touted by Lee as "the largest single installation in water-power development ever undertaken" and dubbed by local residents an awesome "eighth wonder of the world"—exceeded the entire provincial revenue for the year of its completion, 1926. Duke eventually drew to the region the power-intensive aluminum industry in the form of a subsidiary of Alcoa (the Aluminum Company of America, now Rio Tinto Alcan). Alcoa would spawn Alcan, which would in turn complete the Saguenay's hydroelectric development during World War II by constructing the similarly enormous Shipshaw dam downstream near Chicoutimi. This electricity was intended to make aluminum ingot, and to a lesser extent newsprint, both for export to the United States.[6]

Alcan is unusual in Quebec in that it was exempted from the large-scale **nationalization** of hydro resources in the 1960s; but its origins are otherwise typical of the province's major electricity producers. The neighbouring Saint-Maurice valley's hydro–industrial development was begun by two Bostonians: brewer John Joyce and banker John Aldred. Its dams were built by a New York construction firm under the guidance of engineer Wallace Johnson of Massachusetts. At the head of the Montreal Light, Heat and Power Company was the self-made Irish-Canadian railway engineer and business genius Herbert Holt. The Ottawa Valley became the purview of US-based International Paper's Gatineau Power Company. The Southern Canada Power Company, led by Montreal financiers C. J. McCuaig and A. J. Nesbitt, among others, developed the relatively small rivers of the Eastern Townships.

Thus the hydroelectric industry conformed to the other major twentieth-century industries of the Canadian Shield, the so-called "new staples" of hydro, pulpwood, and minerals. All three were exploitable thanks to new technologies developed in the late nineteenth century, which, in turn, granted great new value to this frontier region; and all three were so costly and speculative to develop that new enterprises gravitated to the most capable and powerful American-controlled firms.[7] As historian José Igartua puts it, "the resource regions of Canada were simple pawns on the continental, even global chessboard of American corporate capitalism."[8] "By multiplying and accentuating lines of continental force," historian H. V. Nelles writes, such investments in pulpwood for paper and hard-rock minerals, as well as hydroelectric dams, "drew Canada irresistibly into an ascendant American empire."[9] For its part, the Quebec government acted as a seller of waterfalls to the highest bidder until 1910, and then, stung by nationalist criticism of foreign ownership, as a long-term lessor of waterpower sites; or, through the Quebec Streams Commission (founded in 1910), as the builder of several dams that created holding reservoirs—including the Gouin Reservoir of the upper Saint-Maurice and the Kenogami Reservoir of the Saguenay—which powered the turbines of private corporations.[10]

What did this arrangement between the provincial government and private enterprise yield in the decades before World War II? It certainly attracted foreign capital, which helped Quebec to escape its *retard* (delay) in industrialization. As hydroelectricity was a leading agent of industrial change, it dictated the location of factories and factory towns, as industries set up shop in outlying areas near waterpower, such as Jonquière and Shawinigan Falls and, along the Saint-François River, the Eastern Townships. Thus urban factory life, with its attendant benefits and miseries, began to spread beyond Montreal to the hinterlands. It also dictated the type of industry, since hydroelectricity (unlike coal, the basis of the iron and steel industries) creates power rather than heat; thus Quebec became and remains an important world centre for electricity-intensive industrial processes such as aluminum and magnesium smelting, some chemical production, and pulp and paper manufacturing.

Regional, watershed-based monopolies also grew to dominate Quebec industry according to their control of hydraulic resources; and this pattern of "one river, one company" (as historian John Dales has described it) meant low wholesale electrical rates to large industrial customers and very high retail rates to individual (largely French-Canadian) consumers in need of power and light for households and small businesses. In turn, private power companies may well have helped repress living standards among the French-Canadian majority and fuel growing discontent. To quote Dales: "Through their rate structures, the power companies . . . favored the imposition of twentieth-century big business on a habitant culture—with all that that implies in terms of social and cultural friction."[11] Indeed, the combined circumstances of foreign/Anglo ownership and their excessively high retail profits inspired a nationalist outcry by French Canadians alarmed by their perceived exploitation.

The "Economic Re-conquest" of Quebec

The nationalization of hydroelectricity in Quebec has its roots in the post–World War I unease about urbanization and industrialization among Quebec's French-Canadian petite bourgeoisie, including growing anxiety about foreign and American investments.[12] Such Progressive Era concerns gained popularity and traction during the hard times of the Great Depression. Quebec City dentist Philippe Hamel, an unlikely leader for Quebec's public power movement, denounced the city monopoly held by the Quebec Power Company (a subsidiary of Shawinigan Water and Power) and indeed the entire interconnected "electricity trust"—both in Quebec and beyond—that had already come under attack in the United States. Although Hamel's 1930 fight to municipalize electrical services failed, the cause of public power was embraced by French-Canadian nationalists, such as journalist Ernest Robitaille, university professor J.-E. Grégoire, politician René Chaloult, and Mayor Télesphore-Damien Bouchard, who had successfully municipalized electricity in the town of St-Hyacinthe. Political pressure mounted on the long-ruling Liberal Party, already tainted by the hydropower-related Beauharnois scandal. Premier Taschereau, accused of turning French Canadians into an economic underclass by overly generous concessions in hydro, forestry, and mining, finally sanctioned an Electricity Commission in 1934 to study province-wide nationalization. Still, real reform came to naught. Maurice Duplessis, posing as a progressive nationalist, craftily co-opted the public power movement to seize the premiership in 1936, before adopting the lax and pro-business policies of his predecessor and fully frustrating those who sought more radical intervention.

Only in the brief and enlightened tenure of agronomist turned Liberal politician Premier Adélard Godbout (1939–44) did enduring electricity reform begin in the provincial government's creation of the Hydroelectric Commission of Quebec (Hydro-Québec) to expropriate and operate the energy assets of the Montreal Light, Heat and Power Company (MLHP). Godbout's public statements suggest that this far-reaching decision was made to take control of a corporation that was earning exorbitant profits and charging its Montreal customers unjustifiably high rates.[13] Behind the scenes, the action was also likely embedded in wartime politics as well, as the Godbout administration attempted to fend off criticism of generous concessions to Alcan and court the support of nationalists in an upcoming election.[14] And, of course, the takeover of MLHP was rooted in decades of discontent: French-Canadian nationalist demands to wrest control of the development of crucial hydraulic resources from an anglophone economic elite. Whatever the motives and triggers, Godbout's expropriation of a major Quebec power company (at a cost of $112 million to the province and including the Beauharnois power plant on the St Lawrence River) certainly sealed his reputation as a progressive reformer whose legislative record comprises universal education, rural electrification, and women's suffrage in addition to partial nationalization of the electrical industry.[15]

Hydro-Québec! A political lightning rod since the Quiet Revolution, the electrical behemoth has drawn lavish praise for promoting the economic interests of French Canadians and also ferocious criticism for overlooking the interests of Aboriginal people and the environment, or for assuming the arrogant demeanour and behaviour of "a state within a state."

Amid the hype, it is useful to recall the original and prosaic charge by the Quebec legislature of its Crown corporation in 1944: "to furnish energy to municipalities, industrial or commercial enterprises and to citizens of this province at the lowest possible rates compatible with sound financial administration."[16] Reporting annually to the National Assembly, Hydro-Québec's president and four commissioners had the authority to hire and manage its personnel. With the approval of cabinet (via the minister in charge[17]), the corporation could construct dams, power stations, and transmission lines to generate and transport energy; raise capital in financial markets beyond Quebec; and purchase stock in other energy-related companies (which would pave the way for the second nationalization of the 1960s). Thus was Hydro-Québec fashioned as a public corporation, holding a measure of autonomy from the government to do the will of the provincial electorate.

In the post–World War II economic boom, with energy demand roughly doubling every decade, Quebec's immediate need was to expand electrical production. Through the 1950s, Hydro-Québec twice enlarged the Beauharnois power station just upstream from Montreal on the St Lawrence, built additional dams on the upper Ottawa River, undertook a new project along the Bersimis River of the North Shore, expanded the provincial transmission network to the Gaspé region and elsewhere, and launched the construction of the Carillon dam on the lower Ottawa River. French Canadians had been the primary labour force in provincial dam construction across the century, and only with the establishment of Hydro-Québec did they also become managers and engineers. Carillon was notable in this regard. As Hydro-Québec's official history records with pride, this was "the first grand project for which the direction was given over to French-Canadian engineers"; and despite their youthfulness, as well as the particular technical challenges of the Ottawa River site, they "directed the execution of the works with great dexterity."[18] Hydro-Québec's engineers also surveyed and made plans to build a massive hydroelectric complex along the North Shore's Manicouagan and Outardes rivers. The expansion of power and transmission facilities since 1944 multiplied by six the utility's capacity to generate electricity, keeping pace with consumer demand and lowering rates by as much as one-half in the Montreal area.[19]

In 1960 other watersheds were crossed. In a historic election, Jean Lesage and the Liberal Party defeated the long-reigning Union Nationale (following Duplessis's death in 1959) and were poised to usher in the reforms of the Quiet Revolution. Hydro-Québec would play a major role in this tumultuous period as an instrument of Québécois economic liberation. The man to shape and wield that instrument was the future premier and founder of the Parti Québécois, René Lévesque. Charismatic journalist, spirited and bilingual communicator, independent thinker, and political leftist–nationalist determined to use the power of the state to undo the "economic subordination" of the French-Canadian majority, Lévesque entered politics by accepting a cabinet post in the Lesage government as minister of both public works and, at his insistence, hydraulic resources. Within weeks of taking office, the Lesage government followed through on the Liberal promise to "assure Hydro-Québec the ownership and right to exploit all hydroelectric energy not yet conceded." In this way the corporation was endowed with a rich source of renewable energy for generations hence.

More radically, Lévesque and his economic advisors[20] planned a second and final stage of nationalization. Once again, its purpose was both practical and ideological: to integrate and rationalize what these men deemed "the mess" of multiple power companies and distribution systems, thereby lowering or equalizing electrical rates across regions; to create white-collar managerial jobs in the hydroelectric industry for the rising francophone middle class; and also, as Lévesque explained, to "decolonize the hydro sector" by removing it from the control of "a dozen different principalities" ruled by "feudal barons"—"a clutch of bigwigs, mainly from the West Island and Ontario, who were happy to accept money from our shareholders and consumers but who hewed to the line that outside the 'family compact' there was no chance of promotion by merit, and even less of anyone having a say in running the shop."[21] As this was a momentous and contentious issue, and an expensive proposition, Lesage called an election in the autumn of 1962 to renew his mandate to carry it forward. Its rhetoric was borrowed from a half-century's nationalist critique of Anglo control of the hydro industry. Its campaign slogan *Maîtres chez nous!* ("Masters in our own house!") evoked perfectly a half-century's yearning by French-speaking Quebecers to seize control of their own rocky, river-strewn, northern landscape and its economic potential.

Victorious by a wide margin, the Liberal government authorized Hydro-Québec to purchase the stock of 11 private power companies (all but Alcan) for just over $600 million. Roughly half of this amount was borrowed on US financial markets. With expropriation successfully completed in May 1963, Hydro-Québec had doubled its power-generating capacity and begun to rationalize electricity rates and power transmission province wide. By the mid-1960s, this *colosse en marche* (as *La Presse* journalist Renaude Lapointe dubbed Hydro-Québec) was forging ahead with grand construction projects on the Manicouagan and Outardes rivers, negotiating the joint development of Labrador's Churchill Falls (which would enable the corporation to export huge quantities of power for profit), and had captured the imagination, admiration, and pride of French Canadians by proving that *après tout, on est capable* ("after all, we can do it"). Hydro-Québec's engineers pioneered the world's highest-voltage transmission lines (735 kilovolts, or 735,000 volts) to conduct electricity from the Manic–Outardes complex to urban markets without excessive power loss; and the research laboratory l'Institut de recherche d'Hydro-Québec was founded shortly thereafter to experiment and innovate in long-distance transmission. Visitors to a film theatre at Montreal's Expo '67 could follow construction progress of the beautiful and massive multiple-arched dam at "Manic-5"; more than one French Canadian emerged shedding tears of joy. Songwriter Georges Dor struck a chord with "La Manic," its lyrics a love letter from a lonely construction worker, which proved the most successful record ever by a Quebec songwriter. Revived in the 1990s by Quebec pop singer/heartthrob Bruno Pelletier, the plaintive words and melody still stirred audiences: Si tu savais comme on s'ennuie / A la Manic / Tu m'écrirais bien plus souvent / A la Manicouagan . . . (If you knew how lonely we were, / at the Manic, / You would write me much more often, / At the Manicouagan . . .)

As Hydro-Québec grew ever larger and more visible as a symbol of francophone accomplishment, it also grew more politicized. Robert Boyd has pointed out that when the Manic–Outardes project was publicly launched in 1960, it was announced by Hydro-Québec's commissioners and engineers, as

BIOGRAPHY

René Lévesque: A Little Giant

In a chapter focused on electrical power, it is tempting enough to cast René Lévesque (1922–1987) in the role of "Mr Hydro": the political champion and mobilizing force behind the full-scale nationalization of the electricity industry, principally responsible for the transformation of Hydro-Québec from a Montreal-based public utility to a province-wide engine and instrument of economic development and French-Canadian liberation. True enough. But the moniker hardly does justice to the richness of Lévesque's biography or the full range of his influence. A short, balding man from the Gaspé Peninsula with the husky voice of a lifelong chain smoker, Lévesque was in fact a political giant of twentieth-century Quebec. Any discussion of the Quiet Revolution, or of the political independence movement that followed, must account for his dynamic presence.

René Lévesque, photographed by Yousuf Karsh.

Yousuf Karsh/Library and Archives Canada, e010752248/copyright Estate of Yousuf Karsh

Lévesque spent his youth in the village of New Carlisle, Quebec, in a region originally settled by American Loyalists. Although he later described it as a "prison for my parents . . . on the margin of history,"[22] growing up in this English-speaking pocket of the province gave him a fluent, nearly accent-free English that would open doors to the wider world. The oldest of four children in a middle-class family (Dominic Lévesque was a country lawyer), René obtained a classical education at the Séminaire de Gaspé and then, in Quebec City, at the Collège des Jésuites. From a young age his nationalism was strong and certain: "Never forget that you are French Canadians," he wrote as a student, "that your own people have been stagnating for generations, and that if they, the people, *your* people, do not act, they are lost!"[23]

This passionate young man set out to be a lawyer like his father, but it wouldn't stick. In 1943, at the height of World War II, Lévesque abandoned his legal studies at Laval University to pursue full-time work as a journalist and see the world. He served as a radio war correspondent, reporting from London during the last bombardments by the German Luftwaffe and then with the advancing Allied troops on the continent. Accompanying the first group of American soldiers to liberate the Dachau concentration camp, Lévesque witnessed firsthand one of the darkest images of the war: "We stood there stunned," he recalled, "staring at these phantoms in striped pyjamas who were staggering out of the huts."[24] After the war ended, he reported on politics for the Canadian Broadcasting Corporation's French-language counterpart, Radio-Canada, covering the Korean War of the early 1950s and stories from across Canada and the United States.

Lévesque's journalism career reached its peak between 1956 and 1959 as he hosted a weekly television program for Radio-Canada. *Point de Mire* (*On Target*), a critically acclaimed and hugely popular news program, put the charismatic and cosmopolitan Lévesque in Quebecers' living rooms to explain, using maps, charts, and film footage, such international issues of the day as the Algerian Crisis. A bitter producers' strike at Radio-Canada in the winter of 1959 brought an end to several popular programs, including *Point de Mire*, but Lévesque's leadership role in the union battle gave him a taste for politics. His broad familiarity

continued

as a public figure encouraged him to run for political office.

With Jean Lesage's invitation to join the Liberal cabinet in 1960, Lévesque entered the political arena. When Lesage offered him the Ministry of Public Works, Lévesque apparently rather casually asked for and received the additional file of hydraulic resources (later natural resources). "I was soon to discover," wrote Lévesque in his memoirs, "that under that afterthought hid the goose that laid the golden eggs."[25] Inspired by the calls of Hydro-Québec's commissioners to expand the state's authority over waterpower development, Lévesque assembled the requisite financial feasibility studies. From early in 1962, his strong public advocacy for nationalization split the Lesage cabinet and then forced the premier to stand with him. With the Liberals' election victory in November, Hydro-Québec took possession of Quebec's remaining private utilities.

Lévesque's evolution from Liberal nationalist to committed separatist was gradual. "Slowly and at first subconsciously," Lévesque himself explained, "I became convinced that Quebec should safeguard its identity and develop into an independent political entity."[26] His advocacy of hydro's nationalization already made him the government's most radical spokesperson for French-Canadian autonomy. By 1964, Lévesque's positions in several other policy realms (including greater provincial control over taxation, health and social welfare, and international relations) put him at odds with the majority of the Liberal Party. When the Liberals lost power in 1966, and then refused to discuss a sovereign Quebec at the 1967 party convention, Lévesque leapt and formed a new Movement for Sovereignty-Association (Mouvement Souveraineté-Association, MSA) to advocate a fully pro-independent Quebec that maintained economic ties to the rest of Canada. The MSA was one of several pro-independence factions in Quebec society during the 1960s.

It was in the tumultuous year of 1968 (with violent student protests and political confrontations worldwide) that Lévesque united most of these factions as the Parti Québécois. His political success stemmed from well-crafted policy in addition to his charismatic personality. Faithful to the democratic process, Lévesque rejected violence (and violent fringe groups like the FLQ) as a means of change; and sovereignty-association posed the least possible threat to the economic well-being of the growing French-Canadian middle class. The Parti Québécois steadily gained voter support in the general elections of 1970 (23 per cent) and 1973 (30 per cent). Then in November 1976, taking 41 per cent of the popular vote in a three-way contest with the ruling Liberals and the Union Nationale, in an event that stunned the rest of Canada and suggested to many that the nation itself was splitting apart, the Parti Québécois swept to power.

As premier, Lévesque experienced the soaring highs and disappointing lows of governance. In his victory speech, an ebullient and emotional Lévesque told the party faithful, "I never thought that I could be so proud to be a Quebecer." In the summer of 1977 his government passed Bill 101, the Charter of the French Language, cementing the place of French in provincial education and commercial life. The law remains the centrepiece of Quebec language policy. Achieving independence was more difficult. Lévesque's government called a province-wide referendum on secession from Canada that took place in May of 1980. The question was sufficiently vague in an effort to garner a majority, asking citizens to allow its government "to negotiate a new agreement with the rest of Canada" that would result in "sovereignty" as well as "economic association including a common currency." Still, 60 per cent of the electorate rejected it. Conceding defeat, an emotional Lévesque told Quebecers: "If I have understood you well, you are telling me: until the next time."

There would be no "next time" for Lévesque. He won a second mandate in 1981, with the PQ taking 49 per cent of the popular vote. But the deep recession of the 1980s reduced support for the Parti Québécois. In failing health, Lévesque resigned as party leader in 1985. He died of a heart attack two years later at the age of 65.

What is Lévesque's legacy? To many Canadians outside Quebec, Lévesque represents the fracturing force of Quebec separatism and the misguided belief that Quebecers require their own country to enjoy the full rights of citizenship. Within Quebec, understandably, far more positive impressions linger: a learned and worldly journalist who in midlife turned to politics to defend the rights of French Quebecers; a charismatic visionary who gave spirited voice to a people coming into their own power; a major force of the Quiet Revolution; the father of the Quebec sovereignty movement. Two grand boulevards, one in Quebec City and the other in Montreal, were renamed in his honour. Appropriately, on Montreal's Boulevard René Lévesque stands the headquarters of Hydro-Québec.

was the custom, who spoke to a group of journalists about rising energy needs in terms of megawatts and kilowatt-hours. By 1971, it was Quebec Premier Robert Bourassa who launched the mammoth James Bay Hydroelectric Project as an instrument of job creation and francophone pride in a speech to several thousand Liberal supporters in a Quebec City hockey arena.[27] What Bourassa dubbed "the project of the century," involving world-class dams and power stations and river diversions hundreds of miles north of Montreal, would be celebrated by French Quebecers as an "epic" and "pioneering" achievement by which the North was "conquered and opened to civilization."[28] But it would also be the first major project since Hydro-Québec's creation to be seriously contested within Quebec society.

There were disagreements between the Liberal government and Hydro-Québec's commissioners as to whether the James Bay Project should go forward at that time or perhaps later, followed by an internal struggle over which institution was to manage the project: Hydro-Québec or the Bourassa government's Société de développement de la Baie James (James Bay Development Corporation). Members of the opposition Parti Québécois, who preferred to pursue nuclear energy, raised more public objections. "Just because a river is French-Canadian and Catholic," economist (and later premier) Jacques Parizeau said famously, "it isn't absolutely necessary to put a dam on it."[29] And why, they asked, should Quebec pay an American firm, Bechtel International, to supervise the project when Quebec engineers themselves were capable of it? Another problem concerned organized labour. Nationalization in 1963 had created multiple labour unions (33 originally), a number of which sought primacy to win Hydro-Québec construction contracts, including for the La Grande River work sites. The simmering tensions erupted in 1974 as members of the Fédération des travailleurs du Québec (Quebec Workers Federation) rioted, vandalizing a work camp and halting construction for seven weeks at a cost of some $35 million.[30]

The Rise of First Nations

Far more costly to Hydro-Québec was the rise of **First Nations** activism, beginning with that of the James Bay Crees.

Well before the 1970s, of course, hydroelectric dams had damaged northern Aboriginal lands and lifeways. As the Canadian Shield's resources gained economic value at the end of the 1800s, entrepreneurs and provincial governments alike pushed northward to harvest minerals, forest resources, and hydroelectric energy. And every one of these projects, across the breadth of Canada, disturbed millennia-old societies of hunter-trappers such as the Dene, Cree, Algonquin, and Innu. As hydroelectric projects were often in the vanguard of resource exploitation, they did particular harm. Reservoirs flooded the habitat of beaver and muskrat. Dams cut off salmon (or inland salmon, *ouananiche*) from their spawning grounds, and blocked and altered the flow of rivers, along with the natural arteries for canoe transport and the essential corridors for harvesting fish and game. Perhaps most importantly, access roads built to distant hydro sites opened hitherto inaccessible lands to forest companies as well as non-Aboriginal trappers, sport fishers, and hunters. Forestry operations rolled northward from the beginning of the twentieth century; hunting and fishing clubs proliferated after World War II. Most of these clubs barred Aboriginals from hunting and trapping on their properties and reduced animal and fish populations nearby. "When the White Man touches something, he destroys it," a Montagnais/Innu hunter of the Saguenay watershed said bitterly. "It's only the rocks that the White Man cannot destroy."[31] From the 1950s, it became increasingly difficult, and eventually impossible, to sustain a family from the bounty of the fragile boreal ecosystem. As hydroelectricity also fostered northern industry—whether paper mills or mines—such spinoff projects drew Aboriginals out of the bush to wage labour, permanent settlement on reserves, and dependency on government welfare.

Hydroelectricity is known as a renewable and clean energy, with some justification. Once the dams, powerhouses, and transmission lines are constructed, fossil fuels are no longer required to generate power; with proper maintenance and with adequate rain and snowfall, power production can proceed indefinitely. Thus, "Québec hydropower helps avoid the substantial greenhouse gas emissions resulting from thermal generation."[32] Hydro-Québec has stated on its website that it is "clean and green . . . in harmony with nature." It is ironic, then, that hydroelectricity has been a particularly potent catalyst for social change in the North. The hydro sector has in fact been instrumental in what anthropologist Paul Charest describes as the "sedentarization" of Aboriginal peoples—the quiet Canadian tragedy by which autonomous migratory hunter-trappers were caught in the encroaching industrial frontier and rendered childlike wards of the state.[33]

Aboriginals played no part in the decisions to dam Quebec's rivers at least until the 1970s. During World War II, for example, the Alcan Corporation constructed large reservoirs high in the Saguenay watershed to feed power plants downstream and smelt aluminum for Allied aircraft; and so-called lakes Manouan and Peribonka were fashioned squarely in the middle of the hunting-trapping terrain of the Lac Saint-Jean and Bersimis Montagnais/Innu, who were engaged in the fur trade. In granting its permission to Alcan, the provincial government consulted with forest and paper companies and carefully examined the consequences for French-Canadian farmers and factory workers. Yet Aboriginals, still disenfranchised and powerless in the affairs of the province, were wholly excluded from the political dialogue. Nor were they offered any form of financial compensation.[34] Similarly, for the 1960s Manicouagan project of Hydro-Québec the Montagnais/Innu of the North Shore were neither informed nor compensated. In a moving documentary on this subject by French-born filmmaker Arthur Lamothe, four Innu hunters are interviewed in front of the giant Manic-5 dam. Here, before the pre-eminent symbol of French-Canadian arrival as masters of the provincial house, the camera records the sad and angry hunters and their tales of flooded trapping grounds and cemeteries, of lost livelihoods.[35] In effect, as one Quebec cohort rose to power, others not yet liberated were suffering the consequences. A once downtrodden francophone majority, ironically, rode roughshod over the rights of those weaker than themselves.

"**Red Power**," however, was rising. North American Aboriginal populations rose rapidly in the postwar era due to permanent reserve and village settlement and access to health care. Formal classroom education could be a psychologically dislocating experience, especially in the off-reserve residential schools, but it also groomed the first generation of northern Canadian Aboriginals (whom some called "briefcase Indians"—for example, James Bay Cree leaders Philip Awashish, Billy Diamond, Matthew Coon Come, Ted Moses, and Matthew Mukash) able to deal with the legalistic and bureaucratic language of government and business on its own terms. Rising political strength among Aboriginals was matched by growing North American middle-class sensitivity toward them. Worldwide decolonization and the US civil rights movements led thoughtful citizens to examine their own society's practices of racism or internal colonialism. The American environmental movement beginning in the late 1960s romantically cast Indians in the role of "first ecologists" and increased sympathy for their cause. Environmental consciousness seeped north to Canada. The

"Red Power" movement also spread northward, challenging Canadian First Nations to seize the rights of self-government and the tools of economic development. Canadian politics helped trigger Aboriginal activism in Canada as well: Prime Minister Trudeau's "Just Society" slogan of 1968 raised expectations, but his government's notorious White Paper of 1969—deemed by Aboriginals to be a blueprint for their assimilation into the dominant culture—galvanized Native political organization and resistance.[36]

The Cree resistance to the James Bay Project is by now a well-known story of Quebec and Canadian history, widely disseminated by journalists, academics, activists, and the Cree themselves.[37] Bourassa's government moved to dam the rivers of the James Bay region without consulting or even considering the 5,000 Cree and 3,500 Inuit who occupied that vast terrain. Young Cree leaders sought the advice of their elders and decided to oppose the project. As Ottawa (with jurisdiction over Indian affairs) would do nothing to intervene with Quebecers (fearing the antagonism of the separatist movement), the Crees went to court in Montreal seeking an injunction to halt construction. Aiding them was a batch of sympathetic English-speaking Canadians (the second language of Quebec's Crees and Inuit was English, rather than French, as they had long done business with the British-chartered Hudson's Bay Company), including lawyer James O'Reilly and McGill University–affiliated biologists and anthropologists. They were initially victorious, but the decision of Quebec's Superior Court was overturned on appeal within a week. Still, the court's favourable consideration of the Crees' case, including validation of their title to the land by virtue of continuous occupation and use, forced the government of Quebec to negotiate a settlement.

The resulting James Bay and Northern Quebec Agreement (JBNQA) of 1975, often described as Canada's first modern land-claim settlement, set important precedents in Quebec and Canada. The Crees and Inuit won cash in the form of investment funds for all communities ($20,000–$30,000 per person); additional subsidies for trappers; exclusive hunting, fishing, and trapping rights in a portion of the territory; and significant recognition of Aboriginal self-governance in political, social, and economic affairs: School boards, health and social services, and municipal services, for example, all would continue to be subsidized by Canada but would now be directed by the Crees and Inuit themselves. Moreover, the negotiation process had forged region-wide political institutions (the Grand Council of the Crees, the Northern Quebec Inuit Association) to represent what had been distinct, isolated, and far-flung communities, while other organizations (the Cree Regional Authority, the Makivik Corporation) were fashioned to manage the investment funds deriving from the agreement. Quebec, for its part, had finally met its obligation (dating from the extensions of Quebec's territory northward in 1898 and 1912) to formally recognize the Aboriginal rights of the inhabitants of the North. No longer could any private corporation or government body attempt to develop resources without first resolving Aboriginal claims. And having done so, Hydro-Québec could now legally proceed with its gargantuan hydroelectric complex along the La Grande River.

The struggle, however, was hardly over. Government subsidies do not create a self-supporting revenue base or a sense of accomplishment. It remains unclear whether Crees or Inuit or any other traditional hunting culture, largely dispossessed of their original livelihood and inundated by the material comfort and gadgetry of industrial civilization, can retain or refashion a sense of identity and rootedness. More immediately and practically, the Crees successfully fought Hydro-Québec's second phase of development in the Great Whale River hydro project, claiming that they had only sanctioned the La Grande River complex. They raised objections about the slow pace by which Ottawa and Quebec City met their financial obligations to the 1975 treaty, including job training and employment contracts. Following decades of legal wrangling, Cree Grand Chief Ted Moses and Premier Bernard Landry agreed to the so-called Peace of the Braves (*Paix des Braves*) of 2002, by which the Crees withdrew their lawsuits and relinquished development rights to the mighty Rupert and Eastmain rivers. In exchange they won a lot more money for economic development (at least $70 million annually for 50 years) and the opportunity to become business partners in the logging and mining of their ancestral lands. The *Paix des Braves* broke new ground in recognizing a partnership between a First Nation and a provincial government. Moreover, as the Crees may now benefit from the economic development of the entire traditional territory, the Accord moves ever further away from the treaties of old by which an Aboriginal nation parted with the vast portion of its land in return for fixed financial compensation. Thus did the Crees become "major participants in resource management," Cree Director of Government Relations Romeo Saganash has written, and in fact "the major players with regard to how, when and if development takes place."[38]

The Crees' success in bargaining with Quebec was made possible by excellent historical timing: in an era when non-Aboriginals were forced to pay attention to Aboriginal interests, the Crees still held a trump card of resource-rich land. The Montagnais (or Innu) to the east, whose population slightly exceeds the Crees, were initially less fortunate. Large-scale hydroelectric development invaded their ancestral watersheds—from the Saguenay's Peribonka tributary, northeastward to the Bersimis (Betsiamites), Outardes, and Manicouagan rivers—before the recent era of environmentalism and Aboriginal claims. Still, in the wake of the JBNQA, new agreements were possible for new hydro projects; such negotiations inevitably involved broader Aboriginal settlements as redress for grievances over flooded lands dating back several decades. Thus through the 1990s, at the Peribonka, Sainte-Marguerite, and Toulnustouc rivers, Hydro-Québec negotiated separate multi-million-dollar compensation claims with each of the different Innu bands to be affected by hydroelectric projects, along with "partnership" guarantees of jobs and work contracts. Ongoing and future projects slated farther up the North Shore—on the Romaine, Little-Mecatina, and Labrador's Lower Churchill rivers—must similarly entail Innu partnership and profit sharing. In 2011, for example, the Innu of the Uashat mak Mani-Utenam Band near Sept-Îles agreed to drop legal proceedings against the Romaine project, allowing Hydro-Québec to run transmission lines from the Romaine complex across their ancestral lands. In exchange, the band received $125 million in compensation from Hydro-Québec as well as the Quebec government's commitment to facilitate profit-sharing negotiations between the band and private mining and forestry companies seeking to develop the terrain's resources. Uashat mak Mani-Utenam was the last of five affected Innu communities to sign compensation agreements with Hydro-Québec over the Romaine project. Since the 1970s, the Innu have also sought broader title and rights to their ancestral lands (so-called "comprehensive claims") similar to the JBNQA; and Quebec's strong desire to build new dams and see forest and mineral resources extracted from the Innu homeland have motivated the province to accelerate negotiations with Innu tribal councils on these broader accords. However, no definitive agreements have been reached to date.[39]

From the perspective of the dam builder, "the Aboriginal cause" emerged in the 1980s as one of Hydro-Québec's "thorniest problems."[40] But one party's problem has proved to be another's opportunity. Quebec's Aboriginals, no longer dismissed, today possess an influence over the northern resource economy that they have perhaps not leveraged since the early part of the Canadian fur trade. In the election of 2008, Jean Charest's Liberal government pushed its *Plan Nord* (Plan North), promising resource development in a declining economy via 8,000 new megawatts of electricity by 2035 and accelerated mining and forestry operations in the "last great frontier of Quebec." "We absolutely must occupy our territory," stated Charest. "It's ours. It's our future." But now, the government vows consultation with Aboriginal peoples who, in turn, promise to hold the premier to his word. "Jean Charest now has a chance to make a difference," said Chief of the Assembly of First Nations of Quebec and Labrador Ghislain Picard, "to turn talk into action, to put an end to the colonialist attitude which still prevails in the relationship with the First Nations. We will no longer be ignored." Although Plan Nord was downplayed and scaled back by the Parti Québécois (September 2012–April 2014), it is a stated priority for the new Liberal government of Philippe Couillard, who has declared Quebec to be "back in business." Similarly, Couillard has paid homage to the current political environment by acknowledging the interests of Indigenous peoples, setting aside $100 million in his first budget for education and job training of northern residents and calling for "sustainable northern development" that serves "local communities, First Nations and the Inuit people."[41]

Conclusion

This brief history of hydroelectricity in Quebec illustrates a human struggle to contest and control the province's hydro sector, whether motivated by profit, pride, homeland, or a combination thereof. In fact, the power industry is itself a marvellous bellwether for the sociopolitical history of the province. From the advent of Anglo-directed industrialization, to the rise of French power, to the dawn of Aboriginal claims, harnessing the energy of Quebec's rivers has reflected the aspirations of distinct constituencies. Similarly, it has reflected collective or national self-assertion in other parts of the world: in Soviet Russia and the United States in the 1930s, and in China today with the construction of the gargantuan Three Gorges dam on the Yangtze River. To the thoughtful reader, however, this sketch of hydroelectric development might reveal more than just politics or "power." "Power struggle" is but one of several themes we might identify at this complex intersection of human and environmental history. There are, of course, other ways to trace this story.

Consider *government regulation*. From the outright sale or lease of waterfalls to the creation and growth of the Crown corporation Hydro-Québec, hydro's regulation and management parallels the growth of state bureaucracy and strength in a province that has been dubbed "Quebec Inc." in the last generation. *Technology*, largely overlooked in this chapter, has indeed been an essential strand of hydroelectric history: from the inception of hydro technology to serve urbanizing societies, to the scaling up and refinement of turbine design, dam construction, and long-distance transmission. Along the way, an industry that began by harnessing individual waterfalls grew to amass whole stretches of river and ultimately burst the bounds of individual watersheds—as in the James Bay Project—to generate electricity in ever-larger quantities. In turn, technology to transmit lots of power over long distances permitted Quebec to profitably export its growing surpluses to the United States, beginning in earnest from the completion of the Churchill Falls and James Bay projects in the 1970s, and increasing with the deregulation of US energy markets in the 1990s.

And so, to technology we should add *economy*. Anglo-Americans dominated the earliest third of our chronology before being displaced by French Canadians, yet the influence of American capital or markets never dwindled. Wall Street's reach has been expressed contemporarily by its role in helping to fund the second stage of nationalization in the 1960s as well as the greater part of the James Bay Project. Whether it pursues export contracts with New York or New England, Quebec hydro traces the history of continental finance. With high fixed costs and a dependence on future markets for their return, among hydro's greatest challenges is finding the money to build and sustain its projects.

Hydro's history also takes in the history of the boreal *landscape and environment*. As industrializing human societies reached ever northward for the raw materials deemed necessary for their comfort or survival, they reshaped river valleys and aquatic ecosystems along with the lives and livelihoods of Indigenous peoples. Similarly, hydro's low-priced power (Quebecers pay some of the lowest rates in North America), by limiting the consumer's incentive to conserve energy, poses an environmental–ethical dilemma in an era of rapid, human-induced climate change. In all, turbines and transmission lines form a marvellous and multifaceted lens through which the historian may view the past. Quebec's power history reveals an entire panoply of human phenomena and events.

CASE STUDY

Quebec's Election of 1962: A Referendum on Hydro's Nationalization

Interpreting the Sources

Background

The long and conservative reign of Maurice Duplessis's Union Nationale came to an end in 1960. With the election of the Liberals under Jean Lesage, the stage was set for the multiple and modernizing reforms of the Quiet Revolution, in education, democratic governance, and organized labour. Still, the Liberal rise to power in no way guaranteed that the Quebec government would proceed with the radical and controversial step of full-scale nationalization of the hydro sector.

René Lévesque, Lesage's minister of public works as well as hydraulic resources (later natural resources), certainly intended to "tackle this aspect of our economic subordination"—to seize "the goose that laid the golden egg" (as he wrote in his memoir). Gathering support and economic advice from André Marier, Michel Bélanger, Jacques Parizeau, and others, Lévesque assessed the cost and viability of buying up the remaining 11 private power companies. With the information in hand by January 1962, Lévesque began publicly to call for nationalization, which split the members of Lesage's cabinet and angered the premier himself. In September of 1962, at a Laurentian cabinet retreat at Lac-à-l'épaule, Lévesque finally won Lesage's support for the nationalization project.

Yet Lesage would proceed only with a specific mandate from Quebec voters. So although the Liberals had been in power for only two years, Lesage called for the dissolution of the Assembly and for an election to take place on 14 November 1962. "It is for the people of Quebec to decide, freely and proudly," the premier stated, "whether they wish to take into their hands the most important of all the keys to a progressive economy." The specific origins of the campaign slogan are not clear. What is clear, in retrospect, is that *Maîtres chez nous!* ("Masters in our own house!") struck a powerful chord with the electorate. The Liberals increased their majority in the Assembly substantially, from 51 to 63 seats of the total 95. On 1 May 1963, Hydro-Québec took possession of the remaining electrical utilities of the province at a cost of $604 million.

Questions

The sources below (both visual and written) should permit you to assess the debate between the two major political parties over nationalization that culminated in the election of 1962.

1. What arguments or symbols did the Lesage government employ to coax Quebec voters to vote Liberal?
2. What was the Union Nationale's position on nationalization?
3. Ultimately, what can we reasonably infer about the mood of Quebec society from a close reading of these historical documents?

Sources

1. "1962: Manifeste du parti liberal du Québec" (author's translation)

   The era of economic colonialism is over in Quebec. Now or never, Maîtres chez nous.

   —Jean Lesage

   On June 22, 1960, the electorate approved the platform of the Liberal Party of Quebec by granting to it a mandate to organize national and economic life in such a manner that would favour the well-being of Quebec citizens. Jean Lesage and his team set out resolutely to this task, determined to endow Quebec with social and cultural legislation without precedent. They are doing the same in the domains of education and the economy;

and they are cleaning up governance. At the same time, they have established the *Conseil d'orientation économique* charged with studying the means to bring to reality our economic expansion, which is the essential factor of our social and cultural blossoming. Following serious study, it has become clear that the unification of the electricity network—key to the industrialization of all Quebec regions—is the primary condition for our economic liberation and a policy of full employment. . . . It is up to the Legislative Assembly and the Cabinet to adopt the necessary legislation to bring this task to a conclusion, the largest and most fruitful ever proposed by a government in Quebec since Confederation. . . . We won't replace 30,000 stockholders by more than 5,300,000 without consulting the latter. Jean Lesage and his team calls on the entire population to give them a clear and precise mandate which will permit them to pursue, with renewed vigour, the realization of the Liberal platform of 1960. Now or never

The Liberal Party of Quebec

"maîtres chez nous." Such is the goal of the Liberal Party of Quebec. . . . [Note: the entire Liberal pamphlet is devoted to the issue of nationalization.]

2. Liberal Election Poster (below): "Maintenant ou jamais! Maîtres chez nous."
3. "1962: Programme de l'Union nationale" (author's translation)

The Union Nationale presents to the people a platform based on the following principles: a sense of responsibility . . . social justice . . . [and] regional development . . . For the human being and the family [the UN promises tax reductions, adjustments in health insurance, etc.]; for the farmer [the UN promises aid regarding credit, rural roads, etc.]; for the workers [the UN promises a $1 per hour minimum wage, a pension system, etc.]. . . . [Note: roughly two-fifths of the pamphlet is devoted to these issues.]

For progress and economic emancipation . . . immediate nationalization of the Lower St Lawrence Power Company and of Northern Quebec Power in order to reduce rates and improve service in the regions served by these two companies. Conversion from 25 to 60 cycles in Northwest Quebec; and a referendum, no later than June 30, 1963, on the nationalization of the other private electric companies, in order to permit the population to express itself freely, outside of any partisan consideration and in complete knowledge of the issue. . . . [Note: roughly one-fifth of the pamphlet is devoted to "economic emancipation," of which nationalization forms a part.]

For the municipalities [better collaboration between the province and its towns, more help maintaining winter roads, etc.]; for education and culture [maintain the province's sovereignty in education, maintain the religious character of schools, etc.]; for financial independence and political sovereignty [re-establish financial independence of the province, etc.]." [Note: roughly two-fifths of the pamphlet is devoted to these issues.]

Questions for Critical Thinking

1. Hydro-Québec: What is it, exactly? When was it formed, and why? What would you say have been the milestones of its growth and development? Most broadly, what does this institution suggest or reveal about Quebec history or society?
2. The phrase *power struggle* is employed to describe a century of hydroelectric development in Quebec. Does the evidence support this claim throughout the chapter? Would *national struggle* or *tribal struggle* be more, or perhaps less, appropriate descriptors? Explain.
3. This story of power takes place not in a vacuum, but in a particular place: the province of Quebec. What larger issues or themes of Quebec history and the Quebec experience do you recognize in this chapter?
4. The history of power production in Quebec is but one way to slice the modern history of Quebec. What other subjects does this chapter suggest for further research?

Notes

1. *Webster's New Collegiate Dictionary* (Springfield, MA: Merriam, 1975), 902.
2. Albert Faucher and Maurice Lamontagne, "History of Industrial Development," in *Essais sur le Québec contemporain*, ed. Jean-Claude Falardeau (Quebec: Presses l'Université Laval, 1953).
3. Blodwen Davies, *The Story of Hydro: White Thunder* (Toronto: Ryerson Press, 1931), 12.
4. Quebec Hydro-Electric Commission, *Quebec, The Power Province*, brochure dated circa 1957.
5. Quebec Hydro-Electric Commission, *Quebec, The Power Province*; personal communication with Bernard, November 2008; Louis-Gilles Francoeur, "Rencontre avec Thierry Vandal : la terre des grands barrages," *Le Devoir*, 14–15 June 2003, G5.
6. David Massell, *Amassing Power: J. B. Duke and the Saguenay River, 1897–1927* (Montreal and Kingston: McGill-Queen's University Press, 2000).
7. Morris Zaslow, *The Opening of the Canadian North, 1870–1914* (Toronto: McClelland & Stewart 1971); and *The Northward Expansion of Canada, 1914–1967* (Toronto: McClelland & Stewart, 1988).
8. José Igartua, "'Corporate' Strategy and Locational Decision-Making: The Duke-Price Alcoa Merger, 1925," *Journal of Canadian Studies* 20 (1985–6): 97.
9. H. V. Nelles, *The Politics of Development* (Toronto: Macmillan, 1974), 307.
10. Claude Bellavance, "L'État, la 'houille blanche' et le grand capital : l'aliénation des ressources hydrauliques du domaine public québécois au début du XXe siècle," *Revue d'histoire de l'Amérique française* 51, no. 4 (1998): 487–520; and Massell, *Amassing Power*.
11. John H. Dales, *Hydroelectricity and Industrial Development: Quebec, 1898–1940* (Cambridge, MA: Harvard University Press, 1957), 180.
12. Yves Roby, *Les Québécois et les investissements Américains (1918–1929)* (Quebec: Presses de l'Université Laval, 1976); Susan Mann Trofimenkoff, *The Dream of Nation: A Social and Intellectual History of Quebec* (Toronto: Gage, 1983), ch. 15; Yvan Lamonde, *Histoire sociale des idées au Québec 1896–1929*, vol. 2 (Montreal: Fides, 2004), ch. 7.
13. On the formation of Hydro-Québec, see Clarence Hogue, André Bolduc, and Daniel Larouche, *Québec : un siècle d'électricité* (Montreal: Libre Expression 1979), ch. 7. See also in Yves Bélanger and Robert Comeau, eds., *Hydro-Québec : autres temps, autres défis* (Quebec: Presses de l'Université du Québec, 1995): Gilles Gallichan, "De la Montreal, Light, Heat and Power à Hydro-Québec," 64–70; Claude Bellavance, "Un long mouvement d'appropriation de la première à la seconde nationalization," 71–8; and Robert Boyd, "Cinquante ans au service du consommateur," 97–103.
14. David Massell, *Quebec Hydropolitics: The Peribonka Concessions of the Second World War* (Montreal and Kingston: McGill-Queen's University Press, 2010), ch. 5.
15. Jean-Guy Genest, *Godbout* (Sillery, QC: Les éditions du Septentrion, 1996).
16. Hydro-Québec Act, 17 April 1944.
17. The cabinet minister responsible for Hydro-Québec has changed over the years as the ministries themselves were reorganized, from Terres et Forêts (1944–5), to Ressources hydrauliques (1945–61), to Richesses naturelles (1961–76), to Énergie.
18. Hogue et al., *Québec: un siècle*, 250.
19. Boyd, "Cinquante ans."
20. Principal among Lévesque's advisors regarding nationalization were Michel Bélanger, Jacques Parizeau, Roland Giroux, and André Marier.
21. René Lévesque, *Memoirs* (Toronto: McClelland & Stewart, 1986), 169–72.
22. Ibid., 9.
23. René Lévesque, *My Quebec*, trans. Gaynor Fitzpatrick (Toronto: Methuen, 1979), 4.

24. Lévesque, *Memoirs*, 102.
25. Ibid., 167.
26. Lévesque, *My Quebec*, 6.
27. Boyd was an engineer (from 1945), commissioner (from 1969), and eventually president of Hydro-Québec (1977–82). See his article "Cinquante ans," in *Hydro-Québec : autres temps, autres défis*.
28. Roger Lacasse, *Baie James, une épopée : l'extraordinaire aventure des derniers des pionniers* (Montreal: Libre Expression, 1983), 28–9. Caroline Desbiens analyzes such discourse in *Power from the North: Territory, Identity, and the Culture of Hydroelectricity in Quebec* (Vancouver: UBC Press, 2013).
29. Lacasse, *Baie James*.
30. Ibid., 129, ch. 7, ch. 11.
31. Quoted/translated by Massell, *Quebec Hydropolitics*.
32. Hydro-Québec, *Moving Forward Sustainability Report* (Montreal: Hydro-Québec, 2004), 6.
33. Paul Charest, "Les barrages hydro-électriques en territoire Montagnais et leurs effets sur les communautés amérindiennes," *Recherches amérindiennes au Québec* 9, no. 4 (1980): 323–37; or "Hydroelectric Dam Construction and the Foraging Activities of Eastern Quebec Montagnais," in *Politics and History in Band Societies*, ed. Eleanor Leacock and Richard Lee (Cambridge: Cambridge University Press, 1982), 413–26.
34. Massell, *Hydropolitics*.
35. Arthur Lamothe, *Manicouagan*, Les Ateliers Audio-Visuels du Québec, 1973.
36. Olive Dickason, *Canada's First Nations: A History of Founding Peoples from Earliest Times* (Toronto: McClelland & Stewart, 1992), and J. R. Miller, *Skyscrapers Hide the Heavens: A History of Indian-White Relations in Canada*, 3rd ed. (Toronto: University of Toronto Press, 2000).
37. An accessible and balanced summary of the James Bay Project through the 1980s is found in Sean McCutcheon's *Electric Rivers: The Story of the James Bay Project* (Montreal: Black Rose Books, 1991). More scholarly is Richard Salisbury's *A Homeland for the Cree: Regional Development in James Bay, 1971–1981* (Montreal and Kingston: McGill-Queen's University Press, 1986). More partisan is Boyce Richardson's *Strangers Devour the Land* (Toronto: Macmillan, 1975).
38. Romeo Saganash, "The 'Paix des Braves': An Attempt to Renew Relations with the Cree," in *Power Struggles: Hydro Development and First Nations in Manitoba and Quebec*, ed. Thibault Martin and Steven M. Hoffman (Winnipeg: University of Manitoba Press, 2008), 205–13.
39. "Innu reach deal with Hydro-Québec on $6.5 billion project," *Globe and Mail*, 24 January 2011; "Hydro-Québec and Innu reach final deal on Romaine project," *Postmedia News*, 22 March 2011; Paul Charest, "The Land Claims Negotiations of the Montagnais, or Innu, of the Province of Quebec and the Management of Natural Resources," in *Aboriginal Autonomy and Development in Northern Quebec and Labrador*, ed. Colin H. Scott (Vancouver: UBC Press, 2001), 255–73; and Charest, "More Dams for Nitassinan: New Business Partnerships between Hydro-Québec and Innu Communities," in Martin and Hoffman, *Power Struggles*, 255–79.
40. Boyd, "Cinquante ans," 102.
41. "Charest Unveils Plan for Northern Quebec," *Montreal Gazette*, 28 September 2008; Liberal video "Le Plan Nord," available at www.plq.org/en/PlanNord_energies.php; "Charest's Plan Nord Troublesome News for First Nations," *Montreal Environment*, 8 December 2008. Pre- and post-election coverage of Couillard's Plan Nord relaunch includes "Le gouvernement Couillard relance le Plan Nord," *Ici Radio-Canada*, 4 June 2014; "Couillard announces Plan Nord +, says PQ government 'killed' first Plan Nord," *Forbes*, 15 March 2014; "A Liberal government will re-launch sustainable northern development with the re-launch of Plan Nord," Liberal Party web post, 14 March 2014.

Select Bibliography

Bélanger, Yves, and Robert Comeau, eds. *Hydro-Québec : autres temps, autres défis*. Quebec: Presses de l'Université du Québec, 1995.

Bellavance, Claude. "L'État, la 'houille blanche' et le grand capital : l'aliénation des ressources hydrauliques du domaine public québécois au début du XXe siècle," *Revue d'histoire de l'Amérique française* 51, no. 4 (1998): 487–520.

———. *Shawinigan Water and Power, 1898–1963 : formation et déclin d'un groupe industriel au Québec*. Montreal: Boréal, 1994.

Bourassa, Robert. *Power from the North*. Toronto: Prentice-Hall, 1985.

Charest, Paul. "Les barrages hydro-électriques en territoire Montagnais et leurs effets sur les communautés amérindiennes." *Recherches amérindiennes au Québec* 9, 4 (1980): 323–37.

———. "Hydroelectric Dam Construction and the Foraging Activities of Eastern Quebec Montagnais." In *Politics and History in Band Societies*, edited by Eleanor Leacock and Richard Lee, 413–26. Cambridge: Cambridge University Press, 1982.

———. "The Land Claims Negotiations of the Montagnais, or Innu, of the Province of Quebec and the Management of Natural Resources." In *Aboriginal Autonomy and Development in Northern Quebec and Labrador*, edited by Colin H. Scott. Vancouver: UBC Press, 2001.

Dales, John H. *Hydroelectricity and Industrial Development: Quebec, 1898–1940*. Cambridge, MA: Harvard University Press, 1957.

Dickason, Olive. *Canada's First Nations: A History of Founding Peoples from Earliest Times.* Toronto: McClelland & Stewart, 1992.

Dirks, Patricia. "Dr. Philippe Hamel and the Public Power Movement in Quebec City, 1929–1934: The Failure of a Crusade." *Urban History Review* 10, no. 1 (June 1981): 17–29.

Gagnon, Alain-G., and Guy Rocher, eds. *Reflections on the James Bay and Northern Quebec Agreement.* Montreal: Québec Amérique, 2002.

Genest, Jean-Guy. *Godbout.* Sillery, QC: Les éditions du Septentrion, 1996.

Hogue, Clarence, André Bolduc, and Daniel Larouche. *Québec : un siècle d'électricité.* Montreal: Libre Expression, 1979.

Hydro-Québec : des premiers défis à l'aube de l'an 2000. Montreal: Libre Expression/Forces, 1984.

Igartua, José. "'Corporate' Strategy and Locational Decision-Making: The Duke-Price Alcoa Merger, 1925." *Journal of Canadian Studies* 20 (1985–6): 82–101.

Lacasse, Roger. *Baie James, une épopée : l'extraordinaire aventure des derniers des pionniers.* Montreal: Libre Expression, 1983.

Lévesque, René. *Memoirs.* Translated by Philip Stratford. Toronto: McClelland & Stewart, 1986.

———. *My Quebec.* Translated by Gaynor Fitzpatrick. Toronto: Methuen, 1979.

Martin, Thibault, and Steven M. Hoffman, eds. *Power Struggles: Hydro Development and First Nations in Manitoba and Quebec.* Winnipeg: University of Manitoba Press, 2008.

Massell, David. *Amassing Power: J. B. Duke and the Saguenay River, 1897–1927.* Montreal and Kingston: McGill-Queen's University Press, 2000.

McCutcheon, Sean. *Electric Rivers: The Story of the James Bay Project.* Montreal: Black Rose Books, 1991.

Miller, J. R. *Skyscrapers Hide the Heavens: A History of Indian-White Relations in Canada*, 3rd ed. Toronto: University of Toronto Press, 2000.

Niezen, Ronald. *Power and Dignity: The Social Consequences of Hydroelectric Development for the James Bay Cree.* Toronto: University of Toronto Press, 1993.

Provencher, Jean. *René Lévesque: Portrait of a Québécois.* Translated by David Ellis. Toronto: Gage, 1975.

Regehr, T. D. *The Beauharnois Scandal: A Story of Canadian Entrepreneurship and Politics.* Toronto: University of Toronto Press, 1990.

Richardson, Boyce. *Strangers Devour the Land.* Toronto: Macmillan, 1975.

Salisbury, Richard. *A Homeland for the Cree: Regional Development in James Bay, 1971–1981.* Kingston and Montreal: McGill-Queen's University Press, 1986.

Savard, Stéphane. *Hydro-Québec et l'État québécois, 1944–2005.* Quebec: Septentrion, 2013.

Zaslow, Morris. *The Opening of the Canadian North, 1870–1914.* Toronto: McClelland & Stewart, 1971.

———. *The Northward Expansion of Canada, 1914–1967.* Toronto: McClelland & Stewart, 1988.

23 Health Care in Quebec

Antonia Maioni, McGill University

Timeline

1932 Public health law adopted.

1941 Creation of Ministère de la santé et du bien-être.

1961 Loi sur l'assurance-hospitalisation is adopted.

1963 Fédération des médecins omnipraticiens du Québec is chartered.

1965 Fédération des médecins spécialistes du Québec is chartered.

1966 Castonguay Commission is launched.

1970 Loi sur l'assurance-maladie (Bill 8) is adopted.

Quebec institutes separate payment schedules for generalists and specialists.

Quebec specialist doctors strike.

1971 Loi sur la santé et les services sociaux (Bill 65) is adopted.

1972 Final report of the Castonguay–Nepveu Commission.

1988 Publication of the Rochon Report.

1990 New government initiative: *Une réforme axée sur le citoyen*.

1991 Loi sur les services de santé et les services sociaux is adopted.

1992 Bill 9 (de-insuring certain services) is adopted.

1993 Regional boards (régies régionales) are set up.

2001 Clair Commission Report is released.

2005 Supreme Court decision in *Chaoulli v. Québec*.

2006 Bill 33 is adopted in response to Supreme Court decision.

2015 Major reorganization of the health-care system is introduced: Bill 10 and Bill 20.

Introduction

When Canadians are asked what sets them apart from Americans, many invariably mention the health-care system. In every province, including Quebec, health care is regulated as a "public good," and each provincial government plays a crucial role in ensuring that this good is available to all citizens. The design of health-care policy reflects a commitment to collective responsibility, in which access is universal, coverage comprehensive, and funding primarily assumed by the public sector through general revenues from taxpayers. Although health care remains a popular social program, Canadians are concerned about the overall sustainability of the health-care system.

This is especially true in Quebec, where health reform has been fraught with political struggle. In addition to ideological divisions about the role of the state in society, in Quebec the debate over health reform has always been subject to the larger debate about the role of Quebec in Canada and the complexities of the federal–provincial relationship. In fact, health care has served both as a lightning rod for the tension in this relationship and as a model of how Quebec has been able to develop a unique system within the contours of the federal arrangements.

The development of hospital and medical insurance in Quebec is above all a history of federal–provincial relations superimposed against a landscape of profound socioeconomic and political change. The stories of that relationship and of the period of social change have been well documented and dissected. Yet the place of health reform remains an incomplete picture. The Quebec experience offers not only insights into the health-care dossier per se; it also reveals how health policy making is bounded within specific institutional and ideological environments.

Today in Quebec, as in other Canadian provinces and territories, health care is universally provided—in contrast to the United States—to all its official residents. This system, despite recent, albeit selective, accommodation of private health-care insurance, remains enormously popular. This article examines health policy in Quebec. Why and how has health care in Quebec developed as it has? What key factors have and continue to shape the features and current direction of Quebec health-care policy?

The Historical Antecedents of Health Insurance in Quebec

Prior to 1960, Quebec's health-care system was largely in the hands of the Catholic Church, charitable organizations, and the private sector. With the division of linguistic and religious communities in British North America, and more importantly, that between Quebec and the rest of the colonies, a "marriage of convenience" emerged between the colonial administration and Catholic Church leaders in Quebec, which gave religious authorities substantial power in shaping local poor relief, including hospital care.[1]

Because religious communities were so important in providing social and health-care services, other religious groups did likewise. In the early nineteenth century, the influx of new settlers led to the founding of Protestant hospitals, with the help of merchant benefactors and benevolent societies. Later, the Jewish community developed voluntary relief dispensaries for new immigrants in Montreal.

Confederation reinforced this situation, transferring the responsibility for hospitals to provincial governments, which in turn subsidized local public health initiatives and charity cases in voluntary hospitals. In Quebec, most of these remained church affiliated, and many relied at least in part on municipal funding derived from provincial subsidies. In 1921, the Quebec government formally adopted its first health-care law, la *Loi de l'assistance publique* (Public Assistance Law), which allowed for the direct reimbursement of care provided to "indigents" in Quebec hospitals recognized as charitable institutions. This emphasis on public subsidies of private (religious) charity became the key in maintaining the Catholic Church's autonomous role in social provision within French-Canadian society.[2] The creation of a Ministry of Health in 1936 did little to change this dynamic, since the new ministry was mainly responsible for the coordination of public health departments in the municipalities.

During the 1940s, a new momentum was emerging in Ottawa around health and other social policy matters. The report of the Rowell-Sirois Commission (the Royal Commission on Dominion–Provincial Relations) in 1940 underscored the idea that federal involvement in health insurance was feasible even within the constraints of the British North America Act. The Marsh Report, published in 1943, reinforced this notion of federal leadership in social programs, although it was careful to suggest that medical care would be an exception under provincial administration.[3]

In Quebec, a similar momentum was in play. The Liberal government, led by Prime Minister Mackenzie King's protégé Adélard Godbout, was already interested in moving forward on health insurance. Premier Godbout commissioned a provincial inquiry into hospital care, and the Lessard Commission recommendations, released in 1943, became the centrepiece of the Liberal legislative agenda, receiving the support of union groups and the firm opposition of the clergy in Quebec.[4] When the Union Nationale's Maurice Duplessis returned to power in 1944, his government quickly scuttled plans for such legislation.

Duplessis was likewise less than enthralled with the idea of public financing or any attempt to relinquish religious control of the health sector. And like his influential ally, Ontario's Conservative Premier George Drew, Duplessis was openly critical of the Liberal government in Ottawa and the spectre of increasing burdens on provincial coffers through social policies.[5] Together these two fiscal conservatives were largely responsible for scuttling the social policy promise of the Dominion–Provincial Conference on Reconstruction in 1945 through their refusal to relinquish taxation control. Since health insurance was tied to the plan's fiscal arrangements, the proposals for health insurance expired along with the conference.

BIOGRAPHY

Claude Castonguay: The Quiet Revolutionary

Claude Castonguay is the person responsible for introducing Quebec's first health insurance plan. An actuary by training, he was the epitome of the new generation of technocrats responsible for the rapid modernization of the Quebec state during the Quiet Revolution. For example, Castonguay was part of the team that hammered out the Quebec Pension Plan of 1965, alongside the Canada Pension Plan, a remarkable feat of co-operative federalism.

Claude Castonguay in 1970, as Quebec's Minister of Health.

The Canadian Press/Jacques Boissinot

In the fall of 1965, Premier Jean Lesage appointed Castonguay to head a research committee to develop a medical insurance plan for Quebec. The following year, Premier Daniel Johnson appointed Castonguay to head a public commission of inquiry on health and social services. By the time he reported, Castonguay had become convinced of two essential points: (1) The best way to improve access and to find a more equitable way to finance health care in Quebec would be through the collective pooling of risk and financing through public health insurance; and (2) any new medical insurance plan had to be developed with Quebec's particular context and needs in mind. Castonguay believed that

continued

asymmetry was both necessary and desirable when it came to social programs for Quebec.

In 1970, Castonguay was tapped by Robert Bourassa to develop and implement his own recommendations as the new minister of health and social services. Quebec health-care legislation created a distinctive health-care system in Quebec, based on the integration of health and social services, the creation of CLSCs (local community service centres), public health departments, and regional health boards.

Having accomplished what he set out to do, Castonguay left politics in 1973 to take up a successful career as an insurance executive in Quebec. He was not forgotten, however, as for years Quebecers would fondly refer to their health-care card as *la castonguette*. He re-emerged on the political scene in 1990 when he was appointed to the Canadian Senate by Prime Minister Brian Mulroney. Following the failure of the Meech Lake Accord, he left the Senate in 1992.

More recently, Castonguay was coaxed out of retirement to once again study the Quebec health-care system and make recommendations for a reform agenda. In his *Memoirs of a Quiet Revolutionary*, Castonguay had sharply criticized the inefficiency of Quebec's health-care system and underlined the need for increased private investment in infrastructure and technology. In the May 2007 budget, Quebec Finance Minister Monique Jérôme-Forget announced that Castonguay would lead a task force to find new ways to finance health care and reassess the role of the private sector. He was to be joined by two other members appointed by the opposition parties, well-known journalist Michel Venne for the Parti Québécois and Joanne Marcotte for the Action démocratique du Québec.

The report of the task force, *Getting Our Money's Worth*, was released in early 2008 and covered both organization and financial challenges in the Quebec health-care system. For example, Castonguay's group suggested that the system needed better continuity of care and more investment in primary care and home care, particularly in the context of an aging population. Even though Castonguay's original vision of the Quebec health-care system in the 1970s was based on integrated care, in practice Quebecers have come to rely on specialists, walk-in clinics, and emergency rooms for the kind of care that could be provided much more cost effectively in other settings.

The report also tackled matters of governance and the allocation of resources in the health-care system, criticizing the top-down and overly bureaucratized approach to health-care organization. As for the allocation of resources, Castonguay suggested that money should flow where the patient goes instead of being allocated to health-care establishments on the basis of automatic budgeting. This would mean that even hospitals could be financed according to performance criteria and have more leeway in purchasing services as a way of injecting more competitiveness into the health-care system.

The recommendations on health-care financing proved, however, to be more controversial. Castonguay's main preoccupation was how to control what he considered to be the unsustainable growth in public health expenditures. His remedy was to slow the rate of spending and reduce pressure on public finances by finding alternative sources of financing. The report also suggested that the public system cannot cover all the demands for health-care services, and emphasized that individuals have to adopt more healthy lifestyles. The report also recommended dedicated stabilizing funding and diversifying the financing of health care through an increase in the provincial sales tax, and allowing for deductibles that would encourage individuals to be more responsible in their use of medical services. Finally, the report recommended a widening of the private insurance industry and more flexibility in allowing physicians the ability to practise both in the public system and in the private market.

Although Castonguay's 2008 report stands in sharp contrast to the one he delivered in 1970, in both cases one can see the legacy of a blunt and straightforward technocrat making the case for bold and innovative change. Nevertheless, the political stakes around health reform are still apparent. Quebecers are still not yet ready to swallow such drastic medicine. While public opinion polls show that some Quebecers are in theory open to the idea of private markets, user fees, and the like, when faced with the actual recommendations—and price tags—for such initiatives, they have been less enthusiastic.

Still, Castonguay's diagnosis and prescription are unlikely to fade from public debate. Quebec's health-care reform dilemma is one that resonates in every province. Not only does it provide artillery to proponents of privatization, it also challenges the federal government over the worthiness of the Canada Health Act.

Hospital Insurance: La Réforme malgré tout

During the 1950s, there were nevertheless significant developments that would have an important influence on health care in Quebec. A program of National Health Grants, inaugurated in 1948, provided federal grants-in-aid for the provinces to assist public health measures, medical research, and hospital construction. Hospital construction expanded in Quebec, as did health insurance, particularly private or "voluntary" initiatives supported by the medical profession.[6] Liberal Prime Minister Louis St Laurent, however, also emphasized provincial responsibility in health insurance. During the 1953 election campaign, he framed the issue by insisting it was the provinces that "have to take the initiative" in health insurance "which should, as far as possible, be left to Provincial administration."[7] A special commission on federalism in Quebec, the Tremblay Commission, was set up in 1954 in part as a reaction to this.[8] In its final report, the commission recognized that health, welfare, and education were matters of provincial jurisdiction, and that the federal government's role was to ensure that provinces, in particular Quebec, had the fiscal means to fulfill their responsibilities in this regard.[9]

By this time, given the inauguration of hospital insurance in Saskatchewan, there was considerable discussion of federal involvement through federal grants-in-aid.[10] But the prime minister was reticent, as was Maurice Duplessis, not to mention the Canadian Hospital Council and the Catholic Hospital Conference.[11]

Nevertheless, in 1957 the House of Commons passed the Hospital Insurance and Diagnostic Services Act. Although other provinces soon signed on to this cost-sharing arrangement, the Union Nationale government in Quebec refused to be swayed.[12] Duplessis's last throne speech in November 1958 invoked his "faith" in private health insurance; after his death the following year, his successor Paul Sauvé reiterated the same sentiment.[13]

Quebec's resistance to hospital insurance had been based on the Union Nationale government's aversion to secular, state, and federal intervention in societal issues. Nevertheless, Quebec society was rapidly changing in the postwar era. The labour movement, for example, championed such reform, as did the new middle class emerging from Quebec's universities.[14] The arrival in power of the Liberal Party in 1960, led by former Federal Minister Jean Lesage, signalled an important shift in political thinking about autonomy, society, and the state in Quebec.

During the 1960s, the discourse of federalism in Quebec changed, just as the discourse about the role of the state in society changed. The division of powers was no longer used as a firewall against social reform emanating from the Canadian state; instead, reformers in Quebec would argue that the division of powers gave Quebec the necessary levers to effect social change, and that Quebec's special place in the federation meant that both co-operation and asymmetry could work toward the development of social programs to meet the needs of the Quebec "nation."[15]

The new premier, Jean Lesage, chafed at the conditional nature of federal cost-sharing programs but, having campaigned on the issue of hospital insurance, his government was under pressure to join in with the existing federal–provincial agreement. Thus in 1961, in one of its first legislative actions, the Liberal government signed on to the cost-sharing plan, and in 1962 the *Loi des hôpitaux* (the Hospitals Act) effectively shut out religious communities from the administration of health services in Quebec.[16]

Hospitals remained voluntary institutions, and as elsewhere in Canada they would become "public" institutions as well, in the sense that they would henceforth rely on public funds.[17]

Medical Insurance: The Not-so-Quiet Revolution

As the *Révolution tranquille* (Quiet Revolution) began to rearrange the relationship between state and society in Quebec, this same period was marked by events unfolding in Saskatchewan, as the CCF–NDP government attempted to implement medical insurance against the resistance of the medical lobby there.[18]

In 1964, the Royal Commission studying the issue (the Hall Commission) recommended that the federal government put forward a cost-sharing program for health services.[19] These recommendations were seen by many observers to have ignored constitutional impediments to federal action in this area; nevertheless, public opinion in favour of medical insurance soon intensified in Quebec.[20]

At the 1965 Federal–Provincial Conference, Liberal Prime Minister Lester Pearson outlined a medical insurance program in collaboration with the provinces. Premier Lesage remained wary, emphasizing that any Quebec plan would remain outside the federal government's reach, preferably through opting out in return for sufficient tax points to underwrite the province's own program.[21]

Premier Lesage had already demonstrated a vigorous defence of Quebec's desire for opting out of federal initiatives with financial compensation to develop a Quebec pension plan.[22] Lesage's second-guessing of federal initiatives in social policy, however, was not based on the same resistance as that of the Union Nationale: The question was not about the interference of the *state,* but rather of the *federal* state in these matters. Inside Quebec, the nationalization of hydroelectricity, the swift movement in education reform, and the rise of nationalist sentiment all contributed to an effervescent but volatile situation.[23]

In the fall of 1965, Lesage appointed Claude Castonguay (the actuary who had been a central player in negotiations with the federal government over pension reform) to head a research committee to develop a medical insurance plan for Quebec. Lesage wanted above all to avoid the kind of "improvised" program he had felt compelled to implement with hospital insurance in 1961. Instead, Castonguay's 1966 report stressed that any medical insurance plan should above all respond to the particular context and needs of Quebec, and avoid any "conditions" imposed by Ottawa.[24]

The defeat of the Liberal Party in the provincial elections shortly thereafter did not end the debate over medical insurance. Union Nationale leader Daniel Johnson was above all a practical politician, and he faced immediate problems in the health sector, including a general strike that was paralyzing hospital care in Quebec. He was also aware that, in December 1966, the House of Commons passed federal medical insurance legislation.

Premier Johnson asked Castonguay to head another commission, broadening the mandate to cover not only health but also social services.[25] Castonguay's 1967 report was unveiled to general praise from the media, opinion leaders, general practitioners, the union movement, and the Liberal opposition.[26] However, the recommendation for a public medical insurance program that could pool risk and redistribute care through public financing did not sit well with Premier Johnson, who preferred a system of medical assistance for the indigent.

But Quebec's delay could not last for long once the federal government implemented the medical insurance program in 1968 and imposed a 2 per cent tax hike on Canadian taxpayers to finance it. The new Union Nationale leader (Johnson had died suddenly earlier that year), Jean-Jacques Bertrand, well known in Quebec as an outspoken social and fiscal conservative, vehemently opposed both the tax and the federal intrusion into Quebec's jurisdiction.[27] Still, public opinion in Quebec was reacting favourably to the prospect of medical insurance, and the Quebec government could not sustain its opposition while its taxpayers were being forced to subsidize the program.[28]

Ironically, then, given its long-standing suspicion of the state and social policy, one of the Union Nationale's last political gestures in office was the introduction of the *Loi sur l'assurance-maladie* in 1969, which essentially outlined a universal, publicly funded medical insurance plan for Quebec incorporating the principles of the federal government.

With the return to power of the Liberal Party—under the new leadership of Robert Bourassa—health reform returned to the care of Claude Castonguay, the new minister of health and social services. As minister, Castonguay was able to quickly reformulate the legislation: A significant difference was that it limited the *droit au désengagement* (opting out), and it was the first medical insurance legislation in Canada that prohibited *la surfacturation* (extra billing) for physicians. While the Bourassa government was able to negotiate with general practitioners, dentists, and dental surgeons on the basis of this legislation, the specialists remained intractable.[29] The *Loi sur l'assurance-maladie* was duly adopted in July 1970, but it soon became clear implementation would be difficult. By the first week of October, the **Quebec specialists' strike** began. Even as the sudden and tragic events of the October Crisis began to unfold at the end of that week, the specialists held their position. As the press, the Collège des médecins, and the public, turned against the specialists' federation, the Quebec government passed emergency measures that forced the specialists back to work.[30] Overshadowed by the grim events of that autumn, it was a bitter victory.

The Unfinished Business of Health Reform in Quebec

Although the medical insurance battle was won, health-care reform in Quebec was just beginning on two fronts. The first had to do with the organization of health and health-care services; the second with the financing of these services.

Organization and Reorganization of the Health-Care System

The unfinished business in the reorganization of the health-care system had dogged Castonguay since he began his commission work, underscoring the structural problems in the delivery and financing of health services in Quebec. The work of the Castonguay Commission continued after he became a cabinet minister, with Gérard Nepveu named the new chair. A scathing portrait indeed was emerging.[31] Essentially, the **Castonguay–Nepveu Report** found that, compared to the rest of Canada, Quebec had the lowest rate of hospital use and the highest per capita cost of hospital care. In addition, they found a growing shortage of general practitioners; a hodgepodge distribution of medical specialties; conflict among doctors, hospitals, and administrators; and little coordination or integration of care. As well, the health-care system in Quebec tended to focus on specific diseases, with scant attention to the complexity of conditions or the social determinants of health.[32]

The 1971 *Loi sur la santé et les services sociaux* was intended to address these serious deficiencies and to put into place a distinctive health-care system that included "global medicine" as part of an integrated system of health and social services, and the creation of local community service centres (CLSCs), public health departments, and regional health boards.[33] After considerable legislative debate and amendments, some inspired by Nepveu's final report, the legislation passed in 1972. It was to be Castonguay's crowning achievement (for years after that, Quebecers would refer to their health-care card as *la castonguette*), and one of the lasting legacies of the Quiet Revolution.

The law put into place hospital insurance (Régime d'assurance-hospitalisation du Québec, administered by the Ministry of Health and Social Services) and health-care insurance (Régime d'assurance-maladie, administered by the Régie de l'assurance-maladie du Québec [RAMQ], a public agency responsible to the Ministry). While most hospitals in Quebec are operated as voluntary, not-for-profit institutions (rather than as government owned and operated ones), they are financed by global budgets negotiated with the provincial government. This dependence on public funds means that hospitals are subject to political decisions (either directly by government or through the intermediary of regional boards) about their operation, including closure. As for medical insurance, physicians are paid for their services through a fee schedule negotiated between the RAMQ and the provincial medical federations. Thus, the provision of medical services remains "private" in the sense of an exchange between doctor and patient, but the payment of services is handled through the public purse. The principle of public administration is taken one step further than most provinces by allowing for alternative methods of health-care delivery and physician payment through the CLSCs. Quebec was also the first province to impose limits on physicians by capping the salary of specialists; placing limits on how much physicians can bill the RAMQ; and encouraging new physicians to move to underserviced areas in the province for their first few years of practice, or face limits on the reimbursement of their fees.

Quebec's health-care law was unique in Canada in that it emphasized primary care, made room for the integration of health and social services based on community-centred access, and organized services by region in an explicit attempt to decentralize decision making.[34] Nevertheless, the implementation of this Quebec health-care model proved politically difficult.[35] Physicians retained their "special status" as autonomous professionals in the health sector and remained wary of the network of community health and social service clinics.

Although the CLSC network covered the entire territory and population of Quebec, these clinics were not as successful in reaching out to people in urban areas, where residents had many health-care options to choose from. In fact, many physicians initially boycotted the CLSCs and set up alternative general practice clinics.

In 1988, the Rochon Commission report reminded Quebecers of the gap between the promise of initial reform and the actual progress in the system. Dr. Jean Rochon (who would later become minister of health in the Parti Québécois government) called for a ***virage ambulatoire*** (move toward ambulatory care) that again emphasized regionalization and integration, but the hurdles to such reform remained apparent.[36]

The attempt to "move" health care away from the medicalized model was pre-empted by the fiscal crises of the 1990s. Like most provinces, Quebec cut enrolments in medical schools in 1993 in response to fiscal concerns. And in 1995, the Quebec government announced the closure of several hospitals in an attempt to rein in soaring health-care costs. Despite intense public protest, five acute-care hospitals were closed in the Montreal area, while several others became long-term-care facilities. It also became apparent that access to care was being affected by capacity problems, as emergency rooms became overcrowded and waiting times for certain elective procedures increased.

One of the most important innovations of this era was Quebec's drug insurance plan. Coverage for prescription drugs is not widespread in provincial health-care systems, despite the increase in drug-based therapies and the aging population. In 1997, Quebec introduced the first universal drug insurance plan; it allows Quebecers to choose between a private group insurance (through their employers) and a public plan administered through the RAMQ.

Since 1999, as the fiscal crisis eased, Quebec's governments turned again to the organizational lacunae of the health-care system. The Clair Commission report of 2001 (Michel Clair had also previously served as a PQ health minister) concentrated on the reorganization of front-line services and the creation of new networks of family physician practices. The first projects for these Family Medicine Groups (Groupes de médecine familiale) have been underway since, in tandem with the setting up of a new network of Health and Social Services Centres (Centres de service de santé et des services sociaux). Part of the challenge of this initiative has been the perception of a shortage of general practitioners in Quebec as more and more medical students choose more lucrative specialization.

Quebec Health Care and Fiscal Federalism

One of the key issues in the development of health care in Quebec has been the tension over *chevauchement* (overlapping jurisdiction) between the federal and provincial governments in the financing and orientation of health services. In hospital and medical insurance, Quebec was concerned also with the conditions imposed by Ottawa in return for federal transfers. Already, as early as 1971, Quebec was sensing its isolation vis-à-vis the other provinces and the federal government in this regard.[37]

The original financing formula was a series of conditional federal grants to the provinces for hospital and medical-care insurance. Quebec's health-care plan had to meet certain conditions to qualify for federal funding, but this cost sharing was relatively open-ended in that the federal government covered almost half of provincial expenditures in health. By the mid-1970s, however, a series of fiscal crises almost immediately placed the two levels of government at loggerheads over health-care financing. In 1977, the Established Programs Financing (EPF) formula was introduced, which covered both health care and post-secondary education transfers to the provinces on a per capita basis. Through the 1980s, the Progressive Conservative government would reduce and eventually freeze EPF transfers.[38]

Even as the share of its health-care transfers was being reduced, the federal government moved toward the formalization of conditions on the money through the passage of the **Canada Health Act** (CHA) in 1984. The CHA explicitly listed the five conditions that provincial health plans had to meet to receive federal monies: public administration (the health-care system must be publicly financed and accountable); universality (every legal resident must be eligible for health insurance); comprehensiveness (all "medically necessary" services must be covered); portability (Canadians travelling or moving from one province to another must be covered); and equal access (access to health care must be on "equal terms and conditions" for everyone). To the Quebec government, the imposition of these central norms represented a serious violation of provincial sovereignty. The CHA was considered especially intrusive because Quebec already subscribed to such norms (for example, the equal access provision and the ban on extra billing) within the *Loi sur les services de santé et les services sociaux*.

By the 1990s, the reductions in federal transfers, along with worsening economic conditions, forced the Quebec government to react. In 1995, health-care transfers were consolidated within a larger Canada Health and Social Transfer (CHST), which substantially reduced the cash portion of federal transfers to the provinces. Overall, Quebec governments found themselves in an unpopular political dilemma: reduced federal transfers, increasing deficits, and making cuts to health-care services.

By 1999, the worst seemed to be over, as the federal budget earmarked additional funds to the CHST. In 2000, a health-care funding agreement further increased transfers to the provinces, and in 2003 the Canada Health Transfer (CHT) came into effect, with increased funding provided through a Health Reform Fund that was intended to fund targeted initiatives (primary health care, home care, catastrophic drugs, and diagnostic/medical equipment). While Quebec governments engaged in these federal–provincial arrangements, they remained wary of federal attempts to set the direction of specific health reforms. After extensive negotiations at a high-profile first ministers' meeting in 2004, Quebec still made it clear it would not accept formal conditions and refused to participate in the new Health Council of Canada. The federal government committed to a 10-year plan for increased health-care transfers and a special fund to reduce waiting times, which had become a thorny political issue.

Still, that 10-year funding arrangement is coming to a close, even as health-care spending remains the biggest-ticket item in Quebec's provincial budget. The federal government signalled as early as 2011 that the automatic funding escalator will not be renewed, meaning that Quebec, like the other provinces, will be hard-pressed to make up that difference or find innovative and immediate cost-containment strategies.[39]

The Push for Private Health Care in Quebec

One of the most important events in recent Canadian health-care history was an important court case in Quebec, which emerged during the most difficult years of cutbacks to the provincial health-care system. The case involved an elderly patient, George Zeliotis, who waited over a year for hip-replacement surgery, and a maverick physician, Jacques Chaoulli, who had been trying for over a decade to pressure the Quebec government to allow for more private medicine in the health-care system. In 1997, Zeliotis and Chaoulli claimed that Article 15 of the Quebec Health Insurance Act, which proscribes private insurers from covering publicly funded services, and Article 11 of the Quebec Hospital Insurance Act, which prevents nonparticipating physicians from contracting for services in publicly funded hospitals, were unconstitutional under the Canadian Charter of Rights and Freedoms and the Quebec Charter of Human Rights and Freedoms. The

Primary Source

***Excerpts from Chaoulli v. Quebec (Attorney General),* [2005] 1 S.C.R. 791, 2005 SCC 35.**

Justices Binnie, LeBel, Fish:

> The Quebec health plan shares the policy objectives of the Canada Health Act and the means adopted by Quebec to implement these objectives are not arbitrary. In principle, Quebec wants a health system where access is governed by need rather than wealth or status. To accomplish this objective, Quebec seeks to discourage the growth of private sector delivery of "insured" services based on wealth and insurability. The prohibition is thus rationally connected to Quebec's objective and is not inconsistent with it. In practical terms, Quebec bases the prohibition on the view that private insurance, and a consequent major expansion of private health services, would have a harmful effect on the public system . . . The evidence indicates that a parallel private system will not reduce, and may worsen, the public waiting lists and will likely result in a decrease in government funding for the public system. In light of these findings, it cannot be said that the prohibition against private health insurance "bears no relation to, or is inconsistent with" the preservation of a health system predominantly based on need rather than wealth or status. Prohibition of private insurance is not "inconsistent" with the State interest; still less is it "unrelated" to it. People are free to dispute Quebec's strategy, but it cannot be said that the province's version of a single-tier health system, and the prohibition on private health insurance designed to protect that system, is a legislative choice that has been adopted "arbitrarily" by the Quebec National Assembly.

Justice Deschamps:

> As we enter the 21st century, health care is a constant concern. The public health care system, once a source of national pride, has become the subject of frequent and sometimes bitter criticism. This appeal does not question the appropriateness of the state making health care available to all Quebeckers. On the contrary, all the parties stated that they support this kind of role for the government. Only the state can make available to all Quebeckers the social safety net consisting of universal and accessible health care. The demand for health care is constantly increasing, and one of the tools used by governments to control this increase has been the management of waiting lists. The choice of waiting lists as a management tool falls within the authority of the state and not of the courts. The appellants do not claim to have a solution that will eliminate waiting lists. Rather, they submit that the delays resulting from waiting lists violate their rights . . . they contest the validity of the prohibition in Quebec . . . on private insurance for health care services that are available in the public system. The appellants contend that the prohibition deprives them of access to health care services that do not come with the wait they face in the public system.

Chief Justice McLachlin:

> Access to a waiting list is not access to health care.

initial ruling of the Quebec Superior Court rejected their claims in 2000, as did a subsequent hearing before the Quebec Court of Appeal in 2002.

But the plaintiffs pursued their case to the Supreme Court of Canada, and in 2005 the court invalidated prohibitions against private insurance for core medical services provided through Quebec's public health-care system.[40] The decision, known as *Chaoulli v. Quebec,* was a divided and controversial one involving three separate judgments. The majority decision overturned rulings by the provincial courts and found Quebec's hospital and health insurance legislation to be in violation of the Quebec Charter of Human Rights and Freedoms (the right to life and inviolability of the person).

After requesting a stay of one year, the Quebec government finally drafted a legislative response in June 2006. **Bill 33** opened the provision of core services in the Quebec health-care system to private insurance, but only in three specific areas: hip, knee, and cataract surgery. In 2009, a companion Bill 34 was passed, which expanded the number of elective surgical procedures that could hypothetically be performed in these specialized medical centres (including mastectomies, hysterectomies, and bariatric surgeries) and created certain loopholes to permit some doctors to work in both affiliated and nonaffiliated (private) clinics. At the same time, however, the proposal retains the "wall" between physicians who remain in the public system and those who opt out of it, and introduces a wait time guarantee akin to what the federal government had been trying to persuade provincial governments to implement.

The effect on wait times, the initial cause of the *Chaoulli* case, is still only partial, however. Since 2008, with the implementation of Bill 33, Quebec wait list results have been marginally better for the kinds of surgeries specified in the law, although they have not quite met the benchmarks that were drawn up (90 per cent attainment for surgery within six months of waiting). There remain considerable regional differences as well, since urban areas have been able to better meet these guidelines than more rural or remote areas. As for private ("duplicate") insurance, there has been little to no uptake by insurance companies in this regard in Quebec, at least in part because of the difficulties of trying to coordinate such a limited slice of medical services.[41]

Still, the impact of the *Chaoulli* case has been felt beyond this new legislation as critics of the status quo argued for more private delivery and the creation of supplemental funding instruments to ensure the sustainability of the health-care system. One of them was Claude Castonguay, who had by now become an outspoken critic of the public health-care system he helped create. His 2008 report, commissioned by the Liberal minister of finance and aptly titled *Getting Our Money's Worth*, had two main sets of recommendations.[42] The first dealt with organizational reform, suggesting better continuity of care and more investment in primary care and home care to ensure the "smooth operation" of the system through appropriate treatment and electronic health records. He also borrowed from recent British reforms, suggesting that money should "follow the patient" through the system instead of being allocated to health-care establishments. On the pressing concerns over the rate of growth in public health expenditures, Castonguay urged limiting public spending to the rate of economic growth and moving toward a dedicated health stabilization fund for the rest, plus "diversifying" revenue through user fees, premiums, and deductibles. Since this would be at odds with the Canada Health Act, Castonguay suggested that the "dysfunctional" CHA had to be "adapted to current realities."

The report was not particularly well received at the time, but parts of its recommendations were in evidence in the 2010 Quebec budget, which introduced a new *contribution santé* (health-care premium) of $200 per person.[43] The amounts were modest—just under $1 billion in annual revenues—but the money was to be oriented toward a dedicated "fund" to be allocated to health-care establishments based on their performance in specific criteria. More provocative was the proposal for a *franchise santé*—a retroactive fee assessed on an individual's income tax based on the number and type of "medical visits" during the year. This was never implemented, in part due to the extensive negative reaction to the measure. Still, much of this came home to roost in the 2012 election campaign, when the PQ campaigned hard on the promise of repealing the health premium. The PQ won the election, but instead of repealing the premium it chose to make it a more progressive premium based on income.

Just as the previous Liberal health ministers had been physicians (neurosurgeon Philippe Couillard and family doctor Yves Bolduc), so too was the PQ health minister, Réjean Hébert, a well-known gerontologist. Dr. Hébert's prescription for the Quebec health-care system was directed at "completing" the implementation of primary-care reform and focusing on the needs of an aging population, including home-care services. Although health care did not figure as prominently in the subsequent 2013 election campaign, Dr. Hébert narrowly lost his seat as the PQ government was defeated. Meanwhile, Philippe Couillard had become leader of the Liberal Party and named the outgoing president of the federation of medical specialists, Dr. Gaetan Barrette, as health minister.

A controversial public figure, known for his outspoken opinions and antagonistic attitude, Dr. Barrette lost no time in setting in motion a major reorganization of the health sector: Bill 10, which replaces the existing network of local health agencies with a more streamlined arrangement in which the governing boards will be directly named by the minister; and Bill 20, which redirects incentives for family doctors to take on more patients and for specialists to reduce the wait times for consultations and services.

Conclusion

Health care in Quebec underscores at least two of the fundamental political fault lines in Quebec. The first is the relationship between state and society and the ideological differences about the delineation between private and public spheres in areas such as health care. The insistence on provincial autonomy brandished by the Union Nationale under Duplessis had more to do with resistance against state intrusion and public spending than with federalism. Essentially, the federal government was used as a proxy for state intrusion and secular control. Although that resistance was overlaid by a more specific concern with religious and cultural preservation in Quebec, it was essentially a fundamental struggle about the role of the state in social matters.

While the role of the state characterized this ideological debate, the other enduring fault line is the demarcation of responsibilities between the federal and provincial states. Here the fault lines become more complex. Quebec, during and after the Quiet Revolution, found itself at odds not so much with the federal government's characterization of the role of the state in health and other social matters, but rather with the location of that state power. Successive Quebec governments since the 1960s have wanted the provincial state to wield that power.

In the decades since these pivotal moments in health policy development, both tensions have persisted. Today, reformers such as Claude Castonguay have become outspoken critics of the public system in Quebec and have laid much of the blame for its shortcomings on the absence of private funding and on the rigidity of the Canada Health Act. And the controversy over the landmark *Chaoulli v. Quebec* case and its aftermath indicate the profound societal debate on these matters.

CASE STUDY

The Doctors' Strike in Quebec

The 1970 strike by specialist physicians in Quebec would be one of the most bitter labour disputes in the province, and it would coincide with one of the darkest periods in Quebec history, known as the October Crisis.

In anticipation of the development of public medical insurance in Quebec, two organizations were founded in the 1960s: a federation of general practitioners known as the FMOQ (Fédération des médecins omnipraticiens du Québec) and a federation of specialists known as the FMSQ (Fédération des médecins spécialistes du Québec). They were recognized by government and by professionals as the collective bargaining agents for physicians in Quebec.

This arrangement offers another example of Quebec's distinctiveness vis-à-vis the other provinces. The Association des médecins de langue française du Canada was founded in 1902 as a language-based association of francophone doctors in Quebec and across Canada. This association represented more than the economic and professional interests of its members; it was seen as a vital marker of the identity of its cultural group in Canada and Quebec. As the politics of identity changed, so did the role of traditional professions like physicians. By the 1960s, the Canadian Medical Association had emerged as the most powerful lobby of physicians in Canada, with federated associations in every province, but its representative group in Quebec, the Quebec Medical Association, remained a relatively weak professional association, particularly among francophone doctors. In addition, as the Quebec state began to extend its reach into social and economic life, physicians would become "syndicalized" in a different way than their counterparts in other provinces.

When medical insurance legislation was tabled in Quebec in June 1970 as Bill 8, it soon became apparent that not all physicians relished this new initiative. While the generalists in the FMOQ agreed to negotiate with the provincial government, the specialists' federation refused to sign on to the agreement. The Quebec legislation differed significantly from other provincial initiatives in that it limited the opting-out provisions for physicians and prohibited extra billing altogether.

The FMSQ leaders likened the bill to "conscription," forcing specialists to practise in the public system. The most controversial aspects for specialists were twofold: They wanted a guarantee that they could opt out of the public system and practise on their own, and they wanted to retain the right to bill over and above the fee schedule (extra billing). The specialists argued that this would allow more experienced physicians to charge a differential fee that would reflect their expertise.

Despite the efforts of the Quebec government—including the minister of health, Claude Castonguay—to negotiate with physicians, by the autumn of 1970 Quebec specialists were moving toward strike action. They were widely supported by colleagues throughout Canada. A precedent had been set in Saskatchewan, where in 1962 physicians had gone on strike to protest the implementation of the Saskatchewan medical insurance plan. Although the strike proved to be unpopular, the Saskatchewan government had in effect agreed to allow extra billing by physicians. Note that the two cases were not identical; in Saskatchewan the entire medical community went on strike as opposed to only specialists in Quebec.

With the entry date for the new medical insurance system announced for 1 November 1970, the FMSQ voted for strike action on 8 October. As specialists pulled back their services, leaving patients and medical students without recourse, Quebec was already plunged in an unprecedented political crisis. Just days before, on 5 October, British diplomat James Cross had been kidnapped by members of the Front de libération du Québec (FLQ) and only days later, on 10 October, another FLQ cell would kidnap Quebec Labour Minister Pierre Laporte. As the War Measures Act came into effect and Laporte's murdered body was found, it became clear that the specialists had no hope of winning any public relations battle or labour conflict with the Quebec government. The National Assembly held a special session to pass legislation that forced the specialists to return to work, and on 18 October the strike was officially over. On 11 November, the FMSQ formally signed an agreement with the provincial government that would allow its members to be reimbursed for their services through the Régie de l'Assurance-maladie. Although some concessions were made over fee schedules and paid leave, the ban on extra billing remained in place.

continued

Although the strike was unpopular and coincided with an extraordinary political crisis, the debate over extra billing was not really resolved. Many Quebec specialists voted with their feet and moved out of the province as a consequence. Extra billing remained the Achilles heel for many provincial governments trying to regulate their health-care systems. In 1984, the passage of the Canada Health Act explicitly prohibited extra billing by physicians, forcing several provinces to change their health-care legislation to comply with the new federal statute. A strike by the Ontario Medical Association in 1986 to protest a new ban on extra billing was inspired by the Quebec example. It proved just as unpopular, not only among the public but also among members of the medical community, and ended within a month.

Portions of this chapter appeared in *Parting at the Crossroads: The Emergence of Health Insurance in the United States and Canada*, by Antonia Maioni (Princeton, NJ: Princeton University Press, 1998).

Questions for Critical Thought

1. How have recent events changed the debate around health-care reform in Quebec?
2. Why is health care a central feature of Quebec's Quiet Revolution?
3. What makes federalism so important in the study of health care in Quebec?

Notes

1. Terry Boychuck, *The Making and Meaning of Hospital Policy in the United States and Canada* (Ann Arbor: University of Michigan Press, 1999), 47.
2. Joseph Facal, *Volonté politique et pouvoir médical* (Montreal: Boréal, 2006), 32.
3. Antonia Maioni, "The Marsh Report and the Post-War Welfare State in Canada," *Policy Options/Options politiques* (August 2004): 20–3, 21.
4. Yves Vaillancourt, *L'évolution des politiques sociales au Québec, 1940–1960* (Montreal: Presses de l'Université de Montréal, 1988), 176–7.
5. Ibid., 177–9.
6. House of Commons, *Debates*, 20 June 1951, 4349.
7. Statement by St Laurent broadcast on the CBC on 9 July 1953; reprinted in House of Commons, *Debates*, 19 June 1954, 6302.
8. The official title was *La Commission royale d'enquête sur les problèmes constitutionnels* (Royal Commission on Constitutional Problems).
9. Guy Lachapelle, Gérald Bernier, Daniel Salée, and Luc Bernier, *The Québec Democracy: Structures, Processes and Policies* (Toronto: McGraw-Hill Ryerson, 1993), 380.
10. Public Archives of Canada; Record Group 29; Vol. 1061; 500-3-4 Pt. 1 ("Confidential"); "Working Committee on Health Insurance of the Interdepartmental Committee on Social Security: Final Draft of Report," 14 February 1950.
11. Malcolm G. Taylor, *Health Insurance and Canadian Public Policy: The Seven Decisions that Created the Canadian Health Insurance System and Their Outcomes*, 2nd ed. (Montreal and Kingston: McGill-Queen's University Press, 1987), 193–4. This group had substantial political influence given its regional and linguistic concentration.
12. The other four were Saskatchewan, British Columbia, Alberta, and Newfoundland. On this legislative adventure, see Taylor, *Health Insurance and Canadian Public Policy*, ch. 4; Paul Martin, *A Very Public Life*, vol. 2, *So Many Worlds* (Ottawa: Deneau, 1983), ch. 7.
13. Vaillancourt, *L'évolution des politiques sociales au Québec*, 198–9.
14. Ibid., 200. For a sociological portrait of this changing society, see Marcel Rioux and Yves Martin, eds., *French-Canadian Society*, vol. 1 (Toronto: McClelland & Stewart, 1964).
15. This was the argument made by Jean Lesage at federal-provincial conferences in the 1960s; see Governement du Québec, *Position historique du Québec sur le pouvoir fédéral de dépenser, 1944–1998*, July 1998, 7–9; see also

Alain-G. Gagnon and Mary Beth Montcalm, *Quebec: Beyond the Quiet Revolution* (Toronto: Nelson Canada, 1990).
16. Facal, *Volonté politique et pouvoir médical.*
17. Boychuck, *The Making and Meaning of Hospital Policy*, 98.
18. This story is well told in Edwin A. Tollefson, "The Medicare Dispute," in *Politics in Saskatchewan*, ed. N. Ward and D. Spafford (Toronto: Longmans Canada, 1968); and Robin F. Badgley and Samuel Wolfe, *Doctors' Strike: Medical Care and Conflict in Saskatchewan* (Toronto: Macmillan, 1967).
19. *Report of the Royal Commission on Health Services*, vol. 1, 1964, 19. These services included medical, drug, prosthetic, and home care for all, and dental and optical services for specific groups.
20. Taylor, *Health Insurance and Canadian Public Policy*, 387.
21. Ibid., 386. The four principles were comprehensiveness, universality, portability, and public administration; the fifth, equal access, was eventually added via the 1984 Canada Health Act. For an overview of the birth of Quebec Medicare, see ibid., chapter 7.
22. Richard Simeon, *Federal–Provincial Diplomacy: The Making of Recent Policy in Canada* (Toronto: University of Toronto Press, 2006), 59; Claude Morin, *Mes premiers ministres* (Montreal: Boréal, 1991), 140–2.
23. Réjean Pelletier, "La Révolution tranquille," in *Le Québec en jeu : comprendre les grands défis*, ed. G. Daigle and G. Rocher (Montreal: Presses de l'Université de Montréal, 1992).
24. Claude Castonguay, *Mémoires d'un révolutionnaire tranquille* (Montreal: Boréal, 2006), 48–50.
25. Ibid., 54–6. The extension of the commission's reach to social welfare was apparently a surprise for Castonguay, but it would have far-reaching consequences in the future organization of Quebec's health and social services.
26. Ibid., 59.
27. Taylor, *Health Insurance and Canadian Public Policy*, 391; Facal, *Volonté politique et pouvoir médical*, 42.
28. John Meisel, Guy Rocher, and Arthur Silver, *As I Recall/Si je me souviens bien: Historical Perspectives* (Montreal: Institute for Research on Public Policy, 1999), 149; Taylor, *Health Insurance and Canadian Public Policy*, 392–3.
29. On the left, meanwhile, union leaders pressed for coverage of prescription drugs and other noninsured services; Bill 69, passed the following year, would guarantee prescription drug coverage to the elderly and social welfare recipients, as well as dental care for children (Facal, *Volonté politique et pouvoir médical*, 53).
30. Facal, *Volonté politique et pouvoir médical*, 50–1.
31. See Marc Renaud, "Réforme ou illusion? Une analyse des interventions de l'État québécois dans le domaine de la santé," *Sociologie et sociétés* 9, no. 1 (1977): 127–52.
32. Facal, *Volonté politique et pouvoir médical*, 44–5.
33. See Raynald Pineault, Andre-Pierre Contandriopoulos, and Richard Lessard, "The Quebec Health System: Care Objectives or Health Objectives?" *Journal of Public Health Policy* 6, no. 3 (September 1985): 394–409.
34. Jean Turgeon and Vincent Lemieux, "La décentralisation : panacée ou boîte de Pandore?" in *Le système de santé québécois : un modèle en transformation*, ed. Clermont Bégin et al. (Montreal: Presses de l'Université de Montréal, 1999), 173–94.
35. Renaud, "Réforme ou illusion?"
36. Pierre Bergeron, "La commission Rochon reproduit les solutions de Castonguay-Nepveu," *Recherches sociographiques* 31, no. 3 (1990): 359–80.
37. Morin, *Mes premiers ministres*, 407–8.
38. Miriam Smith and Antonia Maioni, "Health Care and Canadian Federalism," in *New Trends in Canadian Federalism*, ed. François Rocher and Miriam Smith (Peterborough, ON: Broadview Press, 2003).
39. Antonia Maioni, *Health Care in Canada* (Don Mills, ON: Oxford University Press, 2014), ch. 4.
40. Christopher P. Manfredi and Antonia Maioni, "The Last Line of Defence for Citizens: Litigating Private Health Insurance in *Chaoulli v. Quebec*," *Osgoode Hall Law Journal* 44, no. 2 (Fall 2006): 249–71.
41. Colleen Flood, "Canada's Approach to the Public/Private Divide and the Perils of Reform via Court Challenge," *Public Policy Review* 8, no. 2 (2012): 191–214.
42. Claude Castonguay, *Getting Our Money's Worth: Report of the Task Force on the Funding of the Health Care System* (Quebec: Ministry of Finance, 2008).
43. Ministry of Finance, "Budget 2010–11: For a More Efficient and Better Funded Health-Care System" (Quebec: Ministry of Finance, March 2010).

Select Bibliography

Boychuck, Terry. *The Making and Meaning of Hospital Policy in the United States and Canada.* Ann Arbor: University of Michigan Press, 1999.

Castonguay, Claude. *Mémoires d'un révolutionnaire tranquille.* Montreal: Boréal, 2006.

Facal, Joseph. *Volonté politique et pouvoir médical.* Montreal: Boréal, 2006.

Lee, Sidney S. *Quebec's Health System: A Decade of Change, 1967–1977.* Ottawa: Institute of Public Administration of Canada, 1979.

Maioni, Antonia. *Health Care in Canada,* Chapter 4. Don Mills, ON: Oxford University Press, 2014.

Manfredi, Christopher P., and Antonia Maioni. "The Last Line of Defence for Citizens: Litigating Private Health Insurance in *Chaoulli v. Quebec.*" *Osgoode Hall Law Journal* 44, no. 2 (Fall 2006): 249–71.

Smith, Miriam, and Antonia Maioni. "Health Care and Canadian Federalism." In *New Trends in Canadian Federalism,* edited by François Rocher and Miriam Smith. Peterborough, ON: Broadview Press, 2003.

Taylor, Malcolm G. *Health Insurance and Canadian Public Policy: The Seven Decisions that Created the Canadian Health Insurance System and Their Outcomes,* 2nd ed. Montreal and Kingston: McGill-Queen's University Press, 1987.

Vaillancourt, Yves. *L'évolution des politiques sociales au Québec, 1940–1960.* Montreal: Presses de l'Université de Montréal, 1988.

24 Legal Tradition, National Identity, and Quebec Exceptionalism[1]

Daniel Jutras, McGill University

Timeline

1664 French royal edict sets up Custom of Paris as uniform law of New France.

1763 Treaty of Paris is signed. New France becomes a British colony. Royal Proclamation introduces English law and institutions in the colony.

1774 Quebec Act is signed. Civil law re-established in all matters of property and civil rights.

1791 Constitutional Act creating Upper and Lower Canada.

1804 Civil Code is adopted and comes into force in France.

1837–8 Rebellions in Lower and Upper Canada.

1840 Act of Union.

1843 Law courses first dispensed at McGill College in Montreal.

1854 Seigneurial Act and abolition of seigneurial system in Lower Canada.

1857 Act provides for codification of laws of Lower Canada following the style and arrangement of the French Civil Code.

1866 Civil Code of Lower Canada comes into force.

1867 British North American provinces become the Canadian Confederation.

1875 Supreme Court of Canada is established.

1911 Annie Macdonald Langstaff is the first woman to be admitted to a law school in Quebec. She will never be allowed to join the bar.

1940 Women are granted the right to vote in provincial elections in Quebec.

1942 Elizabeth Monk becomes the first woman allowed to join the Quebec Bar.

1955 Duplessis government introduces an act providing for the revision of the Civil Code of Lower Canada.

1964 Married women are granted legal capacity.

continued

1965 Creation of the Civil Code Revision Office.

1966 Major conference in Montreal to mark the 100th anniversary of the Civil Code of Lower Canada.

1971 Consumer Protection Act comes into force.

1975 Quebec Charter of Human Rights and Freedoms is adopted.

1976 Parti Québécois comes to power.

1978 Civil Code Revision Office tables a project for a new Civil Code in the National Assembly.

1980 Referendum on sovereignty-association is held in Quebec.

Family law is overhauled with adoption of a free-standing first chapter of the Civil Code that will come 10 years later.

1987 Meech Lake Accord recognizes Quebec as a distinct society.

1990 Meech Lake Accord fails to gather the necessary ratifications from all provinces.

1991 Civil Code of Quebec is adopted by a unanimous vote of the National Assembly.

1994 Civil Code of Quebec comes into force.

2014 Supreme Court of Canada rules that Federal Court of Appeal Justice Marc Nadon is ineligible for appointment to the Court.

Legal Traditions—in the Plural?

In September 2013, Canadian Prime Minister Stephen Harper announced his intention to appoint Justice Marc Nadon to the Supreme Court of Canada, filling a vacancy created by the retirement of Morris Fish. Justice Nadon's appointment was to take effect on 3 October 2013. It was challenged almost immediately.[2]

Nine judges sit on the highest court in the country. Under the terms of the Canadian *Supreme Court Act*, three of them must come from the province of Quebec, or to be more specific, three must be appointed from among the ranks of Quebec judges or among Quebec lawyers with at least 10 years of experience. Although Justice Nadon had been a member of the Quebec Bar prior to his appointment to the judiciary, his judicial career was spent as a member of a court dealing with federal matters, rather than on a court of general jurisdiction within the province of Quebec. Was he nonetheless eligible for appointment to the Supreme Court of Canada as one of the three Quebec judges? After all, he had been educated in Quebec, had practised law in that province for more than 10 years, and arguably was, in cultural terms, a member of that legal community.

One might think that Justice Nadon's eligibility for appointment depended on some odd idea of continued belonging to a **legal tradition**. But that was not the case, at least not explicitly. In legal terms, the question turned on a difficult issue of interpretation of the *Supreme Court Act*. Ultimately, it was brought to the Supreme Court of Canada on a reference, a process by which the federal government asked for the Court's opinion on this matter. On 21 March 2014, a majority of the Court found that Justice Nadon was not eligible to occupy one of the three Quebec seats on the Court.[3] He was neither a present nor former justice of a Quebec superior court, nor a current member of the Quebec Bar. The Court explained that this narrower construction of the eligibility requirements was consistent with the purpose of the *Supreme Court Act*: "to give effect to the historical compromise aimed at protecting Quebec's legal traditions and social values."[4] Justice Nadon's years on the federal bench had effectively taken him out of the Quebec legal community. Several months later, Prime Minister Harper finally filled the outstanding vacancy on the Supreme Court of Canada with the appointment of Justice Clément Gascon, a member of the Quebec Court of Appeal.

Whether or not the Supreme Court's interpretation of its own constitutive statute is compelling matters less than the ways in which it affirms the distinctiveness of Quebec's legal identity. The Court's decision states that a key element of its composition, the requirement that three judges hail from Quebec, is necessary to protect "both the functioning and the legitimacy of the Supreme Court as a general court of appeal for Canada." The presence of three jurists meeting the strict eligibility requirement ensures that a third of the Court's members understand and reflect "Quebec's distinct legal traditions and social values."[5] The Court's decision also states that this feature of its composition is now constitutionally entrenched, in the sense that it cannot be modified without a constitutional amendment requiring the unanimous consent of Parliament and provincial legislative assemblies. Indeed, in the constitutional negotiations that led to the Meech Lake Accord and the Charlottetown Accord, the constitutional guarantee of Quebec seats on the Supreme Court of Canada had figured prominently. A unique legal tradition was consistently presented as one of the three historical pillars of Quebec's distinct society, along with language and religion. While neither the Meech Lake Accord nor the Charlottetown Accord ever resulted in formal constitutional recognition of this guarantee, the Supreme Court's decision in the Nadon case is only the latest episode in a long line of constitutional events dating back to 1774, underlining the distinctiveness of Quebec's legal tradition and the significance of that fact as a marker of identity and culture.

There is no doubt that, within the Canadian legal order, Quebec's legal system is distinctive. Whereas the other provinces' legal systems are tied to the English **common law** tradition, Quebec's roots are found in the French **civil law** tradition. But Quebec's legal system is also mixed: The present shape of Quebec law is the product of the interplay of common law and civil law in the unique bilingual, **bijural** North American setting of the province of Quebec. There is of course a purely legal dimension to these historical roots of Quebec law. They dictate the configuration of its legal order, the ways in which law is expressed in different sources and texts, and the conceptual structure that determines legal outcomes in the province. But arguably, the significance of Quebec's legal traditions extends far beyond the legal domain into the political, social, and cultural spheres. How do legal traditions come to form part of national identity? Is the amalgamation of legal tradition and national identity anything more than a political slogan? Does it have implications beyond the discourse of legal elites? These questions are explored in the Quebec context in the last section of this essay. But first, we must examine the roots and shape of Quebec's legal system.

BIOGRAPHY

Paul-André Crépeau

Paul-André Crépeau (1926–2011) was the most significant civil law scholar and legal intellectual of the twentieth century in Quebec. Surprisingly, perhaps, he was not born in Quebec. Crépeau grew up in Gravelbourg, Saskatchewan. Abbé Louis-Pierre Gravel, a

Courtesy of the Faculty of Law of McGill University.

Catholic priest, founded this small town in 1906, just 20 years before Crépeau's birth, with the explicit purpose of bringing back to Western Canada the French Canadians who had moved to the United States in search of a better life. Abbé Gravel toured Quebec

continued

and the United States to recruit settlers for his new parish and spent the next 20 years of his life building this French-speaking, Catholic community in southern Saskatchewan.

Paul-André Crépeau's father came to Gravelbourg in 1917. Jean-Baptiste (Jack) Crépeau was an American of French-Canadian descent who was born in Minnesota. As a lawyer in the town he had acquired a certain prominence, but he was also an active Liberal in a very Conservative province. Paul-André Crépeau's mother, Blanche Provencher, was a French-Canadian teacher. She came from Plessisville in Quebec to educate children in Gravelbourg at the request of Abbé Gravel. Their home was bilingual: Crépeau and his four older siblings grew up speaking French to their mother and English to their father. After his father passed away suddenly when Crépeau was eight, the mother and her two daughters struggled to make sure that the three boys would get an education: All three became lawyers like their father, one in Saskatchewan and two in Quebec. Crépeau moved back east with his mother at the age of 17. They settled in Ottawa, where Crépeau obtained degrees in philosophy and economics at the University of Ottawa. Later in life he rarely mentioned his studies in economics, having discovered that his professors had inexplicably ignored the innovative and dominant thought of the "socialist" John Maynard Keynes.

In 1950 Paul-André Crépeau completed his law degree at the University of Montreal, where he had been president of the Law Students Association. He then joined the Quebec Bar—but he was destined for an academic career. Having earned a Rhodes Scholarship, Crépeau set sail for the United Kingdom and completed graduate studies in law at Oxford University. He then moved on to Paris, where he completed a prize-winning doctoral thesis on medical liability. He met his wife-to-be, Nicole, in Jerusalem while on a pilgrimage to the Holy Land. In 1955 he returned to the Faculty of Law at the University of Montreal as a young professor, joining his former classmate Jean Beetz, who later served as a justice of the Supreme Court of Canada. Crépeau became part of an emerging group of young scholars constituting the first generation of full-time French-Canadian legal academics. In 1959 he was recruited by McGill University, moved across the mountain, and began teaching civil law in English. He remained at McGill for the rest of his career, despite an unfruitful attempt by the University of Montreal to bring him back to his alma mater as dean of the Faculty of Law.

Crépeau's career was to take an unexpected turn during the 1960s. The Duplessis years had just ended, and a new Liberal government, led by Jean Lesage, was in power in Quebec City. Crépeau was about to take over the work of revising the Civil Code of Lower Canada. The project had begun rather poorly: In 1957, Duplessis had appointed the former chief justice of Canada Thibaudeau Rinfret to lead the revision of the aging Civil Code. Rinfret had worked on his own, with limited resources, and concluded that piecemeal amendments would suffice, as an overhaul of the Code would be too disruptive. André Nadeau, a prominent lawyer, replaced Rinfret within a few years, but also made limited progress. Crépeau briefly served as Nadeau's secretary before taking over the project: a new legislation, adopted in 1965, created the Civil Code Revision Office. Minister of Justice Claude Wagner named Crépeau president of the office and provided him with resources and a broader mandate, one that was consistent with the discourse of change and social reconstruction that characterized the early 1960s in Quebec. The idea of minimal amendments was abandoned. The entire Code had to be revisited and brought in line with the values of a transformed society. Crépeau's vision for the new Code was always clearly articulated.[6] He saw the Civil Code as the manifestation of a democratic conception of law in which the elected legislative assembly, rather than the judge, is the most important voice. Crépeau also valued the literary quality of the Code, the clarity and elegance of its text, in both French and English. Finally, he imagined the Code as a structured, organic, and coherent expression of the *droit commun* and fundamental values of a community. This vision was eventually captured in the Preliminary Provision of the Civil Code of Quebec.

Efficient, organized, and entrepreneurial, Crépeau set out to complete the task by bringing together and supervising over 40 small committees of experts in each of the areas of law covered by the Code. More than 200 lawyers, notaries, judges, and a new cohort of legal academics and scholars produced reports and draft text for a new Code. The Civil Code Revision Office then organized consultations with civil society on each of the proposals and collated and coordinated the drafts. Within 12 years of intense work that absorbed the creative energies of a generation of private law scholars (and most likely diverted them from more fundamental research and legal theory), the office put together a full project for a new Civil Code of Quebec: 3,288 articles, written in both French and English, accompanied by two volumes of commentaries. In late 1977, Crépeau presented the project to the minister of justice, and in 1978, he brought it to Quebec's National Assembly. It was then that the wheels came off. Crépeau's proposed Civil Code was never adopted as such. It lingered in the bureaucracy of the Ministry of Justice for another 13 years before a somewhat different version was adopted unanimously by the National Assembly in 1991 and came into effect on 1 January 1994.

Several factors explain the slow progress of the proposed Civil Code in the late 1970s through the 1980s. First, while reform of private law was a significant government priority in the mid-sixties when Crépeau assumed the leadership of the Civil Code Revision Office, the legal landscape had changed a decade later. Key pieces of legislation in private law had already been adopted, including the *Consumer Protection Act*, and important amendments to the Code had been made in respect of matrimonial property. The Quebec Charter of Human Rights and Freedoms, originally intended to constitute the first chapter of a new Code, was already in effect as a free-standing statement of fundamental rights and values and seemed more significant than the Code. Indeed, in a report prepared with his McGill colleague Frank Scott, Crépeau himself had paved the way for the adoption of this Charter by the Liberal government.

By the end of the 1970s the political landscape had changed as well. The Parti Québécois was now in power, and its minister of justice was no longer pushing for the comprehensive reform of the Civil Code. The national question was occupying the political foreground. Constitutional law was the order of the day, rather than the reconfiguration of the law of contracts and property. Public law scholars were occupying the limelight, and a referendum on the national question was in the works. Reforming family law was viewed as urgent and could not wait for the entire Code to go through the legislative process. Most significantly, perhaps, the internal bureaucracy of the Ministry of Justice took the view that the Civil Code project could not be abandoned to an unelected group of academics and legal experts. The new Code had to go through the normal deliberative processes of legislation. Hence, somewhat surprisingly, the report that had been carefully prepared by dozens of jurists over 12 years with government funding and support, and with the benefit of broad consultations within civil society, was sent to two experts appointed by the minister for further advice. Over the next 13 years, after several additional internal reports and reviews, legislative redrafting, parliamentary commissions, and on-and-off opposition from the Quebec Bar and Board of Notaries fighting over their respective markets, the Civil Code of Quebec was finally adopted.

Paul-André Crépeau did not participate in this final phase of legislative activity. His work was done with the 1978 report of the Civil Code Revision Office and, gentleman that he was, he stepped aside. After that time he devoted his energies to fundamental scholarship on civil law and legal terminology as the director of a research

continued

centre on private and comparative law that now bears his name at McGill University. His pioneering work on jurilinguistics led to the creation of a bilingual dictionary in private law in several volumes, an ongoing project that earned Crépeau and his team several awards—including two Prix du Québec—and global recognition.

As he approached retirement age, Professor Crépeau became one of the most recognizable figures in international legal circles. He presided over the International Academy of Comparative Law through the 1990s, sat as a member of the Permanent Court of Arbitration at The Hague, and was a leading member of the prestigious working group of Unidroit (the International Institute for the Unification of Private Law). He spent his summers in France, in the Berri region, where his French father-in-law had a property. When he passed away in 2011, at the age of 85, Paul-André Crépeau was still deeply immersed in his scholarship, saving some time for his grandchildren.

Paul-André Crépeau's career is emblematic of the multiple strands of Quebec's legal identity and of the ways in which they were intertwined over the course of the twentieth century. Born in Saskatchewan, enormously proud of his French and Catholic heritage, educated in elite institutions in France and the United Kingdom, Paul-André Crépeau spent his life teaching civil law in French and English at McGill University in Montreal. He lived through the transition of law schools from narrow professional training grounds to research-based higher education. He was the catalyst for and leader of a project to redraft Quebec's Civil Code that galvanized the legal academic community, but failed to capture the imagination of political authorities distracted by the constitutional fate of the province. He was bilingual but most of all culturally connected to France and continental Europe; trained in the civil law and common law but mostly committed to the former. He was, above all, a leading academic deeply engaged in the public sphere of law reform. He embodied the spirit of his time through his pride in the vitality of Quebec civil law and the beauty of its expression in both languages, and the strong faith he had in the capacity of this legal tradition to breathe new life into the highly symbolic legislative exercise that is codification.

Civil Law Roots

The word *tradition* is loaded with negative connotations of static adherence to the ways of the past and reverence for outdated practices and ideas. With this in mind, speaking of Quebec's legal traditions might be mistakenly understood as referring to old rules and customs that still lurk in the present, much as old songs drawn from the folklore of Nouvelle-France still form part of Quebec's musical heritage. But the concept of a legal tradition is more dynamic than this: It refers to the ways in which any contemporary legal order can be understood as both the product and the site of an ongoing conversation about law which began in the distant past. It rests in the historical continuity, transformation, and present relevance—"the changing presence of the past," says H. Patrick Glenn—of a set of normative practices, discourses, and ideas.[7] Some legal traditions, such as the Talmudic or Islamic traditions, have primarily religious origins. Others, like the Western traditions of civil law and common law, emerged in Europe as responses to the imperatives of feudal governance and nation-building. In continental Europe, the civil law tradition grew from scholarly analysis of foundational Roman legal texts, slowly displacing the patchwork of tribal and local customs that were prevalent in that part of the world well into the eighteenth century. English common law, for its part, was built over centuries as the accumulated wisdom and procedural practices of the royal courts of England. Both the civil law and the common law constitute "extensions of the past into the present," ever changing but always recognizable projections of ideas about law, the role of lawmakers and judges, and the connection of rules to rationality and experience. In a pattern of undeniable historical continuity, Quebec's legal order is tied to both of these legal traditions as ongoing conversations. But its roots are firmly planted in the civil law tradition.

The idea of a unified national legal system, with a single set of written laws and an organized judiciary and legal profession, was not yet realized in France as its colony in North America began to grow in the seventeenth century. The law in France was a patchwork of unwritten Germanic customs in the north and a distinct set of legal sources in the south, drawn primarily from Roman legal texts adapted to local conditions. The unification of these different sources of law would only be accomplished later, after the French Revolution, in a Napoleonic codification that was a crucial element in the construction of France as a nation-state. Nonetheless, the Custom of Paris—the set of customary laws that was followed in the great city and its surroundings—was captured in writing in 1580 and had acquired a certain prestige and visibility. In the north of France, it was slowly emerging as the dominant set of rules governing the private interactions of citizens in matters of property, seigneurial land holding, and inheritance. It is this set of customary norms, the Custom of Paris, that was established as the law of New France by a French royal edict of 1664, which sought to provide the colony with a unified legal system as well as the administrative structures of civil government. Formally, that aspiration was realized, although it is probable that the customary norms gave rise to a diversity of legal solutions on the ground as inhabitants and notaries[8] developed their own modulations of the Custom of Paris.

The Custom of Paris came far short of providing a body of rules for all aspects of life. The laws of the Roman Catholic Church, known as canon law, governed family matters. As for the law of contracts and personal obligations, it was significantly influenced by the work of Romanist scholars whose ideas already formed part of the French legal tradition in the seventeenth century as a form of *raison écrite*, or written reason. This interplay of customary, religious, and Romanist sources of law in continental Europe constituted a unique way of doing law—a unique conversation about law that we now know as the civil law tradition.

With the reception of the Custom of Paris, the origin of Quebec's legal tradition was thus determined: It would find its roots in the civil law. Although the substantive content of Quebec law today bears little resemblance to the peculiarities of old French law, key elements of its legal culture can only be fully understood as contemporary manifestations of ideas, debates, and conceptual structures that can be traced back to the Enlightenment, sixteenth-century France, the writings of Renaissance legal scholars, all the way to Roman law as old as the first century BCE.

This heritage was not displaced at the end of the French Regime in 1760. Legal historians describe the period that immediately followed England's military victory and the establishment of a new local government as one of deep uncertainty.[9] The initial intention of English colonial rule was apparently to replace the civil law tradition of the colony with a legal order that was consistent with the laws of England. In this the English Crown was never entirely successful. At the end of military rule, in 1763, new courts were established that were meant to decide cases in accordance with English law. While there is no doubt that the English Crown established English administrative, political, and judicial structures, and introduced English criminal law into the colony, the rules of private law—property, family and the status of persons, inheritance, contracts, obligations, ordinary rules of commerce and trade, and rules of procedure in civil disputes—remained in flux. Local customary juridical practices most likely continued, not necessarily as a form of passive resistance but as a manifestation of the legal pluralism that is inherent in such a complex political and social setting.

The state of unrest in the American colonies and the need to secure the loyalty of French Canadians in this conflict, coupled with persistent uncertainty regarding the status of legal sources in the colony, called into question the wisdom of attempting to displace old French law, at least in respect of the rules governing private interaction. In 1774, English authorities adopted the Quebec Act, which explicitly restored "the laws of Canada" in "Property and Civil Rights." While the Quebec Act reaffirmed the introduction of English criminal law in the colony, preserved the structure of the judiciary along English traditions, and modified important aspects of private law (grounding future land concessions in the rules of English law and recognizing freedom of willing), it essentially reconnected the King's Canadien subjects with their civil law roots and tradition. In the decades that followed, this political strategy produced sustained opposition from many in the English and Scottish elite and merchant class, as well as "inhabitants of British birth and descent" from counties in the Eastern Townships, south of Montreal and close to the US border.[10] Nonetheless, the civil law tradition in Quebec was never eradicated, and its continued existence was reaffirmed at each stage of the construction of Canada in constitutional documents of 1791, 1840, and 1867.

Toward Codification

Over the first half of the nineteenth century, the legal regime of Lower Canada (as it then was) continued as an amalgam of English public law that governed criminal law and the administration of the colony, and old French private law that governed matters closer to the daily lives of its citizens. Through ad hoc legislation and judicial decisions, some elements of old French law were set aside or abandoned, and bits and pieces of English law were adopted, particularly in commercial matters. The legal system remained a quiet battleground between French and English elites, the former protecting its legal customs and privileges against the efforts of the latter to avoid a legal regime they neither understood nor appreciated. But the core of Quebec private law remained civilian in substance and in form.[11]

This said, Quebec law was nothing like French law at the time. By the early nineteenth century France had gone through extraordinary political turmoil and reconstructed its legal system through the adoption of a great **civil code** that was meant to capture, rationally organize, and preserve for all time the foundational principles of a unified national legal order. By virtue of its separation from France, the *Mère Patrie*, Lower Canada had been cut off from these transformations of French legal culture. Local jurists were critical of the radical excesses of the French Revolution and continued to rely on old French law, a legal heritage that was more in line with the conservative, rural, and religious values of French-Canadian society at the time. In other words, sixteenth-century feudal law survived in the North American colony of Lower Canada after it was abandoned in France. But the overall picture of legal sources in Quebec was increasingly complex. In addition to old French law and its arcane interpretation, lawyers and judges had to be familiar with local statutes, ordinances, and judicial decisions as well as some English common law and statutes where applicable. Legal sources were available in English or in French, but rarely in both. The Custom of Paris, in particular, did not exist in English. Legal education was emerging at McGill University and Laval University, but there were no scholars in the grand civilian tradition to organize, synthesize, or rationalize the local civil law vernacular. By the middle of the nineteenth century, in the wake of the rebellion of 1837, the stage was set for major legislative efforts to modernize the legal and political institutions of Canada, with the aim of promoting its economic development and eventual industrialization.

The first step in this transformation involved significant shifts in the laws governing land tenure and registration of land rights. A first measure came in 1841 with an ordinance on the registration of titles to land, which was intended to enhance the security and predictability of land dealings. But the system was not truly universal and did not cure all uncertainties. Then, through the Seigneurial Act of 1854, the rights of the seigneurs over land were abolished and the full ownership of their tenants, known as *censitaires*, was confirmed. With the exception of a small portion of the territory in the Eastern Townships, where land tenure granted after the Conquest had been established on English law, land holding in the province moved away from feudalism. From a regime in which the seigneurs owned the land and collected dues from the local farmers who toiled on it, land holding shifted to a regime in which the farmers themselves owned the land. Seigneurial rights were converted into monetary debts, which were eventually paid off and abolished. In time, a uniform set of property law and a somewhat imperfect land registration system were adopted for the entire province. Land would more easily become the object of commercial speculation and development.

The now defunct seigneurial system had been part of the historical infrastructure of old French law and was for many an essential aspect of the *survivance* of a conservative set of French-Canadian values: religious, rural, and patriarchal. By the middle of the nineteenth century, a new generation of francophone elites viewed its abolition as one piece in the necessary modernization of the legal system. Codification of the laws would be the other foundational piece.[12] The impetus came, in part, from the example of the *Code Civil des Français* adopted in France in 1804 at the initiative of Napoleon. The French Code brought together in a single document, in clear and simple language, all of the rules governing basic legal institutions: the status of persons, family relations, property, successions, contracts, and other obligations. In several respects, it gave effect to liberal values of autonomy, freedom of contract, and unimpeded private ownership that were so important to the emergence of a capitalist market economy. But it was less the set of values embedded in the French Code than its technical advantages that fed the project of codification in Lower Canada.[13] A civil code for Lower Canada would bring an end to the confusion of legal sources, resolve inconsistencies between them, make them all available in both French and English, and do so in a legislative form that reaffirmed the civil law roots of what was to become the province of Quebec. It was politically risky for francophone elites to acknowledge the latter purpose, which explains why the technical benefits were put forward most prominently. Yet the carving out of a law of French origin in an iconic code mirroring its French counterpart no doubt was becoming increasingly important since the project of political unification of Canada into a confederation was gathering strength and support. From a much needed compilation of the laws in force in Quebec at the time, the Code would also come to be imagined as a shield against the threat of harmonization of laws across Canada. It would also stand as a monument to the *grandeur* of the French civil law tradition in North America.

In 1857 a Codification Commission was established by George-Étienne Cartier with a clear mandate to produce a Code that would bring together the law then in force, propose and clearly identify changes wherever necessary, and present the resulting text in an outline that followed, as much as possible, the arrangement of the French Civil Code. The composition of the commission reflected the linguistic and cultural duality of the legal community in Lower Canada.[14] All commissioners were trained in the civil law. The chair of the commission, René-Édouard Caron, was part of the legal establishment in Quebec City, where he had served as mayor. He had built a remunerative legal practice before being appointed to the judiciary. Augustin-Norbert Morin's career was spent in entrepreneurship, nationalist politics, and journalism in Montreal and Quebec City. A lawyer by training, he had served as the first dean of the law faculty established at Université Laval and was appointed to the bench in 1855. As for Charles Dewey Day, he was, according to historian Brian Young, "the intellectual leader of the anglophone community" in Montreal.[15] A prominent judge, he was the chancellor of McGill University, where he had established a law faculty. Through his own practice and family links, he was a long-time member of the city's merchant and legal elite. The three commissioners each took on responsibility for distinct sections of the Code. Without surprise, Day took on the law of obligations and commercial law that mattered most to his community. The francophone commissioners addressed the rules of family law, property, and successions that were most significant to social and cultural life. With the assistance of two distinguished lawyers acting as secretaries, the text of the Code was written, translated, and published in both linguistic versions side by side—a unique legislative practice that is emulated to this day.

The codification project in Quebec was a conservative one: It was not intended to become the cement of a new nation, as had been the case for the French Code. Its orientation was not reformist. As J. E. C. Brierley and R. A. Macdonald point out, "memory was more important than imagination in 1866."[16] The Code's primary purpose was the effective compilation, coherence, and greater accessibility of the law then in existence. Although many portions of the Code were somewhat liberal in orientation, particularly the titles on commercial law and obligations drafted by Charles Dewey Day, there was no rupture with the past. Old French law remained effective in all matters not otherwise addressed in the Code. Nonetheless, the close kinship between the French Civil Code and the Civil Code of Lower Canada in both language and structure opened the door to the use of a vast body of contemporary French legal scholarship that was working out the implications of similar text. And at a symbolic level, the new Code was much more than a compilation of laws. Given its overall structure and arrangement, its style of expression, and its apparent comprehensiveness, the Code was meant to embody the architecture of Quebec private law—timeless, abstract reason for generations to come. The Civil Code of Lower Canada came into force on 1 August 1866, shortly before Canada was reconfigured into a confederation by the British North America Act of 1867. That Code was to last 125 years.

CASE STUDY

Family Law and the Legal Status of Married Women

French Canadians born as late as the 1960s will remember it as a solemn tradition: Every year, on 1 January, the entire family—the mother and her children—would kneel in front of the father, as they would in front of a priest, to be blessed by the head of the family. I remember it being done in my own family. There were variations from one family to the next. In many cases, the eldest child had to request the benediction from the father. Often it was the grandfather who gave the annual benediction, if he was still alive. In some families, only the children received the benediction. After the benediction, family members would exchange their good wishes for the New Year, and the day would continue with a feast and a celebration. The benediction was part of popular religious practices and had no significance in the formal Roman Catholic faith, but its meaning was clear even to small children: The father was the master of the family and all authority resided with him. Within the small kingdom that is the family, mothers occupied a subservient position, barely more autonomous than their children. This family hierarchy was captured in the Civil Code of Lower Canada, enacted in 1866, which crystallized the position of incapacity that old French law and the laws of the Roman Catholic Church had conferred to women.

Indeed, the image of an adult woman kneeling in front of her husband in a family ritual with religious connotations is a rich allegory for the legal status of women over the course of much of Quebec's history. In this chapter I have explored the idea of a legal tradition that governs private life and in so doing comes to embody national identity and values. The rules governing the family, the legal status of women, and their rights within marriage come closest, perhaps, to a true expression of this idea.

Undoubtedly, the regime of family law of the late nineteenth century rested on assumptions that reflected the values of the time. First, family law was deeply religious. Only the Church could celebrate valid marriages, and religious officials had the mandate and authority to keep all records of civil status. Children born out of wedlock had limited rights, if any. The Code contained no provision relating to divorce or adoption. Second, the rules on inheritance were driven by protection of the bloodline, in conformity with what was viewed as the demands of rural life. While the Code recognized freedom of willing, the widow could not become an heir if her husband passed away without having drawn up a will. Land and property that was not specifically attributed to the surviving spouse by a will or by her contract of marriage would pass to children of the marriage or, in their absence, to distant cousins and members of the extended family related by blood. Third, and most significantly, the regime of family law was rigidly patriarchal and grounded in an inequity of status and power. Husbands alone exercised authority over the children. Under the legal regime for matrimonial property, married women had no legal capacity. They could not enter into contracts, or administer their own property or that of the family. They could not perform most acts of civil life without their husband's permission: A woman could not appear in judicial proceedings or carry on an undertaking as a trader without her husband's consent. By the very terms of the Code, the position of men and women was decidedly asymmetrical: Husbands owed protection to their wives, but wives owed obedience to their husbands. A woman's domicile was that chosen by her husband. The wife's adultery was grounds for separation in all cases, but the husband's adultery could only lead to separation if the husband brought his "concubine" to live in the marital home.

Lest it be imagined that this picture of the legal status of women resides in the distant past, it is important to note that most of these rules remained in force until the second half of the twentieth century—less than 50 years ago. It took a long time, extraordinary efforts by Quebec feminists, and deep social transformations before civil law, lagging behind the times, finally recognized the full legal capacity of women and the equality of spouses in marriage and provided effective protection of the property interests of the weaker party upon death or dissolution of the marriage. By 1915 the right of women to be the legal heirs of their deceased spouse was recognized. In 1931 married women subject to the legal regime of community of assets were given the capacity to manage their salary and other proceeds of their own work. In the 1960s and 1970s inequalities between spouses were slowly removed in respect of management of family assets and authority over children, and a more equitable legal regime for matrimonial property was introduced. Following the enactment of the Divorce Act at the federal level, the Civil Code was amended in 1969 to address the consequences of this form of dissolution of marriage.[17] Nonreligious civil marriage made its way into the Code. Finally, in 1980 and building on the work of the Civil Code Revision Office, the National Assembly adopted a comprehensive chapter modernizing family law as a first instalment of the new Civil Code of Quebec that was to come a decade later. The new regime explicitly recognized the equality of spouses, granted equal rights to children born outside of marriage, and provided rules for the fair allocation of the value of family assets and uncompensated enrichment upon dissolution of the marriage.

The slow progress in the transformation of Quebec's family law can be explained, in large measure, by the resistance that came from the local Catholic Church and traditional—particularly rural—elements within the French-Canadian community. Matrimonial property regimes were tied to national identity, in many respects. Until the Civil Code of Lower Canada was amended in 1969, there were essentially two legal regimes governing the property of married spouses. If the spouses had not signed a contract governing their relationship, the Code provided that they had to live in a community of assets, in which the wife was legally incapable and the husband had full control over matrimonial property. These rules could be avoided in a marriage contract through which the spouses could opt for complete separation of assets and women could keep, for the most part, some control over their own property. Community of assets was presented as the natural, almost divine state of affairs—the proper basis for a marital relationship consistent with the dictates of the Church regarding the role of women in the family. Community of assets also came from old French law, and its preservation as the legal regime was connected to the survival of civil law as a distinct legal tradition. Separation of

continued

assets and the full capacity of married women, on the other hand, were viewed as dangerous common law inventions. In the early twentieth century, the most strident critics of the patriarchal legal regime were urban anglophones, including F. P Walton, the dean of the Faculty of Law at McGill University.

Among members of the francophone elites, the strongest advocates for reform of the status of women were feminists like Marie Lacoste Gérin-Lajoie (1867–1945), the brilliant, outspoken, and well-educated reformist who was the daughter of the chief justice of the Court of Appeal, and Thérèse Casgrain (1896–1981), whose exceptional life is described in Chapter 14. For strategic reasons, perhaps, neither of them challenged the need to preserve the connection of family law to its French civil law roots. Gérin-Lajoie, in particular, grounded her reformist activities in a desire to bring her French and Catholic heritage in line with the demands of modern life.[18] Indeed, both women found leverage in the contemporary transformations of French law, inviting Quebec legislators of the early part of the twentieth century to keep pace with the reforms of family law that were taking place at the time. In short, attitudes toward the legal status of women were closely tied to identity, and all the competing demands of gender, class, culture, language, and religious faith found expression in the struggle that took place over the first half of the twentieth century.

It is worth noting that the same period was also defined by the efforts of Quebec feminists to achieve equality in the public sphere, well beyond the capacity of women within marriage. While women could vote in federal elections after 1919, it was not until 1940 that they were finally given this right within the province of Quebec. Over the same period women were also excluded from professional life. Although McGill University first admitted a woman, Annie Macdonald Langstaff (1887–1975), to the Faculty of Law in 1911, the Quebec Bar refused to allow her to join its ranks. Elizabeth Carmichael Monk (1898–1980) finally made it in 1942. Thus, the pace of reform in family law was also dictated by the need to allocate energy and resources to those parallel battles, which occupied several Quebec feminists for decades.[19]

Contemporary family law in Quebec rests on an obligatory, formal egalitarianism that has replaced the patriarchal regime emerging from the 1866 Civil Code of Lower Canada. There is no room for deviation: The equality of spouses is a matter of public order. It would be fair to say that, in this, the state has replaced the Church as the dominant institutional force in Quebec, dictating a single conception of marriage as an economic unit that cannot be abandoned to the autonomy of the parties. Indeed, in principle, regulating property relations between spouses can be accomplished with the state dictating legal rules that achieve appropriate results, or by allowing the spouses to set those rules for themselves through contract, or by a subtle combination of the two.

From the point of view of public policy, one concern is to achieve the right balance between the autonomy that should be left to the parties, on the one hand, and the protection of weaker parties in marital relationships on the other hand. The legal rules governing matrimonial property in 1866 sought to achieve this balance in accordance with the values of that time. Community of assets was a reflection of the family as a productive, fundamental economic and social unit in a rural setting. Within it, in theory, married women exchanged their legal capacity for the continued protection of their husbands and the promise of a share in family assets upon death or dissolution. Setting aside the legal regime and opting for separation of assets, as one was allowed to do, was presented as contrary to Catholic morality and a sound conception of the family. In time, however, the regime of separation of assets came to displace the legal community regime. Spouses opted for it in increasing numbers on the advice of their notaries or for financial reasons that served the stronger party in the couple. While separation of assets appeared to give more respect to the autonomy and capacity of women, it tended to play in their disfavour. Upon dissolution, the spouse without property or income would be left impecunious—and this was the wife in the vast majority of cases. Freedom of contract was playing against their economic equality.

Partly in response to this concern, in the second half of the twentieth century the balance of contractual freedom and regulation shifted again when the new Civil Code of Quebec established an obligatory regime of partition of family assets regardless of the marriage contract formed by the spouses. These rules now govern same-sex marriages and civil unions as well, but the formal equality of the spouses and protective regime of matrimonial property extends only to those who enter those formal institutions, leaving aside those who order their private lives informally. Yet, within Canada, Quebec has the highest proportion of couples living together without getting married or forming a civil union. Thus the dynamic of state regulation and contractual autonomy—sometimes in tension—continues to this day as the effectiveness of family law is measured in relation to other types of intimate relationships. In a stark illustration of this tension, in recent years the policy to extend protection to the economically weaker party in the couple gave rise to a high-profile case that ended up before the Supreme Court of Canada. In this case, an unmarried woman challenged the constitutionality of provisions of the Civil Code to obtain the same protection from her de facto spouse as that guaranteed to married women. Every other Canadian province has extended spousal support to unmarried spouses in diverse statutory regimes. Ultimately, by a slim 5–4 majority, the Supreme Court ruled against the extension of rules requiring support obligations and family property division to unmarried partners in de facto unions in Quebec, favouring the preservation of such spouses' contractual autonomy.[20] Here again, one can pick up the scent of Quebec legal exceptionalism, as implicitly conceived by the Supreme Court of Canada, connecting policy choices embedded in the Code and other legislation to a distinctive national identity and set of social values.

A New Code for the Twentieth Century

Between 1866 and the first half of the twentieth century, the Civil Code of Lower Canada was amended in many respects, primarily in family matters (see the Case Study box), but its overall shape, linguistic style, and organization remained untouched. Legal education and the acculturation of lawyers and notaries were built on it; legal practice turned around it. Francophone legal elites were presenting it as the immutable manifestation of their French legal heritage.[21] Nonetheless, as its centenary was approaching the Code was showing its age. It was still regarded as the foundational text of the legal order, but its centrality was being eroded by proliferating legislation and administrative regulation outside of the Code. For some members of the francophone legal elites, the aging Code was no longer a bulwark against the penetration of common law ideas coming from the rest of Canada and the United States. To serve that purpose, it had to be revitalized. For others, the Code's relevance and modernity was called into question, particularly in respect to the rights of women and children and the legal and financial consequences of marriage and its breakdown. By the 1950s the values that it embodied, reminiscent of a society defined by religious, rural, and paternalistic experience, were no longer in line with those of a community that was embarking on a Quiet Revolution. The dominant position of the Roman Catholic Church was waning as the educational system and social welfare institutions were secularized. A consensus emerged that the Code had to be revised in depth, or even replaced by a new Code reflecting the deep changes in Quebec society.

The work began slowly, in 1955, with legislation creating the conditions for a revision of the Civil Code of Lower Canada. After a decade of limited activity, the recodification project gathered speed and energy. With funding from the Quebec government, and under the leadership of Paul-André Crépeau, a professor of civil law at McGill University (see the Biography box), several dozen experts worked for over a decade in committees and plenaries within the Civil Code Revision Office (CCRO). The CCRO revisited every corner of private law. Its report, presented to the National Assembly in 1978, sought to modernize the Code and the values it embodied. The proposed text was a complete recodification rather than a revision. It proclaimed the Code's role as Quebec's social constitution, and identified within it a few fundamental principles that manifested Quebec's social transformation: the primacy of human dignity, the equality of all human beings, the duty of good faith, the protection of weaker parties in contracts and obligations, and respect for private property.

It would take another decade for the new Civil Code of Quebec to be fully drafted and adopted by the National Assembly.[22] With the Parti Québécois in power, the referendum on secession in 1980, the patriation of the Canadian Constitution without Quebec's consent in 1982, and the constitutional negotiations that followed (and failed) to bring Quebec into the fold, the Quebec government had other priorities. Instead of leading to the direct enactment of a new Code, the report of the CCRO was the object of further reports and expert commentary, as legislative drafters in the Ministry of Justice took bureaucratic control over the process of recodification. The new Code became the site of turf wars between the professional orders of lawyers and notaries, with the latter trying to secure a broader share of the market for legal services. When the Civil Code of Quebec was finally adopted in 1991, it did not follow any model—contrary to the Civil Code of Lower Canada, which had tracked closely the text and outline of the French Civil Code. Quebec's civil law tradition had come to maturity. Its new Code found legal innovations and inspiration in civil law systems from around the world. Unanimous political actors presented it as a new social constitution for the twentieth century—but when it came into force on 1 January 1994 it did not attract much public attention. Neither the media nor civil society received this new Code with fanfare.

Be that as it may, to this day the unique position of the Civil Code within Quebec's legal order continues to underline its deep civil law roots. There is no written source of law with an equivalent stature, significance, or purpose in a common law jurisdiction. As the repository of all private law, a Code is not an ordinary piece of legislation. Its text governs the resolution of all private disputes, the formation of all contracts, and the legal status and juridical rights of all individuals in marriage, family, property, and inheritance. The centrality of this written text, dividing the lived experience into comprehensive, hierarchically organized rules and categories and deriving its architectural features from Romanist and European thought, is the indisputable marker of a civil law tradition. Yet even if Quebec's legal tradition belongs to the civil law, it is also mixed and entrenched within the English common law tradition.

A Mixed Legal Tradition

In its decision regarding the appointment of Justice Nadon, the Supreme Court of Canada states that the strict eligibility requirement to occupy one of the Quebec seats on the Court is justified by the need to preserve and protect Quebec's "legal traditions and values." It is somewhat unusual to refer to Quebec's legal traditions in the plural, but there is no doubt that even when addressed in the singular Quebec's legal tradition is pluralistic, or mixed.

A fuller account of the legal orders that are interacting with one other within the geographic boundaries of Quebec would have to look beyond those that are explicitly tied to the state. It would have to explore the characteristics of Aboriginal legal systems, as well as the semi-autonomous legal practices and institutions of infrastate and transnational organizations, such as religious communities, that do not necessarily accept the priority of laws passed by official authorities in the province. Presumably, it is not this inescapable multiplicity of intertwined legal orders that explains the reference to Quebec's legal traditions, in the plural, in the Supreme Court's reasons.

In fact, Quebec's legal tradition (and system) is mixed in a narrower way that is dictated by its history. While the roots of this tradition lie in the civil law, as we have just seen, Quebec's legal system is also connected to the common law tradition in several respects. At the substantive level, Quebec's private law includes many rules drawn from English law. Some were introduced in the former French colony in the decades that followed the Conquest. For instance, the new English elites favoured freedom of willing over the complex rules of old French law in matters of succession and transmission of property upon death, which tended to protect the interests of the family. Other rules, particularly in the regulation of commerce, were adopted in the nineteenth century at the request of the English merchants, notwithstanding the survival of old French law. As a result of this mixing of legal traditions, some aspects of contemporary Quebec private law are thoroughly original—such as the modified version of the law of trusts, an institution that first emerged in the common law and was, until recently, entirely foreign to continental European legal systems.[23]

Quebec's legal tradition is also mixed at the institutional level. The compromise that was built into the Quebec Act of 1774 reconnected the colony with its civil law roots, but also confirmed that the structure of courts, the status and power of judges, and the ordinary processes for the resolution of legal disputes would be English in character. Jury trials in civil matters, unheard of in France, were held in Quebec well into the twentieth century. To this day, judges in Quebec are appointed from among experienced members of the bar, as is true in the common law world. Although civil procedure in Quebec increasingly relies on the managerial role of judges, the core of litigation and the rules of evidence are still adversarial, and parties and their counsel control most of the events in a trial. Judgments are delivered with extensive written reasons, outlining the sources of law, jurisprudence, and scholarship that support the judge's conclusions. In short, Quebec's administration of justice and dispute resolution practices are embedded in the common law tradition.

The same is true of the substantive rules that govern the activities of the state and public administration as well as political, legislative, and regulatory institutions in Quebec. In administrative law, constitutional law, and criminal law and procedure, the historical sources of law in Quebec reside in the English tradition. In these respects, Quebec's legal system is very much a part of the common law world and is connected to the jurisdictions that surround it in North America. Legal innovations, such as class actions, consumer protection, or judicial enforcement of fundamental rights, have crossed the border from the United States and changed the fabric of Quebec's legal system. In addition, Quebec is also part of the larger Canadian federation. In all areas over which the Parliament has constitutional jurisdiction under the Constitution Act of 1867, the laws in force in Quebec are federal and generally uniform across the country. In the 1990s, following the enactment of the new Civil Code of Quebec, the federal Department of Justice launched a major effort to give fuller effect to Canada's bijuralism and to ensure that federal legislation is interpreted in Quebec in a manner that is consistent with its civil law heritage. As a result, the text of federal legislation now often contains separate references to both civil law and common law concepts, harbouring the potential for divergent results in Quebec and in the common law provinces. Nonetheless, in matters like bankruptcy, banking, or divorce the influence of the common law tradition has been historically significant in Quebec, subtly altering its civil law tradition.

It is fair to say, therefore, that the legal tradition of Quebec is plural—the product of legal *métissage*. Its oldest roots are in the civil law tradition, but its current configuration owes much to the common law tradition. In truth, given the circulation of ideas in the world and the constant exchange of information between cultures and traditions throughout history, no legal tradition is absolutely pure. Every legal tradition is hybrid to a certain degree, much like ethnicity in today's world is necessarily mixed. In legal theory as in ethnography, the discourse of purity and integrity is a political tool that often has limited foundation

Primary Source

Code civil du Québec

Disposition préliminaire

Le Code civil du Québec (L.Q. 1991, c. 64) régit, en harmonie avec la Charte des droits et libertés de la personne (chapitre C-12) et les principes généraux du droit, les personnes, les rapports entre les personnes, ainsi que les biens.

Le Code est constitué d'un ensemble de règles qui, en toutes matières auxquelles se rapportent la lettre, l'esprit ou l'objet de ses dispositions, établit, en termes exprès ou de façon implicite, le droit commun. En ces matières, il constitue le fondement des autres lois qui peuvent elles-mêmes ajouter au code ou y déroger.

Civil Code of Quebec

Preliminary provision

The Civil Code of Quebec (S.Q. 1991, c. 64), in harmony with the Charter of Human Rights and Freedoms (chapter C-12) and the general principles of law, governs persons, relations between persons, and property.

The Civil Code comprises a body of rules which, in all matters within the letter, spirit or object of its provisions, lays down the *jus commune*, expressly or by implication. In these matters, the Code is the foundation of all other laws, although other laws may complement the Code or make exceptions to it.

in reality. Thus, in the political context of Quebec, the hybrid nature of its legal tradition has generally been hidden, ignored, or denied. When Quebec's distinctive legal tradition is identified as a pillar of its national identity, only its civil law heritage is featured. The historical and ongoing encounter and dialogue of the two Western legal traditions has rarely been a source of pride for those who emphasize Quebec's distinctive national identity.[24]

Legal Traditions and National Identity

It may be surprising to note that the elaboration and eventual adoption of a civil code in Quebec attracted almost no popular attention, either in 1866 or in 1991. It was, after all, billed in each case as the centrepiece of the Quebec legal order, a social constitution governing all private interactions in the same way that a state constitution guides and structures all government and legislative activities. Furthermore, the earlier civil codes were associated with the romantic idea that a comprehensive legal text, written in simple language and contained in a book that would fit in one's pocket, could be readily accessible to all citizens and serve as a pedagogical repository of all-important social values. Nonetheless, in substance and perhaps in form as well, the content of a civil code remains highly conceptual. Unlike language or religion, the detailed regulation of legal interactions is not normally part of the daily existence of citizens. Their encounter with the formal laws of their legal tradition is limited to a few major events that punctuate their lives, such as marriage, its breakdown, the death of a family member, the acquisition of a house or a car, or a major dispute with a neighbour or an employer. For this reason, it is difficult to make the case that the actual rules found in a civil code are truly constitutive of a national identity.

Beyond the rules themselves, some of the foundational characteristics of a legal tradition may form part of the implicit conceptions of normativity that define a community. The civil law tradition, for instance, is arguably characterized by strong beliefs in the capacity of written texts to govern behaviour; a distrust of judicial discretion; guarded faith in the power of an enlightened, secular, and elected rule maker to achieve social transformation; and a preference for abstraction over experience. Again, it is difficult to make the case, other than by way of impressionistic anecdotes, that these characteristics shape the normative sensibilities of ordinary members of the Quebec national community.

Nonetheless, the *idea* that one belongs to a different legal tradition is part of the social and political discourse in Quebec in ways that are not replicated elsewhere in Canada. Jurists, but also politicians and—more rarely—social actors, raise the distinctiveness of Quebec's legal tradition as something of value, a unique trait that is worth protecting against encroachments that would alter its essence. Within this legal tradition, the Civil Code, as a readily identifiable, almost physical embodiment of the civil law tradition becomes a political artifact—an object of anxious reverence as well as a powerful tool to shape national identity.

The ways in which the Civil Code and the civil law tradition have been used as elements of Quebec's national identity have shifted over time and taken contradictory directions. A remarkable painting by well-known Quebec artist Jean-Paul Lemieux stands as a perfect metaphor for this ambivalence. In this monumental work completed in 1968, titled *Le Rapide*, Lemieux depicts a winter landscape in rural Quebec. The canvas is almost entirely monochromatic. Different shades of white separate the snowy field from the cloudy sky above the horizon. On the right there is a dark triangle, depicting the approaching figure of a high-speed train, *le rapide*, rushing through the peaceful landscape. Modernity and the traditional ways of life are blended together in this evocative piece. Standing before it, one is at once seized by the beauty of all that is traditional and untouched in its natural state and by the irresistible force of "progress." The themes of *survivance* and modernity are joined in this painting as they are in representations of Quebec's legal traditions as an aspect of its national identity.

The first theme, that of *survivance*, presents the civil law tradition as Quebec's French heritage and connection to the past, and for this reason it tends to be appropriated by the conservative French-speaking elites.[25] In this narrative, Quebec's legal tradition is under threat by the English, by the common law, and by social and juridical innovations coming from outside. Steps must be taken to protect it. In political terms, it tends to be profoundly conservative. Painting with a broad brush, one can see this theme of survival surfacing at least twice in Quebec's history. As outlined in the work of historian Brian Young,[26] the first period of occurrence begins in the late eighteenth century and lasts until the end of the Rebellions, around 1840. In the aftermath of the shift to English colonial rule, there were indeed a number of threats to the economic and political power of established francophone elites, and the politics of assimilation were never far from the surface. The survival of old French law, and of the seigneurial regime in particular, became synonymous with the preservation of the language, religion, and customs of French Canadians. In the face of political and legislative attempts to achieve a union that would overwhelm French culture in Canada, the francophone elites tied the identity of the nation to their seigneurial privileges and traditional legal customs. The resistance was directed at the foreign legal tradition and language, but the target was broader, as Quebec was slowly moving from a rural landscape to a capitalist and industrialized economy. The quashing of the Rebellion, the collapse of the seigneurial regime, and new alliances between emerging francophone and anglophone business elites brought an end to this first period of *survivance*.

This theme resurfaced at the turn of the century in a movement to preserve the integrity of the civil law and the centrality of the Civil Code of Lower Canada against new threats.[27] Indeed, by the beginning of the twentieth century the Code—and through it the entire civil law tradition—had become icons of the French culture in Quebec. Members of the francophone legal elites worried about the threats to its integrity coming from multiple sources. Pierre-Basile Mignault, a former professor at McGill University and long-serving justice of the Supreme Court of Canada, became one of the most powerful voices for this group of defenders of the heritage passed down from their forefathers. From their point of view, the common law judges sitting on the Supreme Court and on the Privy Council in London, which still heard

Canadian appeals, were insufficiently sensitive to the *différence* of Quebec civil law in their rulings.[28] Pressure for harmonization of laws across Canada was mounting. Legislation in federal areas of competence, such as bankruptcy or banking, was jeopardizing the coherence of private law within the province of Quebec. Piecemeal statutes written in the inelegant common law legislative style were addressing matters that naturally fell within the ambit of the Code and threatening to eviscerate it. Here again, the object of *survivance* was the Roman Catholic, francophone national identity as embodied in the venerable Civil Code. But in truth, the primary concern was perhaps less the preservation of the civil law tradition in North America than the safeguarding of traditional values against progressive initiatives of the early twentieth century: the unionization of labour, the protection of injured workers, the emancipation of women, and the liberalization of the economy.

In a civil law tradition, a civil code is an ambivalent instrument. It is at the same time an iconic text that captures the wisdom of the ages and a potent affirmation of legislative authority as a tool for social transformation. Next to the theme of *survivance*, therefore, one can find another theme of modernity and the coexistence of resilience and adaptation pointing in the opposite direction of the rhetorical connection between legal tradition and national identity. In this narrative, the civil law tradition and the Civil Code become optimal vehicles for the construction and growth of a new society. The project is more progressive and less tied to the cultural and ethnic specificity of French Canadians. Again, painting with a broad brush, one can find two moments for this narrative occurring in the decades that preceded the enactment of a civil code: first in the middle of the nineteenth century, culminating with the enactment of the Civil Code of Lower Canada in 1866, and second in the middle of the twentieth century, culminating with the presentation of the report of the Civil Code Revision Office in 1978 that eventually led to the Civil Code of Quebec. In each case legal nationalism is at play—intellectual leaders of the legal community present the enactment of a (new) code as a necessary step in the construction of a new social and economic environment. The existing law is presented as obsolete, out of touch with what are said to be rapid changes in the values and aspirations of the community, lacking in coherence and effectiveness, and standing in the way of progress. Success in the codification project is seen as the manifestation of the dynamism and modernity of Quebec society among the nations sharing in the civil law tradition. The first nation to achieve codification for the twenty-first century, Quebec becomes a model of industriousness and adaptability to evolving and modern legal and social realities—a claim that matches the contemporary image of a globally visible and uniquely creative nation that achieved success in other spheres, from the circus to business to popular music.

Whether under the garb of *survivance* or *modernité*, the connection between Quebec's legal tradition and its national identity is a discourse of the elites, particularly those residing within the legal profession. The fact that lawyers composed a significant proportion of elected members of the legislative assemblies in the province of Quebec well into the twentieth century meant that the preoccupations and discourse of this social group also turned into dominant political discourse. Today, it is difficult to imagine that the Civil Code of Quebec could be seriously represented as the repository of a contemporary national identity, even one grounded on civic—as opposed to ethnic—nationalism. To paraphrase the French legal scholar Jean Carbonnier, modern civil codes are living on the outdated reputation of being a site of memory.[29] In its customary iterations, the civil law may well have been the expression of shared traditions and values embedded in social life. In its modern form, a civil code is an abstract legal text of significant interest mostly to jurists. With the advent of social legislation and administrative bureaucracy, ordinary legal interaction is now more often than not mediated by the state. Within the legal sphere, the Civil Code has been replaced in the role of a foundational text by more recent expressions of collective values. In Quebec, for those who don't belong to the legal professions, the Charter of Human Rights and Freedoms would be more likely than the Civil Code to serve as a social constitution.

Nonetheless, the idea of a now secular, cosmopolitan, and distinct legal tradition forming part of Quebec's national identity endures. Within legal circles, the unique vitality of Quebec's civil law roots within the North American setting continues to feed the notion of a distinct society, and even comes to provide a justification for decisions such as the exclusion of Justice Nadon from the Supreme Court of Canada. Within some nationalist circles, the civil law roots of Quebec attest to its continued link to France, French culture, and even to French conceptions of citizenship and the state. Beyond those circles, the distinctive history of Quebec's legal system serves as the backdrop—but not as explicit justification—for claims of exceptionalism in respect of several social and political issues with legal or normative dimensions: the accommodation of religious minorities, the regulation of crime and possession of firearms, the status of unmarried conjugal relationships, labour relations, the role of the state and bureaucracy in the economy, *et j'en passe*. In time, this legal exceptionalism may well come to be recognized as the "legal traditions and social values" of Quebec that the Supreme Court of Canada was so keen to protect.

Questions for Critical Thinking

1. Do you think a legal tradition that rests on an iconic written text, such as a civil code, is more likely to be resistant to change? Or is the possibility of major shifts in the legal order, brought about when a new code is adopted, a promise of adaptability?
2. How much do you know about the basic laws in your own jurisdiction? Would you say that these rules are constitutive of your national identity? Do you ever hear political actors presenting them as such?
3. In this chapter, Quebec's legal tradition is described as hybrid, or mixed. Is that a meaningful idea in this day and age? In the context of globalization and the mobility of populations, ideas, and cultures, isn't every tradition rooted in multiple cultures? Can there be such a thing as a pure legal tradition or culture?

Notes

1. I wish to thank my colleagues Angela Campbell and Robert Leckey for their comments, and Ms. Aurélie Lanctôt for her diligent research assistance.
2. A court challenge to the prime minister's choice of a Supreme Court judge was historic and unprecedented, and it gives rise to many stories. Some would tell a story about flaws in the selection process by which the executive branch of government can choose judges in a secret, opaque process. Others would tell a story about an arrogant prime minister who is tone-deaf in matters concerning Quebec, a matter exacerbated by a separatist Parti Québécois provincial government keen to pick a fight with Ottawa. Others still would tell a story about a prime minister who fails to respect the institutions of government, including the Supreme Court of Canada. The number of stories and their political and social interest help to explain why the Nadon affair captured media attention over months in Quebec and the rest of Canada. The story relevant for this chapter, however, is one about legal traditions in Quebec and who qualifies to represent them on our country's highest court.
3. *Reference re Supreme Court Act, ss. 5 and 6*, [2014] 1 S.C.R. 433, 2014 SCC 21.
4. Ibid., at par. 49.
5. Ibid.
6. Paul-André Crépeau, "Une certaine conception de la recodification," in *Du Code civil du Québec : contribution à l'histoire immédiate d'une codification réussie*, ed. Serge Lortie, Nicholas Kasirer, and Jean-Guy Belley (Montreal: Thémis, 2005), 28.
7. H. Patrick Glenn, *Legal Traditions of the World*, 5th ed. (Oxford: Oxford University Press, 2014). While many legal scholars use the phrase *legal system* to express the same idea, speaking of *tradition* better captures the sense of intergenerational transmission of information, rhetoric, and storytelling.
8. Within the civil law tradition, two distinct legal professions have emerged. Lawyers typically represent parties before the courts and assist in the resolution of disputes. Notaries are more often involved in noncontentious matters and may well provide advice to both parties forming a contract. Notaries were often members of the local elite in rural Quebec well into the twentieth century and the legal professional that ordinary citizens were most likely to encounter. The division of the profession and mutually exclusive roles of each, established in 1786, continues to

this day. The notarial profession does not exist within common law countries.

9. Evelyn Kolish, *Nationalismes et conflits de droits : le débat du droit privé au Québec, 1760–1840* (Montreal: Hurtubise HMH, 1994); Arnaud Decroix, Michel Morin, and David Gilles, *Les tribunaux d'arbitrage en Nouvelle-France et au Québec de 1740 à 1784* (Montréal: Thémis, 2012); André Morel, "La réaction des Canadiens devant l'administration de la justice : une forme de résistance passive," *Revue du Barreau* 20, no. 2 (1960): 53.
10. Brian Young, *The Politics of Codification* (Montreal and Kingston: McGill-Queen's University Press, 1994), 18–30.
11. On the other hand, legal practice in front of tribunals over the same period was marked by the amalgamation of civil law and common law and the intertwining of French and English. See Jean-Philippe Garneau, "Une culture de l'amalgame au prétoire : Les avocats de Québec et l'élaboration d'un langage juridique commun," *Canadian Historical Review* 88, no. 1 (2007): 113–48. See also, for the later period, David Howes, "From Polyjurality to Mononjurality: The Transformation of Quebec Law, 1875–1929," *McGill Law Journal* 32 (1987): 523–58.
12. John E. C. Brierley and Roderick A. Macdonald, *Quebec Civil Law: An Introduction to Quebec Private Law* (Toronto: Emond Montgomery, 1993), 24–32.
13. John E. C. Brierley, "Quebec's Civil Law Codification—Viewed and Reviewed," *McGill Law Journal* 14 (1968): 522–89.
14. Young, *The Politics of Codification*, 66–140.
15. Ibid., 84.
16. Brierley and Macdonald, *Quebec Civil Law*, 35.
17. Before then there had been no divorce law in Quebec, and divorces could only be achieved through the presentation of a private bill submitted to Parliament.
18. Nicholas Kasirer, "Apostolat Juridique: Teaching Everyday Law in the Life of Marie Lacoste Gérin-Lajoie (1867–1945)," *Osgoode Hall Law Journal* 30, no. 2 (1992): 427–70.
19. Nicole Roy, "La lutte des femmes pour la réforme du droit de la famille 1900–1955," in *Du Code civil du Québec*, ed. Lortie, Kasirer, and Belley, 477–618.
20. *Quebec (Attorney General) v. A*, [2013] 1 S.C.R. 61, 2013 SCC 5.
21. Sylvio Normand, "Le Code civil et l'identité," in *Du Code civil du Québec*, ed. Lortie, Kasirer, and Belley, 618–66.
22. However, throughout the 1980s portions of the draft Code were introduced as sectorial legislation. Most notably, as discussed elsewhere in this chapter, a complete recodification of family law was adopted in 1980 as a free-standing chapter of the new Civil Code of Quebec.
23. The trust, or *fiducie*, is a legal mechanism that enables a person to set aside a group of assets that is then administered by a trustee for a given purpose, such as the benefit of another person (a child, for example). Neither the beneficiary nor the trustee are the owners of the property. The idea of a patrimony without an owner is foreign to the conceptual structure of the civil law tradition. The trust emerged as an equitable institution in the common law tradition. The Quebec *fiducie* is somewhat different from the common law concept from which it was drawn.
24. Hence the historical account of Quebec's legal traditions provided here is not free from controversy, as other accounts significantly downplay the role played by English law and anglophone jurists in shaping contemporary Quebec law.
25. Normand, "Le Code civil et l'identité."
26. Young, *The Politics of Codification.*
27. Sylvio Normand, "Un theme dominant de la pensée juridique traditionnelle au Québec : la sauvegarde de l'intégrité du droit civil," *McGill Law Journal* 32 (1987): 559–601.
28. The Judicial Committee of the Privy Council in London heard appeals from decisions of the Supreme Court of Canada until 1949 as part of its mandate as the court of last resort for the British Empire.
29. Jean Carbonnier, "The French Civil Code," in *Rethinking France : les lieux de mémoire*, vol. 1, ed. Pierre Nora and David P. Jordan (Chicago: University of Chicago Press, 1999). (Originally published in French and translated by Mary Seidman Trouille.)

Select Bibliography

Brierley, John E. C., and Roderick A. Macdonald. *Quebec Civil Law: An Introduction to Quebec Private Law.* Toronto: Emond Montgomery, 1993.

Glenn, H. Patrick. *Legal Traditions of the World*, 5th ed. Oxford: Oxford University Press, 2014.

Lortie, Serge, Nicholas Kasirer, and Jean-Guy Belley, eds. *Du Code civil du Québec : contribution à l'histoire immédiate d'une codification réussie.* Montreal: Thémis, 2005.

Young, Brian. *The Politics of Codification: The Lower Canadian Civil Code of 1866.* Montreal and Kingston: McGill-Queen's University Press, 1994.

Part F
Quebec International

Introduction

This next section of essays, the sixth and final of *Quebec Questions: Quebec Studies for the Twenty-First Century*, seeks to interpret and understand the role and place of Quebec within the larger international community. As such, readers of this section are presented with a core of related inquiries regarding Quebec's "international footprint." How did Quebec become involved in international affairs, and what forces explain Quebec's desire to do so? When did this engagement begin and how has it evolved? Who—which actors—and where—geographically—has Quebec focused attention? And what has Quebec gained from the pursuit of international activities? How has the international community (actors, forces, and ideas) impacted Quebec? What emerges from these contributions is a portrait of an actor that is richly engaged, indeed increasingly so, in myriad significant relationships around the globe.

Martin Papillon's article forcefully demonstrates that Quebec's Indigenous population has been irrevocably shaped and transformed by international forces, peoples, and ideas—the net results of which have been overwhelmingly negative for the Indigenous peoples of Quebec. Initially, French and British exploration, settlement, and war profoundly altered the social, cultural, economic, and political landscape of Quebec's 11 Indigenous nations. In short, Indigenous peoples in Quebec were effectively displaced and marginalized by European colonialism. Aboriginal people were seen by many of European background as unrestrained children and uncivilized—certainly not how they saw themselves. Government policy was based on the European understanding of Aboriginal identities, which resulted in catastrophic ends. The later political formation of Canada (and by extension Quebec), Papillon observes, would not result in enlightened approaches and policies; instead, the post-1867 period can in large measure be characterized as a period of "internal colonialism," where despite episodic changes to federal and provincial policy, Indigenous nations in Quebec have had to "fight" for self-determination. This ongoing commitment to secure Indigenous rights in Quebec, which has been most pronounced over the past 45 years, has been directly informed and influenced by ideas, practices, and trends external to Quebec. The forces of "Third World decolonialization" and the initiatives championed by "similar Indigenous movements in the United States" have propelled the Indigenous nations of Quebec to work to advance and secure their interests. Political arrangements with successive Quebec governments, most notably the James Bay Northern Quebec Agreement and the Paix des Braves, illustrate the determination of Quebec's Indigenous population. "The idea of sovereign Indigenous nations coexisting with the descendants of French and English settlers," according to Papillon, "remains a powerful one."

Geographically, Quebec's most pervasive international role, as Jody Neathery-Castro and Mark Rousseau write, is in the international organization known as La Francophonie. La Francophonie is important to Quebec, the authors point out, not simply because of the rich history and global reach of the organization, but also because it "constitutes the sole international organization to which Quebec belongs where it enjoys full autonomous participation as if it were a sovereign state." In examining the development of La Francophonie, Neathery-Castro and Rousseau raise and address related key questions; among other things, they examine how participation in the organization serves Quebec's international interests and how the organization as a whole works to preserve and promote Quebec's linguistic, cultural, economic, and governance objectives. In so doing, they give us a full picture of La Francophonie, the political context in which it emerged, and its larger organizational structure and mission. The authors conclusively demonstrate how Quebec's participation in La Francophonie has consistently served to advance its interests in the international sphere.

For Louis Balthazar, a pre-eminent academic observer of Quebec–United States political relations, no country—historically or currently—has been as fundamental a priority for Quebec as the United States. Charting the historical development of Quebec's political engagement with the United States, Balthazar explores the motivations and interests behind Quebec's profound desire to engage the United States. These motivations and interests are principally driven, unsurprisingly, by "the promotion of Quebec's economic interests," coupled with a public diplomacy effort to promote and educate the United States about "Quebec's distinctive character, language, and culture." These goals, Balthazar writes, are pursued through a variety of initiatives, most notably the official diplomatic presence of Quebec in the United States. As for Washington's approach to engaging politically with Quebec, while the United States recognizes the distinctiveness of the province, it has purposely sought to avoid—especially when sovereignist challenges have most forcefully emerged in 1980 and 1995—involving itself in what it considers matters internal to Canada.

Michel Biron's examination of the boundaries which inform Quebec literature deftly demonstrates the impact of changes in and expansions to the frontiers used by fictional and poetic writers. More than anything, Biron compellingly illustrates precisely "just how ambiguous the expression 'Quebec literature' can be." Confronted with an ever-changing array of geographic contexts and influences, the literary frontiers of Quebec have been increasingly blurred and less Quebec-centric (be it urban or rural in focus) and instead are informed and shaped by external places including France, the United States, "the French West Indies, the Maghreb, Lebanon, or sub-Saharan Africa." Of these, Biron suggests that Quebec novelists and poets are increasingly fascinated by the American literary tradition, though America continues to be seen as somewhat foreign. While much self-defined Quebec literature shares a language with its former colonial parent, enthusiasm about France is muted. In fact, most Quebec authors have lost any strong feelings (whether love or hate) for France; it is merely one country among many. Contemporary literary Quebec, in Biron's view, is as geographically expansive as it has ever been; jurisdictional boundaries have been permanently transcended and international forces lie at the foundation of much of today's Quebec literature.

The concluding essay in this section, offered by Sylvain Schryburt, explores a key artistic dimension of Quebec's role and place in the international community: the dynamism of Quebec theatre. Only recently, Schryburt writes, is Quebec theatre being promoted, staged, and recognized internationally, as measured by the success of Quebec playwrights, directors, and theatre companies including Michel Tremblay, Robert Lepage, and UBU. To understand Quebec theatre on the international stage, this essay explores the development and growth of theatrical productions squarely focused on identity, the various challenges that emerged as a result, and the movement since 1980 toward greater diversification in theatrical content, form, and presentation. Schryburt's contribution, above all else, provides a clear analytical framework for conceptualizing how best to approach and understand the world of Quebec theatre—a theatre without boundaries, regardless of performer, production, or venue.

25 Indigenous Peoples and Quebec: Competing or Coexisting Nationalisms?

Martin Papillon, Université de Montréal

Timeline

1534 French explorer Jacques Cartier lands on Gaspé Peninsula where he is met by Iroquoians from the St Lawrence Valley.

1701 Great Peace of Montreal. Iroquois establish peace and friendship alliance with the French and their Indigenous allies, ending almost a century of wars.

1763 Royal Proclamation. Colony of Quebec passes to British control. George III limits settlements on Indian lands.

1867 British Parliament adopts the British North America Act, creating the Canadian federation.

1876 First Indian Act adopted by the federal Parliament.

1815–1923 Land cession treaties are negotiated with First Nations in most of Ontario and the Prairie provinces. No such treaties are signed in Quebec.

1969 Federal government's *Statement on Indian Policy* (White Paper) proposes the abolition of the Indian Act and dismantling of the reserve system to further integrate First Nations peoples into mainstream Canadian society.

1975 James Bay Cree and Inuit of Nunavik sign the first "modern treaty," the James Bay and Northern Quebec Agreement, with Quebec and the federal government.

1982 "Aboriginal and Treaty Rights" are recognized in the Constitution Act, 1982.

1990 Oka Crisis. Standoff between Mohawks and Canadian military ends after 78 days.

1989–94 James Bay Cree organize a successful international campaign against the Great Whale hydroelectric project.

1995 Quebec referendum on sovereignty-partnership. Many Indigenous leaders raise the possibility of partition in the event of a "yes" vote.

2001 Quebec and James Bay Cree sign the Paix des Braves agreement.

2008 The Government of Quebec launches Plan Nord, an economic development strategy for northern regions of the province.

2014 The Supreme Court of Canada recognizes the Aboriginal title of the Tsilhqot'in Nation in British Columbia. This decision has direct implications in Quebec, where historic land cession treaties were not negotiated.

Introduction

We often forget that in the early days of Canada, politics was a three-way affair between the French, the British, and the various Indigenous nations who dominated the land beyond the major European settlements. The first inhabitants of the continent were power brokers between British and French forces.[1] They negotiated military and economic alliances with the colonial powers, bargained access to the key fur trade routes, and eventually positioned themselves strategically as key actors in the battles for North America. Of course this trilateral relationship did not last; once the French colonies fell into British hands, Indigenous peoples lost their position as intermediaries between European powers. They were themselves progressively subjected to British colonial rule.

Today, even if Indigenous peoples form a relatively small minority in what has become Canada, the idea of sovereign Indigenous nations coexisting with the descendants of French and English settlers remains a powerful one. Like francophones in Quebec, Indigenous peoples seek to protect their cultures, languages, and distinctive identities. And like many francophone Quebec nationalists, they use the language of **self-determination** to challenge the political foundations, legal institutions, and geographic scope of Canadian sovereignty. Of course, unlike Quebec sovereignists, very few Indigenous nations actually seek complete independence from Canada, given their small size and limited resources. They have nonetheless adopted a similar discourse, seeking greater recognition of their status as distinct polities engaged in a **nation-to-nation relationship** with Canada.

The coexistence of Indigenous and Quebec self-determination movements on a same territory is not always easy. Their respective narratives over the boundaries of the political community often collide. Like any settler state, Quebec is prone to "internalizing" Indigenous peoples onto its own citizenship regime, therefore acting like a colonial state from within. As the core vehicle for francophone nationalism, the provincial government is particularly sensitive to any challenge to its territorial jurisdiction and to the sovereignty of its parliament, the National Assembly. This sensitivity was particularly salient in the years preceding and following the 1995 referendum on sovereignty, but it remains important today as Indigenous peoples challenge Quebec's **Plan Nord**, an economic development strategy focused on facilitating access to resource extraction in the province's northern territories.

But the very presence of Quebec nationalism has also paradoxically opened opportunities for Indigenous peoples, precisely because the very boundaries of the political community and its democratic legitimacy are not settled in Quebec. In a sense, self-determination is part of everyday politics in Quebec as national identities are constantly debated, renegotiated, and challenged in public discourse. This unique context is both a challenge and a fertile ground for Indigenous peoples to carve out their own space for recognition.

After discussing the origins of the Indigenous self-determination movement in the colonial past of the Canadian state, this chapter examines the various moments of tensions between Quebec and Indigenous peoples in the past 40 years, leading to what I define as the contemporary politics of **resources nationalism**—a time when national identities are increasingly negotiated through the politics of resources extraction.

Indigenous Peoples and Colonialism in Canada and Quebec

There are, today, over 1.5 million Indigenous people in Canada, representing 4.3 per cent of the total population. It is a highly diverse population, forming approximately 60 self-defined nations speaking as many as 50 languages.[2] While more than half of Indigenous people in Canada now live in cities and towns, many remain closely attached to the land, which is central to their culture and traditions.

In Quebec, there are approximately 108,000 people who self-identify as Indigenous (or Aboriginal), representing a little over 1.8 per cent of the population of the province. There are 11 Indigenous nations formally recognized by the government of Quebec (see Table 25.1). Most Indigenous people in Quebec live in sparsely populated rural areas that are rich in natural resources. The Inuit live in the northernmost part of the province, where they make up the majority. The Wendat (Huron) and Mohawk nations live in small communities near Quebec City and Montreal, respectively, and have much closer daily interaction with the francophone majority of the province.

There are parallels in the history of Indigenous peoples and French Canadians since both were reduced to minority status within a predominantly British North America. But British colonial rule operated very differently for the two groups. Early on, British colonial authorities saw their interest in maintaining good relationships with the descendants of French settlers. Their religion, legal institutions, and civil society were recognized and protected in the Quebec Act of 1774. Their continued presence as a distinct people was one of the main reasons for the creation of a federal, rather than a unitary, state in 1867. George-Étienne Cartier and other French Canadians played a leading role in the creation of the Canadian federation.

Table 25.1 Indigenous Population in Quebec

Nations	Population
Abenaki	2,577
Algonquin	11,026
Atikamekw	7,032
Cree	17,483
Huron-Wendat	3,845
Innu	18,820
Inuit	11,640
Maliseet	1,102
Mi'kmaq	5,727
Mohawk	18,185
Naskapi	1,117
Total	98,554

Note: These numbers are the officially recognized Indigenous population. In the 2011 *National Household Survey*, 108,342 individuals self-identify as Indigenous in Quebec.

Source: Secrétariat aux affaires autochtones, Gouvernement du Québec, *Statistiques des populations autochtones*, www.autochtones.gouv.qc.ca/nations/population.htm.

Indigenous peoples faced a different reality in British North America. The Royal Proclamation of 1763 recognized their presence and rights to the land, but as subalterns under the protection of the British Crown. In most of what is now Ontario and the Prairie provinces, colonial authorities negotiated land cession treaties through which Indigenous peoples agreed to the presence of settlers on their traditional territories in exchange for smaller tracts of lands reserved for their benefit and protected from the encroachment of settlers. In northern territories, Quebec, most of British Columbia, and the Atlantic provinces, no such treaties were signed; Indigenous peoples were simply ignored and marginalized in the new dominant order.

The Indian Act was adopted in 1876 under the authority of the newly constituted federal government. The act had the explicit objective of facilitating colonial expansion to the West and "preparing" the Indigenous population for its eventual assimilation into the dominant society. The annual report of the Department of the Interior in 1876 illustrates the philosophy behind the Indian Act:

> Our Indian legislation rests on the principle, that the aborigines are to be kept in a condition of tutelage and treated as wards or children of the State. . . . The true interests of the aborigines and of the State alike require that every effort should be made to aid the Red man in lifting himself out of his condition of tutelage . . . and through education and every other means, to prepare him for a higher civilization by encouraging him to assume the privileges and responsibilities of full citizenship.[3]

Until they were judged "emancipated" by the Canadian government, Indigenous peoples were confined to limited reserves, small pieces of lands under federal jurisdiction where they were treated as children under the benevolent protection of the government. Such reserves were first established in what is now Quebec under the French regime, but most isolated Indigenous communities were spared until the federal government systematically applied the policy in the early twentieth century.[4] Many

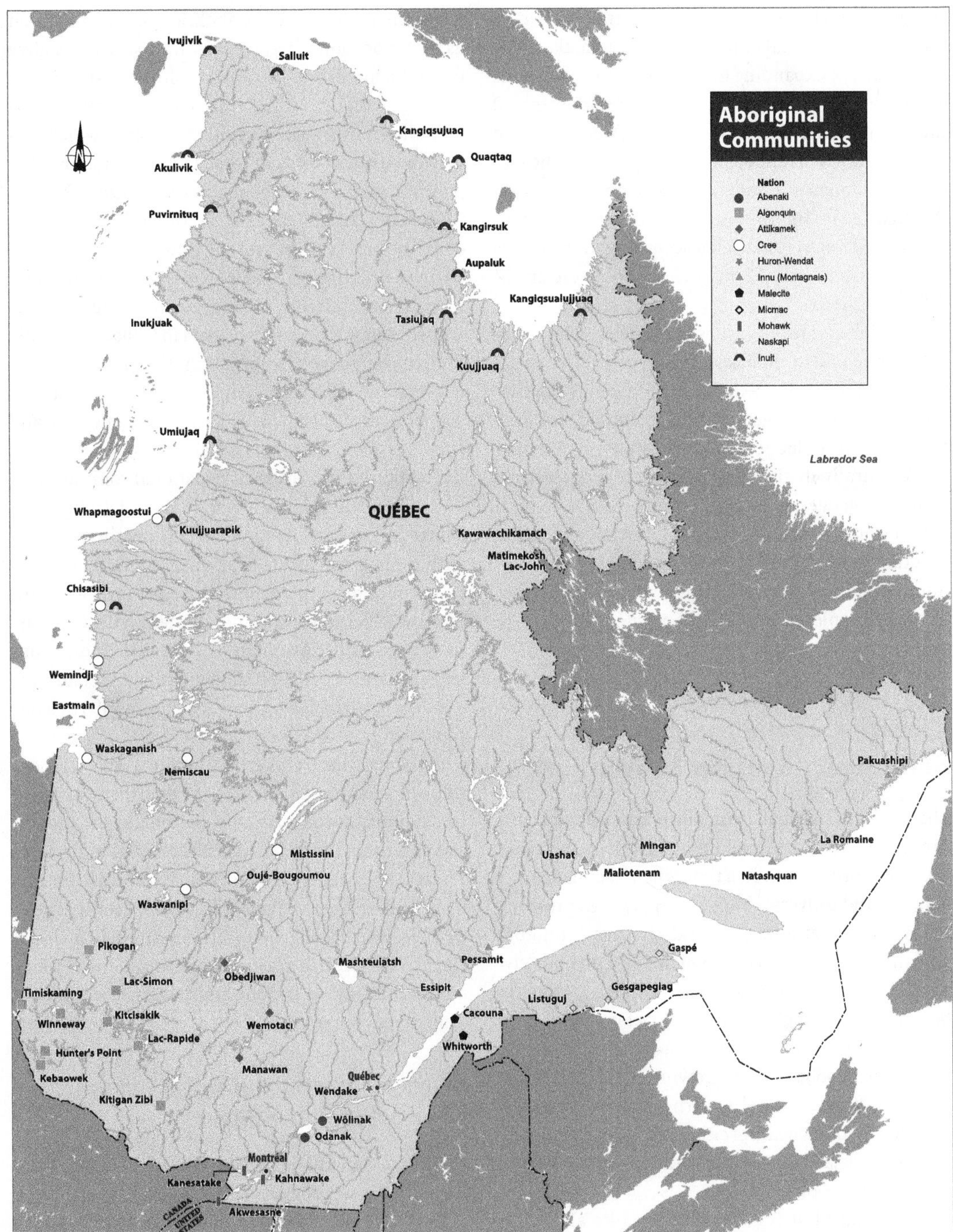

Figure 25.1 Aboriginal Communities in Quebec.

Source: Based on the map "Les Autochtones du Québec," produced by the Secrétariat aux affaires autochtones du Québec, 2008 (www.autochtones.gouv.qc.ca).

Indigenous nations in Quebec were then forced to leave their traditional hunting grounds to make room for the always-expanding Euro-Canadian settlements and economy. The Algonquin, who once dominated the Ottawa River Valley, for example, were confined to remote areas of limited interest to settlers.[5] The federal government also sought to speed up assimilation through the infamous residential schools system, in which children were educated according to the values of Western societies. Many such schools were established in Quebec.

Sociologist Jean-Jacques Simard aptly describes the logic behind the policies and administrative structures set in place to control the Indigenous populations as a process of geographic, economic, cultural, and political "reduction."[6] Previously self-governing and culturally distinct societies were progressively contained geographically, subjugated politically, and forced to adopt the cultural codes, norms, and social practices of the dominant society. Indigenous communities thus became, and largely remain to this day, internal colonies of the Canadian state.

Beyond Colonialism: The Rise of the Indigenous Self-Determination Movement

The model of internal colonialism established in the nineteenth century came under stress in the aftermath of World War II. At a time when liberal ideals of equality and universal human rights were spreading in Canada and around the world, the discriminatory Indian Act and the various policies designed to "civilize" First Nations and other Indigenous peoples became increasingly difficult to defend. The poor socioeconomic conditions in Indigenous communities were also gathering growing media attention. As a result, the federal government progressively expanded most benefits of citizenship—including full access to social programs and the right to vote—to Indigenous people.

Making First Nations citizens like all others was the stated intention behind a now infamous federal *Statement on Indian Policy* (the White Paper) of 1969. To break with its colonial past, the federal government proposed the abolition of the Indian Act as the revocation of treaties that were seen as a source of exclusion from full citizenship. First Nations reacted strongly to the White Paper. Many rejected its philosophy of egalitarian citizenship, which was viewed as a new form of forced assimilation into the majority society. Indigenous organizations started to develop an alternative discourse based not on equality between individuals, but equality among *nations*. Building on examples of Third World decolonization and similar Indigenous movements in the United States, Indigenous leaders in Canada explicitly used the language of international human rights and national self-determination to assert their claims for proper protection of their distinctive cultures and languages, for control over their lands, and for political recognition as distinctive national communities.

Given the relatively small size of Indigenous communities, which now coexist on the territory with a far larger non-Aboriginal population, self-determination is not generally understood as a process by which an independent state with the classic attributes of sovereignty is created. Indigenous self-determination is rather generally understood as a process by which a nation or a community regains control over its own political destiny and renegotiates with the state the terms and conditions of its relationship with and participation in the dominant societies' institutions. Not surprisingly, the federal and provincial governments in Canada have resisted Indigenous assertions of their right to self-determination as a form of shared sovereignty. This is especially true in Quebec, where Indigenous self-determination claims clash with similar claims from another minority nation challenging the boundaries and legitimacy of Canadian sovereignty.

Early Encounters between Indigenous and Quebec Nationalisms

Under the Canadian Constitution (the British North America Act of 1867 and the Canadian Constitution of 1982), the federal government inherited the British Crown's responsibility for relations with "Indians." Indigenous peoples thus have had historically tenuous relationships with Canadian provinces. This is true of Quebec. Until the 1960s, the provincial government showed little interest in establishing its presence in Indigenous communities. Except for Inuit communities in the northernmost part of the province, services in Indigenous communities, including elements of provincial jurisdiction such as education, health, and welfare, were provided through the federal Department of Indian Affairs. The emergence of modern Quebec nationalism in the 1960s transformed this dynamic.

With the Quiet Revolution, the Quebec state became the main vehicle of the newly assertive nationalist francophone elite. Through the provincial government, this elite engaged in a significant nation-building exercise, constantly seeking to consolidate the territorial and social boundaries of the political community and expand the provincial state's influence in various areas of public policy. This was true for Quebec's Aboriginal policy. While elsewhere in Canada provinces are still often unwilling participants in Indigenous governance, the Quebec government adopted an activist stance, seeking simultaneously to assert its authority over Indigenous peoples within its territorial boundaries and gain legitimacy as their primary interlocutor in negotiating the conditions of the exercise of their rights and political autonomy.[7] Not surprisingly, Quebec and Indigenous nationalisms rapidly collided in this context.

A key element of Quebec's national project has been to assert the authority of the provincial state over its resource-rich northern lands, a territory annexed to Quebec in 1912 but largely ignored by subsequent provincial governments. In the words of Quebec Premier Robert Bourassa (premier from 1970–6 and 1985–94), northern Quebec was a "vast reservoir of untapped resources" that "had to be conquered" for the benefit of all Quebecers.[8] Energy production and the expansion of the mining industry were central elements of the province's state-led economic development strategy in the 1960s and 1970s. Linking the remote North to the rest of the province, however, was more than an economic enterprise. In establishing its presence on its entire territory, the Quebec government was also symbolically taking ownership of the land on behalf of the francophone majority.[9] It is in this context that the Bourassa government launched the James Bay hydroelectric project in 1971.

Previously, Quebec had largely ignored the presence of Indigenous peoples on lands and rivers slated for hydroelectric development. For example, Innu communities were simply moved to other locations without any sort of consultation when the large Manicouagan complex was developed on their traditional lands in the 1960s. This time, however, Indigenous communities affected by the James Bay project reacted strongly. A group of young Cree leaders, supported by the Indians of Quebec Association, challenged the legitimacy and legality of Quebec's unilateral action. They won an important court battle to stop the project until their claims to the land were settled. While this court decision was overturned in appeal, it eventually forced Quebec to negotiate a settlement.

This settlement, signed in 1975 by Quebec, Canada, the Crees, and Inuit, became the first **modern treaty** in Canada, the James Bay and Northern Quebec Agreement. This was a significant achievement for Indigenous peoples. Like its federal counterpart, the provincial government was forced to acknowledge not only the existence of Aboriginal rights limiting its territorial sovereignty, but also the political relevance of Indigenous peoples as distinct communities that could not simply be dissolved in the newly assertive provincial nationalism.

Battles over Constitutional Recognition

Indigenous and Quebec nationalisms continued to intersect during the constitutional debates that dominated Canadian politics for most of the 1980s. Indigenous peoples took advantage of Quebec's challenge to the constitutional order to engage in their own form of constitutional politics. They gained sufficient support across Canada for the inclusion in the Constitution Act, 1982 of a general provision for the recognition of Aboriginal and treaty rights. While section 35 is worded very generally, it nonetheless recognizes that Indigenous peoples have specific rights because of their unique status and history in Canada.[10]

Quebec rejected the 1982 constitutional package for reasons that had little to do with the recognition of Aboriginal rights. As a show of goodwill, the Parti Québécois government established 15 principles guiding its relationship with Indigenous peoples. Among others, the Quebec government stated that it

> Recognizes that the Aboriginal peoples of Québec constitute distinct nations, ... having the right to determine the development of their own culture and identity.
>
> Recognizes the right of Aboriginal nations, within the framework of Québec legislation, to govern themselves on lands allocated to them.
>
> Considers that these rights are to be exercised as part of the Québec community and hence could not imply rights of sovereignty that could affect the territorial integrity of Québec.[11]

The policy statement illustrates the ambiguous position of the provincial government on the recognition of Aboriginal rights. On the one hand, Quebec embraced the idea of Indigenous nations as distinct communities. On the other hand, it clearly established the limits of this recognition. Self-government was to be exercised "within Quebec" and was not to affect the territorial integrity of the province. Today this ambiguous position continues to form the backbone of Quebec's Aboriginal policy.

The province's position was put to the test in no small fashion in the following decade as Quebec and Indigenous recognition claims collided again on the constitutional front during the Meech Lake Accord debate, which proposed to recognize Quebec as a distinct society within Canada.

CASE STUDY

The Oka Crisis

What started as a relatively peaceful act of resistance by the Mohawk community of Kanesatake, near Oka, just north of Montreal, against the expansion of a local golf course on their traditional lands, rapidly worsened when the Quebec provincial police intervened to forcibly remove the protesters. Violence erupted, gunfire was exchanged, and a police officer was killed. Militant Mohawks and self-described traditional Warriors of the old Haudenosaunee (Iroquois) Confederacy had erected a barricade on a provincial road nearby, blocking access to many residents of the area. In solidarity, a second group blocked access to a major bridge connecting the island of Montreal to the suburbs near another Mohawk community, Kahnawake.

Tempers flared on both sides of the barricades. Militants and Warriors, some of them armed with semi-automatic weapons and wearing army fatigues, challenged the police force to intervene again, threatening retaliation. Expressions of intolerance from the local non-Aboriginal francophone population were amplified in the media, and the conflict evolved into a bitter battle between two nations, both claiming sovereign authority over the land and ultimately negating the other's legitimacy. The blockade was portrayed in Quebec media as an unlawful action, a challenge to the rule of law by a group of radical militants with ties to organized crime. By contrast, the Mohawk protesters saw themselves as asserting sovereignty; it was a legitimate act of self-defence in the face of an intolerant provincial government. As the conflict dragged on, the Quebec government asked the federal government for military support. During that fateful summer, 2,500 soldiers from the Canadian Armed Forces, a powerful symbol of Canadian sovereignty, were deployed near the barricades and the surrounding areas.

Images of Mohawk children playing near the barricades, a few metres away from Canadian tanks and heavily armed soldiers, received worldwide media attention. The standoff lasted 78 days. On 26 September, after increasing pressure from the military, the remaining protesters left their

Indigenous peoples strongly opposed the agreement because they felt their own recognition claims were being ignored. If there were any distinct society in Canada, they argued, it was the Indigenous peoples, not Quebec.

The collapse of the Meech Lake Accord in 1990 and the ensuing debates over Quebec's and Indigenous peoples' place in the federation resulted in a war of words over boundaries of political communities, nationhood, and democratic legitimacy. Ovide Mercredi, the grand chief of the Assembly of First Nations, one of the main national Aboriginal organizations, declared before Quebec's National Assembly that Quebec did not have the right of self-determination "since it does not constitute a single people." "To deny our right to self-determination in the pursuit of your aspirations," he added, "would be a blatant form of racial discrimination."[12] Quebec Premier Robert Bourassa replied that "no matter Quebec's future, the rights of Aboriginal peoples must be exercised within the jurisdictional boundaries of the National Assembly."[13]

By associating their own claims to self-determination with those of Quebec, Aboriginal leaders positioned themselves as legitimate constitutional actors on par with Quebec and other provinces. Their success in this respect was confirmed in the next round of constitutional negotiations, as major national Indigenous organizations sat at the table as full negotiating partners with the federal government, the provinces, and the territories. The resulting Charlottetown Accord proposed to entrench

compound peacefully and the barricades were dismantled without a clear resolution to the crisis.

Twenty-five years later, the events of Oka still elicit strong emotions in Canada, in Quebec, and especially in Mohawk communities. For many in Canada, the Oka Crisis was an awakening, a realization that a profound gap remained between Indigenous people and other Canadians. The events in Oka led to the federal government's Royal Commission on Aboriginal Peoples, whose 1996 report revisited our shared history, pointed to the painful legacy of past policies, and proposed a radical agenda for change based on the recognition of Indigenous peoples as equal partners in a nation-to-nation relationship with Canada.

In Quebec, especially for nationalists, the episode was a reminder that not everyone agrees on the territorial boundaries of the political community, nor on the role of the provincial state as the legitimate source of authority in that territory. The presence of Indigenous peoples, with their own national aspirations, could no longer be ignored.

For Mohawks, the events of 1990 have left a bitter taste. In both Kanesatake and Kahnawake, the two communities most affected by the crisis, wounds are slowly healing. Tensions with the local non-Aboriginal population are dissipating, 25 years later, but a general distrust of government authority remains. The Quebec police rarely venture into the communities. In Kanesatake, the epicentre of the crisis, the golf course was never built, and some of the disputed land was bought by the federal government for an eventual transfer to the Mohawks. But the Mohawk land is intertwined with non-Aboriginal private properties, making its management as a coherent territory almost impossible and its development difficult. The community is divided on its future course. Sadly, criminal elements are taking advantage of the vacuum created by the divisions and the uncertain legal status of the territory, further complicating reconciliation between the Mohawks and their Québécois neighbours.

Aboriginal peoples' inherent right to self-government in the Canadian Constitution.

Despite the defeat of the Charlottetown Accord in a pan-Canadian referendum, Indigenous peoples gained considerably in the process. They were now considered full constitutional actors, holding what amounts to a de facto political veto on constitutional changes affecting their rights. Their constitutional claims could no longer be simply ignored. In the aftermath of the Charlottetown negotiations, it was clear that any future attempt to change Quebec's status in the Constitution would involve a similar recognition for Indigenous peoples. In many ways, Indigenous peoples succeeded in placing their claims for constitutional recognition on par with those of Quebec, linking their future status in the federation to that of the francophone province.

Competing Sovereignties

If the 1980s were dominated by struggles over recognition in the Canadian Constitution, the 1990s led to more direct conflicts between Indigenous and Quebec self-determination movements over the boundaries of political communities. The Oka Crisis during the summer of 1990 (see the Case Study box) was the first major conflict. When a group of Mohawk activists resisted the construction of a golf course on a traditional cemetery adjacent to the community of Kanesatake, police intervention rapidly turned into an armed standoff lasting several weeks and necessitating the intervention of the Canadian Armed Forces. For the Mohawks, the construction of the golf course without their consent, and the provincial police intervention in support of the construction, were attacks on their authority over the land and their very existence as a distinct nation. Similarly, for Quebec nationalists, the Mohawks' resistance and the ensuing intervention of the Canadian army were reminders of the fragility of their own claim to territorial sovereignty.

The Oka Crisis was fresh in the collective memory when Quebec faced another direct challenge to its territorial authority. The second phase of the James Bay hydroelectric project on the Great Whale River was launched in 1988. The James Bay Cree, who mobilized against the first project in the 1970s, opposed this new development on their traditional hunting grounds. Allied with a network of environmental groups, the Cree put together a highly effective international campaign, portraying the project as "a new Amazonian catastrophe" and decrying Quebec's lack of respect for their rights as the first inhabitants and caretakers of the land.

The Great Whale battle once again pitched Quebec's conception of its territorial sovereignty and economic interests against those of a small group of Indigenous people asserting their own rights and authority on the land. And Quebec lost the international public relations battle. The Quebec state looked just like any other Western capitalist government, obsessed with economic growth and little concerned with the environment and the rights of minorities. Fearing that this negative image would prejudice the international community against an eventual recognition of Quebec sovereignty, the newly elected Parti Québécois government shelved the project on the eve of the 1995 sovereignty referendum.

These conflicts underline the potential volatility of nationalist encounters in Quebec, but also the influence of Indigenous peoples when political boundaries and self-determination are publicly debated. In a sense, while Indigenous peoples face strong resistance to their own self-determination claims in Quebec, they have also taken advantage of the political dynamics caused by Quebec nationalism to make gains of their own.

During the 1995 referendum campaign the tensions between Quebec and Indigenous nationalisms reached their apex. Indigenous representatives boycotted the consultations leading to the referendum, arguing that the province-wide process was a violation of their own right to self-determination.[14] The Crees and Inuit organized their own referendum, while the Mohawks did not allow Quebec election officials onto their territory. Indigenous leaders were again challenging political boundaries and asserting their own notion of their place in Canada through the political debates in Quebec. The will of the majority in Quebec could not be imposed on their people. Matthew Coon Come, the grand chief of the James Bay Cree, put it in plain language at a conference in Washington that received plenty of media attention in the months preceding the referendum:

> We conceive of ourselves as one people, tied together by the land we share and care for. . . . Now, the government of Québec proclaims the Québécois—that is anyone who may presently reside in the province, including Cree—a people. The Parti Québécois claims for that people the right to self-determination, while in the same breath denying the Crees the same right. If the separatists win the referendum, we will stay in Canada with our territory.[15]

As this quote suggests, Indigenous leaders, with the support of some English-Canadian media, also started to evoke the possibility of partition. If Quebec voted "yes" to separation, they argued, Indigenous peoples could very well refuse to join the new independent state and stay in the Canadian federation with their territories. The federal government embraced this argument, thus impressing upon Quebec voters the possible consequences of a "yes" vote.[16]

Contemporary Dynamics: Resource Nationalism

Throughout the 1980s and 1990s, Indigenous peoples challenged the scale and boundaries of the

BIOGRAPHY

Matthew Coon Come

Matthew Coon Come, the long-serving grand chief of the Grand Council of the Crees.

The Canadian Press/Andrew Vaughan

Born in a tent on his father's trapline near the Cree community of Mistissini in 1957, Matthew Coon Come became one of the most recognized and controversial Indigenous leaders in Canada. Like most First Nations children of his generation, Coon Come attended a residential school. He pursued his formal education at Trent and McGill universities where he studied law in the 1980s and became familiar with Canada's legal system and the emerging jurisprudence on Aboriginal and treaty rights. He returned to his community to run for office as a band councillor before he finished his law degree. Part of a young generation of Cree leaders who came of age with the James Bay and Northern Quebec Agreement, Coon Come emerged as a strong advocate of Cree rights. He rapidly distinguished himself as an astute negotiator and political strategist in relations with governments.

Matthew Coon Come was first elected grand chief of the Grand Council of the Crees in 1987. Under his leadership, the Grand Council launched a successful public relations campaign against the second phase of the James Bay hydroelectric project on the Great Whale River. At the heart of the campaign was a clever association of Cree rights on the land to be flooded with the protection of the rivers and forests of northern Quebec, allowing a fruitful alliance with environmentalist groups in Canada

continued

and, perhaps more importantly, in the United States, where the electricity produced by the future hydroelectric complex was to be sold. The highlight of the campaign was a canoe trip down the Hudson River to Manhattan, where Coon Come made a speech in front of thousands of sympathetic New Yorkers on Earth Day in 1991. The ensuing media attention allowed Coon Come to speak to legislators in New York and other New England states about the environmental and human consequences of the hydroelectric project. The Quebec government finally cancelled the Great Whale project in 1994.

Coon Come and the Grand Council of the Crees took advantage of the international network built during the Great Whale campaign to mobilize against yet another project of the nationalist government in Quebec: a referendum on the separation of the province from Canada. While the Parti Québécois assumed that a sovereign Quebec would maintain its existing boundaries, Coon Come argued that the Cree Nation could not be forced to follow Quebec down the path of independence. In a series of speeches at Harvard University, in Washington, and in Europe, Coon Come challenged the legitimacy of Quebec secession from Canada without Cree consent. The Grand Council organized its own consultation on the future of the Cree Nation a few months before the Quebec referendum, and a resounding 96 per cent of those who voted in Cree communities opted to stay in Canada.

Coon Come's politics have certainly put the Crees on the map, but his direct style and colourful language have had consequences. During the referendum campaign, he did not hesitate to accuse Quebec nationalist leaders of racism. He even described the treatment of the Cree Nation by the provincial government as cultural genocide. Not surprisingly, such strong words did not make him a popular figure in Quebec. Francophone media portrayed him as an English-speaking leader with little understanding of Quebec, or—the supreme insult—as an agent of the federal government. Relations with Quebec would remain tense for the duration of his first tenure as grand chief.

After more than 10 years as the head of the Grand Council of the Crees, Matthew Coon Come was elected as grand chief of the Assembly of First Nations (AFN) in 2000. The AFN is the main Aboriginal organization representing the interests of First Nations living on reserves at the federal level in Canada. He narrowly defeated the previous grand chief, Phil Fontaine, by criticizing his conciliatory approach with the federal government. Promising a more assertive and critical leadership, Coon Come focused his energies on treaty rights and the development of a nation-to-nation relationship between the federal government and the AFN. Under his leadership, that relationship rapidly soured and he eventually lost support among the more moderate First Nations leaders, losing his bid for re-election in 2003. After a few years working behind the scenes, Coon Come was again elected grand chief of the Grand Council of the Crees in 2009.

Coon Come is perhaps best described as a Cree nationalist: a nation builder who presided over much of the Crees' own not-so-quiet revolution. Despite his strong political views and sometimes confrontational language, Coon Come is also pragmatic, capable of compromise when necessary. Under his leadership, and despite very public confrontations with Quebec nationalists, the Grand Council of the Crees negotiated several agreements with the provincial government over compensation for hydroelectric development, water contamination resulting from the flooding, and development in the communities. Charismatic in his own way, Coon Come personifies the current generation of Indigenous leaders: educated; astute in using the legal and political resources available to Indigenous peoples; at ease in the hallways of political and economic power in Montreal, Toronto, or New York; but always aware of his roots in the small Cree community where he was born.

Quebec nation. Territorial politics continued to drive the relationship in the aftermath of the 1995 referendum, although the focus became more economic in nature. The late 1990s and early 2000s were a period of unprecedented expansion for Quebec's natural resources extraction economy. The impact of the mining industry on Quebec's gross domestic product (GDP) more than doubled between 1998 and 2008. This massive expansion occurred largely in northern regions, on lands traditionally occupied by Indigenous peoples.

The Quebec government was keen to support this expansion—like many North American regions, it was reeling from a sharp decline in its manufacturing sector. The government sought new sources of income to support its comparatively expansive welfare state associated with the Quebec development model. The natural resource economy had always been key to the province's development, and a return to this more traditional model was only natural in the geopolitical and economic context of the time.

This development strategy is not unique to Quebec. State-led and state-promoted resource-intensive development has become a common economic strategy for governments facing a decline in their manufacturing sectors. And in many places, Indigenous peoples are at the centre of this new resources rush. What is unique in Quebec is the particular association of the extractive industry with the politics of nationalism.

Resource extraction operates in a highly competitive market. The upfront costs of developing a mine are high, and profits are uncertain and mostly in the medium to long term. Investors therefore want certainty and stability. Quebec (and Canada) is generally seen as a "friendly" environment for investments in mining, forestry, and other natural resources. But it can be vulnerable to political and legal uncertainty, especially in the context of the politics of nationalism and Indigenous rights.

Growing tensions over mining, forestry, and hydroelectric development in the late 1990s and early 2000s led the provincial government to change its approach to relations with Indigenous peoples. In a policy orientation document released in 1998, the government reaffirmed its commitment to "reconcile aboriginal aspirations with those of Quebecers as a whole" through the development of bilateral partnerships for economic development.[17] The objective for Quebec was to establish privileged channels with Indigenous nations in order to shift the debate from the political to the economic front.

The most striking development in this respect came in 2001, when Premier Bernard Landry and the grand chief of the James Bay Cree Nation, Ted Moses, announced they had reached an agreement to end the protracted disputes on the interpretation of the James Bay and Northern Quebec Agreement (JBNQA). The Agreement Respecting a New Relationship between the Cree Nation and the Government of Quebec, also known as the Paix des Braves, established the framework for what the parties called a "new era of mutual recognition and nation-to-nation cooperation between the Cree and Quebec."[18]

The Paix des Braves established co-management for the exploitation of forestry, a main area of conflict between the Cree and Quebec. Quebec also agreed to transfer its economic and social development obligations under the JBNQA to Cree authorities. One important innovation of the agreement was the mechanism for transferring economic development funding to the Cree. The basic amount transferred for 50 years ($70 million annually) is indexed to the annual value of natural resource extraction (including forestry, mining, and hydroelectric production) on Cree territory. In exchange, the Cree agreed to withdraw all judicial proceedings against Quebec in matters relating to the agreement, but more importantly they agreed to new hydroelectric developments (the Eastmain-1-A and Rupert diversion project) on their traditional lands.

The Paix des Braves is not revolutionary. It is not a new treaty, nor does it recognize any form of shared sovereignty over the territory. It is essentially an economic development partnership for the region. Quebec was under pressure to open up the territory for resource extraction and obtain guarantees for forestry exploitation and hydroelectric development. But it was clear that Quebec could no longer deal with the Cree as an "administered" group and simply impose its will from above. It had to recognize the mutual nature of the relationship. In this respect, despite their many concessions, the agreement was a victory for the Cree: Their political status and legitimacy as a distinct nation were acknowledged by Quebec.

Building on the success of the Paix des Braves, the provincial government continued to push for new partnerships with other Indigenous nations in the province. In 2009, the Jean Charest government launched Plan Nord, its economic development strategy for the province's northern regions. The plan was part of a five-point strategy to sustain growth in Quebec and reposition the province within the global economy by developing the "mining, energy and tourism potential in the North, in partnership with the northern communities concerned, including the First Nations and Inuit."[19] Indigenous peoples, the premier declared, would be "full partners" in future development projects. While some Indigenous nations, including the James Bay Cree, saw this

Primary Source

Declaration: Affirmation of the Sovereignty of First Nations of Quebec (extracts)

BASED ON the United Nations Declaration on the Rights of Indigenous Peoples, adopted by the United Nations General Assembly, on September 13, 2007;

AFFIRMING the nation-to-nation relationship based on equality and peaceful coexistence;

CONSIDERING THAT our nations possess rights, notably aboriginal title, ancestral rights and rights stemming from treaties, over our traditional territories, which transcend all boundaries;

CONSIDERING THAT our peoples have never renounced their right to sovereignty over these territories and resources;

CONSIDERING THAT First Nations are peoples who possess the right to self-determination as recognized by International Law, particularly by the United Nations Declaration on the Rights of Indigenous Peoples;

CONSIDERING THAT the governments of Quebec and Canada deny, through their actions and/or their inactions, the fundamental rights of First Nations;

CONSIDERING THAT the economy of non-Aboriginal societies was established to the detriment of First Nations while denying their rights;

CONSIDERING THAT the economic autonomy of First Nations is based on genuine sovereignty;

ACKNOWLEDGING the choice of First Nations to engage in nation-to-nation negotiations with federal and provincial governments and recognizing, in the same manner, the Aboriginal rights and territorial rights of First Nations that possess treaties that are solemnly signed with non-Aboriginal nations.

EMPHASIZING the unique contribution of the Elders, youth and women in the governance of our societies, as well as the relationship of equality between women and men within First Nations,

WE, THE CHIEFS OF FIRST NATIONS OF QUEBEC AND LABRADOR UNITED UNDER THE ASSEMBLY OF FIRST NATIONS OF QUEBEC AND LABRADOR, GATHERED IN ASSEMBLY, DECLARE THAT:

The time has come for First Nations of Quebec and Labrador to set in motion a process of unilateral affirmation of their sovereignty over the territory.

ADOPTED IN QUEBEC CITY ON NOVEMBER 27, 2008

Source: Secretariat of the Assembly of the First Nations of Quebec and Labrador, "Declaration on a First Nations of Quebec and Labrador Sovereignty Affirmation Process," www.apnql-afnql.com/en/accueil/img/SOVEREIGNTY-AFFIRMATION.pdf.

development strategy as an opportunity, others were more skeptical.[20]

Their suspicions were heightened given the symbolic politics associated with Plan Nord. In a statement reminiscent of former Premier Robert Bourassa's vision of hydro development as a conquest of the North, Jean Charest declared Plan Nord was "a project to build Quebec, to take ownership of our territory and develop its full economic potential."[21] The association of resources with nation-building is never far behind.

This episode is telling of the complexities of nationalist encounters in Quebec. The government is very much aware it is no longer possible to ignore Indigenous peoples and their collective claims—they are now considered "partners" in development. But it is still difficult for a provincial state that is driven by a classic nation-building project to make space for multiple sources of legitimacy and identities within its territory. For Indigenous peoples, a true partnership would involve community control over the kind of development that is to take place on their traditional lands and the sharing of revenues resulting from resource extraction. Plan Nord was vague in this respect, offering consultation, job creation, and compensation in exchange for Indigenous collaboration. To many Indigenous nations, this was simply not enough.

The Indigenous perspective on nation-to-nation economic partnerships was strengthened in 2014 when the Supreme Court of Canada confirmed that the Tsilhqot'in Nation of British Columbia had title to a 1,750-square-kilometre region that they had historically occupied.[22] The Tsilhqot'in had never signed a cession treaty with the Crown. The Court further held that, with some caveats, the provincial government could no longer authorize resource extraction on Tsilhqot'in lands without their consent. This decision obviously has direct implications in Quebec, where no land cession treaties were signed, with the exception of the James Bay and Northern Quebec Agreement and its sister agreement with the Naskapi. A number of First Nations in Quebec are now arguing that they have a legitimate claim to an Aboriginal title. The provincial government must therefore seek their consent for future development on their traditional lands. The Atikamekw of central Quebec went a step further. Based on the fact that they never signed a treaty with Canadian authorities, let alone Quebec, they officially declared sovereignty over their traditional territories.[23]

While such a unilateral declaration of sovereignty is mostly symbolic, it is a stark reminder that economic development cannot be separated from broader and largely unresolved legal and political issues. The Atikamekw and other Indigenous nations in Quebec do not necessarily oppose development. Instead, they want a real say in when, how, and under what conditions it is taking place. This, they argue, is what a true nation-to-nation partnership should be. The government of Quebec may well have little choice but to accept this new reality if it wants to go ahead with its resource-based economic development strategy.

Conclusion

The encounter of Quebec and Indigenous nationalisms over the past 40 years has resulted in a unique situation. On the one hand, Indigenous peoples and Quebec nationalists compete for recognition, democratic legitimacy, and territorial authority. The boundaries of what are in effect overlapping political communities continue to be the object of protracted battles. On the other hand, Quebec nationalism has created opportunities for Indigenous peoples. Using the same language of self-determination that Quebec nationalists use, Indigenous peoples have forced their way into the national debate. "If Quebec can secede from Canada," they argue, "then why can't we secede from Quebec?"

The decline of popular support for Quebec sovereignty may paradoxically reduce the visibility of Indigenous demands, as their own claims lose their strategic importance for both the federal government and Quebec. But the gains made in recent years remain significant. While Indigenous peoples do not have the jurisdictional tools, resources, and political clout of a large provincial government like Quebec, it is increasingly hard to ignore their claims to self-determination. The Paix des Braves and more recent battles over natural resource development suggest that Indigenous self-determination is alive and well in Quebec.

Questions for Critical Thinking

1. Why are Indigenous peoples challenging the legitimacy of Canadian sovereignty on their lands?
2. What are the sources of the conflict between Indigenous peoples and the Quebec government? How has this conflict evolved in recent decades?
3. What are the similarities and differences between Quebec and Indigenous nationalisms?

Notes

1. In Canada, the term *Aboriginal peoples* is used interchangeably with *Indigenous peoples* to designate the first inhabitants of the land. According to the Constitution Act, 1982, Aboriginal peoples comprise three groups: the First Nations or American Indians, the Inuit, and the Métis. I use both *Indigenous peoples* and *Aboriginal peoples* to refer to all three groups in this text and make the distinction when necessary.
2. For historical details about ancient and contemporary nations, see Volume 1 of the *Final Report of the Royal Commission on Aboriginal Peoples* (RCAP), 1996.
3. Department of the Interior, *Annual Report for the Year Ended 30th June, 1876*, in RCAP, vol. 1, 345.
4. For a historical analysis of reserves in Quebec, see Alain Beaulieu, "La création des réserves indiennes au Québec," in *Les autochtones et le Québec : des premières alliances au Plan Nord*, ed. Alain Beaulieu, Stéphan Gervais, and Martin Papillon (Montreal: Presses de l'Université de Montreal, 2013).
5. For a history of the Algonquin people, see the film *The Invisible Nation* by Richard Desjardins and Robert Monderie, distributed by the National Film Board of Canada.
6. Jean-Jacques Simard, *La reduction : l'autochtone inventé et les Amérindiens d'aujourd'hui* (Sillery, QC: Septentrion, 2003).
7. Daniel Salée, "The Quebec State and Indigenous Peoples," in *Quebec: State and Society*, 3rd ed., ed. Alain-G. Gagnon (Peterborough, ON: Broadview Press, 2004).
8. Robert Bourassa, *La Baie James* (Montreal: Éditions du Jour, 1973), 12.
9. Caroline Desbiens, *Power from the North: Territory, Identity, and the Culture of Hydroelectricity in Quebec* (Vancouver: UBC Press, 2014).
10. Section 35(1) reads: "The existing aboriginal and treaty rights of the aboriginal peoples of Canada are hereby recognized and affirmed." In a later amendment, it was specified that rights defined in a land claim settlement were considered treaty rights under the Constitution.
11. The National Assembly reaffirmed these principles in a motion adopted in 1985.
12. Denis Lessard, "Pour Mercredi, il n'y a pas de peuple québécois," *La Presse*, 12 February 1992, A1.
13. Normand Delisle, "Le droit à l'autonomie gouvernementale ne mène pas à la souveraineté territorial," *La Presse*, 6 March 1992, B14.
14. Philippe Cantin, "Un déni du droit des autochtones," *La Presse*, 7 December 1994, B4.
15. Matthew Coon Come, "The Status and Rights of the James Bay Cree in the Context of Quebec Secession," presented at the Conference of the Centre of International Studies, Washington, September 1994.
16. Ronald Irwin, "Cree Have the Right to Remain Canadians," *Ottawa Citizen*, 24 April 1994, A4.
17. Secrétariat aux affaires autochtones, *Partnership, Development, Achievement* (Quebec: Ministère du Conseil exécutif, Gouvernement du Québec, 1998), 12.
18. Secrétariat aux affaires autochtones, "Signature d'une entente de principe entre le grand conseil des Cris et le Gouvernement du Québec," press release, 23 October 2001.
19. Gouvernement du Québec, *Pour un développement économique socialement responsable et durable* (2009), www.plannord.gouv.qc.ca.
20. Assemblée des Premières Nations du Québec et du Labrador (APNQL), "À quand une opération séduction de toutes les Premières Nations concernées par le Plan Nord?" press release, 30 June 2011, www.cnw.ca/fr/releases/archive/June2011/30/c2601.html.
21. Gouvernement du Québec, *Pour un développement.*
22. *Tsilhqot'in Nation v. British Columbia*, [2014] 2 S.C.R. 257, 2014 SCC 44.
23. *Déclaration de souveraineté d'atikamekw nehirowisiw* (September 2014), www.atikamekwsipi.com/fichiers/File/declaration_souverainete_signe.pdf.

Select Bibliography

Alfred, Taiaike. *Wasáse: Indigenous Pathways of Action and Freedom*. Peterborough, ON: Broadview Press, 2005.

Beaulieu, Alain, Stéphan Gervais, and Martin Papillon, eds. *Les autochtones et le Québec : des premières alliances au*

Plan Nord. Montreal: Presses de l'Université de Montréal, 2013.

Bourassa, Robert. *La Baie James*. Montreal: Éditions du Jour, 1973.

Ciaccia, John. *The Oka Crisis: A Mirror of the Soul*. Dorval, QC: Maren Publications, 2000.

Cairns, Alan. *Citizens Plus*. Vancouver: UBC Press, 2000.

Desbiens, Caroline. *Power from the North: Territory, Identity, and the Culture of Hydroelectricity in Quebec*. Vancouver: UBC Press, 2014.

Dickason, Olive, and David T. McNab. *Canada's First Nations: A History of Founding Peoples from Earliest Times*, 4th ed. Don Mills, ON: Oxford University Press, 2008.

Gélinas, Claude. *Les autochtones dans le Québec post-confédéral, 1867–1960*. Sillery, QC: Septentrion, 2008.

Grand Council of the Crees (of Québec). *Sovereign Injustice: Forcible Inclusion of the James Bay Crees and Cree Territory into a Sovereign Québec*. Nemaska, QC: Grand Council of the Crees, 1995.

Ivison, Doug, Paul Patton, and Will Sanders, eds. *Political Theory and the Rights of Indigenous Peoples*. Cambridge: Cambridge University Press, 2001.

Jenson, Jane, and Martin Papillon. "Challenging the Citizenship Regime: James Bay Cree and Transnational Action." *Politics and Society* 28, no. 2 (2000): 245–64.

Salée, Daniel. "The Quebec State and Indigenous Peoples." In *Quebec: State and Society*, 3rd ed., edited by Alain-G. Gagnon. Peterborough, ON: Broadview Press, 2004.

Simard, Jean-Jacques. *La réduction : l'autochtone inventé et les Amérindiens d'aujourd'hui*. Sillery, QC: Septentrion, 2003.

Royal Commision on Aboriginal Peoples (RCAP). *Final Report*, 4 vols. Ottawa: Canada Communication Group Publishing, 1996.

York, Geoffrey, and Loreen Pindera. *People of the Pines: The Warriors and the Legacy of Oka*. Boston and Toronto: Little, Brown, 1991.

26 Quebec and La Francophonie: The Province as Global Player

Jody Neathery-Castro and Mark Rousseau,
University of Nebraska-Omaha

Timeline

1880 French geographer Onésime Reclus coins *Francophonie* to denote all peoples and countries using French.

1950 UIJPLF (International Union of French-Language Journalists and Press) is initiated by Quebec journalist Émile-Dostaler O'Leary.

1961 AUPELF (Association of Partially or Entirely French-Speaking Universities) is founded in Montreal, on the initiative of Quebec activist and journalist Jean-Marc Léger; now called AUF (University Agency of La Francophonie), it is headquartered in Montreal.

1970 During conference in Niamey, Niger, Canada helps found the first intergovernmental body of Francophonie, ACCT (Agency for Cultural and Technical Cooperation). Jean-Marc Léger becomes its first secretary-general, a title subsequently held by another Quebecer, Jean-Louis Roy, from 1990 to 1997.

1971 Governments of Canada and Quebec agree on terms and conditions for Quebec's participation in institutions, programs, and activities of ACCT with New Brunswick in 1977. They are recognized as participating governments (along with Canadian government) within the OIF (Organisation Internationale de la Francophonie).

1979 AIMF (International Association of Francophone Mayors) is created to serve as Francophonie's urban development wing.

1984 France launches TV5, a global French-language television network. In 1986, CTQC (Consortium de télévision Québec-Canada) is created in Canada to provide the European channel with Canadian programming.

1986 First Summit of La Francophonie held in Paris, France, at the Palace of Versailles.

1987 Second Summit of La Francophonie held in Quebec City, institutionalizing a permanent process of consultation on important international issues. Proposal for Francophonie Games launched at the summit. The Games adopt an original formula, combining sports and cultural events.

1988 IEPF (Francophonie Energy and Environment Institute) is founded. Based in Quebec City, this subsidiary body of OIF helps develop national capacities and partnerships in energy and environmental sectors.

1989 Third Summit of La Francophonie held in Dakar, Senegal, strengthening the organization by reaching into new areas of activity, including education and training, the environment, and legal and judicial co-operation. It confirmed the role of the ACCT as the principal operating agency and key instrument of La Francophonie as a multilateral organization.

1991 Fourth Summit of La Francophonie held in Chaillot, France, creating the Ministerial Conference of La Francophonie and the Permanent Council of La Francophonie and confirming the role of the ACCT as the secretariat of all of the organization's institutions.

1993 Fifth Summit of La Francophonie is held in Mauritius, recognizing the importance of economic issues and calling for increased co-operation among francophone business communities.

1995 Sixth Summit of La Francophonie is held in Cotonou, Benin, marking a major change in the OIF institutions. A secretary-general was appointed and the ACCT became the Intergovernmental Agency of La Francophonie (AIF). Five major co-operation programs of La Francophonie were established for focus: (1) freedom, democracy, and development; (2) culture and communications; (3) knowledge and progress; (4) economics and development; and (5) La Francophonie in the world. This summit also underscored the promotion of cultural diversity as more legitimate and necessary than ever, ascribing it a role in peace building.

1997 Quebec hosts the first Conference of Francophonie Ministers Responsible for the Information Highway. Ministers gather in Montreal to discuss the future of French on the Internet; in 1998, the Francophone Information Highway Fund is created to finance French efforts.

1997 Seventh Francophonie Summit held in Hanoi, Vietnam; election of first secretary-general, Boutros Boutros-Ghali, spokesperson and official representative of La Francophonie internationally. Decision is made to focus efforts on peace and the prevention of conflicts in member countries, and to co-operate with the international community in protecting human rights.

1999 Eighth Francophonie Summit held in Moncton, New Brunswick. Its final declaration marks a milestone in the evolution of La Francophonie, as greater emphasis is placed on peace and security, protection of civilian populations, and human rights. The information highway theme, addressed at Cotonou Summit (1995), becomes a priority in Moncton.

2000 Bamako Declaration, a policy document created at a symposium in Bamako, Mali, enables Francophonie to respond to crisis situations, breakdowns in democracy, and human rights violations. This declaration, a legacy of the Moncton Summit, places Francophonie at the forefront of international and regional organizations working in support of democracy, rights, and freedoms.

2002 Ninth Francophonie Summit held in Beirut, Lebanon. Abdou Diouf, former president of Senegal, succeeds Boutros Boutros-Ghali as secretary-general. The role of culture as an instrument of peace, democracy, and human rights is reaffirmed.

2004 Tenth Francophonie Summit held in Ouagadougou, Burkina Faso, with the theme "Francophonie, showing solidarity toward sustainable development." Ten-year strategic framework is adopted, defining La Francophonie's objectives and means to influence international affairs.

2006 Eleventh Francophonie Summit held in Bucharest, Romania, with a focus on "Information Technologies in Education." Heads of state and government pass five resolutions on (1) the global digital solidarity fund; (2) dumping of toxic waste in Abidjan, Côte d'Ivoire; (3) international migration and development; (4) the positioning of a UN force in the Central African Republic; and (5) climate change. The Ministerial Conference of La Francophonie approves a guide

continued

on the use of the French language in international organizations. The secretary-general, Abdou Diouf, is re-elected to head up La Francophonie for another four-year term.

2008 Ministerial Conference of La Francophonie and Twelfth Francophonie Summit held in Quebec City; focuses on four issues: (1) democracy and rule of law, (2) economic governance, (3) the environment, and (4) the French language.

2011 OIF Secretary-General Abdou Diouf travels to Quebec to speak and to receive the Grand officier de l'Ordre national du Québec.

2012 Quebec City (OIF Canada–Quebec delegation) hosts the first French Language World Forum, bringing together some 2,000 francophone and francophile civil-society participants from 93 countries to think about and discuss the current and future role of the French language.

2012 Fourteenth Francophonie Summit held in Kihshasa, Democratic Republic of the Congo.

2014 Fifteenth Francophonie Summit held in Dakar, Senegal, in October. Former Canadian Governor General Michaëlle Jean wins post as third secretary-general of Francophonie.

Sources: Adapted from Foreign Affairs and International Trade Canada, "Canada in La Francophonie," and "Summits," www.international.gc.ca/franco/evolution.aspx, www.international.gc.ca/franco/summit-sommet.aspx.

Introduction

From the standpoint of a student in the United States or Canada, the number and degree of foreign policy activities carried out by the provincial government of Quebec seems quite extraordinary. In fact, Quebec is one of the most politically powerful subnational units of government in the world, having extensive and varied international relations.[1] L'Organisation Internationale de la Francophonie (abbreviated OIF, or La Francophonie), for example, is the sole international organization to which Quebec belongs where it enjoys full autonomous participation as if it were a sovereign state, as a result of a legal understanding between Quebec and Canada.[2] Within the OIF Quebec represents itself; in other international organizations it is merely a participant observer under Canadian representation. Quebec's autonomous standing in OIF helps it promote Quebec culture and identity internationally.

Quebec has long pursued two primary policy goals: vigorous participation in the global economy and the preservation and promotion of French as the official language within Quebec. Elsewhere in this volume, our fellow authors also point out that, as for many small nations, Quebec's economy depends heavily on international exports, particularly to the United States. At the same time, Quebec (metaphorically) remains a small French-speaking island within English-speaking North America. Its future as a French-speaking society is critical for economic opportunity and advancement for the nearly 80 per cent of Quebecers whose native tongue is French. Because economy and culture mutually influence one another in varied ways, Quebec faces the paradox that its active global economic participation can challenge the maintenance of French within Quebec. As we shall see, OIF participation helps Quebec achieve both of these policy goals by providing a forum and pooled funds for addressing common international policy objectives while promoting the French language among the member countries and internationally.

This chapter addresses one central question: How does Francophonie serve Quebec's foreign policy interests, its economic development goals, the maintenance of the French language, and even Quebec's identity? To answer this question, we will examine how and why La Francophonie developed, how it helps Quebec preserve its language and culture, how it supports Quebec's economic goals, and how it promotes Quebec's interest in **cultural diversity**.

How and Why Did La Francophonie Develop?

L'Organisation Internationale de la Francophonie (OIF) is an **international organization** comprising francophone or French-speaking member-states and governments that aims to enhance the political, economic, and cultural standing of the French language internationally. Francophone meetings, conferences, and associations proliferated in the wake of World War II and global independence movements. France and Quebec were key instigators of the growing alliance among francophone countries. France had suffered traumatic defeat in 1940 and subsequent division and humiliation during the war; its prestige was further diminished in global independence movements (particularly the conflicts in Vietnam and Algeria). French elites feared that a decline in the instrumental value of their language would mean economic losses.[3] Similarly, the Quiet Revolution originated as Quebec nationalism led by francophones who "sensed their relative powerlessness in English-speaking North America; they observed a relative decline in population; they feared an influx of immigrants preferring to learn English; and they realized Anglophones controlled the mass media of communication, thus setting the agenda for problem-solving."[4] Ultimately, elites in French-speaking countries sensed their minority status within states and led the movement that would become Francophonie.[5]

The first francophone organizations evolved out of intergovernmental bodies promoted by the colonial ties between France and Africa, but many elites from Quebec were prominent in their development. In 1950, Quebecer Émile-Dostaler O'Leary founded Union internationale des journalistes et de la presse de langue française (International Union of French-Language Journalists and Press—UIJPLF) to advance co-operation among the francophone media of the world. In 2001 the organization was renamed Union internationale de la presse francophone (Union of the Francophone Press—UPF). From 1950 to 1955, O'Leary served as president of the UPF, which eventually morphed from a convention of French-speaking journalists into a professional union.

L'Association des universités partiellement ou entièrement de langue française (Association of Partially or Entirely French-Speaking Universities—AUPELF) was established at Université de Montréal in 1961 to develop co-operative programs to support international research and education at institutions using French. At the 1989 OIF Dakar Summit it was renamed Agence universitaire de la Francophonie (University Agency of Francophonie—AUF) and today is responsible for linking 692 educational establishments in 81 countries. With an annual budget of more than US$56 million, it provides over 200 grants to qualifying projects every year.

In spite of increased international francophone co-operation, tensions between France and Canada flared in 1967 during French President Charles de Gaulle's triumphant visit to Quebec to pay a visit to Expo 67. In remarks to a crowd of Quebecers at Montreal's city hall, de Gaulle shouted, "*Vive le Quebec libre*" ("long live an independent Quebec"), energizing Quebec's separatists. This direct challenge to Canadian sovereignty was ill received by the Canadian government and most anglophone Canadians.

Tension between Canada and Quebec increased several years later during efforts to develop an international francophone organization, l'Agence de coopération culturelle et technique (Agency for Cultural and Technical Cooperation—ACCT). In 1966 the descendant organization of the colonial French community, OCAM,[6] began to plan a 32-country meeting to take place in 1969 in Niamey, Niger, to establish a multilateral aid organization. At the initial organizing conferences in 1969 and 1970 the question immediately arose of Canadian and Quebec membership. France wanted to exclude Canada from the planned organization, reserving membership solely for Quebec. Canada naturally opposed this proposal, arguing that membership should be open only to countries, not to governments, and that Quebec would participate as a member of the Canadian delegation. France lobbied hard, directly and indirectly, during and after the Niamey conferences for independent membership for Quebec as a French-speaking government. Canada eventually agreed, much to the satisfaction of Quebec, which assumed membership in an international organization for the first time. The signatories thus included 23 countries plus two associated states and one "participating government" (a special category created for Quebec). The 20 March 1970 official founding is now commemorated annually as the Journée internationale de la Francophonie (International Day of Francophonie).[7]

The issue of Quebec's standing in La Francophonie continued to fester for some years, with Canada insisting on a veto over Quebec's actions if necessary. Only with the departure of Canadian Prime Minister Pierre Trudeau from the political scene were Quebec's and New Brunswick's governmental standing in La Francophonie fully accepted and regularized by Ottawa. These early Canada–Quebec disagreements over Quebec's standing in ACCT presaged later battles over such matters as budget and competences in the new organization. In an interesting twist, France nominated Jean-Marc Léger, a Quebec nationalist and francophone internationalist, as the first head of ACCT, which would be headquartered in Paris. After some doubts Canada acceded, believing Léger to be

BIOGRAPHY

Michaëlle Jean

While she had been long rumoured to be interested in the job, the 2014 accession of a federalist Liberal government in Quebec opened the door to the candidacy of Michaëlle Jean to replace Abdou Diouf as secretary-general of La Francophonie. The former governor general of Canada was quoted in the *Globe and Mail* as having heard lukewarm support for her candidacy from the 2012–14 Parti Québécois government of Pauline Marois, which was wary of having Canada's former viceroy running the world's French-language organization. Prime Minister Stephen Harper also seemed to have less-than-enthusiastic support for Jean's candidacy and, after losing a bid for a seat on the UN Security Council, had become wary of endorsing international campaigns and losing. His advisors had long been critical of the stylish Jean. She had been reluctant (but ultimately acquiesced) to endorse the prime minister's plan to prorogue Parliament in 2008 to delay a vote of no confidence against him.

Michaëlle Jean entered the campaign for the secretary-general seat with the declared backing of all three Canadian Francophonie votes—the federal, New Brunswick, and Quebec governments—as well as that of Haiti, her birth country. She also claimed support from several OIF member-states in West and Central Africa. Even so, it was only after a somewhat lengthy process that she was announced as the "consensus choice" for secretary-general of La Francophonie at the start of the 2014 Dakar Summit.

With her compelling personal story as an immigrant from Haiti to Quebec and long career in the public eye, Michaëlle Jean has emerged as one of Quebec's and Canada's most well-known public figures. Jean spent her early years in Port-au-Prince, Haiti, where her father was a private school principal and dissident of the government of François "Papa Doc" Duvalier. The family fled to Canada in the late 1960s after he was arrested and tortured for his politics, settling in Thetford Mines, Quebec. Her parents divorced soon afterward, and Jean has called her father a "broken man," increasingly prone to violence during this period of her life. This experience may have influenced her lifelong interest in women's issues and domestic violence. After finishing her bachelor's degree in Italian and Spanish at the Université de Montréal, Jean began her master's an honest and trustworthy Canadian as well as a Quebecer.

The organizational structure of what is now known as the OIF or La Francophonie has continued to evolve to reflect its increasing interests. Currently the OIF consists of 57 member-states and governments and 20 observer-states for a total membership of 77 states and governments, all having in common the use of the French language. While Canada is an autonomous member, so are its provincial governments of Quebec and New Brunswick. Other members include industrial democracies like France and Belgium, as well as some of the world's poorest and most questionable democracies. In 1986, French President François Mitterrand initiated the first summit of heads of member nations of the OIF, and biennial summits have generally been held ever since. Policy goals and initiatives of the OIF are determined at these biennial summits. While the founding purpose of the OIF was to engage in actions supporting the development and spread of the French language and cultures, its scope of action has expanded in recent years. Under the active leadership of the first two secretaries-general (Boutros Boutros-Ghali, 1997–2002, and Abdou Diouf, 2002–2014), the OIF has developed an agenda to exercise influence in

degree and taught Italian at the same institution. During her studies from 1979 to 1987, Jean worked with Quebec shelters for battered women, actively contributing to the establishment of a network of emergency shelters throughout Quebec and elsewhere in Canada. She was also involved in aid organizations for immigrant women and families, and later worked at Employment and Immigration Canada and at the Conseil des Communautés culturelles du Québec.

Her research on the women of Haiti caught the eye of a National Film Board producer, who invited her to return to Haiti as a researcher and interviewer for a film on the 1987 Haitian elections shown on the French-language Radio-Canada program *Le Point*. Her subsequent hiring by Radio-Canada made her the first black person on French television news in Canada and led to a successful career in journalism on several CBC and RDI programs. In 2004 she was well known enough to francophone Canadians to initiate her own current affairs show on RDI, *Michaëlle*. She was also familiar to English Canadians for her work on CBC Newsworld's documentary programs *The Passionate Eye* and *Rough Cuts*.

Prime Minister Paul Martin appointed Jean as governor general in August 2005, an announcement that sparked some controversy. A Quebec sovereignist publication suggested that Jean and her French-born husband supported the separatist cause, and some documentary evidence seemed to support the assertion. Jean insisted she had never belonged to the separatist movement, and she also renounced her French citizenship (acquired through marriage to her French husband) shortly before taking office. Reflecting on her immigrant experience, Jean argued in her swearing-in that it was time to "eliminate the spectre" of the two solitudes, French and English, which had long vexed Canadian history. In office, Jean championed human rights and the arts, drew attention to socioeconomic problems in the Canadian North, and promoted Canada abroad, particularly in Africa and her native Haiti. Following her tenure as governor general, the Canadian government established the Michaëlle Jean Foundation to promote education, culture, and creativity among youth from rural, northern, and poor communities in Canada. Jean served from 2010–14 as a special envoy to Haiti for UNESCO, fighting poverty and illiteracy and raising international funds. She was appointed by Abdou Diouf, secretary-general of La Francophonie, as the Grand Témoin de la Francophonie for the 2012 London Summer Olympics, tasked with promoting the French language there. She started a term as chancellor of the University of Ottawa in February 2012.

international affairs and tackle some of the challenges of globalization. In particular, the OIF has identified four objectives to pursue in areas where its experience and know-how have already proved their worth:

- promoting the French language and cultural and linguistic diversity
- promoting peace, democracy, and human rights
- supporting education, training, higher education, and research
- developing co-operation for sustainable development and solidarity[8]

In supporting the efforts of the OIF and its components, Quebec favours the issues crucial for the development of member countries: the promotion of the French language, the international protection of cultural diversity, and the affirmation of democratic principles and human rights. The OIF plays an increasingly important role in defending French culture and language globally and in advancing the particular political and economic interests of francophone nations, particularly France and Canada. Quebec has been a major participant in the OIF from the beginning and benefits from OIF's strengthening of French language, culture, and economic interests globally. For Quebec, the OIF is its most important and prominent world arena of participation.

How Does La Francophonie Help Quebec Preserve Its Language and Culture?

As the unique majority French-speaking province in Canada, Quebec has long had two dominant, somewhat contradictory goals: participating actively in the global economy and protecting and deepening its French language and cultural heritage. Growing international trade in the global economy increases economic **interdependence** between nations. Thus, Quebec's active participation in and dependence on the global economy challenges its culture. English has become the primary second language in many nations around the world, diminishing the traditional role of French. Rules of the World Trade Organization (WTO), the regime that regulates international trade, hinder Quebec's ability to subsidize its **cultural industries**, a practice followed in nearly all non-English-speaking nations as well as a number of anglophone nations. As referenced by Daniel Weinstock and Linda Cardinal in this volume, some 80 per cent of Quebec's citizens are native French speakers, and the Quebec government has long been committed to maintaining French as the official language of Quebec. The Quebec government plays an active and decisive role in preserving and promoting the use of French in Quebec as well as internationally. While francophones are a majority in Quebec, they make up only 2 per cent of the North American population. Thus Quebec is an island of French speakers surrounded by an English-language North America, challenging Quebec's ability to maintain French as its national language.

While the Quebec government fosters the maintenance of French within Quebec, it also acknowledges the fragility of the language's position. The government asserts that maintaining the French language is one of its fundamental preoccupations. Participation in the OIF gives Quebec significant support in its efforts to promote French within the province as well as internationally.

Quebec and its partners in the OIF have for many years led the demand for the "cultural exception" in international trade. France, Quebec, and Canada, with the backing of the OIF, argue that culture and cultural goods are unique commodities, unlike steel, personal computers, or cellphones, and should not be subject to the rules of the WTO trade regime. The OIF believes cultural goods represent an aspect of a nation's cultural identity and heritage and that various arts industries (such as publishing, film, and music) need protection in the form of government subsidies to support them from foreign invaders, especially the encroachment of Hollywood on the worldwide film industry.[9] While the cultural exception in trade has remained central to the OIF, it has more recently addressed these concerns under the more inclusive concept of *cultural diversity*, which espouses a state's right and need to promote and subsidize its own cultural industries. This right applies not only to French-speaking nations but also to other language nationalities such as Spanish, Portuguese, and Arabic. While withstanding the dominance of English is a daunting task, Francophonie's expansion of its pro-French stance to one of "plurilingualism"[10] has boosted its international appeal to even non-French speakers.[11]

How Does La Francophonie Support Quebec's Economic Goals?

While defending the French language and culture remains a fundamental preoccupation for Quebec, active participation in the global economy is both a major desire and a necessity. Uniquely, the OIF enhances both of these goals. The OIF allows Quebec to develop its trade, particularly with developing countries in francophone Africa, while demanding pluralism in trade rules and the language of exchange. As Quebec's government acknowledges, "International trade plays a vital role in Quebec's economy and in creating greater wealth for society as a whole."[12] Like that of most small nations, Quebec's economy is highly dependent on exports. Today exports make up some 53 per cent of Quebec's gross domestic product (GDP). While raw materials (forest products, paper, mining, and the like) remain important, diversified advanced industries make an increasingly important contribution. Supported by a high level of research and development activity, Quebec enjoys growing economic production in such advanced sectors of the economy as information technologies, biotechnologies, pharmaceuticals, aerospace, and genomics.[13]

Quebec was an early and staunch supporter of the United States–Canada Free Trade Agreement (FTA) and its successor, the North American Free Trade Agreement (NAFTA). The Quebec government, however, believes that when English serves as the exclusive language of international trade, English-speaking nations have an advantage over non-English-speaking nations. First, businesspeople of non-anglophone nations are obliged to negotiate in a language other than their own. Second, non-anglophone nations must support and finance English-language training, expending funds that English-language nations can invest directly in endeavours like information technologies and science research. As a result, tangible economic advantages accrue to anglophones when English serves as the lingua franca of the WTO and related trade bodies. Quebec believes that non-anglophone nations should push for guaranteed official status in the WTO for all four major New World trade area languages (Spanish, English, Portuguese, and French).

Louise Beaudoin, Quebec's minister of international relations from 1998 to 2003, suggests that Quebec, like many modern nations, finds itself caught between two contrasting goals: "the normal desire of a people to commit itself to globalization and to share in the prosperity of the world around it; the other is that same people's need to preserve an essential part of its personality, namely its cultural distinctiveness, its soul, its unique relationship to the world."[14] While Quebec has been a strong supporter of trade liberalization, like many other non-English-speaking nations it struggles to maintain its own language and culture. Beaudoin observes:

> Our support for **trade liberalization** is, however, not blind and unconditional. . . . Essentially the Quebec government believes that, if care is not taken, the general process of globalization and trade liberalization can threaten the ability of countries and governments to take measures to support culture and cultural diversity. We attach paramount importance to the protection and promotion of culture. Globalization must not deprive countries and governments of all flexibility.[15]

This stance is consistent with the Quebec government's position paper, *Québec's International Policy: Working in Concert* (2006), which seeks to reinforce and strengthen Quebec's international influence and action.

Within the OIF there exists a major divide between the well-developed, wealthy nations of France and Canada and the relatively undeveloped and poor nations of francophone Africa. The OIF's emphasis on economic development thus has

Primary Source

UNESCO Convention on the Protection and Promotion of the Diversity of Cultural Expressions

Article 1—Objectives

The objectives of this Convention are:

(a) to protect and promote the diversity of cultural expressions;
(b) to create the conditions for cultures to flourish and to freely interact in a mutually beneficial manner;
(c) to encourage dialogue among cultures with a view to ensuring wider and balanced cultural exchanges in the world in favour of intercultural respect and a culture of peace;
(d) to foster interculturality in order to develop cultural interaction in the spirit of building bridges among peoples;
(e) to promote respect for the diversity of cultural expressions and raise awareness of its value at the local, national and international levels;
(f) to reaffirm the importance of the link between culture and development for all countries, particularly for developing countries, and to support actions undertaken nationally and internationally to secure recognition of the true value of this link;
(g) to give recognition to the distinctive nature of cultural activities, goods and services as vehicles of identity, values and meaning;
(h) to reaffirm the sovereign rights of States to maintain, adopt and implement policies and measures that they deem appropriate for the protection and promotion of the diversity of cultural expressions on their territory;
(i) to strengthen international cooperation and solidarity in a spirit of partnership with a view, in particular, to enhancing the capacities of developing countries in order to protect and promote the diversity of cultural expressions.

Article 6—Rights of parties at the national level

1. Within the framework of its cultural policies and measures as defined in Article 4.6 and

strong appeal for the poorer, less-developed member nations. The OIF has taken an active role in providing technical assistance to its less-developed members, a task in which Canada, Quebec, and France especially participate. Power in the OIF is heavily concentrated in France and Canada/Quebec, since they provide the bulk of finances for the organization.

With the exception of its participation in La Francophonie, the government of Quebec is not a major provider of developmental aid. It prioritizes its efforts in the areas of its expertise: human resources development and governance capacity-building programs. Quebec has signalled its intent to devote its energies to helping a limited number of countries with those belonging to La Francophonie among its top priorities. An interesting case study is provided by Haiti, where most of Quebec's monetary aid is channelled through La Francophonie, but the effort is multifaceted:

- Some 75 Quebec police officers participate in the UN stabilization mission in Haiti.
- Hydro-Québec supplies technical support for the production, transportation, and transmission of electricity in certain regions.
- With the École nationale d'administration publique (ENAP), the government of Quebec is preparing a project to support the modernization of the Haitian government in collaboration with the Canadian International Development Agency (CIDA).

taking into account its own particular circumstances and needs, each Party may adopt measures aimed at protecting and promoting the diversity of cultural expressions within its territory.

2. Such measures may include the following:
   (a) regulatory measures aimed at protecting and promoting diversity of cultural expressions;
   (b) measures that, in an appropriate manner, provide opportunities for domestic cultural activities, goods and services among all those available within the national territory for the creation, production, dissemination, distribution and enjoyment of such domestic cultural activities, goods and services, including provisions relating to the language used for such activities, goods and services;
   (c) measures aimed at providing domestic independent cultural industries and activities in the informal sector effective access to the means of production, dissemination and distribution of cultural activities, goods and services;
   (d) measures aimed at providing public financial assistance;
   (e) measures aimed at encouraging non-profit organizations, as well as public and private institutions and artists and other cultural professionals, to develop and promote the free exchange and circulation of ideas, cultural expressions and cultural activities, goods and services, and to stimulate both the creative and entrepreneurial spirit in their activities;
   (f) measures aimed at establishing and supporting public institutions, as appropriate;
   (g) measures aimed at nurturing and supporting artists and others involved in the creation of cultural expressions;
   (h) measures aimed at enhancing diversity of the media, including through public service broadcasting.

Source: UNESCO Diversity of Cultural Expressions Section, *Basic Texts of the 2005 Convention on the Protection and Promotion of the Diversity of Cultural Expressions* (2013), http://unesdoc.unesco.org/images/0022/002253/225383E.pdf.

- Since 1997, Quebec has contributed more than $11 million in humanitarian aid and in grants for development projects in Haiti.[16]

Language and cultural ties propel Quebec's active economic and cultural participation in the OIF. At the same time, Quebec's participation in the global economy raises challenges for French-language maintenance and cultural development within Quebec. For economic advancement and upward social mobility, Quebec's largely French-speaking working class needs a Quebec economy that functions in French. At the same time, the French-speaking middle classes (including journalists, academics, writers, and the like) produce French-language cultural products that require a French-speaking audience. Thus the maintenance of French as the national language has broad support. Quebec's leadership across political parties remains committed to French-language protection.[17] For example, former Minister of International Relations Louise Beaudoin stated that "Support for Bill 101 is a bipartisan consensus—the PQ and PLQ agree French must be maintained as the national language. There is support for French as the language of the workplace and economic success."[18] Quebec's membership in the OIF adds legitimacy to these concerns.

During the Quiet Revolution and following, as Quebec built a modern, urban, industrial economy, the standing of French in the workplace took on increasing importance for both the largely French-speaking working class and the middle-class culture producers; the language of business had been less important in Quebec's earlier rural, agricultural economy. Quebec enacted a series of policies to make French the sole official language of the province and ensure its dominance. These efforts culminated in 1977 in the adoption of the Charter of the French Language (Bill 101), requiring the use of French in commerce, the workplace, government, education, and other areas of public life. Quebec's current policies ensure that French remains the sole national language, helping to maintain economic opportunities for the French-speaking working class and the culture-producing, French-speaking middle class.

While Quebec participates vigorously in international trade in the increasingly global economy, some negative consequences result. For example, organized labour in Quebec strongly opposed NAFTA, seeing it as an assault on the Canadian economy by US multinational corporations.[19] In opposing NAFTA, organized labour argued the treaty would diminish Quebec's ability to develop its own cultural policies on language, advertising, and education—such policies would elicit accusations of erecting barriers to bilateral commerce. As subsequent events have shown, these concerns were reasonable. Further, a number of contemporary social analysts have suggested that globalization might more appropriately be labelled "Americanization." George Ritzer argues, "There is no question that exportation of the American means of consumption to the rest of the world involves a process of Americanization."[20] French sociologist Pierre Bourdieu (1930–2002) argued that globalization is essentially imperialism by wealthy countries. He suggests that the ideology of neoliberal economics is propagated under a cloak of modernization and neutrality such that globalization seems inevitable. He believed that while the United States is not the only economically imperialist country, it is in a uniquely powerful position to impose its views on much of the world.[21]

These concerns propel Quebec's active participation in the OIF, where it finds support for its desire to protect and enhance the French language and culture. For these reasons Quebec was among the OIF member nations pushing hard for the adoption of the UNESCO treaty known as the Convention on the Protection and Promotion of the Diversity of Cultural Expressions (see the Primary Source box). Quebec's strong support for the treaty and its activities in OIF helped to achieve the overwhelming adoption of the treaty by UNESCO member nations.

How Does La Francophonie Support Quebec's Interests in Cultural Diversity?

Quebec sees protection of the French language and support for cultural diversity as complementary. While globalization has been widely promoted in recent years, it has also been criticized. Many point to the economic and social costs of international trade policies (particularly those promoted by the WTO) on citizens in developed and developing countries alike. Scholars have pointed to Francophonie as an organization poised to challenge what is often deemed "Americanization."[22]

Along with the federal government, with the backing of the cultural sector in many countries and the concerted efforts of La Francophonie, Quebec encouraged the negotiation of the international Convention on the Protection and Promotion of the Diversity of Cultural Expressions under the auspices of UNESCO. The issue of cultural diversity was one where "Quebec showed its capacity to exert influence on the international scene."[23] By working with experts from civil society, academia, the OIF, and the federal government, Quebec was instrumental in UNESCO's 2005 adoption of the Convention.[24] Currently over 120 countries and the European Union have ratified the Convention.

Countries had begun trying to minimize the WTO's impact on their policy options soon after the creation of the WTO in 1995. In June 1998, Canada's minister of heritage, Sheila Copps, invited culture ministers from 19 other countries to Ottawa to resume a dialogue begun two months earlier at the UNESCO Intergovernmental Conference on Cultural Policies for Development. The result was the International Network on Cultural Policy (INCP), an informal network of ministers of culture who agreed to establish a loose but ongoing association to pursue common concerns involving cultural policy.[25] The INCP has held annual meetings since 1998, and its membership has grown from fewer than 20 countries in 1998 to 69 in 2009 (over one-third of these are either members or observers of the Francophonie). Within the INCP, the Working Group on Cultural Diversity and Globalization, chaired by Canada and comprising government ministers and advisors from member nations, share proposals and advice on policy to promote cultural diversity, both nationally and internationally. The INCP drafted a cultural diversity statement in 2001, which was endorsed by the member ministers of culture and passed on to UNESCO, which used it as the basis for its 2005 Convention.

Similarly, the International Network for Cultural Diversity (INCD) is an international NGO (nongovernmental organization) organized in 1998 by the Canadian Ministry of Heritage to "complement the efforts of the INCP by acting as an umbrella group for individual artists, cultural activists, and cultural NGOs from different countries."[26]

Conferences of OIF professionals were also convened between 1999 and 2001 to discuss and promote a New International Instrument on Cultural Diversity (NIICD). In the final declaration of its Beirut Summit in 2002, the OIF became the first international governmental organization to support the adoption of such an instrument. While skeptics predicted a low likelihood of success for the UNESCO Convention, to date over 120 countries and the EU have ratified it. The contributions of Francophonie to the UNESCO Convention were one of the main achievements of the OIF and demonstrated the increasing political dimension of the organization.[27] Recent OIF summits have regularly confirmed OIF's desire not to let cultural goods and services be reduced to the status of ordinary commodities. Member-states affirm their sovereign rights to define freely their cultural policies and to wield the tools with which to do so.[28] This policy was most recently confirmed at the 2012 Kinshasa Summit.

How does La Francophonie Help Quebec Promote Democracy?

For over 20 years, Quebec has been making the expertise of its public institutions available to French-speaking countries undergoing democratic consolidation or in the process of democratization. Quebec prioritizes the promotion of democratic principles and their dissemination, particularly in the francophone world. These principles include:

- affirming democratic values
- consolidating the rule of law
- holding free and transparent elections
- promoting human rights[29]

Quebec has also strategically used its membership in La Francophonie to leverage a larger role on the international stage to promote democracy and good governance among French-speaking countries—a goal that has increasingly also been on the agenda of La Francophonie itself, as it has expanded its political role in the wake of the 2000 Bamako Declaration. Quebec's chief electoral officer (CEO) both reports to Quebec's National Assembly on provincial electoral issues and also shares democratic electoral expertise with countries and international organizations to promote democracy building and to strengthen electoral systems around the world. Quebec's CEO has participated in 64 electoral missions to date, 22 of them at the initiative of La Francophonie.[30]

In 1999 the Quebec CEO published *Election Observing: Practical Guide for Election Monitoring Missions Abroad*, to be a practical tool to enable international election monitors to quickly gain the skills and cultural skills necessary to function effectively. La Francophonie was one of four international organizations whose electoral observation codes of conduct were incorporated into the guidelines of the manual.[31]

In 2011, the Network of Francophone Electoral Skills was jointly established by the Quebec CEO and La Francophonie, and its headquarters set up in Quebec City. This is an association that brings together electoral commissions and administrations from the francophone world with the aim of sharing research, training, and technical assistance among francophone nations. It holds its own conferences and workshops to disseminate the information, and also partners with other groups to this end. Similarly, Quebec's Commission on Access to Information (CAI) created an international francophone network of structures to protect personal information, particularly in election settings, known as the Association of Data Protection Authorities (ADPA). This network is based in Montreal. In 2014 the Network of Francophone Electoral Skills and the ADPA (with guidance from their Quebec creators) held a seminar in Bamako, Mali, to promote best electoral practices to emerging democracies, and drafted an operational manual to promote the protection of the personal data of voters.[32]

So Quebec's affiliation with La Francophonie has facilitated its capacity for democracy promotion by providing a partner with which to sponsor networks and structures to reach across the francophone world. Such outreach also reinforces Quebec's goal of connecting with French speakers and promoting the French language in the global community.

What Can We Conclude about Quebec and La Francophonie?

Quebec's membership in L'Organisation Internationale de la Francophonie has facilitated its seemingly contradictory goals: to be connected to the global economy and to preserve its cultural heritage and French language. It is through La Francophonie that Quebec most skilfully asserts its priorities in a multinational setting. Quebec enjoys multiple benefits of its OIF participation:

- international prestige deriving from its governmental status that puts it on par with the member-states in OIF
- an important environment in which to consolidate Quebec's influence in multilateral forums like the UN and the Organization of African Unity (OAU)
- an ally with which to partner in reaching out to the francophone world on development and democracy-building measures
- strengthened alliances with the other member countries and governments
- mutually beneficial cultural, economic, and commercial exchanges, including access to emerging markets that play to Quebec's economic strength in the pharmaceutical, telecommunications, energy, and transportation sectors[33]

The OIF, along with other international organizations and countries,[34] has faced the uncertainty of globalization with unease and even hostility, particularly as elements of culture and language are threatened. However, in its strong leadership role within the OIF, Quebec has been instrumental in shaping the organization's increasingly political agenda. In particular, on cultural diversity Quebec has shown its capacity to shape international affairs. Working closely with Francophonie, international groups, and cultural and trade allies, Quebec played a key role in initiating the debate and moving the issue forward to its culmination in the adoption in 2005 of the UNESCO Convention on the Protection and Promotion of the Diversity of Cultural Expressions.[35]

The chapter in this volume by Louis Balthazar shows how Quebec's international ambitions grew, especially with the Quiet Revolution. In some ways the cultural diversity process might be viewed as a "critical test case" of Quebec's international aspirations. While constrained within the Canadian federal framework from pursuing fully its own international agenda, Quebec has leveraged its leadership role within the OIF to expand its international authority. A Quebec government publication lists the following means that it believes will help it attain its ambitions for participating in international organizations:

1. Access to all information and participation during the initial stages of negotiations toward establishing Canada's positions on OIF matters
2. Full member status in Canadian delegations and exclusive responsibility for designating its representative

3. The right to speak for itself at international forums on matters related to its responsibilities
4. Recognition of Quebec's right to give its approval before Canada signs or declares itself bound by a treaty or agreement
5. The right to express its position when Canada appears before supervisory bodies of international organizations for matters involving Quebec or affecting its interests[36]

In 2008, Quebec hosted both the biennial OIF Summit (see the Case Study box) and a Canada–European Union summit to explore integrating Canada's economy with the EU. Both events are indicative of the expanding role in international affairs that Quebec is carving out for itself. Further, with its international ambitions and keen interest in cultural diversity, Quebec negotiated a historic agreement with the Canadian government in 2006[37] to allow Quebec to be an official representative on Canada's Permanent Delegation to UNESCO, not just to observe, but to fully participate in all proceedings and to confer with Canada on matters falling under provincial jurisdiction. Quebec's representative has diplomatic authority to express the opinion of the government of Quebec as distinct from that of Canada's government. In the event of disagreement with Canada, "the Quebec government has the right not to implement conventions, action plans, and other international instruments determined by UNESCO."[38] These extensive successes at the international level illustrate the assertion with which we began this chapter: Among subnational governments, Quebec enjoys multiple international relations that could not be imagined by any state in the United States. L'Organisation Internationale de la Francophonie has made it possible for Quebec to leverage its tremendous ambitions and capacities as it stretches its international wings.

CASE STUDY

Two Francophonie Summits in Quebec: 1987 and 2008

Quebec has hosted two international Francophonie Summits, in 1987 and 2008. The two events, 21 years apart, illustrate the gradual evolution of the OIF from a strictly cultural organization to an international political and economic entity. Both summits also illustrate enduring challenges, such as the ongoing quarrels between the governments of Canada and Quebec and the claim that the organization turns a blind eye to human rights violators among its own membership.

Forty-one OIF states and governments were eligible to participate in the 1987 Francophonie Summit, with Canadian Prime Minister Brian Mulroney and Quebec Premier Robert Bourassa sharing the host's spotlight. The transition in the office of prime minister from Pierre Trudeau to Brian Mulroney was pivotal to the creation of the summit. France had refused to hold a summit in which Quebec was not a full partner, and Trudeau objected to treating a province as a "half-country," refusing to put Quebec on a level footing with sovereign nations. As part of Mulroney's "national reconciliation" and insistence on Quebec's right to "direct and privileged" relations with France, Quebec was given the position as "interlocutor" between Canada as a whole and the French-speaking countries of the world. The understanding was that Quebec could have full participation at the summit on topics under provincial jurisdiction, but would remain an "interested observer" on issues under federal jurisdiction. At both the 1986 inaugural summit in Paris and at the 1987 summit, Quebec Premier Bourassa tested this arrangement by speaking publicly on international issues without the explicit imprimatur of the prime minister. In 1986 Bourassa held a press

continued

conference on international aid without first clearing it with the prime minister, while in 1987 he proposed tying Third World debt to commodity prices—an economic issue clearly under federal, not provincial, jurisdiction (although apparently this proposal had been conveyed to Prime Minister Mulroney in advance).

The 1987 Quebec City Francophonie Summit claimed several successes, notably the announcement of a new energy institute (Institut de l'Énergie et de l'Environnement de la Francophonie) in Quebec dedicated to using hydroelectricity to help solve Third World energy problems, the creation of the Francophone Games sports competition to be held every four years, the forgiving of seven African states' debts to Canada, as well as a variety of co-operative communications and cultural programs. Despite the positive claims of the 1987 meeting, controversies were also highlighted, including human rights protesters angry over Vietnam's inclusion at the summit as well as some concerns over the future of the organization voiced by the spiritual father of La Francophonie, Senegal's former president Léopold Sédar Senghor. Senghor expressed concern that in the rush to emulate the Commonwealth's economic and technical approach to international assistance, the French language was at risk of becoming a mere industrialized tool for doing business.

The 2008 Francophonie Summit in Quebec included representatives from 55 member countries and 13 observer nations. While some of the agenda was overshadowed by concerns about the growing global economic crisis, a milestone on climate change was established, with Francophonie countries pledging to reduce greenhouse gas emissions by 50 per cent by 2050 (with poor countries eligible for some $100 million in Canadian government aid to make the transition).

Once again the 2008 summit was plagued by charges of hypocrisy in its stated commitment to democracy and human rights. Amnesty International issued a report on the eve of the summit deploring the state of human rights in the majority of the developing countries that make up La Francophonie, and blaming the organization for not doing enough to address problems ranging from arbitrary arrest to political violence and torture. In an interview with reporters, Béatrice Vaugrante, director general of the Francophone Canadian branch of Amnesty International, claimed, "They must condemn them, suspend them, simply be much more strict." A spokesperson maintained that Prime Minister Harper believed that leaders of these nations should not be isolated from the rest of the world if they are to be influenced by the organization's norms.

Breaking with France's traditional neutrality on the issue of Quebec sovereignty, French President Nicolas Sarkozy vocalized firm support for Canadian unity. "If anyone tries to tell me that the world today needs an additional division, then they don't have the same read of the world as me," Sarkozy said, with Canadian Prime Minister Harper by his side. "I don't know why a fraternal, familial love of Quebec would have to be nourished through defiance toward Canada." Leaving no room for nuanced interpretation, Sarkozy reinforced his repudiation of Quebec nationalism a few months later in Paris. When it was pointed out that he had just rejected the cornerstone of the French principle toward Quebec nationalism, the policy of "non-interference and non-indifference," Sarkozy replied, "It's not my thing."

Questions for Critical Thinking

1. How do Quebec's goals of preserving/enhancing French and actively trading in the global economy conflict? Does OIF membership benefit Quebec's achievement of either or both goals?
2. If you were making the decision for the Government of Canada, what advantages or disadvantages would you perceive in allowing Quebec to participate as a member government in the OIF?

3. Does the French language constitute enough of a shared bond to facilitate international organizing? If not, on what grounds should such international co-operation be based? In your view, has La Francophonie emerged beyond a language-based organization on the international stage?

Notes

1. Daniel Latouche, "Quebec and Canada: Scenarios for the Future," *Business in the Contemporary World* 3, no. 1 (1990): 58–70.
2. New Brunswick is the only other Canadian province to have this unique independent standing.
3. Brian Weinstein, "Francophonie: A Language-Based Movement in World Politics," *International Organization* 30, no. 3 (1976): 487–8.
4. Ibid., 488.
5. Ibid., 491–3.
6. Organisation Commune Africaine et Malgache.
7. Weinstein, "Francophonie," 496–7.
8. Jody Neathery-Castro and Mark O. Rousseau, "Quebec, Francophonie and Globalization," *Quebec Studies* 32 (2002): 20.
9. Adapted from www.francophonie.org/actions/index.cfm.
10. The notion behind plurilingualism is that a single language (English) is not sufficient for international relations.
11. Jean-Benoît Nadeau and Julie Barlow, *The Story of French* (New York: St Martin's Press, 2006), 349–50.
12. Quebec Ministry of International Relations, *Québec's International Policy: Working in Concert* (Government of Quebec, 2006), 54, available at www.mri.gouv.qc.ca/en/pdf/Politique.pdf.
13. Ibid.
14. Neathery-Castro and Rousseau, "Quebec, Francophonie and Globalization," 23.
15. Ibid., 23–4.
16. Quebec Ministry of International Relations, *Québec's International Policy*, 95–6.
17. Neathery-Castro and Rousseau, "Quebec, Francophonie and Globalization," 25.
18. Louise Beaudoin, Remarks at the Association for Canadian Studies in the United States meetings, Pittsburgh, PA, 18 November 1999.
19. Mark O. Rousseau, "Ethnic Mobilization in Quebec, Federalism in Canada, and the Global Economy," *Research in Social Movements, Conflicts and Change* 21 (1999): 205–23.
20. George Ritzer, *Enchanting a Disenchanted World: Revolutionizing the Means of Consumption* (Thousand Oaks, CA: Pine Forge Press, 2005), 45.
21. Pierre Bourdieu, *Acts of Resistance: Against the Tyranny of the Market* (New York: New Press, 1998); and "Uniting to Better Dominate," *Items and Issues* 2, no. 3–4 (2001): 1–6.
22. Weinstein, "Francophonie," 485; Ritzer, *Enchanting a Disenchanted World*, 51.
23. Quebec Ministry of International Relations, *Québec's International Policy*, 27.
24. Ibid.
25. P. S. Grant and C. Wood, *Blockbusters and Trade Wars: Popular Culture in a Globalized World* (Vancouver: Douglas & McIntyre, 2004), 383.
26. Keith Acheson and Christopher Maule, "Convention on Cultural Diversity," *Journal of Cultural Economics* 28, no. 4 (2004): 246.
27. Jody Neathery-Castro and Mark O. Rousseau, "Does French Matter? France and Francophonie in the Age of Globalization," *French Review* 78, no. 4 (2005): 678–95; Anne-Marie Laulan, "La diversité culturelle à l'UNESCO," *Hermès* 40, *Francophonie et Mondialisation*, ed. Tamatoa Bambridge et al., 44–48 (Paris: CNRS Éditions, 2004).
28. Organisation Internationale de la Francophonie, 2002.
29. Québec, Relations Internationales et Francophonie, "Francophonie: Peace, Democracy and Human Rights," www.mrifce.gouv.qc.ca/en/francophonie/paix-et-democratie.
30. Le Directeur Général des élections du Québec, "List of the Hosting of Delegations and Foreign Visitors," http://www.electionsquebec.qc.ca/english/electoral-experts/dge-list-of-the-hosting-of-delegations-and-foreign-visitors.php?t=m.
31. Le Directeur Général des élections du Québec, *Election Observing: Practical Guide for Members of Election Monitoring Missions Abroad*, www.electionsquebec.qc.ca/documents/pdf/guide-pour-missions-observation-electorale-anglaise.pdf.
32. Québec, Relations Internationales et Francophonie, "Francophonie"; Association Francophone des Autorités de Protection des Données Personnelles, "Le RECEF (administrations électorales) présente ses recommandations aux pays francophones," www.afapdp.org/archives/2375.
33. Quebec Ministry of International Relations, *Québec's International Policy*.
34. Robert W. McChesney, "Global Media, Neoliberalism and Imperialism," *Monthly Review* 52, no. 10 (2001): 16.
35. Quebec Ministry of International Relations, *Québec's International Policy*, 27–9.
36. Ibid., 28.
37. The Conservative government of Stephen Harper followed through on its 2005 election campaign promise

to give Quebec an increased international role and a UNESCO representative.

38. Quebec Ministry of International Relations, *Québec's International Policy*, 28.

Select Bibliography

Acheson, Keith, and Christopher Maule. "Convention on Cultural Diversity." *Journal of Cultural Economics* 28, no. 4 (2004): 243–56.

Beaudoin, Louise. Remarks at the Association for Canadian Studies in the United States meetings. Pittsburgh, PA, 18 November 1999.

Bernier, Ivan, 2001. *La préservation de la diversité linguistique à l'heure de la mondialisation*. Available at www.mcc.gouv.qc.ca/diversite-culturelle/pdf/diversite-linguistique.pdf.

Bourdieu, Pierre. *Acts of Resistance: Against the Tyranny of the Market*. New York: New Press, 1998.

———. "Uniting to Better Dominate." *Items and Issues* 2, no. 3–4 (2001): 1–6.

Duhamel, Ron. "Africa Direct Natural Resources and the 21st Century Economy: The Case for Stronger Canadian-African Collaboration." Speech given in Calgary, 8 May 2000.

Durand, C. "Les menaces de l'«Espéranglais»." *Hermès* 40, *Francophonie et Mondialisation*, edited by Tamatoa Bambridge et al., 222–7. Paris: CNRS Éditions, 2004.

Farchy, Joëlle, and Heritiana Ranaivoson. "La diversité culturelle, soubassements économiques et volonté politique." *Hermès* 40, *Francophonie et Mondialisation*, edited by Tamatoa Bambridge et al., 33–8. Paris: CNRS Éditions, 2004.

Grant, P. S., and C. Wood. *Blockbusters and Trade Wars: Popular Culture in a Globalized World*. Vancouver, Douglas & McIntyre, 2004.

Groupe de travail franco-québécois sur la diversité culturelle. *Évaluation de la faisabilité juridique d'un instrument international sur la diversité culturelle*. 2002. Available at www.diversite-culturelle.qc.ca/fileadmin/documents/pdf/106145_faisabilite.pdf.

Latouche, Daniel. "Quebec and Canada: Scenarios for the Future." *Business in the Contemporary World* 3, no. 1 (1990): 58–70.

Laulan, Anne-Marie. "La diversité culturelle à l'UNESCO." *Hermès* 40, *Francophonie et Mondialisation*, edited by Tamatoa Bambridge et al., 44–48. Paris: CNRS Éditions, 2004.

Léger, Jean-Marc. *La Francophonie : grand dessein, grande ambiguïté*. Montreal: Hurtubise, 1987.

———. "Le Quebec et la Francophonie." In *Le Français au Québec: 400 ans d'histoire et de vie*, edited by Michel Plourde, Hélène Duval, and Pierre Georgeault, 335–42. Quebec: Conseil Supérieur de la langue Française, 2007.

McChesney, Robert W. "Global Media, Neoliberalism and Imperialism." *Monthly Review* 52, no. 10 (2001): 1–19.

Nadeau, Jean-Benoît, and Julie Barlow. *The Story of French*. New York: St Martin's Press, 2006.

Neathery-Castro, Jody, and Mark O. Rousseau. "Quebec, Francophonie and Globalization." *Québec Studies* 32 (2001): 15–35.

———. "Does French Matter? France and Francophonie in the Age of Globalization." *French Review* 78, no. 4 (2005): 678–95.

Organisation Internationale de la Francophonie. *Trois espaces linguistiques face aux défis de la mondialisation*. Actes du Colloque International. Paris, 20–21 March 2001.

Quebec Ministry of International Relations. *Québec's International Policy: Working in Concert*. Government of Quebec, 2006. Available at www.mri.gouv.qc.ca/en/pdf/Politique.pdf.

Ritzer, George. *Enchanting a Disenchanted World: Revolutionizing the Means of Consumption*. Thousand Oaks, CA: Pine Forge Press, 2005.

Rousseau, Mark O. "Ethnic Mobilization in Quebec, Federalism in Canada, and the Global Economy." *Research in Social Movements, Conflicts and Change* 21 (1999): 205–23.

Thérien, Jean-Phillipe. "Cooperation and Conflict in La Francophonie." *International Journal* 48 (1993): 492–526.

UNESCO. *Universal Declaration on Cultural Diversity*. Paris, 2001.

Weinstein, Brian. "Francophonie: A Language-Based Movement in World Politics." *International Organization* 30, no. 3 (1976): 485–507.

27 The Ottawa–Quebec–Washington Dance: The Political Presence of Quebec in the United States

Louis Balthazar, Université Laval

Timeline

1774 Continental Congress sends Address to inhabitants of Province of Quebec.

Quebec Act: recognition of Quebec's civil law and Catholic religion.

1775 American revolutionaries invade Quebec; Richard Montgomery from the south through Montreal and Benedict Arnold from the east through Chaudière River. Quebec City under siege.

1776 End of siege of Quebec. Benjamin Franklin comes to Montreal with Bishop John Carroll and printer Fleury de Mesplet to persuade Quebecers to join the Revolution, with no success.

1837–8 Rebellions in Lower Canada (Quebec). Leader Louis-Joseph Papineau flees to the United States.

1849 Beginning of annexationist movement.

1867 Foundation of modern Canada. British Parliament enacts the British North America Act. United Canada's legislature approves; 60 per cent of Legislative Assembly of Lower Canada approves.

1911 Prime Minister Wilfrid Laurier and President Howard Taft sign a free trade agreement that never materializes after Laurier loses the general election to the protectionist Conservative Party.

1940 Creation of Quebec office in New York City.

1962 New York office becomes a delegation general.

1963 Government of Quebec borrows from Wall Street firms to buy all private hydroelectric companies.

1969 Opening of Chicago delegation.

1970 Opening of delegations in Boston, Lafayette, and Los Angeles.

1971 Premier Robert Bourassa launches the James Bay hydroelectric project.

1973 Founding of Conference of New England Governors and Eastern Canadian Premiers.

1976 In provincial general election, secessionist Parti Québécois takes the majority of seats in Quebec's National Assembly.

1977 Premier René Lévesque presents his sovereignty-association project to the Economic Club of New York; its reception is lukewarm. Quebec government launches a public relations

continued

campaign in the United States. President Jimmy Carter expresses the American position ("mantra") on Quebec sovereignty.

1978 Opening of delegation in Atlanta, bureau in Washington.

1980 Sixty per cent of Quebecers reject a proposition to give a mandate to the government to negotiate sovereignty-association.

1982 Serious economic recession in Quebec.

1984 Brian Mulroney becomes prime minister of Canada.

1985 President Ronald Reagan and Brian Mulroney meet in Quebec City and launch negotiations for the Free Trade Agreement (FTA).

1988 FTA is concluded but not ratified until after the election in Canada on 21 November. Quebec votes overwhelmingly to return Mulroney to power and have the FTA ratified.

1990 Rejection of Meech Lake Accord by Newfoundland and Manitoba, thus failing to obtain the necessary unanimity of all provinces. Subsequently, public opinion polls show that the majority of Quebecers support sovereignty.

1994 PQ regains power under Jacques Parizeau, who promises to conduct a sovereignty referendum.

1995 Referendum held on 30 October on proposed sovereignty-partnership.

Quebecers say "No" by a slim majority of 50.6 per cent. US Ambassador James Blanchard, Secretary of State Warren Christopher, and President Bill Clinton openly supported "No" campaign.

2001 Quebec's National Assembly expresses sympathy for victims of the 11 September attacks. Quebec commits to act on safeguarding the border.

2003 Quebecers protest in great numbers against the invasion of Iraq.

2008 Quebecers applaud the election of Barack Obama as president of United States. Never before has a US electoral campaign been so thoroughly covered by Quebec media.

2010 Release of the Quebec government's US Strategy aimed at the ongoing enhancement of Quebec's position as a leading partner of the United States.

Introduction

From the very beginning, Quebec has been inextricably linked to the American continent. Indeed, the French province's inhabitants and its rulers have always had a deep interest in its immediate neighbours to the south. Especially since World War II, the government of Quebec has maintained a presence in the United States that was, in a variety of ways, reinforced at the time of the Quiet Revolution in the 1960s. Canada's central government has reacted to this political presence sometimes positively, sometimes negatively. Washington's response has been generally prudent and careful to maintain harmonious **relations** with Ottawa and to support Canadian unity, while tacitly recognizing Quebec's distinct character.

In this chapter, we begin by examining the historical background of Quebec's involvement with the United States. Next we deal with the objectives and the instruments of Quebec's representation. Finally, Quebec's political presence in the United States will be considered within the triangle formed between it, the federal government of Canada, and the response from the US government.

Historical Background

French colonials were driven by religious, economic, and imperial desires to expand their presence through the whole of North America (see Chapter 1). With the help of allied Amerindians, explorers travelled the Great Lakes and journeyed south along the Mississippi River to the Gulf of Mexico, founding the large territory that would be called Louisiana. They also travelled west all the way to the Rocky Mountains. Indeed, the first frontiersmen of America were the French!

Permanent Attraction

After the British Conquest of 1760, this continental interest was revived by the insistence of American rebels that Quebec join their Revolution, but two addresses from the Continental Congress met with refusal from the Quebec clerical and feudal elites. Nonetheless, when Quebec was invaded by American militia in the winter of 1775–6, many Quebecers showed some empathy with Yankee soldiers, offering them assistance, food, and shelter.

Later, in 1837, the leader of an aborted rebellion, Louis-Joseph Papineau, fled to the United States, looking for support in the Republic that he admired. He received some help and encouragement among New Englanders, but none in Washington. The government of the United States seemed to be more preoccupied with not offending the former metropolis than in assisting an uncertain revolutionary cause.

American attraction was kept alive in Quebec throughout the nineteenth century by an important minority that was fascinated by the Republic to the point of promoting annexation. Many Quebecers opposed to the 1867 British North America Act were associated with **annexationism.**[1]

Another important development from the mid-nineteenth century to the 1930s was the massive exodus of French Canadians from Quebec to the United States, mainly to the adjacent New England and North Atlantic states. Economic conditions were so harsh in Quebec that many had to leave their homeland to make a living. While the other Canadian provinces were not especially hospitable to Catholic French-speaking Quebecers, the United States was an appealing alternative. There, French Canadians could regroup, form a few parishes, and create for a while what were called "little Canada" enclaves. Almost 1 million Quebecers migrated to the south. During this period, several links were established between Quebec and the United States, especially by the Church but also by Quebec officials who travelled across the border. Two key factors led to the end of this massive migration: First, a new wave of industrialization in Quebec, in great part due to American investment, began around 1910 and provided jobs for those who otherwise would have left; and second, during the 1930s, jobs that had lured French Canadians to the United States disappeared during the Great Depression.

Yet the attraction of the neighbouring country did not recede. Industrialization was frequently coupled with American products and influence, and Quebec governments were generally quite favourable toward American investments. World War II brought Canada closer to the United States because of co-operation in defence and defence production. In 1940, the Quebec Liberal government of Adélard Godbout (1939–45) created a Quebec bureau in New York to promote tourism and boost economic relations.

New Ties in Modern Times

In 1962, Quebec's New York mission was upgraded into a **delegation** general, a quasi-diplomatic mission. One of the main reasons for this was Quebec's need to find capital to finance its various projects, the most spectacular of which was the 1963 nationalization of all hydroelectric companies. Since Canadian investors were lukewarm to this endeavour, Quebec officials turned to Wall Street. This was the beginning of a special relationship between several American brokerage firms and both the Quebec government and its public corporation of Hydro-Québec (see Chapter 22).

Premier Jean Lesage (1960–6) travelled extensively to the United States. Besides his deep interest in promoting investment and trade, he fostered the renewal of old ties between Quebecers and French Canadians in New England and in Louisiana. In 1970, delegations were opened in Boston and in Lafayette, Louisiana. In Boston, the economic dimensions and the promotion of Quebec's modern culture (visual art, music, and theatre, for example) soon took precedence over the cultural relations with traditional French-Canadian associations in New England. In Lafayette, Quebec used its delegation to encourage programs for teaching French among the Cajuns (descended from the French Acadian settlers in what are now Nova Scotia and New Brunswick), but when Quebec policy became dominated by economic interests the delegation was closed in 1986. Other delegations were opened in Chicago (1969), Los Angeles (1970), and Atlanta (1978).

In 1965, when Quebec called for the right to negotiate international treaties in matters under its jurisdiction, Ottawa asserted its claim to be solely responsible for external affairs. This did not prevent the government of Quebec from maintaining its position that on issues within its jurisdiction it had the right not only to implement policy, but also to be party to negotiations of international agreements. This was called the "Gérin-Lajoie doctrine," named after Paul Gérin-Lajoie, minister of education in Lesage's cabinet, who first formulated the claim.

In 1970, Premier Robert Bourassa (1970–6; 1985–94) announced a gigantic project: the construction of huge dams in James Bay (northern Quebec). The James Bay project would substantially increase Hydro-Québec's production of electricity both to satisfy the growing needs of Quebecers and eventually for export to adjacent American states. With this in mind, Bourassa called for massive investment, 60 per cent of which came from American investors managed by the First Boston Corporation.[2] Thus relations with the United States were further enhanced.

In 1976, the Parti Québécois (PQ) came to power in Quebec City with the commitment to hold a referendum on its proposal of sovereignty-association. This produced a shock in the US milieus interested in Canada. In this context of possible political upheaval, one would expect difficult times for Quebec in its relationship with the United States and a downgrading of its political representation. On the contrary, even more than its Liberal predecessor, the PQ government remained open to American investment and sound economic relations. The PQ made it clear that Quebec's proposed new relationship with Canada would occur democratically and peacefully. Several members of this government visited the United States to allay fears and clarify the situation. Quebec soon expanded its influence in Washington, where a bureau was opened in 1978 with the official objective of promoting tourism but also serving as a *pied-à-terre* for officials visiting the capital.

After the defeat of the referendum on sovereignty-association in 1980, the PQ government maintained and reinforced its presence in the United States to the end of its second mandate (1981–5). It was more aggressive than ever in calling for American investment during a period of economic recession.

In 1986, under the Progressive Conservative government of Brian Mulroney in Ottawa, negotiations began for a new trade pact between the United States and Canada. An agreement was concluded in 1988 and was the main reason for the calling of a Canadian federal election in November of that year. Except in Alberta and Quebec, there was strong opposition to this free trade agreement (FTA) throughout Canada. In Quebec, both the Liberal government of Robert Bourassa and the PQ opposition were very favourable toward it, and Quebec provided strong popular support that allowed for the re-election of the Conservatives and the advent of the FTA.

Quebec's political and economic leaders saw in the FTA an opportunity for significant growth. While Ontario was favoured by the 1965 Canada–United States Automobile Agreement (commonly called the Auto Pact) and Western Canada by massive exports of energy, Quebec was seeking larger and freer access to the gigantic US market. Unlike other provinces, it did not feel that its identity was threatened by this economic agreement.

Throughout the 1990s, Quebec remained a champion of the FTA and its successor deal, the North American Free Trade Agreement (NAFTA), which includes Mexico. When the PQ was elected in 1994, the change in government did not alter this policy. It produced another climate of uncertainty, however, as Quebec would go through another referendum on sovereignty in 1995. Yet economic relations were not substantially affected, and Quebec support for NAFTA

Primary Source

Québec's International Policy: Working in Concert

Québec is a federated state invested with the political responsibilities that fall within its purview and whose powers are essentially determined by the Canadian constitutional framework. The Government of Québec has exclusive jurisdiction over natural resources management, health, education, culture, municipal institutions and private law. It also has joint responsibility with the federal government in areas such as agriculture and transportation. It manages its own fiscal system and levies its own taxes. It oversees the administration of the courts and the majority of police and public safety services on its territory, and is responsible for the selection of immigrants to Québec. Although the Canadian Constitution does not address international matters, successive court rulings dating back to the 19th century have established that, in Canada, a federated state is not subordinate to the federal state and that the authority to enact international treaties falls within the jurisdiction of either the federal government or the provinces, according to the internal distribution of powers provided for by the Constitution.

Québec therefore considers itself enabled to exercise the external attributes of the functions it exercises internally. Over the years, it has put into place the appropriate legal and institutional instruments to those ends. It has mandated the Ministère des Relations internationales to lead the Government's international initiatives, coordinate the actions of departments and agencies in this regard, manage a network of representatives abroad, as well as negotiate and enforce international agreements. Today, Québec has nearly thirty delegations, offices, and local representatives in eighteen countries. More than 300 bilateral agreements are now in effect with the national governments and federated states of nearly 80 countries. The Government of Québec is a participating member of La Francophonie and carefully monitors the work of international organizations in matters regarding its jurisdiction and interests. It contributes to the definition of Canadian positions and it ensures the implementation of a number of international agreements concluded under the auspices of the United Nations and other international organizations.

Global changes and international debates have direct consequences for the Government of Québec. For example, its capacity to govern effectively is being increasingly influenced by norms and standards that are established elsewhere. Québec's growth and prosperity are strongly dependent on its foreign trade. The emergence of new security concerns makes it imperative for Québec to collaborate to a greater extent with its international partners. The vitality of its culture and the affirmation of its identity depend on its capacity to reach out to the world. Finally, Québec shares the concerns of the global community when it comes to the huge disparities that still exist between rich and poor countries.

The Government of Québec therefore intends to continue and intensify its international activities. This stems from a view largely shared within the Canadian federation: the strengthening of continental integration and the emergence of new economic giants are weakening the influence of countries with low demographic densities. It is in Canada's interest to pool its international resources and to project an image that truly reflects its federal nature, i.e., the existence of two orders of government working in their respective spheres. The establishment of this new partnership with Canada is founded on the respect and recognition of Québec's jurisdiction, expertise, and unique characteristics.

Source: Government of Québec, *Québec's International Policy: Working in Concert* (2006), 5–6. Available at www.mrif.gouv.qc.ca/Content/documents/en/Politique.pdf.

CASE STUDY

Fall 1988: Confrontation on Free Trade and Language Policy

In the fall of 1988, the US and Canadian governments had agreed on a comprehensive free trade agreement. In Canada, the Mulroney government (1984–93) met with strong opposition as it submitted this agreement to Parliament. The ratification bill gave rise to hot debate in the House of Commons, where both the Liberal Party and the New Democratic Party (NDP) presented strong objections. This was expected from the NDP, but less so from the Liberals, known historically as champions of free trade. Since the 1960s however, under leader and Prime Minister Pierre Elliott Trudeau (1968–79; 1980–4), the Liberals had become more nationalist and had promoted and implemented restrictive policies in the hope of diversifying the Canadian economy, which was considered to be too dependent on the United States. This orientation was still present when, in 1984, John Turner replaced Trudeau as the head of the party and as prime minister but was defeated soon after by the Progressive Conservatives (PC) in a general election.

Yet the idea of a free trade agreement had made significant headway among the Liberals when a Royal Commission, appointed by the Trudeau government and chaired by a prominent Liberal former minister, Donald Macdonald, tabled a report in 1985 favourable to a free trade pact with the United States. Times had changed in the atmosphere of a crumbled economy in the early 1980s, and many in Canada were calling for increasing the flow of goods and capital across the southern border. Thus John Turner, as leader of the Opposition, did not squarely oppose the FTA but claimed that the treaty that was negotiated and signed between Canada and the United States in 1988 was disadvantageous for Canada. His arguments against the agreement were well received by many Canadians, especially among the centre-left and left-wing, in the arts and cultural circles, and in the academic community (except for most economists). It was argued that under the FTA, Canadian identity would be seriously eroded, its social policies jeopardized, and its cultural productions threatened by American competition.

The climate was quite different in Quebec (as it was in Alberta, a province that has always been open to trade with the United States because of its profitable oil and gas exports). With some minor reservations, both major provincial political parties were favourable to the FTA. It was argued that Quebec was left on the sidelines by the Auto Pact of 1965 that was so beneficial to southern Ontario. Quebec's growing economic and business elites were eager to penetrate the large American market. In fact, although it has always sought north–south ties with the United States, Quebec was much less integrated with the American economy than was that of its sister province of Ontario. While Toronto and the Niagara Peninsula are part of a dynamic international Great Lakes area and close to cities like Buffalo, Syracuse, and Rochester in northern New York, Quebec is separated from large American centres by mountains, and its closest neighbours across the border are very small urban centres like Plattsburgh, New York, and Burlington, Vermont. Finally, Quebecers did not deem that their culture would be threatened by American connections because of the language barrier and the strong attachment of its population to its local cultural productions, especially in television.

In spite of the outspoken opposition voiced by the Liberals and the NDP, the legislation to ratify the FTA was passed by the House of Commons, but it still had to be endorsed by the appointed Senate where the Liberals had a majority of seats. Normally, this unelected branch of Parliament may present objections or call for amendments to bills without ever directly opposing the House of Commons. But it has the formal power to delay the adoption of legislation and even recommend its rejection. With the approval of a large part of the population, the Liberal Senate engaged in this unusual procedure over the FTA bill to the point of forcing the prime minister to call a general election. The FTA was, of course, the dominant issue of the campaign.

The election was held on 21 November and returned Mulroney's PCs to power with a substantial majority of 169 seats to 83 for the Liberals and 43 for the NDP. Quebec and Alberta were the only two provinces to vote overwhelmingly for the PC. In other parts of Canada, opposition to the FTA and support for the Liberals and NDP prevailed, notably in all urban centres. Given that Quebec had almost half of the PC seats, one could say that the Quebec vote was responsible for the Conservative victory and the advent of the FTA, which subsequently was implemented in January 1989.

The FTA produced bitter division among Canadians. In academic milieus in particular, some English-speaking intellectuals who had been sympathetic to Quebec's claims—such as those addressed in the Meech Lake Accord, which called for enhanced recognition of the French province and important amendments to the Canadian Constitution—became sour toward Quebecers, accusing them of betraying the cause of an independent Canada. Thus while the whole of English-speaking Canada had shown concern for cultural and social protection against the United States, Quebec was more liberally inclined and open to a stronger connection.

A few weeks later, the Supreme Court of Canada pronounced an important judgment concerning Quebec's Charter of the French Language, commonly referred to as Bill 101. It declared sections of the law related to public signage unconstitutional. According to the Court's compulsory ruling, the practice that all visible signs be exclusively in French was contrary to both Canada's and Quebec's Charters of Rights and Freedoms. Public opinion in Quebec expressed outrage with this ruling, urging its provincial government not to comply, as the language charter was seen as essential to maintaining a distinct Quebec identity and culture. In response, the Quebec government used the notwithstanding clause of the Constitution, which allowed for the suspension of the application of the Charter of Rights and Freedoms in certain special cases. This action was perfectly legal but was radical enough to again provoke bitter reactions in the rest of Canada. This time, it had been Quebec's turn to deem (perhaps wrongly) its language and culture in danger.

These important events of late 1988 show how Quebecers and other Canadians all wanted to protect their role, identity, and place in North America, while disagreeing on what exactly these were. All Canadians have reservations about their belonging to North America, but they express these in clearly different ways.

did not lessen either before or after the referendum (which the PQ lost by a very narrow margin).

For various reasons, the climate of relations would change in the new millennium. Most Quebecers were displeased with the George W. Bush administration. They strongly opposed both the invasion of Iraq in 2003 and, by and large, the conservative tenets of the Republican government. Also at this time Quebec's trade with the United States became less profitable because of the American economic downturn and the strengthening of the Canadian dollar. Nonetheless, Premiers Bernard Landry (2001–3), Jean Charest (2003–12), and Pauline Marois (2012–4) were ardent supporters of harmonious relations with American partners, especially with state governments. Such is the case with Premier Couillard (2014–) as well, although his Liberal government has drastically downgraded Quebec's mission in Atlanta, Georgia, in the context of budget cutting to reduce the government deficit.

An important concern has appeared because of the tightening of the border after 2001: Agreements with the United States on security and facilitation of transborder trade were concluded with both Canada and Quebec. Quite significantly, in a new strategy toward the United States unveiled in 2010, "contributing to the security of the North American continent" was stated as the first objective of the government of Quebec in its relations south of the border.

Through this historical review we see that, especially in the last 50 years, Quebec governments, whatever their political orientation, have always been favourable to a close political relationship with the United States. Why has it been so? What are the principal objectives of successive Quebec governments in seeking ties with the United States?

Quebec's Objectives

Apart from the traditional purpose of maintaining a connection with descendants of French settlers in Louisiana and more recent former Quebecers in the northeast, two main objectives have marked the political presence of Quebec in the United States in modern days: (1) the promotion of Quebec's economic interests, and (2) making known Quebec's distinctive character, language, and culture.

Promotion of Economic Interests

Promoting economic interests means having American capital invested in Quebec, thus creating jobs and technological expertise and opening a large market for Quebec products. Yet, from time to time, nationalists have criticized governments for "selling out" to Americans and "Americanizing" Quebec. Premiers have responded by pointing out the benefits of such investments. Louis-Alexandre Taschereau (1920–36) famously stated: "I prefer importing American dollars than exporting Canadian workers."[3] Quebec leaders have often sought American investment despite attempts by the federal government to restrict it over worries that American investment gave the United States too much influence in Canada.[4]

Especially since the early days of the Quiet Revolution (as we have seen above), Quebec's governments have sought capital to finance its public debt and major semi-autonomous corporations like Hydro-Québec. It is therefore important for Quebec to be on the spot to negotiate with the firms that will float its bonds on the financial market. A presence in the United States is important as well to promote Quebec exports. Small- and medium-sized enterprises in particular appreciate the help of Quebec officials abroad. American markets are by far the most lucrative of all for Quebec producers. This Quebec presence is even more important in the context of the FTA and NAFTA. For example, when Quebec exporters are confronted with countervailing duties on account of public subsidies or anti-dumping duties, Quebec officials and their lawyers can best defend the interests of these exporters in the very places where they are penalized.

To Make Quebec Better Known

The second objective of maintaining close relations with the United States is often referred to by the Ministry of International Relations as the "public affairs mission." The underlying assumption is that

Quebec is not well known. If Canada has reasons to lament that in spite of its proximity and its numerous ties with the United States it is often ignored in the American public agenda and remains unknown except in the border regions, Quebec has even greater cause for concern. Not only are most Americans unaware of the importance of Quebec as a trade partner in the northeast, few are well informed about the distinctiveness of the French province. In most of North America, where the English language is universal, it is difficult to believe that a whole society functions primarily in French. Given the importance of the United States as a trade partner, it is therefore necessary for Quebec to make itself known as a province that is different from the other provinces in Canada.

Since the federal government does not tend to spread abroad an image of national heterogeneity[5] and decentralization, Quebec has to make its case and explain to its American partners why its constitutional **autonomy** is so dear to its population and why it is considered a homeland and "nation" for its large majority. It may also, from time to time, have to explain to Americans why there is an important movement calling for the sovereignty of Quebec.

Quebec officials in the United States must also promote the province's cultural products. In the last 50 years Quebec has been a cauldron of cultural products of all sorts—in literature, music, dance, theatre, and visual arts. It has become a vibrant part of the French-speaking world and an ardent member of the Organisation Internationale de la Francophonie. It is important that Americans be aware that the French language used in Quebec, although it has its own peculiarities, is a species of international French. Quebec literature may therefore be used in teaching French in the United States, and Quebec universities are as well equipped as their counterparts in France, if not better, for the learning of French. In fact the American Association of Teachers of French frequently holds its annual meetings in Quebec. The United States was also home to the first academic association outside of Canada devoted exclusively to Quebec: the American Council for Québec Studies (ACQS), and the first university-based research and teaching centre—the Institute on Québec Studies—established at the State University of New York College at Plattsburgh in 2004.

The Means of a Political Presence

To attain its objectives in its relationship with the United States, Quebec has a limited number of means at its disposal. Although it may claim the right to conduct international activities, the state of Quebec is not a sovereign entity and does not enjoy diplomatic recognition in the United States. The Canadian state officially represents all Canadians and deploys an impressive arsenal of missions to several American cities as well as a large and well-staffed embassy in Washington.

The Quebec government has generally acknowledged that it is well served by Canadian **diplomacy**, but it seeks to play a role of its own to complement and improve this mission for its own interests. Ironically, Quebec representatives, while not being diplomatic agents as such, may at times deploy more diplomacy than Canadian officials; not only is their culture more foreign to Americans, but they must also play on the delicate balance of making the best of Canadian efforts while using their own means.

Quebec is officially recognized by the Foreign Agents Registration Act, an American law that oversees the activities of foreign agents in the United States. In accordance with this law, the Quebec government must submit an annual report to the US Department of Justice. This is done by the New York delegation general, which acts as the voice for all the other delegations. Not surprisingly, it is Quebec's most important mission, in the financial centre and the industrial metropolis of the United States, located just 350 miles, or 563 kilometres, from the border.

Other delegations have equally distinct purposes. The New England delegation, situated in Boston, has a particular relevance. Of the six New England states three share a border with Quebec, and the whole region receives around 17 per cent of Quebec exports (2013 numbers). Boston is also an important centre for scientific and technological research, the home of prestigious universities, and a centre of transnational relations. This delegation also serves as a link to Americans of French-Canadian descent.

In Washington, even though Quebec does not have any official diplomatic contact, the capital is the location of numerous headquarters of national associations, and the delegation there works to bring tourists to Quebec, mainly in the form of large conferences to be held in Montreal and Quebec City. Moreover, Quebec representatives are charged with the valuable mission of monitoring the various think tanks, institutions, and people present within the Beltway on behalf of the New York delegation and the Quebec government.

Atlanta is the hub of the southeast, and the delegation there promotes Quebec's economy in this fast-growing region, which has become extremely important to Quebec as far as trade is concerned; as of 2013, 26 per cent of Quebec exports to the United States went there. Unfortunately, in the spring of 2014 in the context of deficit reduction on the part of the newly elected Couillard government, this most important delegation was downgraded into a small bureau—a choice that is difficult to understand. One has to wonder whether Quebec officials realized that the region covered by the Atlanta mission is the fastest growing in the United States and the destination of the largest proportion of Quebec exports.

Chicago is far away from Quebec, but it is the heart of the greater industrial region of the Midwest, located at the western end of the Great Lakes. Because of its role as a transportation network and the deep interest of Quebec in aeronautics and railway material, having a delegation there is important. The Great Lakes area is also vital for Quebec concerns about water pollution and the environment in general. The volume of trade with this area reached 23 per cent of the total in 2013.

Los Angeles is the city with the largest concentration of aeronautic firms with which Quebec makes contact to promote its own industry. California is also the largest market in the United States and, even if physically remote from Quebec, the state is important for its exports and its cultural relations with Quebec, especially in the film industry. The carbon market (cap and trade) implemented in both California and Quebec is another area of collaboration.

In a country as decentralized as the United States, relations at the state level are inescapable. For Quebec, which is itself autonomous in many jurisdictions as a province in the Canadian federation, these relations are vital and have proved fruitful. Especially in the northeast but also with other large industrial states, contacts have been fostered and intensified, notably since the 1990s. Quebec has been one of the most enthusiastic members of the Conference of New England Governors and Eastern Canadian Premiers since its inception in 1973. This organization deals with several issues concerning New England, the four Atlantic provinces, and Quebec, including the environment, energy, trade, education, and cultural exchanges. The conference meets every year, rotating among the 11 capitals, and has permanent head offices in Boston and Halifax. Quebec also participates in the various activities of the National Conference of State Legislatures and of the Council of State Governments. The latter even held its annual convention in Quebec City in 1999. In addition, Quebec is a member of the Great Lakes Commission and the Council of Great Lakes Governors and Premiers. There is a growing number of such multilateral organizations in which Quebec is more and more active. Worth mentioning are the Southeastern United States-Canadian Provinces (SEUS-CP) Alliance and the Super Corridor Coalition (NASCO), which is devoted to the development of a multimodal transportation system. Finally, several agreements have been signed between Quebec and states as varied as California (the Western Climate Initiative allows for a growing collaboration on carbon limitation), Virginia, and Louisiana on transportation and educational exchange.

With the state of New York, Quebec has a special relationship. Every year, in principle, there is a summit meeting between the governor and the premier to discuss various topics such as the environment, sustainable development projects, taxation, transportation, and trade. This has led to numerous agreements on these various issues.

Living in a Triangle

We have seen that Quebec is connected to the United States in several ways. Yet Quebec is part of Canada and cannot help but take the federal government into account. As a consequence, one can say that Quebec's relations with its American partners take place within a triangle, as of course do those of all Canadian provinces. Canadians are caught between the east–west dimension of their country's history, and the north–south orientation that seems inevitable, as most Canadians live within 150 kilometres of the US border.

Nonetheless the Canadian polity makes for special ties between all provinces. Significant research shows that "borders matter."[6] For example, Canadian cities are more relevant to each other than are American cities of a similar size and distance; Toronto is more important for Montreal than are Boston and New York. Yet on the whole, proximity and size often make the United States more vital for most provinces, notably for Quebec, than the rest of Canada. Thus Quebec may be bound to Ontario in several ways but it is also bound to the United States, as is well illustrated by the fact that during the 1990s Quebec trade with the United States surpassed its trade with other parts of Canada.

This phenomenon has become an argument for nationalists in Quebec, especially for those who advocate sovereignty. They contend that Quebec could bolster exports with the United States, thus strong political ties with Canada would become less important. Trade with Ontario could continue across an international border.

A strong case can be made against this attitude. Isn't there a contradiction between Quebecers' concern for the protection of their identity, culture, and language and accepting American influence? There is no doubt that, in spite of English-speaking Canadians' reluctance to recognize Quebec's distinctive character, this character is much better protected within the Canadian federation than it would be in the United States. The example of the disappearance of the French language in Louisiana speaks for itself. Especially after the Civil War, the pull toward conformity and cultural and linguistic homogeneity has been much stronger in the United States than in Canada. Quebecers are aware of this and generally no longer support annexation to the United States. Yet they tend to consider the United States, since it is a foreign country, as less intrusive than the Canadian government. They feel, rightly or wrongly, that their culture and language make them less susceptible to Americanization than other Canadians.

In fact, English-speaking Canadians have often felt more threatened by the United States than have French-speaking Quebecers.[7] Canadian nationalists have wished to include all Canadians (English, French, and multicultural) in the protection of the Canadian ethos and values against the challenge of Americanization. Quebecers, for their part, have tended to stress that duality and bilingualism make Canada distinct from the United States.

This divergence is somewhat reflected in relations with the southern neighbour. The Government of Canada, devoted to reinforcing Canadian unity, does not always look favourably on the incursions of provincial governments into the United States. It maintains that it is well equipped to represent the interests of all Canadians, including Quebecers. Especially in Washington, where politics are so complex and government is diversified by the separation of powers, Canadian representatives claim that Canada should speak with one voice to be efficient and to properly defend all Canadians' interests. Indeed, the Canadian Embassy has proven to be an impressive organization with a capacity to deal with the various concerns of provinces as well as more general issues.

Yet since the development of the Gérin-Lajoie doctrine, all Quebec governments have emphasized the need for Quebec to defend its own interests and promote its own image. Their claim is that the official image projected by the Canadian government does not reflect Quebec's uniqueness. Especially in matters related to the constitutional debate, they argue that the Quebec point of view and its stand for greater respect of provincial jurisdictions is not well explained or well defended even by French-speaking Canadian diplomats.

It may also frequently happen that typical English-Canadian views of Canada are presented in the United States as if they were American views, because English-speaking Canadians living in the United States are somewhat incognito, hardly recognizable as Canadians. Some journalists from Canada contribute to American media without being identified as Canadians: "Canada is the only country in the world in which the United States networks frame reports by foreigners as if they had been done by United States network staffers."[8]

In spite of Canadian opposition[9] or lukewarm acceptance, Quebec has maintained its presence in the United States, even to a modest extent in its national capital. Furthermore, Quebec representatives have sometimes proved to have enough subtlety and diplomacy to obtain the indispensable co-operation from the extensive network of Canadian missions in the United States to add to its own limited means. The Canadian government, however, has been successful enough to convey a faithful and friendly response from the American government to its claim of being a unique representative.

Response from the United States

For the US executive power, there is only one official interlocutor from Canada: the Canadian government. Canadian provinces are treated by American law as foreign agents on the same level as foreign corporations or institutions operating on US territory. Quebec official representatives are given a special passport but do not enjoy diplomatic immunity. This, however, does not prevent the US State Department and the intelligence community from following developments in Quebec, especially since the rise of the sovereignty movement. At the level of state governments, as mentioned above, Quebec's relations have usually been cordial and without any significant constraint from the central government of either country. Indeed, increasingly, governors and state legislators are interested in dealing with Canadian provinces, notably with Quebec. Some states even include the Quebec delegation or bureau among the consular corps.

The US government has found a way of tacitly recognizing Quebec's distinctiveness through its consulate general in Quebec City. This diplomatic mission has operated without interruption since 1855. In the contemporary era, its existence is not justified by consular affairs; the US consulate general in Montreal is sufficient for that. In other Canadian provinces, the American government is not represented by more than one consulate. The only reason to keep a mission in Quebec City is Quebec's unique political stance within Canada. It is well understood that the purpose of the US consulate general in Quebec City is to establish relations with officials of the Quebec government as well as with members of the Opposition and other political elites in the provincial capital. This does not imply in any way recognition of Quebec as a diplomatic partner. The US consul general in Quebec City is subordinated to the American ambassador in Ottawa, to whom he or she regularly reports. His or her function, not unlike that of the Quebec delegate in Washington, is to monitor and report to the State Department. One US consul general in Quebec City summarized his role as follows:

> We are here to be the eyes and ears of Washington, to try to understand what is going on in Quebec and also to explain our policies to the Quebec government and to Quebec citizens.[10]

The post has been generally occupied by career diplomats of great quality, judgment, and personality who, in all likelihood, have produced fair and well-balanced reports on Quebec. Generally they have enjoyed their stays and the relationships they have developed. In most cases, they have remained friends of Quebec even after their departure.

In no way does this mean that these consulates general have empathized with all tenets of Quebec nationalism, especially with the sovereignty movement. In this respect, they have remained faithful to what has been called the Washington "mantra," articulated for the first time by President Jimmy Carter in 1977 after the election of the PQ. It has been reiterated with very few modifications by all American administrations since then. It has three points:

1. The United States will not intervene in Canadian internal affairs; consequently, it will not take

a stand in the constitutional debate taking place in Canada.

2. The American government considers Canada as a special partner with which it entertains excellent relations. It favours whatever may reinforce Canadian unity and cohesion. It will always express, therefore, its preference for a united Canada as opposed to its fragmentation.
3. Only Canadians can take decisions concerning the future of their country. The United States will respect the popular will of Canadian citizens.

Most American administrations have been very discreet concerning Quebec. President Ronald Reagan, in a memorable visit to Quebec City in 1985, addressed the special character of the French province, and President Bill Clinton gave a well-thought-out speech on the virtues of federalism at a conference in Mont-Tremblant, Quebec, in 1999. George W. Bush visited Quebec City in 2001 for the Third Summit of the Americas in view of a project of continental free trade, but there was no official encounter with the Quebec government.

BIOGRAPHY

Claude Morin

Claude Morin has played a vital role in the development of Quebec's modern international relations, first as a public servant from 1961 to 1971 and second as a member of René Lévesque's PQ government from 1976 to 1982. In this role he constantly favoured strong ties with the United States.

Morin went to work with Jean Lesage soon after the latter became premier in 1960. He directly participated, as a speech writer, in launching the Quiet Revolution. He inspired most of Lesage's declarations, including his significant inroads in the United States. In 1963 he became deputy minister of the new Department of Federal–Provincial Relations. In this function he was at the heart of important negotiations and conflicts with the federal government, notably around Quebec's then-controversial international activities. He contributed substantially in giving a permanent legitimacy to Quebec's international relations and its prominence within La Francophonie. He worked under four successive Quebec premiers: Lesage, Johnson, Bertrand, and Bourassa.

Claude Morin (*right*) waits with Saskatchewan's Roy Romanow (*centre*) and Justice Minister Jean Chrétien (*left*) in August 1980 for a final news conference in Ottawa at the end of official talks on the Constitution.

The Canadian Press/Rod MacIvor.

In part because he had studied at Columbia University in New York, obtaining a master's degree in social welfare in 1956, he was always sensitive to the need for Quebec to maintain strong and meaningful ties with American partners. He was still in office when the Department of Federal–Provincial Relations became the Department of Intergovernmental Affairs in 1969 and when several delegations were opened in the United States: in Lafayette, Boston, Chicago, and Los Angeles.

When he left government in 1971 he went to teach economic policy at École nationale

continued

d'administration publique (National School of Public Administration). He soon joined the Parti Québécois and was a candidate in the 1973 and 1976 elections in the suburban Quebec City riding of Louis-Hébert. He was defeated in 1973, then elected in 1976, the year the PQ formed the government. René Lévesque, predictably enough, chose him to become minister of intergovernmental affairs with the responsibility for international relations.

Among other tasks, he worked to change his party's platform concerning a sovereign Quebec's participation in the organizations created in the context of the Cold War. He understood correctly that Quebec had a strong interest in participating in NATO and NORAD and, as a consequence, he fought to make this clear in his party's program. Along with Premier Lévesque and in contrast to some of his colleagues, he was persuaded that any policy that would prove to be confrontational to the American government would be totally misleading and counterproductive.

He also understood that there was no way his government could persuade American partners of the validity and pertinence of the sovereignty project. Thus he believed that the best Quebec could obtain from the US government would be an attitude of respectful noninterference in the debate on the future status of Quebec. This translated into a campaign to persuade Americans that an independent Quebec would remain friendly to the United States and devoted to a market economy. Under the slogan of "Operation America," his department and the government in general organized several visits of high-level officials in many American cities to broadcast this message.

At the same time, he made sure that Quebec's representatives adhered to their mission of fostering and deepening economic relations while making Quebec better known and its cultural products more widely available, all while refraining from a militant advocacy of sovereignty. Indeed, he went so far as to maintain in office some delegates who did not support sovereignty for Quebec.

After the defeat of the 1980 referendum and the re-election of the PQ in 1981, Morin stayed in office and fought vigorously to maintain an autonomous status for Quebec under the Canadian Constitution. After his efforts proved unsuccessful, he resigned from government.

Claude Morin was above all a pragmatist and always deeply conscious of the limits of political action and diplomacy. He could write a book with the daring title *L'art de l'impossible* (*The Art of the Impossible*, Montreal: Boréal, 1987) to account for the hard-won breakthrough of Quebec on the international scene against all odds and against Ottawa's strong objections. Yet in all of his actions, as bold as he could be at times, he kept believing that politics is the art of the possible and that a halfway compromise was better than total failure.

He favoured strong ties with France, where Quebec always enjoyed a special status. Yet he was always deeply conscious that relations with the United States, although less spectacular, were as important and much more so at the economic level. He always made sure his department would spend as much money and effort in strengthening relations with the United States as it did with France.

Perhaps because he was a pragmatist and a realist, Morin was never very popular in Quebec. Among federalists, he was seen as a promoter of sovereignty and among sovereignists as a lukewarm partisan. He must be counted nonetheless as one of the most valuable architects of the Quiet Revolution and especially as a champion of the development of international relations and meaningful ties with the United States.

Conclusion

Quebecers have constantly striven to assert their identity within North America. This is why, throughout its history, Quebec has sought to establish, maintain, and intensify relations with its southern neighbour. All Quebec governments have sought to reinforce economic ties with the United States while trying to make Americans aware of the existence of a French province north of the border. Quebec has used various means to achieve these goals. In the last 50 years, it has pursued these goals by establishing a network of representatives across the United States and by meeting with state governments and participating in multilateral organizations.

In connecting to the United States, the rest of Canada has not always been on the same wavelength as Quebec. At times the Canadian government has been annoyed by Quebec efforts to stand on its own in the United States, but it has more or less tolerated a Quebec political presence there, provided it is maintained within the framework of Canada's own diplomacy. The US government has responded rather positively to Quebec efforts but would never officially consider the French province as a diplomatic partner.

Quebecers' interest in the United States was certainly reinforced with the election of Barack Obama as president, who was generally much more popular in Quebec than Canadian Prime Minister Stephen Harper. This, however, does not change the nature of the issues at stake. Quebec's relations with the United States are still bound to be as complex as they are essential and vital.

Questions for Critical Thinking

1. What are the main goals of the Quebec government in the United States?
2. Why does Canada object to Quebec's political presence in Washington?
3. In what sense could you possibly say the US government recognizes Quebec's specific character?

Notes

1. The BNA Act sanctioned the union of the three colonies: the Canadas (Upper and Lower Canada, which geographically correspond with southern Ontario and southern Quebec), Nova Scotia, and New Brunswick. The new colony was granted home rule—that is, autonomy in domestic affairs. Canada did not become fully independent until the Statute of Westminster (1931), when it became autonomous in international relations. The Legislative Assembly of Lower Canada voted 60 per cent in favour of the union, called (incorrectly) Confederation.
2. "To put these financial needs in perspective, 1973 estimates of the total cost of the project at Can$9 billion made it the largest project in history." Alexander C. Tomlison, "U.S. Perceptions of Investment Opportunities and Risks in Quebec," in *Problems and Opportunities in U.S-Quebec Relations*, ed. Alfred O. Hero, Jr., and Marcel Daneau (Boulder, CO: Westview Press, 1984), 39.
3. Quoted in Yves Roby, *Les Québécois et les investissements américains, 1918–1927* (Quebec: Presses de l'Université Laval, 1976), 169 (author's translation).
4. Here is how a Quebec minister of intergovernmental affairs, Jacques-Yvan Morin, expressed Quebec's position in 1982: "Quebec does not share Ottawa's viewpoint in foreign investment. We favour a much more open policy . . . .we believe the future lies in the development of a strong north–south economic axis." Lecture to the World Affairs Council of Northern California, San Francisco, 3 June 1982.
5. The image of a multicultural Canada may give the impression that the culture of French-speaking Quebecers is just one of the several subcultures in the Canadian mosaic.
6. John McCallum, "National Borders Matter: Canadian–U.S. Regional Trade Patterns," *American Economic Review* 85, no. 3 (June 1995): 615–23; John F. Helliwell, "Do National Borders Matter for Quebec Trade?" National Bureau of Economic Research Paper no. 5215 (Cambridge, MA: National Bureau of Economic Research, 1996), 5; John F. Helliwell and John McCallum, "National Borders Still Matter for Trade," *Policy Options* 16 (July–August 1995): 45–8.

7. See Chapter 6 by Yvan Lamonde and especially his formula expressing that Quebec is a mixture of a weakened French tradition, British domination, growing American influence, and waning Catholic influence: $Q = -F + GB + US^2 - R$.
8. See Stephen Banker, "How America Sees Quebec," in *Problems and Opportunities in U.S.-Quebec Relations*, ed. Alfred O. Hero, Jr., and Marcel Daneau (Boulder, CO: Westview Press, 1984), 170–80.
9. In Washington, the federal government has often made life difficult for the Quebec representatives by ignoring them or denying residence to their personnel. Ottawa argued that it was better for all Canadians to be represented by a single institution.
10. From an interview done within the framework of a televised course by Louis Balthazar, *Les Américains, le monde et nous*, Université Laval, Direction de la formation continue, 1992.

Select Bibliography

Balthazar, Louis. "A Model for a Ménage à Trois." In *Forgotten Partnership Redux: Canada–U.S. Relations in the 21st Century*, edited by Greg Anderson and Christopher Sands, 471–504. Amherst, NY: Cambria Press, 2011.

———. "Les relations Québec–États-Unis." In *Trente ans de politique extérieure du Québec, 1960–1990*, edited by Louis Balthazar, Louis Bélanger, and Gordon Mace, 65–105. Sillery, QB: Les Éditions du Septentrion, 1993.

———, and Alfred O. Hero, Jr. *Le Québec dans l'espace américain*. Montreal: Québec Amérique, 1999.

Bernier, Luc. *De Paris à Washington : la politique international du Québec*. Sainte-Foy, QB: Presses de l'Université du Québec, 1996.

Bouchard, Gérard, and Yvan Lamonde, eds. *Québécois et Américains : la culture québécoise aux XIXe et XXe siècles*. Montreal: Fides, 1995.

Chartier, Armand. *Histoire des Franco-Américains de la Nouvelle-Angleterre : 1775–1990*. Sillery, QB: Les Éditions du Septentrion, 1991.

Duchacek, Ivo, and Daniel Latouche, eds. *Perforated Sovereignties and International Relations: Trans-Sovereign Contacts of Subnational Governments*. New York: Greenwood Press, 1988.

Fry, Earl H. "Quebec Confronts Globalization: A Model for the Future?" *Quebec Studies*, 30 (2000): 57–69.

———. "Quebec's Relations with the United States." *American Review of Canadian Studies* 32, no. 2 (2002): 323–42.

———. *The Role of Sub-National Governments in North American Integration*. Vol. 3 of *The Art of the State II: Thinking North America*, edited by Thomas J. Courchene, Donald J. Savoie, and Daniel Schwanen. Montreal: Institute for Research on Public Policy, 2005.

Hero, Alfred O., Jr. *Louisiana and Quebec: Bilateral Relations and Comparative Sociopolitical Evolution, 1673–1993*. Tulane Studies in Political Science. Lanham, MD: University Press of America, 1995.

———, and Louis Balthazar. *Contemporary Quebec and the United States: 1960–1985*. Cambridge, MA, and Lanham, MD: Harvard University Center for International Affairs and University Press of America, 1988.

———, and Marcel Daneau, eds. *Problems and Opportunities in U.S.–Quebec Relations*. Boulder, CO: Westview Press, 1984.

Lamonde, Yvan. *Ni avec eux ni sans eux : le Québec et les États-Unis*. Montreal: Nuit Blanche éditeur, 1996.

Lemco, Jonathan. *Turmoil in the Peaceable Kingdom: The Quebec Sovereignty Movement and its Implications for Canada and the United States*. Toronto: University of Toronto Press, 1994.

Lisée, Jean-François. *In the Eye of the Eagle*. Toronto: Harper Collins, 1990.

Morin, David, and Myriam Poliquin. "Governing from the Border? Quebec's Role in North American Security." In *Québec and the World: Foundations, Regions, Actors and Issues*, edited by Stéphan Gervais, Christopher Kirkey, and Stéphane Roussel. Montreal and Kingston: McGill-Queen's University Press (forthcoming).

Quebec, Government of. *The Québec Government's U.S. Strategy* (2010). www.mrifce.gouv.qc.ca/content/documents/en/Sommaire_QC_USA_en.pdf.

Roby, Yves. *Les Franco-Américains de la Nouvelle-Angleterre: rêve et réalité*. Sillery, QB: Septentrion, 2001.

———. *The Franco-Americans of New England: Dreams and Reality*, translated by Mary Ricard. Quebec: Éditions du Septentrion, 2005.

Senécal, André, and Robert Gill. *Plus ou Moins: The State of Quebec Studies in the United States*. Radford, VA: American Council for Québec Studies, 1990.

28 The Frontiers of Quebec Literature

Michel Biron, McGill University

Timeline

	Politics and Culture	Literary Works
1534	Jacques Cartier's first voyage to Canada. He claims territory on behalf of the King of France.	
1632–9		Jesuit Paul Le Jeune writes annual instalments of his *Relation du voyage de la Nouvelle-France*.
1632		Marie de l'Incarnation begins to write her *Écrits spirituels*, which she will complete in 1654.
1744		*Histoire et Description générale de la Nouvelle-France avec le journal historique d'un voyage fait par ordre du roi dans l'Amérique septentrionale* by Pierre-François Xavier de Charlevoix.
1763	Signing of the Treaty of Paris seals Britain's victory in New France.	
1764	*La Gazette de Québec/The Quebec Gazette* is officially launched.	
1806	First issue of *Le Canadien* newspaper begins circulation on 22 November.	
1814	Louis-Joseph Papineau becomes leader of Canadian Party.	
1837–8	Patriote rebellions in Lower Canada occur.	First French-Canadian novel is published: *L'Influence d'un livre* by Philippe Aubert de Gaspé, fils.

continued

	Politics and Culture	Literary Works
1839	After visiting Canada for six months, John George Lambton (Lord Durham) writes a report in which he concludes it is necessary to assimilate French Canadians, "a people with no literature and no history."	
1845–52		*Histoire du Canada depuis sa découverte jusqu'à nos jours* by François-Xavier Garneau published in four volumes.
1860	Beginning of patriotic literature movement in Quebec, spearheaded by Abbé Henri-Raymond Casgrain.	
1862		*Jean Rivard, le défricheur canadien* by Antoine Gérin-Lajoie is published in *Les Soirées canadiennes.*
1863		*Les Anciens Canadiens* by Philippe Aubert de Gaspé, pere.
1873		*Chroniques, humeurs et caprices* by Arthur Buies.
1881		*Angéline de Montbrun* by Laure Conan.
1882		*Œuvres complètes* by Octave Crémazie.
1887		*La Légende d'un peuple* by Louis-Honoré Fréchette.
1895	École littéraire de Montréal is founded.	
1896		*L'Avenir du peuple canadien-français* by Edmond de Nevers.
1904		*Émile Nelligan et son œuvre,* compiled and edited by Louis Dantin.
		Msgr Camille Roy's presentation "La nationalisation de la littérature canadienne" published in *Bulletin du parler français au Canada.*
1916		*Maria Chapdelaine* by Louis Hémon (first released 1914 in *Le Temps* in Paris) published in Quebec.
1918		*Manuel d'histoire de la littérature canadienne-française* by Camille Roy.
1920		*Les Atmosphères* by Jean-Aubert Loranger.
1929		*À l'ombre de l'Orford* by Alfred DesRochers.
1937		*Regards et Jeux dans l'espace* by Hector de Saint-Denys Garneau.

	Politics and Culture	**Literary Works**
1938		*Trente Arpents* by Ringuet.
1944		*Les Îles de la nuit* by Alain Grandbois.
1945		*Bonheur d'occasion* by Gabrielle Roy.
1947		*La France et nous* by Robert Charbonneau.
1948		*Refus global.*
1953	Éditions de l'Hexagone is founded in Quebec.	*Le Tombeau des rois* by Anne Hébert.
1955		*Rue Deschambault* by Gabrielle Roy.
1958		*Agaguk* by Yves Thériault.
		Poèmes de l'Amérique étrangère by Michel van Schendel.
1960		*Le Libraire* by Gérard Bessette.
1962		*Contes du pays incertain* by Jacques Ferron.
1963		*La Ligne du risque* by Pierre Vadeboncœur.
1965	Term *littérature québécoise* featured prominently in *Parti pris* magazine in a manifesto issue entitled "Pour une littérature québécoise."	*Prochain Épisode* by Hubert Aquin.
		L'Âge de la parole by Roland Giguère.
1966	Marie-Claire Blais receives Prix Médicis for her novel *Une saison dans la vie d'Emmanuel.*	*L'Avalée des avalés* by Réjean Ducharme.
1967	On 24 July, General de Gaulle declares "Vive le Québec libre!" from a balcony of Montreal City Hall.	*Salut Galarneau!* by Jacques Godbout.
	Opening of first CEGEPs (collèges d'enseignement général et professionnel).	
1968		Michel Tremblay's *Les Belles-Sœurs* performed for the first time.
		Michèle Lalonde writes poem "Speak White" for *Poèmes et chants de la résistance* show.
1970	In October, the FLQ kidnaps British diplomat James Cross and Quebec Minister of Labour Pierre Laporte. Federal government invokes the War Measures Act. Pierre Laporte is killed.	*L'Homme rapaillé* by Gaston Miron.
		L'Amélanchier by Jacques Ferron.
		Kamouraska by Anne Hébert.
	First *Nuit de la poésie* held on stage of Théâtre Gesù.	
1971		*Le Réel absolu : Poèmes 1948–1965* by Paul-Marie Lapointe.

continued

	Politics and Culture	Literary Works
1972	First Rencontre québécoise internationale des écrivains organized by *Liberté* magazine.	
1973		*L'Hiver de force* by Réjean Ducharme.
1974		From 1974 to 1976, volumes of André Major's *Histoires de déserteurs* successively released.
1976	On 15 November, René Lévesque's Parti Québécois is elected.	*Le Roman à l'imparfait* by Gilles Marcotte.
1977	Union des écrivains québécois (UNEQ) is founded.	
	Hubert Aquin commits suicide.	
1978		*Les Deux Royaumes* by Pierre Vadeboncœur.
		Monsieur Melville by Victor-Lévy Beaulieu.
		La grosse femme d'à côté est enceinte by Michel Tremblay, first novel of Montreal series *Chroniques du Plateau Mont-Royal.*
1979	Antonine Maillet receives Prix Goncourt for *Pélagie-la-Charrette.*	
1981		*Vie et mort du roi boiteux*, play by Jean-Pierre Ronfard.
		Le Matou by Yves Beauchemin.
1982	Anne Hébert wins Prix Femina for *Les Fous de Bassan.*	
1983	*Vice versa*, a magazine about transcultural issues, launched in Montreal.	*Maryse* by Francine Noël.
1984		*Moments fragiles* and *Agonie* by Jacques Brault.
		Volkswagen Blues by Jacques Poulin.
		La Détresse et l'Enchantement, Gabrielle Roy's posthumous autobiography.
		Kaléidoscope ou les Aléas du corps grave by Michel Beaulieu.
1985	First Trois-Rivières International Festival of Poetry.	*Comment faire l'amour avec un nègre sans se fatiguer* by Dany Laferrière.
		La Trilogie des dragons, theatrical show by Robert Lepage.

	Politics and Culture	Literary Works
1986		*Surprendre les voix*, a posthumous essay collection by André Belleau.
		Le Souffle de l'harmattan by Sylvain Trudel.
1988		*L'Écologie du réel* by Pierre Nepveu.
1989		*La rage* by Louis Hamelin.
		Le vieux chagrin by Jacques Poulin.
1990		*Dévadé* by Réjean Ducharme.
1991		*Le Bruit des choses vivantes* by Élise Turcotte.
		L'Obéissance by Suzanne Jacob.
1993		*Genèse de la société québécoise* by Fernand Dumont.
1995		*L'Ingratitude* by Ying Chen.
		Soifs by Marie-Claire Blais.
1996	Poet Gaston Miron dies on 14 December; state funeral services are held.	
1997		*Littoral*, play by Wajdi Mouawad, performed at Théâtre La Licorne.
1998		*La petite fille qui aimait trop les allumettes* by Gaétan Soucy.
		Intérieurs du Nouveau Monde by Pierre Nepveu.
1999		*Mille eaux* by Émile Ollivier.
2001		*Putain* by Nelly Arcan.
		Rouge, mère et fils by Suzanne Jacob.
2005	Opening of Grande Bibliothèque de Montreal.	*Le Siècle de Jeanne* by Yvon Rivard.
2006	Mavis Gallant becomes first anglophone to win Prix Athanase-David.	
2009	Dany Laferrière wins Le Prix Médecis for his novel *L'énigme du retour* (*The Return* in English translation).	
2014	Dany Laferrière becomes the first Canadian to be elected as a member of the Académie française, established in 1635.	

Introduction

When the term *Quebec literature* made its debut in the mid-1960s, it marked a new beginning. Its predecessor, *French-Canadian literature*, had become incompatible with the assertions of the Québécois nationalist project that epitomized the Quiet Revolution. Consequently, *Quebec literature* (*littérature québécoise*) was minted to turn the page on Quebec's former minority status as a national culture vis-à-vis both Canada and France. The name change soon entered into circulation and, by the beginning of the next decade, was widely embraced in intellectual circles, which set about breathing new life into the new nomenclature.

Taught extensively in schools and universities, Quebec literature has since established its institutional legitimacy, but to this day its frontiers remain nebulous. The frontiers of literature, we should keep in mind, do not abide by the same laws as those of politics and are certainly not framed in the same terms. In politics, there are rules that establish who has the right to vote and who is a full-fledged citizen. In literature, these kinds of exclusive rules would be meaningless since the frontiers of national literature are often implicit and shifting.

For example, in the 1970s it would have been unthinkable to include anglophone writers in the history and canon of Quebec literature. A few decades later, anglophone writers like Frank R. Scott, Mavis Gallant, and Mordecai Richler are part of Quebec's literary landscape. Conversely, we might also ask whether Canada's francophone authors living outside of Quebec, such as Acadian poet Gérald Leblanc or Franco-Ontarian novelist Daniel Poliquin, should also be included within the corpus of Quebec literature. Again, in the 1970s this question would have been considered nonsensical. But today, with the emergence of Acadian and Franco-Ontarian literatures, it would be bad form for a literary historian hailing from Quebec to ignore what distinguishes these literatures from Quebec literature. These examples give us an idea of just how ambiguous the expression *Quebec literature* can be, so why even attempt to define **literary frontiers**?

Defining literary frontiers would be of little interest if it simply involved demarcating the limits of a national literature by drawing up a list of what it includes and excludes. But when national frontiers show how a corpus of literary texts interacts with the world around it, frontiers become much more fertile subjects for discussion. In the early days of literary criticism, there was a penchant for linking the distinguishing colours of a literature to its geographical environs. Today, critics who automatically equate a given landscape or climate with specific styles of writing tend to draw bemused smiles. But, setting aside the reductionist/determinist aspects of this early analysis for a moment, it could be argued that a geography of literature exists in conjunction with a sociology of literature. The idea here is not to attach a book to a mighty mountain range or to endless prairie skyland, but to recognize that a literary text bears the imprint of the neighbourhood and community from which it has sprung.

Quebec literature is a particularly salient case in point because its striking geographical frontiers have made a lasting impact on its sociology. Although of the French language, Quebec literature is nonetheless separated from Paris by a vast ocean and has developed independently from its mother literature. Based in North America, it is also isolated by a linguistic frontier and belongs to a tradition that is foreign to the references that inform English-language Canadian and American literatures. Quebec's geographic and linguistic frontiers are often cited by literary critics to explain the twofold marginality of its literature in relation to both France (or La Francophonie) and North America. But there is a third, invisible frontier that gives specific meaning to the ever-shifting relations that Quebec authors have with France and with North America: the legendary frontier to the **North**, which still lies wide open to unknown possibilities. Regardless of their era and the meaning they attributed to this abstract frontier, in their mind's eye Quebec authors have always been able to envision the broad, desert-like expanse of horizon that might allow them to escape and start life with a clean slate elsewhere. There is a part of Quebec literature that simply cannot be understood without getting to know this third side of the triangle.

A Long Way from Paris

As with all other French-language literatures outside of France, Quebec literature has an ambiguous and problematic relationship with Paris. That said, Quebec's relational ambiguities are not the same as those observed in francophone regions to the south, be it the French West Indies, the Maghreb, Lebanon, or sub-Saharan Africa. Unlike these regions, the official language of Quebec is French, the mother tongue of the majority and the dominant language of the culture, as it is in the European Francophonie (Belgium, Luxembourg, and Switzerland). Where language conflicts do exist between France and Quebec, they tend to play out within the French language itself, much as conflicts between American and British English do. Indeed, George Bernard Shaw's famous witticism about the United States and England could be transposed here to describe this relationship: Quebec and France are two nations "separated by the same language."

While the linguistic situation in Quebec and Acadia may be comparable to that of francophone European countries, the geographic distance that separates the North American Francophonie from Paris has, nonetheless, had an obvious and important impact. This cultural distance was already palpable in the days of New France, when the French voyageurs observed a number of unusual characteristics in Quebecers, ranging from their hardy physical endurance to their somewhat casual attitudes regarding social hierarchy. After New France was ceded to Britain in 1763, the effect of distance was amplified and manifested itself in a multitude of ways, most often through various forms of resentment in francophone Canada toward the French motherland. So it was that Louis-Joseph Papineau, the future leader of the rebellious Lower-Canadian nationalist Patriotes, extolled the virtues of the freedoms afforded by British parliamentarianism and was distrustful of the French political model, which he held was prone to serious authoritarian abuses, like France's Reign of Terror in 1793. The same British liberalism influenced François-Xavier Garneau, French Canada's own celebrated "national" historian and author of the four-volume *Histoire du Canada* (1845–52), which emerged as the first great French-language intellectual *oeuvre* in Canada. It has become customary to cite this monumental work as the French-Canadian people's proud collective response to Lord Durham's denigrating report on their society.[4] Garneau is cited far less frequently for the fact that his monumental *Discours préliminaire* was penned for French-Canadian readers rather than for readers in France. His narrative of the burgeoning French-Canadian nation was set within the vast historical framework of the Americas, underscoring Quebec's distance from the *mère-patrie* by placing its people's history under the banner of a new national consciousness.

From a literary perspective, no nineteenth-century French-Canadian work challenged the literary tradition in France. The notion of creating a national literature had occurred to many but was stymied by cultural and demographic realities; despite significant growth in the number of well-read individuals throughout the century, the potential for establishing authorship as a true vocation was still lacking. It was not until the beginning of the twentieth century that Quebecers saw themselves in such vocations, attracted by Paris and European modernism. These were the days when Émile Nelligan became synonymous with French Parisianism. He, better than anyone, exemplified the ideal of the misunderstood poet or bohemian author in Canada. As an imitator of Baudelaire and French symbolism, Nelligan was also out of step with the Parisian works of his time, and hence an unwitting example of the cultural desynchronization that persisted between modern France and Quebec. From 1910 onward (and even more so after World War I), Quebec authors began to sojourn in France and familiarized themselves with contemporary French literature as it was being written. Poets like Jean-Aubert Loranger and Alain Grandbois were directly inspired by modernist poets from France. More often than not, however, relations with France were academic and laden with psychological complexities. It was rare to see a French-Canadian author integrate—much less blend—into French literary life as Belgian or Swiss authors did. It was not until Gaston Miron's generation appeared on the literary scene that personal and professional links with major authors from France were forged. In 1999, Miron was the first Quebec poet

CASE STUDY

Literary Turf War between Montreal and Paris

World War II was a watershed era in the literary evolution of Quebec. During this short interval of time circumstances dramatically changed for French-Canadian authors, leading them to hope they could make a career of their writing. As newspapers and magazines continued to expand their readerships, they solicited the services of French-Canadian writers to attract readers. The radio, very much part of everyday life (having appeared on the scene one decade earlier), allowed many authors to earn additional income by writing radio dramas. Together, these media gave their work a wider distribution than it would ever have had otherwise, given the limited size of the literary community and the weaknesses of editorial infrastructures.

Indeed, from the nineteenth century until the 1930s, literary publishing remained extremely limited in French Canada. In 1936, there were still only six publishers. However, in 1940, when France surrendered to the invading Nazi German forces, the situation quickly changed. As imports originating from enemy or enemy-occupied countries were declared illegal, Canada could no longer import books from France. Canada's Mackenzie King government therefore gave Canadian publishers exceptional licences to reprint all of the French books that were no longer available in Canada, provided they paid for the copyright fees through the Office of the Custodian of Enemy Property. In so doing, it handed over the reins of an immense publishing market to Quebec and brought about a veritable editorial boom.

The first to benefit from this particular situation were a handful of established Montreal publishing houses (for example, Éditions Beauchemin, Éditions Fides, and Éditions Valiquette). But new publishing operations soon sprang up, including Éditions Variétés, Éditions Pony, and notably Éditions de l'Arbre in 1941, followed (between 1943 and 1945) by eight other publishers (Parizeau, Société des Éditions Pascal, Serge, Marquis, Lumen, Mangin, B. D. Simpson, and Pilon). This sudden literary gold rush was followed by an equally swift reversal of fortunes. By the end of the war, licences for new publishing houses were no longer being granted, thereby depriving publishers of their main tool for development and causing about a dozen Quebec publishers to cease operations between 1946 and 1949. Only academic publishers like Beauchemin, Granger et frères, and Librairie générale canadienne survived, along with Éditions Fides (which specialized in religious books). Since literature no longer offered any return on business investment, the annual number of literary publications gradually declined, for lack of a viable market. By the 1950s, as Jacques Michon has noted, an average of 11.9 novels were published annually, a significant drop from the 1940s when the average number of annual releases stood at 14.5.

Despite its brevity, the publishing boom between 1940 and 1946 considerably altered the literary landscape of Quebec. It allowed Montreal publishers to forge direct links with many authors from France who had taken refuge from the war in New York City. At the same time, many writers also chose to take up residence in Montreal, including the likes of Antoine de Saint-Exupéry, Georges Simenon, and Jacques Maritain. Quebec publishers released works by Paul Claudel, Julien Green, François Mauriac, Pierre Emmanuel, Pierre Seghers, Paul Éluard, Georges Bernanos, and many others during this vibrant period. New editions of the classics were re-released. For instance, in 1944, Bernard Valiquette released Victor Hugo's complete poetic works in a single-volume edition. Many other authors whose mass distribution had previously been blocked by the Catholic Church's Index of Forbidden Books were also published. In fact, Balzac, Baudelaire, Verlaine, Rimbaud, Proust, and Gide made their belated literary debuts in Quebec around this time. These books, published in Quebec, were then distributed in many parts of the world.

Montreal publishers, spurred on by the nationalist elite, also published French-Canadian authors. For instance, Roger Lemelin's *Au pied de la pente douce*[1] was released by Éditions de l'Arbre, and Gabrielle Roy's *Bonheur d'occasion*[2] was published by Société des éditions Pascal. Because many of these books appeared side by side with prestigious works formerly published in France, they acquired a newfound legitimacy. Some authors, like Lemelin and Roy, sold very well, proving that there was a market for French-Canadian literature.

But by 1946, during the postwar reconstruction period in France, normal operations were restored and Paris eagerly rushed in to snatch back the reins of French-language publishing. From that time onward, an acrimonious conflict pitted Montreal against Paris—or more precisely, it pitted two clans of intellectuals from French Canada and France against each other. On the one hand, there were those who held that French-Canadian literature existed independently of French literature, while on the other side there were those who believed that Quebec literature was simply a branch of literature originating from France. Very quickly, the debate turned to issues of identity, a sore point that led (by association) to the irksome issues of the autonomy of French-Canadian literature and of French Canada itself in relation to France.

Quebec literary scholars Gilles Marcotte and Élisabeth Nardout-Lafarge recount and analyze the impassioned turf war (*querelle*) that ensued.[3] It began on 8 March 1946, when Louis Aragon, a member of the Comité national des écrivains (CNÉ) in France, launched an attack on Montreal publishers in *Les lettres françaises* (the literary paper of the Resistance in France). Aragon lambasted these Quebec houses for publishing authors from France accused of collaborating with the Nazis during World War II. Secretly founded during the war by an underground group of authors, critics, and anti-fascist Resistance intellectuals, the CNÉ enjoyed considerable legitimacy in the newly liberated postwar France, casting itself as a fearless moral arbiter determined to purge the literary world of its unworthy wartime traitors. But while authors such as Charles Maurras, Pierre Drieu La Rochelle, and Marcel Jouhandeau were being systematically blacklisted in France, they continued to be published in Quebec. It was Quebec's ideological "complacency" toward fascism and Nazi-collaborator authors that Aragon hotly denounced in *Les lettres françaises*.

Robert Charbonneau was the first Quebec publisher to respond to these accusations in Montreal's literary review *La nouvelle relève*, deeming his reputation to be beyond reproach. Charbonneau, who had always opposed Hitler and Nazism, had also belonged to the *Relève* group of authors who had taken a public stand in 1936 in support of the Spanish Republicans fighting the civil war in Spain. Not only did he believe his positions to be ideologically unassailable, but he was speaking to the issue as a publisher who had been victimized by the cavalier actions of his French counterparts, brusquely claiming their market shares after the war with no regard for Quebec publishers. As with almost all new Montreal publishers, Charbonneau's company (Éditions de l'Arbre) had been effectively pushed to the brink of bankruptcy as a result. He emerged embittered and disillusioned by his experiences, concluding that maintaining equitable relations with France was impossible.

In the same breath, the sense of dispossession among French-Canadian authors prompted Charbonneau to argue that French Canada's prospects for development would hinge upon overcoming a number of ingrained, culturally driven preconceptions. He named several, including

continued

the belief that action was more worthwhile than intellectual work; the Jansenist view that the reading of fiction should be held suspect; the Canadian inferiority complex regarding national publications, judged (at that time) to be inferior to foreign offerings; the enduring resonance of Parisianism among French-Canadian authors; and the foregone conclusion that the quality of Quebec French and the province's small literary community made it impossible to create its own homegrown literature.

Charbonneau maintained that the autonomy of French-Canadian literature was no longer tied (as the regionalists would have claimed) to a territory or a race, but more to Joyce, Kafka, Dos Passos, and Faulkner. He also frequently argued that the most innovative literary works, particularly novels, would no longer come from Paris. Looking to France for literary models or examples would therefore be of little interest to French-Canadian authors, in his opinion—they would do better to look elsewhere, beginning with the United States and the rest of Canada. The universalism, or more specifically, the Americanicity that Charbonneau was calling for, was immediately interpreted by Montreal literary critics like René Garneau as an offensive mounted against the culture of France.

The central issue discussed in the collection of articles that Charbonneau assembled about this pitched battle, entitled *La France et nous : Journal d'une querelle*, was Quebec's autonomy. But this rare polemic between intellectuals from Quebec and France also revealed how intensely defensive and centralist reactions became when Quebec authors used their circumstances in North America to stake out their claim on France's time-honoured literary turf. The dashed hope of seeing Quebec culture recognized by France and the strong desire to embrace Americanicity experienced during this conflict established a twofold relationship with literature that continues to haunt Quebec authors to this day.

to be published in the prestigious *Poesie* collection of Gallimard in Paris.

Along with this development, a growing, long-standing malaise was taking hold behind the scenes. Since the end of World War II, Robert Charbonneau and other French-Canadian intellectuals had rejected the metaphor of "the tree and the branch" when discussing the literary relationship between France and French Canada. They contended that literature from Quebec was a tree unto itself, growing far removed from the old tree that gave it life. According to them, in the future the rejuvenation of Quebec literature would have to be nourished by literatures *outside of* France. Strained relations with France manifested themselves in various ways thereafter, notably with the advent of *joual*, which made its sensational literary debut in the 1960s. It was in theatre, with the performance of Michel Tremblay's *Les Belles-Sœurs* (1968) (*The Sisters-in-Law*), that the clash over *joual* reached its most spectacular heights. Among novelists, some authors associated with the magazine *Parti pris* tried (less successfully) to integrate *joual* into their works. Yet another distinctly different linguistic tack was taken by Réjean Ducharme in his first novel (*L'Avalée des avalés*, 1966) (*The Swallower Swallowed*), which he wrote in original, slice-of-life prose that was not *joual*, but that consciously challenged major works in French literature.

After that point, rare were the Quebec authors who would measure their talents against those of their literary contemporaries in France or succeed as brilliantly as Ducharme in their experimentation with linguistic and cultural encounters between the two peoples. Many simply chose to substitute France's language and culture for their own, while a few continued to imitate its literature. Réjean Ducharme was alone in his radical approach, pushing as far as he could the eternal conflict that both separated and united Quebec and France. Gradually, this epic conflict waned as Quebec's progressive detachment from France gained momentum, mitigated by the implementation of reforms in teaching and education at the end of the 1960s, but also by a broader trend toward cultural pluralism in the contemporary world. As times changed,

Primary Source

The Swallower Swallowed

Grown-ups are soft. Children are hard. Grown-ups are to be shunned like quicksands. A kiss given to an adult sinks in, germinates, sends out tentacles that get hold of you and never would snap, a battle-axe would break. A child isn't soft and slimy and fertile, he's hard and dry and sterile as a block of granite. An adult's thighs are flabby. His skin hangs on his bones like masses of white of egg. Constance Cadaverous's forehead gave back my mouth. Her cheeks returned my lips without soiling them, like the two flat golden cheeks of a tree that you've just sawn down. Everything that's slimy and soft soils. Everything ugly makes ugly. One oughtn't to touch what's ugly.

I pick some earth up in my hand, as you pick up a ten of diamonds. What does the earth do? How does it react? If I shake it next to my ear, do I hear bells ringing, in the same way as you hear a noise of pebbles when you shake an empty cylinder? If I throw it against a wall does it bounce back like a ball, as my mouth would have bounced back from Constance Cadaverous's mouth; or does it break as a crystal ball would have done, or the rose-window of a cathedral? If only I could pick up a mosque as you pick up a knave of clubs . . .

I hate grown-ups so much and reject them with such fury that I've laid the foundations of a new language. I used to call them calf's brains and lamb's livers, but the feebleness of these insults mortified me. So by a stroke of genius I cried, emphasising every syllable: "Estanglobular spetermatorinx!" and a new language was born: Bernician. I've borrowed from existing languages, but only very occasionally. When two friends have got separated in the woods and are trying to find each other, they keep calling to one another, using the same word. "Nahanni" is a call calling to another call. When Constance Cadaverous calls me I answer "Nahanni" lengthening and separating each syllable. Bernician has several synonyms. "Bexeroorisidual mounonster" and "Estanglobular spetermatorinx" are synonyms. In Bernician the verb "to be" is always conjugated with the auxiliary "to have."

Source: Réjean Ducharme, *The Swallower Swallowed,* trans. Barbara Bray (London: Hamish Hamilton, 1968), 210.

the focus shifted away from Paris, as demonstrated by *Liberté*, a Quebec arts magazine. Whereas "*Haïr la France?*" (literally, "Hate France?") was emblazoned on the cover of an issue in the early 1980s, some 20 years later the cover headline was purely descriptive: "*Lettres de la France*" ("Letters from France"). The latter issue presented contemporary literature from France just as it would Portuguese or German literature: It was a literature that had become foreign to Quebec. While literature from France was still part of the arts landscape, it incited little debate since it had simply become one point of reference among others.

The view that French literature had become relatively inconsequential for Quebecers was perhaps best expressed by novelist and critic Louis Hamelin (born in 1959), who commented:

> It doesn't happen so often anymore that I take a peek at what is being written over in France. I am reassured by reminding myself that there are people who are paid to do that sort of thing. (*Le Devoir*, 7 January 2004)

In the present era of globalization, commentary about France or French literary personalities involved in literary production is frequent, but in each instance the cultural frontier is clearly evident. Some novelists have even made the figurative distance between Quebec

BIOGRAPHY

Literary Iconoclast Réjean Ducharme

Relatively little is known about Réjean Ducharme's life, apart from the fact that he was born in 1941 in Saint-Félix-de-Valois. Biographical sources do not tell us a great deal about Ducharme and are generally limited to reproducing the information provided by the author himself in a derisory autobiography included with his first novel, *L'Avalée des avalés* (*The Swallower Swallowed*):

Réjean Ducharme, shown in this undated photo, is one of the French language's greatest living literary stylists. He has lived in Montreal as a hermit for more than 30 years. Six of his works have been translated into English.

The Canadian Press

> I was only born once. That was done in Saint-Félix-de-Valois, in the province of Quebec. The next time that I die, it'll be the first time. I want to die vertically, head down and feet up. . . .
>
> I suffered through six months at École Polytechnique de Montréal. At last upon my deliverance [from school], I took myself for an office clerk and still take myself for one today. But the people who hire office clerks don't want to take me for an office clerk. I don't always work and don't always work as an office clerk. One month out of two, I am out of work.
>
> I was in the Arctic with Canadian Aviation, in 1962. No one will believe me. I do not know why. I say, "I was in the Arctic." They answer, "No way." In 1963, 1964 and 1965, I hitch-hiked in Canada, the United States and Mexico. That's tiring.[5]

Well before *L'Avalée des avalés* was released in the fall of 1966, journalists and columnists caught wind of what was in the works: A totally unknown, young, 24-year-old Quebecer was about to publish his first novel with Gallimard, the most prestigious publisher in France. Around that time, publishers in France and Quebec started to cast doubt on the author's true identity, igniting the short-lived "Ducharme affair." It began with a series of outlandish rumours, some intimating that a famous writer was using Ducharme's name as a front. Since the young unknown refused to grant any interviews with the media, the intrigue around his person grew ever thicker, forcing Gallimard to dispatch philosopher Clément Rosset to Ducharme's home to prove that he really existed and was, in fact, the author of his writing. In Quebec, the affair gained even more momentum when it was reported that Ducharme had, at first, unsuccessfully submitted one of his manuscripts (*L'Océantume*) to Montreal publisher Pierre Tisseyre. From that point forward, Quebec critics and journalists could not get enough of the fabulous stories of the young Quebec writer, rejected at home, only to be published in Paris.

In reality, Gallimard had received not one but three manuscripts in the mail, one after the other: *L'Océantume*, *Le nez qui voque*, and *L'Avalée des avalés*. It was this third manuscript that the publishing house chose to release first, sensing that it would be a contender for the Prix Goncourt. Ducharme just missed the mark, but the novel struck an enthusiastic chord with critics on both sides of the Atlantic Ocean.

His success grew the following year with the release of *Le nez qui voque* (1967), which was a clear testament to the novelist's talent. *L'Océantume* (1968) was the next to appear, then a fourth novel, *La fille de Christophe Colomb* (1969, *The Daughter of Christopher Columbus*), written in a bizarre style of verse that demonstrated the extent to which Ducharme's work was moving away from established models and was destabilizing ways of reading.

Like the American authors Thomas Pynchon or J. D. Salinger, Réjean Ducharme has always refused to speak publicly, except at the very beginning of his career when he responded to Pierre Tisseyre's insinuations that his manuscript had been considerably reworked by Gallimard. Since that time, Ducharme has never strayed from his initial line of conduct: "I don't want to be taken for a writer; I never want my face to be recognized."[6] While managing to remain a "phantom" author, he fast became a classic figure in Quebec literature. During the 1970s, Ducharme's reputation continued to flourish, notably after the publication of two other novels, *L'Hiver de force* (1973) (*Wild to Mild*) and *Les enfantômes* (1976), which used the same emotionally charged language, incorporating adult-child characters whose lucid thinking shone a black light on the words and deeds of the society that surrounded them.

During the same period, Ducharme also gained renown as a playwright, scriptwriter, and lyricist. In 1968, he was one of the first playwrights (along with Michel Tremblay) to introduce *joual* into theatre with *Le Cid maghané* (1968), a parody of Corneille's classic. Ten years later, he wrote his strongest play, *HA ha! . . .* (published in English as *HA! HA!*), directed by Jean-Pierre Ronfard. He also wrote several film scripts, including *Bons Débarras* (Francis Mankiewicz, 1980), which became a resounding success. A friend of popular singers Robert Charlebois and Pauline Julien, he wrote the lyrics to a number of their songs.

From 1980 onward, Ducharme became increasingly reclusive, to the point that the media, on constant alert for the slightest rumours about him, wondered what had become of him. As it turned out, he had been holding exhibitions of found-object collages in various Montreal galleries under the pseudonym "Roch Plante." Many of the artist's *trophoux* (a play on the word *trophy* that sounds like *too crazy* in French), as he called them, were a reflection of his taste for punnery, as evidenced by their titles ("Le déjeuner sous l'herbe," "Chemin de fer à repasser").

Ducharme resurfaced in 1990 with his seventh novel, *Dévadé*, to become the first winner of the new Prix Gilles-Corbeil, the highest literary honour in Quebec. True to form, he refused to attend the awards ceremony, once again eliciting a flood of commentary from journalists and critics. The novelist's "big comeback" crystallized in 1994 with the publication of *Va savoir* (*Go Figure*) followed by *Gros mots* in 1999.

Ducharme is primarily known for his inimitable relationship with language. In his literary works, he has never ceased to deconstruct clichés and reinvent the power of emotions. More than any other Quebec writer, Ducharme has profoundly influenced the writers of generations to come. A true iconoclast of his times, he has even been featured as a character in several contemporary novels, including *Le coeur est un muscle involontaire* (2002, *The Heart Is an Involuntary Muscle*) by Monique Proulx and *Ça va aller* (2002) by Catherine Mavrikakis.

and France a prominent theme in their writing. In *Le siècle de Jeanne*, Yvon Rivard creates an author protagonist who writes postcards to his granddaughter from Paris. Rivard himself was well acquainted with France since he, like many Quebec writers, had lived and studied in Paris in his twenties. The protagonist writes as though he has known the people of France forever, introducing them to his granddaughter with a mixture of respect and irony, as an ethnological curiosity.

In *Le manuscrit Phaneuf* by Gilles Marcotte, the narrator describes a Quebec publisher (the central character) and his favourite travel destinations:

> . . . parts of the Middle East and North Africa, a few countries in Europe. With the exception of France, which he had deliberately side-stepped, like a trap, the trap of his fellow creatures, the trap of recognition, of the encounter. Later on, he would have to go to Paris—*profession oblige*—but never stayed around there for long.[7]

This publisher, from a company renowned for its "young" literature, viewed his trips to Paris with marked reluctance. A trip to Paris had become customary practice and no longer elicited any particular expectations in this era of travel beyond the boundaries of the Western world (circa 1985). Indeed, at a time when it was more accessible than it had ever been, the city of lights inspired neither love nor hate: Paris, evermore, was merely "business as usual."

Amérique étrangère: Strangers in Their Own Land

By contrast, in recent decades the draw of the south (meaning, first and foremost, the United States) has grown ever more powerful. France seems to have progressively faded from the collective consciousness of Quebec authors, while the United States and the Americas in general have acquired a captivating cachet in contemporary literary writing. A propos, Louis Hamelin (alluded to earlier) is a contemporary author who has shifted his interest from France to better pursue his passion for American literature, assiduously chronicling its evolution in his columns for publications like *Le Devoir*. Of course, this interest in US culture is nothing new. In the nineteenth century, many French-Canadian journalists, historians, and authors made abundant reference to their neighbours to the south, from François-Xavier Garneau (mentioned earlier) to Antoine Gérin-Lajoie in his two *Jean Rivard* novels (in 1874 and 1876). After the Union Act of 1840, many of French Canada's liberal thinkers even expressed their support for annexing Quebec to the United States. In 1900, essayist Edmond de Nevers devoted a long essay to the American soul (*L'Âme américaine*). In the 1920s and 1930s, while his friend Louis Dantin was living in Cambridge, Massachusetts, poet and journalist Alfred DesRochers became a fan of American poetry. At the same time, Rosaire Dion-Lévesque was translating Walt Whitman. Moreover, after World War II, publisher and novelist Robert Charbonneau proposed that American novelists be translated and published in Montreal rather than in Paris.

By the mid-1960s, the term **Americanicity** had entered into usage at the same time that the expression "Quebec literature" was endorsed and promoted by the young, politicized intellectuals of the magazine *Parti pris*. The concomitance of these concepts was significant, as the initiative to found a "literature of Quebec" was based on an emergent identification of a people with their territory—with a homeland, a nation, and a continent. Quebec authors also began to identify more clearly with the frontier to the south, which had appeared far away and impassable in the time of Louis Hémon's novel, *Maria Chapdelaine* (1914). By the 1930s, the threshold of America was no longer regarded as a threatening entity; it emerged instead as a solution to unemployment. For example, Ringuet's *Trente arpents* (1938, *Thirty Acres*) reaches its conclusion when old Euchariste Moisan, having sold his land, leaves Quebec and finds safe haven with his exiled son, who is living in New England. In *Bonheur d'occasion* (1945, *The Tin Flute*) by Gabrielle Roy, there is no need to leave Quebec to live like an American: Montreal offers all the charms of a modern, American-style metropolis. Even when

Montreal publishing house Éditions de l'Hexagone (founded in 1953) promoted the poetry of Quebec, its "*poésie du pays*" did not constitute a patriotic poetry, but a homegrown poetry of North America. Pierre Nepveu's *Intérieurs du Nouveau Monde*, which would become a landmark essay in Quebec studies, demonstrated the extent to which this poetry (and Quebec literature as a whole) shared with other literatures in the Americas a specific relationship not only with space but also with time, while remaining at arm's length from America itself (like Franco-Belgian poet Michel van Schendel described in *Poèmes de l'Amérique étrangère* [1958]).

Americanicity, strange and fascinating, would begin to enter Quebec literature through every possible avenue in the 1960s. The urban experience (so common to US literature) was the most prevalent Americanized theme to be found in scores of fictional or poetic writing. Jean Basile was among the Quebec novelists who celebrated Montreal's St Lawrence Boulevard—"the Main." In *La jument des Mongols* he declares, "Without the Main, my children, I do believe that I would detest Montreal."[8] Gaston Miron was also among the Quebec poets who would write about his city, expansively proclaiming, "Montreal is as big as universal disorder."[9] Paul-Marie Lapointe associated the city with its most primitive and most modern elements: "small prehistoric men walking / between the buildings / in a rain that is loaded with missiles."[10]

"America" presupposed travelling, a kind of nomadism, manifested as a Kerouacian wanderlust *On the Road*. In *Volkswagen Blues* (1984, Quebec's best-known road novel, by Jacques Poulin), Jack Waterman (the author's alter ego) and an Aboriginal woman cross the entire continent to find Jack's estranged brother who has disappeared without a trace. But the goal of this quest becomes much less important here than the quest itself, a re-enactment (two or three centuries later) of the crossing of the continent by French explorers. In this case, the extreme mobility of Poulin's character is fuelled by his search for his roots. Since no one had ever introduced Jack to his roots, it seemed they had to be retraced and regrown. In contemporary Quebec literature, the characters who disappear into the woodwork are, more often than not, parents who leave their children to fend for themselves.

In parallel with America's beat generation and counterculture, which became mainstays in Quebec's cultural landscape, some Quebec writers also identified with an older literary tradition. In 1978, for instance, novelist Victor-Lévy Beaulieu devoted three volumes to Melville, commenting on his life and works. At one time, Beaulieu even claimed to identify more closely with Melville than with any other French-language writer. Many other Quebec writers found their literary models in American literature. Jacques Poulin's complete works are regarded (by the critics and by himself) as being strongly influenced by the US novel and, more specifically, by the novels of Ernest Hemingway. In *Le vieux chagrin* (1989, *Mr. Blue*), Poulin writes:

> In fact, all I knew about the art of writing I'd picked up from reading interviews with Ernest Hemingway, which I'd actually read before I myself was a writer: at the time I'd been a professor, a Hemingway specialist.[11]

The main thing Poulin learned from Hemingway was a basic rule of writing that he sought to apply to his own works: Always write about the subjects you know best. But in no way could Poulin ever be mistaken for Hemingway himself. Hunting, bullfighting, big cities, female conquests, male camaraderie, military exploits, alcohol, boxing—none of these manly experiences entered into Poulin's world. In his novel, when he asks what the author of *The Old Man and the Sea* would have answered if he found himself before Marika (a mysterious female character), Poulin playfully cites a virile and gallant quip from Hemingway, but only to deride his own inadequacies. In fact, Poulin's copious references to this American author effectively deepen the divide that separates him from Hemingway's America, which remains decidedly foreign, whatever his claims on the subject. The same could also be said of the way in which Victor-Lévy Beaulieu depicts Melville, who is evoked in his novel only to impress upon the reader how hopelessly impossible it is for a Quebec writer to lay full claim to "America."

Up North: The Frontier of Freedom and Solitude

Most curiously, time and again, Quebec authors have turned their backs on the "real American experience," much as they have turned their backs on French literary tradition. It is not that contemporary Quebec authors are trying to cast themselves in a superior light by contrasting their national virtues with those of the United States, as was the case in the era of Abbé Casgrain and Monseigneur Roy. They simply have their characters leave the American experience behind by escaping to the North country. Pierre, the protagonist in Gabrielle Roy's *La montagne secrète* (1961, *The Hidden Mountain*), chooses the silence of the Great White North, and André Major's numerous deserters (*Histoires de déserteurs*, 1974–6) start life anew on the outskirts of the city as marginal members of society. Ducharme's *Dévadé* (1990) paints the individual as a perpetual "de-escapee," trapped, but forever fleeing.

While waves of perception about the Quebec–France and Quebec–US literary frontiers have ebbed and flowed from one era to the next, the frontier of the North has been a bulwark that remained the same, thereby affecting the other frontiers with an equal but invisible force. Two novels, written respectively around the beginning and end of the twentieth century, embody this phenomenon: The first, *Maria Chapdelaine* (an old classic), was ostensibly traditional; the second, *Le vieux chagrin* (*Mr. Blue*), was associated with the renewal of contemporary literature.

Louis Hémon, the author of the first novel, was clearly intrigued by Maria's father, Samuel, a secondary character. Samuel Chapdelaine belongs to the breed of land-clearing pioneers who colonized northern Quebec. The novel transports us northward to the remote region of Lac-Saint-Jean at the end of the nineteenth century, when the tracts of land advertised in a colonization campaign have still only attracted a trickle of settlers. Samuel proves to be an anti-social man who chooses to build a home for his family miles away from the nearest village. His actions are not motivated by a desire to build a fiefdom unto himself, but by an acute aversion to any form of community outside of his immediate family. The *pater familias* Chapdelaine was a pioneer and, as such, could have been one of the most celebrated folk heroes in Quebec's nationalist discourse had he not been possessed by a pining to move (the Anglicism *mouver* is used in the novel) constantly, further and further north. This pining greatly displeased his wife, who had dreamt all her life of living well ensconced in a parish she could call home. When she dies, we see Samuel confess to his daughter his hatred for society—any form of society—and declare that he is insane. Neither France nor the United States nor even his own nation held any attraction for him that could compare to the land of the North, his true home.

In the second novel, Jacques Poulin's *Le vieux chagrin* (*Mr. Blue*), a former professor of literature describes the old frame house that had belonged to his father and was passed down to him. It was an aged, expansive house, and the reader can imagine that it was there the protagonist connects with his roots and childhood memories, much like the characters recounted in *Rue Deschambault* (1955) by Gabrielle Roy (one of Poulin's favourite writers, along with Hemingway). The many patch-ups the house had undergone over the years make it look odd and mismatched—ruins, renovated piecemeal, over and over again. But the strangest part was that the house itself (a home that was never meant to be moved) was literally uprooted by his father, who transported it from one shore of the St Lawrence River over to the other, where there were no people, to get some peace and quiet.

Though the days of Quebec's lumberjacks had passed, when we juxtapose the two stories it becomes clear that the father of Poulin's protagonist is a direct literary descendant of Samuel Chapdelaine, hauling his household far from the village, away from other folks, to get some peace.

Similar examples are easy to find in contemporary Quebec literature. *Va savoir* (*Go Figure*) by Réjean Ducharme introduces us to Rémi Vavasseur. Rémi's wife leaves him and he fills the void by renovating the little place she had just bought in the Laurentians, north of Montreal. In Louis Hamelin's first novel, *La Rage* (1989), which takes place in the same region, the narrator is a former biology student who turns his back on workaday life to become a plane spotter at Mirabel airport. The surrounding countryside looks like the Sahel desert, he tells us. He rides his bicycle around the area in his search for a stream and, showing a blithe disregard for all fences blocking his way, takes hardy possession of this empty territory. The relatively recent *La petite fille qui aimait trop les allumettes* (1998, *The Little Girl Who Was Too Fond of Matches*) by Gaétan Soucy (one of Quebec's most critically acclaimed novels at the time of its release) takes place in an isolated house in the middle of a pine forest, far removed from civilization. Here as well, the father in the story leaves a curious legacy of madness (a paternal death is a frequent motif in contemporary Quebec literature) after raising his two children in seclusion, as though he wanted to shield them from any and all social contact. As in Poulin's novel, the house becomes a retreat and writing space, a kind of postmodern ivory tower crammed with books where reality is shaky. From their respective towers, Poulin cites Hemingway; Ducharme cites Balzac; Soucy cites the Bible, Spinoza, and the dictionary; Hamelin cites Malcolm Lowry, and he too the dictionary—the only book that his character brings on his retreat.

All of these postmodern characters rekindle relationships with old stock figures (for example, the *coureur des bois*) and reactivate the theme of exile that has transcended the history of Quebec literature. Almost invariably, these characters inhabit a barren, marginal space on the fringe of society, where they are guaranteed immense freedom but condemned to solitude. They live in poverty, luxury items being a rarity. They share a common literary culture, which distinguishes them from their predecessors. But most importantly, while going about their business, they observe each other with an inexhaustible curiosity, driven by the desire to give the narrative of their lives an improbable coherence. The traditional poles of identity—including family, friends, social class, generation, or nation—are not enough, nor are they truly determining factors. The past is as vague as the future. Naturally, the open frontier of the North has expanded, but in fact all frontiers are opening up with every step these characters take, pledged to boundless mobility. Regardless of where their focus may lie, they feel highly detached from any form of social life, which they find consistently underwhelming. They are not as attached to others as they are to the signs of their negligible presence. It is as though they are always surveying the land, searching for traces of their origins. In *Lignes aériennes* (2002, *Mirabel*), a prose poem that unfolds like a personal narrative, Pierre Nepveu returns to the expropriated land in the region of Mirabel, where his own family used to live. He talks to himself as though he were alone in the world:

> today it was
> that I bent down
> over my black shoes
> and spoke to them like a pair of dogs,
> ordering them outside
> was scraping over the damp grass,
> I lay down at the foot of a tree,
> although I have few roots
> for probing my life[12]

In fact, the observation in this poem about having "few roots" may be emblematic of all contemporary Quebec literature.

From the nineteenth-century works of Abbé Casgrain to the poetry of the 1960s, the literati who have traditionally described Quebec literature have adopted the vantage point of one people or "*la nation*," often redoubling their efforts to assert its specificity and centricity. But since 1980, the new theme of *dépaysement* or decentring has been redefining Quebec literature as a significant influx of Quebec authors with origins that span the globe are producing what has been called "migrant writing." Bilingual and bicultural Montreal has evolved into multicultural Montreal, as Emile Ollivier, a Haitian novelist, explained to a compatriot:

> I also told him that to really write about Montreal, [he] should begin with contextualizing nomadic discourse, migrant discourse and [the discourse] that both share, discourse from nowhere, discourse from elsewhere, discourse that is not quite from here, not quite from elsewhere; I told him that this city has four solitudes—francophone, anglophone, immigrant and Black—[he] must show how our presence jostles and tropicalizes Montreal, splashes it with bright colours. As Borges said of Buenos Aires, *the only beauties are involuntary.*[13]

In this new space, splashed with bright colours, the very notion of a "frontier" loses part of its meaning. Present-day Montreal no longer bears any resemblance to the Montreal of *Bonheur d'occasion*. Former notions of Quebec's "people" and "nation" now coexist with a growing collective awareness of multifaceted cultural diversity. Without a doubt, Quebec's "national consciousness" is being forced to reconceptualize itself. But even in this vastly altered landscape, some familiar points of reference have remained.

For one thing, the same twofold marginality vis-à-vis France and the United States that has characterized Quebec literature since its inception is still an influential reality. For another, Quebec's northern frontier has kept its exotic magnetic pull. It has repeatedly reconciled Quebecers' sense of *pays* (their people, nation, homeland) with their openness to *dépaysement* (decentring). Indeed, the rapid success of migrant writing in Quebec may be owed to the fact that it confirms (more than it contradicts) this self-made spirit of new beginnings in the open north—a world view shared by generations of Quebec authors.

Questions for Critical Thinking

1. Historically speaking, how would you say France and North America have been diametrically opposed in relation to Quebec literature?
2. Why do Quebec authors often represent "America" as a foreign entity?
3. In what way has the northern frontier marked literary works from Quebec?

Notes

1. Translated as *The Town Below* by Samuel Putnam (Toronto: McClelland & Stewart, 1967).
2. Translated as *The Tin Flute* by Hannah Josephson (Toronto: McClelland & Stewart, 1947).
3. Gilles Marcotte, "Robert Charbonneau, la France, René Garneau et nous . . ." in *Littérature et circonstances*, "Essais" collection (Montreal: L'Hexagone, 1989), 65–84; Élisabeth Nardout-Lafarge, "Histoire d'une querelle," in Robert Charbonneau, *La France et nous: journal d'une querelle* (Montreal: Bibliothèque québécoise, 1993), 7–26.
4. In his report to the Crown, this British emissary suggested that since the French Canadians were a people with no history or literature of their own, they ought to be assimilated.
5. Our translation. Ducharme's autobiography was not included in the English translation of his novel by Barbara Bray (London: Hamish Hamilton, 1968).
6. Our translation of *Le Devoir*, 14 January 1967.
7. Our translation and italics. Gilles Marcotte, *Le Manuscrit Phaneuf* (Montreal: Boréal, 2005), 113–14.
8. Our translation of Jean Basile, *La Jument des Mongols* (Montreal: Éditions du Jour, 1964), 10.
9. Our translation of Gaston Miron, "La marche à l'amour," in *L'Homme rapaillé*, coll. "Poésie" (Paris: Gallimard, 1999), 62.
10. Our translation of Paul-Marie Lapointe, "Le temps tombe," in *Le Réel absolu : poèmes 1948–1965* (Montreal: L'Hexagone, 1971), 220.
11. *Mr. Blue* was translated from the French by Sheila Fischman (Montreal: Vehicle Press, 1993), 22. Original work by Jacques Poulin, *Le vieux chagrin* (Montreal/Arles: Leméac/Actes Sud, 1989), 23.
12. Judith Cowan's translation of *Mirabel* (Montreal: Vehicle Press, 2004), 11. Original by Pierre Nepveu, *Lignes aériennes* (Montreal: Éditions du Noroît, 2002), 11. Excerpt used by permission from *Mirabel* by Pierre Nepveu, translated by Judith Cowan and published by Signal Editions, Véhicule Press.
13. Our italics and translation of Émile Ollivier, *La Brûlerie* (Montreal: Boréal, 2004), 55–6.

Select Bibliography

Biron, Michel. *Le Roman québécois*. Montreal: Boréal, 2012.

Biron, Michel, François Dumont, and Élisabeth Nardout-Lafarge (with the assistance of Martine-Emmanuelle Lapointe). *Histoire de la littérature québécoise*. Montreal: Boréal, 2007.

Bouchard, Chantal. *Méchante langue : la légitimité du français parlé au Québec*. Montreal: Presses de l'Université de Montréal, 2012.

Bourassa, André G. *Surréalisme et littérature québécoise : histoire d'une révolution culturelle*. Montreal: Les Herbes Rouges, 1986.

Brossard, Nicole, and Lisette Girouard, eds. *Anthologie de la poésie des femmes au Québec : des origines à nos jours.* Montreal: Éditions du Remue-ménage, 2003.

Chassay, Jean-François. *L'Ambiguité américaine : le roman québécois face aux États-Unis.* Montreal: XYZ, 1995.

Dumont, François. *La Poésie québécoise.* Montreal: Boréal, 1999.

Gallays, François, Sylvain Simard, and Robert Vigneault, eds. *Le Roman contemporain au Québec (1960–1985).* Archives des lettres canadiennes, Tome VIII. Montreal: Fides, 1992.

Gauvin, Lise, and Gaston Miron. *Écrivains contemporains du Québec : anthologie.* Montreal: L'Hexagone, 1998.

Godin, Jean Cléo, and Dominique Lafon. *Dramaturgies québécoises des années quatre-vingt.* Montreal: Leméac, 1999.

Harel, Simon. *Le Voleur de parcours : identité et cosmopolitisme dans la littérature québécoise contemporaine.* Montréal: XYZ, 1999.

Histoire du livre et de l'imprimé au Canada. Vol. I, Des débuts à 1840, edited by Patricia Fleming, Gilles Gallichan, and Yvan Lamonde, 2004. Vol. *II*, 1840–1918, edited by Yvan Lamonde, Patricia Fleming, and Fiona A. Black, 2006. Vol. *III*, 1918–1980, edited by Carole Gerson and Jacques Michon, 2007. Montreal: Presses de l'Université de Montréal.

Lafon, Dominique, ed. *Théâtre québécois 1975–1995.* Archives des lettres canadiennes, Tome X. Montreal: Fides, 2001.

Lemire, Maurice, Gilles Dorion, and Aurélien Boivin, eds. *Dictionnaire des œuvres littéraires du Québec.* 8 volumes: I (up to 1900), II (1900–1939), III (1940–1959), IV (1960–1969), V (1970–1975), VI (1976–1980), VII (1981–1985), VIII (1986–1989). Montreal: Fides, 1978–2011.

Lemire, Maurice, Denis Saint-Jacques, and Lucie Robert, eds. *La Vie littéraire au Québec.* 6 volumes: I (1764–1805), II (1806–1839), III (1840–1869), IV (1870–1894), V (1895–1918), VI (1919–1933). Québec: Presses de l'Université Laval, 1991–2011.

Lepage, Françoise. *Histoire de la littérature pour la jeunesse (Québec et francophonies du Canada).* Orléans, ON: Éditions David, 2000.

Linteau, Paul-André, René Durocher, Jean-Claude Robert, and François Ricard, *Histoire du Québec contemporain.* Vol. 1, *De la confédération à la Crise*; Vol. 2, *Le Québec depuis 1930.* Montreal: Boréal, 1989.

Lord, Michel. *Anthologie de la science-fiction québécoise contemporaine.* Montreal: Bibliothèque québécoise, 1988.

Mailhot, Laurent. *L'Essai québécois depuis 1845 : étude et anthologie.* Montreal: Hurtubise HMH, 2005.

———. *La Littérature québécoise depuis ses origines.* Montreal: Typo, 1997.

———, and Pierre Nepveu. *La Poésie québécoise, des origines à nos jours. Anthologie.* Montreal: Typo, 2007.

Marcotte, Gilles, ed. *Anthologie de la littérature québécoise.* Vols. 1 and 2 (1534–1895); vols. 3 and 4 (1895–1952). Montreal: L'Hexagone, 1994.

Michon, Jacques, ed. *Histoire de l'édition littéraire au Québec au XXe siècle.* Vol. 1, *La naissance de l'éditeur 1900–1939*; Vol. 2, *Le temps des éditeurs 1940–1959.* Montreal: Fides, 1999, 2004.

Moisan, Clément, and Renate Hildebrand, *Ces étrangers du dedans : une histoire de l'écriture migrante au Québec (1937–1997).* Québec : Nota bene, 2001.

Nepveu, Pierre. *L'Écologie du réel : mort et naissance de la littérature québécoise contemporaine.* Montréal: Boréal, 1999.

———. *Intérieurs du Nouveau Monde : essais sur les littératures du Québec et des Amériques.* Montréal: Boréal, 1998.

New, William H. *A History of Canadian Literature.* Montreal and Kingston: McGill-Queen's University Press, 2003.

Paterson, Janet. *Moments postmodernes dans le roman québécois.* Ottawa: Presses de l'Université d'Ottawa, 1993.

Pellerin, Gilles. *Anthologie de la nouvelle québécoise actuelle.* Quebec: L'Instant même, 2003.

Royer, Jean. *Introduction à la poésie québécoise : les poètes et les œuvres des origines à nos jours.* Montreal: Bibliothèque québécoise, 2009.

Simon, Sherry, et al. *Fictions de l'identitaire au Québec.* Montreal: XYZ, 1991.

Smart, Patricia. *Écrire dans la maison du père : l'émergence du féminin dans la tradition littéraire du Québec.* Montréal: XYZ, 2003.

29 Quebec Theatre: New Dynamics between the Local and the International

Sylvain Schryburt, University of Ottawa

Timeline

1948 Production of *Tit-Coq* by Gratien Gélinas premieres, directed by Fred Barry.

1951 Théâtre du Nouveau Monde presents its first show, Molière's *L'Avare* (*The Miser*), directed by Jean Gascon.

1954 Conservatoire d'art dramatique de Montréal is founded.

Conservatoire d'art dramatique de Québec and National Theatre School of Canada (Montreal) follow in 1957 and 1960, respectively.

1958 Association canadienne du théâtre amateur is founded by Guy Beaulne. Name changed in 1972 to Association québécoise du jeune théâtre.

1965 Centre d'essai des auteurs dramatiques is founded; today it is called Centre des auteurs dramatiques.

1968 *Les Belles-sœurs* by Michel Tremblay premieres, directed by André Brassard.

1981 First Conference on the State of Professional Theatre in Quebec.

1982 Denis Marleau founds Théâtre UBU, today known as UBU compagnie de création.

1985 Festival de théâtre des Amériques (FTA) is founded (later to become Festival TransAmériques in 2007).

1987 Théâtre Repère's *Trilogie des dragons* (*The Dragons' Trilogy*), directed by Robert Lepage, triumphs at second edition of FTA.

1994 Robert Lepage founds Ex Machina.

1995 Usine C, a multidisciplinary creative and stage production space, officially opens. Debut performance is a retrospective of work of Gilles Maheu and his company, Carbone 14 (1981–2005).

1997 Théâtre UBU's *Nathan le Sage* is performed in Cour d'honneur of Palais des Papes at the 51st Festival d'Avignon. Directed by Denis Marleau.

2007 Second Conference on the State of Professional Theatre in Quebec.

2009 Wajdi Mouawad named "Associated Artist" of the 63rd Festival d'Avignon.

Introduction

Because it is a living and therefore transitory art form, the bulk of Quebec theatre, like that of any other national[1] theatre, is rarely seen outside its birthplace. This is true within the province itself, where local Quebec City productions, for example, are seldom performed in Montreal, and vice versa. On a larger, international scale, the same trend has held true in that, apart from a few noteworthy figures, knowledge of Quebec's theatrical activity is still marginal among foreign audiences and scholars alike. Since the 1980s, however, some directors and playwrights have managed to break through onto the world stage. Today, directors like Marie Brassard, Robert Lepage, Gilles Maheu, and Denis Marleau, and playwrights like Daniel Danis, Carole Fréchette, Wajdi Mouawad, Larry Tremblay, and the long-established Michel Tremblay may be said to epitomize Quebec theatre abroad.

This chapter discusses the relatively new phenomenon of the international distribution of Quebec theatre and focuses more specifically on the handful of playwrights and directors who have succeeded in sharing their works through prestigious international venues and distribution networks. To situate our discussion within its wider historical context, we review the far-reaching changes that have taken place in the writing, institutions, and aesthetics of Quebec theatre since the mid-1960s, when it definitively embraced modernity. These points of reference will be helpful in understanding the enduring new dynamics of theatre ushered in during the 1980s: Gradually, the local "theatrical field"[2] in Quebec made links to the international theatrical field, where some of the most respected figures of Quebec contemporary theatre presented their productions and plays, unfettered by borders or local artistic dynamics. By establishing themselves as players both at home (during the regular theatre season in Quebec City and Montreal) and abroad (working within international networks), the most celebrated artists of contemporary Quebec theatre developed simultaneously within these two theatrical fields, a "double social inscription"[3] that will be explored later in this chapter.

From Assertions of Identity to Experiments with Form: 1965 to 1980

Most scholarly works that offer a diachronic reading of Quebec theatre usually bracket part of their research focus between the mid-1960s and the early 1980s. As an institutional marker of this period, one can invoke the Centre d'essai des auteurs dramatiques (CEAD[4]), founded in 1965 and charged with the mandate (which it still maintains today) of supporting, disseminating, and promoting the work of Quebec playwrights. CEAD heralded the genesis of a long dreamt-of autonomous national theatre, theatre that (for a change) would not be derived from models imported from abroad (most notably France) but would resonate with the national assertions of identity that were at the heart of the Quiet Revolution.

The drive to make the language of dramatic literature more autonomous, pioneered by young artists of the baby boom generation, registered its first popular and critical successes with Michel Tremblay's *Les Belles-sœurs* in 1968, followed by the collective creation *T'es pas tannée, Jeanne d'Arc?* by Grand Cirque Ordinaire one year later. On one hand, the 1970s saw the rapid growth of creative theatre collectives in pursuit of "the words to express ourselves,"[5] a goal very typical of the artistic approach of the period in Quebec. The use of ***joual***, a distinctively Québécois French vernacular, previously deemed too unrefined for the theatre, was reclaimed in the scripts of this era as the authentic and legitimate popular voice of Quebec. On the other hand, the unprecedented boom of locally written material was so voluminous that it soon accounted for a good half of all theatre productions on offer across the province.[6] The number of both government-subsidized and private theatre companies[7] also snowballed during this period, putting significantly more plays on Quebec stages. In Montreal alone, theatre productions quadrupled between 1960 and 1980, propelled from 30 to 120 productions per season.[8]

Born of the burgeoning and imperative need for self-expression that reigned during this era, Quebec playwriting was conceptualized as a locus for new creations rather than as a repertoire to invest in and revisit. As a result, of all the playwrights mentioned in Jean Cléo Godin and Laurent Mailhot's two-volume *Le Théâtre québécois* (containing selected plays performed and published from 1940 to 1980), Réjean Ducharme, Claude Gauvreau, and Michel Tremblay are the only authors whose plays are still regularly performed on the contemporary Quebec stage.[9]

At the beginning of the 1980s, following a decade of excitement and somewhat frenzied development, the theatre community was faced with the first growing pains of its history. As their numbers mushroomed, companies soon saturated their limited local markets, underfunded[10] by public authorities who were criticized for their inadequate cultural policies.[11] It was in this chaotic context that the First Conference on the State of Professional Theatre in Quebec was held in November 1981, which culminated in the formation of some 10 professional associations and groupings. These new entities would lay the groundwork for professional practices in Quebec theatre, but they would also splinter the theatre community into pressure groups whose interests sometimes clashed.[12] Whereas the 1970s had been a time of expansion, in the 1980s Quebec theatre would consolidate its institutions and stabilize its assets.

While the intense focus on national identity had lent some measure of uniformity to Quebec playwriting since the Quiet Revolution, it was succeeded in the 1980s and 1990s by a sweeping diversification of aesthetics. From introspective scripts that questioned our roles as individuals in society (Carole Fréchette) and dark, sometimes dreamlike poetical prose (Daniel Danis), to realist or urban writing (François Archambault), fragmented texts with postmodern slants (Normand Chaurette, René-Daniel Dubois), and works about exile verging on the tragic (Wajdi Mouawad), high-profile playwrights of the times used many approaches and spoke with varied voices. Amid all of these voices, the vernacular of *joual,* which had been indispensable to theatre of the 1960s and 1970s, lost much of its subversive powers and came to be regarded as a stylistic device among others.

Along with this diversification of voices in Quebec theatre during the 1980s and beyond, stage directing broke free of the printed script. Some directors (often those who made their mark on the international stage) distanced themselves from strictly script-centric theatrical traditions and made greater use of stage imagery, actors' bodies, new media and technology, intermediality[13] and interdisciplinarity, hybrids of different stage traditions, or compelling and architecturally complex set designs. These artists, who were emblematic of a new conception of theatrical performance, would become the main Quebec players in the international theatre field that was fast emerging.

The Internationalization of Quebec Theatre

Faced with saturated local markets and following the First Conference on the State of Professional Theatre in Quebec (1981), an increasing number of theatre producers started trying their luck abroad. From then onwards, international tours by Quebec companies became commonplace and some began to carve out a niche for themselves.[14] Robert Lepage was among the first directors to distinguish himself to foreign audiences. For 30 years Lepage has been creating compelling **image theatre**, an aesthetic greatly enhanced by the use of new technology (especially video projection) since he founded the Ex Machina production company in 1994 (see the Biography box). Denis Marleau, founding director of the theatre company UBU (1981–), distinguished himself in another vein entirely, with a body of work that initially drew its inspiration from the historical avant-garde movements and used the performative resources of voice, but later focused on major modern European writers (for example, Maeterlinck, Beckett, Bernhard, and Crimp) and used what would become his trademark projections of visuals. Last but not least on this very short list, Gilles Maheu's company, Carbone 14 (1980–2005), stood out as the first Quebec theatre company to commit to interdisciplinarity, producing unequivocally postmodern works that deliberately blurred the boundaries between dance, theatre, and performance.

These three international figureheads of theatre directing have shared world acclaim with a number

BIOGRAPHY

Robert Lepage

Quebec director and actor Robert Lepage in October 2009.

The Canadian Press/Darren Calabrese

Robert Lepage is one of the few directors in Quebec who has made a name for himself well beyond a limited local sphere of aficionados. One of the few truly international theatre superstars, he has piqued interest and stirred enthusiasm in theatre, film, and opera for three decades—a rare achievement in these highly competitive milieus, prone as they are to the whims of fashion and fluttering allegiances. Throughout his career, Lepage has shown an exceptional ability to keep pace with and, at times, outstrip trends in contemporary dramatic arts, making him a popular celebrity in theatre abroad and all the more so at home.

Born 12 December 1957, Lepage earned a certificate in acting from the Conservatoire de Québec (1975–8), rounding out his education under Alain Knapp in Paris. Upon his return to Quebec, he joined Théâtre Repère in 1982 and quickly rose to the position of artistic co-director and principal director. *Circulations* (1984) and the solo work *Vinci* (1986) built his reputation as a director in Quebec. But it was through his second production of *La Trilogie des dragons* (*The Dragons' Trilogy*, 1987), a six-hour saga, that he broke into the relatively closed world of international theatre. Reworked versions of this landmark play toured internationally for five years (and again between 2003 and 2007)—an unparalleled achievement in the history of Quebec theatre that would become the norm for many of Lepage's later works.

Le Polygraphe (*Polygraph*, 1987) and *Plaques tectoniques* (*Tectonic Plates*, 1988) followed, establishing Lepage's modus operandi: the layering of works in progress, the use of improvisation and epic devices in developing shows and playwriting, multilingualism and multiculturalism, experimentation with new technologies, playing with audience perception and perspective, and imagistic theatre. In Lepage's shows, recurring situations and themes also emerge. Leitmotifs include characters from Quebec who set out to discover the world or themselves, historical characters, misunderstood or maladjusted intellectuals, the quest for identity, the intertwining of major historical events and everyday life stories, drug use, and the juxtaposition of pop and high culture.

After leaving the helm at Théâtre Repère, Lepage became artistic director for the Théâtre français from 1989 to 1993 at the National Arts Centre (NAC) in Ottawa. There he presented *Les Aiguilles et l'opium* (*Needles and Opium*, 1991), the second in a series of one-man shows. During this period Lepage made regular forays into the Shakespearean repertoire (for example, French-language versions of *Macbeth*, *Coriolanus*, and *The Tempest*) and multiplied his collaborative efforts with some of the most prestigious theatres in Europe and elsewhere. Indeed, whereas Lepage's previous efforts had been entirely focused on creating new works, during this period he tackled a classic European repertoire, sometimes presenting bold re-readings, such as a 1992 version of *A Midsummer Night's Dream* performed entirely in a sea of mud. Along similar lines, he directed plays by Brecht, Dürrenmatt, and Strindberg, and made his first forays into opera (*Erwartung* [Expectation] and *Le Château de Barbe-Bleue* [*Bluebeard's Castle*], 1992), emphasizing the spectacular aspects of these works.

continued

In 1994, following his tenure with the Théâtre français at the NAC, Lepage founded Ex Machina. The company's first show, *Les Sept branches de la rivière Ota* (*The Seven Streams of the River Ota*, 1994) and a number of later productions with Ex Machina (*Le Polygraphe* [*Polygraph*], 1996, and *La Géométrie des miracles* [*Geometry of Miracles*], 1998), renewed interest in the great collective sagas of Robert Lepage. His solo shows made more complex use of new technologies, as in *Elseneur* (*Elsinore*, 1995), a solo version of *Hamlet* that completed the Shakespearean circle he began some years earlier. Despite Lepage's ever-increasing use of leading-edge technology, the aesthetics of most of the company's productions remained firmly rooted in simple theatricality. His sense of wonder and humour, delight in play, and inventiveness, and his ingenious, understated metonymic devices that seamlessly compress and expand time and space make Lepage an artist who is well appreciated—if not loved—by the masses and aficionados alike.

The fresh start Lepage made by founding Ex Machina also marked his debut as a multidisciplinary artist. Besides his work in opera, still an area of occasional experimentation, he was appointed commissioner of the show *Métissages* (2000) at the Musée de la civilisation de Québec. He directed the Cirque du Soleil show *KÁ* (2004) in Las Vegas and designed *Moulin à images* (*The Image Mill*, 2008), an ambitious outdoor projection in the Port of Québec on an imposing horizon of 81 grain silos to recount Quebec City's 400-year history in sound and images. Lepage has also launched a highly acclaimed career as a filmmaker, directing six films between 1995 and 2013, often adaptations of his stage works.

Throughout his career Lepage has demonstrated a strong attachment to his birthplace, Quebec City. It was there, in 1997, that he opened La Caserne, the creative hub and home to Ex Machina's archives and offices. This facility also includes a stage space where the company's productions in progress are sometimes presented. The numerous awards Lepage has garnered include the Order of Canada (1994), Ordre national du Québec (1999), and the Europe Theatre Prize (2007).

In many respects, Robert Lepage's career path reflects that of contemporary theatre, which has veered away from its "script-centricity" to explore forms that play freely with the boundaries of the dramatic arts. While Lepage's detractors have sometimes justifiably attacked the limits such a pragmatic approach to playwriting may impose on literary qualities, it remains that Lepage's inimitable approach has helped broaden the definition of theatre for audiences and artists alike.

of other theatre artists and companies that tour somewhat regularly abroad, including Marie Brassard's theatre company Infrarouge; Paula de Vasconcelos's theatre-dance troupe, Pigeons International; and the now-defunct Théâtre Ô Parleur, whose former guiding light, Wajdi Mouawad (of Au carré de l'hypoténuse) is now pursuing a solo career. There is also the particularly active sector of theatre for young audiences, spearheaded by Les Deux Mondes, Le Carrousel, Théâtre des Confettis, Théâtre Bouches Décousues, and Théâtre de l'Oeil, whose productions are also seen on their countless regular international tours.

Given the quality of their work and the prestige garnered from their international reach and their endorsement by foreign audiences, most of these companies enjoy exceptional status in the theatrical fields of Montreal and Quebec City. Often cited as examples to prove the vitality of Quebec theatre, these ambassadors of culture—as they are sometimes referred to—have become a source of national pride for Quebec, and their achievements abroad seem to reflect well on the Quebec arts community as a whole. While the international presence of Quebec theatre is a sign of its artistic maturity, this presence also raises the question of how these companies (being part of both the dynamics of regular theatre seasons at home and of the highly competitive environment in major world theatre festivals) are socially inscribed. In other words: How have they established themselves on a sociological level?

To answer this question, we can begin by examining the balance struck between local productions and those designed for international competition. This examination will allow us to analyze and understand the new dynamics that, over and above the artistic merit of these creators, seem to define the distinctive character of contemporary Quebec theatre. Two concepts may be helpful in characterizing the far-reaching paradigm shifts in the dynamics of Quebec theatre: the well-known concept of **field**, as defined by French sociologist Pierre Bourdieu,[15] and what we will call **festival** theatre, which allows us to consider the theatrical means of production, the scope of audience expectations, and the aesthetic parameters that guide the development and appreciation of productions.

Local Theatrical Field–International Theatrical Field

The notion of *field*, as proposed by Pierre Bourdieu, divides society into dynamic spaces in which social agents struggle to impose their views on the economy, politics, culture, and other areas of public life. In the realm of the arts, artists are ultimately struggling to impose their own "legitimate" definition of art and thus define the very boundaries of the field in which they have agency. The notion of field in the realm of theatre (as in dance and other living arts) must take into consideration the fact that performance (by nature a unique and ephemeral event) has no real manifestation or existence outside of the local community of artists and theatre-goers or outside of its occasional dissemination through reviews or rumours. So while we might be tempted to conceptualize Quebec's theatrical field as a function of a "national space," it is more logical to conceptualize it according to the geographical boundaries of its performers, audiences, and main "instances of consecration"[16]—in other words, we should scale back our theatrical field to focus on the major cities likely to produce viable theatre communities. Unlike literature or film, theatre, being a stage-based art, is rarely seen outside the city where it is produced, since touring productions require complex logistics, seasoned distribution networks, and above all financial investment that is often prohibitive. Thus, the province of Quebec really has only two theatrical fields that are sufficiently developed to support a community of theatre professionals and a relatively diversified spectrum of companies: one in Montreal, the other in Quebec City, each with its own flagship institutions, sites of cultural dissemination (performance venues), theatre critics, and publics.

In Montreal, most theatre activity is centred on a dozen or so companies that control their own venue and can therefore be considered major institutions of the local theatrical field. Each occupy a specific market niche, catering to a target public that consists mainly of season-ticket holders. For instance, Théâtre du Rideau Vert (1949–), the doyen of Quebec theatre companies, offers mostly light, popular entertainment (variety shows, comedies, and musicals); Théâtre du Nouveau Monde (1951–), the city's most prestigious theatre, presents mainly classic and modern plays from European repertoires; Théâtre d'Aujourd'hui (1968–) is entirely devoted to the work of Quebec playwrights; the Compagnie Jean Duceppe (1973–) specializes in canonical American drama (for example, Albee and Miller); Théâtre de la Manufacture (1975–) presents realist theatre by English-language playwrights (in translation) and Quebec French-language playwrights; and Espace GO (1990–) leans toward the contemporary, presenting mostly European plays. Today it is the full-time artistic directors of these institutional companies who define their specific aesthetic and "social inscription" rather than the contractual theatre artists hired to produce one of the four or five shows on the season roster.

Alongside these more firmly institutionalized companies we find about a hundred players of varying sizes, some ephemeral, some highly established and consecrated. These last companies are usually founded and run by directors whose respective idiosyncrasies are their sole guarantee of aesthetic specificity. Within the theatrical field of Montreal, their plays are produced in part thanks to the capital provided by national governments,[17] and they compete for media exposure, grant funding, and of course consecration through provincial "instances of legitimation,"[18] such as annual awards from the Association québécoise des critiques de théâtre (1995–) and (previously) the Masques Awards from the Académie québécoise du théâtre (an umbrella organization for all Quebec's theatre professionals from 1993 to 2008). Quebec companies that frequently tour abroad also compete for the same grants, sometimes using the same distribution network, and vie with lesser-known companies from Quebec for the backing of the same instances of legitimation. Indeed, their institutional inscription resembles that of companies whose work is exclusively destined for local consumption.

A local market the size of Montreal has its limitations for most of the few companies whose work, without necessarily being avant-garde, is too innovative or challenging to hope to reach more than a limited audience. At last count in the theatrical field of Montreal, companies like Denis Marleau's UBU, Paula de Vasconcelos's theatre-dance company Pigeons International, and Gilles Maheu's (now-defunct) Carbone 14 depended on a public that rarely exceeded 3,000 or 4,000 spectators, unless they were invited to present their work in a venue that mostly caters to season-ticket holders. The limited opportunities at home partly explain why these producers, while still an integral part of the regular metropolitan theatre season, would also attempt to access the circuit of the international theatrical field for its expanded pool of theatre-goers with "cultivated dispositions," its own sites of dissemination, and distinctive marks of consecration (for example, opening for the illustrious Festival d'Avignon or appearing in special issues of European arts magazines showcasing Quebec theatre artists).

Of course the transition from one theatrical field to another, from the local to the international, is no accident. This transition depends on aesthetic affinities between local Quebec artists and the major international distributors, such as theatre festivals and other specialized performing arts venues. Success abroad also depends on the logistical ability to enter an extremely selective, restricted distribution network and access foreign capital in the form of a co-production, often essential to the complex funding arrangements required for touring abroad. The transition from the local to the international field is all the more daunting since the highly coveted "originality" factor, characteristic of festival theatre, is measured on an international scale, where the struggle to be distinctive is undisputedly fiercer than in the smaller and less competitive environment of Montreal.

The institutional and economic difficulties faced by theatre companies who wish to break into the international touring networks are different from those facing playwrights. Numerous Quebec writers have had their works performed abroad, either in translation or in the original language. For playwrights, penetrating the international market largely depends on individual affinities, since foreign artistic directors or stage directors are generally in charge of choosing which plays they will produce and bankrolling the attendant local costs from their regular operating budgets. Such is not the case for festival theatre, as I define the term.

Festival Theatre

Quebec productions destined for markets abroad may seem edgy and highly innovative when presented at home (compared to the rest of the season's roster), but it is important to understand that they are governed by different standards, as are most of the productions selected for the major festival tours that establish international reputations. Festival theatre has its own funding formulas and networks, sites of dissemination, and instances of legitimation. The shows developed within this framework have the peculiarity of being funded by the national organizations from several countries and are developed as co-productions, courtesy of various instances (for example, festivals or national theatres), some of which later provide venues for tours and may even put their name on the productions they host.

Robert Lepage's one-man play *The Far Side of the Moon* is a case in point. First performed in Quebec City in February 2000, it has now been presented in over 50 cities straddling four continents. Produced by Lepage's company, Ex Machina, which is itself partly funded by federal, provincial, and municipal governments in Canada, *The Far Side of the Moon* also received financial backing from more than 30 foreign co-producers, most of them international festivals.[19] Naturally, all of the festivals involved in subsidizing this venture hosted the production for one of its many stopovers, thereby not only providing financial support for Ex Machina but also guaranteeing the company a sizable distribution network and invaluable logistical assistance to promote the show. Although this may be an extreme example, it is not an isolated case: In reality, local governments are apt to provide only part of the real costs of productions destined for audiences outside of Quebec. Therefore, somewhat predictably, the Quebec theatre productions best known abroad are in fact those supported by international producers and distributors.

But festival theatre cannot be reduced to a sociological phenomenon, an economic fact, or a particularly well-developed **network** for the distribution and dissemination of culture. On an aesthetic level, it generates and upholds specific standards, as evidenced by the similarities among the plays produced in or for the international network. It may even be said that a degree of conformism has been established in these productions, which (as mentioned earlier) are paradoxically seen as quite innovative in the local field. When contemporary Quebec artists move to the international theatrical field, it also reflects the fact that their approach has entered into an aesthetic dialogue that reifies a vision that is shared to some extent with the social agents in this field.

As recent research on postdramatic theatre by Hans-Thies Lehmann makes clear,[20] the international contemporary theatre scene that has welcomed Quebec companies such as Ex Machina, Marie Brassard, Carbone 14, and to a lesser extent UBU favours theatre that incorporates intermediality and interdisciplinarity, the mixing of cultures, traditions, and genres of theatre, using the image as the principle of narrative construction, a non-linear treatment of the plot line (if there is a plot line), multilingualism, and the fragmentation of dramatic action or of the performative aspect of the theatrical event. All of these characteristics apply in varying degrees to both the Quebec companies that tour most frequently abroad and the foreign companies with whom they share billing in the programming of major international theatre festivals. It is precisely this kinship of aesthetic approaches, more than any other factor, that enables Quebec productions to tour abroad, performing in venues receptive to these forms of theatre before audiences more accustomed than others to these codes "of cultivated disposition."

The Presence of the International Theatrical Field within Montreal and Quebec City's Theatrical Fields

Today, the presence of international theatre is not the exception in Quebec but actually represents a new standard that has redefined theatre itself. The reasons behind this paradigm shift are clear. Quebec spectators have had the opportunity to acquaint themselves with the codes of contemporary international theatre because they frequent festivals that feature it almost exclusively. Quebec City and (to a greater extent) Montreal have become part of the vast distribution network of the international theatrical field through two major events: Montreal's Festival TransAmériques (FTA), founded in 1985 as the Festival de Théâtre des Amériques (see the Primary Source box), and Quebec City's more recent Carrefour international de théâtre (CIT), founded in 1991. These events not only enable a select number of hand-picked Quebec producers to present their latest work, but also bring in much of the leading European and American figures on the international circuits, such as Romeo Castellucci, Thomas Ostermeier, Alain Platel, Joël Pommerat, and Frank Castorf.

More recently, Montreal's local theatrical field has included the Usine C stage, which operates like a permanent branch of festival-type theatre. Designed first and foremost as a space for the dissemination and support of new creative work by artists-in-residence, Usine C is now Quebec's primary home-away-from-home for international artists touring on the festival circuits. Since its opening, Usine C has made itself available to the FTA's two-week festival, held from late May to early June, following hot

Primary Source

Marie-Hélène Falcon [on the FTA's founding and initial artistic mandate]

When it came time to tackle this adventure [FTA's founding] we realised we didn't have adequate funding and couldn't travel as much as we initially wished but we still had this desire to discover what was happening in the so close yet so distant and mysterious Americas. This wasn't a strictly geographical choice. For us the Americas also carried an imaginary quality, a dream of sorts. It was a distinct identity; the Americas as a land of refuge or as a runway for take-off. We thought these ideas to be beautiful and claimed to be part of the Americas—plural. FTA's very first edition asserted our wider continental "Americanness"—from the very North to the very South—which includes the reality of First Nations. While travelling I also realised that we all shared similar ties with the old motherlands. The arrival of colonizers and soldiers (French, Spanish or English), for instance, brought with them the theatrical traditions of their respective European metropolis. Then, the birth of national theatres with national playwrights was soon followed by the founding of theatre companies and later the appearance of collective creation, Women's theatre or a return to the classics, starting with the Greeks . . . . It was very interesting to note all these overlapping threads between different societies of the Americas of which we didn't know much. We realised that it was both interesting and fascinating to explore the North-South axis at a time when our theatre mostly focused on East-West exchanges. At the time, I felt it was essential to present what the Americas brought to the world [of performance] and to declare: "Here is the place we can occupy amongst nations." After the 1985 and 1987 editions of our festival, subsequent programming integrated American—in the continental sense of the word—but also European, Asian, African or Australian artists and companies. Indeed it had never been our intent to strictly limit FTA's roster to companies from the Americas. Our focus has always been to look out for what is different, to go towards artists and works that break away from mainstream production—regardless of the country we visited. We were always open to other ways of making theatre whether it be in the Americas or elsewhere around the world.

Gilbert David, "L'art de cultiver le risque sans fin : Entretien avec Marie-Hélène Falcon," *Spirale* 249 (2014): 17.

on the heels of the regular yearly institutional theatre season in Montreal. This multidisciplinary performance space is unusual in that it offers entire seasons of theatre and dance (for which season tickets are available), sometimes featuring celebrated names of the world stage such as Claude Régy or Guy Cassiers. Thanks to Usine C, Montreal's festival theatre public can see shows that not so long ago used to be the exclusive preserve of major international theatre festivals.

Even more importantly for the dynamics in Montreal's theatrical field, Usine C also serves as a dedicated site of dissemination for local companies whose work embraces some of the aesthetic concerns of festival theatre but who have not entirely succeeded, or even attempted, to break into that select circuit. For example, Paula de Vasconcelos's Pigeons International theatre-dance company, which occasionally tours abroad, has been performing regularly at Usine C since 1995. Brigitte Haentjens's company, Sibyllines, which specializes in nontheatrical scripts (adaptations from novels), postmodern works (for example, Heiner Müller), and stage direction that applies extreme plastic rigour, also presents its annual show at Usine C, but has not yet ventured into the international circuit.

Another particularly interesting case is that of Marie Brassard, an actor formerly close to Robert Lepage who has pursued a remarkable solo career since 2001. Her first solo play, *Jimmy, créature de rêve*, like all of Brassard's subsequent productions, was co-produced by the FTA, where it also presented its world premiere. Following the success of this play (which was performed in 40 cities around the world), Brassard's company, Infrarouge, and the FTA have continued to pursue their collaborative efforts along with other distributor-producers, such as the National Arts Centre in Ottawa, Berliner Festspiele in Berlin, and Wiener Festwochen in Vienna.

Thus, sites of dissemination like Usine C and the FTA not only provide windows on new creations in world theatre for Montreal audiences, but also serve as springboards that can help productions from the metropolis access the closed network of international circuits. It is through their choices in co-production and programming that these two atypical institutions from Montreal's theatrical field (one permanent and less prestigious, the other an annual event with strong "specific capital") have acquired bona fide powers to consecrate and sanction, in the local field, legitimate hopefuls or already-consecrated players from the international field.

The Double Institutional Inscription of Contemporary Quebec Theatre

Over and above the outstanding creative minds that have emerged since the early 1980s in the fields of playwriting and (especially) directing, the Quebec theatre community has seen new dynamics emerge, establishing a consecrated double inscription of its best-known productions in both the local and international theatrical fields. At the same time, the contemporary theatre on offer in Quebec has sidelined the paradigm of identity to the point that Quebec theatre is now practically indistinguishable from much pre-eminent European theatre and that of nations whose most challenging fringe theatre shares the same distribution networks and financing structures. In fact, undoubtedly the most striking characteristic of contemporary theatre is that its aesthetic displays an astonishing level of internal conformity, despite the habitual paratext of the modern stage, which thrives on subversion, audacity, and a perpetual quest for original theatrical and dramatic forms and content.

The codes of "festival theatre," or rather the community of aesthetic concerns shared by the principal players of the international circuit (including some of the most highly renowned Quebec companies), are therefore conducive to establishing a common corpus—which is convenient for the international community of theatre scholars. But over time, this common corpus has also empowered the collective impetus of scholars and created expectations to which the productions themselves appear to have conformed. Be they in Montreal, New York, Paris, London, or Berlin, scholars interested in cutting-edge theatre can easily enter into dialogues with their foreign colleagues, who inevitably share their reference corpus, and in so doing also secure a knowledgeable, well-informed readership for their work. Plainly, it is no coincidence that, in Quebec as elsewhere, fashionable research on contemporary theatre includes the avenues of exile, performativity, intermediality, and new technologies. For such are also the aesthetic concerns and tools of "festival theatre," which continues to supply the international university community with ideal case studies, not to mention examples that appear, in turn, to validate academic discourse.

In sum, although Quebec theatre companies that tour abroad remain inscribed in local dynamics, they appeal to foreign scholars and audiences alike—but not because of their specifically national, Québécois characteristics. Quebec theatre's current appeal lies more in its ability to deliver on expectations common to the public, critics, experts, and reviewers who consume or profit by the internationalization of theatrical practice, of which Quebec is now a part. This systemic manifestation of globalization in theatre has therefore sidelined the question of national identities. In their place, we now have an enlarged community, founded on concerns and aesthetic tastes that may be regarded as a new *lingua franca* for theatre professionals and aficionados, both in and beyond Quebec.

CASE STUDY

From Theatre Festivals to Festival Theatre

It was during the darkest days of the Great Depression that the governor general of Canada, Lord Bessborough, first launched the idea of the Dominion Drama Festival (DDF, 1932–9, 1947–78) to support creative theatrical works in Canada.[21] The DDF was a juried, pan-Canadian, officially bilingual (English and French) amateur theatre competition. The jury of professional theatre artists and critics awarded prizes to the best regional productions, which had qualified through local competitions prior to the main event. The festival was a powerful incentive to amateur companies eager to raise their profile by participating in this nationwide contest. Winners included the likes of André Brassard and Paul Buissonneau, directors who would go on to play major roles in Quebec theatre.

The bilingual ideal of the DDF was challenged in 1958 when Guy Beaulne founded the Association canadienne du théâtre amateur (ACTA),[22] which soon attracted the DDF's creative core of amateur francophone theatre talent and set up a competing festival, the Festival-Carrefour de l'ACTA. The first edition of the festival was held in conjunction with the cultural activities of Expo 67, the 1967 World's Fair in Montreal. As a site where theatre artists could gather, discuss, and train (through workshops and seminars), the festival discarded the competitive aspect of the DDF in favour of a more collegial approach and narrowed its scope to French-Canadian cultural space. By its second edition, the rising tide of Quebec nationalism that had reached the theatre community led to massive participation from Quebec French-language theatre troupes, which already dominated both ACTA and its festival. Consequently, the community-based concerns of troupes from outside of Quebec tended to be marginalized. Quebec theatre troupes cast off the theatrical stylings of France in their shows and created collective productions, which grew to become the leading theatrical form among young Quebec theatre artists during this period. Certainly, many theatre hopefuls of this new generation rejected the theatrical traditions of France and taught and promoted in Quebec's major theatre schools,[23] opting instead for theatricality based on playful physical expression (sometimes approaching the bawdy American burlesque) and direct audience interaction. Thus, the sharply defined boundary between amateur and professional practice, drawn a decade earlier with the opening of major theatre schools, was effectively blurred by young artists in Quebec.

It was in this environment that ACTA became the Association québécoise du jeune théâtre (AQJT) in 1972 and turned its back once and for all on the amateur, pan-Canadian vision of the DDF and earlier editions of Festival-Carrefour. The AQJT continued its own annual festival, known as the Festival du jeune théâtre. Entirely devoted to French-language creative works from Quebec, particularly in their socially collective and culturally militant (sometimes openly revolutionary) forms, the new AQJT festival was a space for young Quebec theatre artists to meet and share ideas—and also was a subversive hotbed for debating the sociopolitical issues of the day. Following the tumultuous departure of the most ardently socialist and Marxist elements of the association in 1975, the Festival du jeune théâtre would remain an inward-looking Québécois cultural space, with festival programs shifting progressively toward aesthetic exploration.

The three theatre festivals we have mentioned had specific aims that underwent a number of major paradigm shifts: from official bilingualism to French unilingualism, from amateurism to professionalism, and from a Canadian to a Quebec cultural perspective. The results of the 1980 referendum on Quebec independence effectively marked the end of the Quiet Revolution and a temporary shelving of the nationalist project that had stimulated a great deal of dramatic creation up to that point. Subsequently, the AQJT and its festival spiralled into decline, and in 1985 they both met their demise.

Not coincidentally, the very year the AQJT took its final bow, the Festival de théâtre des Amériques (FTA) made its debut. Initially held every two years,[24] the artistic direction of the FTA was led by Marie-Hélène Falcon, who had earned her stripes with the AQJT and its festival. Emblematic of the increasing openness to outside influences that emerged after 1980 (after Quebec theatre's identity-based paradigm ran out of steam), the FTA was a clear departure from the festivals that had preceded it. International rather than local, multilingual rather than unilingual, the FTA stood out for its high degree of specific consecration, but perhaps most of all for its innovation and its scrupulous formal searches for new, innovative work. Gaining in respectability, the FTA brought together a broad variety of international and local theatre artists as well as foreign critics and distributors. For contemporary theatre artists who wished to access world stages, the FTA, under Marie-Hélène Falcon's and now Martin Faucher's leadership, has become a near-compulsory event if only because it is a rare "site of mediation" that functions as a junction between local and international theatre.

The FTA has introduced production companies from the local field to the aesthetics that have won festival theatre awards and recognition abroad. Inescapably, as the local and international fields get a better look at one another, the situation is not only conducive to building new audiences but also to making comparisons between the limited offering in Montreal and Quebec City's subfields and the best offerings in theatre from abroad.[25] Arranging for both parties to get a better look at each other can inspire a dynamic of striving for excellence and motivate local theatre producers to innovate. Conversely, measuring up to the rhetoric of novelty and creation (that is the lifeblood of this event) is nonetheless an immense challenge for local producers. While foreign shows are individually selected and have already passed muster on stage, Quebec performances are often actually created during the FTA, with all of the perilous risks that such an endeavour involves. So while the FTA has been a launch pad into the international theatre market for a few innovative Quebec theatre artists, many more have failed to be selected by the agents of the international field, yet still remain important local players.

Questions for Critical Thinking

1. What are the characteristics of "festival theatre"?
2. Describe the "double social inscription" that director Robert Lepage and his theatre company, Ex Machina, enjoy.
3. Which factors come into play in crossing over from the local to the international theatrical field?

Notes

1. In the province of Quebec, the word *nation* often refers to Quebec rather than Canada in common parlance (especially in French). Giving voice to the fact that Quebec is a culturally distinct society, Quebec officials have long designated government agencies as "national" bodies.
2. Pierre Bourdieu's concept of *field* will be explained in greater detail in the theoretical portion of this chapter, under the heading "Local Theatrical Field–International Theatrical Field."
3. Also a Bourdieusian term that is explained in the theoretical portion of this chapter.

4. The qualifier *essai* was dropped in 1991, but the acronym (CEAD) remained the same.
5. Jean-Marc Larrue, "La Création collective au Québec," in *Le Théâtre québécois : 1975–1995*, ed. Dominique Lafon (Montreal: Fides, 2001), 155.
6. See Jean Cléo Godin and Laurent Mailhot, "Le théâtre québécois contemporain ou comment devenir classique en une generation," in *Théâtre québécois II : Nouveaux auteurs, autres spectacles*, ed. Jean Cléo Godin and Laurent Mailhot (Montreal: Hurtubise, 1988 [1980]), 20.
7. In the province as a whole, the number of subsidized companies rose from 16 in 1968 to 71 in 1980; see François Colbert, *Le Marché québécois du théâtre* (Quebec: Institut québécois de recherche sur la culture, 1982), 33. This is not counting the 40 or so summer theatres and the large number of companies and small producers such as café theatres that opened their operations without any government funding. At the end of the above-mentioned period, in 1980, the number of theatre companies in Quebec was estimated at 300; see Angèle Dagenais, *Crise de croissance : le théâtre au Québec* (Quebec: Institut québécois de la recherche sur la culture, 1981), 7.
8. See Gilbert David, "Un nouveau territoire théâtral : 1965–1980," in *Le Théâtre au Québec : 1825–1980*, ed. André G. Bourassa, Gilbert David, Jean-Marc Larrue, and Renée Legris (Montreal: VLB éditeur/Société d'histoire du théâtre du Québec/Bibliothèque nationale du Québec, 1988), 144.
9. Authors studied by Godin and Mailhot include Jean Barbeau, Marcel Dubé, Jacques Ferron, Michel Garneau, Gratien Gélinas, Jean-Claude Germain, Éloi de Grandmont, Robert Gurik, Anne Hébert, Jacques Languirand, Françoise Loranger, Yves Sauvageau, and Yves Thériault. Their works are only occasionally performed today, usually for student audiences in venues like the Théâtre Denise-Pelletier for the benefit of the institutions that include them on their academic curriculum.
10. See Colbert, *Le Marché québécois du théâtre*, 70.
11. See David, "Un nouveau territoire théâtral," 164.
12. Some of the most notable groups include the Conseil québécois du théâtre (CQT, 1983), Association des professionnels des arts de la scène du Québec (APASQ, 1984), Théâtres associés inc. (TAI, 1985), Théâtres unis enfance jeunesse inc. (TUEJ, 1986), Association des compagnies de théâtre (ACT, 1989), and the later Association québécoise des auteurs dramatiques (AQAD, 1990), which were added to the older Union des artistes (UDA, 1987) and Centre des auteurs dramatiques (CEAD, 1965).
13. In *intermediality*, scientific and artistic presentation forms are presented together and compared. It is assumed that different media will also yield different findings in each case. This claim is further developed and differentiated in the theory of "Art as Research" within the framework of discussions relating to terms and methods. The comparability of artistic and scientific research is being established in practice through the research of "Intermedial Arts" and within the context of specific artistic projects.
14. See Sylvain Schryburt, *Repère signalétique des productions de compagnies théâtrales du Québec jouées à l'étranger*, cahier de recherche no. 14 (Montreal: CÉTUQ, 1999).
15. See Pierre Bourdieu, *Les règles de l'art : genèse et structure du champ littéraire* (Paris: Éditions du Seuil, 1992).
16. "These consist, on the one hand, of institutions which conserve the capital of symbolic goods, such as museums; and, on the other hand, of institutions (such as the educational system) which ensure the reproduction of agents imbued with the categories of action, expression, conception, imagination, perception, specific to the 'cultivated disposition.'" Pierre Bourdieu, "The Market of Symbolic Goods," in *The Field of Cultural Production: Essays on Art and Literature*, ed. and introd. Randal Johnson (New York: Columbia University Press, 1993), 121.
17. This occurs principally through the Canada Council for the Arts (federal government), Conseil des arts et des lettres du Québec (Quebec provincial government arts council), and the Conseil des arts de Montréal (Montreal municipal government arts council).
18. ". . . by which cultural products are recognised and ranked . . . in public and personal economies of meaning and value." David Peters Corbett and Lara Perry, eds., *English Art, 1860–1914: Modern Artists and Identity*, Barber Institute's Critical Perspectives in Art History series (Manchester: Manchester University Press, 2000), 24.
19. In one of the rare studies on the phenomenon of international tours, Claude des Landes has emphasized the similarities between the funding arrangements required for this kind of venture and those currently in effect in the private sector. See "D'une entreprise nationale au rayonnement planétaire," *L'Annuaire théâtral* 27 (Spring 2000): 41.
20. Hans-Thies Lehmann, *Le Théâtre postdramatique* (Paris: L'Arche, 2002).
21. For a history of the DDF, see Betty Lee, *Love and Whisky: The Story of the Dominion Drama Festival* (Toronto: McClelland & Stewart, 1973).
22. For more on ACTA, refer to the voluminous special issue 15, 1980, of *Cahiers de théâtre Jeu*.
23. Conservatoire d'art dramatique de Montréal (1954–), Conservatoire d'art dramatique de Québec (1958–), and National Theatre School of Canada (1960–).
24. In 2007, the FTA became an annual event, the Festival TransAmériques, a name that reflects the festival's new openness to the world of contemporary dance and, more generally, to performances that play with the boundaries between the living arts.
25. Sometimes this juxtaposition is achieved through more or less separate categories, such as the "Nouvelles scenes" category, launched in 1997 to promote emerging local theatre artists.

Select Bibliography

Beauchamp, Hélène. *Les théâtres de création au Québec, en Acadie et au Canada français.* Montreal: VLB éditeur, 2005.

———, and Gilbert David, eds. *Théâtres québécois et canadiens-français au XXe siècle : Trajectoires et territoires.* Sainte-Foy: Presses de l'Université du Québec, 2003.

Benson, Eugene, and L. W. Conolly, eds. *The Oxford Companion to Canadian Theatre.* Toronto: Oxford University Press, 1989.

Bourdieu, Pierre. *The Field of Cultural Production: Essays on Art and Literature.* Edited with an introduction by Randal Johnson. New York: Columbia University Press, 1993.

Donohoe, Joseph I., Jr., and Jane M. Koustas, eds. *Theatre sans frontières: Essays on the Dramatic Universe of Robert Lepage.* East Lansing: Michigan University Press, 2000.

———, and Jonathan M. Weiss, eds. *Essays on Modern Quebec Theater.* East Lansing: Michigan University Press, 1995.

Godin, Jean Cléo, and Dominique Lafon. *Dramaturgies québécoises des années quatre-vingt : Michel Marc Bouchard, Normand Chaurette, René-Daniel Dubois, Marie Laberge.* Montreal: Leméac, 1999.

———, and Laurent Mailhot. *Le Théâtre québécois I : Introduction à dix dramaturges contemporains.* Montreal: Bibliothèque québécoise, 1995 [1970].

———, and Laurent Mailhot. *Le Théâtre québécois II : Nouveaux auteurs, autres spectacles.* Montreal: Bibliothèque québécoise, 1995 [1980].

Greffard, Madeleine, and Jean-Guy Sabourin. *Le Théâtre québécois.* Montreal: Boréal, 1997.

Hurley, Erin. *National Performance: Representing Quebec from Expo 67 to Céline Dion.* Toronto: University of Toronto Press, 2011.

Ladouceur, Louise. *Dramatic Licence: Translating Theatre from One Official Language to the Other in Canada.* Edmonton: University of Alberta Press, 2012.

Lafon, Dominique, ed. *Le Théâtre québécois : 1975–1995.* Archives des lettres canadiennes. Vol. 10. Montreal: Fides, 2001.

MacDougall, Jill. *Performing Identities on the Stages of Quebec.* New York: Peter Lang, 1997.

Marsden, Peter V. "Social Networks." In *Encyclopedia of Sociology,* 2nd ed., edited by Edgar F. Borgatta and Rhonda J. V. Montgomery, 2727–35. New York: Macmillan, 2000.

Pavis, Patrice. *Dictionary of the Theatre: Terms, Concepts, and Analysis.* Toronto: University of Toronto Press, 1998.

Schoenmakers, Henri. "Festivals, Theatrical Events and Communicative Interactions." In *Festivalising! Theatrical Events, Politics and Culture,* edited by Temple Hauptfleisch, Shulamith Lev-Aladgem, Jacqueline Martin, Willmar Sauter, and Henri Schoenmakers, 27–37. Amsterdam and New York: Rodopi, 2007.

Schryburt, Sylvain. *De l'acteur vedette au théâtre de festival : Histoire des pratiques scéniques montréalaises (1940–1980).* Montreal: Presses de l'Université de Montréal, 2011.

Vaïs, Michel, ed. *Dictionnaire des artistes du théâtre québécois.* Montreal: Cahiers de théâtre Jeu/Québec Amérique, 2008.

Glossary

agenda setting Refers to the ability of the mass media to influence public and political "agendas" by focusing public attention on an event they find to be currently significant. The "pump-priming effect" refers to their ability to influence the importance of different issues. They can impose and shape issues, and thus have the potential to overdetermine the public's choices, notably in electoral matters. *Priming* defines the criteria of political judgment. They not only play the role of "masters of ceremony" by emphasizing problems or issues that merit public debate, but they also alter the criteria by which the public judges political actors by emphasizing a certain issue.

amateur ideal The prevailing view in anglophone Victorian Montreal that organized sport should be played by gentlemen to promote fitness and "manly" character, and the belief that play for pay or any other sort of material reward corrupted the purity and instrumental use of sport.

American Although *American* is most often used to refer to the United States' population, it can also allude to all inhabitants of the Americas.

Americanicity Awareness of a continental sense of belonging removed from a European one that can be traced back to the distinction between the New and Old World. The term first appeared in the 1960s when Montreal's writers and artists started being attracted by the Beat Generation and counterculture. It was a way of redefining Quebec's culture by taking into account the fact that they were living in North America while remaining at arm's length from America itself.

américanité One of a series of shorthand expressions intended to convey a certain essence (see *québécitude* for Quebec, for example). Americanité is increasingly used to signify the cultural importance of the geographical location of Quebec in North America (not to be confused with the narrower definition of America as the United States).

Americanization The transformation of a national culture, or certain aspects of it, by American culture, especially with regard to commercial and media culture. Language is its most important bone of contention.

annexationism This word has had a long career in the history of Canada. Because of proximity, intense relations from one side of the border to the other, and cultural similarities (in spite of linguistic differences in the case of French Canadians), the temptation was strong to propose that Canada join the United States by adding as many states to the Union as there are Canadian provinces. It was an option envisaged by some Quebecers who refused the Confederation project in 1867.

anti-racism A policy or model that promotes the transformation of attitudes and unequal practices through the valorization of concepts like equity, justice, rights, and nondiscrimination.

autonomy An important concept for Quebec. Its governments have generally been eager to defend all the powers that are entitled to provinces according to the Canadian Constitution. Quebec claims to be distinct from the rest of Canada (more distinct from other provinces than any of them are from each other) due to the different language spoken by the majority of its population (its official language) and to a culture that is also specific and different. Quebec insists on the fact that all Canadian provinces are sovereign and not subjugated to the federal government in matters under their jurisdiction. This position has been upheld by Supreme Court jurisprudence.

baby boom Refers to the increase in the birth rate after World War II in the Western world, including Quebec. Some demographers consider that the increase occurred mostly between 1945 and 1960, while others extend the period until 1970. This phenomenon took place not only because women had more children than before or during the war, but also because more women married and had children during this period.

benign neglect Refers to areas of social life where it is felt that no government action is required.

bijural Characterized by the duality of legal traditions to which the legal system is attached. Canada is a bijural jurisdiction, in the sense that Quebec is attached to the civil law tradition whereas the other provinces have their legal roots in the common law tradition. The civil law and common law also come into contact in federal legislation and within federal institutions such as the Supreme Court of Canada. The legal system of Quebec is also bijural by virtue of the influence of both legal traditions in different parts of its law.

Bill 33 As a result of the landmark Supreme Court ruling in 2005 in *Chaoulli v. Quebec*, the government was obliged to modify its existing health-care legislation; passed in 2006, this statute allowed for the emergence of private insurance for specific surgical services including cataract, knee, and hip replacements.

bon usage In the seventeenth century, Claude Favre de Vaugelas, a founding member of the *Académie française*, defined the appropriate use of French, the *bon usage*, as the one used by the most educated members of the court and the writers of the time.

Canada Health Act Passed in 1984, this federal statute amalgamated existing cost-sharing legislation with the provinces for hospital and medical insurance, defined five principles that provincial health plans would have to respect (public administration, portability, universality, comprehensiveness, and equal access), and imposed a specific dollar-for-dollar financial penalty.

Canadiens Generally, descendants of the original pre-Conquest European settlers of Quebec, essentially meaning of French origin, francophone (French-speaking), and Catholic. While forming a relatively homogeneous ethnoreligious group, the characteristics and boundaries of the Canadien population were never absolute. A small number of pre-Conquest French immigrants had been Protestant, for example, and after the Conquest some new immigrants, such as German mercenaries who arrived in the 1770s and 1780s, assimilated into Canadien society.

Castonguay-Nepveu Report Commissioned during the Quiet Revolution era, this commission's report outlined the lacunae of existing health-care services and the specific needs of the Quebec population, and would become the basis for the 1971 *Loi sur les services de santé et les services sociaux* and the design of the Quebec health-care system based on the integration of health and social services.

Catholic cinema A corpus of films representing a Christian concept of the world promoted by the Roman Catholic Church. After the papal encyclical *Vigilanti Cura* was issued in 1936, the prevalence of Catholic cinema increased but, depending on the era and country, its homogeneity varied. In Quebec, a group consisting mainly of traditionalist priests produced a prolific corpus of documentary Catholic propagandist films between 1930 and 1960.

CEGEPs Collèges d'enseignement général et professionnel. Two-year publicly funded junior colleges accessible to all Quebec students after Grade 11. Introduced by the Quebec government in 1967, their purpose was to make postsecondary education more accessible.

chansonnier A term derived from the word *chanson* in French, often translated directly as *song* and *chansonnier* as singer–songwriter. Both translations are inexact: Both *chanson* and *chansonnier* are connected to a tradition emphasizing the primacy of the text or lyrics over musical or pop-culture iconography that are more important in other forms of popular music.

civic pluralism The civic–pluralist conception of identity holds that all inhabitants of Quebec that recognize themselves as Quebecers *are* Quebecers. Being a Quebecer is predicated on neither French-Canadian origin nor assimilation to the majority. Identity choices are left to the individual—it is up to the newcomer to decide whether to keep aspects of his or her cultural origins alive or not. The civic–pluralist vision is at its core a *liberal* one: Individuals have basic human rights that limit what the state can do in the name of the common good (liberalism in this sense relates to the rights and freedoms of individuals, not necessarily leaning toward the left or right side of the political spectrum).

civil code A foundational legal text within a legal system in the civil law tradition. A civil code is a comprehensive, coherent, and structured presentation of the basic rules of legal interaction among persons, such as the laws of the family, property, inheritance, and contracts. A civil code generally has some permanence and stability, giving it a unique stature within a legal system's legislative texts.

civil law A legal tradition derived from Roman law and ecclesiastical and customary laws as reconfigured by scholars and humanist thinkers in continental Europe after the fourteenth century. It is one of the two legal traditions originating from the Western world, in which the primary source of law is legislation (as opposed to case law in the common law tradition). It is often expressed in a Civil Code or analogous iconic text.

Clarity Act Passed in 2000, a federal law that stipulates when the federal government will recognize a province's secession from Canada. It requires a "clear majority" and a "clear question." This law is at odds with the views of more ardent Quebec nationalists who believe that only Quebec itself can determine its own political future.

common law A legal tradition that emerged from the procedures and decisions of the royal courts in England as early as the eleventh century. It is one of the two legal traditions originating from the Western world. It is often characterized by the central role that is played by the judge in giving expression to the law and shaping it.

compact theory A representation of the origins of the Canadian federation that emphasizes the contractarian and aggregative process that led to the creation of the federation. Under this primarily political view, Canada results from an agreement between equal provinces or, alternatively, two founding nations (Quebec and English-speaking Canada). The compact theory is opposed to the formalist representation of the origins of the federation, which instead highlights the federation's legal origins in a British statute.

concertation A process of bargaining between social actors such as unions and business organizations with the goal of finding positive-sum compromises. The word suggests "concerted action" among actors with diverging interests, involving a mixture of conflict and co-operation. In some countries, the results of this process are called "social partnerships."

cultural assimilation A process in which the integration of members of minority ethnocultural groups are expected to be absorbed into a dominant majority culture in a given society. The process often occurs through socialization over time, yet it is sometimes undertaken through more coercive measures by states.

cultural diversity The quality of different or diverse cultures, as opposed to a single or monoculture. The acceleration of globalization and the easy transmission of information around the world raise concerns for some individuals and organizations like UNESCO that cultural meanings and tastes run the risk of becoming homogenized.

cultural industries Sometimes called *creative industries*, these include the creation, production, and distribution of goods and services that are cultural in nature and usually protected by intellectual property rights. In international trade, these typically include arts, publishing, music, television, film, performance, crafts, and design. Critical theorists Theodor Adorno and Max Horkheimer coined the German term *kulturindustrie* to refer to capitalism's negative cultivation of commercially marketed mass culture that crowds out authentic indigenous culture.

cultural pluralism The public recognition of a multitude of cultures coexisting within a bounded society and maintaining their differences. Canadian multiculturalism and Quebec interculturalism are examples of policy choices that have adopted cultural pluralism to varying degrees.

Custom of Paris A legal code used in the Paris region and applied to the colony of New France. While the rest of Canada based its law on English common law, the Custom of Paris formed the basis of Quebec's distinct civil law system as enacted by the Civil Code of Quebec (1866).

decapitation thesis The notion that, immediately after the Conquest, virtually all of Quebec's pre-Conquest elites left, leaving behind a truncated Canadien society with little in the way of an entrepreneurial class. This allowed the new British elites, and notably merchants, to dominate the colony's economy and society. The decapitation thesis has been heavily contested in academic circles but remains strong in popular conceptions of Quebec history.

delegation This term is used to refer to important Quebec government offices abroad. A distinction is made between a *delegation general*, which represents the state of Quebec in a global way in all sectors of activity under its jurisdiction; a *delegation*, which represents Quebec in a defined number of sectors; and a *bureau*, which represents Quebec in a few sectors. In the United States, the only delegation general is in New York. Delegations are found in Boston, Chicago, and Los Angeles and bureaus in Atlanta and Washington, DC.

development model A set of policies affecting a society's wealth generation and distribution. It reflects conflicts about how to organize economic activity to increase the well-being of a society. To call it a *model* is to say that there are a variety of possible ways at any given time to secure development, although with different impacts on wealth generation and distribution.

direct cinema A documentary technique that was spawned by the advent of new technology and contemporary ethical values. World War II brought about a social paradigm shift. In cinema, this shift led to a more critical, transparent documentary approach in direct cinema. Facilitated by the use of lightweight, synchronous equipment, direct cinema film crews moved with ease outside film studios to film protagonists speaking and acting as they did in everyday life. In Quebec, a strong modernist, nationalist movement supported this new documentary technique in the 1960s.

diplomacy Usually refers to the conduct by government officials in negotiations and relations with political officials of other nations. It also refers to the art of conducting such relations and the skills that are applied to it. It also means in practice the art of dealing with people from different cultures. As such, this concept of diplomacy may be applied to Quebec officials abroad, notably in the United States, where they appear as more strikingly different from Americans than English-speaking Canadian officials.

documentary cinema An art form whose materials come from filmed reality rather than fiction, although some fictional treatments may be used in documentary films. Filmmaker John Grierson coined the term *documentary*. He defined it as a "creative treatment of actuality," and this definition has remained valid despite the heterogeneous development of the art form.

economic liberalism An economic ideology that is most concerned with the freedom of individuals to enjoy their property. This translates into a policy of leaving economic decision making to individual property owners and limiting state intervention to the protection of property rights and the enforcement of contracts.

emparons-nous du sport A catch phrase that circulated among French-Canadian promoters of organized sport in 1890s Quebec. "Let us seize sport" was a patriotic call from sports journalists and organizers to young francophone men to use sport as a means to build muscular character and national pride among the francophone community.

Équipe-Québec A movement to establish a Quebec national team that would compete in elite-level international sporting events, particularly in hockey and soccer. The movement has taken shape gradually since the early 1970s, and though popular among separatists in Quebec, it also draws support from others who see in it the potential for a spirited national affirmation.

ethnic group A group of people sharing a putative or real common history, a distinctive social and cultural tradition maintained from generation to generation, and a sense of identification with the group.

federalism A political structure that provided for two levels of government, federal and provincial. The British North America Act (1867) defined the responsibility of each level of government. While it has led to disputes and inefficiencies, federalism permits fundamental policy differences among provinces over social and cultural issues such as education, health services, and language.

feminism Broadly defined as a social and political movement looking to better understand and struggle against women's discrimination and oppression, and as an ideology that denounces the inequalities suffered by women. Some feminist groups mainly want to attain equality with men in every domain of social and private life by transforming the law. More radical feminist collectives aim at eradicating patriarchy as the only way to guarantee women's rights and real equality between the sexes.

festival A festival is an event consisting of several single events or, as Henri Schoenmakers calls it, a meta-event (2007, p. 28; see Chapter 29 Select Bibliography). The single theatrical events are organized and presented within the bigger structure of the festival according to thematic, discipline or genre-based, or other principles.

field "The field of production and circulation of symbolic goods is defined as the system of objective relations among different instances, functionally defined by their role in the division of labour of production, reproduction and diffusion of symbolic goods. The field of production per se owes its own structure to the opposition between the *field of restricted production* as a system producing cultural goods (and the instruments for appropriating these goods) objectively destined for a public of producers of cultural goods, and the *field of large-scale cultural production*, specifically organized with a view to the production of cultural goods destined for non-producers of cultural goods, 'the public at large'" (Pierre Bourdieu, 1984, p. 4; see Chapter 29 Select Bibliography).

First Nations A phrase that refers to the Aboriginal peoples of Canada. In common use since the 1980s, it acknowledges their presence in North America before Europeans while also validating the uniqueness of their traditions and languages. In short, it is a term of respect that seeks to replace Columbus's erroneous "Indians." Nevertheless, "Indians" remains in widespread use among First Nations peoples themselves. Other accepted descriptors include Aboriginals, Native peoples, and indigenous peoples. Also widely used are the names of specific ethnic groups, for example Innu, Algonquin, or Cree.

framing The ability of the mass media to define legitimate contexts of interpretation for a given problem. It refers to the way the media formulate statements (notably problems), select certain aspects to report on, or adopt a particular approach in their treatment of an issue. The designation of a problem influences how the public perceives an issue and the importance it gives to certain points of view.

francization The process, in sport and in all realms of Quebec life, through which the institutions of administrative power in the province gradually became controlled by French-speaking Québécois. In sports organizations, this change began in the middle decades of the twentieth century and reached its height after 1960, when the Quiet Revolution began.

Francophonie An expression having two primary definitions: (1) the ensemble of French-speaking areas of the globe, with some shared cultural reference points, and (2) the Organisation internationale de la Francophonie—an international organization composed of nations interested in collaboration on economical and cultural fronts with varying degrees of attachment to the French language itself.

geopolitics The strategic relationship between geographic, territorial, and economic factors in international relations. New France played an important role in the French empire, despite its relative unprofitability, because of its strategic location and its potential economic benefits to France's enemies.

globalization Refers to the increase and intensification of interaction—economic, cultural, technological, and so on—across national boundaries.

habitants Settlers of New France who became peasant landowners, clearing and farming their land and building houses and other structures to suit their needs. Unlike the French peasants of the seventeenth and eighteenth centuries, they were free landowners and did not need to give a portion of their harvest or their labour—*la corvée*—to cover the needs of others.

hydroelectricity Electricity generated by the power of falling water. The water is impounded by a hydroelectric dam, then released through tubes in the dam called penstocks to drive water wheels called turbines that are housed in a powerhouse. The generators convert the resulting mechanical energy into electric energy that is conveyed by transmission lines to places of use.

iconography *The Oxford Companion to Western Art* defines this term as "the entire descriptive and classificatory investigation of subject matter in the arts . . . [A]part from classifying themes, motifs, attributes, allegories and symbols, iconography also traces their historical development, focusing for example on the perpetuation of certain visual traditions and the resulting standardization of image formulas." The religious imagery used by Catholic missionaries in the seventeenth century depended on iconographic models that render the images intelligible to their viewers; the differing symbolic associations attached by Aboriginal and European visual cultures to certain visual phenomena account for differing iconographic interpretations.

image theatre "[R]efers to a kind of staging that tends to produce stage images, generally of great formal beauty, rather than offering a text or presenting physical actions 'in relief'" (Patrice Pavis, 1998, p. 403; see Chapter 29 Select Bibliography).

immigrant A person who moves voluntarily or involuntarily from one country to another or from one region to another for economic, political, or cultural reasons.

industrialization The process by which industrial production was introduced. Many artisans and craft workers lost independence and became wage labourers while economic activity was increasingly dominated by individuals with capital.

institutional bilingualism Implies the obligation of a government to communicate with its citizens and within its own institutions in the official languages of the citizens' choice.

interculturalism A policy or model that aims to develop an understanding of, respect for, and dialogue between the different cultural groups without negating differences while promoting the construction of a common identity.

interdependence The mutual reliance between actors. Because Quebec participates in the global economy, it is increasingly reliant on the goods and services that trade provides, just as its trade partners are reliant on Quebec's goods and services.

international organization A formal group with an international or global scope. There are two main types: intergovernmental and nongovernmental organizations. The former are composed of sovereign states (WTO, UN) and the latter are nonstate actors (Oxfam, Red Cross).

intersectionality A term first used in an article written by black feminist, legal theorist, and activist Kimberlé Crenshaw to take into account that black women in the United States faced, at the same time, class, race, and gender oppressions and that their social situation was determined by these intersecting oppressions.

Iroquois nations A confederation of six Native nations—Mohawk, Onondaga, Oneida, Cayuga, Seneca, and (after 1722) Tuscarora—living in what is modern-day Quebec, Eastern Ontario, and New York. More than any other people, they shaped the French presence during their first century in New France.

Jesuits Members of the Society of Jesus, a Catholic missionary order established in 1534 by Ignatius of Loyola. In addition to their missionary duties, Jesuits played an important role in cultural and diplomatic relations between French colonists and Native peoples.

joual The name given to the type of working-class language developed in cities among former peasants who became urban labourers and worked under anglophone bosses around the end of the nineteenth century. It originally designated the distinct Québécois French vernacular spoken in urban working-class areas in and around Montreal. By extension it is sometimes used to designate all forms of French vernacular spoken in Quebec, regardless of its social and geographical specificities.

laicization A state-driven political and juridical adjustment process that, by virtue of guaranteeing equal justice for all, seeks to ensure freedom of conscience and religion under a state that is neutral with regard to different coexisting individual moral codes and beliefs about how to live a "good life" in society.

landscape This term can be readily understood as encompassing the realm of drawn, printed, painted, and photographic representations of place, territory, or site for purposes that range from military reconnaissance to civic knowledge and subjective contemplation. It can also be understood as an area of cultural formation in which geographical entities (rivers, mountains, falls, plains, grasslands, hills, cities) are conceived as inherently pictoral or as sources for aesthetic representation. When landscape representations of Quebec became widely circulated, these motifs gained currency as markers of identity and otherness.

language regime The sum of the laws, practices, and conceptions of language and language use framed by state traditions.

legal tradition A distinctive way of thinking about, expressing, and applying the law that has achieved some historical continuity. Different legal traditions accord variable roles to judges, elected legislators, and legal scholars in saying what the law is and how it should evolve. Some legal traditions have religious foundations; others are secular. The legal system of a given country is often described as belonging to one legal tradition or another, within which the circulation of ideas is easier.

liberal democratic Refers to the political ideology that underpins the institutions of most Western states, such as Canada and the United States. According to this theory, policy decisions should be made by institutions representing the will of the majority, subject to constitutional constraints aimed at protecting the rights of individuals and minority groups.

liberal multiculturalism These liberals assert that fairness toward cultural and religious minorities sometimes necessitates differential treatment. Liberal multiculturalists favour, for instance, the reasonable accommodation of minority religious beliefs and practices and the recognition of the collective rights of Aboriginal peoples.

liberal neutralism (*or* difference-blind liberalism) These liberals believe that the state should guarantee the same basic individual rights to every citizen and adopt a "hands-off" approach to culture and identity. They assert that the state ought to fight against ethnic and religious discrimination and promote tolerance, but that it should not put forward what has been called a "politics of recognition" or a policy of multiculturalism that confers special recognition and specific rights to cultural minorities. As civic pluralists, they don't see cultural diversity as a threat that needs to be contained. But they do not think that group-specific rights or policies should be designed for cultural minorities. They see fairness as the identical treatment of all citizens by the state.

linguistic legitimacy When speakers of one language recognize a linguistic variety as valid, conforming to norms and endowed with prestige. Generally, popular and regional varieties of a language have little linguistic legitimacy, while the variety spoken by the upper class is considered as more esteemed.

literary frontiers Based on linguistic and/or geographical boundaries, literary frontiers are not easy to define (as opposed to "real" frontiers that are ruled by law), but they do shape the evolution of any literature.

the long peace The period from 1713 to 1744 marked by a pause in French–British warfare over North America. Although warfare, slave raiding, and dispossession continued in the West, the absence of imperial warfare brought unprecedented growth and prosperity to the colonial settlements of the St Lawrence Valley.

Manifest Destiny A concept first outlined in 1845 that has mostly been tied to the United States, although other societies in the Americas have sought their own version of manifest destiny.

methodological nationalism A nationalist prism through which reality is systematically observed and interpreted and actions are legitimized on the basis of their correspondence with that prism.

modernist In the history of Quebec art, this term is often used to signal the development of artistic practices through which artists established a certain degree of autonomy vis-à-vis the ideological priorities of the dominant political and clerical structures of Quebec society, especially through their choice of stylistic approaches and subject matter. For example, the representations of urban life and the use of colour, line, composition, and application of paint in ways that departed from traditional academic realism are held to be a part of the arrival of *modernité* in Quebec artistic life in the 1920s and 1930s, culminating in the pursuit of lyrical and postpainterly abstraction in the 1940s and 1950s.

modern treaty A contemporary agreement between the federal government (and the provinces when relevant) and an Indigenous nation under which the latter releases its title to the land in exchange for monetary compensation and a specific regime of rights (including self-government) defined in the agreement. The 1975 James Bay and Northern Quebec Agreement was the first modern treaty in Canada.

moral contract A normative aspect of Quebec's model of interculturalism that affirms integration of newcomers is a reciprocal endeavour involving responsibilities not only from immigrants themselves but also from the host society. Newcomers are expected to participate and integrate in the larger society, while members of the receiving society must ensure they are provided with the resources to do so. Rather than structure the process around a hegemonic project that places the onus on newcomers to fully adapt to their new surroundings, the moral contract implies a spirit of mutual recognition.

multiculturalism A policy or model that emphasizes acknowledging the existence of ethnic diversity, and ensures that an individual's right to retain his or her culture goes hand in hand with enjoying full access to, participation in, and adherence to constitutional principles and commonly shared values prevailing in the society.

nationalization When a national government or state seizes or purchases a privately held corporation or industry, creating public ownership and control. In 1938, for example, Mexico expropriated or "nationalized" its oil industry, which was formerly in the hands of foreigners. In the case of Quebec's "nationalization" of electricity corporations in 1944 and 1963, the more accurate but rarely used English term would be "provincialization." In Quebec French, *nationalisation* can be used interchangeably with *étatisation*.

nation-to-nation relationship Relations between Indigenous communities and Canadian authorities based on mutual recognition, equality, and the coexistence of sovereignties.

nested identities The idea that national identities can be overlapping and are not necessarily mutually exclusive. In Quebec, this means that a person can simultaneously identify as a Canadian and a Quebecer without any contradiction in terms.

network In sociology a network is the "structure of relationships linking social actors" (Peter V. Marsden, 2000, p. 2727; see Chapter 29 Select Bibliography). These actors or agents can be either individuals or institutions.

norm A normalized, codified form of language. It is a recurrent phenomenon in the history of languages that the particular version chosen among all others as the language of instruction, of official communication, and of literature is the version spoken by the social class that is in power and comes from the region where this power is exercised.

North The open frontier of the North (synonymous with great liberty, but also with great solitude) has attracted Quebec's writers throughout history. It has repeatedly reconciled Quebecers' sense of *pays* (their people, nation, homeland) with their openness to *dépaysement* (decentring).

Northwest Passage A supposed water route over the top of North America that would allow direct shipping from Europe to Asia via the Atlantic Ocean. The hope for such a passage drew many early explorers, including Verrazzano, Cartier, and Champlain.

official language A language that has received the highest legal status possible in any given polity or jurisdiction.

It is the language used within a government and between a government and its citizens.

open secularism In contrast to restrictive secularism, which seeks to supress the public expression of religious conviction, open secularism views the state as neutral in its relationship to a variety of comprehensive doctrines espoused by individuals. The idea is to allow for the equal flourishing of religious freedoms without undo interference, in some cases even providing accommodations to promote equality. The Bouchard–Taylor Commission outlined four defining principles: the moral equality of persons, freedom of conscience and religion, separation of church and state, and the neutrality of the state with regard to religions and deep-seated secular convictions.

patriarchal society In a feminist sense, a patriarchal society designates a social formation where men hold power and authority in society and in the family and where women are subordinated to men. Men's power is exerted through social, economic, and legal structures, through religious and cultural practices, and through the dissemination of ideologies that legitimate this sociosexual order.

personality principle A principle informed by the idea that individuals have rights, including the right to speak the language of their choice, in particular when in contact with their government.

Plan Nord Quebec's economic development strategy focused on the expansion of resource extraction activities to less accessible northern regions where Indigenous peoples form an important proportion of the population.

postmodern cinema In the world of cinema, *postmodern* indicates a return to the most classic forms of narration, in which the self-referentiality of modernism is replaced by a heterogeneous abundance of intertextual or intermedia references. In postmodern Quebec cinema, the optimistic discourse of modernity was replaced by a relativist apprehension and a rethinking of the unpredictable nature of history—a history in which the aspirations for a sovereign nation-state are confronted with the realities of a society transformed by globalization. In Quebec, the works of Denys Arcand and Robert Lepage are emblematic of postmodern cinema.

postnational cinema The term *postnational* may be used to describe new international situations in which national entities are weakened by globalization. More specifically, the power of nations is challenged by financial international oligarchies while societies are transformed by the intensification of international trade and migration. The storylines of postnational filmmakers are often cosmopolitan, and their films are disseminated widely to international film festivals. Moreover, the work of postnational filmmakers may be better known abroad than in their own country.

public good A good desired by many people but that cannot be produced without government intervention, because even though it is desired by many it can only be produced through the contribution of all or most of the people who will benefit from it. The incentive that all have to not make such a contribution is seen as a major reason for government intervention in the case of public goods.

Quebec Act An act passed by the British Parliament in 1774 that came into effect in Quebec on 1 May 1775 and was meant to provide a new constitutional basis for the government of Quebec. Among other things, it formally did away with most anti-Catholic provisions in the colony; it confirmed the use of French civil law and English criminal law; it continued the colony's autocratic, non-democratic form of government; and it extended the frontiers of Quebec to cover the Great Lakes Basin. It was seen in the American colonies as one of the Intolerable Acts, contributing to the outbreak of the American Revolution, while in Quebec it was presented as a sort of Magna Carta of Canadien liberties (which it was not).

québécitude The ensemble of cultural and linguistic traits understood to constitute the heritage of Quebec.

Quebec specialists' strike In 1970, just days before the October Crisis erupted, Quebec specialist physicians went on strike to protest the government's new medical insurance plan that banned "extra billing," the process by which physicians could charge patients in excess of negotiated fee schedules approved by the provincial government.

Quiet Revolution A period of rapid social and political change in Quebec in the 1960s, characterized by a decline in the social role of the Catholic Church, the development of government institutions, and an increased role of the state in the province's economic, social, and cultural life. This period marked a turn to neonationalism in Quebec, in which the dominant conception of the nation shifted from French-Canadian ethnicity and culture to the territory of Quebec through more civic markers centred on the institutions of the Quebec state.

racializing discursive "slips" A racializing "slip" occurs when an opinion discourse/text by a reader or columnist contains one or more racist rhetorical devices. These sociocognitive devices are implicit or explicit and are often unconscious. They serve to construct, legitimate, reproduce, or contest relations of power and domination within a given sociopolitical context (such as a public debate). Their use attests to a kind of "backlash" against the dominant and normative discourse.

reasonable accommodation A legal obligation that derives from the right to equal treatment and applies in all situations involving discrimination. It entails adapting a standard or practice applied universally to create differential treatment for a person or group who would otherwise be penalized by the application of the standard.

reasoning templates The basic intellectual and cognitive preconceptions that inform how one understands and interprets reality; they also play a significant role in legal interpretation.

Red Power One of several US Civil Rights movements of the 1950s–1970s. It took shape among young, educated, urban American Indians to forge a sense of pan-Indian unity and pride, and to force redress to a long history of racism and government abuse of Indian rights. An important trigger was the 1969 occupation of the former federal prison on Alcatraz Island by a group calling itself the "Indians of All Tribes." Frequently leading subsequent acts of civil disobedience was the American Indian Movement (AIM), founded in Minneapolis in 1968, which also worked to combat police harassment, poverty, and unemployment in "red ghettoes." Like "Black Power," "Red Power" was coined and embraced by the minority itself.

Reference re Secession of Quebec A Supreme Court of Canada ruling presenting the court's legal opinion on whether a province can unilaterally secede from the Canadian federation. While the court ruled that unilateral secession was not legal under Canadian constitutional law, it also stated that the federal government had a responsibility to negotiate with provinces willing to pursue secession.

relations This concept has a special meaning when considered in an international context. What is meant here is more than connections between individual human beings across borders. It refers to communications between official representatives of one state and economic or political agents in another state. It is indeed possible for a government that is not fully sovereign to establish such relations. This is the case of the government of Quebec. Yet its actions abroad are usually mentioned as *international relations* rather than *foreign policy*, a term usually reserved to sovereign nations.

religious accommodation A term that can be used in a narrow way to refer to the legal obligation of reasonable accommodation that requires institutions and organizations (public or private) to modify certain otherwise legitimate rules, practices, and policies, or to exempt certain groups or individuals from those rules, practices, and policies in order to take into account certain religious convictions held by individuals or the specific needs of ethnoreligious groups. It may also be defined more broadly as encompassing not only exemptions to general laws, but also the whole range of measures adopted to enable individuals to freely practise their religion in various social contexts (the workplace, public institutions, etc.).

resources nationalism The promotion of natural resource extraction as a nation-building strategy through the projection of a nationalist narrative on the territorial expansion of the resource economy.

responsible government A system of government in which the executive or cabinet is chosen from members of the party that controls the majority of seats in an elected assembly. Responsible government was granted to Upper and Lower Canada and Nova Scotia in the 1840s.

Richard Riot Also known as *l'Affaire Richard*, this riot occurred when irate fans of the Montreal Canadiens violently protested the season-ending suspension of their hockey hero, Maurice Richard, by NHL President Clarence Campbell on 17 March 1955. Though it started in the Montreal Forum, the riot soon spread into the streets, becoming for many a public demonstration decrying discrimination against Richard and the French-Canadian nation he symbolized.

romantic conservatism The romantic–conservative conception of identity holds that the shift from French-Canadian identity to Quebec identity was not completely positive—something important was lost along the way. It asserts that the "historical majority" (Quebecers of French-Canadian origins) somehow lost its political empowerment and assertiveness as it opened up to plurality. This, according to romantic conservatism, was caused not by conscious and voluntary decisions, but by a combination of the unhappy consciousness of a self-effacing majority that zealously wants to avoid xenophobia and ethnic nationalism and of the successful imposition of a pluralist ideology by the intellectual and political elites.

secularization A process whereby religion progressively loses its relevance as a social and cultural framework for defining moral values and social conduct. Religion may still hold relevance for individuals, but it cannot impose a single moral code prescribing norms for all members of that society.

seigneurialism Introduced into New France and confirmed by Britain after the Conquest, seigneurialism was a landholding system based on the seigneur's cession of land in return for rents and fees. Seigneurs had the obligation to provide mills, but they retained important rights such as waterpower sites.

seigneurial system The feudal form of landholding used in pre-Conquest Quebec. The Crown granted large estates (seigneuries) to members of the elite, who became known as seigneurs; they in turn granted farm lots to settlers, who in return owed a certain number of dues to their seigneur (annual rents, labour, various taxes, and so on). The British continued the seigneurial system after the Conquest, in part as a way of attracting the loyalty of the seigneurs, whom the new colonial masters saw (mistakenly) as the natural leaders of Canadien society.

self-determination The right of a political community to freely decide its political, economic, and cultural future. The right of Indigenous peoples to self-determination is recognized in the *United Nations Declaration on the Rights of Indigenous Peoples.*

social democracy An economic ideology concerned with creating a basis of equality so that all citizens can effectively enjoy their rights and fulfill their duties, and with extending the realm of decisions over which citizens exercise democratic choice. This translates into policies of redistribution and public services to reduce inequality, and forms of public and community ownership to shape investment decisions.

social economy A set of social practices conjugating economic activity with the achievement of social aims. Generally speaking, the social economy includes not-for-profit organizations that run as businesses, but with the goal of employing excluded individuals or of providing services to disadvantaged groups.

souvenir arts In *Trading Identities* (1998), Ruth Phillips explored the vast area of the commodified arts that were produced by Aboriginal men and women for sale to the tourist trade throughout the eighteenth and nineteenth centuries, "combining indigenous materials and techniques such as quillwork, moosehair embroidery, birchbark and basketry with Euro-American genres and styles." The term *souvenir art* encapsulates the notions of having passed through another's territory, of cultural exchange, artistic knowledge, and handcrafting expertise.

sovereignty An expression that has a wide spectrum of connotations in the modern history of Quebec, from actual independence to varying prerogatives in cultural, political, and economic domains. See other chapters in this volume for further discussion.

sovereignty-partnership The idea of making Quebec into a separate country while maintaining some economic and political links with the rest of Canada. Close in spirit to René Lévesque's "sovereignty-association" proposed in the 1980 Quebec referendum. (For more details see the Primary Source box in Chapter 19.)

sponsorship scandal A controversy surrounding plans to raise the profile of the Canadian federal government in Quebec following the 1995 referendum. The Gomery Commission (2004–5) uncovered corruption and misuse of public funds for these promotional programs. While the scandal led to the Conservative Party coming into power in 2006, it had lasting consequences for Liberal Party support at the federal level in Quebec.

sweating system Refers to a system where the workers, usually women and children, worked at home or in very small shops, especially in the garment industry. The employers supplied the material to be sewed, and sometimes the sewing machine, and paid by the piece at a very low rate, forcing the workers to work very long hours to make a barely sufficient salary.

systemic discrimination Notions of prejudicial effect and reasonable accommodation have led to the legal concept of *systemic discrimination*, defined by the Supreme Court in *Action Travail des Femmes v. Canadian National Railway Company* (1987). This concept is based on the idea of an interaction between practices, preconceived ideas, regulations, or norms in matters of recruitment, hiring, promotion, and so on, which creates a vicious circle of discrimination for certain groups. Systemic discrimination thus combines direct and indirect discrimination and must, according to the court, be tackled with systemic *remedies*, such as an employment equity measures.

territoriality principle A principle referring to the idea that a language is a collective good that needs to be protected or reinforced on its own territory.

Test Acts Acts of the British Parliament that imposed severe restrictions on Catholics' ability to hold office, exercise professions, and so on. They were part of broader anti-Catholic measures known as the Penal Laws. Had they been fully enforced in post-Conquest Quebec, they would have excluded Canadiens from many walks of life. However, for largely practical reasons colonial administrators never fully applied the Test Acts in post-Conquest Quebec, even before the Quebec Act effectively shortcircuited their provisions.

Test Oath An oath required by the British regime of Canadian Catholics in which they renounced allegiance to the pope (along with the doctrine of transubstantiation and the cult of the Virgin) if they wanted to hold public office.

trade liberalization The dismantling of trade practices that restrict the free flow of goods and services from one state to another, such as tariffs, restrictive regulations, and quotas. Advocates of liberalization claim that it promotes economic growth, lower prices, and access to more market choices, while critics claim that many types of goods as well as weaker economies and markets may struggle under liberalization, and that governments should have the right to craft their own rules outside of trade regimes like the World Trade Organization.

ultramontanism A Catholic doctrine that made its first appearance during the French Revolution and took root in Quebec between 1820 and 1830. Its followers categorically rejected any compromise between Catholicism and the modern thinking of liberalism. The doctrine promoted that religious society should entirely dominate civil society and that the state should submit to the Church.

le virage ambulatoire The 1988 Rochon Report recommended a move toward ambulatory care to redirect the health-care system toward outpatient services, with an emphasis on preventive measures and primary care as well as regionalized delivery and better integration of services.

visual culture Nicholas Mirzoeff has identified *visual culture* as being "concerned with visual events in which information, meaning or pleasure is sought by the consumer in an interface with visual technology. By visual technology, I mean any form of apparatus designed either to be looked at or to enhance natural vision, from oil painting to television and the Internet (Mirzoeff, 1999, 3). In this chapter, visual culture is taken to broaden these concepts, particularly with respect to the idea of a "consumer," which might be enriched with the notions of "participant," "user," and "maker," especially in the seventeenth century. W. J. T. Mitchell (1995, 542) has identified *visual cultures* as "the visual practices, the ways of seeing and being seen, that make up the world of human visuality."

vocation French Canada's spiritualist and religious vocation is its own version of Manifest Destiny to which it has considered itself as the Athens of a continent defined by the United States' "materialism." This ambition is not unusual, as many cities within the United States were also promoted as such without in fact being named Athens.

world music An expression originally created by music marketers at a loss for how to categorize and sell music created outside the dominant Anglo-Saxon music industries (US/UK). Today it frequently refers to successful fusions of Western pop practice with non-Western music (African, Middle Eastern, West Indian, South Asian).

Index